BLACKSTONE'S

CRIMINAL
PRACTICE

BLACKSTONE'S

CRIMINAL PRACTICE

2024

SUPPLEMENT 2

GENERAL EDITORS

DAVID ORMEROD CBE, KC (HON)

BARRISTER, BENCHER OF MIDDLE TEMPLE,
PROFESSOR OF CRIMINAL JUSTICE,
UNIVERSITY COLLEGE LONDON

DAVID PERRY KC

BARRISTER, 6KBW COLLEGE HILL

SUPPLEMENT EDITOR

WILLIAM HAYS

BARRISTER, 6KBW COLLEGE HILL

ADVISORY EDITORIAL BOARD
THE RT HON SIR BRIAN LEVESON, THE HON SIR HENRY GLOBE,
THE HON MRS JUSTICE BOBBIE CHEEMA-GRUBB, HH ERIC STOCKDALE,
THE RT HON LORD JUSTICE ANDREW EDIS, HHJ MICHAEL BOWES KC,
HH SALLY CAHILL KC, HHJ JONATHAN COOPER,
HHJ MARTIN EDMUNDS KC, HHJ STEVEN EVERETT,
HHJ ANDREW HATTON, HHJ MICHAEL HOPMEIER, HHJ PATRICIA LEES,
HHJ ALISON LEVITT KC, HHJ RICHARD MARKS KC,
HHJ HEATHER NORTON, HH JEFFREY PEGDEN KC, HHJ RAJEEV SHETTY,
HH DEBORAH TAYLOR, HHJ REBECCA TROWLER KC, ELEANOR LAWS KC,
TOM LITTLE KC, TIM OWEN KC, ROBERT SMITH KC,
ADRIAN WATERMAN KC, RICHARD SWALLOW

CONTRIBUTORS
PARAMJIT AHLUWALIA, DUNCAN ATKINSON KC, ALEX BAILIN KC,
DIANE BIRCH OBE, STEVEN BIRD, HHJ JONATHAN COOPER,
NICK DENT, ANAND DOOBAY, HHJ MARTIN EDMUNDS KC,
HHJ STEVEN EVERETT, RUDI FORTSON KC, DANIEL GODDEN,
KATHERINE HARDCASTLE, WILLIAM HAYS, MICHAEL HIRST,
LAURA C. H. HOYANO, PETER HUNGERFORD-WELCH, PAUL JARVIS,
JESSICA JONES, ADRIAN KEANE, SALLY KYD, KARL LAIRD,
MICHAEL LEREGO KC, SIR RICHARD MCMAHON KC, ALEXANDER MILLS,
VALSAMIS MITSILEGAS, TIM MOLONEY KC, AMANDA PINTO KC,
HH PETER ROOK KC, RICHARD D. TAYLOR, MARTIN WASIK CBE

OXFORD

UNIVERSITY PRESS

OXFORD
UNIVERSITY PRESS

Great Clarendon Street, Oxford, OX2 6DP,
United Kingdom

Oxford University Press is a department of the University of Oxford.
It furthers the University's objective of excellence in research, scholarship,
and education by publishing worldwide. Oxford is a registered trade mark of
Oxford University Press in the UK and in certain other countries

Published in the United States of America by Oxford University Press
198 Madison Avenue, New York, NY 10016, United States of America

British Library Cataloguing in Publication Data
Data available

ISBN 978–0–19–889242–7

Printed and bound by
CPI Group (UK) Ltd, Croydon, CR0 4YY

Introduction

This Supplement is the second of three cumulative updating supplements to *Blackstone's Criminal Practice 2024*. It includes updates to the text of *Blackstone's Criminal Practice 2024* taking account of legislative developments and leading cases since the publication of the 2024 edition. These updates are included at the start of the Supplement and follow the headings and the paragraph numbering used in the 2024 edition.

PACE Codes and Other Guidelines

This material is comprised of:

- Codes of Practice under the Police and Criminal Evidence Act 1984
- Attorney-General's Guidelines
- Attorney General's Guidelines on Disclosure for Investigators, Prosecutors and Defence Practitioners
- Code for Crown Prosecutors

Criminal Procedure Rules and Criminal Practice Directions

This Supplement contains the complete text of the Criminal Procedure Rules 2020 (SI 2020 No. 759) as amended by the Criminal Procedure (Amendment) Rules 2021 (SI 2021 No. 40), the Criminal Procedure (Amendment No. 2) Rules 2021 (SI 2021 No. 849), the Criminal Procedure (Amendment) Rules 2022 (SI 2022 No. 45), the Criminal Procedure (Amendment No. 2) Rules 2022 (SI 2022 No. 815), the Criminal Procedure (Amendment) Rules 2023 (SI 2023 No. 44) and the Criminal Procedure (Amendment No. 2) Rules 2023 (SI 2023 No. 786), the latest of which came into force on 2 October 2023.

The Supplement also contains the Criminal Practice Directions 2023, which replaced the previous Criminal Practice Directions 2015 as amended and came into force on 29 May 2023. The first amendment to the Criminal Practice Directions 2023 came into force on 2 October 2023 and it removed references to the temporarily retained sections of the Criminal Practice Directions 2015. Those sections of the 2015 Criminal Practice Directions are not reproduced in this supplement as they have been revoked, effective from 2 October 2023.

Paragraphing: The Criminal Procedure Rules and the Criminal Practice Directions follow the numbering of the primary instruments and make navigation more intuitive for the user.

Criminal Procedure Rules: Paragraphs are prefixed R so that R2.1 in this Supplement is the text of Criminal Procedure Rule 2.1.

Criminal Practice Directions 2023: Paragraphs are prefixed PD so that PD8.4 in this Supplement is the text of Criminal Practice Direction 8.4, Discharge of a juror during trial.

Sentencing Guidelines

The Sentencing Council maintains the latest version of the Sentencing Guidelines on their official website (https://www.sentencingcouncil.org.uk/). Due to the frequency of updates, the Sentencing Guidelines are no longer included in the Supplements. Readers are advised to visit the Sentencing Council's website as the most reliable source of the current guidelines.

Blackstone's Briefing

Please visit the *Blackstone's Criminal Practice 2024* companion website at www.oup.com/blackstones/criminal to view or download *Blackstone's Briefing*, which includes analysis of key developments and feature articles. If you have any queries, please contact blackstonescriminal@oup.com.

Contents

Table of Cases

Table of Statutes

Table of Statutory Instruments

Table of Codes of Conduct

Table of International Treaties and Conventions and other Legal Instruments

Table of European Legislation

Table of Guidelines

Table of Practice Directions

SUPPLEMENT TO PART A
CRIMINAL LAW

Section A3   General Defences

DEFENCES DENYING BASIC ELEMENTS OF LIABILITY

Insanity: General Principles: the M'Naghten Rules

'… or … that he did not know he was doing what was wrong'   The decision in *Keal* [2022]   **A3.33**
EWCA Crim 341 (to the effect that for the defence to succeed under this limb, D must both not
know that what he or she was doing was against the law and also not know that it was wrong by
the standards of reasonable ordinary people) was applied and followed in *Usman* [2023] EWCA
Crim 313. It was also reiterated that the application of the M'Naghten Rules did not involve a
breach of any of the Articles of the ECHR and that any significant change to the law regarding
insanity was a matter for Parliament. Furthermore, it was noted that the Criminal Procedure
(Insanity and Unfitness to Plead) Act 1991, s. 1(1), provides that a jury cannot return a verdict
of not guilty by reason of insanity except on the written or oral evidence of at least two registered
practitioners. This requires supporting evidence from both of them not only as to there being
a disease of the mind but also, as was lacking in this case, as to the other elements of the defence
being satisfied, e.g., as to D either not knowing the nature and quality of his or her act or
alternatively not knowing that it was wrong.

Section A5   Inchoate Offences

INTENTIONALLY ENCOURAGING OR ASSISTING AN OFFENCE

Elements

By s. 51A of the 2007 Act, as amended by the Online Safety Act 2023, s. 44 does not apply to   **A5.12**
an offence under the Suicide Act 1961, s. 2(1) (encouraging or assisting suicide), or to an offence
under the Online Safety Act 2023, s. 184(1) (encouraging or assisting serious self-harm).

ATTEMPT

Definition

The Criminal Attempts Act 1981, s. 1(4) (indictable offences to which s. 1 does not apply) is   **A5.72**
amended by the Online Safety Act 2023, sch. 14, which inserts:

   (d) an offence under section 184(1) of the Online Safety Act 2023 (encouraging or assisting
        serious self-harm).

Section A6   Corporate Liability

RULES OF ATTRIBUTION: PRINCIPLE OF IDENTIFICATION

Seniority and Identification

For the purposes of economic crime, ss. 196 to 198 of the Economic Crime and Corporate   **A6.3**
Transparency Act 2023 (ECCTA) have extended the category of individuals whose criminal
acts and mental state can bind the company to include 'senior management'. Where a senior
manager has committed the relevant offence, the corporate is also guilty. A person is senior
management if they play a significant role in the making of decisions about how the whole or
a substantial part of the company activities are to be managed or organised, or the actual
managing or organising of the whole or a substantial part of those activities (s. 196(4)). In order

3

for liability to attach to the company, the person must be acting within the actual or apparent scope of his or her authority. The definition reflects that found in the CMCHA 2007. The explanatory notes to the CMCHA state that those in the direct chain of management and those in, for example, strategic or regulatory compliance roles are included, and the Ministry of Justice's guidance on the CMCHA 2007 states that regional managers in national organisations and managers of different operational divisions might also be caught. The range of economic crimes affected is set out in the ECCTA 2023, s. 196(2) and sch. 12. As well as expected offences, e.g., under the Fraud Act 2006 and Theft Act 1968, also included in the list are money laundering, terrorist financing and sanctions offences, as well as misleading the market, bribery and customs and excise offences. Although currently limited to economic crime, further offences may be added by regulations and the government has stated its commitment to rolling sch. 12 out more generally. These reforms came into force on 26 December 2023.

SPECIAL RULES OF ATTRIBUTION: STATUTORY CONSTRUCTION

A6.7   Section 199 of the ECCTA 2023 provides a new offence of failure to prevent fraud. An offence is committed by a large organisation ('the relevant body') when a person associated with it commits a fraud offence intending to benefit the organisation or anyone (including their subsidiary) to whom the associate provides services on behalf of the relevant body. By s. 199(2), criminal liability is extended to subsidiaries, where an employee of the parent company commits a fraud offence and the parent company is a large organisation. A large organisation is defined as one which, in the relevant financial year, has two of the following: a turnover of more than £36 million, a balance sheet total of more than £18 million and more than 250 employees. Fraud offences caught are those listed in sch. 13 to the Act. It is a defence for the relevant body to prove that, at the time the fraud offence was committed, the body had 'such prevention procedures in place as it was reasonable in all the circumstances to expect the body to have in place; or it was not reasonable in all the circumstances to expect the body to have any prevention procedures in place' (s. 199(4)). This is an either way offence, and on indictment the punishment is an unlimited fine (s. 199(12)).

PARTNERSHIPS AND OTHER UNINCORPORATED BODIES

Partnerships

A6.15   The extension to liability for economic crime (see **A6.3** in this supplement) is also extended to partnerships by the ECCTA 2023.

Section A8   Territorial and Extra-territorial Jurisdiction

EXTRA-TERRITORIAL JURISDICTION

A8.19   The Online Safety Act 2023 will (once the relevant provisions are brought into force) create further extra-territorial offences.

The offences created by ss. 69, 109, 110, 112 and 138 (providing false information; non-compliance, etc.) are given an extra-territorial ambit by s. 205 of the Act, and if committed outside the UK may be dealt with anywhere in the UK. This includes in some cases extra-territorial liability on the part of directors or other senior officers or managers by virtue of s. 202 or 203 (consent, connivance or neglect by officers of a company or other entity providing a regulated service as defined by s. 4 of the Act).

By s. 185(1) the offences created by ss. 179(1), 181(1) and 183(1) of the Act will apply to acts done outside the UK, but only if the act is done by an individual who is habitually resident in England and Wales or Northern Ireland, or by a body incorporated or constituted under English or Northern Irish law. These are offences of sending false or threatening communications, or communications that include flashing images and are intended to cause harm to epileptics who may view them.

By s. 185(3), a slightly wider ambit is given to the offence of encouraging or assisting serious self-harm, contrary to s. 184. This offence, which also applies to Scotland, and is not limited to online communications, may be committed outside the UK by individuals habitually resident in the UK or by bodies incorporated or constituted anywhere in the UK.

But nothing in the Act brings offences committed wholly in Scotland or Northern Ireland within the ambit of English law or jurisdiction.

A

Part A   Criminal Law

SUPPLEMENT TO PART B
OFFENCES

Section B1   Homicide and Related Offences

MURDER

Elements

Under the King's Peace   The limited extension of extra-territorial jurisdiction for murder, **B1.17** effected by the Domestic Abuse Act 2021, s. 72, has been illustrated by the conviction, for murder committed in Peru, of an individual who was not a British National, and thus not caught by the OAPA 1861, s. 9, but who was habitually resident in England (*Minaya-Garay* (17 July 2023 unreported, Maidstone Crown Court)).

B

Part B   Offences

Section B3   Sexual Offences

SEX OFFENCES AGAINST CHILDREN AGED 13 TO 15

Causing or Inciting a Child to Engage in Sexual Activity

In *BNE* [2023] EWCA Crim 1242, the Court of Appeal quashed the convictions of a person **B3.110** found guilty of offences under the SOA 2003, ss. 10 and 15A, following a 'decoy' operation. The appeal concerned the impact of non-disclosure of the true age of a person whose photograph was used in the construction of a decoy online profile. At trial the appellant had accepted that he had exchanged messages with the decoy officer; that some of their content was sexual; and that some of them incited the recipient to engage in sexual activity. His defence was that he genuinely believed that the person he thought he was communicating with was 16 or over and his belief was not unreasonable. Plainly, therefore, the jury were required to assess what the appellant believed or may have believed in the light of the circumstances known to him. Following an application by the defence for disclosure of the true age of a person shown in four photographs sent to the appellant, the trial judge had ruled that the true age of the person in the photograph was prima facie disclosable but, following a public interest immunity hearing, did not order disclosure. The appellant challenged his convictions on the basis of that ruling. The Court of Appeal accepted that a jury which was shown images in a case of this type may well, without more, assume that they are accurate photographs and true likenesses of a real person of the age stated in the decoy profile, or under 16. A direction not to speculate about that would not cure the position in circumstances where the showing of the images was intended to foster the illusion of contact with an underage child. A defendant could be unfairly prejudiced if such an assumption was made when factually incorrect. The Court provided important detailed guidance as to how courts should approach this issue in future:

> 25. First, if the relevant image is an unaltered photograph of a real person who was in fact aged 16 or over when photographed, it seems to us that the true age of the person, at the time when the photograph was taken, should be disclosed to the defence. In such circumstances, we accept appellant's counsel's submission that the true age of the person depicted is a fact capable of undermining the prosecution case, and/or of assisting the defence case. That is because the jury can properly take the fact, that the image is a true likeness and an accurate portrayal of a real person aged 16 or over, into account when assessing whether a defendant may have believed that he was corresponding with someone aged 16 or over, and/or whether any such belief was reasonable. Moreover, the jury must not be misled by being shown images in circumstances which may give rise to an incorrect assumption about the age of the person depicted…

> 26. It follows that, in this first situation, the prosecution should disclose the actual age of the person shown at the time when the photograph was taken, and not merely the fact that the person was aged 16 or over. It will no doubt often be convenient for that information to be adduced in evidence before the jury in the form of an admission of fact.

> 27. Secondly, what if images have been digitally created, altered or modified in some way, in order to produce images consistent with the decoy profile? In such circumstances, whatever the nature and

9

extent of the process used, its purpose and effect was to create an entirely artificial image or to alter the appearance of the person initially photographed so that it ceases to be a true likeness. In this second situation, the true age and original appearance of any person originally photographed can in our view be of no relevance. The jury are not to be diverted into an examination of the skill with which the digital manufacture of the image has been carried out. Their focus must be on the images seen by the defendant, not on different images which he did not see.

28. It follows that, in this second situation, the prosecution's duty of disclosure does not extend to disclosing the true age of any real person originally photographed or the nature and extent of the digital process which has been used to make the images. It is however necessary that the defence should be informed of the fact that the images have been digitally manufactured, altered or modified so as to make, for the purpose of the decoy profile, images which are not a true likeness of any real person who may originally have been photographed. Subject of course to the precise issues in a particular case, it will generally be appropriate for that limited statement of fact to be adduced in evidence before the jury …

29. Subject again to the precise issues in a particular case, it follows from what we have said that, in a case where there has been no disclosure of the true age of the person shown at the time when the photograph was taken, it will usually be necessary for the jury to hear evidence of the fact that the images were manufactured, altered or modified so as to fit the decoy profile. Where that fact is in evidence, the trial judge should direct the jury that there is no evidence about the true age of any person shown in the images; that there is no evidence about what was done to manufacture, alter or modify them; that they must not speculate about those matters, because they are not relevant to the jury's verdicts; and that they must concentrate on the evidence of the material — the messages and the images — which the defendant received.

Sexual Communication with a Child

B3.139   See *BNE* [2023] EWCA Crim 1242 at **B3.110** in this supplement.

OTHER OFFENCES

Exposure

B3.296   From a date to be appointed, the SOA 2003, s. 66, will be amended by the Online Safety Act 2023, s. 188, to insert four new sections relating to the distribution of photographs or film of genitals and the sharing of other intimate images. Once in force, s. 66A will create a new offence relating to the intentional sending of photographs or film of genitals when either intending that the recipient be caused alarm, distress or humiliation; or doing so for the purpose of sexual gratification and being reckless as to whether the recipient is caused alarm, distress or humiliation. The offence will be triable either way and the maximum sentence on indictment will be one of two years' imprisonment. Section 66B creates an offence relating to the sharing of, or threat to share, intimate photographs or film. The offence may be committed in four different ways:

Sexual Offences Act 2003, s. 66B

(1) A person (A) commits an offence if—
    (a) A intentionally shares a photograph or film which shows, or appears to show, another person (B) in an intimate state,
    (b) B does not consent to the sharing of the photograph or film, and
    (c) A does not reasonably believe that B consents.

(2) A person (A) commits an offence if—
    (a) A intentionally shares a photograph or film which shows, or appears to show, another person (B) in an intimate state,
    (b) A does so with the intention of causing B alarm, distress or humiliation, and
    (c) B does not consent to the sharing of the photograph or film.

(3) A person (A) commits an offence if—
    (a) A intentionally shares a photograph or film which shows, or appears to show, another person (B) in an intimate state,
    (b) A does so for the purpose of A or another person obtaining sexual gratification,
    (c) B does not consent to the sharing of the photograph or film, and
    (d) A does not reasonably believe that B consents.

(4) A person (A) commits an offence if—
  (a) A threatens to share a photograph or film which shows, or appears to show, another person (B) in an intimate state, and
  (b) A does so—
    (i) with the intention that B or another person who knows B will fear that the threat will be carried out, or
    (ii) being reckless as to whether B or another person who knows B will fear that the threat will be carried out.

The offence under s. 66B will also be triable either way and the maximum sentence on indictment will be two years' imprisonment.

New s. 66C provides for exemptions to offences under s. 66B and new s. 66D defines terms found in ss. 66A and 66B.

Offences concerned with 'revenge porn' under ss. 33 to 35 of the CJCA 2015 are also repealed, from a date to be appointed, by the Online Safety Act 2023, s. 190.

PROSECUTION OF HISTORIC SEXUAL OFFENCES

Sentencing in Historic Sexual Cases

Sentencing an Adult in Respect of Offences Committed when a Child   *A* [2023] EWCA   **B3.377**
Crim 1204 is a good illustration of a recent application of the guidance provided in *Ahmed* [2023] EWCA Crim 281 in respect of sentencing defendants who were children at the time of the offending when a different sentencing regime would have applied. In 2023 the appellant (then aged 70) had been sentenced to four years' imprisonment in respect of six sexual offences committed when he was under 18. The lead offence was charged as indecent assault although it would have been an oral rape if committed now. He was also sentenced to nine years' imprisonment (to run consecutively to the four years) in respect of further sexual offences committed against another victim some 20 years later. In respect of the earlier offending, the trial judge noted that by the time the appellant was 16, he would have been liable to a sentence of Borstal training for a maximum of two years. Accordingly, the judge followed the approach in *Ahmed* by treating a sentence of Borstal training for two years, which would have included two years under supervision thereafter, as being equivalent to a sentence of four years' imprisonment. On appeal, it was submitted that, pursuant to the CJA 1961, the maximum custodial sentence available was six months' detention. While Borstal training was an alternative, it could not be treated as equivalent for modern sentencing purposes. The Court of Appeal rejected the argument that this point had not been resolved in *Ahmed*. There was nothing to suggest that the court at that time would have been bound to opt for detention as opposed to Borstal. Furthermore, in *Ahmed*, the Court of Appeal had expressly confirmed that a sentence of Borstal training can properly be reflected in a sentence of up to four years' imprisonment. The Court held that the judge's approach was entirely consistent with that required of the court when faced with historic offending by an offender who was a child at the time, that is to take as the starting point the sentence which it considers was likely to have been imposed at the time.

It was also submitted on appeal that by imposing consecutive sentences in respect of the offending against the two separate victims, the judge failed to have sufficient regard to totality. The Court of Appeal acknowledged that, as had been made clear in *Ahmed*, where the offender has committed offences both as a child and as an adult, it will commonly be the case that the later offending is the most serious aspect of the overall criminality and can be taken as the lead offence, with concurrent sentences for the past offending. In such circumstances the key considerations for the court are likely to be an assessment of the extent to which the offending as a child aggravates the offending as an adult, and the application of the principle of totality. However, the Court of Appeal in *A* pointed out that that did not mandate concurrent sentences in all cases where the offending straddles childhood and adulthood. Concurrent sentences may be appropriate where the offending against the same victim crosses an age threshold or there is some other feature that links the offending over time. Where, however, as in this case, the offending as an adult is entirely separate from that committed as a child, it is open to the judge to impose consecutive sentences. An adjustment for totality may not be required where the offences committed as a child and as an adult were wholly distinct. There was no breach of the totality principle.

Section B18   Offences Involving Writing, Speech or Publication

PUBLISHING, OR HAVING FOR PUBLICATION FOR GAIN, AN OBSCENE ARTICLE

OFCOM Defence

B18.13A   From a date to be appointed, the Online Safety Act 2023 inserts a new s. 2(5A) into the Obscene Publications Act 1959 which provides:

> A person shall not be convicted of an offence against this section of the publication of an obscene article if the person proves that—
>
> (a) at the time of the offence charged, the person was a member of OFCOM, employed or engaged by OFCOM, or assisting OFCOM in the exercise of any of their online safety functions (within the meaning of section 235 of the Online Safety Act 2023), and
>
> (b) the person published the article for the purposes of OFCOM's exercise of any of those functions.

OTHER OFFENCES

Improper Use of Public Electronic Communications Network

B18.27   From a date to be appointed, the Communications Act 2003, s. 127(2)(a) and (b) (sending, or causing to be sent, a message known to be false, for the purpose of causing annoyance etc.), is repealed by the Online Safety Act 2023, s. 189(1).

Instead, there will be a new false communications offence enacted by the Online Safety Act 2023, s. 179, of which the first three subsections are as follows:

Online Safety Act 2023, s. 179

> (1) A person commits an offence if—
>
> (a) the person sends a message (see section 182),
>
> (b) the message conveys information that the person knows to be false,
>
> (c) at the time of sending it, the person intended the message, or the information in it, to cause non-trivial psychological or physical harm to a likely audience, and
>
> (d) the person has no reasonable excuse for sending the message.
>
> (2) For the purposes of this offence an individual is a 'likely audience' of a message if, at the time the message is sent, it is reasonably foreseeable that the individual—
>
> (a) would encounter the message, or
>
> (b) in the online context, would encounter a subsequent message forwarding or sharing the content of the message.
>
> (3) In a case where several or many individuals are a likely audience, it is not necessary for the purposes of subsection (1)(c) that the person intended to cause harm to any one of them in particular (or to all of them).

Section 180 of the 2023 Act provides for exemption from the offence for various regulated enterprises such as news publishers, broadcasters and cinemas. Section 182 explains the meaning of 'sends a message' and also of various other terms used in the definition of the offence. The offence is summary only (see s. 179(5)).

The Communications Act 2003, s. 127(1) (sending messages that are grossly offensive or of an indecent, obscene or menacing character), will remain in force, as will s. 127(2)(c) (persistently using a public electronic communications network for the purpose of causing annoyance etc.).

Indecent or Offensive or Threatening Letters etc.

From a date to be appointed, the offences in the Malicious Communications Act 1988, **B18.30**
s. 1(1)(a)(ii) (threats) and s. 1(1)(a)(iii) (information known or believed to be false) are repealed
by the Online Safety Act 2002, s. 189(2). The false information version of the offence is
replaced by the false communication offence created by the Online Safety Act 2023, s. 179 (see
B18.27 in this supplement). The threats offence is in its turn replaced by a new threatening
communications offence created by the Online Safety Act, s. 181, of which the first four
subsections are as follows:

Online Safety Act 2023, s. 181

(1) A person commits an offence if—
  (a) the person sends a message (see section 182),
  (b) the message conveys a threat of death or serious harm, and
  (c) at the time of sending it, the person—
    (i) intended an individual encountering the message to fear that the threat would be
    carried out (whether or not by the person sending the message), or
    (ii) was reckless as to whether an individual encountering the message would fear that
    the threat would be carried out (whether or not by the person sending the message).
(2) 'Serious harm' means—
  (a) serious injury amounting to grievous bodily harm within the meaning of the Offences
  against the Person Act 1861,
  (b) rape,
  (c) assault by penetration within the meaning of section 2 of the Sexual Offences Act
  2003, or
  (d) serious financial loss.
(3) In proceedings for an offence under this section relating to a threat of serious financial loss,
  it is a defence for the person to show that—
  (a) the threat was used to reinforce a reasonable demand, and
  (b) the person reasonably believed that the use of the threat was a proper means of
  reinforcing the demand.
(4) If evidence is adduced which is sufficient to raise an issue with respect to the defence under
  subsection (3), the court must assume that the defence is satisfied unless the prosecution proves
  beyond reasonable doubt that it is not.

Section 182 explains the meaning of 'sends a message' and also of various other terms used in
the definition of the threatening communication offence in s. 180, just as it does for the s. 179
false communication offence. However, the s. 180 threatening communication offence is
potentially much more serious, being triable either way (s. 180(5)) with a maximum penalty on
indictment of five years' imprisonment.

The Malicious Communications Act 1988, s. 1(1)(a)(iii) (messages that are indecent or grossly
offensive) and s. 1(b) (article or electronic communication, in whole or part, of an indecent or
grossly offensive nature), are not repealed and will remain in force.

Offences of Sending or Showing Flashing Images Electronically

These two completely new offences, designed to protect individuals with epilepsy, will come   **B18.32A**
into force from a date to be appointed and are created by subsections (1) and (8) of the Online
Safety Act 2023, s. 183, which reads as follows:

Online Safety Act 2023, s. 183

(1) A person (A) commits an offence if—
  (a) A sends a communication by electronic means which consists of or includes flashing
  images (see subsection (13)),
  (b) either condition 1 or condition 2 is met, and
  (c) A has no reasonable excuse for sending the communication.
(2) Condition 1 is that—
  (a) at the time the communication is sent, it is reasonably foreseeable that an individual with
  epilepsy would be among the individuals who would view it, and
  (b) A sends the communication with the intention that such an individual will suffer harm
  as a result of viewing the flashing images.

(3) Condition 2 is that, when sending the communication—

  (a) A believes that an individual (B)—

    (i) whom A knows to be an individual with epilepsy, or

    (ii) whom A suspects to be an individual with epilepsy,

       will, or might, view it, and

  (b) A intends that B will suffer harm as a result of viewing the flashing images.

(4) In subsections (2)(a) and (3)(a), references to viewing the communication are to be read as including references to viewing a subsequent communication forwarding or sharing the content of the communication.

(5) The exemptions contained in section 180 apply to an offence under subsection (1) as they apply to an offence under section 179.

(6) For the purposes of subsection (1), a provider of an internet service by means of which a communication is sent is not to be regarded as a person who sends a communication.

(7) In the application of subsection (1) to a communication consisting of or including a hyperlink to other content, references to the communication are to be read as including references to content accessed directly via the hyperlink.

(8) A person (A) commits an offence if—

  (a) A shows an individual (B) flashing images by means of an electronic communications device,

  (b) when showing the images—

    (i) A knows that B is an individual with epilepsy, or

    (ii) A suspects that B is an individual with epilepsy,

  (c) when showing the images, A intends that B will suffer harm as a result of viewing them, and

  (d) A has no reasonable excuse for showing the images.

(9) An offence under subsection (1) or (8) cannot be committed by a healthcare professional acting in that capacity.

(10) A person who commits an offence under subsection (1) or (8) is liable—

  (a) on summary conviction in England and Wales, to imprisonment for a term not exceeding the general limit in a magistrates' court or a fine (or both);

  (b) on summary conviction in Northern Ireland, to imprisonment for a term not exceeding 6 months or a fine not exceeding the statutory maximum (or both);

  (c) on conviction on indictment, to imprisonment for a term not exceeding 5 years or a fine (or both).

(11) It does not matter for the purposes of this section whether flashing images may be viewed at once (for example, a GIF that plays automatically) or only after some action is performed (for example, pressing play).

(12) In this section—

  (a) references to sending a communication include references to causing a communication to be sent;

  (b) references to showing flashing images include references to causing flashing images to be shown.

(13) In this section—

- 'electronic communications device' means equipment or a device that is capable of transmitting images by electronic means;
- 'flashing images' means images which carry a risk that an individual with photosensitive epilepsy who viewed them would suffer a seizure as a result;
- 'harm' means—
  - (a) a seizure, or
  - (b) alarm or distress;
- 'individual with epilepsy' includes, but is not limited to, an individual with photosensitive epilepsy;
- 'send' includes transmit and publish (and related expressions are to be read accordingly).

Offence of Encouraging or Assisting Serious Self-harm

B18.32B   This completely new offence, the core wording of which is not dissimilar to the offence of encouraging or assisting suicide under the Suicide Act 1961, s. 2, comes into force on a date to be appointed and is contained in the Online Safety Act 2023, s. 184, which reads as follows:

Online Safety Act 2023, s. 184

(1) A person (D) commits an offence if—
   (a) D does a relevant act capable of encouraging or assisting the serious self-harm of another person, and
   (b) D's act was intended to encourage or assist the serious self-harm of another person.

(2) D 'does a relevant act' if D—
   (a) communicates in person,
   (b) sends, transmits or publishes a communication by electronic means,
   (c) shows a person such a communication,
   (d) publishes material by any means other than electronic means,
   (e) sends, gives, shows or makes available to a person—
      (i) material published as mentioned in paragraph (d), or
      (ii) any form of correspondence, or
   (f) sends, gives or makes available to a person an item on which data is stored electronically.

(3) 'Serious self-harm' means self-harm amounting to—
   (a) in England and Wales and Northern Ireland, grievous bodily harm within the meaning of the Offences Against the Person Act 1861, and
   (b) in Scotland, severe injury, and includes successive acts of self-harm which cumulatively reach that threshold.

(4) The person referred to in subsection (1)(a) and (b) need not be a specific person (or class of persons) known to, or identified by, D.

(5) D may commit an offence under this section whether or not serious self-harm occurs.

(6) If a person (D1) arranges for a person (D2) to do an act that is capable of encouraging or assisting the serious self-harm of another person and D2 does that act, D1 is to be treated as also having done it.

(7) In the application of subsection (1) to an act by D involving an electronic communication or a publication in physical form, it does not matter whether the content of the communication or publication is created by D (so for example, in the online context, the offence under this section may be committed by forwarding another person's direct message or sharing another person's post).

(8) In the application of subsection (1) to the sending, transmission or publication by electronic means of a communication consisting of or including a hyperlink to other content, the reference in subsection (2)(b) to the communication is to be read as including a reference to content accessed directly via the hyperlink.

(9) In the application of subsection (1) to an act by D involving an item on which data is stored electronically, the reference in subsection (2)(f) to the item is to be read as including a reference to content accessed by means of the item to which the person in receipt of the item is specifically directed by D.

(10) A provider of an internet service by means of which a communication is sent, transmitted or published is not to be regarded as a person who sends, transmits or publishes it.

(11) Any reference in this section to doing an act that is capable of encouraging the serious self-harm of another person includes a reference to doing so by threatening another person or otherwise putting pressure on another person to seriously self-harm.
   'Seriously self-harm' is to be interpreted consistently with subsection (3).

(12) Any reference to an act in this section, except in subsection (3), includes a reference to a course of conduct, and references to doing an act are to be read accordingly.

(13) In subsection (3) 'act' includes omission.

(14) A person who commits an offence under this section is liable—
   (a) on summary conviction in England and Wales, to imprisonment for a term not exceeding the general limit in a magistrates' court or a fine (or both);
   (b) on summary conviction in Scotland, to imprisonment for a term not exceeding 12 months or a fine not exceeding the statutory maximum (or both);
   (c) on summary conviction in Northern Ireland, to imprisonment for a term not exceeding 6 months or a fine not exceeding the statutory maximum (or both);
   (d) on conviction on indictment, to imprisonment for a term not exceeding 5 years or a fine (or both).

Extra-territorial Effect for Individuals Habitually Resident or Bodies Incorporated etc. within the Jurisdiction

B18.32C   The Online Safety Act 2023, s. 185, provides for a degree of extra-territorial application under certain conditions for acts done outside the UK for all the new offences created by ss. 179(1), 181(1), 183(1) and 184(1) (see **B18.27**, **B18.30**, **B18.43** and **B18.44** in this supplement). There is no such provision in relation to the offence created by s. 183(8) (showing flashing images by means of an electronic communications device).

Disclosing or Threatening to Disclose Private Sexual Photographs and Films with Intent to Cause Distress

B18.33   From a date to be appointed this offence under the CJCA 2015, ss. 33 to 35 (commonly referred to as 'revenge pornography') will be repealed by the Online Safety Act 2023, s. 190. In its place will be a new offence of sending etc. a photograph or film of genitals plus four new offences concerned with sharing or threatening to share an intimate photograph or film. These are created by the Online Safety Act 2023, s. 188, which inserts new ss. 66A to 66D into the SOA 2003. These new provisions are now dealt with at **B3.296** where the existing s. 66 offence of exposure of genitals is covered.

Section B20   Offences Relating to Dangerous Dogs and Animal Welfare

OFFENCES UNDER THE DANGEROUS DOGS ACT 1991

Control and Possession of Dogs Bred for Fighting

B20.1   The Dangerous Dogs (Designated Types) (England and Wales) Order 2023 (SI 2023 No. 1164) adds the XL Bully (aka the American Bully XL) to the list of dogs to which the Dangerous Dogs Act 1991, s. 1, applies. The Secretary of State is empowered to make such an Order under s. 1(1)(c) of the Act, in the case of a dog of a type that appears to be bred for fighting or to have the characteristics of a type bred for that purpose.

The Order came into force on 31 December 2023, after which it is an offence to breed, sell, advertise, transfer, offer for sale, gift, abandon or allow such dogs to stray, contrary to s. 1(2) of the Act. It will also be an offence under s. 1(2) for the owner or person in charge of an XL Bully to allow the dog to be in a public place without being muzzled and kept on a lead.

The offence of possessing or having custody of a dog to which s. 1 applies (i.e. the s. 1(3) offence) will not however come into force in respect of XL Bullies until 1 February 2024. A further instrument will specify what owners must do to lawfully possess such a dog after that date. This will no doubt involve obtaining a certificate of exemption under the Dangerous Dogs Exemption Schemes (England and Wales) Order 2015 (SI 2015 No. 138) or some analogous scheme. A scheme will be set up for the payment of compensation to owners of XL Bully types who arrange for them to be destroyed on or before 31 January 2024.

The basic and aggravated s. 3 offences of failing to keep a dog under proper control already (see **B20.5** in the main work) apply to the XL Bully as they do to any other type of dog.

OFFENCES UNDER THE ANIMALS (LOW-WELFARE ACTIVITIES ABROAD) ACT 2023

B20.30   With effect from 18 November 2023 the Animals (Low-Welfare Activities Abroad) Act 2023, s. 1, makes it an offence, within England (and Northern Ireland), to sell, or offer or arrange to sell, any right to observe or participate in an activity which:

(a)   involves an animal,

(b)   takes place outside the UK, and

(c) is of a description specified by regulations made (in respect of England) by the Secretary of State.

Section 2 of the Act also creates offences of advertising such activities, or of distributing such advertisements, etc., within the relevant jurisdiction.

Offences under the Act will be triable summarily anywhere in England and Wales, although the prohibitions do not apply to things done in Wales, and will be punishable by a fine, or by the imposition of a penalty in lieu of prosecution (see s. 4 and sch.).

The activities to which the Act applies have yet to be specified, but it is clear that the Act will be targeted primarily against the promotion of popular tourist shows in which animals such as elephants or bears perform clever but unnatural routines or tricks, having been trained to do so by methods that are cruel or inhumane, and/or are kept in conditions that would be considered unlawful under applicable UK animal welfare legislation. Any non-human vertebrate (including, e.g., a bird, shark, reptile or dolphin) potentially falls within the protection of the Act.

Section B21   Offences Relating to Money Laundering and the Proceeds of Criminal Conduct

OFFENCES UNDER THE PROCEEDS OF CRIME ACT 2002

Offences of Concealment etc.

Sections 182 and 183 of the Economic Crime and Corporate Transparency Act 2023 (ECCTA) **B21.13** create new defences to offences under the POCA 2002, ss. 327 to 329 (see **B21.17** in this supplement). By virtue of the ECCTA 2023, s. 182(2), the following provisions were inserted into s. 327 of the POCA 2002 with effect from 26 October 2023 (ECCTA 2023, s. 219(2)(f)):

Proceeds of Crime Act 2002, s. 327

(2D) A person ('P') who does an act mentioned in subsection (1) does not commit an offence under that subsection if—
(a) P is carrying on business in the regulated sector that is not excluded business,
(b) P does the act, in the course of that business—
(i) in transferring or handing over to the customer or client property of, or owing to, a customer or client, and
(ii) for the purposes of the termination of P's business relationship with 4the customer or client,
(c) the total value of the criminal property so transferred or handed over to the customer or client by P for those purposes is less than the threshold amount determined under section 339A for the act, and
(d) before the act is done, P has complied with the customer due diligence duties.
(2E) For the purposes of subsection (2D)—
(a) business is 'excluded' if it is of a description specified in regulations made by the Secretary of State for the purposes of this subsection;
(b) a reference to property being transferred or handed over to the customer or client includes a reference to property being transferred or handed over to another person at the direction of the customer or client;
(c) 'customer due diligence duties' means all duties imposed on P in relation to the customer or client by regulation 28(2), (3), (3A), (4), (8) or (10) of the Money Laundering, Terrorist Financing and Transfer of Funds (Information on the Payer) Regulations 2017 (S.I. 2017/692) (customer due diligence measures).

By virtue of the ECCTA 2023, s. 183(2), the following provisions were inserted into s. 327 of the POCA 2002 with effect from 15 January 2024 (SI 2023 No. 1206, reg. 3(f)):

Proceeds of Crime Act 2002, s. 327

(2F) A person ('P') who does an act mentioned in paragraph (c), (d) or (e) of subsection (1) does not commit an offence under that subsection if—

(a) P is carrying on business in the regulated sector,

(b) P does the act in the course of that business, on behalf of a customer or client, in operating an account or accounts maintained with P or in connection with holding any property for the customer or client,

(c) at the time of the act, P knows or suspects that part but not all of the funds in the account or accounts, or of the property so held, is criminal property ('the relevant criminal property'),

(d) it is not possible, at the time the act takes place, to identify the part of the funds or property that is the relevant criminal property, and

(e) the value of the funds in the account or accounts, or of the property so held, is not, as a direct or indirect result of the act, less than the value of the relevant criminal property at the time of the act.

(2G) Where subsection (2F) applies—

(a) if P does the act in operating an account or accounts, the funds in the account or accounts immediately after the act are assumed to include the relevant criminal property, and

(b) if P does the act in connection with holding any property for the customer or client, such of that property as is held by P immediately after the act is assumed to include the relevant criminal property.

B21.15 **Procedure and Sentence (Offences under ss. 327, 328 and 329)**   See CrimPD 5.10 (see PD5.10) for the allocation of business within the Crown Court.

B21.17 **Elements**   Two new defences to charges under ss. 327 to 329 were inserted into the POCA 2002 by the ECCTA 2023. The reason for these defences is set out in the explanatory notes to the Bill that became the ECCTA:

> Certain businesses (especially those in the regulated sector, defined in Schedule 9 to POCA) deal with property belonging to clients or customers. Where they suspect money laundering, it is common for those businesses to prevent access to any of that property, even where their suspicion relates only to part of the value of that property. This can result in disproportionate economic hardship to individuals unable to access their property, for example to pay rent or living expenses.

The first defence, inserted by the ECCTA 2023, s. 182, with effect from 26 October 2023 (s. 219(2)(f)), relates to 'exiting and paying away'. When for the purposes of the termination of a business relationship with the customer or client a business in the regulated sector transfers or hands over client property worth £1,000 or more (POCA 2002, s. 339A), no offence under ss. 327 to 329 is committed, as long as the business has complied with its due diligence duties set out in the Money Laundering, Terrorist Financing and Transfer of Funds (Information on the Payer) Regulations 2017 (SI 2017 No. 692), reg. 28.

The second defence, inserted by the ECCTA 2023, s. 183, with effect from 15 January 2024 (SI 2023 No. 1206, reg. 3(f)), relates to 'mixed property transactions' and applies where a business in the regulated sector holds either funds in an account or property, and knows or suspects that part but not all of the funds or property is criminal property but it is not possible to identify the part that represents criminal property. A person acting in the course of the business may carry out an act in respect of the operation of the account or in connection with holding property for the customer or client as long as the act does not reduce the overall value of funds or of the property to below the value of the relevant criminal property. The funds left in an account or the property still held is assumed to include the relevant criminal property.

Money Laundering Arrangements

B21.18 Sections 182 and 183 of the ECCTA 2023 create new defences to offences under ss. 327 to 329 of the POCA 2002 (see **B21.17** in this supplement). By virtue of the ECCTA 2023, s. 182(3), the following provisions were inserted into s. 328 of the POCA 2002 with effect from 26 October 2023 (ECCTA 2023, s. 219(2)(f)):

(6) A person ('P') who does an act mentioned in subsection (1) does not commit an offence under that subsection if—
  (a) P is carrying on business in the regulated sector that is not excluded business,
  (b) P does the act, in the course of that business—
    (i) in transferring or handing over to the customer or client property of, or owing to, a customer or client, and
    (ii) for the purposes of the termination of P's business relationship with the customer or client,
  (c) the total value of the criminal property so transferred or handed over to the customer or client by P for those purposes is less than the threshold amount determined under section 339A for the act, and
  (d) before the act is done, P has complied with the customer due diligence duties.
(7) For the purposes of subsection (6)—
  (a) business is 'excluded' if it is of a description specified in regulations made by the Secretary of State for the purposes of this subsection;
  (b) a reference to property being transferred or handed over to the customer or client includes a reference to property being transferred or handed over to another person at the direction of the customer or client;
  (c) 'customer due diligence duties' means all duties imposed on P in relation to the customer or client by regulation 28(2), (3), (3A), (4), (8) or (10) of the Money Laundering, Terrorist Financing and Transfer of Funds (Information on the Payer) Regulations 2017 (S.I. 2017/692) (customer due diligence measures).

By virtue of the ECCTA 2023, s. 183(3), the following provisions were inserted into s. 328 of the POCA 2002 with effect from 15 January 2024 (SI 2023 No. 1206, reg. 3(f)):

(8) A person ('P') who does an act mentioned in paragraph (c), (d) or (e) of subsection (1) does not commit an offence under that subsection if—
  (a) P is carrying on business in the regulated sector,
  (b) P does the act in the course of that business, on behalf of a customer or client, in operating an account or accounts maintained with P or in connection with holding any property for the customer or client,
  (c) at the time of the act, P knows or suspects that part but not all of the funds in the account or accounts, or of the property so held, is criminal property ('the relevant criminal property'),
  (d) it is not possible, at the time the act takes place, to identify the part of the funds or property that is the relevant criminal property, and
  (e) the value of the funds in the account or accounts, or of the property so held, is not, as a direct or indirect result of the act, less than the value of the relevant criminal property at the time of the act.
(9) Where subsection (8) applies—
  (a) if P does the act in operating an account or accounts, the funds in the account or accounts immediately after the act are assumed to include the relevant criminal property, and
  (b) if P does the act in connection with holding any property for the customer or client, such of that property as is held by P immediately after the act is assumed to include the relevant criminal property.

Offences of Acquisition, Use or Possession

Sections 182 and 183 of the ECCTA 2023 create new defences to offences under ss. 327 to 329 **B21.24** of the POCA 2002 (see **B21.17** in this supplement). By virtue of the ECCTA 2023, s. 182(4), the following provisions were inserted into s. 329 of the POCA 2002 with effect from 26 October 2023 (ECCTA 2023, s. 219(2)(f)):

(2D) A person ('P') who does an act mentioned in subsection (1) does not commit an offence under that subsection if—
  (a) P is carrying on business in the regulated sector that is not excluded business,

(b) P does the act, in the course of that business—
   (i) in transferring or handing over to the customer or client property of, or owing to, a customer or client, and
   (ii) for the purposes of the termination of P's business relationship with the customer or client,

(c) the total value of the criminal property so transferred or handed over to the customer or client by P for those purposes is less than the threshold amount determined under section 339A for the act, and

(d) before the act is done, P has complied with the customer due diligence duties.

(2E) For the purposes of subsection (2D)—
   (a) business is 'excluded' if it is of a description specified in regulations made by the Secretary of State for the purposes of this subsection;
   (b) a reference to property being transferred or handed over to the customer or client includes a reference to property being transferred or handed over to another person at the direction of the customer or client;
   (c) 'customer due diligence duties' means all duties imposed on P in relation to the customer or client by regulation 28(2), (3), (3A), (4), (8) or (10) of the Money Laundering, Terrorist Financing and Transfer of Funds (Information on the Payer) Regulations 2017 (S.I. 2017/692) (customer due diligence measures).

By virtue of the ECCTA 2023, s. 183(4), the following provisions were inserted into s. 329 of the POCA 2002 with effect from 15 January 2024 (SI 2023 No. 1206, reg. 3(f)):

(2F) A person ('P') who does an act mentioned in paragraph (c), (d) or (e) of subsection (1) does not commit an offence under that subsection if—
   (a) P is carrying on business in the regulated sector,
   (b) P does the act in the course of that business, on behalf of a customer or client, in operating an account or accounts maintained with P or in connection with holding any property for the customer or client,
   (c) at the time of the act, P knows or suspects that part but not all of the funds in the account or accounts, or of the property so held, is criminal property ('the relevant criminal property'),
   (d) it is not possible, at the time the act takes place, to identify the part of the funds or property that is the relevant criminal property, and
   (e) the value of the funds in the account or accounts, or of the property so held, is not, as a direct or indirect result of the act, less than the value of the relevant criminal property at the time of the act.

(2G) Where subsection (2F) applies—
   (a) if P does the act in operating an account or accounts, the funds in the account or accounts immediately after the act are assumed to include the relevant criminal property, and
   (b) if P does the act in connection with holding any property for the customer or client, such of that property as is held by P immediately after the act is assumed to include the relevant criminal property.

B21.28 **Sentence** In *Cooper* [2023] EWCA Crim 945, the Court of Appeal gave the following guidance on the approach to totality when sentencing a defendant for 'an offence contrary to the Proceeds of Crime Act 2002 in respect of the criminal benefit from offences for which the defendant also falls to be sentenced':

10. There is a broad spectrum of cases involving the combination of 2002 Act offences and other underlying, primary, offending. At one end of the spectrum, the 2002 Act offence does not involve any additional culpability or harm and does not aggravate the seriousness of the primary offence. At the other end, the offending contrary to the 2002 Act is markedly distinct from the primary offending and involves significant additional culpability and harm, aggravating the primary offence to an extent that would not otherwise be reflected in the sentence for that offence if considered in isolation …

(1) Where the 2002 Act offence adds nothing to the culpability and harm involved in the primary offence then there should be no additional penalty. In such a case it is appropriate to impose concurrent sentences, with no upward adjustment.

(2) Where the 2002 Act offence involves additional criminality (whether increasing the culpability or harm, or both) beyond that involved in the other offences for which sentences are imposed, an additional penalty should be imposed.

The seriousness of the additional criminality is to be assessed by reference to the culpability of the offender and the harm caused by the 2002 Act offending. In such a case the sentencing judge may either impose concurrent sentences with an appropriate upward adjustment, or consecutive sentences, often with a downward adjustment.

11. It is thus important, in each case, to identify whether the 2002 Act offence involves additional culpability and/or harm, and, if so, the extent. Examples of cases where there is such an additional factor include those where the 2002 Act offence:

(1) takes place over a different period from the primary offending.
(2) involves additional or different criminal property, beyond the proceeds of the primary offending.
(3) makes it more difficult to detect the primary offending.
(4) involves dealing with the proceeds of the primary offending in a way which increases the risk that victims will not recover their losses, or that confiscation proceedings will be frustrated.
(5) creates additional victims. This may arise where the proceeds of the primary offending are used to make further transactions which are then thrown into question, resulting in loss to the innocent parties to those transactions.
(6) involves additional planning or sophistication, extending the culpability that might otherwise attach to the primary offending.
(7) assists in the continuation of offending. In this regard, in *Alexander* [[2011] EWCA Crim 89] at [13] Moses LJ drew attention to '[t]he pernicious nature of money laundering and its capacity for enabling the proceeds of drug dealing to be not only concealed but to assist in the continuation of such crimes' …

12. Conversely, where the 2002 Act constitutes nothing more than the continued possession of the proceeds of the primary offence, then there is unlikely to be any additional culpability or harm beyond that reflected in the primary offence. In that event, it would be wrong in principle to impose any additional penalty. If an immediate custodial sentence is imposed for the primary offence this principle requires a sentence for the 2002 offence that runs concurrently with it.

Failure to Disclose Possible Money Laundering

Section 330 of the POCA 2002 was amended by the ECCTA 2023, s. 184, with effect from 26   **B21.32**
October 2023 (s. 219(2)(g)). Subsection 7A was renumbered as subsection 7C. A new subsection 7D has been inserted which provides a defence to the money laundering offences for a person who carries out a status check or immigration check under the Immigration Act 2014. The relevant part of s. 330 now reads as follows:

Proceeds of Crime Act 2002, s. 330

(7C) Nor does a person commit an offence under this section if—
    (a) he knows, or believes on reasonable grounds, that the money laundering is occurring in a particular country or territory outside the United Kingdom, and
    (b) the money laundering—
        (i)   is not unlawful under the criminal law applying in that country or territory, and
        (ii) is not of a description prescribed in an order made by the Secretary of State.
(7D) Nor does a person commit an offence under this section if—
    (a) the information or other matter mentioned in subsection (3) consists of or includes information that was obtained only in consequence of the carrying out of a status check under section 40 of the Immigration Act 2014 or an immigration check under section 40A of that Act or both, and
    (b) but for the information so obtained the person would not have reasonable grounds for knowing or suspecting that another person is engaged in money laundering.

Penalties and Procedure for Offences under ss. 330 to 332 See CrimPD 5.10 (see **PD5.10**) for   **B21.34**
the allocation of business within the Crown Court.

Section B22   Modern Slavery, Trafficking and Immigration Offences

CONSIDERATIONS PRIOR TO PROSECUTION OF VICTIMS OF TRAFFICKING OR SLAVERY

Abuse of Process and Public Interest Considerations for Cases Prior to the Modern Slavery Act 2015

B22.18   In *AJW* [2023] EWCA Crim 803, the Court derived principles for abuse of process pre-dating the MSA 2015 from *AFU* [2023] EWCA Crim 23, at [105]–[113]. *AJW* concerned a sham marriage conspiracy. D was convicted of an offence under the Immigration Act 1971, s. 24A. The facts as accepted at appeal were that D was only 16 at the time of an attempt to marry a 43-year-old man and had a background of having been previously exploited. The Court considered the issue was whether the applicant would or might not have been prosecuted in the public interest. In this case, it was not in the public interest to prosecute and the conviction was unsafe.

National Referral Mechanism

B22.21   The Home Office's *Statutory Guidance for England and Wales for the Modern Slavery Act 2015* was updated on 9 October 2023 (tinyurl.com/4aw9cmvf).

STATUTORY DEFENCE UNDER THE MODERN SLAVERY ACT 2015, s. 45

B22.26   Compulsion is not a requirement under the MSA 2015, s. 45(4), namely the defence that applies to an accused aged under 18 at the time of the offence. In *ADG* [2023] EWCA Crim 1309, convictions were quashed when the jury were wrongly directed with compulsion being referenced in cases involving defendants under 18 years of age at the time of the index allegations. See the *Crown Court Compendium*, ch. 18-6, for the importance of not conflating separate and distinct elements of defence for those aged 18 and older and those under 18 at the time of the acts.

The Home Office's *Statutory Guidance for England and Wales for the Modern Slavery Act 2015* was updated on 9 October 2023 (tinyurl.com/4aw9cmvf).

'Compulsion' or 'compelled': MSA 2015, s. 45(1)(b)

B22.32   Compulsion is not a requirement under the MSA 2015, s. 45(4), when the statutory defence is relied upon for an accused who was under 18 at the time of the index allegation (*ADG* [2023] EWCA Crim 1309).

County Lines Offending

B22.36   The Home Office's *Statutory Guidance for England and Wales for the Modern Slavery Act 2015* was updated on 9 October 2023 (tinyurl.com/4aw9cmvf).

ILLEGAL ENTRY AND OTHER OFFENCES

B22.38   Further sections of the Illegal Migration Act 2023 came into force on 28 September 2023 (Illegal Migration Act 2023 (Commencement No. 1) Regulations 2023 (SI 2023 No. 989)). Key amendments relate to the powers for immigration detention and retention of electronic devices from those liable to be detained. Section 12(1)b of the Act allows for a person to be detained in immigration detention for such period as, in the opinion of the Secretary of State, is reasonably necessary to enable examination or removal to be carried out; for a decision to be made; or for directions to be given. Section 15 confers powers to search people liable to be detained under the Immigration Act 1971, sch. 2, para. 16(2C), as well as vehicles, premises and property for things on which certain information is or may be stored in electronic form. The Illegal Migration Act 2023, sch. 2, para. 8, allows for seizure of a relevant article/electronic device and retention for as long as the Secretary of State considers necessary for a purpose relating to a relevant function.

Sentence

For offences where D knowingly arrives in the UK without a valid entry clearance under the Immigration Act 1971, s. 24(D1), the custody threshold would generally be passed. The Court in *Ginar* [2023] EWCA Crim 1121 considered sentences of 12 months' imprisonment to be appropriate prior to considering credit and other circumstances. The Court provided guidance for sentencing, noting the predominant purpose in sentencing for this type of case was protection of the public, and upheld a sentence of eight months. Key to culpability was that D knew that D was trying to arrive in the UK in an unlawful manner. Culpability would be increased if D provided the means of arrival in the UK; if D tried to involve others (particularly children) in the offence; or if D was seeking to enter to engage in criminal activity.

B22.40

Considerations relevant to harm included the undermining of border control; risk of death or serious injury to D and others; risk and cost to those trying to intercept or rescue and potential disruption of legitimate travel in a busy shipping lane.

Specific aggravating factors included relevant previous convictions, high levels of planning beyond that inherent in an attempt to arrive in the UK and a history of unsuccessful applications for leave to enter. Mitigating factors included where D had become involved due to coercion or pressure; if circumstances included arguable grounds for claiming asylum; if injury has been suffered in crossing, and if D had been misled as to what to expect in the UK.

B

Part B   Offences

SUPPLEMENT TO PART C
ROAD TRAFFIC OFFENCES

Section C7   Sentencing

DISQUALIFICATION GENERALLY

Interim Disqualification

By virtue of the RTOA 1988, s. 26(4), the maximum period of an interim disqualification is six **C7.31** months, so if D is only sentenced after that time, the effect of any interim disqualification is limited to that period (*Marshall* [2023] EWCA Crim 964, where the interim disqualification on D had been imposed around 16 months before D was sentenced). While the sentencing court ought to be aware of the position, the effect of any interim disqualification is dealt with automatically as an administrative exercise under s. 26(12) (see also *Smith (Kenneth)* [2023] EWCA Crim 1097 and *Palmer* [2023] EWCA Crim 1180).

Disqualification Pending Passing of Driving Test

It is unlawful to disqualify until an extended driving test is passed for an offence of driving while **C7.33** disqualified (*Janjua* [2023] EWCA Crim 1172), although disqualifying until an ordinary test is passed is permissible.

Length of Disqualification

For a 21-year-old D sentenced for dangerous driving, driving while disqualified and using a **C7.36** motor vehicle without insurance, disqualification for ten years was regarded as manifestly excessive and five years substituted, which also enabled correction of the *Needham* extension period, which would otherwise have been unavailable as a result of the CAA 1981, s. 11(3) (*Mohammed* [2023] EWCA Crim 1057). This period of disqualification would serve to punish D and protect the public while allowing for D's potential rehabilitation.

The importance of being clear when disqualifying was stressed in *Martin* [2023] EWCA Crim **C7.37** 791, where what had occurred at the sentencing hearing was described as an 'unsatisfactory state of opaque uncertainty'. It was also emphasised that every disqualification takes effect and can only run from the date on which it is imposed.

ENDORSEMENT

A further example of a court falling into error and both disqualifying and incorrectly endorsing **C7.47** penalty points for the same offence is *Janjua* [2023] EWCA Crim 1172.

SUPPLEMENT TO PART D
PROCEDURE

Section D1   Powers of Investigation

ENTRY AND SEARCH UNDER WARRANT

Search Warrant Issued by Judge

The Application   In *R (Metropolitan Police Commissioner) v Kingston-upon-Thames Crown Court* [2023] EWHC 1938 (Admin), the Divisional Court held that the Crown Court was permitted to have recourse to closed material proceedings when hearing a firearms appeal under the FA 1968, s. 44 (following *Al Rawi v Security Service* [2011] UKSC 34, *R (Haralambous) v St Albans Crown Court* [2018] UKSC 1 and *Competition and Markets Authority v Concordia International RX* [2018] EWHC 3158 (Ch)). The Divisional Court found that a Special Advocate could only be appointed during closed material proceedings if there was a 'clear justification for doing so', recognising that such an appointment could add time, complexity and cost to proceedings. However, the Divisional Court declined to find that such an appointment could only be made in 'exceptional circumstances' (see also *R (Terra Services Ltd) v NCA* [2020] EWHC 130 (Admin)). Annex 2 to the judgment sets out the recommended procedure to be followed in appeals pursuant to the FA 1968, s. 44, where an application is made for closed material proceedings.

D1.171

EXTRACTION OF INFORMATION FROM ELECTRONIC DEVICES

The Police, Crime, Sentencing and Courts Act 2022 (Extraction of information from electronic devices) (Amendment of Schedule 3) Regulations 2023 (SI 2023 No. 575) came into force on 26 May 2023. These Regulations amend the PCSCA 2022, sch. 3, part 1 (which is the list of authorised persons in relation to all purposes within the PCSCA 2022, ss. 37 and 41) to include 'a member of the Royal Navy Police, the Royal Military Police or the Royal Air Force Police' (at the same time omitting them from part 2 where they appeared previously).

D1.209

Section D3   Courts, Parties and Abuse of Process

ABUSE OF PROCESS: THE POWER TO STAY PROCEEDINGS

Meaning of 'Abuse of Process'

In *BKR* [2023] EWCA Crim 903, D had pleaded guilty to a number of counts but not guilty to one. The judge asked the prosecution whether they wished to proceed on that count and gave an indication that, if D was convicted on that count, there would be no addition to the overall sentence. The prosecution indicated that, despite no additional sentence being imposed, it was in the public interest — including that of the complainant — that the case should proceed. The judge, who described the case as 'utterly pointless', invited the prosecution to reconsider their position. The prosecution remained of the same view that it was in the public interest to proceed. The judge then stayed the proceedings as an abuse of process, having concluded that a trial would offend the court's sense of justice and propriety (*Horseferry Road Magistrates, ex parte Bennett* [1994] 1 AC 42) or undermine public confidence in the criminal justice system and bring it into disrepute (*Latif* [1996] 1 WLR 104; *Maxwell* [2010] UKSC 48), i.e. a 'limb two' abuse case. The prosecution appealed under the CJA 2003, s. 58, submitting that the judge erred in law. The Court of Appeal allowed the appeal, holding that the judge had no power to refuse to allow a prosecution because, in the judge's view, it ought not to have been brought; a stay could be ordered only if the prosecution was vexatious or oppressive so as to amount an abuse of process.

D3.66

Proceedings cannot be held to amount to an abuse of process merely because the judge takes the view that the prosecution should not be brought (*DPP v Humphrys* [1977] AC 1). The key question in the present case was whether continuation of the prosecution would amount to a 'sufficient affront to the court's sense of justice to enable the court to stay the proceedings' (per Edis LJ, at [41]). His lordship made it clear that the judge was 'quite entitled to express her views on the proper application of the public interest test', and suggested that 'many Crown Court judges, faced with the backlog of serious and important cases waiting to be tried, would probably agree with her that this prosecution was not in the public interest' (at [51]). It was entirely proper for the judge 'to ensure that the decision to continue with the case had been taken at an appropriately senior level and after proper consideration of the Code for Crown Prosecutors'. However, this did not mean that continuation of the prosecution was an abuse of process (at [52]). The decision to prosecute has been 'entrusted by Parliament to the CPS' and, ordinarily, it is 'no part of the function of a judge to say who should be prosecuted and who should not be'. The criticism of the decision to continue the prosecution did not come close to the sort of misconduct by the executive that is required to establish 'limb two' abuse (at [53], [58]).

Delay

D3.81 **Sexual Offences and Delay**   Where D is charged with historic sexual abuse, the judge should (where appropriate on the facts) warn the jury that delays can place D at a material disadvantage and, the longer the delay, the more difficult it is for D to meet those allegations (see, e.g., *PS* [2013] EWCA Crim 992). In *MT* [2023] EWCA Crim 558, the Court of Appeal (at [52]) commended a direction (if warranted on the facts) which tells the jury that they should take the delay into account in D's favour when deciding whether the prosecution have made them sure of guilt.

Failing to Obtain, Losing or Destroying Evidence

D3.83 In *Watson* [2023] EWCA Crim 1016, the investigation into a murder that occurred in 1994 was reopened on the basis of new DNA evidence. The judge rejected a submission of abuse of process on the basis that it would be impossible for D to have a fair trial because of missing exhibits. The Court of Appeal dismissed an appeal against conviction, holding that what might have been revealed by testing which could not be carried out was speculative and there was no demonstrable prejudice suffered by D. The Court noted that, in *Ebrahim* [2001] EWHC Admin 130, Brooke LJ said (at [17]) that a stay should be granted in such cases only in 'exceptional circumstances'. In *Watson*, Holroyde LJ said (at [57]) that this is not a free-standing legal test; rather, 'it reflects the fact that the cases in which it will be possible for an accused to show that a fair trial is impossible, and in which it is appropriate to grant a stay, are very rare'. A stay may be granted 'if — very unusually — the accused can show that the effect of the absence of evidence or exhibits is to make it impossible for him to have a fair trial'.

The Court of Appeal also considered the relevance of fault on the part of the prosecution. In *Ebrahim*, it was held (at [16]) that the power to stay existed only where the prosecution were in breach of a duty to obtain or retain material. This may be taken to suggest that there has to be some fault on the part of the prosecution. However, in *Clay v South Cambridgeshire Justices* [2014] EWHC 321 (Admin), Pitchford LJ said (at [46]) that the question of whether D can have a fair trial 'does not logically depend on whether anyone was "at fault" in causing the exigency that created the unfairness'. In the present case, Holroyde LJ (at [61]) said that the Court regarded Pitchford LJ's approach as clearly correct:

> As we have emphasised, we are concerned here with a type of category 1 abuse of process, where the court must focus on the effect on the fairness of the trial of evidence no longer being available. Cases in which there has been no breach of duty, but a fair trial is impossible because of missing evidence, will be very rare; but we cannot say they will never occur. The staying of proceedings because of a category 1 abuse of the process is not a punitive jurisdiction, and we can see no reason why the exercise of it should necessarily be dependent on a finding of fault. Negligence or deliberate breach of duty on the part of the police or the prosecution may of course be relevant to the court's exercise of its discretion, but it is not a necessary prerequisite of it.

OPEN JUSTICE

Freedom of the Media to Report Court Proceedings

In *R (Marandi) v Westminster Magistrates' Court* [2023] EWHC 587 (Admin), forfeiture **D3.122** proceedings were brought by the NCA against members of a family who were alleged to have been participants in, or beneficiaries of, a complex money-laundering operation. The claimant sought an order that his name be withheld from the public in the proceedings before the court, and for an order under the CCA 1981, s. 11, prohibiting the publication of his name or any information likely to lead to his identification in connection with the proceedings. The judge concluded that it was appropriate and necessary for an order to be made. At the end of the forfeiture proceedings, the judge lifted the reporting restriction order (RRO), being of the opinion that the claimant was not a peripheral figure to the main proceedings. The claimant sought judicial review. The Administrative Court dismissed the claim, holding that the starting point for a judge when determining whether to make a RRO was that, as a general rule, the administration of justice had to be done in public and the media had to be able to report the proceedings fully and contemporaneously, including mentioning names. Any restriction on the usual rules would be exceptional and had to be based on necessity. The threshold question would be whether the measure which allowed the disclosure of the name of a non-party to the proceedings and consequent publicity would amount to a very serious interference with their right to respect for their private and family life. The burden was on the party seeking the RRO to establish it was necessary on the basis of clear and cogent evidence, which had to be closely examined. In the present case, the judge had conducted the necessary balancing process and had determined that the derogation from open justice that anonymity would represent was no longer shown to be justified as both necessary for the protection of the claimant's ECHR, Article 8, rights and proportionate to that aim.

Warby LJ reiterated that the 'starting point is the common law principle of open justice' (at [43(1)]), and that the general principles that '(a) justice is administered in public, and (b) everything said in court is reportable, both encompass the mention of names' (at [43(2)]). When considering an application for derogation from these principles, the appropriate test is one of 'necessity' (at [43(3)]). The 'threshold question' is whether the measure in question (in this case, allowing the disclosure of the claimant's name) would amount to an interference with the claimant's right to respect for his private and family life, the likely effects of which have to be proved (at [43(4)]). The next stage is the 'balancing exercise', namely 'whether the consequences of disclosure would be so serious an interference with the claimant's rights that it was necessary and proportionate to interfere with the ordinary rule of open justice' (at [43(5)]). This requires 'close examination of the weight to be given to the specific rights that are at stake on the facts of the case'; hence the need for 'clear and cogent evidence' (at [43(6)]).

Mostyn J, agreeing with Warby LJ as to the outcome of the case, also noted a number of procedural failures, and summarised (at [85]) what was required in applications for reporting restriction orders:

(i)   An application for a RRO must be accompanied by clear and cogent evidence, which demonstrates that without the order, justice could not be done. The evidence must be admissible. A non-expert opinion expressed in a solicitor's letter is not likely to be worth the paper it is written on.

(ii) Save in situations of great urgency, an application for a RRO should be served no fewer than 3 clear days before the hearing.

(iii) A draft order should be served at the same time.

(iv) It would be good practice to notify the media …

(v)   It would be good practice to permit the press to attend the hearing of the application and to make submissions either through an advocate with rights of audience or in writing.

(vi) Where the evidence is incomplete and findings have not been made, the better course, if the court is satisfied that anonymity should be granted, may be to make a temporary RRO with a return date or other provision for the matter to be reconsidered before finalising the public judgment or shortly following its hand-down.

D

Part D   Procedure

(vii)   The order, whether temporary or final, should delineate its extra-territorial effect and provide for the press and any other affected person to have liberty to apply.

(viii)   If the order made is a final order it should provide for an end-date.

Section D7   Bail

TEXT OF THE BAIL ACT 1976

D7.146   The BA 1976, s. 6(7), as amended by SI 2023 No. 1108, reg. 2(1), with effect from 18 October 2023, now provides:

(7)   A person who is convicted summarily of an offence under subsection (1) or (2) above and is not committed to the Crown Court for sentence shall be liable to imprisonment for a term not exceeding 3 months or to a fine not exceeding level 5 on the standard scale or to both and a person who is so committed for sentence or is dealt with as for such a contempt shall be liable to imprisonment for a term not exceeding 12 months or to a fine or to both.

Section D22   Summary Trial: The Course of the Trial

TRIAL ON THE PAPERS BY A SINGLE JUSTICE

Automatic Online Conviction and Penalty for Certain Summary Offences

D22.34   The MCA 1980, ss. 16G to 16M (automatic online conviction), were brought into force with effect from 7 November 2023 by the Judicial Review and Courts Act 2022 (Commencement No. 4) Regulations 2023 (SI 2023 No. 1194). The offences to which these provisions apply will be specified in subsequent regulations.

Section D23   Sentencing in the Magistrates' Court

COMMITTAL FOR SENTENCE

Committal under the Sentencing Act 2020, s. 20

D23.58   In *Clark* [2023] EWCA Crim 309, D appeared before a magistrates' court charged with assault occasioning actual bodily harm and breach of a restraining order. When the charges were put, he entered a guilty plea to the breach offence, and pleaded not guilty to the assault. Thereafter, both matters were transferred to the Crown Court: however, the sending sheet in the magistrates' court recorded incorrectly that both offences were sent for trial. At the Crown Court, D pleaded guilty to common assault (in place of the actual bodily harm). On appeal, the lawfulness of the sentence passed was raised. The Court of Appeal held that this was not a case where a 'mere administrative error' had occurred. The sending by the magistrates' court was a sending for trial, which was obviously invalid because a guilty plea had been entered, and there was therefore no jurisdiction in the magistrates' court to send the breach offence for trial. The sending sheet did not confirm that the 'plea before venue' procedure had been followed. Moreover, having made the decision to send for trial and recorded it in the sending sheet, the magistrates' court was *functus officio* and any attempts afterwards (even by the magistrates' court itself) to correct the error were a nullity. Any attempt by the Crown Court to exercise powers under the Courts Act 2003, s. 66, would have been equally invalid, since that power did not extend to correcting errors in committals for sentence once the magistrates' court was *functus officio* and no longer had jurisdiction to act. In those circumstances, the sending for trial in respect of the breach offence had to be quashed and a lawful committal effected. The court reconstituted itself as a Divisional Court to set aside the sentence.

However, *Clark* was not followed in *Butt* [2023] EWCA Crim 1131. In that case, D was charged with seven offences. At the magistrates' court, he indicated not guilty pleas to three charges and guilty pleas to the other four. The sending sheet did not reflect these pleas accurately, but the Better Case Management form did.

Edis LJ said that identifying the power exercised by the magistrates' court is a question of fact. The sending sheet is, presumptively, an accurate record of the power that the magistrates' court purported to exercise, but it is not conclusive. It follows that, if there is evidence to suggest that the sending sheet is inaccurate, then a factual issue may have to be resolved as to what power the magistrates' court purported to exercise (at [66]). His lordship added (at [99]) that the Better Case Management form 'will often be a valuable piece of evidence' as to what occurred.

Where D is committed for sentence without first having been convicted, the Crown Court has no jurisdiction to deal with the case (subject to the possibility of correcting the position by use of the Courts Act 2003, s. 66, to take a plea: see [81]). Where the 'plea before venue' procedure required by the MCA 1980, s. 17A, is not followed, that invalidates the subsequent proceedings (see [82]).

So far as remedial action is concerned, Edis LJ said (at [83]) that, if the consequence of the error is that the Crown Court has no jurisdiction, then the matter can be remedied by the magistrates' court using the power under the MCA 1980, s. 142. A judge sitting in the Crown Court can use the Courts Act 2003, s. 66, to exercise the powers of a district judge under the MCA 1980, s. 142. However, even where that power exists, it may not necessarily be appropriate to exercise it.

Turning to the decision in *Clark* [2023] EWCA Crim 309, Edis LJ said (at [90]) that:

> Where the decision in *Clark* is inconsistent with *Ayhan* … is in its decision that the Crown Court was rendered powerless by the defects in the sending sheet. In our judgment, that creates a situation where we are entitled and bound to choose between inconsistent decisions of this court … Given the weight of the authority culminating in *Ayhan* and *Gould*, we consider that we are bound to choose to follow those cases.

Edis LJ concluded (at [91]) that, when confronted with an apparently defective sending sheet (or similar), the Crown Court:

(i)   may hold that the defect is so fundamental that nothing has happened which gives jurisdiction to the Crown Court … If that is so, the case has not left the magistrates' court and the Crown Court judge may lawfully have recourse to the Courts Act 2003 s.66 and deal with the case as a DJ(MC); [or]

(ii) may apply *Ayhan* [2011] EWCA Crim 3184… and deal with the case as validly committed if the magistrates' court had power to commit and the … sending sheet has failed to identify that power …

Edis LJ said (at [95]) that where the magistrates have a power to commit for sentence, which they exercise validly, the mis-recording of that decision as a sending for trial does not invalidate the committal for sentence. It is 'the order which the magistrates make which gives the Crown Court jurisdiction, not the way in which it is recorded'. Where the Crown Court is satisfied that the magistrates made a correct order despite the terms of the sending sheet, then it may proceed to deal with the case.

Edis LJ (at [91(i)]) also observed that, where the original decision of the magistrates' court is a nullity, and so the order by the magistrates' court is treated as being of no effect by the Crown Court (so that the case is deemed to still be in the magistrates' court), it was suggested in *Gould* (at [80]) that a quashing order from the Divisional Court may be required. However, if the Crown Court judge, sitting as a district judge, corrects the original order under the MCA 1980, s. 142, 'the problem does not arise'.

D

Part D   Procedure

The same bench also sat as a Divisional Court to hear the related appeals in *DPP v Luton Crown Court* [2023] EWHC 2464 (Admin). This was an application by the DPP for the quashing of two (unrelated) Crown Court decisions to decline jurisdiction because there had been an error in the procedure adopted by the magistrates' court in sending or committing the case to the Crown Court.

In the first case, the Crown Court judge declined to sentence D for the offences to which he had pleaded guilty but which had been incorrectly sent for trial. Thereafter, a district judge in the magistrates' court, acting under the MCA 1980, s. 142, set aside the original sending sheet and then committed D for sentence (under the SA 2020, s. 14) for the offences to which he had originally indicated guilty pleas. When D appeared again at the Crown Court, the judge ruled that he had no jurisdiction to sentence D for those offences. He considered (following *Clark*) that the only remedy was for the prosecution to seek judicial review to quash the erroneous sending for trial, and that he could not correct the error through the use of the Courts Act 2003, s. 66.

Edis LJ said (at [19]) that, following *Butt*, *Clark* 'should not be followed on this procedural issue because it is inconsistent with a series of authoritative decisions culminating in *Ayhan* and *Gould*'.

The justices' legal adviser made a mistake when recording the outcome of the hearing. The magistrates had not sent for trial the three charges to which D had entered guilty pleas; rather, they had committed him for sentence. Where the error is in the recording of the result, but the magistrates in fact made a correct order (as where the magistrates committed for sentence, but the record shows that they sent for trial), the Crown Court may proceed to deal with the case (at [20]). Alternatively, the Crown Court could have taken the view that a committal for trial (as shown on the court record) where D had entered guilty pleas was 'bad on its face', leaving it open to the Crown Court to hold that the purported order was a nullity and that, in law, the case had 'never left the magistrates' court', which was not therefore *functus officio*, enabling the Crown Court judge to sit as a district judge and make a valid order committing for sentence (at [22]).

In the second case, D was charged with four either way offences and one summary only offence. He was sent for trial for offences that he had admitted in the magistrates' court. In this case, there is no evidence that the court record was created in error and mis-recorded a valid order which the magistrates had made. Edis LJ (at [52]) said that the Crown Court had two choices when dealing with the two charges which had been admitted in the magistrates' court where the record showed they had been sent for trial: either (i) to hold that the record of what had happened in the magistrates' court was bad on its face and that nothing had occurred there which could confer jurisdiction on the Crown Court to deal with these two charges, so the charges remained in the magistrates' court, which was therefore not *functus officio*, thereby enabling the Crown Court judge to sit as a district judge and cure the error through use of the MCA 1980, s. 142; or (ii) hold that it was sufficiently clear from all the evidence that the offences had in fact been committed for sentence and to proceed to sentence on that basis.

Section D24   Trial of Children and Young People

DETERMINING PLACE OF TRIAL OF CHILDREN AND YOUNG PEOPLE

Guidance on the Decision-making process in s. 250 Cases

D24.35 **Sexual Offences in the Youth Court**   CrimPD 5.15 (see **PD5.15**) was amended with effect from 7 November 2023 to make it clear that: 'If it is not practicable for an authorised DJ(MC) to determine venue, any DJ(MC) or any Youth Court Bench may consider that issue'.

Section D31   Extradition

INTRODUCTION

Part 2 Requests

The Extradition Act 2003, s. 194, allows the Secretary of State to enter into special extradition   **D31.3**
relations with a country with which the UK does not have an extradition treaty and, if they do
so, to issue a certificate under s. 70. The Court considered a challenge to the lawfulness of a
certificate issued by the Secretary of State for the first extradition request from Japan to the UK
in *R (Chappell) v Secretary of State for the Home Department* [2022] EWHC 3281 (Admin).

In *Birbeck v Andorra* [2023] EWHC 1740 (Admin), the Court considered whether a requested
person could argue that an extradition request did not comply with the requirements of s. 70(4)
even if the Secretary of State had issued a certificate under s. 70(1), and held that it was open to
the court to consider a challenge brought by the requested person as to the purpose of the
extradition request (at [28]–[34]).

EXTRADITION OFFENCE

In *Bellencs v Hungary* [2023] EWHC 2235 (Admin), the Court considered the application of   **D31.19**
the dual criminality requirement. In *El-Khouri v USA* [2023] EWHC 1878 (Admin), at
[70]–[75], the Divisional Court considered what conduct needs to be transposed in order to
consider whether there is an extradition offence.

BARS TO EXTRADITION

Double Jeopardy

In *Prejoinau v Italy* [2023] EWHC 2378 (Admin), the Court considered the application of the   **D31.23**
double jeopardy bar after the requested person was convicted in Romania and was then subject
to an Italian Part 1 warrant for conduct which was linked to the Romanian conviction.

HUMAN RIGHTS AND PROPORTIONALITY

In *Dujka v Czech Republic* [2023] EWHC 1842 (Admin), the Court found that concern about   **D31.33**
proportionality had been enhanced in the new arrangements, including the TCA, that are in
place after the UK left the EU and this needs to be considered when applying s. 21A(1)(b) (at
[22]–[23]).

In *Prusianu v Romania* [2022] EWHC 1929 (Admin), the Court found that 'on the special   **D31.35**
combination of facts and circumstances' extradition should not take place as it would involve a
violation of Article 8 of the ECHR (at [50]).

ABUSE OF PROCESS

In *Romania v Iancu* [2023] EWHC 1274 (Admin), the Court considered whether a further   **D31.37**
extradition request made after a requested person had been discharged following the failure of
the requesting territory to comply with orders of the court constituted an abuse of process.

APPEALS

The Court considered the approach to be taken in an appeal where there had been a change of   **D31.41**
circumstances or fresh evidence in *Jozsa v Hungary* [2023] EWHC 2404 (Admin), at [18]–[19].

It is possible for a requesting territory to seek to introduce assurances in respect of prison
conditions during an appeal, and the Court set out the principles to be applied in determining
whether they are admissible in *Romania v Szabo* [2023] EWHC 2123 (Admin), at [52]–[53].

D

Part D   Procedure

SUPPLEMENT TO PART E
SENTENCING

Section E1   Sentencing Code and Sentencing Guidelines

SENTENCING GUIDELINES

In *O'Hare* [2023] EWCA Crim 900, the Court of Appeal dealt with a case involving **E1.5** ram-raiding, which had been charged as commercial burglary. Giving the judgment of the Court, Bryan J noted that ram-raiding can be charged as theft, burglary or robbery, but it was not easy to pigeon-hole it within any particular offence guideline. Although in most cases where a guideline applies the citation of appellate authorities is of no assistance, in this situation the judge must consider the appellate cases on ram-raiding, which continue to offer valuable guidance.

For another example of the Court of Appeal providing valuable guidance in relation to **E1.6** sentencing an offence where no definitive guideline is in place and where there is no closely analogous offence, see *Ginair* [2023] EWCA Crim 1121 (offence of attempting to arrive in the UK without valid entry clearance, contrary to the Immigration Act 1971, s. 24(D1)). See further **B22.38** in the main work.

Section E2   Sentencing: General Provisions

REQUIRED REDUCTIONS IN SENTENCE

Reduction in Sentence for Assistance by Offender

In the important case of *Royle* [2023] EWCA Crim 1311, the Court of Appeal gave wide- **E2.6** ranging guidance on the practical operation of the discount accorded to offenders for providing assistance to the authorities. The Court explained and contrasted the statutory and 'text' procedures, and considered with the provision of examples the extent of discount likely to be appropriate across a range of scenarios. Consideration was also given to the general duty upon judges to give reasons for, and to explain the effects of, the sentence passed (SA 2020, s. 52), and how the judge should, in this context, be required to explain the reasons for sentence only in 'general terms'. The statutory duty to explain the sentence will be discharged by the judge making clear (in whatever terms he or she thinks best) that the court has considered all matters of mitigation brought to its attention.

MITIGATION

General Mitigating Factors

The Court of Appeal in *Simmonds* [2023] EWCA Crim 1063 held that where D was a **E2.18** transwoman who had identified as female for about two years, and also had autism and ADHD and a history of self-harm, D was at heightened risk of her mental health deteriorating if she were to serve her custodial sentence in a male prison. Sentence was reduced on appeal for these reasons, the Court adding that 'being a transwoman in a male prison ... will make the experience of imprisonment more arduous'.

Section E13   Custodial Sentences: General Provisions

LENGTH OF SENTENCE

General Provision

E13.11   **Relevance of Prison Conditions**   In *Foster* [2023] EWCA Crim 1196, the Court of Appeal drew attention to the sections of the *Equal Treatment Bench Book* which deal with the impact of imprisonment on women, and added that women held in custody may often be a long distance from their families which can add to the adverse consequences for them and their children. The impact of a woman's imprisonment upon her children or other family members might afford mitigation, but may not do so (*Petherick* [2012] EWCA Crim 2214). Judges should keep in mind that the impact of a custodial sentence is likely to be heavier during the present circumstances of overcrowding in the female estate. Such issues should properly be taken into account, including when deciding whether to suspend a sentence.

See also the decision in *Simmonds* [2023] EWCA Crim 1063, at **E2.18** in this supplement, relating to the sentencing of a transwoman.

Concurrent and Consecutive Determinate Custodial Sentences

E13.22   **Totality Principle**   In *A* [2023] EWCA Crim 1204, D, now aged 70, pleaded guilty to two groups of sexual offences committed against children, the first group occurring when D was himself a child and the second group when D was an adult. The Court of Appeal upheld the judge's decision to pass consecutive sentences for the separate groups of offending and said that in these circumstances there was no need to make the usual downward adjustment to the total sentence, as indicated in the *Totality* guideline. The Court said that such adjustment may be appropriate where the various offences form part of a single overall course of offending, or were part of a linked series. But an adjustment may not be required where, as here, the two groups of offences were wholly distinct. See also **B3.377** in this supplement.

Section E14   Suspended Sentences

POWER TO IMPOSE SUSPENDED SENTENCES

E14.3   The indication in the sentencing guideline, *Imposition of Community and Custodial Sentences*, that the operational period of a suspended sentence should reflect the length of the sentence, and that suspension for up to 12 months might normally be appropriate for a sentence of up to six months, is not an inviolable rule, but is general guidance to be followed, and a judge should provide a reason for departing from it (*Nadeem* [2023] EWCA Crim 408). In that case a maximum operational period of two years was held to be disproportionate to a custodial sentence of 21 weeks which had been suspended in a case of dangerous driving. However, bearing in mind the 'ongoing risk' posed by D the operational period was varied to 18 months.

In the unusual case of *Griffin* [2023] EWCA Crim 1111, D admitted four counts of conspiracy to supply cocaine and heroin. He was sentenced to 22 months' imprisonment. On appeal against sentence the Court of Appeal found that while in many, if not most, cases such offending would mean that appropriate punishment can only be achieved by immediate custody, in this case none of the other Table 1 factors in the guideline were present and all Table 2 factors were in place, including exceptionally strong personal mitigation. The sentence was, accordingly, suspended for two years.

Section E15   Custodial Sentences: Detention and Custody of Offenders under 18

DETERMINING THE AGE OF THE OFFENDER

In *Ahmed* [2023] EWCA Crim 281, the Court of Appeal considered afresh the correct   **E15.3**
approach to sentencing an adult for an offence committed as a child. The issue arose in five
appeals before the Court. The decision provides a clear endorsement of *Limon* [2022] EWCA
Crim 39. As the Court put it, there is no reason why the distinction in levels of culpability
between adult and juvenile offenders should be lost merely because there had been an elapse of
time which meant that the offender was an adult when sentenced for offences committed as a
child. Insofar as *Forbes* [2016] EWCA Crim 1388 took a different line on this central point,
that decision was doubted. It is now clear that what really matters in these cases is the 'likely
sentence' which D would have received if sentenced at the time of the offending. That will
require research by practitioners into the historic sentencing position, but the Court said that
practical difficulty of this kind was outweighed by the importance of the general principle at
stake. Once the historic 'likely sentence' has been determined, the passage of time since the
offending took place may serve to mitigate (where it is clear that the offending was an isolated
occurrence, and D has since led a blameless life) or to aggravate (where the reverse is shown to
be true).

Section E16   Life Sentences, Extended Sentences, Serious Terrorism Sentences and Custodial Sentences for Certain Offenders of 'Particular Concern'

REQUIRED SENTENCE OF IMPRISONMENT FOR LIFE OR CUSTODY FOR LIFE

For a useful decision which rehearses the necessary criteria for the imposition of a life sentence   **E16.6**
under the SA 2020, s. 258, see *Wilder* [2023] EWCA Crim 1295. The Court of Appeal upheld
a life sentence in a case of 'simple arson' directed at property, but where there had been several
incidents orchestrated by D and where no reliable prediction could be made of when D would
cease to be a danger to the public.

Section E18   Minimum Custodial Sentences

MINIMUM CUSTODIAL SENTENCE FOR THIRD CLASS A DRUG OFFENCE

In *Bouhamidi* [2023] EWCA Crim 1066, the Court of Appeal considered the scope of the   **E18.4**
'exceptional circumstances' proviso in relation to the seven year minimum sentence, noting that
the earlier test of 'particular circumstances' had been changed by the PCSCA 2022, with effect
from 28 June 2022. The Court endorsed the principles set out in *Nancarrow* [2019] EWCA
Crim 470, which had previously been applicable to the application of the 'exceptional
circumstances' test in relation to the five year minimum sentence for certain firearms offences.

MINIMUM CUSTODIAL SENTENCE FOR THIRD DOMESTIC BURGLARY

In *Swinbourne* [2023] EWCA Crim 906, the Court of Appeal considered the scope of the   **E18.7**
'exceptional circumstances' proviso in relation to the three year minimum sentence, noting that
the earlier test of 'particular circumstances' had been changed by the PCSCA 2022, with effect

from 28 June 2022. The Court endorsed the principles set out in *Nancarrow* [2019] EWCA Crim 470, which had previously been applicable to the application of the 'exceptional circumstances' test in relation to the five year minimum sentence for certain firearms offences.

Section E21   Exclusions and Disqualifications

RESTRAINING ORDERS

Restraining Order on Acquittal

E21.33   In *Oshosanya* [2022] EWCA Crim 1794, the judge imposed a restraining order for five years under the Protection from Harassment Act 1997, s. 5A, following D's acquittal for an offence of stalking involving fear of violence or serious alarm or distress, the prosecution having offered no evidence at trial. On appeal against that order D argued that the judge had erred in considering whether the evidence established a risk of future harassment, rather than whether there had been a course of conduct amounting to the offence of harassment. The Court of Appeal said that the judge had applied the correct test and had been entitled to make the order, having complied with the procedural requirements of hearing evidence from witnesses and taking account of representations from counsel. When a restraining order is imposed under s. 5A by definition there is no offence or conviction. The issue is not whether harassment has in fact occurred, but whether the order is necessary to protect the complainant(s) from harassment by D in the future.

A restraining order imposed upon an acquittal was quashed by the Court of Appeal in *McCarren* [2023] EWCA Crim 1233, where the prosecution offered no evidence against D at trial, but where there had been several procedural shortcomings, the evidential basis for the order was unclear, and it could not be shown that its imposition was 'necessary'. D's agreement to the order being made was a secondary consideration, and could not dispense with the need for articulation by the judge of the evidence to satisfy the statutory test. The Court rehearsed the relevant authorities, and warned of the dangers of moving too quickly to resolve a contested trial on terms that include a restraining order on acquittal.

Section E24   Rehabilitation of Offenders

REHABILITATION PERIODS

E24.3   The PCSCA 2022, s. 193 (amendment of rehabilitation periods), was brought into effect by the Police, Crime, Sentencing and Courts Act 2022 (Commencement No. 8) Regulations 2023 (SI 2023 No. 1128), as from 28 October 2023. It is important to note that these changes are retrospective in effect, and apply whenever the conviction occurred.

SUPPLEMENT TO PART F
EVIDENCE

Section F1   General Principles of Evidence in Criminal Cases

RELEVANCE

Demeanour of Victim

Lake [2023] EWCA Crim 710, provides further guidance on directions about the evidential **F1.16** value of distress displayed by a complainant when making a complaint or giving evidence. It was held that often the reason why a direction is necessary is that the jury have to consider whether the distress is genuine or feigned. In such a case, factors such as whether the distress has been observed close in time to the circumstances of the alleged offence and whether the complainant was aware that he or she was being observed will often be particularly relevant. In other cases, where there is no suggestion that the distress was feigned, the jury may need to be directed that genuine distress could have been for reasons which did not support D's guilt, for example remorse and anger on the part of the complainant at having allowed matters to progress as they did while affected by alcohol or failure to appreciate signals being sent.

Section F2   Evidence Unlawfully, Improperly or Unfairly Obtained and the Discretion to Exclude Evidence

POLICE AND CRIMINAL EVIDENCE ACT 1984, s. 78

Scope for Exclusion Wider than at Common Law

In *Rowan* [2023] EWCA Crim 205, it was held that where the prosecution decide, on proper **F2.9** grounds, not to charge some of those allegedly involved in a conspiracy, and they are not called as witnesses, evidence of their wrongdoing will not necessarily result in unfairness to those who have been charged. Relevant factors include whether admission of the evidence would impede any of those charged in advancing their defences, whether they would be prejudiced because unable to challenge the evidence of wrongdoing and whether they would have been at risk of being contradicted if those not called as witnesses had been called.

Section F3   Burden and Standard of Proof and Presumptions

BURDEN OF PROOF

Incidence of the Evidential Burden: General Rule

Loss of Self-control   Concerning principle (g) derived from *Gurnipar* [2015] EWCA Crim **F3.39** 178, see, e.g., *Myles* [2023] EWCA Crim 943. D said that he had 'lost it', but various other matters indicated an unlawful attack on a deliberate and considered basis. It was held that the trial judge had properly found that there was no sufficient evidence of loss of self-control.

STANDARD OF PROOF

Usual Direction where Legal Burden on Prosecution

Although a jury must be 'sure' of guilt before returning a verdict of guilty, some statutory **F3.48** provisions continue to use the phrase 'beyond reasonable doubt' as the standard to be met by the prosecution in order to disprove a particular defence (see, e.g., further to the CAJA 2009, s. 54(5), considered at **F3.38** in the main work, the Online Safety Act 2023, ss. 181(4) and 201(2)).

Further to *W* [2014] EWCA Crim 1392 on delay directions, see *MT* [2023] EWCA Crim 558, considered at **D3.81** in this supplement.

Section F5   Corroboration and Care Warnings

CARE WARNINGS

Accomplices Giving Evidence for the Prosecution and Complainants in Sexual Cases

F5.11   'Supporting Material'   Concerning evidence of the complainant's distress, see also *Lake* [2023] EWCA Crim 710, considered at **F1.16** in this supplement.

Section F6   Examination-in-chief

PREVIOUS COMPLAINTS

F6.34   It is submitted that where there are inconsistencies between previous complaints admitted under the CJA 2003, s. 120, and the complainant's evidence at trial, the judge should draw them to the attention of the jury because of their potential to call into question the complainant's reliability as a witness (see *Lake* [2023] EWCA Crim 710, where it is unclear from the report whether the previous complaints were admitted under s. 120 or under the common-law exception to the rule against previous consistent statements).

Section F7   Cross-examination and Re-examination

CROSS-EXAMINATION: GENERAL CONSIDERATIONS

Role of the Judge during Cross-examination

F7.6   In *Lake* [2023] EWCA Crim 710, it was held that the trial judge should not have, in effect, cross-examined D, ending with a flourish, 'So you tell this jury…'. The intervention clearly conveyed that the judge did not believe D's version of events and detracted from the fairness of the trial.

PROTECTION OF COMPLAINANTS IN PROCEEDINGS FOR SEXUAL OFFENCES

Section 41(3) and (4): Evidence or a Question Relating to a Relevant Issue

F7.34   In *Lazzari* [2018] EWCA Crim 1043, evidence of the complainant's behaviour after the alleged offence was admissible to rebut her evidence that she felt scared of D and to advance his case that they enjoyed a normal relationship, which would not be consistent with the offence having taken place shortly beforehand. It was held that s. 41(4) prohibits evidence or questioning which undermines the credibility of the complainant generally as a witness of truth and not that which challenges the complainant's evidence on a specific point in the case. This construction fits in with the underlying rationale of s. 41. See also *VA* [2016] EWCA Crim 1434, where the Court said that the focus of s. 41(4) is questioning or evidence which impugns the credibility of the complainant because of the fact of his or her sexual behaviour, In other words, the subsection prevents the suggestion that such behaviour in itself means that the complainant is not worthy of belief.

Section 41(3)(a): A Relevant Issue Other than Consent

Subject to the restrictions in s. 41(3)(a) and (b), subsection (3) only applies in the case of   **F7.37**
evidence or questioning that relates to a 'relevant issue in the case'. That phrase is defined in
s. 42(1)(a) as 'any issue falling to be proved by the prosecution or defence in the trial of the
accused'. This definition is not restricted to elements of the offence which the Crown has to
prove or something which the defence has to prove, but has a broader meaning that covers any
relevant matter that is in issue at the trial. This interpretation is supported by examples (b), (c),
and (d) of issues falling within s. 41(3)(a) given by Lord Hope in *A (No. 2)* [2001] UKHL 25,
at [79] (*Lazzari* [2018] EWCA Crim 1043).

Section 41(5): Evidence or a Question Relating to Evidence Adduced by the Prosecution

Section 41(5)(a) refers to evidence adduced by the prosecution about 'any sexual behaviour of   **F7.46**
the complainant'. Evidence of a complainant being scared of D is not evidence of sexual
behaviour, notwithstanding that the fear derives from the alleged offence (*Lazzari* [2018]
EWCA Crim 1043).

Section F10   Privilege

PRIVILEGE AGAINST SELF-INCRIMINATION

Statutory Provisions Requiring Answers to Questions

Examples   For another statutory provision similar to the Companies Act 1985, s. 434(5A)   **F10.9**
and (5B), see the Online Safety Act 2003, s. 120. See also the Companies Act 2006, s. 1092C,
as inserted by the Economic Crime and Corporate Transparency Act 2023, s. 83.

Section F11   Opinion Evidence

EXPERT OPINION EVIDENCE

Matters Calling for Expertise

In *Ulas* [2023] EWCA Crim 82, where identification was in issue, an officer was allowed to give   **F11.8**
evidence that he had viewed stills from CCTV footage of the incident in question and that two
days later he had encountered someone whom he recognised as one of the suspects that he had
seen in the stills. Three days after that, he had attended an identification parade and identified
D as the man he had encountered. The decision extends in two ways the principle established
in *Clare* [1995] 2 Cr App R 333. First, whereas in *Clare* the identification was made by
comparing video-recorded images with those in photographs, in *Ulas* the comparison was
between recorded images and the appearance of an actual person. Second, whereas in *Clare* the
officer had spent a substantial amount of time viewing and analysing the video-recorded
images, thereby acquiring special knowledge which the jury did not have, in *Ulas* the officer's
evidence was simply that he had viewed the CCTV stills. It was held that it was open to the trial
judge to infer that the officer had spent time viewing and analysing the images and had thereby
acquired a degree of special knowledge. It was further held that the amount of time or study
required to demonstrate the acquisition of special knowledge depends on the facts; a case
involving a large number of images and a number of different individuals was different from the
present case, where the images involved only three suspects.

F11.9   Concerning expert evidence in relation to footwear marks, see *Dickson* [2023] EWCA
Crim 1002.

Guidance on Scientific Evidence for Judges

F11.45   The primers on scientific evidence for judges have been extended to include a primer on fire
investigation.

Section F12   Admissibility of Previous Verdicts and Findings

CONVICTIONS AS EVIDENCE OF FACTS ON WHICH BASED

Convictions of Persons Other than the Accused

F12.16   **Cases of Conspiracy and Joint Enterprise**   Further to *S* [2007] EWCA Crim 2105, see also
Moore [2023] EWCA Crim 1184. The prosecution case was that D had assisted and/or
encouraged others, including T, to murder the victim, had been with T throughout the day of
the murder, and was present at the scene. The defence was one of alibi. It was held that evidence
of T's conviction for the murder did not fall to be excluded under the PACE 1984, s. 78.
Although its admission may have made D's task more difficult, it did not close off the jury's
consideration of his defence, which remained open to him.

Section F13   Character Evidence: Evidence of Bad Character
of Accused

EXPLANATORY EVIDENCE

Introduction

F13.42   **Evidence of Motive or Intention as Explanatory Evidence**   In *Pierini* [2023] EWCA Crim
1189, the prosecution case against D depended on proof that he knew or suspected that funds
he had acquired in his role as an 'introducer' for a company represented the proceeds of crime.
Bad character evidence was adduced to show that, in a previous role as director of a different
company that had become insolvent, he had proved unfit to act in that capacity and had been
disqualified from doing so, although it was not suggested that he had acted fraudulently. The
argument for admitting the evidence was that a person with the appellant's business experience
might have been expected to spot that the funds he had acquired might be the proceeds of
fraud. The Court of Appeal held that the evidence had correctly been admitted under the CJA
2003, s. 101(1)(c), agreeing with the trial judge's observation that 'to exclude such material
would give the jury a wholly misleading impression of [the appellant's] business experience and
prevent them from being able to properly evaluate his state of mind'. Alternatively, as the Court
of Appeal observes, it could have been admitted under s. 101(1)(d) given that D's state of mind
was the matter in issue.

EVIDENCE OF BAD CHARACTER ADDUCED BY PROSECUTION TO
PROVE GUILT OR UNTRUTHFULNESS

Identifying the Accused by Evidence of Bad Character under the Criminal Justice
Act 2003, s. 101(1)(d)

F13.58   In *Watson* [2023] EWCA Crim 1016, bad character evidence was admitted to support the case
against D in relation to the murder of a young boy in 1994. The defence was that the child's
mother murdered him. The bad character evidence related to a time when D was an adolescent
and was sufficiently close in time to be regarded as contemporaneous with the murder. It tended

to show both a sexual interest in children and that D acted in ways that were similar to unusual actions by the killer. The Court of Appeal held that the evidence had been correctly admitted, and that the jury had been properly directed to take it into account only if they first concluded that the murder was indeed sexually motivated. The Court regarded the evidence as going to the issue of identity rather than propensity, though the distinction was admitted to be a fine one. It would seem that it could equally be regarded as a case where D had a propensity that was relevant to the question whether he, rather than the mother, was the murderer.

Section F20   Inferences From Silence and the Non-Production of Evidence

OUT-OF-COURT SILENCE UNDER THE 1994 ACT

Direction as to Permissible Inferences

Direction where s.34 Not Applicable to Accused's Silence   *McGarry* [1999] 1 Cr App R 377   **F20.27** was considered in *RT* [2023] EWCA Crim 1118. D, who had been invited to attend a police station as a witness, was unexpectedly confronted with serious allegations of historic sexual offences committed when he was between 11 and 16 years of age against a younger boy who was occasionally looked after by D's mother. After speaking to a solicitor, D gave a prepared statement denying all of the allegations, and then answered 'No comment' to specific questions about them. At trial there was a straightforward conflict of evidence between D and his accuser, as witnesses who might have corroborated the accuser's account failed to do so. D was cross-examined about his interview in such a way as to suggest that his evidence at trial might have been a recent fabrication, however the judge and counsel later agreed that the case did not call for a direction under the CJPO 1994, s. 34, as the defence was a bare denial consistent with the statement in interview. The Court of Appeal quashed D's convictions. While it appears from the cases since *McGarry* that the trial judge, in a case to which s. 34 does not apply, has a discretion, rather than an obligation, to give a direction that no adverse inferences should be drawn, the exercise of the discretion was not even considered in the present case. The failure to give a direction to draw no inferences left D, as it did in *McGarry*, in a 'no-man's land' where there was a risk that the jury would regard the failure to answer questions as incriminating. The Court opined that '[a]ny defendant who has this kind of evidence led against him with the challenge of recent fabrication made on the back of it is entitled to a jury direction to protect against the obvious risk of the jury placing unfair weight on that silence'.

Similarly in *Annette-Norman* [2023] EWCA Crim 869, a direction under s. 34 was held to be unnecessary where D's evidence substantially repeated what he had said in the prepared statement given at interview, although he had added some detail to his account as to which he was briefly challenged in cross-examination. The trial judge had mentioned in his summing-up that D had written the prepared statement on legal advice, on the understanding that this was the way things were done. However it would 'arguably have been preferable' for the judge to give the jury a short direction to the effect that, as D had not relied on any material matter at trial which he might have mentioned in his prepared statement, the jury should not hold his 'no comment' answers against him. The judge's failure to do so did not, however, render the convictions unsafe.

FAILURE TO CALL WITNESS OR PROVIDE EVIDENCE

In *Watson* [2023] EWCA Crim 960, the Court of Appeal reviewed authorities regarding   **F20.55** permissible comment on the failure to call witnesses for the defence. The case was one of murder by shooting in which the prosecution alleged that the killer was D and that he had been in possession of a particular phone that was linked to the killing. D declined to give evidence but disputed both points. In closing, prosecution counsel noted that calls had been made to the phone by D's girlfriend and other named acquaintances of his at the relevant time, but none of them had been called to give evidence that they spoke to someone other than D, when they were 'all capable of coming to court' to do so. On appeal it was argued that this undermined the judge's clear direction, immediately prior to the close of evidence, that the jury should not speculate as to why particular witnesses had not been called by either side. The Court of Appeal decided (at [36]) that '[t]here is no *per curiam* authority which prohibits appropriate comment regarding the failure of a defendant to call witnesses'. In the present case, counsel's comments were, in the main, appropriate. It was agreed evidence that the relevant calls had been made, which led to a legitimate inference that they were telephoning D, and it was legitimate to point out that no evidence was called to counter that inference. The comment that the prospective witnesses were all capable of coming to court was without evidential foundation and went too far, particularly in light of the judge's direction to avoid speculation. Any comment should be fair and circumspect. The Court rejected the argument that counsel was not bound by the constraints on comment that applied to the judge. On the contrary, counsel should be careful not to undermine the judge's direction, and an inappropriate comment may require immediate judicial rebuke and challenge.

Codes of Practice under the Police
and Criminal Evidence Act 1984

PACE CODE A

REVISED CODE OF PRACTICE FOR THE EXERCISE BY:

POLICE OFFICERS OF STATUTORY POWERS
OF STOP AND SEARCH

POLICE OFFICERS AND POLICE STAFF OF REQUIREMENTS
TO RECORD PUBLIC ENCOUNTERS

Commencement—Transitional Arrangements

This code applies to any search by a police officer and the recording of public encounters taking place after 00.00 on 17 January 2023.

1.0 General

1.01 This code of practice must be readily available at all police stations for consultation by police officers, police staff, detained persons and members of the public.

1.02 The notes for guidance included are not provisions of this code, but are guidance to police officers and others about its application and interpretation. Provisions in the annexes to the code are provisions of this code.

1.03 This code governs the exercise by police officers of statutory powers to search a person or a vehicle without first making an arrest. The main stop and search powers to which this code applies are set out in Annex A, but that list should not be regarded as definitive (see *Note 1*). In addition, it covers requirements on police officers and police staff to record encounters not governed by statutory powers (see *paragraphs 2.11* and *4.12*). This code does not apply to:

    (a) the powers of stop and search under:

        (i) the Aviation Security Act 1982, section 27(2), and

        (ii) the Police and Criminal Evidence Act 1984 (PACE), section 6(1) (which relates specifically to powers of constables employed by statutory undertakers on the premises of the statutory undertakers);

    (b) searches carried out for the purposes of examination under Schedule 7 to the Terrorism Act 2000 and to which the Code of Practice issued under paragraph 6 of Schedule 14 to the Terrorism Act 2000 applies.

    (c) the powers to search persons and vehicles and to stop and search in specified locations to which the Code of Practice issued under section 47AB of the Terrorism Act 2000 applies.

1 Principles governing stop and search

1.1 Powers to stop and search must be used fairly, responsibly, with respect for people being searched and without unlawful discrimination. Under the Equality Act 2010, section 149, when police officers are carrying out their functions, they also have a duty to have due regard to the need to eliminate unlawful discrimination, harassment and victimisation, to advance equality of opportunity between people who share a 'relevant protected characteristic' and people who do not share it, and to take steps to foster good relations between those persons. (See *Notes 1* and *1A*.) The Children Act 2004, section 11, also requires chief police officers and other specified persons and bodies to ensure that in the discharge of their functions they have regard to the need to safeguard and promote the welfare of all persons under the age of 18.

1.2 The intrusion on the liberty of the person stopped or searched must be brief and detention for the purposes of a search must take place at or near the location of the stop.

1.3 If these fundamental principles are not observed the use of powers to stop and search may be drawn into question. Failure to use the powers in the proper manner reduces their effectiveness. Stop and search can play an important role in the detection and prevention of crime, and using the powers fairly makes them more effective.

1.4   The primary purpose of stop and search powers is to enable officers to allay or confirm suspicions about individuals without exercising their power of arrest. Officers may be required to justify the use or authorisation of such powers, in relation both to individual searches and the overall pattern of their activity in this regard, to their supervisory officers or in court. Any misuse of the powers is likely to be harmful to policing and lead to mistrust of the police. Officers must also be able to explain their actions to the member of the public searched. The misuse of these powers can lead to disciplinary action (see *paragraphs 5.5* and *5.6*).

1.5   An officer must not search a person, even with his or her consent, where no power to search is applicable. Even where a person is prepared to submit to a search voluntarily, the person must not be searched unless the necessary legal power exists, and the search must be in accordance with the relevant power and the provisions of this Code. The only exception, where an officer does not require a specific power, applies to searches of persons entering sports grounds or other premises carried out with their consent given as a condition of entry.

1.6   Evidence obtained from a search to which this Code applies may be open to challenge if the provisions of this Code are not observed.

2 Types of stop and search powers

2.1   This code applies, subject to paragraph 1.03, to powers of stop and search as follows:

(a)   powers which require reasonable grounds for suspicion, before they may be exercised; that articles unlawfully obtained or possessed are being carried such as section 1 of PACE for stolen and prohibited articles and section 23 of the Misuse of Drugs Act 1971 for controlled drugs;

(b)   authorised under section 60 of the Criminal Justice and Public Order Act 1994, based upon a reasonable belief that incidents involving serious violence may take place or that people are carrying dangerous instruments or offensive weapons within any locality in the police area, or that it is expedient to use the powers to find such instruments or weapons that have been used in incidents of serious violence;

(c)   *Not used.*

(d)   the powers in Schedule 5 to the Terrorism Prevention and Investigation Measures (TPIM) Act 2011 to search an individual who has not been arrested, conferred by:

(i)   paragraph 6(2)(a) at the time of serving a TPIM notice;

(ii)   paragraph 8(2)(a) under a search warrant for compliance purposes; and

(iii)   paragraph 10 for public safety purposes.

See *paragraph 2.18A.*

(e)   powers to search a person who has not been arrested in the exercise of a power to search premises (see Code B *paragraph 2.4*).

(a) Stop and search powers requiring reasonable grounds for suspicion — explanation

General

2.2   Reasonable grounds for suspicion is the legal test which a police officer must satisfy before they can stop and detain individuals or vehicles to search them under powers such as section 1 of PACE (to find stolen or prohibited articles) and section 23 of the Misuse of Drugs Act 1971 (to find controlled drugs). This test must be applied to the particular circumstances in each case and is in two parts:

(i)   *Firstly*, the officer must have formed a genuine suspicion in their own mind that they will find the object for which the search power being exercised allows them to search (see *Annex A*, second column, for examples); and

(ii)   *Secondly*, the suspicion that the object will be found must be reasonable. This means that there must be an objective basis for that suspicion based on facts, information and/or intelligence which are relevant to the likelihood that the object in question will be found, so that a reasonable person would be entitled to reach the same conclusion based on the same facts and information and/or intelligence.

Officers must therefore be able to explain the basis for their suspicion by reference to intelligence or information about, or some specific behaviour by, the person concerned (see *paragraphs 3.8(d), 4.6* and *5.5*).

2.2A   The exercise of these stop and search powers depends on the likelihood that the person searched is in possession of an item for which they may be searched; it does not depend on the person concerned being suspected of committing an offence in relation to the object of the search. A police officer who has reasonable grounds to suspect that a person is in innocent possession of a stolen or prohibited article, controlled drug or other item for which the officer is empowered to search, may stop and search the person even though there would be no power of arrest. This would apply when a child under the age of criminal responsibility (10 years) is suspected of carrying any such item, even if they knew they had it. (See Notes *1B* and *1BA*.)

Personal factors can never support reasonable grounds for suspicion

2.2B Reasonable suspicion can never be supported on the basis of personal factors. This means that unless the police have information or intelligence which provides a description of a person suspected of carrying an article for which there is a power to stop and search, the following cannot be used, alone or in combination with each other, or in combination with any other factor, as the reason for stopping and searching any individual, including any vehicle which they are driving or are being carried in:

(a) A person's physical appearance with regard, for example, to any of the 'relevant protected characteristics' set out in the Equality Act 2010, section 149, which are age, disability, gender reassignment, pregnancy and maternity, race, religion or belief, sex and sexual orientation (see *paragraph 1.1* and *Note 1A*), or the fact that the person is known to have a previous conviction; and

(b) Generalisations or stereotypical images that certain groups or categories of people are more likely to be involved in criminal activity.

2.3 *Not used.*

Reasonable grounds for suspicion based on information and/or intelligence

2.4 Reasonable grounds for suspicion should normally be linked to accurate and current intelligence or information, relating to articles for which there is a power to stop and search, being carried by individuals or being in vehicles in any locality. This would include reports from members of the public or other officers describing:

- a person who has been seen carrying such an article or a vehicle in which such an article has been seen.
- crimes committed in relation to which such an article would constitute relevant evidence, for example, property stolen in a theft or burglary, an offensive weapon or bladed or sharply pointed article used to assault or threaten someone or an article used to cause criminal damage to property.

2.4A Searches based on accurate and current intelligence or information are more likely to be effective. Targeting searches in a particular area at specified crime problems not only increases their effectiveness but also minimises inconvenience to law-abiding members of the public. It also helps in justifying the use of searches both to those who are searched and to the public. This does not however prevent stop and search powers being exercised in other locations where such powers may be exercised and reasonable suspicion exists.

2.5 *Not used.*

Reasonable grounds for suspicion and searching groups

2.6 Where there is reliable information or intelligence that members of a group or gang habitually carry knives unlawfully or weapons or controlled drugs, and wear a distinctive item of clothing or other means of identification in order to identify themselves as members of that group or gang, that distinctive item of clothing or other means of identification may provide reasonable grounds to stop and search any person believed to be a member of that group or gang. (See *Note 9.*)

2.6A A similar approach would apply to particular organised protest groups where there is reliable information or intelligence:

(a) that the group in question arranges meetings and marches to which one or more members bring articles intended to be used to cause criminal damage and/or injury to others in support of the group's aims;

(b) that at one or more previous meetings or marches arranged by that group, such articles have been used and resulted in damage and/or injury; and

(c) that on the subsequent occasion in question, one or more members of the group have brought with them such articles with similar intentions.

These circumstances may provide reasonable grounds to stop and search any members of the group to find such articles (see *Note 9A*). See also *paragraphs 2.12* to *2.18*, '*Searches authorised under section 60 of the Criminal Justice and Public Order Act 1994* ', when serious violence is anticipated at meetings and marches.

Reasonable grounds for suspicion based on behaviour, time and location

2.6B Reasonable suspicion may also exist without specific information or intelligence and on the basis of the behaviour of a person. For example, if an officer encounters someone on the street at night who is obviously trying to hide something, the officer may (depending on the other surrounding circumstances) base such suspicion on the fact that this kind of behaviour is often linked to stolen or prohibited articles being carried. An officer who forms the opinion that a person is acting suspiciously or that they appear to be nervous must be able to explain, with reference to specific aspects of the person's behaviour or conduct which they have observed, why they formed that opinion (see *paragraphs 3.8(d)* and *5.5*). A hunch or instinct which cannot be explained or justified to an objective observer can never amount to reasonable grounds.

2.7   *Not used.*

2.8   *Not used.*

Securing public confidence and promoting community relations

2.8A All police officers must recognise that searches are more likely to be effective, legitimate and secure public confidence when their reasonable grounds for suspicion are based on a range of objective factors. The overall use of these powers is more likely to be effective when up-to-date and accurate intelligence or information is communicated to officers and they are well-informed about local crime patterns. Local senior officers have a duty to ensure that those under their command who exercise stop and search powers have access to such information, and the officers exercising the powers have a duty to acquaint themselves with that information (see *paragraphs 5.1 to 5.6*).

Questioning to decide whether to carry out a search

2.9   An officer who has reasonable grounds for suspicion may detain the person concerned in order to carry out a search. Before carrying out the search the officer may ask questions about the person's behaviour or presence in circumstances which gave rise to the suspicion. As a result of questioning the detained person, the reasonable grounds for suspicion necessary to detain that person may be confirmed or, because of a satisfactory explanation, be dispelled. (See *Notes 2* and *3*.) Questioning may also reveal reasonable grounds to suspect the possession of a different kind of unlawful article from that originally suspected. Reasonable grounds for suspicion however cannot be provided retrospectively by such questioning during a person's detention or by refusal to answer any questions asked.

2.10 If, as a result of questioning before a search, or other circumstances which come to the attention of the officer, there cease to be reasonable grounds for suspecting that an article of a kind for which there is a power to stop and search is being carried, no search may take place. (See *Note 3*.) In the absence of any other lawful power to detain, the person is free to leave at will and must be so informed.

2.11 There is no power to stop or detain a person in order to find grounds for a search. Police officers have many encounters with members of the public which do not involve detaining people against their will and do not require any statutory power for an officer to speak to a person (see *paragraph 4.12* and *Note 1*). However, if reasonable grounds for suspicion emerge during such an encounter, the officer may detain the person to search them, even though no grounds existed when the encounter began. As soon as detention begins, and before searching, the officer must inform the person that they are being detained for the purpose of a search and take action in accordance with paragraphs 3.8 to 3.11 under 'Steps to be taken prior to a search'.

(b) Searches authorised under section 60 of the Criminal Justice and Public Order Act 1994

2.12 Authority for a constable in uniform to stop and search under section 60 of the Criminal Justice and Public Order Act 1994 may be given if the authorising officer reasonably believes:
   (a) that incidents involving serious violence may take place in any locality in the officer's police area, and it is expedient to use these powers to prevent their occurrence;
   (b) that persons are carrying dangerous instruments or offensive weapons without good reason in any locality in the officer's police area; or
   (c) that an incident involving serious violence has taken place in the officer's police area, a dangerous instrument or offensive weapon used in the incident is being carried by a person in any locality in that police area, and it is expedient to use these powers to find that instrument or weapon.

2.13 An authorisation under section 60 may only be given by an officer of the rank of inspector or above and in writing, or orally if paragraph 2.12(c) applies and it is not practicable to give the authorisation in writing. The authorisation (whether written or oral) must specify the grounds on which it was given, the locality in which the powers may be exercised and the period of time for which they are in force. The period authorised shall be no longer than appears reasonably necessary to prevent, or seek to prevent incidents of serious violence, or to deal with the problem of carrying dangerous instruments or offensive weapons or to find a dangerous instrument or offensive weapon that has been used. It may not exceed 24 hours. An oral authorisation given where paragraph 2.12(c) applies must be recorded in writing as soon as practicable. (See *Notes 10* to *13*.)

2.14 An inspector who gives an authorisation must, as soon as practicable, inform an officer of or above the rank of superintendent. This officer may direct that the authorisation shall be extended for a further 24 hours, if violence or the carrying of dangerous instruments or offensive weapons has occurred, or is suspected to have occurred, and the continued use of the powers is considered necessary to prevent or deal with further such activity or to find a dangerous instrument or offensive weapon used that has been used. That direction must be given in writing unless it is not practicable to do so, in which case it must be recorded in writing as soon as practicable afterwards. (See *Note 12.*)

2.14A The selection of persons and vehicles under section 60 to be stopped and, if appropriate, searched should reflect an objective assessment of the nature of the incident or weapon in question and the individuals and vehicles thought likely to be associated with that incident or those weapons (see *Notes 10* and *11*). The powers must not be used to stop and search persons and vehicles for reasons unconnected with the purpose of the authorisation. When selecting persons and vehicles to be stopped in response to a specific threat or incident, officers must take care not to discriminate unlawfully against anyone on the grounds of any of the protected characteristics set out in the Equality Act 2010. (See *paragraph 1.1.*)

2.14B The driver of a vehicle which is stopped under section 60 and any person who is searched under section 60 are entitled to a written statement to that effect if they apply within twelve months from the day the vehicle was stopped or the person was searched. This statement is a record which states that the vehicle was stopped or (as the case may be) that the person was searched under section 60 and it may form part of the search record or be supplied as a separate record.

Powers to require removal of face coverings

2.15 Section 60AA of the Criminal Justice and Public Order Act 1994 also provides a power to demand the removal of disguises. The officer exercising the power must reasonably believe that someone is wearing an item wholly or mainly for the purpose of concealing identity. There is also a power to seize such items where the officer believes that a person intends to wear them for this purpose. There is no power to stop and search for disguises. An officer may seize any such item which is discovered when exercising a power of search for something else, or which is being carried, and which the officer reasonably believes is intended to be used for concealing anyone's identity. This power can only be used if an authorisation given under section 60 or under section 60AA, is in force. (See *Note 4.*)

2.16 Authority under section 60AA for a constable in uniform to require the removal of disguises and to seize them may be given if the authorising officer reasonably believes that activities may take place in any locality in the officer's police area that are likely to involve the commission of offences and it is expedient to use these powers to prevent or control these activities.

2.17 An authorisation under section 60AA may only be given by an officer of the rank of inspector or above, in writing, specifying the grounds on which it was given, the locality in which the powers may be exercised and the period of time for which they are in force. The period authorised shall be no longer than appears reasonably necessary to prevent, or seek to prevent the commission of offences. It may not exceed 24 hours. (See *Notes 10* to *13*.)

2.18 An inspector who gives an authorisation must, as soon as practicable, inform an officer of or above the rank of superintendent. This officer may direct that the authorisation shall be extended for a further 24 hours, if crimes have been committed, or are suspected to have been committed, and the continued use of the powers is considered necessary to prevent or deal with further such activity. This direction must also be given in writing at the time or as soon as practicable afterwards. (See *Note 12.*)

(c) Not used

(d) Searches under Schedule 5 to the Terrorism Prevention and Investigation Measures Act 2011

2.18A Paragraph 3 of Schedule 5 to the TPIM Act 2011 allows a constable to detain an individual to be searched under the following powers:
  (i)   paragraph 6(2)(a) when a TPIM notice is being, or has just been, served on the individual for the purpose of ascertaining whether there is anything on the individual that contravenes measures specified in the notice;

    (ii) paragraph 8(2)(a) in accordance with a warrant to search the individual issued by a justice of the peace in England and Wales, a sheriff in Scotland or a lay magistrate in Northern Ireland who is satisfied that a search is necessary for the purpose of determining whether an individual in respect of whom a TPIM notice is in force is complying with measures specified in the notice (see *paragraph 2.20*); and

    (iii) paragraph 10 to ascertain whether an individual in respect of whom a TPIM notice is in force is in possession of anything that could be used to threaten or harm any person.

    See *paragraph 2.1(e)*.

2.19 The exercise of the powers mentioned in *paragraph 2.18A* does not require the constable to have reasonable grounds to suspect that the individual:

    (a) has been, or is, contravening any of the measures specified in the TPIM notice; or

    (b) has on them anything which:
- in the case of the power in sub-paragraph (i), contravenes measures specified in the TPIM notice;
- in the case of the power in sub-paragraph (ii) is not complying with measures specified in the TPIM notice; or
- in the case of the power in sub-paragraph (iii), could be used to threaten or harm any person.

2.20 A search of an individual on warrant under the power mentioned in paragraph 2.18A(ii) must [be] carried out within 28 days of the issue of the warrant and:
- the individual may be searched on one occasion only within that period;
- the search must take place at a reasonable hour unless it appears that this would frustrate the purposes of the search.

2.21 *Not used.*

2.22 *Not used.*

2.23 *Not used.*

2.24 *Not used.*

2.24A *Not used.*

2.25 *Not used.*

2.26 The powers under Schedule 5 allow a constable to conduct a search of an individual only for specified purposes relating to a TPIM notice as set out above. However, anything found may be seized and retained if there are reasonable grounds for believing that it is or it contains evidence of any offence for use at a trial for that offence or to prevent it being concealed, lost, damaged, altered, or destroyed. However, this would not prevent a search being carried out under other search powers if, in the course of exercising these powers, the officer formed reasonable grounds for suspicion.

(e) Powers to search persons in the exercise of a power to search premises

2.27 The following powers to search premises also authorise the search of a person, not under arrest, who is found on the premises during the course of the search:

    (a) section 139B of the Criminal Justice Act 1988 under which a constable may enter school premises and search the premises and any person on those premises for any bladed or pointed article or offensive weapon;

    (b) under a warrant issued under section 23(3) of the Misuse of Drugs Act 1971 to search premises for drugs or documents but only if the warrant specifically authorises the search of persons found on the premises; and

    (c) under a search warrant or order issued under paragraph 1, 3 or 11 of Schedule 5 to the Terrorism Act 2000 to search premises and any person found there for material likely to be of substantial value to a terrorist investigation.

2.28 Before the power under section 139B of the Criminal Justice Act 1988 may be exercised, the constable must have reasonable grounds to suspect that an offence under section 139A or 139AA of the Criminal Justice Act 1988 (having a bladed or pointed article or offensive weapon on school premises) has been or is being committed. A warrant to search premises and persons found therein may be issued under section 23(3) of the Misuse of Drugs Act 1971 if there are reasonable grounds to suspect that controlled drugs or certain documents are in the possession of a person on the premises.

2.29 The powers in paragraph 2.27 do not require prior specific grounds to suspect that the person to be searched is in possession of an item for which there is an existing power to search. However, it is still necessary to ensure that the selection and treatment of those searched under these powers is based upon objective factors connected with the search of the premises, and not upon personal prejudice.

3 Conduct of searches

3.1 All stops and searches must be carried out with courtesy, consideration and respect for the person concerned. This has a significant impact on public confidence in the police. Every reasonable effort must be made to minimise the embarrassment that a person being searched may experience. (See *Note 4*.)

3.2 The co-operation of the person to be searched must be sought in every case, even if the person initially objects to the search. A forcible search may be made only if it has been established that the person is unwilling to co-operate or resists. Reasonable force may be used as a last resort if necessary to conduct a search or to detain a person or vehicle for the purposes of a search.

3.3 The length of time for which a person or vehicle may be detained must be reasonable and kept to a minimum. Where the exercise of the power requires reasonable suspicion, the thoroughness and extent of a search must depend on what is suspected of being carried, and by whom. If the suspicion relates to a particular article which is seen to be slipped into a person's pocket, then, in the absence of other grounds for suspicion or an opportunity for the article to be moved elsewhere, the search must be confined to that pocket. In the case of a small article which can readily be concealed, such as a drug, and which might be concealed anywhere on the person, a more extensive search may be necessary. In the case of searches mentioned in paragraph 2.1(b) and (d), which do not require reasonable grounds for suspicion, officers may make any reasonable search to look for items for which they are empowered to search. (See *Note 5*.)

3.4 The search must be carried out at or near the place where the person or vehicle was first detained. (See *Note 6*.)

3.5 There is no power to require a person to remove any clothing in public other than an outer coat, jacket or gloves, except under section 60AA of the Criminal Justice and Public Order Act 1994 (which empowers a constable to require a person to remove any item worn to conceal identity). (See *Notes 4* and *6*.) A search in public of a person's clothing which has not been removed must be restricted to superficial examination of outer garments. This does not, however, prevent an officer from placing his or her hand inside the pockets of the outer clothing, or feeling round the inside of collars, socks and shoes if this is reasonably necessary in the circumstances to look for the object of the search or to remove and examine any item reasonably suspected to be the object of the search. For the same reasons, subject to the restrictions on the removal of headgear, a person's hair may also be searched in public. (See *paragraphs 3.1* and *3.3*.)

3.6 Where on reasonable grounds it is considered necessary to conduct a more thorough search (e.g. by requiring a person to take off a T-shirt), this must be done out of public view, for example, in a police van unless paragraph 3.7 applies, or police station if there is one nearby (see *Note 6*.) Any search involving the removal of more than an outer coat, jacket, gloves, headgear or footwear, or any other item concealing identity, may only be made by an officer of the same sex as the person searched and may not be made in the presence of anyone of the opposite sex unless the person being searched specifically requests it. (See Code C *Annex L* and *Notes 4* and *7*.)

3.7 Searches involving exposure of intimate parts of the body must not be conducted as a routine extension of a less thorough search, simply because nothing is found in the course of the initial search. Searches involving exposure of intimate parts of the body may be carried out only at a nearby police station or other nearby location which is out of public view (but not a police vehicle). These searches must be conducted in accordance with paragraph 11 of Annex A to Code C except that an intimate search mentioned in paragraph 11(f) of Annex A to Code C may not be authorised or carried out under any stop and search powers. The other provisions of Code C do not apply to the conduct and recording of searches of persons detained at police stations in the exercise of stop and search powers. (See *Note 7*.)

Steps to be taken prior to a search

3.8 Before any search of a detained person or attended vehicle takes place the officer must take reasonable steps, if not in uniform (see *paragraph 3.9*), to show their warrant card to the person to be searched or in charge of the vehicle to be searched and whether or not in uniform, to give that person the following information:

(a) that they are being detained for the purposes of a search;

(b) the officer's name (except in the case of enquiries linked to the investigation of terrorism, or otherwise where the officer reasonably believes that giving their name might put them in danger, in which case a warrant or other identification number shall be given) and the name of the police station to which the officer is attached;

(c) the legal search power which is being exercised, and

  (d) a clear explanation of:
  (i)   the object of the search in terms of the article or articles for which there is a power to search; and
  (ii) in the case of:
  • the power under section 60 of the Criminal Justice and Public Order Act 1994 (see *paragraph 2.1(b))*, the nature of the power, the authorisation and the fact that it has been given;
  • the powers under Schedule 5 to the Terrorism Prevention and Investigation Measures Act 2011 (see *paragraph 2.1(e)* and *2.18A*):
  – the fact that a TPIM notice is in force or, (in the case of paragraph 6(2)(a)) that a TPIM notice is being served;
  – the nature of the power being exercised.
  For a search under paragraph 8 of Schedule 5, the warrant must be produced and the person provided with a copy of it.
  • all other powers requiring reasonable suspicion (see *paragraph 2.1(a)*), the grounds for that suspicion. This means explaining the basis for the suspicion by reference to information and/or intelligence about, or some specific behaviour by, the person concerned (see *paragraph 2.2*).
  (e) that they are entitled to a copy of the record of the search if one is made (see *section 4* below) if they ask within 3 months from the date of the search and:
  (i)   if they are not arrested and taken to a police station as a result of the search and it is practicable to make the record on the spot, that immediately after the search is completed they will be given, if they request, either:
  • a copy of the record; or
  • a receipt which explains how they can obtain a copy of the full record or access to an electronic copy of the record; or
  (ii) if they are arrested and taken to a police station as a result of the search, that the record will be made at the station as part of their custody record and they will be given, if they request, a copy of their custody record which includes a record of the search as soon as practicable whilst they are at the station. (See *Note 16*.)

3.9 Stops and searches under the power mentioned in paragraph 2.1(b) may be undertaken only by a constable in uniform.

3.10 The person should also be given information about police powers to stop and search and the individual's rights in these circumstances.

3.11 If the person to be searched, or in charge of a vehicle to be searched, does not appear to understand what is being said, or there is any doubt about the person's ability to understand English, the officer must take reasonable steps to bring information regarding the person's rights and any relevant provisions of this Code to his or her attention. If the person is deaf or cannot understand English and is accompanied by someone, then the officer must try to establish whether that person can interpret or otherwise help the officer to give the required information.

4 Recording requirements

(a) Searches which do not result in an arrest

4.1 When an officer carries out a search in the exercise of any power to which this Code applies and the search does not result in the person searched or person in charge of the vehicle searched being arrested and taken to a police station, a record must be made of it, electronically or on paper, unless there are exceptional circumstances which make this wholly impracticable (e.g. in situations involving public disorder or when the recording officer's presence is urgently required elsewhere). If a record is to be made, the officer carrying out the search must make the record on the spot unless this is not practicable, in which case, the officer must make the record as soon as practicable after the search is completed. (See *Note 16*.)

4.2 If the record is made at the time, the person who has been searched or who is in charge of the vehicle that has been searched must be asked if they want a copy and if they do, they must be given immediately, either:
  • a copy of the record; or
  • a receipt which explains how they can obtain a copy of the full record or access to an electronic copy of the record.

4.2A An officer is not required to provide a copy of the full record or a receipt at the time if they are called to an incident of higher priority. (See *Note 21*.)

(b) Searches which result in an arrest

4.2B If a search in the exercise of any power to which this Code applies results in a person being arrested and taken to a police station, the officer carrying out the search is responsible for ensuring that a record of the search is made as part of their custody record. The custody officer must then ensure that the person is asked if they want a copy of the record and if they do, that they are given a copy as soon as practicable. (See *Note 16*.)

(c) Record of search

4.3 The record of a search must always include the following information:
  (a) A note of the self defined ethnicity, and if different, the ethnicity as perceived by the officer making the search, of the person searched or of the person in charge of the vehicle searched (as the case may be) (see *Note 18*);
  (b) The date, time and place the person or vehicle was searched (see *Note 6*);
  (c) The object of the search in terms of the article or articles for which there is a power to search;
  (d) In the case of:
    • the power under section 60 of the Criminal Justice and Public Order Act 1994 (see *paragraph 2.1(b)*), the nature of the power, the authorisation and the fact that it has been given (see *Note 17*);
    • the powers under Schedule 5 to the Terrorism Prevention and Investigation Measures Act 2011 (see *paragraphs 2.1(e)* and *2.18A*):
      − the fact that a TPIM notice is in force or, (in the case of paragraph 6(2)(a)), that a TPIM notice is being served;
      − the nature of the power, and
      − for a search under paragraph 8, the date the search warrant was issued, the fact that the warrant was produced and a copy of it provided and the warrant must also be endorsed by the constable executing it to state whether anything was found and whether anything was seized, and
    • all other powers requiring reasonable suspicion (see *paragraph 2.1(a)*), the grounds for that suspicion.
  (e) subject to paragraph 3.8(b), the identity of the officer carrying out the search. (See *Note 15*.)

4.3A For the purposes of completing the search record, there is no requirement to record the name, address and date of birth of the person searched or the person in charge of a vehicle which is searched. The person is under no obligation to provide this information and they should not be asked to provide it for the purpose of completing the record.

4.4 Nothing in paragraph 4.3 requires the names of police officers to be shown on the search record or any other record required to be made under this Code in the case of enquiries linked to the investigation of terrorism or otherwise where an officer reasonably believes that recording names might endanger the officers. In such cases the record must show the officers' warrant or other identification number and duty station.

4.5 A record is required for each person and each vehicle searched. However, if a person is in a vehicle and both are searched, and the object and grounds of the search are the same, only one record need be completed. If more than one person in a vehicle is searched, separate records for each search of a person must be made. If only a vehicle is searched, the self-defined ethnic background of the person in charge of the vehicle must be recorded, unless the vehicle is unattended.

4.6 The record of the grounds for making a search must, briefly but informatively, explain the reason for suspecting the person concerned, by reference to information and/ or intelligence about, or some specific behaviour by, the person concerned (see *paragraph 2.2*).

4.7 Where officers detain an individual with a view to performing a search, but the need to search is eliminated as a result of questioning the person detained, a search should not be carried out and a record is not required. (See *paragraph 2.10* and *Notes 3* and *22A*.)

4.8 After searching an unattended vehicle, or anything in or on it, an officer must leave a notice in it (or on it, if things on it have been searched without opening it) recording the fact that it has been searched.

4.9 The notice must include the name of the police station to which the officer concerned is attached and state where a copy of the record of the search may be obtained and how (if applicable) an electronic copy may be accessed and where any application for compensation should be directed.

4.10 The vehicle must if practicable be left secure.

4.10A *Not used.*

4.10B *Not used.*

Recording of encounters not governed by statutory powers

4.11 *Not used.*

4.12 There is no national requirement for an officer who requests a person in a public place to account for themselves, i.e. their actions, behaviour, presence in an area or possession of anything, to make any record of the encounter or to give the person a receipt. (See *paragraph 2.11* and *Notes 22A* and *22B*.)

4.12A *Not used.*

4.13 *Not used.*

4.14 *Not used.*

4.15 *Not used.*

4.16 *Not used.*

4.17 *Not used.*

4.18 *Not used.*

4.19 *Not used.*

4.20 *Not used.*

5 Monitoring and supervising the use of stop and search powers

General

5.1 Any misuse of stop and search powers is likely to be harmful to policing and lead to mistrust of the police by the local community and by the public in general. Supervising officers must monitor the use of stop and search powers and should consider in particular whether there is any evidence that they are being exercised on the basis of stereotyped images or inappropriate generalisations. Supervising officers must satisfy themselves that the practice of officers under their supervision in stopping, searching and recording is fully in accordance with this Code. Supervisors must also examine whether the records reveal any trends or patterns which give cause for concern, and if so take appropriate action to address this. (See *paragraph 2.8A*.)

5.2 Senior officers with area or force-wide responsibilities must also monitor the broader use of stop and search powers and, where necessary, take action at the relevant level.

5.3 Supervision and monitoring must be supported by the compilation of comprehensive statistical records of stops and searches at force, area and local level. Any apparently disproportionate use of the powers by particular officers or groups of officers or in relation to specific sections of the community should be identified and investigated.

5.4 In order to promote public confidence in the use of the powers, forces, in consultation with police and crime commissioners, must make arrangements for the records to be scrutinised by representatives of the community, and to explain the use of the powers at a local level. (See *Note 19*.)

Suspected misuse of powers by individual officers

5.5 Police supervisors must monitor the use of stop and search powers by individual officers to ensure that they are being applied appropriately and lawfully. Monitoring takes many forms, such as direct supervision of the exercise of the powers, examining stop and search records (particularly examining the officer's documented reasonable grounds for suspicion) and asking the officer to account for the way in which they conducted and recorded particular searches or through complaints about a stop and search that an officer has carried out.

5.6 Where a supervisor identifies issues with the way that an officer has used a stop and search power, the facts of the case will determine whether the standards of professional behaviour as set out in the Code of Ethics (see [https://www.college.police.uk/ethics/code-of-ethics]) have been breached and which formal action is pursued. Improper use might be a result of poor performance or a conduct matter, which will require the supervisor to take appropriate action such as performance or misconduct procedures. It is imperative that supervisors take both timely and appropriate action to deal with all such cases that come to their notice.

Notes for Guidance

Officers exercising stop and search powers

1   *This Code does not affect the ability of an officer to speak to or question a person in the ordinary course of the officer's duties without detaining the person or exercising any element of compulsion. It is not the purpose of the code to prohibit such encounters between the police and the community with the co-operation of the person concerned and neither does it affect the principle that all citizens have a duty to help police officers to prevent crime and discover offenders. This is a civic rather than a legal duty; but when a police officer is trying to discover whether, or by whom, an offence has been committed he or she may question any person from whom useful information might be obtained, subject to the restrictions imposed by Code C. A person's unwillingness to reply does not alter this entitlement, but in the absence of*

a power to arrest, or to detain in order to search, the person is free to leave at will and cannot be compelled to remain with the officer.

1A   In paragraphs 1.1 and 2.2B(a), 'the relevant protected characteristics' are: age, disability, gender reassignment, pregnancy and maternity, race, religion or belief, sex and sexual orientation.

1B   Innocent possession means that the person does [not] have the guilty knowledge that they are carrying an unlawful item which is required before an arrest on suspicion that the person has committed an offence in respect of the item sought (if arrest is necessary — see PACE Code G) and/or a criminal prosecution) can be considered. It is not uncommon for children under the age of criminal responsibility to be used by older children and adults to carry stolen property, drugs and weapons and, in some cases, firearms, for the criminal benefit of others, either:
- in the hope that police may not suspect they are being used for carrying the items; or
- knowing that if they are suspected of being couriers and are stopped and searched, they cannot be arrested or prosecuted for any criminal offence.

Stop and search powers therefore allow the police to intervene effectively to break up criminal gangs and groups that use young children to further their criminal activities.

1BA   Whenever a child under 10 is suspected of carrying unlawful items for someone else, or is found in circumstances which suggest that their welfare and safety may be at risk, the facts should be reported and actioned in accordance with established force safeguarding procedures. This will be in addition to treating them as a potentially vulnerable or intimidated witness in respect of their status as a witness to the serious criminal offence(s) committed by those using them as couriers. Safeguarding considerations will also apply to other persons aged under 18 who are stopped and searched under any of the powers to which this Code applies. See paragraph 1.1 with regard to the requirement under the Children Act 2004, section 11, for chief police officers and other specified persons and bodies, to ensure that in the discharge of their functions, they have regard to the need to safeguard and promote the welfare of all persons under the age of 18.

2   In some circumstances preparatory questioning may be unnecessary, but in general a brief conversation or exchange will be desirable not only as a means of avoiding unsuccessful searches, but to explain the grounds for the stop/search, to gain co-operation and reduce any tension there might be surrounding the stop/search.

3   Where a person is lawfully detained for the purpose of a search, but no search in the event takes place, the detention will not thereby have been rendered unlawful.

4   Many people customarily cover their heads or faces for religious reasons – for example, Muslim women, Sikh men, Sikh or Hindu women, or Rastafarian men or women. A police officer cannot order the removal of a head or face covering except where there is reason to believe that the item is being worn by the individual wholly or mainly for the purpose of disguising identity, not simply because it disguises identity. Where there may be religious sensitivities about ordering the removal of such an item, the officer should permit the item to be removed out of public view. Where practicable, the item should be removed in the presence of an officer of the same sex as the person and out of sight of anyone of the opposite sex (see Code C Annex L).

5   A search of a person in public should be completed as soon as possible.

6   A person may be detained under a stop and search power at a place other than where the person was first detained, only if that place, be it a police station or elsewhere, is nearby. Such a place should be located within a reasonable travelling distance using whatever mode of travel (on foot or by car) is appropriate. This applies to all searches under stop and search powers, whether or not they involve the removal of clothing or exposure of intimate parts of the body (see paragraphs 3.6 and 3.7) or take place in or out of public view. It means, for example, that a search under the stop and search power in section 23 of the Misuse of Drugs Act 1971 which involves the compulsory removal of more than a person's outer coat, jacket or gloves cannot be carried out unless a place which is both nearby the place they were first detained and out of public view, is available. If a search involves exposure of intimate parts of the body and a police station is not nearby, particular care must be taken to ensure that the location is suitable in that it enables the search to be conducted in accordance with the requirements of paragraph 11 of Annex A to Code C.

7   A search in the street itself should be regarded as being in public for the purposes of paragraphs 3.6 and 3.7 above, even though it may be empty at the time a search begins. Although there is no power to require a person to do so, there is nothing to prevent an officer from asking a person voluntarily to remove more than an outer coat, jacket or gloves in public.

8   Not used.

9   Other means of identification might include jewellery, insignias, tattoos or other features which are known to identify members of the particular gang or group.

9A   A decision to search individuals believed to be members of a particular group or gang must be judged on a case by case basis according to the circumstances applicable at the time of the proposed searches and in particular, having regard to:

(a)   the number of items suspected of being carried;

(b)   the nature of those items and the risk they pose; and

(c)   the number of individuals to be searched.

A group search will only be justified if it is a necessary and proportionate approach based on the facts and having regard to the nature of the suspicion in these cases. The extent and thoroughness of the searches must not be excessive.

The size of the group and the number of individuals it is proposed to search will be a key factor and steps should be taken to identify those who are to be searched to avoid unnecessary inconvenience to unconnected members of the public who are also present.

The onus is on the police to be satisfied and to demonstrate that their approach to the decision to search is in pursuit of a legitimate aim, necessary and proportionate.

Authorising officers

10   The powers under section 60 are separate from and additional to the normal stop and search powers which require reasonable grounds to suspect an individual of carrying an offensive weapon (or other article). Their overall purpose is to prevent serious violence and the widespread carrying of weapons which might lead to persons being seriously injured by disarming potential offenders or finding weapons that have been used in circumstances where other powers would not be sufficient. They should not therefore be used to replace or circumvent the normal powers for dealing with routine crime problems. A particular example might be an authorisation to prevent serious violence or the carrying of offensive weapons at a sports event by rival team supporters when the expected general appearance and age range of those likely to be responsible, alone, would not be sufficiently distinctive to support reasonable suspicion (see paragraph 2.6). The purpose of the powers under section 60AA is to prevent those involved in intimidatory or violent protests using face coverings to disguise identity.

11   Authorisations under section 60 require a reasonable belief on the part of the authorising officer. This must have an objective basis, for example: intelligence or relevant information such as a history of antagonism and violence between particular groups; previous incidents of violence at, or connected with, particular events or locations; a significant increase in knife-point robberies in a limited area; reports that individuals are regularly carrying weapons in a particular locality; information following an incident in which weapons were used about where the weapons might be found or in the case of section 60AA previous incidents of crimes being committed while wearing face coverings to conceal identity.

12   It is for the authorising officer to determine the period of time during which the powers mentioned in paragraph 2.1(b) may be exercised. The officer should set the minimum period he or she considers necessary to deal with the risk of violence, the carrying of knives or offensive weapons, or to find dangerous instruments or weapons that have been used. A direction to extend the period authorised under the powers mentioned in paragraph 2.1(b) may be given only once. Thereafter further use of the powers requires a new authorisation.

13   It is for the authorising officer to determine the geographical area in which the use of the powers is to be authorised. In doing so the officer may wish to take into account factors such as the nature and venue of the anticipated incident or the incident which has taken place, the number of people who may be in the immediate area of that incident, their access to surrounding areas and the anticipated or actual level of violence. The officer should not set a geographical area which is wider than that he or she believes necessary for the purpose of preventing anticipated violence, the carrying of knives or offensive weapons, or for finding a dangerous instrument or weapon that has been used or, in the case of section 60AA, the prevention of commission of offences. It is particularly important to ensure that constables exercising such powers are fully aware of the locality within which they may be used. The officer giving the authorisation should therefore specify either the streets which form the boundary of the locality or a divisional boundary if appropriate, within the force area. If the power is to be used in response to a threat or incident that straddles police force areas, an officer from each of the forces concerned will need to give an authorisation.

14   Not used.

Recording

15   Where a stop and search is conducted by more than one officer the identity of all the officers engaged in the search must be recorded on the record. Nothing prevents an officer who is present but not directly involved in searching from completing the record during the course of the encounter.

16   When the search results in the person searched or in charge of a vehicle which is searched being arrested, the requirement to make the record of the search as part of the person's custody record does not apply if the person is granted 'street bail' after arrest (see section 30A of PACE) to attend a police station and is not taken in custody to the police station An arrested person's entitlement to a copy of the search record which is made as part of their custody record does not affect their entitlement to a copy of their custody record or any other provisions of PACE Code C section 2 (Custody records).

17   It is important for monitoring purposes to specify when authority is given for exercising the stop and search power under section 60 of the Criminal Justice and Public Order Act 1994.

18   Officers should record the self-defined ethnicity of every person stopped according to the categories used in the 2001 census question listed in Annex B. The person should be asked to select one of the five main categories representing broad ethnic groups and then a more specific cultural background from within this group. The ethnic classification should be coded for recording purposes using the coding system in Annex B. An additional 'Not stated' box is available but should not be offered to respondents explicitly. Officers should be aware and explain to members of the public, especially where concerns are raised, that this information is required to obtain a true picture of stop and search activity and to help improve ethnic monitoring, tackle discriminatory practice, and promote effective use of the powers. If the person gives what appears to the officer to be an 'incorrect' answer (e.g. a person who appears to be white states that they are black), the officer should record the response that has been given and then record their own perception of the person's ethnic background by using the PNC classification system. If the 'Not stated' category is used the reason for this must be recorded on the form.

19   Arrangements for public scrutiny of records should take account of the right to confidentiality of those stopped and searched. Anonymised forms and/or statistics generated from records should be the focus of the examinations by members of the public. The groups that are consulted should always include children and young persons.

20   Not used.

21   In situations where it is not practicable to provide a written copy of the record or immediate access to an electronic copy of the record or a receipt of the search at the time (see paragraph 4.2A above), the officer should consider giving the person details of the station which they may attend for a copy of the record. A receipt may take the form of a simple business card which includes sufficient information to locate the record should the person ask for copy, for example, the date and place of the search, and a reference number or the name of the officer who carried out the search (unless paragraph 4.4 applies).

22   Not used.

22A   Where there are concerns which make it necessary to monitor any local disproportionality, forces have discretion to direct officers to record the self-defined ethnicity of persons they request to account for themselves in a public place or who they detain with a view to searching but do not search. Guidance should be provided locally and efforts made to minimise the bureaucracy involved. Records should be closely monitored and supervised in line with paragraphs 5.1 to 5.6, and forces can suspend or re-instate recording of these encounters as appropriate.

22B   A person who is asked to account for themselves should, if they request, be given information about how they can report their dissatisfaction about how they have been treated.

Definition of offensive weapon

23   'Offensive weapon' is defined as 'any article made or adapted for use for causing injury to the person, or intended by the person having it with him for such use by him or by someone else'. There are three categories of offensive weapons: those made for causing injury to the person; those adapted for such a purpose; and those not so made or adapted, but carried with the intention of causing injury to the person. A firearm, as defined by section 57 of the Firearms Act 1968, would fall within the definition of offensive weapon if any of the criteria above apply.

24   Not used.

25   Not used.

ANNEX A

SUMMARY OF MAIN STOP AND SEARCH POWERS TO WHICH CODE A APPLIES

This table relates to stop and search powers only. Individual statutes below may contain other police powers of entry, search and seizure.

Power	Object of Search	Extent of Search	Where exercisable
Unlawful articles general			
1. Public Stores Act 1875, s. 6	HM Stores stolen or unlawfully obtained	Persons, vehicles and vessels	Anywhere where the constabulary powers are exercisable
2. Firearms Act 1968, s. 47	Firearms	Persons and vehicles	A public place, or anywhere in the case of reasonable suspicion of offences of carrying firearms with criminal intent or trespassing with firearms
3. Misuse of Drugs Act 1971, s. 23	Controlled drugs	Persons and vehicles	Anywhere
4. Customs and Excise Management Act 1979, s. 163	Goods: (a) on which duty has not been paid; (b) being unlawfully removed, imported or exported; (c) otherwise liable to forfeiture to HM Revenue and Customs	Vehicles and vessels only	Anywhere
5. Aviation Security Act 1982, s. 24B *Note: This power applies throughout the UK but the provisions of this Code will apply only when the power is exercised at an aerodrome situated in England and Wales.*	Stolen articles or articles made, adapted or intended for use in the course of/in connection with conduct which constitutes an offence in the part of the UK where the aerodrome is situated or would so do, if it occurred there.	Persons, vehicles, aircraft. Anything in or on a vehicle or aircraft.	Any part of an aerodrome.
6. Police and Criminal Evidence Act 1984, s. 1	Stolen goods;	Persons and vehicles.	Where there is public access.
	Articles made, adapted or intended for use in the course of or in connection with, certain offences under the Theft Act 1968, Fraud Act and Criminal Damage Act 1971;	Persons and vehicles.	Where there is public access.
	Offensive weapons, bladed or sharply-pointed articles (except folding pocket knives with a bladed cutting edge not exceeding 3 inches);	Persons and vehicles.	Where there is public access.

Power	Object of Search	Extent of Search	Where exercisable
	Fireworks: Category 4 (display grade) fireworks if possession prohibited, Adult fireworks in possession of a person under 18 in a public place.	Persons and vehicles.	Where there is public access.
7. Sporting Events (Control of Alcohol etc.) Act 1985, s. 7	Intoxicating liquor	Persons, coaches and trains	Designated sports grounds or coaches and trains travelling to or from a designated sporting event.
8. Crossbows Act 1987, s. 4	Crossbows or parts of crossbows (except crossbows with a draw weight of less than 1.4 kilograms)	Persons and vehicles	Anywhere except dwellings
9. Criminal Justice Act 1988 s. 139B	Offensive weapons, bladed or sharply pointed article	Persons	School premises
Evidence of game and wildlife offences			
10. Poaching Prevention Act 1862, s. 2	Game or poaching equipment	Persons and vehicles	A public place
11. Deer Act 1991, s. 12	Evidence of offences under the Act	Persons and vehicles	Anywhere except dwellings
12. Conservation of Seals Act 1970, s. 4	Seals or hunting equipment	Vehicles only	Anywhere
13. Protection of Badgers Act 1992, s. 11	Evidence of offences under the Act	Persons and vehicles	Anywhere
14. Wildlife and Countryside Act 1981, s. 19	Evidence of wildlife offences	Persons and vehicles	Anywhere except dwellings
Other			
15. Paragraphs 6 & 8 of Schedule 5 to the Terrorism Prevention and Investigation Measures Act 2011	Anything that contravenes measures specified in a TPIM notice.	Persons in respect of whom a TPIM notice is being served or is in force	Anywhere
16. Paragraph 10 of Schedule 5 to the Terrorism Prevention and Investigation Measures Act 2011	Anything that could be used to threaten or harm any person.	Persons in respect of whom a TPIM notice is in force.	Anywhere
17. *Not used*			
18. *Not used*			
19. Section 60 Criminal Justice and Public Order Act 1994	Offensive weapons or dangerous instruments to prevent incidents of serious violence or to deal with the carrying of such items or find such items which have been used in incidents of serious violence	Persons and vehicles	Anywhere within a locality authorised under subsection (1)

ANNEX B

SELF-DEFINED ETHNIC CLASSIFICATION CATEGORIES

[Omitted.]

ANNEX C

SUMMARY OF POWERS OF COMMUNITY SUPPORT OFFICERS TO SEARCH AND SEIZE

The following is a summary of the search and seizure powers that may be exercised by a community support officer (CSO) who has been designated with the relevant powers in accordance with Part 4 of the Police Reform Act 2002.

When exercising any of these powers, a CSO must have regard to any relevant provisions of this Code, including section 3 governing the conduct of searches and the steps to be taken prior to a search.

1. *Not used*

2. **Powers to search requiring the consent of the person and seizure**

A CSO may detain a person using reasonable force where necessary as set out in Part 1 of Schedule 4 to the Police Reform Act 2002. If the person has been lawfully detained, the CSO may search the person provided that person gives consent to such a search in relation to the following:

Designation	Powers conferred	Object of Search	Extent of Search	Where Exercisable
1. Police Reform Act 2002, Schedule 4, paragraphs 7 and 7A	(a) Criminal Justice and Police Act 2001, s. 12(2)	(a) Alcohol or a container for alcohol	(a) Persons	(a) Designated public place
	(b) Confiscation of Alcohol (Young Persons) Act 1997, s. 1	(b) Alcohol	(b) Persons under 18 years old	(b) Public place
	(c) Children and Young Persons Act 1933, s. 7(3)	(c) Tobacco or cigarette papers	(c) Persons under 16 years old found smoking	(c) Public place

3. **Powers to search not requiring the consent of the person and seizure**

A CSO may detain a person using reasonable force where necessary as set out in Part 1 of Schedule 4 to the Police Reform Act 2002. If the person has been lawfully detained, the CSO may search the person without the need for that person's consent in relation to the following:

Designation	Power conferred	Object of Search	Extent of Search	Where Exercisable
Police Reform Act 2002, Schedule 4, paragraph 2A	Police and Criminal Evidence Act 1984, s. 32	(a) Objects that might be used to cause physical injury to the person or the CSO. (b) Items that might be used to assist escape.	Persons made subject to a requirement to wait.	Any place where the requirement to wait has been made

4. **Powers to seize without consent**

This power applies when drugs are found in the course of any search mentioned above.

Designation	Power conferred	Object of Seizure	Where Exercisable
Police Reform Act 2002, Schedule 4, paragraph 7B	Police Reform Act 2002, Schedule 4, paragraph 7B	Controlled drugs in a person's possession.	Any place where the person is in possession of the drug.

Annex D – Deleted

Annex E – Deleted

Annex F – Establishing Gender of Persons for the Purpose of Searching

See Code C *Annex L*

Annex G

Searches under Section 342E of the Sentencing Code in Relation to Offenders
Subject to A Serious Violence Reduction Order (SVRO)

Additions of Paragraphs 2.30–2.39 and Modifications that Apply to Paragraphs 3.3, 3.8, 4.3 and Annex A of this Code.

1.   This Annex applies to any search under Section 342E of the Sentencing Code in relation to offenders subject to a Serious Violence Reduction Order (SVRO) by a police officer and the recording of public encounters taking place.
2.   This Annex shall apply from 00.00 on 17 January 2023 to 23.59 on 17 July 2025 for the purpose of the pilot for SVROs. This period covers the 24 months pilot period plus an additional 6-month transitional period.
3.   The 6-month transitional period allows for SVROs which take effect before the end of the pilot period to remain 'live' for 6 months after the end of the pilot, but it will not be possible to apply for new SVROs or renew existing SVROs once the pilot period ends. This allows courts to issue an SVRO on the last day of the pilot for the minimum duration of the order (6 months).
4.   For the avoidance of doubt, the expiry of the period in paragraph 2 does not affect any other provisions of this Code which shall continue to apply.
5.   This Annex outlines the powers under Section 324E of the Sentencing Code and the considerations police officers should make when deciding to conduct a search on individuals subject to an SVRO.
6.   SVROs are being piloted in Thames Valley, Sussex, West Midlands and Merseyside police force areas before a decision is made on full roll out of the powers across England and Wales.
7.   SVROs can be issued in the pilot force areas only. This Annex shall, however, be enforceable across England and Wales, for the purpose of the pilot. The powers to stop and search under section 342E of the Sentencing Code are exercisable by a constable across England and Wales.
8.   During the period for which this Annex applies, its provisions should be read in conjunction with all other provisions of Code A that apply during the same period.
9.   This Annex should be read in conjunction with the Statutory Guidance on SVROs which sets out background, police processes, evidential considerations, court procedure and information on using SVROs alongside other orders and interventions. The Statutory Guidance can be found on gov.uk.

Types of Stop and Search Powers

This Annex inserts searches under Section 342E of the Sentencing Code in relation to individuals subject to an SVRO into Paragraph 2 of Code A (Types of Stop and Search Power) in particular:

Addition of Paragraph 2.1(F)

f)   Searches under Section 342E of the Sentencing Code in relation to individuals subject to a Serious Violence Reduction Order

Addition of Paragraphs 2.30–2.39

The additions of paragraph 2.30–2.39 to Code A outline the considerations police officers should make when deciding to conduct a search on individuals subject to an SVRO. In particular:

2.30 Section 342A to 342K of the Sentencing Code provides for Serious Violence Reduction Orders, a civil order made in respect of an offender convicted of an offence involving a bladed article or offensive weapons.
2.31 Section 342E of the Sentencing Code provides the police with the power to search a person subject to an SVRO, to ascertain if they have a bladed article or offensive weapon with them and to detain them for the purpose of carrying out that search, provided that person is in a public place.
2.32 The exercise of the powers mentioned in paragraph 2.31 do not require the constable to have prior reasonable grounds to suspect that the person to be searched is in possession of an item for which there is an existing power to search. However, it is still necessary to ensure that the treatment of those searched under this power is based upon that individual being subject to an SVRO, and not upon personal prejudice.
2.33 Officers must ensure that any stop and search under the power mentioned in paragraph 2.31 is conducted on an individual who is subject to an SVRO only. In most cases, it is expected that individuals subject to an SVRO will be known to the police in the police force area where the individual lives and offenders will have notified the police in that area of their address through the

notification requirements. Therefore, officers should be able to identify the offender before conducting a search. Where an officer is unsure of an offender's identity, they should seek to confirm that offender's identity and whether they have an SVRO. Officers may wish to confirm the order is in place via PNC.

2.34 This means that unless officers are able to confirm the individual is subject to an SVRO, the power mentioned in paragraph 2.31 cannot be used and it would be unlawful if an individual without an SVRO is searched.

2.35 There must always be an objective and rational basis for conducting a stop and search. In these circumstances this is based on the fact that an SVRO is in force in relation to the individual. However, the use of the power mentioned in paragraph 2.31 is also discretionary and police officers are expected to use their judgement as to when deciding, in what circumstances and how many times an individual who is subject to an SVRO is stopped and searched.

2.36 Searches must be conducted in a public place and the power does not provide officers with any grounds to search anyone else accompanying that person. A person accompanying an individual that has an SVRO should not be searched unless a constable has the relevant reasonable grounds for suspicion.

2.37 The power does not provide officers with the grounds to search vehicles. However, Section 342E(7) of the Sentencing Code provides that this power may be used in addition to existing powers held by the police under common law or by virtue of any other enactment.

2.38 Police officers may seize and retain, in accordance with regulations made by the Secretary of State under section 342F of the Sentencing Code Items found in the course of the search which they reasonably suspect to be a bladed article or an offensive weapon.

2.39 The Statutory Guidance on SVROs which sets out background on SVROs, police processes, evidential considerations, court procedure and information on using SVROs alongside other orders and interventions can be found on gov.uk.

Conduct of Searches

Addition to Paragraph 3.3

This Annex makes an addition to paragraph 3.3 of Code A (Conduct of Searches). This addition outlines that:

> In the case of searches mentioned in paragraph 2.1(b), (d) and (f) (searches in relation to SVROs), which do not require reasonable grounds for suspicion, officers may make any reasonable search to look for items for which they are empowered to search.

Steps to be taken prior to a search

Addition to Paragraph 3.8

This Annex makes an addition to paragraph 3.8 of Code A (steps to be taken prior to a search). This annex provides that an officer must provide a detained person with the officer's name, the legal search power which is being exercised, a clear explanation of the object of the search in terms of the article or articles for which there is a power to search; and in the case of:

> searches under Section 342E of the Sentencing Code in relation to individuals subject to a Serious Violence Reduction Order,
>
> — the fact that a Serious Violence Reduction Order is in force.

Record of Search

Addition to paragraph 4.3(d)

In this Annex, in accordance with paragraph 4.3, a record of a search must always include, in the case of:

> searches powers under Section 342E of the Sentencing Code in relation to individuals subject to a Serious Violence Reduction Order:
>
> — the fact that a Serious Violence Reduction Order is in force
>
> — whether anything was found and whether anything was seized

Annex A — Summary of Main Stop And Search Powers to Which Code A Applies

Addition to Annex A

This Annex makes additions to the table at Annex A (summary of main stop and search powers to which Code A applies) to include searches under Section 342E of the Sentencing Code in relation to individuals subject to a Serious Violence Reduction Order (SVRO).

Power	Object of search	Extent of search	Where exercisable
20. Sentencing Act 2020 ('the Sentencing Code') s.342E	Bladed articles or offensive weapon	Persons	A public place

PACE CODE B

REVISED CODE OF PRACTICE FOR SEARCHES OF PREMISES BY POLICE OFFICERS AND THE SEIZURE OF PROPERTY FOUND BY POLICE OFFICERS ON PERSONS OR PREMISES

Commencement—Transitional Arrangements

This code applies to applications for warrants made after 00.00 on 27 October 2013 and to searches and seizures taking place after 0.00 on 27 October 2013.

1 Introduction

1.1 This Code of Practice deals with police powers to:
- search premises
- seize and retain property found on premises and persons

1.1A These powers may be used to find:
- property and material relating to a crime
- wanted persons
- children who abscond from local authority accommodation where they have been remanded or committed by a court

1.2 A justice of the peace may issue a search warrant granting powers of entry, search and seizure, e.g. warrants to search for stolen property, drugs, firearms and evidence of serious offences. Police also have powers without a search warrant. The main ones provided by the Police and Criminal Evidence Act 1984 (PACE) include powers to search premises:
- to make an arrest
- after an arrest

1.3 The right to privacy and respect for personal property are key principles of the Human Rights Act 1998. Powers of entry, search and seizure should be fully and clearly justified before use because they may significantly interfere with the occupier's privacy. Officers should consider if the necessary objectives can be met by less intrusive means.

1.3A Powers to search and seize must be used fairly, responsibly, with respect for people who occupy premises being searched or are in charge of property being seized and without unlawful discrimination. Under the Equality Act 2010, section 149, when police officers are carrying out their functions, they also have a duty to have due regard to the need to eliminate unlawful discrimination, harassment and victimisation, to advance equality of opportunity between people who share a relevant protected characteristic and people who do not share it, and to take steps to foster good relations between those persons. (See *Note 1A*).

1.4 In all cases, police should therefore:
- exercise their powers courteously and with respect for persons and property
- only use reasonable force when this is considered necessary and proportionate to the circumstances

1.5 If the provisions of PACE and this Code are not observed, evidence obtained from a search may be open to question.

Note for Guidance

1A *In paragraph 1.3A, 'relevant protected characteristic' includes: age, disability, gender reassignment, pregnancy and maternity, race, religion/belief, sex and sexual orientation.*

2 General

2.1 This Code must be readily available at all police stations for consultation by:
- police officers
- police staff

- detained persons
- members of the public

2.2 The Notes for Guidance included are not provisions of this Code.

2.3 This Code applies to searches of premises:
   (a) by police for the purposes of an investigation into an alleged offence, with the occupier's consent, other than:
      - routine scene of crime searches;
      - calls to a fire or burglary made by or on behalf of an occupier or searches following the activation of fire or burglar alarms or discovery of insecure premises;
      - searches when paragraph 5.4 applies;
      - bomb threat calls;
   (b) under powers conferred on police officers by PACE, sections 17, 18 and 32;
   (c) undertaken in pursuance of search warrants issued to and executed by constables in accordance with PACE, sections 15 and 16 (see *Note 2A*);
   (d) subject to paragraph 2.6, under any other power given to police to enter premises with or without a search warrant for any purpose connected with the investigation into an alleged or suspected offence. (See *Note 2B*.)
   For the purposes of this Code, 'premises' as defined in PACE, section 23, includes any place, vehicle, vessel, aircraft, hovercraft, tent or movable structure and any offshore installation as defined in the Mineral Workings (Offshore Installations) Act 1971, section 1. (See *Note 2D*.)

2.4 A person who has not been arrested but is searched during a search of premises should be searched in accordance with Code A. (See *Note 2C*.)

2.5 This Code does not apply to the exercise of a statutory power to enter premises or to inspect goods, equipment or procedures if the exercise of that power is not dependent on the existence of grounds for suspecting that an offence may have been committed and the person exercising the power has no reasonable grounds for such suspicion.

2.6 This Code does not affect any directions or requirements of a search warrant, order or other power to search and seize lawfully exercised in England or Wales that any item or evidence seized under that warrant, order or power be handed over to a police force, court, tribunal, or other authority outside England or Wales. For example, warrants and orders issued in Scotland or Northern Ireland (see *Note 2B(f)*) and search warrants and powers provided for in sections 14 to 17 of the Crime (International Co-operation) Act 2003.

2.7 When this Code requires the prior authority or agreement of an officer of at leastinspector or superintendent rank, that authority may be given by a sergeant or chief inspector authorised to perform the functions of the higher rank under PACE, section 107.5

2.8 Written records required under this Code not made in the search record shall, unless otherwise specified, be made:
   - in the recording officer's pocket book ('pocket book' includes any official report book issued to police officers) or
   - on forms provided for the purpose

2.9 Nothing in this Code requires the identity of officers, or anyone accompanying them during a search of premises, to be recorded or disclosed:
   (a) in the case of enquiries linked to the investigation of terrorism; or
   (b) if officers reasonably believe recording or disclosing their names might put them in danger.
   In these cases officers should use warrant or other identification numbers and the name of their police station. Police staff should use any identification number provided to them by the police force. (See *Note 2E*.)

2.10 The 'officer in charge of the search' means the officer assigned specific duties and responsibilities under this Code. Whenever there is a search of premises to which this Code applies one officer must act as the officer in charge of the search. (See *Note 2F*.)

2.11 In this Code:
   (a) 'designated person' means a person other than a police officer, designated under the Police Reform Act 2002, Part 4 who has specified powers and duties of police officers conferred or imposed on them. (See *Note 2G*.)
   (b) any reference to a police officer includes a designated person acting in the exercise or performance of the powers and duties conferred or imposed on them by their designation.
   (c) a person authorised to accompany police officers or designated persons in the execution of a warrant has the same powers as a constable in the execution of the warrant and the search and

seizure of anything related to the warrant. These powers must be exercised in the company and under the supervision of a police officer. (See *Note 3C*.)

2.12 If a power conferred on a designated person:

    (a) allows reasonable force to be used when exercised by a police officer, a designated person exercising that power has the same entitlement to use force;

    (b) includes power to use force to enter any premises, that power is not exercisable by that designated person except:

        (i) in the company and under the supervision of a police officer; or

        (ii) for the purpose of:

            • saving life or limb; or

            • preventing serious damage to property.

2.13 Designated persons must have regard to any relevant provisions of the Codes of Practice.

Notes for Guidance

2A   *PACE sections 15 and 16 apply to all search warrants issued to and executed by constables under any enactment, e.g. search warrants issued by a:*

    (a) justice of the peace under the:

       • Theft Act 1968, section 26 – stolen property;

       • Misuse of Drugs Act 1971, section 23 – controlled drugs;

       • PACE, section 8 – evidence of an indictable offence;

       • Terrorism Act 2000, Schedule 5, paragraph 1;

       • Terrorism Prevention and Investigation Measures Act 2011, Schedule 5, paragraph 8(2)(b) search of premises for compliance purposes (see paragraph 10.1).

    (b) Circuit judge under:

       • PACE, Schedule 1;

       • Terrorism Act 2000, Schedule 5, paragraph 11.

2B   *Examples of the other powers in paragraph 2.3(d) include:*

    (a) Road Traffic Act 1988, section 6E(1) giving police power to enter premises under section 6E(1) to:

       • require a person to provide a specimen of breath; or

       • arrest a person following:

          – a positive breath test;

          – failure to provide a specimen of breath;

    (b) Transport and Works Act 1992, section 30(4) giving police powers to enter premises mirroring the powers in (a) in relation to specified persons working on transport systems to which the Act applies;

    (c) Criminal Justice Act 1988, section 139B giving police power to enter and search school premises for offensive weapons, bladed or pointed articles;

    (d) Terrorism Act 2000, Schedule 5, paragraphs 3 and 15 empowering a superintendent in urgent cases to give written authority for police to enter and search premises for the purposes of a terrorist investigation;

    (e) Explosives Act 1875, section 73(b) empowering a superintendent to give written authority for police to enter premises, examine and search them for explosives;

    (f) search warrants and production orders or the equivalent issued in Scotland or Northern Ireland endorsed under the Summary Jurisdiction (Process) Act 1881 or the Petty Sessions (Ireland) Act 1851 respectively for execution in England and Wales.

    (g) Terrorism Prevention and Investigation Measures Act 2011, Schedule 5, paragraphs 5(1), 6(2)(b) and 7(2), searches relating to TPIM notices (see paragraph 10.1).

2C   *The Criminal Justice Act 1988, section 139B provides that a constable who has reasonable grounds to suspect an offence under the Criminal Justice Act 1988, section 139A or 139AA has or is being committed may enter school premises and search the premises and any persons on the premises for any bladed or pointed article or offensive weapon. Persons may be searched under a warrant issued under the Misuse of Drugs Act 1971, section 23(3) to search premises for drugs or documents only if the warrant specifically authorises the search of persons on the premises. Powers to search premises under certain terrorism provisions also authorise the search of persons on the premises, for example, under paragraphs 1, 2, 11 and 15 of Schedule 5 to the Terrorism Act 2000 and section 52 of the Anti-terrorism, Crime and Security Act 2001.*

2D   *The Immigration Act 1971, Part III and Schedule 2 gives immigration officers powers to enter and search premises, seize and retain property, with and without a search warrant. These are similar to the powers available to police under search warrants issued by a justice of the peace and without a warrant under PACE, sections 17, 18, 19 and 32 except they only apply to specified offences under the Immigration Act 1971 and immigration control powers. For certain types of investigations and enquiries these powers avoid the need for the Immigration Service to rely on police officers becoming directly involved. When exercising these powers, immigration officers are required by the Immigration and Asylum Act 1999, section 145 to have regard to this Code's corresponding provisions. When immigration officers are dealing with persons or property at police stations, police officers should give appropriate assistance to help them discharge their specific duties and responsibilities.*

2E   *The purpose of paragraph 2.9(b) is to protect those involved in serious organised crime investigations or arrests of particularly violent suspects when there is reliable information that those arrested or their associates may threaten or cause harm to the officers or anyone accompanying them during a search of premises. In cases of doubt, an officer of inspector rank or above should be consulted.*

2F   *For the purposes of paragraph 2.10, the officer in charge of the search should normally be the most senior officer present. Some exceptions are:*

    (a) a supervising officer who attends or assists at the scene of a premises search may appoint an officer of lower rank as officer in charge of the search if that officer is:
- *more conversant with the facts;*
- *a more appropriate officer to be in charge of the search;*

    (b) when all officers in a premises search are the same rank. The supervising officer if available, must make sure one of them is appointed officer in charge of the search, otherwise the officers themselves must nominate one of their number as the officer in charge;

    (c) a senior officer assisting in a specialist role. This officer need not be regarded as having a general supervisory role over the conduct of the search or be appointed or expected to act as the officer in charge of the search.

    Except in (c), nothing in this Note diminishes the role and responsibilities of a supervisory officer who is present at the search or knows of a search taking place.

2G   *An officer of the rank of inspector or above may direct a designated investigating officer not to wear a uniform for the purposes of a specific operation.*

3 Search warrants and production orders

(a) Before making an application

3.1   When information appears to justify an application, the officer must take reasonable steps to check the information is accurate, recent and not provided maliciously or irresponsibly. An application may not be made on the basis of information from an anonymous source if corroboration has not been sought. (See *Note 3A*.)

3.2   The officer shall ascertain as specifically as possible the nature of the articles concerned and their location.

3.3   The officer shall make reasonable enquiries to:

    (i)   establish if:
- anything is known about the likely occupier of the premises and the nature of the premises themselves;
- the premises have been searched previously and how recently;

    (ii) obtain any other relevant information.

3.4   An application:

    (a)   to a justice of the peace for a search warrant or to a Circuit judge for a search warrant or production order under PACE, Schedule 1 must be supported by a signed written authority from an officer of inspector rank or above:

        Note: If the case is an urgent application to a justice of the peace and an inspector or above is not readily available, the next most senior officer on duty can give the written authority.

    (b)   to a circuit judge under the Terrorism Act 2000, Schedule 5 for:
- a production order;
- search warrant; or
- an order requiring an explanation of material seized or produced under such a warrant or production order, must be supported by a signed written authority from an officer of superintendent rank or above.

3.5   Except in a case of urgency, if there is reason to believe a search might have an adverse effect on relations between the police and the community, the officer in charge shall consult the local police/community liaison officer:
- before the search; or
- in urgent cases, as soon as practicable after the search

(b) Making an application

3.6   A search warrant application must be supported in writing, specifying:
    (a) the enactment under which the application is made (see *Note 2A*);
    (b) (i) whether the warrant is to authorise entry and search of:
        • one set of premises; or
        • if the application is under PACE section 8, or Schedule 1, paragraph 12, more than one
         set of specified premises or all premises occupied or controlled by a specified person,
         and
        (ii) the premises to be searched;
    (c) the object of the search (see *Note 3B*);
    (d) the grounds for the application, including, when the purpose of the proposed search is to find
      evidence of an alleged offence, an indication of how the evidence relates to the investigation;
    (da) Where the application is under PACE section 8, or Schedule 1, paragraph 12 for a single
      warrant to enter and search:
      (i) more than one set of specified premises; the officer must specify each set of premises which
        it is desired to enter and search;
      (ii) all premises occupied or controlled by a specified person; the officer must specify;
        • as many sets of premises which it is desired to enter and search as it is reasonably
         practicable to specify;
        • the person who is in occupation or control of those premises and any others which it is
         desired to search;
        • why it is necessary to search more premises than those which can be specified, and
        • why it is not reasonably practicable to specify all the premises which it is desired to enter
         and search;
    (db) Whether an application under PACE section 8 is for a warrant authorising entry and search on
      more than one occasion, and if so, the officer must state the grounds for this and whether the
      desired number of entries authorised is unlimited or a specified maximum;
    (e) That there are no reasonable grounds to believe the material to be sought, when making
      application to a:
      (i) justice of the peace or a Circuit judge consists of or includes items subject to legal
        privilege;
      (ii) justice of the peace, consists of or includes excluded material or special procedure material;
      Note: this does not affect the additional powers of seizure in the Criminal Justice and Police Act
      2001, Part 2 covered in paragraph 7.7 (see *Note 3B*).
    (f) if applicable, a request for the warrant to authorise a person or persons to accompany the officer
      who executes the warrant. (See *Note 3C*.)
3.7   A search warrant application under PACE, Schedule 1, paragraph 12(a), shall if appropriate indicate
    why it is believed service of notice of an application for a production order may seriously prejudice
    the investigation. Applications for search warrants under the Terrorism Act 2000, Schedule 5,
    paragraph 11 must indicate why a production order would not be appropriate.
3.8   If a search warrant application is refused, a further application may not be made for those premises
    unless supported by additional grounds.

Notes for Guidance

*3A   The identity of an informant need not be disclosed when making an application, but the officer should be
    prepared to answer any questions the magistrate or judge may have about:*
    • the accuracy of previous information from that source, and
    • any other related matters
*3B   The information supporting a search warrant application should be as specific as possible, particularly in
    relation to the articles or persons being sought and where in the premises it is suspected they may be found.
    The meaning of 'items subject to legal privilege', 'excluded material' and 'special procedure material' are
    defined by PACE, sections 10, 11 and 14 respectively.*
*3C   Under PACE, section 16(2), a search warrant may authorise persons other than police officers to
    accompany the constable who executes the warrant. This includes, e.g. any suitably qualified or skilled
    person or an expert in a particular field whose presence is needed to help accurately identify the material
    sought or to advise where certain evidence is most likely to be found and how it should be dealt with. It does
    not give them any right to force entry, but it gives them the right to be on the premises during the search
    and to search for or seize property without the occupier's permission.*

4 Entry without warrant – particular powers

(a) Making an arrest etc

4.1   The conditions under which an officer may enter and search premises without a warrant are set out in PACE, section 17. It should be noted that this section does not create or confer any powers of arrest. See other powers in *Note 2B(a)*.

(b) Search of premises where arrest takes place or the arrested person was immediately before arrest

4.2   When a person has been arrested for an indictable offence, a police officer has power under PACE, section 32 to search the premises where the person was arrested or where the person was immediately before being arrested.

(c) Search of premises occupied or controlled by the arrested person

4.3   The specific powers to search premises which are occupied or controlled by a person arrested for an indictable offence are set out in PACE, section 18. They may not be exercised, except if section 18(5) applies, unless an officer of inspector rank or above has given written authority. That authority should only be given when the authorising officer is satisfied that the premises are occupied or controlled by the arrested person and that the necessary grounds exist. If possible the authorising officer should record the authority on the Notice of Powers and Rights and, subject to paragraph 2.9, sign the Notice. The record of the grounds for the search and the nature of the evidence sought as required by section 18(7) of the Act should be made in:

- the custody record if there is one, otherwise
- the officer's pocket book, or
- the search record

5 Search with consent

5.1   Subject to paragraph 5.4, if it is proposed to search premises with the consent of a person entitled to grant entry the consent must, if practicable, be given in writing on the Notice of Powers and Rights before the search. The officer must make any necessary enquiries to be satisfied the person is in a position to give such consent. (See *Notes 5A* and *5B*.)

5.2   Before seeking consent the officer in charge of the search shall state the purpose of the proposed search and its extent. This information must be as specific as possible, particularly regarding the articles or persons being sought and the parts of the premises to be searched. The person concerned must be clearly informed they are not obliged to consent, that any consent given can be withdrawn at any time, including before the search starts or while it is underway and anything seized may be produced in evidence. If at the time the person is not suspected of an offence, the officer shall say this when stating the purpose of the search.

5.3   An officer cannot enter and search or continue to search premises under paragraph 5.1 if consent is given under duress or withdrawn before the search is completed.

5.4   It is unnecessary to seek consent under paragraphs 5.1 and 5.2 if this would cause disproportionate inconvenience to the person concerned. (See *Note 5C*.)

Notes for Guidance

5A   *In a lodging house, hostel or similar accommodation, every reasonable effort should be made to obtain the consent of the tenant, lodger or occupier. A search should not be made solely on the basis of the landlord's consent.*

5B   *If the intention is to search premises under the authority of a warrant or a power of entry and search without warrant, and the occupier of the premises co-operates in accordance with paragraph 6.4, there is no need to obtain written consent.*

5C   *Paragraph 5.4 is intended to apply when it is reasonable to assume innocent occupiers would agree to, and expect, police to take the proposed action, e.g. if:*

- *a suspect has fled the scene of a crime or to evade arrest and it is necessary quickly to check surrounding gardens and readily accessible places to see if the suspect is hiding, or*
- *police have arrested someone in the night after a pursuit and it is necessary to make a brief check of gardens along the pursuit route to see if stolen or incriminating articles have been discarded.*

6 Searching premises – general considerations

(a) Time of searches

6.1   Searches made under warrant must be made within three calendar months of the date the warrant is issued or within the period specified in the enactment under which the warrant is issued if this is shorter.

6.2   Searches must be made at a reasonable hour unless this might frustrate the purpose of the search.

6.3   When the extent or complexity of a search mean it is likely to take a long time, the officer in charge of the search may consider using the seize and sift powers referred to in section 7.

6.3A A warrant under PACE, section 8 may authorise entry to and search of premises on more than one occasion if, on the application, the justice of the peace is satisfied that it is necessary to authorise multiple entries in order to achieve the purpose for which the warrant is issued. No premises may be entered or searched on any subsequent occasions without the prior written authority of an officer of the rank of inspector who is not involved in the investigation. All other warrants authorise entry on one occasion only.

6.3B Where a warrant under PACE section 8, or Schedule 1, paragraph 12 authorises entry to and search of all premises occupied or controlled by a specified person, no premises which are not specified in the warrant may be entered and searched without the prior written authority of an officer of the rank of inspector who is not involved in the investigation.

(b) Entry other than with consent

6.4   The officer in charge of the search shall first try to communicate with the occupier, or any other person entitled to grant access to the premises, explain the authority under which entry is sought and ask the occupier to allow entry, unless:
   (i)   the search premises are unoccupied;
   (ii)   the occupier and any other person entitled to grant access are absent;
   (iii) there are reasonable grounds for believing that alerting the occupier or any other person entitled to grant access would frustrate the object of the search or endanger officers or other people.

6.5   Unless sub-paragraph 6.4(iii) applies, if the premises are occupied the officer, subject to paragraph 2.9, shall, before the search begins:
   (i)   identify him or herself, show their warrant card (if not in uniform) and state the purpose of, and grounds for, the search, and
   (ii)   Identify and introduce any person accompanying the officer on the search (such persons should carry identification for production on request) and briefly describe that person's role in the process.

6.6   Reasonable and proportionate force may be used if necessary to enter premises if the officer in charge of the search is satisfied the premises are those specified in any warrant, or in exercise of the powers described in paragraphs 4.1 to 4.3, and if:
   (i)   the occupier or any other person entitled to grant access has refused entry;
   (ii)   it is impossible to communicate with the occupier or any other person entitled to grant access; or
   (iii) any of the provisions of paragraph 6.4 apply.

(c) Notice of Powers and Rights

6.7   If an officer conducts a search to which this Code applies the officer shall, unless it is impracticable to do so, provide the occupier with a copy of a Notice in a standard format:
   (i)   specifying if the search is made under warrant, with consent, or in the exercise of the powers described in paragraphs 4.1 to 4.3. Note: the notice format shall provide for authority or consent to be indicated (see *paragraphs 4.3* and *5.1*);
   (ii)   summarising the extent of the powers of search and seizure conferred by PACE and other relevant legislation as appropriate;
   (iii) explaining the rights of the occupier and the owner of the property seized;
   (iv)   explaining compensation may be payable in appropriate cases for damages caused entering and searching premises, and giving the address to send a compensation application (see *Note 6A*), and
   (v)   stating this Code is available at any police station.

6.8   If the occupier is:
   • present; copies of the Notice and warrant shall, if practicable, be given to them before the search begins, unless the officer in charge of the search reasonably believes this would frustrate the object of the search or endanger officers or other people;
   • not present; copies of the Notice and warrant shall be left in a prominent place on the premises or appropriate part of the premises and endorsed, subject to paragraph 2.9 with the name of the officer in charge of the search, the date and time of the search
   The warrant shall be endorsed to show this has been done.

(d) Conduct of searches

6.9 Premises may be searched only to the extent necessary to achieve the purpose of the search, having regard to the size and nature of whatever is sought.

6.9A A search may not continue under:
- a warrant's authority once all the things specified in that warrant have been found;
- any other power once the object of that search has been achieved.

6.9B No search may continue once the officer in charge of the search is satisfied whatever is being sought is not on the premises (see *Note 6B*). This does not prevent a further search of the same premises if additional grounds come to light supporting a further application for a search warrant or exercise or further exercise of another power. For example, when, as a result of new information, it is believed articles previously not found or additional articles are on the premises.

6.10 Searches must be conducted with due consideration for the property and privacy of the occupier and with no more disturbance than necessary. Reasonable force may be used only when necessary and proportionate because the co-operation of the occupier cannot be obtained or is insufficient for the purpose. (See *Note 6C*.)

6.11 A friend, neighbour or other person must be allowed to witness the search if the occupier wishes unless the officer in charge of the search has reasonable grounds for believing the presence of the person asked for would seriously hinder the investigation or endanger officers or other people. A search need not be unreasonably delayed for this purpose. A record of the action taken should be made on the premises search record including the grounds for refusing the occupier's request.

6.12 A person is not required to be cautioned prior to being asked questions that are solely necessary for the purpose of furthering the proper and effective conduct of a search, (see Code C, *paragraph 10.1(c)*). For example, questions to discover the occupier of specified premises, to find a key to open a locked drawer or cupboard or to otherwise seek co-operation during the search or to determine if a particular item is liable to be seized.

6.12A If questioning goes beyond what is necessary for the purpose of the exemption in Code C, the exchange is likely to constitute an interview as defined by Code C, paragraph 11.1A and would require the associated safeguards included in Code C, section 10.

(e) Leaving premises

6.13 If premises have been entered by force, before leaving the officer in charge of the search must make sure they are secure by:
- arranging for the occupier or their agent to be present;
- any other appropriate means.

(f) Searches under PACE Schedule 1 or the Terrorism Act 2000, Schedule 5

6.14 An officer shall be appointed as the officer in charge of the search (see *paragraph 2.10*), in respect of any search made under a warrant issued under PACE Act 1984, Schedule 1 or the Terrorism Act 2000, Schedule 5. They are responsible for making sure the search is conducted with discretion and in a manner that causes the least possible disruption to any business or other activities carried out on the premises.

6.15 Once the officer in charge of the search is satisfied material may not be taken from the premises without their knowledge, they shall ask for the documents or other records concerned. The officer in charge of the search may also ask to see the index to files held on the premises, and the officers conducting the search may inspect any files which, according to the index, appear to contain the material sought. A more extensive search of the premises may be made only if:
- the person responsible for them refuses to:
  - produce the material sought, or
  - allow access to the index.
- it appears the index is:
  - inaccurate, or
  - incomplete.
- for any other reason the officer in charge of the search has reasonable grounds for believing such a search is necessary in order to find the material sought.

Notes for Guidance

6A   *Whether compensation is appropriate depends on the circumstances in each case. Compensation for damage caused when effecting entry is unlikely to be appropriate if the search was lawful, and the force used can be shown to be reasonable, proportionate and necessary to effect entry. If the wrong premises are searched by mistake everything possible should be done at the earliest opportunity to allay any sense of grievance and there should normally be a strong presumption in favour of paying compensation.*

6B   *It is important that, when possible, all those involved in a search are fully briefed about any powers to be exercised and the extent and limits within which it should be conducted.*

6C   *In all cases the number of officers and other persons involved in executing the warrant should be determined by what is reasonable and necessary according to the particular circumstances.*

7 Seizure and retention of property

(a) Seizure

7.1   Subject to paragraph 7.2, an officer who is searching any person or premises under any statutory power or with the consent of the occupier may seize anything:
      (a) covered by a warrant;
      (b) the officer has reasonable grounds for believing is evidence of an offence or has been obtained in consequence of the commission of an offence but only if seizure is necessary to prevent the items being concealed, lost, disposed of, altered, damaged, destroyed or tampered with;
      (c) covered by the powers in the Criminal Justice and Police Act 2001, Part 2 allowing an officer to seize property from persons or premises and retain it for sifting or examination elsewhere.
      See *Note 7B*.

7.2   No item may be seized which an officer has reasonable grounds for believing to be subject to legal privilege, as defined in PACE, section 10, other than under the Criminal Justice and Police Act 2001, Part 2.

7.3   Officers must be aware of the provisions in the Criminal Justice and Police Act 2001, section 59, allowing for applications to a judicial authority for the return of property seized and the subsequent duty to secure in section 60. (See *paragraph 7.12(iii)*.)

7.4   An officer may decide it is not appropriate to seize property because of an explanation from the person holding it but may nevertheless have reasonable grounds for believing it was obtained in consequence of an offence by some person. In these circumstances, the officer should identify the property to the holder, inform the holder of their suspicions and explain the holder may be liable to civil or criminal proceedings if they dispose of, alter or destroy the property.

7.5   An officer may arrange to photograph, image or copy, any document or other article they have the power to seize in accordance with paragraph 7.1. This is subject to specific restrictions on the examination, imaging or copying of certain property seized under the Criminal Justice and Police Act 2001, Part 2. An officer must have regard to their statutory obligation to retain an original document or other article only when a photograph or copy is not sufficient.

7.6   If an officer considers information stored in any electronic form and accessible from the premises could be used in evidence, they may require the information to be produced in a form:
      • which can be taken away and in which it is visible and legible, or
      • from which it can readily be produced in a visible and legible form.

(b) Criminal Justice and Police Act 2001: Specific procedures for seize and sift powers

7.7   The Criminal Justice and Police Act 2001, Part 2 gives officers limited powers to seize property from premises or persons so they can sift or examine it elsewhere. Officers must be careful they only exercise these powers when it is essential and they do not remove any more material than necessary. The removal of large volumes of material, much of which may not ultimately be retainable, may have serious implications for the owners, particularly when they are involved in business or activities such as journalism or the provision of medical services. Officers must carefully consider if removing copies or images of relevant material or data would be a satisfactory alternative to removing originals. When originals are taken, officers must be prepared to facilitate the provision of copies or images for the owners when reasonably practicable. (See *Note 7C*.)

7.8   Property seized under the Criminal Justice and Police Act 2001, sections 50 or 51 must be kept securely and separately from any material seized under other powers. An examination under section 53 to determine which elements may be retained must be carried out at the earliest practicable time, having due regard to the desirability of allowing the person from whom the property was seized, or a person with an interest in the property, an opportunity of being present or represented at the examination.

7.8A All reasonable steps should be taken to accommodate an interested person's request to be present, provided the request is reasonable and subject to the need to prevent harm to, interference with, or unreasonable delay to the investigatory process. If an examination proceeds in the absence of an interested person who asked to attend or their representative, the officer who exercised the relevant seizure power must give that person a written notice of why the examination was carried out in those circumstances. If it is necessary for security reasons or to maintain confidentiality officers may exclude interested persons from decryption or other processes which facilitate the examination but do not form part of it. (See *Note 7D*.)

7.9   It is the responsibility of the officer in charge of the investigation to make sure property is returned in accordance with sections 53 to 55. Material which there is no power to retain must be:
- separated from the rest of the seized property, and
- returned as soon as reasonably practicable after examination of all the seized property.

7.9A   Delay is only warranted if very clear and compelling reasons exist, for example:
- the unavailability of the person to whom the material is to be returned, or
- the need to agree a convenient time to return a large volume of material

7.9B   Legally privileged, excluded or special procedure material which cannot be retained must be returned:
- as soon as reasonably practicable, and
- without waiting for the whole examination.

7.9C   As set out in section 58, material must be returned to the person from whom it was seized, except when it is clear some other person has a better right to it. (See *Note 7E*.)

7.10   When an officer involved in the investigation has reasonable grounds to believe a person with a relevant interest in property seized under section 50 or 51 intends to make an application under section 59 for the return of any legally privileged, special procedure or excluded material, the officer in charge of the investigation should be informed as soon as practicable and the material seized should be kept secure in accordance with section 61. (See *Note 7C*.)

7.11   The officer in charge of the investigation is responsible for making sure property is properly secured. Securing involves making sure the property is not examined, copied, imaged or put to any other use except at the request, or with the consent, of the applicant or in accordance with the directions of the appropriate judicial authority. Any request, consent or directions must be recorded in writing and signed by both the initiator and the officer in charge of the investigation. (See *Notes 7F* and *7G*.)

7.12   When an officer exercises a power of seizure conferred by sections 50 or 51 they shall provide the occupier of the premises or the person from whom the property is being seized with a written notice:
   (i)   specifying what has been seized under the powers conferred by that section;
   (ii)   specifying the grounds for those powers;
   (iii) setting out the effect of sections 59 to 61 covering the grounds for a person with a relevant interest in seized property to apply to a judicial authority for its return and the duty of officers to secure property in certain circumstances when an application is made, and
   (iv) specifying the name and address of the person to whom:
- notice of an application to the appropriate judicial authority in respect of any of the seized property must be given;
- an application may be made to allow attendance at the initial examination of the property.

7.13   If the occupier is not present but there is someone in charge of the premises, the notice shall be given to them. If no suitable person is available, so the notice will easily be found it should either be:
- left in a prominent place on the premises, or
- attached to the exterior of the premises.

(c) Retention

7.14   Subject to paragraph 7.15, anything seized in accordance with the above provisions may be retained only for as long as is necessary. It may be retained, among other purposes:
   (i)   for use as evidence at a trial for an offence;
   (ii)   to facilitate the use in any investigation or proceedings of anything to which it is inextricably linked (see *Note 7H*);
   (iii) for forensic examination or other investigation in connection with an offence;
   (iv) in order to establish its lawful owner when there are reasonable grounds for believing it has been stolen or obtained by the commission of an offence.

7.15   Property shall not be retained under paragraph 7.14(i), (ii) or (iii) if a copy or image would be sufficient.

(d) Rights of owners etc

7.16   If property is retained, the person who had custody or control of it immediately before seizure must, on request, be provided with a list or description of the property within a reasonable time.

7.17   That person or their representative must be allowed supervised access to the property to examine it or have it photographed or copied, or must be provided with a photograph or copy, in either case within a reasonable time of any request and at their own expense, unless the officer in charge of an investigation has reasonable grounds for believing this would:

    (i)   prejudice the investigation of any offence or criminal proceedings; or

    (ii) lead to the commission of an offence by providing access to unlawful material such as pornography;

A record of the grounds shall be made when access is denied.

Notes for Guidance

7A   *Any person claiming property seized by the police may apply to a magistrates' court under the Police (Property) Act 1897 for its possession and should, if appropriate, be advised of this procedure.*

7B   *The powers of seizure conferred by PACE, sections 18(2) and 19(3) extend to the seizure of the whole premises when it is physically possible to seize and retain the premises in their totality and practical considerations make seizure desirable. For example, police may remove premises such as tents, vehicles or caravans to a police station for the purpose of preserving evidence.*

7C   *Officers should consider reaching agreement with owners and/or other interested parties on the procedures for examining a specific set of property, rather than awaiting the judicial authority's determination. Agreement can sometimes give a quicker and more satisfactory route for all concerned and minimise costs and legal complexities.*

7D   *What constitutes a relevant interest in specific material may depend on the nature of that material and the circumstances in which it is seized. Anyone with a reasonable claim to ownership of the material and anyone entrusted with its safe keeping by the owner should be considered.*

7E   *Requirements to secure and return property apply equally to all copies, images or other material created because of seizure of the original property.*

7F   *The mechanics of securing property vary according to the circumstances; 'bagging up', i.e. placing material in sealed bags or containers and strict subsequent control of access is the appropriate procedure in many cases.*

7G   *When material is seized under the powers of seizure conferred by PACE, the duty to retain it under the Code of Practice issued under the Criminal Procedure and Investigations Act 1996 is subject to the provisions on retention of seized material in PACE, section 22.*

7H   *Paragraph 7.14 (ii) applies if inextricably linked material is seized under the Criminal Justice and Police Act 2001, sections 50 or 51. Inextricably linked material is material it is not reasonably practicable to separate from other linked material without prejudicing the use of that other material in any investigation or proceedings. For example, it may not be possible to separate items of data held on computer disk without damaging their evidential integrity. Inextricably linked material must not be examined, imaged, copied or used for any purpose other than for proving the source and/or integrity of the linked material.*

8 Action after searches

8.1   If premises are searched in circumstances where this Code applies, unless the exceptions in paragraph 2.3(a) apply, on arrival at a police station the officer in charge of the search shall make or have made a record of the search, to include:

    (i)   the address of the searched premises;

    (ii) the date, time and duration of the search;

    (iii) the authority used for the search:
- if the search was made in exercise of a statutory power to search premises without warrant, the power which was used for the search:
- if the search was made under a warrant or with written consent;
  - a copy of the warrant and the written authority to apply for it, see *paragraph 3.4*; or
  - the written consent;

  shall be appended to the record or the record shall show the location of the copy warrant or consent;

    (iv) subject to paragraph 2.9, the names of:
- the officer(s) in charge of the search;
- all other officers and authorised persons who conducted the search;

    (v)   the names of any people on the premises if they are known;

    (vi) any grounds for refusing the occupier's request to have someone present during the search, see *paragraph 6.11*;

    (vii) a list of any articles seized or the location of a list and, if not covered by a warrant, the grounds for their seizure;

    (viii) whether force was used, and the reason;

    (ix) details of any damage caused during the search, and the circumstances;

    (x)   if applicable, the reason it was not practicable;

        (a) to give the occupier a copy of the Notice of Powers and Rights, see *paragraph 6.7*;

    (b) before the search to give the occupier a copy of the Notice, see *paragraph 6.8*;

  (xi) when the occupier was not present, the place where copies of the Notice of Powers and Rights and search warrant were left on the premises, see *paragraph 6.8*.

8.2 On each occasion when premises are searched under warrant, the warrant authorising the search on that occasion shall be endorsed to show:

  (i) if any articles specified in the warrant were found and the address where found;

  (ii) if any other articles were seized;

  (iii) the date and time it was executed and if present, the name of the occupier or if the occupier is not present the name of the person in charge of the premises;

  (iv) subject to *paragraph 2.9*, the names of the officers who executed it and any authorised persons who accompanied them, and

  (v) if a copy, together with a copy of the Notice of Powers and Rights was:
- handed to the occupier, or
- endorsed as required by paragraph 6.8; and left on the premises and where.

8.3 Any warrant shall be returned within three calendar months of its issue or sooner on completion of the search(es) authorised by that warrant, if it was issued by a:
- justice of the peace, to the designated officer for the local justice area in which the justice was acting when issuing the warrant; or
- judge, to the appropriate officer of the court concerned.

9 Search registers

9.1 A search register will be maintained at each sub-divisional or equivalent police station. All search records required under paragraph 8.1 shall be made, copied, or referred to in the register. (See *Note 9A*.)

Note for Guidance

9A *Paragraph 9.1 also applies to search records made by immigration officers. In these cases, a search register must also be maintained at an immigration office. (See also Note 2D.)*

10 Searches under Schedule 5 to the Terrorism Prevention and Investigation Measures Act 2011

10.1 This Code applies to the powers of constables under Schedule 5 to the Terrorism Prevention and Investigation Measures Act 2011 relating to TPIM notices to enter and search premises subject to the modifications in the following paragraphs.

10.2 In paragraph 2.3(d), the reference to the investigation into an alleged or suspected offence include the enforcement of terrorism prevention and investigation measures which may be imposed on an individual by a TPIM notice in accordance with the Terrorism Prevention and Investigation Measures Act 2011.

10.3 References to the purpose and object of the entry and search of premises, the nature of articles sought and what may be seized and retained include (as appropriate):

  (a) in relation to the power to search without a search warrant in paragraph 5 (for purposes of serving TPIM notice), finding the individual on whom the notice is to be served.

  (b) in relation to the power to search without a search warrant in paragraph 6 (at time of serving TPIM notice), ascertaining whether there is anything in the premises, that contravenes measures specified in the notice. (See *Note 10A*.)

  (c) in relation to the power to search without a search warrant under paragraph 7 (suspected absconding), ascertaining whether a person has absconded or if there is anything on the premises which will assist in the pursuit or arrest of an individual in respect of whom a TPIM notice is force who is reasonably suspected of having absconded.

  (d) in relation to the power to search under a search warrant issued under paragraph 8 (for compliance purposes), determining whether an individual in respect of whom a TPIM notice is in force is complying with measures specified in the notice. (See *Note 10A*.)

Note for Guidance

10A *Searches of individuals under Schedule 5, paragraphs 6(2)(a) (at time of serving TPIM notice) and 8(2)(a) (for compliance purposes) must be conducted and recorded in accordance with Code A. (See Code A paragraph 2.18A for details.)*

POLICE AND CRIMINAL EVIDENCE ACT 1984
(PACE) — CODE C

REVISED CODE OF PRACTICE FOR THE DETENTION, TREATMENT AND QUESTIONING OF PERSONS BY POLICE OFFICERS

Commencement—Transitional Arrangements

This Code applies to people in police detention after 00.00 on 21 August 2019, notwithstanding that their period of detention may have commenced before that time.

1 General

1.0 The powers and procedures in this Code must be used fairly, responsibly, with respect for the people to whom they apply and without unlawful discrimination. Under the Equality Act 2010, section 149 (Public sector Equality Duty), police forces must, in carrying out their functions, have due regard to the need to eliminate unlawful discrimination, harassment, victimisation and any other conduct which is prohibited by that Act, to advance equality of opportunity between people who share a relevant protected characteristic and people who do not share it, and to foster good relations between those persons. The Equality Act *also* makes it unlawful for police officers to discriminate against, harass or victimise any person on the grounds of the 'protected characteristics' of age, disability, gender reassignment, race, religion or belief, sex and sexual orientation, marriage and civil partnership, pregnancy and maternity, when using their powers. See *Notes 1A* and *1AA*.

1.1 All persons in custody must be dealt with expeditiously, and released as soon as the need for detention no longer applies.

1.1A A custody officer must perform the functions in this Code as soon as practicable. A custody officer will not be in breach of this Code if delay is justifiable and reasonable steps are taken to prevent unnecessary delay. The custody record shall show when a delay has occurred and the reason. See *Note 1H.*

1.2 This Code of Practice must be readily available at all police stations for consultation by:
- police officers;
- police staff;
- detained persons;
- members of the public.

1.3 The provisions of this Code:
- include the Annexes
- do not include the Notes for Guidance *which* form guidance to police officers and others about its application and interpretation.

1.4 If at any time an officer has any reason to suspect that a person of any age may be vulnerable (see *paragraph 1.13(d)*), in the absence of clear evidence to dispel that suspicion, that person shall be treated as such for the purposes of this Code and to establish whether any such reason may exist in relation to a person suspected of committing an offence (see *paragraph 10.1* and *Note 10A*), the custody officer in the case of a detained person, or the officer investigating the offence in the case of a person who has not been arrested or detained, shall take, or cause to be taken, (see *paragraph 3.5* and *Note 3F*) the following action:

(a) reasonable enquiries shall be made to ascertain what information is available that is relevant to any of the factors described in *paragraph 1.13(d)* as indicating that the person may be vulnerable might apply;

(b) a record shall be made describing whether any of those factors appear to apply and provide any reason to suspect that the person may be vulnerable or (as the case may be) may not be vulnerable; and

(c) the record mentioned in sub-paragraph (b) shall be made available to be taken into account by police officers, police staff and any others who, in accordance with the provisions of this or any other Code, are required or entitled to communicate with the person in question. This would include any solicitor, appropriate adult and healthcare professional and is particularly relevant to communication by telephone or by means of a live link (see *paragraphs 12.9A* (interviews), *13.12* (interpretation), and *15.3C, 15.11A, 15.11B, 15.11C* and *15.11D* (reviews and extension of detention)).

See *Notes 1G, 1GA, 1GB* and *1GC.*

1.5   Anyone who appears to be under 18, shall, in the absence of clear evidence that they are older, be treated as a juvenile for the purposes of this Code and any other Code. See *Note 1L*.

1.5A *Not used.*

1.6   If a person appears to be blind, seriously visually impaired, deaf, unable to read or speak or has difficulty orally because of a speech impediment, they shall be treated as such for the purposes of this Code in the absence of clear evidence to the contrary.

1.7   'The appropriate adult' means, in the case of a:
   (a) juvenile:
      (i)   the parent, guardian or, if the juvenile is in the care of a local authority or voluntary organisation, a person representing that authority or organisation (see *Note 1B*);
      (ii)   a social worker of a local authority (see *Note 1C*);
      (iii) failing these, some other responsible adult aged 18 or over who is *not*:
         • a police officer;
         • employed by the police;
         • under the direction or control of the chief officer of a police force; or
         • a person who provides services under contractual arrangements (but without being employed by the chief officer of a police force), to assist that force in relation to the discharge of its chief officer's functions, whether or not they are on duty at the time. See *Note 1F*.
   (b) a person who is vulnerable (see *paragraph 1.4* and *Note 1D*):
      (i)   a relative, guardian or other person responsible for their care or custody;
      (ii)   someone experienced in dealing with vulnerable persons but who is *not*:
         • a police officer;
         • employed by the police;
         • under the direction or control of the chief officer of a police force; or
         • a person who provides services under contractual arrangements (but without being employed by the chief officer of a police force), to assist that force in relation to the discharge of its chief officer's functions, whether or not they are on duty at the time.
      (iii) failing these, some other responsible adult aged 18 or over who is other than a person described in the bullet points in *sub-paragraph (b)(ii)* above. See *Note 1F*.

1.7A The role of the appropriate adult is to safeguard the rights, entitlements and welfare of juveniles and vulnerable persons (see *paragraphs 1.4* and *1.5*) to whom the provisions of this and any other Code of Practice apply. For this reason, the appropriate adult is expected, amongst other things, to:
   • support, advise and assist them when, in accordance with this Code or any other Code of Practice, they are given or asked to provide information or participate in any procedure;
   • observe whether the police are acting properly and fairly to respect their rights and entitlements, and inform an officer of the rank of inspector or above if they consider that they are not;
   • assist them to communicate with the police whilst respecting their right to say nothing unless they want to as set out in the terms of the caution (see *paragraphs 10.5* and *10.6*);
   • help them to understand their rights and ensure that those rights are protected and respected (see *paragraphs 3.15, 3.17, 6.5A* and *11.17*).

1.8   If this Code requires a person be given certain information, they do not have to be given it if at the time they are incapable of understanding what is said, are violent or may become violent or in urgent need of medical attention, but they must be given it as soon as practicable.

1.9   References to a custody officer include any police officer who, for the time being, is performing the functions of a custody officer.

1.9A When this Code requires the prior authority or agreement of an officer of at least inspector or superintendent rank, that authority may be given by a sergeant or chief inspector authorised to perform the functions of the higher rank under the Police and Criminal Evidence Act 1984 (PACE), section 107.

1.10 Subject to *paragraph 1.12*, this Code applies to people in custody at police stations in England and Wales, whether or not they have been arrested, and to those removed to a police station as a place of safety under the Mental Health Act 1983, sections 135 and 136, as amended by the Policing and Crime Act 2017 (see *paragraph 3.16*). *Section 15* applies solely to people in police detention, e.g. those brought to a police station under arrest or arrested at a police station for an offence after going there voluntarily.

1.11 No part of this Code applies to a detained person:
   (a) to whom PACE Code H applies because:

- they are detained following arrest under section 41 of the Terrorism Act 2000 (TACT) and not charged; or
- an authorisation has been given under section 22 of the Counter-Terrorism Act 2008 (CTACT) (post-charge questioning of terrorist suspects) to interview them.

(b) to whom the Code of Practice issued under paragraph 6 of Schedule 14 to TACT applies because they are detained for examination under Schedule 7 to TACT.

1.12 This Code does not apply to people in custody:

(i) arrested by officers under the Criminal Justice and Public Order Act 1994, section 136(2) on warrants issued in Scotland, or arrested or detained without warrant under section 137(2) by officers from a police force in Scotland. In these cases, police powers and duties and the person's rights and entitlements whilst at a police station in England or Wales are the same as those in Scotland;

(ii) arrested under the Immigration and Asylum Act 1999, section 142(3) in order to have their fingerprints taken;

(iii) whose detention has been authorised under Schedules 2 or 3 to the Immigration Act 1971 or section 62 of the Nationality, Immigration and Asylum Act 2002;

(iv) who are convicted or remanded prisoners held in police cells on behalf of the Prison Service under the Imprisonment (Temporary Provisions) Act 1980;

(v) Not used.

(vi) detained for searches under stop and search powers except as required by Code A.

The provisions on conditions of detention and treatment in *sections 8* and *9* must be considered as the minimum standards of treatment for such detainees.

1.13 In this Code:

(a) 'designated person' means a person other than a police officer, who has specified powers and duties conferred or imposed on them by designation under section 38 or 39 of the Police Reform Act 2002;

(b) reference to a police officer includes a designated person acting in the exercise or performance of the powers and duties conferred or imposed on them by their designation;

(c) if there is doubt as to whether the person should be treated, or continued to be treated, as being male or female in the case of:

(i) a search carried out or observed by a person of the same sex as the detainee; or

(ii) any other procedure which requires action to be taken or information to be given that depends on whether the person is to be treated as being male or female;

then the gender of the detainee and other parties concerned should be established and recorded in line with *Annex L* of this Code.

(d) 'vulnerable' applies to any person who, because of a mental health condition or mental disorder (see *Notes 1G and 1GB*):

(i) may have difficulty understanding or communicating effectively about the full implications for them of any procedures and processes connected with:

- their arrest and detention; or (as the case may be)
- their voluntary attendance at a police station or their presence elsewhere (see *paragraph 3.21*), for the purpose of a voluntary interview; and
- the exercise of their rights and entitlements.

(ii) does not appear to understand the significance of what they are told, of questions they are asked or of their replies:

(iii) appears to be particularly prone to:

- becoming confused and unclear about their position;
- providing unreliable, misleading or incriminating information without knowing or wishing to do so;
- accepting or acting on suggestions from others without consciously knowing or wishing to do so; or
- readily agreeing to suggestions or proposals without any protest or question.

(e) 'Live link' means:

(i) for the purpose of *paragraph 12.9A;* an arrangement by means of which the *interviewing officer* who is not present at the police station where the detainee is held, is able to see and hear, and to be seen and heard by, the detainee concerned, the detainee's solicitor, appropriate adult and interpreter (as applicable) and the officer who has custody of that detainee (see *Note 1N*).

(ii) for the purpose of *paragraph 15.9A;* an arrangement by means of which the *review officer* who is not present at the police station where the detainee is held, is able to see and hear, and to be seen and heard by, the detainee concerned and the detainee's solicitor, appropriate adult and interpreter (as applicable) (see *Note 1N*). The use of live link for decisions about detention under *section 45A of PACE* is subject to regulations made by the Secretary of State being in force.

(iii) for the purpose of *paragraph 15.11A*; an arrangement by means of which the *authorising officer* who is not present at the police station where the detainee is held, is able to see and hear, and to be seen and heard by, the detainee concerned and the detainee's solicitor, appropriate adult and interpreter (as applicable) (see *Note 1N*).

(iv) for the purpose of *paragraph 15.11C*; an arrangement by means of which the *detainee* when not present in the court where the hearing is being held, is able to see and hear, and to be seen and heard by, the court during the hearing (see *Note 1N*).

Note: Chief officers must be satisfied that live link used in their force area for the above purposes provides for accurate and secure communication between the detainee, the detainee's solicitor, appropriate adult and interpreter (as applicable). This includes ensuring that at any time during which the live link is being used: a person cannot see, hear or otherwise obtain access to any such communications unless so authorised or allowed by the custody officer or, in the case of an interview, the interviewer and that as applicable, the confidentiality of any private consultation between a suspect and their solicitor and appropriate adult is maintained.

1.14 Designated persons are entitled to use reasonable force as follows:

(a) when exercising a power conferred on them which allows a police officer exercising that power to use reasonable force, a designated person has the same entitlement to use force; and

(b) at other times when carrying out duties conferred or imposed on them that also entitle them to use reasonable force, for example:

- when at a police station carrying out the duty to keep detainees for whom they are responsible under control and to assist any police officer or designated person to keep any detainee under control and to prevent their escape;
- when securing, or assisting any police officer or designated person in securing, the detention of a person at a police station;
- when escorting, or assisting any police officer or designated person in escorting, a detainee within a police station;
- for the purpose of saving life or limb; or
- preventing serious damage to property.

1.15 Nothing in this Code prevents the custody officer, or other police officer or designated person (see *paragraph 1.13(a)*) given custody of the detainee by the custody officer, from allowing another person (see *(a)* and *(b)* below) to carry out individual procedures or tasks at the police station if the law allows. However, the officer or designated person given custody remains responsible for making sure the procedures and tasks are carried out correctly in accordance with the Codes of Practice (see *paragraph 3.5* and *Note 3F*). The other person who is allowed to carry out the procedures or tasks must be someone who *at that time*, is:

(a) under the direction and control of the chief officer of the force responsible for the police station in question; or

(b) providing services under contractual arrangements (but without being employed by the chief officer the police force), to assist a police force in relation to the discharge of its chief officer's functions.

1.16 Designated persons and others mentioned in *sub-paragraphs (a)* and *(b)* of *paragraph 1.15*, must have regard to any relevant provisions of the Codes of Practice.

1.17 In any provision of this or any other Code which allows or requires police officers or police staff to make a record in their report book, the reference to report book shall include any official report book or electronic recording device issued to them that enables the record in question to be made and dealt with in accordance with that provision. References in this and any other Code to written records, forms and signatures include electronic records and forms and electronic confirmation that identifies the person making the record or completing the form. Chief officers must be satisfied as to the integrity and security of the devices, records and forms to which this *paragraph* applies and that use of those devices, records and forms satisfies relevant data protection legislation.

Notes for Guidance

1A   Although certain sections of this Code apply specifically to people in custody at police stations, a person who attends a police station or other location voluntarily to assist with an investigation should be treated with no less consideration, e.g. offered or allowed refreshments at appropriate times, and enjoy an absolute right to obtain legal advice or communicate with anyone outside the police station or other location (see paragraphs 3.21 and 3.22).

1AA In paragraph 1.0, under the Equality Act 2010, section 149, the 'relevant protected characteristics' are age, disability, gender reassignment, pregnancy and maternity, race, religion/belief and sex and sexual orientation. For further detailed guidance and advice on the Equality Act, see: https://www.gov.uk/guidance/equality-act-2010-guidance.

1B A person, including a parent or guardian, should not be an appropriate adult if they:
- are:
  - suspected of involvement in the offence;
  - the victim;
  - a witness;
  - involved in the investigation.
- received admissions prior to attending to act as the appropriate adult.

Note: If a juvenile's parent is estranged from the juvenile, they should not be asked to act as the appropriate adult if the juvenile expressly and specifically objects to their presence.

1C If a juvenile admits an offence to, or in the presence of, a social worker or member of a youth offending team other than during the time that person is acting as the juvenile's appropriate adult, another appropriate adult should be appointed in the interest of fairness.

1D In the case of someone who is vulnerable, it may be more satisfactory if the appropriate adult is someone experienced or trained in their care rather than a relative lacking such qualifications. But if the person prefers a relative to a better qualified stranger or objects to a particular person their wishes should, if practicable, be respected.

1E A detainee should always be given an opportunity, when an appropriate adult is called to the police station, to consult privately with a solicitor in the appropriate adult's absence if they want. An appropriate adult is not subject to legal privilege.

1F An appropriate adult who is not a parent or guardian in the case of a juvenile, or a relative, guardian or carer in the case of a vulnerable person, must be independent of the police as their role is to safeguard the person's rights and entitlements. Additionally, a solicitor or independent custody visitor who is present at the police station and acting in that capacity, may not be the appropriate adult.

1G A person may be vulnerable as a result of a having a mental health condition or mental disorder. Similarly, simply because an individual does not have, or is not known to have, any such condition or disorder, does not mean that they are not vulnerable for the purposes of this Code. It is therefore important that the custody officer in the case of a detained person or the officer investigating the offence in the case of a person who has not been arrested or detained, as appropriate, considers on a case by case basis, whether any of the factors described in paragraph 1.13(d) might apply to the person in question. In doing so, the officer must take into account the particular circumstances of the individual and how the nature of the investigation might affect them and bear in mind that juveniles, by virtue of their age will always require an appropriate adult.

1GA For the purposes of paragraph 1.4(a), examples of relevant information that may be available include:
- the behaviour of the adult or juvenile;
- the mental health and capacity of the adult or juvenile;
- what the adult or juvenile says about themselves;
- information from relatives and friends of the adult or juvenile;
- information from police officers and staff and from police records;
- information from health and social care (including liaison and diversion services) and other professionals who know, or have had previous contact with, the individual and may be able to contribute to assessing their need for help and support from an appropriate adult. This includes contacts and assessments arranged by the police or at the request of the individual or (as applicable) their appropriate adult or solicitor.

1GB The Mental Health Act 1983 Code of Practice at page 26 describes the range of clinically recognised conditions which can fall with the meaning of mental disorder for the purpose of paragraph 1.13(d). The Code is published here: https://www.gov.uk/government/publications/code-of-practice-mental-health-act-1983.

1GC When a person is under the influence of drink and/or drugs, it is not intended that they are to be treated as vulnerable and requiring an appropriate adult for the purpose of paragraph 1.4 unless other information indicates that any of the factors described in paragraph 1.13(d) may apply to that person. When the person has recovered from the effects of drink and/or drugs, they should be re-assessed in accordance with paragraph 1.4. See paragraph 15.4A for application to live link

1H Paragraph 1.1A is intended to cover delays which may occur in processing detainees e.g. if:
- a large number of suspects are brought into the station simultaneously to be placed in custody;

- *interview rooms are all being used;*
- *there are difficulties contacting an appropriate adult, solicitor or interpreter.*

1I   *The custody officer must remind the appropriate adult and detainee about the right to legal advice and record any reasons for waiving it in accordance with section 6.*

1J   *Not used.*

1K   *This Code does not affect the principle that all citizens have a duty to help police officers to prevent crime and discover offenders. This is a civic rather than a legal duty; but when police officers are trying to discover whether, or by whom, offences have been committed they are entitled to question any person from whom they think useful information can be obtained, subject to the restrictions imposed by this Code. A person's declaration that they are unwilling to reply does not alter this entitlement.*

1L   *Paragraph 1.5 reflects the statutory definition of 'arrested juvenile' in section 37(15) of PACE. This section was amended by section 42 of the Criminal Justice and Courts Act 2015 with effect from 26 October 2015, and includes anyone who appears to be under the age of 18. This definition applies for the purposes of the detention and bail provisions in sections 34 to 51 of PACE. With effect from 3 April 2017, amendments made by the Policing and Crime Act 2017 require persons under the age of 18 to be treated as juveniles for the purposes of all other provisions of PACE and the Codes.*

1M   *Not used.*

1N   *For the purpose of the provisions of PACE that allow a live link to be used, any impairment of the detainee's eyesight or hearing is to be disregarded. This means that if a detainee's eyesight or hearing is impaired, the arrangements which would be needed to ensure effective communication if all parties were physically present in the same location, for example, using sign language, would apply to the live link arrangements.*

2 Custody records

2.1A   When a person:
- is brought to a police station under arrest;
- is arrested at the police station having attended there voluntarily; or
- attends a police station to answer bail;

they must be brought before the custody officer as soon as practicable after their arrival at the station or if applicable, following their arrest after attending the police station voluntarily. This applies to both designated and non-designated police stations. A person is deemed to be 'at a police station' for these purposes if they are within the boundary of any building or enclosed yard which forms part of that police station.

2.1   A separate custody record must be opened as soon as practicable for each person brought to a police station under arrest or arrested at the station having gone there voluntarily or attending a police station in answer to street bail. All information recorded under this Code must be recorded as soon as practicable in the custody record unless otherwise specified. Any audio or video recording made in the custody area is not part of the custody record.

2.2   If any action requires the authority of an officer of a specified rank, subject to *paragraph 2.6A*, their name and rank must be noted in the custody record.

2.3   The custody officer is responsible for the custody record's accuracy and completeness and for making sure the record or copy of the record accompanies a detainee if they are transferred to another police station. The record shall show the:
- time and reason for transfer;
- time a person is released from detention.

2.3A   If a person is arrested and taken to a police station as a result of a search in the exercise of any stop and search power to which PACE Code A (Stop and search) or the 'search powers code' issued under TACT applies, the officer carrying out the search is responsible for ensuring that the record of that stop and search is made as part of the person's custody record. The custody officer must then ensure that the person is asked if they want a copy of the search record and if they do, that they are given a copy as soon as practicable. The person's entitlement to a copy of the search record which is made as part of their custody record is in addition to, and does not affect, their entitlement to a copy of their custody record or any other provisions of section 2 (Custody records) of this Code. (See Code A, *paragraph 4.2B* and the TACT search powers code *paragraph 5.3.5*).

2.4   The detainee's solicitor and appropriate adult must be permitted to inspect the whole of the detainee's custody record as soon as practicable after their arrival at the station and at any other time on request, whilst the person is detained. This includes the following *specific* records relating to the reasons for the detainee's arrest and detention and the offence concerned to which *paragraph 3.1(b)* refers:

(a) The information about the circumstances and reasons for the detainee's arrest as recorded in the custody record in accordance with *paragraph 4.3* of Code G. This applies to any further offences for which the detainee is arrested whilst in custody;

(b) The record of the grounds for each authorisation to keep the person in custody. The authorisations to which this applies are the same as those described at items *(i)(a)* to *(d)* in the table in *paragraph 2 of Annex M* of this Code.

Access to the records in *sub-paragraphs (a)* and *(b)* is *in addition* to the requirements in *paragraphs 3.4(b), 11.1A, 15.0, 15,7A(c) and 16.7A* to make certain documents and materials available and to provide information about the offence and the reasons for arrest and detention.

Access to the custody record for the purposes of this paragraph must be arranged and agreed with the custody officer and may not unreasonably interfere with the custody officer's duties. A record shall be made when access is allowed and whether it includes the records described in *sub-paragraphs (a)* and *(b)* above.

2.4A When a detainee leaves police detention or is taken before a court they, their legal representative or appropriate adult shall be given, on request, a copy of the custody record as soon as practicable. This entitlement lasts for 12 months after release.

2.5 The detainee, appropriate adult or legal representative shall be permitted to inspect the original custody record after the detainee has left police detention provided they give reasonable notice of their request. Any such inspection shall be noted in the custody record.

2.6 Subject to *paragraph 2.6A*, all entries in custody records must be timed and signed by the maker. Records entered on computer shall be timed and contain the operator's identification.

2.6A Nothing in this Code requires the identity of officers or other police staff to be recorded or disclosed:

(a) *Not used.*

(b) if the officer or police staff reasonably believe recording or disclosing their name might put them in danger.

In these cases, they shall use their warrant or other identification numbers and the name of their police station. See *Note 2A.*

2.7 The fact and time of any detainee's refusal to sign a custody record, when asked in accordance with this Code, must be recorded.

Note for Guidance

2A *The purpose of paragraph 2.6A(b) is to protect those involved in serious organised crime investigations or arrests of particularly violent suspects when there is reliable information that those arrested or their associates may threaten or cause harm to those involved. In cases of doubt, an officer of inspector rank or above should be consulted.*

3 Initial action

(A) Detained persons — normal procedure

3.1 When a person is brought to a police station under arrest or arrested at the station having gone there voluntarily, the custody officer must make sure the person is told clearly about:

(a) the following continuing rights, which may be exercised at any stage during the period in custody:

(i) their right to consult privately with a solicitor and that free independent legal advice is available as in *section 6*;

(ii) their right to have someone informed of their arrest as in *section 5*;

(iii) their right to consult the Codes of Practice (see *Note 3D*); and

(iv) if applicable, their right to interpretation and translation (see *paragraph 3.12*) and their right to communicate with their High Commission, Embassy or Consulate (see *paragraph 3.12A*).

(b) their right to be informed about the offence and (as the case may be) any further offences for which they are arrested whilst in custody and why they have been arrested and detained in accordance with *paragraphs 2.4, 3.4(a)* and *11.1A* of this Code and *paragraph 3.3* of Code G.

3.2 The detainee must also be given a written notice, which contains information:

(a) to allow them to exercise their rights by setting out:

(i) their rights under *paragraph 3.1, paragraph 3.12* and *3.12A*;

(ii) the arrangements for obtaining legal advice, see *section 6*;

(iii) their right to a copy of the custody record as in *paragraph 2.4A*;

(iv) their right to remain silent as set out in the caution in the terms prescribed in *section 10*;

(v) their right to have access to materials and documents which are essential to effectively challenging the lawfulness of their arrest and detention for any offence and (as the case may be) any further offences for which they are arrested whilst in custody, in accordance with *paragraphs 3.4(b)*, *15.0*, *15.7A(c)* and *16.7A* of this Code;

    (vi) the maximum period for which they may be kept in police detention without being charged, when detention must be reviewed and when release is required;

    (vii) their right to medical assistance in accordance with *section 9* of this Code;

    (viii) their right, if they are prosecuted, to have access to the evidence in the case before their trial in accordance with the Criminal Procedure and Investigations Act 1996, the Attorney General's Guidelines on Disclosure, the common law and the Criminal Procedure Rules; and

  (b) briefly setting out their other entitlements while in custody, by:

    (i) mentioning:
- the provisions relating to the conduct of interviews;
- the circumstances in which an appropriate adult should be available to assist the detainee and their statutory rights to make representations whenever the need for their detention is reviewed;

    (ii) listing the entitlements in this Code, concerning;
- reasonable standards of physical comfort;
- adequate food and drink;
- access to toilets and washing facilities, clothing, medical attention, and exercise when practicable.
- Personal needs relating to health, hygiene and welfare concerning the provision of menstrual and any other health, hygiene and welfare products needed by the detainee in question and speaking about these in private to a member of the custody staff (see *paragraphs 9.3A* and *9.3B*).

     See *Note 3A*.

3.2A The detainee must be given an opportunity to read the notice and shall be asked to sign the custody record to acknowledge receipt of the notice. Any refusal to sign must be recorded on the custody record.

3.3   *Not used.*

3.3A An 'easy read' illustrated version should also be provided if available (see *Note 3A*).

3.4   (a) The custody officer shall:
- record the offence(s) that the detainee has been arrested for and the reason(s) for the arrest on the custody record. See *paragraph 10.3* and Code G, *paragraphs 2.2 and 4.3*;
- note on the custody record any comment the detainee makes in relation to the arresting officer's account but shall not invite comment. If the arresting officer is not physically present when the detainee is brought to a police station, the arresting officer's account must be made available to the custody officer remotely or by a third party on the arresting officer's behalf. If the custody officer authorises a person's detention, subject to *paragraph 1.8*, that officer must record the grounds for detention in the detainee's presence and at the same time, inform them of the grounds. The detainee must be informed of the grounds for their detention before they are questioned about any offence;
- note any comment the detainee makes in respect of the decision to detain them but shall not invite comment;
- not put specific questions to the detainee regarding their involvement in any offence, nor in respect of any comments they may make in response to the arresting officer's account or the decision to place them in detention. Such an exchange is likely to constitute an interview as in *paragraph 11.1A* and require the associated safeguards in *section 11*.

     Note: This sub-paragraph also applies to any further offences and grounds for detention which come to light whilst the person is detained.

     See *paragraph 11.13* in respect of unsolicited comments.

  (b) Documents and materials which are essential to effectively challenging the lawfulness of the detainee's arrest and detention must be made available to the detainee or their solicitor. Documents and materials will be 'essential' for this purpose if they are capable of undermining the reasons and grounds which make the detainee's arrest and detention *necessary*. The decision about whether particular documents or materials must be made available for the purpose of this requirement therefore rests with the custody officer who determines whether detention is necessary, in consultation with the investigating officer who has the knowledge of the documents and materials in a particular case necessary to inform that decision. A note should be made in the detainee's custody record of the *fact* that documents or materials have been made available under this sub-paragraph and when. The investigating officer should make a separate note of what is made available and how it is made available in a particular case. This sub-paragraph also applies (with modifications) for the purposes of *sections 15 (Reviews and extensions of detention)* and *16 (Charging detained persons)*. See *Note 3ZA* and *paragraphs 15.0* and *16.7A*.

3.5   The custody officer or other custody staff as directed by the custody officer shall:
    (a) ask the detainee whether at this time, they:
       (i)   would like legal advice, see *paragraph 6.5*;
       (ii)   want someone informed of their detention, see *section 5*;
    (b) ask the detainee to sign the custody record to confirm their decisions in respect of (*a*);
    (c) determine whether the detainee:
       (i)   is, or might be, in need of medical treatment or attention, see *section 9*;
       (ii)   is a juvenile and/or vulnerable and therefore requires an appropriate adult (see *paragraphs 1.4, 1.5*, and *3.15*);
       (iia) wishes to speak in private with a member of the custody staff who may be of the same sex about any matter concerning their personal needs relating to health, hygiene and welfare (see *paragraph 9.3A*)
       (iii) requires:
          • help to check documentation (see *paragraph 3.20*);
          • an interpreter (see *paragraph 3.12* and *Note 13B*).
    (ca) if the detainee is a female aged 18 or over, ask if they require or are likely to require any menstrual products whilst they are in custody (see *paragraph 9.3B*). For girls under 18, see *paragraph 3.20A*;
    (d) record the decision and actions taken as applicable in respect of (*c*) and (ca).
    Where any duties under this paragraph have been carried out by custody staff at the direction of the custody officer, the outcomes shall, as soon as practicable, be reported to the custody officer who retains overall responsibility for the detainee's care and treatment and ensuring that it complies with this Code. See *Note 3F*.

3.6   When the needs mentioned in *paragraph 3.5(c)* are being determined, the custody officer is responsible for initiating an assessment to consider whether the detainee is likely to present specific risks to custody staff, any individual who may have contact with detainee (e.g. legal advisers, medical staff) or themselves. This risk assessment must include the taking of reasonable steps to establish the detainee's identity and to obtain information about the detainee that is relevant to their safe custody, security and welfare and risks to others. Such assessments should therefore always include a check on the Police National Computer (PNC), to be carried out as soon as practicable, to identify any risks that have been highlighted in relation to the detainee. Although such assessments are primarily the custody officer's responsibility, it may be necessary for them to consult and involve others, e.g. the arresting officer or an appropriate healthcare professional, see *paragraph 9.13*.
    Other records held by or on behalf of the police and other UK law enforcement authorities that might provide information relevant to the detainee's safe custody, security and welfare and risk to others and to confirming their identity should also be checked. Reasons for delaying the initiation or completion of the assessment must be recorded.

3.7   Chief officers should ensure that arrangements for proper and effective risk assessments required by *paragraph 3.6* are implemented in respect of all detainees at police stations in their area.

3.8   Risk assessments must follow a structured process which clearly defines the categories of risk to be considered and the results must be incorporated in the detainee's custody record. The custody officer is responsible for making sure those responsible for the detainee's custody are appropriately briefed about the risks. If no specific risks are identified by the assessment, that should be noted in the custody record. See *Note 3E* and *paragraph 9.14*.

3.8A The content of any risk assessment and any analysis of the level of risk relating to the person's detention is not required to be shown or provided to the detainee or any person acting on behalf of the detainee. But information should not be withheld from any person acting on the detainee's behalf, for example, an appropriate adult, solicitor or interpreter, if to do so might put that person at risk.

3.9   The custody officer is responsible for implementing the response to any specific risk assessment, e.g.:
    • reducing opportunities for self harm;
    • calling an appropriate healthcare professional;
    • increasing levels of monitoring or observation;
    • reducing the risk to those who come into contact with the detainee.

See *Note 3E*.

3.10 Risk assessment is an ongoing process and assessments must always be subject to review if circumstances change.

3.11 If video cameras are installed in the custody area, notices shall be prominently displayed showing cameras are in use. Any request to have video cameras switched off shall be refused.

(B) Detained persons — special groups

3.12 If the detainee appears to be someone who does not speak or understand English or who has a hearing or speech impediment, the custody officer must ensure:

(a) that without delay, arrangements (*see paragraph 13.1ZA*) are made for the detainee to have the assistance of an interpreter in the action under *paragraphs 3.1 to 3.5*. If the person appears to have a hearing or speech impediment, the reference to 'interpreter' includes appropriate assistance necessary to comply with *paragraphs 3.1 to 3.5*. See *paragraph 13.1C* if the detainee is in Wales. See *section 13* and *Note 13B*;

(b) that in addition to the continuing rights set out in *paragraph 3.1(a)(i) to (iv)*, the detainee is told clearly about their right to interpretation and translation;

(c) that the written notice given to the detainee in accordance with *paragraph 3.2* is in a language the detainee understands and includes the right to interpretation and translation together with information about the provisions in *section 13* and *Annex M*, which explain how the right applies (see *Note 3A*); and

(d) that if the translation of the notice is not available, the information in the notice is given through an interpreter and a written translation provided without undue delay.

3.12A If the detainee is a citizen of an independent Commonwealth country or a national of a foreign country, including the Republic of Ireland, the custody officer must ensure that in addition to the continuing rights set out in *paragraph 3.1(a)(i) to (iv)*, they are informed as soon as practicable about their rights of communication with their High Commission, Embassy or Consulate set out in *section 7*. This right must be included in the written notice given to the detainee in accordance with *paragraph 3.2*.

3.13 If the detainee is a juvenile, the custody officer must, if it is practicable, ascertain the identity of a person responsible for their welfare. That person:

• may be:
  - the parent or guardian;
  - if the juvenile is in local authority or voluntary organisation care, or is otherwise being looked after under the Children Act 1989, a person appointed by that authority or organisation to have responsibility for the juvenile's welfare;
  - any other person who has, for the time being, assumed responsibility for the juvenile's welfare.

• must be informed as soon as practicable that the juvenile has been arrested, why they have been arrested and where they are detained. This right is in addition to the juvenile's right in *section 5* not to be held incommunicado. See *Note 3C*.

3.14 If a juvenile is known to be subject to a court order under which a person or organisation is given any degree of statutory responsibility to supervise or otherwise monitor them, reasonable steps must also be taken to notify that person or organisation (the 'responsible officer'). The responsible officer will normally be a member of a Youth Offending Team, except for a curfew order which involves electronic monitoring when the contractor providing the monitoring will normally be the responsible officer.

3.15 If the detainee is a juvenile or a vulnerable person, the custody officer must, as soon as practicable, ensure that:

• the detainee is informed of the decision that an appropriate adult is required and the reason for that decision (see *paragraph 3.5(c)(ii)*) and;

• the detainee is advised:
  - of the duties of the appropriate adult as described in *paragraph 1.7A;* and
  - that they can consult privately with the appropriate adult at any time.

• the appropriate adult, who in the case of a juvenile may or may not be a person responsible for their welfare, as in *paragraph 3.13*, is informed of:
  - the grounds for their detention;
  - their whereabouts; and

• the attendance of the appropriate adult at the police station to see the detainee is secured.

3.16 It is imperative that a person detained under the Mental Health Act 1983, section 135 or 136, be assessed as soon as possible within the permitted period of detention specified in that Act. A police station may only be used as a place of safety in accordance with The Mental Health Act 1983 (Places of Safety) Regulations 2017. If that assessment is to take place at the police station, an approved mental health professional and a registered medical practitioner shall be called to the station as soon as possible to carry it out. See *Note 9D*. The appropriate adult has no role in the assessment process and their presence is not required. Once the detainee has been assessed and suitable arrangements made for their treatment or care, they can no longer be detained under section 135 or 136. A detainee must be immediately discharged from detention if a registered medical practitioner, having examined them, concludes they are not mentally disordered within the meaning of the Act.

3.17 If the appropriate adult is:
- already at the police station, the provisions of *paragraphs 3.1* to *3.5* must be complied with in the appropriate adult's presence;
- not at the station when these provisions are complied with, they must be complied with again in the presence of the appropriate adult when they arrive,

and a copy of the notice given to the detainee in accordance with *paragraph 3.2*, shall also be given to the appropriate adult.

3.17A The custody officer must ensure that at the time the copy of the notice is given to the appropriate adult, or as soon as practicable thereafter, the appropriate adult is advised of the duties of the appropriate adult as described in *paragraph 1.7A*.

3.18 *Not used.*

3.19 If the detainee, or appropriate adult on the detainee's behalf, asks for a solicitor to be called to give legal advice, the provisions of *section 6* apply (see *paragraph 6.5A* and *Note 3H*).

3.20 If the detainee is blind, seriously visually impaired or unable to read, the custody officer shall make sure their solicitor, relative, appropriate adult or some other person likely to take an interest in them and not involved in the investigation is available to help check any documentation. When this Code requires written consent or signing the person assisting may be asked to sign instead, if the detainee prefers. This paragraph does not require an appropriate adult to be called solely to assist in checking and signing documentation for a person who is not a juvenile, or is not vulnerable (see *paragraph 3.15* and *Note 13C*).

3.20A The Children and Young Persons Act 1933, section 31, requires that arrangements must be made for ensuring that a girl under the age of 18, while detained in a police station, is under the care of a woman. The custody officer must ensure that the woman under whose care the girl is, makes the enquiries and provides the information concerning personal needs relating to their health, hygiene and welfare described in *paragraph 9.3A* and menstrual products described in *paragraph 9.3B*. See *Note 3G*. The section also requires that arrangements must be made for preventing any person under 18, while being detained in a police station, from associating with an adult charged with any offence, unless that adult is a relative or the adult is jointly charged with the same offence as the person under 18.

(C) Detained persons – Documentation

3.20B The grounds for a person's detention shall be recorded, in the person's presence if practicable. See *paragraph 1.8*.

3.20C Action taken under *paragraphs 3.12* to *3.20A* shall be recorded.

(D) Persons attending a police station or elsewhere voluntarily

3.21 Anybody attending a police station or other location (see *paragraph 3.22* and *Note 3I*) voluntarily to assist police with the investigation of an offence may leave at will unless arrested. See *Notes 1A* and *1K*. The person may only be prevented from leaving at will if their arrest on suspicion of committing the offence is necessary in accordance with Code G. See Code G *Note 2G*.

Action if arrest becomes necessary

   (a) If during a person's voluntary attendance at a police station or other location it is decided for any reason that their arrest is necessary, they must:
- be informed at once that they are under arrest and of the grounds and reasons as required by Code G, and
- be brought before the custody officer at the police station where they are arrested or (as the case may be) at the police station to which they are taken after being arrested elsewhere. The custody officer is then responsible for making sure that a custody record is opened and that they are notified of their rights in the same way as other detainees as required by this Code.

Information to be given when arranging a voluntary interview:

(b) If the suspect's arrest is not necessary but they are cautioned as required in *section 10*, the person who, after describing the nature and circumstances of the suspected offence, gives the caution must at the same time, inform them that they are not under arrest and that they are not obliged to remain at the station or other location (see *paragraph 3.22* and *Note 3I*). The rights, entitlements and safeguards that apply to the conduct and recording of interviews with suspects are not diminished simply because the interview is arranged on a voluntary basis. For the purpose of arranging a voluntary interview (see *Code G Note 2F*), the duty of the interviewer reflects that of the custody officer with regard to detained suspects. As a result:

    (i) the requirement in *paragraph 3.5(c)(ii)* to determine whether a detained suspect requires an appropriate adult, help to check documentation or an interpreter shall apply equally to a suspect who has not been arrested; and

    (ii) the suspect must not be asked to give their informed consent to be interviewed until *after* they have been informed of the rights, entitlements and safeguards that apply to voluntary interviews. These are set out in *paragraph 3.21A* and the interviewer is responsible for ensuring that the suspect is so informed and for explaining these rights, entitlements and safeguards.

3.21A The interviewer must inform the suspect that the purpose of the voluntary interview is to question them to obtain evidence about their involvement or suspected involvement in the offence(s) described when they were cautioned and told that they were not under arrest. The interviewer shall then inform the suspect that the following matters will apply if they agree to the voluntary interview proceeding:

(a) Their right to information about the offence(s) in question by providing sufficient information to enable them to understand the nature of any such offence(s) and why they are suspected of committing it. This is in order to allow for the effective exercise of the rights of the defence as required by *paragraph 11.1A*. It applies whether or not they ask for legal advice and includes any further offences that come to light and are pointed out during the voluntary interview and for which they are cautioned.

(b) Their right to free *(see Note 3J)* legal advice by:

    (i) explaining that they may obtain free and independent legal advice if they want it, and that this includes the right to speak with a solicitor on the telephone and to have the solicitor present during the interview;

    (ii) asking if they want legal advice and recording their reply; and

    (iii) if the person requests advice, securing its provision before the interview by contacting the Defence Solicitor Call Centre and explaining that the time and place of the interview will be arranged to enable them to obtain advice and that the interview will be delayed until they have received the advice unless, in accordance with *paragraph 6.6(c)* (Nominated solicitor not available and duty solicitor declined) or *paragraph 6.6(d)* (Change of mind), an officer of the rank of inspector or above agrees to the interview proceeding; or

    (iv) if the person declines to exercise the right, asking them why and recording any reasons given (see *Note 6K*).

Note:When explaining the right to legal advice and the arrangements, the interviewer must take care not to indicate, except to answer a direct question, that the time taken to arrange and complete the voluntary interview might be reduced if:

    • the suspect does not ask for legal advice or does not want a solicitor present when they are interviewed; or

    • the suspect asks for legal advice or (as the case may be) asks for a solicitor to be present when they are interviewed, but changes their mind and agrees to be interviewed without waiting for a solicitor.

(c) Their right, if in accordance with *paragraph 3.5(c)(ii)* the interviewer determines:

    (i) that they are a juvenile or are vulnerable; or

    (ii) that they need help to check documentation (see *paragraph 3.20*),

to have the appropriate adult present or (as the case may be) to have the necessary help to check documentation; and that the interview will be delayed until the presence of the appropriate adult or the necessary help, is secured.

(d) If they are a juvenile or vulnerable and do not want legal advice, their appropriate adult has the right to ask for a solicitor to attend if this would be in their best interests and the appropriate adult must be so informed. In this case, action to secure the provision of advice if so requested by their appropriate adult will be taken without delay in the same way as if requested by the person (see *sub-paragraph (b)(iii)*). However, they cannot be forced to see the solicitor if they are adamant that they do not wish to do so (see *paragraphs 3.19* and *6.5A*).

(e) Their right to an interpreter, if in accordance with, *paragraphs 3.5(c)(ii)* and *3.12*, the interviewer determines that they require an interpreter and that if they require an interpreter, making the necessary arrangements in accordance with *paragraph 13.1ZA* and that the interview will be delayed to make the arrangements.

(f) That interview will be arranged for a time and location (see *paragraph 3.22* and *Note 3I*) that enables:

    (i) the suspect's rights described above to be fully respected; and

    (ii) the whole of the interview to be recorded using an authorised recording device in accordance with Code E (Code of Practice on Audio recording of interviews with suspects) or (as the case may be) Code F (Code of Practice on visual recording with sound of interviews with suspects); and

(g) That their agreement to take part in the interview also signifies their agreement for that interview to be audio-recorded or (as the case may be) visually recorded with sound.

3.21B The provision by the interviewer of factual information described in *paragraph 3.21A* and, if asked by the suspect, further such information, does not constitute an interview for the purpose of this Code and *when that information is provided*:

(a) the interviewer must remind the suspect about the caution as required in *section 10* but must not *invite* comment about the offence or put specific questions to the suspect regarding their involvement in any offence, nor in respect of any comments they may make when given the information. Such an exchange is itself likely to constitute an interview as in *paragraph 11.1A* and require the associated interview safeguards in *section 11*.

(b) Any comment the suspect makes when the information is given which might be relevant to the offence, must be recorded and dealt with in accordance with *paragraph 11.13*.

(c) The suspect must be given a notice summarising the matters described in *paragraph 3.21A* and which includes the arrangements for obtaining legal advice. If a specific notice is not available, the notice given to detained suspects with references to detention-specific requirements and information redacted, may be used.

(d) For juvenile and vulnerable suspects (see *paragraphs 1.4* and *1.5*):

    (i) the information must be provided or (as the case may be) provided again, together with the notice, in the presence of the appropriate adult;

    (ii) if cautioned in the absence of the appropriate adult, the caution must be repeated in the appropriate adult's presence (see *paragraph 10.12*);

    (iii) the suspect must be informed of the decision that an appropriate is required and the reason (see *paragraph 3.5(c)(ii)*);

    (iv) the suspect *and* the appropriate adult shall be advised:

        • that the duties of the appropriate adult include giving advice and assistance in accordance with *paragraphs 1.7A* and *11.17*; and

        • that they can consult privately at any time.

    (v) their informed agreement to be interviewed voluntarily must be sought and given in the presence of the appropriate adult and for a juvenile, the agreement of a parent or guardian of the juvenile is also required.

3.22 If the other location mentioned in *paragraph 3.21* is any place or premises for which the interviewer requires the informed consent of the suspect and/or occupier (if different) to remain, for example, the suspect's home (see *Note 3I*), then the references that the person is 'not obliged to remain' and that they 'may leave at will' mean that the suspect and/or occupier (if different) may also withdraw their consent and require the interviewer to leave.

Commencement of voluntary interview – general

3.22A Before asking the suspect any questions about their involvement in the offence they are suspected of committing, the interviewing officer must ask them to confirm that they agree to the interview proceeding. This confirmation shall be recorded in the interview record made in accordance with section 11 of this Code (written record) or Code E or Code F.

Documentation

3.22B Action taken under *paragraphs 3.21A* to *3.21B* shall be recorded. The record shall include the date time and place the action was taken, who was present and anything said to or by the suspect and to or by those present.

3.23 *Not used.*

3.24 *Not used.*

(E) Persons answering street bail

3.25　When a person is answering street bail, the custody officer should link any documentation held in relation to arrest with the custody record. Any further action shall be recorded on the custody record in accordance with *paragraphs 3.20B* and *3.20C* above.

(F) Requirements for suspects to be informed of certain rights

3.26　The provisions of this section identify the information which must be given to suspects who have been cautioned in accordance with *section 10* of this Code according to whether or not they have been arrested and detained. It includes information required by *EU Directive 2012/13* on the right to information in criminal proceedings. If a complaint is made by or on behalf of such a suspect that the information and (as the case may be) access to records and documents has not been provided as required, the matter shall be reported to an inspector to deal with as a complaint for the purposes of *paragraph 9.2*, or *paragraph 12.9* if the challenge is made during an interview. This would include, for example:

(a)　in the case of a detained suspect:
- not informing them of their rights (see *paragraph 3.1*);
- not giving them a copy of the Notice (see *paragraph 3.2(a)*);
- not providing an opportunity to read the notice (see *paragraph 3.2A*);
- not providing the required information (see *paragraphs 3.2(a), 3.12(b)* and, *3.12A*);
- not allowing access to the custody record (see *paragraph 2.4*);
- not providing a translation of the Notice (see *paragraph 3.12(c)* and *(d)*); and

(b)　in the case of a suspect who is not detained:
- not informing them of their rights or providing the required information (see *paragraphs 3.21(b)* to *3.21B*).

Notes for Guidance

3ZA　For the purposes of paragraphs 3.4(b) and 15.0:

(a)　*Investigating officers are responsible for bringing to the attention of the officer who is responsible for authorising the suspect's detention or (as the case may be) continued detention (before or after charge), any documents and materials in their possession or control which appear to undermine the need to keep the suspect in custody. In accordance with Part IV of PACE, this officer will be either the custody officer, the officer reviewing the need for detention before or after charge (PACE, section 40), or the officer considering the need to extend detention without charge from 24 to 36 hours (PACE, section 42) who is then responsible for determining, which, if any, of those documents and materials are capable of undermining the need to detain the suspect and must therefore be made available to the suspect or their solicitor.*

(b)　*the way in which documents and materials are 'made available', is a matter for the investigating officer to determine on a case by case basis and having regard to the nature and volume of the documents and materials involved. For example, they may be made available by supplying a copy or allowing supervised access to view. However, for view only access, it will be necessary to demonstrate that sufficient time is allowed for the suspect and solicitor to view and consider the documents and materials in question.*

3A　*For access to currently available notices, including 'easy-read' versions, see https://www.gov.uk/guidance/notice-of-rights-and-entitlements-a-persons-rights-in-police-detention.*

3B　*Not used.*

3C　*If the juvenile is in local authority or voluntary organisation care but living with their parents or other adults responsible for their welfare, although there is no legal obligation to inform them, they should normally be contacted, as well as the authority or organisation unless they are suspected of involvement in the offence concerned. Even if the juvenile is not living with their parents, consideration should be given to informing them.*

3D　*The right to consult the Codes of Practice does not entitle the person concerned to delay unreasonably any necessary investigative or administrative action whilst they do so. Examples of action which need not be delayed unreasonably include:*
- *procedures requiring the provision of breath, blood or urine specimens under the Road Traffic Act 1988 or the Transport and Works Act 1992;*
- *searching detainees at the police station;*
- *taking fingerprints, footwear impressions or non-intimate samples without consent for evidential purposes.*

3E　*The Detention and Custody Authorised Professional Practice (APP) produced by the College of Policing (see http://www.app.college.police.uk) provides more detailed guidance on risk assessments and identifies* key risk areas which should always be considered. See Home Office Circular 34/2007 (Safety of solicitors and probationary representatives at police stations).

3F   A custody officer or other officer who, in accordance with this Code, allows or directs the carrying out of any task or action relating to a detainee's care, treatment, rights and entitlements to another officer or any other person, must be satisfied that the officer or person concerned is suitable, trained and competent to carry out the task or action in question.

3G   Guidance for police officers and police staff on the operational application of section 31 of the Children and Young Persons Act 1933 has been published by the College of Policing and is available at: https://www.app.college.police.uk/app-content/detention-and-custody-2/detainee-care/children-and-yo ung-persons/#girls.

3H   The purpose of the provisions at paragraphs 3.19 and 6.5A is to protect the rights of juvenile and vulnerable persons who may not understand the significance of what is said to them. They should always be given an opportunity, when an appropriate adult is called to the police station, to consult privately with a solicitor in the absence of the appropriate adult if they want.

3I   An interviewer who is not sure, or has any doubt, about whether a place or location elsewhere than a police station is suitable for carrying out a voluntary interview, particularly in the case of a juvenile or vulnerable person, should consult an officer of the rank of sergeant or above for advice. Detailed guidance for police officers and staff concerning the conduct and recording of voluntary interviews is being developed by the College of Policing.

It follows a review of operational issues arising when voluntary interviews need to be arranged. The aim is to ensure the effective implementation of the safeguards in paragraphs 3.21 to 3.22B particularly concerning the rights of suspects, the location for the interview and supervision.

3J   For voluntary interviews conducted by non-police investigators, the provision of legal advice is set out by the Legal Aid Agency at paragraph 9.54 of the 2017 Standard Crime Contract Specification. This is published at https://www.gov.uk/government/publications/standard-crime-contract-2017 and the rules mean that a non-police interviewer who does not have their own statutory power of arrest would have to inform the suspect that they have a right to seek legal advice if they wish, but payment would be a matter for them to arrange with the solicitor.

4 Detainee's property

(A) Action

4.1   The custody officer is responsible for:
   (a)   ascertaining what property a detainee:
      (i)   has with them when they come to the police station, whether on:
         • arrest or re-detention on answering to bail;
         • commitment to prison custody on the order or sentence of a court;
         • lodgement at the police station with a view to their production in court from prison custody;
         • transfer from detention at another station or hospital;
         • detention under the Mental Health Act 1983, section 135 or 136;
         • remand into police custody on the authority of a court.
      (ii)   might have acquired for an unlawful or harmful purpose while in custody;
   (b)   the safekeeping of any property taken from a detainee which remains at the police station.
   The custody officer may search the detainee or authorise their being searched to the extent they consider necessary, provided a search of intimate parts of the body or involving the removal of more than outer clothing is only made as in *Annex A*. A search may only be carried out by an officer of the same sex as the detainee. See *Note 4A* and *Annex L*.

4.2   Subject to *paragraph 4.3A*, detainees may retain clothing and personal effects at their own risk unless the custody officer considers they may use them to cause harm to themselves or others, interfere with evidence, damage property, effect an escape or they are needed as evidence. In this event the custody officer may withhold such articles as they consider necessary and must tell the detainee why.

4.3   Personal effects are those items a detainee may lawfully need, use or refer to while in detention but do not include cash and other items of value.

4.3A For the purpose of *paragraph 4.2*, the reference to clothing and personal effects shall be treated as including menstrual and any other health, hygiene and welfare products needed by a detainee in question (see *paragraphs 9.3A* and *9.3B*) and a decision to withhold any such products must be subject to a further specific risk assessment.

(B) Documentation

4.4 It is a matter for the custody officer to determine whether a record should be made of the property a detained person has with him or had taken from him on arrest. Any record made is not required to be kept as part of the custody record but the custody record should be noted as to where such a record exists and that record shall be treated as being part of the custody record for the purpose of this and any other Code of Practice (see *paragraphs 2.4, 2.4A* and *2.5*). Whenever a record is made the detainee shall be allowed to check and sign the record of property as correct. Any refusal to sign shall be recorded.

4.5 If a detainee is not allowed to keep any article of clothing or personal effects, the reason must be recorded.

Notes for Guidance

4A *PACE, Section 54(1) and paragraph 4.1 require a detainee to be searched when it is clear the custody officer will have continuing duties in relation to that detainee or when that detainee's behaviour or offence makes an inventory appropriate. They do not require every detainee to be searched, e.g. if it is clear a person will only be detained for a short period and is not to be placed in a cell, the custody officer may decide not to search them. In such a case the custody record will be endorsed 'not searched', paragraph 4.4 will not apply, and the detainee will be invited to sign the entry. If the detainee refuses, the custody officer will be obliged to ascertain what property they have in accordance with paragraph 4.1.*

4B *Paragraph 4.4 does not require the custody officer to record on the custody record property in the detainee's possession on arrest if, by virtue of its nature, quantity or size, it is not practicable to remove it to the police station.*

4C *Paragraph 4.4 does not require items of clothing worn by the person to be recorded unless withheld by the custody officer as in paragraph 4.2.*

5 Right not to be held incommunicado

(A) Action

5.1 Subject to *paragraph 5.7B*, any person arrested and held in custody at a police station or other premises may, on request, have one person known to them or likely to take an interest in their welfare informed at public expense of their whereabouts as soon as practicable. If the person cannot be contacted the detainee may choose up to two alternatives. If they cannot be contacted, the person in charge of detention or the investigation has discretion to allow further attempts until the information has been conveyed. See *Notes 5C* and *5D*.

5.2 The exercise of the above right in respect of each person nominated may be delayed only in accordance with *Annex B*.

5.3 The above right may be exercised each time a detainee is taken to another police station.

5.4 If the detainee agrees, they may at the custody officer's discretion, receive visits from friends, family or others likely to take an interest in their welfare, or in whose welfare the detainee has an interest. See *Note 5B*.

5.5 If a friend, relative or person with an interest in the detainee's welfare enquires about their whereabouts, this information shall be given if the suspect agrees and *Annex B* does not apply. See *Note 5D*.

5.6 The detainee shall be given writing materials, on request, and allowed to telephone one person for a reasonable time, see *Notes 5A* and *5E*. Either or both of these privileges may be denied or delayed if an officer of inspector rank or above considers sending a letter or making a telephone call may result in any of the consequences in:

(a) *Annex B, paragraphs 1* and *2* and the person is detained in connection with an indictable offence;

(b) *Not used.*

Nothing in this paragraph permits the restriction or denial of the rights in *paragraphs 5.1* and *6.1*.

5.7 Before any letter or message is sent, or telephone call made, the detainee shall be informed that what they say in any letter, call or message (other than in a communication to a solicitor) may be read or listened to and may be given in evidence. A telephone call may be terminated if it is being abused. The costs can be at public expense at the custody officer's discretion.

5.7A Any delay or denial of the rights in this section should be proportionate and should last no longer than necessary.

5.7B In the case of a person in police custody for specific purposes and periods in accordance with a direction under the *Crime (Sentences) Act 1997, Schedule 1* (productions from prison etc.), the exercise of the rights in this section shall be subject to any additional conditions specified in the direction for the purpose of regulating the detainee's contact and communication with others whilst in police custody. See *Note 5F.*

(B) Documentation

5.8   A record must be kept of any:
  (a) request made under this section and the action taken;
  (b) letters, messages or telephone calls made or received or visit received;
  (c) refusal by the detainee to have information about them given to an outside enquirer. The detainee must be asked to countersign the record accordingly and any refusal recorded.

Notes for Guidance

5A   *A person may request an interpreter to interpret a telephone call or translate a letter.*

5B   *At the custody officer's discretion and subject to the detainee's consent, visits should be allowed when possible, subject to having sufficient personnel to supervise a visit and any possible hindrance to the investigation.*

5C   *If the detainee does not know anyone to contact for advice or support or cannot contact a friend or relative, the custody officer should bear in mind any local voluntary bodies or other organisations who might be able to help. Paragraph 6.1 applies if legal advice is required.*

5D   *In some circumstances it may not be appropriate to use the telephone to disclose information under paragraphs 5.1 and 5.5.*

5E   *The telephone call at paragraph 5.6 is in addition to any communication under paragraphs 5.1 and 6.1.*

5F   *Prison Service Instruction 26/2012 (Production of Prisoners at the Request of Warranted Law Enforcement Agencies) provides detailed guidance and instructions for police officers and Governors and Directors of Prisons regarding applications for prisoners to be transferred to police custody and their safe custody and treatment while in police custody.*

6 Right to legal advice

(A) Action

6.1   Unless *Annex B* applies, all detainees must be informed that they may at any time consult and communicate privately with a solicitor, whether in person, in writing or by telephone, and that free independent legal advice is available. See *paragraph 3.1, Notes 1I, 6B and 6J.*

6.2   *Not used.*

6.3   A poster advertising the right to legal advice must be prominently displayed in the charging area of every police station. See *Note 6H.*

6.4   No police officer should, at any time, do or say anything with the intention of dissuading any person who is entitled to legal advice in accordance with this Code, whether or not they have been arrested and are detained, from obtaining legal advice. See *Note 6ZA.*

6.5   The exercise of the right of access to legal advice may be delayed only as in *Annex B*. Whenever legal advice is requested, and unless *Annex B* applies, the custody officer must act without delay to secure the provision of such advice. If the detainee has the right to speak to a solicitor in person but declines to exercise the right the officer should point out that the right includes the right to speak with a solicitor on the telephone. If the detainee continues to waive this right, or a detainee whose right to free legal advice is limited to telephone advice from the Criminal Defence Service (CDS) Direct (see *Note 6B*) declines to exercise that right, the officer should ask them why and any reasons should be recorded on the custody record or the interview record as appropriate. Reminders of the right to legal advice must be given as in *paragraphs 3.5, 11.2, 15.4, 16.4, 16.5, 2B of Annex A, 3 of Annex K and 5 of Annex M* of this Code and Code D, *paragraphs 3.17(ii) and 6.3.* Once it is clear a detainee does not want to speak to a solicitor in person or by telephone they should cease to be asked their reasons. See *Note 6K.*

6.5A In the case of a person who is a juvenile or is vulnerable, an appropriate adult should consider whether legal advice from a solicitor is required. If such a detained person wants to exercise the right to legal advice, the appropriate action should be taken and should not be delayed until the appropriate adult arrives. If the person indicates that they do not want legal advice, the appropriate adult has the right to ask for a solicitor to attend if this would be in the best interests of the person and must be so informed. In this case, action to secure the provision of advice if so requested by the appropriate adult shall be taken without delay in the same way as when requested by the person. However, the person cannot be forced to see the solicitor if they are adamant that they do not wish to do so.

6.6   A detainee who wants legal advice may not be interviewed or continue to be interviewed until they have received such advice unless:

(a) *Annex B* applies, when the restriction on drawing adverse inferences from silence in *Annex C* will apply because the detainee is not allowed an opportunity to consult a solicitor; or

(b) an officer of superintendent rank or above has reasonable grounds for believing that:

    (i) the consequent delay might:
- lead to interference with, or harm to, evidence connected with an offence;
- lead to interference with, or physical harm to, other people;
- lead to serious loss of, or damage to, property;
- lead to alerting other people suspected of having committed an offence but not yet arrested for it;
- hinder the recovery of property obtained in consequence of the commission of an offence.

See *Note 6A*

    (ii) when a solicitor, including a duty solicitor, has been contacted and has agreed to attend, awaiting their arrival would cause unreasonable delay to the process of investigation.

Note: In these cases the restriction on drawing adverse inferences from silence in *Annex C* will apply because the detainee is not allowed an opportunity to consult a solicitor.

(c) the solicitor the detainee has nominated or selected from a list:

    (i) cannot be contacted;
    (ii) has previously indicated they do not wish to be contacted; or
    (iii) having been contacted, has declined to attend; and
- the detainee has been advised of the Duty Solicitor Scheme but has declined to ask for the duty solicitor;
- in these circumstances the interview may be started or continued without further delay provided an officer of inspector rank or above has agreed to the interview proceeding.

Note: The restriction on drawing adverse inferences from silence in *Annex C* will not apply because the detainee is allowed an opportunity to consult the duty solicitor;

(d) the detainee changes their mind about wanting legal advice or (as the case may be) about wanting a solicitor present at the interview and states that they no longer wish to speak to a solicitor. In these circumstances, the interview may be started or continued without delay provided that:

    (i) an officer of inspector rank or above:
- speaks to the detainee to enquire about the reasons for their change of mind (see *Note 6K*), and
- makes, or directs the making of, reasonable efforts to ascertain the solicitor's expected time of arrival and to inform the solicitor that the suspect has stated that they wish to change their mind and the reason (if given);

    (ii) the detainee's reason for their change of mind (if given) and the outcome of the action in (i) are recorded in the custody record;

    (iii) the detainee, after being informed of the outcome of the action in (i) above, confirms in writing that they want the interview to proceed without speaking or further speaking to a solicitor or (as the case may be) without a solicitor being present and do not wish to wait for a solicitor by signing an entry to this effect in the custody record;

    (iv) an officer of inspector rank or above is satisfied that it is proper for the interview to proceed in these circumstances and:
- gives authority in writing for the interview to proceed and, if the authority is not recorded in the custody record, the officer must ensure that the custody record shows the date and time of the authority and where it is recorded, and
- takes, or directs the taking of, reasonable steps to inform the solicitor that the authority has been given and the time when the interview is expected to commence and records or causes to be recorded, the outcome of this action in the custody record.

    (v) When the interview starts and the interviewer reminds the suspect of their right to legal advice (see *paragraph 11.2*, Code E *paragraph 4.5* and Code F *paragraph 4.5*), the interviewer shall then ensure that the following is recorded in the written interview record or the interview record made in accordance with Code E or F:
- confirmation that the detainee has changed their mind about wanting legal advice or (as the case may be) about wanting a solicitor present and the reasons for it if given;
- the fact that authority for the interview to proceed has been given and, subject to *paragraph 2.6A*, the name of the authorising officer;

- that if the solicitor arrives at the station before the interview is completed, the detainee will be so informed without delay and *a break will be taken* to allow them to speak to the solicitor if they wish, unless *paragraph 6.6(a)* applies, and
- that at any time during the interview, the detainee may again ask for legal advice and that if they do, a break will be taken to allow them to speak to the solicitor, unless *paragraph 6.6(a), (b), or (c)* applies.

Note: In these circumstances, the restriction on drawing adverse inferences from silence in *Annex C* will not apply because the detainee is allowed an opportunity to consult a solicitor if they wish.

6.7   If *paragraph 6.6(a)* applies, where the reason for authorising the delay ceases to apply, there may be no further delay in permitting the exercise of the right in the absence of a further authorisation unless *paragraph 6.6(b), (c)* or *(d)* applies. If *paragraph 6.6(b)(i)* applies, once sufficient information has been obtained to avert the risk, questioning must cease until the detainee has received legal advice unless *paragraph 6.6(a), (b)(ii), (c)* or *(d)* applies.

6.8   A detainee who has been permitted to consult a solicitor shall be entitled on request to have the solicitor present when they are interviewed unless one of the exceptions in *paragraph 6.6* applies.

6.9   The solicitor may only be required to leave the interview if their conduct is such that the interviewer is unable properly to put questions to the suspect. See *Notes 6D* and *6E*.

6.10 If the interviewer considers a solicitor is acting in such a way, they will stop the interview and consult an officer not below superintendent rank, if one is readily available, and otherwise an officer not below inspector rank not connected with the investigation. After speaking to the solicitor, the officer consulted will decide if the interview should continue in the presence of that solicitor. If they decide it should not, the suspect will be given the opportunity to consult another solicitor before the interview continues and that solicitor given an opportunity to be present at the interview. See *Note 6E*.

6.11 The removal of a solicitor from an interview is a serious step and, if it occurs, the officer of superintendent rank or above who took the decision will consider if the incident should be reported to the Solicitors Regulatory Authority. If the decision to remove the solicitor has been taken by an officer below superintendent rank, the facts must be reported to an officer of superintendent rank or above, who will similarly consider whether a report to the Solicitors Regulatory Authority would be appropriate. When the solicitor concerned is a duty solicitor, the report should be both to the Solicitors Regulatory Authority and to the Legal Aid Agency.

6.12 'Solicitor' in this Code means:
- a solicitor who holds a current practising certificate;
- an accredited or probationary representative included on the register of representatives maintained by the Legal Aid Agency.

6.12A An accredited or probationary representative sent to provide advice by, and on behalf of, a solicitor shall be admitted to the police station for this purpose unless an officer of inspector rank or above considers such a visit will hinder the investigation and directs otherwise. Hindering the investigation does not include giving proper legal advice to a detainee as in *Note 6D*. Once admitted to the police station, *paragraphs 6.6* to *6.10* apply.

6.13 In exercising their discretion under *paragraph 6.12A*, the officer should take into account in particular:
- whether:
  – the identity and status of an accredited or probationary representative have been satisfactorily established;
  – they are of suitable character to provide legal advice, e.g. a person with a criminal record is unlikely to be suitable unless the conviction was for a minor offence and not recent.
- any other matters in any written letter of authorisation provided by the solicitor on whose behalf the person is attending the police station. See *Note 6F*.

6.14 If the inspector refuses access to an accredited or probationary representative or a decision is taken that such a person should not be permitted to remain at an interview, the inspector must notify the solicitor on whose behalf the representative was acting and give them an opportunity to make alternative arrangements. The detainee must be informed and the custody record noted.

6.15 If a solicitor arrives at the station to see a particular person, that person must, unless *Annex B* applies, be so informed whether or not they are being interviewed and asked if they would like to see the solicitor. This applies even if the detainee has declined legal advice or, having requested it, subsequently agreed to be interviewed without receiving advice. The solicitor's attendance and the detainee's decision must be noted in the custody record.

(B) Documentation

6.16 Any request for legal advice and the action taken shall be recorded.

6.17 A record shall be made in the interview record if a detainee asks for legal advice and an interview is begun either in the absence of a solicitor or their representative, or they have been required to leave an interview.

Notes for Guidance

6ZA *No police officer or police staff shall indicate to any suspect, except to answer a direct question, that the period for which they are liable to be detained, or if not detained, the time taken to complete the interview, might be reduced:*
   • *if they do not ask for legal advice or do not want a solicitor present when they are interviewed; or*
   • *if they have asked for legal advice or (as the case may be) asked for a solicitor to be present when they are interviewed but change their mind and agree to be interviewed without waiting for a solicitor.*

6A   *In considering if paragraph 6.6(b) applies, the officer should, if practicable, ask the solicitor for an estimate of how long it will take to come to the station and relate this to the time detention is permitted, the time of day (i.e. whether the rest period under paragraph 12.2 is imminent) and the requirements of other investigations. If the solicitor is on their way or is to set off immediately, it will not normally be appropriate to begin an interview before they arrive. If it appears necessary to begin an interview before the solicitor's arrival, they should be given an indication of how long the police would be able to wait before 6.6(b) applies so there is an opportunity to make arrangements for someone else to provide legal advice.*

6B   *A detainee has a right to free legal advice and to be represented by a solicitor. This Note for Guidance explains the arrangements which enable detainees to obtain legal advice. An outline of these arrangements is also included in the Notice of Rights and Entitlements given to detainees in accordance with paragraph 3.2. The arrangements also apply, with appropriate modifications, to persons attending a police station or other location (see paragraph 3.22 and Notes 3I and 3J) voluntarily who are cautioned prior to being interviewed. See paragraph 3.21.*

   When a detainee asks for free legal advice, the Defence Solicitor Call Centre (DSCC) must be informed of the request.

   Free legal advice will be limited to telephone advice provided by CDS Direct if a detainee is:
   • *detained for a non-imprisonable offence;*
   • *arrested on a bench warrant for failing to appear and being held for production at court (except where the solicitor has clear documentary evidence available that would result in the client being released from custody);*
   • *arrested for drink driving (driving/in charge with excess alcohol, failing to provide a specimen, driving/in charge whilst unfit through drink), or*
   • *detained in relation to breach of police or court bail conditions*
   unless one or more exceptions apply, in which case the DSCC should arrange for advice to be given by a solicitor at the police station, for example:
   • *the police want to interview the detainee or carry out an eye-witness identification procedure;*
   • *the detainee needs an appropriate adult;*
   • *the detainee is unable to communicate over the telephone;*
   • *the detainee alleges serious misconduct by the police;*
   • *the investigation includes another offence not included in the list,*
   • *the solicitor to be assigned is already at the police station.*
   When free advice is not limited to telephone advice, a detainee can ask for free advice from a solicitor they know or if they do not know a solicitor or the solicitor they know cannot be contacted, from the duty solicitor.

   To arrange free legal advice, the police should telephone the DSCC. The call centre will decide whether legal advice should be limited to telephone advice from CDS Direct, or whether a solicitor known to the detainee or the duty solicitor should speak to the detainee.

   When a detainee wants to pay for legal advice themselves:
   • *the DSCC will contact a solicitor of their choice on their behalf;*
   • *they may, when free advice is only available by telephone from CDS Direct, still speak to a solicitor of their choice on the telephone for advice, but the solicitor would not be paid by legal aid and may ask the person to pay for the advice;*
   • *they should be given an opportunity to consult a specific solicitor or another solicitor from that solicitor's firm. If this solicitor is not available, they may choose up to two alternatives. If these alternatives are not available, the custody officer has discretion to allow further attempts until a solicitor has been contacted and agreed to provide advice;*

- *they are entitled to a private consultation with their chosen solicitor on the telephone or the solicitor may decide to come to the police station;*
- *If their chosen solicitor cannot be contacted, the DSCC may still be called to arrange free legal advice. Apart from carrying out duties necessary to implement these arrangements, an officer must not advise the suspect about any particular firm of solicitors.*

6B1 *Not used.*

6B2 *Not used.*

6C *Not used.*

6D *The solicitor's only role in the police station is to protect and advance the legal rights of their client. On occasions this may require the solicitor to give advice which has the effect of the client avoiding giving evidence which strengthens a prosecution case. The solicitor may intervene in order to seek clarification, challenge an improper question to their client or the manner in which it is put, advise their client not to reply to particular questions, or if they wish to give their client further legal advice. Paragraph 6.9 only applies if the solicitor's approach or conduct prevents or unreasonably obstructs proper questions being put to the suspect or the suspect's response being recorded. Examples of unacceptable conduct include answering questions on a suspect's behalf or providing written replies for the suspect to quote.*

6E *An officer who takes the decision to exclude a solicitor must be in a position to satisfy the court the decision was properly made. In order to do this they may need to witness what is happening.*

6F *If an officer of at least inspector rank considers a particular solicitor or firm of solicitors is persistently sending probationary representatives who are unsuited to provide legal advice, they should inform an officer of at least superintendent rank, who may wish to take the matter up with the Solicitors Regulation Authority.*

6G *Subject to the constraints of Annex B, a solicitor may advise more than one client in an investigation if they wish. Any question of a conflict of interest is for the solicitor under their professional code of conduct. If, however, waiting for a solicitor to give advice to one client may lead to unreasonable delay to the interview with another, the provisions of paragraph 6.6(b) may apply.*

6H *In addition to a poster in English, a poster or posters containing translations into Welsh, the main minority ethnic languages and the principal European languages should be displayed wherever they are likely to be helpful and it is practicable to do so.*

6I *Not used.*

6J *Whenever a detainee exercises their right to legal advice by consulting or communicating with a solicitor, they must be allowed to do so in private. This right to consult or communicate in private is fundamental. If the requirement for privacy is compromised because what is said or written by the detainee or solicitor for the purpose of giving and receiving legal advice is overheard, listened to, or read by others without the informed consent of the detainee, the right will effectively have been denied. When a detainee speaks to a solicitor on the telephone, they should be allowed to do so in private unless this is impractical because of the design and layout of the custody area or the location of telephones. However, the normal expectation should be that facilities will be available, unless they are being used, at all police stations to enable detainees to speak in private to a solicitor either face to face or over the telephone.*

6K *A detainee is not obliged to give reasons for declining legal advice and should not be pressed to do so.*

7 Citizens of independent Commonwealth countries or foreign nationals

(A) Action

7.1 A detainee who is a citizen of an independent Commonwealth country or a national of a foreign country, including the Republic of Ireland, has the right, upon request, to communicate at any time with the appropriate High Commission, Embassy or Consulate. That detainee must be informed as soon as practicable of this right and asked if they want to have their High Commission, Embassy or Consulate told of their whereabouts and the grounds for their detention. Such a request should be acted upon as soon as practicable. See *Note 7A.*

7.2 A detainee who is a citizen of a country with which a bilateral consular convention or agreement is in force requiring notification of arrest must also be informed that subject to *paragraph 7.4,* notification of their arrest will be sent to the appropriate High Commission, Embassy or Consulate as soon as practicable, whether or not they request it. A list of the countries to which this requirement currently applies and contact details for the relevant High Commissions, Embassies and Consulates can be obtained from the Consular Directorate of the Foreign and Commonwealth Office (FCO) as follows:
- from the FCO web pages:
  - *https://gov.uk/government/publications/table-of-consular-conventions-and-mandatory-notification-obligations,* and

    – *https://www.gov.uk/government/publications/foreign-embassies-in-the-uk*
- by telephone to 020 7008 3100,
- by email to *fcocorrespondence@fco.gov.uk*.
- by letter to the Foreign and Commonwealth Office, King Charles Street, London, SW1A 2AH.

7.3   Consular officers may, if the detainee agrees, visit one of their nationals in police detention to talk to them and, if required, to arrange for legal advice. Such visits shall take place out of the hearing of a police officer.

7.4   Notwithstanding the provisions of consular conventions, if the detainee claims that they are a refugee or have applied or intend to apply for asylum, the custody officer must ensure that UK Visas and Immigration (UKVI) (formerly the UK Border Agency) is informed as soon as practicable of the claim. UKVI will then determine whether compliance with relevant international obligations requires notification of the arrest to be sent and will inform the custody officer as to what action police need to take.

(B) Documentation

7.5   A record shall be made:
- when a detainee is informed of their rights under this section and of any requirement in *paragraph 7.2*;
- of any communications with a High Commission, Embassy or Consulate, and
- of any communications with UKVI about a detainee's claim to be a refugee or to be seeking asylum and the resulting action taken by police.

Note for Guidance

7A   *The exercise of the rights in this section may not be interfered with even though Annex B applies.*

8 Conditions of detention

(A) Action

8.1   So far as it is practicable, not more than one detainee should be detained in each cell. See *Note 8C*.

8.2   Cells in use must be adequately heated, cleaned and ventilated. They must be adequately lit, subject to such dimming as is compatible with safety and security to allow people detained overnight to sleep. No additional restraints shall be used within a locked cell unless absolutely necessary and then only restraint equipment, approved for use in that force by the chief officer, which is reasonable and necessary in the circumstances having regard to the detainee's demeanour and with a view to ensuring their safety and the safety of others. If a detainee is deaf or a vulnerable person, particular care must be taken when deciding whether to use any form of approved restraints.

8.3   Blankets, mattresses, pillows and other bedding supplied shall be of a reasonable standard and in a clean and sanitary condition. See *Note 8A*.

8.4   Access to toilet and washing facilities must be provided. This must take account of the dignity of the detainee. See *Note 8D*.

8.5   If it is necessary to remove a detainee's clothes for the purposes of investigation, for hygiene, health reasons or cleaning, removal shall be conducted with proper regard to the dignity, sensitivity and vulnerability of the detainee and replacement clothing of a reasonable standard of comfort and cleanliness shall be provided. A detainee may not be interviewed unless adequate clothing has been offered.

8.6   At least two light meals and one main meal should be offered in any 24-hour period. See *Note 8B*. Drinks should be provided at meal times and upon reasonable request between meals. Whenever necessary, advice shall be sought from the appropriate healthcare professional, see *Note 9A*, on medical and dietary matters. As far as practicable, meals provided shall offer a varied diet and meet any specific dietary needs or religious beliefs the detainee may have. The detainee may, at the custody officer's discretion, have meals supplied by their family or friends at their expense. See *Note 8A*.

8.7   Brief outdoor exercise shall be offered daily if practicable.

8.8   A juvenile shall not be placed in a police cell unless no other secure accommodation is available and the custody officer considers it is not practicable to supervise them if they are not placed in a cell or that a cell provides more comfortable accommodation than other secure accommodation in the station. A juvenile may not be placed in a cell with a detained adult.

(B) Documentation

8.9   A record must be kept of replacement clothing and meals offered.

8.10 If a juvenile is placed in a cell, the reason must be recorded.

8.11 The use of any restraints on a detainee whilst in a cell, the reasons for it and, if appropriate, the arrangements for enhanced supervision of the detainee whilst so restrained, shall be recorded. See *paragraph 3.9.*

Notes for Guidance

8A   *The provisions in paragraph 8.3 and 8.6 respectively are of particular importance in the case of a person likely to be detained for an extended period. In deciding whether to allow meals to be supplied by family or friends, the custody officer is entitled to take account of the risk of items being concealed in any food or package and the officer's duties and responsibilities under food handling legislation.*

8B   *Meals should, so far as practicable, be offered at recognised meal times, or at other times that take account of when the detainee last had a meal.*

8C   *The Detention and Custody Authorised Professional Practice (APP) produced by the College of Policing (see http://www.app.college.police.uk) provides more detailed guidance on matters concerning detainee healthcare and treatment and associated forensic issues which should be read in conjunction with sections 8 and 9 of this Code.*

8D   *In cells subject to CCTV monitoring, privacy in the toilet area should be ensured by any appropriate means and detainees should be made aware of this when they are placed in the cell. If a detainee or appropriate adult on their behalf, expresses doubt about the effectiveness of the means used, reasonable steps should be taken to allay those doubts, for example, by explaining or demonstrating the means used.*

9 Care and treatment of detained persons

(A) General

9.1   Nothing in this section prevents the police from calling an appropriate healthcare professional to examine a detainee for the purposes of obtaining evidence relating to any offence in which the detainee is suspected of being involved. See *Notes 9A* and *8C.*

9.2   If a complaint is made by, or on behalf of, a detainee about their treatment since their arrest, or it comes to notice that a detainee may have been treated improperly, a report must be made as soon as practicable to an officer of inspector rank or above not connected with the investigation. If the matter concerns a possible assault or the possibility of the unnecessary or unreasonable use of force, an appropriate healthcare professional must also be called as soon as practicable.

9.3   Subject to *paragraph 9.6* in the case of a person to whom The Mental Health Act 1983 (Places of Safety) Regulations 2017 apply, detainees should be visited at least every hour. If no reasonably foreseeable risk was identified in a risk assessment, see *paragraphs 3.6 to 3.10*, there is no need to wake a sleeping detainee. Those suspected of being under the influence of drink or drugs or both or of having swallowed drugs, see *Note 9CA*, or whose level of consciousness causes concern must, subject to any clinical directions given by the appropriate healthcare professional, see *paragraph 9.13*:
   • be visited and roused at least every half hour;
   • have their condition assessed as in *Annex H*;
   • and clinical treatment arranged if appropriate.
   See *Notes 9B, 9C* and *9H*

9.3A *As soon as practicable after arrival at the police station, each detainee must be given an opportunity to speak in private with a member of the custody staff who if they wish may be of the same sex as the detainee (see paragraph 1.13(c)), about any matter concerning the detainee's personal needs relating to their health, hygiene and welfare that might affect or concern them whilst in custody. If the detainee wishes to take this opportunity, the necessary arrangements shall be made as soon as practicable. In the cases of a juvenile or vulnerable person, the appropriate adult must be involved in accordance with paragraph 3.17 and in the case of a girl under 18, see paragraph 3.20A (see Note 9CB).*

9.3B *Each female detainee aged 18 or over shall be asked in private if possible and at the earliest opportunity, if they require or are likely to require any menstrual products whilst they are in custody. They must be told that they will be provided free of charge and that replacement products are available. At the custody officer's discretion, detainees may have menstrual products supplied by their family or friends at their expense (see Note 9CC). For girls under 18, see paragraph 3.20A.*

9.4   When arrangements are made to secure clinical attention for a detainee, the custody officer must make sure all relevant information which might assist in the treatment of the detainee's condition is made available to the responsible healthcare professional. This applies whether or not the healthcare professional asks for such information. Any officer or police staff with relevant information must inform the custody officer as soon as practicable.

(B) Clinical treatment and attention

9.5 The custody officer must make sure a detainee receives appropriate clinical attention as soon as reasonably practicable if the person:

(a) appears to be suffering from physical illness; or

(b) is injured; or

(c) appears to be suffering from a mental disorder; or

(d) appears to need clinical attention.

9.5A This applies even if the detainee makes no request for clinical attention and whether or not they have already received clinical attention elsewhere. If the need for attention appears urgent, e.g. when indicated as in *Annex H*, the nearest available healthcare professional or an ambulance must be called immediately.

9.5B The custody officer must also consider the need for clinical attention as set out in *Note 9C* in relation to those suffering the effects of alcohol or drugs.

9.6 *Paragraph 9.5* is not meant to prevent or delay the transfer to a hospital if necessary of a person detained under the Mental Health Act 1983, sections 135 and 136, as amended by the Policing and Crime Act 2017. See *Note 9D*. When an assessment under that Act is to take place at a police station (see *paragraph 3.16*) the custody officer must also ensure that in accordance with *The Mental Health Act 1983 (Places of Safety) Regulations 2017*, a health professional is present and available to the person throughout the period they are detained at the police station and that at the welfare of the detainee is checked by the health professional at least once every thirty minutes and any appropriate action for the care and treatment of the detainee taken.

9.7 If it appears to the custody officer, or they are told, that a person brought to a station under arrest may be suffering from an infectious disease or condition, the custody officer must take reasonable steps to safeguard the health of the detainee and others at the station. In deciding what action to take, advice must be sought from an appropriate healthcare professional. See *Note 9E*. The custody officer has discretion to isolate the person and their property until clinical directions have been obtained.

9.8 If a detainee requests a clinical examination, an appropriate healthcare professional must be called as soon as practicable to assess the detainee's clinical needs. If a safe and appropriate care plan cannot be provided, the appropriate healthcare professional's advice must be sought. The detainee may also be examined by a medical practitioner of their choice at their expense.

9.9 If a detainee is required to take or apply any medication in compliance with clinical directions prescribed before their detention, the custody officer must consult the appropriate healthcare professional before the use of the medication. Subject to the restrictions in *paragraph 9.10*, the custody officer is responsible for the safekeeping of any medication and for making sure the detainee is given the opportunity to take or apply prescribed or approved medication. Any such consultation and its outcome shall be noted in the custody record.

9.10 No police officer may administer or supervise the self-administration of medically prescribed controlled drugs of the types and forms listed in the Misuse of Drugs Regulations 2001, Schedule 2 or 3. A detainee may only self-administer such drugs under the personal supervision of the registered medical practitioner authorising their use or other appropriate healthcare professional. The custody officer may supervise the self-administration of, or authorise other custody staff to supervise the self-administration of, drugs listed in Schedule 4 or 5 if the officer has consulted the appropriate healthcare professional authorising their use and both are satisfied self-administration will not expose the detainee, police officers or anyone else to the risk of harm or injury.

9.11 When appropriate healthcare professionals administer drugs or authorise the use of other medications, supervise their self-administration or consult with the custody officer about allowing self-administration of drugs listed in Schedule 4 or 5, it must be within current medicines legislation and the scope of practice as determined by their relevant statutory regulatory body.

9.12 If a detainee has in their possession, or claims to need, medication relating to a heart condition, diabetes, epilepsy or a condition of comparable potential seriousness then, even though *paragraph 9.5* may not apply, the advice of the appropriate healthcare professional must be obtained.

9.13 Whenever the appropriate healthcare professional is called in accordance with this section to examine or treat a detainee, the custody officer shall ask for their opinion about:

• any risks or problems which police need to take into account when making decisions about the detainee's continued detention;

• when to carry out an interview if applicable; and

• the need for safeguards.

9.14 When clinical directions are given by the appropriate healthcare professional, whether orally or in writing, and the custody officer has any doubts or is in any way uncertain about any aspect of the directions, the custody officer shall ask for clarification. It is particularly important that directions concerning the frequency of visits are clear, precise and capable of being implemented. See *Note 9F.*

(C) Documentation

9.15 A record must be made in the custody record of:

(a) the arrangements made for an examination by an appropriate healthcare professional under *paragraph 9.2* and of any complaint reported under that paragraph together with any relevant remarks by the custody officer;

(b) any arrangements made in accordance with *paragraph 9.5*;

(c) any request for a clinical examination under *paragraph 9.8* and any arrangements made in response;

(d) the injury, ailment, condition or other reason which made it necessary to make the arrangements in (*a*) to (*c*); See *Note 9G.*

(e) any clinical directions and advice, including any further clarifications, given to police by a healthcare professional concerning the care and treatment of the detainee in connection with any of the arrangements made in (*a*) to (*c*); See *Notes 9E* and *9F.*

(f) if applicable, the responses received when attempting to rouse a person using the procedure in *Annex H.* See *Note 9H.*

9.16 If a healthcare professional does not record their clinical findings in the custody record, the record must show where they are recorded. See *Note 9G.* However, information which is necessary to custody staff to ensure the effective ongoing care and well being of the detainee must be recorded openly in the custody record, see *paragraph 3.8* and *Annex G, paragraph 7.*

9.17 Subject to the requirements of *Section 4*, the custody record shall include:

• a record of all medication a detainee has in their possession on arrival at the police station;

• a note of any such medication they claim to need but do not have with them.

Notes for Guidance

9A   A 'healthcare professional' means a clinically qualified person working within the scope of practice as determined by their relevant statutory regulatory body. Whether a healthcare professional is 'appropriate' depends on the circumstances of the duties they carry out at the time.

9B   Whenever possible, detained juveniles and vulnerable persons should be visited more frequently.

9C   A detainee who appears drunk or behaves abnormally may be suffering from illness, the effects of drugs or may have sustained injury, particularly a head injury which is not apparent. A detainee needing or dependent on certain drugs, including alcohol, may experience harmful effects within a short time of being deprived of their supply. In these circumstances, when there is any doubt, police should always act urgently to call an appropriate healthcare professional or an ambulance. Paragraph 9.5 does not apply to minor ailments or injuries which do not need attention. However, all such ailments or injuries must be recorded in the custody record and any doubt must be resolved in favour of calling the appropriate healthcare professional.

9CA Paragraph 9.3 would apply to a person in police custody by order of a magistrates' court under the Criminal Justice Act 1988, section 152 (as amended by the Drugs Act 2005, section 8) to facilitate the recovery of evidence after being charged with drug possession or drug trafficking and suspected of having swallowed drugs. In the case of the healthcare needs of a person who has swallowed drugs, the custody officer, subject to any clinical directions, should consider the necessity for rousing every half hour. This does not negate the need for regular visiting of the suspect in the cell.

9D   Except as allowed for under The Mental Health Act 1983 (Places of Safety) Regulations 2017, a police station must not be used as a place of safety for persons detained under section 135 or 136 of that Act. Chapter 16 of the Mental Health Act 1983 Code of Practice (as revised), provides more detailed guidance about arranging assessments under the Mental Health Act and transferring detainees from police stations to other places of safety. Additional guidance in relation to amendments made to the Mental Health Act in 2017 are published at https://www.gov.uk/government/publications/mental-health-act-1983-implem enting-changes-to-police-powers.

9E   It is important to respect a person's right to privacy and information about their health must be kept confidential and only disclosed with their consent or in accordance with clinical advice when it is necessary to protect the detainee's health or that of others who come into contact with them.

9F   The custody officer should always seek to clarify directions that the detainee requires constant observation or supervision and should ask the appropriate healthcare professional to explain precisely what action needs to be taken to implement such directions.

9G   Paragraphs 9.15 and 9.16 do not require any information about the cause of any injury, ailment or condition to be recorded on the custody record if it appears capable of providing evidence of an offence.

9H   The purpose of recording a person's responses when attempting to rouse them using the procedure in Annex H is to enable any change in the individual's consciousness level to be noted and clinical treatment arranged if appropriate.

10 Cautions

(A) When a caution must be given

10.1 A person whom there are grounds to suspect of an offence, see *Note 10A*, must be cautioned before any questions about an offence, or further questions if the answers provide the grounds for suspicion, are put to them if either the suspect's answers or silence, (i.e. failure or refusal to answer or answer satisfactorily) may be given in evidence to a court in a prosecution. A person need not be cautioned if questions are for other necessary purposes, e.g.:
   (a) solely to establish their identity or ownership of any vehicle;
   (b) to obtain information in accordance with any relevant statutory requirement, see *paragraph 10.9*;
   (c) in furtherance of the proper and effective conduct of a search, e.g. to determine the need to search in the exercise of powers of stop and search or to seek co-operation while carrying out a search; or
   (d) to seek verification of a written record as in *paragraph 11.13*.
   (e) *Not used.*

10.2 Whenever a person not under arrest is initially cautioned, or reminded that they are under caution, that person must at the same time be told they are not under arrest and must be informed of the provisions of *paragraphs 3.21 to 3.21B* which explain that they need to agree to be interviewed, how they may obtain legal advice according to whether they are at a police station or elsewhere and the other rights and entitlements that apply to a voluntary interview. See *Note 10C*.

10.3 A person who is arrested, or further arrested, must be informed at the time if practicable or, if not, as soon as it becomes practicable thereafter, that they are under arrest and of the grounds and reasons for their arrest, see *paragraph 3.4, Note 10B* and Code G, *paragraphs 2.2 and 4.3*.

10.4 As required by Code G, *section 3*, a person who is arrested, or further arrested, must also be cautioned unless:
   (a) it is impracticable to do so by reason of their condition or behaviour at the time;
   (b) they have already been cautioned immediately prior to arrest as in *paragraph 10.1*.

(B) Terms of the cautions

10.5 The caution which must be given on:
   (a) arrest; or
   (b) all other occasions before a person is charged or informed they may be prosecuted; see *section 16*,
   should, unless the restriction on drawing adverse inferences from silence applies, see *Annex C*, be in the following terms:
   'You do not have to say anything. But it may harm your defence if you do not mention when questioned something which you later rely on in Court. Anything you do say may be given in evidence.'
   Where the use of the Welsh Language is appropriate, a constable may provide the caution directly in Welsh in the following terms:
   'Does dim rhaid i chi ddweud dim byd. Ond gall niweidio eich amddiffyniad os na fyddwch chi'n sôn, wrth gael eich holi, am rywbeth y byddwch chi'n dibynnu arno nes ymlaen yn y Llys. Gall unrhyw beth yr ydych yn ei ddweud gael ei roi fel tystiolaeth.'
   See *Note 10G*.

10.6 *Annex C, paragraph 2* sets out the alternative terms of the caution to be used when the restriction on drawing adverse inferences from silence applies.

10.7 Minor deviations from the words of any caution given in accordance with this Code do not constitute a breach of this Code, provided the sense of the relevant caution is preserved. See *Note 10D*.

10.8 After any break in questioning under caution, the person being questioned must be made aware they remain under caution. If there is any doubt the relevant caution should be given again in full when the interview resumes. See *Note 10E*.

10.9 When, despite being cautioned, a person fails to co-operate or to answer particular questions which may affect their immediate treatment, the person should be informed of any relevant consequences and that those consequences are not affected by the caution. Examples are when a person's refusal to provide:
- their name and address when charged may make them liable to detention;
- particulars and information in accordance with a statutory requirement, e.g. under the Road Traffic Act 1988, may amount to an offence or may make the person liable to a further arrest.

(C) Special warnings under the Criminal Justice and Public Order Act 1994, sections 36 and 37

10.10 When a suspect interviewed at a police station or authorised place of detention after arrest fails or refuses to answer certain questions, or to answer satisfactorily, after due warning, see *Note 10F,* a court or jury may draw such inferences as appear proper under the Criminal Justice and Public Order Act 1994, sections 36 and 37. Such inferences may only be drawn when:
- (a) the restriction on drawing adverse inferences from silence, see *Annex C,* does not apply; and
- (b) the suspect is arrested by a constable and fails or refuses to account for any objects, marks or substances, or marks on such objects found:
  - on their person;
  - in or on their clothing or footwear;
  - otherwise in their possession; or
  - in the place they were arrested;
- (c) the arrested suspect was found by a constable at a place at or about the time the offence for which that officer has arrested them is alleged to have been committed, and the suspect fails or refuses to account for their presence there.

When the restriction on drawing adverse inferences from silence applies, the suspect may still be asked to account for any of the matters in *(b)* or *(c)* but the special warning described in *paragraph 10.11* will not apply and must not be given.

10.11 For an inference to be drawn when a suspect fails or refuses to answer a question about one of these matters or to answer it satisfactorily, the suspect must first be told in ordinary language:
- (a) what offence is being investigated;
- (b) what fact they are being asked to account for;
- (c) this fact may be due to them taking part in the commission of the offence;
- (d) a court may draw a proper inference if they fail or refuse to account for this fact; and
- (e) a record is being made of the interview and it may be given in evidence if they are brought to trial.

(D) Juveniles and vulnerable persons

10.11A The information required in *paragraph 10.11* must not be given to a suspect who is a juvenile or a vulnerable person unless the appropriate adult is present.

10.12 If a juvenile or a vulnerable person is cautioned in the absence of the appropriate adult, the caution must be repeated in the appropriate adult's presence.

10.12A *Not used.*

(E) Documentation

10.13 A record shall be made when a caution is given under this section, either in the interviewer's report book or in the interview record.

Notes for Guidance

10A *There must be some reasonable, objective grounds for the suspicion, based on known facts or information which are relevant to the likelihood the offence has been committed and the person to be questioned committed it.*

10B *An arrested person must be given sufficient information to enable them to understand that they have been deprived of their liberty and the reason they have been arrested, e.g. when a person is arrested on suspicion of committing an offence they must be informed of the suspected offence's nature, when and where it was committed. The suspect must also be informed of the reason or reasons why the arrest is considered necessary. Vague or technical language should be avoided.*

10C *The restriction on drawing inferences from silence, see Annex C, paragraph 1, does not apply to a person who has not been detained and who therefore cannot be prevented from seeking legal advice if they want, see paragraph 3.21.*

10D *If it appears a person does not understand the caution, the person giving it should explain it in their own words.*

10E *It may be necessary to show to the court that nothing occurred during an interview break or between interviews which influenced the suspect's recorded evidence. After a break in an interview or at the beginning of a subsequent interview, the interviewer should summarise the reason for the break and confirm this with the suspect.*

10F *The Criminal Justice and Public Order Act 1994, sections 36 and 37 apply only to suspects who have been arrested by a constable or an officer of Revenue and Customs and are given the relevant warning by the police or Revenue and Customs officer who made the arrest or who is investigating the offence. They do not apply to any interviews with suspects who have not been arrested.*

10G *Nothing in this Code requires a caution to be given or repeated when informing a person not under arrest they may be prosecuted for an offence. However, a court will not be able to draw any inferences under the Criminal Justice and Public Order Act 1994, section 34, if the person was not cautioned.*

11 Interviews — general

(A) Action

11.1A An interview is the questioning of a person regarding their involvement or suspected involvement in a criminal offence or offences which, under *paragraph 10.1*, must be carried out under caution. Before a person is interviewed, they and, if they are represented, their solicitor must be given sufficient information to enable them to understand the nature of any such offence, and why they are suspected of committing it (see *paragraphs 3.4(a)* and *10.3*), in order to allow for the effective exercise of the rights of the defence. However, whilst the information must always be sufficient for the person to understand the nature of any offence (see *Note 11ZA*), this does not require the disclosure of details at a time which might prejudice the criminal investigation. The decision about what needs to be disclosed for the purpose of this requirement therefore rests with the investigating officer who has sufficient knowledge of the case to make that decision. The officer who discloses the information shall make a record of the information disclosed and when it was disclosed. This record may be made in the interview record, in the officer's report book or other form provided for this purpose. Procedures under the Road Traffic Act 1988, section 7 or the Transport and Works Act 1992, section 31 do not constitute interviewing for the purpose of this Code.

11.1 Following a decision to arrest a suspect, they must not be interviewed about the relevant offence except at a police station or other authorised place of detention, unless the consequent delay would be likely to:
   (a) lead to:
      • interference with, or harm to, evidence connected with an offence;
      • interference with, or physical harm to, other people; or
      • serious loss of, or damage to, property;
   (b) lead to alerting other people suspected of committing an offence but not yet arrested for it; or
   (c) hinder the recovery of property obtained in consequence of the commission of an offence.
   Interviewing in any of these circumstances shall cease once the relevant risk has been averted or the necessary questions have been put in order to attempt to avert that risk.

11.2 Immediately prior to the commencement or re-commencement of any interview at a police station or other authorised place of detention, the interviewer should remind the suspect of their entitlement to free legal advice and that the interview can be delayed for legal advice to be obtained, unless one of the exceptions in *paragraph 6.6* applies. It is the interviewer's responsibility to make sure all reminders are recorded in the interview record.

11.3 *Not used.*

11.4 At the beginning of an interview the interviewer, after cautioning the suspect, see *section 10*, shall put to them any significant statement or silence which occurred in the presence and hearing of a police officer or other police staff before the start of the interview and which have not been put to the suspect in the course of a previous interview. See *Note 11A*. The interviewer shall ask the suspect whether they confirm or deny that earlier statement or silence and if they want to add anything.

11.4A A significant statement is one which appears capable of being used in evidence against the suspect, in particular a direct admission of guilt. A significant silence is a failure or refusal to answer a question or answer satisfactorily when under caution, which might, allowing for the restriction on drawing adverse inferences from silence, see *Annex C*, give rise to an inference under the Criminal Justice and Public Order Act 1994, Part III.

11.5 No interviewer may try to obtain answers or elicit a statement by the use of oppression. Except as in *paragraph 10.9*, no interviewer shall indicate, except to answer a direct question, what action will be taken by the police if the person being questioned answers questions, makes a statement or refuses to do either. If the person asks directly what action will be taken if they answer questions, make a statement or refuse to do either, the interviewer may inform them what action the police propose to take provided that action is itself proper and warranted.

11.6 The interview or further interview of a person about an offence with which that person has not been charged or for which they have not been informed they may be prosecuted, must cease when:

(a) the officer in charge of the investigation is satisfied all the questions they consider relevant to obtaining accurate and reliable information about the offence have been put to the suspect, this includes allowing the suspect an opportunity to give an innocent explanation and asking questions to test if the explanation is accurate and reliable, e.g. to clear up ambiguities or clarify what the suspect said;

(b) the officer in charge of the investigation has taken account of any other available evidence; and

(c) the officer in charge of the investigation, or in the case of a detained suspect, the custody officer, see *paragraph 16.1*, reasonably believes there is sufficient evidence to provide a realistic prospect of conviction for that offence. See *Note 11B*.

This paragraph does not prevent officers in revenue cases or acting under the confiscation provisions of the Criminal Justice Act 1988 or the Drug Trafficking Act 1994 from inviting suspects to complete a formal question and answer record after the interview is concluded.

(B) Interview records

11.7 (a) An accurate record must be made of each interview, whether or not the interview takes place at a police station.

(b) The record must state the place of interview, the time it begins and ends, any interview breaks and, subject to *paragraph 2.6A*, the names of all those present; and must be made on the forms provided for this purpose or in the interviewer's report book or in accordance with Codes of Practice E or F.

(c) Any written record must be made and completed during the interview, unless this would not be practicable or would interfere with the conduct of the interview, and must constitute either a verbatim record of what has been said or, failing this, an account of the interview which adequately and accurately summarises it.

11.8 If a written record is not made during the interview it must be made as soon as practicable after its completion.

11.9 Written interview records must be timed and signed by the maker.

11.10 If a written record is not completed during the interview the reason must be recorded in the interview record.

11.11 Unless it is impracticable, the person interviewed shall be given the opportunity to read the interview record and to sign it as correct or to indicate how they consider it inaccurate. If the person interviewed cannot read or refuses to read the record or sign it, the senior interviewer present shall read it to them and ask whether they would like to sign it as correct or make their mark or to indicate how they consider it inaccurate. The interviewer shall certify on the interview record itself what has occurred. See *Note 11E*.

11.12 If the appropriate adult or the person's solicitor is present during the interview, they should also be given an opportunity to read and sign the interview record or any written statement taken down during the interview.

11.13 A record shall be made of any comments made by a suspect, including unsolicited comments, which are outside the context of an interview but which might be relevant to the offence. Any such record must be timed and signed by the maker. When practicable the suspect shall be given the opportunity to read that record and to sign it as correct or to indicate how they consider it inaccurate. See *Note 11E*.

11.14 Any refusal by a person to sign an interview record when asked in accordance with this Code must itself be recorded.

(C) Juveniles and vulnerable persons

11.15 A juvenile or vulnerable person must not be interviewed regarding their involvement or suspected involvement in a criminal offence or offences, or asked to provide or sign a written statement under caution or record of interview, in the absence of the appropriate adult unless *paragraphs 11.1* or *11.18 to 11.20* apply. See *Note 11C*.

11.16 Juveniles may only be interviewed at their place of education in exceptional circumstances and only when the principal or their nominee agrees. Every effort should be made to notify the parent(s) or other person responsible for the juvenile's welfare and the appropriate adult, if this is a different person, that the police want to interview the juvenile and reasonable time should be allowed to enable the appropriate adult to be present at the interview. If awaiting the appropriate adult would cause unreasonable delay, and unless the juvenile is suspected of an offence against the educational establishment, the principal or their nominee can act as the appropriate adult for the purposes of the interview.

11.17 If an appropriate adult is present at an interview, they shall be informed:
- that they are not expected to act simply as an observer; and
- that the purpose of their presence is to:
  - advise the person being interviewed;
  - observe whether the interview is being conducted properly and fairly; and
  - facilitate communication with the person being interviewed.

See paragraph 1.7A.

11.17A The appropriate adult may be required to leave the interview if their conduct is such that the interviewer is unable properly to put questions to the suspect. This will include situations where the appropriate adult's approach or conduct prevents or unreasonably obstructs proper questions being put to the suspect or the suspect's responses being recorded (see *Note 11F*). If the interviewer considers an appropriate adult is acting in such a way, they will stop the interview and consult an officer not below superintendent rank, if one is readily available, and otherwise an officer not below inspector rank not connected with the investigation. After speaking to the appropriate adult, the officer consulted must remind the adult that their role under *paragraph 11.17* does not allow them to obstruct proper questioning and give the adult an opportunity to respond. The officer consulted will then decide if the interview should continue without the attendance of that appropriate adult. If they decide it should, another appropriate adult must be obtained before the interview continues, unless the provisions of *paragraph 11.18* below apply.

(D) Vulnerable suspects — urgent interviews at police stations

11.18 The following interviews may take place only if an officer of superintendent rank or above considers delaying the interview will lead to the consequences in *paragraph 11.1(a)* to *(c)*, and is satisfied the interview would not significantly harm the person's physical or mental state (see *Annex G*):
(a) an interview of a detained juvenile or vulnerable person without the appropriate adult being present (see *Note 11C*);
(b) an interview of anyone detained other than in *(a)* who appears unable to:
- appreciate the significance of questions and their answers; or
- understand what is happening because of the effects of drink, drugs or any illness, ailment or condition;
(c) an interview, without an interpreter having been arranged, of a detained person whom the custody officer has determined requires an interpreter (see *paragraphs 3.5(c)(ii)* and *3.12*) which is carried out by an interviewer speaking the suspect's own language or (as the case may be) otherwise establishing effective communication which is sufficient to enable the necessary questions to be asked and answered in order to avert the consequences. See *paragraphs 13.2* and *13.5*.

11.19 These interviews may not continue once sufficient information has been obtained to avert the consequences in *paragraph 11.1(a)* to *(c)*.

11.20 A record shall be made of the grounds for any decision to interview a person under *paragraph 11.18*.

(E) Conduct and recording of Interviews at police stations — use of live link

11.21 When a suspect in police detention is interviewed using a live link by a police officer who is not at the police station where the detainee is held, the provisions of this section that govern the conduct and making a written record of that interview, shall be subject to *paragraph 12.9B* of this Code.

(F) Witnesses

11.22 The provisions of this Code and Codes E and F which govern the conduct and recording of interviews do not apply to interviews with, or taking statements from, witnesses.

Notes for Guidance

11ZA *The requirement in paragraph 11.1A for a suspect to be given sufficient information about the offence applies prior to the interview and whether or not they are legally represented. What is sufficient will depend on the circumstances of the case, but it should normally include, as a minimum, a description of the facts relating to the suspected offence that are known to the officer, including the time and place in question. This aims to avoid suspects being confused or unclear about what they are supposed to have done and to help an innocent suspect to clear the matter up more quickly.*

11A *Paragraph 11.4 does not prevent the interviewer from putting significant statements and silences to a suspect again at a later stage or a further interview.*

11B   The Criminal Procedure and Investigations Act 1996 Code of Practice, paragraph 3.5 states 'In conducting an investigation, the investigator should pursue all reasonable lines of enquiry, whether these point towards or away from the suspect. What is reasonable will depend on the particular circumstances.' Interviewers should keep this in mind when deciding what questions to ask in an interview.

11C   Although juveniles or vulnerable persons are often capable of providing reliable evidence, they may, without knowing or wishing to do so, be particularly prone in certain circumstances to providing information that may be unreliable, misleading or self- incriminating. Special care should always be taken when questioning such a person, and the appropriate adult should be involved if there is any doubt about a person's age, mental state or capacity. Because of the risk of unreliable evidence it is also important to obtain corroboration of any facts admitted whenever possible. Because of the risks, which the presence of the appropriate adult is intended to minimise, officers of superintendent rank or above should exercise their discretion under paragraph 11.18(a) to authorise the commencement of an interview in the appropriate adult's absence only in exceptional cases, if it is necessary to avert one or more of the specified risks in paragraph 11.1.

11D   Juveniles should not be arrested at their place of education unless this is unavoidable. When a juvenile is arrested at their place of education, the principal or their nominee must be informed.

11E   Significant statements described in paragraph 11.4 will always be relevant to the offence and must be recorded. When a suspect agrees to read records of interviews and other comments and sign them as correct, they should be asked to endorse the record with, e.g. 'I agree that this is a correct record of what was said' and add their signature. If the suspect does not agree with the record, the interviewer should record the details of any disagreement and ask the suspect to read these details and sign them to the effect that they accurately reflect their disagreement. Any refusal to sign should be recorded.

11F   The appropriate adult may intervene if they consider it is necessary to help the suspect understand any question asked and to help the suspect to answer any question. Paragraph 11.17A only applies if the appropriate adult's approach or conduct prevents or unreasonably obstructs proper questions being put to the suspect or the suspect's response being recorded. Examples of unacceptable conduct include answering questions on a suspect's behalf or providing written replies for the suspect to quote. An officer who takes the decision to exclude an appropriate adult must be in a position to satisfy the court the decision was properly made. In order to do this they may need to witness what is happening and give the suspect's solicitor (if they have one) who witnessed what happened, an opportunity to comment.

12 Interviews in police stations

(A) Action

When interviewer and suspect are present at the same police station

12.1   If a police officer wants to interview or conduct enquiries which require the presence of a detainee, the custody officer is responsible for deciding whether to deliver the detainee into the officer's custody. An investigating officer who is given custody of a detainee takes over responsibility for the detainee's care and safe custody for the purposes of this Code until they return the detainee to the custody officer when they must report the manner in which they complied with the Code whilst having custody of the detainee.

12.2   Except as below, in any period of 24 hours a detainee must be allowed a continuous period of at least 8 hours for rest, free from questioning, travel or any interruption in connection with the investigation concerned. This period should normally be at night or other appropriate time which takes account of when the detainee last slept or rested. If a detainee is arrested at a police station after going there voluntarily, the period of 24 hours runs from the time of their arrest and not the time of arrival at the police station. The period may not be interrupted or delayed, except:
   (a)   when there are reasonable grounds for believing not delaying or interrupting the period would:
        (i)   involve a risk of harm to people or serious loss of, or damage to, property;
        (ii)   delay unnecessarily the person's release from custody; or
        (iii) otherwise prejudice the outcome of the investigation;
   (b)   at the request of the detainee, their appropriate adult or legal representative;
   (c)   when a delay or interruption is necessary in order to:
        (i)   comply with the legal obligations and duties arising under *section 15*; or
        (ii)   to take action required under *section 9* or in accordance with medical advice.
   If the period is interrupted in accordance with *(a)*, a fresh period must be allowed. Interruptions under *(b)* and *(c)* do not require a fresh period to be allowed.

12.3   Before a detainee is interviewed, the custody officer, in consultation with the officer in charge of the investigation and appropriate healthcare professionals as necessary, shall assess whether the detainee is fit enough to be interviewed. This means determining and considering the risks to the detainee's physical and mental state if the interview took place and determining what safeguards are needed to allow the interview to take place. See *Annex G.* The custody officer shall not allow a detainee to be interviewed if the custody officer considers it would cause significant harm to the detainee's physical or mental state. Vulnerable suspects listed at *paragraph 11.18* shall be treated as always being at some risk during an interview and these persons may not be interviewed except in accordance with *paragraphs 11.18* to *11.20.*

12.4 As far as practicable interviews shall take place in interview rooms which are adequately heated, lit and ventilated.

12.5 A suspect whose detention without charge has been authorised under PACE because the detention is necessary for an interview to obtain evidence of the offence for which they have been arrested may choose not to answer questions but police do not require the suspect's consent or agreement to interview them for this purpose. If a suspect takes steps to prevent themselves being questioned or further questioned, e.g. by refusing to leave their cell to go to a suitable interview room or by trying to leave the interview room, they shall be advised that their consent or agreement to be interviewed is not required. The suspect shall be cautioned as in *section 10*, and informed if they fail or refuse to co-operate, the interview may take place in the cell and that their failure or refusal to co-operate may be given in evidence. The suspect shall then be invited to co-operate and go into the interview room. If they refuse and the custody officer considers, on reasonable grounds, that the interview should not be delayed, the custody officer has discretion to direct that the interview be conducted in a cell.

12.6 People being questioned or making statements shall not be required to stand.

12.7 Before the interview commences each interviewer shall, subject to *paragraph 2.6A*, identify themselves and any other persons present to the interviewee.

12.8 Breaks from interviewing should be made at recognised meal times or at other times that take account of when an interviewee last had a meal. Short refreshment breaks shall be provided at approximately two hour intervals, subject to the interviewer's discretion to delay a break if there are reasonable grounds for believing it would:
  (i) involve a:
     • risk of harm to people;
     • serious loss of, or damage to, property;
  (ii) unnecessarily delay the detainee's release; or
  (iii) otherwise prejudice the outcome of the investigation.
  See *Note 12B.*

12.9 If during the interview a complaint is made by or on behalf of the interviewee concerning the provisions of any of the Codes, or it comes to the interviewer's notice that the interviewee may have been treated improperly, the interviewer should:
  (i) record the matter in the interview record; and
  (ii) inform the custody officer, who is then responsible for dealing with it as in *section 9.*

Interviewer not present at the same station as the detainee — use of live link

12.9A Amendments to PACE, section 39, allow a person in police detention to be interviewed using a live link (see *paragraph 1.13(e)(i)*) by a police officer who is not at the police station where the detainee is held. Subject to *sub-paragraphs (a)* to *(f)* below, the custody officer is responsible for deciding on a case by case basis whether a detainee is fit to be interviewed (see *paragraph 12.3*) and should be delivered into the physical custody of an officer who is not involved in the investigation, for the purpose of enabling another officer who is investigating the offence for which the person is detained and who is not at the police station where the person is detained, to interview the detainee by means of a live link (see *Note 12ZA*).
  (a) The custody officer must be satisfied that the live link to be used provides for accurate and secure communication with the suspect. The provisions of *paragraph 13.13* shall apply to communications between the interviewing officer, the suspect and anyone else whose presence at the interview or, (as the case may be) whose access to any communications between the suspect and the interviewer, has been authorised by the custody officer or the interviewing officer.
  (b) Each decision must take account of the age, gender and vulnerability of the suspect, the nature and circumstances of the offence and the investigation and the impact on the suspect of carrying out the interview by means of a live link. For this reason, the custody officer must consider whether the ability of the particular suspect, to communicate confidently and effectively for the purpose of the interview is likely to be adversely affected or otherwise undermined or limited if the interviewing officer is not physically present and a live-link is used (see *Note 12ZB*). Although a suspect for whom an appropriate adult is required may be more

likely to be adversely affected as described, it is important to note that a person who does not require an appropriate adult may also be adversely impacted if interviewed by means of a live link.

(c) If the custody officer is satisfied that interviewing the detainee by means of a live link *would not* adversely affect or otherwise undermine or limit the suspect's ability to communicate confidently and effectively for the purpose of the *interview*, the officer must so inform the suspect, their solicitor and (if applicable) the appropriate adult. At the same time, the operation of the live-link must be explained and demonstrated to them (see *Note 12ZC*), they must be advised of the chief officer's obligations concerning the security of live-link communications under *paragraph 13.13* and they must be asked if they wish to make representations that the live-link should not be used or if they require more information about the operation of the arrangements. They must also be told that at any time live-link is in use, they may make representations to the custody officer or the interviewer that its operation should cease and that the physical presence of the interviewer should be arranged.

When the authority of an inspector is required

(d) If:
   (i)   representations are made that a live-link should not be used to carry out the interview, or that at any time it is in use, its operation should cease and the physical presence of the interviewer arranged; and
   (ii) the custody officer in consultation with the interviewer is unable to allay the concerns raised;
   then live-link may not be used, or (as the case may be) continue to be used, unless authorised in writing by an officer of the rank of inspector or above in accordance with *sub-paragraph (e)*.

(e) Authority may be given if the officer is satisfied that interviewing the detainee by means of a live link is necessary and justified. In making this decision, the officer must have regard to:
   (i)   the circumstances of the suspect;
   (ii)   the nature and seriousness of the offence;
   (iii) the requirements of the investigation, including its likely impact on both the suspect and any victim(s);
   (iv)   the representations made by the suspect, their solicitor and (if applicable) the appropriate adult that a live-link should not be used (see *sub-paragraph (b)*);
   (v)   the impact on the investigation of making arrangements for the physical presence of the interviewer (see *Note 12ZD*); and
   (vi)   the risk if the interpreter is not *physically* present, evidence obtained using link interpretation might be excluded in subsequent criminal proceedings; and
   (vii) the likely impact on the suspect and the investigation of any consequential delay to arrange for the interpreter to be *physically* present with the suspect.

(f) The officer given custody of the detainee *and* the interviewer take over responsibility for the detainee's care, treatment and safe custody for the purposes of this Code until the detainee is returned to the custody officer. On that return, both must report the manner in which they complied with the Code during period in question.

12.9B When a suspect detained at a police station is interviewed using a live link in accordance with *paragraph 12.9A*, the officer given custody of the detainee at the police station *and* the interviewer who is not present at the police station, take over responsibility for ensuring compliance with the provisions of *sections 11* and *12* of this Code, or *Code E* (Audio recording) or *Code F* (Audio visual recording) that govern the conduct and recording of that interview. In these circumstances:

(a) *the interviewer who is not at the police station where the detainee is held* must direct the officer having physical custody of the suspect at the police station, to take the action required by those provisions and which the interviewer would be required to take if they were present at the police station.

(b) *the officer having physical custody of the suspect at the police station* must take the action required by those provisions and which would otherwise be required to be taken by the interviewer if they were present at the police station. This applies whether or not the officer has been so directed by the interviewer but in such a case, the officer must inform the interviewer of the action taken.

(c) *during the course of the interview*, the officers in (a) and (b) may consult each other as necessary to clarify any action to be taken and to avoid any misunderstanding. Such consultations must, if in the hearing of the suspect and any other person present with the suspect (for example, a solicitor, appropriate adult or interpreter) be recorded in the interview record.

(B) Documentation

12.10 A record must be made of the:
- time a detainee is not in the custody of the custody officer, and why
- reason for any refusal to deliver the detainee out of that custody.

12.11 A record shall be made of the following:
  (a) the reasons it was not practicable to use an interview room;
  (b) any action taken as in *paragraph 12.5*; and
  (c) the actions, decisions, authorisations, representations and outcomes arising from the requirements of *paragraphs 12.9A* and *12.9B*.

The record shall be made on the custody record or in the interview record for action taken whilst an interview record is being kept, with a brief reference to this effect in the custody record.

12.12 Any decision to delay a break in an interview must be recorded, with reasons, in the interview record.

12.13 All written statements made at police stations under caution shall be written on forms provided for the purpose.

12.14 All written statements made under caution shall be taken in accordance with *Annex D*. Before a person makes a written statement under caution at a police station, they shall be reminded about the right to legal advice. See *Note 12A*.

Notes for Guidance

12ZA 'Live link' means an arrangement by means of which the interviewing officer who is not at the police station is able to see and hear, and to be seen and heard by, the detainee concerned, the detainee's solicitor, any appropriate adult present and the officer who has custody of that detainee. See paragraphs 13.12 to 13.14 and Annex N for application to live-link interpretation.

12ZB In considering whether the use of the live link is appropriate in a particular case, the custody officer, in consultation with the interviewer, should make an assessment of the detainee's ability to understand and take part in the interviewing process and make a record of the outcome. If the suspect has asked for legal advice, their solicitor should be involved in the assessment and in the case of a juvenile or vulnerable person, the appropriate adult should be involved.

12ZC The explanation and demonstration of live-link interpretation is intended to help the suspect, solicitor and appropriate adult make an informed decision and to allay any concerns they may have.

12ZD Factors affecting the arrangements for the interviewer to be physically present will include the location of the police station where the interview would take place and the availability of an interviewer with sufficient knowledge of the investigation who can attend that station and carry out the interview.

12A It is not normally necessary to ask for a written statement if the interview was recorded in writing and the record signed in accordance with paragraph 11.11 or audibly or visually recorded in accordance with Code E or F. Statements under caution should normally be taken in these circumstances only at the person's express wish. A person may however be asked if they want to make such a statement.

12B Meal breaks should normally last at least 45 minutes and shorter breaks after two hours should last at least 15 minutes. If the interviewer delays a break in accordance with paragraph 12.8 and prolongs the interview, a longer break should be provided. If there is a short interview and another short interview is contemplated, the length of the break may be reduced if there are reasonable grounds to believe this is necessary to avoid any of the consequences in paragraph 12.8(i) to (iii).

13 Interpreters

(A) General

13.1 Chief officers are responsible for making arrangements (see *paragraph 13.1ZA*) to provide appropriately qualified independent persons to act as interpreters and to provide translations of essential documents for:
  (a) detained suspects who, in accordance with *paragraph 3.5(c)(ii)*, the custody officer has determined require an interpreter, and
  (b) suspects who are not under arrest but are cautioned as in *section 10* who, in accordance with *paragraph 3.21(b)*, the interviewer has determined require an interpreter. In these cases, the responsibilities of the custody officer are, if appropriate, assigned to the interviewer. An interviewer who has any doubts about whether and what arrangements for an interpreter must be made or about how the provisions of this section should be applied to a suspect who is not under arrest should seek advice from an officer of the rank of sergeant or above.

If the suspect has a hearing or speech impediment, references to 'interpreter' and 'interpretation' in this Code include arrangements for appropriate assistance necessary to establish effective communication with that person. See *paragraph 13.1C* below if the person is in Wales.

13.1ZA References in *paragraph 13.1* above and elsewhere in this Code (see *paragraphs 3.12(a), 13.2, 13.2A, 13.5, 13.6, 13.9, 13.10, 13.10A, 13.10D* and *13.11* below and in any other Code, to making arrangements for an interpreter to assist a suspect, mean making arrangements for the interpreter to be *physically* present in the same location as the suspect *unless* the provisions in *paragraph 13.12* below, and Part 1 of *Annex N*, allow live-link interpretation to be used.

13.1A The arrangements *must* comply with the minimum requirements set out in *Directive 2010/64/EU* of the European Parliament and of the Council of 20 October 2010 on the right to interpretation and translation in criminal proceedings (see *Note 13A*). The provisions *of this* Code implement the requirements for those to whom this Code applies. These requirements include the following:

- That the arrangements made and the quality of interpretation and translation provided shall be sufficient to 'safeguard the fairness of the proceedings, in particular by ensuring that suspected or accused persons have knowledge of the cases against them and are able to exercise their right of defence'. This term which is used by the Directive means that the suspect must be able to understand their position and be able to communicate effectively with police officers, interviewers, solicitors and appropriate adults as provided for by this and any other Code in the same way as a suspect who can speak and understand English and who does not have a hearing or speech impediment and who would therefore not require an interpreter. See *paragraphs 13.12* to *13.14* and *Annex N* for application to live-link interpretation.
- The provision of a written translation of all documents considered essential for the person to exercise their right of defence and to 'safeguard the fairness of the proceedings' as described above. For the purposes of this Code, this includes any decision to authorise a person to be detained and details of any offence(s) with which the person has been charged or for which they have been told they may be prosecuted, see *Annex M*.
- Procedures to help determine:
  - whether a suspect can speak and understand English and needs the assistance of an interpreter, see *paragraph 13.1* and *Notes 13B* and *13C*; and
  - whether another interpreter should be arranged or another translation should be provided when a suspect complains about the quality of either or both, see *paragraphs 13.10A* and *13.10C*.

13.1B All reasonable attempts should be made to make the suspect understand that interpretation and translation will be provided at public expense.

13.1C With regard to persons in Wales, nothing in this or any other Code affects the application of the Welsh Language Schemes produced by police and crime commissioners in Wales in accordance with the Welsh Language Act 1993. See *paragraphs 3.12* and *13.1*.

(B) Interviewing suspects — foreign languages

13.2 Unless *paragraphs 11.1* or *11.18(c)* apply, a suspect who for the purposes of this Code requires an interpreter because they do not appear to speak or understand English (see *paragraphs 3.5(c)(ii)* and *3.12*) must not be interviewed unless arrangements are made for a person capable of interpreting to assist the suspect to understand and communicate.

13.2A If a person who is a juvenile or a vulnerable person is interviewed and the person acting as the appropriate adult does not appear to speak or understand English, arrangements must be made for an interpreter to assist communication between the person, the appropriate adult and the interviewer, unless the interview is urgent and *paragraphs 11.1* or *11.18(c)* apply.

13.3 When a written record of the interview is made (see *paragraph 11.7*), the interviewer shall make sure the interpreter makes a note of the interview at the time in the person's language for use in the event of the interpreter being called to give evidence, and certifies its accuracy. The interviewer should allow sufficient time for the interpreter to note each question and answer after each is put, given and interpreted. The person should be allowed to read the record or have it read to them and sign it as correct or indicate the respects in which they consider it inaccurate. If an audio or visual record of the interview is made, the arrangements in Code E or F shall apply. See *paragraphs 13.12* to *13.14* and *Annex N* for application to live-link interpretation.

13.4 In the case of a person making a statement under caution (see *Annex D*) to a police officer or other police staff in a language other than English:
  (a) the interpreter shall record the statement in the language it is made;
  (b) the person shall be invited to sign it;

(c)   an official English translation shall be made in due course. See *paragraphs 13.12* to *13.14* and *Annex N* for application to live-link interpretation.

(C)   Interviewing suspects who have a hearing or speech impediment

13.5   Unless *paragraphs 11.1* or *11.18(c)* (urgent interviews) apply, a suspect who for the purposes of this Code requires an interpreter or other appropriate assistance to enable effective communication with them because they appear to have a hearing or speech impediment (see *paragraphs 3.5(c)(ii)* and *3.12*) must not be interviewed without arrangements having been made to provide an independent person capable of interpreting or of providing other appropriate assistance.

13.6   An interpreter should also be arranged if a person who is a juvenile or a vulnerable person is interviewed and the person who is present as the appropriate adult, appears to have a hearing or speech impediment, unless the interview is urgent and *paragraphs 11.1* or *11.18(c)* apply.

13.7   If a written record of the interview is made, the interviewer shall make sure the interpreter is allowed to read the record and certify its accuracy in the event of the interpreter being called to give evidence. If an audio or visual recording is made, the arrangements in Code E or F apply.
See *paragraphs 13.12* to *13.14* and *Annex N* for application to live-link interpretation.

(D)   Additional rules for detained persons

13.8   *Not used.*

13.9   If *paragraph 6.1* applies and the detainee cannot communicate with the solicitor because of language, hearing or speech difficulties, arrangements must be made for an interpreter to enable communication. A police officer or any other police staff may not be used for this purpose.

13.10   After the custody officer has determined that a detainee requires an interpreter (see *paragraph 3.5(c)(ii)*) and following the initial action in *paragraphs 3.1* to *3.5*, arrangements must also be made for an interpreter to:
- explain the grounds and reasons for any authorisation for their *continued* detention, before or after charge and any information about the authorisation given to them by the authorising officer and which is recorded in the custody record. See *paragraphs 15.3, 15.4* and *15.16(a)* and *(b)*;
- to provide interpretation at the magistrates' court for the hearing of an application for a warrant of further detention or any extension or further extension of such warrant to explain any grounds and reasons for the application and any information about the authorisation of their further detention given to them by the court (see PACE, sections 43 and 44 and *paragraphs 15.2* and *15.16(c)*); and
- explain any offence with which the detainee is charged or for which they are informed they may be prosecuted and any other information about the offence given to them by or on behalf of the custody officer, see *paragraphs 16.1* and *16.3*.

13.10A   If a detainee complains that they are not satisfied with the quality of interpretation, the custody officer or (as the case may be) the interviewer, is responsible for deciding whether to make arrangements for a different interpreter in accordance with the procedures set out in the arrangements made by the chief officer, see *paragraph 13.1A*.

(E)   Translations of essential documents

13.10B   Written translations, oral translations and oral summaries of essential documents in a language the detainee understands shall be provided in accordance with *Annex M* (Translations of documents and records).

13.10C   If a detainee complains that they are not satisfied with the quality of the translation, the custody officer or (as the case may be) the interviewer, is responsible for deciding whether a further translation should be provided in accordance with the procedures set out in the arrangements made by the chief officer, see *paragraph 13.1A*.

(F)   Decisions not to provide interpretation and translation.

13.10D   If a suspect challenges a decision:
- made by the custody officer or (as the case may be) by the interviewer, in accordance with this Code (see *paragraphs 3.5(c)(ii)* and *3.21(b)*) that they do not require an interpreter, or
- made in accordance with *paragraphs 13.10A, 13.10B* or *13.10C* not to make arrangements to provide a different interpreter or another translation or not to translate a requested document,
the matter shall be reported to an inspector to deal with as a complaint for the purposes of *paragraph 9.2* or *paragraph 12.9* if the challenge is made during an interview.

(G) Documentation

13.11   The following must be recorded in the custody record or, as applicable, the interview record:

(a)   Action taken to arrange for an interpreter, including the live-link requirements in *Annex N* as applicable;

(b)   Action taken when a detainee is not satisfied about the standard of interpretation or translation provided, see *paragraphs 13.10A* and *13.10C*;

(c)   When an urgent interview is carried out in accordance with *paragraph 13.2* or *13.5* in the absence of an interpreter;

(d)   When a detainee has been assisted by an interpreter for the purpose of providing or being given information or being interviewed;

(e)   Action taken in accordance with *Annex M* when:

- a written translation of an essential document is provided;
- an oral translation or oral summary of an essential document is provided instead of a written translation and the authorising officer's reason(s) why this would not prejudice the fairness of the proceedings (see *Annex M, paragraph 3*);
- a suspect waives their right to a translation of an essential document (see *Annex M, paragraph 4*);
- when representations that a document which is not included in the table is essential and that a translation should be provided are refused and the reason for the refusal (see *Annex M, paragraph 8*).

(H) Live-link interpretation

13.12   In this section and in *Annex N*, 'live-link interpretation' means an arrangement to enable communication between the suspect and an interpreter who is not *physically* present with the suspect. The arrangement must ensure that anything said by any person in the suspect's presence and hearing can be interpreted in the same way as if the interpreter was physically present at that time. The communication must be by audio *and* visual means for the purpose of an interview, and for all other purposes it may be *either*, by audio and visual means, or by audio means *only*, as follows:

(a)   **Audio and visual communication**

This applies for the purposes of an interview conducted and recorded in accordance with Code E (Audio recording) or Code F (Visual recording) and during that interview, live link interpretation must *enable*:

(i)   the suspect, the interviewer, solicitor, appropriate adult and any other person *physically* present with the suspect at any time during the interview and an interpreter who is not *physically* present, to *see* and *hear* each other; and

(ii)   the interview to be conducted and recorded in accordance with the provisions of Codes C, E and F, subject to the modifications in Part 2 of *Annex N*.

(b)   **Audio and visual or audio without visual communication.**

This applies to communication for the purposes of any provision of this or any other Code except as described in (a), which requires or permits information to be given to, sought from, or provided by a suspect, whether orally or in writing, which would include communication between the suspect and their solicitor and/or appropriate adult, and for these cases, live link interpretation must:

(i)   *enable* the suspect, the person giving or seeking that information, any other person *physically* present with the suspect at that time and an interpreter who is not so present, to either *see* and *hear* each other, or to *hear without seeing* each other (for example by using a telephone); and

(ii)   enable that information to be given to, sought from, or provided by, the suspect in accordance with the provisions of this or any other Code that apply to that information, as modified for the purposes of the live-link, by Part 2 of *Annex N*.

13.12A   The requirement in *sub-paragraphs 13.12(a)(ii)* and *(b)(ii)*, that live-link interpretation must enable compliance with the relevant provisions of the Codes C, E and F, means that the arrangements must provide for any written or electronic record of what the suspect says in their own language which is made by the interpreter, to be securely transmitted without delay so that the suspect can be invited to read, check and if appropriate, sign or otherwise confirm that the record is correct or make corrections to the record.

13.13   Chief officers must be satisfied that live-link interpretation used in their force area for the purposes of *paragraphs 3.12(a)* and *(b)*, provides for accurate and secure communication with the suspect. This includes ensuring that at any time during which live link interpretation is being used: a person cannot see, hear or otherwise obtain access to any communications between the suspect and interpreter or communicate with the suspect or interpreter unless so authorised or allowed by the custody officer or, in the case of an interview, the interviewer and that as applicable, the confidentiality of any private consultation between a suspect and their solicitor and appropriate adult (see *paragraphs 13.2A*, *13.6* and *13.9*) is maintained. See *Annex N paragraph 4*.

Notes for Guidance

13A *Chief officers have discretion when determining the individuals or organisations they use to provide interpretation and translation services for their forces provided that these are compatible with the requirements of the Directive. One example which chief officers may wish to consider is the Ministry of Justice commercial agreements for interpretation and translation services.*

13B *A procedure for determining whether a person needs an interpreter might involve a telephone interpreter service or using cue cards or similar visual aids which enable the detainee to indicate their ability to speak and understand English and their preferred language. This could be confirmed through an interpreter who could also assess the extent to which the person can speak and understand English.*

13C *There should also be a procedure for determining whether a suspect who requires an interpreter requires assistance in accordance with paragraph 3.20 to help them check and if applicable, sign any documentation.*

14 Questioning — special restrictions

14.1 If a person is arrested by one police force on behalf of another and the lawful period of detention in respect of that offence has not yet commenced in accordance with PACE, section 41, no questions may be put to them about the offence while they are in transit between the forces except to clarify any voluntary statement they make.

14.2 If a person is in police detention at a hospital, they may not be questioned without the agreement of a responsible doctor. See *Note 14A*.

Notes for Guidance

14A *If questioning takes place at a hospital under paragraph 14.2, or on the way to or from a hospital, the period of questioning concerned counts towards the total period of detention permitted.*

15 Reviews and extensions of detention

(A) Persons detained under PACE

15.0 The requirement in *paragraph 3.4(b)* that documents and materials essential to challenging the lawfulness of the detainee's arrest and detention must be made available to the detainee or their solicitor, applies for the purposes of this section as follows:

   (a) The officer reviewing the need for detention without charge (PACE, section 40), or (as the case may be) the officer considering the need to extend detention without charge from 24 to 36 hours (PACE, section 42), is responsible, in consultation with the investigating officer, for deciding which documents and materials are essential and must be made available.

   (b) When *paragraph 15.7A* applies (application for a warrant of further detention or extension of such a warrant), the officer making the application is responsible for deciding which documents and materials are essential and must be made available *before* the hearing. See *Note 3ZA*.

15.1 The review officer is responsible under PACE, section 40 for periodically determining if a person's detention, before or after charge, continues to be necessary. This requirement continues throughout the detention period and, except when a telephone or a live link is used in accordance with *paragraphs 15.9* to *15.11C*, the review officer must be present at the police station holding the detainee. See *Notes 15A* and *15B*.

15.2 Under PACE, section 42, an officer of superintendent rank or above who is responsible for the station holding the detainee may give authority any time after the second review to extend the maximum period the person may be detained without charge by up to 12 hours. Except when a live link is used as in *paragraph 15.11A*, the superintendent must be present at the station holding the detainee. Further detention without charge may be authorised only by a magistrates' court in accordance with PACE, sections 43 and 44 and unless the court has given a live link direction as in *paragraph 15.11B*, the detainee must be brought before the court for the hearing. See *Notes 15C, 15D* and *15E*.

15.2A An authorisation under section 42(1) of PACE extends the maximum period of detention permitted before charge for indictable offences from 24 hours to 36 hours. Detaining a juvenile or a vulnerable person for longer than 24 hours will be dependent on the circumstances of the case and with regard to the person's:

   (a) special vulnerability;

   (b) the legal obligation to provide an opportunity for representations to be made prior to a decision about extending detention;

    (c)   the need to consult and consider the views of any appropriate adult; and

    (d)   any alternatives to police custody.

15.3 Before deciding whether to authorise continued detention the officer responsible under *paragraph 15.1* or *15.2* shall give an opportunity to make representations about the detention to:

    (a)   the detainee, unless in the case of a review as in *paragraph 15.1*, the detainee is asleep;

    (b)   the detainee's solicitor if available at the time; and

    (c)   the appropriate adult if available at the time.

    See *Note 15CA.*

15.3A Other people having an interest in the detainee's welfare may also make representations at the authorising officer's discretion.

15.3B Subject to *paragraph 15.10*, the representations may be made orally in person or by telephone or in writing. The authorising officer may, however, refuse to hear oral representations from the detainee if the officer considers them unfit to make representations because of their condition or behaviour. See *Note 15C.*

15.3C The decision on whether the review takes place in person or by telephone or by live link (see *paragraph 1.13(e)(ii)*) is a matter for the review officer. In determining the form the review may take, the review officer must always take full account of the needs of the person in custody. The benefits of carrying out a review in person should always be considered, based on the individual circumstances of each case with specific additional consideration if the person is:

    (a)   a juvenile (and the age of the juvenile); or

    (b)   a vulnerable person; or

    (c)   in need of medical attention for other than routine minor ailments; or

    (d)   subject to presentational or community issues around their detention.

15.4 Before conducting a review or determining whether to extend the maximum period of detention without charge, the officer responsible must make sure the detainee is reminded of their entitlement to free legal advice, see *paragraph 6.5*, unless in the case of a review the person is asleep. When determining whether to extend the maximum period of detention without charge, it should also be pointed out that for the purposes of *paragraph 15.2*, the superintendent or (as the case may be) the court, responsible for authorising any such extension, will not be able to use a live link unless the detainee has *received* legal advice on the use of the live link (see *paragraphs 15.11A(ii)* and *15.11C(ii)*) and given consent to its use (see *paragraphs 15.11A(iii)* and *15.11C(iii)*). The detainee must also be given information about how the live link is used.

15.4A Following sections 45ZA and 45ZB of PACE, when the reminder and information concerning legal advice and about the use of the live link is given and the detainee's consent is sought, the presence of an appropriate adult is required if the detainee in question is a juvenile (see *paragraph 1.5*) or is a *vulnerable adult* by virtue of being a person aged 18 or over who, because of a mental disorder established in accordance *paragraphs 1.4* and *1.13(d)* or for *any other reason* (see *paragraph 15.4B*), may have difficulty understanding the purpose of:

    (a)   an authorisation under section 42 of PACE or anything that occurs in connection with a decision whether to give it (see *paragraphs 15.2* and *15.2A*); or

    (b)   a court hearing under section 43 or 44 of PACE or what occurs at the hearing it (see *paragraphs 15.2* and *15.7A*).

15.4B For the purpose of using a live link in accordance with sections 45ZA and 45ZB of PACE to authorise detention without charge (see *paragraphs 15.11A* and *15.11C*), the reference to '*any other reason*' would extend to difficulties in understanding the purposes mentioned in *paragraph 15.4A* that might arise if the person happened to be under the influence of drink or drugs at the time the live link is to be used. This does not however apply for the purposes of *paragraphs 1.4* and *1.13(d)* (see *Note 1GC*).

15.5 If, after considering any representations, the review officer under *paragraph 15.1* decides to keep the detainee in detention or the superintendent under *paragraph 15.2* extends the maximum period for which they may be detained without charge, then any comment made by the detainee shall be recorded. If applicable, the officer shall be informed of the comment as soon as practicable. See also *paragraphs 11.4* and *11.13*.

15.6 No officer shall put specific questions to the detainee:

    • regarding their involvement in any offence; or

    • in respect of any comments they may make:

       – when given the opportunity to make representations; or

     – in response to a decision to keep them in detention or extend the maximum period of detention.

Such an exchange could constitute an interview as in *paragraph 11.1A* and would be subject to the associated safeguards in *section 11* and, in respect of a person who has been charged, *paragraph 16.5*. See also *paragraph 11.13*.

15.7   A detainee who is asleep at a review, see *paragraph 15.1*, and whose continued detention is authorised must be informed about the decision and reason as soon as practicable after waking.

15.7A When an application is made to a magistrates' court under PACE, section 43 for a warrant of further detention to extend detention without charge of a person arrested for an *indictable offence*, or under section 44, to extend or further extend that warrant, the detainee:

    (a)   must, unless the court has given a live link direction as in *paragraph 15.11C*, be brought to court for the hearing of the application (see *Note 15D*);

    (b)   is entitled to be legally represented if they wish, in which case, *Annex B* cannot apply; and

    (c)   must be given a copy of the information which supports the application and states:

        (i)   the nature of the offence for which the person to whom the application relates has been arrested;

        (ii)   the general nature of the evidence on which the person was arrested;

        (iii)   what inquiries about the offence have been made and what further inquiries are proposed;

        (iv)   the reasons for believing continued detention is necessary for the purposes of the further inquiries;

Note: A warrant of further detention can only be issued or extended if the court has reasonable grounds for believing that the person's further detention is necessary for the purpose of obtaining evidence of an indictable offence for which the person has been arrested and that the investigation is being conducted diligently and expeditiously.

See *paragraph 15.0(b)*.

15.8   *Not used.*

(B) Review of detention by telephone or by using a live link (section 40A and 45A)

15.9   PACE, section 40A provides that the officer responsible under section 40 for reviewing the detention of a person who has not been charged, need not attend the police station holding the detainee and may carry out the review by telephone.

15.9A PACE, section 45A(2) provides that the officer responsible under section 40 for reviewing the detention of a person who has not been charged, need not attend the police station holding the detainee and may carry out the review using a live link. See *paragraph 1.13(e)(ii)*.

15.9B A telephone review is not permitted where facilities for review using a live link exist and it is practicable to use them.

15.9C The review officer can decide at any stage that a telephone review or review by live link should be terminated and that the review will be conducted in person. The reasons for doing so should be noted in the custody record. See *Note 15F*.

15.10 When a review is carried out by telephone or by using a live link, an officer at the station holding the detainee shall be required by the review officer to fulfil that officer's obligations under PACE, section 40 and this Code by:

    (a)   making any record connected with the review in the detainee's custody record;

    (b)   if applicable, making the record in (*a*) in the presence of the detainee; and

    (c)   for a review by telephone, giving the detainee information about the review.

15.11 When a review is carried out by telephone or by using a live link, or the requirement in *paragraph 15.3* will be satisfied:

    (a)   if facilities exist for the immediate transmission of written representations to the review officer, e.g. fax or email message, by allowing those who are given the opportunity to make representations, to make their representations:

        (i)   orally by telephone or (as the case may be) by means of the live link; or

        (ii)   in writing using the facilities for the immediate transmission of written representations; and

    (b)   in all other cases, by allowing those who are given the opportunity to make representations, to make their representations orally by telephone or by means of the live link.

(C) Authorisation to extend detention using live link (sections 45ZA and 45ZB)

15.11A For the purpose of *paragraphs 15.2* and *15.2A*, a superintendent who is not present at the police station where the detainee is being held but who has access to the use of a live link (see *paragraph 1.13(e)(iii)*) may, using that live link, give authority to extend the maximum period of detention permitted before charge, if, and only if, the following conditions are satisfied:
- (i) the custody officer considers that the use of the live link is appropriate (see *Note 15H*);
- (ii) the detainee in question has requested and received legal advice on the use of the live link (see *paragraph 15.4*).
- (iii) the detainee has given their consent to the live link being used (see *paragraph 15.11D*)

15.11B When a live link is used:
- (a) the authorising superintendent shall, with regard to any record connected with the authorisation which PACE, section 42 and this Code require to be made by the authorising officer, require an officer at the station holding the detainee to make that record in the detainee's custody record;
- (b) the requirement in *paragraph 15.3* (allowing opportunity to make representations) will be satisfied:
  - (i) if facilities exist for the immediate transmission of written representations to the authorising officer, e.g. fax or email message, by allowing those who are given the opportunity to make representations, to make their representations:
    - in writing by means of those facilities or
    - orally by means of the live link; or
  - (ii) in all other cases, by allowing those who are given the opportunity to make representations, to make their representations orally by means of the live link.
- (c) The authorising officer can decide at any stage to terminate the live link and attend the police station where the detainee is held to carry out the procedure in person. The reasons for doing so should be noted in the custody record.

15.11C For the purpose of *paragraph 15.7A* and the hearing of an application to a magistrates' court under PACE, section 43 for a warrant of further detention to extend detention without charge of a person arrested for an *indictable offence*, or under PACE, section 44, to extend or further extend that warrant, the magistrates' court may give a direction that a live link (see *paragraph 1.13(e)(iv)*) be used for the purposes of the hearing if, and only if, the following conditions are satisfied:
- (i) the custody officer considers that the use of the live link for the purpose of the hearing is appropriate (see *Note 15H*);
- (ii) the detainee in question has requested and received legal advice on the use of the live link (see *paragraph 15.4*);
- (iii) the detainee has given their consent to the live link being used (see *paragraph 15.11D*); and
- (iv) it is not contrary to the interests of justice to give the direction.

15.11D References in *paragraphs 15.11A(iii)* and *15.11C(iii)* to the consent of the detainee mean:
- (a) if detainee is aged 18 or over, the consent of that detainee;
- (b) if the detainee is aged 14 and under 18, the consent of the detainee and their parent or guardian; and
- (c) if the detainee is aged under 14, the consent of their parent or guardian.

15.11E The consent described in *paragraph 15.11D* will only be valid if:
- (i) in the case of a detainee aged 18 or over *who is a vulnerable adult* as described in *paragraph 15.4A*), information about how the live link is used and the reminder about their right to legal advice mentioned in *paragraph 15.4* and their consent, are given in the *presence of the appropriate adult*; and
- (ii) in the case of a *juvenile:*
  - if information about how the live link is used and the reminder about their right to legal advice mentioned in *paragraph 15.4* are given in the *presence of the appropriate adult* (who may or may not be their parent or guardian); and
  - if the juvenile is aged 14 or over, their consent is given in the *presence of the appropriate adult* (who may or may not be their parent or guardian).

  Note: If the juvenile is aged under 14, the consent of their parent or guardian is sufficient in its own right (see *Note 15I*).

(D) Documentation

15.12 It is the officer's responsibility to make sure all reminders given under *paragraph 15.4* are noted in the custody record.

15.13 The grounds for, and extent of, any delay in conducting a review shall be recorded.

15.14 When a review is carried out by telephone or video conferencing facilities, a record shall be made of:
    (a) the reason the review officer did not attend the station holding the detainee;
    (b) the place the review officer was;
    (c) the method representations, oral or written, were made to the review officer, see *paragraph 15.11.*

15.15 Any written representations shall be retained.

15.16 A record shall be made as soon as practicable of:
    (a) the outcome of each review of detention before or after charge, and if *paragraph 15.7* applies, of when the person was informed and by whom;
    (b) the outcome of any determination under PACE, section 42 by a superintendent whether to extend the maximum period of detention without charge beyond 24 hours from the relevant time. If an authorisation is given, the record shall state the number of hours and minutes by which the detention period is extended or further extended.
    (c) the outcome of each application under PACE, section 43, for a warrant of further detention or under section 44, for an extension or further extension of that warrant. If a warrant for further detention is granted under section 43 or extended or further extended under 44, the record shall state the detention period authorised by the warrant and the date and time it was granted or (as the case may be) the period by which the warrant is extended or further extended.

Note: Any period during which a person is released on bail does not count towards the maximum period of detention without charge allowed under PACE, sections 41 to 44.

Notes for Guidance

15A *Review officer for the purposes of:*
    • *PACE, sections 40, 40A and 45A means, in the case of a person arrested but not charged, an officer of at least inspector rank not directly involved in the investigation and, if a person has been arrested and charged, the custody officer.*

15B *The detention of persons in police custody not subject to the statutory review requirement in paragraph 15.1 should still be reviewed periodically as a matter of good practice. Such reviews can be carried out by an officer of the rank of sergeant or above. The purpose of such reviews is to check the particular power under which a detainee is held continues to apply, any associated conditions are complied with and to make sure appropriate action is taken to deal with any changes. This includes the detainee's prompt release when the power no longer applies, or their transfer if the power requires the detainee be taken elsewhere as soon as the necessary arrangements are made. Examples include persons:*
    (a) *arrested on warrant because they failed to answer bail to appear at court;*
    (b) *arrested under the Bail Act 1976, section 7(3) for breaching a condition of bail granted after charge;*
    (c) *in police custody for specific purposes and periods under the Crime (Sentences) Act 1997, Schedule 1;*
    (d) *convicted, or remand prisoners, held in police stations on behalf of the Prison Service under the Imprisonment (Temporary Provisions) Act 1980, section 6;*
    (e) *being detained to prevent them causing a breach of the peace;*
    (f) *detained at police stations on behalf of Immigration Enforcement (formerly the UK Immigration Service);*
    (g) *detained by order of a magistrates' court under the Criminal Justice Act 1988, section 152 (as amended by the Drugs Act 2005, section 8) to facilitate the recovery of evidence after being charged with drug possession or drug trafficking and suspected of having swallowed drugs.*
  The detention of persons remanded into police detention by order of a court under the Magistrates' Courts Act 1980, section 128 is subject to a statutory requirement to review that detention. This is to make sure the detainee is taken back to court no later than the end of the period authorised by the court or when the need for their detention by police ceases, whichever is the sooner.

15C *In the case of a review of detention, but not an extension, the detainee need not be woken for the review. However, if the detainee is likely to be asleep, e.g. during a period of rest allowed as in paragraph 12.2, at the latest time a review or authorisation to extend detention may take place, the officer should, if the legal obligations and time constraints permit, bring forward the procedure to allow the detainee to make representations. A detainee not asleep during the review must be present when the grounds for their continued detention are recorded and must at the same time be informed of those grounds unless the review officer considers the person is incapable of understanding what is said, violent or likely to become violent or in urgent need of medical attention.*

15CA *In paragraph 15.3(b) and (c), 'available' includes being contactable in time to enable them to make representations remotely by telephone or other electronic means or in person by attending the station.*

Reasonable efforts should therefore be made to give the solicitor and appropriate adult sufficient notice of the time the decision is expected to be made so that they can make themselves available.

15D   *An application to a Magistrates' Court under PACE, sections 43 or 44 for a warrant of further detention or its extension should be made between 10am and 9pm, and if possible during normal court hours. It will not usually be practicable to arrange for a court to sit specially outside the hours of 10am to 9pm. If it appears a special sitting may be needed outside normal court hours but between 10am and 9pm, the clerk to the justices should be given notice and informed of this possibility, while the court is sitting if possible.*

15E   *In paragraph 15.2, the officer responsible for the station holding the detainee includes a superintendent or above who, in accordance with their force operational policy or police regulations, is given that responsibility on a temporary basis whilst the appointed long-term holder is off duty or otherwise unavailable.*

15F   *The provisions of PACE, section 40A allowing telephone reviews do not apply to reviews of detention after charge by the custody officer. When use of a live link is not required, they allow the use of a telephone to carry out a review of detention before charge.*

15G   *Not used.*

15H   *In considering whether the use of the live link is appropriate in the case of a juvenile or vulnerable person, the custody officer and the superintendent should have regard to the detainee's ability to understand the purpose of the authorisation or (as the case may be) the court hearing, and be satisfied that the suspect is able to take part effectively in the process (see paragraphs 1.4(c)). The appropriate adult should always be involved.*

15I   *For the purpose of paragraphs 15.11D and 15.11E, the consent required from a parent or guardian may, for a juvenile in the care of a local authority or voluntary organisation, be given by that authority or organisation. In the case of a juvenile, nothing in paragraphs 15.11D and 15.11E require the parent, guardian or representative of a local authority or voluntary organisation to be present with the juvenile to give their consent, unless they are acting as the appropriate adult. However, it is important that the parent, guardian or representative of a local authority or voluntary organisation who is not present is fully informed before being asked to consent. They must be given the same information as that given to the juvenile and the appropriate adult in accordance with paragraph 15.11E. They must also be allowed to speak to the juvenile and the appropriate adult if they wish. Provided the consent is fully informed and is not withdrawn, it may be obtained at any time before the live link is used.*

16 Charging detained persons

(A) Action

16.1   When the officer in charge of the investigation reasonably believes there is sufficient evidence to provide a realistic prospect of conviction for the offence (see *paragraph 11.6)*, they shall without delay, and subject to the following qualification, inform the custody officer who will be responsible for considering whether the detainee should be charged. See *Notes 11B* and *16A.* When a person is detained in respect of more than one offence it is permissible to delay informing the custody officer until the above conditions are satisfied in respect of all the offences, but see *paragraph 11.6.* If the detainee is a juvenile or a vulnerable person, any resulting action shall be taken in the presence of the appropriate adult if they are present at the time. See *Notes 16B* and *16C.*

16.1A Where guidance issued by the Director of Public Prosecutions under PACE, section 37A is in force the custody officer must comply with that Guidance in deciding how to act in dealing with the detainee. See *Notes 16AA* and *16AB.*

16.1B Where in compliance with the DPP's Guidance the custody officer decides that the case should be immediately referred to the CPS to make the charging decision, consultation should take place with a Crown Prosecutor as soon as is reasonably practicable. Where the Crown Prosecutor is unable to make the charging decision on the information available at that time, the detainee may be released without charge and on bail (with conditions if necessary) under section 37(7)(a). In such circumstances, the detainee should be informed that they are being released to enable the Director of Public Prosecutions to make a decision under section 37B.

16.2   When a detainee is charged with or informed they may be prosecuted for an offence, see *Note 16B*, they shall, unless the restriction on drawing adverse inferences from silence applies, see *Annex C*, be cautioned as follows:

'*You do not have to say anything. But it may harm your defence if you do not mention now something which you later rely on in court. Anything you do say may be given in evidence.*'

Where the use of the Welsh Language is appropriate, a constable may provide the caution directly in Welsh in the following terms:

> *'Does dim rhaid i chi ddweud dim byd. Ond gall niweidio eich amddiffyniad os na fyddwch chi'n sôn, yn awr, am rywbeth y byddwch chi'n dibynnu arno nes ymlaen yn y llys. Gall unrhyw beth yr ydych yn ei ddweud gael ei roi fel tystiolaeth.'*

Annex C, paragraph 2 sets out the alternative terms of the caution to be used when the restriction on drawing adverse inferences from silence applies.

16.3   When a detainee is charged they shall be given a written notice showing particulars of the offence and, subject to *paragraph 2.6A*, the officer's name and the case reference number. As far as possible the particulars of the charge shall be stated in simple terms, but they shall also show the precise offence in law with which the detainee is charged. The notice shall begin:

> *'You are charged with the offence(s) shown below.'* Followed by the caution.

If the detainee is a juvenile, mentally disordered or otherwise mentally vulnerable, a copy of the notice should also be given to the appropriate adult.

16.4   If, after a detainee has been charged with or informed they may be prosecuted for an offence, an officer wants to tell them about any written statement or interview with another person relating to such an offence, the detainee shall either be handed a true copy of the written statement or the content of the interview record brought to their attention. Nothing shall be done to invite any reply or comment except to:

(a)   caution the detainee, *'You do not have to say anything, but anything you do say may be given in evidence.'*;

Where the use of the Welsh Language is appropriate, caution the detainee in the following terms:

> *'Does dim rhaid i chi ddweud dim byd, ond gall unrhyw beth yr ydych yn ei ddweud gael ei roi fel tystiolaeth.'*
> and

(b)   remind the detainee about their right to legal advice.

16.4A If the detainee:
- cannot read, the document may be read to them;
- is a juvenile, mentally disordered or otherwise mentally vulnerable, the appropriate adult shall also be given a copy, or the interview record shall be brought to their attention.

16.5   A detainee may not be interviewed about an offence after they have been charged with, or informed they may be prosecuted for it, unless the interview is necessary:
- to prevent or minimise harm or loss to some other person, or the public
- to clear up an ambiguity in a previous answer or statement
- in the interests of justice for the detainee to have put to them, and have an opportunity to comment on, information concerning the offence which has come to light since they were charged or informed they might be prosecuted

Before any such interview, the interviewer shall:

(a)   caution the detainee, *'You do not have to say anything, but anything you do say may be given in evidence.'*

Where the use of the Welsh Language is appropriate, the interviewer shall caution the detainee: *'Does dim rhaid i chi ddweud dim byd, ond gall unrhyw beth yr ydych yn ei ddweud gael ei roi fel tystiolaeth.'*

(b)   remind the detainee about their right to legal advice.

See *Note 16B*

16.6   The provisions of *paragraphs 16.2* to *16.5* must be complied with in the appropriate adult's presence if they are already at the police station. If they are not at the police station then these provisions must be complied with again in their presence when they arrive unless the detainee has been released. See *Note 16C*.

16.7   When a juvenile is charged with an offence and the custody officer authorises their continued detention after charge, the custody officer must make arrangements for the juvenile to be taken into the care of a local authority to be detained pending appearance in court *unless* the custody officer certifies in accordance with PACE, section 38(6), that:

(a)   for any juvenile; it is impracticable to do so and the reasons why it is impracticable must be set out in the certificate that must be produced to the court; or,

(b) in the case of a juvenile of at least 12 years old, no secure accommodation is available and other accommodation would not be adequate to protect the public from serious harm from that juvenile. See *Note 16D*.

Note: Chief officers should ensure that the operation of these provisions at police stations in their areas is subject to supervision and monitoring by an officer of the rank of inspector or above. See *Note 16E*.

16.7A The requirement in *paragraph 3.4(b)* that documents and materials essential to effectively challenging the lawfulness of the detainee's arrest and detention must be made available to the detainee and, if they are represented, their solicitor, applies for the purposes of this section and a person's detention after charge. This means that the custody officer making the bail decision (PACE, section 38) or reviewing the need for detention after charge (PACE, section 40), is responsible for determining what, if any, documents or materials are essential and must be made available to the detainee or their solicitor. See *Note 3ZA*.

(B) Documentation

16.8 A record shall be made of anything a detainee says when charged.

16.9 Any questions put in an interview after charge and answers given relating to the offence shall be recorded in full during the interview on forms for that purpose and the record signed by the detainee or, if they refuse, by the interviewer and any third parties present. If the questions are audibly recorded or visually recorded the arrangements in Code E or F apply.

16.10 If arrangements for a juvenile's transfer into local authority care as in *paragraph 16.7* are not made, the custody officer must record the reasons in a certificate which must be produced before the court with the juvenile. See *Note 16D*.

Notes for Guidance

16A *The custody officer must take into account alternatives to prosecution under the Crime and Disorder Act 1998 applicable to persons under 18, and in national guidance on the cautioning of offenders applicable to persons aged 18 and over.*

16AA *When a person is arrested under the provisions of the Criminal Justice Act 2003 which allow a person to be re-tried after being acquitted of a serious offence which is a qualifying offence specified in Schedule 5 to that Act and not precluded from further prosecution by virtue of section 75(3) of that Act the detention provisions of PACE are modified and make an officer of the rank of superintendent or above who has not been directly involved in the investigation responsible for determining whether the evidence is sufficient to charge.*

16AB *Where Guidance issued by the Director of Public Prosecutions under section 37B is in force, a custody officer who determines in accordance with that Guidance that there is sufficient evidence to charge the detainee, may detain that person for no longer than is reasonably necessary to decide how that person is to be dealt with under PACE, section 37(7)(a) to (d), including, where appropriate, consultation with the Duty Prosecutor. The period is subject to the maximum period of detention before charge determined by PACE, sections 41 to 44. Where in accordance with the Guidance the case is referred to the CPS for decision, the custody officer should ensure that an officer involved in the investigation sends to the CPS such information as is specified in the Guidance.*

16B *The giving of a warning or the service of the Notice of Intended Prosecution required by the Road Traffic Offenders Act 1988, section 1 does not amount to informing a detainee they may be prosecuted for an offence and so does not preclude further questioning in relation to that offence.*

16C *There is no power under PACE to detain a person and delay action under paragraphs 16.2 to 16.5 solely to await the arrival of the appropriate adult. Reasonable efforts should therefore be made to give the appropriate adult sufficient notice of the time the decision (charge etc.) is to be implemented so that they can be present. If the appropriate adult is not, or cannot be, present at that time, the detainee should be released on bail to return for the decision to be implemented when the adult is present, unless the custody officer determines that the absence of the appropriate adult makes the detainee unsuitable for bail for this purpose. After charge, bail cannot be refused, or release on bail delayed, simply because an appropriate adult is not available, unless the absence of that adult provides the custody officer with the necessary grounds to authorise detention after charge under PACE, section 38.*

16D *Except as in paragraph 16.7, neither a juvenile's behaviour nor the nature of the offence provides grounds for the custody officer to decide it is impracticable to arrange the juvenile's transfer to local authority care. Impracticability concerns the transport and travel requirements and the lack of secure accommodation which is provided for the purposes of restricting liberty does not make it impracticable to transfer the juvenile. Rather, 'impracticable' should be taken to mean that exceptional circumstances render movement of the child impossible or that the juvenile is due at court in such a short space of time that transfer would deprive them of rest or cause them to miss a court appearance. When the reason for not transferring the juvenile is an imminent court appearance, details of the travelling and court appearance times which justify the decision should be included in the certificate. The availability of secure accommodation is only a factor in relation to a juvenile aged 12 or over when other local authority accommodation would not be adequate to protect the public from serious harm from them. The obligation to transfer a juvenile to local authority accommodation applies as much to a juvenile charged during the daytime as to a juvenile to be held overnight, subject to a requirement to bring the juvenile before a court under PACE, section 46.*

16E   *The Concordat on Children in Custody published by the Home Office in 2017 provides detailed guidance with the aim of preventing the detention of children in police stations following charge. It is available here: https://www.gov.uk/government/publications/concordat-on-children-in-custody.*

17 Testing persons for the presence of specified Class A drugs

(A) Action

17.1 This section of Code C applies only in selected police stations in police areas where the provisions for drug testing under section 63B of PACE (as amended by section 5 of the Criminal Justice Act 2003 and section 7 of the Drugs Act 2005) are in force and in respect of which the Secretary of State has given a notification to the relevant chief officer of police that arrangements for the taking of samples have been made. Such a notification will cover either a police area as a whole or particular stations within a police area. The notification indicates whether the testing applies to those arrested or charged or under the age of 18 as the case may be and testing can only take place in respect of the persons so indicated in the notification. Testing cannot be carried out unless the relevant notification has been given and has not been withdrawn. See *Note 17F.*

17.2 A sample of urine or a non-intimate sample may be taken from a person in police detention for the purpose of ascertaining whether they have any specified Class A drug in their body only where they have been brought before the custody officer and:
(a) either the arrest condition, see *paragraph 17.3*, or the charge condition, see *paragraph 17.4* is met;
(b) the age condition see *paragraph 17.5*, is met;
(c) the notification condition is met in relation to the arrest condition, the charge condition, or the age condition, as the case may be. (Testing on charge and/or arrest must be specifically provided for in the notification for the power to apply. In addition, the fact that testing of under 18s is authorised must be expressly provided for in the notification before the power to test such persons applies.). See *paragraph 17.1*; and
(d) a police officer has requested the person concerned to give the sample (the request condition).

17.3 The arrest condition is met where the detainee:
(a) has been arrested for a trigger offence, see *Note 17E*, but not charged with that offence; or
(b) has been arrested for any other offence but not charged with that offence and a police officer of inspector rank or above, who has reasonable grounds for suspecting that their misuse of any specified Class A drug caused or contributed to the offence, has authorised the sample to be taken.

17.4 The charge condition is met where the detainee:
(a) has been charged with a trigger offence, or
(b) has been charged with any other offence and a police officer of inspector rank or above, who has reasonable grounds for suspecting that the detainee's misuse of any specified Class A drug caused or contributed to the offence, has authorised the sample to be taken.

17.5 The age condition is met where:
(a) in the case of a detainee who has been arrested but not charged as in *paragraph 17.3*, they are aged 18 or over;
(b) in the case of a detainee who has been charged as in *paragraph 17.4*, they are aged 14 or over.

17.6 Before requesting a sample from the person concerned, an officer must:
(a) inform them that the purpose of taking the sample is for drug testing under PACE. This is to ascertain whether they have a specified Class A drug present in their body;
(b) warn them that if, when so requested, they fail without good cause to provide a sample they may be liable to prosecution;
(c) where the taking of the sample has been authorised by an inspector or above in accordance with *paragraph 17.3(b)* or *17.4(b)* above, inform them that the authorisation has been given and the grounds for giving it;

   (d) remind them of the following rights, which may be exercised at any stage during the period in custody:
      (i) the right to have someone informed of their arrest [see *section 5*];
      (ii) the right to consult privately with a solicitor and that free independent legal advice is available [see *section 6*]; and
      (iii) the right to consult these Codes of Practice [see *section 3*].

17.7 In the case of a person who has not attained the age specified in section 63B(5A) of PACE—
   (a) the making of the request for a sample under *paragraph 17.2(d)* above;
   (b) the giving of the warning and the information under *paragraph 17.6* above; and
   (c) the taking of the sample, may not take place except in the presence of an appropriate adult. See *Note 17G*.

17.8 Authorisation by an officer of the rank of inspector or above within *paragraph 17.3(b)* or *17.4(b)* may be given orally or in writing but, if it is given orally, it must be confirmed in writing as soon as practicable.

17.9 If a sample is taken from a detainee who has been arrested for an offence but not charged with that offence as in *paragraph 17.3*, no further sample may be taken during the same continuous period of detention. If during that same period the charge condition is also met in respect of that detainee, the sample which has been taken shall be treated as being taken by virtue of the charge condition, see *paragraph 17.4*, being met.

17.10 A detainee from whom a sample may be taken may be detained for up to six hours from the time of charge if the custody officer reasonably believes the detention is necessary to enable a sample to be taken. Where the arrest condition is met, a detainee whom the custody officer has decided to release on bail without charge may continue to be detained, but not beyond 24 hours from the relevant time (as defined in section 41(2) of PACE), to enable a sample to be taken.

17.11 A detainee in respect of whom the arrest condition is met, but not the charge condition, see *paragraphs 17.3* and *17.4*, and whose release would be required before a sample can be taken had they not continued to be detained as a result of being arrested for a further offence which does not satisfy the arrest condition, may have a sample taken at any time within 24 hours after the arrest for the offence that satisfies the arrest condition.

(B) Documentation

17.12 The following must be recorded in the custody record:
   (a) if a sample is taken following authorisation by an officer of the rank of inspector or above, the authorisation and the grounds for suspicion;
   (b) the giving of a warning of the consequences of failure to provide a sample;
   (c) the time at which the sample was given; and
   (d) the time of charge or, where the arrest condition is being relied upon, the time of arrest and, where applicable, the fact that a sample taken after arrest but before charge is to be treated as being taken by virtue of the charge condition, where that is met in the same period of continuous detention. See *paragraph 17.9*.

(C) General

17.13 A sample may only be taken by a prescribed person. See *Note 17C*.

17.14 Force may not be used to take any sample for the purpose of drug testing.

17.15 The terms 'Class A drug' and 'misuse' have the same meanings as in the Misuse of Drugs Act 1971. 'Specified' (in relation to a Class A drug) and 'trigger offence' have the same meanings as in Part III of the Criminal Justice and Court Services Act 2000.

17.16 Any sample taken:
   (a) may not be used for any purpose other than to ascertain whether the person concerned has a specified Class A drug present in his body; and
   (b) can be disposed of as clinical waste unless it is to be sent for further analysis in cases where the test result is disputed at the point when the result is known, including on the basis that medication has been taken, or for quality assurance purposes.

(D) Assessment of misuse of drugs

17.17 Under the provisions of Part 3 of the Drugs Act 2005, where a detainee has tested positive for a specified Class A drug under section 63B of PACE a police officer may, at any time before the person's release from the police station, impose a requirement on the detainee to attend an initial assessment of their drug misuse by a suitably qualified person and to remain for its duration. Where such a requirement is imposed, the officer must, at the same time, impose a second requirement on the detainee to attend and remain for a follow-up assessment. The officer must inform the detainee that the second requirement will cease to have effect if, at the initial assessment they are informed that a follow-up assessment is not necessary These requirements may only be imposed on a person if:

(a) they have reached the age of 18

(b) notification has been given by the Secretary of State to the relevant chief officer of police that arrangements for conducting initial and follow-up assessments have been made for those from whom samples for testing have been taken at the police station where the detainee is in custody.

17.18 When imposing a requirement to attend an initial assessment and a follow-up assessment the police officer must:

(a) inform the person of the time and place at which the initial assessment is to take place;

(b) explain that this information will be confirmed in writing; and

(c) warn the person that they may be liable to prosecution if they fail without good cause to attend the initial assessment and remain for its duration and if they fail to attend the follow-up assessment and remain for its duration (if so required).

17.19 Where a police officer has imposed a requirement to attend an initial assessment and a follow-up assessment in accordance with *paragraph 17.17*, he must, before the person is released from detention, give the person notice in writing which:

(a) confirms their requirement to attend and remain for the duration of the assessments; and

(b) confirms the information and repeats the warning referred to in *paragraph 17.18*.

17.20 The following must be recorded in the custody record:

(a) that the requirement to attend an initial assessment and a follow-up assessment has been imposed; and

(b) the information, explanation, warning and notice given in accordance with *paragraphs 17.17* and *17.19*.

17.21 Where a notice is given in accordance with *paragraph 17.19*, a police officer can give the person a further notice in writing which informs the person of any change to the time or place at which the initial assessment is to take place and which repeats the warning referred to in *paragraph 17.18(c)*.

17.22 Part 3 of the Drugs Act 2005 also requires police officers to have regard to any guidance issued by the Secretary of State in respect of the assessment provisions.

Notes for Guidance

17A *When warning a person who is asked to provide a urine or non-intimate sample in accordance with paragraph 17.6(b), the following form of words may be used:*

'You do not have to provide a sample, but I must warn you that if you fail or refuse without good cause to do so, you will commit an offence for which you may be imprisoned, or fined, or both'.

Where the Welsh language is appropriate, the following form of words may be used:

'Does dim rhaid i chi roi sampl, ond mae'n rhaid i mi eich rhybuddio y byddwch chi'n cyflawni trosedd os byddwch chi'n methu neu yn gwrthod gwneud hynny heb reswm da, ac y gellir, oherwydd hynny, eich carcharu, eich dirwyo, neu'r ddau.'

17B *A sample has to be sufficient and suitable. A sufficient sample is sufficient in quantity and quality to enable drug-testing analysis to take place. A suitable sample is one which by its nature, is suitable for a particular form of drug analysis.*

17C *A prescribed person in paragraph 17.13 is one who is prescribed in regulations made by the Secretary of State under section 63B(6) of the Police and Criminal Evidence Act 1984. [The regulations are currently contained in regulation SI 2001 No. 2645, the Police and Criminal Evidence Act 1984 (Drug Testing Persons in Police Detention) (Prescribed Persons) Regulations 2001.]*

17D *Samples, and the information derived from them, may not be subsequently used in the investigation of any offence or in evidence against the persons from whom they were taken.*

17E *Trigger offences are:*

1. *Offences under the following provisions of the Theft Act 1968:*

    section 1   *(theft)*
    section 8   *(robbery)*
    section 9   *(burglary)*
    section 10   *(aggravated burglary)*
    section 12   *(taking a motor vehicle or other conveyance without authority)*
    section 12A   *(aggravated vehicle-taking)*

        section 22   *(handling stolen goods)*
        section 25   *(going equipped for stealing etc.)*

2. *Offences under the following provisions of the Misuse of Drugs Act 1971, if committed in respect of a specified Class A drug:–*
    section 4   *(restriction on production and supply of controlled drugs)*
    section 5(2)   *(possession of a controlled drug)*
    section 5(3)   *(possession of a controlled drug with intent to supply)*

3. *Offences under the following provisions of the Fraud Act 2006: section 1 (fraud)*
    section 6   *(possession etc. of articles for use in frauds)*
    section 7   *(making or supplying articles for use in frauds)*

3A. *An offence under section 1(1) of the Criminal Attempts Act 1981 if committed in respect of an offence under:*

   (a) *any of the following provisions of the Theft Act 1968:*
       section 1   *(theft)*
       section 8   *(robbery)*
       section 9   *(burglary)*
       section 22   *(handling stolen goods)*
   (b) *section 1 of the Fraud Act 2006 (fraud)*

4. *Offences under the following provisions of the Vagrancy Act 1824:*
       section 3   *(begging)*
       section 4   *(persistent begging)*

17F *The power to take samples is subject to notification by the Secretary of State that appropriate arrangements for the taking of samples have been made for the police area as a whole or for the particular police station concerned for whichever of the following is specified in the notification:*

   (a) *persons in respect of whom the arrest condition is met;*
   (b) *persons in respect of whom the charge condition is met;*
   (c) *persons who have not attained the age of 18.*

  Note: Notification is treated as having been given for the purposes of the charge condition in relation to a police area, if testing (on charge) under section 63B(2) of PACE was in force immediately before section 7 of the Drugs Act 2005 was brought into force; and for the purposes of the age condition, in relation to a police area or police station, if immediately before that day, notification that arrangements had been made for the taking of samples from persons under the age of 18 (those aged 14-17) had been given and had not been withdrawn.

17G *Appropriate adult in paragraph 17.7 means the person's–*
   (a) *parent or guardian or, if they are in the care of a local authority or voluntary organisation, a person representing that authority or organisation; or*
   (b) *a social worker of a local authority; or*
   (c) *if no person falling within (a) or (b) above is available, any responsible person aged 18 or over who is not:*
      • *a police officer;*
      • *employed by the police;*
      • *under the direction or control of the chief officer of police force; or*
      • *a person who provides services under contractual arrangements (but without being employed by the chief officer of a police force), to assist that force in relation to the discharge of its chief officer's functions;*
  whether or not they are on duty at the time.

Annex A

Intimate and Strip Searches

A Intimate search

1. An intimate search consists of the physical examination of a person's body orifices other than the mouth. The intrusive nature of such searches means the actual and potential risks associated with intimate searches must never be underestimated.

(a) Action

2. Body orifices other than the mouth may be searched only:
   (a) if authorised by an officer of inspector rank or above who has reasonable grounds for believing that the person may have concealed on themselves:

      (i)   anything which they could and might use to cause physical injury to themselves or others at the station; or

      (ii) a Class A drug which they intended to supply to another or to export;

      and the officer has reasonable grounds for believing that an intimate search is the only means of removing those items; and

  (b) if the search is under *paragraph 2(a)(ii)* (a drug offence search), the detainee's appropriate consent has been given in writing.

2A.   Before the search begins, a police officer or designated detention officer, must tell the detainee:-

  (a) that the authority to carry out the search has been given;

  (b) the grounds for giving the authorisation and for believing that the article cannot be removed without an intimate search.

2B.   Before a detainee is asked to give appropriate consent to a search under *paragraph 2(a)(ii)* (a drug offence search) they must be warned that if they refuse without good cause their refusal may harm their case if it comes to trial, see *Note A6*. This warning may be given by a police officer or member of police staff. In the case of a juvenile or a vulnerable person, the seeking and giving of consent must take place in the presence of the appropriate adult. A juvenile's consent is only valid if their parent's or guardian's consent is also obtained unless the juvenile is under 14, when their parent's or guardian's consent is sufficient in its own right. A detainee who is not legally represented must be reminded of their entitlement to have free legal advice, see Code C, *paragraph 6.5*, and the reminder noted in the custody record.

3.   An intimate search may only be carried out by a registered medical practitioner or registered nurse, unless an officer of at least inspector rank considers this is not practicable and the search is to take place under *paragraph 2(a)(i)*, in which case a police officer may carry out the search. See *Notes A1 to A5*.

3A.   Any proposal for a search under *paragraph 2(a)(i)* to be carried out by someone other than a registered medical practitioner or registered nurse must only be considered as a last resort and when the authorising officer is satisfied the risks associated with allowing the item to remain with the detainee outweigh the risks associated with removing it. See *Notes A1 to A5*.

4.   An intimate search under:

  • *paragraph 2(a)(i)* may take place only at a hospital, surgery, other medical premises or police station;

  • *paragraph 2(a)(ii)* may take place only at a hospital, surgery or other medical premises and must be carried out by a registered medical practitioner or a registered nurse.

5.   An intimate search at a police station of a juvenile or vulnerable person may take place only in the presence of an appropriate adult of the same sex (see *Annex L*), unless the detainee specifically requests a particular appropriate adult of the opposite sex who is readily available. In the case of a juvenile, the search may take place in the absence of the appropriate adult only if the juvenile signifies in the presence of the appropriate adult they do not want the appropriate adult present during the search and the appropriate adult agrees. A record shall be made of the juvenile's decision and signed by the appropriate adult.

6.   When an intimate search under *paragraph 2(a)(i)* is carried out by a police officer, the officer must be of the same sex as the detainee (see *Annex L*). A minimum of two people, other than the detainee, must be present during the search. Subject to *paragraph 5*, no person of the opposite sex who is not a medical practitioner or nurse shall be present, nor shall anyone whose presence is unnecessary. The search shall be conducted with proper regard to the dignity, sensitivity and vulnerability of the detainee including in particular their health, hygiene and welfare needs to which *paragraphs 9.3A and 9.3B* apply.

(b) Documentation

7.   In the case of an intimate search, the following shall be recorded as soon as practicable in the detainee's custody record:

  (a) for searches under *paragraphs 2(a)(i)* and *(ii)*;

     • the authorisation to carry out the search;

     • the grounds for giving the authorisation;

     • the grounds for believing the article could not be removed without an intimate search;

     • which parts of the detainee's body were searched;

     • who carried out the search;

     • who was present;

     • the result.

  (b) for searches under *paragraph 2(a)(ii)*:

- the giving of the warning required by *paragraph 2B*;
- the fact that the appropriate consent was given or (as the case may be) refused, and if refused, the reason given for the refusal (if any).

8.   If an intimate search is carried out by a police officer, the reason why it was impracticable for a registered medical practitioner or registered nurse to conduct it must be recorded.

B   Strip search

9.   A strip search is a search involving the removal of more than outer clothing. In this Code, outer clothing includes shoes and socks.

(a) Action

10. A strip search may take place only if it is considered necessary to remove an article which a detainee would not be allowed to keep and the officer reasonably considers the detainee might have concealed such an article. Strip searches shall not be routinely carried out if there is no reason to consider that articles are concealed.

The conduct of strip searches

11. When strip searches are conducted:
     (a) a police officer carrying out a strip search must be the same sex as the detainee (see *Annex L*);
     (b) the search shall take place in an area where the detainee cannot be seen by anyone who does not need to be present, nor by a member of the opposite sex (see *Annex L*) except an appropriate adult who has been specifically requested by the detainee;
     (c) except in cases of urgency, where there is risk of serious harm to the detainee or to others, whenever a strip search involves exposure of intimate body parts, there must be at least two people present other than the detainee, and if the search is of a juvenile or vulnerable person, one of the people must be the appropriate adult. Except in urgent cases as above, a search of a juvenile may take place in the absence of the appropriate adult only if the juvenile signifies in the presence of the appropriate adult that they do not want the appropriate adult to be present during the search and the appropriate adult agrees. A record shall be made of the juvenile's decision and signed by the appropriate adult. The presence of more than two people, other than an appropriate adult, shall be permitted only in the most exceptional circumstances;
     (d) the search shall be conducted with proper regard to the dignity, sensitivity and vulnerability of the detainee in these circumstances, including in particular, their health, hygiene and welfare needs to which *paragraphs 9.3A* and *9.3B* apply. Every reasonable effort shall be made to secure the detainee's co-operation, maintain their dignity, and minimise embarrassment. Detainees who are searched shall not normally be required to remove all their clothes at the same time, e.g. a person should be allowed to remove clothing above the waist and redress before removing further clothing;
     (e) if necessary to assist the search, the detainee may be required to hold their arms in the air or to stand with their legs apart and bend forward so a visual examination may be made of the genital and anal areas provided no physical contact is made with any body orifice;
     (f) if articles are found, the detainee shall be asked to hand them over. If articles are found within any body orifice other than the mouth, and the detainee refuses to hand them over, their removal would constitute an intimate search, which must be carried out as in *Part A*;
     (g) a strip search shall be conducted as quickly as possible, and the detainee allowed to dress as soon as the procedure is complete.

(b) Documentation

12. A record shall be made on the custody record of a strip search including the reason it was considered necessary, those present and any result.

Notes for Guidance

A1   *Before authorising any intimate search, the authorising officer must make every reasonable effort to persuade the detainee to hand the article over without a search. If the detainee agrees, a registered medical practitioner or registered nurse should whenever possible be asked to assess the risks involved and, if necessary, attend to assist the detainee.*

A2   *If the detainee does not agree to hand the article over without a search, the authorising officer must carefully review all the relevant factors before authorising an intimate search. In particular, the officer must consider whether the grounds for believing an article may be concealed are reasonable.*

A3   *If authority is given for a search under paragraph 2(a)(i), a registered medical practitioner or registered nurse shall be consulted whenever possible. The presumption should be that the search will be conducted by the registered medical practitioner or registered nurse and the authorising officer must make every reasonable effort to persuade the detainee to allow the medical practitioner or nurse to conduct the search.*

A4   *A constable should only be authorised to carry out a search as a last resort and when all other approaches have failed. In these circumstances, the authorising officer must be satisfied the detainee might use the article for one or more of the purposes in paragraph 2(a)(i) and the physical injury likely to be caused is sufficiently severe to justify authorising a constable to carry out the search.*

A5   *If an officer has any doubts whether to authorise an intimate search by a constable, the officer should seek advice from an officer of superintendent rank or above.*

A6   *In warning a detainee who is asked to consent to an intimate drug offence search, as in paragraph 2B, the following form of words may be used:*

   'You do not have to allow yourself to be searched, but I must warn you that if you refuse without good cause, your refusal may harm your case if it comes to trial.'

   Where the use of the Welsh Language is appropriate, the following form of words may be used:

   'Nid oes rhaid i chi roi caniatâd i gael eich archwilio, ond mae'n rhaid i mi eich rhybuddio os gwrthodwch heb reswm da, y gallai eich penderfyniad i wrthod wneud niwed i'ch achos pe bai'n dod gerbron llys.'

ANNEX B

DELAY IN NOTIFYING ARREST OR ALLOWING ACCESS TO LEGAL ADVICE

A   Persons detained under PACE

1.   The exercise of the rights in *Section 5* or *Section 6*, or both, may be delayed if the person is in police detention, as in PACE, section 118(2), in connection with an indictable offence, has not yet been charged with an offence and an officer of superintendent rank or above, or inspector rank or above only for the rights in *Section 5*, has reasonable grounds for believing their exercise will:
   (i)   lead to:
      • interference with, or harm to, evidence connected with an indictable offence; or
      • interference with, or physical harm to, other people; or
   (ii) lead to alerting other people suspected of having committed an indictable offence but not yet arrested for it; or
   (iii) hinder the recovery of property obtained in consequence of the commission of such an offence.
2.   These rights may also be delayed if the officer has reasonable grounds to believe that:
   (i)   the person detained for an indictable offence has benefited from their criminal conduct (decided in accordance with Part 2 of the Proceeds of Crime Act 2002); and
   (ii) the recovery of the value of the property constituting that benefit will be hindered by the exercise of either right.
3.   Authority to delay a detainee's right to consult privately with a solicitor may be given only if the authorising officer has reasonable grounds to believe the solicitor the detainee wants to consult will, inadvertently or otherwise, pass on a message from the detainee or act in some other way which will have any of the consequences specified under *paragraphs 1 or 2*. In these circumstances, the detainee must be allowed to choose another solicitor. See *Note B3*.
4.   If the detainee wishes to see a solicitor, access to that solicitor may not be delayed on the grounds they might advise the detainee not to answer questions or the solicitor was initially asked to attend the police station by someone else. In the latter case, the detainee must be told the solicitor has come to the police station at another person's request, and must be asked to sign the custody record to signify whether they want to see the solicitor.
5.   The fact the grounds for delaying notification of arrest may be satisfied does not automatically mean the grounds for delaying access to legal advice will also be satisfied.
6.   These rights may be delayed only for as long as grounds exist and in no case beyond 36 hours after the relevant time as in PACE, section 41. If the grounds cease to apply within this time, the detainee must, as soon as practicable, be asked if they want to exercise either right, the custody record must be noted accordingly, and action taken in accordance with the relevant section of the Code.
7.   A detained person must be permitted to consult a solicitor for a reasonable time before any court hearing.

B Not used

C Documentation

13.   The grounds for action under this Annex shall be recorded and the detainee informed of them as soon as practicable.

14.   Any reply given by a detainee under *paragraphs 6* or *11* must be recorded and the detainee asked to endorse the record in relation to whether they want to receive legal advice at this point.

D Cautions and special warnings

15.   When a suspect detained at a police station is interviewed during any period for which access to legal advice has been delayed under this Annex, the court or jury may not draw adverse inferences from their silence.

Notes for Guidance

B1   Even if Annex B applies in the case of a juvenile, or a vulnerable person, action to inform the appropriate adult and the person responsible for a juvenile's welfare, if that is a different person, must nevertheless be taken as in paragraph 3.13 and 3.15.

B2   In the case of Commonwealth citizens and foreign nationals, see Note 7A.

B3   A decision to delay access to a specific solicitor is likely to be a rare occurrence and only when it can be shown the suspect is capable of misleading that particular solicitor and there is more than a substantial risk that the suspect will succeed in causing information to be conveyed which will lead to one or more of the specified consequences.

ANNEX C

RESTRICTION ON DRAWING ADVERSE INFERENCES FROM SILENCE AND TERMS OF
THE CAUTION WHEN THE RESTRICTION APPLIES

(a) The restriction on drawing adverse inferences from silence

1.   The Criminal Justice and Public Order Act 1994, sections 34, 36 and 37 as amended by the Youth Justice and Criminal Evidence Act 1999, section 58 describe the conditions under which adverse inferences may be drawn from a person's failure or refusal to say anything about their involvement in the offence when interviewed, after being charged or informed they may be prosecuted. These provisions are subject to an overriding restriction on the ability of a court or jury to draw adverse inferences from a person's silence. This restriction applies:

(a)   to any detainee at a police station, see *Note 10C*, who, before being interviewed, see *section 11* or being charged or informed they may be prosecuted, see *section 16*, has:

(i)   asked for legal advice, see *section 6, paragraph* 6.1;

(ii)   not been allowed an opportunity to consult a solicitor, including the duty solicitor, as in this Code; and

(iii)   not changed their mind about wanting legal advice, see *section 6, paragraph 6.6(d)*.

Note the condition in (ii) will:

• apply when a detainee who has asked for legal advice is interviewed before speaking to a solicitor as in *section 6, paragraph 6.6(a)* or *(b)*;

• not apply if the detained person declines to ask for the duty solicitor, see *section 6, paragraphs 6.6(c)* and *(d)*.

(b)   to any person charged with, or informed they may be prosecuted for, an offence who:

(i)   has had brought to their notice a written statement made by another person or the content of an interview with another person which relates to that offence, see *section 16, paragraph 16.4*;

(ii)   is interviewed about that offence, see *section 16, paragraph 16.5*; or

(iii)   makes a written statement about that offence, see *Annex D, paragraphs 4* and *9*.

(b) Terms of the caution when the restriction applies

2.   When a requirement to caution arises at a time when the restriction on drawing adverse inferences from silence applies, the caution shall be:

'*You do not have to say anything, but anything you do say may be given in evidence.*'

Where the use of the Welsh Language is appropriate, the caution may be used directly in Welsh in the following terms:

'*Does dim rhaid i chi ddweud dim byd, ond gall unrhyw beth yr ydych chi'n ei ddweud gael ei roi fel tystiolaeth.*'

3.   Whenever the restriction either begins to apply or ceases to apply after a caution has already been given, the person shall be re-cautioned in the appropriate terms. The changed position on drawing inferences and that the previous caution no longer applies shall also be explained to the detainee in ordinary language. See *Note C2*.

Notes for Guidance

C1   *The restriction on drawing inferences from silence does not apply to a person who has not been detained and who therefore cannot be prevented from seeking legal advice if they want to, see paragraphs 10.2 and 3.21.*

C2   *The following is suggested as a framework to help explain changes in the position on drawing adverse inferences if the restriction on drawing adverse inferences from silence:*

      (a) *begins to apply:*

      'The caution you were previously given no longer applies. This is because after that caution:

      (i)   you asked to speak to a solicitor but have not yet been allowed an opportunity to speak to a solicitor. See paragraph 1(a); or

      (ii) you have been charged with/informed you may be prosecuted. See paragraph 1(b).

      'This means that from now on, adverse inferences cannot be drawn at court and your defence will not be harmed just because you choose to say nothing. Please listen carefully to the caution I am about to give you because it will apply from now on. You will see that it does not say anything about your defence being harmed.'

      (b) *ceases to apply before or at the time the person is charged or informed they may be prosecuted, see paragraph 1(a);*

      'The caution you were previously given no longer applies. This is because after that caution you have been allowed an opportunity to speak to a solicitor. Please listen carefully to the caution I am about to give you because it will apply from now on. It explains how your defence at court may be affected if you choose to say nothing.'

Annex D

Written Statements under Caution

(a) Written by a person under caution

1.   A person shall always be invited to write down what they want to say.

2.   A person who has not been charged with, or informed they may be prosecuted for, any offence to which the statement they want to write relates, shall:

      (a) unless the statement is made at a time when the restriction on drawing adverse inferences from silence applies, see *Annex C*, be asked to write out and sign the following before writing what they want to say:

           '*I make this statement of my own free will. I understand that I do not have to say anything but that it may harm my defence if I do not mention when questioned something which I later rely on in court. This statement may be given in evidence.*';

      (b) if the statement is made at a time when the restriction on drawing adverse inferences from silence applies, be asked to write out and sign the following before writing what they want to say;

           '*I make this statement of my own free will. I understand that I do not have to say anything. This statement may be given in evidence.*'

3.   When a person, on the occasion of being charged with or informed they may be prosecuted for any offence, asks to make a statement which relates to any such offence and wants to write it they shall:

      (a) unless the restriction on drawing adverse inferences from silence, see *Annex C*, applied when they were so charged or informed they may be prosecuted, be asked to write out and sign the following before writing what they want to say:

           '*I make this statement of my own free will. I understand that I do not have to say anything but that it may harm my defence if I do not mention when questioned something which I later rely on in court. This statement may be given in evidence.*';

      (b) if the restriction on drawing adverse inferences from silence applied when they were so charged or informed they may be prosecuted, be asked to write out and sign the following before writing what they want to say:

           '*I make this statement of my own free will. I understand that I do not have to say anything. This statement may be given in evidence.*'

4.   When a person who has already been charged with or informed they may be prosecuted for any offence asks to make a statement which relates to any such offence and wants to write it, they shall be asked to write out and sign the following before writing what they want to say:

> '*I make this statement of my own free will. I understand that I do not have to say anything. This statement may be given in evidence.*';

5.   Any person writing their own statement shall be allowed to do so without any prompting except a police officer or other police staff may indicate to them which matters are material or question any ambiguity in the statement.

(b) Written by a police officer or other police staff

6.   If a person says they would like someone to write the statement for them, a police officer, or other police staff shall write the statement.

7.   If the person has not been charged with, or informed they may be prosecuted for, any offence to which the statement they want to make relates they shall, before starting, be asked to sign, or make their mark, to the following:

(a)   unless the statement is made at a time when the restriction on drawing adverse inferences from silence applies, see *Annex C*:

> '*I, ..., wish to make a statement. I want someone to write down what I say. I understand that I do not have to say anything but that it may harm my defence if I do not mention when questioned something which I later rely on in court. This statement may be given in evidence.*';

(b)   if the statement is made at a time when the restriction on drawing adverse inferences from silence applies:

> '*I, ..., wish to make a statement. I want someone to write down what I say. I understand that I do not have to say anything. This statement may be given in evidence.*'

8.   If, on the occasion of being charged with or informed they may be prosecuted for any offence, the person asks to make a statement which relates to any such offence they shall before starting be asked to sign, or make their mark to, the following:

(a)   unless the restriction on drawing adverse inferences from silence applied, see *Annex C*, when they were so charged or informed they may be prosecuted:

> '*I, ..., wish to make a statement. I want someone to write down what I say. I understand that I do not have to say anything but that it may harm my defence if I do not mention when questioned something which I later rely on in court. This statement may be given in evidence.*';

(b)   if the restriction on drawing adverse inferences from silence applied when they were so charged or informed they may be prosecuted:

> '*I, ..., wish to make a statement. I want someone to write down what I say. I understand that I do not have to say anything. This statement may be given in evidence.*'

9.   If, having already been charged with or informed they may be prosecuted for any offence, a person asks to make a statement which relates to any such offence they shall before starting, be asked to sign, or make their mark to:

> '*I, ..., wish to make a statement. I want someone to write down what I say. I understand that I do not have to say anything. This statement may be given in evidence.*'

10.   The person writing the statement must take down the exact words spoken by the person making it and must not edit or paraphrase it. Any questions that are necessary, e.g. to make it more intelligible, and the answers given must be recorded at the same time on the statement form.

11.   When the writing of a statement is finished the person making it shall be asked to read it and to make any corrections, alterations or additions they want. When they have finished reading they shall be asked to write and sign or make their mark on the following certificate at the end of the statement:

> '*I have read the above statement, and I have been able to correct, alter or add anything I wish. This statement is true. I have made it of my own free will.*'

12.   If the person making the statement cannot read, or refuses to read it, or to write the above mentioned certificate at the end of it or to sign it, the person taking the statement shall read it to them and ask them if they would like to correct, alter or add anything and to put their signature or make their mark at the end. The person taking the statement shall certify on the statement itself what has occurred.

ANNEX E

SUMMARY OF PROVISIONS RELATING TO MENTALLY DISORDERED AND OTHERWISE
MENTALLY VULNERABLE PEOPLE

1.   If at any time, an officer has reason to suspect that a person of any age may be vulnerable (see
       paragraph 1.13(d)), in the absence of clear evidence to dispel that suspicion that person shall be
       treated as such for the purposes of this Code and to establish whether any such reason may exist in
       relation to a person suspected of committing an offence (see *paragraph 10.1* and *Note 10A*), the
       custody officer in the case of a detained person, or the officer investigating the offence in the case of
       a person who has not been arrested or detained, shall take, or cause to be taken, (see *paragraph 3.5*
       and *Note 3F*) the following action:
       (a)   reasonable enquiries shall be made to ascertain what information is available that is relevant to
             any of the factors described in *paragraph 1.13(d)* as indicating that the person may be
             vulnerable might apply;
       (b)   a record shall be made describing whether any of those factors appear to apply and provide any
             reason to suspect that the person may be vulnerable or (as the case may be) may not be
             vulnerable; and
       (c)   the record mentioned in sub-paragraph (b) shall be made available to be taken into account by
             police officers, police staff and any others who, in accordance with the provisions of this or any
             other Code, are entitled to communicate with the person in question. This would include any
             solicitor, appropriate adult and healthcare professional and is particularly relevant to commu-
             nication by telephone or by means of a live link (see *paragraphs 12.9A* (interviews), *13.12*
             (interpretation), and *15.3C, 15.11A, 15.11B, 15.11C* and *15.11D* (reviews and extension of
             detention)).
       See Notes 1G, E5, E6 and *E7.*
2.   In the case of a person who is vulnerable, 'the appropriate adult' means:
       (i)   a relative, guardian or other person responsible for their care or custody;
       (ii)   someone experienced in dealing with vulnerable persons but who is not:
              • a police officer;
              • employed by the police;
              • under the direction or control of the chief officer of a police force;
              • a person who provides services under contractual arrangements (but without being employed
                by the chief officer of a police force), to assist that force in relation to the discharge of its chief
                officer's functions, whether or not they are on duty at the time.
       (iii) failing these, some other responsible adult aged 18 or over who is other than a person described
              in the bullet points in *sub-paragraph (ii)* above.
       See *paragraph 1.7(b)* and *Notes 1D* and *1F.*
2A   The role of the appropriate adult is to safeguard the rights, entitlements and welfare of 'vulnerable
       persons' (see *paragraph 1*) to whom the provisions of this and any other Code of Practice apply. For
       this reason, the appropriate adult is expected, amongst other things, to:
       • support, advise and assist them when, in accordance with this Code or any other Code of Practice,
         they are given or asked to provide information or participate in any procedure;
       • observe whether the police are acting properly and fairly to respect their rights and entitlements,
         and inform an officer of the rank of inspector or above if they consider that they are not;
       • assist them to communicate with the police whilst respecting their right to say nothing unless they
         want to as set out in the terms of the caution (see *paragraphs 10.5* and *10.6*); and
       • help them understand their rights and ensure that those rights are protected and respected (see
         paragraphs 3.15, 3.17, 6.5A and *11.17*).
       See *paragraph 1.7A.*
3.   If the custody officer authorises the detention of a vulnerable person, the custody officer must as
       soon as practicable inform the appropriate adult of the grounds for detention and the person's
       whereabouts, and secure the attendance of the appropriate adult at the police station to see the
       detainee. If the appropriate adult:
       • is already at the station when information is given as in *paragraphs 3.1* to *3.5* the information must
         be given in their presence;
       • is not at the station when the provisions of *paragraph 3.1* to *3.5* are complied with these provisions
         must be complied with again in their presence once they arrive.
       See *paragraphs 3.15 to 3.17*

4.   If the appropriate adult, having been informed of the right to legal advice, considers legal advice should be taken, the provisions of *section 6* apply as if the vulnerable person had requested access to legal advice. See *paragraphs 3.19, 6.5A* and *Note E1*.

5.   The custody officer must make sure a person receives appropriate clinical attention as soon as reasonably practicable if the person appears to be suffering from a mental disorder or in urgent cases immediately call the nearest appropriate healthcare professional or an ambulance. See Code C *paragraphs 3.16, 9.5* and *9.6* which apply when a person is detained under the Mental Health Act 1983, sections 135 and 136, as amended by the Policing and Crime Act 2017.

6.   *Not used.*

7.   If a vulnerable person is cautioned in the absence of the appropriate adult, the caution must be repeated in the appropriate adult's presence. See *paragraph 10.12*.

8.   A vulnerable person must not be interviewed or asked to provide or sign a written statement in the absence of the appropriate adult unless the provisions of *paragraphs 11.1* or *11.18 to 11.20* apply. Questioning in these circumstances may not continue in the absence of the appropriate adult once sufficient information to avert the risk has been obtained. A record shall be made of the grounds for any decision to begin an interview in these circumstances. See *paragraphs 11.1, 11.15* and *11.18 to 11.20*.

9.   If the appropriate adult is present at an interview, they shall be informed they are not expected to act simply as an observer and the purposes of their presence are to:
      • advise the interviewee;
      • observe whether or not the interview is being conducted properly and fairly;
      • facilitate communication with the interviewee.
      See *paragraph 11.17*.

10.   If the detention of a vulnerable person is reviewed by a review officer or a superintendent, the appropriate adult must, if available at the time, be given an opportunity to make representations to the officer about the need for continuing detention. See *paragraph 15.3*.

11.   If the custody officer charges a vulnerable person with an offence or takes such other action as is appropriate when there is sufficient evidence for a prosecution this must be carried out in the presence of the appropriate adult if they are at the police station. A copy of the written notice embodying any charge must also be given to the appropriate adult. See *paragraphs 16.1 to 16.4A*.

12.   An intimate or strip search of a vulnerable person may take place only in the presence of the appropriate adult of the same sex, unless the detainee specifically requests the presence of a particular adult of the opposite sex. A strip search may take place in the absence of an appropriate adult only in cases of urgency when there is a risk of serious harm to the detainee or others. See *Annex A, paragraphs 5* and *11(c)*.

13.   Particular care must be taken when deciding whether to use any form of approved restraints on a vulnerable person in a locked cell. See *paragraph 8.2*.

Notes for Guidance

E1   *The purpose of the provisions at paragraphs 3.19 and 6.5A is to protect the rights of a vulnerable person who does not understand the significance of what is said to them. A vulnerable person should always be given an opportunity, when an appropriate adult is called to the police station, to consult privately with a solicitor in the absence of the appropriate adult if they want.*

E2   *Although vulnerable persons are often capable of providing reliable evidence, they may, without knowing or wanting to do so, be particularly prone in certain circumstances to provide information that may be unreliable, misleading or self-incriminating. Special care should always be taken when questioning such a person, and the appropriate adult should be involved if there is any doubt about a person's mental state or capacity. Because of the risk of unreliable evidence, it is important to obtain corroboration of any facts admitted whenever possible.*

E3   *Because of the risks referred to in Note E2, which the presence of the appropriate adult is intended to minimise, officers of superintendent rank or above should exercise their discretion to authorise the commencement of an interview in the appropriate adult's absence only in exceptional cases, if it is necessary to avert one or more of the specified risks in paragraph 11.1. See paragraphs 11.1 and 11.18 to 11.20.*

E4   *When a person is detained under section 136 of the Mental Health Act 1983 for assessment, the appropriate adult has no role in the assessment process and their presence is not required.*

E5   *For the purposes of Annex E paragraph 1, examples of relevant information that may be available include:*
      • *the behaviour of the adult or juvenile;*
      • *the mental health and capacity of the adult or juvenile;*
      • *what the adult or juvenile says about themselves;*
      • *information from relatives and friends of the adult or juvenile;*

- *information from police officers and staff and from police records;*
- *information from health and social care (including liaison and diversion services) and other professionals who know, or have had previous contact with, the individual and may be able to contribute to assessing their need for help and support from an appropriate adult. This includes contacts and assessments arranged by the police or at the request of the individual or (as applicable) their appropriate adult or solicitor.*

E6   *The Mental Health Act 1983 Code of Practice at page 26 describes the range of clinically recognised conditions which can fall with the meaning of mental disorder for the purpose of paragraph 1.13(d). The Code is published here: https://www.gov.uk/government/publications/code-of-practice-mental-health-act-1983.*

E7   *When a person is under the influence of drink and/or drugs, it is not intended that they are to be treated as vulnerable and requiring an appropriate adult for the purpose of Annex E paragraph 1 unless other information indicates that any of the factors described in paragraph 1.13(d) may apply to that person. When the person has recovered from the effects of drink and/or drugs, they should be re-assessed in accordance with Annex E paragraph 1. See paragraph 15.4A for application to live link.*

ANNEX F

Not Used

ANNEX G

FITNESS TO BE INTERVIEWED

1.   This Annex contains general guidance to help police officers and healthcare professionals assess whether a detainee might be at risk in an interview.

2.   A detainee may be at risk in a interview if it is considered that:
    (a) conducting the interview could significantly harm the detainee's physical or mental state;
    (b) anything the detainee says in the interview about their involvement or suspected involvement in the offence about which they are being interviewed **might** be considered unreliable in subsequent court proceedings because of their physical or mental state.

3.   In assessing whether the detainee should be interviewed, the following must be considered:
    (a) how the detainee's physical or mental state might affect their ability to understand the nature and purpose of the interview, to comprehend what is being asked and to appreciate the significance of any answers given and make rational decisions about whether they want to say anything;
    (b) the extent to which the detainee's replies may be affected by their physical or mental condition rather than representing a rational and accurate explanation of their involvement in the offence;
    (c) how the nature of the interview, which could include particularly probing questions, might affect the detainee.

4.   It is essential healthcare professionals who are consulted consider the functional ability of the detainee rather than simply relying on a medical diagnosis, e.g. it is possible for a person with severe mental illness to be fit for interview.

5.   Healthcare professionals should advise on the need for an appropriate adult to be present, whether reassessment of the person's fitness for interview may be necessary if the interview lasts beyond a specified time, and whether a further specialist opinion may be required.

6.   When healthcare professionals identify risks they should be asked to quantify the risks. They should inform the custody officer:
- whether the person's condition:
  - is likely to improve;
  - will require or be amenable to treatment; and

indicate how long it may take for such improvement to take effect.

7.   The role of the healthcare professional is to consider the risks and advise the custody officer of the outcome of that consideration. The healthcare professional's determination and any advice or recommendations should be made in writing and form part of the custody record.

8.   Once the healthcare professional has provided that information, it is a matter for the custody officer to decide whether or not to allow the interview to go ahead and if the interview is to proceed, to determine what safeguards are needed. Nothing prevents safeguards being provided in addition to those required under the Code. An example might be to have an appropriate healthcare professional present during the interview, in addition to an appropriate adult, in order constantly to monitor the person's condition and how it is being affected by the interview.

Annex H

Detained Person: Observation List

1. If any detainee fails to meet any of the following criteria, an appropriate healthcare professional or an ambulance must be called.
2. When assessing the level of rousability, consider:
    Rousability — can they be woken?
    *   go into the cell
    *   call their name
    *   shake gently
    Response to questions — can they give appropriate answers to questions such as:
    *   What's your name?
    *   Where do you live?
    *   Where do you think you are?
    Response to commands — can they respond appropriately to commands such as:
    *   Open your eyes!
    *   Lift one arm, now the other arm!
3. Remember to take into account the possibility or presence of other illnesses, injury, or mental condition; a person who is drowsy and smells of alcohol may also have the following:
    *   Diabetes
    *   Epilepsy
    *   Head injury
    *   Drug intoxication or overdose
    *   Stroke

Annex I

Not used

Annex J

Not used

Annex K

X-Rays and Ultrasound Scans

(a) Action

1. PACE, section 55A allows a person who has been arrested and is in police detention to have an X-ray taken of them or an ultrasound scan to be carried out on them (or both) if:
    (a) authorised by an officer of inspector rank or above who has reasonable grounds for believing that the detainee:
        (i)   may have swallowed a Class A drug; and
        (ii) was in possession of that Class A drug with the intention of supplying it to another or to export; and
    (b) the detainee's appropriate consent has been given in writing.
2. Before an x-ray is taken or an ultrasound scan carried out, a police officer or designated detention officer must tell the detainee:-
    (a) that the authority has been given; and
    (b) the grounds for giving the authorisation.
3. Before a detainee is asked to give appropriate consent to an x-ray or an ultrasound scan, they must be warned that if they refuse without good cause their refusal may harm their case if it comes to trial, see *Notes K1* and *K2*. This warning may be given by a police officer or member of police staff. In the case of juveniles and vulnerable persons, the seeking and giving of consent must take place in the presence of the appropriate adult. A juvenile's consent is only valid if their parent's or guardian's consent is also obtained unless the juvenile is under 14, when their parent's or guardian's consent is sufficient in its own right. A detainee who is not legally represented must be reminded of their entitlement to have free legal advice, see Code C, *paragraph 6.5*, and the reminder noted in the custody record.
4. An x-ray may be taken, or an ultrasound scan may be carried out, only by a registered medical practitioner or registered nurse, and only at a hospital, surgery or other medical premises.

(b) Documentation

5.   The following shall be recorded as soon as practicable in the detainee's custody record:
      (a)   the authorisation to take the x-ray or carry out the ultrasound scan (or both);
      (b)   the grounds for giving the authorisation;
      (c)   the giving of the warning required by *paragraph 3*; and
      (d)   the fact that the appropriate consent was given or (as the case may be) refused, and if refused, the reason given for the refusal (if any); and
      (e)   if an x-ray is taken or an ultrasound scan carried out:
            • where it was taken or carried out;
            • who took it or carried it out;
            • who was present;
            • the result.

6   *Not used.*

Notes for Guidance

K1   *If authority is given for an x-ray to be taken or an ultrasound scan to be carried out (or both), consideration should be given to asking a registered medical practitioner or registered nurse to explain to the detainee what is involved and to allay any concerns the detainee might have about the effect which taking an x-ray or carrying out an ultrasound scan might have on them. If appropriate consent is not given, evidence of the explanation may, if the case comes to trial, be relevant to determining whether the detainee had a good cause for refusing.*

K2   *In warning a detainee who is asked to consent to an X-ray being taken or an ultrasound scan being carried out (or both), as in paragraph 3, the following form of words may be used:*

      'You do not have to allow an x-ray of you to be taken or an ultrasound scan to be carried out on you, but I must warn you that if you refuse without good cause, your refusal may harm your case if it comes to trial.'

      Where the use of the Welsh Language is appropriate, the following form of words may be provided in Welsh:

      'Does dim rhaid i chi ganiatáu cymryd sgan uwchsain neu belydr-x (neu'r ddau) arnoch, ond mae'n rhaid i mi eich rhybuddio os byddwch chi'n gwrthod gwneud hynny heb reswm da, fe allai hynny niweidio eich achos pe bai'n dod gerbron llys.'

Annex L

Establishing Gender of Persons for the Purpose of Searching

1.   Certain provisions of this and other PACE Codes explicitly state that searches and other procedures may only be carried out by, or in the presence of, persons of the same sex as the person subject to the search or other procedure or require action to be taken or information to be given which depends on whether the detainee is treated as being male or female. See *Note L1*.

2.   All such searches, procedures and requirements must be carried out with courtesy, consideration and respect for the person concerned. Police officers should show particular sensitivity when dealing with transgender individuals (including transsexual persons) and transvestite persons (see *Notes L2, L3 and L4*).

(a) Consideration

3.   In law, the gender (and accordingly the sex) of an individual is their gender as registered at birth unless they have been issued with a Gender Recognition Certificate (GRC) under the Gender Recognition Act 2004 (GRA), in which case the person's gender is their acquired gender. This means that if the acquired gender is the male gender, the person's sex becomes that of a man and, if it is the female gender, the person's sex becomes that of a woman and they must be treated as their acquired gender.

4.   When establishing whether the person concerned should be treated as being male or female for the purposes of these searches, procedures and requirements, the following approach which is designed to maintain their diginity, minimise embarrassment and secure their co-operation should be followed:
      (a)   The person must not be asked whether they have a GRC (see *paragraph 8*);
      (b)   If there is no doubt as to as to whether the person concerned should be treated as being male or female, they should be dealt with as being of that sex.

(c)   If at any time (including during the search or carrying out the procedure or requirement) there is doubt as to whether the person should be treated, or continue to be treated, as being male or female:

   (i)   the person should be asked what gender they consider themselves to be. If they express a preference to be dealt with as a particular gender, they should be asked to indicate and confirm their preference by signing the custody record or, if a custody record has not been opened, the search record or the officer's notebook. Subject to (ii) below, the person should be treated according to their preference except with regards to the requirements to provide that person with information concerning menstrual products and their personal needs relating to health, hygiene and welfare described in *paragraph 3.20A* (if aged under 18) and *paragraphs 9.3A* and *9.3B* (if aged 18 or over). In these cases, a person whose confirmed preference is to be dealt with as being male should be asked in private whether they wish to speak in private with a member of the custody staff of a gender of their choosing about the provision of menstrual products and their personal needs, notwithstanding their confirmed preference (see *Note L3A*).

   (ii)   if there are grounds to doubt that the preference in (i) accurately reflects the person's predominant lifestyle, for example, if they ask to be treated as a woman but documents and other information make it clear that they live predominantly as a man, or vice versa, they should be treated according to what appears to be their predominant lifestyle and not their stated preference;

   (iii)   If the person is unwilling to express a preference as in (i) above, efforts should be made to determine their predominant lifestyle and they should be treated as such. For example, if they appear to live predominantly as a woman, they should be treated as being female except with regard to the requirements to provide that person with information concerning menstrual products and their personal needs relating to health, hygiene and welfare described in *paragraph 3.20A* (if aged under 18) and *paragraphs 9.3A* and *9.3B* (if aged 18 or over). In these cases, a person whose predominant lifestyle has been determined to be male should be asked in private whether they wish to speak in private with a member of the custody staff of a gender of their choosing about the provision of menstrual products and their personal needs, notwithstanding their determined predominant lifestyle (see *Note L3A*); or

   (iv)   if none of the above apply, the person should be dealt with according to what reasonably appears to have been their sex as registered at birth.

5.   Once a decision has been made about which gender an individual is to be treated as, each officer responsible for the search procedure or requirement should where possible be advised before the search or procedure starts of any doubts as to the person's gender and the person informed that the doubts have been disclosed. This is important so as to maintain the dignity of the person and any officers concerned.

(b) Documentation

6.   The person's gender as established under *paragraph 4(c)(i)* to *(iv)* above must be recorded in the person's custody record or, if a custody record has not been opened, on the search record or in the officer's notebook.

7.   Where the person elects which gender they consider themselves to be under *paragraph 4(b)(i)* but, following *4(b)(ii)* is not treated in accordance with their preference, the reason must be recorded in the search record, in the officer's notebook or, if applicable, in the person's custody record.

(c) Disclosure of information

8.   Section 22 of the GRA defines any information relating to a person's application for a GRC or to a successful applicant's gender before it became their acquired gender as 'protected information'. Nothing in this Annex is to be read as authorising or permitting any police officer or any police staff who has acquired such information when acting in their official capacity to disclose that information to any other person in contravention of the GRA. Disclosure includes making a record of 'protected information' which is read by others.

Notes for Guidance

L1   *Provisions to which paragraph 1 applies include:*
   • *In Code C; paragraphs 3.20A, 4.1 and Annex A paragraphs 5, 6, and 11 (searches, strip and intimate searches of detainees under sections 54 and 55 of PACE) and 9.3B;*
   • *In Code A; paragraphs 2.8 and 3.6 and Note 4;*

- In Code D; paragraph 5.5 and Note 5F (searches, examinations and photographing of detainees under section 54A of PACE) and paragraph 6.9 (taking samples);
- In Code H; paragraphs 3.21, 4.1 and Annex A paragraphs 6, 7 and 12 (searches, strip and intimate searches under sections 54 and 55 of PACE of persons arrested under section 41 of the Terrorism Act 2000) and 9.4B.

L2   While there is no agreed definition of transgender (or trans), it is generally used as an umbrella term to describe people whose gender identity (self-identification as being a woman, man, neither or both) differs from the sex they were registered as at birth. The term includes, but is not limited to, transsexual people.

L3   Transsexual means a person who is proposing to undergo, is undergoing or has undergone a process (or part of a process) for the purpose of gender reassignment, which is a protected characteristic under the Equality Act 2010 (see paragraph 1.0), by changing physiological or other attributes of their sex. This includes aspects of gender such as dress and title. It would apply to a woman making the transition to being a man and a man making the transition to being a woman, as well as to a person who has only just started out on the process of gender reassignment and to a person who has completed the process. Both would share the characteristic of gender reassignment with each having the characteristics of one sex, but with certain characteristics of the other sex.

L3A The reason for the exception is to modify the same sex/gender approach for searching to acknowledge the possible needs of transgender individuals in respect of menstrual products and other personal needs relating to health, hygiene and welfare and ensure that they are not overlooked.

L4   Transvestite means a person of one gender who dresses in the clothes of a person of the opposite gender. However, a transvestite does not live permanently in the gender opposite to their birth sex.

L5   Chief officers are responsible for providing corresponding operational guidance and instructions for the deployment of transgender officers and staff under their direction and control to duties which involve carrying out, or being present at, any of the searches and procedures described in paragraph 1. The guidance and instructions must comply with the Equality Act 2010 and should therefore complement the approach in this Annex.

Annex M
Documents and Records to be Translated

1.   For the purposes of Directive 2010/64/EU of the European Parliament and of the Council of 20 October 2010 and this Code, essential documents comprise records required to be made in accordance with this Code which are relevant to decisions to deprive a person of their liberty, to any charge and to any record considered necessary to enable a detainee to defend themselves in criminal proceedings and to safeguard the fairness of the proceedings. Passages of essential documents which are not relevant need not be translated. See Note M1.

2.   The table below lists the documents considered essential for the purposes of this Code and when (subject to paragraphs 3 to 7) written translations must be created and provided. See paragraphs 13.12 to 13.14 and Annex N for application to live-link interpretation.

Table of essential documents:

	Essential Documents for the Purposes of this Code	When Translation to be Created	When Translation to be Provided
(i)	The grounds for each of the following authorisations to keep the person in custody as they are described and referred to in the custody record: (a) Authorisation for detention before and after charge given by the custody officer and by the review officer, see Code C, paragraphs 3.4 and 15.16(a).	As soon as practicable after each authorisation has been recorded in the custody record.	As soon as practicable after the translation has been created, whilst the person is detained or afters they have been releases (see Note M3).

	Essential Documents for the Purposes of this Code	When Translation to be Created	When Translation to be Provided
	(b) Authorisation to extend detention without charge beyond 24 hours given by a superintendent, see Code C, *paragraph 15.16(b)*. (c) A warrant of further detention issued by a magistrates' court and any extension(s) of the warrant, see Code C, *paragraph 15.16(c)*. (d) An authority to detain in accordance with the directions in a warrant of arrest issued in connection with criminal proceedings including the court issuing the warrant.		
(ii)	Written notice showing particulars of the offence charged required by Code C, *paragraph 16.3* or the offence for which the suspect has been told they may be prosecuted.	As soon as practicable after the person has been charged or reported.	
(iii)	Written interview records: Code C, 11.11, 13.3, 13.4 and Code E4.7 Written statement under caution: Code C, *Annex D*.	To be created contemporaneously by the interpreter for the person to check and sign.	As soon as practicable after the person has been charged or told they may be prosecuted.

3. The custody officer may authorise an oral translation or oral summary of documents (i) to (ii) in the table (but not (iii)) to be provided (through an interpreter) instead of a written translation. Such an oral translation or summary may only be provided if it would not prejudice the fairness of the proceedings by in any way adversely affecting or otherwise undermining or limiting the ability of the suspect in question to understand their position and to communicate effectively with police officers, interviewers, solicitors and appropriate adults with regard to their detention and the investigation of the offence in question and to defend themselves in the event of criminal proceedings. The quantity and complexity of the information in the document should always be considered and specific additional consideration given if the suspect is vulnerable or is a juvenile (see Code C, *paragraph 1.5*). The reason for the decision must be recorded (see *paragraph 13.11(e)*).

4. Subject to *paragraphs 5 to 7* below, a suspect may waive their right to a written translation of the essential documents described in the table but only if they do so voluntarily after receiving legal advice or having full knowledge of the consequences and give their unconditional and fully informed consent in writing (see *paragraph 9*).

5. The suspect may be asked if they wish to waive their right to a written translation and before giving their consent, they must be reminded of their right to legal advice and asked whether they wish to speak to a solicitor.

6. No police officer or police staff should do or say anything with the intention of persuading a suspect who is entitled to a written translation of an essential document to waive that right. See *Notes M2* and *M3*.

7. For the purpose of the waiver:
    (a) the consent of a vulnerable person is only valid if the information about the circumstances under which they can waive the right and the reminder about their right to legal advice mentioned in *paragraphs 3 to 5* and their consent is given in the presence of the appropriate adult.

(b) the consent of a juvenile is only valid if their parent's or guardian's consent is also obtained unless the juvenile is under 14, when their parent's or guardian's consent is sufficient in its own right and the information and reminder mentioned in *subparagraph (a)* above and their consent is also given in the presence of the appropriate adult (who may or may not be a parent or guardian).

8.   The detainee, their solicitor or appropriate adult may make representations to the custody officer that a document which is not included in the table is essential and that a translation should be provided. The request may be refused if the officer is satisfied that the translation requested is not essential for the purposes described in *paragraph 1* above.

9.   If the custody officer has any doubts about
   • providing an oral translation or summary of an essential document instead of a written translation (see *paragraph 3*);
   • whether the suspect fully understands the consequences of waiving their right to a written translation of an essential document (see *paragraph 4*), or
   • about refusing to provide a translation of a requested document (see *paragraph 7*),
   the officer should seek advice from an inspector or above.

Documentation

10.   Action taken in accordance with this Annex shall be recorded in the detainee's custody record or interview record as appropriate (see Code C *paragraph 13.11(e)*).

Notes for Guidance

M1   *It is not necessary to disclose information in any translation which is capable of undermining or otherwise adversely affecting any investigative processes, for example, by enabling the suspect to fabricate an innocent explanation or to conceal lies from the interviewer.*

M2   *No police officer or police staff shall indicate to any suspect, except to answer a direct question, whether the period for which they are liable to be detained or if not detained, the time taken to complete the interview, might be reduced:*
   • *if they do not ask for legal advice before deciding whether they wish to waive their right to a written translation of an essential document; or*
   • *if they decide to waive their right to a written translation of an essential document.*

M3   *There is no power under PACE to detain a person or to delay their release solely to create and provide a written translation of any essential document.*

Annex N

Live-Link Interpretation (Para. 13.12)

Part 1: When the physical presence of the interpreter is not required.

1.   EU Directive 2010/64 (see *paragraph 13.1*), Article 2(6) provides 'Where appropriate, communication technology such as videoconferencing, telephone or the Internet may be used, unless the physical presence of the interpreter is required in order to safeguard the fairness of the proceedings.' This Article permits, but does not require the use of a live-link, and the following provisions of this Annex determine whether the use of a live-link is appropriate in any particular case.

2.   Decisions in accordance with this Annex that the physical presence of the interpreter is not required and to permit live-link interpretation, must be made on a case by case basis. Each decision must take account of the age, gender and vulnerability of the suspect, the nature and circumstances of the offence and the investigation and the impact on the suspect according to the particular purpose(s) for which the suspect requires the assistance of an interpreter and the time(s) when that assistance is required (see *Note N1*). For this reason, the custody officer in the case of a detained suspect, or in the case of a suspect who has not been arrested, the interviewer (subject to *paragraph 13.1(b)*), must consider whether the ability of the particular suspect, to communicate confidently and effectively for the purpose in question (see *paragraph 3*) is likely to be adversely affected or otherwise undermined or limited if the interpreter is not physically present and live-link interpretation is used. Although a suspect for whom an appropriate adult is required may be more likely to be adversely affected as described, it is important to note that a person who does not require an appropriate adult may also be adversely impacted by the use of live-link interpretation.

3.   Examples of purposes referred to in *paragraph 2* include:
   (a) understanding and appreciating their position having regard to any information given to them, or sought from them, in accordance with this or any other Code of Practice which, in particular, include:

- the caution (see *paragraphs C10.1* and *10.12*).
- the special warning (see *paragraphs 10.10* to *10.12*).
- information about the offence (see *paragraphs 10.3, 11.1A* and *Note 11ZA*).
- the grounds and reasons for detention (see *paragraphs 13.10* and *13.10A*).
- the translation of essential documents (see *paragraph 13.10B* and *Annex M*).
- their rights and entitlements (see *paragraph 3.12 and C3.21(b)*).
- intimate and non-intimate searches of detained persons at police stations.
- provisions and procedures to which Code D (Identification) applies concerning, for example, eye-witness identification, taking fingerprints, samples and photographs.

(b) understanding and seeking clarification from the interviewer of questions asked during an interview conducted and recorded in accordance with Code E or Code F and of anything else that is said by the interviewer and answering the questions.

(c) consulting privately with their solicitor and (if applicable) the appropriate adult (see *paragraphs 3.18, 13.2A, 13.6 and 13.9*):
   (i)   to help decide whether to answer questions put to them during interview; and
   (ii) about any other matter concerning their detention and treatment whilst in custody.

(d) communicating with practitioners and others who have some formal responsibility for, or an interest in, the health and welfare of the suspect. Particular examples include appropriate healthcare professionals (see *section 9* of this Code), Independent Custody Visitors and drug arrest referral workers.

4. If the custody officer or the interviewer (subject to *paragraph 13.1(b)*) is satisfied that for a particular purpose as described in *paragraphs 2 and 3 above*, the live-link interpretation *would not* adversely affect or otherwise undermine or limit the suspect's ability to communicate confidently and effectively for *that* purpose, they must so inform the suspect, their solicitor and (if applicable) the appropriate adult. At the same time, the operation of live-link interpretation must be explained and demonstrated to them, they must be advised of the chief officer's obligations concerning the security of live-link communications under *paragraph 13.13* (see *Note N2*) and they must be asked if they wish to make representations that live-link interpretation should not be used or if they require more information about the operation of the arrangements. They must also be told that at any time live-link interpretation is in use, they may make representations to the custody officer or the interviewer that its operation should cease and that the physical presence of an interpreter should be arranged.

When the authority of an inspector is required

5. If
   (i)   representations are made that live-link interpretation should not be used, or that at any time live-link interpretation is in use, its operation should cease and the physical presence of an interpreter arranged; and
   (ii) the custody officer or interviewer (subject to *paragraph 13.1(b)*) is unable to allay the concerns raised;
   then live-link interpretation may not be used, or (as the case may be) continue to be used, unless authorised in writing by an officer of the rank of inspector or above, in accordance with *paragraph 6*.

6. Authority may be given if the officer is satisfied that for the purpose(s) in question at the time an interpreter is required, live-link interpretation is necessary and justified. In making this decision, the officer must have regard to:
   (a) the circumstances of the suspect;
   (b) the nature and seriousness of the offence;
   (c) the requirements of the investigation, including its likely impact on both the suspect and any victim(s);
   (d) the representations made by the suspect, their solicitor and (if applicable) the appropriate adult that live-link interpretation should not be used (see *paragraph 5*);
   (e) the availability of a suitable interpreter to be *physically* present compared with the availability of a suitable interpreter for live-link interpretation (see *Note N3*); and
   (f) the risk if the interpreter is not *physically* present, evidence obtained using link interpretation might be excluded in subsequent criminal proceedings; and
   (g) the likely impact on the suspect and the investigation of any consequential delay to arrange for the interpreter to be *physically* present with the suspect.

7. For the purposes of Code E and live-link interpretation, there is no requirement to make a visual recording which shows the interpreter as viewed by the suspect and others present at the interview.

The audio recording required by that Code is sufficient. However, the authorising officer, in consultation with the officer in charge of the investigation, may direct that the interview is conducted and recorded in accordance with Code F. This will require the visual record to show the live-link interpretation arrangements and the interpreter as seen and experienced by the suspect during the interview. This should be considered if it appears that the admissibility of interview evidence might be challenged because the interpreter was not *physically* present or if the suspect, solicitor or appropriate adult make representations that Code F should be applied.

Documentation

8.   A record must be made of the actions, decisions, authorisations and outcomes arising from the requirements of this Annex. This includes representations made in accordance with *paragraphs 4* and *7*.

Part 2: Modifications for live-link interpretation

9.   The following modification shall apply for the purposes of live-link interpretation:

(a) **Code C paragraph 13.3:**

For the third sentence, substitute: 'A clear legible copy of the complete record shall be sent without delay via the live-link to the interviewer. The interviewer, after confirming with the suspect that the copy is legible and complete, shall allow the suspect to read the record, or have the record read to them by the interpreter and to sign the copy as correct or indicate the respects in which they consider it inaccurate. The interviewer is responsible for ensuring that that the signed copy and the original record made by the interpreter are retained with the case papers for use in evidence if required and must advise the interpreter of their obligation to keep the original record securely for that purpose.';

(b) **Code C paragraph 13.4:**

For sub-paragraph (b), substitute: 'A clear legible copy of the complete statement shall be sent without delay via the live-link to the interviewer. The interviewer, after confirming with the suspect that the copy is legible and complete, shall invite the suspect to sign it. The interviewer is responsible for ensuring that that the signed copy and the original record made by the interpreter are retained with the case papers for use in evidence if required and must advise the interpreter of their obligation to keep the original record securely for that purpose.';

(c) **Code C paragraph 13.7:**

After the first sentence, insert: 'A clear legible copy of the certified record must be sent without delay via the live-link to the interviewer. The interviewer is responsible for ensuring that the original certified record and the copy are retained with the case papers for use as evidence if required and must advise the interpreter of their obligation to keep the original record securely for that purpose.'

(d) **Code C paragraph 11.2, Code E paragraphs 3.4 and 4.3 and Code F paragraph 2.5 interviews**

At the beginning of each paragraph, insert: 'Before the interview commences, the operation of live-link interpretation shall be explained and demonstrated to the suspect, their solicitor and appropriate adult, unless it has been previously explained and demonstrated (see Code C *Annex N paragraph 4*).'

(e) **Code E, paragraph 3.20 (signing master recording label)**

After the third sentence, insert, 'If live-link interpretation has been used, the interviewer should ask the interpreter to observe the removal and sealing of the master recording and to confirm in writing that they have seen it sealed and signed by the interviewer. A clear legible copy of the confirmation signed by the interpreter must be sent via the live-link to the interviewer. The interviewer is responsible for ensuring that the original confirmation and the copy are retained with the case papers for use in evidence if required and must advise the interpreter of their obligation to keep the original confirmation securely for that purpose.'

Note: By virtue of *paragraphs 2.1* and *2.3 of Code F*, this applies when a visually recording to which Code F applies is made.

Notes for Guidance

N1   *For purposes other than an interview, audio-only live-link interpretation, for example by telephone (see Code C, paragraph 13.12(b)) may provide an appropriate option until an interpreter is physically present or audio-visual live-link interpretation becomes available. A particular example would be the initial action required when a detained suspect arrives at a police station to inform them of, and to explain, the reasons for their arrest and detention and their various rights and entitlements. Another example would be to inform the suspect by telephone, that an interpreter they will be able to see and hear is being arranged.*

In these circumstances, telephone live-link interpretation may help to allay the suspect's concerns and contribute to the completion of the risk assessment (see Code C, paragraph 3.6).

N2   *The explanation and demonstration of live-link interpretation is intended to help the suspect, solicitor and appropriate adult make an informed decision and to allay any concerns they may have.*

N3   *Factors affecting availability of a suitable interpreter will include the location of the police station and the language and type of interpretation (oral or sign language) required.*

PACE CODE D

CODE OF PRACTICE FOR THE IDENTIFICATION OF PERSONS BY POLICE OFFICERS

Commencement—Transitional Arrangements

This code has effect in relation to any identification procedure carried out after 00:00 on 23 February 2017.

1 Introduction

1.1   This Code of Practice concerns the principal methods used by police to identify people in connection with the investigation of offences and the keeping of accurate and reliable criminal records. The powers and procedures in this code must be used fairly, responsibly, with respect for the people to whom they apply and without unlawful discrimination. Under the Equality Act 2010, section 149 (Public sector Equality Duty), police forces must, in carrying out their functions, have due regard to the need to eliminate unlawful discrimination, harassment, victimisation and any other conduct which is prohibited by that Act, to advance equality of opportunity between people who share a relevant protected characteristic and people who do not share it, and to foster good relations between those persons. The Equality Act also makes it unlawful for police officers to discriminate against, harass or victimise any person on the grounds of the 'protected characteristics' of age, disability, gender reassignment, race, religion or belief, sex and sexual orientation, marriage and civil partnership, pregnancy and maternity when using their powers. See *Note 1A*.

1.2   In this Code, identification by an eye-witness arises when a witness who has seen the offender committing the crime and is given an opportunity to identify a person suspected of involvement in the offence in a video identification, identification parade or similar procedure. These eye-witness identification procedures which are in Part A of section 3 below, are designed to:
   • test the eye-witness' ability to identify the suspect as the person they saw on a previous occasion
   • provide safeguards against mistaken identification.
   While this Code concentrates on visual identification procedures, it does not prevent the police making use of aural identification procedures such as a 'voice identification parade', where they judge that appropriate. See *Note 1B*.

1.2A   In this Code, separate provisions in Part B of section 3 below, apply when any person, including a police officer, is asked if they recognise anyone they see in an image as being someone who is known to them and to test their claim that they recognise that person. These separate provisions are not subject to the eye-witnesses identification procedures described in *paragraph 1.2*.

1.2B   Part C applies when a film, photograph or image relating to the offence or any description of the suspect is broadcast or published in any national or local media or on any social networking site or on any local or national police communication systems.

1.3   Identification by fingerprints applies when a person's fingerprints are taken to:
   • compare with fingerprints found at the scene of a crime
   • check and prove convictions
   • help to ascertain a person's identity.

1.3A   Identification using footwear impressions applies when a person's footwear impressions are taken to compare with impressions found at the scene of a crime.

1.4   Identification by body samples and impressions includes taking samples such as a cheek swab, hair or blood to generate a DNA profile for comparison with material obtained from the scene of a crime, or a victim.

1.5   Taking photographs of arrested people applies to recording and checking identity and locating and tracing persons who:
   • are wanted for offences
   • fail to answer their bail.

1.6 Another method of identification involves searching and examining detained suspects to find, e.g., marks such as tattoos or scars which may help establish their identity or whether they have been involved in committing an offence.

1.7 The provisions of the Police and Criminal Evidence Act 1984 (PACE) and this Code are designed to make sure fingerprints, samples, impressions and photographs are taken, used and retained, and identification procedures carried out, only when justified and necessary for preventing, detecting or investigating crime. If these provisions are not observed, the application of the relevant procedures in particular cases may be open to question.

1.8 The provisions of this Code do not authorise, or otherwise permit, fingerprints or samples to be taken from a person detained solely for the purposes of assessment under section 136 of the Mental Health Act 1983.

Note for Guidance

1A *In paragraph 1.1, under the Equality Act 1949, section 149, the 'relevant protected characteristics' are: age, disability, gender reassignment, pregnancy and maternity, race, religion/belief, sex and sexual orientation. For further detailed guidance and advice on the Equality Act, see: https://www.gov.uk/guidance/equality-act-2010-guidance.*

1B *See Home Office Circular 57/2003 'Advice on the use of voice identification parades'.*

2 General

2.1 This Code must be readily available at all police stations for consultation by:
- police officers and police staff
- detained persons
- members of the public

2.2 The provisions of this Code:
- include the Annexes
- do not include the Notes for guidance.

2.3 Code C, *paragraph 1.4* and the *Notes for guidance* applicable to those provisions apply to this Code with regard to a suspected person who may be mentally disordered or otherwise mentally vulnerable.

2.4 Code C, *paragraphs 1.5* and *1.5A* and the *Notes for guidance* applicable to those provisions apply to this Code with regard to a suspected person who appears to be under the age of 18.

2.5 Code C, *paragraph 1.6* applies to this Code with regard to a suspected person who appears to be blind, seriously visually impaired, deaf, unable to read or speak or has difficulty communicating orally because of a speech impediment.

2.6 In this Code:
- 'appropriate adult' means the same as in Code C, *paragraph 1.7*
- 'solicitor' means the same as in Code C, *paragraph 6.12* and the *Notes for guidance* applicable to those provisions apply to this Code.
- where a search or other procedure under this Code may only be carried out or observed by a person of the same sex as the person to whom the search or procedure applies, the gender of the detainee and other persons present should be established and recorded in line with *Annex L* of Code C.

2.7 References to a custody officer include any police officer who, for the time being, is performing the functions of a custody officer, see *paragraph 1.9* of Code C.

2.8 When a record of any action requiring the authority of an officer of a specified rank is made under this Code, subject to *paragraph 2.18*, the officer's name and rank must be recorded.

2.9 When this Code requires the prior authority or agreement of an officer of at least inspector or superintendent rank, that authority may be given by a sergeant or chief inspector who has been authorised to perform the functions of the higher rank under PACE, section 107.

2.10 Subject to *paragraph 2.18*, all records must be timed and signed by the maker.

2.11 Records must be made in the custody record, unless otherwise specified. In any provision of this Code which allows or requires police officers or police staff to make a record in their report book, the reference to 'report book' shall include any official report book or electronic recording device issued to them that enables the record in question to be made and dealt with in accordance with that provision. References in this Code to written records, forms and signatures include electronic records and forms and electronic confirmation that identifies the person completing the record or form. Chief officers must be satisfied as to the integrity and security of the devices, records and forms to which this *paragraph* applies and that use of those devices, records and forms satisfies relevant data protection legislation. (taken from *Code C, paragraph 1.17*).

2.12 If any procedure in this Code requires a person's consent, the consent of a:

- mentally disordered or otherwise mentally vulnerable person is only valid if given in the presence of the appropriate adult
- juvenile is only valid if their parent's or guardian's consent is also obtained unless the juvenile is under 14, when their parent's or guardian's consent is sufficient in its own right. If the only obstacle to an identification procedure in *section 3* is that a juvenile's parent or guardian refuses consent or reasonable efforts to obtain it have failed, the identification officer may apply the provisions of *paragraph 3.21* (suspect known but not available). See *Note 2A*.

2.13 If a person is blind, seriously visually impaired or unable to read, the custody officer or identification officer shall make sure their solicitor, relative, appropriate adult or some other person likely to take an interest in them and not involved in the investigation is available to help check any documentation. When this Code requires written consent or signing, the person assisting may be asked to sign instead, if the detainee prefers. This paragraph does not require an appropriate adult to be called solely to assist in checking and signing documentation for a person who is not a juvenile, or mentally disordered or otherwise mentally vulnerable (see *Note 2B* and Code C, *paragraph 3.15*).

2.14 If any procedure in this Code requires information to be given to or sought from a suspect, it must be given or sought in the appropriate adult's presence if the suspect is mentally disordered, otherwise mentally vulnerable or a juvenile. If the appropriate adult is not present when the information is first given or sought, the procedure must be repeated in the presence of the appropriate adult when they arrive. If the suspect appears deaf or there is doubt about their hearing or speaking ability or ability to understand English, the custody officer or identification officer must ensure that the necessary arrangements in accordance with Code C are made for an interpreter to assist the suspect.

2.15 Any procedure in this Code involving the participation of a suspect who is mentally disordered, otherwise mentally vulnerable or a juvenile must take place in the presence of the appropriate adult. See Code C, *paragraph 1.4*.

2.15A Any procedure in this Code involving the participation of a witness who is or appears to be mentally disordered, otherwise mentally vulnerable or a juvenile should take place in the presence of a pre-trial support person unless the witness states that they do not want a support person to be present. A support person must not be allowed to prompt any identification of a suspect by a witness. See *Note 2AB*.

2.16 References to:
- 'taking a photograph', include the use of any process to produce a single, still or moving, visual image
- 'photographing a person', should be construed accordingly
- 'photographs', 'films', 'negatives' and 'copies' include relevant visual images recorded, stored, or reproduced through any medium
- 'destruction' includes the deletion of computer data relating to such images or making access to that data impossible

2.17 This Code does not affect or apply to, the powers and procedures:
  (i) for requiring and taking samples of breath, blood and urine in relation to driving offences, etc, when under the influence of drink, drugs or excess alcohol under the:
  - Road Traffic Act 1988, sections 4 to 11
  - Road Traffic Offenders Act 1988, sections 15 and 16
  - Transport and Works Act 1992, sections 26 to 38;
  (ii) under the Immigration Act 1971, Schedule 2, paragraph 18, for taking photographs, measuring and identifying and taking biometric information (not including DNA) from persons detained or liable to be detained under that Act, Schedule 2, paragraph 16 (Administrative Provisions as to Control on Entry etc.); or for taking fingerprints in accordance with the Immigration and Asylum Act 1999, sections 141 and 142(4), or other methods for collecting information about a person's external physical characteristics provided for by regulations made under that Act, section 144;
  (iii) under the Terrorism Act 2000, Schedule 8, for taking photographs, fingerprints, skin impressions, body samples or impressions from people:
  - arrested under that Act, section 41,
  - detained for the purposes of examination under that Act, Schedule 7, and to whom the Code of Practice issued under that Act, Schedule 14, paragraph 6, applies ('the terrorism provisions')
  (iv) for taking photographs, fingerprints, skin impressions, body samples or impressions from people who have been:

- arrested on warrants issued in Scotland, by officers exercising powers mentioned in Part X of the Criminal Justice and Public Order Act 1994;
- arrested or detained without warrant by officers from a police force in Scotland exercising their powers of arrest or detention mentioned in Part X of the Criminal Justice and Public Order Act 1994.

Note: In these cases, police powers and duties and the person's rights and entitlements whilst at a police station in England and Wales are the same as if the person had been arrested in Scotland by a Scottish police officer.

2.18   Nothing in this Code requires the identity of officers or police staff to be recorded or disclosed:

(a)   in the case of enquiries linked to the investigation of terrorism;

(b)   if the officers or police staff reasonably believe recording or disclosing their names might put them in danger.

In these cases, they shall use their warrant or other identification numbers and the name of their police station. *See Note 2D.*

2.19   In this Code:

(a)   'designated person' means a person other than a police officer, who has specified powers and duties conferred or imposed on them by designation under section 38 or 39 of the Police Reform Act 2002;

(b)   any reference to a police officer includes a designated person acting in the exercise or performance of the powers and duties conferred or imposed on them by their designation.

2.20   If a power conferred on a designated person:

(a)   allows reasonable force to be used when exercised by a police officer, a designated person exercising that power has the same entitlement to use force;

(b)   includes power to use force to enter any premises, that power is not exercisable by that designated person except:

(i)   in the company, and under the supervision, of a police officer; or

(ii)   for the purpose of:

- saving life or limb; or
- preventing serious damage to property.

2.21   In the case of a detained person, nothing in this Code prevents the custody officer, or other police officer or designated person given custody of the detainee by the custody officer for the purposes of the investigation of an offence for which the person is detained, from allowing another person (see *(a)* and *(b)* below) to carry out individual procedures or tasks at the police station if the law allows. However, the officer or designated person given custody remains responsible for making sure the procedures and tasks are carried out correctly in accordance with the Codes of Practice. The other person who is allowed to carry out the procedures or tasks must be *someone who at that time* is:

(a)   under the direction and control of the chief officer of the force responsible for the police station in question; or

(b)   providing services under contractual arrangements (but without being employed by the chief officer [of] the police force), to assist a police force in relation to the discharge of its chief officer's functions.

2.22   Designated persons and others mentioned in *sub-paragraphs (a)* and *(b)* of *paragraph 2.21* must have regard to any relevant provisions of the Codes of Practice.

Notes for Guidance

2A   *For the purposes of paragraph 2.12, the consent required from a parent or guardian may, for a juvenile in the care of a local authority or voluntary organisation, be given by that authority or organisation. In the case of a juvenile, nothing in paragraph 2.12 requires the parent, guardian or representative of a local authority or voluntary organisation to be present to give their consent, unless they are acting as the appropriate adult under paragraphs 2.14 or 2.15. However, it is important that a parent or guardian not present is fully informed before being asked to consent. They must be given the same information about the procedure and the juvenile's suspected involvement in the offence as the juvenile and appropriate adult. The parent or guardian must also be allowed to speak to the juvenile and the appropriate adult if they wish. Provided the consent is fully informed and is not withdrawn, it may be obtained at any time before the procedure takes place.*

2AB   *The Youth Justice and Criminal Evidence Act 1999 guidance 'Achieving Best Evidence in Criminal Proceedings' indicates that a pre-trial support person should accompany a vulnerable witness during any identification procedure unless the witness states that they do not want a support person to be present. It states that this support person should not be (or not be likely to be) a witness in the investigation.*

2B   *People who are seriously visually impaired or unable to read may be unwilling to sign police documents. The alternative, i.e. their representative signing on their behalf, seeks to protect the interests of both police and suspects.*

2C   *Not used*

2D   *The purpose of paragraph 2.18(b) is to protect those involved in serious organised crime investigations or arrests of particularly violent suspects when there is reliable information that those arrested or their associates may threaten or cause harm to the officers. In cases of doubt, an officer of inspector rank or above should be consulted.*

3 Identification and recognition of suspects

Part (A)   *Identification of a suspect by an eye-witness*

3.0   This part applies when an eye-witness has seen a person committing a crime or in any other circumstances which tend to prove or disprove the involvement of the person they saw in a crime, for example, close to the scene of the crime, immediately before or immediately after it was committed. It sets out the procedures to be used to test the ability of that eye-witness to identify a person suspected of involvement in the offence ('the suspect') as the person they saw on the previous occasion. This part does not apply to the procedure described in Part B (see *Note 3AA*) which is used to test the ability of someone who is not an eye-witness, to recognise anyone whose image they see.

3.1   A record shall be made of the description of the suspect as first given by the eye-witness .This record must:

(a)   be made and kept in a form which enables details of that description to be accurately produced from it, in a visible and legible form, which can be given to the suspect or the suspect's solicitor in accordance with this Code; and

(b)   unless otherwise specified, be made before the eye-witness takes part in any identification procedures under *paragraphs 3.5 to 3.10, 3.21, 3.23* or *Annex E* (Showing Photographs to Eye-Witnesses).

A copy of the record shall where practicable, be given to the suspect or their solicitor before any procedures under *paragraphs 3.5 to 3.10, 3.21 or 3.23* are carried out. See *Note 3E*.

3.1A References in this Part:

(a)   to the identity of the suspect being 'known' mean that there is sufficient information known to the police to establish, in accordance with Code G (Arrest), that there are reasonable grounds to suspect a particular person of involvement in the offence;

(b)   to the suspect being 'available' mean that the suspect is immediately available, or will be available within a reasonably short time, in order that they can be invited to take part in at least one of the eye-witness identification procedures under *paragraphs 3.5 to 3.10* and it is practicable to arrange an effective procedure under *paragraphs 3.5 to 3.10*; and

(c)   to the eye-witness identification procedures under *paragraphs 3.5 to 3.10* mean:
- Video identification (*paragraphs 3.5* and *3.6*);
- Identification parade (*paragraphs 3.7* and *3.8*); and
- Group identification (*paragraphs 3.9* and *3.10*).

(a) Cases when the suspect's identity is not known

3.2   In cases when the suspect's identity is not known, an eye-witness may be taken to a particular neighbourhood or place to see whether they can identify the person they saw on a previous occasion. Although the number, age, sex, race, general description and style of clothing of other people present at the location and the way in which any identification is made cannot be controlled, the principles applicable to the formal procedures under *paragraphs 3.5 to 3.10* shall be followed as far as practicable. For example:

(a)   where it is practicable to do so, a record should be made of the eye-witness' description of the person they saw on the previous occasion, as in *paragraph 3.1(a)*, before asking the eye-witness to make an identification;

(b)   Care must be taken not [to] provide the eye-witness with any information concerning the description of the suspect (if such information is available) and not to direct the eyewitness' attention to any individual unless, taking into account all the circumstances, this cannot be avoided. However, this does not prevent an eye-witness being asked to look carefully at the people around at the time or to look towards a group or in a particular direction, if this appears necessary to make sure that the witness does not overlook a possible suspect simply because the eye-witness is looking in the opposite direction and also to enable the eye-witness to make comparisons between any suspect and others who are in the area;

(c) where there is more than one eye-witness, every effort should be made to keep them separate and eye-witnesses should be taken to see whether they can identify a person independently;

(d) once there is sufficient information to establish, in accordance with *paragraph 3.1A(a)*, that the suspect is 'known', e.g. after the eye-witness makes an identification, the provisions set out from *paragraph 3.4* onwards shall apply for that and any other eyewitnesses in relation to that individual;

(e) the officer or police staff accompanying the eye-witness must record, in their report book, the action taken as soon as practicable and in as much detail, as possible. The record should include:

(i) the date, time and place of the relevant occasion when the eye-witness claims to have previously seen the person committing the offence in question or in any other circumstances which tend to prove or disprove the involvement of the person they saw in a crime (see *paragraph 3.0*); and

(ii) where any identification was made:
- how it was made and the conditions at the time (e.g., the distance the eyewitness was from the suspect, the weather and light);
- if the eye-witness's attention was drawn to the suspect; the reason for this;
- and anything said by the eye-witness or the suspect about the identification or the conduct of the procedure.

See *Note 3F.*

3.3 An eye-witness must not be shown photographs, computerised or artist's composite likenesses or similar likenesses or pictures (including 'E-fit' images) if in accordance with *paragraph 3.1A*, the identity of the suspect is known and they are available to take part in one of the procedures under *paragraphs 3.5 to 3.10*. If the suspect's identity is not known, the showing of any such images to an eye-witness to see if they can identify a person whose image they are shown as the person they saw on a previous occasion must be done in accordance with *Annex E.*

(b) Cases when the suspect is known and available

3.4 If the suspect's identity is known to the police (see *paragraph 3.1A(a)*) and they are available (see *paragraph 3.1A(b)*), the identification procedures that may be used are set out in *paragraphs 3.5 to 3.10* below as follows:

(i) video identification;
(ii) identification parade; or
(iii) group identification.

(i) Video identification

3.5 A 'video identification' is when the eye-witness is shown images of a known suspect, together with similar images of others who resemble the suspect. *Moving* images must be used unless the conditions in *sub-paragraph (a)* or *(b)* below apply:

(a) this sub-paragraph applies if:

(i) the identification officer, in consultation with the officer in charge of the investigation, is satisfied that because of aging, or other physical changes or differences, the appearance of the suspect has significantly changed since the previous occasion when the eye-witness claims to have seen the suspect (see *paragraph 3.0* and *Note 3ZA*);

(ii) an image (moving or still) is available which the identification officer and the officer in charge of the investigation reasonably believe shows the appearance of the suspect as it was at the time the suspect was seen by the eye-witness; and

(iii) having regard to the extent of change and the purpose of eye-witness identification procedures (see *paragraph 3.0*), the identification officer believes that that such an image should be shown to the eye-witness.

In such a case, the identification officer may arrange a video identification procedure using the image described in (ii). In accordance with the 'Notice to suspect' (see *paragraph 3.17(vi)*), the suspect must first be given an opportunity to provide their own image(s) for use in the procedure but it is for the identification officer and officer in charge of the investigation to decide whether, following (ii) and (iii), any image(s) provided by the suspect should be used.

A video identification using an image described above may, at the discretion of the identification officer be arranged in addition to, or as an alternative to, a video identification using *moving* images taken after the suspect has been given the information and notice described in *paragraphs 3.17* and *3.18*.

See *paragraph 3.21* and *Note 3D* in any case where the suspect deliberately takes steps to frustrate the eye-witness identification arrangements and procedures.

(b) this sub-paragraph applies if, in accordance with *paragraph 2A* of *Annex A* of this Code, the identification officer does not consider that replication of a physical feature or concealment of the location of the feature can be achieved using a moving image. In these cases, still images may be used.

3.6   Video identifications must be carried out in accordance with *Annex A*.

(ii) Identification parade

3.7   An 'identification parade' is when the eye-witness sees the suspect in a line of others who resemble the suspect.

3.8   Identification parades must be carried out in accordance with *Annex B*.

(iii) Group identification

3.9   A 'group identification' is when the eye-witness sees the suspect in an informal group of people.

3.10   Group identifications must be carried out in accordance with *Annex C*.

Arranging eye-witness identification procedures – duties of identification officer

3.11   Except as provided for in *paragraph 3.19*, the arrangements for, and conduct of, the eyewitness identification procedures in *paragraphs 3.5* to *3.10* and circumstances in which any such identification procedure must be held shall be the responsibility of an officer not below inspector rank who is not involved with the investigation ('the identification officer'). The identification officer may direct another officer or police staff, see *paragraph 2.21*, to make arrangements for, and to conduct, any of these identification procedures and except as provided for in *paragraph 7* of *Annex A*, any reference in this section to the identification officer includes the officer or police staff to whom the arrangements for, and/or conduct of, any of these procedure has been delegated. In delegating these arrangements and procedures, the identification officer must be able to supervise effectively and either intervene or be contacted for advice. Where any action referred to in this paragraph is taken by another officer or police staff at the direction of the identification officer, the outcome shall, as soon as practicable, be reported to the identification officer. For the purpose of these procedures, the identification officer retains overall responsibility for ensuring that the procedure complies with this Code and in addition, in the case of detained suspect, their care and treatment until returned to the custody officer. Except as permitted by this Code, no officer or any other person involved with the investigation of the case against the suspect may take any part in these procedures or act as the identification officer.

This paragraph does not prevent the identification officer from consulting the officer in charge of the investigation to determine which procedure to use. When an identification procedure is required, in the interest of fairness to suspects and eye-witnesses, it must be held as soon as practicable.

Circumstances in which an eye-witness identification procedure must be held

3.12   If, before any identification procedure set out in *paragraphs 3.5* to *3.10* has been held
(a)   an eye-witness has identified a suspect or purported to have identified them; or
(b)   there is an eye-witness available who expresses an ability to identify the suspect; or
(c)   there is a reasonable chance of an eye-witness being able to identify the suspect,
and the eye-witness in (a) to (c) has not been given an opportunity to identify the suspect in any of the procedures set out in *paragraphs 3.5* to *3.10*, then an identification procedure shall be held if the suspect disputes being the person the eye-witness claims to have seen on a previous occasion (see *paragraph 3.0*), unless:
(i)   it is not practicable to hold any such procedure; or
(ii)   any such procedure would serve no useful purpose in proving or disproving whether the suspect was involved in committing the offence, for example
• where the suspect admits being at the scene of the crime and gives an account of what took place and the eye-witness does not see anything which contradicts that; or
• when it is not disputed that the suspect is already known to the eye-witness who claims to have recognised them when seeing them commit the crime.

3.13   An eye-witness identification procedure may also be held if the officer in charge of the investigation, after consultation with the identification officer, considers it would be useful.

Selecting an eye-witness identification procedure

3.14 If, because of *paragraph 3.12*, an identification procedure is to be held, the suspect shall initially be invited to take part in a video identification unless:

(a) a video identification is not practicable; or

(b) an identification parade is both practicable and more suitable than a video identification; or

(c) *paragraph 3.16* applies.

The identification officer and the officer in charge of the investigation shall consult each other to determine which option is to be offered. An identification parade may not be practicable because of factors relating to the witnesses, such as their number, state of health, availability and travelling requirements. A video identification would normally be more suitable if it could be arranged and completed sooner than an identification parade. Before an option is offered the suspect must also be reminded of their entitlement to have free legal advice, see Code C, *paragraph 6.5*.

3.15 A suspect who refuses the identification procedure in which the suspect is first invited to take part shall be asked to state their reason for refusing and may get advice from their solicitor and/or if present, their appropriate adult. The suspect, solicitor and/or appropriate adult shall be allowed to make representations about why another procedure should be used. A record should be made of the reasons for refusal and any representations made. After considering any reasons given, and representations made, the identification officer shall, if appropriate, arrange for the suspect to be invited to take part in an alternative which the officer considers suitable and practicable. If the officer decides it is not suitable and practicable to invite the suspect to take part in an alternative identification procedure, the reasons for that decision shall be recorded.

3.16 A suspect may initially be invited to take part in a group identification if the officer in charge of the investigation considers it is more suitable than a video identification or an identification parade and the identification officer considers it practicable to arrange.

Notice to suspect

3.17 Unless *paragraph 3.20* applies, before any eye-witness identification procedure set out in *paragraphs 3.5* to *3.10* is arranged, the following shall be explained to the suspect:

(i) the purpose of the procedure (see *paragraph 3.0*);

(ii) their entitlement to free legal advice; see Code C, *paragraph 6.5*;

(iii) the procedures for holding it, including their right, subject to *Annex A, paragraph 9*, to have a solicitor or friend present;

(iv) that they do not have to consent to or co-operate in the procedure;

(v) that if they do not consent to, and co-operate in, a procedure, their refusal may be given in evidence in any subsequent trial and police may proceed covertly without their consent or make other arrangements to test whether an eye-witness can identify them, see *paragraph 3.21*;

(vi) whether, for the purposes of a video identification procedure, images of them have previously been obtained either:

• in accordance with *paragraph 3.20*, and if so, that they may co-operate in providing further, suitable images to be used instead; or

• in accordance with *paragraph 3.5(a)*, and if so, that they may provide their own images for the identification officer to consider using.

(vii) if appropriate, the special arrangements for juveniles;

(viii) if appropriate, the special arrangements for mentally disordered or otherwise mentally vulnerable people;

(ix) that if they significantly alter their appearance between being offered an identification procedure and any attempt to hold an identification procedure, this may be given in evidence if the case comes to trial, and the identification officer may then consider other forms of identification, see *paragraph 3.21* and *Note 3C*;

(x) that a moving image or photograph may be taken of them when they attend for any identification procedure;

(xi) whether, before their identity became known, the eye-witness was shown photographs, a computerised or artist's composite likeness or similar likeness or image by the police, see *Note 3B*;

(xii) that if they change their appearance before an identification parade, it may not be practicable to arrange one on the day or subsequently and, because of the appearance change, the identification officer may consider alternative methods of identification, see *Note 3C*;

(xiii) that they or their solicitor will be provided with details of the description of the suspect as first given by any eye-witnesses who are to attend the procedure or confrontation, see *paragraph 3.1.*

3.18 This information must also be recorded in a written notice handed to the suspect. The suspect must be given a reasonable opportunity to read the notice, after which, they should be asked to sign a copy of the notice to indicate if they are willing to co-operate with the making of a video or take part in the identification parade or group identification. The signed copy shall be retained by the identification officer.

3.19 In the case of a detained suspect, the duties under *paragraphs 3.17* and *3.18* may be performed by the custody officer or by another officer or police staff not involved in the investigation as directed by the custody officer, if:

(a) it is proposed to release the suspect in order that an identification procedure can be arranged and carried out and an inspector is not available to act as the identification officer, see *paragraph 3.11*, before the suspect leaves the station; or

(b) it is proposed to keep the suspect in police detention whilst the procedure is arranged and carried out and waiting for an inspector to act as the identification officer, see *paragraph 3.11*, would cause unreasonable delay to the investigation.

The officer concerned shall inform the identification officer of the action taken and give them the signed copy of the notice. See *Note 3C.*

3.20 If the identification officer and officer in charge of the investigation suspect, on reasonable grounds that if the suspect was given the information and notice as in *paragraphs 3.17* and *3.18*, they would then take steps to avoid being seen by a witness in any identification procedure, the identification officer may arrange for images of the suspect suitable for use in a video identification procedure to be obtained before giving the information and notice. If suspect's images are obtained in these circumstances, the suspect may, for the purposes of a video identification procedure, co-operate in providing new images which if suitable, would be used instead, see *paragraph 3.17(vi).*

(c) Cases when the suspect is known but not available

3.21 When a known suspect is not available or has ceased to be available, see *paragraph 3.1A*, the identification officer may make arrangements for a video identification (see *paragraph 3.5* and *Annex A*). If necessary, the identification officer may follow the video identification procedures using any suitable moving or still images and these may be obtained covertly if necessary. Alternatively, the identification officer may make arrangements for a group identification without the suspect's consent (see *Annex C, paragraph 34*). See *Note 3D.* These provisions may also be applied to juveniles where the consent of their parent or guardian is either refused or reasonable efforts to obtain that consent have failed (see *paragraph 2.12*).

3.22 Any covert activity should be strictly limited to that necessary to test the ability of the eyewitness to identify the suspect as the person they saw on the relevant previous occasion.

3.23 The identification officer may arrange for the suspect to be confronted by the eye-witness if none of the options referred to in *paragraphs 3.5* to *3.10* or *3.21* are practicable. A 'confrontation' is when the suspect is directly confronted by the eye-witness. A confrontation does not require the suspect's consent. Confrontations must be carried out in accordance with *Annex D.*

3.24 Requirements for information to be given to, or sought from, a suspect or for the suspect to be given an opportunity to view images before they are shown to an eye-witness, do not apply if the suspect's lack of co-operation prevents the necessary action.

(d) Documentation

3.25 A record shall be made of the video identification, identification parade, group identification or confrontation on forms provided for the purpose.

3.26 If the identification officer considers it is not practicable to hold a video identification or identification parade requested by the suspect, the reasons shall be recorded and explained to the suspect.

3.27 A record shall be made of a person's failure or refusal to co-operate in a video identification, identification parade or group identification and, if applicable, of the grounds for obtaining images in accordance with *paragraph 3.20.*

(e) Not used

3.28 *Not used.*

3.29 *Not used.*

(f) Destruction and retention of photographs taken or used in eye-witness identification procedures

3.30 PACE, section 64A, see *paragraph 5.12*, provides powers to take photographs of suspects and allows these photographs to be used or disclosed only for purposes related to the prevention or detection of crime, the investigation of offences or the conduct of prosecutions by, or on behalf of, police or other law enforcement and prosecuting authorities inside and outside the United Kingdom or the enforcement of a sentence. After being so used or disclosed, they may be retained but can only be used or disclosed for the same purposes.

3.31 Subject to *paragraph 3.33*, the photographs (and all negatives and copies), of suspects *not* taken in accordance with the provisions in *paragraph 5.12* which are taken for the purposes of, or in connection with, the identification procedures in *paragraphs 3.5 to 3.10, 3.21* or *3.23* must be destroyed unless the suspect:

(a) is charged with, or informed they may be prosecuted for, a recordable offence;

(b) is prosecuted for a recordable offence;

(c) is cautioned for a recordable offence or given a warning or reprimand in accordance with the Crime and Disorder Act 1998 for a recordable offence; or

(d) gives informed consent, in writing, for the photograph or images to be retained for purposes described in *paragraph 3.30*.

3.32 When *paragraph 3.31* requires the destruction of any photograph, the person must be given an opportunity to witness the destruction or to have a certificate confirming the destruction if they request one within five days of being informed that the destruction is required.

3.33 Nothing in *paragraph 3.31* affects any separate requirement under the Criminal Procedure and Investigations Act 1996 to retain material in connection with criminal investigations.

Part (B) *Recognition by controlled showing of films, photographs and images*

3.34 This Part of this section applies when, for the purposes of obtaining evidence of recognition, arrangements are made for a person, including a police officer, who is not an eye-witness (see *Note 3AA*):

(a) to view a film, photograph or any other visual medium; and

(b) on the occasion of the viewing, to be asked whether they recognise anyone whose image is shown in the material as someone who is known to them.

The arrangements for such viewings may be made by the officer in charge of the relevant investigation. Although there is no requirement for the identification officer to make the arrangements or to be consulted about the arrangements, nothing prevents this. See *Notes 3AA* and *3G*.

3.35 To provide safeguards against mistaken recognition and to avoid any possibility of collusion, on the occasion of the viewing, the arrangements should ensure:

(a) that the films, photographs and other images are shown on an individual basis;

(b) that any person who views the material;

(i) is unable to communicate with any other individual to whom the material has been, or is to be, shown;

(ii) is not reminded of any photograph or description of any individual whose image is shown or given any other indication as to the identity of any such individual;

(iii) is not . . . told whether a previous witness has recognised any one;

(c) that immediately before a person views the material, they are told that:

(i) an individual who is known to them may, or may not, appear in the material they are shown and that if they do not recognise anyone, they should say so;

(ii) at any point, they may ask to see a particular part of the material frozen for them to study and there is no limit on how many times they can view the whole or any part or parts of the material; and

(d) that the person who views the material is not asked to make any decision as to whether they recognise anyone whose image they have seen as someone known to them until they have seen the whole of the material at least twice, unless the officer in charge of the viewing decides that because of the number of images the person has been invited to view, it would not be reasonable to ask them to view the whole of the material for a second time. A record of this decision must be included in the record that is made in accordance with *paragraph 3.36*. (see *Note 3G*).

3.36 A record of the circumstances and conditions under which the person is given an opportunity to recognise an individual must be made and the record must include:

(a) whether the person knew or was given information concerning the name or identity of any suspect;

(b) what the person has been told *before* the viewing about the offence, the person(s) depicted in the images or the offender and by whom;

(c) how and by whom the witness was asked to view the image or look at the individual;

(d) whether the viewing was alone or with others and if with others, the reason for it;

(e) the arrangements under which the person viewed the film or saw the individual and by whom those arrangements were made;

(f) subject to *paragraph 2.18*, the name and rank of the officer responsible for deciding that the viewing arrangements should be made in accordance with this Part;

(g) the date time and place images were viewed or further viewed or the individual was seen;

(h) the times between which the images were viewed or the individual was seen;

(i) how the viewing of images or sighting of the individual was controlled and by whom;

(j) whether the person was familiar with the location shown in any images or the place where they saw the individual and if so, why;

(k) whether or not, on this occasion, the person claims to recognise any image shown, or any individual seen, as being someone known to them, and if they do:

    (i) the reason;

    (ii) the words of recognition;

    (iii) any expressions of doubt; and

    (iv) what features of the image or the individual triggered the recognition.

3.37 The record required under *paragraph 3.36* may be made by the person who views the image or sees the individual and makes the recognition; and if applicable, by the officer or police staff in charge of showing the images to that person or in charge of the conditions under which that person sees the individual. The person must be asked to read and check the completed record and as applicable, confirm that it is correctly and accurately reflects the part they played in the viewing (see *Note 3H*).

Part (C) *Recognition by uncontrolled viewing of films, photographs and images*

3.38 This Part applies when, for the purpose of identifying and tracing suspects, films and photographs of incidents or other images are:

(a) shown to the public (which may include police officers and police staff as well as members of the public) through the national or local media or any social media networking site; or

(b) circulated through local or national police communication systems for viewing by police officers and police staff; and the viewing is not formally controlled and supervised as set out in Part B.

3.39 A copy of the relevant material released to the national or local media for showing as described in *sub-paragraph 3.38(a)*, shall be kept. The suspect or their solicitor shall be allowed to view such material before any eye-witness identification procedure under *paragraphs 3.5* to *3.10*, *3.21* or *3.23* of Part A are carried out, provided it is practicable and would not unreasonably delay the investigation. This paragraph does not affect any separate requirement under the Criminal Procedure and Investigations Act 1996 to retain material in connection with criminal investigations that might apply to *sub-paragraphs 3.38(a)* and *(b)*.

3.40 Each eye-witness involved in any eye-witness identification procedure under *paragraphs 3.5* to *3.10*, *3.21* or *3.23* shall be asked, *after they have taken part*, whether they have seen any film, photograph or image relating to the offence or any description of the suspect which has been broadcast or published as described in *paragraph 3.38(a)* and their reply recorded. If they have, they should be asked to give details of the circumstances and subject to the eye-witness's recollection, the record described in *paragraph 3.41* should be completed.

3.41 As soon as practicable after an individual (member of the public, police officer or police staff) indicates in response to a viewing that they may have information relating to the identity and whereabouts of anyone they have seen in that viewing, arrangements should be made to ensure that they are asked to give details of the circumstances and, subject to the individual's recollection, a record of the circumstances and conditions under which the viewing took place is made. This record shall be made in accordance with the provisions of *paragraph 3.36* insofar as they can be applied to the viewing in question (*see Note 3H*).

Notes for Guidance

3AA *The eye-witness identification procedures in Part A should not be used to test whether a witness can recognise a person as someone they know and would be able to give evidence of recognition along the lines that 'On (describe date, time, location and circumstances) I saw an image of an individual who I recognised as AB.' In these cases, the procedures in Part B shall apply if the viewing is controlled and the procedure in Part C shall apply if the viewing is not controlled.*

3ZA   *In paragraph 3.5(a)(i), examples of physical changes or differences that the identification officer may wish to consider include hair style and colour, weight, facial hair, wearing or removal of spectacles and tinted contact lenses, facial injuries, tattoos and makeup.*

3A   *Except for the provisions of Annex E, paragraph 1, a police officer who is a witness for the purposes of this part of the Code is subject to the same principles and procedures as a civilian witness.*

3B   *When an eye-witness attending an identification procedure has previously been shown photographs, or been shown or provided with computerised or artist's composite likenesses, or similar likenesses or pictures, it is the officer in charge of the investigation's responsibility to make the identification officer aware of this.*

3C   *The purpose of paragraph 3.19 is to avoid or reduce delay in arranging identification procedures by enabling the required information and warnings, see sub-paragraphs 3.17(ix) and 3.17(xii), to be given at the earliest opportunity.*

3D   *Paragraph 3.21 would apply when a known suspect becomes 'unavailable' and thereby delays or frustrates arrangements for obtaining identification evidence. It also applies when a suspect refuses or fails to take part in a video identification, an identification parade or a group identification, or refuses or fails to take part in the only practicable options from that list. It enables any suitable images of the suspect, moving or still, which are available or can be obtained, to be used in an identification procedure. Examples include images from custody and other CCTV systems and from visually recorded interview records, see Code F Note for Guidance 2D.*

3E   *When it is proposed to show photographs to a witness in accordance with Annex E, it is the responsibility of the officer in charge of the investigation to confirm to the officer responsible for supervising and directing the showing, that the first description of the suspect given by that eye-witness has been recorded. If this description has not been recorded, the procedure under Annex E must be postponed, see Annex E, paragraph 2.*

3F   *The admissibility and value of identification evidence obtained when carrying out the procedure under paragraph 3.2 may be compromised if:*
      (a) before a person is identified, the eye-witness' attention is specifically drawn to that person; or
      (b) the suspect's identity becomes known before the procedure.

3G   *The admissibility and value of evidence of recognition obtained when carrying out the procedures in Part B may be compromised if, before the person is recognised, the witness who has claimed to know them is given or is made, or becomes aware of, information about the person which was not previously known to them personally but which they have purported to rely on to support their claim that the person is in fact known to them.*

3H   *It is important that the record referred to in paragraphs 3.36 and 3.41 is made as soon as practicable after the viewing and whilst it is fresh in the mind of the individual who makes the recognition.*

4 *Identification by fingerprints and footwear impressions*

(A) *Taking fingerprints in connection with a criminal investigation*

(a) General

4.1   References to 'fingerprints' means any record, produced by any method, of the skin pattern and other physical characteristics or features of a person's:
      (i)   fingers; or
      (ii) palms.

(b) Action

4.2   A person's fingerprints may be taken in connection with the investigation of an offence only with their consent or if *paragraph 4.3* applies. If the person is at a police station, consent must be in writing.

4.3   PACE, section 61, provides powers to take fingerprints without consent from any person aged ten or over as follows:
      (a) under *section 61(3)*, from a person detained at a police station in consequence of being arrested for a recordable offence, see *Note 4A*, if they have not had their fingerprints taken in the course of the investigation of the offence unless those previously taken fingerprints are not a complete set or some or all of those fingerprints are not of sufficient quality to allow satisfactory analysis, comparison or matching.
      (b) under *section 61(4)*, from a person detained at a police station who has been charged with a recordable offence, see *Note 4A*, or informed they will be reported for such an offence if they have not had their fingerprints taken in the course of the investigation of the offence unless those previously taken fingerprints are not a complete set or some or all of those fingerprints are not of sufficient quality to allow satisfactory analysis, comparison or matching.

(c) under *section 61(4A)*, from a person who has been bailed to appear at a court or police station if the person:

  (i)   has answered to bail for a person whose fingerprints were taken previously and there are reasonable grounds for believing they are not the same person; or

  (ii) who has answered to bail claims to be a different person from a person whose fingerprints were previously taken;

  and in either case, the court or an officer of inspector rank or above, authorises the fingerprints to be taken at the court or police station (an inspector's authority may be given in writing or orally and confirmed in writing, as soon as practicable);

(ca) under *section 61(5A)* from a person who has been arrested for a recordable offence and released if the person:

  (i)   is on bail and has not had their fingerprints taken in the course of the investigation of the offence, or;

  (ii) has had their fingerprints taken in the course of the investigation of the offence, but they do not constitute a complete set or some, or all, of the fingerprints are not of sufficient quality to allow satisfactory analysis, comparison or matching.

(cb) under *section 61(5B)* from a person not detained at a police station who has been charged with a recordable offence or informed they will be reported for such an offence if:

  (i)   they have not had their fingerprints taken in the course of the investigation; or

  (ii) their fingerprints have been taken in the course of the investigation of the offence but either:

  • they do not constitute a complete set or some, or all, of the fingerprints are not of sufficient quality to allow satisfactory analysis, comparison or matching; or

  • the investigation was discontinued but subsequently resumed and, before the resumption, their fingerprints were destroyed pursuant to section 63D(3).

(d) under *section 61(6)*, from a person who has been:

  (i)   convicted of a recordable offence; or

  (ii) given a caution in respect of a recordable offence (see *Note 4A*) which, at the time of the caution, the person admitted;

    if, since being convicted or cautioned:

  • their fingerprints have not been taken; or

  • their fingerprints which have been taken do not constitute a complete set or some, or all, of the fingerprints are not of sufficient quality to allow satisfactory analysis, comparison or matching;

  and in either case, an officer of inspector rank or above is satisfied that taking the fingerprints is necessary to assist in the prevention or detection of crime and authorises the taking;

(e) under *section 61(6A)* from a person a constable reasonably suspects is committing or attempting to commit, or has committed or attempted to commit, any offence if either:

  (i)   the person's name is unknown to, and cannot be readily ascertained by, the constable; or

  (ii) the constable has reasonable grounds for doubting whether a name given by the person as their name is their real name.

  Note: fingerprints taken under this power are not regarded as having been taken in the course of the investigation of an offence. [See *Note 4C*]

(f) under *section 61(6D)* from a person who has been convicted outside England and Wales of an offence which if committed in England and Wales would be a qualifying offence as defined by PACE, section 65A (see *Note 4AB*) if:

  (i)   the person's fingerprints have not been taken previously under this power or their fingerprints have been so taken on a previous occasion but they do not constitute a complete set or some, or all, of the fingerprints are not of sufficient quality to allow satisfactory analysis, comparison or matching; and

  (ii) a police officer of inspector rank or above is satisfied that taking fingerprints is necessary to assist in the prevention or detection of crime and authorises them to be taken.

4.4   PACE, section 63A(4) and Schedule 2A provide powers to:

(a) make a requirement (in accordance with *Annex G*) for a person to attend a police station to have their fingerprints taken in the exercise of one of the following powers (described in *paragraph 4.3* above) within certain periods as follows:

  (i)   *section 61(5A)* – Persons arrested for a recordable offence and released, see *paragraph 4.3(ca)*: In the case of a person whose fingerprints were taken in the course of the investigation but those fingerprints do not constitute a complete set or some, or all, of the fingerprints are not of sufficient quality, the requirement may not be made more than six months from the day the investigating officer was informed that the fingerprints previously taken were incomplete or below standard. In the case of a person whose fingerprints were destroyed prior to the resumption of the investigation, the requirement may not be made more than six months from the day on which the investigation resumed.

(ii) *section 61(5B)* – Persons not detained at a police station charged etc. with a recordable offence, see *paragraph 4.3(cb)*: The requirement may not be made more than six months from:

- the day the person was charged or informed that they would be reported,
- if fingerprints have not been taken in the course of the investigation of the offence; or
- the day the investigating officer was informed that the fingerprints previously taken were incomplete or below standard, if fingerprints have been taken in the course of the investigation but those fingerprints do not constitute a complete set or some, or all, of the fingerprints are not of sufficient quality; or
- the day on which the investigation was resumed, in the case of a person whose fingerprints were destroyed prior to the resumption of the investigation.

(iii) *section 61(6)* – Persons convicted or cautioned for a recordable offence in England and Wales, see *paragraph 4.3(d)*: Where the offence for which the person was convicted or cautioned is a qualifying offence (see *Note 4AB*), there is no time limit for the exercise of this power. Where the conviction or caution is for a recordable offence which is not a qualifying offence, the requirement may not be made more than two years from:

- in the case of a person who has not had their fingerprints taken since the conviction or caution, the day on which the person was convicted or cautioned, or, if later, the day on which Schedule 2A came into force (March 7, 2011), ; or
- in the case of a person whose fingerprints have been taken in the course of the investigation but those fingerprints do not constitute a complete set or some, or all, of the fingerprints are not of sufficient quality, the day on which an officer from the force investigating the offence was informed that the fingerprints previously taken were incomplete or below standard, or, if later, the day on which Schedule 2A came into force (March 7, 2011).

(iv) *section 61(6D)* – A person who has been convicted of a qualifying offence (see *Note 4AB*) outside England and Wales, see *paragraph 4.3(g)*: There is no time limit for making the requirement.

Note: A person who has had their fingerprints taken under any of the powers in section 61 mentioned in *paragraph 4.3* on two occasions in relation to any offence may not be required under Schedule 2A to attend a police station for their fingerprints to be taken again under section 61 in relation to that offence, unless authorised by an officer of inspector rank or above. The fact of the authorisation and the reasons for giving it must be recorded as soon as practicable.

(b) arrest, without warrant, a person who fails to comply with the requirement.

4.5 A person's fingerprints may be taken, as above, electronically.

4.6 Reasonable force may be used, if necessary, to take a person's fingerprints without their consent under the powers as in *paragraphs 4.3* and *4.4*.

4.7 Before any fingerprints are taken:

(a) without consent under any power mentioned in *paragraphs 4.3* and *4.4* above, the person must be informed of:

(i) the reason their fingerprints are to be taken;
(ii) the power under which they are to be taken; and
(iii) the fact that the relevant authority has been given if any power mentioned in *paragraph 4.3(c)*, *(d)* or *(f)* applies

(b) with or without consent at a police station or elsewhere, the person must be informed:

(i) that their fingerprints may be subject of a speculative search against other fingerprints, see *Note 4B*; and
(ii) that their fingerprints may be retained in accordance with *Annex F, Part (a)* unless they were taken under the power mentioned in *paragraph 4.3(e)* when they must be destroyed after they have being checked (see *Note 4C*).

(c) Documentation

4.8A A record must be made as soon as practicable after the fingerprints are taken, of:

- the matters in *paragraph 4.7(a)(i)* to *(iii)* and the fact that the person has been informed of those matters; and
- the fact that the person has been informed of the matters in *paragraph 4.7(b)(i)* and *(ii)*.

The record must be made in the person's custody record if they are detained at a police station when the fingerprints are taken.

4.8 If force is used, a record shall be made of the circumstances and those present.

4.9 *Not used*

(B) *Not used*

4.10 *Not used*
4.11 *Not used*
4.12 *Not used*
4.13 *Not used*
4.14 *Not used*
4.15 *Not used*

(C) *Taking footwear impressions in connection with a criminal investigation*

(a) Action

4.16 Impressions of a person's footwear may be taken in connection with the investigation of an offence only with their consent or if *paragraph 4.17* applies. If the person is at a police station consent must be in writing.

4.17 PACE, section 61A, provides power for a police officer to take footwear impressions without consent from any person over the age of ten years who is detained at a police station:

(a) in consequence of being arrested for a recordable offence, see *Note 4A*; or if the detainee has been charged with a recordable offence, or informed they will be reported for such an offence; and

(b) the detainee has not had an impression of their footwear taken in the course of the investigation of the offence unless the previously taken impression is not complete or is not of sufficient quality to allow satisfactory analysis, comparison or matching (whether in the case in question or generally).

4.18 Reasonable force may be used, if necessary, to take a footwear impression from a detainee without consent under the power in *paragraph 4.17*.

4.19 Before any footwear impression is taken with, or without, consent as above, the person must be informed:

(a) of the reason the impression is to be taken;

(b) that the impression may be retained and may be subject of a speculative search against other impressions, see *Note 4B*, unless destruction of the impression is required in accordance with *Annex F, Part B.*

(b) Documentation

4.20 A record must be made, as soon as possible, of the reason for taking a person's footwear impressions without consent. If force is used, a record shall be made of the circumstances and those present.

4.21 A record shall be made when a person has been informed under the terms of *paragraph 4.19(b)*, of the possibility that their footwear impressions may be subject of a speculative search.

Notes for Guidance

4A   References to 'recordable offences' in this Code relate to those offences for which convictions or cautions may be recorded in national police records. See PACE, section 27(4). The recordable offences current at the time when this Code was prepared, are any offences which carry a sentence of imprisonment on conviction (irrespective of the period, or the age of the offender or actual sentence passed) as well as the non-imprisonable offences under the Vagrancy Act 1824 sections 3 and 4 (begging and persistent begging), the Street Offences Act 1959, section 1 (loitering or soliciting for purposes of prostitution), the Road Traffic Act 1988, section 25 (tampering with motor vehicles), the Criminal Justice and Public Order Act 1994, section 167 (touting for hire car services) and others listed in the National Police Records (Recordable Offences) Regulations 2000 as amended.

4AB A qualifying offence is one of the offences specified in PACE, section 65A. These include offences which involve the use or threat of violence or unlawful force against persons, sexual offences, offences against children and other offences, for example:

- murder, false imprisonment, kidnapping contrary to Common law

- *manslaughter, conspiracy to murder, threats to kill, wounding with intent to cause grievous bodily harm (GBH), causing GBH and assault occasioning actual bodily harm contrary to the Offences Against the Person Act 1861;*
- *criminal possession or use of firearms contrary to sections 16 to 18 of the Firearms Act 1968;*
- *robbery, burglary and aggravated burglary contrary to sections 8, 9 or 10 of the Theft Act 1968 or an offence under section 12A of that Act involving an accident which caused a person's death;*
- *criminal damage required to be charged as arson contrary to section 1 of the Criminal Damage Act 1971;*
- *taking, possessing and showing indecent photographs of children contrary to section 1 of the Protection of Children Act 1978;*
- *rape, sexual assault, child sex offences, exposure and other offences contrary to the Sexual Offences Act 2003.*

4B   *Fingerprints, footwear impressions or a DNA sample (and the information derived from it) taken from a person arrested on suspicion of being involved in a recordable offence, or charged with such an offence, or informed they will be reported for such an offence, may be subject of a speculative search. This means the fingerprints, footwear impressions or DNA sample may be checked against other fingerprints, footwear impressions and DNA records held by, or on behalf of, the police and other law enforcement authorities in, or outside, the UK, or held in connection with, or as a result of, an investigation of an offence inside or outside the UK.*

4C   *The power under section 61(6A) of PACE described in paragraph 4.3(e) allows fingerprints of a suspect who has not been arrested, and whose name is not known or cannot be ascertained, or who gave a doubtful name, to be taken in connection with any offence (whether recordable or not) using a mobile device and then checked on the street against the database containing the national fingerprint collection. Fingerprints taken under this power cannot be retained after they have been checked. The results may make an arrest for the suspected offence based on the name condition unnecessary (see Code G, paragraph 2.9(a)) and enable the offence to be disposed of without arrest, for example, by summons/charging by post, penalty notice or words of advice. If arrest for a non-recordable offence is necessary for any other reasons, this power may also be exercised at the station. Before the power is exercised, the officer should:*
- *inform the person of the nature of the suspected offence and why they are suspected of committing it.*
- *give them a reasonable opportunity to establish their real name before deciding that their name is unknown and cannot be readily ascertained or that there are reasonable grounds to doubt that a name they have given is their real name.*
- *as applicable, inform the person of the reason why their name is not known and cannot be readily ascertained or of the grounds for doubting that a name they have given is their real name, including, for example, the reason why a particular document the person has produced to verify their real name, is not sufficient.*

4D   *Not used.*

5 *Examinations to establish identity and the taking of photographs*

(A) *Detainees at police stations*

(a) Searching or examination of detainees at police stations

5.1   PACE, section 54A(1), allows a detainee at a police station to be searched or examined or both, to establish:

(a)   whether they have any marks, features or injuries that would tend to identify them as a person involved in the commission of an offence and to photograph any identifying marks, see *paragraph 5.5*; or

(b)   their identity, see *Note 5A*.

A person detained at a police station to be searched under a stop and search power, see Code A, is not a detainee for the purposes of these powers.

5.2   A search and/or examination to find marks under section 54A(1)(a) may be carried out without the detainee's consent, see *paragraph 2.12*, only if authorised by an officer of at least inspector rank when consent has been withheld or it is not practicable to obtain consent, see *Note 5D*.

5.3   A search or examination to establish a suspect's identity under section 54A (1) (b) may be carried out without the detainee's consent, see *paragraph 2.12*, only if authorised by an officer of at least inspector rank when the detainee has refused to identify themselves or the authorising officer has reasonable grounds for suspecting the person is not who they claim to be.

5.4   Any marks that assist in establishing the detainee's identity, or their identification as a person involved in the commission of an offence, are identifying marks. Such marks may be photographed with the detainee's consent, see *paragraph 2.12*; or without their consent if it is withheld or it is not practicable to obtain it, see *Note 5D*.

5.5   A detainee may only be searched, examined and photographed under section 54A, by a police officer of the same sex.

5.6   Any photographs of identifying marks, taken under section 54A, may be used or disclosed only for purposes related to the prevention or detection of crime, the investigation of offences or the conduct of prosecutions by, or on behalf of, police or other law enforcement and prosecuting authorities inside, and outside, the UK. After being so used or disclosed, the photograph may be retained but must not be used or disclosed except for these purposes, see *Note 5B*.

5.7   The powers, as in *paragraph 5.1*, do not affect any separate requirement under the Criminal Procedure and Investigations Act 1996 to retain material in connection with criminal investigations.

5.8   Authority for the search and/or examination for the purposes of *paragraphs 5.2* and *5.3* may be given orally or in writing. If given orally, the authorising officer must confirm it in writing as soon as practicable. A separate authority is required for each purpose which applies.

5.9   If it is established a person is unwilling to co-operate sufficiently to enable a search and/or examination to take place or a suitable photograph to be taken, an officer may use reasonable force to:
(a)   search and/or examine a detainee without their consent; and
(b)   photograph any identifying marks without their consent.

5.10 The thoroughness and extent of any search or examination carried out in accordance with the powers in section 54A must be no more than the officer considers necessary to achieve the required purpose. Any search or examination which involves the removal of more than the person's outer clothing shall be conducted in accordance with Code C, *Annex A, paragraph 11*.

5.11 An intimate search may not be carried out under the powers in section 54A.

(b) Photographing detainees at police stations and other persons elsewhere than at a police station

5.12 Under PACE, section 64A, an officer may photograph:
(a)   any person whilst they are detained at a police station; and
(b)   any person who is elsewhere than at a police station and who has been:
    (i)   arrested by a constable for an offence;
    (ii)   taken into custody by a constable after being arrested for an offence by a person other than a constable;
    (iii) made subject to a requirement to wait with a community support officer under paragraph 2(3) or (3B) of Schedule 4 to the Police Reform Act 2002;
    (iiia) given a direction by a constable under section 27 of the Violent Crime Reduction Act 2006.
    (iv)   given a penalty notice by a constable in uniform under Chapter 1 of Part 1 of the Criminal Justice and Police Act 2001, a penalty notice by a constable under section 444A of the Education Act 1996, or a fixed penalty notice by a constable in uniform under section 54 of the Road Traffic Offenders Act 1988;
    (v)   given a notice in relation to a relevant fixed penalty offence (within the meaning of paragraph 1 of Schedule 4 to the Police Reform Act 2002) by a community support officer by virtue of a designation applying that paragraph to him;
    (vi)   given a notice in relation to a relevant fixed penalty offence (within the meaning of paragraph 1 of Schedule 5 to the Police Reform Act 2002) by an accredited person by virtue of accreditation specifying that that paragraph applies to him; or
    (vii) given a direction to leave and not return to a specified location for up to 48 hours by a police constable (under section 27 of the Violent Crime Reduction Act 2006).

5.12A Photographs taken under PACE, section 64A:
(a)   may be taken with the person's consent, or without their consent if consent is withheld or it is not practicable to obtain their consent, see *Note 5E*; and
(b)   may be used or disclosed only for purposes related to the prevention or detection of crime, the investigation of offences or the conduct of prosecutions by, or on behalf of, police or other law enforcement and prosecuting authorities inside and outside the United Kingdom or the enforcement of any sentence or order made by a court when dealing with an offence. After being so used or disclosed, they may be retained but can only be used or disclosed for the same purposes. See *Note 5B*.

5.13 The officer proposing to take a detainee's photograph may, for this purpose, require the person to remove any item or substance worn on, or over, all, or any part of, their head or face. If they do not comply with such a requirement, the officer may remove the item or substance.

5.14 If it is established the detainee is unwilling to co-operate sufficiently to enable a suitable photograph to be taken and it is not reasonably practicable to take the photograph covertly, an officer may use reasonable force, see *Note 5F.*

   (a) to take their photograph without their consent; and

   (b) for the purpose of taking the photograph, remove any item or substance worn on, or over, all, or any part of, the person's head or face which they have failed to remove when asked.

5.15 For the purposes of this Code, a photograph may be obtained without the person's consent by making a copy of an image of them taken at any time on a camera system installed anywhere in the police station.

(c) Information to be given

5.16 When a person is searched, examined or photographed under the provisions as in *paragraph 5.1* and *5.12*, or their photograph obtained as in *paragraph 5.15*, they must be informed of the:

   (a) purpose of the search, examination or photograph;

   (b) grounds on which the relevant authority, if applicable, has been given; and

   (c) purposes for which the photograph may be used, disclosed or retained. This information must be given before the search or examination commences or the photograph is taken, except if the photograph is:

      (i) to be taken covertly;

     (ii) obtained as in *paragraph 5.15*, in which case the person must be informed as soon as practicable after the photograph is taken or obtained.

(d) Documentation

5.17 A record must be made when a detainee is searched, examined, or a photograph of the person, or any identifying marks found on them, are taken. The record must include the:

   (a) identity, subject to *paragraph 2.18*, of the officer carrying out the search, examination or taking the photograph;

   (b) purpose of the search, examination or photograph and the outcome;

   (c) detainee's consent to the search, examination or photograph, or the reason the person was searched, examined or photographed without consent;

   (d) giving of any authority as in *paragraphs 5.2* and *5.3*, the grounds for giving it and the authorising officer.

5.18 If force is used when searching, examining or taking a photograph in accordance with this section, a record shall be made of the circumstances and those present.

(B) *Persons at police stations not detained*

5.19 When there are reasonable grounds for suspecting the involvement of a person in a criminal offence, but that person is at a police station **voluntarily** and not detained, the provisions of *paragraphs 5.1* to *5.18* should apply, subject to the modifications in the following paragraphs.

5.20 References to the 'person being detained' and to the powers mentioned in *paragraph 5.1* which apply only to detainees at police stations shall be omitted.

5.21 Force may not be used to:

   (a) search and/or examine the person to:

      (i) discover whether they have any marks that would tend to identify them as a person involved in the commission of an offence; or

     (ii) establish their identity, see *Note 5A*;

   (b) take photographs of any identifying marks, see *paragraph 5.4*; or

   (c) take a photograph of the person.

5.22 Subject to *paragraph 5.24*, the photographs of persons or of their identifying marks which are not taken in accordance with the provisions mentioned in *paragraphs 5.1* or *5.12*, must be destroyed (together with any negatives and copies) unless the person:

   (a) is charged with, or informed they may be prosecuted for, a recordable offence;

   (b) is prosecuted for a recordable offence;

   (c) is cautioned for a recordable offence or given a warning or reprimand in accordance with the Crime and Disorder Act 1998 for a recordable offence; or

   (d) gives informed consent, in writing, for the photograph or image to be retained as in *paragraph 5.6*.

5.23 When *paragraph 5.22* requires the destruction of any photograph, the person must be given an opportunity to witness the destruction or to have a certificate confirming the destruction provided they so request the certificate within five days of being informed the destruction is required.

5.24 Nothing in *paragraph 5.22* affects any separate requirement under the Criminal Procedure and Investigations Act 1996 to retain material in connection with criminal investigations.

Notes for Guidance

5A   The conditions under which fingerprints may be taken to assist in establishing a person's identity, are described in Section 4.

5B   Examples of purposes related to the prevention or detection of crime, the investigation of offences or the conduct of prosecutions include:

(a)   checking the photograph against other photographs held in records or in connection with, or as a result of, an investigation of an offence to establish whether the person is liable to arrest for other offences;

(b)   when the person is arrested at the same time as other people, or at a time when it is likely that other people will be arrested, using the photograph to help establish who was arrested, at what time and where;

(c)   when the real identity of the person is not known and cannot be readily ascertained or there are reasonable grounds for doubting a name and other personal details given by the person, are their real name and personal details. In these circumstances, using or disclosing the photograph to help to establish or verify their real identity or determine whether they are liable to arrest for some other offence, e.g. by checking it against other photographs held in records or in connection with, or as a result of, an investigation of an offence;

(d)   when it appears any identification procedure in section 3 may need to be arranged for which the person's photograph would assist;

(e)   when the person's release without charge may be required, and if the release is:

(i)   on bail to appear at a police station, using the photograph to help verify the person's identity when they answer their bail and if the person does not answer their bail, to assist in arresting them; or

(ii)   without bail, using the photograph to help verify their identity or assist in locating them for the purposes of serving them with a summons to appear at court in criminal proceedings;

(f)   when the person has answered to bail at a police station and there are reasonable grounds for doubting they are the person who was previously granted bail, using the photograph to help establish or verify their identity;

(g)   when the person arrested on a warrant claims to be a different person from the person named on the warrant and a photograph would help to confirm or disprove their claim;

(h)   when the person has been charged with, reported for, or convicted of, a recordable offence and their photograph is not already on record as a result of (a) to (f) or their photograph is on record but their appearance has changed since it was taken and the person has not yet been released or brought before a court.

5C   There is no power to arrest a person convicted of a recordable offence solely to take their photograph. The power to take photographs in this section applies only where the person is in custody as a result of the exercise of another power, e.g. arrest for fingerprinting under PACE, Schedule 2A, paragraph 17.

5D   Examples of when it would not be practicable to obtain a detainee's consent, see paragraph 2.12, to a search, examination or the taking of a photograph of an identifying mark include:

(a)   when the person is drunk or otherwise unfit to give consent;

(b)   when there are reasonable grounds to suspect that if the person became aware a search or examination was to take place or an identifying mark was to be photographed, they would take steps to prevent this happening, e.g. by violently resisting, covering or concealing the mark etc and it would not otherwise be possible to carry out the search or examination or to photograph any identifying mark;

(c)   in the case of a juvenile, if the parent or guardian cannot be contacted in sufficient time to allow the search or examination to be carried out or the photograph to be taken.

5E   Examples of when it would not be practicable to obtain the person's consent, see paragraph 2.12, to a photograph being taken include:

(a)   when the person is drunk or otherwise unfit to give consent;

(b)   when there are reasonable grounds to suspect that if the person became aware a photograph, suitable to be used or disclosed for the use and disclosure described in paragraph 5.6, was to be taken, they would take steps to prevent it being taken, e.g. by violently resisting, covering or distorting their face etc, and it would not otherwise be possible to take a suitable photograph;

(c)   when, in order to obtain a suitable photograph, it is necessary to take it covertly; and

    (d) *in the case of a juvenile, if the parent or guardian cannot be contacted in sufficient time to allow the photograph to be taken.*

5F   *The use of reasonable force to take the photograph of a suspect elsewhere than at a police station must be carefully considered. In order to obtain a suspect's consent and cooperation to remove an item of religious headwear to take their photograph, a constable should consider whether in the circumstances of the situation the removal of the headwear and the taking of the photograph should be by an officer of the same sex as the person. It would be appropriate for these actions to be conducted out of public view (see paragraph 1.1 and Note 1A).*

6 Identification by body samples and impressions

(A) *General*

6.1   References to:

    (a) an 'intimate sample' mean a dental impression or sample of blood, semen or any other tissue fluid, urine, or pubic hair, or a swab taken from any part of a person's genitals or from a person's body orifice other than the mouth;

    (b) a 'non-intimate sample' means:

       (i)   a sample of hair, other than pubic hair, which includes hair plucked with the root, see *Note 6A*;

       (ii) a sample taken from a nail or from under a nail;

       (iii) a swab taken from any part of a person's body other than a part from which a swab taken would be an intimate sample;

       (iv) saliva;

       (v) a skin impression which means any record, other than a fingerprint, which is a record, in any form and produced by any method, of the skin pattern and other physical characteristics or features of the whole, or any part of, a person's foot or of any other part of their body.

(B) *Action*

(a) *Intimate samples*

6.2   PACE, section 62, provides that intimate samples may be taken under:

    (a) section 62(1), from a person in police detention only:

       (i)   if a police officer of inspector rank or above has reasonable grounds to believe such an impression or sample will tend to confirm or disprove the suspect's involvement in a recordable offence, see *Note 4A*, and gives authorisation for a sample to be taken; and

       (ii) with the suspect's written consent;

    (b) section 62(1A), from a person not in police detention but from whom two or more non-intimate samples have been taken in the course of an investigation of an offence and the samples, though suitable, have proved insufficient if:

       (i)   a police officer of inspector rank or above authorises it to be taken; and

       (ii) the person concerned gives their written consent. See *Notes 6B* and *6C*.

    (c) section 62(2A), from a person convicted outside England and Wales of an offence which if committed in England and Wales would be qualifying offence as defined by PACE, section 65A (see *Note 4AB*) from whom two or more non-intimate samples taken under section 63(3E) (see *paragraph 6.6(h)* have proved insufficient if:

       (i)   a police officer of inspector rank or above is satisfied that taking the sample is necessary to assist in the prevention or detection of crime and authorises it to be taken; and

       (ii) the person concerned gives their written consent.

6.2A PACE, section 63A(4) and Schedule 2A provide powers to:

    (a) make a requirement (in accordance with *Annex G*) for a person to attend a police station to have an intimate sample taken in the exercise of one of the following powers (see *paragraph 6.2*):

       (i)   *section 62(1A)* – Persons from whom two or more non-intimate samples have been taken and proved to be insufficient, see *paragraph 6.2(b)*: There is no time limit for making the requirement.

       (ii) *section 62(2A)* – Persons convicted outside England and Wales from whom two or more non-intimate samples taken under section 63(3E) (see *paragraph 6.6(g)* have proved insufficient, see *paragraph 6.2(c)*: There is no time limit for making the requirement.

    (b) arrest without warrant a person who fails to comply with the requirement.

6.3   Before a suspect is asked to provide an intimate sample, they must be:

    (a) informed:

     (i)   of the reason, including the nature of the suspected offence (except if taken under *paragraph 6.2(c)* from a person convicted outside England and Wales.

     (ii) that authorisation has been given and the provisions under which given;

     (iii) that a sample taken at a police station may be subject of a speculative search;

  (b) warned that if they refuse without good cause their refusal may harm their case if it comes to trial, see *Note 6D*. If the suspect is in police detention and not legally represented, they must also be reminded of their entitlement to have free legal advice, see Code C, *paragraph 6.5*, and the reminder noted in the custody record. If *paragraph 6.2(b)* applies and the person is attending a station voluntarily, their entitlement to free legal advice as in Code C, *paragraph 3.21* shall be explained to them.

6.4   Dental impressions may only be taken by a registered dentist. Other intimate samples, except for samples of urine, may only be taken by a registered medical practitioner or registered nurse or registered paramedic.

(b) Non-intimate samples

6.5   A non-intimate sample may be taken from a detainee only with their written consent or if *paragraph 6.6* applies.

6.6   A non-intimate sample may be taken from a person without the appropriate consent in the following circumstances:

  (a) under *section 63(2A)* from a person who is in police detention as a consequence of being arrested for a recordable offence and who has not had a non-intimate sample of the same type and from the same part of the body taken in the course of the investigation of the offence by the police or they have had such a sample taken but it proved insufficient.

  (b) Under *section 63(3)* from a person who is being held in custody by the police on the authority of a court if an officer of at least the rank of inspector authorises it to be taken. An authorisation may be given:

     (i)   if the authorising officer has reasonable grounds for suspecting the person of involvement in a recordable offence and for believing that the sample will tend to confirm or disprove that involvement, and

     (ii) in writing or orally and confirmed in writing, as soon as practicable; but an authorisation may not be given to take from the same part of the body a further non-intimate sample consisting of a skin impression unless the previously taken impression proved insufficient

  (c) under *section 63(3ZA)* from a person who has been arrested for a recordable offence and released if:

     (i)   in the case of a person who is on bail, they have not had a sample of the same type and from the same part of the body taken in the course of the investigation of the offence, or;

     (ii) in any case, the person has had such a sample taken in the course of the investigation of the offence, but either:

       • it was not suitable or proved insufficient; or

       • the investigation was discontinued but subsequently resumed and before the resumption, any DNA profile derived from the sample was destroyed and the sample itself was destroyed pursuant to section 63R(4), (5) or (12).

  (d) under *section 63(3A)*, from a person (whether or not in police detention or held in custody by the police on the authority of a court) who has been charged with a recordable offence or informed they will be reported for such an offence if the person:

     (i)   has not had a non-intimate sample taken from them in the course of the investigation of the offence; or

     (ii) has had a sample so taken, but it was not suitable or proved insufficient, see *Note 6B*; or

     (iii) has had a sample taken in the course of the investigation of the offence and the sample has been destroyed and in proceedings relating to that offence there is a dispute as to whether a DNA profile relevant to the proceedings was derived from the destroyed sample.

  (e) under *section 63(3B)*, from a person who has been:

     (i)   convicted of a recordable offence; or

     (ii) given a caution in respect of a recordable offence which, at the time of the caution, the person admitted;

    if, since their conviction or caution a non-intimate sample has not been taken from them or a sample which has been taken since then was not suitable or proved insufficient and in either case, an officer of inspector rank or above, is satisfied that taking the fingerprints is necessary to assist in the prevention or detection of crime and authorises the taking;

(f)   under *section 63(3C)* from a person to whom section 2 of the Criminal Evidence (Amendment) Act 1997 applies (persons detained following acquittal on grounds of insanity or finding of unfitness to plead).

(g)   under *section 63(3E)* from a person who has been convicted outside England and Wales of an offence which if committed in England and Wales would be a qualifying offence as defined by PACE, section 65A (see *Note 4AB*) if:

(i)   a non-intimate sample has not been taken previously under this power or unless a sample was so taken but was not suitable or proved insufficient; and

(ii)   a police officer of inspector rank or above is satisfied that taking a sample is necessary to assist in the prevention or detection of crime and authorises it to be taken.

6.6A PACE, *section 63A(4)* and *Schedule 2A* provide powers to:

(a)   make a requirement (in accordance with *Annex G*) for a person to attend a police station to have a non-intimate sample taken in the exercise of one of the following powers (see *paragraph 6.6* above) within certain time limits as follows:

(i)   *section 63(3ZA)* – Persons arrested for a recordable offence and released, see *paragraph 6.6(c)*: In the case of a person from whom a non-intimate sample was taken in the course of the investigation but that sample was not suitable or proved insufficient, the requirement may not be made more than six months from the day the investigating officer was informed that the sample previously taken was not suitable or proved insufficient. In the case of a person whose DNA profile and sample was destroyed prior to the resumption of the investigation, the requirement may not be made more than six months from the day on which the investigation resumed.

(ii)   *section 63(3A)* – Persons charged etc. with a recordable offence, see *paragraph 6.6(d)*: The requirement may not be made more than six months from:

• the day the person was charged or informed that they would be reported, if a sample has not been taken in the course of the investigation;

• the day the investigating officer was informed that the sample previously taken was not suitable or proved insufficient, if a sample has been taken in the course of the investigation but the sample was not suitable or proved insufficient; or

• the day on which the investigation was resumed, in the case of a person whose DNA profile and sample were destroyed prior to the resumption of the investigation.

(iii)   *section 63(3B)* – Person convicted or cautioned for a recordable offence in England and Wales, see *paragraph 6.6(e)*: Where the offence for which the person was convicted etc. is also a qualifying offence (see *Note 4AB*), there is no time limit for the exercise of this power. Where the conviction etc. was for a recordable offence that is not a qualifying offence, the requirement may not be made more than two years from:

• in the case of a person whose sample has not been taken since they were convicted or cautioned, the day the person was convicted or cautioned, or, if later. the day Schedule 2A came into force (March 7 2011); or

• in the case of a person whose sample has been taken but was not suitable or proved insufficient, the day an officer from the force investigating the offence was informed that the sample previously taken was not suitable or proved insufficient or, if later, the day Schedule 2A came into force (March 7 2011).

(iv)   *section 63(3E)* – A person who has been convicted of qualifying offence (see *Note 4AB*) outside England and Wales, see *paragraph 6.6(h)*: There is no time limit for making the requirement.

Note: A person who has had a non-intimate sample taken under any of the powers in section 63 mentioned in *paragraph 6.6* on two occasions in relation to any offence may not be required under Schedule 2A to attend a police station for a sample to be taken again under section 63 in relation to that offence, unless authorised by an officer of inspector rank or above. The fact of the authorisation and the reasons for giving it must be recorded as soon as practicable.

(b)   arrest, without warrant, a person who fails to comply with the requirement.

6.7   Reasonable force may be used, if necessary, to take a non-intimate sample from a person without their consent under the powers mentioned in *paragraph 6.6*.

6.8   Before any non-intimate sample is taken:

(a)   without consent under any power mentioned in *paragraphs 6.6* and *6.6A*, the person must be informed of:

(i)   the reason for taking the sample;

(ii)   the power under which the sample is to be taken;

       (iii) the fact that the relevant authority has been given if any power mentioned in *paragraph 6.6(b), (e)* or *(g)* applies, including the nature of the suspected offence (except if taken under *paragraph 6.6(e)* from a person convicted or cautioned, or under *paragraph 6.6(g)* if taken from a person convicted outside England and Wales;

   (b) with or without consent at a police station or elsewhere, the person must be informed:

       (i) that their sample or information derived from it may be subject of a speculative search against other samples and information derived from them, see *Note 6E*, and

       (ii) that their sample and the information derived from it may be retained in accordance with *Annex F*, Part (a).

(c) Removal of clothing

6.9 When clothing needs to be removed in circumstances likely to cause embarrassment to the person, no person of the opposite sex who is not a registered medical practitioner or registered health care professional shall be present, (unless in the case of a juvenile, mentally disordered or mentally vulnerable person, that person specifically requests the presence of an appropriate adult of the opposite sex who is readily available) nor shall anyone whose presence is unnecessary. However, in the case of a juvenile, this is subject to the overriding proviso that such a removal of clothing may take place in the absence of the appropriate adult only if the juvenile signifies in their presence, that they prefer the adult's absence and they agree.

(c) Documentation

6.10 A record must be made as soon as practicable after the sample is taken of:
- The matters in *paragraph 6.8(a)(i)* to *(iii)* and the fact that the person has been informed of those matters; and
- The fact that the person has been informed of the matters in *paragraph 6.8(b)(i)* and *(ii)*.

6.10A If force is used, a record shall be made of the circumstances and those present.

6.11 A record must be made of a warning given as required by *paragraph 6.3*.

6.12 *Not used*

Notes for Guidance

6A   *When hair samples are taken for the purpose of DNA analysis (rather than for other purposes such as making a visual match), the suspect should be permitted a reasonable choice as to what part of the body the hairs are taken from. When hairs are plucked, they should be plucked individually, unless the suspect prefers otherwise and no more should be plucked than the person taking them reasonably considers necessary for a sufficient sample.*

6B   *(a) An insufficient sample is one which is not sufficient either in quantity or quality to provide information for a particular form of analysis, such as DNA analysis. A sample may also be insufficient if enough information cannot be obtained from it by analysis because of loss, destruction, damage or contamination of the sample or as a result of an earlier, unsuccessful attempt at analysis.*

      (b) An unsuitable sample is one which, by its nature, is not suitable for a particular form of analysis.

6C   *Nothing in paragraph 6.2 prevents intimate samples being taken for elimination purposes with the consent of the person concerned but the provisions of paragraph 2.12 relating to the role of the appropriate adult, should be applied. Paragraph 6.2(b) does not, however, apply where the non-intimate samples were previously taken under the Terrorism Act 2000, Schedule 8, paragraph 10.*

6D   *In warning a person who is asked to provide an intimate sample as in paragraph 6.3, the following form of words may be used:*

      'You do not have to provide this sample/allow this swab or impression to be taken, but I must warn you that if you refuse without good cause, your refusal may harm your case if it comes to trial.'

6E   *Fingerprints or a DNA sample and the information derived from it taken from a person arrested on suspicion of being involved in a recordable offence, or charged with such an offence, or informed they will be reported for such an offence, may be subject of a speculative search. This means they may be checked against other fingerprints and DNA records held by, or on behalf of, the police and other law enforcement authorities in or outside the UK or held in connection with, or as a result of, an investigation of an offence inside or outside the UK.*

      See Annex F regarding the retention and use of fingerprints and samples taken with consent for elimination purposes.

6F   *Samples of urine and non-intimate samples taken in accordance with sections 63B and 63C of PACE may not be used for identification purposes in accordance with this Code. See Code C Note for guidance 17D.*

Annex A

Video Identification

(a) General

1. The arrangements for obtaining and ensuring the availability of a suitable set of images to be used in a video identification must be the responsibility of an identification officer (see *paragraph 3.11* of this Code) who has no direct involvement with the case.

2. The set of images must include the suspect and at least eight other people who, so far as possible, and subject to *paragraph 7*, resemble the suspect in age, general appearance and position in life. Only one suspect shall appear in any set unless there are two suspects of roughly similar appearance, in which case they may be shown together with at least twelve other people.

2A If the suspect has an unusual physical feature, e.g., a facial scar, tattoo or distinctive hairstyle or hair colour which does not appear on the images of the other people that are available to be used, steps may be taken to:

    (a) conceal the location of the feature on the images of the suspect and the other people; or
    (b) replicate that feature on the images of the other people.

    For these purposes, the feature may be concealed or replicated electronically or by any other method which it is practicable to use to ensure that the images of the suspect and other people resemble each other. The identification officer has discretion to choose whether to conceal or replicate the feature and the method to be used.

2B If the identification officer decides that a feature should be concealed or replicated, the reason for the decision and whether the feature was concealed or replicated in the images shown to any eye-witness shall be recorded.

2C If the eye-witness requests to view any image where an unusual physical feature has been concealed or replicated without the feature being concealed or replicated, the identification officer has discretion to allow the eye-witness to view such image(s) if they are available.

3. The images used to conduct a video identification shall, as far as possible, show the suspect and other people in the same positions or carrying out the same sequence of movements. They shall also show the suspect and other people under identical conditions unless the identification officer reasonably believes:

    (a) because of the suspect's failure or refusal to co-operate or other reasons, it is not practicable for the conditions to be identical; and
    (b) any difference in the conditions would not direct an eye-witness' attention to any individual image.

4. The reasons identical conditions are not practicable shall be recorded on forms provided for the purpose.

5. Provision must be made for each person shown to be identified by number.

6. If police officers are shown, any numerals or other identifying badges must be concealed. If a prison inmate is shown, either as a suspect or not, then either all, or none of, the people shown should be in prison clothing.

7. The suspect or their solicitor, friend, or appropriate adult must be given a reasonable opportunity to see the complete set of images before it is shown to any eye-witness. If the suspect has a reasonable objection to the set of images or any of the participants, the suspect shall be asked to state the reasons for the objection. Steps shall, if practicable, be taken to remove the grounds for objection. If this is not practicable, the suspect and/or their representative shall be told why their objections cannot be met and the objection, the reason given for it and why it cannot be met shall be recorded on forms provided for the purpose. The requirement in *paragraph 2* that the images of the other people 'resemble' the suspect does not require the images to be identical or extremely similar (see *Note A1*).

8. Before the images are shown in accordance with *paragraph 7*, the suspect or their solicitor shall be provided with details of the first description of the suspect by any eye-witnesses who are to attend the video identification. When a broadcast or publication is made, as in *paragraph 3.38(a)*, the suspect or their solicitor must also be allowed to view any material released to the media by the police for the purpose of recognising or tracing the suspect, provided it is practicable and would not unreasonably delay the investigation.

9. No unauthorised people may be present when the video identification is conducted. The suspect's solicitor, if practicable, shall be given reasonable notification of the time and place the video identification is to be conducted. The suspect's solicitor may only be present at the video identification on request and with the prior agreement of the identification officer, if the officer is satisfied that the solicitor's presence will not deter or distract any eye-witness from viewing the

images and making an identification. If the identification officer is not satisfied and does not agree to the request, the reason must be recorded. The solicitor must be informed of the decision and the reason for it. and that they may then make representations about why they should be allowed to be present. The representations may be made orally or in writing, in person or remotely by electronic communication and must be recorded. These representations must be considered by an officer of at least the rank of inspector who is not involved with the investigation and responsibility for this may not be delegated under *paragraph 3.11*. If, after considering the representations, the officer is satisfied that the solicitor's presence will deter or distract the eye-witness, the officer shall inform the solicitor of the decision and reason for it and ensure that any response by the solicitor is also recorded. If allowed to be present, the solicitor is not entitled to communicate in any way with an eye-witness during the procedure but this does not prevent the solicitor from communicating with the identification officer. The suspect may not be present when the images are shown to any eye-witness and is not entitled to be informed of the time and place the video identification procedure is to be conducted. The video identification procedure itself shall be recorded on video with sound. The recording must show all persons present within the sight or hearing of the eye-witness whilst the images are being viewed and must include what the eye-witness says and what is said to them by the identification officer and by any other person present at the video identification procedure. A supervised viewing of the recording of the video identification procedure by the suspect and/or their solicitor may be arranged on request, at the discretion of the investigating officer. Where the recording of the video identification procedure is to be shown to the suspect and/or their solicitor, the investigating officer may arrange for anything in the recording that might allow the eye-witness to be identified to be concealed if the investigating officer considers that this is justified (see *Note A2*). In accordance with *paragraph 2.18*, the investigating officer may also arrange for anything in that recording that might allow any police officers or police staff to be identified to be concealed.

(b) Conducting the video identification

10.   The identification officer is responsible for making the appropriate arrangements to make sure, before they see the set of images, eye-witnesses are not able to communicate with each other about the case, see any of the images which are to be shown, see, or be reminded of, any photograph or description of the suspect or be given any other indication as to the suspect's identity, or overhear an eye-witness who has already seen the material. There must be no discussion with the eye-witness about the composition of the set of images and they must not be told whether a previous eye-witness has made any identification.

11.   Only one eye-witness may see the set of images at a time. Immediately before the images are shown, the eye-witness shall be told that the person they saw on a specified earlier occasion may, or may not, appear in the images they are shown and that if they cannot make an identification, they should say so. The eye-witness shall be advised that at any point, they may ask to see a particular part of the set of images or to have a particular image frozen for them to study. Furthermore, it should be pointed out to the eye-witness that there is no limit on how many times they can view the whole set of images or any part of them. However, they should be asked not to make any decision as to whether the person they saw is on the set of images until they have seen the whole set at least twice.

12.   Once the eye-witness has seen the whole set of images at least twice and has indicated that they do not want to view the images, or any part of them, again, the eye-witness shall be asked to say whether the individual they saw in person on a specified earlier occasion has been shown and, if so, to identify them by number of the image. The eye-witness will then be shown that image to confirm the identification, see *paragraph 17*.

13.   Care must be taken not to direct the eye-witness' attention to any one individual image or give any indication of the suspect's identity. Where an eye-witness has previously made an identification by photographs, or a computerised or artist's composite or similar likeness, they must not be reminded of such a photograph or composite likeness once a suspect is available for identification by other means in accordance with this Code. Nor must the eyewitness be reminded of any description of the suspect.

13A. If after the video identification procedure has ended, the eye-witness informs any police officer or police staff involved in the post-viewing arrangements that they wish to change their decision about their identification, or they have not made an identification when in fact they could have made one, an accurate record of the words used by the eye-witness and of the circumstances immediately after the procedure ended, shall be made. If the eyewitness has not had an opportunity to communicate with other people about the procedure, the identification officer has the discretion to allow the eye-witness a second opportunity to make an identification by repeating the video identification procedure using the same images but in different positions.

14. After the procedure, action required in accordance with *paragraph 3.40* applies.

(c) Image security and destruction

15. Arrangements shall be made for all relevant material containing sets of images used for specific identification procedures to be kept securely and their movements accounted for. In particular, no-one involved in the investigation shall be permitted to view the material prior to it being shown to any witness.

16. As appropriate, *paragraph 3.30* or *3.31* applies to the destruction or retention of relevant sets of images.

(d) Documentation

17. A record must be made of all those participating in, or seeing, the set of images whose names are known to the police.

18. A record of the conduct of the video identification must be made on forms provided for the purpose. This shall include anything said by the witness about any identifications or the conduct of the procedure and any reasons it was not practicable to comply with any of the provisions of this Code governing the conduct of video identifications. This record is in addition to any statement that is taken from any eye-witness after the procedure.

Note for Guidance

A1 *The purpose of the video identification is to test the eye-witness' ability to distinguish the suspect from others and it would not be a fair test if all the images shown were identical or extremely similar to each other. The identification officer is responsible for ensuring that the images shown are suitable for the purpose of this test.*

A2 *The purpose of allowing the identity of the eye-witness to be concealed is to protect them in cases when there is information that suspects or their associates, may threaten the witness or cause them harm or when the investigating officer considers that special measures may be required to protect their identity during the criminal process.*

ANNEX B

IDENTIFICATION PARADES

(a) General

1. A suspect must be given a reasonable opportunity to have a solicitor or friend present, and the suspect shall be asked to indicate on a second copy of the notice whether or not they wish to do so.

2. An identification parade may take place either in a normal room or one equipped with a screen permitting witnesses to see members of the identification parade without being seen. The procedures for the composition and conduct of the identification parade are the same in both cases, subject to *paragraph 8* (except that an identification parade involving a screen may take place only when the suspect's solicitor, friend or appropriate adult is present or the identification parade is recorded on video).

3. Before the identification parade takes place, the suspect or their solicitor shall be provided with details of the first description of the suspect by any witnesses who are attending the identification parade. When a broadcast or publication is made as in *paragraph 3.38(a)*, the suspect or their solicitor should also be allowed to view any material released to the media by the police for the purpose of identifying and tracing the suspect, provided it is practicable to do so and would not unreasonably delay the investigation.

(b) Identification parades involving prison inmates

4. If a prison inmate is required for identification, and there are no security problems about the person leaving the establishment, they may be asked to participate in an identification parade or video identification.

5. An identification parade may be held in a Prison Department establishment but shall be conducted, as far as practicable under normal identification parade rules. Members of the public shall make up the identification parade unless there are serious security, or control, objections to their admission to the establishment. In such cases, or if a group or video identification is arranged within the establishment, other inmates may participate. If an inmate is the suspect, they are not required to wear prison clothing for the identification parade unless the other people taking part are other inmates in similar clothing, or are members of the public who are prepared to wear prison clothing for the occasion.

(c) Conduct of the identification parade

6.   Immediately before the identification parade, the suspect must be reminded of the procedures governing its conduct and cautioned in the terms of Code C, *paragraphs 10.5* or *10.6*, as appropriate.

7.   All unauthorised people must be excluded from the place where the identification parade is held.

8.   Once the identification parade has been formed, everything afterwards, in respect of it, shall take place in the presence and hearing of the suspect and any interpreter, solicitor, friend or appropriate adult who is present (unless the identification parade involves a screen, in which case everything said to, or by, any witness at the place where the identification parade is held, must be said in the hearing and presence of the suspect's solicitor, friend or appropriate adult or be recorded on video).

9.   The identification parade shall consist of at least eight people (in addition to the suspect) who, so far as possible, resemble the suspect in age, height, general appearance and position in life. Only one suspect shall be included in an identification parade unless there are two suspects of roughly similar appearance, in which case they may be paraded together with at least twelve other people. In no circumstances shall more than two suspects be included in one identification parade and where there are separate identification parades, they shall be made up of different people.

10.   If the suspect has an unusual physical feature, e.g., a facial scar, tattoo or distinctive hairstyle or hair colour which cannot be replicated on other members of the identification parade, steps may be taken to conceal the location of that feature on the suspect and the other members of the identification parade if the suspect and their solicitor, or appropriate adult, agree. For example, by use of a plaster or a hat, so that all members of the identification parade resemble each other in general appearance.

11.   When all members of a similar group are possible suspects, separate identification parades shall be held for each unless there are two suspects of similar appearance when they may appear on the same identification parade with at least twelve other members of the group who are not suspects. When police officers in uniform form an identification parade any numerals or other identifying badges shall be concealed.

12.   When the suspect is brought to the place where the identification parade is to be held, they shall be asked if they have any objection to the arrangements for the identification parade or to any of the other participants in it and to state the reasons for the objection. The suspect may obtain advice from their solicitor or friend, if present, before the identification parade proceeds. If the suspect has a reasonable objection to the arrangements or any of the participants, steps shall, if practicable, be taken to remove the grounds for objection. When it is not practicable to do so, the suspect shall be told why their objections cannot be met and the objection, the reason given for it and why it cannot be met, shall be recorded on forms provided for the purpose.

13.   The suspect may select their own position in the line, but may not otherwise interfere with the order of the people forming the line. When there is more than one witness, the suspect must be told, after each witness has left the room, that they can, if they wish, change position in the line. Each position in the line must be clearly numbered, whether by means of a number laid on the floor in front of each identification parade member or by other means.

14.   Appropriate arrangements must be made to make sure, before witnesses attend the identification parade, they are not able to:

(i)   communicate with each other about the case or overhear a witness who has already seen the identification parade;

(ii)   see any member of the identification parade;

(iii) see, or be reminded of, any photograph or description of the suspect or be given any other indication as to the suspect's identity; or

(iv)   see the suspect before or after the identification parade.

15.   The person conducting a witness to an identification parade must not discuss with them the composition of the identification parade and, in particular, must not disclose whether a previous witness has made any identification.

16.   Witnesses shall be brought in one at a time. Immediately before the witness inspects the identification parade, they shall be told the person they saw on a specified earlier occasion may, or may not, be present and if they cannot make an identification, they should say so. The witness must also be told they should not make any decision about whether the person they saw is on the identification parade until they have looked at each member at least twice.

17.   When the officer or police staff (see *paragraph 3.11*) conducting the identification procedure is satisfied the witness has properly looked at each member of the identification parade, they shall ask

the witness whether the person they saw on a specified earlier occasion is on the identification parade and, if so, to indicate the number of the person concerned, see *paragraph 28*.

18. If the witness wishes to hear any identification parade member speak, adopt any specified posture or move, they shall first be asked whether they can identify any person(s) on the identification parade on the basis of appearance only. When the request is to hear members of the identification parade speak, the witness shall be reminded that the participants in the identification parade have been chosen on the basis of physical appearance only. Members of the identification parade may then be asked to comply with the witness' request to hear them speak, see them move or adopt any specified posture.

19. If the witness requests that the person they have indicated remove anything used for the purposes of *paragraph 10* to conceal the location of an unusual physical feature, that person may be asked to remove it.

20. If the witness makes an identification after the identification parade has ended, the suspect and, if present, their solicitor, interpreter or friend shall be informed. When this occurs, consideration should be given to allowing the witness a second opportunity to identify the suspect.

21 After the procedure, action required in accordance with *paragraph 3.40* applies.

22. When the last witness has left, the suspect shall be asked whether they wish to make any comments on the conduct of the identification parade.

(d) Documentation

23. A video recording must normally be taken of the identification parade. If that is impracticable, a colour photograph must be taken. A copy of the video recording or photograph shall be supplied, on request, to the suspect or their solicitor within a reasonable time.

24. As appropriate, *paragraph 3.30* or *3.31*, should apply to any photograph or video taken as in *paragraph 23*.

25. If any person is asked to leave an identification parade because they are interfering with its conduct, the circumstances shall be recorded.

26. A record must be made of all those present at an identification parade whose names are known to the police.

27. If prison inmates make up an identification parade, the circumstances must be recorded.

28. A record of the conduct of any identification parade must be made on forms provided for the purpose. This shall include anything said by the witness or the suspect about any identifications or the conduct of the procedure, and any reasons it was not practicable to comply with any of this Code's provisions.

Annex C

Group Identification

(a) General

1. The purpose of this Annex is to make sure, as far as possible, group identifications follow the principles and procedures for identification parades so the conditions are fair to the suspect in the way they test the witness' ability to make an identification.

2. Group identifications may take place either with the suspect's consent and co-operation or covertly without their consent.

3. The location of the group identification is a matter for the identification officer, although the officer may take into account any representations made by the suspect, appropriate adult, their solicitor or friend.

4. The place where the group identification is held should be one where other people are either passing by or waiting around informally, in groups such that the suspect is able to join them and be capable of being seen by the witness at the same time as others in the group. For example people leaving an escalator, pedestrians walking through a shopping centre, passengers on railway and bus stations, waiting in queues or groups or where people are standing or sitting in groups in other public places.

5. If the group identification is to be held covertly, the choice of locations will be limited by the places where the suspect can be found and the number of other people present at that time. In these cases, suitable locations might be along regular routes travelled by the suspect, including buses or trains or public places frequented by the suspect.

6. Although the number, age, sex, race and general description and style of clothing of other people present at the location cannot be controlled by the identification officer, in selecting the location the officer must consider the general appearance and numbers of people likely to be present. In particular, the officer must reasonably expect that over the period the witness observes the group,

they will be able to see, from time to time, a number of others whose appearance is broadly similar to that of the suspect.

7. A group identification need not be held if the identification officer believes, because of the unusual appearance of the suspect, none of the locations it would be practicable to use, satisfy the requirements of *paragraph 6* necessary to make the identification fair.

8. Immediately after a group identification procedure has taken place (with or without the suspect's consent), a colour photograph or video should be taken of the general scene, if practicable, to give a general impression of the scene and the number of people present. Alternatively, if it is practicable, the group identification may be video recorded.

9. If it is not practicable to take the photograph or video in accordance with *paragraph 8*, a photograph or film of the scene should be taken later at a time determined by the identification officer if the officer considers it practicable to do so.

10. An identification carried out in accordance with this Code remains a group identification even though, at the time of being seen by the witness, the suspect was on their own rather than in a group.

11. Before the group identification takes place, the suspect or their solicitor shall be provided with details of the first description of the suspect by any witnesses who are to attend the identification. When a broadcast or publication is made, as in *paragraph 3.38(a)*, the suspect or their solicitor should also be allowed to view any material released by the police to the media for the purposes of identifying and tracing the suspect, provided that it is practicable and would not unreasonably delay the investigation.

12. After the procedure, action required in accordance with *paragraph 3.40* applies.

(b) Identification with the consent of the suspect

13. A suspect must be given a reasonable opportunity to have a solicitor or friend present. They shall be asked to indicate on a second copy of the notice whether or not they wish to do so.

14. The witness, the person carrying out the procedure and the suspect's solicitor, appropriate adult, friend or any interpreter for the witness, may be concealed from the sight of the individuals in the group they are observing, if the person carrying out the procedure considers this assists the conduct of the identification.

15. The person conducting a witness to a group identification must not discuss with them the forthcoming group identification and, in particular, must not disclose whether a previous witness has made any identification.

16. Anything said to, or by, the witness during the procedure about the identification should be said in the presence and hearing of those present at the procedure.

17. Appropriate arrangements must be made to make sure, before witnesses attend the group identification, they are not able to:
   (i) communicate with each other about the case or overhear a witness who has already been given an opportunity to see the suspect in the group;
   (ii) see the suspect; or
   (iii) see, or be reminded of, any photographs or description of the suspect or be given any other indication of the suspect's identity.

18. Witnesses shall be brought one at a time to the place where they are to observe the group. Immediately before the witness is asked to look at the group, the person conducting the procedure shall tell them that the person they saw on a specified earlier occasion may, or may not, be in the group and that if they cannot make an identification, they should say so. The witness shall be asked to observe the group in which the suspect is to appear. The way in which the witness should do this will depend on whether the group is moving or stationary.

Moving group

19. When the group in which the suspect is to appear is moving, e.g. leaving an escalator, the provisions of *paragraphs 20 to 24* should be followed.

20. If two or more suspects consent to a group identification, each should be the subject of separate identification procedures. These may be conducted consecutively on the same occasion.

21. The person conducting the procedure shall tell the witness to observe the group and ask them to point out any person they think they saw on the specified earlier occasion.

22. Once the witness has been informed as in *paragraph 21* the suspect should be allowed to take whatever position in the group they wish.

23. When the witness points out a person as in *paragraph 21* they shall, if practicable, be asked to take a closer look at the person to confirm the identification. If this is not practicable, or they cannot

confirm the identification, they shall be asked how sure they are that the person they have indicated is the relevant person.

24. The witness should continue to observe the group for the period which the person conducting the procedure reasonably believes is necessary in the circumstances for them to be able to make comparisons between the suspect and other individuals of broadly similar appearance to the suspect as in *paragraph 6.*

Stationary groups

25. When the group in which the suspect is to appear is stationary, e.g. people waiting in a queue, the provisions of *paragraphs 26* to *29* should be followed.

26. If two or more suspects consent to a group identification, each should be subject to separate identification procedures unless they are of broadly similar appearance when they may appear in the same group. When separate group identifications are held, the groups must be made up of different people.

27. The suspect may take whatever position in the group they wish. If there is more than one witness, the suspect must be told, out of the sight and hearing of any witness, that they can, if they wish, change their position in the group.

28. The witness shall be asked to pass along, or amongst, the group and to look at each person in the group at least twice, taking as much care and time as possible according to the circumstances, before making an identification. Once the witness has done this, they shall be asked whether the person they saw on the specified earlier occasion is in the group and to indicate any such person by whatever means the person conducting the procedure considers appropriate in the circumstances. If this is not practicable, the witness shall be asked to point out any person they think they saw on the earlier occasion.

29. When the witness makes an indication as in *paragraph 28*, arrangements shall be made, if practicable, for the witness to take a closer look at the person to confirm the identification. If this is not practicable, or the witness is unable to confirm the identification, they shall be asked how sure they are that the person they have indicated is the relevant person.

All cases

30. If the suspect unreasonably delays joining the group, or having joined the group, deliberately conceals themselves from the sight of the witness, this may be treated as a refusal to co-operate in a group identification.

31. If the witness identifies a person other than the suspect, that person should be informed what has happened and asked if they are prepared to give their name and address. There is no obligation upon any member of the public to give these details. There shall be no duty to record any details of any other member of the public present in the group or at the place where the procedure is conducted.

32. When the group identification has been completed, the suspect shall be asked whether they wish to make any comments on the conduct of the procedure.

33. If the suspect has not been previously informed, they shall be told of any identifications made by the witnesses.

(c) Identification without the suspect's consent

34. Group identifications held covertly without the suspect's consent should, as far as practicable, follow the rules for conduct of group identification by consent.

35. A suspect has no right to have a solicitor, appropriate adult or friend present as the identification will take place without the knowledge of the suspect.

36. Any number of suspects may be identified at the same time.

(d) Identifications in police stations

37. Group identifications should only take place in police stations for reasons of safety, security or because it is not practicable to hold them elsewhere.

38. The group identification may take place either in a room equipped with a screen permitting witnesses to see members of the group without being seen, or anywhere else in the police station that the identification officer considers appropriate.

39. Any of the additional safeguards applicable to identification parades should be followed if the identification officer considers it is practicable to do so in the circumstances.

(e) Identifications involving prison inmates

40. A group identification involving a prison inmate may only be arranged in the prison or at a police station.

41.   When a group identification takes place involving a prison inmate, whether in a prison or in a police station, the arrangements should follow those in *paragraphs 37 to 39*. If a group identification takes place within a prison, other inmates may participate. If an inmate is the suspect, they do not have to wear prison clothing for the group identification unless the other participants are wearing the same clothing.

(f) Documentation

42.   When a photograph or video is taken as in *paragraph 8 or 9*, a copy of the photograph or video shall be supplied on request to the suspect or their solicitor within a reasonable time.

43.   *Paragraph 3.30 or 3.31*, as appropriate, shall apply when the photograph or film taken in accordance with *paragraph 8 or 9* includes the suspect.

44.   A record of the conduct of any group identification must be made on forms provided for the purpose. This shall include anything said by the witness or suspect about any identifications or the conduct of the procedure and any reasons why it was not practicable to comply with any of the provisions of this Code governing the conduct of group identifications.

ANNEX D

CONFRONTATION BY A WITNESS

1.   Before the confrontation takes place, the eye-witness must be told that the person they saw on a specified earlier occasion may, or may not, be the person they are to confront and that if they are not that person, then the witness should say so.

2.   Before the confrontation takes place the suspect or their solicitor shall be provided with details of the first description of the suspect given by any eye-witness who is to attend. When a broadcast or publication is made, as in *paragraph 3.38(a)*, the suspect or their solicitor should also be allowed to view any material released to the media for the purposes of recognising or tracing the suspect, provided it is practicable to do so and would not unreasonably delay the investigation.

3.   Force may not be used to make the suspect's face visible to the eye-witness.

4.   Confrontation must take place in the presence of the suspect's solicitor, interpreter or friend unless this would cause unreasonable delay.

5.   The suspect shall be confronted independently by each eye-witness, who shall be asked 'Is this the person?'. If the eye-witness identifies the person but is unable to confirm the identification, they shall be asked how sure they are that the person is the one they saw on the earlier occasion.

6.   The confrontation should normally take place in the police station, either in a normal room or one equipped with a screen permitting the eye-witness to see the suspect without being seen. In both cases, the procedures are the same except that a room equipped with a screen may be used only when the suspect's solicitor, friend or appropriate adult is present or the confrontation is recorded on video.

7.   After the procedure, action required in accordance with *paragraph 3.40* applies.

ANNEX E

SHOWING PHOTOGRAPHS

(a) Action

1.   An officer of sergeant rank or above shall be responsible for supervising and directing the showing of photographs. The actual showing may be done by another officer or police staff, see *paragraph 3.11*.

2.   The supervising officer must confirm the first description of the suspect given by the eyewitness has been recorded before they are shown the photographs. If the supervising officer is unable to confirm the description has been recorded they shall postpone showing the photographs.

3.   Only one eye-witness shall be shown photographs at any one time. Each witness shall be given as much privacy as practicable and shall not be allowed to communicate with any other eye-witness in the case.

4.   The eye-witness shall be shown not less than twelve photographs at a time, which shall, as far as possible, all be of a similar type.

5.   When the eye-witness is shown the photographs, they shall be told the photograph of the person they saw on a specified earlier occasion may, or may not, be amongst them and if they cannot make an identification, they should say so. The eye-witness shall also be told they should not make a decision until they have viewed at least twelve photographs. The eye-witness shall not be prompted or guided in any way but shall be left to make any selection without help.

6.   If an eye-witness makes an identification from photographs, unless the person identified is otherwise eliminated from enquiries or is not available, other eye-witnesses shall not be shown photographs. But both they, and the eye-witness who has made the identification, shall be asked to attend a video identification, an identification parade or group identification unless there is no dispute about the suspect's identification.

7.   If the eye-witness makes a selection but is unable to confirm the identification, the person showing the photographs shall ask them how sure they are that the photograph they have indicated is the person they saw on the specified earlier occasion.

8.   When the use of a computerised or artist's composite or similar likeness has led to there being a known suspect who can be asked to participate in a video identification, appear on an identification parade or participate in a group identification, that likeness shall not be shown to other potential eye-witnesses.

9.   When an eye-witness attending a video identification, an identification parade or group identification has previously been shown photographs or computerised or artist's composite or similar likeness (and it is the responsibility of the officer in charge of the investigation to make the identification officer aware that this is the case), the suspect and their solicitor must be informed of this fact before the identification procedure takes place.

10. None of the photographs shown shall be destroyed, whether or not an identification is made, since they may be required for production in court. The photographs shall be numbered and a separate photograph taken of the frame or part of the album from which the eye-witness made an identification as an aid to reconstituting it.

(b) Documentation

11. Whether or not an identification is made, a record shall be kept of the showing of photographs on forms provided for the purpose. This shall include anything said by the eye-witness about any identification or the conduct of the procedure, any reasons it was not practicable to comply with any of the provisions of this Code governing the showing of photographs and the name and rank of the supervising officer.

12. The supervising officer shall inspect and sign the record as soon as practicable.

Annex F

Fingerprints, Samples and Footwear Impressions — Destruction and Speculative Searches

Part A: Fingerprints and samples

Paragraphs 1 to 12 summarise and update information which is available at: https://www.gov.uk/ government/publications/protection-of-freedoms-act-2012-dna-and-fingerprintprovisions/protection-of-freedoms-act-2012-how-dna-and-fingerprint-evidence-is-protected-in-law

DNA samples

1.   A DNA sample is an individual's biological material, containing all of their genetic information. The Act requires all DNA samples to be destroyed within 6 months of being taken. This allows sufficient time for the sample to be analysed and a DNA profile to be produced for use on the database.

2.   The only exception to this is if the sample is or may be required for disclosure as evidence, in which case it may be retained for as long as this need exists under the Criminal Procedure and Investigations Act 1996.

DNA profiles and fingerprints

3.   A DNA profile consists of a string of 16 pairs of numbers and 2 letters (XX for women, XY for men) to indicate gender. This number string is stored on the National DNA Database (NDNAD). It allows the person to be identified if they leave their DNA at a crime scene.

4.   Fingerprints are usually scanned electronically from the individual in custody and the images stored on IDENT1, the national fingerprint database.

Retention Periods: Fingerprints and DNA profiles

5.   The retention period depends on the outcome of the investigation of the recordable offence in connection with which the fingerprints and DNA samples was taken, the age of the person at the time the offence was committed and whether the *recordable* offence is a qualifying offence and whether it is an excluded offence (see Table *Notes (a)* to *(c)*), as follows:

Table – Retention periods

(a) Convictions

Age when offence committed	Outcome	Retention Period
Any age	Convicted or given a caution or youth caution for a recordable offence which is also a qualifying offence	INDEFINITE
18 or over	Convicted or given a caution for a recordable offence which is NOT a qualifying offence	INDEFINITE
Under 18	Convicted or given a youth caution for a recordable offence which is NOT a qualifying offence.	1st conviction or youth caution – 5 years plus length of any prison sentence. Indefinite if prison sentence 5 years or more 2nd conviction or youth caution: Indefinite

(b) Non-Convictions

Age when offence committed	Outcome	Retention Period
Any age	Charged but not convicted of a recordable qualifying offence.	3 years plus a 2 year extension if granted by a District Judge (or indefinite if the individual has a previous conviction for a recordable offence which is not excluded)
Any age	Arrested for, but not charged with, a recordable qualifying offence	3 years if granted by the Biometrics Commissioner plus a 2 year extension if granted by a District Judge (or indefinite if the individual has a previous conviction for a recordable offence which is not excluded)
Any age	Arrested for or charged with a recordable offence which is not a qualifying offence.	Indefinite if the person has a previous conviction for a recordable offence which is not excluded otherwise NO RETENTION
18 or over	Given Penalty Notice for Disorder for recordable offence	2 years

Table Notes:

(a)   *A 'recordable' offence is one for which the police are required to keep a record. Generally speaking, these are imprisonable offences; however, it also includes a number of non-imprisonable offences such as begging and taxi touting. The police are not able to take or retain the DNA or fingerprints of an individual who is arrested for an offence which is not recordable.*

(b)   *A 'qualifying' offence is one listed under section 65A of the Police and Criminal Evidence Act 1984 (the list comprises sexual, violent, terrorism and burglary offences).*

(c)   *An 'excluded' offence is a recordable offence which is not a qualifying offence, was committed when the individual was under 18, for which they received a sentence of fewer than 5 years imprisonment and is the only recordable offence for which the person has been convicted.*

Speculative searches

6.   Where the retention framework above requires the deletion of a person's DNA profile and fingerprints, the Act first allows a *speculative search* of their DNA and fingerprints against DNA and fingerprints obtained from crime scenes which are stored on NDNAD and IDENT1. Once the speculative search has been completed, the profile and fingerprints are deleted unless there is a match, in which case they will be retained for the duration of any investigation and thereafter in

accordance with the retention framework (e.g. if that investigation led to a conviction for a qualifying offence, they would be retained indefinitely).

Extensions of retention period

7.   For qualifying offences, PACE allows chief constables to apply for extensions to the given retention periods for DNA profiles and fingerprints if considered necessary for prevention or detection of crime.

8.   Section 20 of the Protection of Freedoms Act 2012 established the independent office of Commissioner for the Retention and Use of Biometric Material ('the 'Biometrics Commissioner'). For details, see https://www.gov.uk/government/organisations/biometrics-commissioner.

9.   Where an individual is arrested for, but not charged with, a qualifying offence, their DNA profile and fingerprint record will normally be deleted. However, the police can apply to the Biometrics Commissioner for permission to retain their DNA profile and fingerprint record for a period of 3 years. The application must be made within 28 days of the decision not to proceed with a prosecution.

10.   If the police make such an application, the Biometrics Commissioner would first give both them and the arrested individual an opportunity to make written representations and then, taking into account factors including the age and vulnerability of the victim(s) of the alleged offences, and their relationship to the suspect, make a decision on whether or not retention is appropriate.

11.   If after considering the application, the Biometrics Commissioner decides that retention is not appropriate, the DNA profile and fingerprint record in question must be destroyed.

12.   If the Biometrics Commissioner agrees to allow retention, the police will be able to retain that individual's DNA profile and fingerprint record for a period of 3 years from the date the samples were taken. At the end of that period, the police will be able to apply to a District Judge (Magistrates' Courts) for a single 2 year extension to the retention period. If the application is rejected, the force must then destroy the DNA profile and fingerprint record.

Part B: Footwear impressions

13.   Footwear impressions taken in accordance with section 61A of PACE (see *paragraphs 4.16 to 4.21*) may be retained for as long as is necessary for purposes related to the prevention or detection of crime, the investigation of an offence or the conduct of a prosecution.

Part C: Fingerprints, samples and footwear impressions taken in connection with a criminal investigation from a person not suspected of committing the offence under investigation for elimination purposes.

14.   When fingerprints, footwear impressions or DNA samples are taken from a person in connection with an investigation and the person is *not suspected of having committed the offence*, see *Note F1*, they must be destroyed as soon as they have fulfilled the purpose for which they were taken unless:

      (a) they were taken for the purposes of an investigation of an offence for which a person has been convicted; and

      (b) fingerprints, footwear impressions or samples were also taken from the convicted person for the purposes of that investigation.

      However, subject to *paragraph 14*, the fingerprints, footwear impressions and samples, and the information derived from samples, may not be used in the investigation of any offence or in evidence against the person who is, or would be, entitled to the destruction of the fingerprints, footwear impressions and samples, see *Note F2*.

15.   The requirement to destroy fingerprints, footwear impressions and DNA samples, and information derived from samples and restrictions on their retention and use in *paragraph 14* do not apply if the person gives their written consent for their fingerprints, footwear impressions or sample to be retained and used after they have fulfilled the purpose for which they were taken, see *Note F1*. This consent can be withdrawn at any time.

16.   When a person's fingerprints, footwear impressions or sample are to be destroyed:

      (a) any copies of the fingerprints and footwear impressions must also be destroyed; and

      (b) neither the fingerprints, footwear impressions, the sample, or any information derived from the sample, may be used in the investigation of any offence or in evidence against the person who is, or would be, entitled to its destruction.

Notes for Guidance

F1   *Fingerprints, footwear impressions and samples given voluntarily for the purposes of elimination play an important part in many police investigations. It is, therefore, important to make sure innocent volunteers are not deterred from participating and their consent to their fingerprints, footwear impressions and DNA being used for the purposes of a specific investigation is fully informed and voluntary. If the police or volunteer seek to have the fingerprints, footwear impressions or samples retained for use after the specific investigation ends, it is important the volunteer's consent to this is also fully informed and voluntary. The volunteer must be told that they may withdraw their consent at any time. The consent must be obtained in writing using current nationally agreed forms provided for police use according to the purpose for which the consent is given. This purpose may be either:*

- *DNA/fingerprints/footwear impressions — to be used only for the purposes of a specific investigation; or*
- *DNA/fingerprints/footwear impressions — to be used in the specific investigation **and** retained by the police for future use.*

To minimise the risk of confusion:
- *if a police officer or member of police staff has any doubt about:*
  - *how the consent forms should be completed and signed, or*
  - *whether a consent form they propose to use and refer to is fully compliant with the current nationally agreed form,*

  the relevant national police helpdesk (for DNA or fingerprints) should be contacted.
- *in each case, the meaning of consent should be explained orally and care taken to ensure the oral explanation accurately reflects the contents of the written form the person is to be asked to sign.*

F2   *The provisions for the retention of fingerprints, footwear impressions and samples in paragraph 15 allow for all fingerprints, footwear impressions and samples in a case to be available for any subsequent miscarriage of justice investigation.*

Annex G

Requirement for a Person to Attend a Police Station for Fingerprints and Samples
(Paragraphs 4.4, 6.2A and 6.6A)

1.   A requirement under Schedule 2A for a person to attend a police station to have fingerprints or samples taken:
      (a) must give the person a period of at least seven days within which to attend the police station; and
      (b) may direct them to attend at a specified time of day or between specified times of day.

2.   When specifying the period and times of attendance, the officer making the requirements must consider whether the fingerprints or samples could reasonably be taken at a time when the person is required to attend the police station for any other reason. See *Note G1*.

3.   An officer of the rank of inspector or above may authorise a period shorter than 7 days if there is an urgent need for person's fingerprints or sample for the purposes of the investigation of an offence. The fact of the authorisation and the reasons for giving it must be recorded as soon as practicable.

4.   The constable making a requirement and the person to whom it applies may agree to vary it so as to specify any period within which, or date or time at which, the person is to attend. However, variation shall not have effect for the purposes of enforcement, unless it is confirmed by the constable in writing.

Notes for Guidance

G1   *The specified period within which the person is to attend need not fall within the period allowed (if applicable) for making the requirement.*

G2   *To justify the arrest without warrant of a person who fails to comply with a requirement, (see paragraphs 4.4(b) and 6.7(b) above), the officer making the requirement, or confirming a variation, should be prepared to explain how, when and where the requirement was made or the variation was confirmed and what steps were taken to ensure the person understood what to do and the consequences of not complying with the requirement.*

PACE CODE E

REVISED CODE OF PRACTICE ON AUDIO RECORDING INTERVIEWS WITH SUSPECTS

[Omitted: see D1.90. The full text of Code E is freely available at tinyurl.com/ybm87hfr]

PACE CODE F

REVISED CODE OF PRACTICE ON VISUAL RECORDING WITH SOUND OF INTERVIEWS WITH SUSPECTS

[Omitted: see D1.90. The full text of Code F is freely available at tinyurl.com/y930995g]

PACE CODE G

CODE OF PRACTICE FOR THE STATUTORY POWER OF ARREST BY POLICE OFFICERS

Commencement — Transitional Arrangements

This Code applies to any arrest made by a police officer after midnight on 12 November 2012.

1. Introduction

1.1   This Code of Practice deals with the statutory power of police to arrest a person who is involved, or suspected of being involved, in a criminal offence. The power of arrest must be used fairly, responsibly, with respect for people suspected of committing offences and without unlawful discrimination. The Equality Act 2010 makes it unlawful for police officers to discriminate against, harass or victimise any person on the grounds of the 'protected characteristics' of age, disability, gender reassignment, race, religion or belief, sex and sexual orientation, marriage and civil partnership, pregnancy and maternity when using their powers. When police forces are carrying out their functions they also have a duty to have regard to the need to eliminate unlawful discrimination, harassment and victimisation and to take steps to foster good relations.

1.2   The exercise of the power of arrest represents an obvious and significant interference with the Right to liberty and security under Article 5 of the European Convention on Human Rights set out in Part I of Schedule 1 to the Human Rights Act 1998.

1.3   The use of the power must be fully justified and officers exercising the power should consider if the necessary objectives can be met by other, less intrusive means. Absence of justification for exercising the power of arrest may lead to challenges should the case proceed to court. It could also lead to civil claims against police for unlawful arrest and false imprisonment. When the power of arrest is exercised it is essential that it is exercised in a non-discriminatory and proportionate manner which is compatible with the Right to liberty under Article 5. See *Note 1B*.

1.4   Section 24 of the Police and Criminal Evidence Act 1984 (as substituted by section 110 of the Serious Organised Crime and Police Act 2005) provides the statutory power for a constable to arrest without warrant for all offences. If the provisions of the Act and this Code are not observed, both the arrest and the conduct of any subsequent investigation may be open to question.

1.5   This Code of Practice must be readily available at all police stations for consultation by police officers and police staff, detained persons and members of the public.

1.6   The notes for guidance are not provisions of this code.

2. Elements of arrest under section 24 PACE

2.1   A lawful arrest requires two elements:

A person's involvement or suspected involvement or attempted involvement in the commission of a criminal offence;

AND

Reasonable grounds for *believing* that the person's arrest is necessary.

- both elements must be satisfied, and
- it can never be necessary to arrest a person unless there are reasonable grounds to suspect them of committing an offence.

2.2   The arrested person must be informed that they have been arrested, even if this fact is obvious, and of the relevant circumstances of the arrest in relation to both the above elements. The custody officer must be informed of these matters on arrival at the police station. See *paragraphs 2.9, 3.3 and Note 3 and Code C paragraph 3.4.*

(a) Involvement in the commission of an offence'

2.3   A constable may arrest without warrant in relation to any offence (see *Notes 1 and 1A*) anyone:
- who is about to commit an offence or is in the act of committing an offence;
- whom the officer has reasonable grounds for suspecting is about to commit an offence or to be committing an offence;
- whom the officer has reasonable grounds to suspect of being guilty of an offence which he or she has reasonable grounds for suspecting has been committed;
- anyone who is guilty of an offence which has been committed or anyone whom the officer has reasonable grounds for suspecting to be guilty of that offence.

2.3A There must be some reasonable, objective grounds for the suspicion, based on known facts and information which are relevant to the likelihood the offence has been committed and the person liable to arrest committed it. See *Notes 2 and 2A.*

(b) Necessity criteria

2.4   The power of arrest is only exercisable if the constable has reasonable grounds for *believing* that it is necessary to arrest the person. The statutory criteria for what may constitute necessity are set out in paragraph 2.9 and it remains an operational decision at the discretion of the constable to decide:
- which one or more of the necessity criteria (if any) applies to the individual; and
- if any of the criteria do apply, whether to arrest, grant street bail after arrest, report for summons or for charging by post, issue a penalty notice or take any other action that is open to the officer.

2.5   In applying the criteria, the arresting officer has to be satisfied that at least one of the reasons supporting the need for arrest is satisfied.

2.6   Extending the power of arrest to all offences provides a constable with the ability to use that power to deal with any situation. However applying the necessity criteria requires the constable to examine and justify the reason or reasons why a person needs to be arrested or (as the case may be) further arrested, for an offence for the custody officer to decide whether to authorise their detention for that offence. See *Note 2C*

2.7   The criteria in paragraph 2.9 below which are set out in section 24 of PACE as substituted by section 110 of the Serious Organised Crime and Police Act 2005 are exhaustive. However, the circumstances that may satisfy those criteria remain a matter for the operational discretion of individual officers. Some examples are given to illustrate what those circumstances might be and what officers might consider when deciding whether arrest is necessary.

2.8   In considering the individual circumstances, the constable must take into account the situation of the victim, the nature of the offence, the circumstances of the suspect and the needs of the investigative process.

2.9   When it is practicable to tell a person why their arrest is necessary (as required by paragraphs 2.2, 3.3 and *Note 3*), the constable should outline the facts, information and other circumstances which provide the grounds for believing that their arrest is necessary and which the officer considers satisfy one or more of the statutory criteria in sub-paragraphs (a) to (f), namely:

(a)   to enable the name of the person in question to be ascertained (in the case where the constable does not know, and cannot readily ascertain, the person's name, or has reasonable grounds for doubting whether a name given by the person as his name is his real name):

An officer might decide that a person's name cannot be readily ascertained if they fail or refuse to give it when asked, particularly after being warned that failure or refusal is likely to make their arrest necessary (see *Note 2D*). Grounds to doubt a name given may arise if the person appears reluctant or hesitant when asked to give their name or to verify the name they have given.

Where mobile fingerprinting is available and the suspect's name cannot be ascertained or is doubted, the officer should consider using the power under section 61(6A) of PACE (see *Code D paragraph 4.3(e)*) to take and check the fingerprints of a suspect as this may avoid the need to arrest solely to enable their name to be ascertained.

(b) correspondingly as regards the person's address:

An officer might decide that a person's address cannot be readily ascertained if they fail or refuse to give it when asked, particularly after being warned that such a failure or refusal is likely to make their arrest necessary. See *Note 2D*. Grounds to doubt an address given may arise if the person appears reluctant or hesitant when asked to give their address or is unable to provide verifiable details of the locality they claim to live in.

When considering reporting to consider summons or charging by post as alternatives to arrest, an address would be satisfactory if the person will be at it for a sufficiently long period for it to be possible to serve them with the summons or requisition and charge; or, that some other person at that address specified by the person will accept service on their behalf. When considering issuing a penalty notice, the address should be one where the person will be in the event of enforcement action if the person does not pay the penalty or is convicted and fined after a court hearing.

(c) to prevent the person in question:
   (i) causing physical injury to himself or any other person;
      This might apply where the suspect has already used or threatened violence against others and it is thought likely that they may assault others if they are not arrested. See *Note 2D*.
   (ii) suffering physical injury;
      This might apply where the suspect's behaviour and actions are believed likely to provoke, or have provoked, others to want to assault the suspect unless the suspect is arrested for their own protection. See *Note 2D*.
   (iii) causing loss or damage to property;
      This might apply where the suspect is a known persistent offender with a history of serial offending against property (theft and criminal damage) and it is thought likely that they may continue offending if they are not arrested.
   (iv) committing an offence against public decency (only applies where members of the public going about their normal business cannot reasonably be expected to avoid the person in question);
      This might apply when an offence against public decency is being committed in a place to which the public have access and is likely to be repeated in that or some other public place at a time when the public are likely to encounter the suspect. See *Note 2D*.
   (v) causing an unlawful obstruction of the highway;
      This might apply to any offence where its commission causes an unlawful obstruction which it is believed may continue or be repeated if the person is not arrested, particularly if the person has been warned that they are causing an obstruction. See *Note 2D*.

(d) to protect a child or other vulnerable person from the person in question.
   This might apply when the health (physical or mental) or welfare of a child or vulnerable person is likely to be harmed or is at risk of being harmed, if the person is not arrested in cases where it is not practicable and appropriate to make alternative arrangements to prevent the suspect from having any harmful or potentially harmful contact with the child or vulnerable person.

(e) to allow the prompt and effective investigation of the offence or of the conduct of the person in question. See *Note 2E*.
   This may arise when it is thought likely that unless the person is arrested and then either taken in custody to the police station or granted 'street bail' to attend the station later, see *Note 2J*, further action considered necessary to properly investigate their involvement in the offence would be frustrated, unreasonably delayed or otherwise hindered and therefore be impracticable. Examples of such actions include:
   (i) *interviewing the suspect* on occasions when the person's voluntary attendance is not considered to be a practicable alternative to arrest, because for example:
      • it is thought unlikely that the person would attend the police station voluntarily to be interviewed.
      • it is necessary to interview the suspect about the outcome of other investigative action for which their arrest is necessary, see (ii) to (v) below.
      • arrest would enable the special warning to be given in accordance with Code C paragraphs 10.10 and 10.11 when the suspect is found:
         – in possession of incriminating objects, or at a place where such objects are found;
         – at or near the scene of the crime at or about the time it was committed.
      • the person has made false statements and/or presented false evidence;

- it is thought likely that the person:
  - may steal or destroy evidence;
  - may collude or make contact with, co-suspects or conspirators;
  - may intimidate or threaten or make contact with, witnesses.

  See *Notes 2F and 2G*.

   (ii)   when considering arrest in connection with the investigation of an *indictable offence* (see *Note 6*), there is a need:

- to enter and search without a search warrant any premises occupied or controlled by the arrested person or where the person was when arrested or immediately before arrest;
- to prevent the arrested person from having contact with others;
- to detain the arrested person for more than 24 hours before charge.

   (iii)   when considering arrest in connection with any *recordable offence* and it is necessary to secure or preserve evidence of that offence by taking fingerprints, footwear impressions or samples from the suspect for evidential comparison or matching with other material relating to that offence, for example, from the crime scene. See *Note 2H*.

   (iv)   when considering arrest in connection with any offence and it is necessary to search, examine or photograph the person to obtain evidence. See *Note 2H*.

   (v)   when considering arrest in connection with an offence to which the statutory Class A drug testing requirements in Code C section 17 apply, to enable testing when it is thought that drug misuse might have caused or contributed to the offence. See *Note 2I*.

(f)   to prevent any prosecution for the offence from being hindered by the disappearance of the person in question.

This may arise when it is thought that:

- if the person is not arrested they are unlikely to attend court if they are prosecuted;
- the address given is not a satisfactory address for service of a summons or a written charge and requisition to appear at court because the person will not be at it for a sufficiently long period for the summons or charge and requisition to be served and no other person at that specified address will accept service on their behalf.

3. Information to be given on arrest

(a) Cautions —when a caution must be given

3.1   Code C paragraphs 10.1 and 10.2 set out the requirement for a person whom there are grounds to suspect of an offence (see *Note 2*) to be cautioned before being questioned or further questioned about an offence.

3.2   *Not used.*

3.3   A person who is arrested, or further arrested, must be informed at the time if practicable, or if not, as soon as it becomes practicable thereafter, that they are under arrest and of the grounds and reasons for their arrest, see paragraphs 2.2 and *Note 3*.

3.4   A person who is arrested, or further arrested, must be cautioned unless:

   (a) it is impracticable to do so by reason of their condition or behaviour at the time;

   (b) they have already been cautioned immediately prior to arrest as in *paragraph 3.1*.

(b) Terms of the caution (Taken from Code C section 10)

3.5   The caution, which must be given on arrest, should be in the following terms:

> 'You do not have to say anything. But it may harm your defence if you do not mention when questioned something which you later rely on in Court. Anything you do say may be given in evidence.'

Where the use of the Welsh Language is appropriate, a constable may provide the caution directly in Welsh in the following terms:

> *'Does dim rhaid i chi ddweud dim byd. Ond gall niweidio eich amddiffyniad os na fyddwch chi'n sôn, wrth gael eich holi, am rywbeth y byddwch chi'n dibynnu arno nes ymlaen yn y Llys. Gall unrhyw beth yr ydych yn ei ddweud gael ei roi fel tystiolaeth.'*

See *Note 5*

3.6   Minor deviations from the words of any caution given in accordance with this Code do not constitute a breach of this Code, provided the sense of the relevant caution is preserved. See *Note 6*

3.7   *Not used.*

4. Records of arrest

(a) General

4.1 The arresting officer is required to record in his pocket book or by other methods used for recording information:
  - the nature and circumstances of the offence leading to the arrest;
  - the reason or reasons why arrest was necessary;
  - the giving of the caution; and
  - anything said by the person at the time of arrest.

4.2 Such a record should be made at the time of the arrest unless impracticable to do so. If not made at that time, the record should then be completed as soon as possible thereafter.

4.3 On arrival at the police station or after being first arrested at the police station, the arrested person must be brought before the custody officer as soon as practicable and a custody record must be opened in accordance with section 2 of Code C. The information given by the arresting officer on the circumstances and reason or reasons for arrest shall be recorded as part of the custody record. Alternatively, a copy of the record made by the officer in accordance with paragraph 4.1 above shall be attached as part of the custody record. See *paragraph 2.2* and *Code C paragraphs 3.4 and 10.3*.

4.4 The custody record will serve as a record of the arrest. Copies of the custody record will be provided in accordance with paragraphs 2.4 and 2.4A of Code C and access for inspection of the original record in accordance with paragraph 2.5 of Code C.

(b) Interviews and arrests

4.5 Records of interview, significant statements or silences will be treated in the same way as set out in sections 10 and 11 of Code C and in Codes E and F (audio and visual recording of interviews).

Notes for Guidance

1 *For the purposes of this Code, 'offence' means any statutory or common law offence for which a person may be tried by a magistrates' court or the Crown court and punished if convicted. Statutory offences include assault, rape, criminal damage, theft, robbery, burglary, fraud, possession of controlled drugs and offences under road traffic, liquor licensing, gambling and immigration legislation and local government byelaws. Common law offences include murder, manslaughter, kidnapping, false imprisonment, perverting the course of justice and escape from lawful custody.*

1A *This code does not apply to powers of arrest conferred on constables under any arrest warrant, for example, a warrant issued under the Magistrates' Courts Act 1980, sections 1 or 13, or the Bail Act 1976, section 7(1), or to the powers of constables to arrest without warrant other than under section 24 of PACE for an offence. These other powers to arrest without warrant do not depend on the arrested person committing any specific offence and include:*
  - *PACE, section 46A, arrest of person who fails to answer police bail to attend police station or is suspected of breaching any condition of that bail for the custody officer to decide whether they should be kept in police detention which applies whether or not the person commits an offence under section 6 of the Bail Act 1976 (e.g. failing without reasonable cause to surrender to custody);*
  - *Bail Act 1976, section 7(3), arrest of person bailed to attend court who is suspected of breaching, or is believed likely to breach, any condition of bail to take them to court for bail to be re-considered;*
  - *Children & Young Persons Act 1969, section 32(1A) (absconding) —arrest to return the person to the place where they are required to reside;*
  - *Immigration Act 1971, Schedule 2 to arrest a person liable to examination to determine their right to remain in the UK;*
  - *Mental Health Act 1983, section 136 to remove person suffering from mental disorder to place of safety for assessment;*
  - *Prison Act 1952, section 49, arrest to return person unlawfully at large to the prison etc. where they are liable to be detained;*
  - *Road Traffic Act 1988, section 6D arrest of driver following the outcome of a preliminary roadside test requirement to enable the driver to be required to provide an evidential sample;*
  - *Common law power to stop or prevent a Breach of the Peace — after arrest a person aged 18 or over may be brought before a justice of the peace court to show cause why they should not be bound over to keep the peace — not criminal proceedings.*

1B *Juveniles should not be arrested at their place of education unless this is unavoidable. When a juvenile is arrested at their place of education, the principal or their nominee must be informed. (From Code C Note 11D)*

2 *Facts and information relevant to a person's suspected involvement in an offence should not be confined to those which tend to indicate the person has committed or attempted to commit the offence. Before making*

a decision to arrest, a constable should take account of any facts and information that are available, including claims of innocence made by the person, that might dispel the suspicion.

2A   Particular examples of facts and information which might point to a person's innocence and may tend to dispel suspicion include those which relate to the statutory defence provided by the Criminal Law Act 1967, section 3(1) which allows the use of reasonable force in the prevention of crime or making an arrest and the common law of self-defence. This may be relevant when a person appears, or claims, to have been acting reasonably in defence of themselves or others or to prevent their property or the property of others from being stolen, destroyed or damaged, particularly if the offence alleged is based on the use of unlawful force, e.g. a criminal assault. When investigating allegations involving the use of force by school staff, the power given to all school staff under the Education and Inspections Act 2006, section 93, to use reasonable force to prevent their pupils from committing any offence, injuring persons, damaging property or prejudicing the maintenance of good order and discipline may be similarly relevant. The Association of Chief Police Officers and the Crown Prosecution Service have published joint guidance to help the public understand the meaning of reasonable force and what to expect from the police and CPS in cases which involve claims of self defence. Separate advice for school staff on their powers to use reasonable force is available from the Department for Education

2B   If a constable who is dealing with an allegation of crime and considering the need to arrest becomes an investigator for the purposes of the Code of Practice under the Criminal Procedure and Investigations Act 1996, the officer should, in accordance with paragraph 3.5 of that Code, 'pursue all reasonable lines of inquiry, whether these point towards or away from the suspect. What is reasonable in each case will depend on the particular circumstances.'

2C   For a constable to have reasonable grounds for believing it necessary to arrest, he or she is not required to be satisfied that there is no viable alternative to arrest. However, it does mean that in all cases, the officer should consider that arrest is the practical, sensible and proportionate option in all the circumstances at the time the decision is made. This applies equally to a person in police detention after being arrested for an offence who is suspected of involvement in a further offence and the necessity to arrest them for that further offence is being considered.

2D   Although a warning is not expressly required, officers should if practicable, consider whether a warning which points out their offending behaviour, and explains why, if they do not stop, the resulting consequences may make their arrest necessary. Such a warning might:
   • if heeded, avoid the need to arrest, or
   • if it is ignored, support the need to arrest and also help prove the mental element of certain offences, for example, the person's intent or awareness, or help to rebut a defence that they were acting reasonably.
   A person who is warned that they may be liable to arrest if their real name and address cannot be ascertained, should be given a reasonable opportunity to establish their real name and address before deciding that either or both are unknown and cannot be readily ascertained or that there are reasonable grounds to doubt that a name and address they have given is their real name and address. They should be told why their name is not known and cannot be readily ascertained and (as the case may be) of the grounds for doubting that a name and address they have given is their real name and address, including, for example, the reason why a particular document the person has produced to verify their real name and/or address, is not sufficient.

2E   The meaning of 'prompt' should be considered on a case by case basis taking account of all the circumstances. It indicates that the progress of the investigation should not be delayed to the extent that it would adversely affect the effectiveness of the investigation. The arresting officer also has discretion to release the arrested person on 'street bail' as an alternative to taking the person directly to the station. See Note 2J.

2F   An officer who believes that it is necessary to interview the person suspected of committing the offence must then consider whether their arrest is necessary in order to carry out the interview. The officer is not required to interrogate the suspect to determine whether they will attend a police station voluntarily to be interviewed but they must consider whether the suspect's voluntary attendance is a practicable alternative for carrying out the interview. If it is, then arrest would not be necessary. Conversely, an officer who considers this option but is not satisfied that it is a practicable alternative, may have reasonable grounds for deciding that the arrest is necessary at the outset 'on the street'. Without such considerations, the officer would not be able to establish that arrest was necessary in order to interview.
   Circumstances which suggest that a person's arrest 'on the street' would not be necessary to interview them might be where the officer:
   • is satisfied as to their identity and address and that they will attend the police station voluntarily to be interviewed, either immediately or by arrangement at a future date and time; and

- *is not aware of any other circumstances which indicate that voluntary attendance would not be a practicable alternative. See paragraph 2.9(e)(i) to (v).*

When making arrangements for the person's voluntary attendance, the officer should tell the person:

- *that to properly investigate their suspected involvement in the offence they must be interviewed under caution at the police station, but in the circumstances their arrest for this purpose will not be necessary if they attend the police station voluntarily to be interviewed;*
- *that if they attend voluntarily, they will be entitled to free legal advice before, and to have a solicitor present at, the interview;*
- *that the date and time of the interview will take account of their circumstances and the needs of the investigation; and*
- *that if they do not agree to attend voluntarily at a time which meets the needs of the investigation, or having so agreed, fail to attend, or having attended, fail to remain for the interview to be completed, their arrest will be necessary to enable them to be interviewed.*

2G   *When the person attends the police station voluntarily for interview by arrangement as in Note 2F above, their arrest on arrival at the station prior to interview would only be justified if:*

- *new information coming to light after the arrangements were made indicates that from that time, voluntary attendance ceased to be a practicable alternative and the person's arrest became necessary; and*
- *it was not reasonably practicable for the person to be arrested before they attended the station.*

If a person who attends the police station voluntarily to be interviewed decides to leave before the interview is complete, the police would at that point be entitled to consider whether their arrest was necessary to carry out the interview. The possibility that the person might decide to leave during the interview is therefore not a valid reason for arresting them before the interview has commenced. See Code C paragraph 3.21.

2H   *The necessity criteria do not permit arrest solely to enable the routine taking, checking (speculative searching) and retention of fingerprints, samples, footwear impressions and photographs when there are no prior grounds to believe that checking and comparing the fingerprints etc. or taking a photograph would provide relevant evidence of the person's involvement in the offence concerned or would help to ascertain or verify their real identity.*

2I   *The necessity criteria do not permit arrest for an offence solely because it happens to be one of the statutory drug testing 'trigger offences' (see Code C Note 17E) when there is no suspicion that Class A drug misuse might have caused or contributed to the offence.*

2J   *Having determined that the necessity criteria have been met and having made the arrest, the officer can then consider the use of street bail on the basis of the effective and efficient progress of the investigation of the offence in question. It gives the officer discretion to compel the person to attend a police station at a date/time that best suits the overall needs of the particular investigation. Its use is not confined to dealing with child care issues or allowing officers to attend to more urgent operational duties and granting street bail does not retrospectively negate the need to arrest.*

3   *An arrested person must be given sufficient information to enable them to understand they have been deprived of their liberty and the reason they have been arrested, as soon as practicable after the arrest, e.g. when a person is arrested on suspicion of committing an offence they must be informed of the nature of the suspected offence and when and where it was committed. The suspect must also be informed of the reason or reasons why arrest is considered necessary. Vague or technical language should be avoided. When explaining why one or more of the arrest criteria apply, it is not necessary to disclose any specific details that might undermine or otherwise adversely affect any investigative processes. An example might be the conduct of a formal interview when prior disclosure of such details might give the suspect an opportunity to fabricate an innocent explanation or to otherwise conceal lies from the interviewer.*

4   *Nothing in this Code requires a caution to be given or repeated when informing a person not under arrest they may be prosecuted for an offence. However, a court will not be able to draw any inferences under the Criminal Justice and Public Order Act 1994, section 34, if the person was not cautioned.*

5   *If it appears a person does not understand the caution, the person giving it should explain it in their own words.*

6   *Certain powers available as the result of an arrest — for example, entry and search of premises, detention without charge beyond 24 hours, holding a person incommunicado and delaying access to legal advice — only apply in respect of indictable offences and are subject to the specific requirements on authorisation as set out in PACE and the relevant Code of Practice.*

PACE CODE H

REVISED CODE OF PRACTICE IN CONNECTION WITH: THE DETENTION, TREATMENT AND QUESTIONING BY POLICE OFFICERS OF PERSONS IN POLICE DETENTION UNDER SECTION 41 OF, AND SCHEDULE 8 TO, THE TERRORISM ACT 2000 THE TREATMENT AND QUESTIONING BY POLICE OFFICERS OF DETAINED PERSONS IN RESPECT OF WHOM AN AUTHORISATION TO QUESTION AFTER CHARGE HAS BEEN GIVEN UNDER SECTION 22 OF THE COUNTER-TERRORISM ACT 2008

[Code H is not reproduced. The full text of Code H is freely available at tinyurl.com/vt22x6g.]

Attorney-General's Guidelines

JURY VETTING: RIGHT OF STAND BY GUIDELINES

Updated: 30 November 2012

Exercise by the Crown of its Right of Stand by

1. Although the law has long recognised the right of the Crown to exclude a member of a jury panel from sitting as a juror by the exercise in open court of the right to request a stand by or, if necessary, by challenge for cause, it has been customary for those instructed to prosecute on behalf of the Crown to assert that right only sparingly and in exceptional circumstances. It is generally accepted that the prosecution should not use its right in order to influence the overall composition of a jury or with a view to tactical advantage.

2. The approach outlined above is founded on the principles that:
   a. the members of a jury should be selected at random from the panel subject to any rule of law as to right of challenge by the defence, and
   b. the Juries Act 1974 identifies those classes of persons who alone are disqualified from or ineligible for service on a jury. No other class of person may be treated as disqualified or ineligible.

3. The enactment by Parliament of s. 118 of the Criminal Justice Act 1988 abolishing the right of defendants to remove jurors by means of peremptory challenge makes it appropriate that the Crown should assert its right to stand by only on the basis of clearly defined and restrictive criteria. Derogation from the principle that members of a jury should be selected at random should be permitted only where it is essential.

4. Primary responsibility for ensuring that an individual does not serve on a jury if he is not competent to discharge properly the duties of a juror rests with the appropriate court officer and, ultimately the trial judge. Current legislation provides, in ss. 9 to s.10 of the Juries Act 1974, fairly wide discretion to excuse, defer or discharge jurors.

5. The circumstances in which it would be proper for the Crown to exercise its right to stand by a member of a jury panel are:
   a. where a jury check authorised in accordance with the Attorney-General's Guidelines on Jury Checks reveals information justifying exercise of the right to stand by in accordance with para.11 of the guidelines below [under **Jury Checks**] and the Attorney-General personally authorises the exercise of the right to stand by; or
   b. where a person is about to be sworn as a juror who is manifestly unsuitable and the defence agree that, accordingly, the exercise by the prosecution of the right to stand by would be appropriate. An example of the sort of exceptional circumstances which might justify stand by is where it becomes apparent that, despite the provisions mentioned in para. 4 above, a juror selected for service to try a complex case is in fact illiterate.

Jury Checks

1. The principles which are generally to be observed are:
   a. that members of a jury should be selected at random from the panel,
   b. the Juries Act 1974 identifies those classes of persons who alone are either disqualified from or ineligible for service on a jury; no other class of person may be treated as disqualified or ineligible,
   c. the correct way for the Crown to seek to exclude a member of the panel from sitting as a juror is by the exercise in open court of the right to request a stand by or, if necessary, to challenge for cause.

2. Parliament has provided safeguards against jurors who may be corrupt or biased. In addition to the provision for majority verdicts, there is the sanction of a criminal offence for a disqualified person to serve on a jury. The omission of a disqualified person from the panel is a matter for court officials—they will check criminal records for the purpose of ascertaining whether or not a potential juror is a disqualified person.

3. There are, however, certain exceptional types of case of public importance for which the provisions as to majority verdicts and the disqualification of jurors may not be sufficient to ensure the proper administration of justice. In such cases it is in the interests of both justice and the public that there

should be further safeguards against the possibility of bias and in such cases checks which go beyond the investigation of criminal records may be necessary.

4. These classes of case may be defined broadly as (a) cases in which national security is involved and part of the evidence is likely to be heard in camera, and (b) security and terrorist cases in which a juror's extreme beliefs could prevent a fair trial.

5. The particular aspects of these cases which may make it desirable to seek extra precautions are:

    a. in security cases a danger that a juror, either voluntarily or under pressure, may make an improper use of evidence which, because of its sensitivity, has been given in camera,

    b. in both security and terrorist cases the danger that a juror's personal beliefs are so biased as to go beyond normally reflecting the broad spectrum of views and interests in the community to reflect the extreme views of sectarian interest or pressure group to a degree which might interfere with his fair assessment of the facts of the case or lead him to exert improper pressure on his fellow jurors.

6. In order to ascertain whether in exceptional circumstances of the above nature either of these factors might seriously influence a potential juror's impartial performance of his duties or his respecting the secrecy of evidence given in camera, it may be necessary to conduct a limited investigation of the panel. In general, such further investigation beyond one of criminal records made for disqualifications may only be made with the records of the police. However, a check may, additionally be made against the records of the Security Service. No checks other than on these sources and no general inquiries are to be made save to the limited extent that they may be needed to confirm the identity of a juror about whom the initial check has raised serious doubts.

7. No further investigation, as described in para. 6 above, should be made save with the personal authority of the Attorney-General on the application of the Director of Public Prosecutions and such checks are hereafter referred to as 'authorised checks'. When a chief officer of police or the prosecutor has reason to believe that it is likely that an authorised check may be desirable and proper in accordance with these guidelines, he should refer the matter to the Director of Public Prosecutions. In those cases in which the Director of Public Prosecutions believes authorised checks are both proportionate and necessary, the Director will make an application to the Attorney-General.

8. The Director of Public Prosecutions will provide the Attorney-General with all relevant information in support of the requested authorised checks. The Attorney-General will consider personally the request and, if appropriate, authorise the check.

9. The result of any authorised check will be sent to the Director of Public Prosecutions. The Director will then decide, having regard to the matters set out in para. 5 above, what information ought to be brought to the attention of prosecuting counsel. The Director will also provide the Attorney-General with the result of the authorised check.

10. Although the right of stand by and the decision to authorise checks are wholly within the discretion of the Attorney-General, when the Attorney-General has agreed to an authorised check being conducted, the Director of Public Prosecutions will write to the Presiding Judge for the area to advise him that this is being done.

11. No right of stand by should be exercised by counsel for the Crown on the basis of information obtained as a result of an authorised check save with the personal authority of the Attorney-General and unless the information is such as, having regard to the facts of the case and the offences charged, to afford strong reason for believing that a particular juror might be a security risk, be susceptible to improper approaches or be influenced in arriving at a verdict for the reasons given above.

12. Information revealed in the course of an authorised check must be considered in line with the normal rules on disclosure.

13. A record is to be kept by the Director of Public Prosecutions of the use made by counsel of the information passed to him and of the jurors stood by or challenged by the parties to the proceedings. A copy of this record is to be forwarded to the Attorney-General for the sole purpose of enabling him to monitor the operation of these guidelines.

14. No use of the information obtained as a result of an authorised check is to be made except as may be necessary in direct relation to or arising out of the trial for which the check was authorised. The information may, however, be used for the prevention of crime or as evidence in a future criminal prosecution, save that material obtained from the Security Service may only be used in those circumstances with the authority of the Security Service.

THE ACCEPTANCE OF PLEAS AND THE PROSECUTOR'S ROLE IN THE SENTENCING EXERCISE

Updated: 30 November 2012

A. Foreword

A1. Prosecutors have an important role in protecting the victim's interests in the criminal justice process, not least in the acceptance of pleas and the sentencing exercise. The basis of plea, particularly in a case that is not contested, is the vehicle through which the victim's voice is heard. Factual inaccuracies in pleas in mitigation cause distress and offence to victims, the families of victims and witnesses. This can take many forms but may be most acutely felt when the victim is dead and the family hears inaccurate assertions about the victim's character or lifestyle. Prosecution advocates are reminded that they are required to adhere to the standards set out in the Victim's Charter, which places the needs of the victim at the heart of the criminal justice process, and that they are subject to a similar obligation in respect of the Code of Practice for Victims of Crime.

A2. The principle of fairness is central to the administration of justice. The implementation of Human Rights Act 1998 in October 2000 incorporated into domestic law the principle of fairness to the accused articulated in the European Convention on Human Rights. Accuracy and reasonableness of plea plays an important part in ensuring fairness both to the accused and to the victim.

A3. The Attorney General's Guidelines on the Acceptance of Pleas issued on December 7, 2000 highlighted the importance of transparency in the conduct of justice. The basis of plea agreed by the parties in a criminal trial is central to the sentencing process. An illogical or unsupported basis of plea can lead to an unduly lenient sentence being passed, and has a consequential effect where consideration arises as to whether to refer the sentence to the Court of Appeal under section 36 of the Criminal Justice Act 1988.

A4. These Guidelines, which replace the Guidelines issued in October 2005, give guidance on how prosecutors should meet these objectives of protection of victims' interests and of securing fairness and transparency in the process. They take into account paragraphs IV.45.4 and following of the Consolidated Criminal Practice Direction, amended May 2009 and the guidance issued by the Court of Appeal (Criminal) Division in *R v Beswick* [1996] 1 Cr App R 343, *R v Tolera* [1999] 1 Cr App R 25 and *R v Underwood* [2005] 1 Cr App R 178. They complement the Bar Council Guidance on Written Standards for the Conduct of Professional Work issued with the 7th edition of the Code of Conduct for the Bar of England and Wales and the Law Society's Professional Conduct Rules. When considering the acceptance of a guilty plea prosecution advocates are also reminded of the need to apply 'The Farquharson Guidelines on The Role and Responsibilities of the Prosecution Advocate'.

A5. The Guidelines should be followed by all prosecutors and those persons designated under section 7 of the Prosecution of Offences Act 1985 (designated caseworkers) and apply to prosecutions conducted in England and Wales.

B. General Principles

B1. Justice in this jurisdiction, save in the most exceptional circumstances, is conducted in public. This includes the acceptance of pleas by the prosecution and sentencing.

B2. The Code for Crown Prosecutors governs the prosecutor's decision-making prior to the commencement of the trial hearing and sets out the circumstances in which pleas to a reduced number of charges, or less serious charges, can be accepted.

B3. When a case is listed for trial and the prosecution form the view that the appropriate course is to accept a plea before the proceedings commence or continue, or to offer no evidence on the indictment or any part of it, the prosecution should whenever practicable speak to the victim or the victim's family, so that the position can be explained. The views of the victim or the family may assist in informing the prosecutor's decision as to whether it is the public interest, as defined by the Code for Crown Prosecutors, to accept or reject the plea. The victim or victim's family should then be kept informed and decisions explained once they are made at court.

B4. The appropriate disposal of a criminal case after conviction is as much a part of the criminal justice process as the trial of guilt or innocence. The prosecution advocate represents the public interest, and should be ready to assist the court to reach its decision as to the appropriate sentence. This will include drawing the court's attention to:
- any victim personal statement or other information available to the prosecution advocate as to the impact of the offence on the victim;
- where appropriate, to any evidence of the impact of the offending on a community;
- any statutory provisions relevant to the offender and the offences under consideration;

- any relevant sentencing guidelines and guideline cases; and
- the aggravating and mitigating factors of the offence under consideration.

B5.   The prosecution advocate may also offer assistance to the court by making submissions, in the light of all these factors, as to the appropriate sentencing range. In all cases, it is the prosecution advocate's duty to apply for appropriate ancillary orders, such as anti-social behaviour orders and confiscation orders. When considering which ancillary orders to apply for, prosecution advocates must always have regard to the victim's needs, including the question of his or her future protection.

C. The Basis of Plea

C1.   The basis of a guilty plea must not be agreed on a misleading or untrue set of facts and must take proper account of the victim's interests. An illogical or insupportable basis of plea will inevitably result in the imposition of an inappropriate sentence and is capable of damaging public confidence in the criminal justice system. In cases involving multiple defendants the bases of plea for each defendant must be factually consistent with each other.

C2.   When the defendant indicates an acceptable plea, the defence advocate should reduce the basis of the plea to writing. This must be done in all cases save for those in which the defendant has indicated that the guilty plea has been or will be tendered on the basis of the prosecution case.

C3.   The written basis of plea must be considered with great care, taking account of the position of any other relevant defendant where appropriate. The prosecution should not lend itself to any agreement whereby a case is presented to the sentencing judge on a misleading or untrue set of facts or on a basis that is detrimental to the victim's interests. There will be cases where a defendant seeks to mitigate on the basis of assertions of fact which are outside the scope of the prosecution's knowledge. A typical example concerns the defendant's state of mind. If a defendant wishes to be sentenced on this basis, the prosecution advocate should invite the judge not to accept the defendant's version unless he or she gives evidence on oath to be tested in cross-examination. Paragraph IV.45.14 of the Consolidated Criminal Practice Direction states that in such circumstances the defence advocate should be prepared to call the defendant and, if the defendant is not willing to testify, subject to any explanation that may be given, the judge may draw such inferences as appear appropriate.

C4.   The prosecution advocate should show the prosecuting authority any written record relating to the plea and agree with them the basis on which the case will be opened to the court. If, as may well be the case, the basis of plea differs in its implications for sentencing or the making of ancillary orders from the case originally outlined by the prosecution, the prosecution advocate must ensure that such differences are accurately reflected in the written record prior to showing it to the prosecuting authority.

C5.   It is the responsibility of the prosecution advocate thereafter to ensure that the defence advocate is aware of the basis on which the plea is accepted by the prosecution and the way in which the prosecution case will be opened to the court.

C6.   In all cases where it is likely to assist the court where the sentencing issues are complex or unfamiliar the prosecution must add to the written outline of the case which is served upon the court a summary of the key considerations. This should take the form of very brief notes on:
- any relevant statutory limitations
- the names of any relevant sentencing authorities or guidelines
- the scope for any ancillary orders (e.g., concerning anti-social behaviour, confiscation or deportation will need to be considered).
- The outline should also include the age of the defendant and information regarding any outstanding offences.

C7.   It remains open to the prosecutor to provide further written information (for example to supplement and update the analysis at later stages of the case) where he or she thought that likely to assist the court, or if the judge requests it.

C8.   When the prosecution advocate has agreed the written basis of plea submitted by the defence advocate, he or she should endorse the document accordingly. If the prosecution advocate takes issue with all or part of the written basis of plea, the procedure set out in the Consolidated Criminal Practice Direction (and in [r. 25.16] of the Criminal Procedure Rules) should be followed. The defendant's basis of plea must be set out in writing identifying what is in dispute; the court may invite the parties to make representations about whether the dispute is material to sentence; and if the court decides that it is a material dispute, the court will invite further representations or evidence as it may require and decide the dispute in accordance with the principles set out in *R v Newton* 77 Cr App R13, CA. The signed original document setting out the disputed factual matters should be made available to the trial judge and thereafter lodged with the court papers, as it will form part of the record of the hearing.

C9. Where the basis of plea cannot be agreed and the discrepancy between the two accounts is such as to have a potentially significant effect on the level of sentence, it is the duty of the defence advocate so to inform the court before the sentencing process begins. There remains an overriding duty on the prosecution advocate to ensure that the sentencing judge is made aware of the discrepancy and of the consideration which must be given to holding a *Newton* hearing to resolve the issue. The court should be told where a derogatory reference to a victim, witness or third party is not accepted, even though there may be no effect on sentence.

C10. As emphasised in paragraph IV.45.10 of the Consolidated Criminal Practice Direction, whenever an agreement as to the basis of plea is made between the prosecution and defence, any such agreement will be subject to the approval of the trial judge, who may of his or her own motion disregard the agreement and direct that a *Newton* hearing should be held to determine the proper basis on which sentence should be passed.

C11. Where a defendant declines to admit an offence that he or she previously indicated should be taken into consideration, the prosecution advocate should indicate to the defence advocate and the court that, subject to further review, the offence may now form the basis of a new prosecution.

D. Sentence Indications

D1. Only in the Crown Court may sentence indications be sought. Advocates there are reminded that indications as to sentence should not be sought from the trial judge unless issues between the prosecution and defence have been addressed and resolved. Therefore, in difficult or complicated cases, no less than seven days' notice in writing of an intention to seek an indication should normally be given to the prosecution and the court. When deciding whether the circumstances of a case require such notice to be given, defence advocates are reminded that prosecutors should not agree a basis of plea unless and until the necessary consultation has taken place first with the victim and/or the victim's family and second, in the case of an independent prosecution advocate, with the prosecuting authority.

D2. If there is no final agreement about the plea to the indictment, or the basis of plea, and the defence nevertheless proceeds to seek an indication of sentence, which the judge appears minded to give, the prosecution advocate should remind him or her of the guidance given in *R v Goodyear (Karl)* [2005] EWCA 888 that normally speaking an indication of sentence should not be given until the basis of the plea has been agreed or the judge has concluded that he or she can properly deal with the case without the need for a trial of the issue.

D3. If an indication is sought, the prosecution advocate should normally enquire whether the judge is in possession of or has access to all the evidence relied on by the prosecution, including any victim personal statement, as well as any information about relevant previous convictions recorded against the defendant.

D4. Before the judge gives the indication, the prosecution advocate should draw the judge's attention to any minimum or mandatory statutory sentencing requirements. Where the prosecution advocate would be expected to offer the judge assistance with relevant guideline cases or the views of the Sentencing Guidelines Council, he or she should invite the judge to allow them to do so. Where it applies, the prosecution advocate should remind the judge that the position of the Attorney General to refer any sentencing decision as unduly lenient is unaffected. In any event, the prosecution advocate should not say anything which may create the impression that the sentence indication has the support or approval of the Crown.

E. Pleas In Mitigation

E1. The prosecution advocate must challenge any assertion by the defence in mitigation which is derogatory to a person's character, (for instance, because it suggests that his or her conduct is or has been criminal, immoral or improper) and which is either false or irrelevant to proper sentencing considerations. If the defence advocate persists in that assertion, the prosecution advocate should invite the court to consider holding a *Newton* hearing to determine the issue.

E2. The defence advocate must not submit in mitigation anything that is derogatory to a person's character without giving advance notice in writing so as to afford the prosecution advocate the opportunity to consider their position under paragraph E1. When the prosecution advocate is so notified they must take all reasonable steps to establish whether the assertions are true. Reasonable steps will include seeking the views of the victim. This will involve seeking the views of the victim's family if the victim is deceased, and the victim's parents or legal guardian where the victim is a child. Reasonable steps may also include seeking the views of the police or other law enforcement authority, as appropriate. An assertion which is derogatory to a person's character will rarely amount to mitigation unless it has a causal connection to the circumstances of the offence or is otherwise relevant to proper sentencing considerations.

E3. Where notice has not been given in accordance with paragraph E2, the prosecution advocate must not acquiesce in permitting mitigation which is derogatory to a person's character. In such circumstances, the prosecution advocate should draw the attention of the court to the failure to give advance notice and seek time, and if necessary, an adjournment to investigate the assertion in the same way as if proper notice had been given. Where, in the opinion of the prosecution advocate, there are substantial grounds for believing that such an assertion is false or irrelevant to sentence, he or she should inform the court of their opinion and invite the court to consider making an order under section 58(8) of the Criminal Procedure and Investigations Act 1996, preventing publication of the assertion.

E4.   Where the prosecution advocate considers that the assertion is, if true, relevant to sentence, or the court has so indicated, he or she should seek time, and if necessary an adjournment, to establish whether the assertion is true. If the matter cannot be resolved to the satisfaction of the parties, the prosecution advocate should invite the court to consider holding a *Newton* hearing to determine the issue.

THE USE OF THE COMMON LAW OFFENCE OF CONSPIRACY TO DEFRAUD

Updated: 29 November 2012

Summary

1.   This guidance concerns the issues which the Attorney General asks prosecuting authorities in England and Wales to consider before using the common law offence of conspiracy to defraud, in the light of the implementation of the Fraud Act 2006. It may be supplemented by Departmental-specific guidance issued by individual Directors of the prosecuting authorities.

Background

2.   When the Fraud Act 2006 comes into force on 15 January 2007, the prosecution will be able to use modern and flexible statutory offences of fraud. The 2006 Act replaces the deception offences contained in the Theft Acts 1968–1996 with a general offence of fraud that can be committed in three ways:
 • fraud by false representation;
 • fraud by failing to disclose information; and
 • fraud by abuse of position.
 It also introduces other offences which can be used in particular circumstances, notably:
 • new offences to tackle the possession and supply of articles for use in fraud; and
 • a new offence of fraudulent trading applicable to sole traders and other businesses not caught by the existing offence in section 458 of the Companies Act 1985.

3.   The new offences are designed to catch behaviour that previously fell through gaps in the Theft Acts and could only be prosecuted as conspiracy to defraud. Indeed the Act is based on a Law Commission report (Cm 5560) which also recommended the abolition of the common law offence of conspiracy to defraud. The argument is that the offence is unfairly uncertain, and wide enough to have the potential to catch behaviour that should not be criminal. Furthermore it can seem anomalous that what is legal if performed by one person should be criminal if performed by many.

4.   However, consultations showed a widespread view in favour of retention of common law conspiracy to defraud, and the Government decided to retain it for the meantime, but accepted the case for considering repeal in the longer term. Whether there is a continuing need for retention of the common law offence is one of the issues that will be addressed in the Home Office review of the operation of the Fraud Act 2006, which will take place 3 years after its implementation.

5.   In 2003, 14,928 defendants were proceeded against in England and Wales for crimes of fraud; 1018 of these were charged with the common law crime of conspiracy to defraud of which 44% were found guilty (compared with 71% for the statutory fraud offences). The expectation now is that the common law offence will be used to a significantly lesser extent once the Fraud Act 2006 has come into force.

Issues to be considered in using the common law offence

6.   In selecting charges in fraud cases, the prosecutor should first consider:
 • whether the behaviour could be prosecuted under statute—whether under the Fraud Act 2006 or another Act or as a statutory conspiracy; and
 • whether the available statutory charges adequately reflect the gravity of the offence.

7.   Statutory conspiracy to commit a substantive offence should be charged if the alleged agreement satisfies the definition in section 1 of the Criminal Law Act 1977, provided that there is no wider dishonest objective that would be important to the presentation of the prosecution case in reflecting the gravity of the case.

8. Section 12 of the Criminal Justice Act 1987 provides that common law conspiracy to defraud may be charged even if the conduct agreed upon will involve the commission of a statutory offence. However, Lord Bingham said in *R v Rimmington* and *R v Goldstein* [(2005) UKHL 63]:

    'I would not go to the length of holding that conduct may never be lawfully prosecuted as a generally-expressed common law crime where it falls within the terms of a specific statutory provision, *but good practice and respect for the primacy of statute do in my judgment require that conduct falling within the terms of a specific statutory provision should be prosecuted under that provision unless there is good reason for doing otherwise.*'

9. In the Attorney General's view the common law charge may still be appropriate in the type of cases set out in paragraphs 12–15, but in order to understand the circumstances under which conspiracy to defraud is used *prosecutors should make a record of the reasons for preferring that charge.*

Records of decisions

10. Where a charge of common law conspiracy to defraud is proposed the case lawyer must consider and set out in writing in the review note:
    - how much such a charge will add to the amount of evidence likely to be called both by the prosecution and the defence; and
    - the justification for using the charge, and why specific statutory offences are inadequate or otherwise inappropriate.
    - Thereafter, and before charge, the use of this charge should be specifically approved by a supervising lawyer experienced in fraud cases. Equivalent procedures to ensure proper consideration of the charge and recording of the decision should be applied by all prosecuting authorities in their case review processes.

11. Information from these records will be collected retrospectively for the review to be conducted in 3 years. It will enable the identification of where and why the common law offence has been used. It could then also form the basis for any future work on whether, and if so how, to replace the common law or whether it can simply and safely be repealed. It is expected that in 3 years the Government will be able to review the situation in the light of the practical operation not only of the new fraud offences, but of other relevant changes. These include the Lord Chief Justice's protocol on the control and management of heavy fraud cases, and the sample count provisions in the Domestic Violence, Crime and Victims Act 2004. Any actual or proposed changes to the law on assisting and encouraging crime in the light of the Law Commission's study of that issue [Cm 6878, published in July 2006] will also be taken into account.

A. Conduct that can more effectively be prosecuted as conspiracy to defraud

12. There may be cases where the interests of justice can only be served by presenting to a court an overall picture which cannot be achieved by charging a series of substantive offences or statutory conspiracies. Typically, such cases will involve some, but not necessarily all of the following:
    - evidence of several significant but different kinds of criminality;
    - several jurisdictions;
    - different types of victims, e.g., individuals, banks, web site administrators, credit card companies;
    - organised crime networks.

13. The proper presentation of such cases as statutory conspiracies could lead to:
    - large numbers of separate counts to reflect the different conspiracies;
    - severed trials for single or discrete groups of conspiracies;
    - evidence in one severed trial being deemed inadmissible in another.

14. If so, the consequences might be that no one court would receive a cohesive picture of the whole case which would allow sentencing on a proper basis. In contrast a single count of common law conspiracy to defraud might, in such circumstances, reflect the nature and extent of criminal conduct in a way that prosecuting the underlying statutory offences or conspiracies would fail to achieve.

B. Conduct that can only be prosecuted as conspiracy to defraud

15. Examples of such conduct might include but are not restricted to agreements to the following courses of action:
    - The dishonest obtaining of land and other property which cannot be stolen such as intellectual property not protected by the Copyright, Designs and Patents Act 1988 and the Trademarks Act 1994, and other confidential information. The Fraud Act will bite where there is intent to make a gain or cause a loss through false representation, failure to disclose information where there is a legal obligation to do so, or the abuse of position;
    - Dishonestly infringing another's right; for example the dishonest exploitation of another's patent in the absence of a legal duty to disclose information about its existence;
    - Where it is intended that the final offence be committed by someone outside the conspiracy; and

- Cases where the accused cannot be proved to have had the necessary degree of knowledge of the substantive offence to be perpetrated;

SCHEDULE 3 OF THE INVESTIGATORY POWERS ACT 2016

Updated: 21 April 2022

Schedule 3 IPA: Prosecutor's Guidelines

1. These Guidelines concern the approach to be taken by prosecutors in applying Schedule 3 to the Investigatory Powers Act (IPA) in England and Wales. Paragraph 21 of Schedule 3 provides that disclosure to the prosecutor can be permitted during criminal proceedings so that the prosecutor can determine what action to take in order to ensure that the prosecution is fair. The paragraph also allows disclosure to a judge where the judge considers there are exceptional circumstances making the disclosure essential in the interests of justice.[1]

Background

2. It has been long-standing Government policy that the fact that interception of communications has taken place in any particular case should remain secret and not be disclosed to the subject. This is because of the need to protect the continuing value of interception as a vital means of gathering intelligence about serious crime and activities which threaten national security. The Government judges that if the use of the technique in particular cases were to be confirmed, the value of the technique would be diminished because targets would either know, or could deduce, when their communications might be intercepted and so could take avoiding action by using other, more secure means of communication.

3. In the context of legal proceedings, the policy that the fact of interception should remain secret is implemented by section 56 of IPA. Section 56 provides that no evidence may be adduced, question asked, assertion or disclosure made or other thing done in, for the purposes of, or in connection with, any legal proceedings or Inquiries Act proceedings which discloses, in circumstances from which its origin in interception-related conduct may be inferred, any (i) content of an intercepted communication, (ii) any secondary data obtained from a communication, or (iii) tends to suggest that any interception-related conduct has or may have occurred or may be going to occur.

4. The effect of section 56 is that the fact of interception of the subject's communications and the product of that interception cannot be relied upon or referred to by either party to the proceedings. This is given further effect by sections 3(7), 7A(9) and 8(6) of the Criminal Procedure and Investigations Act 1996 (as amended). This protects the continuing value of interception whilst also creating a 'level playing-field', in that neither side can gain any advantage from the interception. In the context of criminal proceedings, this means that the defendant cannot be prejudiced by the existence in the hands of the prosecution of intercept material which is adverse to his interests.

Detailed Analysis

First Stage: action to be taken by the prosecutor

5. Paragraph 21(1) of Schedule 3 to IPA provides:

    Nothing in section 56(1) prohibits:

    (a) a disclosure to a person ('P') conducting a criminal that is made for the purpose only of enabling P to determine what is required of P by P's duty to secure the fairness of the prosecution, or

    (b) a disclosure to a relevant judge in a case in which the judge has ordered the disclosure to be made to the judge alone.

    If protected information is disclosed to a prosecutor, as permitted by paragraph 18(1)(a), the first step that should be taken by the prosecutor is to review any information regarding an interception that remains extant at the time that he or she has conduct of the case.[2] In reviewing it, the prosecutor should seek to identify any information whose existence, if no

---

[1] Disclosure in the context of RIPA/IPA action is distinct from disclosure under the Criminal Procedure and Investigations Act (CPIA) 1996, CPIA Code of Practice, the Attorney General's Disclosure Guidelines (AGDG), and Director's Guidance on Charging Sixth Edition (DG6).

[2] Section 53 of IPA provides that it is the duty of the issuing authority to ensure that arrangements are in place to ensure that (amongst other matters) intercept material is retained by the intercepting agencies only for as long as is necessary for any of the authorised purposes. The authorised purposes include retention which, 'is necessary to ensure that a person ('P') who is conducting a criminal prosecution has the information P needs to determine what is required of P by P's duty to secure the fairness of the prosecution' (section 53(3)(d)).

action was taken by the Crown, might result in unfairness. Experience suggests that the most likely example of such potential unfairness is where the evidence in the case is such that the jury may draw an inference which intercept shows to be wrong, and to leave this uncorrected will result in the defence being disadvantaged.

6.   If in the view of the prosecutor to take no action would render the proceedings unfair, the prosecutor should, first consulting with the relevant prosecution agency, take such steps as are available to him or her to secure the fairness of the proceedings provided these steps do not contravene paragraph 21(4). In the example given above, such steps could include:

    (i)   putting the prosecution case in such a way to ensure that a potentially misleading inference is not drawn by the jury;

    (ii) not relying upon the evidence which makes the information relevant;

    (iii) discontinuing that part of the prosecution case in relation to which the protected information is relevant, by amending a charge or count on the indictment or offering no evidence on such a charge or count; or

    (iv) making an admission of fact.[3]

There is no requirement for the prosecutor to notify the judge of the action that they have taken or propose to take. Such a course should only be taken by the prosecutor if they [consider] it essential in the interests of justice to do so (see below).

Second Stage: disclosure to the judge

7.   There may be some cases (although these are likely to be rare) where the prosecutor considers that they cannot secure the fairness of the proceedings without assistance from the relevant judge. In recognition of this, paragraph 21(1)(b) of Schedule 3 provides that in certain limited circumstances, the prosecutor may invite the judge to order a disclosure of the protected information to the judge.

8.   If the prosecutor considers that they require the assistance of the trial judge to ensure the fairness of the proceedings, or they are in doubt as to whether the result of taking the steps outlined at para 6 above would ensure fairness, they must apply to see the judge *ex parte*. Under paragraph 21(2), a judge shall not order a disclosure to themselves except where the judge is satisfied that the exceptional circumstances of the case make that disclosure essential in the interests of justice. Before the judge is in a position to order such disclosure the prosecutor will need to impart to the judge such information, but only such information, as is necessary to demonstrate that exceptional circumstances mean that the prosecutor acting alone cannot secure the fairness of the proceedings. Experience suggests that exceptional circumstances in the course of a trial justifying disclosure to a judge arise only in the following two situations:

(1) Where the judge's assistance is necessary to ensure the fairness of the trial

This situation may arise in the example given at paragraph 5 above, where there is a risk that the jury might draw an inference from certain facts, which protected information shows would be the wrong inference, and the prosecutor is unable to ensure that the jury will not draw this inference by the prosecutor's actions alone. The purpose in informing the judge is so that the judge will then be in a position to ensure fairness by:

    (i)   summing up in a way which will ensure that the wrong inference is not drawn;

    (ii) giving appropriate directions to the jury; or,

    (iii) requiring the Crown to make an admission of fact which the judge thinks *essential in the interests of justice* if the judge is of the opinion that *exceptional circumstances* require the judge to make such a direction (paragraph 21(3)). However, such a direction **must not** authorise or require anything to be done which discloses any of the contents of an intercepted communication or related data or tends to suggest that anything falling within section 56(2) has or may have occurred or be going to occur (paragraph 21(4)). Situations where an admission of fact is required are likely to be rare. The judge must be of the view that proceedings could not be continued unless an admission of fact is made (and the conditions in paragraph 21(3) are satisfied). There may be other ways in which it is possible for a judge to ensure fairness, such as those outlined at (i) and (ii) above.

In practice, no question of taking the action at (i)–(iii) arises if the protected information is already contained in a separate document in another form that has been or can be disclosed without contravening section 56(1), and this disclosure will secure the fairness of the proceedings.

'is necessary to ensure that a person conducting a criminal prosecution has the information he needs to determine what is required of him by his duty to secure the fairness of the prosecution' (section 15(4)(d)).

3 This is acceptable as long as to do so would not contravene section 17 i.e. reveal the existence of an interception warrant. Prosecutors must bear in mind that such a breach might conceivably occur not only from the factual content of the admission, but also from the circumstances in which it is made.

(2) **Where the judge requires knowledge of the protected material for some other purpose**

This situation may arise where, usually in the context of a PII application, the true significance of, or duty of disclosure in relation to, other material being considered for disclosure by a judge, cannot be appraised by the judge without reference to protected information. Disclosure to the judge of the protected information without more may be sufficient to enable the judge to appraise the material, but once he has seen the protected information the judge may also conclude that the conditions in paragraph 21(3) are satisfied so that an admission of fact by the Crown is required in addition to or instead of disclosure of the non-protected material.

Another example is a case where protected information underlies operational decisions which are likely to be the subject of cross-examination and it is necessary to inform the judge of the existence of the protected information to enable the judge to deal with the issue when the questions are first posed in a way which ensures section 56(1) is not contravened.

What if the actions of the prosecutor and/or the judge cannot ensure the fairness of the proceedings?

9. There may be very rare cases in which no action taken by the prosecutor and/or judge can prevent the continuation of the proceedings being unfair, e.g. where the requirements of fairness could only be met if the Crown were to make an admission, but it cannot do so without contravening paragraph 21(4). In that situation the prosecutor will have no option but to offer no evidence on the charge in question, or to discontinue the proceedings in their entirety.

Responding to questions about interception

10. Prosecutors are sometimes placed in a situation in which they are asked by the court or by the defence whether interception has taken place or whether protected information exists. Whether or not interception has taken place or protected information exists, an answer in the following terms, or similar should be given:

'I am not in a position to answer that, but I am aware of section 56 of and Schedule 3 to the Investigatory Powers Act 2016 and the Attorney General's Guidelines on the Disclosure of Information in Exceptional Circumstances under Schedule 3'.

In a case where interception has taken place or protected information exists, an answer in these terms will avoid a breach of the prohibition in section 56 while providing assurance that the prosecutor is aware of his obligations.

11. For the avoidance of doubt, any notification or disclosure of information to the judge in accordance with paragraphs 7–10 must be *ex parte*. It will never be appropriate for prosecutors to volunteer, either *inter partes* or to the Court *ex parte*, that interception has taken place or that protected information exists, save in accordance with paragraph 21(1) of Schedule 3 of IPA as elaborated in these Guidelines.

Further Assistance

12. Should a prosecutor be unsure as to the application of these guidelines in any particular case, further guidance should be sought from those instructing him or her. In those cases where a prosecutor has been instructed by the Crown Prosecution Service, the relevant CPS prosecutor must seek appropriate guidance from the relevant casework division in CPS Headquarters.

APPLICATIONS FOR WITNESS ANONYMITY ORDERS: THE PROSECUTOR'S ROLE

Updated: 30 November 2012

A. Foreword

A1. Every defendant has a right to a fair trial. An important aspect of a fair trial is the right of the defendant to be confronted by, and to challenge, those who accuse him or her.

A2. Making an application for a witness anonymity order is therefore a serious step, to be taken by the prosecutor only where there are genuine grounds to believe that the court would not otherwise hear evidence that should be available to it in the interests of justice; that other measures falling short of anonymity would not be sufficient; and that the defendant will have a fair trial if the order is made.

A3. Anonymous witness testimony is not necessarily incompatible with Article 6, even when it is the sole or decisive evidence against the accused. But whether the measures used to allow a witness to give evidence anonymously in any particular case would make the trial unfair has to be evaluated with care on the facts of each case.

A4.   When assessing whether and in what terms to make an application for a witness anonymity order, prosecutors have overriding duties to be fair, independent and objective. These guidelines set out the overarching principles by which a prosecutor should consider, and if appropriate apply for, a witness anonymity order in accordance with the considerations set out in the Criminal Evidence (Witness Anonymity) Act 2008.

B.   The Prosecutor's Duties

B1.   The effect of a witness anonymity order is to prevent the defendant from knowing the identity of a witness. Without this information the defendant's ability to investigate and challenge the accuracy or credibility of the witness's evidence may be limited.

B2.   When considering whether to make a witness anonymity order the court will consider to what extent the defendant needs to know the identity of the witness in order to challenge the witness's evidence effectively. This question will often be central to the question of whether, having regard to all the circumstances, the witness anonymity order sought would be consistent with a fair trial.

B3.   The prosecutor's role is:
   • To act with scrupulous fairness.
   • To examine with care, and probe where appropriate, the material provided in support of the application and the evidential basis for it. Prosecutors should in particular objectively assess any statement made by the witness or witnesses in question and the grounds on which it is based.
   • To be satisfied before making the application that, viewed objectively, it can properly be said that the order is necessary and in the interests of justice and that the defendant can receive a fair trial.
   • To put before the court all material that is relevant to the application. Courts will rely to a significant extent upon the prosecutor and the investigator to provide relevant material. Material will be relevant if the prosecutor relies upon it to support the application, or if it may tend to undermine or qualify the justification for making the order at all, or for making it in the form sought by the prosecutor. Material is particularly relevant if credibility is or may be in issue, for example if there is a known link between the witness and the defendant or a co-accused.
   • To disclose as much relevant material to the defence as possible without identifying the witness, including material that may tend to cast doubt on the credibility, reliability or accuracy of the witness's evidence.

B4.   The role of the prosecutor as an independent and impartial minister of justice is of paramount importance. Applications should only be authorised by prosecutors at an appropriately senior level within the prosecuting authority.

B5.   The interests of justice include the interests of the victim or victims, the interests of the witness or witnesses, the interests of the defendant and any co-defendants and the wider public interest.

B6.   Prosecutors should take all necessary and reasonable steps consistent with a fair trial and the interests of justice to ensure the safety of a witness or the avoidance of real harm to the public interest or the protection of property.

C.   Applications by Defendants

C1.   The Act permits a defendant (as well as a prosecutor) to apply for a Witness Anonymity Order. Prosecutors should respond to such applications independently and objectively. Prosecutors should examine critically, but fairly, the basis for any application and any material put forward in support of any application.

C2.   The prosecutor should provide the court with all material within the prosecutor's possession or control that is relevant to the defendant's application.

D.   Appointment and Role of Special Counsel in Applications for Witness Anonymity

D1.   The Act makes no statutory provision for the appointment of Special Counsel.

D2.   A criminal court may invite the Attorney General to appoint Special Counsel.[4] However, in line with authority, such an appointment:
   • Should be regarded as '… exceptional, never automatic, a course of last and never first resort.' *R v H* and *R v C* [2004] UKHL 3. The need for Special Counsel has to be shown.
   • The court will take account of the seriousness of the issue that the court has to determine in the particular case. Whether credibility is at issue is likely to be an important consideration. The court will also need to consider the extent to which Special Counsel could further the defendant's case.
   • The court itself can be expected to perform a role of testing and probing the case which is presented on the application. When coupled with the prosecutor's duty to put all relevant material

3 Most recently, *Shiv Malik and Manchester Crown Court and Chief Constable of Greater Manchester Police, Constable and Robinson Ltd and Attorney General as interested parties* [2008] EWHC 1362 (Admin).

before the court, this may often be sufficient to enable a fair and informed decision to be reached without the need to appoint Special Counsel.

D3. Where appointed, the role of Special Counsel is to make representations on behalf of the accused in any closed proceedings.

D4. The Attorney General will consider each invitation to appoint Special Counsel on its merits, having regard to all the relevant circumstances of the case. In particular, in this context, to the basis of the application, whether it is opposed, the basis upon which it is opposed and the particular considerations that the court wishes Special Counsel to address.

D5. A prosecutor making an application for a witness anonymity order should always be prepared to assist the court to consider whether the circumstances are such that exceptionally the appointment of Special Counsel may be called for. When appropriate a prosecutor should draw to the attention of the court any aspect of an application for a witness anonymity order or any aspect of the case that may, viewed objectively, call for the appointment of Special Counsel.

D6. When a court decides to invite the Attorney General to appoint Special Counsel the prosecutor should (regardless of any steps taken by the court or any defendant) ensure that the Attorney General's Office is promptly notified; and assist in ensuring that the Attorney General receives all the information needed to take a decision.

D7. Where Special Counsel is appointed, he or she will initially be provided by the prosecutor with any open material made available to the accused regarding the application (and any other open material requested by Special Counsel). Special Counsel may then seek instructions from the defendant and his legal representatives. Only then will Special Counsel be provided by the prosecutor with the closed or un-redacted material provided to the court.

PLEA DISCUSSIONS IN CASES OF SERIOUS OR COMPLEX FRAUD

Updated: 29 November 2012

A. Foreword

A1. These Guidelines set out a process by which a prosecutor may discuss an allegation of serious or complex fraud with a person who he or she is prosecuting or expects to prosecute, or with that person's legal representative. They come into force on the 5th day of May 2009 and apply to plea discussions initiated on or after that date.

A2. The Guidelines will be followed by all prosecutors in England and Wales when conducting plea discussions in cases of serious or complex fraud. For the purposes of the Guidelines, fraud means any financial, fiscal or commercial misconduct or corruption which is contrary to the criminal law. Fraud may be serious or complex if at least two of the following factors are present:
- The amount obtained or intended to be obtained is alleged to exceed £500,000;
- There is a significant international dimension;
- The case requires specialised knowledge of financial, commercial, fiscal or regulatory matters such as the operation of markets, banking systems, trusts or tax regimes;
- The case involves allegations of fraudulent activity against numerous victims;
- The case involves an allegation of substantial and significant fraud on a public body;
- The case is likely to be of widespread public concern;
- The alleged misconduct endangered the economic well-being of the United Kingdom, for example by undermining confidence in financial markets.

Taking account of these matters, it is for the prosecutor to decide whether or not a case is one of fraud, and whether or not it is serious or complex.

A3. The decision whether a person should be charged with a criminal offence rests with the prosecutor. In selecting the appropriate charge or charges, the prosecutor applies principles set out in the Code for Crown Prosecutors ('the Code'). Charges should reflect the seriousness and extent of the offending, give the court adequate sentencing powers and enable the case to be presented in a clear and simple way. The Code also states that prosecutors should not go ahead with more charges to encourage a defendant to plead guilty to a few; equally, prosecutors should not charge a more serious offence to encourage a defendant to plead to a less serious one.

A4. Once proceedings are instituted, the accused may plead guilty to all of the charges selected. If the defendant will plead guilty to some, but not all, of the charges or to a different, possibly less serious charge, the Code states that a prosecutor is entitled to accept such pleas if he or she assesses that the court could still pass an adequate sentence. In taking these decisions the prosecutor also applies the Attorney General's Guidelines on the Acceptance of Pleas and the Prosecutor's Role in the Sentencing Exercise ('the Acceptance of Pleas Guidelines').

A5.   The purpose of plea discussions is to narrow the issues in the case with a view to reaching a just outcome at the earliest possible time, including the possibility of reaching an agreement about acceptable pleas of guilty and preparing a joint submission as to sentence.

A6.   The potential benefits of plea discussions are that:
- Early resolution of the case may reduce the anxiety and uncertainty for victims and witnesses, and provide earlier clarity for accused persons who admit their guilt (subject to the court's power to reject the agreement);
- The issues in dispute may be narrowed so that even if the case proceeds to trial, it can be managed more efficiently in accordance with Rule 3.2 of the Criminal Procedure Rules 2005. If pleas are agreed, litigation can be kept to a minimum.

A7.   Where plea discussions take place prior to the commencement of proceedings, the charges brought by the prosecutor will reflect those agreed, rather than those that the prosecutor would necessarily have preferred if no agreement had been reached. Also, any criminal investigation may not be complete when these discussions take place. For these reasons it is important that the procedures followed should command public and judicial confidence; that any agreement reached is reasonable, fair and just; that there are safeguards to ensure that defendants are not under improper pressure to make admissions; and that there are proper records of discussions that have taken place.

A8.   The Guidelines are not intended to prevent or discourage existing practices by which prosecutors and prosecuting advocates discuss cases with defence legal representatives after charge, in order to narrow the issues or to agree a basis of plea. Neither do they affect the existing practice of judicial sentence indications at the plea and case management hearing or later in accordance with the guidance in *R v Goodyear (Karl)* [2005] EWCA 888 (see also the Acceptance of Pleas Guidelines). They complement, and do not detract from or replace, the Code and the Acceptance of Pleas Guidelines, or any other relevant guidance such as the Prosecutor's Pledge, the Victim's Charter and the Code of Practice for Victims of Crime.

A9.   Where a plea agreement is reached, it remains entirely a matter for the court to decide how to deal with the case.

B. General Principles

B1.   In conducting plea discussions and presenting a plea agreement to the court, the prosecutor must act openly, fairly and in the interests of justice.

B2.   Acting in the interests of justice means ensuring that the plea agreement reflects the seriousness and extent of the offending, gives the court adequate sentencing powers, and enables the court, the public and the victims to have confidence in the outcome. The prosecutor must consider carefully the impact of a proposed plea or basis of plea on the community and the victim, and on the prospects of successfully prosecuting any other person implicated in the offending. The prosecutor must not agree to a reduced basis of plea which is misleading, untrue or illogical.

B3.   Acting fairly means respecting the rights of the defendant and of any other person who is being or may be prosecuted in relation to the offending. The prosecutor must not put improper pressure on a defendant in the course of plea discussions, for example by exaggerating the strength of the case in order to persuade the defendant to plead guilty, or to plead guilty on a particular basis.

B4.   Acting openly means being transparent with the defendant, the victim and the court. The prosecutor must:
- Ensure that a full and accurate record of the plea discussions is prepared and retained;
- Ensure that the defendant has sufficient information to enable him or her to play an informed part in the plea discussions;
- Communicate with the victim before accepting a reduced basis of plea, wherever it is practicable to do so, so that the position can be explained; and
- Ensure that the plea agreement placed before the court fully and fairly reflects the matters agreed. The prosecutor must not agree additional matters with the defendant which are not recorded in the plea agreement and made known to the court.

C. Initiating Plea Discussions

When and with whom discussions should be initiated and conducted

C1.   Where he or she believes it advantageous to do so, the prosecutor may initiate plea discussions with any person who is being prosecuted or investigated with a view to prosecution in connection with a serious or complex fraud, and who is legally represented. The prosecutor will not initiate plea discussions with a defendant who is not legally represented. If the prosecutor receives an approach from such a defendant, he or she may enter into discussions if satisfied that it is appropriate to do so.

C2.   Where proceedings have not yet been instituted, the prosecutor should not initiate plea discussions until he or she and the investigating officer are satisfied that the suspect's criminality is known. This will not usually be the case until after the suspect has been interviewed under caution.

C3.   The prosecutor should be alert to any attempt by the defendant to use plea discussions as a means of delaying the investigation or prosecution, and should not initiate or continue discussions where the defendant's commitment to the process is in doubt. The prosecutor should ensure that the position is preserved during plea discussions by, for example, restraining assets in anticipation of the making of a confiscation order. Where a defendant declines to take part in plea discussions, the prosecutor should not make a second approach unless there is a material change in circumstances.

Invitation letter

C4.   In order to initiate the plea discussions, the prosecutor will send the defendant's representatives a letter which:
   • Asks whether the defence wish to enter into discussions in accordance with these Guidelines; and
   • Sets a deadline for a response from the defence.

Terms and conditions letter

C5.   Where the defence agree to engage in plea discussions, the prosecutor should send them a letter setting out the way in which the discussions will be conducted. This letter should deal with:
   • The confidentiality of information provided by the prosecutor and defendant in the course of the plea discussions;
   • The use which may be made by the prosecutor of information provided by the defendant; and
   • The practical means by which the discussions will be conducted.

Confidentiality and use of information

C6.   In relation to confidentiality, the prosecutor will indicate that he or she intends to provide an undertaking to the effect that the fact that the defendant has taken part in the plea discussions, and any information provided by the defence in the course of the plea discussions will be treated as confidential and will not be disclosed to any other party other than for the purposes of the plea discussions and plea agreement (applying these Guidelines), or as required by law. The undertaking will make it clear that the law in relation to the disclosure of unused material may require the prosecutor to provide information about the plea discussions to another defendant in criminal proceedings.

C7.   The prosecutor will require the defendant's legal representative to provide an undertaking to the effect that information provided by the prosecutor in the course of the plea discussions will be treated as confidential and will not be disclosed to any other party, other than for the purposes of the plea discussion and plea agreement or as required by law.

C8.   In relation to the use of information, the prosecutor will indicate that he or she intends to undertake not to rely upon the fact that the defendant has taken part in the plea discussions, or any information provided by the defendant in the course of the discussions, as evidence in any prosecution of that defendant for the offences under investigation, should the discussions fail. However, this undertaking will make it clear that the prosecutor is not prevented from:
   • Relying upon a concluded and signed plea agreement as confession evidence or as admissions;
   • Relying upon any evidence obtained from enquiries made as a result of the provision of information by the defendant;
   • Relying upon information provided by the defendant as evidence against him or her in any prosecution for an offence other than the fraud which is the subject of the plea discussion and any offence which is consequent upon it, such as money laundering; and
   • Relying upon information provided by the defendant in a prosecution of any other person for any offence (so far as the rules of evidence allow).

C9.   In exceptional circumstances the prosecutor may agree to different terms regarding the confidentiality and use of information. However, the prosecutor must not surrender the ability to rely upon a concluded and signed plea agreement as evidence against the defendant. The prosecutor may reserve the right to bring other charges (additional to those to which the defendant has indicated a willingness to plead guilty) in specific circumstances, for example if substantial new information comes to light at a later stage, the plea agreement is rejected by the court, or the defendant fails to honour the agreement.

C10. Until the issues of confidentiality and use of information have been agreed to the satisfaction of both parties, and the agreement reflected in signed undertakings, the prosecutor must not continue with the substantive plea discussions.

D. Conducting Plea Discussions

Statement of case

D1.   Where plea discussions take place prior to proceedings being instituted, the prosecutor will provide a statement of case to the defence. This is a written summary of the nature of the allegation against the suspect and the evidence which has been obtained, or is expected to be obtained, to support it.

The statement of case should include a list of the proposed charges. Material in support of the statement of case may also be provided, whether or not in the form of admissible evidence. However, the prosecutor is not obliged to reveal to the suspect all of the information or evidence supporting his case, provided that this does not mislead the suspect to his or her prejudice.

D2. Where plea discussions are initiated after proceedings have been commenced, but before the prosecutor has provided the defence with a case summary or opening note, the prosecutor may provide a statement of case to assist the defendant in understanding the evidence and identifying the issues.

Unused material

D3. These Guidelines do not affect the prosecutor's existing duties in relation to the disclosure of unused material. Where plea discussions take place prior to the institution of proceedings, the prosecutor should ensure that the suspect is not misled as to the strength of the prosecution case. It will not usually be necessary to provide copies of unused material in order to do this.

Conducting and recording the discussions

D4. Having provided the defence with the statement of case and supporting material, the parties will then be in a position to conduct the plea discussion proper. Whether this is done by correspondence, by face-to-face meetings or by a combination of the two is a matter for the parties to decide in the individual case.

D5. It is essential that a full written record is kept of every key action and event in the discussion process, including details of every offer or concession made by each party, and the reasons for every decision taken by the prosecutor. Meetings between the parties should be minuted and the minutes agreed and signed. Particular care should be taken where the defendant is not legally represented. The prosecutor should only meet with a defendant who is not legally represented if the defendant agrees to the meeting being recorded, or to the presence of an independent third party.

[King's] Evidence

D6. If the defendant offers at any stage to provide information, or to give evidence about the criminal activities of others, any such offer will be dealt with in accordance with sections 71 to 75 of the Serious Organised Crime and Police Act 2005 ('SOCPA'), the judgment of the Court of Appeal in *R v P, R v Blackburn* [2007] EWCA Crim 2290 and the guidance agreed and issued by the Director of Public Prosecutions, the Director of the Serious Fraud Office and the Director of Revenue and Customs Prosecutions.

Discussion of pleas

D7. In deciding whether or not to accept an offer by the defendant to plead guilty, the prosecutor will follow sections 7 and 10 of the Code relating to the selection of charges and the acceptance of guilty pleas. The prosecutor should ensure that:
- The charges reflect the seriousness and extent of the offending;
- They give the court adequate powers to sentence and impose appropriate post-conviction orders;
- They enable the case to be presented in a clear and simple way (bearing in mind that many cases of fraud are necessarily complex);
- The basis of plea enables the court to pass a sentence that matches the seriousness of the offending, particularly if there are aggravating features;
- The interests of the victim, and where possible any views expressed by the victim, are taken into account when deciding whether it is in the public interest to accept the plea; and
- The investigating officer is fully appraised of developments in the plea discussions and his or her views are taken into account.

D8. In reaching an agreement on pleas, the parties should resolve any factual issues necessary to allow the court to sentence the defendant on a clear, fair and accurate basis. Before agreeing to proposed pleas, the prosecutor should satisfy him or herself that the Full Code Test as set out in the Code will be made out in respect of each charge. In considering whether the evidential stage of the test will be met, the prosecutor should assume that the offender will sign a plea agreement amounting to an admission to the charge.

Discussion of sentence

D9. Where agreement is reached as to pleas, the parties should discuss the appropriate sentence with a view to presenting a joint written submission to the court. This document should list the aggravating and mitigating features arising from the agreed facts, set out any personal mitigation available to the defendant, and refer to any relevant sentencing guidelines or authorities. In the light of all of these factors, it should make submissions as to the applicable sentencing range in the relevant guideline. The prosecutor must ensure that the submissions are realistic, taking full account of all relevant material and considerations.

D10. The prosecutor should bear in mind all of the powers of the court, and seek to include in the joint submission any relevant ancillary orders. It is particularly desirable that measures should be included that achieve redress for victims (such as compensation orders) and protection for the public (such as directors' disqualification orders, serious crime prevention orders or financial reporting orders).

D11. Due regard should be had to the court's asset recovery powers and the desirability of using these powers both as a deterrent to others and as a means of preventing the defendant from benefiting from the proceeds of crime or funding future offending. The Proceeds of Crime Act 2002 requires the Crown Court to proceed to the making of a confiscation order against a convicted defendant who has benefited from his criminal conduct where the prosecutor asks the court to do so, or the court believes that it is appropriate to do so. Fraud is an acquisitive crime, and the expectation in a fraud case should be that a confiscation order will be sought by the prosecutor reflecting the full benefit to the defendant. However, in doing so it is open to the prosecutor to take a realistic view of the likely approach of the court to the determination of any points in dispute (such as the interest of a third party in any property).

D12. In the course of the plea discussions the prosecutor must make it clear to the defence that the joint submission as to sentence (including confiscation) is not binding on the court.

Liaison with another prosecutor or regulator

D13. The prosecutor may become aware that another prosecuting authority or regulatory body (either in England and Wales or elsewhere) has an interest in the defendant. The prosecutor should liaise with the other agency, in accordance with the Prosecutors' Convention and any other relevant agreement or guidance. The other agency may wish to take part in the plea discussions, or they may authorise the prosecutor to discuss with the defendant the matters which they are interested in, with a view to resolving all matters in one plea agreement. The prosecutor should warn the defendant that a plea agreement will not bind any other agency which is not a party to it.

E. The Written Plea Agreement

E1. All matters agreed between the prosecutor and the defence must be reduced to writing as a plea agreement and signed by both parties. The plea agreement will include:
- A list of the charges;
- A statement of the facts; and
- A declaration, signed by the defendant personally, to the effect that he or she accepts the stated facts and admits he or she is guilty of the agreed charges.

E2. Any agreement under the SOCPA regarding the giving of assistance to the prosecutor by the defendant should be in a separate document accompanying the plea agreement.

E3. Once a plea agreement is signed in a case where proceedings have not yet been commenced, the prosecutor will review the case in accordance with the Code and, assuming the evidential stage of the Full Code Test is satisfied on the basis of the signed plea agreement and the other available evidence, will arrange for proceedings to be instituted by summons or charge.

E4. In advance of the defendant's first appearance in the Crown Court, the prosecutor should send the court sufficient material to allow the judge to understand the facts of the case and the history of the plea discussions, to assess whether the plea agreement is fair and in the interests of justice, and to decide the appropriate sentence. This will include:
- The signed plea agreement;
- A joint submission as to sentence and sentencing considerations;
- Any relevant sentencing guidelines or authorities;
- All of the material provided by the prosecution to the defendant in the course of the plea discussions;
- Any material provided by the defendant to the prosecution, such as documents relating to personal mitigation; and
- The minutes of any meetings between the parties and any correspondence generated in the plea discussions.

E5. It will then be for the court to decide how to deal with the plea agreement. In particular, the court retains an absolute discretion as to whether or not it sentences in accordance with the joint submission from the parties.

F. Failure of Plea Discussions

F1. There are several circumstances in which plea discussions may result in an outcome other than the defendant pleading guilty in accordance with a plea agreement. The prosecutor or the defendant may break off the discussions. They may be unable to reach an agreement. They may reach an agreement, but intervening events may lead the prosecutor to decide that proceedings should not be instituted. Proceedings may be instituted but the court may reject the plea agreement. The defendant may decline to plead guilty in accordance with the plea agreement, either as a result of a sentence indication given under the procedure set out in *R v Goodyear*, or for some other reason.

F2.   If any of these situations arises, the prosecutor may wish for further enquiries to be made with a view to bringing or completing proceedings against the defendant. If proceedings have already been instituted, the prosecutor will use the appropriate means to delay them — either discontinuing under section 23 or 23A of the Prosecution of Offences Act 1985 or (if the indictment has already been preferred) applying for an adjournment or stay of the proceedings. The prosecutor and the defendant's representatives will continue to be bound by the preliminary undertakings made in relation to the confidentiality and use of information provided in the course of the plea discussions.

F3.   Where plea discussions have broken down for any reason, it will be rare that the prosecutor will wish to re-open them, but he or she may do so if there is a material change in circumstances which warrants it.

Disclosure

ATTORNEY-GENERAL'S GUIDELINES ON DISCLOSURE FOR INVESTIGATORS, PROSECUTORS AND DEFENCE PRACTITIONERS

EFFECTIVE FROM 25th July 2022

Introduction

These Guidelines are issued by the Attorney-General for investigators, prosecutors and defence practitioners on the application of the disclosure regime contained in the Criminal Procedure and Investigations Act 1996 ('CPIA') Code of Practice Order 2020.

These Guidelines replace the existing Attorney-General's Guidelines on Disclosure issued in 2013 and the Supplementary Guidelines on Digital Material issued in 2013, which is an annex to the general guidelines.

The Guidelines outline the high-level principles which should be followed when the disclosure regime is applied throughout England and Wales. They are not designed to be an unequivocal statement of the law at any one time, nor are they a substitute for a thorough understanding of the relevant legislation, codes of practice, case law and procedure.

Important principles

Disclosure process, with judicial oversight

Investigators
Pursue all reasonable lines of inquiry and keep a record of all material relevant to the case, including that which will not be used as evidence in the prosecution case. Investigators prepare disclosure schedules for review by the prosecution.

Prosecution
Engage with the investigators and advise on reasonable lines of inquiry. Ensure investigators provide disclosure schedules, and review these. Apply the test for disclosure set out in CPIA 1996.

Defence
Engage with prosecution (including pre-charge where appropriate). Serve a defence statement setting out the nature of the defence, and request any material which could reasonably assist their case. Participate in process for completing a disclosure management document.

Prosecution advocates
Review schedules and disclosed material, advise the prosecution where advice is sought and at any rate where deficiencies in disclosure are apparent.

Ongoing evaluation
Disclosure is subject to continuous review throughout the lifetime of a case. All parties should reassess as new information or material becomes available and the case progresses.

1. Every accused person has a right to a fair trial. This right is a fundamental part of our legal system and is guaranteed by Article 6 of the European Convention on Human Rights (ECHR). The disclosure process secures the right to a fair trial.

2. The statutory framework for criminal investigations and disclosure is contained in the Criminal Procedure and Investigations Act 1996 (the CPIA 1996). The CPIA 1996 is an important part of the system that ensures criminal investigations and trials are conducted in a fair, objective and thorough manner. The roles, responsibilities and terminology used in this document therefore mirror the definitions given in the CPIA 1996 and its Code of Practice.

3. A fair trial does not require consideration of irrelevant material. It does not require irrelevant material to be obtained or reviewed. It should not involve spurious applications or arguments which aim to divert the trial process from examining the real issues before the court.

4. The statutory disclosure regime does not require the prosecutor to make available to the accused either neutral material or material which is adverse to the accused[1]. This material may be listed on the schedule, alerting the accused to its existence, but does not need to be disclosed: prosecutors should not disclose material which they are not required to, as this would overburden the participants in the trial process, divert attention away from the relevant issues and may lead to unjustifiable delays. **Disclosure should be completed in a thinking manner,[2] in light of the issues in the case, and not simply as a schedule completing exercise.**[3] Prosecutors need to think about what the case is about, what the likely issues for trial are going to be and how this affects the reasonable lines of inquiry, what material is relevant, and whether material meets the test for disclosure.

5. There will always be a number of participants in prosecutions and investigations. Communication within the prosecution team is vital to ensure that all disclosure issues are given sufficient attention by the right person. The respective roles of an investigator, the officer in charge of an investigation, disclosure officer, and prosecutor are set out in the CPIA Code.[4]

6. A full log of disclosure decisions and the reasons for those decisions must be kept on file and made available to the prosecution team. Any prosecutor must be able to see and understand previous disclosure decisions before carrying out their continuous review function.

7. The role of the reviewing lawyer is central to ensuring that all members of the prosecution team are aware of their role and their duties. Where prosecution advocates are instructed, they should be provided with clear written instructions about disclosure and provided with copies of any unused material which has been disclosed to the defence.

8. Investigators and disclosure officers must be fair and objective and must work together with prosecutors to ensure that disclosure obligations are met. Investigators and disclosure officers should be familiar with the CPIA Code of Practice[5] - in particular their obligations to **retain and record** the relevant material, to **review** it and to **reveal** it to the prosecutor (see paragraphs 3–7 of the Code).

9. Investigators and disclosure officers should be deployed on cases which are commensurate with their training, skills and experience. The conduct of an investigation provides the foundation for the entire case, and may even impact on linked cases. The specific strategy and approach to disclosure that will be taken must always be considered at the start of each investigation.

10. Where there are a number of disclosure officers assigned to a case there should be a lead disclosure officer who is the focus for enquiries and whose responsibility it is to ensure that the investigator's disclosure obligations are complied with. Regular case conferences should be held, as required, to ensure that prosecutors are apprised of all relevant developments. Full records, including detailed minutes, should be kept of any such meetings. The parties involved should agree at the outset whose responsibility it will be to record the case conferences.

The balance between the right to a fair trial (Article 6 of the European Convention of Human Rights) and the right to private and family life (Article 8 of the European Convention of Human Rights)

11. Investigators and prosecutors need to be aware of the delicate questions which arise when both the right to a fair trial and the privacy of complainants and witnesses are engaged.[6]

12. Fulfilling disclosure obligations is part of ensuring a fair trial in accordance with Article 6 of the ECHR. To comply with Article 6, during the course of an investigation, the investigator or

---

[1] *R v H and others* [2004] UKHL 3, [2004] 2 AC 134 paras. [17] and [35]

[2] "Not undertaking the process in a mechanical manner...keeping the issues in mind...being alive to the countervailing points of view...considering the impact of disclosure decisions...keeping disclosure decisions under review". *R v Olu, Wilson and Brooks* [2010] EWCA Crim 2975, [2011] 1 Cr. App. R. 33 [42]–[44]

[3] *R v Olu, Wilson and Brooks* [2010] EWCA Crim 2975, [2011] 1 Cr. App. R. 33 [42]–[44]

[4] The CPIA Code (n2) para. 2.1

[5] Ministry of Justice, *Criminal Procedure and Investigations Act 1996 Code of Practice* (2020) (the CPIA Code)

[6] Guidance is given by the Court of Appeal in *Bater-James and Mohammed* [2020] EWCA Crim 790

prosecutor may decide that it is necessary to request and/or process personal or private information from a complainant or witness to pursue a reasonable line of inquiry; this includes, but is not limited to, digital material.

13. When seeking to obtain and review such material, investigators and prosecutors should be aware that these lines of inquiry may engage that individual's Article 8 rights and those rights in respect of other parties within that material. Such material may also include sensitive data.[7] When seeking to satisfy their disclosure obligations in these circumstances, investigators and prosecutors should apply the following principles:

   a. Collecting and/or processing personal or private material can only be done when in accordance with the law, strictly necessary,[8] and proportionate.

   b. In order to be in accordance with the law and necessary, an investigator must be pursuing a reasonable line of inquiry in seeking to obtain the material. What constitutes a reasonable line of inquiry may be informed by others, including the prosecutor and the defendant. Seeking the personal or private information of a complainant or witness will not be a reasonable line of inquiry in every case – an assessment of reasonableness is required (see below for an example).

   c. The assessment of reasonableness must be made on a case-by-case basis and regard may be had to:

     (i) the prospect of obtaining relevant material; and

     (ii) what the perceived relevance of that material is, having regard to the identifiable facts and issues in the individual case;

   d. If, by following a reasonable line of inquiry, it becomes necessary to obtain personal or private material, investigators will also need to consider:

     (i) what review is required;

     (ii) how the review of this material should be conducted;

     (iii) what is the least intrusive method which will nonetheless secure relevant material;

     (iv) are particular parameters for searching best suited to the identification of relevant material;

     (v) is provision of the material in its entirety to the investigator strictly necessary; or alternatively, could the material be obtained from other sources, or by the investigator viewing and/or capturing the material in situ? An incremental approach should be taken to the degree of intrusion.

   e. The rationale for pursuing the reasonable line of inquiry and the scope of the review it necessitates should be open and transparent. It should be capable of articulation by the investigator making the decision. It should provide the basis for:

     (i) consultation with the prosecutor,

     (ii) engagement with the defence and,

     (iii) the provision of information to the witness about how their material is to be handled.

   f. The refusal by a witness to provide private or personal material requires an investigator and prosecutor to consider the information the witness has been provided (and could be provided) with regard to the use of their personal material, the reasons for refusal, and how the trial process could address the absence of the material.

   g. Disclosure of such material to the defence is in accordance with the law and necessary if, but only if, the material meets the disclosure test in the CPIA 1996.
Personal information which does not meet this test but is contained within the material to be disclosed should be redacted.

   h. Where there is a conflict between both of these rights, investigators and prosecutors should bear in mind that the right to a fair trial is an absolute right. Where prosecutors and investigators work within the framework provided by the CPIA, any unavoidable intrusion into privacy rights is likely to be justified, so long as any intrusion is no more than necessary.

For retention of data, see paragraphs 21–25 of Annex A on Digital Material and paragraph 5(a) and (b) of the Code.

---

7 See s.35(8) of the Data Protection Act 2018 for data that requires sensitive processing
8 The processing must relate to a pressing social need, and where the investigator or prosecutor cannot reasonably achieve it through less intrusive means. See Part 3 and sch.8 of the Data Protection Act 2018

Example

There will be cases where there is no requirement for the police to take the devices of a complainant/ witness or others at all, and no requirement for any examination to be undertaken.

Examples of this could include sexual offences committed opportunistically against strangers, or historic allegations where there is considered to be no prospect that the complainant's phone will contain any material relevant to the period in which the conduct is said to have occurred and/or the complainant through age or other circumstances did not have access to a phone at that time.

However, decisions will depend on the facts of the case in question. For example, in the case of a sexual offence committed opportunistically against a stranger, a mobile phone could contain first complaint evidence. Investigators should always carefully consider what is relevant for the case in question.

A case might, for example, involve a complainant contacting the police to make an allegation of an offence against a person they had met that same day. The suspect may accept that they met the complainant but deny the allegation. The complainant and suspect communicated on a single medium. The investigator may consider it is a reasonable line of enquiry to view the messages from the day on which the two persons met as, before and after, they are highly likely to be relevant. They may contain material about what was expected or not expected when the complainant and suspect met, the nature of their relationship, and the response after they met, all of which may cast light on the complainant's account and the suspect's account. That is unlikely to require the investigator taking custody of the phone or obtaining a large volume of data. If, by way of example and contrast, the complainant alleged coercive and controlling behaviour over a period of years, including manipulative conduct over various platforms, a larger quantity of data may be relevant and require review and retention by the investigator by different means.

The investigation

14.   Consideration of disclosure issues is an integral part of an investigation and is not something that should be considered in isolation.

15.   Investigators should approach the investigation with a view to establishing what actually happened. They are to be fair and objective.

16.   The following diagram illustrates how material that forms part of an investigation may be categorised and consequently treated. Further information on sensitive material can be found at here.

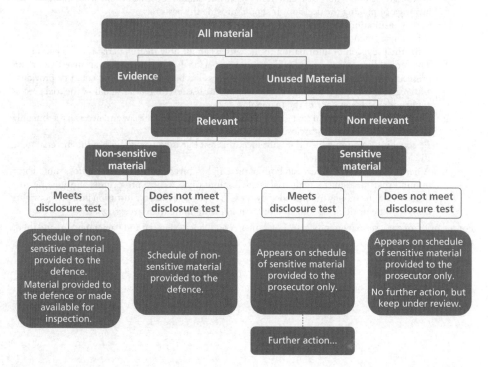

17. Investigators should ensure that all reasonable lines of inquiry are investigated, whether they point towards or away from the suspect. What is 'reasonable' will depend on the context of the case. A fair investigation does not mean an endless investigation. Investigators and disclosure officers must give thought to defining and articulating the limits of the scope of their investigations. When assessing what is reasonable, thought should be given to what is likely to be obtained as a result of the line of inquiry and how it can be obtained. An investigator may seek the advice of the prosecutor when considering which lines of inquiry should be pursued where appropriate.

18. When conducting an investigation, an investigator should always have in mind their obligation to retain and record all relevant material.[9] Material which is presumed to meet the test for disclosure, as set out in the dedicated section of these guidelines, must always be retained and recorded. All relevant material must be retained, whereas non- relevant material does not need to be retained.

Definitions

Relevant Material

Material may be relevant to an investigation if it appears to an investigator, or to the officer in charge of an investigation, or to the disclosure officer, that it has some bearing on any offence under investigation or any person being investigated, or on the surrounding circumstances of the case, unless it is incapable of having any impact on the case.[10]

Reasonable Line of Inquiry

A reasonable line of inquiry is that which points either towards or away from the suspect. What is reasonable will depend on the circumstances of the case and consideration should be had of the prospect of obtaining relevant material, and the perceived relevance of that material.

Disclosure Test

Material that might reasonably be considered capable of undermining the case for the prosecution against the accused, or of assisting the case for the accused.

All definitions correspond to the CPIA and CPIA Code of Practice

19. The decision as to relevance requires an exercise of judgment and, although some material may plainly be relevant or non-relevant, ultimately this requires a decision by the disclosure officer or investigator.

20. Disclosure officers and/or investigators must inspect, view, listen to, or search all relevant material. The disclosure officer must provide a personal declaration that this task has been completed. In some cases a detailed examination of every item of material seized would be disproportionate. In such cases the disclosure officer can apply search techniques using the principles contained in Annex A. Whatever the approach taken by disclosure officers in examining material, it is crucial that disclosure officers record their reasons for a particular approach in writing. Where third party material is under consideration, reference should be made to paragraphs 26 et seq. of these Guidelines.

21. Disclosure officers should seek the advice and assistance of prosecutors when in doubt as to their responsibility as early as possible. They must deal expeditiously with requests by the prosecutor for further information on material, which may lead to disclosure.

22. Where prosecutors have reason to believe that the disclosure officer has not inspected, viewed, listened to or searched relevant material, or has not done so sufficiently or has not articulated a reason for doing so, they should raise this issue with the disclosure officer and request that it is addressed. Prosecutors should also assist disclosure officers and investigators in defining the parameters of review and the methodology to be adopted.

23. It may become apparent to an investigator that some material obtained in the course of an investigation, either because it was considered to be potentially relevant, or because it was inextricably linked to material that was relevant, is in fact incapable of impacting on the case.[11] It is not necessary to retain such material. However, the investigator should also exercise considerable caution in reaching that conclusion. The investigator should be particularly mindful of the fact that some investigations continue over some time. Material that is incapable of impact may change over time and it may not be possible to foresee what the issues in the case will be. The advice of the prosecutor may be sought where necessary. Ultimately, however, the decision on whether to retain material is one for the investigator, and should always be based on their assessment of the relevance of the material and the likelihood of it having any impact on the case in future.

---

9 CPIA Code paras.4 and 5
10 CPIA Code para.2
11 CPIA (s.23(1))

24. Prosecutors must be alert to the need to provide advice to and, where necessary, probe actions taken by the investigator to ensure that disclosure obligations are capable of being met. This should include advice on potential further reasonable lines of inquiry. There should be no aspects of an investigation about which prosecutors are unable to ask probing questions.

25. In some investigations it may be appropriate for the officer in charge of the investigation to seek engagement with the defence at the pre-charge stage. This is likely to be where it is possible that such engagement will lead to the defence volunteering additional information which may assist in identifying new lines of inquiry. Annex B sets out the process for any such pre-charge engagement.

Third party material

26. Third party material is material held by a person, organisation, or government department other than the investigator and prosecutor, either within the UK or outside the UK. Third parties are not directly involved in the case in question but may hold information relevant to it.

27. The CPIA addresses material once it has come into the possession of an investigator or prosecutor. These guidelines prescribe the approach to be taken to disclosure of material held by third parties, either when it comes into the possession of the investigator or prosecutor or remains in the possession of the third party.

Principles of accessing third party material

Step 1: Establishing a Reasonable Line of Inquiry

28. The CPIA Code and these guidelines make clear the obligation on the investigator to pursue all reasonable lines of inquiry in relation to any offence under investigation, its surrounding circumstances or any person being investigated. This requires the investigator to pursue all lines of inquiry, whether they point towards or away from the suspect, that may reveal material **relevant**[12] to the investigation or the likely issues at trial. This obligation is the same in respect of material held by third parties within the UK.

29. It is for investigators, in consultation or discussion with prosecutors where appropriate, to identify and pursue all reasonable lines of inquiry. Prosecutors can advise on additional reasonable lines of inquiry and should satisfy themselves that such reasonable lines of inquiry have been pursued.

Step 2: Establishing Relevance

30. Third party material should only be requested in an individual case if it has been identified as relevant to an issue in the case. This will depend on the circumstances of the individual case, including any potential defence, and any other information informing the direction of the case. Access to third party material should never occur as a matter of course. It should never be assumed that because of the nature of an offence that is being investigated that particular types of material will need to be accessed. There will be cases where no investigation of third party material is necessary at all, and others where detailed scrutiny is needed. There must be a properly identifiable foundation for the inquiry, not mere conjecture or speculation.[13]

31. A written record must be made of any decision to access third party material in the Investigation or Disclosure Management Document as appropriate. This record must also detail the underlying basis or rationale for the decision to access third party material. Disclosure Management Documents should be drafted to include the lines of inquiry pursued relating to third party material. This will assist in demonstrating to the defence and court the steps that have or have not been taken and why.

32. Investigators and prosecutors, when deciding whether third party material should be requested in an individual case, should consider the following, although this list is not exhaustive, and the considerations will vary depending on the circumstances of the case:

 i.   What relevant information is the material believed to contain?

 ii. Why is it believed that the material contains that relevant information? If it is likely that no relevant information will be contained within the material, a request should not be made.

 iii. Will the request for the material intrude on a complainant's or witness's privacy?

 iv. If the material requested does amount to an invasion of privacy, is it a proportionate and justifiable request to make in the circumstances of the individual case and any known issues? Consider vi. below or whether the information which may result in access amounting to an invasion of privacy can be redacted to remove anything that does not meet the disclosure test.[14]

 v.   Depending on the stage of the case, does the material need to be obtained or would a request to preserve the material suffice until more information is known?

---

[12] For the definition of 'relevant' please refer to the definitions section of these Guidelines
[13] *Bater-James and Mohammed* [2020] EWCA Crim 790 at [77]
[14] See Annex D on Redaction for further information

vi. Is there an alternative way of readily accessing the information such as open-source searches, searches of material obtained from the suspect, or speaking directly to a witness, that does not require a request to a third party?

vii. Consider the scope of the material required, for example are the entirety of an individual's medical records required or would a particular month or year be sufficient? Ensure the request is focused so that only relevant information is being sought.

viii. The process of disclosure and its role in the justice system should be clearly and understandably expressed to the third party. They must be kept appraised of any ongoing disclosure decisions that are made with regard to their material.

Step 3: Balancing Rights

33. If as a result of the duty to pursue all reasonable lines of inquiry, the investigator or prosecutor obtains or receives material from a third party, then it must be dealt with in accordance with the CPIA 1996, (i.e. the prosecutor must disclose material only if it meets the disclosure test, subject to any public interest immunity claim). The person who has an interest in the material (the third party) may make representations to the court concerning public interest immunity (see section 16 of the CPIA 1996).

34. In some cases, third party material may reveal intimate, personal or delicate information. Prosecutors should give close scrutiny to such material and only disclose it where absolutely necessary. Further guidance and best practice on obtaining third party material can be found in the Joint Protocol on Third Party Material and Chapter 5 of the CPS Disclosure Manual. Investigators and prosecutors must also comply with data protection law when accessing third party material which contains personal information; they must consider closely how to balance the right to fair trial and right to privacy as set out at paragraphs 11 et seq. For more information, please consult Annex A on Digital Material and Annex D on Redaction.

Material held by Government departments

35. During an investigation or prosecution it may become apparent that a Government department or another Crown body has material that may be relevant to an issue in the case. Investigators or prosecutors should seek access to this material if and only if they have met **the principles for accessing third party material** as set out above. Any access must be in accordance with those principles.

36. The investigator or prosecutor should inform the Government department or Crown body at the earliest opportunity of the nature of the case and the relevant issues in the case, and ask whether it has any relevant material. They should assist the Government department or Crown body in understanding what may be relevant in the context of the case in question.

37. Crown Servants have a duty to support the administration of justice and should take reasonable steps to identify and consider such material. This extends to revealing to the investigator or prosecutor the extent of the searches conducted and the existence of any information which they believe may be relevant to the issues in the case, to supply them with that information unless it is protected to the issues in the case, and to supply them with that information unless it is protected in law, subject to legal professional privilege or attracts public interest immunity.

38. If access is denied to relevant material, the investigator or prosecutor should consider the reasons given by the Government department or Crown body and what, if any, further steps might be taken to obtain the material. The final decision on further steps rests with the prosecutor.

39. Investigators and prosecutors cannot be regarded to be in constructive possession of material held by Government departments or Crown bodies simply by virtue of their status as Government departments or Crown bodies.

40. The steps taken to identify and obtain relevant material held by a Government department or Crown body should be recorded by the investigator and the prosecutor.

41. Where appropriate, the defence should be informed of the steps taken to obtain material and the results of the line of inquiry.

Other domestic bodies

42. If an investigator, disclosure officer or a prosecutor considers a third party (for example a local authority, social services department, hospital, doctor, school, provider of forensic services, or CCTV operator) has material or information that is relevant to an issue in the case, they should seek access to this material if and only if they have met **the principles for accessing third party material** as set out above. A third party has no obligation under the CPIA to reveal material to investigators or prosecutors. There is also no duty on the third party to retain material which may be relevant to the investigation and, in some circumstances, the third party may not be aware of the investigation or prosecution.

43. If access to the material is refused and, despite the reasons given for refusal of access, it is still believed that it is reasonable to seek production of the material or information and that the requirements of

a witness summons[15],[16] are satisfied (or any other relevant power), then the prosecutor or investigator should apply for the summons causing a representative of the third party to produce the material to court. A witness summons is only available once a case has been charged. If the material is sought pre-charge, investigators and prosecutors should request that the third party preserve the material. This request should be documented.

44. When the third party material in question is personal data, investigators and prosecutors must refer to paragraphs 11–13 of these guidelines to ensure that there is no unjust intrusion of privacy.

45. The defence should be informed of what steps have been taken to obtain material and what the results of the inquiry have been. Disclosure Management Documents should be used in Crown Court cases.

International enquiries

46. The obligations under the CPIA Code to pursue all reasonable lines of inquiry apply to material held overseas.

47. Where it appears that there is material relevant to an issue in the case held overseas, the investigator or prosecutor should seek access to this material if and only if they have met **the principles for accessing third party material** as set out above. If this standard is met, they must take reasonable steps to obtain it while acting in accordance with the principles. Investigators or prosecutors may do so either informally or by making use of the powers contained in the Crime (International Co-operation) Act 2003, the Criminal Justice (European Investigation Order) Regulations 2017 and any international conventions.

48. There may be cases where a foreign state or court refuses to make the material available to the investigator or prosecutor. There may be other cases where the foreign state, though willing to show the material to investigators, will not allow the material to be copied or otherwise made available and the courts of the foreign state will not order its provision.

49. It is for these reasons that there is no absolute duty on the prosecutor to disclose relevant material held overseas by entities not subject to the jurisdiction of the courts in England and Wales. However, consideration should be given to whether the type of material believed to be held can be provided to the defence.

50. The obligation on the investigator and prosecutor under the CPIA Code is to take reasonable steps. Where investigators are allowed to examine the files of a foreign state but are not allowed to take copies, take notes or list the documents held, there is no breach by the prosecution in its duty of disclosure by reason of its failure to obtain such material, provided reasonable steps have been taken to try and obtain it. Prosecutors have a margin of consideration as to what steps are appropriate in the particular case, but prosecutors must be alive to their duties and there may be some circumstances where these duties cannot be met. Whether or not a prosecutor has taken reasonable steps is for the court to determine in each case if the matter is raised.

51. Where it is apparent during the investigation that there may be relevant material held overseas then investigators and prosecutors should consider engaging with the defence at the pre-charge stage, applying the principles contained in Annex B, to ensure that all reasonable lines of inquiry are followed.

52. It is important that the position taken in relation to any material held overseas is clearly set out in a document such as a disclosure management document (DMD) so that the court and the defence know what the position is. Further information on DMDs can be found below.

53. In the DMD, investigators and prosecutors must record and explain the situation and set out, insofar as they are permitted by the foreign state, such information as they can and the steps they have taken to obtain it.

54. The defence should be informed of what steps have been taken to obtain material and what the results of the enquiry have been.

Electronic material

55. The exponential increase in the use of technology in society means that many routine investigations are increasingly likely to have to engage with digital material of some form. It is not only in large and complex investigations where there may be large quantities of such material. When dealing with large quantities of digital material prosecutors and investigators should apply the principles contained in Annex A to these guidelines.

56. Where investigations involve a large quantity of digital material it may be impossible for investigators to examine every item of such material individually. Therefore there should be no expectation that this should happen. Investigators and disclosure officers will need to decide how best to pursue a reasonable line of inquiry in relation to the relevant digital material, and ensure that the extent and

---

[15] Criminal Procedure (Attendance of Witnesses) Act 1965, s.2
[16] Magistrates' Court Act 1980, s.97

manner of the examination are appropriate to the issues in the case. In reaching any such decisions, investigators and disclosure officers must bear in mind the overriding obligation to ensure a fair trial of any suspect who is charged and the requirement to provide disclosure in the trial process.

57. Prosecutors and investigators must ensure that any line of inquiry pursued in relation to the digital devices of victims and witnesses are reasonable in the context of the likely issues in the case. Digital devices should not be obtained as a matter of course and the decision to obtain and examine a digital device will be a fact-specific decision to be made in each and every case.[17] Where digital devices are obtained, if it becomes apparent that they do not contain relevant material they should be returned at the earliest opportunity.

58. Prosecutors should be consulted, where appropriate, to agree a strategy for dealing with digital material. This strategy should be set out in a disclosure management document (DMD) and shared with the defence at the appropriate time.

Revelation of material to a prosecutor

59. Prosecutors only have knowledge of the matters which are revealed to them by investigators and disclosure officers. The schedules are the means by which that revelation takes place. Therefore it is crucial that the schedules detail all of the relevant material and that the material is adequately described. This process will also enable defence practitioners to become apprised of relevant material at the appropriate stage of the investigation. More detail on what constitutes relevant material can be found in the definitions section .

60. Schedules must be completed in a form which not only reveals sufficient information to the prosecutor, but which demonstrates a transparent and thinking approach to the disclosure exercise. The speed with which the schedule is produced should not reduce the quality of the material contained therein.

61. Descriptions on the schedules must be clear and accurate and must contain sufficient detail to enable the prosecutor to make an informed decision on disclosure. Abbreviations and acronyms should be avoided as they risk significant material being overlooked.

62. Investigators and disclosure officers must ensure that material which is presumed to meet the test for disclosure, as set out in paragraph 86 of these guidelines and paragraph 6.6 of the CPIA Code, is placed on the schedules. The requirement to schedule this material is in addition to the requirement to schedule all other relevant unused material.

63. Where relevant unused material has been omitted from the schedule or where material is not described sufficiently, and the prosecutor asks the disclosure officer to rectify the schedule, the disclosure officer must comply with this request in a timely manner.

64. Disclosure officers must bring to the prosecutor's attention any material which is potentially capable of meeting the test for disclosure. This material should be provided to the prosecutor along with the reasons why it is thought to meet the test.

65. Disclosure officers must also draw material to the attention of the prosecutor for consideration where they have doubt as to whether it might reasonably be considered capable of undermining the prosecution case or of assisting the case for the accused.

Revelation of sensitive material

What is sensitive material?

66. Sensitive material is material that, if disclosed, would give rise to a real risk of serious prejudice to an important public interest. Investigators must ensure that all relevant unused sensitive material is retained, reviewed and revealed to the prosecutor. Sensitive material should be revealed to a prosecutor on a separate schedule to the non-sensitive material.

Examples of sensitive material can be found in paragraph 6.14 of the CPIA Code.

Sensitive material as defined by the CPIA Code of Practice is distinct from personal information requiring strict necessity processing under the Data Protection Act 2018, which is sometimes referred to as 'sensitive personal information/data.'

67. When making a decision about the sensitivity of an item, investigators should have regard to the types of material listed in paragraph 6.14 of the CPIA Code. The disclosure officer must ensure that the sensitive material schedule includes the reasons why it is asserted that items on the schedule are considered sensitive.

68. Where a document contains a mix of sensitive and non-sensitive material, the sensitive material must be redacted, with a copy of the redacted document placed on the non- sensitive unused material schedule and the original placed on the sensitive schedule.

---

[17] *R v E* [2018] EWCA 2426 (Crim)

69. Investigators must ensure that the descriptions of sensitive unused material are sufficiently clear to enable the prosecutor to make an informed decision as to whether or not the material itself should be viewed, to the extent possible without compromising the confidentiality of the information.

70. Prosecutors must carefully review the sensitive unused material schedule in order to be satisfied that there are no omissions, that the items have been correctly identified as sensitive, and that the items are adequately described. If a prosecutor identifies that a schedule is inadequate, the investigator must provide an adequate schedule as soon as possible. This may involve items being moved from the sensitive unused material schedule to the non-sensitive unused material schedule.

The timing of revelation

71. In order to support prosecutors' assessment of the impact of unused material on any proposed prosecution, it is essential that prosecutors are provided with the schedule of unused material at an early stage, as well as any material which the disclosure officer considers potentially capable of meeting the test for disclosure. This will allow for a thorough review of the case and enable the prosecutor to consider what the disclosure strategy should be.

72. The timing of revelation of material should be in accordance with paragraph 7.1 of the Code. The point at which the case file is submitted to the CPS will depend on the circumstances of the charging decision and on the anticipated plea:

   a. Where the police are seeking a charging decision under the Full Code Test from the CPS, and it is anticipated that the defendant will plead not guilty, the unused material schedules should be provided to the prosecutor by the disclosure officer at the same time as seeking this charging decision.

   b. Where the police have charged a suspect on the Full Code Test under the arrangements contained in the Director's Guidance on Charging, and a not guilty plea is anticipated, then the unused material schedule should be provided to the prosecutor at the point at which the case file is submitted to the CPS.

   c. In all other cases the disclosure officer must provide the schedules as soon as possible after a not guilty plea has either been indicated or entered.

73. There may be instances where an investigator is seeking a charging decision on the Full Code Test and anticipating a not guilty plea, but where it is not feasible to provide the unused material schedules to the prosecutor at the same time as seeking a charging decision. This may be the case where an arrest is not planned, and the suspect cannot be bailed.

74. For large and complex investigations, particularly those conducted by the Serious Fraud Office, it is recognised that the preparation of schedules continues beyond the point of charge due to the quantity and complexity of data to be analysed, and that it may not be feasible or necessary to provide the schedules at the same time that a charging decision is sought.

75. Disclosure officers should apply the criteria contained in the Director's Guidance on Charging when making a decision about a suspect's likely plea and must follow any additional guidance provided by the prosecutor.

The charging decision

76. Prosecutors must ensure that all reasonable lines of inquiry likely to affect the application of the Full Code Test have been pursued before the Test is applied, unless the prosecutor is satisfied that any further evidence or material is unlikely to affect the application of the Full Code Test[18]. The failure to pursue reasonable lines of inquiry may result in the application of the Full Code Test being deferred, or in a decision that the Test cannot be met.

77. If a decision is made to charge a case under the Threshold Test, then prosecutors and investigators need to be proactive in ensuring that any outstanding lines of inquiry are pursued and that the case is kept under continuous review.

Common law disclosure

78. A prosecutor's statutory duty of disclosure applies from the point of a not guilty plea in the magistrates' court and from the point a case is sent to the Crown Court.[19] However, prosecutors must also consider their duties under the common law which apply at all stages of a case, from charge to sentence and post-conviction (see paragraphs 139 and 140) and regardless of anticipated or actual plea.

79. These duties may require the prosecutor to disclose material to the accused outside the statutory scheme in accordance with the interests of justice and fairness. An example of this is where it would assist the accused in the preparation of the defence case, prior to plea and regardless of anticipated plea. This would include material which would assist in the making of a bail application, material

---

18 Crown Prosecution Service, *The Code for Crown Prosecutors* para.4.3
19 Criminal Procedure and Investigations Act 1996 (CPIA 1996), s.1(1)(a) and (2)(cc)

which may enable the accused to make an early application to stay the proceedings as an abuse of process, material which may enable the accused to make representations about the trial venue or a lesser charge, or material which would enable an accused to prepare for trial effectively.[20]

Initial disclosure

80. The defence must be provided with copies of, or access to, any prosecution material not previously disclosed, which might reasonably be considered capable of undermining the case for the prosecution against the accused, or of assisting the case for the accused.[21] Paragraphs 101 et seq. of these Guidelines contain guidance as to when initial disclosure should be served.

81. In order for the prosecutor to comply with their duty of initial disclosure they must analyse the case for the prosecution, the defence case, and the likely trial issues. A prosecutor can anticipate the likely issues on the basis of information available (such as any explanation provided by the accused in interview).

82. The prosecutor and defence are both under a duty to engage promptly in order to aid understanding of the defence case and the likely issues for trial at an early stage. This engagement assists in ensuring compliance with the overriding objective of the Criminal Procedure Rules[22, 23] and that any further reasonable lines of inquiry can be identified and pursued. Without engagement from defence at an early stage, the accuracy of disclosure can be compromised. Significant cooperation should be a regular occurrence and all parties should consider the Criminal Practice Direction CPD1, para 1A.1 which includes the statement of Lord Justice Auld that *a criminal trial is not a game under which a guilty defendant should be provided with a sporting chance. It is a search for truth in accordance with the twin principles that the prosecution must prove its case and that a defendant is not obliged to inculpate himself*.

83. Prosecutors must review schedules prepared by disclosure officers thoroughly at an early stage and must be alert to the possibility that relevant material may exist which has not been revealed to them or material included which should not have been. If no schedules are provided, if there are apparent omissions from the schedules, or if documents or other items are inadequately described or are unclear, the prosecutor must request properly completed schedules from the investigator. Investigators must comply with any such request. A log of such communications should be kept by the prosecutor.

84. In deciding whether material satisfies the disclosure test, consideration should include:
     a. The use that might be made of it in cross-examination;
     b. Its capacity to support submissions that could lead to:
         i.   The exclusion of evidence;
         ii.   A stay of proceedings, where the material is required to allow a proper application to be made;
         iii. A court or tribunal finding that any public authority had acted incompatibly with the accused's rights under the European Convention of Human Rights;
     c. Its capacity to suggest an explanation or partial explanation of the accused's actions;
     d. Its capacity to undermine the reliability or credibility of a prosecution witness;
     e. The capacity of the material to have a bearing on scientific or medical evidence in the case.

85. Material relating to the accused's mental or physical health, intellectual capacity, or to any ill treatment which the accused may have suffered when in the investigator's custody is likely to meet the test for disclosure.
     Material should not be viewed in isolation as, whilst items taken alone may not be reasonably considered capable of undermining the prosecution case or assisting the case for the accused, several items together can have that effect.

Material which is likely to meet the test for disclosure

86. The following material, which is produced and obtained in the majority of investigations is likely to include information which meets the test for disclosure:
     a) records which are derived from tapes or recordings of telephone messages (for example 999 calls) containing descriptions of an alleged offence or offender;
     b) any incident logs relating to the allegation;
     c) **crime reports and crime report forms**, or where not already contained within the crime report:
         - an investigation log;

---

20 *R v DPP, ex p. Lee* [1999] 1 WLR 1950 [1962]–[1963]
21 CPIA 1996, s. 3
22 The Criminal Procedure Rules 2020 (SI No. 759) (L.19) (the CrimPR), Part 1
23 *R v R and others* [2015] EWCA Crim 1941, [2016] 1 WLR 1872, para. [35]

- any record or note made by an investigator (including police notebook entries and other handwritten notes) on which they later make a statement or which relates to contact with suspects, victims or witnesses;
- an account of an incident or information relevant to an incident noted by an investigator in manuscript or electronically;
- records of actions carried out by officers (such as house-to- house interviews, CCTV or forensic enquiries) noted by a police officer in manuscript or electronically;
- CCTV footage, or other imagery, of the incident in action;
d) the defendant's custody record or voluntary attendance record;
e) any previous accounts made by a complainant or by any other witnesses;
f) interview records (written records, or audio or video tapes, of interviews with actual or potential witnesses or suspects);
g) any material casting doubt on the reliability of a witness e. g. relevant previous convictions and relevant cautions of any prosecution witnesses and any co-accused.

87. When providing CCTV footage, or other imagery, of the incident in action as material which is likely to meet the test for disclosure, investigators should include all **relevant** body-worn footage that is not provided as evidence. It may be that the entirety of the footage contains both relevant and irrelevant material. Irrelevant footage should not be provided to prosecutors in the first instance. It may be the footage requires clipping or editing to achieve this. Where multiple body worn cameras capture the same content, it may be that only one set of footage needs be provided. The remainder should be listed clearly on the unused material schedule. This decision must be made on a case-by-case basis, as it may be that similar but distinct footage has been captured, in which case multiple sets of footage should be provided.

88. This list is reflected in paragraphs 5.4 and 6.6 of the Code. This material, in addition to all other material which may be relevant to an investigation, must, in the first instance, be **retained** and **listed** on the schedule by the investigator. It is likely that some of this material will need to be redacted (see paragraph 6(c) of the Code and the sensitive material provisions of these guidelines for redaction and revelation of sensitive material.)

Assessment by the Investigator

89. Before any of this material is provided to the prosecutor, investigators should apply the disclosure test to the material to ascertain if in fact it is disclosable. When providing the material to the prosecutor the investigator should highlight the material they consider is disclosable and why.

Assessment by the Prosecutor

90. Once the material has been provided to the prosecutor, as this material is likely to contain information which meets the test for disclosure, prosecutors should start their review of the material with a presumption that this material should be disclosed to the defence. However, in every instance the disclosure test should be applied in a thinking manner.

91. After applying the disclosure test, a prosecutor must record on the unused material schedule whether each item of this material does or does not meet the test for disclosure and they must record the reason for that decision.

92. This list of material is not intended to cause automatic disclosure – investigators and prosecutors should always apply the disclosure test and consider each list of material carefully in the context of the case in question. Defence should not expect to be provided with this material as of right in every case. The material is always subject to the disclosure test first before any material is provided.

Disclosure management document (DMD)

What is a disclosure management document?

93. A disclosure management document (DMD) outlines the strategy and approach taken in relation to disclosure and should be served to the defence and the court at an early stage. DMDs will require careful preparation and presentation which is tailored to the individual case. The investigator should provide information for use in the DMD and the prosecutor should prepare it.

94. A DMD is a living document which should be amended in light of developments in the case and kept up to date as the case progresses. DMDs are intended to assist the court in case management and will also enable the defence to engage from an early stage with the prosecution's proposed approach to disclosure.

95. DMDs may set out:
   a. Where prosecutors and investigators operate in an integrated office, an explanation as to how the disclosure responsibilities have been managed.

b. A brief summary of the prosecution case and a statement outlining how the prosecutor's general approach will comply with the CPIA 1996 regime and these guidelines

c. The prosecutor's understanding of the defence case, including information revealed during interview. The prosecutor may wish to explain their understanding of what is in dispute and what is not in dispute, the lines of inquiry that have been pursued in light of these issues, and specific disclosure decisions that have been taken.

d. An outline of the prosecution's general approach to disclosure, which may include detail relating to:

  i.   The lines of inquiry pursued, particularly those which may assist the defence.
  ii.   The timescales for disclosure and, where relevant, how the review of unused material has been prioritised.
  iii. The method and extent of examination of digital material, in accordance with the Annex A to these guidelines.
  iv.   Any potential video footage.
  v.   Any linked investigations, including an explanation of the nexus between investigations and any memoranda of understanding and disclosure agreements between investigators.
  vi.   Any third party material, including the steps taken to obtain the material.
  vii. Any international material, including the steps taken to obtain the material.
  viii. Credibility of prosecution witnesses (including professional witnesses).

96. In cases heard in the magistrates' court and the youth court, prosecutors should always consider whether or not a disclosure management document (DMD) would be beneficial. DMDs are most likely to be beneficial in cases with the following features:
a. Substantial or complex third party material;
b. Digital material in which parameters of search, examination or analysis have been set;
c. Cases involving international enquiries;
d. Cases where there are linked operations;
e. Non-recent offending;
f. Cases involving material held or sought by the investigation that is susceptible to a claim of legal professional privilege.

97. DMDs should be prepared in all Crown Court cases.
98. In order for the prosecutor to complete a DMD at an early stage, the investigator should, at the point of or prior to charge, provide written details as to the lines of inquiry that have been pursued.
99. Where a DMD has been prepared, it should be served at the same time as initial disclosure.
100. An example template for a DMD is contained in Annex C.

The timing of initial disclosure

101. In all cases it is essential that the prosecution takes a grip on the case and its disclosure requirements at an early stage. Prosecutors must adopt a considered and appropriately resourced approach to providing initial disclosure. Initial disclosure in this context refers to the period post-charge; more detailed timings for this are set out below.

Cases expected to be tried in the magistrates' courts

102. Where a case is charged on the Full Code Test and a not guilty plea is anticipated, initial disclosure should be served in advance of the first hearing.
103. Where a guilty plea was originally anticipated but a not guilty plea is entered then initial disclosure should be served as soon as possible after a not guilty plea is entered.
104. Where a case is charged on the Threshold Test, initial disclosure should be served as soon as possible after the Full Code Test is applied and in accordance with any order made by the court.

Cases sent to the Crown Court for trial

105. Where it is expected that the accused will maintain a not guilty plea, it is encouraged as a matter of best practice for initial disclosure to be served prior to the Plea and Trial Preparation Hearing (PTPH).
106. It is accepted that it may not be appropriate or possible to serve initial disclosure prior to the PTPH for cases charged on the Threshold Test. Where initial disclosure has not been served at the PTPH it should be served as soon as possible after that hearing and in accordance with any direction made by the court.
107. In cases prosecuted by the Serious Fraud Office, or other similarly large or complex cases, it is accepted that full initial disclosure may not be capable of being served prior to the PTPH. In such cases, best practice is to adopt a phased approach to disclosure, ensuring that robust judicial case management during Further Case Management Hearings, and in line with the Criminal Procedure

Rules and Criminal Practice Directions, manages the on-going disclosure process. Utilising an initial DMD at the PTPH which outlines the intended plan for onwards staged disclosure of remaining materials and associated schedules, can be an effective mechanism for this approach and is to adopted where possible.

108. Nothing in these guidelines should undermine the established principles of the Better Case Management Framework.

Case management

109. In order for the statutory disclosure regime to work effectively all parties should ensure compliance with the Criminal Procedure Rules. The rules require the court to actively manage the case by identifying the real issues.[24] Each party is obliged to assist the court with this duty.[25]

110. It is important that prosecutors keep a record of all correspondence which relates to disclosure and keep a record of any disclosure decisions made.

111. Any party who takes the view that another party is not complying with their obligations under the disclosure regime should bring this to the attention of the court as soon as possible.

Magistrates' court

112. Following a not guilty plea being entered in the magistrates' court, the defence must ensure that the trial issues are clearly identified both in court and on the preparation for effective trial form. Prosecutors should ensure that any issues of dispute that are raised are noted on file. The preparation for effective trial form should be carefully reviewed, alongside the DMD (where this exists). Consideration of any issues raised in court or on the form will assist in deciding whether any further material undermines the prosecution case or assists the accused.

Crown Court

113. A focus of the Plea and Trial Preparation Hearing (PTPH) must be on the disclosure strategy. This will involve the defence identifying the likely trial issues, a discussion of any additional lines of inquiry, and scrutiny of the DMD.

114. Prosecutors must ensure that the disclosure strategy and any disclosure decisions taken previously are reviewed in light of any issues raised at the PTPH and on the plea and trial preparation form.

115. Where the defence do not feel that the prosecution have adequately discharged their obligations then this must be brought to the court's attention at an early stage. The defence should be proactive in ensuring that any issue is addressed, and must not delay raising these issues until a late stage in the proceedings. The DMD may be relevant in any challenge raised.

116. Where any party has not complied with their obligations, the court will consider giving any direction appropriate to ensure compliance and progression of the case.

Applications for non-disclosure in the public interest

117. The CPIA 1996 allows prosecutors to apply to the court for an order to withhold material which would otherwise fall to be disclosed if disclosure would give rise to a real risk of serious prejudice to an important public interest. Before making such an application, prosecutors should aim to disclose as much of the material as they properly can (for example, by giving the defence redacted or edited copies or summaries). Neutral material or material damaging to the defendant should <u>not</u> be disclosed and should <u>not</u> be brought to the attention of the court. Only in truly borderline cases should the prosecution seek a judicial ruling on whether material in its possession should be disclosed.

118. Prior to the hearing, the prosecutor and the prosecution advocate must examine all material which is the subject matter of the application and make any necessary enquiries of the investigator. There is an additional duty of candour on the advocate at this hearing, given the defendant will not be present. In order to assist the court, it is best practice for the advocate to prepare a note that is either written in conjunction, or agreed with, the prosecutor and disclosure officer.

119. The investigator must also be frank with the prosecutor about the full extent of the sensitive material. Prior to, or at the hearing, the court must be provided with full and accurate information about the material.

120. The prosecutor and/or investigator should attend such applications. Section 16 of the CPIA 1996 allows a person claiming to have an interest in the sensitive material to apply to the court for the opportunity to be heard at the application.

121. The prosecutor should carefully consider the series of questions contained in paragraph 36 of *R v H and others* [2004] UKHL 3. These are the questions that the court must address before it makes a decision to withhold material. It is essential that these principles are scrupulously adhered to, to

---

24 CrimPR, r.3.2(2)(a)
25 CrimPR, r.3.3(1)(a)

ensure that the procedure for examination of material in the absence of the accused is compliant with Article 6 of the ECHR.

122. If the prosecutor concludes that a fair trial cannot take place because material which satisfies the test for disclosure cannot be disclosed and that this cannot be remedied by an application for non-disclosure in the public interest, through altering the presentation of the case or by any other means, then they should not continue with the case.

The defence statement

123. Defence statements are an integral part of the statutory disclosure regime. A defence statement should help to focus the attention of the prosecutor, court and co-defendants on the relevant issues in order to identify material which may meet the test for disclosure. The defence must serve their defence statement in a timely manner, in accordance with any court directions made.

124. There is no requirement for a defence statement to be served in the magistrates' court but it should be noted that if one is not provided the court does not have a power to hear an application for further prosecution disclosure under section 8 of the CPIA 1996.[26]

125. Defence practitioners must ensure that defence statements are drafted in accordance with the requirements in the CPIA 1996.[27] Defence statements must not make general and unspecified allegations in order to seek far reaching disclosure[28] and should not describe the defence in ambiguous or limited terms (such as self-defence, mistaken identify, consent).

126. It is vital that prosecutors consider defence statements thoroughly. Prosecutors should challenge the lack of (in the Crown Court) or inadequate defence statements in writing, copying the document to the court and the defence and seeking directions from the court to require the provision of an adequate defence statement from the defence as soon as possible.

127. Prosecutors must send a copy of the defence statement to the investigator as soon as reasonably practicable after receipt and, at the same time, provide guidance to the disclosure officer about the key issues. The advice should contain guidance on whether any further reasonable lines of inquiry need to be pursued, guidance on what to look for when reviewing the unused material and guidance on what further material may need to be disclosed. On receipt of a defence statement, disclosure officers must re-review retained unused material and draw to the attention of the prosecutor any material which is potentially capable of meeting the test for disclosure and consider whether any further reasonable lines of inquiry need to be pursued. They should address the matters raised in guidance given by the prosecutor.

128. Defence requests for further disclosure should ordinarily only be answered by the prosecution if the request is relevant to, and directed to, an issue identified in the defence statement. If it is not, then a further or amended defence statement should be sought and obtained by the prosecutor before considering the request for further disclosure.

Continuing disclosure

129. The obligation of continuing disclosure is crucial and particular attention must be paid to understanding the significance of developments in the case on the unused material and earlier disclosure decisions. After service of initial disclosure, a prosecutor must keep under review whether or not there is prosecution material which might reasonably be considered capable of undermining the case for the prosecution against the accused, or of assisting the case for the accused, which has not been previously been disclosed. This obligation is a continuous one,[29] and it can be beneficial for it to take place in tranches, particularly in large and/or complex cases.

130. In particular, prosecutors should consider any issues raised by the defence at the first hearing in the magistrates' court or the PTPH in the Crown Court, as well as during any further hearings and after receipt of a defence statement. Any matters raised on the preparation for effective trial form or the PTPH form should also be carefully considered.

Applications for disclosure under Section 8 of the CPIA

131. An application for disclosure can only be made if the defence have provided an **adequate** defence statement. [30]

132. Any application for disclosure must describe the material which is subject to the application and explain why there is reasonable cause to believe that the prosecutor has the material and why it meets the test for disclosure. There must not be any speculative requests for material.

---

26 CPIA 1996, s.8(1)
27 CPIA 1996, s.6A
28 *R v H and others* [2004] UKHL 3
29 CPIA 1996, s.7A
30 CPIA 1996, s.5 and Part 15 Criminal Procedure Rules may be considered for a more detailed examination of the meaning of 'adequate'.

133. Prosecutors must carefully review any application for disclosure and consider whether any items described in the application meet the test for disclosure. This may require the prosecutor asking the disclosure officer for copies of the items or inspecting the items.

The trial

134. Prosecutors must ensure that advocates in court are provided with sufficient instructions regarding the disclosure strategy and any disclosure decisions taken.

135. Prosecution advocates should ensure that all material which ought to be disclosed under the CPIA 1996 is disclosed to the defence. Prosecution advocates must ensure that they are fully informed about disclosure so that they are able to make decisions. Prosecution advocates must consider, in every case, whether they can be satisfied that they are in possession of all relevant documentation and that they have been fully instructed regarding disclosure matters. If the advocate considers that further information or action is required then written advice should be provided setting out the aspects that need clarification or action.

136. All decisions regarding disclosure must be kept under review until the conclusion of the trial, whenever possible in consultation with the reviewing prosecutor. The prosecution advocate must in every case specifically consider whether they can satisfactorily discharge the duty of continuing review on the basis of the material supplied already, or whether it is necessary to reconsider the unused material schedule and/or unused material.

137. Prosecution advocates must not abrogate their responsibility under the CPIA 1996 by disclosing material which does not pass the test for disclosure. This is especially so where it is proposed to disclose material engaging Article 8 rights.

138. There is no basis in practice or law for counsel-to-counsel disclosure. It is of critical importance that, even where prosecution counsel is advising and leading on disclosure, the duty to disclose material that meets the test for disclosure remains with the prosecutor. A record of material disclosed made must be kept, not least in the event of an appeal or a re-trial.

Material relevant to sentence

139. At sentence, the prosecutor should disclose any material which might reasonably be considered capable of ensuring fairness in the sentencing process. This material could include information which might mitigate the seriousness of the offence or the level of the defendant's involvement.

Post-conviction

140. Where, at any stage after the conclusion of the proceedings, material comes to light which might reasonably be considered capable of casting doubt upon the safety of the conviction, the prosecutor should disclose such material.

Confiscation Proceedings

141. The disclosure regime in the CPIA ceases to have effect post-conviction and the continuing duty of disclosure does not apply to confiscation proceedings (see section 7A(1)(b) of the CPIA).

142. Part 2 of the Proceeds of Crime Act 2002 provides the legislative scheme for confiscation in the Crown Court following a conviction. The prosecutor is required to set out relevant matters in accordance with Section 16 of the Proceeds of Crime Act 2002 apply and the disclosure requirements at common law also apply meaning that there may be a requirement to disclose material in the interests of justice and fairness in the proceedings.

ANNEX A

DIGITAL MATERIAL

1. This annex is intended to supplement the Attorney-General's Guidelines on Disclosure. It is not intended to be a detailed operational guide but is intended to set out a common approach to be adopted when seeking to obtain and handle digital material, whether that be from a suspect or from a complainant. This annex aims to set out how relevant material and consequently material satisfying the test for disclosure can best be identified, revealed and if necessary disclosed to the defence without imposing unrealistic or disproportionate demands on the investigator and prosecutor. This annex also seeks to recognise the considerations investigators and prosecutors should have when obtaining and handling sensitive personal information, in accordance with obligations under data protection legislation.

2. In cases involving large amounts of digital material, investigators should complete an investigation management document (IMD) which will inform the disclosure management document (DMD) that prosecutors should complete. The DMD allows prosecutors to be open and transparent with the defence and the court about how the prosecution has approached complying with its disclosure obligations in the specific context of the individual case.

3. In cases where there may be a large amount of digital material, the investigator should consult the prosecutor, ideally before it is seized, and in turn they may consider seeking the advice of a digital forensic specialist on the strategy for the identification and review of digital material, including potential timings for this.

4. The defence must also play their part in defining the real issues in the case. This is required by the overriding objective of the Criminal Procedure Rules[31]. The defence should be invited by the prosecution at an early stage to participate in defining the scope of the reasonable searches that may be made of digital material in order to identify material that might reasonably be expected to undermine the prosecution case or assist the case for the defence.

5. This approach enables the court to use its case management powers robustly to ensure that the prosecution's obligation of disclosure is discharged effectively.

General principles for investigators

6. These general principles must be followed by investigators in handling and examining digital material:[32]
    a. No action should be taken which changes data on a device which may subsequently be relied upon in court.
    b. If it is necessary to access original data then that data should only be accessed by someone who is competent to do so and is able to explain the relevance and implications of their actions to a court.
    c. An audit trail should be kept of all processes followed. Another practitioner should be able to follow the audit trail and achieve the same results.
    d. The investigator in charge of the investigation has responsibility for ensuring that the law and these principles are followed.

7. Where an investigator has reasonable grounds for believing that digital material may contain material subject to legal professional privilege then this may not be seized unless the provisions of the Criminal Justice and Police Act 2001 apply. This is addressed in more detail later on in this Annex.

8. The legal obligations in relation to seizure, relevance and retention are found in the Police and Criminal Evidence Act 1984, the Criminal Justice and Police Act 2001 and the Criminal Procedure and Investigations Act 1996.

Obtaining devices by seizure or co-operation

9. Digital material may be seized from suspects using legal powers but this material may be obtained from suspects and witnesses with their co-operation as well. Before searching a suspect's premises where digital material is likely to be found, consideration must be given to:
    a. What sort of material is likely to be found, and in what volume;
    b. Whether it is likely that relevant material at the location will be able to be viewed and copied; and
    c. What should be seized.

10. Investigators will need to consider the practicalities of requesting/seizing digital devices, especially where there are a large number of devices. They will also need to consider the effect that taking possession/seizure will have on a business, organisation or individual; and where it is not feasible to obtain an image of the digital material, the likely timescale for returning the obtained items.

11. In deciding whether to obtain and retain digital material, it is important that the investigator either complies with the procedure under the relevant statutory authority, relying on statutory powers or a search warrant, or obtains the owner's permission.

12. When seeking to obtain digital material, whether from a suspect or a witness/complainant, investigators should be guided by the principles set out in paragraphs 11–13 in the Attorney General's Guidelines. Any intrusion into the personal and private lives of individuals should be carried out only where deemed necessary and using the least intrusive means possible to obtain the material required, adopting an incremental approach. Further guidance has been published by the CPS which has been endorsed by the Court of Appeal.[33]

13. A computer hard drive is a single storage entity. This means that if any digital material found on the hard drive can lawfully be obtained or seized, the computer hard drive may, if appropriate, be seized or imaged. In some circumstances investigators may wish to image specific folders, files or categories of data where it is feasible to do so without seizing the hard drive or other media. Digital material may also be contained across a number of digital devices and so more than one device may be required in order to access the information sought.

14. Digital material must not be requested or seized if an investigator has reasonable grounds for believing it is subject to legal professional privilege, other than where sections 50 or 51 of the

---

31 CrimPR, Part 1
32 Association of Chief Police Officers, *ACPO Good Practice Guide for Digital Evidence* (2012), para.2.1
33 CPS Guidance on 'Reasonable lines of Enquiry and Communications Evidence' and 'Disclosure – Guidance on Communications Evidence', endorsed in the case of *R v E* [2018] EWCA 2426 (Crim).

Criminal Justice and Police Act 2001 apply. If such material is seized it must be isolated from other seized material and any other investigation material in the possession of the investigation authority.

The Police and Criminal Evidence Act 1984

15.   The Police and Criminal Evidence Act 1984 provides the power to seize anything from a suspect in the following circumstances:

    a.   Where a search has been authorised pursuant to a warrant – the search must fall within the scope of the warrant issued;[34]

    b.   After arrest;[35]

    c.   Where evidence or anything used in the commission of an offence is on a premises and it is necessary to seize it to prevent it being concealed, lost, altered or destroyed.[36]

16.   An image of the digital material may be taken at the location of the search. Where an image is taken the original does not need to be seized. Where it is not possible to image the digital material it will need to be removed from the location for examination elsewhere. This allows the investigator to seize and sift material for the purpose of identifying material which meets the test of retention.[37] If digital material is seized in its original form, investigators must be prepared to copy or image the material for the owners of that material when reasonably practicable.[38]

The Criminal Justice and Police Act 2001

17.   The additional powers of seizure in sections 50 and 51 of the Criminal Justice and Police Act 2001 (CJPA 2001) only extend the scope of existing powers of search and seizure under the Police and Criminal Evidence Act 1984 and other specified statutory authorities[39] where the relevant conditions and circumstances specified in the legislation apply.

18.   Investigators must be careful to only exercise powers under the CJPA 2001 when it is necessary and to not remove any more material than is justified. The removal of large volumes of material, much of which may not ultimately be retainable, may have serious consequences for the owner of the material, particularly when they are involved in business or other commercial activities.

19.   A written notice must be given to the occupier of the premises where items are seized under sections 50 and 51.[40]

20.   Until material seized under the CJPA 2001 has been examined, it must be kept securely and separately from any material seized under other powers. Any such material must be examined as soon as reasonably practicable to determine which elements may be retained and which should be returned. Consideration should be given as to whether the person from whom the property was seized, or a person with interest in the property, should be given an opportunity of being present or represented at the examination.

Retention

21.   Where material is seized under the powers conferred by PACE 1984 the duty to retain it under the Code is subject to the provisions on retention under section 22 of PACE 1984. Material seized under sections 50 and 51 of the CJPA 2001 may be retained or returned in accordance with sections 53 to 58 of the CJPA 2001. Where material is obtained through co-operation and not using powers conferred on investigators by legislation, these principles should also be observed, including retaining the material for only as long as is necessary (see paragraph 5(b) of the Code).

22.   Retention is limited to evidence and relevant material (as defined in the CPIA Code). Where either evidence or relevant material is inextricably linked to non-relevant material which it is not reasonably practicable to separate from the other linked material without prejudicing the use of that other material in any investigation or proceedings, that material can also be retained.

23.   However, inextricably linked material must not be examined, imaged, copied or used for any purpose other than for providing the source of or the integrity of the linked material.

24.   There are four categories of material that may be retained:

    a.   Material that is evidence or potential evidence in the case. Where material is retained for evidential purposes there will be a strong argument that the whole thing (or an authenticated image or copy) should be retained for the purpose of proving provenance and continuity.

---

34 The Police and Criminal Evidence Act 1984 (PACE 1984), s.8
35 PACE 1984, s.18
36 PACE 1984, s.19
37 Special provision exists for investigators conducted by [His] Majesty's Revenue and Customs in the application of their powers under PACE 1984 (see s.114(2)(b) of PACE and the CJPA).
38 The Home Office, *PACE 1984 Codes of Practice Code B* (2013), para.7.17.
39 Criminal Justice and Police Act 2001 (CJPA 2001), sch.1
40 CJPA 2001, s.52

    b. Where evidential material has been retained, inextricably linked non-relevant material which it is not reasonably practicable to separate can also be retained (PACE Code B paragraph 7).

    c. An investigator should retain material that is relevant to the investigation and required to be scheduled as unused material. This is broader than but includes the duty to retain material which may satisfy the test for prosecution disclosure. The general duty to retain relevant material is set out in the CPIA Code at paragraph 5.

    d. Material which is inextricably linked to relevant unused material which of itself may not be relevant material. Such material should be retained (PACE Code B paragraph 7).

25.   The balance of any digital material should be returned in accordance with sections 53–55 of the CJPA 2001 if seized under that Act.

Legal professional privilege

26.   No digital material may be requested or seized which an investigator has reasonable grounds for believing to be subject to legal professional privilege (LPP), other than under the additional powers of seizure in the CJPA 2001.

27.   The CJPA 2001 enables an investigator to seize relevant items which contain LPP material where it is not reasonably practicable on the search premises to separate LPP material from non-LPP material.

28.   Where LPP material or material suspected of containing LPP is seized, it must be isolated from the other material which has been seized in the investigation. Where suspected LPP material is discovered when reviewing material, and it was not anticipated that this material existed, again it must be isolated from the other material and the steps outlined below taken. The prosecution will need to decide on a case by case basis if the material is LPP material or not – defence may be able to assist with this.

29.   Where material has been identified as potentially containing LPP it must be reviewed by a lawyer independent of the prosecuting authority. No member of the investigative or prosecution team involved in either the current investigation or, if the LPP material relates to other criminal proceedings, in those proceedings should have sight of or access to the LPP material.

30.   If the material is voluminous, search terms or other filters may have to be used to identify the LPP material. If so this will also have to be done by someone independent and not connected with the investigation.

31.   It is essential that anyone dealing with LPP material maintains proper records showing the way in which the material has been handled and those who have had access to it, as well as decisions taken in relation to that material.

32.   LPP material can only be retained in specific circumstances in accordance with section 54 of the CJPA 2001. It can only be retained where the property which comprises the LPP material has been lawfully seized and it is not reasonably practicable for the item to be separated from the rest of the property without prejudicing the use of the rest of the property. LPP material which cannot be retained must be returned as soon as practicable after the seizure without waiting for the whole examination of the seized material.

Excluded and special procedure material

33.   Similar principles to those that apply to LPP material apply to excluded or special procedure material.[41,42] By way of example, this may include material a journalist holds in confidence from a source.

Encryption

34.   Part III of the Regulation of Investigatory Powers Act 2000 (RIPA 2000) and the Investigation of Protected Electronic Information Code of Practice govern encryption.

35.   RIPA enables specified law enforcement agencies to compel individuals or companies to provide passwords or encryption keys for the purpose of rendering protected material readable. Failure to comply with RIPA 2000 Part III orders is a criminal offence. The Code of Practice provides guidance when exercising powers under RIPA, to require disclosure of protected electronic data in an intelligible form or to acquire the means by which protected electronic data may be accessed or put in an intelligible form.

Sifting and examination

36.   In complying with its duty of disclosure, the prosecution should follow the procedure as outlined below.

---

41 CJPA 2001, s.55

42 Special provision exists for investigators conducted by [His] Majesty's Revenue and Customs in the application of their powers under PACE 1984 (see s.114(2)(b) of PACE and the CJPA).

37. Where digital material is examined, the extent and manner of inspecting, viewing or listening will depend on the nature of the material and its form.

38. It is important for investigators and prosecutors to remember that the duty under the CPIA Code is to "pursue all reasonable lines of inquiry including those that point away from the suspect".

39. Lines of inquiry, of whatever kind, should be pursued only if they are reasonable in the context of the individual case. It is not the duty of the prosecution to comb through all the material in its possession (e.g. every word or byte of computer material) on the lookout for anything which might conceivably or speculatively undermine the case or assist the defence. The duty of the prosecution is to disclose material which might reasonably be considered capable of undermining its case or assisting the case for the accused which they become aware of, or to which their attention is drawn.

40. In some cases, the sift may be conducted by an investigator and/or disclosure officer manually assessing the content of the computer or other digital material from its directory and determining which files are relevant and should be retained for evidence or unused material.

41. In other cases, such an approach may not be feasible. Where there is a large volume of material, it is perfectly proper for the investigator and/or disclosure officer to search by sample, key words, or other appropriate search tools or analytical techniques to locate relevant passages, phrases and identifiers. For the avoidance of any doubt, mobile phones are capable of storing a large volume of material. Technology that takes the form of search tools which use unambiguous calculations to perform problem-solving operations, such as algorithms or predictive coding, are an acceptable method of examining and reviewing material for disclosure purposes.

42. In cases involving very large quantities of data, the person in charge of the investigation will develop a strategy setting out how the material should be analysed or searched to identify categories of data. This strategy may include an initial scoping exercise of the material obtained to ascertain the most effective strategy for reviewing relevant material. Any such strategy should be agreed with the prosecutor and communicated to the court and defence using a DMD

43. Where search terms are to be used, investigators and prosecutors should consider whether engagement with the defence at the pre-charge stage would assist in the identification of relevant search terms. It will usually be appropriate to provide to the accused and their legal representative with a copy of the reasonable search terms used, or to be used, and to invite them to suggest any further reasonable search terms. If search terms are suggested which the investigator or prosecutor believes will not be productive, for example where the use of common words is likely to identify a mass of irrelevant material, the investigator or prosecutor should discuss the issues with the defence in order to agree sensible refinements.

44. The digital strategy must be set out in an IMD and subsequently a DMD. This should include the details of any sampling techniques used (including key word searches) and how the material identified as a result was examined.

45. It may be necessary to carry out sampling and searches on more than one occasion, especially as there is a duty on the prosecutor to keep duties of disclosure under review. To comply with this duty, further sampling and searches may be appropriate (and should be considered) where:
    a. Further evidence or unused material is obtained in the course of the investigation; and/or
    b. The defence statement is served on the prosecutor; and/or
    c. The defendant makes an application under section 8 of the CPIA 1996 for disclosure; and/or
    d. The defendant requests that further sampling or searches be carried out (provided it is a reasonable line of inquiry).

Record keeping

46. A record or log must be made of all digital material seized or imaged and subsequently retained as relevant to the investigation.

47. In cases involving large quantities of data where the person in charge of the investigation has developed a strategy setting out how the material should be analysed or searched to identify categories of data, a record should be made of the strategy and the analytical techniques used to search the data, including the software used. The record should include details of the person who has carried out the process and the date and time it was carried out. In such cases the strategy should record the reasons why certain categories have been searched for (such as names, companies, dates etc).

48. It is important that any searching or analytical processing of digital material, as well as the data identified by that process, is properly recorded. So far as is practicable, what is required is a record of the terms of the searches or processing that has been carried out. This means that in principle the following details may be recorded:
    a. A record of all searches carried out, including the date of each search and the person(s) who conducted it.

b. A record of all search words or terms used on each search. However, where it is impracticable to record each word or term it will usually be sufficient to record each broad category of search.

c. A log of the key judgements made while refining the search strategy in light of what is found, or deciding not to carry out further searches.

d. Where material relating to a "hit" is not examined, the decision not to examine should be explained in the record of examination or in a statement. For instance, a large number of "hits" may be obtained in relation to a particular search word or term, but material relating to the "hits" is not examined because they do not appear to be relevant to the investigation. Any subsequent refinement of the search terms and further hits should also be noted and explained as above.

49. Just as it is not necessary for the investigator or prosecutor to produce records of every search made of hard copy material, it is not necessary to produce records of what may be many hundreds of searches or analyses that have been carried out on digitally stored material simply to demonstrate that these have been done. Instead, the investigator and the prosecutor should ensure that they are able to explain how the disclosure exercise has been approached and to give the accused or suspect's legal representative an opportunity to participate in defining the reasonable searches to be made, as described in the section on sifting/examination.

Scheduling

50. The disclosure officer should ensure that scheduling of relevant material is carried out in accordance with the CPIA Code of Practice. This may require each item of unused material to be listed separately on the unused material schedule and numbered consecutively (which may include numbering by volume and sub-volume). The description of each item should make clear the nature of the item and should contain sufficient detail to enable the prosecutor to decide whether they need to inspect the material before deciding whether or not it should be disclosed.

51. It will generally be disproportionate in cases involving large quantities of digital data to list each item of material separately. Unless it is necessary or otherwise appropriate to separately list each item, the material should be listed in a block or blocks and described by quantity and generic title. Where the material is listed in a block or blocks, the search terms used and any items of material which might satisfy the disclosure test should be listed and described separately. In practical terms this will mean, where appropriate, cross referencing the schedules to the DMD.

52. Where material has been listed in a block and metadata is available for the material within the block, consideration should be given to creating a file of that metadata and listing this separately and linked to the block listing to which it relates.

53. Where continuation sheets of the unused material schedule are used, or additional schedules are sent subsequently, the item numbering must be, where possible, sequential to all other items on earlier schedules. This may include numbering by volume or sub-volume.

Annex B

Pre-charge engagement

The scope of pre-charge engagement

1. These Guidelines are intended to assist prosecutors, investigators, suspects and suspect's legal representatives who wish to enter into discussions about an investigation at any time after the first PACE interview, up until the commencement of criminal proceedings.

2. These Guidelines are not intended to cover discussions regarding pleas to an allegation of serious or complex fraud. Nor do they apply to formal agreements relating to the provision of information or evidence about the criminal activities of others. In such cases, where appropriate, the parties should refer to the relevant guidance and follow the advised procedures:

a. In cases of serious or complex fraud, see the Attorney-General's Guidelines on Plea discussions in cases of serious or complex fraud.

b. In cases where the suspect wishes to enter into a formal agreement to provide information or evidence, see sections 71–75 of the Serious Organised Crime and Police Act (SOCPA) 2005 and the CPS legal guidance on SOCPA 2005 – Queen's Evidence.

What is pre-charge engagement?

3. Pre-charge engagement in these guidelines refers to voluntary engagement between the parties to an investigation after the first PACE interview, and before any suspect has been formally charged. Pre-charge engagement is a voluntary process and it may be terminated at any time. It does not refer to engagement between the parties to an investigation by way of further PACE interviews, and none

of the guidance in this Annex is intended to apply to such circumstances. Should a defendant choose not to engage at this stage, that decision should not be held against him at a later stage in the proceedings.

4. Pre-charge engagement may, among other things, involve:
    a. Giving the suspect the opportunity to comment on any proposed further lines of inquiry.
    b. Ascertaining whether the suspect can identify any other lines of inquiry.
    c. Asking whether the suspect is aware of, or can provide access to, digital material that has a bearing on the allegation.
    d. Discussing ways to overcome barriers to obtaining potential evidence, such as revealing encryption keys.
    e. Agreeing any key word searches of digital material that the suspect would like carried out.
    f. Obtaining a suspect's consent to access medical records.
    g. The suspect identifying and providing contact details of any potential witnesses.
    h. Clarifying whether any expert or forensic evidence is agreed and, if not, whether the suspect's representatives intend to instruct their own expert, including timescales for this.

5. Pre-charge engagement is encouraged by the Code for Crown Prosecutors and may impact decisions as to charge.[43]

When is pre-charge engagement appropriate?

6. It may take place whenever it is agreed between the parties that it may assist the investigation. Where a suspect is not yet represented, an investigator should take care to ensure that the suspect understands their right to legal advice before the pre charge engagement process commences. Sufficient time should be given to enable a suspect to access this advice if they wish to do so.

7. Pre-charge engagement should not, however, be considered a replacement to a further interview with a suspect. Investigators and prosecutors should be conscious that adverse inferences under section 34 of the Criminal Justice and Public Order Act 1994 are not available at trial where a suspect failed to mention a fact when asked about a matter in pre-charge engagement. An adverse inference may only be drawn where the suspect failed to mention a fact while being questioned under caution by a constable trying to discover whether or by whom the offence had been committed. Moreover, investigators and prosecutors should be aware of the advantages of holding a further formal interview, including the fact that suspects will have been appropriately cautioned and that any answers given will be recorded.

8. Accordingly, investigators and prosecutors should not seek to initiate, or agree to, pre- charge engagement in respect of matters where they are likely to seek to rely on the contents of the suspect's answers as evidence at trial. Pre-charge engagement should not therefore be used for putting new summaries of the case to the defence, and where deemed necessary such accounts should be put to the suspect in a further interview.

9. A no comment interview does not preclude the possibility of pre-charge engagement. When taking into account paragraph 8 above, while a no comment interview may limit the scope of any such discussions, pre-charge engagement may still be pursued where appropriate, but consideration should be given to a further PACE interview with the suspect before there is any agreement to engage in pre-charge engagement.

10. There are a number of potential benefits that may arise from pre-charge engagement:
    a. Suspects who maintain their innocence will be aided by early identification of lines of inquiry which may lead to evidence or material that points away from the suspect or points towards another suspect.
    b. Pre-charge engagement can help inform a prosecutor's charging decision. It might avoid a case being charged that would otherwise be stopped later in proceedings, when further information becomes available.
    c. The issues in dispute may be narrowed, so that unnecessary inquiries are not pursued, and if a case is charged and proceeds to trial, it can be managed more efficiently.
    d. Early resolution of a case may reduce anxiety and uncertainty for suspects and complainants.
    e. The cost of the matter to the criminal justice system may be reduced, including potentially avoiding or mitigating the cost of criminal proceedings.

Who may initiate and conduct pre-charge engagement?

11. Depending on the circumstances, it may be appropriate for an investigator, the prosecutor, the suspect's representative or an unrepresented suspect to initiate pre- charge engagement.

12. When referring a case to a prosecutor, the investigator should inform the prosecutor if any pre-charge engagement has already taken place and should indicate if they believe pre-charge engagement would benefit the case.

---

[43] The Code for Crown Prosecutors, para.3.4

13. The prosecutor may advise the investigator to initiate and carry out pre-charge engagement, or do so themselves.

14. In cases in which statutory time limits on charging apply, it will usually be more practical for the investigator, rather than the prosecutor, to initiate and conduct pre-charge engagement.

15. Prosecutors and investigators should be alert to use of pre-charge engagement as a means to frustrate or delay the investigation unnecessarily. Engagement should not be initiated or continued where this is apparent. In particular, pre-charge engagement is not intended to provide an opportunity for the suspect to make unfounded allegations against the complainant, so that the complainant becomes unjustly subject to investigation. Prosecutors and investigators should be alert to prevent this happening and investigators are not obliged to follow any line of inquiry suggested by the suspect's representative: a line of inquiry should be reasonable in the circumstances of the case. What is reasonable is a matter for an investigator to decide, with the assistance of a prosecutor if required. Refer to Annex A and paragraphs 11–13 for more guidance on reasonable lines of inquiry, particularly in relation to the obtaining of a complainant's mobile or other personal devices.

Information on pre-charge engagement

16. The investigator should provide information on pre-charge engagement to the suspect or their representative either before or after interview.

17. The pre-charge engagement process should be explained orally or in writing, in simple terms.

18. The explanation may include the aim and benefits of the process, any relevant timescales and a police point of contact to make any future representations at the pre- charge stage.

Conducting pre-charge engagement

19. Pre-charge engagement discussions may take place face to face or via correspondence.

20. It need not always be undertaken via a formal process, but a written record should always be made and kept. For instance, the process may be initiated immediately after interview, when the investigator and suspect's representative may agree on the further lines of inquiry that have arisen from interview.

21. However, in some circumstances the parties will require a more formal mechanism to enable them to begin the process at any stage post-interview and before charge. This may be done by the investigator, prosecutor or suspect's representative sending a letter of invitation to the other party, which:

   a. Asks whether the other party wishes to enter into pre-charge engagement in accordance with these Guidelines.

   b. Explains in what way the engagement may assist the investigation. The prosecutor or investigator may wish to include the information sought, or sought to be discussed.

Disclosure during Pre-Charge Engagement

22. Since pre-charge engagement takes place prior to the institution of any proceedings, the statutory disclosure rules will not be engaged. However, disclosure of unused material must be considered as part of the pre-charge engagement process, to ensure that the discussions are fair and that the suspect is not misled as to the strength of the prosecution case.

23. Accordingly, before, during and after pre-charge engagement, the investigator/prosecutor should consider whether any further material, additional to that contained in the summary of the allegation, falls to be disclosed to the suspect. The investigator/prosecutor should at all stages bear in mind the potential need to cease pre- charge engagement and to put further evidence to the suspect in a PACE interview.

24. As the suspect provides information during the process, the investigator/prosecutor should continually be alive to the potential need to make any further disclosure.

Recording the discussions

25. A full written, signed record of the pre-charge engagement discussions should be made.

26. Additionally, the prosecutor and/or investigator should record every key action involved in the process, such as the provision of written information on pre-charge engagement to the suspect, any informal discussions with the suspect's representative about entering into the process, or any formal letter of invitation sent or received.

27.   A record should be made of all information provided by the suspect's representative, such as potential lines of inquiry, suggested key word searches of digital material and any witness details.

28.   The law may require the prosecutor to disclose any information provided by the suspect's representative to another party, including a defendant in criminal proceedings.

29.   A record should also be made of all information and material provided to the suspect's representative, including any disclosure material.

30.   The prosecutor and investigator should ensure that the records of the pre-charge engagement are provided to each other. Information or material generated by the process will need to be assessed for evidential and disclosure purposes.

Annex C

Disclosure Management Documents (DMDs)

Template "Disclosure Management Document"

This Disclosure Management Document sets out the approach of the prosecution to relevant non-sensitive material in this case. Unless otherwise indicated, all the material on the non-sensitive schedule has been inspected by the disclosure officer.

R v [Name]

Prosecutor:

Disclosure officer:

Prosecution counsel instructed:

1.   Reasonable lines of inquiry

The rationale for the identification and scheduling of relevant material is based upon the reasonable lines of inquiry that were conducted within this investigation. The Disclosure Officer's understanding of the defence case is as follows;

- [What explanation has been offered by the accused, whether in formal interview, defence statement or otherwise. How has this been followed up? This should be set out.]
- [What are the identified/likely issues in the case e.g identification, alibi, factual dispute, no intention etc]
- [Insert summary of reasonable lines of inquiry pursued, particularly those that point away from the suspect, or which may assist the defence]
- The time frame selected is considered to be a reasonable line of inquiry, and represents [e.g. the date that the victim first met the suspect to a month after the suspect's arrest]

2.   Electronic material

This section should cover the following issues:

- What mobile telephones/communication devices/computers were seized during the investigation (from all suspects, complainants, witnesses).
- Identify the items with reference to the schedule of materials – i.e. telephone, download
- Have the devices been downloaded? If not, why not. If so, what type of download?
- Set out the method of examination of each download – were key words deployed, was the entire download inspected, were date parameters employed?
- What social media accounts of suspect/complaint/witness have been considered a reasonable line of inquiry.
- Were any phones from the complainant or suspect not seized? If not, why not?
- Set out the method by which the defence will be given disclosure of material that satisfies the disclosure test explaining, if relevant, why the whole item is not being provided.
- What CCTV/multi-media evidence has been seized and how it has been examined?

A suggested presentation and wording of the information is set out below:

Exhibit ref	Description	Inquiry undertaken	Result
AB/1	*I-phone seized from defendant*	*This telephone has been downloaded using the XRY software. This has resulted in 40,000 pages of data which includes telephone calls to and from the suspect, contact list, text messages, WhatsApp messages and internet search history. No further data has been downloaded from the phone.* *The internet search history does not appear to be relevant to the issues in the case and has not been reviewed.* *The contact list has been reviewed to identify whether the complainant is a contact, no further checks have been made.* *The telephone call list has been reviewed for any contact between the suspect and complainant between dates x and Y. All identified contact has been produced as exhibit AB/2.* *Text messages and WhatsApp messages have been searched using the following keywords [A, B, C, D] all responsive messages which correspond with the keywords have been disclosed.*	*Relevant evidential material has been served.* *Material which has been identified through keyword searching has been collated and scheduled. The defence are invited to identify any further keywords which might represent a reasonable line of inquiry. If further interrogation of the telephone is considered to be necessary the defence are invited to identify what enquiries should be undertaken and identify the relevance of such enquiries to the issues in this case.*
		No further checks have been conducted upon the phone.	

3. Third Party Material

   The prosecution believe that the following third parties have relevant non sensitive material that might satisfy the disclosure test if it were in the possession of the prosecution (e.g. Medical and dental records, Records held by other agencies, Records/material held by Social Services or local authority):

   The reason for this belief is …

   The type of relevant material is…

   The following steps have been taken to obtain this material:

   The defence have a critical role in ensuring that the prosecution are directed to material that meets the disclosure test. Any representations by the defence on the contents of this document, including identifying issues in the case and why material meets the test for disclosure should be received by *[insert date/ timescale]*

   Signed:

   Dated:

ANNEX D

REDACTION

Overview

1. This annex relates to the obligation on investigators to redact material provided to the CPS when a charging decision is sought. While it focuses on unused material at the pre-charge stage, the principles may also apply to evidence and to other stages of the prosecution process. The term redaction in this annex refers to any way of obscuring personal data, including but not limited to redaction, clipping, pixelization, anonymisation or pseudonymisation.
2. Providing data to the CPS or any other party from the police is an action regulated by data protection law. There may be a number of reasons why data is processed: if it is for law enforcement purposes it will fall under the Data Protection Act 2018, Part 3; otherwise, it may fall within the UK GDPR and other parts of the DPA 2018.
3. Redaction is a vital tool, mandated by law, to protect fundamental rights when personal data is handled.
4. It is not an automatic legal requirement that every piece of data passed by the police to the CPS must be redacted of all personal data. Cases need to be considered on their own facts.

The Redaction Decision-Making Process

Reviewing for Relevance

5.   The first consideration must be to review the material and assess its relevance.
6.   The investigator should review the material and decide if it is relevant to seeking a charging decision. This does not need to be weighed to a nicety but requires a clear idea of why the material is to be provided to the CPS and what is relevant. Irrelevant material is neither evidential nor disclosable and does not need to be provided to the CPS.

Establishing the Data is Personal

7.   Once the relevant data is identified the next consideration before redacting is to decide whether that data requires protecting.
8.   Personal data is information which relates to an identified or identifiable individual. If the data is not personal data, it will not need redacting for UK GDPR/DPA 2018 reasons (there may be other grounds for redaction such as sensitivity).
9.   Where the information is personal data, but the person does not have a reasonable expectation of privacy, it will not need to be redacted.
     a.   Typically, helicopter or drone footage of people in public locations, vehicle registrations on public roads, staff and customers in shops and openly recorded interviews of witnesses would not likely fall to be redacted.[44]
     b.   Typically, covert recordings, recordings in a domestic setting or footage of other persons detained at a police station would likely fall to be redacted.

Applying the Necessity Test

10. Where the data is relevant, personal and there is a reasonable expectation of privacy, investigators will need to go on to consider whether it is nonetheless necessary or strictly necessary to provide it to the CPS in an unredacted form for the purposes of making a charging decision. Where it is necessary or strictly necessary to do so, the data need not be redacted; where data does not meet this standard, it should be redacted.

> Officers should have, at the front of their minds, the purpose for which the data is being provided. In the case of this annex, the purpose is for the CPS to make a charging decision.
>
> For example: Footage of an assault may capture a number of people's faces. While this will be personal information, it is highly likely that this information will be necessary to provide — this is likely to be the case whether the assault is in public or private. The faces of any suspects and complainants will be necessary for the CPS to identify key figures in the video. The faces of witnesses will likely be necessary for the CPS to assess whether they have provided witness statements, their proximity to the incident, their involvement in the incident, and to verify any statements made are plausible in the context of the person's actions in the footage.
>
> A considered approach is needed from investigators to make an informed judgement about whether data will be necessary to provide. These decisions must take account of the full context of the case and not be based on standardised processes.

11. Necessity tests are a balancing exercise, the reasons in favour of disclosing must outweigh those against. This balance should be assessed objectively and on a case-by-case basis. The purpose of the data being used must always be at the centre of any decision. Whether the test is of necessity or strict necessity will not change this approach. However, a strict necessity standard requires a greater evidential basis to justify providing the data unredacted.
     • 'Necessity' has its natural meaning. It does not mean there is absolutely no other possible option. Investigators must balance the rights of the individual(s) involved with the legitimate public interest in an informed charging decision.
     • 'Strict necessity' is a higher standard than necessary and applies to sensitive personal data. Data about criminal convictions and offences is sensitive and so is any data which is categorised as sensitive by the UK GDPR. This is:
          i.   personal data revealing racial or ethnic origin;
          ii.   personal data revealing political opinions;
          iii. personal data revealing religious or philosophical beliefs;
          iv.   personal data revealing trade union membership;
          v.   genetic data;
          vi.   biometric data (where used for identification purposes);

---

44 Remember that some public footage will need special consideration, such as places of worship, polling stations or political protests.

       vii.   data concerning health;

      viii.   data concerning a person's sex life; and

       ix.   data concerning a person's sexual orientation.

12.   When deciding whether data is necessary or strictly necessary to provide unredacted, investigators should take into consideration the balance of rights and legitimate need.

- The greater the expectation of privacy over the data, the more likely it is to require redaction.
  - o For example, greater consideration will likely need to be given to whether to provide medical or financial data unredacted than names or dates of birth.
- The greater the detriment to a person if their privacy is not maintained, the more likely it is to require redaction.
  - o For example, information which is of an intimate or revealing nature will need greater consideration than that which is not.
- The greater the value of the data to the function being undertaken, the less likely it is to require redaction.
  - o For example, the date of birth of a person in a prosecution may be critical (e.g. to proving an offence where the prosecution must show the victim was under a certain age), important (e.g. to illustrate the relative age of two persons in the case) or of no apparent importance.

13.   In some instances, redaction of the data may not be proportionate. Where this is the case the data may be provided to the CPS unredacted – subject to the standards set out below.

Providing Material that is Disproportionate to Redact

14.   If an officer suspects that the exercise of reviewing material and redacting it will be disproportionate, they should seek approval of that assessment by an officer of inspector rank or higher[45] and record it, ideally in communication with the CPS.

15.   Disproportionate means: the resources (having regard to volume, time and/or expense) required to redact clearly outweigh the merits of redaction. If it would be disproportionate to conduct a review and redaction exercise, that can justify not redacting. Practical considerations such as time and resourcing **will likely only be relevant in marginal cases**, where there is not an obvious reason for or against redacting. The greater the impact on resource considerations such as time, money and delay, the stronger the reasons for not redacting.

16.   The scope for redaction to be considered disproportionate is by no means unlimited and **a blanket approach can never be adopted**. Individual cases must always be considered on their own facts.

17.   Any decision on proportionality will need to closely consider the following non-exhaustive range of factors:

- The scope for finding redaction disproportionate is limited.
- The greater the expectation of privacy, the more likely it is proportionate to redact it.
- Where in an individual case it is agreed with the CPS and there are restrictions ensuring the material will only be provided to, and be capable of being accessed by, the CPS, it may be proportionate to provide material unredacted.
- Where, in an individual case, protections have been put in place against onwards disclosure. For example, secure computer systems or password protection may significantly enhance the proportionality of not redacting. They mean the CPS does not take possession of personal data without the scope for it being accessed being very reduced and controlled.

18.   Where data is provided to the CPS unredacted for a charging decision due to being disproportionate, it will need to be reviewed when the charging decision is made. The responsibility for additional redaction of such material which then becomes necessary remains with the party that provided the data to the CPS initially. Where data is instead provided to the CPS unredacted because it is necessary or strictly necessary to provide it, the CPS has responsibility for any additional redaction (e.g., where required before disclosure to the defence).

Example 1

The police are called to an address to respond to an allegation of assault. The investigating officer preparing a charging decision file for the CPS has an electronic file containing body worn footage from one of the officers attending the address.

Reviewing for Relevance

The investigating officer reviews the file. It contains a quantity of footage from the attending officer's day. The investigating officer decides that this is not all relevant: only the footage of the response to the incident is relevant. The footage is clipped to reduce it to just this section. The officer has not reached a

---

[45] Or a person of equivalent rank in other organisations.

final conclusion about the evidential value of the footage but is clear that the prosecutor must see the scene captured as part of the charging decision, including:

(i)   the reaction of the persons present, and

(ii)   items which are strewn around and damaged.

Establish the Data is Personal

The footage captures images of persons on the street. It captures the image of a witness to whom the attending officer speaks, who is informed that a recording is being made. This is unlikely to need redaction as there is no realistic expectation of privacy. The officer then enters a dwelling. The images of the persons inside may be personal.

Applying the Necessity Test

The investigating officer considers the images of the persons in the dwelling and decides that the necessity test is met. The officer decides the prosecutor does need to see the reactions of those present because they are probative of an assault having taken place, they are therefore provided unredacted. The officer decides that the images of items on the floor is not personal data so does not need to be redacted.

The attending officer also enters a bedroom. There is material present relating to a person's political opinions, including a party membership card, books, posters and leaflets. It may not be necessary to provide this material if the scene in the bedroom is unrelated to the assault. If it is necessary, for instance because the complainant's political opinions are relevant backdrop to why the assault took place, it may not be strictly necessary, because the prosecutor could understand what was present from witnesses including the attending officer without needing to see all of the detail captured in the footage.

Providing Material that is Disproportionate to Redact

The investigating officer considers that the prosecutor does not strictly need to see the material from the bedroom. Having regard to the time and expense of redacting a small part of the body worn footage, and the fact that the decision is a marginal one – the material is something it is necessary for the prosecutor to see given it forms the background to the incident – the investigating officer concludes that redaction would be disproportionate.

Example 2

Officers respond to the theft of a car from the driveway of a residential property. Although the owner of the property was at work, a local resident calls the police and provides an eye-witness account of the theft. The investigator is preparing a file for submission to the CPS. She has the transcript of the 999 call. The call describes the events that occurred and gives a description of the thief; the caller gives their own name, date of birth and address to the call handler. They also provide the names and addresses of three other neighbours, who they believe might have witnessed the theft. The caller goes on to provide a statement which is consistent with the descriptions given on the calls. It later becomes apparent that none of the neighbours saw or heard anything related to the theft.

Reviewing for Relevance

The investigating officer comes to the conclusion that the witness statement will form part of the evidence in the case, but that the call is not required. Nonetheless, the call remains relevant as it contains content which clearly relates to the offending. She is also aware the call will need to be provided to the CPS as material likely to be disclosable as a contemporaneous record of the incident.

Establishing the Data is Personal

The call transcript contains personal details, of both the caller and their neighbours, given in the context of reporting an offence. It is capable of identifying living persons who have a reasonable expectation of privacy. On a first assessment, it may need redacting. The investigator considers the type of information and realises the strict necessity standard does not apply to the personal data involved.

Applying the Necessity Test

The investigator assesses that the personal details of the caller, including their name, address and date of birth are necessary to provide to the CPS to identify them as the witness. The personal details of the neighbours are not likely to be important to the CPS charging decision, as they are unrelated to the substance of the offence being investigated. The investigator contacts the prosecutor in the case, who agrees that these names wouldn't be necessary for him to know. As there is no need for the CPS to know the personal information, it is likely that this material will require redaction.

Providing Material that is Disproportionate to Redact

While assessing the transcript, the investigating officer considers the disclosure test. She knows that material only needs to be disclosed where it is not already available to the defence. As the witness statement will be available to the defence, the investigating officer decides that the CPS are unlikely to disclose the transcript – it will be listed on the unused material schedule instead. As the transcript is only likely to be assessed by the CPS, and the time and resources required to provide redacted copies would be significant, she decides it would not be proportionate to redact the details of the other neighbours. She confirms this with the CPS prosecutor and provides the transcript unredacted.

The Code for Crown Prosecutors

Introduction

1.1 The Code for Crown Prosecutors (the Code) is issued by the Director of Public Prosecutions (DPP) under section 10 of the Prosecution of Offences Act 1985. This is the eighth edition of the Code and replaces all earlier versions.

1.2 The DPP is the head of the Crown Prosecution Service (CPS), which is the principal public prosecution service for England and Wales. The DPP operates independently, under the superintendence of the Attorney General who is accountable to Parliament for the work of the CPS.

1.3 The Code gives guidance to prosecutors on the general principles to be applied when making decisions about prosecutions. The Code is issued primarily for prosecutors in the CPS but other prosecutors follow the Code, either through convention or because they are required to do so by law.

1.4 In this Code:
- 'Suspect' is used to describe a person who is under consideration as the subject of formal criminal proceedings;
- 'Defendant' is used to describe a person who has been charged or summonsed;
- 'Offender' is used to describe a person who has admitted guilt as to the commission of an offence, or who has been found guilty in a court of law;
- 'Victim' is used to describe a person against whom an offence has been committed, or the complainant in a case being considered or prosecuted by the CPS.

General Principles

2.1 The independence of the prosecutor is central to the criminal justice system of a democratic society. Prosecutors are independent from persons or agencies that are not part of the prosecution decision-making process. CPS prosecutors are also independent from the police and other investigators. Prosecutors must be free to carry out their professional duties without political interference and must not be affected by improper or undue pressure or influence from any source.

2.2 It is not the function of the CPS to decide whether a person is guilty of a criminal offence, but to make assessments about whether it is appropriate to present charges for the criminal court to consider. The CPS assessment of any case is not in any sense a finding of, or implication of, any guilt or criminal conduct. A finding of guilt can only be made by a court.

2.3 Similarly, a decision not to bring criminal charges does not necessarily mean that an individual has not been a victim of crime. It is not the role of the CPS to make such determinations.

2.4 The decision to prosecute or to recommend an out-of-court disposal is a serious step that affects suspects, victims, witnesses and the public at large and must be undertaken with the utmost care.

2.5 It is the duty of prosecutors to make sure that the right person is prosecuted for the right offence and to bring offenders to justice wherever possible. Casework decisions taken fairly, impartially and with integrity help to secure justice for victims, witnesses, suspects, defendants and the public. Prosecutors must ensure that the law is properly applied, that relevant evidence is put before the court and that obligations of disclosure are complied with.

2.6 Although each case must be considered on its own facts and on its own merits, there are general principles that apply in every case.

2.7 When making decisions, prosecutors must be fair and objective. They must not let any personal views about the ethnic or national origin, gender, disability, age, religion or belief, sexual orientation or gender identity of the suspect, defendant, victim or any witness influence their decisions. Neither must they be motivated by political considerations. Prosecutors must always act in the interests of justice and not solely for the purpose of obtaining a conviction.

2.8 Prosecutors must be even-handed in their approach to every case, and have a duty to protect the rights of suspects and defendants, while providing the best possible service to victims.

2.9 The CPS is a public authority for the purposes of current, relevant equality legislation. Prosecutors are bound by the duties set out in this legislation.

2.10 Prosecutors must apply the principles of the European Convention on Human Rights, in accordance with the Human Rights Act 1998, at each stage of a case. They must comply with any guidelines issued by the Attorney General and with the policies and guidance of the CPS issued on behalf of the DPP, unless it is determined that there are exceptional circumstances. CPS guidance contains further evidential and public interest factors for specific offences and offenders and is available for the public to view on the CPS website. Prosecutors must also comply with the Criminal

Procedure Rules and Criminal Practice Directions, and have regard to the Sentencing Council Guidelines and the obligations arising from international conventions.

2.11 The CPS prosecutes on behalf of some other Government departments. In such cases, prosecutors should have regard to any relevant enforcement policies of those departments.

2.12 Some offences may be prosecuted by either the CPS or by other prosecutors in England and Wales. When making decisions in these cases, CPS prosecutors may, where they think it appropriate, have regard to any relevant enforcement or prosecution policy or code of the other prosecutor.

2.13 Where the law differs in England and Wales prosecutors must apply the Code and have regard to any relevant policy, guidance or charging standard.

The Decision Whether to Prosecute

3.1 In more serious or complex cases, prosecutors decide whether a person should be charged with a criminal offence and, if so, what that offence should be. Prosecutors may also advise on or authorise out-of-court disposals as an alternative to prosecution. They make their decisions in accordance with this Code, the DPP's Guidance on Charging and any relevant legal guidance or policy. The police apply the same principles in deciding whether to start criminal proceedings against a person in those cases for which they are responsible.

3.2 The police and other investigators are responsible for conducting inquiries into any alleged crime and for deciding how to deploy their resources. This includes decisions to start or continue an investigation and on the scope of the investigation. Prosecutors should advise the police and other investigators about possible reasonable lines of inquiry, evidential requirements, pre-charge procedures, disclosure management and the overall investigation strategy. This can include decisions to refine or narrow the scope of the criminal conduct and the number of suspects under investigation. Such advice assists the police and other investigators to complete the investigation within a reasonable period of time and to build the most effective prosecution case.

3.3 Prosecutors cannot direct the police or other investigators. However, prosecutors must have regard to the impact of any failure to pursue an advised reasonable line of inquiry or to comply with a request for information, when deciding whether the application of the Full Code Test should be deferred or whether the test can be met at all.

3.4 Prosecutors should identify and, where possible, seek to rectify evidential weaknesses but, subject to the Threshold Test (see section 5), they should quickly stop cases which do not meet the evidential stage of the Full Code Test (see section 4) and which cannot be strengthened by further investigation, or where the public interest clearly does not require a prosecution (see section 4). Although prosecutors primarily consider the evidence and information supplied by the police and other investigators, the suspect or those acting on their behalf may also submit evidence or information to the prosecutor, before or after charge, to help inform the prosecutor's decision. In appropriate cases, the prosecutor may invite the suspect or their representative to do so.

3.5 Prosecutors should not start or continue a prosecution where their view is that it is highly likely that a court will rule that a prosecution is an abuse of its process, and stay the proceedings.

3.6 Prosecutors review every case they receive from the police or other investigators. Review is a continuing process and prosecutors must take account of any change in circumstances that occurs as the case develops. This includes what becomes known of the defence case, any further reasonable lines of inquiry that should be pursued, and receipt of any unused material that may undermine the prosecution case or assist the defence case, to the extent that charges should be altered or discontinued or the prosecution should not proceed. If a case is to be stopped, care should be taken when choosing the method of termination, as this can affect the victim's position under the Victims' Right to Review scheme. Wherever possible, prosecutors should consult the investigator when considering changing the charges or stopping the case. Prosecutors and investigators work closely together, but the final responsibility for the decision whether or not a case should go ahead rests with the CPS.

3.7 Parliament has decided that a limited number of offences should only be taken to court with the agreement of the DPP. These are called consent cases. In such cases the DPP, or a prosecutor acting on their behalf, applies the Code in deciding whether to give consent to a prosecution.

3.8 There are also certain offences that can only be taken to court with the consent of the Attorney General. Prosecutors must follow current guidance when referring any such cases to the Attorney General. Some offences require the consent of a Secretary of State before a prosecution is started. Prosecutors must obtain such consent prior to charge and apply any relevant guidance in these cases. Additionally, the Attorney General will be kept informed of certain cases as part of their superintendence of the CPS and accountability to Parliament for its actions.

The Full Code Test

4.1   Prosecutors must only start or continue a prosecution when the case has passed both stages of the Full Code Test. The exception is when the Threshold Test may be applied (see section 5).

4.2   The Full Code Test has two stages: (i) the evidential stage; followed by (ii) the public interest stage.

4.3   The Full Code Test should be applied:

    a.   when all outstanding reasonable lines of inquiry have been pursued; or

    b.   prior to the investigation being completed, if the prosecutor is satisfied that any further evidence or material is unlikely to affect the application of the Full Code Test, whether in favour of or against a prosecution.

4.4   In most cases prosecutors should only consider whether a prosecution is in the public interest after considering whether there is sufficient evidence to prosecute. However, there will be cases where it is clear, prior to reviewing all the evidence, that the public interest does not require a prosecution. In these instances, prosecutors may decide that the case should not proceed further.

4.5   Prosecutors should only take such a decision when they are satisfied that the broad extent of the criminality has been determined and that they are able to make a fully informed assessment of the public interest. If prosecutors do not have sufficient information to take such a decision, the investigation should continue and a decision taken later in accordance with the Full Code Test set out in this section.

The Evidential Stage

4.6   Prosecutors must be satisfied that there is sufficient evidence to provide a realistic prospect of conviction against each suspect on each charge.[*] They must consider what the defence case may be, and how it is likely to affect the prospects of conviction. A case which does not pass the evidential stage must not proceed, no matter how serious or sensitive it may be.

4.7   The finding that there is a realistic prospect of conviction is based on the prosecutor's objective assessment of the evidence, including the impact of any defence and any other information that the suspect has put forward or on which they might rely. It means that an objective, impartial and reasonable jury or bench of magistrates or judge hearing a case alone, properly directed and acting in accordance with the law, is more likely than not to convict the defendant of the charge alleged. This is a different test from the one that the criminal courts themselves must apply. A court may only convict if it is sure that the defendant is guilty.

4.8   When deciding whether there is sufficient evidence to prosecute, prosecutors should ask themselves the following:

Can the evidence be used in court?

Prosecutors should consider whether there is any question over the admissibility of certain evidence. In doing so, prosecutors should assess:

• the likelihood of that evidence being held as inadmissible by the court; and
• the importance of that evidence in relation to the evidence as a whole.

Is the evidence reliable?

Prosecutors should consider whether there are any reasons to question the reliability of the evidence, including its accuracy or integrity.

Is the evidence credible?

Prosecutors should consider whether there are any reasons to doubt the credibility of the evidence.

Is there any other material that might affect the sufficiency of evidence?

Prosecutors must consider at this stage and throughout the case whether there is any material that may affect the assessment of the sufficiency of evidence, including examined and unexamined material in the possession of the police, and material that may be obtained through further reasonable lines of inquiry.

The Public Interest Stage

4.9   In every case where there is sufficient evidence to justify a prosecution or to offer an out-of-court disposal, prosecutors must go on to consider whether a prosecution is required in the public interest.

4.10   It has never been the rule that a prosecution will automatically take place once the evidential stage is met. A prosecution will usually take place unless the prosecutor is satisfied that there are public

---

[*] For the purposes of the Code for Crown Prosecutors, 'conviction' includes a finding that 'the person did the act or made the omission' in circumstances where the person is likely to be found not guilty on the grounds of insanity.

interest factors tending against prosecution which outweigh those tending in favour. In some cases the prosecutor may be satisfied that the public interest can be properly served by offering the offender the opportunity to have the matter dealt with by an out-of-court disposal rather than bringing a prosecution.

4.11 When deciding the public interest, prosecutors should consider each of the questions set out below in paragraphs 4.14 a) to g) so as to identify and determine the relevant public interest factors tending for and against prosecution. These factors, together with any public interest factors set out in relevant guidance or policy issued by the DPP, should enable prosecutors to form an overall assessment of the public interest.

4.12 The explanatory text below each question in paragraphs 4.14 a) to g) provides guidance to prosecutors when addressing each particular question and determining whether it identifies public interest factors for or against prosecution. The questions identified are not exhaustive, and not all the questions may be relevant in every case. The weight to be attached to each of the questions, and the factors identified, will also vary according to the facts and merits of each case.

4.13 It is quite possible that one public interest factor alone may outweigh a number of other factors which tend in the opposite direction. Although there may be public interest factors tending against prosecution in a particular case, prosecutors should consider whether nonetheless a prosecution should go ahead and those factors put to the court for consideration when sentence is passed.

4.14 Prosecutors should consider each of the following questions:

a) *How serious is the offence committed?*
- The more serious the offence, the more likely it is that a prosecution is required.
- When assessing the seriousness of an offence, prosecutors should include in their consideration the suspect's culpability and the harm caused, by asking themselves the questions at b) and c).

b) *What is the level of culpability of the suspect?*
- The greater the suspect's level of culpability, the more likely it is that a prosecution is required.
- Culpability is likely to be determined by:
    i. the suspect's level of involvement;
    ii. the extent to which the offending was premeditated and/or planned;
    iii. the extent to which the suspect has benefitted from criminal conduct;
    iv. whether the suspect has previous criminal convictions and/or out-of-court disposals and any offending whilst on bail or whilst subject to a court order;
    v. whether the offending was or is likely to be continued, repeated or escalated;
    vi. the suspect's age and maturity (see paragraph d below).
- A suspect is likely to have a much lower level of culpability if the suspect has been compelled, coerced or exploited, particularly if they are the victim of a crime that is linked to their offending.
- Prosecutors should also have regard to whether the suspect is, or was at the time of the offence, affected by any significant mental or physical ill health or disability, as in some circumstances this may mean that it is less likely that a prosecution is required. However, prosecutors will also need to consider how serious the offence was, whether the suspect is likely to re-offend and the need to safeguard the public or those providing care to such persons.

c) *What are the circumstances of and the harm caused to the victim?*
- The circumstances of the victim are highly relevant. The more vulnerable the victim's situation, or the greater the perceived vulnerability of the victim, the more likely it is that a prosecution is required.
- This includes where a position of trust or authority exists between the suspect and victim.
- A prosecution is also more likely if the offence has been committed against a victim who was at the time a person serving the public.
- It is more likely that prosecution is required if the offence was motivated by any form of prejudice against the victim's actual or presumed ethnic or national origin, gender, disability, age, religion or belief, sexual orientation or gender identity; or if the suspect targeted or exploited the victim, or demonstrated hostility towards the victim, based on any of those characteristics.
- Prosecutors also need to consider if a prosecution is likely to have an adverse effect on the victim's physical or mental health, always bearing in mind the seriousness of the offence, the availability of special measures and the possibility of a prosecution without the participation of the victim.
- Prosecutors should take into account the views expressed by the victim about the impact that the offence has had. In appropriate cases, this may also include the views of the victim's family.
- However, the CPS does not act for victims or their families in the same way as solicitors act for their clients, and prosecutors must form an overall view of the public interest.

d) *What was the suspect's age and maturity at the time of the offence?*

- The criminal justice system treats children and young people differently from adults and significant weight must be attached to the age of the suspect if they are a child or young person under 18.
- The best interests and welfare of the child or young person must be considered, including whether a prosecution is likely to have an adverse impact on their future prospects that is disproportionate to the seriousness of the offending. Prosecutors must have regard to the principal aim of the youth justice system, which is to prevent offending by children and young people. Prosecutors must also have regard to the obligations arising under the United Nations 1989 Convention on the Rights of the Child.
- Prosecutors should consider the suspect's maturity, as well as their chronological age, as young adults will continue to mature into their mid-twenties.
- As a starting point, the younger the suspect, the less likely it is that a prosecution is required.
- However, there may be circumstances which mean that, notwithstanding the fact that the suspect is under 18 or lacks maturity, a prosecution is in the public interest. These include where:
    i. the offence committed is serious;
    ii. the suspect's past record suggests that there are no suitable alternatives to prosecution; and
    iii. the absence of an admission means that out-of-court disposals that might have addressed the offending behaviour are not available.

e) *What is the impact on the community?*

- The greater the impact of the offending on the community, the more likely it is that a prosecution is required.
- The prevalence of an offence in a community may cause particular harm to that community, increasing the seriousness of the offending.
- Community is not restricted to communities defined by location and may relate to a group of people who share certain characteristics, experiences or backgrounds, including an occupational group.
- Evidence of impact on a community may be obtained by way of a Community Impact Statement.

f) *Is prosecution a proportionate response?*

- In considering whether prosecution is proportionate to the likely outcome, the following may be relevant:
    i. The cost to the CPS and the wider criminal justice system, especially where it could be regarded as excessive when weighed against any likely penalty. Prosecutors should not decide the public interest on the basis of this factor alone. It is essential that regard is also given to the public interest factors identified when considering the other questions in paragraphs 4.14 a) to g), but cost can be a relevant factor when making an overall assessment of the public interest.
    ii. Cases should be prosecuted in accordance with principles of effective case management. For example, in a case involving multiple suspects, prosecution might be reserved for the main participants in order to avoid excessively long and complex proceedings.

g) *Do sources of information require protecting?*

- In cases where public interest immunity does not apply, special care should be taken when proceeding with a prosecution where details may need to be made public that could harm sources of information, ongoing investigations, international relations or national security. It is essential that such cases are kept under continuing review.

The Threshold Test

5.1   In limited circumstances, where the Full Code Test is not met, the Threshold Test may be applied to charge a suspect. The seriousness or circumstances of the case must justify the making of an immediate charging decision, and there must be substantial grounds to object to bail.

5.2   There must be a rigorous examination of the five conditions of the Threshold Test, to ensure that it is only applied when necessary and that cases are not charged prematurely. All five conditions must be met before the Threshold Test can be applied. Where any of the conditions are not met, there is no need to consider any of the other conditions, as the Threshold Test cannot be applied and the suspect cannot be charged.

First condition—There are reasonable grounds to suspect that the person to be charged has committed the offence

5.3   Prosecutors must be satisfied, on an objective assessment of the evidence, that there are reasonable grounds to suspect that the person to be charged has committed the offence. The assessment must consider the impact of any defence or information that the suspect has put forward or on which they might rely.

5.4   In determining whether there are reasonable grounds to suspect, prosecutors must consider all of the material or information available, whether in evidential format or otherwise. Prosecutors must be satisfied that the material to be relied on at this stage is capable of being:
  • put into an admissible format for presentation in court;
  • reliable; and
  • credible.

Second condition—further evidence can be obtained to provide a realistic prospect of conviction

5.5   Prosecutors must be satisfied that there are reasonable grounds to believe that the continuing investigation will provide further evidence, within a reasonable period of time, so that when all the evidence is considered together, including material which may point away from as well as towards a particular suspect, it is capable of establishing a realistic prospect of conviction in accordance with the Full Code Test.
5.6   The likely further evidence must be identifiable and not merely speculative.
5.7   In reaching this decision prosecutors must consider:
  • the nature, extent and admissibility of any likely further evidence and the impact it will have on the case;
  • the charges that all the evidence will support;
  • the reasons why the evidence is not already available;
  • the time required to obtain the further evidence, including whether it could be obtained within any available detention period; and
  • whether the delay in applying the Full Code Test is reasonable in all the circumstances.

Third condition—The seriousness or the circumstances of the case justifies the making of an immediate charging decision

5.8   The seriousness and the circumstances of the case should be assessed in relation to the alleged offending and should be linked to the level of risk created by granting bail.

Fourth condition—There are continuing substantial grounds to object to bail in accordance with the Bail Act 1976 and in all the circumstances of the case it is proper to do so

5.9   This determination must be based on a proper risk assessment, which reveals that the suspect is not suitable to be bailed, even with substantial conditions. For example, a dangerous suspect who poses a serious risk of harm to a particular person or the public, or a suspect who poses a serious risk of absconding or interfering with witnesses. Prosecutors should not accept, without careful enquiry, any unjustified or unsupported assertions about risk if release on bail were to take place.

Fifth condition—It is in the public interest to charge the suspect

5.10 Prosecutors must apply the public interest stage of the Full Code Test based on the information available at that time.

Reviewing the Threshold Test

5.11 A decision to charge under the Threshold Test must be kept under review. The prosecutor should be proactive to secure from the police the identified outstanding evidence or other material in accordance with an agreed timetable. The evidence must be regularly assessed to ensure that the charge is still appropriate and that continued objection to bail is justified. The Full Code Test must be applied as soon as the anticipated further evidence or material is received and, in any event, in Crown Court cases, usually before the formal service of the prosecution case.

Selection of Charges

6.1   Prosecutors should select charges which:
  • reflect the seriousness and extent of the offending;
  • give the court adequate powers to sentence and impose appropriate post-conviction orders;
  • allow a confiscation order to be made in appropriate cases, where a defendant has benefitted from criminal conduct; and
  • enable the case to be presented in a clear and simple way.
6.2   This means that prosecutors may not always choose or continue with the most serious charge where there is a choice and the interests of justice are met by selecting the lesser charge.
6.3   Prosecutors should never proceed with more charges than are necessary just to encourage a defendant to plead guilty to a few. In the same way, they should never proceed with a more serious charge just to encourage a defendant to plead guilty to a less serious one.

6.4   Prosecutors should not change the charge simply because of the decision made by the court or the defendant about where the case will be heard.

6.5   Prosecutors must take account of any relevant change in circumstances as the case progresses after charge.

Out-of-Court Disposals

7.1   An out-of-court disposal may take the place of a prosecution if it is an appropriate response to the offender and/or the seriousness and consequences of the offending.

7.2   Prosecutors must follow any relevant guidance when asked to advise on or authorise an out-of-court disposal, including any appropriate regulatory proceedings, a punitive or civil penalty, or other disposal. They should ensure that the appropriate evidential standard for the specific out-of-court disposal is met including, where required, a clear admission of guilt, and that the public interest would be properly served by such a disposal.

Court Venue

8.1   Prosecutors must have regard to the guidelines on sentencing and allocation when making submissions to the magistrates' court about where the defendant should be tried.

8.2   Speed must never be the only reason for asking for a case to stay in the magistrates' court. But prosecutors should consider the effect of any likely delay if a case is sent to the Crown Court, including the possible effect on any victim or witness.

8.3   Prosecutors should bear in mind that if confiscation proceedings are required, these may only take place in the Crown Court. Summary proceedings may be committed for that purpose, where appropriate.

Venue for trial in cases involving Children and Young People

8.4   Prosecutors must bear in mind that children and young people (under 18s) should be tried in the youth court wherever possible. It is the court which is best designed to meet their specific needs. A trial of a child or young person in the Crown Court should be reserved for the most serious cases or where the interests of justice require a child or young person to be jointly tried with an adult.

Accepting Guilty Pleas

9.1   Defendants may want to plead guilty to some, but not all, of the charges. Alternatively, they may want to plead guilty to a different, possibly less serious, charge because they are admitting only part of the crime.

9.2   Prosecutors should only accept the defendant's plea if:
   • the court is able to pass a sentence that matches the seriousness of the offending, particularly where there are aggravating features;
   • it enables the court to make a confiscation order in appropriate cases, where a defendant has benefitted from criminal conduct; and
   • it provides the court with adequate powers to impose other ancillary orders, bearing in mind that these can be made with some offences but not with others.

9.3   Particular care must be taken when considering pleas which would enable the defendant to avoid the imposition of a mandatory minimum sentence.

9.4   Prosecutors must never accept a guilty plea just because it is convenient.

9.5   In considering whether the pleas offered are acceptable, prosecutors should ensure that the interests and, where possible, the views of the victim, or in appropriate cases the views of the victim's family, are taken into account when deciding whether it is in the public interest to accept the plea. However, the decision rests with the prosecutor.

9.6   It must be made clear to the court on what basis any plea is advanced and accepted. In cases where a defendant pleads guilty to the charges but on the basis of facts that are different from the prosecution case, and where this may significantly affect sentence, the court should be invited to hear evidence to determine what happened, and then sentence on that basis.

9.7   Where a defendant has previously indicated that they will ask the court to take an offence into consideration when sentencing, but then declines to admit that offence at court, prosecutors will consider whether a prosecution is required for that offence. Prosecutors should explain to the defence advocate and the court that the prosecution of that offence may be subject to further review, in consultation with the police or other investigators wherever possible.

Reconsidering a Prosecution Decision

10.1 People should be able to rely on decisions taken by the CPS. Normally, if the CPS tells a suspect or defendant that there will not be a prosecution, or that the prosecution has been stopped, the case will not start again. But occasionally there are cases where the CPS will overturn a decision not to prosecute or to deal with the case by way of an out-of-court disposal or when it will restart the prosecution, particularly if the case is serious.

10.2 These cases include:

- cases where a further review of the original decision shows that it was wrong and, in order to maintain confidence in the criminal justice system, a prosecution should be brought despite the earlier decision;
- cases which are stopped so that further anticipated evidence, which is likely to become available in the fairly near future, can be collected and prepared. In these cases, the prosecutor will tell the defendant that the prosecution may well start again;
- cases which are not prosecuted or are stopped because of a lack of evidence but where more significant evidence is discovered later; and
- cases involving a death in which a review following the findings of an inquest concludes that a prosecution should be brought, notwithstanding any earlier decision not to prosecute.

10.3 Victims may seek a review of certain CPS decisions not to start a prosecution or to stop a prosecution, under the Victims' Right to Review Scheme.

CRIMINAL PROCEDURE RULES

Criminal Procedure Rules 2020 (SI 2020 No. 759 (L. 19))

Criminal Procedure Rules 2020 (SI 2020 No. 759 (L. 19))

Criminal Procedure Rules 2020 (SI 2020 No. 759) as amended by the Criminal Procedure (Amendment) Rules 2021 (SI 2021 No. 40), the Criminal Procedure (Amendment No. 2) Rules 2021 (SI 2021 No. 849), the Criminal Procedure (Amendment) Rules 2022 (SI 2022 No. 45), the Criminal Procedure (Amendment No. 2) Rules 2022 (SI 2022 No. 815), the Criminal Procedure (Amendment) Rules 2023 (SI 2023 No. 44), and the Criminal Procedure (Amendment No. 2) Rules 2023 (SI 2023 No. 786), the latest of which came into force on 2 October 2023.

The Rules and the Practice Directions have been designed and structured to provide, in combination, an effective procedural framework. Where in previous supplements, the Practice Directions were arranged so as to correspond so far as practicable with the related parts of the Criminal Procedure Rules, the introduction of the new 2023 Practice Directions necessitates a change in layout. The Practice Directions are now presented in a separate section following the 2020 Rules (as amended by the 2021, 2022 and 2023 Amendment Rules).

The text of the Rules is presented as laid, accompanied by a corresponding paragraph number (e.g. **R3.26** indicates **Rule 3.26—Commencement of preparatory hearing**).

Note on statutory powers

The Criminal Procedure Rule Committee noted that in making the Rules listed in the first column of this table, it exercises also the powers listed in the corresponding entry in the second column—

Rule	Power
2.4, 2.5, 2.6, 2.7, 2.8 and 2.9	Section 67B(1) of the Courts Act 2003[1]
2.11	Section 2 of the Commissioners for Oaths Act 1889[2]
3.16	Section 86A(2) of the Courts Act 2003[3]
3.21	Section 86A(2) of the Courts Act 2003
3.32	Section 77(1) of the Senior Courts Act 1981[4]
4.1 and 4.12	Section 12(1) and (3) of the Road Traffic Offenders Act 1988[5]
5.5	Section 32(1) of the Criminal Appeal Act 1968[6]
Part 8	Section 48(1) of the Criminal Law Act 1977[7]
9.2	Section 86A(2) of the Courts Act 2003
Part 10	Section 2 of the Indictments Act 1915[8] and section 2(6) of the Administration of Justice (Miscellaneous Provisions) Act 1933[9]
14.6	Section 5B(9) of the Bail Act 1976[10]
16.4	Section 9(2A) of the Criminal Justice Act 1967[11]
19.3	Section 81(1) of the Police and Criminal Evidence Act 1984[12] and section 20(3) of the Criminal Procedure and Investigations Act 1996[13]
20.4	Section 132(4) of the Criminal Justice Act 2003[14]
Part 23	Sections 37(5) and 38(6) and (7) of the Youth Justice and Criminal Evidence Act 1999[15]
24.9	Section 52(4) of the Sentencing Act 2020[16]
24.11	Section 52(4) of the Sentencing Act 2020[17]
24.14	Section 12(7ZA) of the Magistrates' Courts Act 1980[18]
25.16	Section 52(4) of the Sentencing Act 2020[19]
28.4	Section 385(7) of the Sentencing Act 2020
33.7, 33.37, 33.39 and 33.40	Section 91 of the Proceeds of Crime Act 2002[20]
33.47	Section 52(1) of the Senior Courts Act 1981[21]
34.11	Sections 73(2) and 74(2), (3) and (4) of the Senior Courts Act 1981[22]

Rule	Power
36.8	Section 87(4) of the Senior Courts Act 1981[23]
37.6	Section 49(1) of the Criminal Justice Act 2003
38.9	Section 73(2) of the Criminal Justice Act 2003
40.8	Section 159(6) of the Criminal Justice Act 1988[24]
42.8	Section 141(2) of the Sentencing Act 2020
42.14, 42.18, 42.19 and 42.20	Section 91 of the Proceeds of Crime Act 2002
44.2	Section 30(1) of the Criminal Justice Act 2003[25] and section 2 of the Commissioners for Oaths Act 1889[26]
45.6 and 45.7	Section 52(1) of the Senior Courts Act 1981
47.4 and 47.10; 47.24 and 47.30	Paragraph 15A of Schedule 1 to the Police and Criminal Evidence Act 1984[27]
47.4 and 47.11 to 47.16 inclusive	Paragraph 10(2) of Schedule 5, paragraph 14(2) of Schedule 5A, paragraph 4(1) of Schedule 6 and paragraph 5(1) of Schedule 6A to the Terrorism Act 2000[28]
47.4 and 47.17 to 47.22 inclusive	Sections 351(2), 362(2), 369(2) and 375(1) of the Proceeds of Crime Act 2002[29]
47.4 and 47.23	Section 157(9) of the Extradition Act 2003[30]
47.24 and 47.31	Paragraph 11(5) of Schedule 5 to the Terrorism Act 2000[31]
47.24 and 47.32	Section 352(8) of the Proceeds of Crime Act 2002[32]
47.24 and 47.33	Section 160(10) of the Extradition Act 2003[33]
47.35 and 47.38	Section 59(13) of the Criminal Justice and Police Act 2001[34]
47.49	Section 74(3) of the Senior Courts Act 1981[35]
47.63 to 47.68	Sections 11(1) and 18(2) of the Crime (Overseas Production Orders) Act 2019[36]
48.16	Section 19 of the Criminal Procedure and Investigations Act 1996[37]
50.17	Section 67 of the Senior Courts Act 1981[38]
50.23	Sections 36A(4), 36B(3), 118A(4) and 118B(3) of the Extradition Act 2003[39]
50.30	Sections 19(3) and 66(1) of the Senior Courts Act 1981[40]

[1] 2003 c. 39; section 67B was inserted by section 3 of, and paragraph 32 of the Schedule to, the Courts and Tribunals (Judiciary and Functions of Staff) Act 2018 (c. 33).

[2] 1889 c. 10; section 2 was amended by section 59 of, and paragraph 15 of Schedule 11 to, the Constitutional Reform Act 2005 (c. 4).

[3] 2003 c. 39; section 86A was inserted by section 162 of the Policing and Crime Act 2017 (c. 3).

[4] 1981 c. 54; section 77 was amended by section 15 of, and paragraph 11 of Schedule 2 to, the Criminal Justice Act 1987 (c. 38), section 168 of, and paragraph 18 of Schedule 9 to, the Criminal Justice and Public Order Act 1994 (c. 33), section 41 of, and paragraph 54 of Schedule 3 to, the Criminal Justice Act 2003 (c. 44) and article 3 of, and paragraphs 11 and 13 of the Schedule to, SI 2004/2035. It is further amended by section 31 of, and paragraph 11 of Schedule 1 and Schedule 2 to, the Prosecution of Offences Act 1985 (c. 23) with effect from a date to be appointed.

[5] 1988 c. 53; section 12 was amended by article 3 of, and paragraphs 29 and 30 of the Schedule to, S.I. 2004/2035.

[6] 1968 c. 19.

[7] 1977 c. 45; section 48 was amended by paragraph 190 of Schedule 8 to the Courts Act 2003 (c. 39).

[8] 1915 c. 90; section 2 was amended by section 19 of the Criminal Justice Administration Act 1956 (c. 34) and sections 56 and 109 of, and paragraph 67 of Schedule 8 and Schedule 11 to, the Courts Act 2003 (c. 39).

[9] 1933 c. 36; section 2(6) was amended by Part IV of Schedule 11 to the Courts Act 1971 (c. 23), paragraph 1 of the Schedule to S.I. 2004/2035 and section 82 of the Deregulation Act 2015 (c. 20).

[10] 1976 c. 63; section 5B(9) was inserted by section 30 of the Criminal Justice and Public Order Act 1994 (c. 33) and amended by paragraph 183 of Schedule 8 to the Courts Act 2003 (c. 39).

[11] 1967 c. 80; section 9(2A) was inserted by section 80 of the Deregulation Act 2015 (c. 20).

[12] 1984 c. 60; section 81 was amended by paragraph 286 of Schedule 8 to, the Courts Act 2003 (c. 39).

[13] 1996 c. 25; section 20(3) was amended by paragraph 378 of Schedule 8 to the Courts Act 2003 (c. 39).

[14] 2003 c. 44; section 132 was amended by article 3 of, and paragraphs 45 and 51 of the Schedule to, S.I. 2004/2035.

[15] 1999 c. 23; section 37(5) and section 38(6), (7) were amended by section 109 of, and paragraph 384 of Schedule 8 to, the Courts Act 2003 (c. 39).

[16] 1980 c. 43; section 16K is inserted by section 3 of the Judicial Review and Courts Act 2022 (c. 35) with effect from a date to be appointed.
[17] 2020 c. 17.
[18] 1980 c. 43; section 12(7ZA) was inserted by section 81 of the Deregulation Act 2015 (c. 20).
[19] 2020 c. 17.
[20] 2002 c. 29; section 91 was amended by section 109(1) of, and paragraph 410 of Schedule 8 to, the Courts Act 2003 (c. 39).
[21] 1981 c. 54; section 52 was amended by section 31 of, and Part II of Schedule 1 to, the Prosecution of Offences Act 1985 (c. 23), section 4 of the Courts and Legal Services Act 1990 (c. 41), article 3 and paragraphs 11 and 12(a) of the Schedule to S.I. 2004/2035 and section 59 of, and paragraph 26 of Schedule 11 to, the Constitutional Reform Act 2005 (c. 4).
[22] 1981 c. 54; section 73(2) was amended by article 3 of, and paragraphs 11 and 12(b) of the Schedule to, S.I. 2004/2035. Section 74(2) and (3) was amended by article 3 of, and paragraphs 11 and 12(c) of the Schedule to, S.I. 2004/2035.
[23] 1981 c. 54; section 87(4) was amended by articles 2 and 3 of, and paragraphs 11 and 17 of the Schedule to, S.I. 2004/2035.
[24] 1988 c. 33; section 159(6) was amended by S.I. 2004/2035.
[25] 2003 c. 44; section 30 was amended by article 3 of, and paragraphs 45 and 46 of the Schedule to, S.I. 2004/2035.
[26] 1889 c. 10; section 2 was amended by section 59 of, and paragraph 15 of Schedule 11 to, the Constitutional Reform Act 2005 (c. 4).
[27] 1984 c. 60; paragraph 15A of Schedule 1 was inserted by section 82 of the Deregulation Act 2015 (c. 20).
[28] 2000 c. 11; paragraph 10 of Schedule 5 was amended by section 109(1) of, and paragraph 389 of Schedule 8 to, the Courts Act 2003 (c. 39) and it is further amended by section 65 of, and paragraph 9 of Schedule 4 to, the Courts Act 2003 (c. 39), with effect from a date to be appointed. Paragraph 4 of Schedule 6 was amended by section 109(1) of, and paragraph 390 of Schedule 8 to, the Courts Act 2003 (c. 39). Schedule 6A was inserted by section 3 of, and paragraph 1(1) and (3) of Part 1 of Schedule 2 to, the Anti-terrorism, Crime and Security Act 2001 (c. 24).
[29] 2002 c. 29.
[30] 2003 c. 41; section 157(9) was inserted by section 174 of the Anti-social Behaviour, Crime and Policing Act 2014 (c. 12).
[31] 2000 c. 11; paragraph 11(5) of Schedule 5 was inserted by section 82 of the Deregulation Act 2015 (c. 20).
[32] 2002 c. 29; section 352(8) was inserted by section 82 of the Deregulation Act 2015 (c. 20).
[33] 2003 c. 41; section 160(10) was inserted by section 174 of the Anti-social Behaviour, Crime and Policing Act 2014 (c. 12).
[34] 2001 c. 16; section 59(13) was inserted by section 82 of the Deregulation Act 2015 (c. 20).
[35] 1981 c. 54; section 74(3) was amended by article 3 of, and paragraphs 11 and 12(c) of the Schedule to, S.I. 2004/2035. The Act's title was amended by section 59(5) of, and paragraph 1 of Schedule 11 to, the Constitutional Reform Act 2005 (c. 4).
[36] 2019 c. 5.
[37] 1996 c. 25; section 19 was amended by section 109 of, and paragraph 377 of Schedule 8 to, the Courts Act 2003 (c. 39), section 331 of, and paragraphs 20 and 34 of Schedule 36 to, the Criminal Justice Act 2003 (c. 44) and section 15 of, and paragraph 251 of Schedule 4 to, the Constitutional Reform Act 2005 (c. 4).
[38] 1981 c. 54.
[39] 2003 c. 41; sections 36A, 36B, 118A and 118B were inserted by section 161 of the Anti-social Behaviour, Crime and Policing Act 2014 (c. 12).
[40] 1981 c. 54.

CRIMINAL PROCEDURE RULES   PART 1   THE OVERRIDING OBJECTIVE

The overriding objective   R1.1

1.1   (1) The overriding objective of this procedural code is that criminal cases be dealt with justly.
      (2) Dealing with a criminal case justly includes—
           (a) acquitting the innocent and convicting the guilty;
           (b) treating all participants with politeness and respect;
           (c) dealing with the prosecution and the defence fairly;
           (d) recognising the rights of a defendant, particularly those under Article 6 of the European Convention on Human Rights;
           (e) respecting the interests of witnesses, victims and jurors and keeping them informed of the progress of the case;
           (f) dealing with the case efficiently and expeditiously;
           (g) ensuring that appropriate information is available to the court when bail and sentence are considered; and
           (h) dealing with the case in ways that take into account—
               (i) the gravity of the offence alleged,
               (ii) the complexity of what is in issue,
               (iii) the severity of the consequences for the defendant and others affected, and
               (iv) the needs of other cases.

The duty of the participants in a criminal case   R1.2

1.2   (1) Each participant, in the conduct of each case, must—
           (a) prepare and conduct the case in accordance with the overriding objective;
           (b) comply with these Rules, practice directions and directions made by the court; and
           (c) at once inform the court and all parties of any significant failure (whether or not that participant is responsible for that failure) to take any procedural step required by these Rules, any practice direction or any direction of the court. A failure is significant if it might hinder the court in furthering the overriding objective.

(2) Anyone involved in any way with a criminal case is a participant in its conduct for the purposes of this rule.

R1.3   **The application by the court of the overriding objective**

1.3   The court must further the overriding objective in particular when—

(a) exercising any power given to it by legislation (including these Rules);

(b) applying any practice direction; or

(c) interpreting any rule or practice direction.

CRIMINAL PROCEDURE RULES   PART 2   UNDERSTANDING AND APPLYING THE RULES; POWERS AND DUTIES OF COURT OFFICERS AND JUSTICES' LEGAL ADVISERS

Understanding and applying the Rules

R2.1   **When the Rules apply**

2.1   (1) In general, the Criminal Procedure Rules apply—

(a) in all criminal cases in magistrates' courts and in the Crown Court;

(b) in extradition cases in the High Court; and

(c) in all cases in the criminal division of the Court of Appeal.

(2) If a rule applies only in one or some of those courts, the rule makes that clear.

(3) These Rules apply on and after 5th October, 2020, but unless the court otherwise directs, they do not affect a right or duty existing under the Criminal Procedure Rules 2015.[1]

(4) The amendments to Part 14 of these Rules (Bail and custody time limits) made by rule 7(a) and (b) of the Criminal Procedure (Amendment) Rules 2023 do not apply in relation to a defendant arrested before 28th October, 2022, for an offence, or in relation to such a defendant who on or after that date is arrested again in relation to that offence under—

(a) section 46A of the Police and Criminal Evidence Act 1984[2] (arrest for failure to attend at a police station as required by police bail, or failure to comply with a condition of such bail); or

(b) section 24A of the Criminal Justice Act 2003[3] (arrest for failure to comply with a condition attached to a conditional caution).

[Note. The rules replaced by the first Criminal Procedure Rules (the Criminal Procedure Rules 2005[4]) were revoked when those Rules came into force by provisions of the Courts Act 2003, the Courts Act 2003 (Consequential Amendments) Order 2004 and the Courts Act 2003 (Commencement No. 6 and Savings) Order 2004[5]. The first Criminal Procedure Rules reproduced the substance of all the rules they replaced. Amendments made by the Police, Crime, Sentencing and Courts Act 2022[6] to the pre-charge bail provisions of the Police and Criminal Evidence Act 1984 came into force on 28th October, 2022.[7] Under section 45(3) of the 2022 Act, those amendments do not apply in the circumstances described in paragraph (4) of this rule.]

R2.2   **Definitions**

2.2   (1) In these Rules, unless the context makes it clear that something different is meant:

'advocate' means a person who is entitled to exercise a right of audience in the court under section 13 of the Legal Services Act 2007[8];

'authorised court officer' has the meaning given by rule 2.4;

'business day' means any day except Saturday, Sunday, Christmas Day, Boxing Day, Good Friday, Easter Monday or a bank holiday;

---

[1] S.I. 2015/1490; amended by S.I. 2016/120, 2016/705, 2017/144, 2017/282, 2017/755, 2017/915, 2018/132, 2018/847, 2019/143, 2019/908, 2019/1119, 2020/32, 2020/417.

[2] 1984 c. 60; section 46A was inserted by section 29 of the Criminal Justice and Public Order Act 1994 (c. 33) and amended by section 28 of, and paragraphs 1 and 5 of Schedule 2 to, the Criminal Justice Act 2003 (c. 44), section 46 of the Police and Justice Act 2006 (c. 48), section 108 of the Coroners and Justice Act 2009 (c. 25), section 61 of the Policing and Crime Act 2017 (c. 3) and paragraph 4 of Schedule 20 to the Police, Crime, Sentencing and Courts Act 2022 (c. 32).

[3] 2002 c. 44; section 24A was inserted by section 18 of the Police and Justice Act 2006 (c. 48) and amended by sections 60 and 64 of the Policing and Crime Act 2017 (c. 3) and paragraphs 14 and 15 of Schedule 4 to the Police, Crime, Sentencing and Courts Act 2022 (c. 32). It is repealed with effect from a date to be appointed by section 118 of that latter Act.

[4] S.I. 2005/384; amended by S.I. 2006/353, 2006/2636, 2007/699, 2007/2317, 2007/3662, 2008/2076, 2008/3269 and 2009/2087.

[5] S.I. 2004/2066.

[6] 2022 c. 32.

[7] See S.I. 2022/1075.

[8] 2007 c. 29.

'court' means a tribunal with jurisdiction over criminal cases. It includes a judge, recorder, District Judge (Magistrates' Court), lay justice and, when exercising their judicial powers, the Registrar of Criminal Appeals, and an authorised court officer;

'court officer' means the appropriate member of the staff of a court;

'justices' legal adviser' means a person authorised under section 28 of the Courts Act 2003[9] to give advice about law to justices of the peace;

'legal representative' means:

    (i)   the person for the time being named as a party's representative in any legal aid representation order made under section 16 of the Legal Aid, Sentencing and Punishment of Offenders Act 2012[10], or

    (ii) subject to that, the person named as a party's representative in any notice for the time being given under rule 46.2 (Notice of appointment, etc. of legal representative: general rules) provided that person is entitled to conduct litigation in the court under section 13 of the Legal Services Act 2007;

'live link' means a live audio link or a live video link and:

    (i)   'live audio link' means a live telephone link or other arrangement by which a person taking part in a hearing can hear, and be heard by, everyone else who is taking part and who is not in the same place as that person,

    (ii) 'live video link' means a live television link or other arrangement by which a person taking part in a hearing can see and hear, and be seen and heard by, everyone else who is taking part and who is not in the same place as that person;

'live link direction' means a direction that requires or permits a person to take part through a live audio link or a live video link in the proceedings listed in section 51(3) of the Criminal Justice Act 2003[11];

'Practice Direction' means the Lord Chief Justice's Criminal Practice Directions, as amended, and 'Criminal Costs Practice Direction' means the Lord Chief Justice's Practice Direction (Costs in Criminal Proceedings), as amended;

'public interest ruling' means a ruling about whether it is in the public interest to disclose prosecution material under sections 3(6), 7A(8) or 8(5) of the Criminal Procedure and Investigations Act 1996[12]; and

'Registrar' means the Registrar of Criminal Appeals or a court officer exercising a function of the Registrar.

(2) Special definitions and definitions of some other expressions are in the rules in which they apply.

[Note. The glossary at the end of the Rules is a guide to the meaning of certain legal expressions used in them.]

References to legislation, including these Rules   R2.3

2.3   (1) In these Rules, where a rule refers to an Act of Parliament or to subordinate legislation by title and year, subsequent references to that Act or to that legislation in the rule are shortened: so, for example, after a reference to the Criminal Procedure and Investigations Act 1996[13] that Act is called 'the 1996 Act'; and after a reference to the Criminal Procedure and Investigations Act 1996 (Defence Disclosure Time Limits) Regulations 2011[14] those Regulations are called 'the 2011 Regulations'.

    (2) In the courts in which these Rules apply—

       (a) unless the context makes it clear that something different is meant, a reference to the Criminal Procedure Rules, without reference to a year, is a reference to the Criminal Procedure Rules in force at the date on which the event concerned occurs or occurred;

       (b) a reference to the Criminal Procedure Rules may be abbreviated to 'CrimPR'; and

       (c) a reference to a Part or rule in the Criminal Procedure Rules may be abbreviated to, for example, 'CrimPR Part 3' or 'CrimPR 3.5'.

---

[9] 2003 c. 39; section 28 is substituted by section 3 of, and paragraph 26 of the Schedule to, the Courts and Tribunals (Judiciary and Functions of Staff) Act 2018 (c. 33).

[10] 2012 c. 10.

[11] 2003 c. 44; section 51 was substituted by section 200 of the Police, Crime, Sentencing and Courts Act 2022 (c. 32).

[12] 1996 c. 25; section 7A was inserted by section 37 of the Criminal Justice Act 2003 (c. 44).

[13] 1996 c. 25.

[14] S.I. 2011/209.

Powers of authorised court officers

R2.4 **Exercise of court's functions by authorised court officers: general rules**

2.4 (1) This rule and rules 2.5, 2.6, 2.7, 2.8 and 2.9 provide for the exercise of relevant judicial functions within the meaning of section 67A of the Courts Act 2003[15] —

    (a) in a court in which these Rules apply;

    (b) by a person authorised for the purpose by the Lord Chief Justice under section 67B of that Act[16].

(2) In this rule and in rules 2.5, 2.6, 2.7, 2.8 and 2.9—

    (a) 'authorised court officer' means any such person;

    (b) a reference to an authorised court officer who is legally qualified is a reference to one who has such qualifications as are for the time being prescribed by regulations made under section 28(3) of the Courts Act 2003.

(3) No court officer may—

    (a) authorise a person's committal to prison;

    (b) authorise a person's arrest (but that exclusion does not apply to the issue of a warrant of arrest, whether or not endorsed for bail, to secure that a person attends court proceedings relating to an offence of which the person has been accused or convicted in a case in which no objection is made by or on behalf of that person to the issue of the warrant);

    (c) grant or withhold bail, except to the extent that rule 2.6 or rule 2.8 allows;

    (d) adjudicate on guilt, or on the act or omission with which a defendant is charged, except to the extent of—

        (i) acquitting a defendant against whom the prosecutor offers no evidence,

        (ii) convicting a defendant who pleads guilty, or

        (iii) giving a prosecutor permission to withdraw a case;

    (e) determine the admissibility of evidence;

    (f) set ground rules for the conduct of questioning where rule 3.8(6), (7) (directions for the appropriate treatment and questioning of a witness or the defendant) applies;

    (g) make findings of fact for the purpose of sentence, defer or pass sentence, impose a penalty or commit a defendant to the Crown Court for sentence;

    (h) make an order for a party or other person to pay costs, unless that party or person agrees;

    (i) make any other order consequent upon acquittal, conviction or a finding that the accused did the act or made the omission charged, except to the extent that rule 2.8 allows;

    (j) vary, discharge, remit, remove, revoke, review or suspend a sentence, penalty or other order consequent on acquittal or conviction, except to the extent that rule 2.8 allows;

    (k) order the search, confiscation, restraint, detention or seizure of property except to the extent that rule 2.8 allows;

    (l) determine an appeal or reference to an appeal court, or an application for permission to appeal or refer, except to the extent that rule 2.6 allows; or

    (m) determine an allegation of contempt of court.

(4) An authorised court officer may exercise a relevant judicial function for which rule 2.5, 2.6, 2.7, 2.8 or 2.9 provides—

    (a) only subject to the same conditions as apply to its exercise by the court or person whose function it is; and

    (b) where a party affected by the exercise of that function is entitled to make representations before its exercise, only if each such party has had a reasonable opportunity to make such representations—

        (i) in writing, or

        (ii) at a hearing (whether or not that party in fact attends).

(5) Unless the context makes it clear that something different is meant, provision in rule 2.5, 2.6, 2.7, 2.8 or 2.9 permitting the exercise of a relevant judicial function by an authorised court officer includes a power to decline to exercise that function.

[Note. Under section 67A of the Courts Act 2003, 'relevant judicial function' means a function of a court to which the general duty of the Lord Chancellor under section 1 of that Act applies and a judicial function of a person holding an office that entitles the person to exercise functions of such a court, but does not include in a court in which Criminal Procedure Rules apply—

    (a) any function so far as its exercise involves authorising a person's committal to prison; or

---

[15] 2003 c. 39; section 67A is inserted by section 3 of, and paragraph 32 of the Schedule to, the Courts and Tribunals (Judiciary and Functions of Staff) Act 2018 (c. 33).

[16] 2003 c. 39; section 67B is inserted by section 3 of, and paragraph 32 of the Schedule to, the Courts and Tribunals (Judiciary and Functions of Staff) Act 2018 (c. 33).

(b) *any function so far as its exercise involves authorising a person's arrest, except the issue of a warrant of arrest (whether or not endorsed for bail) to secure that a person attends court proceedings relating to an offence of which the person has been accused or convicted in a case in which no objection is made by or on behalf of that person to the issue of the warrant.*

Under section 67B of the 2003 Act, in a court in which Criminal Procedure Rules apply the Rules may provide for the exercise of relevant judicial functions by persons who are appointed under section 2(1) of that Act and who satisfy any requirements specified in the Rules as to qualifications or experience. Such a person may exercise such a function only if authorised to do so by the Lord Chief Justice.

Section 28 of the 2003 Act provides for persons authorised by the Lord Chief Justice to give advice to justices of the peace about matters of law. Such a person may be authorised for that purpose only if appointed under section 2(1) of that Act and possessed of such qualifications as may be prescribed by regulations made under section 28. See also rule 2.2 (Definitions).]

Exercise of functions of the Court of Appeal   R2.5

2.5   (1) This rule provides for the exercise by an authorised court officer of relevant judicial functions of—
        (a) the criminal division of the Court of Appeal; and
        (b) the Registrar of Criminal Appeals.
      (2) Subject to rule 2.4, an authorised court officer may exercise—
        (a) any function of the criminal division of the Court of Appeal that may be exercised by the Registrar of Criminal Appeals; and
        (b) any other judicial function of the Registrar.
      (3) Where an authorised court officer exercises a function of the court—
        (a) the same provision as that made by section 31A(4) or section 31C(3), as the case may be, of the Criminal Appeal Act 1968[17] applies as if that function had been exercised by the Registrar; and
        (b) rule 36.5 (Renewing an application refused by a judge or the Registrar) applies.

[Note. See also rule 2.4, which makes general rules about the exercise of judicial functions by authorised court officers.

For the functions of the criminal division of the Court of Appeal that may be exercised by the Registrar of Criminal Appeals, see sections 31A and 31B of the Criminal Appeal Act 1968[18]. For other functions of the Registrar, see section 21 of that Act[19].

Sections 31A(4) and 31C(3) of the 1968 Act provide for the reconsideration by a judge of a decision by the Registrar to which those provisions apply.]

Exercise of functions of the High Court   R2.6

2.6   (1) This rule provides for the exercise by an authorised court officer of relevant judicial functions of the High Court in relation to its jurisdiction under the Extradition Act 2003[20].
      (2) An authorised court officer may exercise any such function of the High Court to which the rules in Section 3 of Part 50 apply (Extradition; Appeal to the High Court), subject to—
        (a) rule 2.4; and
        (b) paragraph (3) of this rule.
      (3) No court officer may—
        (a) grant or withhold bail;
        (b) impose or vary a condition of bail; or
        (c) reopen a decision which determines an appeal or an application for permission to appeal, unless paragraph (4) applies.
      (4) If making a decision to which the parties have agreed in writing, an authorised court officer may—
        (a) give or refuse permission to appeal;
        (b) determine an appeal;
        (c) grant or withhold bail; or
        (d) impose or vary a condition of bail.

---

[17] 1968 c. 19; section 31A was inserted by section 6 of the Criminal Appeal Act 1995 (c. 35) and amended by sections 87 and 109 of, and Schedule 10 to, the Courts Act 2003 (c. 39) and paragraphs 86 and 88 of Schedule 36 to the Criminal Justice Act 2003 (c. 44). Section 31C was inserted by section 87 of the Courts Act 2003 (c. 39) and amended by sections 47 and 149 of, and paragraphs 1 and 12 of Schedule 8 and part 3 of Schedule 28 to, the Criminal Justice and Immigration Act 2008 (c. 4).
[18] 1968 c. 19; section 31B was inserted by section 87 of the Courts Act 2003 (c. 39).
[19] 1968 c. 19.
[20] 2003 c. 41.

(5) Paragraph (6) of this rule—

  (a) applies where a party wants a judge to reconsider a decision made by an authorised court officer;

  (b) does not apply where such an officer agrees to postpone the date on which the required period for extradition begins under section 36(3) of the Extradition Act 2003[21].

(6) Such a party must—

  (a) apply for such a reconsideration as soon as reasonably practicable, and in any event no later than the earlier of—

    (i) the next hearing before a judge, or

    (ii) the fifth business day after the date on which notice of the decision is served on the applicant;

  (b) unless the application is made at a hearing, serve the application on—

    (i) the court officer, and

    (ii) each other party (if any) affected by the decision; and

  (c) in the application—

    (i) specify the decision in issue,

    (ii) explain why it is appropriate for the decision to be reconsidered and what decision the applicant thinks would be appropriate, and

    (iii) ask for a hearing, if one is wanted, and explain why it is needed.

(7) The judge may determine the application—

  (a) at a hearing (which may be in public or private), or without a hearing;

  (b) in the absence of—

    (i) the applicant,

    (ii) each other party (if any) affected by the decision.

(8) But the judge must not determine the application in the absence of an affected party unless that party has had—

  (a) such notice as the nature and urgency of the application permits; and

  (b) a reasonable opportunity to make representations.

[Note. See also—

  (a) rule 2.4, which makes general rules about the exercise of judicial functions by authorised court officers;

  (b) rule 2.10, which provides for extension of the time limit under this rule;

  (c) rule 3.6 (Application to vary a direction); and

  (d) rule 50.18 (Case management in the High Court).

For the functions of the High Court for which this rule provides, see the introductory note to Section 3 of Part 50. See also rule 50.30 for the constitution of the High Court when exercising the powers to which that Section of that Part applies.

Under section 36 of the Extradition Act 2003, where an extradition order has been made under Part 1 of the Act and the outcome of an appeal by the defendant is that he or she is to be extradited then (a) the defendant must be removed to the requesting territory within 10 days starting with the day on which the decision of the relevant court on the appeal becomes final or proceedings on the appeal are discontinued, unless (b) the requesting authority and the High Court agree to postpone that starting date.]

R2.7   Exercise of functions of the Crown Court

2.7 (1) This rule provides for the exercise by an authorised court officer of relevant judicial functions of the Crown Court in a criminal cause or matter.

(2) Subject to rule 2.4 and to paragraph (3) of this rule, an authorised court officer may—

  (a) determine an application to extend a time limit set by a rule or by a judge, including a time limit for the conduct of confiscation proceedings, unless the effect would be—

    (i) to affect the date of any hearing that has been fixed, including a trial, or

    (ii) significantly to affect the progress of the case in any other way;

  (b) give a live link direction under section 51 of the Criminal Justice Act 2003 for the participation of a defendant in custody in a preliminary hearing, a sentencing hearing or an enforcement hearing; and

  (c) exercise the court's functions listed in rule 23.2 (Appointment of advocate to cross-examine witness) and select such an advocate as that rule describes (but a court officer may not decline to select such an advocate where that rule applies).

(3) An authorised court officer may not exercise a function of the court in a case in which a judge so directs.

[21] 2003 c. 41; section 36 was amended by section 40 of, and paragraph 81 of Schedule 9 to, the Constitutional Reform Act 2005 (c. 4).

(4) Paragraph (5) of this rule applies where a party or an advocate appointed under rule 23.2 (Appointment of advocate to cross-examine witness) wants a judge to reconsider a decision made by an authorised court officer.

(5) Such a party or advocate must—

    (a) apply for such a reconsideration as soon as reasonably practicable, and in any event no later than the earlier of—

        (i) the next hearing before a judge, or

        (ii) the tenth business day after the date on which notice of the decision is served on the applicant;

    (b) unless the application is made at a hearing, serve the application on—

        (i) the court officer, and

        (ii) each other party (if any) affected by the decision; and

    (c) in the application—

        (i) specify the decision in issue,

        (ii) explain why it is appropriate for the decision to be reconsidered and what decision the applicant thinks would be appropriate, and

        (iii) ask for a hearing, if one is wanted, and explain why it is needed.

(6) The judge may determine the application—

    (a) at a hearing (which may be in public or private), or without a hearing;

    (b) in the absence of—

        (i) the applicant,

        (ii) each other party (if any) affected by the decision.

(7) But the judge must not determine the application in the absence of an affected party unless that party has had—

    (a) such notice as the nature and urgency of the application permits; and

    (b) a reasonable opportunity to make representations.

[Note. See also—

    (a) rule 2.4, which makes general rules about the exercise of judicial functions by authorised court officers;

    (b) rule 2.10, which provides for extension of the time limit under this rule; and

    (c) rule 3.6 (Application to vary a direction).

For the constitution and powers of the Crown Court, see the note to rule 25.1 (Trial and sentence in the Crown Court; When this Part applies).]

Exercise of functions of a magistrates' court   **R2.8**

2.8 (1) This rule provides for the exercise by an authorised court officer of relevant judicial functions of a magistrates' court in a criminal cause or matter.

    (2) Subject to rule 2.4 and to paragraph (12) of this rule, an authorised court officer may—

        (a) fix, cancel or vary the date, time or place for a hearing, including a trial, or adjourn a hearing;

        (b) adjourn, remit or transfer proceedings from one local justice area to another;

        (c) determine an application to extend a time limit set by a rule or by the court, unless the effect would be—

            (i) to affect the date of any hearing that has been fixed, including a trial, or

            (ii) significantly to affect the progress of the case in any other way;

        (d) issue a summons at the request of a public prosecutor, or under section 16B of the Magistrates' Courts Act 1980[22] (Cases not tried in accordance with section 16A) or section 83 of that Act[23] (Process for securing attendance of offender);

        (e) give a prosecutor permission to withdraw a case;

        (f) grant bail where the defendant already is on bail and—

            (i) the conditions, if any, to which that bail is subject will remain the same, or

            (ii) bail conditions will be varied or imposed with both parties' agreement;

        (g) give consent for another magistrates' court to deal with a defendant for an offence in respect of which the defendant, when an adult, was discharged conditionally;

        (h) order a convicted defendant to produce his or her driving licence;

        (i) require a statement of the defendant's assets and other financial circumstances;

---

[22] 1980 c. 43; section 16B was inserted by section 48 of the Criminal Justice and Courts Act 2015 (c. 2).
[23] 1980 c. 43; section 83 was amended by articles 46 and 47 of S.I. 2006/1737 and sections 97(2) and 106 of, and Part V (table 8) of Schedule 15 to, the Access to Justice Act 1999 (c. 22).

    (j) amend an attendance centre order to—
       (i) vary the day or hour specified in that order for the defendant's first attendance, or
       (ii) substitute an alternative centre;
    (k) amend the local justice area or responsible officer named in an order of the court;
    (l) amend a sentence or order by requiring it to be completed in Northern Ireland or Scotland;
    (m) extend the time for service of a statutory declaration to which applies—
       (i) rule 44.2 (Statutory declaration of ignorance of proceedings), or
       (ii) rule 29.4 (Statutory declaration to avoid fine after fixed penalty notice);
    (n) fix a later time at which a defendant must attend court for the purposes of an enquiry or hearing under section 82 of the Magistrates' Courts Act 1980[24] (Restriction on power to impose imprisonment for default);
    (o) conduct a means enquiry;
    (p) make a collection order;
    (q) issue a warrant of control;
    (r) extend the time for payment of a fine or sum to which Part 30 (Enforcement of fines and other orders for payment) applies;
    (s) vary an order for the payment by instalments of such a fine or sum;
    (t) make a transfer of fine order;
    (u) make a disclosure order under section 125CA Magistrates' Courts Act 1980[25] (Power to make disclosure order) for the purposes of securing the execution of a warrant;
    (v) make an attachment of earnings order;
    (w) make or withdraw an application for deductions to be made from a defendant's benefit payments; and
    (x) take any step listed in paragraph 38 of Schedule 5 to the Courts Act 2003[26] (range of further steps available against defaulters).

(3) In addition to the functions listed in paragraph (2), subject to rule 2.4 and to paragraph (12) of this rule an authorised court officer who is legally qualified may exercise the other functions of a magistrates' court listed in paragraphs (4) to (11).

(4) In connection with the rules about general matters (Parts 1 to 6)—
    (a) exercising the powers to which section 50 of the Crime and Disorder Act 1998[27] (Early administrative hearings) refers, where that section applies and subject to the restrictions that it contains;
    (b) giving, varying or revoking a live link direction under sections 51 and 52 of the Criminal Justice Act 2003[28] for the participation of a defendant in custody in a preliminary hearing, a sentencing hearing or an enforcement hearing;
    (c) determining an application to extend a time limit set by a rule or by the court;
    (d) giving, varying or revoking an order for separate or joint trials in respect of two or more defendants or two or more offences, if all parties agree;
    (e) giving, varying or revoking directions for the conduct of proceedings, including—
       (i) the timetable for the case,
       (ii) the attendance of the parties,

---

[24] 1980 c. 43; section 82 was amended by section 77 of, and paragraph 52 of Schedule 14 to, the Criminal Justice Act 1982 (c. 48), sections 61 and 123 of, and paragraphs 1 and 2 of Schedule 8 to, the Criminal Justice Act 1988 (c. 33), section 55 of and paragraph 10 of Schedule 4 to the Crime (Sentences) Act 1997 (c. 43), paragraph 220 of Schedule 8 to the Courts Act 2003 (c. 39), section 62 of, and paragraphs 45 and 51 of Schedule 13 to, the Tribunals, Courts and Enforcement Act 2007 (c. 15) and section 179 of the Anti-social Behaviour, Crime and Policing Act 2014 (c. 12) and section 54 of, and paragraphs 2 and 3 of Schedule 12 to, the Criminal Justice and Courts Act 2015 (c. 2). It is further amended by paragraphs 58 and 63 of Part II of Schedule 7 to the Criminal Justice and Court Services Act 2000 (c. 43) and Part 7 of Schedule 37 to the Criminal Justice Act 2003 (c. 44), with effect from dates to be appointed.
[25] 1980 c. 43; section 125CA was inserted by section 28 of the Domestic Violence, Crime and Victims Act 2004 (c. 28) and amended by section 62 of, and paragraphs 45 and 60 of Schedule 13 to, the Tribunals, Courts and Enforcement Act 2007 (c. 15).
[26] 2003 c. 39; paragraph 38 of Schedule 5 was amended by articles 2, 4 and 26 of S.I. 2006/1737, section 62 of, and paragraphs 148 and 149 of Schedule 13 to, the Tribunals, Courts and Enforcement Act 2007 (c. 15), section 80 of the Criminal Justice and Immigration Act 2008 (c. 4) and section 88 of the Legal Aid, Sentencing and Punishment of Offenders Act 2012 (c. 10).
[27] 1998 c. 37; section 50 was amended by section 106 of, and Schedule 15 to, the Access to Justice Act 1999 (c. 22), sections 41 and 332 of, and paragraphs 15 and 16 of Schedule 3 and Part 4 of Schedule 37 to, the Criminal Justice Act 2003 (c. 44), regulation 8 of S.I. 2006/2493 and section 39 of, and paragraphs 46 and 47 of Schedule 5 to, the Legal Aid, Sentencing and Punishment of Offenders Act 2012 (c. 10). It is further amended by section 3 of, and paragraphs 20 and 22 of the Schedule to, the Courts and Tribunals (Judiciary and Functions of Staff) Act 2018 (c. 33).
[28] 2003 c. 44; section 52 was substituted by paragraph 1 of Schedule 20 to the Police, Crime, Sentencing and Courts Act 2022 (c. 32).

Criminal Procedure Rules

        (iii) the service of documents (including summaries of any legal arguments relied on by the parties),

        (iv) the manner in which evidence is to be given, insofar as this rule makes no other provision and except the making, varying or revocation of a witness anonymity order;

    (f) where rule 5.10 applies (Request for information determined by the court)—

        (i) directing service of a request under rule 5.10(2)(a)(ii) (service on a person not specified by the rule),

        (ii) extending the period for objection under rule 5.10(3), and

        (iii) determining a request referred to the court under rule 5.9(7) (Request for information by a party or person directly affected by a case) where no notice of objection is given within the time for which rule 5.10(3) provides;

    (g) imposing a reporting restriction under section 45 of the Youth Justice and Criminal Evidence Act 1999[29] (identity of a person under 18) where there is no objection to the order;

    (h) giving permission for proceedings to be recorded; and

    (i) asking a court security officer to remove a person from a courtroom.

(5) In connection with the rules about preliminary proceedings (Parts 7 to 12)—

    (a) issuing a summons and giving directions for service;

    (b) under section 4 of the Summary Jurisdiction (Process) Act 1881[30], endorsing a summons or warrant issued by a court in Scotland;

    (c) giving a prosecutor permission to withdraw a charge;

    (d) dismissing a prosecution where the prosecutor offers no evidence;

    (e) amending a charge; and

    (f) sending a defendant to the Crown Court for trial where the only condition for sending is—

        (i) that prescribed by section 51(2)(a), of the Crime and Disorder Act 1998[31] (offence triable only on indictment other than one in respect of which notice is given under section 51B or 51C of that Act[32]), or

        (ii) the service of a notice under section 51B or 51C of that Act (prosecutor's notice requiring sending for trial in a case of serious or complex fraud or a case in which a child is to be called as a witness).

(6) In connection with the rules about custody and bail (Parts 13 and 14)—

    (a) issuing or withdrawing a warrant for a person's arrest to secure that the person attends court proceedings relating to an offence of which the person has been accused or convicted in a case in which no objection is made by or on behalf of that person to the issue of the warrant; and

    (b) granting bail where—

        (i) the defendant is present,

        (ii) the prosecutor agrees to the grant of bail, and

        (iii) the conditions, if any, to which that bail will be subject will remain the same as before, or will be varied or imposed with the parties' agreement.

(7) In connection with the rules about evidence (Parts 16 to 23)—

    (a) requiring a person who has made a written statement to attend before the court to give evidence;

    (b) issuing a witness summons and giving directions for its service; and

    (c) exercising the court's functions listed in rule 23.2 (Appointment of advocate to cross-examine witness) and appointing such an advocate as that rule describes (but a court officer may not decline to appoint such an advocate where that rule applies).

(8) In connection with the rules about trial (Parts 24 to 27)—

    (a) convicting a defendant who has pleaded guilty;

    (b) requesting a pre-sentence report where a defendant pleads guilty; and

    (c) directing the commissioning of a medical report.

---

[29] 1999 c. 23.

[30] 1881 c. 24.

[31] 1998 c. 37; section 51 was substituted by paragraphs 15 and 18 of Schedule 3 to the Criminal Justice Act 2003 (c. 44) and amended by section 52 of the Criminal Justice and Courts Act 2015 (c. 2).

[32] 1998 c. 37; sections 51B and 51C were inserted by paragraphs 15 and 18 of Schedule 3 to the Criminal Justice Act 2003 (c. 44). Section 51B was amended by section 50 of, and paragraph 69 of Schedule 4 to, the Commissioners for Revenue and Customs Act 2005 (c. 11), paragraphs 46 and 48 of Schedule 5 to the Legal Aid, Sentencing and Punishment of Offenders Act 2012 (c. 10) and article 3 of, and paragraphs 14 and 15 of Schedule 2 to, S.I. 2014/834. Section 51C was modified by section 63 of, and paragraph 36 of Schedule 6 to, the Serious Crime Act 2007 (c. 27) and amended by regulations 8 and 9 of S.I. 2016/244.

(9) In connection with the rules about appeal (Parts 34 to 44)—
   (a) stating a case for the opinion of the High Court where the decision under appeal was made by an authorised court officer; and
   (b) requiring the appellant to enter into a recognizance under section 114 of the Magistrates' Courts Act 1980[33] on an application to state a case for the opinion of the High Court.
(10) In connection with the rules about costs (Part 45)—
   (a) making or varying an order for a party to pay costs, if both parties agree;
   (b) making or varying an order for another person to pay costs, if that person agrees; and
   (c) making a costs order to which rule 45.4 (Costs out of central funds) applies.
(11) In connection with the rules about other proceedings (Parts 46 to 50)—
   (a) making a legal aid representation order on an appeal against a refusal of legal aid (but a court officer may not decline to make such an order); and
   (b) determining an application for a change of legal representative.
(12) An authorised court officer who is not a justices' legal adviser may not exercise a function of the court in a case in which a District Judge (Magistrates' Courts), a lay justice or a justices' legal adviser so directs.

[Note. See also—

   (a) rule 2.4, which makes general rules about the exercise of judicial functions by authorised court officers; and
   (b) rule 3.6 (Application to vary a direction).

Under section 148 of the Magistrates' Courts Act 1980[34], the expression 'magistrates' court' means any justice or justices of the peace acting under any enactment or by virtue of their commission or under the common law. For a court's power to try an allegation of an offence, see the note to rule 24.1 (Trial and sentence in a magistrates' court; When this Part applies).

Under section 50 of the Crime and Disorder Act 1998[35], where a defendant has been charged with an offence at a police station the magistrates' court before whom he or she appears or is brought for the first time in relation to the charge may consist of a single justice; and where on such an occasion the powers of a single justice are exercised by an authorised court officer that court officer may not remand the defendant in custody or, without the consent of the prosecutor and the defendant, remand the defendant on bail on conditions other than those (if any) previously imposed.

Under section 8B(3) of the Magistrates' Courts Act 1980[36], a magistrates' court may discharge or vary (or further vary) a pre-trial ruling within the meaning of section 8A of that Act[37] if the court has given the parties an opportunity to be heard and if, among other things, there has been a material change of circumstances since the ruling was made or, if a previous application has been made, since the application (or last application) was made.

Under section 53(4) of the Courts Act 2003[38], a court security officer acting in the execution of that officer's duty may remove any person from a courtroom at the request of a judge or a justice of the peace.]

R2.9 **Exercise of functions of a District Judge (Magistrates' Courts) in extradition cases**
2.9 (1) This rule provides for the exercise by an authorised court officer of relevant judicial functions of a District Judge (Magistrates' Courts) in a case to which Part 50 (Extradition) applies.
   (2) Subject to rule 2.4, an authorised court officer who is legally qualified may—
      (a) fix, cancel or vary the date, time or place for a hearing, including an extradition hearing; and

[33] 1980 c. 43; section 114 was amended by section 90 of, and paragraphs 95 and 113 of Schedule 13 to, the Access to Justice Act 1999 (c. 22) and section 109 of, and paragraph 235 of Schedule 8 to, the Courts Act 2003 (c. 39). It is further amended by section 3 of, and paragraphs 5 and 7 of the Schedule to, the Courts and Tribunals (Judiciary and Functions of Staff) Act 2018 (c 33).
[34] 1980 c. 43; section 148 was amended by section 109 of, and paragraph 248 of Schedule 8 to, the Courts Act 2003 (c. 39).
[35] 1998 c. 37; section 50 was amended by section 106 of, and Schedule 15 to, the Access to Justice Act 1999 (c. 22), sections 41 and 332 of, and paragraphs 15 and 16 of Schedule 3 and Part 4 of Schedule 37 to, the Criminal Justice Act 2003 (c. 44), regulation 8 of S.I. 2006/2493 and section 39 of, and paragraphs 46 and 47 of Schedule 5 to, the Legal Aid, Sentencing and Punishment of Offenders Act 2012 (c. 10). It is further amended by section 3 of, and paragraphs 20 and 22 of the Schedule to, the Courts and Tribunals (Judiciary and Functions of Staff) Act 2018 (c. 33).
[36] 1980 c. 43; section 8B was inserted by section 45 of, and Schedule 3 to, the Courts Act 2003 (c. 39) and amended by paragraph 51 of Schedule 3, and Part 4 of Schedule 37, to the Criminal Justice Act 2003 (c. 44).
[37] 1980 c. 43; section 8A was inserted by section 45 of, and Schedule 3 to, the Courts Act 2003 (c. 39) and amended by SI 2006/2493 and paragraphs 12 and 14 of Schedule 5 to the Legal Aid, Sentencing and Punishment of Offenders Act 2012 (c. 10).
[38] 2003 c. 39.

(b) determine an application to extend a time limit set by a rule or by the court, unless the effect would be—

    (i) to affect the date of any hearing that has been fixed, including an extradition hearing, or

    (ii) significantly to affect the progress of the case in any other way.

(3) An authorised court officer who is not a justices' legal adviser may not exercise a function of the court in a case in which a District Judge (Magistrates' Courts) or a justices' legal adviser so directs.

[Note. See also—

    (a) rule 2.4, which makes general rules about the exercise of judicial functions by authorised court officers;

    (b) rule 3.6 (Application to vary a direction); and

    (c) rule 50.4 (Case management in the magistrates' court and duty of court officer).]

Court's power to extend time under rule 2.6 or rule 2.7   R2.10

2.10 (1) The court may extend (even after it has expired) a time limit under rule 2.6 (Exercise of functions of the High Court) or rule 2.7 (Exercise of functions of the Crown Court).

(2) A party who wants an extension of time must—

    (a) apply when serving the application for which it is needed; and

    (b) explain the delay.

Powers of court officers to take statutory declarations

Taking of statutory declarations by court officers   R2.11

2.11 (1) This rule applies to a statutory declaration required by—

    (a) rule 29.4 (Statutory declaration to avoid fine after fixed penalty notice); or

    (b) rule 44.2 (Statutory declaration of ignorance of proceedings).

(2) A court officer may take a statutory declaration to which this rule applies if that officer is—

    (a) a justices' legal adviser;

    (b) nominated for the purpose by a justices' legal adviser; or

    (c) authorised to exercise the function to which rule 2.8(2)(m) refers (extending time for the service of a statutory declaration).

[Note. Section 2 of the Commissioners for Oaths Act 1889[39] allows rules that regulate the procedure of a court to authorise the taking of a statutory declaration by an officer of that court.]

Justices' legal advisers

Duties of justices' legal adviser   R2.12

2.12 (1) This rule applies in relation to a magistrates' court, including a youth court, that comprises a lay justice or lay justices.

(2) A justices' legal adviser—

    (a) must provide the court with any legal advice that it needs to carry out its functions, whether the court asks for that advice or not, including advice about—

        (i)   questions of law,

        (ii)   questions of mixed law and fact,

        (iii)   matters of practice and procedure,

        (iv)   relevant judicial decisions that bind the court,

        (v)   the process to be followed to reach a decision,

        (vi)   the process to be followed when sentencing,

        (vii) the range of penalties and orders available when sentencing and the matters to be taken into account, in accordance with any sentencing guideline that applies, and

        (viii) any other matter relevant to the case before the court;

    (b) must allow the parties, if present, an opportunity to make representations to the court about that advice;

    (c) may ask questions of a party or witness on the court's behalf to clarify representations and evidence;

    (d) if necessary must assist the court with the formulation and recording of reasons for its decisions; and

---

[39] 1889 c. 10; section 2 was amended by section 59 of, and paragraph 15 of Schedule 11 to, the Constitutional Reform Act 2005 (c. 4).

     (e) may make announcements on the court's behalf, other than an announcement of—
        (i)   an allocation or sending decision,
        (ii) an indication of likely sentence, or
        (iii) a verdict or sentence.

(3) To provide the legal advice required by paragraph (2)(a) a justices' legal adviser must—
     (a) if necessary, attend the members of the court outside the courtroom; and
     (b) in that event, inform the parties, if present, of any such advice given there.

(4) A justices' legal adviser must assist a party who has no legal representative—
     (a) to understand what the court requires and why;
     (b) to provide information required by the court to prepare for trial or to carry out its other functions; and
     (c) if necessary, to make representations to the court or to give evidence.

(5) In performing the functions for which these Rules provide a justices' legal adviser—
     (a) must avoid the appearance of advocacy for a party;
     (b) must adhere to the same principles that apply to courts of independence, impartiality, integrity, propriety, competence, diligence and ensuring fair treatment; and
     (c) may consult with other justices' legal advisers.

[Note. Section 28 of the Courts Act 2003[40] provides for persons authorised by the Lord Chief Justice to give advice to justices of the peace about matters of law. Such a person may be authorised for that purpose only if appointed under section 2(1) of that Act and possessed of such qualifications as may be prescribed. Section 29 of the 2003 Act[41] provides that the Lord Chief Justice may give directions to such a person but that, apart from that, such a person is not subject to the direction of the Lord Chancellor or anyone else when exercising functions under section 28.

See also rule 2.2 (Definitions).

The following rules impose specific duties on a justices' legal adviser in addition to those listed in this rule—

     (a) rule 9.4 (duty of justices' legal adviser during allocation and sending for trial);
     (b) rule 14.3 (duty of justices' legal adviser in proceedings about bail and custody time limits);
     (c) rule 24.14 (duty of justices' legal adviser during trial and sentence in a magistrates' court);
     (d) rule 30.2 ((duty of justices' legal adviser in proceedings about the enforcement of fines and other orders for payment);
     (e) rule 35.4 (duty of justices' legal adviser on an application to a magistrates' court to state a case for the High Court); and
     (f) rule 47.25 (duty of justices' legal adviser on an application to a magistrates' court for a search warrant).]

CRIMINAL PROCEDURE RULES   PART 3   CASE MANAGEMENT

General rules

R3.1   **When this Part applies**

3.1   (1) Rules 3.1 to 3.15 apply to the management of each case in a magistrates' court and in the Crown Court (including an appeal to the Crown Court) until the conclusion of that case.

(2) Rules 3.16 to 3.18 apply where the case must be tried in a magistrates' court, or the court orders trial there.
     (a) the court sends the defendant for trial in the Crown Court; or
     (b) the case is one to which rule 24.8 or rule 24.9 applies (Written guilty plea: special rules; Single justice procedure: special rules).

(3) Rules 3.19 to 3.34 apply where—
     (a) the defendant is sent to the Crown Court for trial;
     (b) a High Court or Crown Court judge gives permission to serve a draft indictment; or
     (c) the Court of Appeal orders a retrial.

(4) Rules 3.35 to 3.39 apply where the court can give a live link direction.

---

[40] 2003 c. 39; section 28 was substituted by section 3 of, and paragraphs 25 and 26 of the Schedule to, the Courts and Tribunals (Judiciary and Functions of Staff) Act 2018 (c. 33).
[41] 2003 c. 39; section 29 was substituted by section 3 of, and paragraphs 25 and 26 of the Schedule to, the Courts and Tribunals (Judiciary and Functions of Staff) Act 2018 (c. 33).

[Note. Rules that apply to procedure in the Court of Appeal are in Parts 36 to 42 of these Rules.

At the first hearing in a magistrates' court the court may (and in some cases must) order trial in that court, or may (and in some cases must) send the defendant to the Crown Court for trial under section 51 or 51A of the Crime and Disorder Act 1998[1]. See Part 9 (Allocation and sending for trial) for the procedure. The decision depends upon—

(a) *the classification of the offence (and the general rule, subject to exceptions, is that an offence classified as triable only on indictment must be sent to the Crown Court for trial; an offence classified as triable only summarily must be tried in a magistrates' court; and an offence classified as triable either way, on indictment or summarily, must be allocated to one or the other court for trial, subject to the defendant's right to choose Crown Court trial: see in particular sections 50A, 51 and 51A of the 1998 Act[2] and section 19 of the Magistrates' Courts Act 1980[3]);*

(b) *the defendant's age (and the general rule, subject to exceptions, is that an offence alleged against a defendant under 18 must be tried in a magistrates' court sitting as a youth court: see in particular sections 24 and 24A of the 1980 Act[4]) ;*

(c) *whether the defendant is awaiting Crown Court trial for another offence;*

(d) *whether another defendant, charged with the same offence, is awaiting Crown Court trial for that offence;*

(e) *in some cases (destroying or damaging property; aggravated vehicle taking), whether the value involved is more or less than £5,000; and*

(f) *in a case of low-value shoplifting, whether the defendant chooses Crown Court trial: see section 22A of the 1980 Act[5].*

Under paragraph 2(1) of Schedule 17 to the Crime and Courts Act 2013[6] and section 2 of the Administration of Justice (Miscellaneous Provisions) Act 1933[7], the Crown Court may give permission to serve a draft indictment where it approves a deferred prosecution agreement. See Part 11 for the rules about that procedure and Part 10 for the rules about indictments.

The procedure for applying for the permission of a High Court judge to serve a draft indictment is in rule 10.9 (Application to a High Court judge for permission to serve a draft indictment).

---

[1] 1998 c. 37; section 51 was substituted by paragraphs 15 and 18 of Schedule 3 to the Criminal Justice Act 2003 (c. 44) and amended by section 59 of, and paragraph 1 of Schedule 11 to, the Constitutional Reform Act 2005 (c. 4). Section 51A was inserted by paragraphs 15 and 18 of Schedule 3 to the Criminal Justice Act 2003 (c. 44) and amended by section 49 of, and paragraph 5 of Schedule 1 to, the Violent Crime Reduction Act 2006 (c. 38) and paragraph 6 of Schedule 21 to the Legal Aid, Sentencing and Punishment of Offenders Act 2012 (c. 10).

[2] 1998 c. 37; section 50A was inserted by paragraphs 15 and 17 of Schedule 3 to the Criminal Justice Act 2003 (c. 44).

[3] 1980 c. 43; section 19 was substituted by paragraphs 1 and 5 of Schedule 3 to the Criminal Justice Act 2003 (c. 44) and amended by sections 144, 177 and 178 of, and paragraph 4 of Schedule 17, paragraph 80 of Schedule 21 and Part 5 of Schedule 23 to, the Coroners and Justice Act 2009 (c. 25).

[4] 1980 c. 43; section 24 was amended by paragraph 47 of Schedule 14 to the Criminal Justice Act 1982 (c. 48), sections 17, 68 and 101 of, and paragraph 6 of Schedule 8 and Schedule 13 to, the Criminal Justice Act 1991 (c. 53), paragraph 40 of Schedule 10, and Schedule 11, to the Criminal Justice and Public Order Act 1994 (c. 33), sections 47 and 119 of, and paragraph 40 of Schedule 8, to the Crime and Disorder Act 1998 (c. 37), paragraph 64 of Schedule 9 to the Powers of Criminal Courts (Sentencing) Act 2000 (c. 6), section 42 of, and paragraphs 1 and 9 of Schedule 3, and Part 4 of Schedule 37, to the Criminal Justice Act 2003 (c. 44) and sections 49 and 65 of, and paragraph 1 of Schedule 1 and Schedule 5 to, the Violent Crime Reduction Act 2006 (c. 38). Section 24A was inserted by paragraphs 1 and 10 of Schedule 3 to the Criminal Justice Act 2003 (c. 44).

[5] 1980 c. 43; section 22A was inserted by section 176 of the Anti-social Behaviour, Crime and Policing Act 2014 (c. 12) and amended by section 52 of the Criminal Justice and Courts Act 2015 (c. 2).

[6] 2013 c. 22.

[7] 1933 c. 36; section 2 was amended by Part IV of Schedule 11 to, the Courts Act 1971 (c. 23), Schedule 5 to, the Senior Courts Act 1981 (c. 54), Schedule 2 to the Prosecution of Offences Act 1985 (c. 23), paragraph 1 of Schedule 2 to the Criminal Justice Act 1987 (c. 38), paragraph 10 of Schedule 15 to the Criminal Justice Act 1988 (c. 33), paragraph 8 of Schedule 6 to the Criminal Justice Act 1991 (c. 53), Schedule 1 to the Statute Law (Repeals Act 1993, paragraph 17 of Schedule 1 to the Criminal Procedure and Investigations Act 1996 (c. 25), paragraph 5 of Schedule 8 to the Crime and Disorder Act 1998 (c. 37), paragraph 34 of Schedule 3 and Part 4 of Schedule 37 to the Criminal Justice Act 2003 (c. 44), paragraph 1 of the Schedule to S.I. 2004/2035, section 12 of, and paragraph 7 of Schedule 1 to, the Constitutional Reform Act 2005 (c. 4), sections 116 and 178 of, and Part 3 of Schedule 23 to, the Coroners and Justice Act 2009 (c. 25), paragraph 32 of Schedule 17 to the Crime and Courts Act 2013 (c. 22) and section 82 of the Deregulation Act 2015 (c. 20).

The Court of Appeal may order a retrial under section 8 of the Criminal Appeal Act 1968[8] (on a defendant's appeal against conviction) or under section 77 of the Criminal Justice Act 2003[9] (on a prosecutor's application for the retrial of a serious offence after acquittal). Section 8 of the 1968 Act, section 84 of the 2003 Act and rules 27.6 and 39.14 require the arraignment of a defendant within 2 months.]

R3.2   The duty of the court

3.2   (1)   The court must further the overriding objective by actively managing the case.

(2)   Active case management includes—

(a)   the early identification of the real issues;

(b)   the early identification of the needs of witnesses;

(c)   achieving certainty as to what must be done, by whom, and when, in particular by the early setting of a timetable for the progress of the case;

(d)   monitoring the progress of the case and compliance with directions;

(e)   ensuring that evidence, whether disputed or not, is presented in the shortest and clearest way;

(f)   discouraging delay, dealing with as many aspects of the case as possible on the same occasion, and avoiding unnecessary hearings;

(g)   encouraging the participants to co-operate in the progression of the case; and

(h)   making use of technology.

(3)   The court must actively manage the case by giving any direction appropriate to the needs of that case as early as possible.

(4)   Where appropriate live links are available, making use of technology for the purposes of this rule includes giving a live link direction for a person's participation—

(a)   under a power to which rule 3.35 applies (Live link direction: exercise of court's powers); and

(b)   whether an application for such a direction is made or not.

(5)   At the first hearing in a case the court must require a defendant who is present—

(a)   to provide—

(i)   the defendant's name and date of birth; and

(ii)   at least one address at which documents may be served on the defendant under rule 4.4 (Service by leaving or posting a document), including any address at which the defendant resides, in order to facilitate effective communication between the court and the defendant; and

(b)   further to assist communication between the court and the defendant, to provide any—

(i)   electronic address by means of which written messages may be sent to the defendant, and

(ii)   telephone number by means of which oral messages may be given to or left for the defendant.

(6)   At any hearing after the first in a case the court may require a defendant who is present to provide or confirm the information required under paragraph (5).

(7)   Information required under paragraph (5)(a) must be provided in public unless on an application under rule 6.4 (Reporting and access restrictions) the court otherwise directs.

(8)   If the defendant fails to comply with a requirement to provide name and date of birth—

(a)   the court that imposed the requirement—

(i)   may invite the prosecutor there and then to start a prosecution in respect of that failure, in accordance with the rules in Part 7 (Starting a prosecution in a magistrates' court),

(ii)   must apply to any such prosecution the rules in Part 24 (Trial and sentence in a magistrates' court), and

(iii)   in any such prosecution may receive evidence from court staff but must not, as a general rule, receive evidence from the defendant's legal representative (if any) or from a member of the court; and

(b)   for the purposes of this paragraph the rules in Parts 7 and 24 apply in the Crown Court as well as in a magistrates' court.

---

[8]   1968 c. 19; section 8 was amended by Section 12 of, and paragraph 38 of Schedule 2 to, the Bail Act 1976 (c. 63), section 56 of, and Part IV of Schedule 11 to, the Courts Act 1971 (c. 23), section 65 of, and paragraph 36 of Schedule 3 to, the Mental Health (Amendment Act 1982 (c. 51), section 148 of, and paragraph 23 of Schedule 4 to, the Mental Health Act 1983 (c. 20), section 43 of the Criminal Justice Act 1988 (c. 33), section 168 of, and paragraph 19 of Schedule 10 to, the Criminal Justice and Public Order Act 1994 (c. 33), section 58 of the Access to Justice Act 1999 (c. 22), sections 41 and 332 of, and paragraph 43 of Schedule 3 to, and Part 4 of Schedule 37 to, the Criminal Justice Act 2003 (c. 44) and section 32 of, and paragraph 2 of Schedule 4 to, the Mental Health Act 2007 (c. 12).

[9]   2003 c. 44.

[Note. Under section 51 of the Criminal Justice Act 2003, the court may require or permit any person to take part through a live audio or video link in the pre-trial, trial, sentencing, enforcement and appeal proceedings listed in that section. Under section 52A of the Act[10]*, a person who takes part in accordance with a live link direction is to be treated as present in court.*

Under section 86A of the Courts Act 2003[11]*, Criminal Procedure Rules must specify stages of proceedings at which the court must require the defendant to provide name and date of birth and may specify other stages of proceedings at which such a requirement may be imposed. Under section 86A(3) a person commits an offence if, without reasonable excuse, that person fails to comply with such a requirement, whether by providing false or incomplete information or by providing no information. Under section 86A(6) the court before which a person is required to provide that information may deal with any suspected such offence at the same time as dealing with the offence for which the person was already before the court.]*

The duty of the parties   **R3.3**

3.3   (1) Each party must—
    (a) actively assist the court in fulfilling its duty under rule 3.2, without or if necessary with a direction; and
    (b) apply for a direction if needed to further the overriding objective.
   (2) Active assistance for the purposes of this rule includes—
    (a) at the beginning of the case, communication between the prosecutor and the defendant at the first available opportunity and in any event no later than the beginning of the day of the first hearing;
    (b) after that, communication between the parties and with the court officer until the conclusion of the case;
    (c) by such communication establishing, among other things—
      (i)   whether the defendant is likely to plead guilty or not guilty,
      (ii) what is agreed and what is likely to be disputed,
      (iii) what information, or other material, is required by one party of another, and why, and
      (iv) what is to be done, by whom, and when (without or if necessary with a direction);
    (d) reporting on that communication to the court—
      (i)   at the first hearing, and
      (ii) after that, as directed by the court;
    (e) alerting the court to any reason why—
      (i)   a live link direction should not be given, or
      (ii) such a direction should be varied or rescinded;
    (f) alerting the court to any potential impediment to the defendant's effective participation in the trial;
    (g) alerting the court to any potential need for a witness to be accompanied while giving evidence, and in that event?
      (i)   identifying a proposed companion,
      (ii) naming that person, if possible, and
      (iii) explaining why that person would be an appropriate companion for the witness, including the witness' own views; and
    (h) alerting the court to any related family proceedings or anticipated such proceedings as soon as reasonably practicable after becoming aware of them.

Case progression officers and their duties   **R3.4**

3.4   (1) At the beginning of the case each party must, unless the court otherwise directs—
    (a) nominate someone responsible for progressing that case; and
    (b) tell other parties and the court who that is and how to contact that person.
   (2) In fulfilling its duty under rule 3.2, the court must where appropriate—
    (a) nominate a court officer responsible for progressing the case; and
    (b) make sure the parties know who that is and how to contact that court officer.
   (3) In this Part a person nominated under this rule is called a case progression officer.
   (4) A case progression officer must—
    (a) monitor compliance with directions;
    (b) make sure that the court is kept informed of events that may affect the progress of that case;
    (c) make sure that he or she can be contacted promptly about the case during ordinary business hours;

---

[10] 2003 c. 44; section 52A was inserted by paragraph 1 of Schedule 20 to the Police, Crime, Sentencing and Courts Act 2022 (c. 32).
[11] 2003 c. 39; section 86A was inserted by section 162 of the Policing and Crime Act 2017 (c. 3).

(d) act promptly and reasonably in response to communications about the case; and

(e) if he or she will be unavailable, appoint a substitute to fulfil his or her duties and inform the other case progression officers.

R3.5 **The court's case management powers**

3.5 (1) In fulfilling its duty under rule 3.2 the court may give any direction and take any step actively to manage a case unless that direction or step would be inconsistent with legislation, including these Rules.

(2) In particular, the court may—

(a) nominate a judge, magistrate or justices' legal adviser to manage the case;

(b) give a direction on its own initiative or on application by a party;

(c) ask or allow a party to propose a direction;

(d) receive applications, notices, representations and information by letter, by live link, by email or by any other means of electronic communication, and conduct a hearing by live link or other such electronic means;

(e) give a direction—

    (i) at a hearing, in public or in private, or

    (ii) without a hearing;

(f) fix, postpone, bring forward, extend, cancel or adjourn a hearing;

(g) shorten or extend (even after it has expired) a time limit fixed by a direction;

(h) require that issues in the case should be—

    (i) identified in writing,

    (ii) determined separately, and decide in what order they will be determined;

(i) specify the consequences of failing to comply with a direction.

(j) request information from a court dealing with family proceedings by—

    (i) making the request itself, or

    (ii) directing the court officer or a party to make the request on the criminal court's behalf; and

(k) supply information to a court dealing with family proceedings as if a request had been made under rule 5.8(7) (Request for information about a case) by—

    (i) supplying the information itself, or

    (ii) directing the court officer or a party to supply that information on the criminal court's behalf.

(3) A magistrates' court may give a direction that will apply in the Crown Court if the case is to continue there.

(4) The Crown Court may give a direction that will apply in a magistrates' court if the case is to continue there.

(5) Any power to give a direction under this Part includes a power to vary or revoke that direction.

(6) If a party fails to comply with a rule or a direction, the court may—

(a) fix, postpone, bring forward, extend, cancel or adjourn a hearing;

(b) exercise its powers to make a costs order; and

(c) impose such other sanction as may be appropriate.

(7) In deciding whether to postpone, cancel or adjourn a hearing the court must take into account—

(a) the likelihood that delay would be contrary to the court's duty under rule 1.3 (The application by the court of the overriding objective);

(b) the court's duty under rule 3.8 (Case preparation and progression);

(c) the availability of a substitute hearing date;

(d) the need for compelling reasons, and especially where an application to postpone, cancel or adjourn is made at or shortly before the hearing;

(e) the nature and gravity of any failure to comply with a rule or direction, or to take some other step, where that failure prompts the proposed postponement, cancellation or adjournment; and

(f) the evidence of unfitness to attend, where a participant's ill-health prompts the proposed postponement, cancellation or adjournment, and in particular the extent to which any medical certificate satisfactorily—

    (i) identifies the date of the participant's examination,

    (ii) describes the participant's injury, illness or condition, the activity or activities which that ill-health impedes and the likely duration of that impediment, and

    (iii) explains how that ill-health renders the participant unfit to attend the hearing.

[Note. Depending upon the nature of a case and the stage that it has reached, its progress may be affected by other Criminal Procedure Rules and by other legislation. The note at the end of this Part lists other rules and legislation that may apply.

See also rule 3.8 (Case preparation and progression).

The court may require expert evidence in support of an application to postpone, cancel or adjourn a hearing by reason of ill-health, in particular from the medical practitioner who provided a certificate in support of the application. See also Part 19 (Expert evidence).

The court may make a costs order under—

      (a) section 19 of the Prosecution of Offences Act 1985[12], where the court decides that one party to criminal proceedings has incurred costs as a result of an unnecessary or improper act or omission by, or on behalf of, another party;

      (b) section 19A of that Act[13], where the court decides that a party has incurred costs as a result of an improper, unreasonable or negligent act or omission on the part of a legal representative;

      (c) section 19B of that Act[14], where the court decides that there has been serious misconduct by a person who is not a party.

Under some other legislation, including Parts 19, 20 and 21 of these Rules, if a party fails to comply with a rule or a direction then in some circumstances—

      (a) the court may refuse to allow that party to introduce evidence;

      (b) evidence that that party wants to introduce may not be admissible;

      (c) the court may draw adverse inferences from the late introduction of an issue or evidence.

See also—

      (a) section 81(1) of the Police and Criminal Evidence Act 1984[15] and section 20(3) of the Criminal Procedure and Investigations Act 1996[16] (advance disclosure of expert evidence);

      (b) section 11(5) of the Criminal Procedure and Investigations Act 1996[17] (faults in disclosure by accused);

      (c) section 132(5) of the Criminal Justice Act 2003[18] (failure to give notice of hearsay evidence).]

Application to vary a direction

    R3.6

3.6 (1) A party may apply to vary a direction if—

    (a) the court gave it without a hearing;

    (b) the court gave it at a hearing in that party's absence; or

    (c) circumstances have changed.

    (2) A party who applies to vary a direction must—

    (a) apply as soon as practicable after becoming aware of the grounds for doing so; and

    (b) give as much notice to the other parties as the nature and urgency of the application permits.

Agreement to vary a time limit fixed by a direction

    R3.7

3.7 (1) The parties may agree to vary a time limit fixed by a direction, but only if—

    (a) the variation will not—

        (i) affect the date of any hearing that has been fixed, or

        (ii) significantly affect the progress of the case in any other way;

    (b) the court has not prohibited variation by agreement; and

    (c) the court's case progression officer is promptly informed.

---

[12] 1985 c. 23; section 19 was amended by section 166 of the Criminal Justice Act 1988 (c. 33), section 45 of, and Schedule 6 to, the Legal Aid Act 1988 (c. 34), section 7 of, and paragraph 8 of Schedule 3 to, the Criminal Procedure (Insanity and Unfitness to Plead Act 1991 (c. 25), section 24 of, and paragraphs 27 and 28 of Schedule 4 to, the Access to Justice Act 1999 (c. 22), sections 40 and 67 of, and paragraph 4 of Schedule 7 to, the Youth Justice and Criminal Evidence Act 1999 (c. 23), section 165 of, and paragraph 99 of Schedule 9 to, the Powers of Criminal Courts (Sentencing Act 2000 (c. 6), section 378 of, and paragraph 107 of Schedule 16 to, the Armed Forces Act 2006 (c. 52), section 6 of, and paragraph 32 of Schedule 4 and paragraphs 1 and 5 of Schedule 27 to, the Criminal Justice and Immigration Act 2008 (c. 4) and paragraphs 22 and 23 of Schedule 5, and paragraphs 1 and 5 and Part 4 of Schedule 7, to the Legal Aid, Sentencing and Punishment of Offenders Act 2012 (c. 10).

[13] 1985 c. 23; section 19A was inserted by section 111 of the Courts and Legal Services Act 1990 (c. 41).

[14] 1985 c. 23; section 19B was inserted by section 93 of the Courts Act 2003 (c. 39).

[15] 1984 c. 60; section 81(1) was amended by section 109(1) of, and paragraph 286 of Schedule 8 to, the Courts Act 2003 (c.39).

[16] 1996 c. 25; section 20(3) was amended by section 109(1) of, and paragraph 378 of Schedule 8 to, the Courts Act 2003 (c.39).

[17] 1996 c. 25; section 11 was substituted by section 39 of the Criminal Justice Act 2003 (c. 44) and amended by section 60 of the Criminal Justice and Immigration Act 2008 (c. 4).

[18] 2003 c. 44.

(2) The court's case progression officer must refer the agreement to the court if in doubt that the condition in paragraph (1)(a) is satisfied.

R3.8   Case preparation and progression

3.8   (1) At every hearing, if a case cannot be concluded there and then the court must give directions so that it can be concluded at the next hearing or as soon as possible after that.

(2) At every hearing the court must, where relevant—

     (a) if the defendant is absent, decide whether to proceed nonetheless;

     (b) take the defendant's plea (unless already done) or if no plea can be taken then find out whether the defendant is likely to plead guilty or not guilty;

     (c) set, follow or revise a timetable for the progress of the case, which may include a timetable for any hearing including the trial or (in the Crown Court) the appeal;

     (d) in giving directions, ensure continuity in relation to the court and to the parties' representatives where that is appropriate and practicable; and

     (e) where a direction has not been complied with, find out why, identify who was responsible, and take appropriate action.

(3) In order to prepare for the trial, the court must take every reasonable step—

     (a) to encourage and to facilitate the attendance of witnesses when they are needed; and

     (b) to facilitate the participation of any person, including the defendant.

(4) Facilitating the participation of the defendant includes finding out whether the defendant needs interpretation because—

     (a) the defendant does not speak or understand English; or

     (b) the defendant has a hearing or speech disorder.

(5) Where the defendant needs interpretation—

     (a) the court officer must arrange for interpretation to be provided at every hearing which the defendant is due to attend;

     (b) interpretation may be by an intermediary where the defendant has a speech disorder, without the need for a defendant's evidence direction;

     (c) on application or on its own initiative, the court may require a written translation to be provided for the defendant of any document or part of a document, unless—

         (i) translation of that document, or part, is not needed to explain the case against the defendant, or

         (ii) the defendant agrees to do without and the court is satisfied that the agreement is clear and voluntary and that the defendant has had legal advice or otherwise understands the consequences; and

     (d) on application by the defendant, the court must give any direction which the court thinks appropriate, including a direction for interpretation by a different interpreter, where —

         (i) no interpretation is provided,

         (ii) no translation is ordered or provided in response to a previous application by the defendant, or

         (iii) the defendant complains about the quality of interpretation or of any translation.

(6) Facilitating the participation of any person includes—

     (a) giving directions for someone to accompany a witness while the witness gives evidence, including directions about seating arrangements for that companion; and

     (b) giving directions for the appropriate treatment and questioning of a witness or the defendant, especially where the court directs that such questioning is to be conducted through an intermediary.

(7) Where directions for appropriate treatment and questioning are required, the court must—

     (a) invite representations by the parties and by any intermediary; and

     (b) set ground rules for the conduct of the questioning, which rules may include—

         (i) a direction relieving a party of any duty to put that party's case to a witness or a defendant in its entirety,

         (ii) directions about the manner of questioning,

         (iii) directions about the duration of questioning,

         (iv) if necessary, directions about the questions that may or may not be asked,

         (v) directions about the means by which any intermediary may intervene in questioning, if necessary,

         (vi) where there is more than one defendant, the allocation among them of the topics about which a witness may be asked, and

         (vii) directions about the use of models, plans, body maps or similar aids to help communicate a question or an answer.

[Note. Part 18 (Measures to assist a witness or defendant to give evidence) contains rules about an application for a defendant's evidence direction under (among other provisions) sections 33BA and 33BB of the Youth Justice and Criminal Evidence Act 1999[19].

Where a trial in a magistrates' court will take place in Wales, a participant may use the Welsh language: see rule 3.18. Where a trial in the Crown Court will take place in Wales and a participant wishes to use the Welsh language, see rule 3.34.]

Ground rules hearing   R3.9

3.9 (1) This rule applies where the court exercises the powers to which rule 3.8(6) and (7) apply (directions for appropriate treatment and questioning of a witness or defendant).

(2) At a pre-trial case management hearing convened for the purpose—
   (a) the parties and any intermediary must—
      (i) attend, unless the court otherwise directs, and
      (ii) actively assist the court in setting ground rules and giving directions;
   (b) the court must—
      (i) discuss proposed ground rules and directions with the parties and any intermediary,
      (ii) set ground rules for the conduct of questioning of the witness or defendant, as applicable, and
      (iii) give such other directions as may be required to facilitate the effective participation of that witness or defendant; and
   (c) despite rule 3.14(b) (court officer's duty to make a record of directions), the court may require the parties—
      (i) to make a record of those ground rules and directions, and
      (ii) to serve that record on each other, on any intermediary and on the court officer.

(3) In setting such ground rules and giving such directions, the court must have regard to—
   (a) any intermediary's report;
   (b) the parties' representations; and
   (c) such other information or advice as the court requires.

(4) The ground rules for questioning set by the court may include any listed in rule 3.8(7)(b).

(5) The directions given by the court may include any about—
   (a) the timetable for the submission of proposed questions;
   (b) the timetable for the trial, including the taking of breaks during proceedings;
   (c) seating arrangements in the court room for the defendant, the defendant's advocate and legal representative, any intermediary and any parent, guardian or other companion of the defendant; and
   (d) any explanation to be given to the jury, if there is one, of—
      (i) the witness' or the defendant's communication needs and behaviour, as applicable, and
      (ii) the role of the intermediary, if there is one.

[Note. See also rule 3.16 (Pre-trial hearings in a magistrates' court: general rules) and rule 3.21 (Pre-trial hearings in the Crown Court: general rules).]

Directions for commissioning medical reports, other than for sentencing purposes   R3.10

3.10 (1) This rule applies where, because of a defendant's suspected mental ill-health—
   (a) a magistrates' court requires expert medical opinion about the potential suitability of a hospital order under section 37(3) of the Mental Health Act 1983[20] (hospital order without convicting the defendant);
   (b) the Crown Court requires expert medical opinion about the defendant's fitness to participate at trial, under section 4 of the Criminal Procedure (Insanity) Act 1964[21]; or
   (c) a magistrates' court or the Crown Court requires expert medical opinion to help the court determine a question of intent or insanity,
   other than such opinion introduced by a party.

(2) A court may exercise the power to which this rule applies on its own initiative having regard to—

---

[19] 1999 c. 23; sections 33BA and 33BB are inserted by section 104 of the Coroners and Justice Act 2009 (c. 25), with effect from a date to be appointed.
[20] 1983 c. 20; section 37(3) was amended by sections 1 and 55 of, and paragraphs 1 and 7 of Schedule 1 and Schedule 11 to, the Mental Health Act 2007 (c. 12).
[21] 1964 c. 84; section 4 was substituted, together with section 4A, for section 4 as originally enacted, by section 2 of the Criminal Procedure (Insanity and Unfitness to Plead Act 1991 (c. 25), and amended by section 22 of the Domestic Violence, Crime and Victims Act 2004 (c. 28).

Criminal Procedure Rules

    (a) an assessment of the defendant's health by a mental health practitioner acting independently of the parties to assist the court;

    (b) representations by a party; or

    (c) observations by the court.

(3) A court that requires expert medical opinion to which this rule applies must—

    (a) identify each issue in respect of which the court requires such opinion and any legislation applicable;

    (b) specify the nature of the expertise likely to be required for giving such opinion;

    (c) identify each party or participant by whom a commission for such opinion must be prepared, who may be—

        (i) a party (or party's representative) acting on that party's own behalf,

        (ii) a party (or party's representative) acting on behalf of the court, or

        (iii) the court officer acting on behalf of the court;

    (d) where there are available to the court arrangements with the National Health Service under which an assessment of a defendant's mental health may be prepared, give such directions as are needed under those arrangements for obtaining the expert report or reports required;

    (e) where no such arrangements are available to the court, or they will not be used, give directions for the commissioning of an expert report or expert reports, including—

        (i) such directions as can be made about supplying the expert or experts with the defendant's medical records,

        (ii) directions about the other information, about the defendant and about the offence or offences alleged to have been committed by the defendant, which is to be supplied to each expert, and

        (iii) directions about the arrangements that will apply for the payment of each expert;

    (f) set a timetable providing for—

        (i) the date by which a commission is to be delivered to each expert,

        (ii) the date by which any failure to accept a commission is to be reported to the court,

        (iii) the date or dates by which progress in the preparation of a report or reports is to be reviewed by the court officer, and

        (iv) the date by which each report commissioned is to be received by the court; and

    (g) identify the person (each person, if more than one) to whom a copy of a report is to be supplied, and by whom.

(4) A commission addressed to an expert must—

    (a) identify each issue in respect of which the court requires expert medical opinion and any legislation applicable;

    (b) include—

        (i) the information required by the court to be supplied to the expert,

        (ii) details of the timetable set by the court, and

        (iii) details of the arrangements that will apply for the payment of the expert;

    (c) identify the person (each person, if more than one) to whom a copy of the expert's report is to be supplied; and

    (d) request confirmation that the expert from whom the opinion is sought—

        (i) accepts the commission, and

        (ii) will adhere to the timetable.

[Note. See also rule 28.8 (Directions for commissioning medical reports for sentencing purposes).

The court may request a medical examination of the defendant and a report under—

    (a) section 4 of the Criminal Procedure (Insanity) Act 1964, under which the Crown Court may determine a defendant's fitness to plead;

    (b) section 35 of the Mental Health Act 1983[22], under which the court may order the defendant's detention in hospital to obtain a medical report;

    (c) section 36 of the 1983 Act[23], under which the Crown Court may order the defendant's detention in hospital instead of in custody pending trial or sentence;

---

[22] 1983 c. 20; section 35 was amended by sections 1(4) and 10(1) and (2) of, and paragraphs 1 and 5 of Schedule 1 to, the Mental Health Act 2007 (c. 12) and section 208(1) of, and paragraphs 53 and 54 of Schedule 21 to, the Legal Services Act 2007 (c. 29).

[23] 1983 c. 20; section 36 was amended by sections 1(4), 5(1) and (2) and 10(1) and (3) of, and paragraphs 1 and 6 of Schedule 1 to, the Mental Health Act 2007 (c. 12) and section 208(1) of, and paragraphs 53 and 55 of Schedule 21 to, the Legal Services Act 2007 (c. 29).

(d) *section 37 of the 1983 Act*[24]*, under which the court may order the defendant's detention and treatment in hospital, or make a guardianship order, instead of disposing of the case in another way (section 37(3) allows a magistrates' court to make such an order without convicting the defendant if satisfied that the defendant did the act or made the omission charged);*

(e) *section 38 of the 1983 Act*[25]*, under which the court may order the defendant's temporary detention and treatment in hospital instead of disposing of the case in another way;*

(f) *section 157 of the Criminal Justice Act 2003*[26]*, under which the court must usually obtain and consider a medical report before passing a custodial sentence if the defendant is, or appears to be, mentally disordered;*

(g) *section 207 of the 2003 Act*[27] *(in the case of a defendant aged 18 or over), or section 1(1)(k) of the Criminal Justice and Immigration Act 2008*[28] *(in the case of a defendant who is under 18), under which the court may impose a mental health treatment requirement.*

For the purposes of the legislation listed in (a), (c), (d) and (e) above, the court requires the written or oral evidence of at least two registered medical practitioners, at least one of whom is approved as having special experience in the diagnosis or treatment of mental disorder. For the purposes of (b), (f) and (g), the court requires the evidence of one medical practitioner so approved.

Under section 11 of the Powers of Criminal Courts (Sentencing) Act 2000[29]*, a magistrates' court may adjourn a trial to obtain medical reports.*

Part 19 (Expert evidence) contains rules about the content of expert medical reports.

For the authorities from whom the court may require information about hospital treatment or guardianship, see sections 39 and 39A of the 1983 Act[30]*.*

The Practice Direction includes a timetable for the commissioning and preparation of a report or reports which the court may adopt with such adjustments as the court directs.

Payments to medical practitioners for reports and for giving evidence are governed by section 19(3) of the Prosecution of Offences Act 1985[31] *and by the Costs in Criminal Cases (General) Regulations 1986*[32]*, regulation 17 (Determination of rates or scales of allowances payable out of central funds), regulation 20 (Expert witnesses, etc.) and regulation 25 (Written medical reports). The rates and scales of allowances payable under those Regulations are determined by the Lord Chancellor.]*

---

[24] 1983 c. 20; section 37 was amended by sections 55 and 56 of, and paragraph 12 of Schedule 4 and Schedule 6 to, the Crime (Sentences Act 1997 (c. 43), section 67 of, and paragraph 11 of Schedule 4 to, the Youth Justice and Criminal Evidence Act 1999 (c. 23), paragraph 90 of Schedule 9 to the Powers of Criminal Courts (Sentencing Act 2000 (c. 6), section 304 of, and paragraphs 37 and 38 of Schedule 32 to, the Criminal Justice Act 2003 (c. 44), sections 49 and 65 of, and paragraph 2 of Schedule 1 and Schedule 5 to, the Violent Crime Reduction Act 2006 (c. 38), sections 1, 4, 10, 55 and paragraphs 1 and 7 of Schedule 1, and Part 1 of Schedule 11 to, the Mental Health Act 2007 (c. 12), sections 6 and 149 of, and paragraph 30 of Schedule 4, and Schedule 28 to, the Criminal Justice and Immigration Act 2008 (c. 4), sections 122 and 142 of, and paragraph 1 of Schedule 19 and paragraph 2 of Schedule 26 to, the Legal Aid, Sentencing and Punishment of Offenders Act 2012 (c. 10) and section 28 of, and paragraph 1 of Schedule 5 to, the Criminal Justice and Courts Act 2015 (c. 2). It is further amended by section 148 of, and paragraph 8 of Schedule 26 to, the Criminal Justice and Immigration Act 2008 (c. 4) with effect from a date to be appointed.

[25] 1983 c. 20; section 38 was amended by section 49(1) of the Crime (Sentences Act 1997 (c. 43), sections 1(4) and 10(1) and (5) of, and paragraphs 1 and 8 of Schedule 1 to, the Mental Health Act 2007 (c. 12) and section 208(1) of, and paragraphs 53 and 56 of Schedule 21 to, the Legal Services Act 2007 (c. 29).

[26] 2003 c. 44; section 157 was amended by section 38 of the Health and Social Care Act 2012 (c. 7).

[27] 2003 c. 44; section 207 was amended by article 4(2) of, and paragraph 7 of Schedule 5 to, S.I. 2009/1182, article 14(a and (b of, and Part 1 of Schedule 5 to, S.I. 2010/813, section 72 of the Health and Social Care Act 2012 (c. 7), section 73 of the Legal Aid, Sentencing and Punishment of Offenders Act 2012 (c. 10) and section 62 of, and paragraph 48 of Schedule 5 to, the Children and Social Work Act 2017 (c. 16).

[28] 2008 c. 4.

[29] 2000 c. 6.

[30] 1983 c. 20; section 39 was amended by sections 2(1) and 5(1) of, and paragraph 107 of Schedule 1 and Schedule 3 to, the Health Authorities Act 1995 (c. 17), section 2(5) of, and paragraphs 42 and 46 of Schedule 2 to, the National Health Service Reform and Health Care Professions Act 2002 (c. 17), section 31(1) and (2) of the Mental Health Act 2007 (c. 12), article 3 of, and paragraph 13 of the Schedule to, S.I. 2007/961 and section 55 of, and paragraphs 24 and 28 of Schedule 5 to, the Health and Social Care Act 2012 (c. 7). Section 39A was inserted by section 27(1) of the Criminal Justice Act 1991 (c. 53).

[31] 1985 c. 23; section 19(3) was amended by section 166 of the Criminal Justice Act 1988 (c. 33), section 7 of, and paragraph 8 of Schedule 3 to, the Criminal Procedure (Insanity and Unfitness to Plead Act 1991 (c. 25), sections 40 and 67 of, and paragraph 4 of Schedule 7 to, the Youth Justice and Criminal Evidence Act 1999 (c. 23), section 165 of, and paragraph 99 of Schedule 9 to, the Powers of Criminal Courts (Sentencing Act 2000 (c. 6) and section 378 of, and paragraph 107 of Schedule 16 to, the Armed Forces Act 2006 (c. 52).

[32] S.I. 1986/1335; regulation 17 was amended by regulations 2 and 13 of S.I. 2008/2448, regulation 20 was amended by regulations 2 and 14 of S.I. 2008/2448 and by regulations 4 and 7 of S.I. 2012/1804, and regulation 25 was amended by regulations 2 and 10 of S.I. 2009/2720.

R3.11   **Hearing to inform the court of sensitive material**

3.11 (1) This rule applies where the prosecutor has, or is aware of, material—

(a) the revelation of which to the public or to the defendant the prosecutor thinks would give rise to a real risk of serious prejudice to an important public interest;

(b) to which the prosecutor does not think the obligation to disclose prosecution material applies, under Part I of the Criminal Procedure and Investigations Act 1996; but

(c) of the existence of which the prosecutor thinks it necessary to inform the court to avoid—

(i)   potential unfairness to the defendant in the conduct of the trial,

(ii) potential prejudice to the fair management of the trial, or

(iii) potential prejudice to that public interest.

(2) Such a prosecutor must—

(a) ask for a hearing so to inform the court; and

(b) notify the defendant of that request only to such extent, if any, and at such time, if at all, as the court directs.

(3) At or before the hearing the prosecutor must—

(a) explain—

(i)   why the hearing is necessary, and

(ii) why it is necessary for the hearing to take place in the defendant's absence;

(b) explain to what extent, if any, and when, if at all, the defendant should be informed—

(i)   of the hearing, and

(ii) of the material of which the prosecutor wants to inform the court; and

(c) provide or describe the material to the court—

(i)   only to the extent needed to achieve the purpose for which the hearing is convened, and

(ii) in such manner as the court directs.

(4) Unless the court otherwise directs—

(a) any such hearing—

(i)   must be in private, and

(ii) must take place in the defendant's absence;

(b) the court officer must not give notice to anyone other than the prosecutor of—

(i)   the court's decision on the request for a hearing,

(ii) the arrangements for any such hearing, and

(iii) any directions given at such a hearing; and

(c) the court officer may—

(i)   keep any written representations or material received under this rule, or

(ii) arrange for the whole or any part to be kept by some other appropriate person, subject to any conditions that the court may impose.

R3.12   **Readiness for trial or appeal**

3.12 (1) This rule applies to a party's preparation for trial or appeal, and in this rule and rule 3.13 'trial' includes any hearing at which evidence will be introduced.

(2) In fulfilling the duty under rule 3.3, each party must—

(a) comply with directions given by the court;

(b) take every reasonable step to make sure that party's witnesses will attend when they are needed;

(c) make appropriate arrangements to present any written or other material; and

(d) promptly inform the court and the other parties of anything that may—

(i)   affect the date or duration of the trial or appeal, or

(ii) significantly affect the progress of the case in any other way.

(3) The court may require a party to give a certificate of readiness.

R3.13   **Conduct of a trial or an appeal**

3.13 In order to manage trial or an appeal, the court—

(a) must establish, with the active assistance of the parties, what are the disputed issues;

(b) must consider setting a timetable that—

(i)   takes account of those issues and any timetable proposed by a party, and

(ii) may limit the duration of any stage of the hearing;

(c) may require a party to identify—

(i)   which witnesses that party wants to give evidence in person,

(ii) the order in which that party wants those witnesses to give their evidence,

(iii) whether that party requires an order compelling the attendance of a witness,

(iv) what arrangements are desirable to facilitate the giving of evidence by a witness,

(v)   what arrangements are desirable to facilitate the participation of any other person, including the defendant,

(vi)   what written evidence that party intends to introduce,

(vii)   what other material, if any, that person intends to make available to the court in the presentation of the case, and

(viii)   whether that party intends to raise any point of law that could affect the conduct of the trial or appeal; and

(d)   may limit—

(i)   the examination, cross-examination or re-examination of a witness, and

(ii)   the duration of any stage of the hearing.

[Note. See also rules 3.5 (The court's case management powers) and 3.8 (Case preparation and progression).]

Duty of court officer   R3.14

3.14   The court officer must—

(a)   where a person is entitled or required to attend a hearing, give as much notice as reasonably practicable to—

(i)   that person, and

(ii)   that person's custodian (if any);

(b)   where the court gives directions, promptly make a record available to the parties.

[Note. See also rule 5.9 (Request for information by a party or person directly affected by a case).]

Court's power to vary requirements under this Part   R3.15

3.15   (1)   The court may—

(a)   shorten or extend (even after it has expired) a time limit set by this Part; and

(b)   allow an application or representations to be made orally.

(2)   A person who wants an extension of time must—

(a)   apply when serving the application or representations for which it is needed; and

(b)   explain the delay.

Preparation for trial in a magistrates' court

Pre-trial hearings in a magistrates' court: general rules   R3.16

3.16   (1)   A magistrates' court—

(a)   must conduct a preparation for trial hearing unless—

(i)   under rule 9.11 or rule 9.13 (Adult defendant: allocation for magistrates' court trial; Young defendant) the defendant indicates an intention to plead guilty, or

(ii)   the case is one to which rule 24.8 or rule 24.9 applies (Written guilty plea: special rules; Single justice procedure: special rules);

(b)   may conduct a further pre-trial case management hearing (and if necessary more than one such hearing) only where—

(i)   the court anticipates a guilty plea,

(ii)   it is necessary to conduct such a hearing in order to give directions for an effective trial, or

(iii)   such a hearing is required to set ground rules for the conduct of the questioning of a witness or defendant.

(2)   At a preparation for trial hearing the court must give directions for an effective trial.

(3)   At a preparation for trial hearing, if the defendant is present—

(a)   the court must satisfy itself that there has been explained to the defendant, in terms the defendant can understand (with help, if necessary), that the defendant will receive credit for a guilty plea;

(b)   the court may explain, in terms the defendant can understand (with help, if necessary), that the defendant may ask the court for an indication of whether a custodial or non-custodial sentence is more likely in the event of a guilty plea there and then, but the court need not give such an indication;

(c)   whether the court gives such an explanation or not the defendant may ask the court for such an indication;

(d)   if the defendant asks the court for such an indication, the prosecutor must—

(i)   provide any information relevant to sentence not yet served but which is available there and then, and

(ii)   identify any other matter relevant to sentence, including the legislation applicable, any sentencing guidelines or guideline cases and aggravating and mitigating factors;

(e)   the court must take the defendant's plea or if no plea can be taken then find out whether the defendant is likely to plead guilty or not guilty; and

(f) unless the defendant pleads guilty, the court must satisfy itself that there has been explained to the defendant, in terms the defendant can understand (with help, if necessary), that at the trial—

(i) the defendant will have the right to give evidence after the court has heard the prosecution case,

(ii) if the defendant does not attend, the trial is likely to take place in the defendant's absence, and

(iii) where the defendant is released on bail, failure to attend court when required is an offence for which the defendant may be arrested and punished and bail may be withdrawn.

(4) A pre-trial case management hearing must be in public, as a general rule, but all or part of the hearing may be in private if the court so directs.

[Note. Under sections 8A and 8B of the Magistrates' Courts Act 1980[33], a pre-trial ruling about the admissibility of evidence or any other question of law is binding unless it later appears to the court in the interests of justice to discharge or vary that ruling.]

R3.17 Place of magistrates' court trial

3.17 The court officer must arrange for a magistrates' court trial to take place in a courtroom provided by the Lord Chancellor, unless—

(a) the court otherwise directs; or

(b) the case is one to which rule 24.9 (Single justice procedure: special rules) applies.

[Note. See section 3 of the Courts Act 2003[34] and section 16A of the Magistrates' Courts Act 1980[35].

In some circumstances the court may conduct all or part of the hearing outside a courtroom. The members of the court may discuss the verdict and sentence outside the courtroom.]

R3.18 Use of Welsh language at magistrates' court trial

3.18 Where a magistrates' court trial takes place in Wales—

(a) any party or witness may use the Welsh language; and

(b) if practicable, at least one member of the court must be Welsh-speaking.

[Note. See section 3 of the Courts Act 2003[36] and section 22 of the Welsh Language Act 1993[37].]

Preparation for trial in the Crown Court

R3.19 Service of prosecution evidence

3.19 (1) This rule applies where—

(a) a magistrates' court sends the defendant to the Crown Court for trial; and

(b) the prosecutor serves on the defendant copies of the documents containing the evidence on which the prosecution case relies.

(2) The prosecutor must at the same time serve copies of those documents on the Crown Court officer.

[Note. See the Crime and Disorder Act 1998 (Service of Prosecution Evidence) Regulations 2005[38]. The time for service of the prosecution evidence is prescribed by regulation 2. It is—

(a) not more than 50 days after sending for trial, where the defendant is in custody; and

(b) not more than 70 days after sending for trial, where the defendant is on bail.]

R3.20 Application to dismiss offence sent for Crown Court trial

3.20 (1) This rule applies where a defendant wants the Crown Court to dismiss an offence sent for trial there.

(2) The defendant must—

(a) apply in writing—

(i) not more than 20 business days after service of the prosecution evidence, and

---

[33] 1980 c. 43; section 8A was inserted by section 45 of, and Schedule 3 to, the Courts Act 2003 (c. 39) and amended by SI 2006/2493 and paragraphs 12 and 14 of Schedule 5 to the Legal Aid, Sentencing and Punishment of Offenders Act 2012 (c. 10). Section 8B was inserted by section 45 of, and Schedule 3 to, the Courts Act 2003 (c. 39) and amended by paragraph 51 of Schedule 3, and Part 4 of Schedule 37, to the Criminal Justice Act 2003 (c. 44).

[34] 2003 c. 39.

[35] 1980 c. 43; section 16A was inserted by section 48 of the Criminal Justice and Courts Act 2015 (c. 2).

[36] 2003 c. 39.

[37] 1993 c. 38.

[38] S.I. 2005/902; amended by S.I. 2012/1345.

  (ii) before the defendant's arraignment under rule 3.32 (Arraigning the defendant on the indictment);
  (b) serve the application on—
   (i) the Crown Court officer, and
   (ii) each other party; and
  (c) in the application—
   (i) explain why the prosecution evidence would not be sufficient for the defendant to be properly convicted,
   (ii) ask for a hearing, if the defendant wants one, and explain why it is needed,
   (iii) identify any witness whom the defendant wants to call to give evidence in person, with an indication of what evidence the witness can give,
   (iv) identify any material already served that the defendant thinks the court will need to determine the application, and
   (v) include any material not already served on which the defendant relies.
 (3) A prosecutor who opposes the application must—
  (a) serve notice of opposition, not more than 10 business days after service of the defendant's notice, on—
   (i) the Crown Court officer, and
   (ii) each other party; and
  (b) in the notice of opposition—
   (i) explain the grounds of opposition,
   (ii) ask for a hearing, if the prosecutor wants one, and explain why it is needed,
   (iii) identify any witness whom the prosecutor wants to call to give evidence in person, with an indication of what evidence the witness can give,
   (iv) identify any material already served that the prosecutor thinks the court will need to determine the application, and
   (v) include any material not already served on which the prosecutor relies.
 (4) The court may determine an application under this rule—
  (a) at a hearing, in public or in private, or without a hearing; and
  (b) in the absence of—
   (i) the defendant who made the application, and
   (ii) the prosecutor, if the prosecutor has had at least 10 business days in which to serve notice opposing the application.
 (5) The court may—
  (a) shorten or extend (even after it has expired) a time limit under this rule; and
  (b) allow a witness to give evidence in person even if that witness was not identified in the defendant's application or in the prosecutor's notice.

[Note. Under paragraph 2 of Schedule 3 to the Crime and Disorder Act 1998[39], on an application by the defendant the Crown Court must dismiss an offence charged if it appears to the court that the evidence would not be sufficient for the applicant to be properly convicted.]

Pre-trial hearings in the Crown Court: general rules   R3.21

3.21 (1) The Crown Court—
  (a) may, and in some cases must, conduct a preparatory hearing where rule 3.22 applies;
  (b) must conduct a plea and trial preparation hearing; and
  (c) may conduct a further pre-trial case management hearing (and if necessary more than one such hearing) only where—
   (i) the court anticipates a guilty plea,
   (ii) it is necessary to conduct such a hearing in order to give directions for an effective trial, or
   (iii) such a hearing is required to set ground rules for the conduct of the questioning of a witness or defendant.
 (2) At the plea and trial preparation hearing the court must—
  (a) satisfy itself that there has been explained to the defendant, in terms the defendant can understand (with help, if necessary), that the defendant will receive credit for a guilty plea;
  (b) take the defendant's plea in accordance with rule 3.24 (Arraigning the defendant on the indictment) or if no plea can be taken then find out whether the defendant is likely to plead guilty or not guilty;

---

[39] 1998 c. 37; paragraph 2 of Schedule 3 was amended by paragraphs 15 and 20 of Schedule 3, paragraph 73 of Schedule 36 and Part 4 of Schedule 37 to the Criminal Justice Act 2003 (c. 44) and SI 2004/2035.

(c) unless the defendant pleads guilty, satisfy itself that there has been explained to the defendant, in terms the defendant can understand (with help, if necessary), that at the trial—

    (i) the defendant will have the right to give evidence after the court has heard the prosecution case,

    (ii) if the defendant does not attend, the trial may take place in the defendant's absence,

    (iii) if the trial takes place in the defendant's absence, the judge may inform the jury of the reason for that absence, and

    (iv) where the defendant is released on bail, failure to attend court when required is an offence for which the defendant may be arrested and punished and bail may be withdrawn; and

(d) give directions for an effective trial.

(3) A pre-trial case management hearing—

    (a) must be in public, as a general rule, but all or part of the hearing may be in private if the court so directs; and

    (b) must be recorded, in accordance with rule 5.5 (Recording and transcription of proceedings in the Crown Court).

(4) Where the court determines a pre-trial application in private, it must announce its decision in public.

[Note. See also the general rules in the first section of this Part (rules 3.1 to 3.15) and the other rules in this section.

The Practice Direction lists the circumstances in which a further pre-trial case management hearing is likely to be needed in order to give directions for an effective trial.

There are rules relevant to applications which may be made at a pre-trial hearing in Part 6 (Reporting, etc. restrictions), Part 14 (Bail and custody time limits), Part 15 (Disclosure), Part 17 (Witness summonses, warrants and orders), Part 18 (Measures to assist a witness or defendant to give evidence), Part 19 (Expert evidence), Part 20 (Hearsay evidence), Part 21 (Evidence of bad character), Part 22 (Evidence of a complainant's previous sexual behaviour) and Part 23 (Restriction on cross-examination by a defendant).

On an application to which Part 14 (Bail and custody time limits) applies, rule 14.2 (exercise of court's powers under that Part) may require the defendant's presence, which may be by live link. Where rule 14.10 applies (Consideration of bail in a murder case), the court officer must arrange for the Crown Court to consider bail within 2 business days of the first hearing in the magistrates' court.

Under section 40 of the Criminal Procedure and Investigations Act 1996[40], a pre-trial ruling about the admissibility of evidence or any other question of law is binding unless it later appears to the court in the interests of justice to discharge or vary that ruling.]

R3.22 **Preparatory hearing**

3.22 (1) This rule applies where the Crown Court—

    (a) can order a preparatory hearing, under—

        (i) section 7 of the Criminal Justice Act 1987[41] (cases of serious or complex fraud), or

        (ii) section 29 of the Criminal Procedure and Investigations Act 1996[42] (other complex, serious or lengthy cases);

    (b) must order such a hearing, to determine an application for a trial without a jury, under—

        (i) section 44 of the Criminal Justice Act 2003[43] (danger of jury tampering), or

        (ii) section 17 of the Domestic Violence, Crime and Victims Act 2004[44] (trial of sample counts by jury, and others by judge alone); and

    (c) must order such a hearing, under section 29 of the 1996 Act, where section 29(1B) or (1C) applies (cases in which a terrorism offence is charged, or other serious cases with a terrorist connection).

(2) The court may decide whether to order a preparatory hearing—

    (a) on an application or on its own initiative;

    (b) at a hearing (in public or in private), or without a hearing; and

---

[40] 1996 c. 25.

[41] 1987 c. 38; section 7 is amended by paragraph 30 of Schedule 9 to the Criminal Justice and Public Order Act 1994 (c. 33), sections 72 and 80 of, paragraph 2 of Schedule 3 to, and Schedule 5 to, the Criminal Procedure and Investigations Act 1996 (c. 25) and sections 45 and 310 of, and paragraphs 52 and 53 of Schedule 36 to, the Criminal Justice Act 2003 (c. 44).

[42] 1996 c. 25; section 29 is amended by sections 45, 309 and 310 of, and paragraphs 65 and 66 of Schedule 36 to, the Criminal Justice Act 2003 (c. 44) and section 16 of the Terrorism Act 2006 (c. 11).

[43] 2003 c. 44.

[44] 2004 c. 28.

(c) in a party's absence, if that party—
    (i)   applied for the order, or
    (ii) has had at least 10 business days in which to make representations.

[Note. See also section 45(2) of the Criminal Justice Act 2003 and section 18(1) of the Domestic Violence, Crime and Victims Act 2004.

At a preparatory hearing, the court may—

    (a) require the prosecution to set out its case in a written statement, to arrange its evidence in a form that will be easiest for the jury (if there is one) to understand, to prepare a list of agreed facts, and to amend the case statement following representations from the defence (section 9(4) of the 1987 Act, section 31(4) of the 1996 Act); and
    (b) require the defence to give notice of any objection to the prosecution case statement, and to give notice stating the extent of agreement with the prosecution as to documents and other matters and the reason for any disagreement (section 9(5) of the 1987 Act, section 31(6), (7), (9) of the 1996 Act).

Under section 10 of the 1987 Act[45], and under section 34 of the 1996 Act[46], if either party later departs from the case or objections disclosed by that party, then the court, or another party, may comment on that, and the court may draw such inferences as appear proper.]

Application for preparatory hearing

R3.23

3.23 (1) A party who wants the court to order a preparatory hearing must—
    (a) apply in writing—
        (i)   as soon as reasonably practicable, and in any event
        (ii) not more than 10 business days after the defendant pleads not guilty; and
    (b) serve the application on—
        (i)   the court officer, and
        (ii) each other party.
    (2) The applicant must—
    (a) if relevant, explain what legislation requires the court to order a preparatory hearing; or
    (b) explain—
        (i)   what makes the case complex or serious, or makes the trial likely to be long,
        (ii) why a substantial benefit will accrue from a preparatory hearing, and
        (iii) why the court's ordinary powers of case management are not adequate.
    (3) A prosecutor who wants the court to order a trial without a jury must explain—
    (a) where the prosecutor alleges a danger of jury tampering—
        (i)   what evidence there is of a real and present danger that jury tampering would take place,
        (ii) what steps, if any, reasonably might be taken to prevent jury tampering, and
        (iii) why, notwithstanding such steps, the likelihood of jury tampering is so substantial as to make it necessary in the interests of justice to order such a trial; or
    (b) where the prosecutor proposes trial without a jury on some counts on the indictment—
        (i)   why a trial by jury involving all the counts would be impracticable,
        (ii) how the counts proposed for jury trial can be regarded as samples of the others, and
        (iii) why it would be in the interests of justice to order such a trial.

Application for non-jury trial containing information withheld from a defendant

R3.24

3.24 (1) This rule applies where—
    (a) the prosecutor applies for an order for a trial without a jury because of a danger of jury tampering; and
    (b) the application includes information that the prosecutor thinks ought not be revealed to a defendant.
    (2) The prosecutor must—
    (a) omit that information from the part of the application that is served on that defendant;
    (b) mark the other part to show that, unless the court otherwise directs, it is only for the court; and
    (c) in that other part, explain why the prosecutor has withheld that information from that defendant.
    (3) The hearing of an application to which this rule applies—
    (a) must be in private, unless the court otherwise directs; and

Criminal Procedure Rules

(b) if the court so directs, may be, wholly or in part, in the absence of a defendant from whom information has been withheld.

(4) At the hearing of an application to which this rule applies—

    (a) the general rule is that the court will receive, in the following sequence—

        (i) representations first by the prosecutor and then by each defendant, in all the parties' presence, and then

        (ii) further representations by the prosecutor, in the absence of a defendant from whom information has been withheld; but

    (b) the court may direct other arrangements for the hearing.

(5) Where, on an application to which this rule applies, the court orders a trial without a jury—

    (a) the general rule is that the trial will be before a judge other than the judge who made the order; but

    (b) the court may direct other arrangements.

R3.25   Representations in response to application for preparatory hearing

3.25 (1) This rule applies where a party wants to make representations about—

    (a) an application for a preparatory hearing;

    (b) an application for a trial without a jury.

(2) Such a party must—

    (a) serve the representations on—

        (i) the court officer, and

        (ii) each other party;

    (b) do so not more than 10 business days after service of the application; and

    (c) ask for a hearing, if that party wants one, and explain why it is needed.

(3) Where representations include information that the person making them thinks ought not to be revealed to another party, that person must—

    (a) omit that information from the representations served on that other party;

    (b) mark the information to show that, unless the court otherwise directs, it is only for the court; and

    (c) with that information include an explanation of why it has been withheld from that other party.

(4) Representations against an application for an order must explain why the conditions for making it are not met.

R3.26   Commencement of preparatory hearing

3.26 At the beginning of a preparatory hearing, the court must—

    (a) announce that it is such a hearing; and

    (b) take the defendant's plea under rule 3.32 (Arraigning the defendant on the indictment), unless already done.

[Note. See section 8 of the Criminal Justice Act 1987[47] and section 30 of the Criminal Procedure and Investigations Act 1996[48].]

R3.27   Defence trial advocate

3.27 (1) The defendant must notify the court officer of the identity of the intended defence trial advocate—

    (a) as soon as practicable, and in any event no later than the day of the plea and trial preparation hearing; and

    (b) in writing, or orally at that hearing.

(2) The defendant must notify the court officer in writing of any change in the identity of the intended defence trial advocate as soon as practicable, and in any event not more than 5 business days after that change.

R3.28   Application to stay case for abuse of process

3.28 (1) This rule applies where a defendant wants the Crown Court to stay the case on the grounds that the proceedings are an abuse of the court, or otherwise unfair.

(2) Such a defendant must—

    (a) apply in writing—

        (i) as soon as practicable after becoming aware of the grounds for doing so,

        (ii) at a pre-trial hearing, unless the grounds for the application do not arise until trial, and

---

[47] 1987 c. 38.
[48] 1996 c. 25.

(iii) in any event, before the defendant pleads guilty or the jury (if there is one) retires to consider its verdict at trial;

   (b) serve the application on—
      (i) the court officer, and
      (ii) each other party; and

   (c) in the application—
      (i) explain the grounds on which it is made,
      (ii) include, attach or identify all supporting material,
      (iii) specify relevant events, dates and propositions of law, and
      (iv) identify any witness the applicant wants to call to give evidence in person.

(3) A party who wants to make representations in response to the application must serve the representations on—
   (a) the court officer; and
   (b) each other party,

not more than 10 business days after service of the application.

Application for joint or separate trials, etc.   **R3.29**

3.29 (1) This rule applies where a party wants the Crown Court to order—
   (a) the joint trial of—
      (i) offences charged by separate indictments, or
      (ii) defendants charged in separate indictments;
   (b) separate trials of offences charged by the same indictment;
   (c) separate trials of defendants charged in the same indictment; or
   (d) the deletion of a count from an indictment.

(2) Such a party must—
   (a) apply in writing—
      (i) as soon as practicable after becoming aware of the grounds for doing so, and
      (ii) before the trial begins, unless the grounds for the application do not arise until trial;
   (b) serve the application on—
      (i) the court officer, and
      (ii) each other party; and
   (c) in the application—
      (i) specify the order proposed, and
      (ii) explain why it should be made.

(3) A party who wants to make representations in response to the application must serve the representations on—
   (a) the court officer; and
   (b) each other party,
not more than 10 business days after service of the application.

(4) Where the same indictment charges more than one offence, the court may exercise its power to order separate trials of those offences if of the opinion that—
   (a) the defendant otherwise may be prejudiced or embarrassed in his or her defence (for example, where the offences to be tried together are neither founded on the same facts nor form or are part of a series of offences of the same or a similar character); or
   (b) for any other reason it is desirable that the defendant should be tried separately for any one or more of those offences.

[Note. See section 5 of the Indictments Act 1915[49]. Rule 10.2 (The indictment: general rules) governs the form and content of an indictment.

Any issue arising from a decision under this rule may be subject to appeal to the Court of Appeal. Part 37 (Appeal to the Court of Appeal against ruling at preparatory hearing), Part 38 (Appeal to the Court of Appeal against ruling adverse to prosecution) and Part 39 (Appeal to the Court of Appeal about conviction or sentence) each contains relevant rules. The powers of the Court of Appeal on an appeal to which Part 39 applies are set out in sections 2, 3 and 7 of the Criminal Appeal Act 1968[50].]

[49] 1915 c. 90; section 5 was amended by section 12 of, and paragraph 8 of Schedule 2 to, the Bail Act 1976 (c. 63), section 31 of, and Schedule 2 to, the Prosecution of Offences Act 1985 (c. 23) and section 331 of, and paragraph 40 of Schedule 36 to, the Criminal Justice Act 2003 (c. 44).
[50] 1968 c. 19; section 2 was amended by section 2 of the Criminal Appeal Act 1995 (c. 35). Section 3 was amended by section 316 of the Criminal Justice Act 2003 (c. 44). Section 7 was amended by sections 43 and 170 of, and Schedule 16 to, the Criminal Justice Act 1988 (c. 33) and paragraph 44 of Schedule 36 to the Criminal Justice Act 2003 (c. 44).

R3.30 **Order for joint or separate trials, or amendment of the indictment**

3.30 (1) This rule applies where the Crown Court makes an order—

   (a) on an application under rule 3.29 applies (Application for joint or separate trials, etc.); or

   (b) amending an indictment in any other respect.

(2) Unless the court otherwise directs, the court officer must endorse any paper copy of each affected indictment made for the court with—

   (a) a note of the court's order; and

   (b) the date of that order.

R3.31 **Application for indication of sentence**

3.31 (1) This rule applies where a defendant wants the Crown Court to give an indication of the maximum sentence that would be passed if a guilty plea were entered when the indication is sought.

(2) Such a defendant must—

   (a) apply in writing as soon as practicable; and

   (b) serve the application on—

      (i) the court officer, and

      (ii) the prosecutor.

(3) The application must—

   (a) specify—

      (i) the offence or offences to which it would be a guilty plea, and

      (ii) the facts on the basis of which that plea would be entered; and

   (b) include the prosecutor's agreement to, or representations on, that proposed basis of plea.

(4) The prosecutor must—

   (a) provide information relevant to sentence, including—

      (i) any previous conviction of the defendant, and the circumstances where relevant, and

      (ii) any statement of the effect of the offence on the victim, the victim's family or others; and

   (b) identify any other matter relevant to sentence, including—

      (i) the legislation applicable,

      (ii) any sentencing guidelines, or guideline cases, and

      (iii) aggravating and mitigating factors.

(5) The hearing of the application—

   (a) may take place in the absence of any other defendant; and

   (b) must be attended by—

      (i) the applicant defendant's legal representatives (if any), and

      (ii) the prosecution advocate.

R3.32 **Arraigning the defendant**

3.32 (1) In order to take the defendant's plea, the Crown Court must—

   (a) if more than one indictment has been preferred or proposed, or more than one draft indictment has been presented where rule 10.3 applies—

      (i) identify the indictment or indictments that the prosecutor wants to be read to or placed before the defendant under this rule, and

      (ii) identify any draft indictment, indictment or count in an indictment on which the prosecutor does not want to proceed;

   (b) obtain the prosecutor's confirmation, in writing or orally—

      (i) that each indictment (or draft indictment, as the case may be) that the prosecutor wants to be read to or placed before the defendant sets out a statement of each offence that the prosecutor wants the court to try and such particulars of the conduct constituting the commission of each such offence as the prosecutor relies upon to make clear what is alleged, and

      (ii) of the order in which the prosecutor wants the defendants' names to be listed in each indictment, if the prosecutor proposes that more than one defendant should be tried at the same time;

   (c) ensure that the defendant is correctly identified by each indictment or draft indictment that the prosecutor wants to be read to or placed before the defendant;

   (d) satisfy itself that each allegation has been explained to the defendant, in terms the defendant can understand (with help, if necessary); and

   (e) in respect of each count on which the prosecutor wants to proceed—

      (i) read the count aloud to the defendant, or arrange for it to be read aloud or placed before the defendant in writing,

      (ii) ask whether the defendant pleads guilty or not guilty to the offence charged by that count, and

      (iii) take the defendant's plea.

(2) Where a count is read which is substantially the same as one already read aloud, then only the materially different details need be read aloud.

(3) Where a count is placed before the defendant in writing, the court must summarise its gist aloud.

(4) In respect of each count in an indictment read to or placed before the defendant—

    (a) if the defendant declines to enter a plea, the court must treat that as a not guilty plea unless rule 25.10 applies (Defendant unfit to plead);

    (b) if the defendant pleads not guilty to the offence charged by that count but guilty to another offence of which the court could convict on that count—

        (i) if the prosecutor and the court accept that plea, the court must treat the plea as one of guilty of that other offence, but

        (ii) otherwise, the court must treat the plea as one of not guilty; and

    (c) if the defendant pleads a previous acquittal or conviction of the offence charged by that count—

        (i) the defendant must identify that acquittal or conviction in writing, explaining the basis of that plea, and

        (ii) the court must exercise its power to decide whether that plea disposes of that count.

(5) In a case in which a magistrates' court sends the defendant for trial, the Crown Court must take the defendant's plea—

    (a) not less than 10 business days after the date on which that sending takes place, unless the parties otherwise agree; and

    (b) more than 80 business days after that date, unless the court otherwise directs (either before or after that period expires).

(6) Unless the court otherwise directs, no further proceedings may be taken on a draft indictment, indictment or count in an indictment on which under this rule the prosecutor chooses not to proceed.

[Note. See section 6 of the Criminal Law Act 1967[51], section 77 of the Senior Courts Act 1981[52] and section 122 of the Criminal Justice Act 1988[53]. Part 10 contains rules about the content and service of indictments: see in particular rule 10.2 (The indictment: general rules).

Under section 6(2) of the 1967 Act, on an indictment for murder a defendant may instead be convicted of manslaughter or another offence specified by that provision. Under section 6(3) of that Act, on an indictment for an offence other than murder or treason a defendant may instead be convicted of another offence if—

    (a) the allegation in the indictment amounts to or includes an allegation of that other offence; and

    (b) the Crown Court has power to convict and sentence for that other offence.]

Place of Crown Court trial   **R3.33**

3.33 (1) Unless the court otherwise directs, the court officer must arrange for a Crown Court trial to take place in a courtroom provided by the Lord Chancellor.

    (2) The court officer must arrange for the court and the jury (if there is one) to view any place required by the court.

[Note. See section 3 of the Courts Act 2003[54] and section 14 of the Juries Act 1974[55].

In some circumstances the court may conduct all or part of the hearing outside a courtroom.]

Use of Welsh language at Crown Court trial   **R3.34**

3.34 Where a Crown Court trial will take place in Wales and a participant wishes to use the Welsh language—

    (a) that participant must serve notice on the court officer, or arrange for such a notice to be served on that participant's behalf—

        (i) at or before the plea and trial preparation hearing, or

        (ii) in accordance with any direction given by the court; and

    (b) if such a notice is served, the court officer must arrange for an interpreter to attend.

---

[51] 1967 c. 58; section 6 was amended by paragraph 41 of Schedule 36 to the Criminal Justice Act 2003 (c. 44) and section 11 of the Domestic Violence, Crime and Victims Act 2004 (c. 28).

[52] 1981 c. 54; section 77 was amended by section 15 of, and paragraph 11 of Schedule 2 to, the Criminal Justice Act 1987 (c. 38), section 168 of, and paragraph 18 of Schedule 9 to, the Criminal Justice and Public Order Act 1994 (c. 33), section 41 of, and paragraph 54 of Schedule 3 to, the Criminal Justice Act 2003 (c. 44) and article 3 of, and paragraphs 11 and 13 of the Schedule to, SI 2004/2035. It is further amended by section 31 of, and paragraph 11 of Schedule 1 and Schedule 2 to, the Prosecution of Offences Act 1985 (c. 23) with effect from a date to be appointed.

[53] 1988 c. 33.

[54] 2003 c. 39.

[55] 1974 c. 23; section 14 was amended by paragraph 173 of Schedule 8 to the Courts Act 2003 (c. 39).

Criminal Procedure Rules

[Note. See section 22 of the Welsh Language Act 1993[56].]

Other provisions affecting case management

Case management may be affected by the following other rules and legislation:

Criminal Procedure Rules
Part 8 Initial details of the prosecution case
Part 9 Allocation and sending for trial
Part 10 The indictment
Part 15 Disclosure
Parts 16 – 23: the rules that deal with evidence
Part 24 Trial and sentence in a magistrates' court
Part 25 Trial and sentence in the Crown Court

Regulations
The Prosecution of Offences (Custody Time Limits) Regulations 1987[57]
The Crime and Disorder Act 1998 (Service of Prosecution Evidence) Regulations 2005[58]
The Criminal Procedure and Investigations Act 1996 (Defence Disclosure Time Limits) Regulations 2011[59]

Acts of Parliament
Sections 10 and 18, Magistrates' Courts Act 1980[60] : powers to adjourn hearings
Sections 128 and 129, Magistrates' Courts Act 1980[61] : remand in custody by magistrates' courts
Sections 19 and 24A, Magistrates' Courts Act 1980[62] and sections 51 and 51A, Crime and Disorder Act 1998[63] : allocation and sending for trial
Section 2, Administration of Justice (Miscellaneous Provisions) Act 1933[64] : procedural conditions for trial in the Crown Court
Sections 8A and 8B, Magistrates' Courts Act 1980[65] : pre-trial hearings in magistrates' courts

---

[56] 1993 c. 38.
[57] S.I. 1987/299; amended by sections 71 and 80 of, and paragraph 8 of Schedule 5 to, the Criminal Procedure and Investigations Act 1996 (c. 25) and S.I. 1989/767, 1991/1515, 1995/555, 1999/2744, 2000/3284, 2012/1344.
[58] S.I. 2005/902; amended by S.I. 2012/1345.
[59] S.I. 2011/209.
[60] 1980 c. 43; section 10 was amended by section 59 of, and paragraph 1 of Schedule 9 to, the Criminal Justice Act 1982 (c. 48), section 68 of, and paragraph 6 of Schedule 8 to, the Criminal Justice Act 1991 (c. 53) and section 47 of the Crime and Disorder Act 1998 (c. 37). Section 18 was amended by section 59 of, and paragraph 1 of Schedule 9 to, the Criminal Justice Act 1982 (c. 48), section 68 of, and paragraph 6 of Schedule 8 to, the Criminal Justice Act 1991 (c. 53), section 49 of the Criminal Procedure and Investigations Act 1996 (c. 25), and paragraphs 1 and 4 of Schedule 3 to the Criminal Justice Act 2003 (c. 44).
[61] 1980 c. 43; section 128 was amended by section 59 to, and paragraphs 2, 3 and 4 of Schedule 9 to, the Criminal Justice Act 1982 (c. 48), section 48 of the Police and Criminal Evidence Act 1984 (c. 60), section 170(1) of, and paragraphs 65 and 69 of Schedule 15 to, the Criminal Justice Act 1988 (c. 33), section 125(3) of, and paragraph 25 of Schedule 18 to, the Courts and Legal Services Act 1990 (c. 41), sections 49, 52 and 80 of, and Schedule 5 to, the Criminal Procedure and Investigations Act 1996 (c. 25), paragraph 75 of Schedule 9 to the Powers of Criminal Courts (Sentencing) Act 2000 (c. 6) and paragraph 51 of Schedule 3 and Part 4 of Schedule 37 to the Criminal Justice Act 2003 (c. 44). It is modified by section 91(5) of the Legal Aid, Sentencing and Punishment of Offenders Act 2012 (c. 10). Section 129 was amended by paragraph 51 of Schedule 3 to the Criminal Justice Act 2003 (c. 44).
[62] 1980 c. 43; section 19 was substituted by paragraphs 1 and 5 of Schedule 3 to the Criminal Justice Act 2003 (c. 44) and amended by sections 144, 177 and 178 of, and paragraph 4 of Schedule 17, paragraph 80 of Schedule 21 and Part 5 of Schedule 23 to, the Coroners and Justice Act 2009 (c. 25).
[63] 1998 c. 37; section 51 was substituted by paragraphs 15 and 18 of Schedule 3 to the Criminal Justice Act 2003 (c. 44) and amended by section 59 of, and paragraph 1 of Schedule 11 to, the Constitutional Reform Act 2005 (c. 4). Section 51A was inserted by paragraphs 15 and 18 of Schedule 3 to the Criminal Justice Act 2003 (c. 44) and amended by section 49 of, and paragraph 5 of Schedule 1 to, the Violent Crime Reduction Act 2006 (c. 38) and paragraph 6 of Schedule 21 to the Legal Aid, Sentencing and Punishment of Offenders Act 2012 (c. 10).
[64] 1933 c. 36; section 2 was amended by Part IV of Schedule 11 to, the Courts Act 1971 (c. 23), Schedule 5 to, the Senior Courts Act 1981 (c. 54), Schedule 2 to the Prosecution of Offences Act 1985 (c. 23), paragraph 1 of Schedule 2 to the Criminal Justice Act 1987 (c. 38), paragraph 10 of Schedule 15 to the Criminal Justice Act 1988 (c. 33), paragraph 8 of Schedule 6 to the Criminal Justice Act 1991 (c. 53), Schedule 1 to the Statute Law (Repeals) Act 1993, paragraph 17 of Schedule 1 to the Criminal Procedure and Investigations Act 1996 (c. 25), paragraph 5 of Schedule 8 to the Crime and Disorder Act 1998 (c. 37), paragraph 34 of Schedule 3 and Part 4 of Schedule 37 to the Criminal Justice Act 2003 (c. 44), paragraph 1 of the Schedule to S.I. 2004/2035, section 12 of, and paragraph 7 of Schedule 1 to, the Constitutional Reform Act 2005 (c. 4), sections 116 and 178 of, and Part 3 of Schedule 23 to, the Coroners and Justice Act 2009 (c. 25), paragraph 32 of Schedule 17 to the Crime and Courts Act 2013 (c. 22) and section 82 of the Deregulation Act 2015 (c. 20).
[65] 1980 c. 43; section 8A was inserted by section 45 of, and Schedule 3 to, the Courts Act 2003 (c. 39) and amended by SI 2006/2493 and paragraphs 12 and 14 of Schedule 5 to the Legal Aid, Sentencing and Punishment of Offenders Act 2012 (c. 10). Section 8B was inserted by section 45 of, and Schedule 3 to, the Courts Act 2003 (c. 39) and amended by paragraph 51 of Schedule 3, and Part 4 of Schedule 37, to the Criminal Justice Act 2003 (c. 44).

Section 7, Criminal Justice Act 1987[66]; Parts III and IV, Criminal Procedure and Investigations Act 1996: pre-trial and preparatory hearings in the Crown Court
Section 9, Criminal Justice Act 1967[67] : proof by written witness statement
Part 1, Criminal Procedure and Investigations Act 1996[68] : disclosure.]

Live Links

Live link direction: exercise of court's powers   R3.35

3.35   (1)   The court may exercise its power to give, vary or rescind a live link direction under sections 51 and 52 of the Criminal Justice Act 2003[69] —

    (a)   at a hearing, in public or in private, or without a hearing; and

    (b)   on an application under rule 3.36 (Content of application for a live link direction) or on its own initiative.

  (2)   Whether it acts on an application or on its own initiative, the court must not give, vary or rescind a live link direction unless—

    (a)   the court is satisfied that it is in the interests of justice to do so; and

    (b)   each party and (if applicable) any representative of the youth offending team whose functions are exercisable in relation to a defendant—

      (i)   is present, or

      (ii)   has had an opportunity to make representations.

  (3)   In deciding whether to give a live link direction the court must consider—

    (a)   any guidance given by the Lord Chief Justice under section 51(5)(a) of the Criminal Justice Act 2003; and

    (b)   all the circumstances of the case.

  (4)   Those circumstances include in particular—

    (a)   the availability of the proposed participant by live link;

    (b)   any potential need for that person to attend in person instead of by live link;

    (c)   any views which that person may have expressed;

    (d)   the suitability of the facilities at the place where that person would take part by live link if the direction were given;

    (e)   that person's ability to take part effectively if the direction were given (and see paragraph (5));

    (f)   if the proposed direction is for a person to give evidence by live link—

      (i)   the importance of that person's evidence to the case, and

      (ii)   any potential for the proposed direction to inhibit a party from effectively testing that evidence; and

    (g)   arrangements for members of the public to see and hear proceedings at which a person takes part by live link (and see paragraph (6)).

  (5)   In assessing a person's ability to take part effectively by live link, where that person is a defendant the court must have regard to, among other things—

    (a)   whether that defendant will be represented at the hearing for which the live link is proposed; and

    (b)   what other assistance will be available to that defendant at that hearing (for example, an intermediary).

  (6)   In assessing arrangements for members of the public to see and hear proceedings the court must have regard to, among other things, the terms of any direction under section 85A of the Courts Act 2003[70] (Remote observation and recording of proceedings by direction of the court).

  (7)   Where the court refuses an application to give, vary or rescind a live link direction the court must announce in public its reasons for doing so.

---

[66] 1987 c. 38; section 7 was amended by section 168(1) of, and paragraph 30 of Schedule 9 to, the Criminal Justice and Public Order Act 1994 (c. 33), section 80 of, and paragraph 2 of Schedule 3 and Schedule 5 to, the Criminal Procedure and Investigations Act 1996 (c. 25) and sections 45 and 310 of, and paragraphs 52 and 53 of Schedule 36 to, the Criminal Justice Act 2003 (c. 44). The amendment made by section 45 of the Criminal Justice Act 2003 (c. 44) is in force for certain purposes; for remaining purposes it has effect from a date to be appointed.
[67] 1967 c. 80; section 9 was amended by section 56 of, and paragraph 49 of Schedule 8 to, the Courts Act 1971 (c. 23), section 168 of, and paragraph 6 of Schedule 9 to, the Criminal Justice and Public Order Act 1994 (c. 33), section 69 of the Criminal Procedure and Investigations Act 1996 (c. 25), regulation 9 of, and paragraph 4 of Schedule 5 to, S.I. 2001/1090, paragraph 43 of Schedule 3 and Part 4 of Schedule 37 to the Criminal Justice Act 2003 (c. 44), section 26 of, and paragraph 7 of Schedule 2 to, the Armed Forces Act 2011 (c. 18) and section 80 of the Deregulation Act 2015 (c. 20). It is further amended by section 72 of, and paragraph 55 of Schedule 5 to, the Children and Young Persons Act 1969 (c. 54) and section 65 of, and paragraph 1 of Schedule 4 to, the Courts Act 2003 (c. 39), with effect from dates to be appointed.
[68] 1996 c. 25.
[69] 2003 c. 44; section 51 was substituted by section 200 of, and section 52 was substituted by paragraph 1 of Schedule 20 to, the Police, Crime, Sentencing and Courts Act 2022 (c. 32).
[70] 2003 c. 44; section 85A was inserted by section 198 of the Police, Crime, Sentencing and Courts Act 2022 (c. 32).

[Note. See sections 51, 52, 52A and 53 of the Criminal Justice Act 2003[71].]

R3.36   **Content of application for a live link direction**

3.36   (1)   An applicant for a live link direction under section 51 of the Criminal Justice Act 2003 must—

   (a)   apply in writing as soon as reasonably practicable;
   (b)   serve the application on—
      (i)   the court officer, and
      (ii)   each other party; and
   (c)   ask for a hearing of the application, if the applicant wants one, and explain why it is needed.

   (2)   The application must—

   (a)   specify the hearing or hearings in respect of which the applicant wants the direction to apply;
   (b)   identify each person to whom the applicant wants the direction to apply and specify—
      (i)   each one whom the applicant wants to give evidence by live link, and
      (ii)   each one whom the applicant wants to take part by live link without giving evidence;
   (c)   in respect of each such person, specify the type of live link proposed (either video or audio);
   (d)   unless the court otherwise directs, identify the place where each such person will take part if the direction is given;
   (e)   identify any material circumstances relating to—
      (i)   the availability of the proposed participant by live link,
      (ii)   any potential need for that participant to attend in person, not by live link,
      (iii)   any views which that participant may have expressed,
      (iv)   the suitability of the facilities at the place where that participant would take part by live link if the direction were given,
      (v)   any permission needed from a court or other authority in a place outside the United Kingdom from where, if the direction were given, the participant would take part by live link, and
      (vi)   that participant's ability to take part effectively if the direction were given;
   (f)   if the proposed direction is for a person to give evidence by live link, identify any material circumstances relating to—
      (i)   the importance of that person's evidence to the case, and
      (ii)   any potential for the proposed direction to inhibit a party from effectively testing that evidence;
   (g)   explain why it is in the interests of justice for each proposed participant by live link to take part by those means; and
   (h)   if the applicant wants a witness to be accompanied by another person while giving evidence–
      (i)   name that other person, if possible, and
      (ii)   explain why it is appropriate for that witness to be accompanied, including the witness' own views.

R3.37   **Application to vary or rescind a live link direction**

3.37   (1)   A party who wants the court to vary or rescind a live link direction must—

   (a)   apply in writing, as soon as reasonably practicable after becoming aware of the grounds for doing so; and
   (b)   serve the application on—
      (i)   the court officer, and
      (ii)   each other party.

   (2)   The applicant must—

   (a)   explain what material circumstances have changed since the direction was given;
   (b)   explain why it is in the interests of justice to vary or rescind the direction; and
   (c)   ask for a hearing, if the applicant wants one, and explain why it is needed.

[Note. See section 52 of the Criminal Justice Act 2003.]

R3.38   **Application containing information withheld from another party**

3.38   (1)   This rule applies where—

   (a)   an applicant serves an application for a live link direction, or for its variation or rescission; and

---

[71] 2003 c. 44; section 53 was amended by paragraph 1 of Schedule 20 to the Police, Crime, Sentencing and Courts Act 2022 (c. 32).

(b) the application includes information that the applicant thinks ought not to be revealed to another party.

(2) The applicant must—

    (a) omit that information from the part of the application that is served on that other party;

    (b) mark the other part to show that, unless the court otherwise directs, it is only for the court; and

    (c) in that other part, explain why the applicant has withheld that information from that other party.

(3) Any hearing of an application to which this rule applies—

    (a) must be in private, unless the court otherwise directs; and

    (b) if the court so directs, may be, wholly or in part, in the absence of a party from whom information has been withheld.

(4) At any hearing of an application to which this rule applies—

    (a) the general rule is that the court must consider, in the following sequence—

        (i) representations first by the applicant and then by each other party, in all the parties' presence, and then

        (ii) further representations by the applicant, in the absence of a party from whom information has been withheld; but

    (b) the court may direct other arrangements for the hearing.

Representations in response   R3.39

3.39 (1) This rule applies where a party wants to make representations about an application for a live link direction or for the variation or rescission of such a direction.

(2) Such a party must—

    (a) serve the representations on—

        (i) the court officer, and

        (ii) each other party;

    (b) do so not more than 10 business days after service of the application; and

    (c) ask for a hearing, if that party wants one, and explain why it is needed.

(3) Representations must explain why it is not in the interests of justice for the direction to be given, varied or rescinded, as the case may be.

CRIMINAL PROCEDURE RULES   PART 4   SERVICE OF DOCUMENTS

When this Part applies   R4.1

4.1 (1) The rules in this Part apply to the service of—

    (a) every document in a case to which these Rules apply; and

    (b) any document which other legislation allows or requires to be served in accordance with these Rules.

(2) The rules apply subject to any special rules in other legislation (including other Parts of these Rules) or in the Practice Direction.

(3) In this Part, 'the relevant court office' means—

    (a) in relation to a case in a magistrates' court or in the Crown Court, an office—

        (i) at which that court's business is administered, and

        (ii) the address or electronic address of which is advertised by the Lord Chancellor at the date of service as that at which that type of document must be served;

    (b) in relation to an application to a High Court judge for permission to serve a draft indictment—

        (i) in London, the [King's] Bench Listing Office, Royal Courts of Justice, Strand, London WC2A 2LL,

        (ii) elsewhere, the office at which court staff administer the business of any court then constituted of a High Court judge, and

        (iii) in either case, the electronic address which is advertised by the Lord Chancellor at the date of service as that at which such an application must be served;

    (c) in relation to an extradition appeal case in the High Court—

        (i) the Administrative Court Office, Royal Courts of Justice, Strand, London WC2A 2LL, and

        (ii) the electronic address which is advertised by the Lord Chancellor at the date of service as that at which that type of document must be served; and

    (d) where the recipient is the Registrar of Criminal Appeals—

        (i) the Criminal Appeal Office, Royal Courts of Justice, Strand, London WC2A 2LL, and

(ii) the electronic address which is advertised by the Lord Chancellor at the date of service as that at which that type of document must be served.

[Note. The following provisions allow or require the service of documents in accordance with Criminal Procedure Rules—

(a) *section 243 of the Road Traffic Act 1960[1] (notice requiring identification of driver);*

(b) *section 29(A1) of the Misuse of Drugs Act 1971[2] (notice or other document required by Act to be served);*

(c) *paragraph 8(3) of the Schedule to the Prices Act 1974[3] (notice of intended prosecution);*

(d) *paragraph 10 of Schedule 4 to the Salmon and Freshwater Fisheries Act 1975[4] (surrender of licence to court officer);*

(e) *section 5(1) of the Isle of Man Act 1979[5] (summons or process requiring a person in the Isle of Man to attend a criminal court in England and Wales);*

(f) *section 82(5F) of the Magistrates' Courts Act 1980[6] (notice of hearing to consider issue of warrant of commitment);*

(g) *section 72 of the Public Passenger Vehicles Act 1981[7] (notice requiring identification of driver);*

(h) *section 19(4A) of the Video Recordings Act 1984[8] (copy of certificate of examination);*

(i) *section 83(4) of the Weights and Measures Act 1985[9] (notice of intended prosecution for offence);*

(j) *sections 164(10) and 172(7) of the Road Traffic Act 1988[10] (notice requiring verification of date of birth; notice requiring identification of driver);*

(k) *sections 1(1ZA), 12(1) and (3), 16(6), 25(7) and 85(A2) of the Road Traffic Offenders Act 1988[11] (notice of intended prosecution; notice requiring identification of driver; analyst's certificate; notice requiring attendance of analyst; notice requiring verification of date of birth; other specified documents);*

(l) *section 35(7) of the Transport and Works Act 1992[12] (documentary evidence as to breath and other specimens);*

(m) *section 60(11) of, and paragraphs 4(5) and 5(3) of Schedule 5 to, the Powers of Criminal Courts (Sentencing) Act 2000[13] (attendance centre order); and*

(n) *section 27(1) of the Criminal Justice and Police Act 2001[14] (notice in connection with proposed closure of premises).]*

R4.2 Methods of service

4.2 (1) A document may be served by any of the methods described in rules 4.3 to 4.6 (subject to rules 4.7 and 4.10), or in rule 4.8.

(2) Where a document may be served by electronic means under rule 4.6, the general rule is that the person serving it must use that method.

---

[1] 1960 c. 16; section 243 was amended by section 109 of, and paragraph 107 of Schedule 8 to, the Courts Act 2003 (c. 39) and paragraph 1 of Schedule 1 to the Judicial Review and Courts Act 2022 (c. 35).
[2] 1971 c. 38; section 29(A1) was inserted by paragraph 2 of Schedule 1 to the Judicial Review and Courts Act 2022 (c. 35).
[3] 1974 c. 24; paragraph 8(3) of the Schedule was amended by paragraph 3 of Schedule 1 to the Judicial Review and Courts Act 2022 (c. 35).
[4] 1975 c. 51; paragraph 10 of Schedule 4 was amended by section 233 of, and paragraphs 1 and 17 of Schedule 16 to, the Marine and Coastal Access Act 2009 (c. 23), section 90 of, and paragraph 86 of Schedule 13 to, the Access to Justice Act 1999 (c. 22) and paragraph 4 of Schedule 1 to the Judicial Review and Courts Act 2022 (c. 35).
[5] 1979 c. 58; section 5(1) was amended by paragraph 5 of Schedule 1 to the Judicial Review and Courts Act 2022 (c. 35).
[6] 1980 c. 43; section 82(5F) was inserted by section 61 of the Criminal Justice Act 1988 (c. 33) and amended by paragraph 6 of Schedule 1 to the Judicial Review and Courts Act 2022 (c. 35).
[7] 1981 c. 14; section 72 was amended by section 139 of, and Schedule 8 to, the Transport Act 1985 (c. 67) and paragraph 7 of Schedule 1 to the Judicial Review and Courts Act 2022 (c. 35).
[8] 1984 c. 39; section 19(4A) was inserted by paragraph 8 of Schedule 1 to the Judicial Review and Courts Act 2022 (c. 35).
[9] 1985 c. 72; section 83(4) was amended by paragraph 9 of Schedule 1 to the Judicial Review and Courts Act 2022 (c. 35).
[10] 1988 c. 52; sections 164(10) and 172(7) were amended by paragraph 10 of Schedule 1 to the Judicial Review and Courts Act 2022 (c. 35).
[11] 1988 c. 53; sections 1(1ZA) and 85(A2) were inserted, and sections 12(1) and (3), 16(6) and 25(7) were amended, by paragraph 11 of Schedule 1 to the Judicial Review and Courts Act 2022 (c. 35).
[12] 1992 c. 42; section 35(7) was amended by paragraph 12 of Schedule 1 to the Judicial Review and Courts Act 2022 (c. 35).
[13] 2000 c. 6; section 60(11) was amended by S.I. 2001/618 and S.I. 2005/866. Paragraph 5(3) of Schedule 5 was amended by S.I. 2005/866. Those two provisions and paragraph 4(5) of Schedule 5 all were amended by paragraph 13 of Schedule 1 to the Judicial Review and Courts Act 2022 (c. 35).
[14] 2001 c. 16; section 27(1) was amended by paragraph 14 of Schedule 1 to the Judicial Review and Courts Act 2022 (c. 35).

Service by handing over a document

4.3   (1) A document may be served on—
(a) an individual by handing it to him or her;
(b) a corporation by handing it to a person holding a senior position in that corporation;
(c) an individual or corporation who is legally represented in the case by handing it to that legal representative;
(d) the prosecution by handing it to the prosecutor or to the prosecution representative; and
(e) the court officer or the Registrar of Criminal Appeals by handing it to a court officer with authority to accept it at the relevant court office.

(2) If an individual is under 18, a copy of a document served under paragraph (1)(a) must be handed to his or her parent, or another appropriate adult, unless no such person is readily available.

(3) Unless the court otherwise directs, for the purposes of paragraph (1)(c) or (d) (service by handing a document to a party's representative) 'representative' includes an advocate appearing for that party at a hearing.

[Note. Some legislation treats a body that is not a corporation as if it were one for the purposes of rules about service of documents. See for example section 143 of the Adoption and Children Act 2002[15].]

Service by leaving or posting a document

4.4   (1) A document may be served by addressing it to the person to be served and leaving it at the appropriate address for service under this rule, or by sending it to that address by first class post or by the equivalent of first class post.

(2) The address for service under this rule on—
(a) an individual is an address where it is reasonably believed that he or she will receive it;
(b) a corporation is its principal office, and if there is no readily identifiable principal office then any place where it carries on its activities or business;
(c) an individual or corporation who is legally represented in the case is that legal representative's office;
(d) the prosecution is the prosecutor's office;
(e) the court officer or the Registrar of Criminal Appeals is the relevant court office.

[Note. In addition to service in England and Wales for which these rules provide, service outside England and Wales may be allowed under other legislation. See—

(a) section 39 of the Criminal Law Act 1977[16] (service of summons, etc. in Scotland and Northern Ireland);

(b) section 1139(4) of the Companies Act 2006[17] (service of copy summons, etc. on company's registered office in Scotland and Northern Ireland);

(c) sections 3, 4, 4A and 4B of the Crime (International Co-operation) Act 2003[18] (service of summons, etc. outside the United Kingdom) and rules 49.1 and 49.2; and

(d) section 1139(2) of the Companies Act 2006 (service on overseas company).]

Service by document exchange

4.5   (1) This rule applies where—
(a) the person to be served—
(i)   has given a document exchange (DX) box number, and
(ii) has not refused to accept service by DX; or
(b) the person to be served is legally represented in the case and the legal representative has given a DX box number.

(2) A document may be served by—
(a) addressing it to that person or legal representative, as appropriate, at that DX box number; and
(b) leaving it at—
(i)   the document exchange at which the addressee has that DX box number, or
(ii) a document exchange at which the person serving it has a DX box number.

---

[15] 2002 c. 38.
[16] 1977 c. 45; sub-section (1) was substituted by section 331 of, and paragraph 6 of Schedule 36 to, the Criminal Justice Act 2003 (c. 44). Sub-section (3) was amended by section 83 of, and paragraph 79 of Schedule 7 to, the Criminal Justice (Scotland) Act 1980 (c. 62).
[17] 2006 c. 46.
[18] 2003 c. 32; sections 4A and 4B were inserted by section 331 of, and paragraph 16 of Schedule 36 to, the Criminal Justice Act 2003 (c. 44).

(3) Where the person to be served under this rule is the court officer, the address for service is the relevant court office.

R4.6 Service by electronic means

4.6 (1) This rule applies where—
    (a) the person to be served—
        (i) has given an electronic address and has not refused to accept service at that address, or
        (ii) is given access to an electronic address at which a document may be deposited and has not refused to accept service by the deposit of a document at that address; or
    (b) the person to be served is legally represented in the case and the legal representative—
        (i) has given an electronic address, or
        (ii) is given access to an electronic address at which a document may be deposited.

(2) A document may be served—
    (a) by sending it by electronic means to the address which the recipient has given; or
    (b) by depositing it at an address to which the recipient has been given access and—
        (i) in every case, making it possible for the recipient to read the document, or view or listen to its content, as the case may be,
        (ii) unless the court otherwise directs, making it possible for the recipient to make and keep an electronic copy of the document, and
        (iii) notifying the recipient of the deposit of the document (which notice may be given by electronic means).

(3) Where the person to be served under this rule is the court officer—
    (a) the address for service is the relevant court office; and
    (b) if service is by deposit under paragraph (2)(b), notice of that deposit—
        (i) must be given only where arrangements for use of the electronic address advertised under rule 4.1(3) so require, and
        (ii) if so required, must be given in accordance with those arrangements.

(4) Where a document is served under this rule the person serving it need not provide a paper copy as well.

R4.7 Documents that must be served by specified methods

4.7 An application or written statement, and notice, under rule 48.9 alleging contempt of court may be served—
    (a) on an individual, only under rule 4.3(1)(a) (by handing it to him or her); and
    (b) on a corporation, only under rule 4.3(1)(b) (by handing it to a person holding a senior position in that corporation).

R4.8 Service by person in custody

4.8 (1) A person in custody may serve a document by handing it to the custodian addressed to the person to be served.
(2) The custodian must—
    (a) endorse it with the time and date of receipt;
    (b) record its receipt; and
    (c) forward it promptly to the addressee.

R4.9 Service by another method

4.9 (1) The court may allow service of a document by a method—
    (a) other than those described in rules 4.3 to 4.6 and in rule 4.8; and
    (b) other than one specified by rule 4.7, where that rule applies.
(2) An order allowing service by another method must specify—
    (a) the method to be used; and
    (b) the date on which the document will be served.

R4.10 Documents that may not be served on a legal representative

4.10 Unless the court otherwise directs, service on a party's legal representative of any of the following documents is not service of that document on that party—
    (a) a summons, requisition, single justice procedure notice or witness summons;
    (b) notice of an order under section 25 of the Road Traffic Offenders Act 1988[19];

---

[19] 1988 c. 53; section 25 was amended by section 90 of, and paragraphs 140 and 142 of Schedule 13 to, the Access to Justice Act 1999 (c. 22), section 165 of, and paragraph 118 of Schedule 9 to, the Powers of Criminal Courts (Sentencing) Act 2000 (c. 6) and section 109 of, and paragraph 311 of Schedule 8 to, the Courts Act 2003 (c. 39).

(c) a notice of registration under section 71(6) of that Act[20],

(d) notice of a hearing to review the postponement of the issue of a warrant of detention or imprisonment under section 77(6) of the Magistrates' Courts Act 1980[21],

(e) notice under section 86 of that Act[22] of a revised date to attend a means inquiry;

(f) any notice or document served under Part 14 (Bail and custody time limits);

(g) notice under rule 24.15(a) of when and where an adjourned hearing will resume;

(h) notice under rule 28.5(3) of an application to vary or discharge a compensation order;

(i) notice under rule 28.10(2)(c) of the location of the sentencing or enforcing court;

(j) a collection order, or notice requiring payment, served under rule 30.2(a); or

(k) an application or written statement, and notice, under rule 48.9 alleging contempt of court.

Date of service

R4.11

4.11 (1) A document served under rule 4.3 or rule 4.8 is served on the day it is handed over.

(2) Unless something different is shown, a document served on a person by any other method is served—

(a) in the case of a document left at an address, on the next business day after the day on which it was left;

(b) in the case of a document sent by first class post or by the equivalent of first class post, on the second business day after the day on which it was posted or despatched;

(c) in the case of a document served by document exchange, on the second business day after the day on which it was left at a document exchange allowed by rule 4.5;

(d) in the case of a document served by electronic means —

(i) on the day on which it is sent under rule 4.6(2)(a), if that day is a business day and if it is sent by no later than 2.30pm that day (or 4.30pm that day, in an extradition appeal case in the High Court or 5pm that day if it is an application for permission to refer a sentencing case to which Part 41 (Reference to the Court of Appeal of point of law or unduly lenient sentencing) applies),

(ii) on the day on which notice of its deposit is given under rule 4.6(2)(b), if that day is a business day and if that notice is given by no later than 2.30pm that day (or 4.30pm that day, in an extradition appeal case in the High Court, or 5pm that day if it is an application for permission to refer a sentencing case to which Part 41 (Reference to the Court of Appeal of point of law or unduly lenient sentencing) applies),

(iii) on the day of its deposit under rule 4.6(2)(b), if that day is a business day and if under rule 4.6(3)(b) no notice of deposit is required, or

(iv) otherwise, on the next business day after it was sent, deposited or such notice was given; and

(e) in any case, on the day on which the addressee responds to it, if that is earlier.

(3) Unless something different is shown, a document produced by a computer system for dispatch by post is to be taken as having been sent by first class post, or by the equivalent of first class post, to the addressee on the business day after the day on which it was produced.

(4) Where a document is served on or by the court officer or the Registrar of Criminal Appeals, 'business day' does not include a day on which the relevant court office is closed.

Proof of service

R4.12

4.12 The person who serves a document may prove that by signing a certificate explaining how and when it was served.

Court's power to give directions about service

R4.13

4.13 (1) The court may specify the time as well as the date by which a document must be—

(a) served under rule 4.3 (Service by handing over a document) or rule 4.8 (Service by person in custody); or

(b) sent or deposited by electronic means, if it is served under rule 4.6.

(2) The court may treat a document as served if the addressee responds to it even if it was not served in accordance with the rules in this Part.

---

[20] 1988 c. 53; section 71(6) was amended by section 109 of, and paragraph 317 of Schedule 8 to, the Courts Act 2003 (c. 39).

[21] 1980 c. 43; section 77(6) was substituted by section 109 of, and paragraph 218 of Schedule 8 to, the Courts Act 2003 (c. 39).

[22] 1980 c. 43; section 86 was amended by section 51(2) of the Criminal Justice Act 1982 (c. 48) and section 97(3) of the Access to Justice Act 1999 (c. 22).

Criminal Procedure Rules   Part 5   Forms and Court Records

Forms

R5.1   Applications, etc. by forms or electronic means

5.1   (1) This rule applies where a rule, a practice direction or the court requires a person to—
(a) make an application or give a notice;
(b) supply information for the purposes of case management by the court; or
(c) supply information needed for other purposes by the court.
(2) Unless the court otherwise directs, such a person must—
(a) use such electronic arrangements as the court officer may make for that purpose, in accordance with those arrangements; or
(b) if no such arrangements have been made, use the appropriate form issued under the Practice Direction or the Criminal Costs Practice Direction, in accordance with those Directions.

R5.2   Forms in Welsh

5.2   (1) Any Welsh language form issued under the Practice Direction or the Criminal Costs Practice Direction, is for use in connection with proceedings in courts in Wales.
(2) Both a Welsh form and an English form may be contained in the same document.
(3) Where only a Welsh form, or only the corresponding English form, is served—
(a) the following words in Welsh and English must be added:
"Darperir y ddogfen hon yn Gymraeg / Saesneg os bydd arnoch ei heisiau. Dylech wneud cais yn ddi-oed i (swyddog y llys) (rhodder yma'r cyfeiriad)
This document will be provided in Welsh / English if you require it. You should apply immediately to (the court officer) (address)"; and
(b) the court officer, or the person who served the form, must, on request, supply the corresponding form in the other language to the person served.

R5.3   Signature of forms

5.3   (1) This rule applies where a form provides for its signature.
(2) Unless other legislation otherwise requires, or the court otherwise directs, signature may be by any written or electronic authentication of the form by, or with the authority of, the signatory.

[Note. Section 7 of the Electronic Communications Act 2000[1] provides for the use of an electronic signature in an electronic communication.]

Court Records

R5.4   Duty to make records

5.4   (1) For each case, as appropriate, the court officer must record, by such means as the Lord Chancellor directs—
(a) each charge or indictment against the defendant;
(b) the defendant's plea to each charge or count;
(c) each acquittal, conviction, sentence, determination, direction or order;
(d) each decision about bail;
(e) the power exercised where the court commits or adjourns the case to another court—
(i) for sentence, or
(ii) for the defendant to be dealt with for breach of a community order, a deferred sentence, a conditional discharge, or a suspended sentence of imprisonment, imposed by that other court;
(f) the court's reasons for a decision, where legislation requires those reasons to be recorded;
(g) any appeal;
(h) each party's presence or absence at each hearing;
(i) any consent that legislation requires before the court can proceed with the case, or proceed to a decision;
(j) in a magistrates' court—
(i) any indication of sentence given by the court, and
(ii) the registration of a fixed penalty notice for enforcement as a fine, and any related endorsement on a driving record;
(iii) the power exercised where the court sends the defendant to the Crown Court for trial for an offence,

---

[1] 2000 c. 7.

      (iv) any statement made by the court under section 70(5) of the Proceeds of Crime Act 200[2] (statement that if the court were not committing the defendant for consideration of a confiscation order then it would have committed the defendant to the Crown Court for sentence for an offence under section 14, 16 or 16A of the Sentencing Act 2020[3]),

      (v) any opinion given by the court under section 18(4) or 19(3) of the Sentencing Act 2020 (opinion that if the court were not committing the defendant for sentence under section 18 or 19 of the 2020 Act then it could, or would be required to, commit the defendant to the Crown Court for sentence for the offence under one of sections 14, 15, 16, 16A or 17 of that Act), and

      (vi) the exercise of a power to which paragraph (3) applies (judges exercising powers of District Judges (Magistrates' Courts));

   (k) in the Crown Court—

      (i) any request for assistance or other communication about the case received from a juror,

      (ii) the date and time at which the court gives the jury directions about the law under rule 25.14(2) or (3)(a),

      (iii) the date and time at which the court gives the jury other assistance in writing under rule 25.14(5), and

      (iv) the date, time and subject matter of submissions and rulings that relate to such directions and assistance;

   (l) the identity of—

      (i) the prosecutor,

      (ii) the defendant,

      (iii) any other applicant to whom these Rules apply,

      (iv) any interpreter or intermediary,

      (v) the parties' legal representatives, if any, and

      (vi) the judge, magistrate or magistrates, justices' legal adviser or other person who made each recorded decision;

   (m) where a defendant is entitled to attend a hearing, any agreement by the defendant to waive that right; and

   (n) where interpretation is required for a defendant, any agreement by that defendant to do without the written translation of a document.

(2) Such records must include—

   (a) each party's and representative's address, including any electronic address and telephone number available;

   (b) the defendant's date of birth, if available; and

   (c) the date of each event and decision recorded.

(3) Where a judge acting under section 66 of the Courts Act 2003[4] (Judges having powers of District Judges (Magistrates' Courts)) exercises the power of a magistrates' court, the court officer then assisting that judge must—

   (a) record, by such means as the Lord Chancellor directs, the magistrates' court power exercised by that judge; and

   (b) as soon as practicable arrange the transmission to the magistrates' court of—

      (i) that record, and

      (ii) a record of the circumstances in which that power was exercised.

[Note. For the duty to keep court records, see sections 5 and 8 of the Public Records Act 1958[5].

Requirements to record the court's reasons for its decision are contained in: section 5 of the Bail Act 1976[6]; section 47(1) of the Road Traffic Offenders Act 1988[7]; sections 20, 33A and 33BB of the Youth Justice and Criminal Evidence Act 1999[8]; section 174 of the Criminal Justice Act 2003[9]; and rule 6.8.

---

[2] 2002 c. 29; section 70 was amended by section 41 of, and paragraph 75 of Schedule 3 to, the Criminal Justice Act 2003 (c. 44), section 410 of, and paragraphs 181 and 195 of Schedule 24 to, the Sentencing Act 2020 (c. 17) and section 46 of, and paragraph 19 of Schedule 13 to, the Counter-Terrorism and Sentencing Act 2021 (c. 11).

[3] 2020 c. 17; section 16A was inserted by section 46 of, and paragraph 26 of Schedule 13 to, the Counter-Terrorism and Sentencing Act 2021 (c. 11).

[4] 2003 c. 39; section 66 was amended by section 32 of, and paragraph 6 of Schedule 2 to, the Armed Forces Act 2011 (c. 18) and section 61 of, and paragraph 90 of Schedule 10 and paragraph 4 of Schedule 14 to, the Crime and Courts Act 2013 (c. 22).

[5] 1958 c. 51; section 5 was amended by sections 67 and 86 of, and paragraph 2 of Schedule 5 to, the Freedom of Information Act 2000 (c. 36); and section 8 was amended by sections 27 and 35 of, and Schedule 2 to, the Administration of Justice Act 1969 (c. 58), section 1 of, and paragraph 19 of Schedule 2 to, the Administration of Justice Act 1970 (c. 31), section 56 of, and

The prosecution of some offences requires the consent of a specified authority. Requirements for the defendant's consent to proceedings in his or her absence are contained in sections 23 and 128 of the Magistrates' Courts Act 1980[10].

In the circumstances for which it provides, section 20 of the Magistrates' Courts Act 1980[11] allows the court to give an indication of whether a custodial or non-custodial sentence is more likely in the event of a guilty plea at trial in that court.

See also rule 9.11(3). Rules 3.16 and 9.13 provide for sentencing indications in other circumstances in magistrates' courts.

Under section 66 of the Courts Act 2003, every holder of a judicial office listed in that section has the powers of a justice of the peace who is a District Judge (Magistrates' Courts) in relation to criminal causes and matters. The list includes Circuit judges and judges of the High Court and Court of Appeal.]

R5.5 **Recording and transcription of proceedings in the Crown Court**

5.5	(1)	Where someone may appeal to the Court of Appeal, paragraphs (2) to (4) apply and the court officer must—

(a)	arrange for the recording of the proceedings in the Crown Court, unless the court otherwise directs; and

(b)	arrange for the transcription of such a recording if—

(i)	the Registrar wants such a transcript, or

(ii)	anyone else wants such a transcript (but that is subject to the restrictions in paragraph (2)).

(2)	Unless the court otherwise directs, a person who transcribes a recording of proceedings under such arrangements—

(a)	may only supply a transcript of a recording of a hearing in private to—

(i)	the Registrar, or

(ii)	an individual who was present at that hearing;

(b)	if the recording of a hearing in public contains information to which reporting restrictions apply, may only supply a transcript containing that information to—

(i)	the Registrar, or

(ii)	a recipient to whom that supply will not contravene those reporting restrictions; but

(c)	subject to paragraph (2)(a) and (b), must supply any person with any transcript for which that person asks—

(i)	in accordance with the transcription arrangements made by the court officer, and

(ii)	on payment by that person of any fee prescribed.

(3)	A party who wants to hear a recording of proceedings must—

(a)	apply—

(i)	in writing to the Registrar, if an appeal notice has been served where Part 36 applies (Appeal to the Court of Appeal: general rules), or

(ii)	orally or in writing to the Crown Court officer;

Schedule 11 to, the Courts Act 1971 (c. 23), section 152 of, and Schedule 7 to, the Senior Courts Act 1981 (c. 54) and sections 56 and 59 of, and Schedule 11 to, the Constitutional Reform Act 2005 (c. 4).

[6] 1976 c. 63; section 5 was amended by section 65 of, and Schedule 12 to, the Criminal Law Act 1977 (c. 45), section 60 of the Criminal Justice Act 1982 (c. 48), paragraph 1 of Schedule 3 to the Criminal Justice and Public Order Act 1994 (c. 33), paragraph 53 of Schedule 9 to the Powers of Criminal Courts (Sentencing) Act 2000 (c. 6), section 129(1) of the Criminal Justice and Police Act 2001 (c. 16), paragraph 182 of Schedule 8 to the Courts Act 2003 (c. 39), paragraph 48 of Schedule 3, paragraphs 1 and 2 of Schedule 36, and Parts 2, 4 and 12 of Schedule 37 to the Criminal Justice Act 2003 (c. 44) and section 208 of, and paragraphs 33 and 35 of Schedule 21 to, the Legal Services Act 2007 (c. 27).

[7] 1988 c. 53.

[8] 1999 c. 23; section 20(6) was amended by paragraph 384(a) of Schedule 8 to the Courts Act 2003 (c. 39); section 33A was inserted by section 47 of the Police and Justice Act 2006 (c. 48). Section 33BB is inserted by section 104(1) of the Coroners and Justice Act 2009, with effect from a date to be appointed.

[9] 2003 c. 44; section 174 was substituted by section 64 of the Legal Aid, Sentencing and Punishment of Offenders Act 2012 (c. 10).

[10] 1980 c. 43; section 23 was amended by section 125 of, and paragraph 25 of Schedule 18 to, the Courts and Legal Services Act 1990 (c. 41) and paragraphs 1 and 8 of Schedule 3 to the Criminal Justice Act 2003 (c. 44). Section 128 was amended by section 59 to, and paragraphs 2, 3 and 4 of Schedule 9 to, the Criminal Justice Act 1982 (c. 48), section 48 of the Police and Criminal Evidence Act 1984 (c. 60), section 170(1) of, and paragraphs 65 and 69 of Schedule 15 to, the Criminal Justice Act 1988 (c. 33), section 125(3) of, and paragraph 25 of Schedule 18 to, the Courts and Legal Services Act 1990 (c. 41), sections 49, 52 and 80 of, and Schedule 5 to, the Criminal Procedure and Investigations Act 1996 (c. 25), paragraph 75 of Schedule 9 to the Powers of Criminal Courts (Sentencing) Act 2000 (c. 6) and paragraph 51 of Schedule 3 and Part 4 of Schedule 37 to the Criminal Justice Act 2003 (c. 44). It is modified by section 91(5) of the Legal Aid, Sentencing and Punishment of Offenders Act 2012 (c. 10).

[11] 1980 c. 43; section 20 was amended by section 100 of, and paragraph 25 of Schedule 11 to, the Criminal Justice Act 1991 (c. 53), paragraph 63 of Schedule 9 to the Powers of Criminal Courts (Sentencing) Act 2000 (c. 6) and paragraphs 1 and 6 of Schedule 3 to the Criminal Justice Act 2003 (c. 44).

       (b) explain the reasons for the request; and

       (c) pay any fee prescribed.

(4) If the Crown Court or the Registrar so directs, the Crown Court officer must allow that party to hear a recording of—

       (a) a hearing in public; and

       (b) a hearing in private, if the applicant was present at that hearing.

(5) Where the court exercises at a hearing a power to which Part 47 applies (Investigation orders and warrants)—

       (a) the court officer must arrange for the recording of that hearing unless the court otherwise directs; and

       (b) paragraphs (6) to (9) apply.

(6) A party or person affected by the exercise of that power who wants to hear such a recording or who wants a transcript of such a recording must—

       (a) apply in writing to the court officer;

       (b) explain the reasons for the request; and

       (c) pay any fee prescribed.

(7) On an application under paragraph (6) to hear a recording the court officer may allow the applicant to do so—

       (a) where the hearing was in public;

       (b) where the hearing was in private only if the applicant was present at that hearing; and

       (c) subject to any direction by the court.

(8) On an application under paragraph (6) for a transcript of a recording the court officer may arrange for transcription—

       (a) where the hearing was in public;

       (b) where the hearing was in private only if the applicant was present at that hearing; and

       (c) subject to any direction by the court.

(9) A person who transcribes such a recording—

       (a) must supply a transcript of a hearing in public to any applicant under paragraph (6), subject to paragraph (9)(b);

       (b) if the recording of a hearing in public contains information to which reporting restrictions apply, may only supply a transcript containing that information to a recipient to whom that supply will not contravene those restrictions;

       (c) may only supply a transcript of a hearing in private to a recipient who was present at that hearing; and

       (d) must supply any such transcript—

          (i) in accordance with the transcription arrangements made by the court officer, and

          (ii) on payment of any fee prescribed.

[Note. Under section 32 of the Criminal Appeal Act 1968[12] Criminal Procedure Rules may provide for the making of a record of any proceedings in respect of which an appeal lies to the Court of Appeal and for the making and supply of a transcript of such a record.

For the circumstances in which reporting restrictions may apply, see the provisions listed in the note to rule 6.1. In summary, reporting restrictions prohibit the publication of the information to which they apply where that publication is likely to lead members of the public to acquire the information concerned.]

Custody of case materials   R5.6

5.6   Unless the court otherwise directs, in respect of each case the court officer must—

       (a) keep—

          (i) any evidence, application, representation or other material served by the parties, and

          (ii) any evidence or other material prepared for the court; or

       (b) arrange for the whole or any part to be kept by some other appropriate person, subject to—

          (i) any condition imposed by the court, and

          (ii) the rules in Part 34 (Appeal to the Crown Court) and Part 36 (Appeal to the Court of Appeal: general rules) about keeping exhibits pending any appeal.

Access to Information in Court Records

The open justice principle   R5.7

5.7   (1) Where rules 5.8, 5.9, 5.10 and 5.11 apply, as well as furthering the overriding objective in accordance with rules 1.2 and 1.3 the court officer and the court must have regard to the importance of—

       (a) dealing with criminal cases in public;

___
[12] 1968 c. 19.

(b) allowing a public hearing to be reported to the public; and

(c) the rights of a person affected by a direction or order made, or warrant issued, by the court to understand why that decision was made.

(2) In rules 5.10 and 5.11 this requirement is called 'the open justice principle'.

R5.8   **Request for information about a case**

5.8   (1) This rule—

(a) applies where anyone, including a member of the public or a reporter, requests information about a case including information contained in materials kept by the court officer for the purposes of the case; but

(b) does not apply if rule 5.12 applies (Request for certificate, extract or information under other legislation).

(2) A person requesting information must—

(a) ask the court officer;

(b) specify the information requested; and

(c) pay any fee prescribed.

(3) The request—

(a) may be made orally or in writing, and need not explain why the information is requested, if this rule requires the court officer to supply that information; but

(b) must be in writing, unless the court otherwise permits, and must explain why the information is requested, if this rule does not so require.

(4) Subject to paragraph (5), the court officer must supply to the person making the request—

(a) the date of a hearing in public;

(b) each alleged offence and any plea entered;

(c) the court's decision—

(i) at a hearing in public,

(ii) to grant or withhold bail, or to impose or vary a bail condition, or

(iii) about the committal, sending or transfer of the case to another court;

(d) whether the case is under appeal;

(e) the outcome of the case;

(f) the identity of—

(i) the prosecutor,

(ii) the defendant, including the defendant's date of birth,

(iii) the parties' representatives, including their addresses, and

(iv) the judge, magistrate or magistrates, or justices' legal adviser by whom a decision at a hearing in public was made;

(g) such other information about the case as is required by arrangements to which paragraph (6)(c) refers,

(h) details of any reporting or access restriction ordered by the court; and

(i) notice that reporting restrictions may apply to the publication of information supplied under this rule.

(5) The court officer must not supply the information requested if—

(a) the supply of that information is prohibited by a reporting restriction;

(b) that information is—

(i) the date of a hearing in public of which a party has yet to be notified, or

(ii) a recording arranged under rule 5.5 (Recording and transcription of proceedings in the Crown Court), or a copy or transcript of such a recording;

(c) that information concerns a trial in which the verdict was more than 6 months ago; or

(d) that information is not readily available to the court officer (for example, because of the location or conditions of its storage).

(6) Where the court officer must supply the information requested the supply may be—

(a) by word of mouth;

(b) in writing, including by written certificate or extract from a court record; or

(c) by such other arrangements as the Lord Chancellor directs, including supply by electronic means.

(7) Where this rule does not require the court officer to supply the information requested then unless that information can be supplied under rule 5.9—

(a) the court officer must refer the request to the court; and

(b) rule 5.10 applies.

[Note. See also rule 5.7 (The open justice principle).]

Request for information by a party or person directly affected by a case

5.9   (1) This rule applies where a party, or a person directly affected by a direction or order made or warrant issued by the court, wants information about their case including information contained in materials kept by the court officer for the purposes of that case.

      (2) Such a party or person must—
         (a) ask the court officer;
         (b) specify the information requested; and
         (c) pay any fee prescribed.

      (3) The request—
         (a) may be made orally or in writing, and need not explain why the information is requested, if this rule requires the court officer to supply that information; but
         (b) must be in writing, unless the court otherwise permits, and must explain why the information is requested, if this rule does not so require.

      (4) Subject to paragraph (5), the court officer must supply to the party or person making the request—
         (a) information about the terms of any direction or order made, or warrant issued, which was—
            (i)   served on, or addressed or directed to, that party or person, or
            (ii) made on an application by that party or person; and
         (b) information received from that party or person (which might be, for example, to establish what information the court holds, or in case of a loss of that information by the party or person making the request).

      (5) The court officer must not supply the information requested if that information—
         (a) concerns the grounds on which a direction or order was made, or a warrant issued, in the absence of the party or person making the request;
         (b) is a recording arranged under rule 5.5 (Recording and transcription of proceedings in the Crown Court), or a copy or transcript of such a recording; or
         (c) is not readily available to the court officer (for example, because of the location or conditions of its storage).

      (6) Where the court officer must supply the information requested the supply may be, at the choice of the party or person making the request—
         (a) by word of mouth;
         (b) in writing, including by written certificate or extract from a court record; or
         (c) by a copy of a document served by, or on, that party or person (but not of a document not so served).

      (7) Where this rule does not require the court officer to supply the information requested—
         (a) the court officer must refer the request to the court; and
         (b) rule 5.10 applies.

[Note. See also rule 5.7 (The open justice principle).]

Request for information determined by the court

5.10   (1) This rule applies where the court officer refers to the court a request for information under rule 5.8 (Request for information about a case) or rule 5.9 (Request for information by a party or person directly affected by a case).

      (2) The court officer must—
         (a) serve the request on—
            (i)   the applicant for any direction, order or warrant that the request concerns which was made or issued in the absence of the party or person making the request, and
            (ii) anyone else, and to such extent, as the court directs; and
         (b) notify the party or person making the request of—
            (i)   the date of its service under this rule, and
            (ii) the identity of each person served with it, if the court so directs.

      (3) If a party or person served with the request objects to the supply of information requested the objector must—
         (a) give notice of the objection not more than 20 business days after service of the request, or within any longer period allowed by the court;
         (b) serve that notice on the court officer and on the party or person making the request; and
         (c) if the objector wants a hearing, explain why one is needed.

      (4) A notice of objection must explain—
         (a) whether the objection is to the supply of the whole of the information requested, or only to the supply of a specified part or specified parts;

(b) whether the objection applies without limit of time, or only for a specified period (for example, until a date or event specified by the objector); and

(c) the grounds of the objection.

(5) Where a notice of objection includes material that the objector thinks ought not be revealed to the party or person making the request, the objector must—

(a) omit that material from the notice served on that party or person;

(b) mark the material to show that it is only for the court; and

(c) with that material include an explanation of why it has been withheld.

(6) The court must not determine the request, and information requested must not be supplied, until—

(a) each party or person served with the request has had at least 20 business days, or any longer period allowed by the court, in which to object or make other representations; and

(b) the court is satisfied that in all the circumstances every such party or person has had a reasonable opportunity to do so.

(7) The court may determine the request—

(a) without a hearing; or

(b) at a hearing, which—

(i) may be in public or private, but

(ii) must be in private, unless the court otherwise directs, where the request concerns a direction, order or warrant made or issued in the absence of the party or person making the request.

(8) Where a notice of objection includes material that the objector thinks ought not be revealed to the party or person making the request—

(a) any hearing of the request may take place, wholly or in part, in the absence of the party or person making it; and

(b) at any such hearing the general rule is that the court must consider, in the following sequence—

(i) representations first by the party or person making the request and then by the objector, in the presence of both, and then

(ii) further representations by the objector, in the absence of the party or person making the request

but the court may direct other arrangements for the hearing.

(9) In deciding whether to order the supply of the information requested the court must have regard to—

(a) the open justice principle;

(b) any reporting restriction;

(c) rights and obligations under other legislation;

(d) the importance of any public interest in the withholding of that information, or in its supply only in part or subject to conditions (which public interest might be, for example, in preventing injustice, protecting others' rights, protecting the confidentiality of a criminal investigation or protecting national security); and

(e) the extent to which that information is otherwise available to the party or person making the request.

(10) Where the court orders the supply of the information requested the supply may be, at the court's direction and on such terms as the court directs—

(a) by word of mouth;

(b) in writing, including by written certificate or extract from a court record;

(c) by a copy of a document; or

(d) by allowing access to a document, including a recording (other than a recording to which rule 5.5 applies (Recording and transcription of proceedings in the Crown Court)).

[Note. See also rule 5.7 (The open justice principle).

The court's decision under this rule may be affected by—

(a) *a reporting restriction imposed by legislation or by the court (Part 6 lists the reporting restrictions that might apply);*

(b) *Articles 6, 8 and 10 of the European Convention on Human Rights;*

(c) *the Rehabilitation of Offenders Act 1974[13] (section 5 of the Act[14] lists sentences and rehabilitation periods);*

---

[13] 1974 c. 53.

[14] 1974 c. 53; section 5 was amended by section 15 of, and paragraphs 77 and 78 of Schedule 4 to, the Constitutional Reform Act 2005 (c. 4) and by sections 126 and 139 of, and paragraph 2 of Schedule 21 to, the Legal Aid, Sentencing and Punishment of Offenders Act 2012 (c. 10).

(d) section 18 of the *Criminal Procedure and Investigations Act 1996*[15], which affects the supply of information about material, other than evidence, disclosed by the prosecutor;

(e) Part 3 of the *Data Protection Act 2018*[16] (sections 43(3) and 117 of which make exceptions for criminal proceedings from some other provisions of that Act); and

(f) sections 33, 34 and 35 of the *Legal Aid, Sentencing and Punishment of Offenders Act 2012*[17], which affect the supply of information about applications for legal aid.]

Publication of information about court hearings, etc.

5.11 (1) Where a case is due to be heard in public, the court officer must—
  (a) publish the information listed in paragraph (2)—
    (i) if that information is available to the court officer, and
    (ii) unless the publication of that information is prohibited by a reporting restriction; and
  (b) publish that information for no longer than 5 business days—
    (i) by notice displayed somewhere prominent in the vicinity of a court room in which the hearing is due to take place, and
    (ii) by such arrangements as the Lord Chancellor directs, including arrangements for publication by electronic means, but only to the extent needed to comply with the open justice principle.
  (2) The information that paragraph (1) requires the court officer to publish is—
  (a) the date, time and place of the hearing;
  (b) the identity of the defendant;
  (c) by notice under paragraph (1)(b)(i), such other information as it may be practicable to publish concerning—
    (i) the type of hearing,
    (ii) the identity of the prosecutor,
    (iii) the identity of the court, and
    (iv) any reporting or access restriction that applies; and
  (d) by arrangements under paragraph (1)(b)(ii), such other information as it may be practicable to publish concerning—
    (i) the details listed in paragraph (2)(c), and
    (ii) the offence or offences alleged.
  (3) Where 15 business days have expired after service on the defendant of a written charge and other documents under rule 24.9 (Single justice procedure: special rules), the court officer must—
  (a) publish the information listed in paragraph (4) if—
    (i) the information is available to the court officer, and
    (ii) the publication of the information is not prohibited by a reporting restriction; and
  (b) publish that information for no longer than 5 business days by such arrangements as the Lord Chancellor directs, including arrangements for publication by electronic means, but only to the extent needed to comply with the open justice principle.
  (4) The information that paragraph (3) requires the court officer to publish is—
  (a) the identity of the defendant;
  (b) the identity of the prosecutor;
  (c) the offence or offences alleged; and
  (d) such other information as it may be practicable to publish about any reporting restriction that applies.
  (5) If it is not practicable to publish the information about reporting or access restrictions that this rule requires then the court officer must publish a notice or notices by such arrangements as the Lord Chancellor directs—
  (a) warning that such restrictions may apply to a case information about which is published under this rule;
  (b) explaining the general effect of such restrictions; and
  (c) explaining how further information about such restrictions may be obtained, generally and in relation to an individual case.

[Note. See also rule 5.7 (The open justice principle).]

Criminal Procedure Rules

R5.12   Request for certificate, extract or information under other legislation

5.12 (1) This rule applies where legislation other than these Rules—

(a) allows a certificate of conviction or acquittal, or an extract from records kept by the court officer, to be introduced in evidence in criminal proceedings; or

(b) requires or permits information about a case, including information contained in materials kept by the court officer for the purposes of the case, to be supplied by the court officer to a specified person for a specified purpose.

(2) A person who wants such a certificate or extract, or such information, must—

(a) apply in writing to the court officer;

(b) specify the certificate, extract or information required;

(c) explain under what legislation and for what purpose it is required; and

(d) pay any fee prescribed.

(3) If the application satisfies the requirements of that legislation, the court officer must supply the certificate, extract or information requested—

(a) to a party; and

(b) unless the court otherwise directs, to any other applicant.

[Note. Under sections 73 to 75 of the Police and Criminal Evidence Act 1984[18], a certificate of conviction or acquittal, and certain other details from records to which this Part applies, may be admitted in evidence in criminal proceedings.

Examples of legislation to which paragraph (1)(b) of this rule applies include (this is not a complete list)—

(a) section 17 of the Criminal Appeal Act 1995[19], under which information may be required by the Criminal Cases Review Commission;

(b) section 115 of the Crime and Disorder Act 1998[20], under which information may be supplied to specified authorities for the purposes of that Act; and

(c) section 14 of the Offender Management Act 2007[21], under which information may be supplied to specified persons for offender management purposes; and

(d) article 7 of the Age of Criminal Responsibility (Scotland) Act 2019 (Consequential Provisions and Modifications) Order 2021[22], under which information may be required to assist in a review of Scottish criminal records concerning a time at which the subject of those records was under 12 years old.

Under section 92 of the Sexual Offences Act 2003[23], a certificate which records a conviction for an offence and a statement by the convicting court that that offence is listed in Schedule 3 to the Act is evidence of those facts for certain purposes of that Act.

A certificate of conviction or acquittal, and certain other information, required for other purposes, may be obtained from the Secretary of State under sections 112, 113A and 113B of the Police Act 1997[24].

---

[18] 1984 c. 60; section 73 was amended by section 90(1) of, and paragraphs 125 and 128 of Schedule 13 to, the Access to Justice Act 1999 (c. 22), paragraph 285 of Schedule 8 to the Courts Act 2003 (c. 39) and paragraph 13 of Schedule 17 to the Coroners and Justice Act 2009 (c. 25); and section 74 was amended by paragraph 85 of Schedule 36, and Part 5 of Schedule 37, to the Criminal Justice Act 2003 (c. 44) and paragraph 14 of Schedule 17 to the Coroners and Justice Act 2009 (c. 25).

[19] 1995 c. 35; section 17 was amended by section 1 of the Criminal Cases Review Commission (Information) Act 2016 (c. 17).

[20] 1998 c. 37; section 115 was amended by paragraphs 150 and 151 of Schedule 7 to the Criminal Justice and Court Services Act 2000 (c. 43), paragraph 35 of Schedule 1 to S.I. 2000/90, section 97 of the Police Reform Act 2002 (c. 30), paragraph 25 of Schedule 1 to S.I. 2002/2469, section 219 of the Housing Act 2004 (c. 34), section 22 of, and paragraphs 1 and 7 of Schedule 9 to, the Police and Justice Act 2006 (c. 48), paragraph 29 of the Schedule to S.I. 2007/961, section 29 of the Transport for London Act 2008 (c. i), paragraph 13 of Schedule 1 to S.I. 2008/912, paragraphs 109 and 111 of Schedule 2 to S.I. 2010/866, section 98 of, and paragraphs 231 and 238 of Schedule 16 to, the Police Reform and Social Responsibility Act 2011 (c. 13), paragraphs 83 and 90 of Schedule 5 to the Health and Social Care Act 2012 (c. 7), article 26 of, and paragraph 30 of Schedule 2 to, S.I. 2013/602, paragraphs 78 and 80 of Schedule 1 and paragraphs 103 and 106 of Schedule 2 to the Policing and Crime Act 2017 (c. 3) and paragraph 1 of Schedule 1 and paragraphs 51 and 57 of Schedule 4 to the Health and Care Act 2022 (c. 31).

[21] 2007 c. 21; section 14 was amended by sections 38 and 39 of, and paragraphs 24 and 26 of Schedule 9 and paragraph 37 of Schedule 10 to, the Criminal Justice and Courts Act 2015 (c. 2).

[22] S.I. 2021/1458.

[23] 2003 c. 42.

[24] 1997 c. 50; section 112 was amended by section 50 of the Criminal Justice and Immigration Act 2008 (c. 4), sections 93, 97 and 112 of, and Part 8 of Schedule 8 to, the Policing and Crime Act 2009 (c. 26) and sections 80 and 84 of the Protection of Freedoms Act 2012 (c. 9). Section 113A was added by section 163(2) of the Serious Organised Crime and Police Act 2005 (c. 15), modified by regulation 4 of S.I. 2010/1146, and amended by paragraph 14 of Schedule 9 to the Safeguarding Vulnerable Groups Act 2006 (c. 47), section 50 of the Criminal Justice and Immigration Act 2008 (c. 4), sections 97 and 112 of, and Part 8 of Schedule 8 to, the Policing and Crime Act 2009 (c. 26), sections 80 and 115 of, and paragraphs 35 and 36 of Schedule 9 and Part 5 of Schedule 10 to, the Protection of Freedoms Act 2012 (c. 9), articles 2 and 3 of S.I. 2009/203 and

This rule applies where certificates or extracts from court records are required for use in evidence or for some other purpose specified in legislation. Where this rule does not apply, information about a case may be obtained under rule 5.8.]

CRIMINAL PROCEDURE RULES   PART 6   REPORTING, ETC. RESTRICTIONS

General rules

When this Part applies   R6.1

6.1   (1)   This Part applies where the court can—
    (a)   impose a restriction on—
        (i)   reporting what takes place at a public hearing, or
        (ii)   public access to what otherwise would be a public hearing;
    (b)   vary or remove a reporting or access restriction that is imposed by legislation;
    (c)   withhold information from the public during a public hearing;
    (d)   order a trial in private; or
    (e)   allow there to take place during a hearing—
        (i)   sound recording, or
        (ii)   communication by electronic means.
    (2)   This Part does not apply to arrangements required by legislation, or directed by the court, in connection with—
    (a)   sound recording during a hearing, or the transcription of such a recording; or
    (b)   measures to assist a witness or defendant to give evidence.

[Note. The court can impose reporting restrictions under—

    (a)   section 4(2) of the Contempt of Court Act 1981[1] (postponed report of public hearing);

    (b)   section 11 of the Contempt of Court Act 1981 (matter withheld from the public during a public hearing);

    (c)   section 58 of the Criminal Procedure and Investigations Act 1996[2] (postponed report of derogatory assertion in mitigation);

    (d)   section 45 of the Youth Justice and Criminal Evidence Act 1999[3] (identity of a person under 18);

    (e)   section 45A of the Youth Justice and Criminal Evidence Act 1999[4] (identity of a witness or victim under 18);

    (f)   section 46 of the Youth Justice and Criminal Evidence Act 1999[5] (identity of a vulnerable adult witness);

    (g)   section 82 of the Criminal Justice Act 2003[6] (order for retrial after acquittal); or

    (h)   section 75 of the Serious Organised Crime and Police Act 2005[7] (identity of a defendant who assisted the police).

There are reporting restrictions imposed by legislation that the court can vary or remove, under—

    (a)   section 49 of the Children and Young Persons Act 1933[8] (youth court proceedings);

articles 36 and 37 of S.I. 2012/3006. Section 113B was added by section 163(2) of the Serious Organised Crime and Police Act 2005 (c. 15), modified by regulations 5 to 7 of S.I. 2010/1146, and amended by paragraph 14 of Schedule 9 to the Safeguarding Vulnerable Groups Act 2006 (c. 47), paragraph 149 of Schedule 16 to the Armed Forces Act 2006 (c. 52), section 50 of the Criminal Justice and Immigration Act 2008 (c. 4), sections 97 and 112 of, and Part 8 of Schedule 8 to, the Policing and Crime Act 2009 (c. 26), sections 79, 80, 82 and 115 of, and paragraphs 35 and 37 of Schedule 9 and Parts 5 and 6 of Schedule 10 to, the Protection of Freedoms Act 2012 (c. 9), articles 2 and 4 of S.I. 2009/203, regulation 8 of S.I. 2010/1146 and articles 36, 37 and 39 of S.I. 2012/3006.

[1]   1981 c. 49.
[2]   1996 c. 25.
[3]   1999 c. 23.
[4]   1999 c. 23; section 45A was inserted by section 78 of the Criminal Justice and Courts Act 2015 (c. 2).
[5]   1999 c. 23.
[6]   2003 c. 44.
[7]   2005 c. 15.
[8]   1933 c. 12; section 49 was substituted by section 49 of the Criminal Justice and Public Order Act 1994 (c. 33) and amended by section 45 of the Crime (Sentences) Act 1997 (c. 43), section 119 of, and paragraph 1 of Schedule 8 to, the Crime and Disorder Act 1998 (c. 37), section 165 of, and paragraph 2 of Schedule 9 to, the Powers of Criminal Courts (Sentencing) Act 2000 (c. 6), paragraph 2 of Schedule 32 to, the Criminal Justice Act 2003 (c. 44), sections 208 and 210 of, and paragraphs 15 and 19 of Schedule 21, and Schedule 23 to, the Legal Services Act 2007 (c. 29) and section 6 of, and paragraphs 1, 3 and 100 of Schedule 4 to, the Criminal Justice and Immigration Act 2008 (c. 4). It is further amended by section 48 of, and paragraphs 1 and 3 of Schedule 2 to, the Youth Justice and Criminal Evidence Act 1999 (c. 23), section 74 of, and paragraph 5 of Schedule 7 to, the Criminal Justice and Court Services Act 2000 (c. 43) and sections 6 and 149 of, and paragraphs 1 and 3 of Schedule 4 and Schedule 28 to, the Criminal Justice and Immigration Act 2008 (c. 4), with effect from dates to be appointed.

    (b)   *section 8C of the Magistrates' Courts Act 1980[9] (pre-trial ruling in magistrates' courts);*

    (c)   *section 11 of the Criminal Justice Act 1987[10] (preparatory hearing in the Crown Court);*

    (d)   *section 1 of the Sexual Offences (Amendment) Act 1992[11] (identity of complainant of sexual offence);*

    (e)   *section 37 of the Criminal Procedure and Investigations Act 1996[12] (preparatory hearing in the Crown Court);*

    (f)   *section 41 of the Criminal Procedure and Investigations Act 1996[13] (pre-trial ruling in the Crown Court);*

    (g)   *section 52A of, and paragraph 3 of Schedule 3 to, the Crime and Disorder Act 1998[14] (allocation and sending for trial proceedings);*

    (h)   *section 47 of the Youth Justice and Criminal Evidence Act 1999[15] (special measures direction);*

    (i)   *section 141F of the Education Act 2002[16] (restrictions on reporting alleged offences by teachers);*

    (j)   *section 71 of the Criminal Justice Act 2003[17] (prosecution appeal against Crown Court ruling); and*

    (k)   *section 4A of, and paragraph 1 of Schedule 1 to, the Female Genital Mutilation Act 2003[18] (identity of person against whom a female genital mutilation offence is alleged to have been committed).*

There are reporting restrictions imposed by legislation that the court has no power to vary or remove, under—

    (a)   *section 1 of the Judicial Proceedings (Regulation of Reports) Act 1926[19] (indecent or medical matter);*

    (b)   *section 2 of the Contempt of Court Act 1981[20] (risk of impeding or prejudicing active proceedings).*

Access to a youth court is restricted under section 47 of the Children and Young Persons Act 1933[21]. See also rule 24.2 (Trial and sentence in a magistrates' court – general rules).

Under section 36 of the Children and Young Persons Act 1933[22], no-one under 14 may be present in court when someone else is on trial, or during proceedings preliminary to a trial, unless that person is required as a witness, or for the purposes of justice, or the court permits.

The court can restrict access to the courtroom under—

---

[9] 1980 c. 43; section 8C was inserted by section 45 of, and Schedule 3 to, the Courts Act 2003 (c. 39) and amended by paragraphs 12 and 15 of Schedule 5 to the Legal Aid, Sentencing and Punishment of Offenders Act 2012 (c. 10).

[10] 1987 c. 38; section 11 was amended by paragraphs 1 and 6 of Schedule 3 to the Criminal Procedure and Investigations Act 1996 (c. 25), section 24 of, and paragraphs 38 and 40 of Schedule 4 to, the Access to Justice Act 1999 (c. 22), section 311 of, and paragraph 58 of Schedule 3 and Part 4 of Schedule 37 to, the Criminal Justice Act 2003 (c. 44) and section 40(4) of, and paragraph 46 of Schedule 9 to, the Constitutional Reform Act 2005 (c. 4).

[11] 1992 c. 34; section 1 was amended by section 48 of, and paragraphs 6 and 7 of Schedule 2 to, the Youth Justice and Criminal Evidence Act 1999 (c. 23).

[12] 1996 c. 25; section 37 was amended by section 24 of, and paragraph 49 of Schedule 4 to, the Access to Justice Act 1999 (c. 22), section 311 of the Criminal Justice Act 2003 (c. 44) and section 40(4) of, and paragraph 61 of Schedule 9 to, the Constitutional Reform Act 2005 (c. 4).

[13] 1996 c. 25; section 41 was amended by section 311 of the Criminal Justice Act 2003 (c. 44).

[14] 1998 c. 37; section 52A was inserted by paragraphs 15 and 19 of Schedule 3 to the Criminal Justice Act 2003 (c. 44) and amended by paragraphs 46 and 47 of Schedule 5 to the Legal Aid, Sentencing and Punishment of Offenders Act 2012 (c. 10). Paragraph 3 of Schedule 3 was amended by section 24 of, and paragraphs 53 and 55 of Schedule 4 to, the Access to Justice Act 1999 (c. 22), paragraphs 68 and 71 of Schedule 3 to the Criminal Justice Act 2003 (c. 44) and paragraphs 46 and 50 of Schedule 5 to the Legal Aid, Sentencing and Punishment of Offenders Act 2012 (c. 10).

[15] 1999 c. 23; section 47 was amended by section 52 of, and paragraph 37 of Schedule 14 to, the Police and Justice Act 2006 (c. 48).

[16] 2002 c. 32; section 141F was inserted by section 13 of the Education Act 2011 (c. 21).

[17] 2003 c. 44; section 71 was amended by section 40(4) of, and paragraph 82 of Schedule 9 to, the Constitutional Reform Act 2005 (c. 4) and paragraph 65 of Schedule 5 to the Legal Aid, Sentencing and Punishment of Offenders Act 2012 (c. 10).

[18] 2003 c. 31; section 4A and Schedule 1 were inserted by section 71 of the Serious Crime Act 2015 (c. 9).

[19] 1926 c. 61; section 1 was amended by sections 38 and 46 of the Criminal Justice Act 1982 (c. 48), paragraph 2 of Schedule 8 to the Family Law Act 1996 (c. 27) and paragraph 8 of Schedule 27 to the Civil Partnership Act 2004 (c. 33). It is further amended by paragraph 7 of Schedule 26 to the Criminal Justice Act 2003 (c. 44), with effect from a date to be appointed.

[20] 1981 c. 49; section 2 was amended by paragraph 31 of Schedule 20 to the Broadcasting Act 1990 (c. 42).

[21] 1933 c. 12; section 47 was amended by Parts II and III of Schedule 7 to the Justices of the Peace Act 1949 (c. 101), paragraph 40 of Schedule 11 to the Criminal Justice Act 1991 (c. 53), sections 47(7) and 120(2) of, and Schedule 10 to, the Crime and Disorder Act 1998 (c. 37) and paragraphs 15 and 18 of Schedule 21 to the Legal Services Act 2007 (c. 29). It is further amended by paragraph 2 of Schedule 4 to the Youth Justice and Criminal Evidence Act 1999 (c. 23), with effect from a date to be appointed.

[22] 1933 c. 12; section 36 was amended by section 73 of, and Part III of Schedule 15 to, the Access to Justice Act 1999 (c. 22).

(a) *section 8(4) of the Official Secrets Act 1920[23], during proceedings for an offence under the Official Secrets Acts 1911 and 1920;*

(b) *section 37 of the Children and Young Persons Act 1933[24], where the court receives evidence from a person under 18;*

(c) *section 75 of the Serious Organised Crime and Police Act 2005[25], where the court reviews a sentence passed on a defendant who assisted an investigation.*

The court has an inherent power, in exceptional circumstances—

(a) *to allow information, for example a name or address, to be withheld from the public at a public hearing;*

(b) *to restrict public access to what otherwise would be a public hearing, for example to control disorder;*

(c) *to hear a trial in private, for example for reasons of national security.*

Under section 9(1) of the Contempt of Court Act 1981[26], it is a contempt of court without the court's permission to—

(a) *use in court, or bring into court for use, a device for recording sound;*

(b) *publish a recording of legal proceedings made by means of such a device; or*

(c) *use any such recording in contravention of any condition on which permission was granted.*

Under section 41 of the Criminal Justice Act 1925[27], it is an offence to take or attempt to take a photograph, or with a view to publication to make or attempt to make a portrait or sketch, of any judge, juror, witness or party, in the courtroom, or in the building or in the precincts of the building in which the court is held, or while that person is entering or leaving the courtroom, building or precincts; or to publish such a photograph, portrait or sketch.

Section 32 of the Crime and Courts Act 2013[28] (Enabling the making, and use, of films and other recordings of proceedings) allows for exceptions to be made to the prohibitions imposed by section 9 of the 1981 Act and section 41 of the 1925 Act.

By reason of sections 15 and 45 of the Senior Courts Act 1981[29], the Court of Appeal and the Crown Court each has an inherent power to deal with a person for contempt of court for disrupting the proceedings. Under section 12 of the Contempt of Court Act 1981[30], a magistrates' court has a similar power.

See also—

(a) *rule 5.5, under which the court officer must make arrangements for recording proceedings in the Crown Court;*

(b) *Part 18, which applies to live links and other measures to assist a witness or defendant to give evidence;*

(c) *rule 45.10, which applies to costs orders against a non-party for serious misconduct; and*

(d) *Part 48, which contains rules about contempt of court.]*

Exercise of court's powers to which this Part applies   R6.2

6.2   (1)   When exercising a power to which this Part applies, as well as furthering the overriding objective, in accordance with rule 1.3, the court must have regard to the importance of—

(a)   dealing with criminal cases in public; and

(b)   allowing a public hearing to be reported to the public.

(2)   The court may determine an application or appeal under this Part—

(a)   at a hearing, in public or in private; or

(b)   without a hearing.

---

[23] 1920 c. 75; section 8 was amended by section 32 of the Magistrates' Courts Act 1980 (c. 43).

[24] 1933 c. 12; section 37 was amended by paragraphs 15 and 16 of Schedule 21 to the Legal Services Act 2007 (c. 29) and is further amended by paragraph 2 of Schedule 4 to the Youth Justice and Criminal Evidence Act 1999 (c. 23), with effect from a date to be appointed.

[25] 2005 c. 15.

[26] 1981 c. 49.

[27] 1925 c. 86; section 41 was amended by section 56(4) of, and Part IV of Schedule 11 to, the Courts At 1971 (c. 23), sections 38 and 46 of the Criminal Justice Act 1982 (c. 48) and section 47 of the Constitutional Reform Act 2005 (c. 4).

[28] 2013 c. 22.

[29] 1981 c. 54.

[30] 1981 c. 49; section 12 was amended by section 78 of, and Schedule 16 to, the Criminal Justice Act 1982 (c. 48), section 17(3) of, and Part I of Schedule 4 to, the Criminal Justice Act 1991 (c. 53); section 65(3) and (4) of, and paragraph 6(4) of Schedule 3 to, the Criminal Justice Act 1993 (c. 36) and section 165 of, and paragraph 83 of Schedule 9 to, the Powers of Criminal Courts (Sentencing) Act 2000 (c. 6).

(3) But the court must not exercise a power to which this Part applies unless each party and any other person directly affected—

    (a) is present; or

    (b) has had an opportunity—

      (i) to attend, or

      (ii) to make representations.

[Note. See also section 121 of the Magistrates' Courts Act 1980[31] and rule 24.2 (general rules about trial and sentence in a magistrates' court).]

R6.3 Court's power to vary requirements under this Part

6.3 (1) The court may—

    (a) shorten or extend (even after it has expired) a time limit under this Part;

    (b) require an application to be made in writing instead of orally;

    (c) consider an application or representations made orally instead of in writing; and

    (d) dispense with a requirement to—

      (i) give notice, or

      (ii) serve an application.

(2) Someone who wants an extension of time must—

    (a) apply when making the application or representations for which it is needed; and

    (b) explain the delay.

Reporting and access restrictions

R6.4 Reporting and access restrictions

6.4 (1) This rule applies where the court can—

    (a) impose a restriction on—

      (i) reporting what takes place at a public hearing, or

      (ii) public access to what otherwise would be a public hearing; or

    (b) withhold information from the public during a public hearing.

(2) Unless other legislation otherwise provides, the court may do so—

    (a) on application by a party; or

    (b) on its own initiative.

(3) A party who wants the court to do so must—

    (a) apply as soon as reasonably practicable;

    (b) notify—

      (i) each other party, and

      (ii) such other person (if any) as the court directs;

    (c) specify the proposed terms of the order, and for how long it should last;

    (d) explain—

      (i) what power the court has to make the order, and

      (ii) why an order in the terms proposed is necessary;

    (e) where the application is for a reporting direction under section 45A of the Youth Justice and Criminal Evidence Act 1999[32] (Power to restrict reporting of criminal proceedings for lifetime of witnesses and victims under 18), explain—

      (i) how the circumstances of the person whose identity is concerned meet the conditions prescribed by that section, having regard to the factors which that section lists; and

      (ii) why such a reporting direction would be likely to improve the quality of any evidence given by that person, or the level of co-operation given by that person to any party in connection with the preparation of that party's case, taking into account the factors listed in that section; and

    (f) where the application is for a reporting direction under section 46 of the Youth Justice and Criminal Evidence Act 1999[33] (Power to restrict reports about certain adult witnesses in criminal proceedings), explain—

      (i) how the witness is eligible for assistance, having regard to the factors listed in that section, and

      (ii) why such a reporting direction would be likely to improve the quality of the witness' evidence, or the level of co-operation given by the witness to the applicant in

---

[31] 1980 c. 43; section 121 was amended by section 61 of the Criminal Justice Act 1988 (c. 33), section 92 of, and paragraph 8 of Schedule 11 to, the Children Act 1989 (c. 41), section 109 of, and paragraph 237 of Schedule 8 and Schedule 10 to, the Courts Act 2003 (c. 39).
[32] 1999 c. 23; section 45A was inserted by section 78 of the Criminal Justice and Courts Act 2015 (c. 2).
[33] 1999 c. 23.

connection with the preparation of the applicant's case, taking into account the factors which that section lists.

[Note. Under section 45A(10) or section 46(9) of the Youth Justice and Criminal Evidence Act 1999, if the conditions prescribed by those sections are met the court may make an excepting direction dispensing, to any extent specified, with the restrictions imposed by a reporting direction made under those sections.]

Varying or removing restrictions   R6.5

6.5 (1) This rule applies where the court can vary or remove a reporting or access restriction.
   (2) Unless other legislation otherwise provides, the court may do so—
      (a) on application by a party or person directly affected; or
      (b) on its own initiative.
   (3) A party or person who wants the court to do so must—
      (a) apply as soon as reasonably practicable;
      (b) notify—
         (i)   each other party, and
         (ii) such other person (if any) as the court directs;
      (c) specify the restriction; and
      (d) explain, as appropriate, why it should be varied or removed.
   (4) A person who wants to appeal to the Crown Court under section 141F of the Education Act 2002[34] must—
      (a) serve an appeal notice on—
         (i)   the Crown Court officer, and
         (ii) each other party;
      (b) serve on the Crown Court officer, with the appeal notice, a copy of the application to the magistrates' court;
      (c) serve the appeal notice not more than 15 business days after the magistrates' court's decision against which the appellant wants to appeal; and
      (d) in the appeal notice, explain, as appropriate, why the restriction should be maintained, varied or removed.
   (5) Rule 34.11 (Constitution of the Crown Court) applies on such an appeal.

[Note. Under section 141F(7) of the Education Act 2002, a party to an application to a magistrates' court to remove the statutory restriction on reporting an alleged offence by a teacher may appeal to the Crown Court against the decision of the magistrates' court. With the Crown Court's permission, any other person may appeal against such a decision.]

Trial in private   R6.6

6.6 (1) This rule applies where the court can order a trial in private.
   (2) A party who wants the court to do so must—
      (a) apply in writing not less than 5 business days before the trial is due to begin; and
      (b) serve the application on—
         (i)   the court officer, and
         (ii) each other party.
   (3) The applicant must explain—
      (a) the reasons for the application;
      (b) how much of the trial the applicant proposes should be in private; and
      (c) why no measures other than trial in private will suffice, such as—
         (i)   reporting restrictions,
         (ii) an admission of facts,
         (iii) the introduction of hearsay evidence,
         (iv) a direction for a special measure under section 19 of the Youth Justice and Criminal Evidence Act 1999,
         (v)   a witness anonymity order under section 86 of the Coroners and Justice Act 2009, or
         (vi) arrangements for the protection of a witness.
   (4) Where the application includes information that the applicant thinks ought not be revealed to another party, the applicant must—
      (a) omit that information from the part of the application that is served on that other party;
      (b) mark the other part to show that, unless the court otherwise directs, it is only for the court; and
      (c) in that other part, explain why the applicant has withheld that information from that other party.

[34] 2002 c. 32; section 141F was inserted by section 13 of the Education Act 2011 (c. 21).

(5) The court officer must at once—

    (a) display notice of the application somewhere prominent in the vicinity of the courtroom; and

    (b) give notice of the application to reporters by such other arrangements as the Lord Chancellor directs.

(6) The application must be determined at a hearing which—

    (a) must be in private, unless the court otherwise directs;

    (b) if the court so directs, may be, wholly or in part, in the absence of a party from whom information has been withheld; and

    (c) in the Crown Court, must be after the defendant is arraigned but before the jury is sworn.

(7) At the hearing of the application—

    (a) the general rule is that the court must consider, in the following sequence—

        (i) representations first by the applicant and then by each other party, in all the parties' presence, and then

        (ii) further representations by the applicant, in the absence of a party from whom information has been withheld; but

    (b) the court may direct other arrangements for the hearing.

(8) The court must not hear a trial in private until—

    (a) the business day after the day on which it orders such a trial, or

    (b) the disposal of any appeal against, or review of, any such order, if later.

R6.7 Representations in response

6.7 (1) This rule applies where a party, or person directly affected, wants to make representations about an application or appeal.

    (2) Such a party or person must—

        (a) serve the representations on—

            (i) the court officer,

            (ii) the applicant,

            (iii) each other party, and

            (iv) such other person (if any) as the court directs;

        (b) do so as soon as reasonably practicable after notice of the application; and

        (c) ask for a hearing, if that party or person wants one, and explain why it is needed.

    (3) Representations must—

        (a) explain the reasons for any objection; and

        (b) specify any alternative terms proposed.

R6.8 Order about restriction or trial in private

6.8 (1) This rule applies where the court—

        (a) orders, varies or removes a reporting or access restriction; or

        (b) orders a trial in private.

    (2) The court officer must—

        (a) record the court's reasons for the decision; and

        (b) as soon as reasonably practicable, arrange for notice of the decision to be—

            (i) displayed somewhere prominent in the vicinity of the courtroom, and

            (ii) communicated to reporters by such other arrangements as the Lord Chancellor directs.

Sound recording and electronic communication

R6.9 Sound recording and electronic communication

6.9 (1) This rule applies where the court can give permission to—

        (a) bring into a hearing for use, or use during a hearing, a device for—

            (i) recording sound, or

            (ii) communicating by electronic means; or

        (b) publish a sound recording made during a hearing.

    (2) The court may give such permission—

        (a) on application; or

        (b) on its own initiative.

    (3) A person who wants the court to give such permission must—

        (a) apply as soon as reasonably practicable;

        (b) notify—

            (i) each party, and

            (ii) such other person (if any) as the court directs; and

        (c) explain why the court should permit the use or publication proposed.

(4) As a condition of the applicant using such a device, the court may direct arrangements to minimise the risk of its use—
  (a) contravening a reporting restriction;
  (b) disrupting the hearing; or
  (c) compromising the fairness of the hearing, for example by affecting—
    (i) the evidence to be given by a witness, or
    (ii) the verdict of a jury.
(5) Such a direction may require that the device is used only—
  (a) in a specified part of the courtroom;
  (b) for a specified purpose;
  (c) for a purpose connected with the applicant's activity as a member of a specified group, for example representatives of news-gathering or reporting organisations; or
  (d) at a specified time, or in a specified way.

Forfeiture of unauthorised sound recording   R6.10

6.10 (1) This rule applies where someone without the court's permission—
  (a) uses a device for recording sound during a hearing; or
  (b) publishes a sound recording made during a hearing.
(2) The court may exercise its power to forfeit the device or recording—
  (a) on application by a party, or on its own initiative; and
  (b) provisionally, despite rule 6.2(3), to allow time for representations.
(3) A party who wants the court to forfeit a device or recording must—
  (a) apply as soon as reasonably practicable;
  (b) notify—
    (i) as appropriate, the person who used the device, or who published the recording, and
    (ii) each other party; and
  (c) explain why the court should exercise that power.

[Note. Under section 9(3) of the Contempt of Court Act 1981[35], the court can forfeit any device or recording used or made in contravention of section 9(1) of the Act.]

CRIMINAL PROCEDURE RULES   PART 7   STARTING A PROSECUTION IN A MAGISTRATES' COURT

When this Part applies   R7.1

7.1 (1) This Part applies in a magistrates' court where—
  (a) a prosecutor wants the court to issue a summons or warrant under section 1 of the Magistrates' Courts Act 1980[1];
  (b) a prosecutor with the power to do so issues—
    (i) a written charge and requisition, or
    (ii) a written charge and single justice procedure notice under section 29 of the Criminal Justice Act 2003[2]; or
  (c) a person who is in custody is charged with an offence; or
  (d) the prosecutor alleges an offence against a defendant who is due to attend, or attends, the court in response to another allegation.
(2) In this Part, 'authorised prosecutor' means a prosecutor authorised under section 29 of the Criminal Justice Act 2003 to issue a written charge and requisition or single justice procedure notice.

[Note. Under section 1 of the Magistrates' Courts Act 1980, on receiving a formal statement (described in that section as an 'information') alleging that someone has committed an offence, the court may issue—

  (a) a summons requiring that person to attend court; or

---

[35] 1981 c. 49.

[1] 1980 c. 43; section 1 was amended by section 68 of, and paragraph 6 of Schedule 8 to, the Criminal Justice Act 1991 (c. 53), sections 43 and 109 of, and Schedule 10 to, the Courts Act 2003 (c. 39), section 31 of, and paragraph 12 of Schedule 7 to, the Criminal Justice Act 2003 (c. 44) and section 153 of the Police Reform and Social Responsibility Act 2011. It is further amended by paragraphs 7 and 8 of Schedule 36 to, the Criminal Justice Act 2003 (c. 44), with effect from a date to be appointed.

[2] 2003 c. 44; section 29 has been brought into force for certain purposes only (see S.I. 2007/1999, 2008/1424, 2009/2879, 2010/3005, 2011/2188, 2012/825 and 2014/633). It was amended by section 50 of, and paragraph 130 of Schedule 4 to, the Commissioners for Revenue and Customs Act 2005 (c. 11), section 59 of, and paragraph 196 of Schedule 4 to, the Serious Organised Crime and Police Act 2005 (c. 15), section 15 of, and paragraph 187 of Schedule 8 to, the Crime and Courts Act 2013 (c. 22), S.I. 2014/834 and section 46 of the Criminal Justice and Courts Act 2015 (c. 2).

> (b) a warrant for that person's arrest, if—
>> (i)   the alleged offence must or may be tried in the Crown Court,
>> (ii) the alleged offence is punishable with imprisonment, or
>> (iii) the person's address cannot be established sufficiently clearly to serve a summons or requisition.
>
> The powers of the court to which this Part applies may be exercised by a single justice of the peace.
>
> Under section 29 of the Criminal Justice Act 2003, a prosecutor authorised under that section may issue a written charge alleging that someone has committed an offence, and either—
>
>> (a) a requisition requiring that person to attend court; or
>> (b) a notice that the single justice procedure under section 16A of the Magistrates' Courts Act 1980[3] and rule 24.9 of these Rules applies.
>
> Section 30 of the 2003 Act[4] contains other provisions about written charges, requisitions and single justice procedure notices.
>
> A person detained under a power of arrest may be charged if the custody officer decides that there is sufficient evidence to do so. See sections 37 and 38 of the Police and Criminal Evidence Act 1984[5].]

R7.2 Application for summons, etc.

7.2 (1) A prosecutor who wants the court to issue a summons must—
    (a) serve on the court officer a written application; or
    (b) unless other legislation prohibits this, present an application orally to the court, with a written statement of the allegation or allegations made by the prosecutor.

    (2) A prosecutor who wants the court to issue a warrant must—
    (a) serve on the court officer—
      (i)   a written application, or
      (ii) a copy of a written charge that has been issued; or
    (b) present to the court either of those documents.

    (3) An application for the issue of a summons or warrant must—
    (a) set out the allegation or allegations made by the applicant in terms that comply with rule 7.3(1) (Allegation of offence in application or charge); and
    (b) demonstrate—
      (i)   that the application is made in time, if legislation imposes a time limit, and
      (ii) that the applicant has the necessary consent, if legislation requires it.

    (4) As well as complying with paragraph (3), an application for the issue of a warrant must—
    (a) demonstrate that the offence or offences alleged can be tried in the Crown Court;
    (b) demonstrate that the offence or offences alleged can be punished with imprisonment; or
    (c) concisely outline the applicant's grounds for asserting that the defendant's address is not sufficiently established for a summons to be served.

    (5) Paragraph (6) applies unless the prosecutor is—
    (a) a public authority within the meaning of section 17 of the Prosecution of Offences Act 1985[6]; or
    (b) a person acting—
      (i)   on behalf of such an authority, or
      (ii) in that person's capacity as an official appointed by such an authority.

    (6) Where this paragraph applies, as well as complying with paragraph (3), and with paragraph (4) if applicable, an application for the issue of a summons or warrant must—

---

[3] 1980 c. 43; section 16A was inserted by section 48 of the Criminal Justice and Courts Act 2015 (c. 2).
[4] 2003 c. 44; section 30 has been brought into force for certain purposes only (see S.I. 2007/1999, 2008/1424, 2009/2879, 2010/3005, 2011/2188, 2012/825 and 2014/633). It was amended by article 3 of, and paragraphs 45 and 46 of the Schedule to, S.I. 2004/2035 and section 47 of the Criminal Justice and Courts Act 2015 (c. 2).
[5] 1984 c. 60; section 37 was amended by section 108(7) of, and Schedule 15 to, the Children Act 1989 (c. 41), sections 72 and 101(2) of, and Schedule 13 to, the Criminal Justice Act 1991 (c. 53), sections 29(4) and 168(3) of, and Schedule 11 to, the Criminal Justice and Public Order Act 1994 (c. 33), section 28 of, and paragraphs 1 and 2 of Schedule 2 to, the Criminal Justice Act 2003 (c. 44), section 23(1) of, and paragraphs 1 and 2 of Schedule 1 to, the Drugs Act 2005 (c. 17) and sections 11 and 52 of, and paragraph 9 of Schedule 14 to, the Police and Justice Act 2006 (c. 48).
Section 38 was amended by section 108(5) of, and paragraph 53 of Schedule 13 to, the Children Act 1989 (c. 41), section 59 of the Criminal Justice Act 1991 (c. 53), sections 24, 28 and 168(2) of, and paragraph 54 of Schedule 10 to, the Criminal Justice and Public Order Act 1994 (c. 33), section 57 of the Criminal Justice and Court Services Act 2000 (c. 43), section 5 of, and paragraph 44 of Schedule 32 and paragraph 5 of Schedule 36 to, the Criminal Justice Act 2003 (c. 44), section 23 of, and paragraphs 1 and 3 of Schedule 1 to, the Drugs Act 2005 (c. 17) and paragraph 34 of Schedule 11 to the Legal Aid, Sentencing and Punishment of Offenders Act 2012 (c. 10).
[6] 1985 c. 23; section 17 was amended by section 40 of, and paragraph 41 of Schedule 9 to, the Constitutional Reform Act 2005 (c. 4) and paragraphs 1 and 4 and Part 4 of Schedule 7 to the Legal Aid, Sentencing and Punishment of Offenders Act 2012 (c. 10).

Criminal Procedure Rules

(a) concisely outline the grounds for asserting that the defendant has committed the alleged offence or offences;

(b) disclose—

    (i) details of any previous such application by the same applicant in respect of any allegation now made, and

    (ii) details of any current or previous proceedings brought by another prosecutor in respect of any allegation now made; and

(c) include a statement that to the best of the applicant's knowledge, information and belief—

    (i) the allegations contained in the application are substantially true,

    (ii) the evidence on which the applicant relies will be available at the trial,

    (iii) the details given by the applicant under paragraph (6)(b) are true, and

    (iv) the application discloses all the information that is material to what the court must decide

(7) Where the statement required by paragraph (6)(c) is made orally—

    (a) the statement must be on oath or affirmation, unless the court otherwise directs; and

    (b) the court must arrange for a record of the making of the statement.

(8) An authorised prosecutor who issues a written charge must notify the court officer immediately.

(9) A single document may contain—

    (a) more than one application; or

    (b) more than one written charge.

(10) Where an offence can be tried only in a magistrates' court, then unless other legislation otherwise provides—

    (a) a prosecutor must serve an application for the issue of a summons or warrant on the court officer or present it to the court; or

    (b) an authorised prosecutor must issue a written charge, not more than 6 months after the offence alleged.

(11) Where an offence can be tried in the Crown Court then—

    (a) a prosecutor must serve an application for the issue of a summons or warrant on the court officer or present it to the court; or

    (b) an authorised prosecutor must issue a written charge, within any time limit that applies to that offence.

(12) The court may determine an application to issue or withdraw a summons or warrant—

    (a) without a hearing, as a general rule, or at a hearing (which must be in private unless the court otherwise directs);

    (b) in the absence of—

        (i) the prosecutor,

        (ii) the defendant; and

    (c) with or without representations by the defendant.

(13) If the court so directs, a party to an application to issue or withdraw a summons or warrant may attend a hearing by live link.

(14) The court may decline to issue a summons or warrant if, for example—

    (a) a court has previously determined an application by the same prosecutor which alleged the same or substantially the same offence against the same defendant on the same or substantially the same asserted facts;

    (b) the prosecutor fails to disclose all the information that is material to what the court must decide;

    (c) the prosecutor has—

        (i) reached a binding agreement with the defendant not to prosecute, or

        (ii) made representations that no prosecution would be brought, on which the defendant has acted to the defendant's detriment;

    (d) the prosecutor asserts facts incapable of proof in a criminal court as a matter of law;

    (e) the prosecution would constitute an assertion that the decision of another court or authority was wrong where that decision has been, or could have been, or could be, questioned in other proceedings or by other lawful means; or

    (f) the prosecutor's dominant motive would render the prosecution an abuse of the process of the court.

[Note. In some legislation, including the Magistrates' Courts Act 1980, an application for the issue of a summons or warrant is described as an 'information' and serving an application on the court officer or presenting it to the court is described as 'laying' that information.

Where an offence can be tried only in a magistrates' court the general time limit for serving or presenting an application for a summons or warrant, and for issuing a written charge, is prescribed by section 127 of the Magistrates' Courts Act 1980[7] and section 30(5) of the Criminal Justice Act 2003[8]. However, the legislation that creates the offence may prescribe a different time limit, which may be calculated by reference to the date of the offence or by reference to another event specified by that legislation. If the application contains insufficient information to show that it is in time the court may refuse to issue a summons or warrant.

In section 17 of the Prosecution of Offences Act 1985 'public authority' means (a) a police force as defined by that Act, (b) the Crown Prosecution Service or any other government department, (c) a local authority or other authority or body constituted for purposes of the public service or of local government, or carrying on under national ownership any industry or undertaking or part of an industry or undertaking, or (d) any other authority or body whose members are appointed by [His] Majesty or by any Minister of the Crown or government department or whose revenues consist wholly or mainly of money provided by Parliament.

Part 46 (Representatives) contains rules allowing a member, officer or employee of a prosecutor, on the prosecutor's behalf, to—

(a) serve on the court officer or present to the court an application for the issue of a summons or warrant; or

(b) issue a written charge and requisition.

See Part 3 for the court's general powers of case management, including power to consider applications and give directions for (among other things) the amendment of an allegation or charge and for separate trials.

See also Part 32 (Breach, revocation and amendment of community and other orders). Rule 32.2(2) (Application by responsible officer) applies rules 7.2 to 7.4 to the procedure with which that rule deals.

The Practice Direction sets out a form of application for use in connection with rule 7.2(6).]

R7.3 Allegation of offence

7.3 (1) An allegation of an offences in an application for the issue of a summons or warrant or in a charge must contain—
    (a) a statement of the offence that—
      (i) describes the offence in ordinary language, and
      (ii) identifies any legislation that creates it; and
    (b) such particulars of the conduct constituting the commission of the offence as to make clear what the prosecutor alleges against the defendant, including the value of any damage or theft alleged where that value is known and where it affects the exercise of the court's powers.
    (2) More than one incident of the commission of the offence may be included in the allegation if those incidents taken together amount to a course of conduct having regard to the time, place or purpose of commission.
    (3) Where rule 7.1(1)(d) applies (additional allegation in existing prosecution), the prosecutor must—
    (a) set out the additional allegation in terms that comply with paragraph (1);
    (b) as soon as practicable—
      (i) serve the additional allegation on the court officer and the defendant, or
      (ii) present the additional allegation orally to the court, with a written statement of that allegation;
    (c) demonstrate that the allegation is made in time, if legislation imposes a time limit; and
    (d) demonstrate that the prosecutor has the necessary consent, if legislation requires it.

[Note. In some circumstances the court may allow the prosecutor to amend an allegation of an offence, including to allege a different offence. In those circumstances the allegation may be amended after any time limit for prosecuting the different offence has expired if the amendment is based on substantially the same facts as the allegation first made. See Part 3 for the court's general powers of case management, including power to consider an application and give directions for (among other things) the amendment of an allegation.]

R7.4 Summons, warrant and requisition

7.4 (1) A summons, warrant or requisition may be issued in respect of more than one offence.
    (2) A summons or requisition must—
    (a) contain notice of when and where the defendant is required to attend the court;
    (b) specify each offence in respect of which it is issued;
    (c) in the case of a summons, identify—

---

[7] 1980 c. 43.
[8] 2003 c. 44; section 30(5) was amended by section 47 of the Criminal Justice and Courts Act 2015 (c. 2).

(i)   the court that issued it, unless that is otherwise recorded by the court officer,

(ii) the court office for the court that issued it, and

(iii) the prosecutor, unless the prosecutor is a public authority; and

(d) in the case of a requisition, identify the person under whose authority it is issued.

(3) A summons may be contained in the same document as an application for the issue of that summons.

(4) A requisition may be contained in the same document as a written charge.

(5) Where the court issues a summons—

(a) the prosecutor must—

(i)   serve it on the defendant, and

(ii) notify the court officer; or

(b) the court officer must—

(i)   serve it on the defendant, and

(ii) notify the prosecutor.

(6) Where an authorised prosecutor issues a requisition that prosecutor must—

(a) serve on the defendant—

(i)   the requisition, and

(ii) the written charge; and

(b) serve a copy of each on the court officer.

(7) Unless it would be inconsistent with other legislation, a replacement summons or requisition may be issued without a fresh application or written charge where the one replaced—

(a) was served under rule 4.4 (Service by leaving or posting a document); but

(b) is shown not to have been received by the addressee.

(8) Where a summons or requisition is served on a defendant under 18—

(a) the prosecutor or court officer who serves it must serve a copy on a parent or guardian of the defendant as well, and

(b) if the court requires the parent or guardian to attend, the copy may impose that requirement or a separate summons or requisition may be issued for that purpose.

[Note. Part 13 contains other rules about warrants.

Section 47 of the Magistrates' Courts Act 1980[9] and section 30(5) of the Criminal Justice Act 2003 make special provision about time limits under other legislation for the issue and service of a summons or requisition, where service by post is not successful.

Under section 34A of the Children and Young Persons Act 1933[10] unless the court is satisfied that it would be unreasonable to require such attendance having regard to the circumstances of the case (i) the court may require the parent or guardian of a defendant under 18 to attend court with the defendant, and (ii) the court must do so if the defendant is under 16.]

Notice of defendant in custody   R7.5

7.5   (1) This rule and rule 7.6 (Arrangements for court to receive defendant in custody) apply where—

(a) a defendant in custody must be brought before a court—

(i)   under section 46 of the Police and Criminal Evidence Act 1984[11] (Detention after charge), or

(ii) after arrest on a warrant issued under section 1 of the Magistrates' Courts Act 1980 (Issue of summons to accused or warrant for his arrest); and

(b) a police custody officer so notifies the court officer.

(2) The police custody officer must provide the court officer with—

(a) the defendant's name and date of birth;

(b) the offence charged and confirmation of the date and time of charge;

(c) confirmation that the information required by rule 8.3 (Content of initial details) is available and will be served before the defendant's case is heard;

(d) confirmation that the prosecutor has been notified;

(e) confirmation that the following have been notified and are available—

(i)   any interpreter required,

(ii) the defendant's legal representative, if any, and

(iii) any local or other authority, including any youth offending team, responsible for the defendant's care or welfare;

---

[9] 1980 c. 43; section 47 was amended by section 109(1) of, and paragraph 207 of Schedule 8 to, the Courts Act 2003 (c. 39).

[10] 1933 c. 12; section 34A was inserted by section 56 of the Criminal Justice Act 1991 (c. 53) and amended by section 107 of, and paragraph 1 of Schedule 5 to, the Local Government Act 2000 (c. 22) and regulations 3 and 5 of S.I. 2016/413.

[11] 1984 c. 60; section 46 was amended by section 109 of, and paragraph 282 of Schedule 8 to, the Courts Act 2003 (c. 39).

    (f) the police custody officer's proposal for the means by which the defendant will be brought before the court, either by live link or in person, and—

       (i) if the proposal is for the defendant to attend court by live link, details of any material circumstance listed in rule 3.35 (Live link direction: exercise of court's powers), or

       (ii) if the proposal is for the defendant to attend court in person, the identity of the authority responsible for transporting the defendant and the expected time of arrival; and

    (g) details of any disability or other vulnerability of the defendant of which the police custody officer is aware and which is not apparent from other information supplied.

[Note. Under section 46 of the Police and Criminal Evidence Act 1984 a defendant who is charged with an offence and, after being charged, is kept in police or local authority detention must be brought before a magistrates' court as soon as is practicable that day, or the next day which is not Christmas Day, Good Friday or a Sunday.]

R7.6   **Arrangements for court to receive defendant in custody**

7.6   (1) Subject to paragraph (3), the court officer must arrange for a defendant of whom notice is given under rule 7.5 (Notice of defendant in custody) to be brought before a court in person or by live link as soon as is practicable that day and in any event—

    (a) by 3.30pm if that day is a business day;

    (b) by 12.30pm if that day is a Saturday or a bank holiday; or

    (c) in either case, later if, but only if, a disability or vulnerability of the defendant so requires.

   (2) In making the arrangements required by paragraph (1) the court officer must—

    (a) consult with those affected including—

       (i) the police custody officer,

       (ii) court members,

       (iii) justices' legal advisers and other court officers, and

       (iv) the prosecutor; and

    (b) as far as is practicable rearrange court business to ensure that the time available will allow all cases heard that day to conclude by 4.30pm (or later if, but only if, a disability or vulnerability of the defendant the subject of this rule so requires).

   (3) If the arrangements otherwise required by paragraph (1) cannot practicably be made then the court officer must arrange for the defendant to be brought before a court as soon as is practicable on the next day which is not Christmas Day, Good Friday or a Sunday.

   (4) When arrangements for the defendant to be brought before a court have been made the court officer promptly must so inform—

    (a) the police custody officer; and

    (b) as applicable, others consulted under paragraph (2)(a).

CRIMINAL PROCEDURE RULES   PART 8   INITIAL DETAILS OF THE PROSECUTION CASE

R8.1   **When this Part applies**

8.1   This Part applies in a magistrates' court.

R8.2   **Providing initial details of the prosecution case**

8.2   (1) The prosecutor must serve initial details of the prosecution case on the court officer—

    (a) as soon as practicable; and

    (b) in any event, no later than the beginning of the day of the first hearing.

   (2) Where a defendant requests those details, the prosecutor must serve them on the defendant—

    (a) as soon as practicable; and

    (b) in any event, no later than the beginning of the day of the first hearing.

   (3) Where a defendant does not request those details, the prosecutor must make them available to the defendant at, or before, the beginning of the day of the first hearing.

R8.3   **Content of initial details**

8.3   Initial details of the prosecution case must include—

    (a) where, immediately before the first hearing in the magistrates' court, the defendant was in police custody for the offence charged—

       (i) a summary of the circumstances of the offence, and

       (ii) the defendant's criminal record, if any; or

    (b) where paragraph (a) does not apply—

       (i) a summary of the circumstances of the offence,

       (ii) any account given by the defendant in interview, whether contained in that summary or in another document,

       (iii) any written witness statement or exhibit that the prosecutor then has available and considers material to plea, or to the allocation of the case for trial, or to sentence,

       (iv) the defendant's criminal record, if any, and

       (v) any available statement of the effect of the offence on a victim, a victim's family or others.

Use of initial details   R8.4

8.4   (1) This rule applies where—

      (a) the prosecutor wants to introduce information contained in a document listed in rule 8.3; and

      (b) the prosecutor has not—

        (i) served that document on the defendant, or

        (ii) made that information available to the defendant.

   (2) The court must not allow the prosecutor to introduce that information unless the court first allows the defendant sufficient time to consider it.

CRIMINAL PROCEDURE RULES   PART 9   ALLOCATION AND SENDING FOR TRIAL

General rules

When this Part applies   R9.1

9.1   (1) This Part applies to—

      (a) the allocation and sending of cases to the Crown Court for trial under—

        (i) sections 17A to 26 of the Magistrates' Courts Act 1980[1], and

        (ii) sections 50A to 52 of the Crime and Disorder Act 1998[2]; and

      (b) the sending back or referring of cases to a magistrates' court for trial under—

        (i) section 46ZA of the Senior Courts Act 1981[3], and

        (ii) paragraph 6 of Schedule 3 to the Crime and Disorder Act 1998[4].

   (2) Rules 9.6 and 9.7 apply in a magistrates' court where the court must, or can, send a defendant to the Crown Court for trial, without allocating the case for trial there.

   (3) Rules 9.8 to 9.14 apply in a magistrates' court where the court must allocate the case to a magistrates' court or to the Crown Court for trial.

   (4) Rule 9.15 applies in a magistrates' court where, after applying other rules in this Part, the court can commit for sentence to the Crown Court a defendant who pleads guilty to an offence related to one sent for trial there.

   (5) Rule 9.16 applies in the Crown Court where the court can send back or refer a defendant to a magistrates' court for trial.

[Note. At the first hearing in a magistrates' court the court may (and in some cases must) order trial in that court, or may (and in some cases must) send the defendant to the Crown Court for trial under section 51 or 51A of the Crime and Disorder Act 1998[5]. The decision depends upon—

---

[1] 1980 c. 43; sections 17A to 17C were inserted by section 49 of the Criminal Procedure and Investigations Act 1996 (c. 25). Sections 17A, 17D, 17E, 18 to 21 and 23 to 26 were amended or inserted by Schedule 3 to the Criminal Justice Act 2003 (c. 44). Sections 17A, 17D, 20, 20A, 24 and 24A were further amended by paragraphs 44, 45, 46, 47, 48 and 49 respectively of Schedule 24 to the Sentencing Act 2020 (c. 17). Section 19 was further amended by section 378 of, and paragraph 88 of Schedule 16 to, the Armed Forces Act 2006 (c. 52), sections 144, 177 and 178 of, and paragraph 4 of Schedule 17, paragraph 80 of Schedule 21 and Schedule 23 to, the Coroners and Justice Act 2009 (c. 25) and S.I. 2019/780. Section 22 was amended by sections 38 and 170 of, and Schedule 16 to, the Criminal Justice Act 1988 (c. 33), section 68 of, and paragraph 6 of Schedule 8 to, the Criminal Justice Act 1991 (c. 53), section 2 of the Aggravated Vehicle-Taking Act 1992 (c. 11) and sections 46 and 168 of, and Schedule 11 to, the Criminal Justice and Public Order Act 1994 (c. 33). Section 22A was inserted by section 176 of the Anti-social Behaviour, Crime and Policing Act 2014 (c. 12) and amended by section 52 of the Criminal Justice and Courts Act 2015 (c. 2).

[2] 1998 c. 37; sections 50A to 52 were inserted or amended by Schedule 3 to the Criminal Justice Act 2003 (c. 44). Section 51 was further amended by section 52 of the Criminal Justice and Courts Act 2015 (c. 2). Section 51A was further amended by sections 49 and 65 of, and paragraph 5 of Schedule 1 and Schedule 5 to, the Violent Crime Reduction Act 2006 (c. 38) and paragraph 156 of Schedule 24 to the Sentencing Act 2020 (c. 17). Section 51B was further amended by section 50 of, and paragraph 69 of Schedule 4 to, the Commissioners for Revenue and Customs Act 2005 (c. 11), section 39 of, and paragraphs 46 and 48 of Schedule 5 to, the Legal Aid, Sentencing and Punishment of Offenders Act 2012 (c. 10) and S.I. 2014/834. Section 51C was further amended by S.I. 2006/244. Section 52 was further amended by section 177 of, and paragraph 78 of Schedule 21 to, the Coroners and Justice Act 2009 (c. 25).

[3] 1981 c. 54; section 46ZA was inserted by section 11 of the Judicial Review and Courts Act 2022 (c. 35).

[4] 1998 c. 37; paragraph 6 of Schedule 3 was amended by sections 90 and 106 of, and paragraph 179 of Schedule 13 and Schedule 15 to, the Access to Justice Act 1999 (c. 22), sections 41 of, and paragraphs 15 and 20 of Schedule 3 to, the Criminal Justice Act 2003 (c. 44), S.I. 2005/886 and paragraphs 20 and 23 of the Schedule to the Courts and Tribunals (Judiciary and Functions of Staff) Act 2018 (c. 33).

[5] 1998 c. 37; section 51 was substituted by paragraphs 15 and 18 of Schedule 3 to the Criminal Justice Act 2003 (c. 44) and amended by section 59 of, and paragraph 1 of Schedule 11 to, the Constitutional Reform Act 2005 (c. 4). Section 51A was inserted by paragraphs 15 and 18 of Schedule 3 to the Criminal Justice Act 2003 (c. 44) and amended by section 49 of, and

(a) *the classification of the offence (and the general rule, subject to exceptions, is that an offence classified as triable only on indictment must be sent to the Crown Court for trial; an offence classified as triable only summarily must be tried in a magistrates' court; and an offence classified as triable either way, on indictment or summarily, must be allocated to one or the other court for trial, subject to the defendant's right to choose Crown Court trial: see in particular sections 50A, 51 and 51A of the 1998 Act[6] and section 19 of the Magistrates' Courts Act 1980[7]);*

(b) *the defendant's age (and the general rule, subject to exceptions, is that an offence alleged against a defendant under 18 must be tried in a magistrates' court sitting as a youth court: see in particular sections 24 and 24A of the 1980 Act[8];*

(c) *whether the defendant is awaiting Crown Court trial for another offence;*

(d) *whether another defendant, charged with the same offence, is awaiting Crown Court trial for that offence;*

(e) *in some cases (destroying or damaging property; aggravated vehicle taking), whether the value involved is more or less than £5,000; and*

(f) *in a case of low-value shoplifting, whether the defendant chooses Crown Court trial: see section 22A of the 1980 Act[9].*

A magistrates' court's powers of sending and allocation, including its powers (i) to receive a defendant's indication of an intention to plead guilty (see rules 9.7, 9.8 and 9.13) and (ii) to give an indication of likely sentence (see rule 9.11), may be exercised by a single justice: see sections 51 and 51A(11) of the 1998 Act, and sections 17E, 18(5) and 24D of the 1980 Act[10],

The circumstances in which the Crown Court can send back or refer a case for magistrates' court trial are summarised in the note to rule 9.16.]

R9.2   **Exercise of magistrates' court's powers**

9.2   (1) This rule applies to the exercise of a magistrates' court's powers to which this Part applies.

     (2) The general rule is that the court must exercise its powers at a hearing in public, but it may exercise any power it has to—

       (a) where rule 9.7 (Sending for Crown Court trial) applies, if the defendant is represented;

       (b) withhold information from the public; or

       (c) order a hearing in private.

     (3) The general rule is that the court must exercise its powers in the defendant's presence, but it may exercise the powers to which the following rules apply in the defendant's absence on the conditions specified—

       (a) where rule 9.7 (Sending for Crown Court trial) applies, if the defendant is represented;

       (b) where rule 9.8 (Adult defendant: request for plea), rule 9.9 (Adult defendant: guilty plea) or rule 9.13 (Young defendant) applies, if—

         (i) the defendant is represented, and

         (ii) the defendant's disorderly conduct makes his or her presence in the courtroom impracticable;

       (c) where rule 9.10 (Adult defendant: not guilty plea) or rule 9.11 (Adult defendant: allocation for magistrates' court trial) applies, if—

         (i) the defendant is represented and waives the right to be present, or

         (ii) the defendant's disorderly conduct makes his or her presence in the courtroom impracticable; and

paragraph 5 of Schedule 1 to, the Violent Crime Reduction Act 2006 (c. 38) and paragraph 6 of Schedule 21 to the Legal Aid, Sentencing and Punishment of Offenders Act 2012 (c. 10).

[6] 1998 c. 37; section 50A was inserted by paragraphs 15 and 17 of Schedule 3 to the Criminal Justice Act 2003 (c. 44).

[7] 1980 c. 43; section 19 was substituted by paragraphs 1 and 5 of Schedule 3 to the Criminal Justice Act 2003 (c. 44) and amended by sections 144, 177 and 178 of, and paragraph 4 of Schedule 17, paragraph 80 of Schedule 21 and Part 5 of Schedule 23 to, the Coroners and Justice Act 2009 (c. 25).

[8] 1980 c. 43; section 24 was amended by paragraph 47 of Schedule 14 to the Criminal Justice Act 1982 (c. 48), sections 17, 68 and 101 of, and paragraph 6 of Schedule 8 and Schedule 13 to, the Criminal Justice Act 1991 (c. 53), paragraph 40 of Schedule 10, and Schedule 11, to the Criminal Justice and Public Order Act 1994 (c. 33), sections 47 and 119 of, and paragraph 40 of Schedule 8, to the Crime and Disorder Act 1998 (c. 37), paragraph 64 of Schedule 9 to the Powers of Criminal Courts (Sentencing) Act 2000 (c. 6), section 42 of, and paragraphs 1 and 9 of Schedule 3, and Part 4 of Schedule 37, to the Criminal Justice Act 2003 (c. 44) and sections 49 and 65 of, and paragraph 1 of Schedule 1 and Schedule 5 to, the Violent Crime Reduction Act 2006 (c. 38). Section 24A was inserted by paragraphs 1 and 10 of Schedule 3 to the Criminal Justice Act 2003 (c. 44).

[9] 1980 c. 43; section 22A was inserted by section 176 of the Anti-social Behaviour, Crime and Policing Act 2014 (c. 12) and amended by section 52 of the Criminal Justice and Courts Act 2015 (c. 2).

[10] 1980 c. 43; section 17E was inserted by paragraphs 1 and 3 of Schedule 3 to the Criminal Justice Act 2003 (c. 44). Section 18 was amended by section 59 of, and paragraph 1 of Schedule 9 to, the Criminal Justice Act 1982 (c. 48), section 68 of, and paragraph 6 of Schedule 8 to, the Criminal Justice Act 1991 (c. 53), section 49 of the Criminal Procedure and Investigations Act 1996 (c. 25), and paragraphs 1 and 4 of Schedule 3 to the Criminal Justice Act 2003 (c. 44). Section 24D was inserted by paragraphs 1 and 10 of Schedule 3 to the Criminal Justice Act 2003 (c. 44).

    (d) where rule 9.15 (Committal for sentence for offence related to an offence sent for trial) applies, unless—

        (i) it appears to the court to be contrary to the interests of justice to do so, and

        (ii) the court considers that there is an acceptable reason for the defendant's absence.

(4) The court may exercise its power to adjourn—

    (a) if either party asks; or

    (b) on its own initiative.

(5) Where the court on the same occasion deals with two or more offences alleged against the same defendant, the court must deal with those offences in the following sequence—

    (a) any to which rule 9.6 applies (Prosecutor's notice requiring Crown Court trial);

    (b) any to which rule 9.7 applies (sending for Crown Court trial, without allocation there), in this sequence—

        (i) any the court must send for trial, then

        (ii) any the court can send for trial; and

    (c) any to which rule 9.14 applies (Allocation and sending for Crown Court trial).

(6) Where the court on the same occasion deals with two or more defendants charged jointly with an offence that can be tried in the Crown Court then in the following sequence—

    (a) the court must explain, in terms each defendant can understand (with help, if necessary), that if the court sends one of them to the Crown Court for trial then the court must send for trial in the Crown Court, too, any other of them—

        (i) who is charged with the same offence as the defendant sent for trial, or with an offence which the court decides is related to that offence,

        (ii) who does not wish to plead guilty to each offence with which he or she is charged, and

        (iii) (if that other defendant is under 18, and the court would not otherwise have sent him or her for Crown Court trial) where the court decides that sending is necessary in the interests of justice

        even if the court by then has decided to allocate that other defendant for magistrates' court trial; and

    (b) the court may ask the defendants questions to help it decide in what order to deal with them.

(7) After following paragraph (5), if it applies, where the court on the same occasion—

    (a) deals with two or more defendants charged jointly with an offence that can be tried in the Crown Court;

    (b) allocates any of them to a magistrates' court for trial; and

    (c) then sends another one of them to the Crown Court for trial,

    the court must deal again with each one whom, on that occasion, it has allocated for magistrates' court trial.

[Note. See sections 50A, 51, 51A and 52 of the Crime and Disorder Act 1998[11] and sections 17A, 17B, 17C, 18, 23, 24A, 24B and 24C of the Magistrates' Courts Act 1980[12].

Under sections 57A to 57E of the 1998 Act[13], the court may require a defendant to attend by live link a hearing to which this Part applies.

Where a defendant waives the right to be present then the court may nonetheless require his or her attendance by summons or warrant: see section 26 of the 1980 Act[14].

Under section 52A of the 1998 Act[15], reporting restrictions apply to the proceedings to which rules 9.6 to 9.14 apply.

Part 46 contains rules allowing a representative to act on a defendant's behalf for the purposes of these Rules.

Part 3 contains rules about the court's powers of case management.]

[11] 1998 c. 37; section 52 was amended by paragraphs 68 and 69 of Schedule 3 to the Criminal Justice Act 2003 (c. 44).

[12] 1980 c. 43; sections 17A, 17B and 17C were inserted by section 49 of the Criminal Procedure and Investigations Act 1996 (c. 25). Section 17A was amended by paragraph 62 of Schedule 9 to the Powers of Criminal Courts (Sentencing Act 2000 (c. 6) and paragraphs 1 and 2 of Schedule 3 to the Criminal Justice Act 2003 (c. 44). Section 23 was amended by section 125 of, and paragraph 25 of Schedule 18 to, the Courts and Legal Services Act 1990 (c. 41) and paragraphs 1 and 8 of Schedule 3 to the Criminal Justice Act 2003 (c. 44). Sections 24A, 24B and 24C were inserted by paragraphs 1 and 10 of Schedule 3 to the Criminal Justice Act 2003 (c. 44).

[13] 1998 c. 37; sections 57A to 57E were substituted for section 57 as originally enacted by section 45 of the Police and Justice Act 2006 (c. 48), and amended by sections 106, 109 and 178 of, and Part 3 of Schedule 23 to, the Coroners and Justice Act 2009 (c. 25). Section 57A was further amended by paragraphs 36 and 39 of Schedule 12 to the Legal Aid, Sentencing and Punishment of Offenders Act 2012 (c. 10).

[14] 1980 c. 43; section 26 was amended by paragraphs 1 and 12 of Schedule 3 to the Criminal Justice Act 2003 (c. 44).

[15] 1998 c. 37; section 52A was inserted by paragraphs 15 and 19 of Schedule 3 to the Criminal Justice Act 2003 (c. 44) and amended by paragraphs 46 and 47 of Schedule 5 to the Legal Aid, Sentencing and Punishment of Offenders Act 2012 (c. 10).

R9.3   **Matters to be specified on sending for trial**

9.3   (1) Where the court sends a defendant to the Crown Court for trial, it must specify—
             (a) each offence to be tried;
             (b) in respect of each, the power exercised to send the defendant for trial for that offence; and
             (c) the Crown Court centre at which the trial will take place.
        (2) In a case in which the prosecutor serves a notice to which rule 9.6(1)(a) applies (notice requiring Crown Court trial in a case of serious or complex fraud), the court must specify the Crown Court centre identified by that notice.
        (3) In any other case, in deciding the Crown Court centre at which the trial will take place, the court must take into account—
             (a) the convenience of the parties and witnesses;
             (b) how soon a suitable courtroom will be available; and
             (c) the directions on the allocation of Crown Court business contained in the Practice Direction.

[Note. See sections 51 and 51D of the Crime and Disorder Act 1998[17].]

R9.4   **Duty of justices' legal adviser**

9.4   (1) This rule applies—
             (a) only in a magistrates' court; and
             (b) unless the court—
                  (i)   includes a District Judge (Magistrates' Courts), and
                  (ii) otherwise directs.
        (2) On the court's behalf, a justices' legal adviser may—
             (a) read the allegation of the offence to the defendant; and
             (b) give any explanation and ask any question required by the rules in this Part.

[Note. For the functions of a justices' legal adviser, see sections 28 and 29 of the Courts Act 2003[18]. See also rule 2.12 (Duties of justices' legal adviser).]

R9.5   **Duty of magistrates' court officer**

9.5   (1) The magistrates' court officer must—
             (a) serve notice of a sending for Crown Court trial on—
                  (i)   the Crown Court officer, and
                  (ii) the parties;
             (b) in that notice record—
                  (i)   the matters specified by the court under rule 9.3 (Matters to be specified on sending for trial),
                  (ii)   any decision by the defendant under rule 9.7 (Sending for Crown Court trial) to require Crown Court trial for low-level shoplifting,
                  (iii) any indication given by the defendant under rule 9.7 of intended guilty plea
                  (iv)   any decision by the defendant under rule 9.11 (Adult defendant: allocation to magistrates' court for trial) to decline magistrates' court trial,
                  (v)   any opinion stated by the court under rule 9.15 (Committal for sentence for offence related to an offence sent for trial), and
                  (vi)   the date on which any custody time limit will expire;
             (c) record any indication of likely sentence to which rule 9.11 or rule 9.13 applies; and
             (d) give the court such other assistance as it requires.
        (2) The magistrates' court officer must include with the notice served on the Crown Court officer—
             (a) the initial details of the prosecution case served by the prosecutor under rule 8.2;
             (b) a record of any—
                  (i)   listing or case management direction affecting the Crown Court,
                  (ii)   direction about reporting restrictions,
                  (iii) decision about bail, for the purposes of section 5 of the Bail Act 1976[19],

---

[17] 1998 c. 37; section 51D was inserted by paragraphs 15 and 18 of Schedule 3 to the Criminal Justice Act 2003 (c. 44) and amended by section 59 of, and paragraph 1 of Schedule 11 to, the Constitutional Reform Act 2005 (c. 4).
[18] 2003 c. 39; section 28 was amended by section 15 of, and paragraphs 308 and 327 of Schedule 4 to, the Constitutional Reform Act 2005 (c. 4).
[19] 1976 c. 63; section 5 was amended by section 65 of, and Schedule 12 to, the Criminal Law Act 1977 (c. 45), section 60 of the Criminal Justice Act 1982 (c. 48), paragraph 1 of Schedule 3 to the Criminal Justice and Public Order Act 1994 (c. 33), paragraph 53 of Schedule 9 to the Powers of Criminal Courts (Sentencing Act 2000 (c. 6), section 129(1) of the Criminal Justice and Police Act 2001 (c. 16), paragraph 182 of Schedule 8 to the Courts Act 2003 (c. 39), paragraph 48 of Schedule 3,

(iv) recognizance given by a surety, or

(v) representation order; and

(c) if relevant, any available details of any—

(i) interpreter,

(ii) intermediary, or

(iii) other supporting adult, where the defendant is assisted by such a person.

[Note. See sections 51 and 51D of the Crime and Disorder Act 1998[20], and section 20A of the Magistrates' Courts Act 1980[21].]

Sending without allocation for Crown Court trial

Prosecutor's notice requiring Crown Court trial   **R9.6**

9.6 (1) This rule applies where a prosecutor with power to do so requires a magistrates' court to send for trial in the Crown Court—

(a) a case of serious or complex fraud; or

(b) a case which will involve a child witness.

(2) The prosecutor must serve notice of that requirement—

(a) on the magistrates' court officer and on the defendant; and

(b) before trial in a magistrates' court begins under Part 24 (Trial and sentence in a magistrates' court).

(3) The notice must identify—

(a) the power on which the prosecutor relies; and

(b) the Crown Court centre at which the prosecutor wants the trial to take place.

(4) The prosecutor—

(a) must, when choosing a Crown Court centre, take into account the matters listed in rule 9.3(3) (court deciding to which Crown Court centre to send a case); and

(b) may change the centre identified before the case is sent for trial.

[Note. Under section 51B of the Crime and Disorder Act 1998[22], the Director of Public Prosecutions or a Secretary of State may require the court to send a case for trial in the Crown Court if, in that prosecutor's opinion, the evidence of the offence charged—

(a) is sufficient for the person charged to be put on trial for the offence; and

(b) reveals a case of fraud of such seriousness or complexity that it is appropriate that the management of the case should without delay be taken over by the Crown Court.

Under section 51C of the Crime and Disorder Act 1998[23], the Director of Public Prosecutions may require the court to send for trial in the Crown Court a case involving one of certain specified violent or sexual offences if, in the Director's opinion—

(a) the evidence of the offence would be sufficient for the person charged to be put on trial for that offence;

(b) a child would be called as a witness at the trial; and

(c) for the purpose of avoiding any prejudice to the welfare of the child, the case should be taken over and proceeded with without delay by the Crown Court.

'Child' for these purposes is defined by section 51C(7) of the 1998 Act.]

Sending for Crown Court trial   **R9.7**

9.7 (1) This rule applies where a magistrates' court must, or can, send a defendant to the Crown Court for trial without first allocating the case for trial there.

(2) The court must read the allegation of the offence to the defendant.

(3) The court must explain, in terms the defendant can understand (with help, if necessary)—

(a) the allegation, unless it is self-explanatory;

paragraphs 1 and 2 of Schedule 36, and Parts 2, 4 and 12 of Schedule 37 to the Criminal Justice Act 2003 (c. 44) and section 208 of, and paragraphs 33 and 35 of Schedule 21 to, the Legal Services Act 2007 (c. 27).

[20] 1998 c. 37; section 51 was substituted and section 51D inserted by paragraphs 15 and 18 of Schedule 3 to the Criminal Justice Act 2003 (c. 44). They were amended by section 59 of, and paragraph 1 of Schedule 11 to, the Constitutional Reform Act 2005 (c. 4).

[21] 1980 c. 43; section 20A was inserted by paragraphs 1 and 6 of Schedule 3 to the Criminal Justice Act 2003 (c. 44).

[22] 1998 c. 37; section 51B was inserted by paragraphs 15 and 18 of Schedule 3 to the Criminal Justice Act 2003 (c. 44) and amended by section 50 of, and paragraph 69 of Schedule 4 to, the Commissioners for Revenue and Customs Act 2005 (c. 11) and paragraphs 46 and 48 of Schedule 5 to the Legal Aid, Sentencing and Punishment of Offenders Act 2012 (c. 10).

[23] 1998 c. 37; section 51C was inserted by paragraphs 15 and 18 of Schedule 3 to the Criminal Justice Act 2003 (c. 44) and modified by section 63 of, and paragraph 36 of Schedule 6 to, the Serious Crime Act 2007 (c. 27).

(b) that the offence is one for which the court, as appropriate—

    (i) must send the defendant to the Crown Court for trial because the offence is one which can only be tried there or because the court for some other reason is required to send that offence for trial,

    (ii) may send the defendant to the Crown Court for trial if the magistrates' court decides that the offence is related to one already sent for trial there; or

    (iii) (where the offence is low-value shoplifting and the defendant is 18 or over) must send the defendant to the Crown Court for trial if the defendant wants to be tried there; and

(c) that reporting restrictions apply, which the defendant may ask the court to vary or remove.

(4) In the following sequence, the court must then—

    (a) invite the prosecutor to—

        (i) identify the court's power to send the defendant to the Crown Court for trial for the offence, and

        (ii) make representations about any ancillary matters, including bail and directions for the management of the case in the Crown Court;

    (b) invite the defendant to make representations about—

        (i) the court's power to send the defendant to the Crown Court, and

        (ii) any ancillary matters;

    (c) (where the offence is low-value shoplifting and the defendant is 18 or over) offer the defendant the opportunity to require trial in the Crown Court; and

    (d) decide whether or not to send the defendant to the Crown Court for trial.

(5) If the court sends the defendant to the Crown Court for trial, it must—

    (a) ask whether the defendant intends to plead guilty in the Crown Court and—

        (i) if the answer is 'yes', make arrangements for the Crown Court to take the defendant's plea as soon as possible, or

        (ii) if the defendant does not answer, or the answer is 'no', make arrangements for a case management hearing in the Crown Court; and

    (b) give any other ancillary directions.

[Note. See sections 51, 51A and 51E of the Crime and Disorder Act 1998[24], and sections 22A and 24A of the Magistrates' Courts Act 1980[25].

See also Part 6 (Reporting, etc. restrictions).]

Allocation for magistrates' court or Crown Court trial

R9.8   Adult defendant: request for plea

9.8   (1) This rule applies where—

    (a) the defendant is 18 or over; and

    (b) the court must decide whether a case is more suitable for trial in a magistrates' court or in the Crown Court.

(2) The court must read the allegation of the offence to the defendant.

(3) The court must explain, in terms the defendant can understand (with help, if necessary)—

    (a) the allegation, unless it is self-explanatory;

    (b) that the offence is one which can be tried in a magistrates' court or in the Crown Court;

    (c) that the court is about to ask whether the defendant intends to plead guilty;

    (d) that if the answer is 'yes', then the court must treat that as a guilty plea and must sentence the defendant, or commit the defendant to the Crown Court for sentence;

    (e) that if the defendant does not answer, or the answer is 'no', then—

        (i) the court must decide whether to allocate the case to a magistrates' court or to the Crown Court for trial,

        (ii) the value involved may require the court to order trial in a magistrates' court (where the offence is one to which section 22 of the Magistrates' Courts Act 1980[26] applies), and

---

[24] 1998 c. 37; section 51 was substituted, and sections 51A and 51E inserted, by paragraphs 15 and 18 of Schedule 3 to the Criminal Justice Act 2003 (c. 44). Section 51 was amended by section 59 of, and paragraph 1 of Schedule 11 to, the Constitutional Reform Act 2005 (c. 4). Section 51A was amended by section 49 of, and paragraph 5 of Schedule 1 to, the Violent Crime Reduction Act 2006 (c. 38) and paragraph 6 of Schedule 21 to the Legal Aid, Sentencing and Punishment of Offenders Act 2012 (c. 10).

[25] 1980 c. 43; section 24A was inserted by paragraphs 1 and 10 of Schedule 3 to the Criminal Justice Act 2003 (c. 44). Section 22A was inserted by section 176 of the Anti-social Behaviour, Crime and Policing Act 2014 (c. 12).

[26] 1980 c. 43; section 22 was amended by sections 38 and 170(2) of, and Schedule 16 to, the Criminal Justice Act 1988 (c. 33), section 68 of, and paragraph 6 of Schedule 8 to, the Criminal Justice Act 1991 (c. 53), section 2(2) of the Aggravated Vehicle Taking Act 1992 (c. 11) and sections 46 and 168(3) of, and Schedule 11 to, the Criminal Justice and Public Order Act 1994 (c. 33).

       (iii) if the court allocates the case to a magistrates' court for trial, the defendant can nonetheless require trial in the Crown Court (unless the offence is one to which section 22 of the Magistrates' Courts Act 1980 applies and the value involved requires magistrates' court trial); and

  (f) that reporting restrictions apply, which the defendant may ask the court to vary or remove.

(4) The court must then ask whether the defendant intends to plead guilty.

[Note. See section 17A of the Magistrates' Courts Act 1980[27].

For the circumstances in which a magistrates' court may (and, in some cases, must) commit a defendant to the Crown Court for sentence after that defendant has indicated an intention to plead guilty where this rule applies see sections 18 and 20 of the Sentencing Act 2020[28].

See also Part 6 (Reporting, etc. restrictions).]

Adult defendant: guilty plea   **R9.9**

9.9 (1) This rule applies where—

  (a) rule 9.8 applies; and

  (b) the defendant indicates an intention to plead guilty.

(2) The court must exercise its power to deal with the case—

  (a) as if the defendant had just pleaded guilty at a trial in a magistrates' court; and

  (b) in accordance with rule 24.11 (Procedure if the court convicts).

[Note. See section 17A of the Magistrates' Courts Act 1980.]

Adult defendant: not guilty plea   **R9.10**

9.10 (1) This rule applies where—

  (a) rule 9.8 applies; and

  (b) the defendant—

    (i) indicates an intention to plead not guilty, or

    (ii) gives no indication of intended plea.

(2) In the following sequence, the court must then—

  (a) where the offence is one to which section 22 of the Magistrates' Courts Act 1980 applies, explain in terms the defendant can understand (with help, if necessary) that—

    (i) if the court decides that the value involved clearly is less than £5,000, the court must order trial in a magistrates' court,

    (ii) if the court decides that it is not clear whether that value is more or less than £5,000, then the court will ask whether the defendant agrees to be tried in a magistrates' court, and

    (iii) if the answer to that question is 'yes', then the court must order such a trial and if the defendant is convicted then the maximum sentence is limited;

  (b) invite the prosecutor to—

    (i) identify any previous convictions of which it can take account, and

    (ii) make representations about how the court should allocate the case for trial, including representations about the value involved, if relevant;

  (c) invite the defendant to make such representations;

  (d) where the offence is one to which section 22 of the Magistrates' Courts Act 1980 applies—

    (i) if it is not clear whether the value involved is more or less than £5,000, ask whether the defendant agrees to be tried in a magistrates' court,

    (ii) if the defendant's answer to that question is 'yes', or if that value clearly is less than £5,000, order a trial in a magistrates' court,

    (iii) if the defendant does not answer that question, or the answer is 'no', or if that value clearly is more than £5,000, apply paragraph (2)(e); and

  (e) exercise its power to allocate the case for trial, taking into account—

    (i) the adequacy of a magistrates' court's sentencing powers,

    (ii) any representations by the parties, and

    (iii) any allocation guidelines issued by the Sentencing Council.

Criminal Procedure Rules

---

[27] 1980 c. 43; section 17A was inserted by section 49 of the Criminal Procedure and Investigations Act 1996 (c. 25) and amended by paragraph 62 of Schedule 9 to the Powers of Criminal Courts (Sentencing Act 2000 (c. 6) and paragraphs 1 and 2 of Schedule 3 to the Criminal Justice Act 2003 (c. 44).

[28] 2020 c. 17.

[Note. See sections 17A, 18, 19, 22 and 24A of the Magistrates' Courts Act 1980[29].

Under section 22 of the 1980 Act, some offences, which otherwise could be tried in a magistrates' court or in the Crown Court, must be tried in a magistrates' court in the circumstances described in this rule.

The convictions of which the court may take account are those specified by section 19 of the 1980 Act.

The Sentencing Council may issue allocation guidelines under section 122 of the Coroners and Justice Act 2009[30]. The definitive allocation guideline which took effect on 1st March, 2016 provides:

(1) In general, either way offences should be tried summarily unless—

    (a) the outcome would clearly be a sentence in excess of the court's powers for the offence(s) concerned after taking into account personal mitigation and any potential reduction for a guilty plea; or

    (b) for reasons of unusual legal, procedural or factual complexity, the case should be tried in the Crown Court. This exception may apply in cases where a very substantial fine is the likely sentence. Other circumstances where this exception will apply are likely to be rare and case specific; the court will rely on the submissions of the parties to identify relevant cases.

(2) In cases with no factual or legal complications the court should bear in mind its power to commit for sentence after a trial and may retain jurisdiction notwithstanding that the likely sentence might exceed its powers.

(3) Cases may be tried summarily even where the defendant is subject to a Crown Court Suspended Sentence Order or Community Order.

(4) All parties should be asked by the court to make representations as to whether the case is suitable for summary trial. The court should refer to definitive guidelines (if any) to assess the likely sentence for the offence in the light of the facts alleged by the prosecution case, taking into account all aspects of the case including those advanced by the defence, including any personal mitigation to which the defence wish to refer.

Where the court decides that the case is suitable to be dealt with in the magistrates' court, it must warn the defendant that all sentencing options remain open and, if the defendant consents to summary trial and is convicted by the court or pleads guilty, the defendant may be committed to the Crown Court for sentence.]

R9.11   Adult defendant: allocation for magistrates' court trial

9.11   (1)   This rule applies where—

    (a)   rule 9.10 applies; and

    (b)   the court allocates the case to a magistrates' court for trial.

(2)   The court must explain, in terms the defendant can understand (with help, if necessary) that—

    (a)   the court considers the case more suitable for trial in a magistrates' court than in the Crown Court;

    (b)   if the defendant is convicted at a magistrates' court trial, then in some circumstances the court may commit the defendant to the Crown Court for sentence;

    (c)   if the defendant does not agree to a magistrates' court trial, then the court must send the defendant to the Crown Court for trial; and

    (d)   before deciding whether to accept magistrates' court trial, the defendant may ask the court for an indication of whether a custodial or non-custodial sentence is more likely in the event of a guilty plea at such a trial, but the court need not give such an indication.

(3)   If the defendant asks for such an indication of sentence and the court gives such an indication—

    (a)   the court must then ask again whether the defendant intends to plead guilty;

    (b)   if, in answer to that question, the defendant indicates an intention to plead guilty, then the court must exercise its power to deal with the case—

        (i)   as if the defendant had just pleaded guilty to an offence that can be tried only in a magistrates' court, and

        (ii)   in accordance with rule 24.11 (Procedure if the court convicts); and

    (c)   if, in answer to that question, the defendant indicates an intention to plead not guilty, or gives no indication of intended plea, in the following sequence the court must then—

---

[29]   1980 c. 43; section 18 was amended by section 59 of, and paragraph 1 of Schedule 9 to, the Criminal Justice Act 1982 (c. 48), section 68 of, and paragraph 6 of Schedule 8 to, the Criminal Justice Act 1991 (c. 53), section 49 of the Criminal Procedure and Investigations Act 1996 (c. 25), and paragraphs 1 and 4 of Schedule 3 to the Criminal Justice Act 2003 (c. 44). Section 19 was substituted by paragraphs 1 and 5 of Schedule 3 to the Criminal Justice Act 2003 (c. 44) and amended by sections 144, 177 and 178 of, and paragraph 4 of Schedule 17, paragraph 80 of Schedule 21 and Part 5 of Schedule 23 to, the Coroners and Justice Act 2009 (c. 25).

[30]   2009 c. 25.

Criminal Procedure Rules

      (i) ask whether the defendant agrees to trial in a magistrates' court,

      (ii) if the defendant's answer to that question is 'yes', order such a trial, and

      (iii) if the defendant does not answer that question, or the answer is 'no', apply rule 9.14.

(4) If the defendant asks for an indication of sentence but the court gives none, or if the defendant does not ask for such an indication, in the following sequence the court must then—

  (a) ask whether the defendant agrees to trial in a magistrates' court;

  (b) if the defendant's answer to that question is 'yes', order such a trial; and

  (c) if the defendant does not answer that question, or the answer is 'no', apply rule 9.14.

[Note. See section 20 of the Magistrates' Courts Act 1980[31].

For the circumstances in which a magistrates' court may (and, in some cases, must) commit a defendant to the Crown Court for sentence after that defendant has been convicted at a magistrates' court trial, see sections 14, 15, 17 and 20 of the Sentencing Act 2020[32].

For the circumstances in which an indication of sentence to which this rule applies restricts the sentencing powers of a court, see section 20A of the 1980 Act[33].

Where the court orders trial in a magistrates' court, see also rules 3.16 to 3.18 about preparation for trial.]

Adult defendant: prosecutor's application for Crown Court trial   R9.12

9.12 (1) This rule applies where—

  (a) rule 9.11 applies;

  (b) the defendant agrees to trial in a magistrates' court; but

  (c) the prosecutor wants the court to exercise its power to send the defendant to the Crown Court for trial instead.

(2) The prosecutor must—

  (a) apply before trial in a magistrates' court begins under Part 24 (Trial and sentence in a magistrates' court); and

  (b) notify—

      (i) the defendant, and

      (ii) the magistrates' court officer.

(3) The court must determine an application to which this rule applies before it deals with any other pre-trial application.

[Note. See sections 8A and 25 of the Magistrates' Courts Act 1980[34]. Under section 25(2B), the court may grant an application to which this rule applies only if it is satisfied that the sentence which a magistrates' court would have power to impose would be inadequate.]

Young defendant   R9.13

9.13 (1) This rule applies where—

  (a) the defendant is under 18; and

  (b) the court must decide whether to send the defendant for Crown Court trial instead of ordering trial in a youth court.

(2) The court must read the allegation of the offence to the defendant.

(3) The court must explain, in terms the defendant can understand (with help, if necessary)—

  (a) the allegation, unless it is self-explanatory;

  (b) that the offence is one which can be tried in the Crown Court instead of in a youth court;

  (c) that the court is about to ask whether the defendant intends to plead guilty;

  (d) that if the answer is 'yes', then the court must treat that as a guilty plea and must sentence the defendant, or commit the defendant to the Crown Court for sentence;

  (e) that if the defendant does not answer, or the answer is 'no', then the court must decide whether to send the defendant for Crown Court trial instead of ordering trial in a youth court;

---

[31] 1980 c. 43; section 20 was amended by section 100 of, and paragraph 25 of Schedule 11 to, the Criminal Justice Act 1991 (c. 53), paragraph 63 of Schedule 9 to the Powers of Criminal Courts (Sentencing Act 2000 (c. 6) and paragraphs 1 and 6 of Schedule 3 to the Criminal Justice Act 2003 (c. 44).

[32] 2020 c. 17.

[33] 1980 c. 43; section 20A was inserted by paragraphs 1 and 6 of Schedule 3 to the Criminal Justice Act 2003 (c. 44).

[34] 1980 c. 43; section 8A was inserted by section 45 of, and Schedule 3 to, the Courts Act 2003 (c. 39) and amended by SI 2006/2493 and paragraphs 12 and 14 of Schedule 5 to the Legal Aid, Sentencing and Punishment of Offenders Act 2012 (c. 10). Section 25 was amended by section 31 of, and paragraph 3 of Schedule 1 and Schedule 2, to the Prosecution of Offences Act 1985 (c. 23), paragraph 6 of Schedule 8 to the Criminal Justice Act 1991 (c. 53), paragraphs 1 and 5 of Schedule 1 to the Criminal Procedure and Investigations Act 1996 (c. 25), section 42 of the Criminal Justice Act 2003 (c. 44) and paragraphs 1 and 11 of Schedule 3, and Part 4 of Schedule 37, to the Criminal Justice Act 2003 (c. 44).

(f) that before answering and at any time until the court decides whether to send the
defendant for Crown Court trial or order trial in a youth court—

    (i) the defendant may ask the court for an indication of whether a custodial or
non-custodial sentence is more likely in the event of a guilty plea there and then, but

    (ii) the court need not give such an indication; and

(g) that reporting restrictions apply, which the defendant may ask the court to vary or remove.

(4) The defendant may then ask the court for such an indication of sentence,

(5) Whether the defendant asks for and the court gives such an indication or not, the court must
then ask whether the defendant intends to plead guilty.

(6) If the defendant's answer to that question is 'yes', the court must exercise its power to deal with
the case—

(a) as if the defendant had just pleaded guilty at a trial in a youth court; and

(b) in accordance with rule 24.11 (Procedure if the court convicts).

(7) If the defendant does not answer that question, or the answer is 'no', in the following sequence
the court must then—

(a) invite the prosecutor to make representations about whether Crown Court or youth court
trial is more appropriate;

(b) invite the defendant to make such representations; and

(c) exercise its power to allocate the case for trial in the Crown Court or a youth court, taking
into account—

    (i) the offence and the circumstances of the offence,

    (ii) the suitability of a youth court's sentencing powers,

    (iii) where the defendant is jointly charged with an adult, whether it is necessary in the
interests of justice for them to be tried together in the Crown Court, and

    (iv) any representations by the parties.

[Note. See section 24A of the Magistrates' Courts Act 1980[35].

*For the circumstances in which a magistrates' court may (and, in some cases, must) commit a defendant who is
under 18 to the Crown Court for sentence after that defendant has indicated a guilty plea, sections 16, 17, 19
and 20 of the Sentencing Act 2020[36].*

Where the court orders trial in a youth court, see also rules 3.16 to 3.18 about preparation for trial.]

R9.14   **Allocation and sending for Crown Court trial**

    9.14 (1) This rule applies where—

    (a) under rule 9.10 or rule 9.13, the court allocates the case to the Crown Court for trial;

    (b) under rule 9.11, the defendant does not agree to trial in a magistrates' court; or

    (c) under rule 9.12, the court grants the prosecutor's application for Crown Court trial.

    (2) In the following sequence, the court must—

    (a) invite the prosecutor to make representations about any ancillary matters, including bail
and directions for the management of the case in the Crown Court;

    (b) invite the defendant to make any such representations; and

    (c) exercise its powers to—

        (i) send the defendant to the Crown Court for trial, and

        (ii) give any ancillary directions.

*[Note. See sections 21 and 24A of the Magistrates' Courts Act 1980[37] and section 51 of the Crime and Disorder
1998[38]. See also rule 9.3 (matters to be specified on sending for trial).]*

Committal for Sentence in Connection with Sending for Trial

R9.15   **Committal for sentence for offence related to an offence sent for trial**

    9.15 (1) This rule applies where—

    (a) on a previous occasion the court has sent the defendant to the Crown Court for trial for
an offence in exercise of a power to which rule 9.7, 9.13 or 9.14 applies;

    (b) on the present occasion, under rule 9.9 or 9.13 the defendant indicates an intention to
plead guilty to, and is convicted of, an offence which the court decides is related to the
offence for which the defendant was previously sent for trial;

---

[35] 1980 c. 43; section 24A was inserted by paragraphs 1 and 10 of Schedule 3 to the Criminal Justice Act 2003 (c. 44).

[36] 2020 c. 17.

[37] 1980 c. 43; section 21 was amended by paragraphs 1 and 7 of Schedule 3 to the Criminal Justice Act 2003 (c. 44).

[38] 1998 c. 37; section 51 was substituted by paragraphs 15 and 18 of Schedule 3 to the Criminal Justice Act 2003 (c. 44) and
amended by section 59 of, and paragraph 1 of Schedule 11 to, the Constitutional Reform Act 2005 (c. 4).

    (c) the court decides to commit the defendant to the Crown Court for sentence for the related offence under—

      (i) section 18 of the Sentencing Act 2020[39], if the defendant is over 18, or

      (ii) section 19 of the 2020 Act[40], if the defendant is under 18; and

    (d) in the court's opinion, if it were not committing the defendant for sentence under section 18 or 19 of the 2020 Act then it could, or would be required to, commit the defendant to the Crown Court for sentence for the related offence under—

      (i) section 14 or 15 of that Act, if the defendant is over 18, or

      (ii) section 16, 16A or 17 of that Act[41], if the defendant is under 18.

(2) The court must state that opinion for the Crown Court.

[Note. See sections 18(4) and 19(3) of the Sentencing Act 2020 for the court's powers to state the opinion to which this rule refers.

Under section 51E of the Crime and Disorder Act 1998[42] —

    (a) an offence classified as triable either way is related to an offence for which a defendant has been sent for trial in the Crown Court if both offences are based on the same prosecution evidence (and see rule 10.2(4)(c) in the rules about indictments); and

    (b) an offence classified as triable only summarily is related to an offence for which a defendant has been sent for trial in the Crown Court if both offences arise out of the same or connected circumstances.

Under section 51 of the 1998 Act[43] —

    (a) if a magistrates' court sends a defendant to the Crown Court for trial for an offence and on the same occasion deals with a related offence then the general rule is that the court must send the defendant to the Crown Court for trial for the related offence, too; but

    (b) if the court sends a defendant to the Crown Court for trial for an offence on one occasion and on a later occasion deals with a related offence then it may send the defendant to the Crown Court for trial for the related offence, too, or it may finish dealing with that offence itself and, if it convicts the defendant, may commit the defendant for sentence to the Crown Court instead.

For the circumstances in which a magistrates' court may (and, in some cases, must) commit a defendant to the Crown Court for sentence or for the making of other orders beyond a magistrates' court's powers, see sections 14, 15, 16, 16A, 17, 18, 19, 20 and 24 of the Sentencing Act 2020 and paragraph 11 of Schedule 16 to that Act. See also rules 24.11 (Procedure if the court convicts) and 28.12 (Sentencing, etc. after committal to the Crown Court). The note to rule 28.12 summarises the statutory provisions that apply.]

Sending back, etc. for magistrates' court trial

Sending back or referring case for magistrates' court trial   **R9.16**

9.16 (1) This rule applies where a magistrates' court sends the defendant to the Crown Court for trial and—

    (a) under section 46ZA of the Senior Courts Act 1981, the Crown Court can send the defendant back to a magistrates' court for trial for a summary offence or for an offence triable either way; or

    (b) under paragraph 6 of Schedule 3 to the Crime and Disorder Act 1998, where a summary offence remains outstanding the Crown Court must so inform the magistrates' court.

  (2) Where paragraph (1)(a) applies—

    (a) the Crown Court may exercise its power to send back—

      (i) at a hearing, in public or in private, or without a hearing,

      (ii) in the defendant's absence, but only if the defendant consents to being absent on its exercise, and

      (iii) in the prosecutor's absence, but only if the prosecutor has had at least 5 business days in which to make representations; and

    (b) if the defendant is under 18, the Crown Court must—

      (i) consider sending the defendant back, and

      (ii) explain why, if it does not do so.

---

[39] 2020 c. 17.

[40] 2020 c. 17; section 19 was amended by section 46 of, and paragraph 26 of Schedule 13 to, the Counter-Terrorism and Sentencing Act 2021 (c. 11).

[41] 2020 c. 17; section 16A was inserted by section 46 of, and paragraph 26 of Schedule 13 to, the Counter-Terrorism and Sentencing Act 2021 (c. 11).

[42] 1998 c. 37; section 51E was substituted by paragraphs 15 and 18 of Schedule 3 to the Criminal Justice Act 2003 (c. 44).

[43] 1998 c. 37; section 51 was substituted by paragraphs 15 and 18 of Schedule 3 to the Criminal Justice Act 2003 (c. 44) and amended by section 52 of the Criminal Justice and Courts Act 2015 (c. 2).

(3) Where paragraph (1)(a) applies and the Crown Court sends the defendant back—
   (a) the Crown Court must—
      (i)   specify the date on which the defendant must attend at or be taken to the magistrates' court, and
      (ii) decide whether to grant or withhold bail;
   (b) the Crown Court officer must make available to the magistrates' court officer a record of the Crown Court's order under paragraph (3)(a) and details of any—
      (i)   case management direction affecting the magistrates' court,
      (ii)   direction about reporting restrictions,
      (iii) period for which the defendant was in custody during proceedings in the Crown Court,
      (iv)   decision about bail, for the purposes of section 5 of the Bail Act 1976[44],
      (v)   recognizance given by a surety,
      (vi)   representation order,
      (vii) interpreter, intermediary, or supporting adult, and
      (viii) information supplied by the parties for the purposes of case management by the court; and
   (c) the Crown Court officer must at the same time serve on each party notice of the sending back and of the Crown Court's order, unless that party was present when the order was made.
(4) Where paragraph (1)(b) applies—
   (a) the Crown Court must exercise its power at a hearing; and
   (b) unless the defendant pleads guilty to the summary offence, the Crown Court officer must notify the magistrates' court officer of the outcome of the proceedings.

[Note. An offence may be classified as triable only on indictment; triable only summarily (a summary offence); or triable either way (on indictment or summarily). Offences classified either as triable only on indictment or as triable either way collectively are described as indictable offences.

Under section 46ZA(2) of the Senior Courts Act 1981 the Crown Court cannot send the defendant back to a magistrates' court for trial—

   (a) where the defendant is 18 or over, or is a corporation, and the offence is triable only on indictment; or
   (b) where the defendant is under 18 and the offence is homicide or one of the other offences listed in section 51A(12) of the Crime and Disorder Act 1998.

Under section 46ZA(3) of the 1981 Act the Crown Court cannot send an adult or corporate defendant back to a magistrates' court for trial for an offence triable either way unless the defendant consents.

Under section 46ZA(5) of the 1981 Act, in deciding whether to send a defendant back the Crown Court must take into account (a) any other related offence before the Crown Court (whether the same, or a different, person is accused or has been convicted of the other offence), and (b) any allocation guideline.

Under section 46ZA(6) of the 1981 Act, on sending a defendant back the Crown Court may give such directions as appear to be necessary with respect to the custody of the defendant or for the defendant's release on bail until the defendant can appear or be brought before the magistrates' court.

Under paragraph 6(7) of Schedule 3 to the Crime and Disorder Act 1998, the Crown Court must inform the magistrates' court of the outcome of the proceedings in the Crown Court where—

   (a) the offences for which the defendant was sent for trial include a summary offence;
   (b) that summary offence is not tried in the Crown Court under a power to do so;
   (c) in the Crown Court the defendant is convicted of an indictable offence;
   (d) the Crown Court considers that the summary offence is related to any indictable offence for which the defendant was sent for trial;
   (e) under paragraph 6(4), the defendant does not plead guilty in the Crown Court to the summary offence; and
   (f) under paragraph 6(6), the prosecutor does not wish to withdraw the prosecution for that offence.

[44] 1976 c. 63; section 5 was amended by section 65 of, and Schedule 12 to, the Criminal Law Act 1977 (c. 45), section 60 of the Criminal Justice Act 1982 (c. 48), paragraph 1 of Schedule 3 to the Criminal Justice and Public Order Act 1994 (c. 33), paragraph 53 of Schedule 9 to the Powers of Criminal Courts (Sentencing) Act 2000 (c. 6), section 129(1) of the Criminal Justice and Police Act 2001 (c. 16), paragraph 182 of Schedule 8 to the Courts Act 2003 (c. 39), paragraph 48 of Schedule 3, paragraphs 1 and 2 of Schedule 36, and Parts 2, 4 and 12 of Schedule 37 to the Criminal Justice Act 2003 (c. 44) and section 208 of, and paragraphs 33 and 35 of Schedule 21 to, the Legal Services Act 2007 (c. 27).

Under paragraph 6(5) of Schedule 3 to the 1998 Act, the Crown Court then has no other powers, for example to send the defendant back to the magistrates' court on bail or in custody.

See also rule 28.10 (Committal or remission, etc. for sentence), which applies to the exercise of the Crown Court's powers under sections 25, 25A and 26 of the Sentencing Act 2020[45] to remit a convicted defendant to a magistrates' court for sentence.]

CRIMINAL PROCEDURE RULES   PART 10   THE INDICTMENT

When this Part applies

R10.1

10.1   This Part applies where—

(a)   a magistrates' court sends a defendant to the Crown Court for trial under section 51 or section 51A of the Crime and Disorder Act 1998[1];

(b)   a prosecutor wants a High Court judge's permission to serve a draft indictment;

(c)   the Crown Court approves a proposed indictment under paragraph 2 of Schedule 17 to the Crime and Courts Act 2013[2] and rule 11.4 (Deferred prosecution agreements: Application to approve the terms of an agreement);

(d)   a prosecutor wants to re-institute proceedings in the Crown Court under section 22B of the Prosecution of Offences Act 1985[3]; or

(e)   the Court of Appeal orders a retrial, under section 8 of the Criminal Appeal Act 1968[4] or under section 77 of the Criminal Justice Act 2003[5].

[Note. See also sections 3, 4 and 5 of the Indictments Act 1915[6] and section 2 of the Administration of Justice (Miscellaneous Provisions) Act 1933[7]. Under section 2(1) of the 1933 Act, a draft indictment (in the Act, a 'bill of indictment') becomes an indictment when it is 'preferred' in accordance with these rules. See rule 10.2.

Part 3 contains rules about the court's general powers of case management, including power to consider applications and give directions for (among other things) the amendment of an indictment and for separate trials under section 5 of the Indictments Act 1915. See in particular rule 3.29 (Application for joint or separate trials, etc.).

---

[45] 2020 c. 17; section 25 was amended and section 25A was inserted by section 11 of the Judicial Review and Courts Act 2022 (c. 35). Section 26 was amended by paragraph 14 of Schedule 2 to that 2022 Act.

[1] 1998 c. 37; section 51 was substituted by paragraphs 15 and 18 of Schedule 3 to the Criminal Justice Act 2003 (c. 44) and amended by section 59 of, and paragraph 1 of Schedule 11 to, the Constitutional Reform Act 2005 (c. 4). Section 51A was inserted by paragraphs 15 and 18 of Schedule 3 to the Criminal Justice Act 2003 (c. 44) and amended by section 49 of, and paragraph 5 of Schedule 1 to, the Violent Crime Reduction Act 2006 (c. 38) and paragraph 6 of Schedule 21 to the Legal Aid, Sentencing and Punishment of Offenders Act 2012 (c. 10).

[2] 2013 c. 22.

[3] 1985 c. 23; section 22B was inserted by section 45 of the Crime and Disorder Act 1998 (c. 37) and amended by paragraph 17 of Schedule 36 to the Criminal Justice Act 2003 (c. 44) and section 112 of, and Part 13 of Schedule 8 to, the Policing and Crime Act 2009 (c. 26).

[4] 1968 c. 19; section 8 was amended by Section 12 of, and paragraph 38 of Schedule 2 to, the Bail Act 1976 (c. 63), section 56 of, and Part IV of Schedule 11 to, the Courts Act 1971 (c. 23), section 65 of, and paragraph 36 of Schedule 3 to, the Mental Health (Amendment) Act 1982 (c. 51), section 148 of, and paragraph 23 of Schedule 4 to, the Mental Health Act 1983 (c. 20), section 43 of the Criminal Justice Act 1988 (c. 33), section 168 of, and paragraph 19 of Schedule 10 to, the Criminal Justice and Public Order Act 1994 (c. 33), section 58 of the Access to Justice Act 1999 (c. 22), sections 41 and 332 of, and paragraph 43 of Schedule 3 to, and Part 4 of Schedule 37 to, the Criminal Justice Act 2003 (c. 44) and section 32 of, and paragraph 2 of Schedule 4 to, the Mental Health Act 2007 (c. 12).

[5] 2003 c. 44.

[6] 1915 c. 90; section 4 was amended by section 83 of, and Part I of Schedule 10 to, the Criminal Justice Act 1948 (c. 58) and section 10 of, and Part III of Schedule 3 to, the Criminal Law Act 1967 (c. 58). Section 5 was amended by section 12 of, and paragraph 8 of Schedule 2 to, the Bail Act 1976 (c. 63), section 31 of, and Schedule 2 to, the Prosecution of Offences Act 1985 (c. 23) and section 331 of, and paragraph 40 of Schedule 36 to, the Criminal Justice Act 2003 (c. 44).

[7] 1933 c. 36; section 2 was amended by Part IV of Schedule 11 to, the Courts Act 1971 (c. 23), Schedule 5 to, the Senior Courts Act 1981 (c. 54), Schedule 2 to the Prosecution of Offences Act 1985 (c. 23), paragraph 1 of Schedule 2 to the Criminal Justice Act 1987 (c. 38), paragraph 10 of Schedule 15 to the Criminal Justice Act 1988 (c. 33), paragraph 8 of Schedule 6 to the Criminal Justice Act 1991 (c. 53), Schedule 1 to the Statute Law (Repeals) Act 1993, paragraph 17 of Schedule 1 to the Criminal Procedure and Investigations Act 1996 (c. 25), paragraph 5 of Schedule 8 to the Crime and Disorder Act 1998 (c. 37), paragraph 34 of Schedule 3 and Part 4 of Schedule 37 to the Criminal Justice Act 2003 (c. 44), paragraph 1 of the Schedule to S.I. 2004/2035, section 12 of, and paragraph 7 of Schedule 1 to, the Constitutional Reform Act 2005 (c. 4), sections 116 and 178 of, and Part 3 of Schedule 23 to, the Coroners and Justice Act 2009 (c. 25), paragraph 32 of Schedule 17 to the Crime and Courts Act 2013 (c. 22) and section 82 of the Deregulation Act 2015 (c. 20).

Under section 51D of the Crime and Disorder Act 1998[8], the magistrates' court must notify the Crown Court of the offence or offences for which the defendant is sent for trial. Part 9 (Allocation and sending for trial) contains relevant rules.

A Crown Court judge may approve a proposed indictment on approving a deferred prosecution agreement. Part 11 (Deferred prosecution agreements) contains relevant rules.

A prosecutor may apply to a High Court judge for permission to serve a draft indictment under rule 10.9.

Under section 22B of the Prosecution of Offences Act 1985, one of the prosecutors listed in that section may re-institute proceedings that have been stayed under section 22(4) of that Act[9] on the expiry of an overall time limit (where such a time limit has been prescribed). Section 22B(2) requires the service of a draft indictment within 3 months of the date on which the Crown Court ordered the stay, or within such longer period as the court allows.

The Court of Appeal may order a retrial under section 8 of the Criminal Appeal Act 1968 (on a defendant's appeal against conviction) or under section 77 of the Criminal Justice Act 2003 (on a prosecutor's application for the retrial of a serious offence after acquittal). Section 8 of the 1968 Act and section 84 of the 2003 Act require the arraignment of a defendant within 2 months. See also rules 27.7 and 39.14.

Where a magistrates' court sends a defendant to the Crown Court for trial under section 51 or 51A of the Crime and Disorder Act 1998, in some circumstances the Crown Court may try the defendant for other offences: see section 2(2) of the Administration of Justice (Miscellaneous Provisions) Act 1933 (indictable offences founded on the prosecution evidence), section 40 of the Criminal Justice Act 1988[10] (specified summary offences founded on that evidence) and paragraph 6 of Schedule 3 to the Crime and Disorder Act 1998 (power of Crown Court to deal with related summary offence sent to that court). An offence of theft under section 1 of the Theft Act 1968 which is low-value shoplifting under section 22A of the Magistrates' Courts Act 1980[11] is a summary offence unless the defendant chooses to be tried in the Crown Court.]

R10.2　The indictment: general rules

10.2 (1) The indictment on which the defendant is arraigned under rule 3.32 (Arraigning the defendant on the indictment) must be in writing and must contain, in a paragraph called a 'count'—

　(a) a statement of the offence charged that—

　　(i) describes the offence in ordinary language, and

　　(ii) identifies any legislation that creates it; and

　(b) such particulars of the conduct constituting the commission of the offence as to make clear what the prosecutor alleges against the defendant.

(2) More than one incident of the commission of the offence may be included in a count if those incidents taken together amount to a course of conduct having regard to the time, place or purpose of commission.

(3) The counts must be numbered consecutively.

(4) An indictment may contain—

　(a) any count charging substantially the same offence as one for which the defendant was sent for trial;

　(b) any count contained in a draft indictment served with the permission of a High Court judge or at the direction of the Court of Appeal; and

　(c) any other count charging an offence that the Crown Court can try and which is based on the prosecution evidence that has been served, including a summary offence to which section 40 of the Criminal Justice Act 1988 applies.

[8] 1998 c. 37; section 51D was inserted by paragraphs 15 and 18 of Schedule 3 to the Criminal Justice Act 2003 (c. 44) and amended by section 59 of, and paragraph 1 of Schedule 11 to, the Constitutional Reform Act 2005 (c. 4).
[9] 1985 c. 23; section 22 was amended by paragraph 104 of Schedule 15 to the Criminal Justice Act 1988 (c. 33), section 43 of the Crime and Disorder Act 1998 (c. 37), paragraph 36 of Schedule 11 to the Criminal Justice Act 1991 (c. 53), paragraph 27 of Schedule 9 to the Criminal Justice and Public Order Act 1994 (c. 33), section 71 of the Criminal Procedure and Investigations Act 1996 (c. 25), section 67(3) of the Access to Justice Act 1999 (c. 22), section 70 of, and paragraph 57 of Schedule 3 and paragraphs 49 and 51 of Schedule 36 to, the Criminal Justice Act 2003 (c. 44), section 59 of, and paragraph 1 of Schedule 11 to, the Constitutional Reform Act 2005 (c. 4) and paragraph 22 of Schedule 12 to the Legal Aid, Sentencing and Punishment of Offenders Act 2012 (c. 10).
[10] 1988 c. 33; section 40 was amended by section 4 of, and paragraph 39 of Schedule 3 to, the Road Traffic (Consequential Provisions) Act 1988 (c. 54), section 168 of, and paragraph 35 of Schedule 9 to, the Criminal Justice and Public Order Act 1994 (c. 33), section 47 of, and paragraph 34 of Schedule 1 to, the Criminal Procedure and Investigations Act 1996 (c. 25), section 119 of, and paragraph 66 of Schedule 8 to, the Crime and Disorder Act 1998 (c. 37) and paragraph 60 of Schedule 3 and Part 4 of Schedule 37 to the Criminal Justice Act 2003 (c. 44).
[11] 1980 c. 43; section 22A was inserted by section 176 of the Anti-social Behaviour, Crime and Policing Act 2014 (c. 12).

(5) For the purposes of section 2 of the Administration of Justice (Miscellaneous Provisions) Act 1933—
  (a) a draft indictment constitutes a bill of indictment; and
  (b) the draft, or bill, is preferred before the Crown Court and becomes the indictment—
    (i) where rule 10.3 applies (Draft indictment generated electronically on sending for trial), immediately before the first count (or the only count, if there is only one) is read to or placed before the defendant to take the defendant's plea under rule 3.32(1)(e),
    (ii) when the prosecutor serves the draft indictment on the Crown Court officer, where rule 10.4 (Draft indictment served by the prosecutor after sending for trial), rule 10.5 (Draft indictment served by the prosecutor with a High Court judge's permission), rule 10.7 (Draft indictment served by the prosecutor on re-instituting proceedings) or rule 10.8 (Draft indictment served by the prosecutor at the direction of the Court of Appeal) applies,
    (iii) when the Crown Court approves the proposed indictment, where rule 10.6 applies (Draft indictment approved by the Crown Court with deferred prosecution agreement), or
    (iv) when the prosecutor serves on the Crown Court officer a draft indictment to which rule 25.16(3)(e) applies (substituted indictment for sentencing purposes).
(6) An indictment—
  (a) must be in one of the forms set out in the Practice Direction unless—
    (i) rule 10.3 applies, or
    (ii) the Crown Court otherwise directs; and
  (b) must include at the head of the document in which it is set out the date of that document and a statement that it contains, as appropriate—
    (i) the first indictment in the case,
    (ii) a proposed amended indictment,
    (iii) a substituted indictment,
    (iv) an additional indictment,
    (v) a trial indictment, or
    (vi) an indictment required by rule 25.16(3)(e) (substituted indictment for sentencing purposes).
(7) Unless the Crown Court otherwise directs, the court officer must—
  (a) endorse any paper copy of the indictment made for the court with—
    (i) a note to identify it as a copy of the indictment, and
    (ii) the date on which the draft indictment became the indictment under paragraph (5); and
  (b) where rule 10.4, 10.5, 10.7 or 10.8 applies, serve a copy of the indictment on all parties.
(8) The Crown Court may extend the time limit under rule 10.4, 10.5, 10.7 or 10.8, even after it has expired.

[Note. Under section 2(6) of the Administration of Justice (Miscellaneous Provisions) Act 1933, Criminal Procedure Rules may provide for the manner in which and the time at which 'bills of indictment' are to be 'preferred'.

Under rule 3.29 (Application for joint or separate trials, etc.), the court may order separate trials of counts in the circumstances listed in that rule.]

Draft indictment generated electronically on sending for trial   R10.3
10.3 (1) Unless the Crown Court otherwise directs before the defendant is arraigned, this rule applies where—
  (a) a magistrates' court sends a defendant to the Crown Court for trial;
  (b) the magistrates' court officer serves on the Crown Court officer the notice required by rule 9.5 (Duty of magistrates' court officer); and
  (c) by means of such electronic arrangements as the court officer may make for the purpose, there is presented to the Crown Court as a count—
    (i) each allegation of an indictable offence specified in the notice, and
    (ii) each allegation specified in the notice to which section 40 of the Criminal Justice Act 1988 applies (specified summary offences founded on the prosecution evidence).
(2) Where this rule applies—
  (a) each such allegation constitutes a count;
  (b) the allegation or allegations so specified together constitute a draft indictment;

(c) before the draft indictment so constituted is preferred before the Crown Court under rule 10.2(5)(b)(i) the prosecutor may substitute for any count an amended count to the same effect and charging the same offence;

(d) if under rule 3.19 (Service of prosecution evidence) the prosecutor has served copies of the documents containing the evidence on which the prosecution case relies then, before the draft indictment is preferred before the Crown Court under rule 10.2(5)(b)(i), the prosecutor may substitute or add—

    (i) any count charging substantially the same offence as one specified in the notice, and

    (ii) any other count charging an offence which the Crown Court can try and which is based on the prosecution evidence so served; and

(e) a prosecutor who substitutes or adds a count under paragraph (2)(c) or (d) must serve that count on the Crown Court officer and the defendant.

[Note. An 'indictable offence' is (i) an offence classified as triable on indictment exclusively, or (ii) an offence classified as triable either on indictment or summarily. See also the note to rule 9.1 (Allocation and sending for trial: When this Part applies).

Section 40 of the Criminal Justice Act 1988 lists summary offences which may be included in an indictment if the charge—

    (a) is founded on the same facts or evidence as a count charging an indictable offence; or

    (b) is part of a series of offences of the same or similar character as an indictable offence which is also charged.]

R10.4 Draft indictment served by the prosecutor after sending for trial

10.4 (1) This rule applies where—

    (a) a magistrates' court sends a defendant to the Crown Court for trial; and

    (b) rule 10.3 (Draft indictment generated electronically on sending for trial) does not apply.

(2) The prosecutor must serve a draft indictment on the Crown Court officer not more than 20 business days after serving under rule 3.19 (Service of prosecution evidence) copies of the documents containing the evidence on which the prosecution case relies.

R10.5 Draft indictment served by the prosecutor with a High Court judge's permission

10.5 (1) This rule applies where—

    (a) the prosecutor applies to a High Court judge under rule 10.9 (Application to a High Court judge for permission to serve a draft indictment); and

    (b) the judge gives permission to serve a proposed indictment.

(2) Where this rule applies—

    (a) that proposed indictment constitutes the draft indictment; and

    (b) the prosecutor must serve the draft indictment on the Crown Court officer not more than 20 business days after the High Court judge's decision.

R10.6 Draft indictment approved with deferred prosecution agreement

10.6 (1) This rule applies where—

    (a) the prosecutor applies to the Crown Court under rule 11.4 (Deferred prosecution agreements: Application to approve the terms of an agreement); and

    (b) the Crown Court approves the proposed indictment served with that application.

(2) Where this rule applies, that proposed indictment constitutes the draft indictment.

R10.7 Draft indictment served by the prosecutor on re-instituting proceedings

10.7 (1) This rule applies where the prosecutor wants to re-institute proceedings in the Crown Court under section 22B of the Prosecution of Offences Act 1985.

(2) The prosecutor must serve a draft indictment on the Crown Court officer not more than 3 months after the proceedings were stayed under section 22(4) of that Act[12].

R10.8 Draft indictment served by the prosecutor at the direction of the Court of Appeal

10.8 (1) This rule applies where the Court of Appeal orders a retrial.

(2) The prosecutor must serve a draft indictment on the Crown Court officer not more than 28 days after that order.

R10.9 Application to a High Court judge for permission to serve a draft indictment

10.9 (1) This rule applies where a prosecutor wants a High Court judge's permission to serve a draft indictment.

---

[12] 1985 c. 23; section 22(4) was amended by section 43 of the Crime and Disorder Act 1998 (c. 37).

(2) Such a prosecutor must—
   (a) apply in writing;
   (b) serve the application on—
      (i) the court officer, and
      (ii) the proposed defendant, unless the judge otherwise directs; and
   (c) ask for a hearing, if the prosecutor wants one, and explain why it is needed.
(3) The application must—
   (a) attach—
      (i) the proposed indictment,
      (ii) copies of the documents containing the evidence on which the prosecutor relies, including any written witness statement or statements complying with rule 16.2 (Content of written witness statement) and any documentary exhibit to any such statement,
      (iii) a copy of any indictment on which the defendant already has been arraigned, and
      (iv) if not contained in such an indictment, a list of any offence or offences for which the defendant already has been sent for trial;
   (b) include—
      (i) a concise statement of the circumstances in which, and the reasons why, the application is made, and
      (ii) a concise summary of the evidence contained in the documents accompanying the application, identifying each passage in those documents said to evidence each offence alleged by the prosecutor and relating that evidence to each count in the proposed indictment; and
   (c) contain a statement that, to the best of the prosecutor's knowledge, information and belief—
      (i) the evidence on which the prosecutor relies will be available at the trial, and
      (ii) the allegations contained in the application are substantially true
   unless the application is made by or on behalf of the Director of Public Prosecutions or the Director of the Serious Fraud Office.
(4) A proposed defendant served with an application who wants to make representations to the judge must—
   (a) serve the representations on the court officer and on the prosecutor;
   (b) do so as soon as practicable, and in any event within such period as the judge directs; and
   (c) ask for a hearing, if the proposed defendant wants one, and explain why it is needed.
(5) The judge may determine the application—
   (a) without a hearing, or at a hearing in public or in private; and
   (b) with or without receiving the oral evidence of any proposed witness.
(6) At any hearing, if the judge so directs a statement required by paragraph (3)(c) must be repeated on oath or affirmation.
(7) If the judge gives permission to serve a draft indictment, the decision must be recorded in writing and endorsed on, or annexed to, the proposed indictment.

[Note. See section 2(6) of the Administration of Justice (Miscellaneous Provisions) Act 1933[13].]

CRIMINAL PROCEDURE RULES   PART 11   DEFERRED PROSECUTION AGREEMENTS

When this Part applies   R11.1

11.1 (1) This Part applies to proceedings in the Crown Court under Schedule 17 to the Crime and Courts Act 2013.[1]
   (2) In this Part—
      (a) 'agreement' means a deferred prosecution agreement under paragraph 1 of that Schedule;
      (b) 'prosecutor' means a prosecutor designated by or under paragraph 3 of that Schedule; and
      (c) 'defendant' means the corporation, partnership or association with whom the prosecutor proposes to enter, or enters, an agreement.

[Note. Under Schedule 17 to the Crime and Courts Act 2013, a designated prosecutor may make a deferred prosecution agreement with a defendant, other than an individual, whom the prosecutor is considering prosecuting for an offences or offences listed in that Schedule. Under such an agreement, the defendant agrees to

---

[13] 1933 c. 36; section 2(6) was amended by Part IV of Schedule 11 to the Courts Act 1971 (c. 23), paragraph 1 of the Schedule to S.I. 2004/2035 and section 82 of the Deregulation Act 2015 (c. 20).
[1] 2013 c. 22.

comply with its terms and the prosecutor agrees that, if the Crown Court approves those terms, then paragraph 2 of the Schedule will apply and —

   (a) *the prosecutor will serve a draft indictment charging the defendant with the offence or offences the subject of the agreement;*

   (b) *the prosecution will be suspended under that paragraph, and the suspension may not be lifted while the agreement is in force; and*

   (c) *no-one may prosecute the defendant for the offence or offences charged while the agreement is in force, or after it expires if the defendant complies with it.*

The Code for prosecutors issued under paragraph 6 of that Schedule contains guidance on the exercise of prosecution functions in relation to a deferred prosecution agreement.]

R11.2   **Exercise of court's powers**

11.2 (1) The court must determine an application to which this Part applies at a hearing, which—

   (a) must be in private, under rule 11.3 (Application to approve a proposal to enter an agreement);

   (b) may be in public or private, under rule 11.4 (Application to approve the terms of an agreement), rule 11.6 (Application to approve a variation of the terms of an agreement) or rule 11.9 (Application to postpone the publication of information by the prosecutor); and

   (c) must be in public, under rule 11.5 (Application on breach of agreement) or rule 11.7 (Application to lift suspension of prosecution), unless the court otherwise directs.

(2) If at a hearing in private to which rule 11.4 or rule 11.6 applies the court approves the agreement or the variation proposed, the court must announce its decision and reasons at a hearing in public.

(3) The court must not determine an application under rule 11.3, rule 11.4 or rule 11.6 unless—

   (a) both parties are present;

   (b) the prosecutor provides the court with a written declaration that, for the purposes of the application—

     (i) the investigator enquiring into the alleged offence or offences has certified that no information has been supplied which the investigator knows to be inaccurate, misleading or incomplete, and

     (ii) the prosecutor has complied with the prosecution obligation to disclose material to the defendant; and

   (c) the defendant provides the court with a written declaration that, for the purposes of the application—

     (i) the defendant has not supplied any information which the defendant knows to be inaccurate, misleading or incomplete, and

     (ii) the individual through whom the defendant makes the declaration has made reasonable enquiries and believes the defendant's declaration to be true.

(4) The court must not determine an application under rule 11.5 or rule 11.7—

   (a) in the prosecutor's absence; or

   (b) in the absence of the defendant, unless the defendant has had at least 20 business days in which to make representations.

(5) If the court approves a proposal to enter an agreement—

   (a) the general rule is that any further application to which this Part applies must be made to the same judge; but

   (b) the court may direct other arrangements.

(6) The court may adjourn a hearing—

   (a) if either party asks, or on its own initiative; and

   (b) in particular, if the court requires more information about—

     (i) the facts of an alleged offence,

     (ii) the terms of a proposal to enter an agreement, or of a proposed agreement or variation of an agreement, or

     (iii) the circumstances in which the prosecutor wants the court to decide whether the defendant has failed to comply with the terms of an agreement.

(7) The court may—

   (a) hear an application under rule 11.4 immediately after an application under rule 11.3, if the court approves a proposal to enter an agreement; and

   (b) hear an application under rule 11.7 immediately after an application under rule 11.5, if the court terminates an agreement.

[Note. See paragraphs 7(4), 8(5), (6) and 10(5), (6) of Schedule 17 to the Crime and Courts Act 2013.

The Code for prosecutors issued under paragraph 6 of that Schedule contains guidance on fulfilling the prosecution duty of disclosure.]

Application to approve a proposal to enter an agreement   R11.3

11.3 (1) This rule applies where a prosecutor wants the court to approve a proposal to enter an agreement.

(2) The prosecutor must—

(a) apply in writing after the commencement of negotiations between the parties but before the terms of agreement have been settled; and

(b) serve the application on—

(i)   the court officer, and

(ii) the defendant.

(3) The application must—

(a) identify the parties to the proposed agreement;

(b) attach a proposed indictment setting out such of the offences listed in Part 2 of Schedule 17 to the Crime and Courts Act 2013 as the prosecutor is considering;

(c) include or attach a statement of facts proposed for inclusion in the agreement, which must give full particulars of each alleged offence, including details of any alleged financial gain or loss;

(d) include any information about the defendant that would be relevant to sentence in the event of conviction for the offence or offences;

(e) specify the proposed expiry date of the agreement;

(f) describe the proposed terms of the agreement, including details of any—

(i)   monetary penalty to be paid by the defendant, and the time within which any such penalty is to be paid,

(ii) compensation, reparation or donation to be made by the defendant, the identity of the recipient of any such payment and the time within which any such payment is to be made,

(iii) surrender of profits or other financial benefit by the defendant, and the time within which any such sum is to be surrendered,

(iv) arrangement to be made in relation to the management or conduct of the defendant's business,

(v)   co-operation required of the defendant in any investigation related to the offence or offences,

(vi) other action required of the defendant,

(vii) arrangement to monitor the defendant's compliance with a term,

(viii) consequence of the defendant's failure to comply with a term, and

(ix) prosecution costs to be paid by the defendant, and the time within which any such costs are to be paid;

(g) in relation to those terms, explain how they comply with—

(i)   the requirements of the code issued under paragraph 6 of Schedule 17 to the Crime and Courts Act 2013, and

(ii) any sentencing guidelines or guideline cases which apply;

(h) contain or attach the defendant's written consent to the proposal; and

(i) explain why—

(i)   entering into an agreement is likely to be in the interests of justice, and

(ii) the proposed terms of the agreement are fair, reasonable and proportionate.

(4) If the proposed statement of facts includes assertions that the defendant does not admit, the application must—

(a) specify the facts that are not admitted; and

(b) explain why that is immaterial for the purposes of the proposal to enter an agreement.

[Note. See paragraphs 5 and 7 of Schedule 17 to the Crime and Courts Act 2013.]

Application to approve the terms of an agreement   R11.4

11.4 (1) This rule applies where—

(a) the court has approved a proposal to enter an agreement on an application under rule 11.3; and

(b) the prosecutor wants the court to approve the terms of the agreement.

(2) The prosecutor must—

(a) apply in writing as soon as practicable after the parties have settled the terms; and

(b) serve the application on—

(i)   the court officer, and

(ii) the defendant.

    (3) The application must—
- (a) attach the agreement;
- (b) indicate in what respect, if any, the terms of the agreement differ from those proposed in the application under rule 11.3;
- (c) contain or attach the defendant's written consent to the agreement;
- (d) explain why—
  - (i) the agreement is in the interests of justice, and
  - (ii) the terms of the agreement are fair, reasonable and proportionate;
- (e) attach a draft indictment, charging the defendant with the offence or offences the subject of the agreement; and
- (f) include any application for the hearing to be in private.

    (4) If the court approves the agreement and the draft indictment, the court officer must—
- (a) endorse any paper copy of the indictment made for the court with—
  - (i) a note to identify it as the indictment approved by the court, and
  - (ii) the date of the court's approval; and
- (b) treat the case as if it had been suspended by order of the court.

[Note. See paragraph 8 of Schedule 17 to the Crime and Courts Act 2013. See also rule 11.9 (Application to postpone the publication of information by the prosecutor).

Under paragraph 2(1) of Schedule 17 to the 2013 Act and section 2 of the Administration of Justice (Miscellaneous Provisions) Act 1933[2], the draft indictment to which this rule applies becomes an indictment when the court approves the agreement and consents to the service of that draft. Part 10 contains rules about indictments.

Under paragraph 2(2) of Schedule 17 to the 2013 Act, on approval of the draft indictment the proceedings are automatically suspended.

Under paragraph 13(2) of Schedule 17 to the 2013 Act, where the court approves an agreement the statement of facts contained in that agreement is to be treated as an admission by the defendant under section 10 of the Criminal Justice Act 1967[3] (proof by formal admission) in any criminal proceedings against the defendant for the alleged offence.]

R11.5   Application on breach of agreement

  11.5 (1) This rule applies where—
- (a) the prosecutor believes that the defendant has failed to comply with the terms of an agreement; and
- (b) the prosecutor wants the court to decide—
  - (i) whether the defendant has failed to comply, and
  - (ii) if so, whether to terminate the agreement, or to invite the parties to agree proposals to remedy that failure.

    (2) The prosecutor must—
- (a) apply in writing, as soon as practicable after becoming aware of the grounds for doing so; and
- (b) serve the application on—
  - (i) the court officer, and
  - (ii) the defendant.

    (3) The application must—
- (a) specify each respect in which the prosecutor believes the defendant has failed to comply with the terms of the agreement, and explain the reasons for the prosecutor's belief; and
- (b) attach a copy of any document containing evidence on which the prosecutor relies.

    (4) A defendant who wants to make representations in response to the application must serve the representations on—
- (a) the court officer; and
- (b) the prosecutor,

---

[2] 1933 c. 36; section 2 was amended by Part IV of Schedule 11 to, the Courts Act 1971 (c. 23), Schedule 5 to, the Senior Courts Act 1981 (c. 54), Schedule 2 to the Prosecution of Offences Act 1985 (c. 23), paragraph 1 of Schedule 2 to the Criminal Justice Act 1987 (c. 38), paragraph 10 of Schedule 15 to the Criminal Justice Act 1988 (c. 33), paragraph 8 of Schedule 6 to the Criminal Justice Act 1991 (c. 53), Schedule 1 to the Statute Law (Repeals) Act 1993, paragraph 17 of Schedule 1 to the Criminal Procedure and Investigations Act 1996 (c. 25), paragraph 5 of Schedule 8 to the Crime and Disorder Act 1998 (c. 37), paragraph 34 of Schedule 3 and Part 4 of Schedule 37 to the Criminal Justice Act 2003 (c. 44), paragraph 1 of the Schedule to S.I. 2004/2035, section 12 of, and paragraph 7 of Schedule 1 to, the Constitutional Reform Act 2005 (c. 4), sections 116 and 178 of, and Part 3 of Schedule 23 to, the Coroners and Justice Act 2009 (c. 25), paragraph 32 of Schedule 17 to the Crime and Courts Act 2013 (c. 22) and section 82 of the Deregulation Act 2015 (c. 20).

[3] 1967 c. 80.

not more than 20 business days after service of the application.

[Note. See paragraph 9 of Schedule 17 to the Crime and Courts Act 2013. See also rule 11.9 (Application to postpone the publication of information by the prosecutor).]

Application to approve a variation of the terms of an agreement

R11.6

11.6 (1) This rule applies where the parties have agreed to vary the terms of an agreement because—

    (a) on an application under rule 11.5 (Application on breach of agreement), the court has invited them to do so; or

    (b) variation of the agreement is necessary to avoid a failure by the defendant to comply with its terms in circumstances that were not, and could not have been, foreseen by either party at the time the agreement was made.

(2) The prosecutor must—

    (a) apply in writing, as soon as practicable after the parties have settled the terms of the variation; and

    (b) serve the application on—

        (i) the court officer, and

        (ii) the defendant.

(3) The application must—

    (a) specify each variation proposed;

    (b) contain or attach the defendant's written consent to the variation;

    (c) explain why—

        (i) the variation is in the interests of justice, and

        (ii) the terms of the agreement as varied are fair, reasonable and proportionate; and

    (d) include any application for the hearing to be in private.

[Note. See paragraph 10 of Schedule 17 to the Crime and Courts Act 2013. See also rule 11.9 (Application to postpone the publication of information by the prosecutor).]

Application to lift suspension of prosecution

R11.7

11.7 (1) This rule applies where—

    (a) the court terminates an agreement before its expiry date; and

    (b) the prosecutor wants the court to lift the suspension of the prosecution that applied when the court approved the terms of the agreement.

(2) The prosecutor must—

    (a) apply in writing, as soon as practicable after the termination of the agreement; and

    (b) serve the application on—

        (i) the court officer, and

        (ii) the defendant.

(3) A defendant who wants to make representations in response to the application must serve the representations on—

    (a) the court officer; and

    (b) the prosecutor,

not more than 20 business days after service of the application.

[Note. See paragraphs 2(3) and 9 of Schedule 17 to the Crime and Courts Act 2013.]

Notice to discontinue prosecution

R11.8

11.8 (1) This rule applies where an agreement expires—

    (a) on its expiry date, or on a date treated as its expiry date; and

    (b) without having been terminated by the court.

(2) The prosecutor must—

    (a) as soon as practicable give notice in writing discontinuing the prosecution on the indictment approved by the court under rule 11.4 (Application to approve the terms of an agreement); and

    (b) serve the notice on—

        (i) the court officer, and

        (ii) the defendant.

[Note. See paragraph 11 of Schedule 17 to the Crime and Courts Act 2013.]

Application to postpone the publication of information by the prosecutor

R11.9

11.9 (1) This rule applies where the prosecutor—

    (a) makes an application under rule 11.4 (Application to approve the terms of an agreement), rule 11.5 (Application on breach of agreement) or rule 11.6 (Application to approve a variation of the terms of an agreement);

    (b) decides not to make an application under rule 11.5, despite believing that the defendant has failed to comply with the terms of the agreement; or

    (c) gives a notice under rule 11.8 (Notice to discontinue prosecution).

(2) A party who wants the court to order that the publication of information by the prosecutor about the court's or the prosecutor's decision should be postponed must—

    (a) apply in writing, as soon as practicable and in any event before such publication occurs;

    (b) serve the application on—

      (i) the court officer, and

      (ii) the other party; and

    (c) in the application—

      (i) specify the proposed terms of the order, and for how long it should last, and

      (ii) explain why an order in the terms proposed is necessary.

[Note. See paragraph 12 of Schedule 17 to the Crime and Courts Act 2013.

Part 6 of these Rules contains rules about applications for a restriction on reporting what takes place at a public hearing, or public access to what otherwise would be a public hearing.]

R11.10 Duty of court officer, etc.

11.10 (1) Unless the court otherwise directs, the court officer must—

    (a) arrange for the recording of proceedings on an application to which this Part applies; and

    (b) arrange for the transcription of such a recording if—

      (i) a party wants such a transcript, or

      (ii) anyone else wants such a transcript (but that is subject to the restrictions in paragraph (2)).

(2) Unless the court otherwise directs, a person who transcribes a recording of proceedings under such arrangements—

    (a) must not supply anyone other than a party with a transcript of a recording of—

      (i) a hearing in private, or

      (ii) a hearing in public to which reporting restrictions apply; but

    (b) subject to that, must supply any person with any transcript for which that person asks—

      (i) in accordance with the transcription arrangements made by the court officer, and

      (ii) on payment by that person of any fee prescribed.

(3) The court officer must not identify either party to a hearing in private under rule 11.3 (Application to approve a proposal to enter an agreement) or rule 11.4 (Application to approve the terms of an agreement)—

    (a) in any notice displayed in the vicinity of the courtroom; or

    (b) in any other information published by the court officer.

R11.11 Court's power to vary requirements under this Part

11.11 (1) The court may—

    (a) shorten or extend (even after it has expired) a time limit under this Part; and

    (b) allow there to be made orally—

      (i) an application under rule 11.4 (Application to approve the terms of an agreement), or

      (ii) an application under rule 11.7 (Application to lift suspension of prosecution)

where the court exercises its power under rule 11.2(7) to hear one application immediately after another.

(2) A party who wants an extension of time must—

    (a) apply when serving the application or notice for which it is needed; and

    (b) explain the delay.

CRIMINAL PROCEDURE RULES   PART 12   DISCONTINUING A PROSECUTION

R12.1 When this Part applies

12.1 (1) This Part applies where—

    (a) the Director of Public Prosecutions can discontinue a case in a magistrates' court, under section 23 of the Prosecution of Offences Act 1985;[1] or

---

[1] 1985 c. 23; section 23 was amended by section 119 of, and paragraph 63 of Schedule 8 to, the Crime and Disorder Act 1998 (c. 37), paragraph 290 of Schedule 8 to the Courts Act 2003 (c. 39) and paragraph 57 of Schedule 3 to the Criminal Justice Act 2003 (c. 44).

(b) the Director of Public Prosecutions, or another public prosecutor, can discontinue a case sent for trial in the Crown Court, under section 23A of the Prosecution of Offences Act 1985.[2]

(2) In this Part, 'prosecutor' means one of those authorities.

[Note. Under section 23 of the Prosecution of Offences Act 1985, the Director of Public Prosecutions may discontinue proceedings in a magistrates' court, before the court—

(a) sends the defendant for trial in the Crown Court; or

(b) begins to hear the prosecution evidence, at a trial in the magistrates' court.

Under section 23(4) of the 1985 Act, the Director may discontinue proceedings where a person charged is in custody but has not yet been brought to court.

Under section 23 of the 1985 Act, the defendant has a right to require the proceedings to continue. See rule 12.3.

Under section 23A of the 1985 Act, the Director of Public Prosecutions, or a public authority within the meaning of section 17 of that Act[3], may discontinue proceedings where the defendant was sent for trial in the Crown Court under section 51 of the Crime and Disorder Act 1998[4]. In such a case—

(a) the prosecutor must discontinue before a draft indictment becomes an indictment under rule 10.2(5); and

(b) the defendant has no right to require the proceedings to continue.

Where a prosecution does not proceed, the court has power to order the payment of the defendant's costs out of central funds. See rule 45.4.]

Discontinuing a case   R12.2

12.2 (1) A prosecutor exercising a power to which this Part applies must serve notice on—
  (a) the court officer;
  (b) the defendant; and
  (c) any custodian of the defendant.

(2) Such a notice must—
  (a) identify—
    (i) the defendant and each offence to which the notice relates,
    (ii) the person serving the notice, and
    (iii) the power that that person is exercising; and
  (b) explain—
    (i) in the copy of the notice served on the court officer, the reasons for discontinuing the case,
    (ii) that the notice brings the case to an end,
    (iii) if the defendant is in custody for any offence to which the notice relates, that the defendant must be released from that custody, and
    (iv) if the notice is under section 23 of the 1985 Act, that the defendant has a right to require the case to continue.

(3) Where the defendant is on bail, the court officer must notify—
  (a) any surety; and
  (b) any person responsible for monitoring or securing the defendant's compliance with a condition of bail.

Defendant's notice to continue   R12.3

12.3 (1) This rule applies where a prosecutor serves a notice to discontinue under section 23 of the 1985 Act.

(2) A defendant who wants the case to continue must serve notice—
  (a) on the court officer; and
  (b) not more than 25 business days after service of the notice to discontinue.

(3) If the defendant serves such a notice, the court officer must—
  (a) notify the prosecutor; and
  (b) refer the case to the court.

---

[2] 1985 c. 23; section 23A was inserted by section 119 of, and paragraph 64 of Schedule 8 to, the Crime and Disorder Act 1998 (c. 37) and amended by paragraph 57 of Schedule 3, and Part 4 of Schedule 37, to the Criminal Justice Act 2003 (c. 44).
[3] 1985 c. 23; section 17 was amended by section 40 of, and paragraph 41 of Schedule 9 to, the Constitutional Reform Act 2005 (c. 4) and paragraphs 1 and 4 and Part 4 of Schedule 7 to the Legal Aid, Sentencing and Punishment of Offenders Act 2012 (c. 10).
[4] 1998 c. 37; section 51 was substituted by paragraphs 15 and 18 of Schedule 3 to the Criminal Justice Act 2003 (c. 44) and amended by section 59 of, and paragraph 1 of Schedule 11 to, the Constitutional Reform Act 2005 (c. 4).

CRIMINAL PROCEDURE RULES   PART 13   WARRANTS FOR ARREST,
DETENTION OR IMPRISONMENT

[Note. Part 30 contains rules about warrants to take goods to pay fines, etc.]

R13.1 **When this Part applies**

13.1 (1) This Part applies where the court can issue a warrant for arrest, detention or imprisonment.
(2) In this Part, 'defendant' means anyone against whom such a warrant is issued.

R13.2 **Terms of a warrant for arrest**

13.2 A warrant for arrest must require each person to whom it is directed to arrest the defendant and—
(a) bring the defendant to a court—
(i) specified in the warrant, or
(ii) required or allowed by law; or
(b) release the defendant on bail (with conditions or without) to attend court at a date, time and place—
(i) specified in the warrant, or
(ii) to be notified by the court.

[Note. The principal provisions under which the court can issue a warrant for arrest are—

(a) section 4 of the Criminal Procedure (Attendance of Witnesses) Act 1965[1];
(b) section 7 of the Bail Act 1976[2];
(c) sections 1 and 97 of the Magistrates' Courts Act 1980[3]; and
(d) sections 79, 80 and 81(4), (5) of the Senior Courts Act 1981[4].

See also section 27A of the Magistrates' Courts Act 1980[5] (power to transfer criminal proceedings) and section 78(2) of the Senior Courts Act 1981[6] (adjournment of Crown Court case to another place).]

R13.3 **Terms of a warrant for detention or imprisonment**

13.3 (1) A warrant for detention or imprisonment must—
(a) require each person to whom it is directed to detain the defendant and—
(i) take the defendant to any place specified in the warrant or required or allowed by law, and
(ii) deliver the defendant to the custodian of that place; and
(b) require that custodian to detain the defendant, as ordered by the court, until in accordance with the law—
(i) the defendant is delivered to the appropriate court or place, or
(ii) the defendant is released.
(2) Where a magistrates' court remands a defendant to police detention under section 128(7)[7] or section 136[8] of the Magistrates' Courts Act 1980, or to customs detention under section 152 of the Criminal Justice Act 1988[9], the warrant it issues must—
(a) be directed, as appropriate, to—

[1] 1965 c. 69; section 4 was amended by section 56 of, and paragraph 45 of Schedule 8 to, the Courts Act 1971 (c. 23) and sections 65, 66, 67 and 80 of, and Schedule 5 to, the Criminal Procedure and Investigations Act 1996 (c. 25).
[2] 1976 c. 63; section 7(1A) and (1B) were inserted section 198 of the Extradition Act 2003 (c. 41).
[3] 1980 c. 43; section 1 was amended by section 68 of, and paragraph 6 of Schedule 8 to, the Criminal Justice Act 1991 (c. 53), sections 43 and 109 of, and Schedule 10 to, the Courts Act 2003 (c. 39), section 31 of, and paragraph 12 of Schedule 7 to, the Criminal Justice Act 2003 (c. 44) and section 153 of the Police Reform and Social Responsibility Act 2011. It is further amended by paragraphs 7 and 8 of Schedule 36 to, the Criminal Justice Act 2003 (c. 44), with effect from a date to be appointed. Section 97 was amended by sections 13 and 14 of, and paragraph 7 of Schedule 2 to, the Contempt of Court Act 1981 (c. 47), section 31 of, and paragraph 2 of Schedule 4 to, the Criminal Justice (International Co-operation) Act 1990 (c. 5), sections 17 and 65 of, and paragraph 6 of Schedule 3 and Part I of Schedule 4 to, the Criminal Justice Act 1991 (c. 53), section 51 of the Criminal Procedure and Investigations Act 1996 (c. 25) and section 169 of the Serious Organised Crime and Police Act 2005 (c. 15).
[4] 1981 c. 54; section 80 was amended by paragraph 54 of Schedule 3 to the Criminal Justice Act 2003 (c. 44).
[5] 1980 c. 43; section 27A was inserted by section 46 of the Courts Act 2003 (c. 39).
[6] 1981 c. 54.
[7] 1980 c. 43; section 128(7) was amended by section 48 of the Police and Criminal Evidence Act 1984 (c. 60). It is modified by section 91(5) of the Legal Aid, Sentencing and Punishment of Offenders Act 2012 (c. 10).
[8] 1980 c. 43; section 136 was amended by section 77 of, and paragraph 58 of Schedule 14 to, the Criminal Justice Act 1982 (c. 48), section 68 of, and paragraph 6 of Schedule 8 to, the Criminal Justice Act 1991(c. 53), section 95(2) of the Access to Justice Act 1999 (c. 22) and section 165(1) of, and paragraph 78 of Schedule 9 to, the Powers of Criminal Courts (Sentencing) Act 2000 (c. 6). It is further amended by sections 74 and 75 of, and paragraphs 58 and 68 of Schedule 7, and Schedule 8 to, the Criminal Justice and Court Services Act 2000 (c. 43), with effect from a date to be appointed.
[9] 1988 c. 33; section 152 was amended by paragraphs 1 and 17 of Schedule 11 to, the Proceeds of Crime Act 2002 (c. 29) and section 8 of the Drugs Act 2005 (c. 17).

(i)   a constable, or
(ii) an officer of [His] Majesty's Revenue and Customs; and
(b)   require that constable or officer to detain the defendant—
(i)   for a period (not exceeding the maximum permissible) specified in the warrant, or
(ii) until in accordance with the law the defendant is delivered to the appropriate court or place.
(3) Where a magistrates' court sentences a defendant to imprisonment or detention and section 11(3) of the Magistrates' Courts Act 1980[10] applies (custodial sentence imposed in the defendant's absence), the warrant it issues must—
(a)   require each person to whom the warrant is directed—
(i)   to arrest the defendant and bring him or her to a court specified in the warrant, and
(ii) unless the court then otherwise directs, after that to act as required by paragraph (1)(a) of this rule; and
(b)   require the custodian to whom the defendant is delivered in accordance with that paragraph to act as required by paragraph (1)(b) of this rule.

[Note. Under section 128(7) of the Magistrates' Courts Act 1980, a magistrates' court can remand a defendant to police detention for not more than 3 clear days, if the defendant is an adult, or for not more than 24 hours if the defendant is under 18.

Under section 136 of the 1980 Act, a magistrates' court can order a defendant's detention in police custody until the following 8am for non-payment of a fine, etc.

Under section 152 of the Criminal Justice Act 1988, a magistrates' court can remand a defendant to customs detention for not more than 192 hours if the defendant is charged with a drug trafficking offence.]

Information to be included in a warrant

R13.4

13.4 (1) A warrant must identify—
(a)   each person to whom it is directed;
(b)   the defendant against whom it was issued;
(c)   the reason for its issue;
(d)   the court that issued it, unless that is otherwise recorded by the court officer; and
(e)   the court office for the court that issued it.
(2) A warrant for detention or imprisonment must contain a record of any decision by the court under—
(a)   section 91 of the Legal Aid, Sentencing and Punishment of Offenders Act 2012[11] (remands of children otherwise than on bail), including in particular—
(i)   whether the defendant must be detained in local authority accommodation or youth detention accommodation,
(ii) the local authority designated by the court,
(iii) any requirement imposed by the court on that authority,
(iv) any condition imposed by the court on the defendant, and
(v)   the reason for any such requirement or condition;
(b)   section 80 of the Magistrates' Courts Act 1980[12] (application of money found on defaulter to satisfy sum adjudged); or
(c)   section 82(1) or (4) of the 1980 Act[13] (conditions for issue of a warrant).
(3) A warrant for detention or imprisonment must include such an indication of the defendant's physical and mental health as may be needed to alert those to whom the warrant is directed—
(a)   to any vulnerability of the defendant; and
(b)   to any risk to others that may be posed by the defendant.

---

[10] 1980 c. 43; section 11(3) was amended by section 123 of, and paragraph 1 of Schedule 8 to, the Criminal Justice Act 1988 (c. 33), section 168 of, and paragraph 39 of Schedule 10 to, the Criminal Justice and Public Order Act 1994 (c. 33), section 119 of, and paragraph 39 of Schedule 8 to, the Crime and Disorder Act 1998 (c. 37), section 304 of, and paragraphs 25 and 26 of Schedule 32 to, the Criminal Justice Act 2003 (c. 44) and section 54 of the Criminal Justice and Immigration Act 2008 (c. 4).
[11] 2012 c. 10.
[12] 1980 c. 43; section 80 was amended by section 33(1) of, and paragraph 83 of Schedule 2 to, the Family Law Reform Act 1987 (c. 42) and section 62(3) of, and paragraphs 45 and 49 of the Tribunals, Courts and Enforcement Act 2007 (c. 15).
[13] 1980 c. 43; section 82 was amended by section 77 of, and paragraph 52 of Schedule 14 to, the Criminal Justice Act 1982 (c. 48), sections 61 and 123 of, and paragraphs 1 and 2 of Schedule 8 to, the Criminal Justice Act 1988 (c. 33), section 55 of and paragraph 10 of Schedule 4 to the Crime (Sentences) Act 1997 (c. 43), paragraph 220 of Schedule 8 to the Courts Act 2003 (c. 39), section 62 of, and paragraphs 45 and 51 of Schedule 13 to, the Tribunals, Courts and Enforcement Act 2007 (c. 15) and section 179 of the Anti-social Behaviour, Crime and Policing Act 2014 (c. 12) and section 54 of, and paragraphs 2 and 3 of Schedule 12 to, the Criminal Justice and Courts Act 2015 (c. 2). It is further amended by paragraphs 58 and 63 of Part II of Schedule 7 to the Criminal Justice and Court Services Act 2000 (c. 43) and Part 7 of Schedule 37 to the Criminal Justice Act 2003 (c. 44), with effect from dates to be appointed.

(4) The indication required by paragraph (3) may be given by reference to an accompanying document.

(5) A warrant that contains an error is not invalid, as long as—

    (a) it was issued in respect of a lawful decision by the court; and

    (b) it contains enough information to identify that decision.

[Note. See sections 93(7) and 102(5) of the Legal Aid, Sentencing and Punishment of Offenders Act 2012. Under section 91 of the Act, instead of granting bail to a defendant under 18 the court may—

    (a) remand him or her to local authority accommodation and, after consulting with that authority, impose on the defendant a condition that the court could impose if granting bail; or

    (b) remand him or her to youth detention accommodation, if the defendant is at least 12 years old and the other conditions, about the offence and the defendant, prescribed by the Act are met.

Under section 80 of the Magistrates' Courts Act 1980, the court may decide that any money found on the defendant must not be applied towards payment of the sum for which a warrant is issued under section 76 of that Act (enforcement of sums adjudged to be paid).

See section 82(6) of the 1980 Act. Under section 82(1) and (4), the court may only issue a warrant for the defendant's imprisonment for non-payment of a sum due where it finds that the prescribed conditions are met.

Under section 123 of the 1980 Act[14], "no objection shall be allowed to any ... warrant to procure the presence of the defendant, for any defect in it in substance or in form ...".]

R13.5   Execution of a warrant

13.5 (1) A warrant may be executed—

    (a) by any person to whom it is directed; or

    (b) if the warrant was issued by a magistrates' court, by anyone authorised to do so by section 125[15] (warrants), 125A[16] (civilian enforcement officers) or 125B[17] (execution by approved enforcement agency) of the Magistrates' Courts Act 1980.

(2) The person who executes a warrant must—

    (a) explain, in terms the defendant can understand, what the warrant requires, and why;

    (b) show the defendant the warrant, if that person has it; and

    (c) if the defendant asks—

        (i) arrange for the defendant to see the warrant, if that person does not have it, and

        (ii) show the defendant any written statement of that person's authority required by section 125A or 125B of the 1980 Act.

(3) The person who executes a warrant of arrest that requires the defendant to be released on bail must—

    (a) make a record of—

        (i) the defendant's name,

        (ii) the reason for the arrest,

        (iii) the defendant's release on bail, and

        (iv) when and where the warrant requires the defendant to attend court; and

    (b) serve the record on—

        (i) the defendant, and

        (ii) the court officer.

(4) The person who executes a warrant of detention or imprisonment must—

    (a) take the defendant—

        (i) to any place specified in the warrant, or

        (ii) if that is not immediately practicable, to any other place at which the defendant may be lawfully detained (and the warrant then has effect as if it specified that place);

    (b) obtain a receipt from the custodian; and

    (c) notify the court officer that the defendant has been taken to that place.

---

[14] 1980 c. 43.

[15] 1980 c. 43; section 125 was amended by section 33 of the Police and Criminal Evidence Act 1984 (c. 60), section 65(1) of the Criminal Justice Act 1988 (c. 33), sections 95(1), 97(4) and 106 of, and Part V of Schedule 15 and Table (8) to, the Access to Justice Act 1999 (c. 22), section 109(1) of, and paragraph 238 of Schedule 8 to, the Courts Act 2003 (c. 39) and sections 62(3), 86 and 146 of and paragraphs 45 and 57 of Schedule 23 to, the Tribunals, Courts and Enforcement Act 2007 (c. 15).

[16] 1980 c. 43; section 125A was inserted by section 92 of the Access to Justice Act 1999 (c. 22) and amended by articles 46 and 52 of S.I. 2006/1737 and article 8 of, and paragraph 5 of the Schedule to, S.I. 2007/2128 and section 62 of, and paragraphs 45 and 58 of Schedule 13 to, the Tribunals, Courts and Enforcement Act 2007 (c. 15).

[17] 1980 c. 43; section 125A was inserted by section 92 of the Access to Justice Act 1999 (c. 22) and amended by articles 46 and 52 of S.I. 2006/1737 and article 8 of, and paragraph 5 of the Schedule to, S.I. 2007/2128 and section 62 of, and paragraphs 45 and 58 of Schedule 13 to, the Tribunals, Courts and Enforcement Act 2007 (c. 15).

[Note. Under section 125 of the Magistrates' Courts Act 1980, a warrant issued by a magistrates' court may be executed by any person to whom it is directed or by any constable acting within that constable's police area.

Certain warrants issued by a magistrates' court may be executed anywhere in England and Wales by a civilian enforcement officer, under section 125A of the 1980 Act; or by an approved enforcement agency, under section 125B of the Act. In either case, the person executing the warrant must, if the defendant asks, show a written statement indicating: that person's name; the authority or agency by which that person is employed, or in which that person is a director or partner; that that person is authorised to execute warrants; and, where section 125B applies, that the agency is registered as one approved by the Lord Chancellor.

See also section 125D of the 1980 Act[18], under which—

> *(a) a warrant to which section 125A applies may be executed by any person entitled to execute it even though it is not in that person's possession at the time; and*
>
> *(b) certain other warrants, including any warrant to arrest a person in connection with an offence, may be executed by a constable even though it is not in that constable's possession at the time.]*

Warrants that cease to have effect on payment   R13.6

13.6 (1) This rule applies to a warrant issued by a magistrates' court under any of the following provisions of the Magistrates' Courts Act 1980—

> (a) section 76[19] (enforcement of sums adjudged to be paid);
>
> (b) section 83[20] (process for securing attendance of offender);
>
> (c) section 86[21] (power of magistrates' court to fix day for appearance of offender at means inquiry, etc.);
>
> (d) section 136[22] (committal to custody overnight at police station for non-payment of sum adjudged by conviction).

[Note. See sections 79[23] and 125(1) of the Magistrates' Courts Act 1980.]

> (2) The warrant no longer has effect if—
>
> (a) the sum in respect of which the warrant was issued is paid to the person executing it;
>
> (b) that sum is offered to, but refused by, that person; or
>
> (c) that person is shown a receipt for that sum given by—
>
> > (i) the court officer, or
> >
> > (ii) the authority to which that sum is due.

Warrant issued when the court office is closed   R13.7

13.7 (1) This rule applies where the court issues a warrant when the court office is closed.

> (2) The applicant for the warrant must, not more than 72 hours later, serve on the court officer—
>
> (a) a copy of the warrant; and
>
> (b) any written material that was submitted to the court.

CRIMINAL PROCEDURE RULES   PART 14   BAIL AND CUSTODY TIME LIMITS

General rules

When this Part applies   R14.1

14.1 (1) This Part applies where a magistrates' court or the Crown Court can—

> (a) grant or withhold bail, or impose or vary a condition of bail; and

---

[18] 1980 c. 43; section 125D was inserted by section 96 of the Access to Justice Act 1999 (c. 22) and amended by sections 62 and 146 of, and paragraphs 45 and 61 of Schedule 13 to, the Tribunals, Courts and Enforcement Act 2007 (c. 15).

[19] 1980 c. 43: section 76 was amended by section 7 of the Maintenance Enforcement Act 1991 (c. 17); section 78 of, and Schedule 16 to, the Criminal Justice Act 1982 (c. 48), and section 62(3) of, and paragraphs 45 and 46 of Schedule 13 to, the Tribunals, Courts and Enforcement Act 2007 (c. 15).

[20] 1980 c. 43; section 83 was amended by articles 46 and 47 of S.I. 2006/1737 and sections 97(2) and 106 of, and Part V (table 8) of Schedule 15 to, the Access to Justice Act 1999 (c. 22).

[21] 1980 c. 43; section 86 was amended by section 51(2) of the Criminal Justice Act 1982 (c. 48) and section 97(3) of the Access to Justice Act 1999 (c. 22).

[22] 1980 c. 43; section 82 was amended by section 77 of, and paragraph 52 of Schedule 14 to, the Criminal Justice Act 1982 (c. 48), sections 61 and 123 of, and paragraphs 1 and 2 of Schedule 8 to, the Criminal Justice Act 1988 (c. 33), section 55 of and paragraph 10 of Schedule 4 to the Crime (Sentences) Act 1997 (c. 43), paragraph 220 of Schedule 8 to the Courts Act 2003 (c. 39), section 62 of, and paragraphs 45 and 51 of Schedule 13 to, the Tribunals, Courts and Enforcement Act 2007 (c. 15), section 179 of the Anti-social Behaviour, Crime and Policing Act 2014 (c. 12) and section 54 of, and paragraphs 2 and 3 of Schedule 12 to, the Criminal Justice and Courts Act 2015 (c. 2). It is further amended by paragraphs 58 and 63 of Part II of Schedule 7 to the Criminal Justice and Court Services Act 2000 (c. 43) and Part 7 of Schedule 37 to the Criminal Justice Act 2003 (c. 44), with effect from dates to be appointed.

[23] 1980 c. 43; section 79 was amended by paragraph 219 of Schedule 8 to the Courts Act 2003 (c. 39) and section 62 of, and paragraphs 45, 47 and 48 of Schedule 13 to, the Tribunals, Courts and Enforcement Act 2007 (c. 15).

(b) where bail has been withheld, extend a custody time limit.

(2) Rules 14.18, 14.19 and 14.20 apply where a magistrates' court can authorise an extension of the period for which a defendant is released on bail before being charged with an offence.

(3) In this Part, 'defendant' includes a person who has been granted bail by a police officer.

[Note. See in particular—

(a) the Bail Act 1976[1];

(b) section 128 of the Magistrates' Courts Act 1980[2] (general powers of magistrates' courts in relation to bail);

(c) section 81 of the Senior Courts Act 1981[3] (general powers of the Crown Court in relation to bail);

(d) section 115 of the Coroners and Justice Act 2009[4] (exclusive power of the Crown Court to grant bail to a defendant charged with murder);

(e) section 22 of the Prosecution of Offences Act 1985[5] (provision for custody time limits);

(f) the Prosecution of Offences (Custody Time Limits) Regulations 1987[6] (maximum periods during which a defendant may be kept in custody pending trial); and

(g) sections 47ZF and 47ZG of the Police and Criminal Evidence Act 1984[7] (extensions by court of pre-charge bail time limit).

At the end of this Part there is a summary of the general entitlement to bail and of the exceptions to that entitlement

R14.2   Exercise of court's powers: general

14.2 (1) The court must not make a decision to which this Part applies unless—

(a) each party to the decision and any surety directly affected by the decision—
  (i) is present, in person or by live link, or
  (ii) has had an opportunity to make representations;

(b) on an application for bail by a defendant who is absent and in custody, the court is satisfied that the defendant—
  (i) has waived the right to attend, or
  (ii) was present when a court withheld bail in the case on a previous occasion and has been in custody continuously since then;

(c) on a prosecutor's appeal against a grant of bail, application to extend a custody time limit or appeal against a refusal to extend such a time limit—
  (i) the court is satisfied that a defendant who is absent has waived the right to attend, or
  (ii) the court is satisfied that it would be just to proceed even though the defendant is absent; and

(d) the court is satisfied that sufficient time has been allowed—
  (i) for the defendant to consider the information provided by the prosecutor under rule 14.5(2), and

---

[1] 1976 c. 63.

[2] 1980 c. 43; section 128 was amended by section 59 to, and paragraphs 2, 3 and 4 of Schedule 9 to, the Criminal Justice Act 1982 (c. 48), section 48 of the Police and Criminal Evidence Act 1984 (c. 60), section 170(1) of, and paragraphs 65 and 69 of Schedule 15 to, the Criminal Justice Act 1988 (c. 33), section 125(3) of, and paragraph 25 of Schedule 18 to, the Courts and Legal Services Act 1990 (c. 41), sections 49, 52 and 80 of, and Schedule 5 to, the Criminal Procedure and Investigations Act 1996 (c. 25), paragraph 75 of Schedule 9 to the Powers of Criminal Courts (Sentencing) Act 2000 (c. 6) and paragraph 51 of Schedule 3 and Part 4 of Schedule 37 to the Criminal Justice Act 2003 (c. 44). It is modified by section 91(5) of the Legal Aid, Sentencing and Punishment of Offenders Act 2012 (c. 10).

[3] 1981 c. 54; section 81(1) was amended by sections 29 and 60 of the Criminal Justice Act 1982 (c. 48), section 15 of, and paragraph 2 of Schedule 12 to, the Criminal Justice Act 1987 (c. 38), section 168 of, and paragraph 19 of Schedule 9 and paragraph 48 of Schedule 10 to, the Criminal Justice and Public Order Act 1994 (c. 33), section 119 of, and paragraph 48 of Schedule 8 and Schedule 10 to, the Crime and Disorder Act 1998 (c. 37), section 165 of, and paragraph 87 of Schedule 9 and Schedule 12 to, the Powers of Criminal Courts (Sentencing) Act 2000 (c. 6), paragraph 54 of Schedule 3, paragraph 4 of Schedule 36 and Part 4 of Schedule 37 to the Criminal Justice Act 2003 (c. 44), articles 2 and 6 of S.I. 2004/1033 and section 177(1) of, and paragraph 76 of Schedule 21 to, the Coroners and Justice Act 2009 (c. 25).

[4] 2009 c. 25.

[5] 1985 c. 23; section 22 was amended by paragraph 104 of Schedule 15 to the Criminal Justice Act 1988 (c. 33), section 43 of the Crime and Disorder Act 1998 (c. 37), paragraph 36 of Schedule 11 to the Criminal Justice Act 1991 (c. 53), paragraph 27 of Schedule 9 to the Criminal Justice and Public Order Act 1994 (c. 33), section 71 of the Criminal Procedure and Investigations Act 1996 (c. 25), section 67(3) of the Access to Justice Act 1999 (c. 22), section 70 of, and paragraph 57 of Schedule 3 and paragraphs 49 and 51 of Schedule 36 to, the Criminal Justice Act 2003 (c. 44), section 59 of, and paragraph 1 of Schedule 11 to, the Constitutional Reform Act 2005 (c. 4) and paragraph 22 of Schedule 12 to the Legal Aid, Sentencing and Punishment of Offenders Act 2012 (c. 10).

[6] S.I. 1987/299; amended by sections 71 and 80 of, and paragraph 8 of Schedule 5 to, the Criminal Procedure and Investigations Act 1996 (c. 25) and S.I. 1989/767, 1991/1515, 1995/555, 1999/2744, 2000/3284, 2012/1344.

[7] 1984 c. 60; sections 47ZF and 47ZG were inserted by section 63 of the Policing and Crime Act 2017 (c. 3).

(ii) for the court to consider the parties' representations and make the decision required.

(2) The court may make a decision to which this Part applies at a hearing, in public or in private.

(3) The court may determine without a hearing an application to vary a condition of bail if—

    (a) the parties to the application have agreed the terms of the variation proposed; or

    (b) on an application by a defendant, the court determines the application no sooner than the fifth business day after the application was served.

(4) The court may adjourn a determination to which this Part applies, if that is necessary to obtain information sufficient to allow the court to make the decision required.

(5) At any hearing at which the court makes one of the following decisions, the court must announce in terms the defendant can understand (with help, if necessary), and by reference to the circumstances of the defendant and the case, its reasons for—

    (a) withholding bail, or imposing or varying a bail condition;

    (b) granting bail, where the prosecutor opposed the grant; or

    (c) where the defendant is under 18—

        (i) imposing or varying a bail condition when ordering the defendant to be detained in local authority accommodation, or

        (ii) ordering the defendant to be detained in youth detention accommodation.

(6) At any hearing at which the court grants bail, the court must—

    (a) tell the defendant where and when to surrender to custody; or

    (b) arrange for the court officer to give the defendant, as soon as practicable, notice of where and when to surrender to custody.

(7) This rule does not apply on an application to a magistrates' court to authorise an extension of pre-charge bail.

[Note. See section 5 of the Bail Act 1976 and sections 93(7) and 102(4) of the Legal Aid, Sentencing and Punishment of Offenders Act 2012[8].

Under sections 57A and 57B of the Crime and Disorder Act 1998[9], a defendant is to be treated as present in court when, by virtue of a live link direction within the meaning of those provisions, he or she attends a hearing through a live link.

Under section 91 of the 2012 Act, instead of granting bail to a defendant under 18 the court may—

    (a) remand him or her to local authority accommodation and, after consulting with that authority, impose on the defendant a condition that the court could impose if granting bail; or

    (b) remand him or her to youth detention accommodation, if the defendant is at least 12 years old and the other conditions, about the offence and the defendant, prescribed by the Act are met.

See also rule 14.18 (Exercise of court's powers: extension of pre-charge bail).]

Duty of justices' legal adviser

R14.3

14.3 (1) This rule applies—

    (a) only in a magistrates' court; and

    (b) unless the court—

        (i) includes a District Judge (Magistrates' Courts), and

        (ii) otherwise directs.

(2) A justices' legal adviser must ask such questions as may be needed to obtain information sufficient to allow the court to make such decisions as are required.

[Note. For the functions of a justices' legal adviser, see sections 28 and 29 of the Courts Act 2003[10]. See also rule 2.12 (Duties of justices' legal adviser).]

General duties of court officer

R14.4

14.4 (1) The court officer must arrange for a note or other record to be made of—

    (a) the parties' representations about bail; and

    (b) the court's reasons for a decision—

        (i) to withhold bail, or to impose or vary a bail condition,

        (ii) to grant bail, where the prosecutor opposed the grant or,

---

[8] 2012 c. 10.

[9] 1998 c. 37; sections 57A to 57E were substituted for section 57 as originally enacted by section 45 of the Police and Justice Act 2006 (c. 48), and amended by sections 106, 109 and 178 of, and Part 3 of Schedule 23 to, the Coroners and Justice Act 2009 (c. 25). Section 57A was further amended by paragraphs 36 and 39 of Schedule 12 to the Legal Aid, Sentencing and Punishment of Offenders Act 2012 (c. 10).

[10] 2003 c. 39; section 28 was amended by section 15 of, and paragraphs 308 and 327 of Schedule 4 to, the Constitutional Reform Act 2005 (c. 4).

        (iii) on an application to which rule 14.19 applies (Application to authorise extension of pre-charge bail).

(2) The court officer must serve notice of a decision about bail on—

    (a) the defendant (but, in the Crown Court, only where the defendant's legal representative asks for such a notice, or where the defendant has no legal representative);

    (b) the prosecutor (but only where the court granted bail, the prosecutor opposed the grant, and the prosecutor asks for such a notice);

    (c) a party to the decision who was absent when it was made;

    (d) a surety who is directly affected by the decision;

    (e) the defendant's custodian, where the defendant is in custody and the decision requires the custodian—

        (i) to release the defendant (or will do so, if a requirement ordered by the court is met), or

        (ii) to transfer the defendant to the custody of another custodian; and

    (f) the court officer for any other court at which the defendant is required by that decision to surrender to custody.

(3) Where the court postpones the date on which a defendant who is on bail must surrender to custody, the court officer must serve notice of the postponed date on—

    (a) the defendant; and

    (b) any surety.

(4) Where a magistrates' court withholds bail in a case to which section 5(6A)[11] of the Bail Act 1976 applies (remand in custody after hearing full argument on an application for bail), the court officer must serve on the defendant a certificate that the court heard full argument.

(5) Where the court determines without a hearing an application to which rule 14.21 applies (Application to authorise extension of pre-charge bail), the court officer must—

    (a) if the court allows the application, notify the applicant; and

    (b) if the court refuses the application, notify the applicant and the defendant.

[Note. See section 5 of the Bail Act 1976[12]; section 43 of the Magistrates' Courts Act 1980[13]; and section 52 of the Mental Health Act 1983[14].]

Bail

R14.5   **Prosecutor's representations about bail**

14.5 (1) This rule applies whenever the court can grant or withhold bail.

(2) The prosecutor must as soon as practicable—

    (a) provide the defendant with all the information in the prosecutor's possession which is material to what the court must decide; and

    (b) provide the court with the same information.

(3) A prosecutor who opposes the grant of bail must specify—

    (a) each exception to the general right to bail on which the prosecutor relies; and

    (b) each consideration that the prosecutor thinks relevant.

(4) A prosecutor who wants the court to impose a condition on any grant of bail must—

    (a) specify each condition proposed; and

    (b) explain what purpose would be served by such a condition.

[Note. A summary of the general entitlement to bail and of the exceptions to that entitlement is at the end of this Part.]

R14.6   **Reconsideration of police bail by magistrates' court**

14.6 (1) This rule applies where—

---

[11] 1976 c. 63; section 5(6A) was inserted by section 60 of the Criminal Justice Act 1982 (c. 48) and amended by section 165 of, and paragraph 53 of Schedule 9 to, the Powers of Criminal Courts (Sentencing) Act 2000 (c. 6) and by paragraph 48 of Schedule 3, paragraphs 1 and 2 of Schedule 36, and Part 4 of Schedule 37 to the Criminal Justice Act 2003 (c. 44).

[12] 1976 c. 63; section 5 was amended by section 65 of, and Schedule 12 to, the Criminal Law Act 1977 (c. 45), section 60 of the Criminal Justice Act 1982 (c. 48), paragraph 1 of Schedule 3 to the Criminal Justice and Public Order Act 1994 (c. 33), paragraph 53 of Schedule 9 to the Powers of Criminal Courts (Sentencing) Act 2000 (c. 6), section 129(1) of the Criminal Justice and Police Act 2001 (c. 16), paragraph 182 of Schedule 8 to the Courts Act 2003 (c. 39), paragraph 48 of Schedule 3, paragraphs 1 and 2 of Schedule 36, and Parts 2, 4 and 12 of Schedule 37 to the Criminal Justice Act 2003 (c. 44) and section 208 of, and paragraphs 33 and 35 of Schedule 21 to, the Legal Services Act 2007 (c. 27).

[13] 1980 c. 43; section 43 was substituted by section 47 of the Police and Criminal Evidence Act 1984 (c. 60) and amended by paragraph 43 of Schedule 10 to the Criminal Justice and Public Order Act 1994 (c. 33) and paragraph 206 of Schedule 8 to the Courts Act 2003 (c. 39).

[14] 1983 c. 20; section 52 was amended by paragraph 55 of Schedule 3 and Schedule 37 to the Criminal Justice Act 2003 (c. 44), section 11 of the Mental Health Act 2007 (c. 12) and paragraphs 53 and 57 of Schedule 21 to the Legal Services Act 2007 (c. 29).

    (a) a party wants a magistrates' court to reconsider a bail decision by a police officer after the defendant is charged with an offence; and

    (b) a defendant wants a magistrates' court to reconsider a bail condition imposed by a police officer before the defendant is charged with an offence.

(2) An application under this rule must be made to—

    (a) the magistrates' court to whose custody the defendant is under a duty to surrender, if any; or

    (b) any magistrates' court acting for the police officer's local justice area, in any other case.

(3) The applicant party must—

    (a) apply in writing; and

    (b) serve the application on—

        (i)   the court officer,

        (ii) the other party, and

        (iii) any surety affected or proposed.

(4) The application must—

    (a) specify—

        (i)   the decision that the applicant wants the court to make,

        (ii) each offence charged, or for which the defendant was arrested, and

        (iii) the police bail decision to be reconsidered and the reasons given for it;

    (b) explain, as appropriate—

        (i)   why the court should grant bail itself, or withdraw it, or impose or vary a condition, and

        (ii) if the applicant is the prosecutor, what material information has become available since the police bail decision was made;

    (c) propose the terms of any suggested condition of bail; and

    (d) if the applicant wants an earlier hearing than paragraph (7) requires, ask for that, and explain why it is needed.

(5) A prosecutor who applies under this rule must serve on the defendant, with the application, notice that the court has power to withdraw bail and, if the defendant is absent when the court makes its decision, order the defendant's arrest.

(6) A party who opposes an application must—

    (a) so notify the court officer and the applicant at once; and

    (b) serve on each notice of the reasons for opposition.

(7) Unless the court otherwise directs, the court officer must arrange for the court to hear the application as soon as practicable and in any event—

    (a) if it is an application to withdraw bail, no later than the second business day after it was served; and

    (b) in any other case, no later than the fifth business day after it was served.

(8) The court may—

    (a) vary or waive a time limit under this rule;

    (b) allow an application to be in a different form to one set out in the Practice Direction; and

    (c) if rule 14.2 allows, determine without a hearing an application to vary a condition.

[Note. The Practice Direction sets out a form of application for use in connection with this rule.

Under section 5B of the Bail Act 1976[15] —

    (a) where a defendant has been charged with an offence which can be tried in the Crown Court; or

    (b) in an extradition case,

on application by the prosecutor a magistrates' court may withdraw bail granted by a constable, impose conditions of bail, or vary conditions of bail. See also sections 37, 37C(2)(b), 37CA(2)(b), 46A and 47(1B) of the Police and Criminal Evidence Act 1984[16].

---

[15] 1976 c. 63; section 5B was inserted by section 30 of the Criminal Justice and Public Order Act 1994 (c. 33) and amended by section 129(3) of the Criminal Justice and Police Act 2001 (c. 16), section 109 of, and paragraph 183 of Schedule 8 and Schedule 10 to, the Courts Act 2003 (c. 39) and section 198 of the Extradition Act 2003 (c. 41).

[16] 1984 c. 60; section 37 was amended by section 108(7) of, and Schedule 15 to, the Children Act 1989 (c. 41), sections 72 and 101(2) of, and Schedule 13 to, the Criminal Justice Act 1991 (c. 53), sections 29(4) and 168(3) of, and Schedule 11 to, the Criminal Justice and Public Order Act 1994 (c. 33), section 28 of, and paragraphs 1 and 2 of Schedule 2 to, the Criminal Justice Act 2003 (c. 44), section 23(1) of, and paragraphs 1 and 2 of Schedule 1 to, the Drugs Act 2005 (c. 17) and sections 11 and 52 of, and paragraph 9 of Schedule 14 to, the Police and Justice Act 2006 (c. 48). Section 37C was inserted by section 28 of, and paragraphs 1 and 3 of Schedule 2 to, the Criminal Justice Act 2003 (c. 44). Section 37CA was inserted by section 10 of, and paragraphs 1 and 8 of Schedule 6 to, the Police and Justice Act 2006 (c. 48). Section 46A was inserted by section 29 of the Criminal Justice and Public Order Act 1994 (c. 33), and amended by section 28 of, and paragraphs 1 and 5 of Schedule 2 to, the Criminal Justice Act 2003 (c. 44), sections 10 and 46 of, and paragraphs 1 and 7 of Schedule 6 to, the Police and Justice

Under section 43B of the Magistrates' Courts Act 1980[17], where a defendant has been charged with an offence, on application by the defendant a magistrates' court may grant bail itself, in substitution for bail granted by a custody officer, or vary the conditions of bail granted by a custody officer. See also sections 37, 37C(2)(b), 37CA(2)(b), 46A and 47(1C), (1D) of the Police and Criminal Evidence Act 1984[18].

Under section 47(1E) of the Police and Criminal Evidence Act 1984[19], where a defendant has been released on bail by a custody officer without being charged with an offence, on application by the defendant a magistrates' court may vary any conditions of that bail. See also sections 37, 37C(2)(b), 37CA(2)(b), 46A and 47(1C) of the Act.]

R14.7   Notice of application to consider bail

14.7   (1)   This rule applies where—

(a)   in a magistrates' court—

(i)   a prosecutor wants the court to withdraw bail granted by the court, or to impose or vary a condition of such bail, or

(ii)   a defendant wants the court to reconsider such bail before the next hearing in the case; and

(b)   in the Crown Court,

(i)   a party wants the court to grant bail that has been withheld, or to withdraw bail that has been granted, or to impose a new bail condition or to vary a present one, or

(ii)   a prosecutor wants the court to consider whether to grant or withhold bail, or impose or vary a condition of bail, under section 88 or section 89 of the Criminal Justice Act 2003[20] (bail and custody in connection with an intended application to the Court of Appeal to which Part 27 (Retrial after acquittal) applies).

(2)   Such a party must—

(a)   apply in writing;

(b)   serve the application on—

(i)   the court officer,

(ii)   the other party, and

(iii)   any surety affected or proposed; and

(c)   serve the application not less than 2 business days before any hearing in the case at which the applicant wants the court to consider it, if such a hearing is already due.

(3)   The application must—

(a)   specify—

(i)   the decision that the applicant wants the court to make,

(ii)   each offence charged, and

(iii)   each relevant previous bail decision and the reasons given for each;

(b)   if the applicant is a defendant, explain—

(i)   as appropriate, why the court should not withhold bail, or why it should vary a condition, and

(ii)   what further information or legal argument, if any, has become available since the most recent previous bail decision was made;

(c)   if the applicant is the prosecutor, explain—

(i)   as appropriate, why the court should withdraw bail, or impose or vary a condition, and

(ii)   what material information has become available since the most recent previous bail decision was made;

(d)   propose the terms of any suggested condition of bail; and

(e)   if the applicant wants an earlier hearing than paragraph (6) requires, ask for that, and explain why it is needed.

Act 2006 (c. 48) and sections 107 and 178 of, and Part 3 of Schedule 3 to, the Coroners and Justice Act 2009 (c. 25). Section 47(1B) was inserted by section 28 of, and paragraphs 1 and 6 of Schedule 2 to, the Criminal Justice Act 2003 (c. 44) and amended by section 10 of, and paragraphs 1 and 11 of Schedule 6 to, the Police and Justice Act 2006 (c. 48).

[17]   1980 c. 43; section 43B was inserted by section 27 of, and paragraph 3 of Schedule 3 to, the Criminal Justice and Public Order Act 1994 (c. 33).

[18]   1984 c. 60; section 47(1C) and (1D) were inserted by section 28 of, and paragraphs 1 and 6 of Schedule 2 to, the Criminal Justice Act 2003 (c. 44), and section 47(1C) was amended by section 10 of, and paragraphs 1 and 11 of Schedule 6 to, the Police and Justice Act 2006 (c. 48).

[19]   1984 c. 60; section 47(1E) was inserted by section 28 of, and paragraphs 1 and 6 of Schedule 2 to, the Criminal Justice Act 2003 (c. 44).

[20]   2003 c. 44; section 88 is amended by section 148 of, and paragraphs 59 and 63 of Schedule 26 to, the Criminal Justice and Immigration Act 2008 (c. 4), with effect from a date to be appointed. Section 89 was amended by section 59 of, and paragraph 1 of Schedule 11 to, the Constitutional Reform Act 2005 (c. 4). It is further amended by section 148 of, and paragraphs 59 and 63 of Schedule 26 to, the Criminal Justice and Immigration Act 2008 (c. 4), with effect from a date to be appointed.

(4) A prosecutor who applies under this rule must serve on the defendant, with the application, notice that the court has power to withdraw bail and, if the defendant is absent when the court makes its decision, order the defendant's arrest.

(5) A party who opposes an application must—
(a) so notify the court officer and the applicant at once; and
(b) serve on each notice of the reasons for opposition.

(6) Unless the court otherwise directs, the court officer must arrange for the court to hear the application as soon as practicable and in any event—
(a) if it is an application to grant or withdraw bail, no later than the second business day after it was served; and
(b) if it is an application to impose or vary a condition, no later than the fifth business day after it was served.

(7) The court may—
(a) vary or waive a time limit under this rule;
(b) allow an application to be in a different form to one set out in the Practice Direction, or to be made orally; and
(c) if rule 14.2 allows, determine without a hearing an application to vary a condition.

[Note. The Practice Direction sets out a form of application for use in connection with this rule,

In addition to the court's general powers in relation to bail—

(a) under section 3(8) of the Bail Act 1976(), on application by either party the court may impose a bail condition or vary a condition it has imposed. Until the Crown Court makes its first bail decision in the case, a magistrates' court may vary a condition which it imposed on committing or sending a defendant for Crown Court trial.

(b) under section 5B of the Bail Act 1976(), where the defendant is on bail and the offence is one which can be tried in the Crown Court, or in an extradition case, on application by the prosecutor a magistrates' court may withdraw bail, impose conditions of bail or vary the conditions of bail.

(c) under sections 88 and 89 of the Criminal Justice Act 2003, the Crown Court may remand in custody, or grant bail to, a defendant pending an application to the Court of Appeal for an order for retrial under section 77 of that Act.

Under Part IIA of Schedule 1 to the Bail Act 1976(), if the court withholds bail then at the first hearing after that the defendant may support an application for bail with any argument as to fact or law, whether or not that argument has been advanced before. At subsequent hearings, the court need not hear arguments which it has heard previously.]

Defendant's application or appeal to the Crown Court after magistrates' court bail decision   R14.8

14.8 (1) This rule applies where a defendant wants to—
(a) apply to the Crown Court for bail after a magistrates' court has withheld bail; or
(b) appeal to the Crown Court after a magistrates' court has refused to vary a bail condition as the defendant wants.

(2) The defendant must—
(a) apply to the Crown Court in writing as soon as practicable after the magistrates' court's decision; and
(b) serve the application on—
(i) the Crown Court officer,
(ii) the magistrates' court officer,
(iii) the prosecutor, and
(iv) any surety affected or proposed.

(3) The application must—
(a) specify—
(i) the decision that the applicant wants the Crown Court to make, and
(ii) each offence charged;
(b) explain—
(i) as appropriate, why the Crown Court should not withhold bail, or why it should vary the condition under appeal, and
(ii) what further information or legal argument, if any, has become available since the magistrates' court's decision;
(c) propose the terms of any suggested condition of bail;
(d) if the applicant wants an earlier hearing than paragraph (6) requires, ask for that, and explain why it is needed; and
(e) on an application for bail, attach a copy of the certificate of full argument served on the defendant under rule 14.4(4).

(4) The magistrates' court officer must as soon as practicable serve on the Crown Court officer—
  (a) a copy of the note or record made under rule 14.4(1) in connection with the magistrates' court's decision; and
  (b) the date of the next hearing, if any, in the magistrates' court.
(5) A prosecutor who opposes the application must—
  (a) so notify the Crown Court officer and the defendant at once; and
  (b) serve on each notice of the reasons for opposition.
(6) Unless the Crown Court otherwise directs, the court officer must arrange for the court to hear the application or appeal as soon as practicable and in any event no later than the business day after it was served.
(7) The Crown Court may vary a time limit under this rule.

[Note. The Practice Direction sets out a form of application for use in connection with this rule.

Under section 81 of the Senior Courts Act 1981[21], the Crown Court may grant bail in a magistrates' court case in which the magistrates' court has withheld bail.

Under section 16 of the Criminal Justice Act 2003[22], a defendant may appeal to the Crown Court against a bail condition imposed by a magistrates' court only where—

(a) the condition is one that the defendant must—
  (i) live and sleep at a specified place, or away from a specified place,
  (ii) give a surety or a security,
  (iii) stay indoors between specified hours,
  (iv) comply with electronic monitoring requirements, or
  (v) make no contact with a specified person; and
(b) the magistrates' court has determined an application by either party to vary that condition.

In an extradition case, where a magistrates' court withholds bail or imposes bail conditions, on application by the defendant the High Court may grant bail, or vary the conditions, under section 22 of the Criminal Justice Act 1967[23]. For the procedure in the High Court, see Schedule 1 to the Civil Procedure Rules 1998 (RSC Order 79)[24].]

R14.9 Prosecutor's appeal against grant of bail

14.9 (1) This rule applies where a prosecutor wants to appeal—
  (a) to the Crown Court against a grant of bail by a magistrates' court, in a case in which the defendant has been charged with, or convicted of, an offence punishable with imprisonment; or
  (b) to the High Court against a grant of bail—
    (i) by a magistrates' court, in an extradition case, or
    (ii) by the Crown Court, in a case in which the defendant has been charged with, or convicted of, an offence punishable with imprisonment (but not in a case in which the Crown Court granted bail on an appeal to which paragraph (1)(a) applies).
(2) The prosecutor must tell the court which has granted bail of the decision to appeal—
  (a) at the end of the hearing during which the court granted bail; and
  (b) before the defendant is released on bail.
(3) The court which has granted bail must exercise its power to remand the defendant in custody pending determination of the appeal.
(4) The prosecutor must serve an appeal notice—
  (a) on the court officer for the court which has granted bail and on the defendant; and
  (b) not more than 2 hours after telling that court of the decision to appeal.

[21] 1981 c. 54; section 81(1) was amended by sections 29 and 60 of the Criminal Justice Act 1982 (c. 48), section 15 of, and paragraph 2 of Schedule 12 to, the Criminal Justice Act 1987 (c. 38), section 168 of, and paragraph 19 of Schedule 9 and paragraph 48 of Schedule 10 to, the Criminal Justice and Public Order Act 1994 (c. 33), section 119 of, and paragraph 48 of Schedule 8 and Schedule 10 to, the Crime and Disorder Act 1998 (c. 37), section 165 of, and paragraph 87 of Schedule 9 and Schedule 12 to, the Powers of Criminal Courts (Sentencing) Act 2000 (c. 6), paragraph 54 of Schedule 3, paragraph 4 of Schedule 36 and Part 4 of Schedule 37 to the Criminal Justice Act 2003 (c. 44), articles 2 and 6 of S.I. 2004/1033 and section 177(1) of, and paragraph 76 of Schedule 21 to, the Coroners and Justice Act 2009 (c. 25).
[22] 2003 c. 44.
[23] 1967 c. 80; section 22 was amended by section 56 of, and paragraph 48 of Schedule 8 and Schedule 11 to, the Courts Act 1971 (c. 23), section 12 of, and paragraphs 36 and 37 of Schedule 2 and Schedule 3 to, the Bail Act 1976 (c. 63), section 65 of, and Schedules 12 and 13 to, the Criminal Law Act 1977 (c. 45), paragraph 15 of Schedule 10 to the Criminal Justice and Public Order Act 1994 (c. 33), sections 17 and 332 of, and Schedule 37 to, the Criminal Justice Act 2003 (c. 44) and section 42 of, and paragraph 27 of Schedule 13 to, the Police and Justice Act 2006 (c. 48).
[24] S.I. 1998/3132; Schedule 1 RSC Order 79 was amended by S.I. 1999/1008, 2001/256, 2003/3361 and 2005/617.

(5) The appeal notice must specify—
   (a) each offence with which the defendant is charged;
   (b) the decision under appeal;
   (c) the reasons given for the grant of bail; and
   (d) the grounds of appeal.
(6) On an appeal to the Crown Court, the magistrates' court officer must, as soon as practicable, serve on the Crown Court officer—
   (a) the appeal notice;
   (b) a copy of the note or record made under rule 14.4(1) (record of bail decision); and
   (c) notice of the date of the next hearing in the court which has granted bail.
(7) If the Crown Court so directs, the Crown Court officer must arrange for the defendant to be assisted by the Official Solicitor in a case in which the defendant—
   (a) has no legal representative; and
   (b) asks for such assistance.
(8) On an appeal to the Crown Court, the Crown Court officer must arrange for the court to hear the appeal as soon as practicable and in any event no later than the second business day after the appeal notice was served.
(9) The prosecutor—
   (a) may abandon an appeal to the Crown Court without the court's permission, by serving a notice of abandonment, signed by or on behalf of the prosecutor, on—
      (i) the defendant,
      (ii) the Crown Court officer, and
      (iii) the magistrates' court officer
      before the hearing of the appeal begins; but
   (b) after the hearing of the appeal begins, may only abandon the appeal with the Crown Court's permission.
(10) The court officer for the court which has granted bail must instruct the defendant's custodian to release the defendant on the bail granted by that court, subject to any condition or conditions of bail imposed, if—
   (a) the prosecutor fails to serve an appeal notice within the time to which paragraph (4) refers; or
   (b) the prosecutor serves a notice of abandonment under paragraph (9).

[Note. See section 1 of the Bail (Amendment) Act 1993[25]. The time limit for serving an appeal notice is prescribed by section 1(5) of the Act. It may be neither extended nor shortened.

For the procedure in the High Court, see Schedule 1 to the Civil Procedure Rules 1998 (RSC Order 79, rule 9) and the Practice Direction which supplements that Order. Under those provisions, the prosecutor must file in the High Court, among other things—

   (a) a copy of the appeal notice served by the prosecutor under rule 14.9(4);
   (b) notice of the Crown Court decision to grant bail served on the prosecutor under rule 14.4(2); and
   (c) notice of the date of the next hearing in the Crown Court.]

Consideration of bail in a murder case   R14.10

14.10 (1) This rule applies in a case in which—
   (a) the defendant is charged with murder; and
   (b) the Crown Court has not yet considered bail.
   (2) The magistrates' court officer must arrange with the Crown Court officer for the Crown Court to consider bail as soon as practicable and in any event no later than the second business day after—
   (a) a magistrates' court sends the defendant to the Crown Court for trial; or
   (b) the first hearing in the magistrates' court, if the defendant is not at once sent for trial.

[Note. See section 115 of the Coroners and Justice Act 2009[26].]

Condition of residence   R14.11

14.11 (1) The defendant must notify the prosecutor of the address at which the defendant will live and sleep if released on bail with a condition of residence—
   (a) as soon as practicable after the institution of proceedings, unless already done; and
   (b) as soon as practicable after any change of that address.

---

[25] 1993 c. 26; section 1 was amended by sections 200 and 220 of, and Schedule 4 to, the Extradition Act 2003 (c. 41), section 18 of the Criminal Justice Act 2003 (c. 44), section 15 of, and paragraph 231 of Schedule 4 to, the Constitutional Reform Act 2005 (c. 4), section 42 of, and paragraph 28 of Schedule 13 to, the Police and Justice Act 2006 (c. 48) and paragraph 32 of Schedule 11 to the Legal Aid, Sentencing and Punishment of Offenders Act 2012 (c. 10).
[26] 2009 c. 25.

(2) The prosecutor must help the court to assess the suitability of an address proposed as a condition of residence.

R14.12   Electronic monitoring requirements

14.12 (1) This rule applies where the court imposes electronic monitoring requirements, where available, as a condition of bail.

(2) The court officer must—

(a) inform the person responsible for the monitoring ('the monitor') of—

(i) the defendant's name, and telephone number if available,

(ii) each offence with which the defendant is charged,

(iii) details of the place at which the defendant's presence must be monitored,

(iv) the period or periods during which the defendant's presence at that place must be monitored, and

(v) if fixed, the date on which the defendant must surrender to custody;

(b) inform the defendant and, where the defendant is under 16, an appropriate adult, of the monitor's identity and the means by which the monitor may be contacted; and

(c) notify the monitor of any subsequent—

(i) variation or termination of the electronic monitoring requirements, or

(ii) fixing or variation of the date on which the defendant must surrender to custody.

[Note. Under section 3(6ZAA) of the Bail Act 1976[27], the conditions of bail that the court may impose include requirements for the electronic monitoring of a defendant's compliance with other bail conditions, for example a curfew. Sections 3AA and 3AB of the 1976 Act[28] set out conditions for imposing such requirements.

Under section 3AC of the 1976 Act[29], where the court imposes electronic monitoring requirements they must provide for the appointment of a monitor.]

R14.13   Accommodation or support requirements

14.13 (1) This rule applies where the court imposes as a condition of bail a requirement, where available, that the defendant must—

(a) reside in accommodation provided for that purpose by, or on behalf of, a public authority; or

(b) receive bail support provided by, or on behalf of, a public authority.

(2) The court officer must—

(a) inform the person responsible for the provision of any such accommodation or support ('the service provider') of—

(i) the defendant's name, and telephone number if available,

(ii) each offence with which the defendant is charged,

(iii) details of the requirement,

(iv) any other bail condition, and

(v) if fixed, the date on which the defendant must surrender to custody;

(b) inform the defendant and, where the defendant is under 16, an appropriate adult, of—

(i) the service provider's identity and the means by which the service provider may be contacted, and

(ii) the address of any accommodation in which the defendant must live and sleep; and

(c) notify the service provider of any subsequent—

(i) variation or termination of the requirement,

(ii) variation or termination of any other bail condition, and

(iii) fixing or variation of the date on which the defendant must surrender to custody.

R14.14   Requirement for a surety or payment, etc.

14.14 (1) This rule applies where the court imposes as a condition of bail a requirement for—

(a) a surety;

---

[27] 1976 c. 63; 1976 c. 63; section 3(6ZAA) was substituted, with sub-section (6ZAB), for sub-section (6ZAA) as inserted by section 131 of the Criminal Justice and Police Act 2001 (c. 16) by section 51 of, and paragraphs 1 and 2 of Schedule 11 to, the Criminal Justice and Immigration Act 2008 (c. 4) and amended by paragraphs 1 and 3 of Schedule 11 to the Legal Aid, Sentencing and Punishment of Offenders Act 2012 (c. 10).

[28] 1976 c. 63; section 3AA was inserted by section 131 of the Criminal Justice and Police Act 2001 (c. 16) and amended by sections 51 and 149 of, and paragraphs 1 and 3 of Schedule 11 to, and Part 4 of Schedule 28 to, the Criminal Justice and Immigration Act 2008 (c. 4) and paragraph 4 of Schedule 11 to the Legal Aid, Sentencing and Punishment of Offenders Act 2012 (c. 10).

[29] 1976 c. 63; section 3AC was inserted by section 51 of, and paragraphs 1 and 4 of Schedule 11 to, the Criminal Justice and Immigration Act 2008 (c. 4) and amended by paragraphs 1 and 7 of Schedule 11 to the Legal Aid, Sentencing and Punishment of Offenders Act 2012 (c. 10).

(b)   a payment; or

(c)   the surrender of a document or thing.

(2)   The court may direct how such a condition must be met.

(3)   Unless the court otherwise directs, if any such condition or direction requires a surety to enter into a recognizance—

    (a)   the recognizance must specify—

        (i)   the amount that the surety will be required to pay if the purpose for which the recognizance is entered is not fulfilled, and

        (ii)   the date, or the event, upon which the recognizance will expire;

    (b)   the surety must enter into the recognizance in the presence of—

        (i)   the court officer,

        (ii)   the defendant's custodian, where the defendant is in custody, or

        (iii)   someone acting with the authority of either; and

    (c)   the person before whom the surety enters into the recognizance must at once serve a copy on—

        (i)   the surety, and

        (ii)   as appropriate, the court officer and the defendant's custodian.

(4)   Unless the court otherwise directs, if any such condition or direction requires someone to make a payment, or surrender a document or thing—

    (a)   that payment, document or thing must be made or surrendered to—

        (i)   the court officer,

        (ii)   the defendant's custodian, where the defendant is in custody, or

        (iii)   someone acting with the authority of either; and

    (b)   the court officer or the custodian, as appropriate, must serve immediately on the other a statement that the payment, document or thing has been made or surrendered.

(5)   The custodian must release the defendant when each requirement ordered by the court has been met.

[Note. See also section 119 of the Magistrates' Courts Act 1980[30].]

Forfeiture of a recognizance given by a surety   R14.15

14.15 (1)   This rule applies where the court imposes as a condition of bail a requirement that a surety enter into a recognizance and, after the defendant is released on bail,—

    (a)   the defendant fails to surrender to custody as required, or

    (b)   it appears to the court that the surety has failed to comply with a condition or direction.

(2)   The court officer must serve notice on—

    (a)   the surety; and

    (b)   each party to the decision to grant bail,

of the hearing at which the court will consider the forfeiture of the recognizance.

(3)   The court must not forfeit the recognizance less than 5 business days after service of notice under paragraph (2).

[Note. If the purpose for which a recognizance is entered is not fulfilled, that recognizance may be forfeited by the court. If the court forfeits a surety's recognizance, the sum promised by that person is then payable to the Crown. See also section 120 of the Magistrates' Courts Act 1980[31].]

Notice of arrest for breach of bail   R14.16

14.16 (1)   This rule and rule 14.17 (Arrangements for court to receive defendant arrested for breach of bail) apply where—

    (a)   a defendant arrested for breach of bail must be brought before a court under section 7 of the Bail Act 1976[32] (Liability to arrest for absconding or breaking conditions of bail); and

    (b)   a police custody officer so notifies the court officer.

(2)   The police custody officer must provide the court officer with—

    (a)   the defendant's name and date of birth;

---

[30]   1980 c. 43; section 119 was amended by section 77 of, and paragraph 55 of Schedule 14 to, the Criminal Justice Act 1982 (c. 48).

[31]   1980 c. 43; section 120 was amended by section 55 of the Crime and Disorder Act 1998 (c. 37) and section 62 of, and paragraphs 45 and 56 of Schedule 13 to, the Tribunals, Courts and Enforcement Act 2007 (c. 15).

[32]   1976 c. 63; section 7 was amended by section 65 of, and Schedule 12 to, the Criminal Law Act 1977 (c. 45), section 109 of, and paragraph 185 of Schedule 8 and Schedule 10 to, the Courts Act 2003 (c. 39), sections 198 and 220 of, and Schedule 4 to, the Extradition Act 2003 (c. 41), section 177 of, and paragraph 74 of Schedule 21 to, the Coroners and Justice Act 2009 (c. 25) and sections 90 and 105 of, and paragraphs 1 and 8 of Schedule 11 and paragraphs 14 and 16 of Schedule 12 to, the Legal Aid, Sentencing and Punishment of Offenders Act 2012 (c. 10).

(b) details of—
   (i)   the warrant under which the defendant was arrested, or
   (ii) the reasons for an arrest without a warrant;
(c) confirmation that the prosecutor has been notified;
(d) confirmation that the following have been notified and are available—
   (i)   any interpreter required,
   (ii) the defendant's legal representative, if any, and
   (iii) any local or other authority, including any youth offending team, responsible for the defendant's care or welfare;
(e) the police custody officer's proposal for the means by which the defendant will be brought before the court, either by live link or in person, and—
   (i)   if the proposal is for the defendant to attend court by live link, details of any material circumstance listed in rule 3.35 (Live link direction: exercise of court's powers), or
   (ii) if the proposal is for the defendant to attend court in person, the identity of the authority responsible for transporting the defendant and the expected time of arrival; and
(f) details of any disability or other vulnerability of the defendant of which the police custody officer is aware and which is not apparent from other information supplied.

[Note. The court may issue a warrant for the defendant's arrest—

(a) under section 7(1) of the Bail Act 1976 where the defendant was released on bail under a duty to surrender into the custody of the court and fails to do so when required; or
(b) under section 7(2) of the Act where the defendant was released on bail, surrenders into the custody of the court, and then leaves without the court's permission before the hearing begins or resumes.

Under section 7(3) of the 1976 Act a defendant who has been released on bail and is under a duty to surrender into the custody of a court may be arrested and detained without a warrant by a constable—

(a) who has reasonable grounds for believing that the defendant is not likely to surrender to custody,
(b) who has reasonable grounds for believing that the defendant is likely to break any of the conditions of bail,
(c) who has reasonable grounds for suspecting that the defendant has broken any of those conditions, or
(d) where a surety for that bail notifies the constable in writing that the defendant is unlikely to surrender to custody and for that reason the surety wishes to be relieved of the obligations of a surety.

Under section 7(4) of the 1976 Act, subject to the exceptions to which rule 14.17(2) refers a defendant arrested under section 7(3) must be brought before a magistrates' court as soon as practicable and in any event within 24 hours after the arrest, omitting any part of a day which is Christmas Day, Good Friday or a Sunday.

Under section 81(5) of the Senior Courts Act 1981[33] a defendant arrested under a warrant issued by the Crown Court must be brought forthwith before—

(a) the Crown Court if the defendant is charged with murder, or with murder and one or more other offences; or
(b) the Crown Court or a magistrates' court in any other case.]

R14.17   Arrangements for court to receive defendant arrested for breach of bail

14.17 (1) The court officer must arrange for a defendant of whose arrest the police custody officer gives notice under rule 14.16 (Notice of arrest for breach of bail)—
   (a) if the arrest was under a Crown Court warrant, to be brought at once before—
      (i)   the Crown Court, if the defendant is charged with murder or with murder and one or more other offences, or
      (ii) if the defendant is not so charged, the Crown Court as a general rule and otherwise a magistrates' court;
   (b) if the arrest was under a magistrates' court warrant, to be brought as soon as practicable before a magistrates' court; and

---

[33] 1981 c. 54; section 81 was amended by sections 29 and 60 of the Criminal Justice Act 1982 (c. 48), section 7 of, and paragraph 6 of Schedule 3 to, the Criminal Procedure (Insanity and Unfitness to Plead) Act 1991 (c. 25), section 168 of, and paragraph 19 of Schedule 9 and paragraph 48 of Schedule 10 to, the Criminal Justice and Public Order Act 1994 (c. 33), section 119 of, and paragraph 48 of Schedule 8 to, the Crime and Disorder Act 1998 (c. 37), section 165 of, and paragraph 87 of Schedule 9 and Part I of Schedule 12 to, the Powers of Criminal Courts (Sentencing) Act 2000 (c. 6), sections 41, 331 and 332 of, and paragraph 54 of Schedule 3, paragraph 4 of Schedule 36 and Parts 2 and 4 of Schedule 37 to, the Criminal Justice Act 2003 (c. 44), section 58 of, and paragraph 15 of Schedule 10 to, the Domestic Violence, Crime and Victims Act 2004 (c. 28), articles 2, 3 and 6 of, and paragraphs 12 and 14 of the Schedule to, S.I. 2004/1033 and section 177 of, and paragraph 76 of Schedule 21 to, the Coroners and Justice Act 2009 (c. 25).

(c) if the arrest was without a warrant, subject to paragraph (2) to be brought as soon as practicable before a magistrates' court—

    (i)   by 3.30pm that day if that day is a business day,

    (ii) by 12.30pm that day if that day is a Saturday or a bank holiday,

    (iii) in either case, later if, but only if, a disability or vulnerability of the defendant so requires, and in any event

    (iv) within 24 hours after the arrest (but omitting from that period any part of a day which is Christmas Day, Good Friday or a Sunday).

(2) Where a defendant of whose arrest the police custody officer gives notice under rule 14.16 was arrested without a warrant—

  (a) if the arrest was within 24 hours of the time at which that defendant was due to surrender into the custody of a court then the court officer must arrange for the defendant to be brought before that court; and

  (b) if the defendant is charged with murder or with murder and one or more other offences then—

    (i)   the court officer must arrange for the defendant to be brought before the Crown Court as soon as practicable and in any event within 24 hours after the arrest (but omitting from that period any part of a day which is not a business day), and

    (ii) in paragraph (3) the reference to justices' legal advisers is omitted.

(3) In making the arrangements required by paragraph (1) the court officer must—

  (a) consult with those affected including—

    (i)   the police custody officer,

    (ii) court members,

    (iii) justices' legal advisers and other court officers, and

    (iv) the prosecutor; and

  (b) as far as is practicable rearrange court business to ensure that the time available will allow all cases heard that day to conclude by 4.30pm (or later if, but only if, a disability or vulnerability of the defendant the subject of this rule so requires).

(4) When arrangements for the defendant to be brought before a court have been made the court officer promptly must so inform—

  (a) the police custody officer; and

  (b) as applicable, others consulted under paragraph (3)(a).

(5) The court before which the defendant is brought under this rule must—

  (a) deal there and then with the alleged breach of bail; and

  (b) as far as is practicable take the next steps required in the defendant's case in accordance with rule 3.8 (Case preparation and progression).

Extension of bail before charge

Exercise of court's powers: extension of pre-charge bail   R14.18

14.18 (1) The court must determine an application to which rule 14.19 (Application to authorise extension of pre-charge bail) applies—

  (a) without a hearing, subject to paragraph (2); and

  (b) as soon as practicable, but as a general rule no sooner than the fifth business day after the application was served.

(2) The court must determine an application at a hearing where—

  (a) if the application succeeds, its effect will be to extend the period for which the defendant is on bail to 24 months or less from the day after the defendant's arrest for the offence and the court considers that the interests of justice require a hearing;

  (b) if the application succeeds, its effect will be to extend that period to more than 24 months from that day and the applicant or the defendant asks for a hearing; or

  (c) it is an application to withhold information from the defendant and the court considers that the interests of justice require a hearing.

(3) Any hearing must be in private.

(4) Subject to rule 14.20 (Application to withhold information from the defendant), at a hearing the court may determine an application in the absence of—

  (a) the applicant; and

  (b) the defendant, if the defendant has had at least 5 business days in which to make representations.

(5) If the court so directs, a party to an application may attend a hearing by live link.

(6) The court must not authorise an extension of the period for which a defendant is on bail before being charged unless—

  (a) the applicant states, in writing or orally, that to the best of the applicant's knowledge and belief—

         (i)   the application discloses all the information that is material to what the court must decide, and

        (ii) the content of the application is true; or

    (b) the application includes a statement by an investigator of the suspected offence that to the best of that investigator's knowledge and belief those requirements are met.

(7) Where the statement required by paragraph (6) is made orally—

    (a) the statement must be on oath or affirmation, unless the court otherwise directs; and

    (b) the court must arrange for a record of the making of the statement.

(8) The court may shorten or extend (even after it has expired) a time limit imposed by this rule or by rule 14.19 (Application to authorise extension of pre-charge bail).

[Note. For the definition of 'defendant' for the purposes of this rule and rules 14.19 and 14.20, see rule 14.1(3).

Sections 47ZA and 47ZB of the Police and Criminal Evidence Act 1984[34] limit the period during which a defendant who has been arrested for an offence may be on bail after being released without being charged. That period ('the applicable bail period') is—

    (a) *6 months from the day after the day on which the defendant was arrested (the defendant's 'bail start date') in an 'FCA', 'HMRC', 'NCA' or 'SFO' case (that is, a case, as defined by section 47ZB, being investigated by the Financial Conduct Authority, an officer of Revenue and Customs, the National Crime Agency or the Serious Fraud Office, as applicable); and*

    (b) *3 months from the defendant's bail start date in any other case ('a standard case').*

Under section 47ZDB of the 1984 Act[35], in an FCA, HMRC, NCA or SFO case the applicable bail period may be extended on the authority of the appropriate decision maker until the end of 12 months from the bail start date. 'Appropriate decision maker' is defined as, in summary, a senior officer of the relevant authority.

Under sections 47ZC and 47ZD of the 1984 Act[36], in a standard case the applicable bail period may be extended on the authority of a police officer of the rank of inspector or above until the end of 6 months from the bail start date. Under section 47ZDA[37] the applicable bail period may be further extended on the authority of a police officer of the rank of superintendent or above until the end of 9 months from the bail start date.

Under sections 47ZC and 47ZE of the 1984 Act[38], if the case is designated by the Director of Public Prosecutions as exceptionally complex (a 'designated case') the applicable bail period may be further extended on the authority of one of the senior officers listed in section 47ZE until the end of 12 months from the bail start date.

Under section 47ZF of the 1984 Act[39], on an application made before the date on which the applicable bail period ends by a constable, a member of staff of the Financial Conduct Authority of the description designated by its Chief Executive, an officer of Revenue and Customs, a National Crime Agency officer, a member of the Serious Fraud Office or a Crown Prosecutor, a magistrates' court may authorise an extension of that period—

    (a) *from a previous total of 9 months to a new total of 12 months or, if the investigation is unlikely to be completed or a police charging decision made within a lesser period, a new total of 18 months (following extension under section 47ZDA of the Act);*

    (b) *from a previous total of 12 months to a new total of 18 months or, if the investigation is unlikely to be completed or a police charging decision made within a lesser period, a new total of 24 months (following extension under section 47ZDB or 47ZE of the Act),*

where the conditions listed in that section are met.

Under section 47ZL of the Act[40], the running of the applicable bail period does not begin (in the case of a first release on bail) or is suspended (in any other case) where—

[34] 1984 c. 60; sections 47ZA and 47ZB were inserted by section 63 of the Policing and Crime Act 2017 (c. 3). Section 47ZB was amended by amended by paragraphs 24 and 26 of Schedule 4 to the Police, Crime, Sentencing and Courts Act 2022 (c. 32).

[35] 1984 c. 60; section 47ZDB was inserted by paragraphs 24 and 29 of Schedule 4 to the Police, Crime, Sentencing and Courts Act 2022 (c. 32).

[36] 1984 c. 60; section 47ZC was inserted by section 63 of the Policing and Crime Act 2017 (c. 3) and amended by paragraphs 1, 12, 24 and 27 of Schedule 4 to the Police, Crime, Sentencing and Courts Act 2022 (c. 32). Section 47ZD was inserted by section 63 of the Policing and Crime Act 2017 (c. 3) and amended by paragraphs 24 and 28 of Schedule 4 to the Police, Crime, Sentencing and Courts Act 2022 (c. 32).

[37] 1984 c. 60; section 47ZDA was inserted by paragraphs 24 and 29 of Schedule 4 to the Police, Crime, Sentencing and Courts Act 2022 (c. 32).

[38] 1984 c. 60; section 47ZE was inserted by section 63 of the Policing and Crime Act 2017 (c. 3) and amended by paragraphs 24 and 30 of Schedule 4 to the Police, Crime, Sentencing and Courts Act 2022 (c. 32).

[39] 1984 c. 60; section 47ZF was inserted by section 63 of the Policing and Crime Act 2017 (c. 3) and amended by paragraphs 24 and 31 of Schedule 4 to the Police, Crime, Sentencing and Courts Act 2022 (c. 32).

[40] 1984 c. 60; section 47ZL was inserted by section 63 of the Policing and Crime Act 2017 (c. 3).

Criminal Procedure Rules

(a) *the defendant is released on bail to await a charging decision by the Director of Public Prosecutions under section 37B of the Act; or*

(b) *following arrest for breach of such bail the defendant is again released on bail.*

The court's authority therefore is not required for an extension of an applicable bail period the running of which is postponed or suspended pending a Director's charging decision. However—

(a) *time runs in any period during which information requested by the Director is being obtained; and*

(b) *if the Director requests information less than 7 days before the applicable bail period otherwise would end then the running of that period is further suspended until the end of 7 days beginning with the day on which the Director's request is made.*

See also section 47ZI of the Police and Criminal Evidence Act 198[41] (Sections 47ZF to 47ZH: proceedings in magistrates' courts). The requirement for the court except in specified circumstances to determine an application without a hearing is prescribed by that section. Under that section the court must comprise a single justice of the peace unless a hearing is convened, when it must comprise two or more justices.]

Application to authorise extension of pre-charge bail   R14.19

14.19 (1) This rule applies where an applicant wants the court to authorise an extension of the period for which a defendant is released on bail before being charged with an offence.

(2) The applicant must—

(a) apply in writing before the date on which the defendant's pre-charge bail is due to end;

(b) demonstrate that the applicant is entitled to apply as a constable, an officer of Revenue and Customs, a National Crime Agency officer, a member of staff of the Financial Conduct Authority, a member of the Serious Fraud Office or a Crown Prosecutor;

(c) serve the application on—

(i) the court officer, and

(ii) the defendant; and

(d) serve on the defendant, with the application, a form of response notice for the defendant's use.

(3) The application must specify—

(a) the offence or offences for which the defendant was arrested;

(b) the date on which the defendant's pre-charge bail began;

(c) the date and period of any previous extension of that bail;

(d) the date on which that bail is due to end;

(e) the conditions of that bail; and

(f) if different, the bail conditions which are to be imposed if the court authorises an extension, or further extension, of the period for which the defendant is released on pre-charge bail.

(4) The application must explain—

(a) the grounds for believing that, as applicable—

(i) further investigation is needed of any matter in connection with the offence or offences for which the defendant was released on bail, or

(ii) further time is needed for making a decision as to whether to charge the defendant with that offence or those offences;

(b) the grounds for believing that, as applicable—

(i) the investigation into the offence or offences for which the defendant was released on bail is being conducted diligently and expeditiously, or

(ii) the decision as to whether to charge the defendant with that offence or those offences is being made diligently and expeditiously; and

(c) the grounds for believing that the defendant's further release on bail is necessary and proportionate in all the circumstances having regard, in particular, to any conditions of bail imposed.

(5) The application must—

(a) indicate whether the applicant wants the court to authorise an extension of the defendant's bail for 3 months or for 6 months; and

(b) if for 6 months, explain why the investigation is unlikely to be completed or the charging decision made, as the case may be, within 3 months.

(6) The application must explain why it was not made earlier where—

(a) the application is made before the date on which the defendant's bail is due to end; but

(b) it is not likely to be practicable for the court to determine the application before that date.

---

[41] 1984 c. 60; section 47ZI was inserted by section 63 of the Policing and Crime Act 2017 (c. 3).

(7) A defendant who objects to the application must—
    (a) serve notice on—
        (i)   the court officer, and
        (ii) the applicant, not more than 5 business days after service of the application; and
    (b) in the notice explain the grounds of the objection.

[Note. The Practice Direction sets out forms of application and response notice for use in connection with this rule.

See sections 47ZF (Applicable bail period: first extension of limit by the court), 47ZG (Applicable bail period: subsequent extensions of limit by the court) and 47ZJ (Sections 47ZF and 47ZG: late applications to magistrates' court) of the Police and Criminal Evidence Act 1984[42].

The time limit for making an application is prescribed by section 47ZF(2) and by section 47ZG(2) of the 1984 Act. It may be neither extended nor shortened. Under section 47ZJ(2) of the Act, if it is not practicable for the court to determine the application before the applicable bail period ends then the court must determine the application as soon as practicable. Under section 47ZJ(3), the applicable bail period is treated as extended until the application is determined. Under section 47ZJ(4), if it appears to the court that it would have been reasonable for the application to have been made in time for it to be determined by the court before the end of the applicable bail period then the court may refuse the application.]

R14.20   **Application to withhold information from the defendant**

14.20 (1) This rule applies where an application to authorise an extension of pre-charge bail includes an application to withhold information from the defendant.
    (2) The applicant must—
        (a) omit that information from the part of the application that is served on the defendant;
        (b) mark the other part to show that, unless the court otherwise directs, it is only for the court; and
        (c) in that other part, explain the grounds for believing that the disclosure of that information would have one or more of the following results—
            (i)   evidence connected with an indictable offence would be interfered with or harmed,
            (ii) a person would be interfered with or physically injured,
            (iii) a person suspected of having committed an indictable offence but not yet arrested for the offence would be alerted, or
            (iv) the recovery of property obtained as a result of an indictable offence would be hindered.
    (3) At any hearing of an application to which this rule applies—
        (a) the court must first determine the application to withhold information, in the defendant's absence and that of any legal representative of the defendant; and
        (b) if the court allows the application to withhold information, then in the following sequence—
            (i)   the court must consider representations first by the applicant and then by the defendant, in the presence of both, and
            (ii) the court may consider further representations by the applicant in the defendant's absence and that of any legal representative of the defendant, if satisfied that there are reasonable grounds for believing that information withheld from the defendant would be disclosed during those further representations.
    (4) If the court refuses an application to withhold information from the defendant, the applicant may withdraw the application to authorise an extension of pre-charge bail.

[Note. See sections 47ZH and 47ZI(5), (6), (8) of the Police and Criminal Evidence Act 1984[43] (withholding sensitive information; proceedings in magistrates' courts: determination of applications to withhold sensitive information).]

Summary of the general entitlement to bail and of the exceptions

The court must consider bail whenever it can order the defendant's detention pending trial or sentencing, or in an extradition case, and whether an application is made or not. Under section 4 of the Bail Act 1976[44], the general rule, subject to exceptions, is that a defendant must be granted bail. Under Part IIA of Schedule 1 to the Act[45], if the court decides not to grant the defendant bail then at each subsequent hearing the court must consider whether to grant bail.

---

[42] 1984 c. 60; section 47ZJ was inserted by section 63 of the Policing and Crime Act 2017 (c. 3).
[43] 1984 c. 60; sections 47ZH and 47ZI were inserted by section 63 of the Policing and Crime Act 2017 (c. 3).
[44] 1976 c. 63; section 4 was amended by section 154 of, and paragraph 145 of Schedule 7 to, the Magistrates' Courts Act 1980 (c. 43), section 168 of, and paragraphs 32 and 33 of Schedule 10 to, the Criminal Justice and Public Order Act 1994 (c. 33),

Section 3 of the Bail Act 1976[46] allows the court, before granting bail, to require a surety or security to secure the defendant's surrender to custody; and allows the court, on granting bail, to impose such requirements as appear to the court to be necessary—

    (a) to secure that the defendant surrenders to custody;

    (b) to secure that the defendant does not commit an offence while on bail;

    (c) to secure that the defendant does not interfere with witnesses or otherwise obstruct the course of justice whether in relation to the defendant or any other person;

    (d) for the defendant's own protection or, if a child or young person, for the defendant's welfare or in the defendant's own interests;

    (e) to secure the defendant's availability for the purpose of enabling enquiries or a report to be made to assist the court in dealing with the defendant for the offence;

    (f) to secure that before the time appointed for surrender to custody the defendant attends an interview with a legal representative.

Under section 3 of the Bail Act 1976, a person granted bail in criminal proceedings is under a duty to surrender to custody as required by that bail. Under section 6 of the Act, such a person who fails without reasonable cause so to surrender commits an offence and, under section 7, may be arrested.

Exceptions to the general right to bail are listed in Schedule 1 to the Bail Act 1976[47]. They differ according to the category of offence concerned. Under section 4(2B) of the 1976 Act[48], in an extradition case there is no general right to bail where the defendant is alleged to have been convicted in the territory requesting extradition.

Under Part I of Schedule 1 to the 1976 Act, where the offence is punishable with imprisonment, and is not one that can be tried only in a magistrates' court, or in an extradition case—

    (a) the defendant need not be granted bail if the court is satisfied that—

        (i) there are substantial grounds for believing that, if released on bail (with or without conditions), the defendant would fail to surrender to custody, would commit an offence, or would interfere with witnesses or otherwise obstruct the course of justice,

        (ii) there are substantial grounds for believing that, if released on bail (with or without conditions), the defendant would commit an offence by engaging in conduct that would, or would be likely to, cause physical or mental injury to an associated person (within the meaning of section 33 of the Family Law Act 1996[49]), or cause that person to fear injury,

        (iii) the defendant should be kept in custody for his or her own protection or welfare, or

---

section 58 of the Criminal Justice and Court Services Act 2000 (c. 43), sections 198 and 220 of, and Schedule 4 to, the Extradition Act 2003 (c. 41), section 304 of, and paragraphs 20 and 22 of Schedule 32 to, the Criminal Justice Act 2003 (c. 44), section 42 of, and paragraph 34 of Schedule 13 to, the Police and Justice Act 2006 (c. 48), sections 6 and 148 of, and paragraphs 23 and 102 of Schedule 4 and Part 1 of Schedule 28 to, the Criminal Justice and Immigration Act 2008 (c. 4) and paragraph 19 of Schedule 7, and Schedule 8, to the Policing and Crime Act 2009 (c. 26).

[45] 1976 c. 63; Schedule 1, Part IIA was added by section 154 of the Criminal Justice Act 1988 (c. 33).

[46] 1976 c. 63; section 3 was amended by section 65 of, and Schedule 12 to, the Criminal Law Act 1977 (c. 45), section 34 of the Mental Health (Amendment) Act 1982 (c. 51), paragraph 46 of Schedule 4 to the Mental Health Act 1983 (c. 20), section 15 of, and paragraph 9 of Schedule 2 to, the Criminal Justice Act 1987 (c. 38), section 131 of the Criminal Justice Act 1988 (c. 33), sections 27 and 168 of, and paragraph 12 of Schedule 9 and Schedule 11 to, the Criminal Justice and Public Order Act 1994 (c. 33), sections 54 and 120 of, and paragraph 37 of Schedule 8 and Schedule 10 to, the Crime and Disorder Act 1998 (c. 37), paragraph 51 of Schedule 9 to the Powers of Criminal Courts (Sentencing) Act 2000 (c. 6), section 131 of the Criminal Justice and Police Act 2001 (c. 16), sections 13 and 19 of, and paragraph 48 of Schedule 3 and Schedule 37 to, the Criminal Justice Act 2003 (c. 44), paragraphs 33 and 34 of Schedule 21 to the Legal Services Act 2007 (c. 29) and paragraphs 1 and 2 of Schedule 11, paragraphs 1 and 2 of Schedule 12, to the Criminal Justice and Immigration Act 2008 (c. 4) and paragraphs 1 to 4 of Schedule 11, and paragraphs 14 and 15 of Schedule 12, to the Legal Aid, Sentencing and Punishment of Offenders Act 2012 (c. 10).

[47] 1976 c. 63; Schedule 1 was amended by section 34 of the Mental Health (Amendment) Act 1982 (c. 51), sections 153, 154 and 155 of the Criminal Justice Act 1988 (c. 33), paragraph 22 of Schedule 11 to the Criminal Justice Act 1991 (c. 53), section 26 of the Criminal Justice and Public Order Act 1994 (c. 33), paragraph 38 of Schedule 8 to the Crime and Disorder Act 1998 (c. 37), paragraph 54 of Schedule 9 to the Powers of Criminal Courts (Sentencing) Act 2000 (c. 6), sections 129 and 137 of, and Schedule 7 to, the Criminal Justice and Police Act 2001 (c. 16), section 198 of the Extradition Act 2003 (c. 41), sections 13, 14, 15, 19 and 20 of, and paragraphs 20 and 23 of Schedule 32 and paragraphs 1 and 3 of Schedule 36 to, the Criminal Justice Act 2003 (c. 44), paragraph 40 of the Schedule to S.I. 2005/886, paragraph 78 of Schedule 16, and Schedule 17, to the Armed Forces Act 2006 (c. 52), paragraphs 1, 4, 5 and 6 of Schedule 12 to the Criminal Justice and Immigration Act 2008 (c. 4), section 114 of the Coroners and Justice Act 2009 (c. 25) and paragraphs 10 to 31 of Schedule 11, and paragraphs 14 and 17 of Schedule 12, to the Legal Aid, Sentencing and Punishment of Offenders Act 2012 (c. 10).

[48] 1976 c. 63; section 4(2B) was inserted by section 198 of the Extradition Act 2003 (c. 41) and amended by paragraph 34 of Schedule 13 to the Police and Justice Act 2006 (c. 48).

[49] 1996 c. 27; section 33 was amended by section 82 of, and paragraph 4 of Schedule 9 to, the Civil Partnership Act 2004 (c. 33).

    (iv) it has not been practicable, for want of time since the institution of the proceedings, to obtain sufficient information for the court to take the decisions required;

(b) the defendant need not be granted bail if it appears to the court that the defendant was on bail at the time of the offence (this exception does not apply in an extradition case);

(c) the defendant need not be granted bail if, having been released on bail in the case on a previous occasion, the defendant since has been arrested for breach of bail;

(d) the defendant need not be granted bail if in custody pursuant to a sentence;

(e) the defendant need not be granted bail if it appears to the court that it would be impracticable to complete enquiries or a report for which the case is to be adjourned without keeping the defendant in custody;

(f) the defendant may not be granted bail if charged with murder, unless the court is of the opinion that there is no significant risk of the defendant committing an offence while on bail that would, or would be likely to, cause physical or mental injury to some other person;

(g) the defendant in an extradition case need not be granted bail if he or she was on bail on the date of the alleged offence and that offence is not one that could be tried only in a magistrates' court if it were committed in England or Wales.

Exceptions (a)(i), (b) and (c) do not apply where—

(a) the defendant is 18 or over;

(b) the defendant has not been convicted of an offence in those proceedings; and

(c) it appears to the court that there is no real prospect that the defendant will be sentenced to a custodial sentence in those proceedings.

In deciding whether an exception to the right to bail applies the court must have regard to any relevant consideration, including—

(a) the nature and seriousness of the offence, and the probable method of dealing with the defendant for it;

(b) the character, antecedents, associations and community ties of the defendant;

(c) the defendant's record of fulfilling obligations imposed under previous grants of bail; and

(d) except where the case is adjourned for enquires or a report, the strength of the evidence of the defendant having committed the offence.

Under Part IA of Schedule 1 to the 1976 Act, where the offence is punishable with imprisonment, and is one that can be tried only in a magistrates' court—

(a) the defendant need not be granted bail if it appears to the court that—

    (i) having previously been granted bail in criminal proceedings, the defendant has failed to surrender as required and, in view of that failure, the court believes that, if released on bail (with or without conditions), the defendant would fail to surrender to custody, or

    (ii) the defendant was on bail on the date of the offence and the court is satisfied that there are substantial grounds for believing that, if released on bail (with or without conditions), the defendant would commit an offence while on bail;

(b) the defendant need not be granted bail if the court is satisfied that—

    (i) there are substantial grounds for believing that, if released on bail (with or without conditions), the defendant would commit an offence while on bail by engaging in conduct that would, or would be likely to, cause physical or mental injury to some other person, or cause some other person to fear such injury,

    (ii) the defendant should be kept in custody for his or her own protection or welfare, or

    (iii) it has not been practicable, for want of time since the institution of the proceedings, to obtain sufficient information for the court to take the decisions required;

(c) the defendant need not be granted bail if in custody pursuant to a sentence;

(d) the defendant need not be granted bail if, having been released on bail in the case on a previous occasion, the defendant since has been arrested for breach of bail, and the court is satisfied that there are substantial grounds for believing that, if released on bail (with or without conditions), the defendant would fail to surrender to custody, would commit an offence, or would interfere with witnesses or otherwise obstruct the course of justice.

Exceptions (a) and (d) do not apply where—

(a) the defendant is 18 or over;

(b) the defendant has not been convicted of an offence in those proceedings; and

(c) it appears to the court that there is no real prospect that the defendant will be sentenced to a custodial sentence in those proceedings.

Under Part II of Schedule 1 to the 1976 Act, where the offence is not punishable with imprisonment—

(a) *the defendant need not be granted bail if it appears to the court that having previously been granted bail in criminal proceedings, the defendant has failed to surrender as required and, in view of that failure, the court believes that, if released on bail (with or without conditions), the defendant would fail to surrender to custody;*

(b) *the defendant need not be granted bail if the court is satisfied that the defendant should be kept in custody for his or her own protection or welfare;*

(c) *the defendant need not be granted bail if in custody pursuant to a sentence;*

(d) *the defendant need not be granted bail if, having been released on bail in the case on a previous occasion, the defendant since has been arrested for breach of bail, and the court is satisfied that there are substantial grounds for believing that, if released on bail (with or without conditions), the defendant would fail to surrender to custody, would commit an offence, or would interfere with witnesses or otherwise obstruct the course of justice;*

(e) *the defendant need not be granted bail if, having been released on bail in the case on a previous occasion, the defendant since has been arrested for breach of bail, and the court is satisfied that there are substantial grounds for believing that, if released on bail (with or without conditions), the defendant would commit an offence while on bail by engaging in conduct that would, or would be likely to, cause physical or mental injury to an associated person (within the meaning of section 33 of the Family Law Act 1996), or to cause that person to fear such injury.*

Exceptions (a) and (d) apply only where—

(a) *the defendant is under 18; and*

(b) *the defendant has been convicted in those proceedings.*

Further exceptions to the general right to bail are set out in section 25 of the Criminal Justice and Public Order Act 1994[50], under which a defendant charged with murder, attempted murder, manslaughter, rape or another sexual offence specified in that section, and who has been previously convicted of such an offence, may be granted bail only if there are exceptional circumstances which justify it.

Custody time limits

Application to extend a custody time limit   **R14.21**

14.21 (1) This rule applies where the prosecutor gives notice of application to extend a custody time limit.

(2) The court officer must arrange for the court to hear that application as soon as practicable after the expiry of—

(a) 5 days from the giving of notice, in the Crown Court; or

(b) 2 days from the giving of notice, in a magistrates' court.

(3) The court may shorten a time limit under this rule.

[Note. See regulation 7 of the Prosecution of Offences (Custody Time Limits) Regulations 1987[51].

Under regulations 4 and 5 of the 1987 Regulations[52], unless the court extends the time limit the maximum period during which the defendant may be in pre-trial custody is—

(a) *in a case which can be tried only in a magistrates' court, 56 days pending the beginning of the trial;*

(b) *in a magistrates' court, in a case which can be tried either in that court or in the Crown Court—*

(i) *70 days, pending the beginning of a trial in the magistrates' court, or*

(ii) *56 days, pending the beginning of a trial in the magistrates' court, if the court decides on such a trial during that period;*

---

[50] 1994 c. 33; section 25 was amended by section 56 of the Crime and Disorder Act 1998 (c. 37), paragraph 160 of Schedule 9 to the Powers of Criminal Courts (Sentencing) Act 2000 (c. 6), paragraph 32 of Schedule 6 to the Sexual Offences Act 2003 (c. 42), paragraph 67 of Schedule 32 and Schedule 37 to the Criminal Justice Act 2003 (c. 44), article 16 of S.I. 2008/1779, paragraph 3 of Schedule 17, and Schedule 23, to the Coroners and Justice Act 2009 (c. 25) and paragraph 33 of Schedule 11 to the Legal Aid, Sentencing and Punishment of Offenders Act 2012 (c. 10).

[51] S.I. 1987/299; regulation 7 was amended by S.I. 1989/767.

[52] S.I. 1987/299; regulation 4 was amended by section 71 of the Criminal Procedure and Investigations Act 1996 (c. 25) and S.I. 1989/767, 1991/1515, 1999/2744. Regulation 5 was amended by sections 71 and 80 of, and paragraph 8 of Schedule 5 to, the Criminal Procedure and Investigations Act 1996 (c. 25) and S.I. 1989/767, 1991/1515, 2000/3284, 2012/1344.

(c) in the Crown Court, pending the beginning of the trial, 182 days from the sending of the defendant for trial, less any period or periods during which the defendant was in custody in the magistrates' court.

Under section 22(3) of the Prosecution of Offences Act 1985[53], the court cannot extend a custody time limit which has expired, and must not extend such a time limit unless satisfied—

(a) that the need for the extension is due to—

(i) the illness or absence of the accused, a necessary witness, a judge or a magistrate,

(ii) a postponement which is occasioned by the ordering by the court of separate trials in the case of two or more defendants or two or more offences, or

(iii) some other good and sufficient cause; and

(b) that the prosecution has acted with all due diligence and expedition.]

R14.22 Appeal against custody time limit decision

14.22 (1) This rule applies where—

(a) a defendant wants to appeal to the Crown Court against a decision by a magistrates' court to extend a custody time limit; or

(b) a prosecutor wants to appeal to the Crown Court against a decision by a magistrates' court to refuse to extend a custody time limit.

(2) The appellant must serve an appeal notice—

(a) on—

(i) the other party to the decision,

(ii) the Crown Court officer, and

(iii) the magistrates' court officer;

(b) in a defendant's appeal, as soon as practicable after the decision under appeal; and

(c) in a prosecutor's appeal—

(i) as soon as practicable after the decision under appeal, and

(ii) before the relevant custody time limit expires.

(3) The appeal notice must specify—

(a) each offence with which the defendant is charged;

(b) the decision under appeal;

(c) the date on which the relevant custody time limit will expire;

(d) on a defendant's appeal, the date on which the relevant custody time limit would have expired but for the decision under appeal; and

(e) the grounds of appeal.

(4) The Crown Court officer must arrange for the Crown Court to hear the appeal as soon as practicable and in any event no later than the second business day after the appeal notice was served.

(5) The appellant—

(a) may abandon an appeal without the Crown Court's permission, by serving a notice of abandonment, signed by or on behalf of the appellant, on—

(i) the other party,

(ii) the Crown Court officer, and

(iii) the magistrates' court officer

before the hearing of the appeal begins; but

(b) after the hearing of the appeal begins, may only abandon the appeal with the Crown Court's permission.

[Note. See section 22(7), (8), (9) of the Prosecution of Offences Act 1985[54].]

CRIMINAL PROCEDURE RULES   PART 15   DISCLOSURE

R15.1 When this Part applies

15.1 This Part applies in a magistrates' court and in the Crown Court where Parts I and II of the Criminal Procedure and Investigations Act 1996 apply.

[53] 1985 c. 23; section 22 was amended by paragraph 104 of Schedule 15 to the Criminal Justice Act 1988 (c. 33), section 43 of the Crime and Disorder Act 1998 (c. 37), paragraph 36 of Schedule 11 to the Criminal Justice Act 1991 (c. 53), paragraph 27 of Schedule 9 to the Criminal Justice and Public Order Act 1994 (c. 33), section 71 of the Criminal Procedure and Investigations Act 1996 (c. 25), section 67(3) of the Access to Justice Act 1999 (c. 22), section 70 of, and paragraph 57 of Schedule 3 and paragraphs 49 and 51 of Schedule 36 to, the Criminal Justice Act 2003 (c. 44), section 59 of, and paragraph 1 of Schedule 11 to, the Constitutional Reform Act 2005 (c. 4) and paragraph 22 of Schedule 12 to the Legal Aid, Sentencing and Punishment of Offenders Act 2012 (c. 10).
[54] 1985 c. 23; section 22(7) and (8) was amended by section 43 of the Crime and Disorder Act 1998 (c. 37).

[Note. A summary of the disclosure requirements of the Criminal Procedure and Investigations Act 1996 is at the end of this Part.]

Prosecution disclosure

15.2 (1) This rule applies in the Crown Court where, under section 3 of the Criminal Procedure and Investigations Act 1996[1], the prosecutor—

  (a) discloses prosecution material to the defendant; or

  (b) serves on the defendant a written statement that there is no such material to disclose.

(2) The prosecutor must at the same time so inform the court officer.

[Note. See section 3 of the Criminal Procedure and Investigations Act 1996 and paragraph 10 of the Code of Practice accompanying the Criminal Procedure and Investigations Act 1996 (Code of Practice) Order 2015[2].]

Prosecutor's application for public interest ruling

15.3 (1) This rule applies where—

  (a) without a court order, the prosecutor would have to disclose material; and

  (b) the prosecutor wants the court to decide whether it would be in the public interest to disclose it.

(2) The prosecutor must—

  (a) apply in writing for such a decision; and

  (b) serve the application on—

    (i) the court officer,

    (ii) any person who the prosecutor thinks would be directly affected by disclosure of the material, and

    (iii) the defendant, but only to the extent that serving it on the defendant would not disclose what the prosecutor thinks ought not be disclosed.

(3) The application must—

  (a) describe the material, and explain why the prosecutor thinks that—

    (i) it is material that the prosecutor would have to disclose,

    (ii) it would not be in the public interest to disclose that material, and

    (iii) no measure such as the prosecutor's admission of any fact, or disclosure by summary, extract or edited copy, adequately would protect both the public interest and the defendant's right to a fair trial;

  (b) omit from any part of the application that is served on the defendant anything that would disclose what the prosecutor thinks ought not be disclosed (in which case, paragraph (4) of this rule applies); and

  (c) explain why, if no part of the application is served on the defendant.

(4) Where the prosecutor serves only part of the application on the defendant, the prosecutor must—

  (a) mark the other part, to show that it is only for the court; and

  (b) in that other part, explain why the prosecutor has withheld it from the defendant.

(5) Unless already done, the court may direct the prosecutor to serve an application on—

  (a) the defendant; and

  (b) any other person who the court considers would be directly affected by the disclosure of the material.

(6) The court must determine the application at a hearing which—

  (a) must be in private, unless the court otherwise directs; and

  (b) if the court so directs, may take place, wholly or in part, in the defendant's absence.

(7) At a hearing at which the defendant is present—

  (a) the general rule is that the court must consider, in the following sequence—

    (i) representations first by the prosecutor and any other person served with the application, and then by the defendant, in the presence of them all, and then

    (ii) further representations by the prosecutor and any such other person in the defendant's absence; but

  (b) the court may direct other arrangements for the hearing.

(8) The court may only determine the application if satisfied that it has been able to take adequate account of—

  (a) such rights of confidentiality as apply to the material; and

  (b) the defendant's right to a fair trial.

---

[1] 1996 c. 25; section 3 was amended by section 82 of, and paragraph 7 of Schedule 4 to, the Regulation of Investigatory Powers Act 2000 (c. 23) and section 32 and section 331 of, and paragraphs 20 and 21 of Schedule 36 to, the Criminal Justice Act 2003 (c. 44).

[2] S.I. 2015/861.

(9) Unless the court otherwise directs, the court officer—

    (a) must not give notice to anyone other than the prosecutor—

        (i) of the hearing of an application under this rule, unless the prosecutor served the application on that person, or

        (ii) of the court's decision on the application; and

    (b) may—

        (i) keep a written application or representations, or

        (ii) arrange for the whole or any part to be kept by some other appropriate person, subject to any conditions that the court may impose.

[Note. The court's power to order that it is not in the public interest to disclose material is provided for by sections 3(6), 7(6) (where the investigation began between 1ˢᵗ April, 1997 and 3ʳᵈ April, 2005) and 7A(8) (where the investigation began on or after 4ᵗʰ April, 2005) of the Criminal Procedure and Investigations Act 1996[3].

See also sections 16 and 19 of the 1996 Act[4].]

R15.4   **Defence disclosure**

15.4 (1) This rule applies where—

    (a) under section 5 or 6 of the Criminal Procedure and Investigations Act 1996[5], the defendant gives a defence statement; and

    (b) under section 6C of the 1996 Act[6], the defendant gives a defence witness notice.

  (2) The defendant must serve such a statement or notice on—

    (a) the court officer; and

    (b) the prosecutor.

[Note. The Practice Direction sets out forms of—

    (a) defence statement; and

    (b) defence witness notice.

Under section 5 of the 1996 Act, in the Crown Court the defendant must give a defence statement. Under section 6 of the Act, in a magistrates' court the defendant may give such a statement but need not do so.

Under section 6C of the 1996 Act, in the Crown Court and in magistrates' courts the defendant must give a defence witness notice indicating whether he or she intends to call any witnesses (other than him or herself) and, if so, identifying them.]

R15.5   **Defendant's application for prosecution disclosure**

15.5 (1) This rule applies where the defendant—

    (a) has served a defence statement given under the Criminal Procedure and Investigations Act 1996; and

    (b) wants the court to require the prosecutor to disclose material.

  (2) The defendant must serve an application on—

    (a) the court officer; and

    (b) the prosecutor.

  (3) The application must—

    (a) describe the material that the defendant wants the prosecutor to disclose;

    (b) explain why the defendant thinks there is reasonable cause to believe that—

        (i) the prosecutor has that material, and

        (ii) it is material that the Criminal Procedure and Investigations Act 1996 requires the prosecutor to disclose; and

    (c) ask for a hearing, if the defendant wants one, and explain why it is needed.

  (4) The court may determine an application under this rule—

    (a) at a hearing, in public or in private; or

    (b) without a hearing.

---

[3] 1996 c. 25; section 7 was repealed by sections 331 and 332 of, and paragraphs 20 and 25 of Schedule 36 and Part 3 of Schedule 37 to, the Criminal Justice Act 2003 (c. 44), with transitional provisions for certain offences in article 2 of S.I. 2005/1817. Section 7A was inserted by section 37 of the Criminal Justice Act 2003 (c. 44).

[4] 1996 c. 25; section 16 was amended by section 331 of, and paragraphs 20 and 32 of Schedule 36 to, the Criminal Justice Act 2003 (c. 44). Section 19 was amended by section 109 of, and paragraph 377 of Schedule 8 to, the Courts Act 2003 (c. 39), section 331 of, and paragraphs 20 and 34 of Schedule 36 to, the Criminal Justice Act 2003 (c. 44) and section 15 of, and paragraph 251 of Schedule 4 to, the Constitutional Reform Act 2005 (c. 4).

[5] 1996 c. 25; section 5 was amended by section 33 of, and paragraph 66 of Schedule 3, paragraphs 20 and 23 of Schedule 36 and Parts 3 and 4 of Schedule 37 to, the Criminal Justice Act 2003 (c. 44). It was further amended by section 119 of, and paragraph 126 of Schedule 8 to, the Crime and Disorder Act 1998 (c. 37) in respect of certain proceedings only.

[6] 1996 c. 25; section 6C was inserted by section 34 of the Criminal Justice Act 2003 (c. 44).

(5) The court must not require the prosecutor to disclose material unless the prosecutor—
  (a) is present; or
  (b) has had at least 10 business days in which to make representations.

[Note. The Practice Direction sets out a form of application for use in connection with this rule.

Under section 8 of the Criminal Procedure and Investigations Act 1996[7], a defendant may apply for prosecution disclosure only if the defendant has given a defence statement.]

Review of public interest ruling

15.6 (1) This rule applies where the court has ordered that it is not in the public interest to disclose material that the prosecutor otherwise would have to disclose, and—
  (a) the defendant wants the court to review that decision; or
  (b) the Crown Court reviews that decision on its own initiative.
  (2) Where the defendant wants the court to review that decision, the defendant must—
  (a) serve an application on—
    (i) the court officer, and
    (ii) the prosecutor; and
  (b) in the application—
    (i) describe the material that the defendant wants the prosecutor to disclose, and
    (ii) explain why the defendant thinks it is no longer in the public interest for the prosecutor not to disclose it.
  (3) The prosecutor must serve any such application on any person who the prosecutor thinks would be directly affected if that material were disclosed.
  (4) The prosecutor, and any such person, must serve any representations on—
  (a) the court officer; and
  (b) the defendant, unless to do so would in effect reveal something that either thinks ought not be disclosed.
  (5) The court may direct—
  (a) the prosecutor to serve any such application on any person who the court considers would be directly affected if that material were disclosed; and
  (b) the prosecutor and any such person to serve any representations on the defendant.
  (6) The court must review a decision to which this rule applies at a hearing which—
  (a) must be in private, unless the court otherwise directs; and
  (b) if the court so directs, may take place, wholly or in part, in the defendant's absence.
  (7) At a hearing at which the defendant is present—
  (a) the general rule is that the court must consider, in the following sequence—
    (i) representations first by the defendant, and then by the prosecutor and any other person served with the application, in the presence of them all, and then
    (ii) further representations by the prosecutor and any such other person in the defendant's absence; but
  (b) the court may direct other arrangements for the hearing.
  (8) The court may only conclude a review if satisfied that it has been able to take adequate account of—
  (a) such rights of confidentiality as apply to the material; and
  (b) the defendant's right to a fair trial.

[Note. The court's power to review a public interest ruling is provided for by sections 14 and 15 of the Criminal Procedure and Investigations Act 1996[8]. Under section 14 of the Act, a magistrates' court may reconsider an order for non-disclosure only if a defendant applies. Under section 15, the Crown Court may do so on an application, or on its own initiative.

See also sections 16 and 19 of the 1996 Act.]

Defendant's application to use disclosed material

15.7 (1) This rule applies where a defendant wants the court's permission to use disclosed prosecution material—
  (a) otherwise than in connection with the case in which it was disclosed; or
  (b) beyond the extent to which it was displayed or communicated publicly at a hearing.

---

[7] 1996 c. 25; section 8 was amended by section 82 of, and paragraph 7 of Schedule 4 to, the Regulation of Investigatory Powers Act 2000 (c. 23) and section 38 of the Criminal Justice Act 2003 (c. 44).
[8] 1996 c. 25; section 14 was amended by section 331 of, and paragraphs 20 and 30 of Schedule 36 to, the Criminal Justice Act 2003 (c. 44) and section 15 was amended by section 331 of, and paragraphs 20 and 31 of Schedule 36 to, the Criminal Justice Act 2003 (c. 44).

(2) The defendant must serve an application on—
   (a) the court officer; and
   (b) the prosecutor.
(3) The application must—
   (a) specify what the defendant wants to use or disclose; and
   (b) explain why.
(4) The court may determine an application under this rule—
   (a) at a hearing, in public or in private; or
   (b) without a hearing.
(5) The court must not permit the use of such material unless—
   (a) the prosecutor has had at least 20 business days in which to make representations; and
   (b) the court is satisfied that it has been able to take adequate account of any rights of confidentiality that may apply to the material.

[Note. The court's power to allow a defendant to use disclosed material is provided for by section 17 of the Criminal Procedure and Investigations Act 1996[9].]

R15.8   Unauthorised use of disclosed material

15.8 (1) This rule applies where a person is accused of using disclosed prosecution material in contravention of section 17 of the Criminal Procedure and Investigations Act 1996.
   (2) A party who wants the court to exercise its power to punish that person for contempt of court must comply with the rules in Part 48 (Contempt of court).
   (3) The court must not exercise its power to forfeit material used in contempt of court unless—
      (a) the prosecutor; and
      (b) any other person directly affected by the disclosure of the material.
      is present, or has had at least 14 days in which to make representations.

[Under section 18 of the 1996 Act, the court can punish for contempt of court any other use of disclosed prosecution material. See also section 19 of the 1996 Act.]

R15.9   Court's power to vary requirements under this Part

15.9 The court may—
   (a) shorten or extend (even after it has expired) a time limit under this Part;
   (b) allow a defence statement, or a defence witness notice, to be in a different written form to one set out in the Practice Direction, as long as it contains what the Criminal Procedure and Investigations Act 1996 requires;
   (c) allow an application under this Part to be in a different form to one set out in the Practice Direction, or to be presented orally; and
   (d) specify the period within which—
      (i) any application under this Part must be made, or
      (ii) any material must be disclosed, on an application to which rule 15.5 applies (Defendant's application for prosecution disclosure).

Summary of disclosure requirements of Criminal Procedure and Investigations Act 1996

The Criminal Procedure and Investigations Act 1996 came into force on 1st April, 1997. It does not apply where the investigation began before that date. With effect from 4th April, 2005, the Criminal Justice Act 2003 made changes to the 1996 Act that do not apply where the investigation began before that date.

In some circumstances, the prosecutor may be required to disclose material to which the 1996 Act does not apply: see sections 1 and 21[10].

Part I of the 1996 Act contains sections 1 to 21A. Part II, which contains sections 22 to 27, requires an investigator to record information relevant to an investigation that is obtained during its course. See also the Criminal Procedure and Investigations Act 1996 (Code of Practice) (No. 2) Order 1997[11], the Criminal

---

[9] 1996 c. 25; section 17 was amended by section 331 of, and paragraphs 20 and 33 of Schedule 36 to, the Criminal Justice Act 2003 (c. 44).

[10] 1996 c. 25; section 1 was amended by section 119 of, and paragraph 125 of Schedule 8 to, the Crime and Disorder Act 1998 (c. 37), paragraph 66 of Schedule 3 and Part 4 of Schedule 37 to the Criminal Justice Act 2003 (c. 44) and paragraph 37 of Schedule 17 to the Crime and Courts Act 2013 (c. 22). It was amended in respect of certain proceedings only by section 119 of, and paragraph 125(a) of Schedule 8 to, the Crime and Disorder Act 1998 (c. 37). It is further amended by section 9 of the Sexual Offences (Protected Material) Act 1997 (c. 39), with effect from a date to be appointed. Section 21 was amended by paragraph 66 of Schedule 3 to the Criminal Justice Act 2003 (c. 44).

[11] S.I. 1997/1033; this Order was revoked by S.I. 2005/985.

Procedure and Investigations Act 1996 (Code of Practice) Order 2005[12] and the Criminal Procedure and Investigations Act 1996 (Code of Practice) Order 2015[13] issued under sections 23 to 25 of the 1996 Act.

Prosecution disclosure

Where the investigation began between 1st April, 1997, and 3rd April, 2005, sections 3 and 7 of the 1996 Act require the prosecutor—

    (a) to disclose material not previously disclosed that in the prosecutor's opinion might undermine the case for the prosecution against the defendant—

        (i) in a magistrates' court, as soon as is reasonably practicable after the defendant pleads not guilty, and

        (ii) in the Crown Court, as soon as is reasonably practicable after the case is committed or transferred for trial, or after the evidence is served where the case is sent for trial; and

    (b) as soon as is reasonably practicable after service of the defence statement, to disclose material not previously disclosed that might be reasonably expected to assist the defendant's case as disclosed by that defence statement; or in either event

    (c) if there is no such material, then to give the defendant a written statement to that effect.

Where the investigation began on or after 4th April, 2005, sections 3 and 7A of the 1996 Act[14] require the prosecutor—

    (a) to disclose prosecution material not previously disclosed that might reasonably be considered capable of undermining the case for the prosecution against the defendant or of assisting the case for the defendant—

        (i) in a magistrates' court, as soon as is reasonably practicable after the defendant pleads not guilty, or

        (ii) in the Crown Court, as soon as is reasonably practicable after the case is committed or transferred for trial, or after the evidence is served where the case is sent for trial, or after a count is added to the indictment; and in either case

    (b) if there is no such material, then to give the defendant a written statement to that effect; and after that

    (c) in either court, to disclose any such material—

        (i) whenever there is any, until the court reaches its verdict or the prosecutor decides not to proceed with the case, and

        (ii) in particular, after the service of the defence statement.

Sections 2 and 3 of the 1996 Act define material, and prescribe how it must be disclosed.

In some circumstances, disclosure is prohibited by section 17 of the Regulation of Investigatory Powers Act 2000.

The prosecutor must not disclose material that the court orders it would not be in the public interest to disclose: see sections 3(6), 7(6) and 7A(8) of the 1996 Act.

Sections 12 and 13 of the 1996 Act prescribe the time for prosecution disclosure. Under paragraph 10 of the Code of Practice accompanying the Criminal Procedure and Investigations Act 1996 (Code of Practice) Order 2015, in a magistrates' court the prosecutor must disclose any material due to be disclosed at the hearing where a not guilty plea is entered, or as soon as possible following a formal indication from the accused or representative that a not guilty plea will be entered at that hearing.

See also sections 1, 4 and 10 of the 1996 Act.

Defence disclosure

Under section 5 of the 1996 Act[15], in the Crown Court the defendant must give a defence statement. Under section 6 of the Act, in a magistrates' court the defendant may give such a statement but need not do so.

Under section 6C of the 1996 Act[16], in the Crown Court and in magistrates' courts the defendant must give a defence witness notice indicating whether he or she intends to call any witnesses (other than him or herself) and, if so, identifying them.

---

[12] S.I. 2005/985.
[13] S.I. 2015/861.
[14] 1996 c. 25; section 3 was amended by section 82 of, and paragraph 7 of Schedule 4 to, the Regulation of Investigatory Powers Act 2000 (c. 23) and section 32 and section 331 of, and paragraphs 20 and 21 of Schedule 36 to, the Criminal Justice Act 2003 (c. 44). Section 7A was inserted by section 37 of the Criminal Justice Act 2003 (c. 44).
[15] 1996 c. 25; section 5 was amended by section 33 of, and paragraph 66 of Schedule 3, paragraphs 20 and 23 of Schedule 36 and Parts 3 and 4 of Schedule 37 to, the Criminal Justice Act 2003 (c. 44). It was further amended by section 119 of, and paragraph 126 of Schedule 8 to, the Crime and Disorder Act 1998 (c. 37) in respect of certain proceedings only.
[16] 1996 c. 25; section 6C was inserted by section 34 of the Criminal Justice Act 2003 (c. 44).

The time for service of a defence statement is prescribed by section 12 of the 1996 Act[17] and by the Criminal Procedure and Investigations Act 1996 (Defence Disclosure Time Limits) Regulations 2011[18]. It is—

    (a) in a magistrates' court, not more than 14 days after the prosecutor—
        (i) discloses material under section 3 of the 1996 Act, or
        (ii) serves notice that there is no such material to disclose;
    (b) in the Crown Court, not more than 28 days after either of those events, if the prosecution evidence has been served on the defendant.

The requirements for the content of a defence statement are set out in—

    (a) section 5 of the 1996 Act, where the investigation began between 1st April, 1997 and 3rd April, 2005;
    (b) section 6A of the 1996 Act[19], where the investigation began on or after 4th April, 2005. See also section 6E of the Act[20].

Where the investigation began between 1st April, 1997 and 3rd April, 2005, the defence statement must—

    (a) set out in general terms the nature of the defence;
    (b) indicate the matters on which the defendant takes issue with the prosecutor, and, in respect of each, explain why;
    (c) if the defence statement discloses an alibi, give particulars, including—
        (i) the name and address of any witness whom the defendant believes can give evidence in support (that is, evidence that the defendant was in a place, at a time, inconsistent with having committed the offence),
        (ii) where the defendant does not know the name or address, any information that might help identify or find that witness.

Where the investigation began on or after 4th April, 2005, the defence statement must—

    (a) set out the nature of the defence, including any particular defences on which the defendant intends to rely;
    (b) indicate the matters of fact on which the defendant takes issue with the prosecutor, and, in respect of each, explain why;
    (c) set out particulars of the matters of fact on which the defendant intends to rely for the purposes of the defence;
    (d) indicate any point of law that the defendant wants to raise, including any point about the admissibility of evidence or about abuse of process, and any authority relied on; and
    (e) if the defence statement discloses an alibi, give particulars, including—
        (i) the name, address and date of birth of any witness whom the defendant believes can give evidence in support (that is, evidence that the defendant was in a place, at a time, inconsistent with having committed the offence),
        (ii) where the defendant does not know any of those details, any information that might help identify or find that witness.

The time for service of a defence witness notice is prescribed by section 12 of the 1996 Act and by the Criminal Procedure and Investigations Act 1996 (Defence Disclosure Time Limits) Regulations 2011. The time limits are the same as those for a defence statement.

A defence witness notice that identifies any proposed defence witness (other than the defendant) must—

    (a) give the name, address and date of birth of each such witness, or as many of those details as are known to the defendant when the notice is given;
    (b) provide any information in the defendant's possession which might be of material assistance in identifying or finding any such witness in whose case any of the details mentioned in paragraph (a) are not known to the defendant when the notice is given; and
    (c) amend any earlier such notice, if the defendant—
        (i) decides to call a person not included in an earlier notice as a proposed witness,
        (ii) decides not to call a person so included, or

---

[17] 1996 c. 25; section 12 was amended by sections 331 of, and paragraphs 20 and 28 of Schedule 36 to, the Criminal Justice Act 2003 (c. 44).
[18] S.I. 2011/209.
[19] 1996 c. 25; section 6A was inserted by section 33 of the Criminal Justice Act 2003 (c. 44) and amended by section 60 of the Criminal Justice and Immigration Act 2008 (c. 4).
[20] 1996 c. 25; section 6E was inserted by section 36 of the Criminal Justice Act 2003 (c. 44).

(iii) discovers any information which the defendant would have had to include in an earlier notice, if then aware of it.

Under section 11 of the 1996 Act[21], if a defendant—

    (a) fails to disclose what the Act requires;
    (b) fails to do so within the time prescribed;
    (c) at trial, relies on a defence, or facts, not mentioned in the defence statement;
    (d) at trial, introduces alibi evidence without having given in the defence statement—
        (i) particulars of the alibi, or
        (ii) the details of the alibi witness, or witnesses, required by the Act; or
    (e) at trial, calls a witness not identified in a defence witness notice,

then the court or another party at trial may comment on that, and the court may draw such inferences as appear proper in deciding whether the defendant is guilty.

Under section 6E(2) of the 1996 Act, if before trial in the Crown Court it seems to the court that section 11 may apply, then the court must warn the defendant.

CRIMINAL PROCEDURE RULES   PART 16   WRITTEN WITNESS STATEMENTS

When this Part applies   **R16.1**

16.1   This Part applies where a party wants to introduce a written witness statement in evidence under section 9 of the Criminal Justice Act 1967[1].

[Note. Under section 9 of the Criminal Justice Act 1967, if the conditions specified in that section are met the written statement of a witness is admissible in evidence to the same extent as if that witness gave evidence in person.]

Content of written witness statement   **R16.2**

16.2   The statement must contain—
    (a) at the beginning—
        (i) the witness' name, and
        (ii) the witness' age, if under 18;
    (b) a declaration by the witness that—
        (i) it is true to the best of the witness' knowledge and belief, and
        (ii) the witness knows that if it is introduced in evidence, then it would be an offence wilfully to have stated in it anything that the witness knew to be false or did not believe to be true;
    (c) if the witness cannot read the statement, a signed declaration by someone else that that person read it to the witness; and
    (d) the witness' signature.

[Note. The Practice Direction sets out a form of written statement for use in connection with this rule.]

Reference to exhibit   **R16.3**

16.3   Where the statement refers to a document or object as an exhibit, it must identify that document or object clearly.

[Note. See section 9(7) of the Criminal Justice Act 1967[2].]

Written witness statement in evidence   **R16.4**

16.4   (1) A party who wants to introduce in evidence a written witness statement must—
    (a) before the hearing at which that party wants to introduce it, serve a copy of the statement on—
        (i) the court officer, and
        (ii) each other party; and

---

[21] 1996 c. 25; section 11 was substituted by section 39 of the Criminal Justice Act 2003 (c. 44) and amended by section 60(2) of the Criminal Justice and Immigration Act 2008 (c. 4).
[1] 1967 c. 80; section 9 was amended by section 56 of, and paragraph 49 of Schedule 8 to, the Courts Act 1971 (c. 23), section 168 of, and paragraph 6 of Schedule 9 to, the Criminal Justice and Public Order Act 1994 (c. 33), section 69 of the Criminal Procedure and Investigations Act 1996 (c. 25), regulation 9 of, and paragraph 4 of Schedule 5 to, S.I. 2001/1090, paragraph 43 of Schedule 3 and Part 4 of Schedule 37 to the Criminal Justice Act 2003 (c. 44), section 26 of, and paragraph 7 of Schedule 2 to, the Armed Forces Act 2011 (c. 18) and section 80 of the Deregulation Act 2015 (c. 20). It is further amended by section 72 of, and paragraph 55 of Schedule 5 to, the Children and Young Persons Act 1969 (c. 54) and section 65 of, and paragraph 1 of Schedule 4 to, the Courts Act 2003 (c. 39), with effect from dates to be appointed.
[2] 1967 c. 80.

   (b) at or before that hearing, serve on the court officer the statement or an authenticated
       copy.
(2) If that party relies on only part of the statement, that party must mark the copy in such a way
    as to make that clear.
(3) A prosecutor must serve on a defendant, with the copy of the statement, a notice—
   (a) of the right to object to the introduction of the statement in evidence instead of the
       witness giving evidence in person;
   (b) of the time limit for objecting under this rule; and
   (c) that if the defendant does not object in time, the court—
       (i) can nonetheless require the witness to give evidence in person, but
       (ii) may decide not to do so.
(4) A party served with a written witness statement who objects to its introduction in evidence
    must—
   (a) serve notice of the objection on—
       (i) the party who served it, and
       (ii) the court officer; and
   (b) serve the notice of objection not more than 5 business days after service of the statement
       unless—
       (i) the court extends that time limit, before or after the statement was served,
       (ii) rule 24.8 (Written guilty plea: special rules) applies, in which case the time limit is the
            later of 5 business days after service of the statement or 5 business days before the
            hearing date, or
       (iii) rule 24.9 (Single justice procedure: special rules) applies, in which case the time limit
             is 15 business days after service of the statement.
(5) The court may exercise its power to require the witness to give evidence in person—
   (a) on application by any party; or
   (b) on its own initiative.
(6) A party entitled to receive a copy of a statement may waive that entitlement by so informing—
   (a) the party who would have served it; and
   (b) the court.

*[Note. The Practice Direction sets out a form of written witness statement and a form of notice for use in
connection with this rule.*

*Under section 9(2A) of the Criminal Justice Act 1967[3], Criminal Procedure Rules may prescribe the period
within which a party served with a written witness statement must object to its introduction in evidence, subject
to a minimum period of 7 days from its service.*

*Under section 133 of the Criminal Justice Act 2003[4], where a statement in a document is admissible as evidence
in criminal proceedings, the statement may be proved by producing either (a) the document, or (b) (whether or
not the document exists) a copy of the document or of the material part of it, authenticated in whatever way the
court may approve. By section 134 of the 2003 Act, 'document' means anything in which information of any
description is recorded.]*

CRIMINAL PROCEDURE RULES   PART 17   WITNESS SUMMONSES, WARRANTS AND ORDERS

R17.1   **When this Part applies**

17.1 (1) This Part applies in magistrates' courts and in the Crown Court where—
             (a) a party wants the court to issue a witness summons, warrant or order under—
                 (i) section 97 of the Magistrates' Courts Act 1980[1],
                 (ii) paragraph 4 of Schedule 3 to the Crime and Disorder Act 1998[2],

[3] 1967 c. 80; section 9(2A) was inserted by section 80 of the Deregulation Act 2015 (c. 20).
[4] 2003 c. 44.
[1] 1980 c. 43; section 97 was amended by sections 13 and 14 of, and paragraph 7 of Schedule 2 to, the Contempt of Court Act 1981 (c. 47), section 31 of, and paragraph 2 of Schedule 4 to, the Criminal Justice (International Co-operation) Act 1990 (c. 5), sections 17 and 65 of, and paragraph 6 of Schedule 3 and Part I of Schedule 4 to, the Criminal Justice Act 1991 (c. 53), section 51 of the Criminal Procedure and Investigations Act 1996 (c. 25) and section 169 of the Serious Organised Crime and Police Act 2005 (c. 15).
[2] 1998 c. 37; paragraph 4 of Schedule 3 was amended by paragraphs 15, 20, 68 and 72 of Schedule 3 to the Criminal Justice Act 2003 (c. 44), section 169 of the Serious Organised Crime and Police Act 2005 (c. 15), article 3 of, and paragraphs 35 and 37 of the Schedule to, S.I. 2004/2035 and article 2 of, and paragraph 61 of the Schedule to, S.I. 2005/886.

      (iii) section 2 of the Criminal Procedure (Attendance of Witnesses) Act 1965[3], or

      (iv) section 7 of the Bankers' Books Evidence Act 1879[4];

  (b) the court considers the issue of such a summons, warrant or order on its own initiative as if a party had applied; or

  (c) one of those listed in rule 17.7 wants the court to withdraw such a summons, warrant or order.

(2) A reference to a 'witness' in this Part is a reference to a person to whom such a summons, warrant or order is directed.

[Note. A magistrates' court may require the attendance of a witness to give evidence or to produce in evidence a document or thing by a summons, or in some circumstances a warrant for the witness' arrest, under section 97 of the Magistrates' Courts Act 1980 or under paragraph 4 of Schedule 3 to the Crime and Disorder Act 1998. The Crown Court may do so under sections 2, 2D, 3 and 4 of the Criminal Procedure (Attendance of Witnesses) Act 1965. Either court may order the production in evidence of a copy of an entry in a banker's book without the attendance of an officer of the bank, under sections 6 and 7 of the Bankers' Books Evidence Act 1879. See section 2D of the Criminal Procedure (Attendance of Witnesses) Act 1965 for the Crown Court's power to issue a witness summons on the court's own initiative.

See Part 3 for the court's general powers to consider an application and to give directions.]

Issue etc. of summons, warrant or order with or without a hearing   R17.2

17.2 (1) The court may issue or withdraw a witness summons, warrant or order with or without a hearing.

      (2) A hearing under this Part must be in private unless the court otherwise directs.

[Note. If rule 17.5 applies, a person served with an application for a witness summons will have an opportunity to make representations about whether there should be a hearing of that application before the witness summons is issued.]

Application for summons, warrant or order: general rules   R17.3

17.3 (1) A party who wants the court to issue a witness summons, warrant or order must apply as soon as practicable after becoming aware of the grounds for doing so.

      (2) A party applying for a witness summons or order must—

        (a) identify the proposed witness;

        (b) explain—

          (i) what evidence the proposed witness can give or produce,

          (ii) why it is likely to be material evidence, and

          (iii) why it would be in the interests of justice to issue a summons, order or warrant as appropriate.

      (3) A party applying for an order to be allowed to inspect and copy an entry in bank records must—

        (a) identify the entry;

        (b) explain the purpose for which the entry is required; and

        (c) propose—

          (i) the terms of the order, and

          (ii) the period within which the order should take effect, if 3 days from the date of service of the order would not be appropriate.

      (4) The application may be made orally unless—

        (a) rule 17.5 applies; or

        (b) the court otherwise directs.

      (5) The applicant must serve any order made on the witness to whom, or the bank to which, it is directed.

[Note. The court may issue a warrant for a witness' arrest if that witness fails to obey a witness summons directed to him: see section 97(3) of the Magistrates' Courts Act 1980, paragraph 4(5) of Schedule 3 to the Crime and Disorder Act 1998 and section 4 of the Criminal Procedure (Attendance of Witnesses) Act 1965. Before a magistrates' court may issue a warrant under section 97(3) of the 1980 Act, the witness must first be paid or offered a reasonable amount for costs and expenses.]

---

[3] 1965 c. 69; section 2 was substituted, together with sections 2 A to 2E, by section 66 of the Criminal Procedure and Investigations Act 1996 (c. 25) and amended by section 119 of, and paragraph 8 of Schedule 8 to, the Crime and Disorder Act 1998 (c. 37), section 109 of, and paragraph 126 of Schedule 8 to, the Courts Act 2003 (c. 39), paragraph 42 of Schedule 3 and Part 4 of Schedule 37 to the Criminal Justice Act 2003 (c. 44), section 169 of the Serious Organised Crime and Police Act 2005 (c. 15) and paragraph 33 of Schedule 17 to the Crime and Courts Act 2013 (c. 22).

[4] 1879 c. 11; section 6 has been amended; none is relevant to these rules.

R17.4 **Written application: form and service**

17.4 (1) An application in writing under rule 17.3 must be in the form set out in the Practice Direction, containing the same declaration of truth as a witness statement.

(2) The party applying must serve the application—

(a) in every case, on the court officer and as directed by the court; and

(b) as required by rule 17.5, if that rule applies.

[Note. Declarations of truth in witness statements are required by section 9 of the Criminal Justice Act 1967[5]. Section 89 of the 1967 Act[6] makes it an offence to make a written statement under section 9 of that Act which the person making it knows to be false or does not believe to be true.]

R17.5 **Application for summons to produce a document, etc.: special rules**

17.5 (1) This rule applies to an application under rule 17.3 for a witness summons requiring the proposed witness—

(a) to produce in evidence a document or thing; or

(b) to give evidence about information apparently held in confidence, that relates to another person.

(2) The application must be in writing in the form required by rule 17.4.

(3) The party applying must serve the application—

(a) on the proposed witness, unless the court otherwise directs; and

(b) on one or more of the following, if the court so directs—

(i) a person to whom the proposed evidence relates, and

(ii) another party.

(4) The court must not issue a witness summons where this rule applies unless—

(a) everyone served with the application has had at least 10 business days in which to make representations, including representations about whether there should be a hearing of the application before the summons is issued; and

(b) the court is satisfied that it has been able to take adequate account of the duties and rights, including rights of confidentiality, of the proposed witness and of any person to whom the proposed evidence relates.

(5) This rule does not apply to an application for an order to produce in evidence a copy of an entry in bank records.

[Note. Under section 2A of the Criminal Procedure (Attendance of Witnesses) Act 1965[7]), a witness summons to produce a document or thing issued by the Crown Court may require the witness to produce it for inspection by the applicant before producing it in evidence.]

R17.6 **Application for summons to produce a document, etc.: court's assessment of relevance and confidentiality**

17.6 (1) This rule applies where a person served with an application for a witness summons requiring the proposed witness to produce in evidence a document or thing objects to its production on the ground that—

(a) it is not likely to be material evidence; or

(b) even if it is likely to be material evidence, the duties or rights, including rights of confidentiality, of the proposed witness or of any person to whom the document or thing relates, outweigh the reasons for issuing a summons.

(2) The court may require the proposed witness to make the document or thing available for the objection to be assessed.

(3) The court may invite—

(a) the proposed witness or any representative of the proposed witness; or

(b) a person to whom the document or thing relates or any representative of such a person, to help the court assess the objection.

[5] 1967 c. 80; section 9 was amended by section 56 of, and paragraph 49 of Schedule 8 to, the Courts Act 1971 (c. 23), section 168 of, and paragraph 6 of Schedule 9 to, the Criminal Justice and Public Order Act 1994 (c. 33), section 69 of the Criminal Procedure and Investigations Act 1996 (c. 25), regulation 9 of, and paragraph 4 of Schedule 5 to, S.I. 2001/1090, paragraph 43 of Schedule 3 and Part 4 of Schedule 37 to the Criminal Justice Act 2003 (c. 44), section 26 of, and paragraph 7 of Schedule 2 to, the Armed Forces Act 2011 (c. 18) and section 80 of the Deregulation Act 2015 (c. 20). It is further amended by section 72 of, and paragraph 55 of Schedule 5 to, the Children and Young Persons Act 1969 (c. 54) and section 65 of, and paragraph 1 of Schedule 4 to, the Courts Act 2003 (c. 39), with effect from dates to be appointed.
[6] 1967 c. 80; section 89 was amended by section 154 of, and Schedule 9 to, the Magistrates' Courts Act 1980 (c. 43).
[7] 1965 c. 69; section 2A was substituted, together with sections 2, 2 B, 2D and 2E, for existing section 2 by section 66(1) and (2) of the Criminal Procedure and Investigations Act 1996 (c. 25).

Application to withdraw a summons, warrant or order   R17.7

17.7 (1) The court may withdraw a witness summons, warrant or order if one of the following applies
            for it to be withdrawn—
      (a) the party who applied for it, on the ground that it no longer is needed;
      (b) the witness, on the grounds that the court received no representations by the witness
          before the summons, warrant or order was issued and, in the Crown Court, the witness
          had had no notice of any application for a summons, and—
          (i) the witness cannot give or produce evidence likely to be material evidence, or
          (ii) even if the witness could do so, the witness' duties or rights, including rights of
               confidentiality, or those of any person to whom the evidence relates, outweigh the
               reasons for the issue of the summons, warrant or order; or
      (c) any person to whom the proposed evidence relates, on the grounds that the court received
          no representations by that person before the summons, warrant or order was issued,
          and—
          (i) that evidence is not likely to be material evidence, or
          (ii) even if it is, that person's duties or rights, including rights of confidentiality, or those
               of the witness, outweigh the reasons for the issue of the summons, warrant or order.
      (2) A person applying under this rule must—
      (a) apply in writing as soon as practicable after becoming aware of the grounds for doing so,
          explaining why the court should withdraw the summons, warrant or order; and
      (b) serve the application on the court officer and as appropriate on—
          (i)   the witness,
          (ii) the party (if any) who applied for the summons, warrant or order, and
          (iii) any other person who was served with the application for the summons, warrant or
                order.
      (3) Rule 17.6 applies to an application under this rule that concerns a document or thing to be
           produced in evidence.

*[Note. See sections 2B, 2C and 2E of the Criminal Procedure (Attendance of Witnesses) Act 1965[8] for the Crown
Court's powers to withdraw a witness summons, including the power to order costs.]*

Court's power to vary requirements under this Part   R17.8

17.8 (1) The court may—
      (a) shorten or extend (even after it has expired) a time limit under this Part; and
      (b) where a rule or direction requires an application under this Part to be in writing, allow that
          application to be made orally instead.
      (2) Someone who wants the court to allow an application to be made orally under paragraph (1)(b)
           of this rule must—
      (a) give as much notice as the urgency of the application permits to those on whom the
          application otherwise should be served; and
      (b) in doing so explain the reasons for the application and for wanting the court to consider
          it orally.

CRIMINAL PROCEDURE RULES   PART 18   MEASURES TO ASSIST A
WITNESS OR DEFENDANT TO GIVE EVIDENCE OR OTHERWISE PARTICIPATE

General rules

When this Part applies   R18.1

18.1 This Part applies—
      (a) where the court can give a direction (a 'special measures direction'), under section 19 of the
          Youth Justice and Criminal Evidence Act 1999[1], on an application or on its own initiative, for
          any of the following measures—
          (i) preventing a witness from seeing the defendant (section 23 of the 1999 Act),
          (ii) allowing a witness to give evidence by live link (section 24 of the 1999 Act[2]),

Criminal Procedure Rules

---

[8] 1965 c. 69; sections 2B, 2C and 2E were substituted with section 2 and 2A, for the existing section 2 by section 66(1) and
(2) of the Criminal Procedure and Investigations Act 1996 (c. 25) and amended by section 109 of, and paragraph 126 of
Schedule 8 to, the Courts Act 2003 (c. 39).
[1] 1999 c. 23.
[2] 1999 c. 23; section 24 was amended by paragraph 385 of Schedule 8 to, and Schedule 10 to, the Courts Act 2003 (c. 39) and
section 102(1) of the Coroners and Justice Act 2009 (c. 25).

      (iii) hearing a witness' evidence in private (section 25 of the 1999 Act[3]),

      (iv) dispensing with the wearing of wigs and gowns (section 26 of the 1999 Act),

      (v) admitting video recorded evidence (sections 27 and 28 of the 1999 Act[4]),

      (vi) questioning a witness through an intermediary (section 29 of the 1999 Act[5]),

      (vii) using a device to help a witness communicate (section 30 of the 1999 Act);

   (b) where the court can vary or discharge such a direction, under section 20 of the 1999 Act[6];

   (c) where the court can give, vary or discharge a direction (a 'defendant's evidence direction') for a defendant to give evidence through an intermediary, under sections 33BA and 33BB of the 1999 Act[7] ;

   (d) where the court can—

      (i) make a witness anonymity order, under section 86 of the Coroners and Justice Act 2009[8], or

      (ii) vary or discharge such an order, under section 91, 92 or 93 of the 2009 Act;

   (e) (i) appoint an intermediary to facilitate a defendant's effective participation in that defendant's trial, when the defendant gives evidence or at any other time, or

      (ii) vary or discharge such an appointment; and

   (f) where the court can exercise any other power it has to give, make, vary, rescind, discharge or revoke a direction for a measure to help a witness to give evidence or to help a defendant to participate in that defendant's trial.

[Note. At the end of this Part there is a summary of the circumstances in which a witness or defendant may be eligible for the assistance of one of the measures to which this Part applies.]

R18.2   **Meaning of 'witness' and 'live link'**

   18.2   In this Part—

      (a) 'witness' means anyone (other than a defendant) for whose benefit an application, direction or order is made; and

      (b) 'live link', in relation to a witness, means a live television link or other arrangement by which a witness who is absent from the courtroom or other place where the proceedings are being held is able to see and hear a person there and to be seen and heard by—

      (i) the judge or justices (or both) and the jury (if there is one),

      (ii) legal representatives acting in the proceedings, and

      (iii) any interpreter or other person appointed (in pursuance of the direction or otherwise) to assist the witness.

[Note. See section 24(8) of the Youth Justice and Criminal Evidence Act 1999[9].]

R18.3   **Meaning of 'intermediary' and 'intermediary's report'**

   18.3   (a) 'intermediary' means a person who is—

      (i) approved by the court for the purposes of section 29 of the Youth Justice and Criminal Evidence Act 1999[10] (Examination of witness through intermediary),

      (ii) approved by the court for the purposes of section 33BA of the 1999 Act[11] (Examination of accused through intermediary),

      (iii) asked to assess a defendant's communication needs, or

      (iv) appointed by the court to facilitate a defendant's effective participation in the trial, when the defendant gives evidence or at any other time, where otherwise that defendant's communication needs would impede such participation; and

      (b) a reference to 'an intermediary's report' means a report by such a person which complies with rule 18.28.

---

[3] 1999 c. 23; section 25 was amended by paragraphs 1 and 3 of the Schedule to S.I. 2013/554 and section 46 of the Modern Slavery Act 2015 (c. 30).

[4] 1999 c. 23; section 27 was amended by paragraph 384 of Schedule 8 to the Courts Act 2003 (c. 39), paragraph 73 of Schedule 3 and Part 4 of Schedule 37 to the Criminal Justice Act 2003 (c. 44) and sections 102(2), 103(1), (3), (4) and (5), 177(1) and (2) and 178 of, and paragraph 73 of Schedule 21, paragraph 23 of Schedule 22 and Part 3 of Schedule 23 to, the Coroners and Justice Act 2009 (c. 25).

[5] 1999 c. 23; section 29 was amended by paragraph 384(d) of Schedule 8 to the Courts Act 2003 (c. 39).

[6] 1999 c. 23; section 20(6) was amended by paragraph 384(a) of Schedule 8 to the Courts Act 2003 (c. 39).

[7] 1999 c. 23; sections 33BA and 33BB are inserted by section 104 of the Coroners and Justice Act 2009 (c. 25), with effect from a date to be appointed.

[8] 2009 c. 25.

[9] 1999 c. 23.

[10] 1999 c. 23; section 29 was amended by paragraph 384 of Schedule 8 to the Courts Act 2003 (c. 39).

[11] 1999 c. 23; section 33BA is inserted by section 104(1) of the Coroners and Justice Act 2009 (c. 25), with effect from a date to be appointed.

Making an application for a direction or order   R18.4

18.4   A party who wants the court to exercise its power to give or make a direction or order must—

    (a) apply in writing as soon as reasonably practicable, and in any event not more than—

        (i)   20 business days after the defendant pleads not guilty, in a magistrates' court, or

        (ii) 10 business days after the defendant pleads not guilty, in the Crown Court; and

    (b) serve the application on—

        (i)   the court officer, and

        (ii) each other party.

[Note. See also rule 18.10 (Content of application for a special measures direction), rule 18.15 (Content of application for a defendant's evidence direction), rule 18.19 (Content and conduct of application for a witness anonymity order) and rule 18.23 (Appointment of intermediary to facilitate a defendant's participation).

The Practice Direction sets out a form for use in connection with an application under rule 18.10 for a special measures direction.]

Decisions and reasons   R18.5

18.5   (1) A party who wants to introduce the evidence of a witness who is the subject of an application, direction or order must—

    (a) inform the witness of the court's decision as soon as reasonably practicable; and

    (b) explain to the witness the arrangements that as a result will be made for him or her to give evidence.

    (2) The court must—

    (a) promptly determine an application; and

    (b) allow a party sufficient time to comply with the requirements of—

        (i)   paragraph (1), and

        (ii) the code of practice issued under section 32 of the Domestic Violence, Crime and Victims Act 2004[12].

    (3) The court must announce, at a hearing in public before the witness gives evidence or the defendant's trial begins (as the case may be), the reasons for a decision—

    (a) to give, make, vary or discharge—

        (i)   a special measures direction for a witness, or

        (ii) a direction to help a defendant to participate in that defendant's trial; or

    (b) to refuse to do so.

    (4) Where the court can give, vary or rescind a live link direction the court must—

    (a) announce the reasons for a decision not to give such a direction; and

    (b) in the case of a live link direction for a sentencing hearing, announce the reasons for a decision to rescind that direction.

    (5) Where the court gives a direction for everyone taking part in a hearing to do so by live link the court must announce the reasons for a decision—

    (a) not to direct that the proceedings are to be broadcast, within the meaning of section 85A of the Courts Act 2003[13] (Enabling the public to see and hear proceedings); or

    (b) not to direct that a recording of the proceedings is to be made, within the meaning of that section of that Act.

[Note. See sections 20(5) and 33BB(4) of the Youth Justice and Criminal Evidence Act 1999[14], sections 57B(6), 57E(8) and 57F(9) of the Crime and Disorder Act 1998 and section 51(8) of the Criminal Justice Act 2003.

Under section 32 of the Domestic Violence, Crime and Victims Act 2004, the Secretary of State for Justice must issue a code of practice as to the services to be provided by specified persons to a victim of criminal conduct.]

Under section 85A of the Courts Act 2003, if the court directs that proceedings are to be conducted wholly by live video or live audio link the court may direct (i) that the proceedings are to be broadcast for the purpose of enabling members of the public to see and hear, or to hear, those proceedings (as the case may be), and (ii) that a recording of the proceedings is to be made for the purpose of enabling the court to keep an audio-visual, or audio, record of the proceedings (as the case may be).]

Criminal Procedure Rules

---

[12] 2004 c. 28; section 32 was amended by article 8 of, and paragraph 10 of the Schedule to, S.I. 2007/2128.

[13] 2003 c. 39; section 85A was temporarily inserted by section 55 of, and paragraph 1 of Schedule 25 to, the Coronavirus Act 2020 (c. 7).

[14] 1999 c. 23; section 20 was amended by paragraph 384(a) of Schedule 8 to the Courts Act 2003 (c. 39). Section 33A was inserted by section 47 of the Police and Justice Act 2006 (c. 48). Section 33BB is inserted by section 104 of the Coroners and Justice Act 2009 (c. 25), with effect from a date to be appointed.

R18.6   **Court's power to vary requirements under this Part**

18.6 (1) The court may—

    (a) shorten or extend (even after it has expired) a time limit under this Part; and

    (b) allow an application or representations to be made in a different form to one set out in the Practice Direction, or to be made orally.

  (2) A person who wants an extension of time must—

    (a) apply when serving the application or representations for which it is needed; and

    (b) explain the delay.

R18.7   **Custody of documents**

18.7 Unless the court otherwise directs, the court officer may—

    (a) keep a written application or representations; or

    (b) arrange for the whole or any part to be kept by some other appropriate person, subject to any conditions that the court may impose.

Special measures directions

R18.8   **Exercise of court's powers**

18.8 (1) The court may decide whether to give, vary or discharge a special measures direction—

    (a) at a hearing, in public or in private, or without a hearing; and

    (b) in a party's absence, if that party—

      (i) applied for the direction, variation or discharge, or

      (ii) has had at least 10 business days in which to make representations.

  (2) Where a direction provides for evidence to be admitted under section 28 of the Youth Justice and Criminal Evidence Act 1999[15] (Video recorded cross-examination or re-examination) the court must set a timetable that provides for—

    (a) the date of any ground rules hearing under rule 3.9;

    (b) the date on which the cross-examination and any re-examination will be recorded; and

    (c) the date by which any application under section 28(5) of the 1999 Act must be made for a direction for further cross-examination or re-examination.

R18.9   **Special measures direction without application**

18.9 (1) This rule applies where—

    (a) a party notifies the court that a witness is eligible for assistance under section 16 or section 17 of the Youth Justice and Criminal Evidence Act 1999;

    (b) the notice is given at—

      (i) a preparation for trial hearing in a magistrates' court, or

      (ii) a plea and trial preparation hearing in the Crown Court; and

    (c) no other party opposes the giving of a special measures direction for the benefit of that witness.

  (2) The court may exercise its power to give a special measures direction without requiring an application under rule 18.10.

  (3) The party who gives the notice must—

    (a) provide any information that the court may need to assess—

      (i) the measure or measures likely to maximise so far as practicable the quality of the witness' evidence, and

      (ii) the witness' own views; and

    (b) where a direction provides for video recorded evidence to be admitted under section 27 of the Youth Justice and Criminal Evidence Act 1999, as soon as reasonably practicable serve such evidence on—

      (i) the court officer, and

      (ii) each other party.

[Note. Under sections 21 and 22 of the Youth Justice and Criminal Evidence Act 1999, a 'child witness' is one who is under 18, and a 'qualifying witness' is one who was a child witness when interviewed.

Under those sections, the 'primary rule' requires the court to give a direction—

    (a) for the evidence of a child witness or of a qualifying witness to be admitted—

    (b) by means of a video recording of an interview with the witness, in the place of examination-in-chief, and

    (c) after that, by live link; or

    (d) if one or both of those measures is not taken, for the witness while giving evidence to be screened from seeing the defendant.

[15] 1999 c. 23; section 8 was amended by section 109 of, and paragraph 384 of Schedule 8 to, the Courts Act 2003 (c. 39).

The primary rule always applies unless—

   (a) *the witness does not want it to apply, and the court is satisfied that to omit a measure usually required by that rule would not diminish the quality of the witness' evidence; or*
   (b) *the court is satisfied that to direct one of the measures usually required by that rule would not be likely to maximise, so far as practicable, the quality of the witness' evidence.]*

Content of application for a special measures direction   R18.10

18.10 An applicant for a special measures direction must—
   (a) explain how the witness is eligible for assistance;
   (b) explain why special measures would be likely to improve the quality of the witness' evidence;
   (c) propose the measure or measures that in the applicant's opinion would be likely to maximise, so far as practicable, the quality of that evidence;
   (d) report any views that the witness has expressed about—
      (i) his or her eligibility for assistance,
      (ii) the likelihood that special measures would improve the quality of his or her evidence, and
      (iii) the measure or measures proposed by the applicant;
   (e) in a case in which a child witness or a qualifying witness does not want the primary rule to apply, provide any information that the court may need to assess the witness' views;
   (f) in a case in which the applicant proposes that the witness should give evidence by live link—
      (i) identify someone to accompany the witness while the witness gives evidence,
      (ii) name that person, if possible, and
      (iii) explain why that person would be an appropriate companion for the witness, including the witness' own views;
   (g) in a case in which the applicant proposes the admission of video recorded evidence, identify—
      (i) the date and duration of the recording, and
      (ii) which part the applicant wants the court to admit as evidence, if the applicant does not want the court to admit all of it;
   (h) attach any other material on which the applicant relies; and
   (i) if the applicant wants a hearing, ask for one, and explain why it is needed.

[Note. The Practice Direction sets out a form of application for use in connection with this rule.]

Application to vary or discharge a special measures direction   R18.11

18.11 (1) A party who wants the court to vary or discharge a special measures direction must—
   (a) apply in writing, as soon as reasonably practicable after becoming aware of the grounds for doing so; and
   (b) serve the application on—
      (i) the court officer, and
      (ii) each other party.
   (2) The applicant must—
   (a) explain what material circumstances have changed since the direction was given (or last varied, if applicable);
   (b) explain why the direction should be varied or discharged; and
   (c) ask for a hearing, if the applicant wants one, and explain why it is needed.

[Note. Under section 20 of the Youth Justice and Criminal Evidence Act 1999, the court can vary or discharge a special measures direction—

   (a) *on application, if there has been a material change of circumstances; or*
   (b) *on the court's own initiative.]*

Application containing information withheld from another party   R18.12

18.12 (1) This rule applies where—
   (a) an applicant serves an application for a special measures direction, or for its variation or discharge; and
   (b) the application includes information that the applicant thinks ought not be revealed to another party.
   (2) The applicant must—
   (a) omit that information from the part of the application that is served on that other party;
   (b) mark the other part to show that, unless the court otherwise directs, it is only for the court; and
   (c) in that other part, explain why the applicant has withheld that information from that other party.
   (3) Any hearing of an application to which this rule applies—
   (a) must be in private, unless the court otherwise directs; and

(b) if the court so directs, may be, wholly or in part, in the absence of a party from whom information has been withheld.

(4) At any hearing of an application to which this rule applies—

    (a) the general rule is that the court must consider, in the following sequence—

        (i) representations first by the applicant and then by each other party, in all the parties' presence, and then

        (ii) further representations by the applicant, in the absence of a party from whom information has been withheld; but

    (b) the court may direct other arrangements for the hearing.

[Note. See section 20 of the Youth Justice and Criminal Evidence Act 1999.]

R18.13 **Representations in response**

18.13 (1) This rule applies where a party wants to make representations about—

    (a) an application for a special measures direction;

    (b) an application for the variation or discharge of such a direction; or

    (c) a direction, variation or discharge that the court proposes on its own initiative.

(2) Such a party must—

    (a) serve the representations on—

        (i) the court officer, and

        (ii) each other party;

    (b) do so not more than 10 business days after, as applicable—

        (i) service of the application, or

        (ii) notice of the direction, variation or discharge that the court proposes; and

    (c) ask for a hearing, if that party wants one, and explain why it is needed.

(3) Where representations include information that the person making them thinks ought not be revealed to another party, that person must—

    (a) omit that information from the representations served on that other party;

    (b) mark the information to show that, unless the court otherwise directs, it is only for the court; and

    (c) with that information include an explanation of why it has been withheld from that other party.

(4) Representations against a special measures direction must explain, as appropriate—

    (a) why the witness is not eligible for assistance;

    (b) if the witness is eligible for assistance, why—

        (i) no special measure would be likely to improve the quality of the witness' evidence,

        (ii) the proposed measure or measures would not be likely to maximise, so far as practicable, the quality of the witness' evidence, or

        (iii) the proposed measure or measures might tend to inhibit the effective testing of that evidence; and

    (c) in a case in which the admission of video recorded evidence is proposed, why it would not be in the interests of justice for the recording, or part of it, to be admitted as evidence.

(5) Representations against the variation or discharge of a special measures direction must explain why it should not be varied or discharged.

[Note. Under sections 21 and 22 of the Youth Justice and Criminal Evidence Act 1999, where the witness is a child witness or a qualifying witness the special measures that the court usually must direct must be treated as likely to maximise, so far as practicable, the quality of the witness' evidence, irrespective of representations to the contrary.]

Defendant's evidence directions

R18.14 **Exercise of court's powers**

18.14 The court may decide whether to give, vary or discharge a defendant's evidence direction—

    (a) at a hearing, in public or in private, or without a hearing; and

    (b) in a party's absence, if that party—

        (i) applied for the direction, variation or discharge, or

        (ii) has had at least 10 business days in which to make representations.

R18.15 **Content of application for a defendant's evidence direction**

18.15 An applicant for a defendant's evidence direction must—

    (a) explain how the proposed direction meets the conditions prescribed by the Youth Justice and Criminal Evidence Act 1999; and

    (b) ask for a hearing, if the applicant wants one, and explain why it is needed.

[Note. See section 33BA of the Youth Justice and Criminal Evidence Act 1999.]

Application to vary or discharge a defendant's evidence direction   R18.16

18.16 (1) A party who wants the court to vary or discharge a defendant's evidence direction must—

    (a) apply in writing, as soon as reasonably practicable after becoming aware of the grounds for doing so; and

    (b) serve the application on—

      (i) the court officer, and

      (ii) each other party.

(2) The applicant must—

    (a) on an application to discharge a direction for an intermediary, explain why it is no longer necessary in order to ensure that the defendant receives a fair trial;

    (b) on an application to vary a direction for an intermediary, explain why it is necessary for the direction to be varied in order to ensure that the defendant receives a fair trial; and

    (c) ask for a hearing, if the applicant wants one, and explain why it is needed.

[Note. See section 33BB of the Youth Justice and Criminal Evidence Act 1999.]

Representations in response   R18.17

18.17 (1) This rule applies where a party wants to make representations about—

    (a) an application for a defendant's evidence direction;

    (b) an application for the variation or discharge of such a direction; or

    (c) a direction, variation or discharge that the court proposes on its own initiative.

(2) Such a party must—

    (a) serve the representations on—

      (i) the court officer, and

      (ii) each other party;

    (b) do so not more than 10 business days after, as applicable—

      (i) service of the application, or

      (ii) notice of the direction, variation or discharge that the court proposes; and

    (c) ask for a hearing, if that party wants one, and explain why it is needed.

(3) Representations against a direction, variation or discharge must explain why the conditions prescribed by the Youth Justice and Criminal Evidence Act 1999 are not met.

Witness anonymity orders

Exercise of court's powers   R18.18

18.18 (1) The court may decide whether to make, vary or discharge a witness anonymity order—

    (a) at a hearing (which must be in private, unless the court otherwise directs), or without a hearing (unless any party asks for one); and

    (b) in the absence of a defendant.

(2) The court must not exercise its power to make, vary or discharge a witness anonymity order, or to refuse to do so—

    (a) before or during the trial, unless each party has had an opportunity to make representations;

    (b) on an appeal by the defendant to which applies Part 34 (Appeal to the Crown Court) or Part 39 (Appeal to the Court of Appeal about conviction or sentence), unless in each party's case—

      (i) that party has had an opportunity to make representations, or

      (ii) the appeal court is satisfied that it is not reasonably practicable to communicate with that party;

    (c) after the trial and any such appeal are over, unless in the case of each party and the witness—

      (i) each has had an opportunity to make representations, or

      (ii) the court is satisfied that it is not reasonably practicable to communicate with that party or witness.

Content and conduct of application for a witness anonymity order   R18.19

18.19 (1) An applicant for a witness anonymity order must—

    (a) include in the application nothing that might reveal the witness' identity;

    (b) describe the measures proposed by the applicant;

    (c) explain how the proposed order meets the conditions prescribed by section 88 of the Coroners and Justice Act 2009[16];

    (d) explain why no measures other than those proposed will suffice, such as—

      (i) an admission of the facts that would be proved by the witness,

---

[16] 2009 c. 25.

(ii) an order restricting public access to the trial,

(iii) reporting restrictions, in particular under sections 45, 45A or 46 of the Youth Justice and Criminal Evidence Act 1999[17],

(iv) a direction for a special measure under section 19 of the Youth Justice and Criminal Evidence Act 1999,

(v) introduction of the witness' written statement as hearsay evidence, under section 116 of the Criminal Justice Act 2003[18], or

(vi) arrangements for the protection of the witness;

(e) attach to the application—

(i) a witness statement setting out the proposed evidence, edited in such a way as not to reveal the witness' identity,

(ii) where the prosecutor is the applicant, any further prosecution evidence to be served, and any further prosecution material to be disclosed under the Criminal Procedure and Investigations Act 1996, similarly edited, and

(iii) any defence statement that has been served, or as much information as may be available to the applicant that gives particulars of the defence; and

(f) ask for a hearing, if the applicant wants one.

(2) At any hearing of the application, the applicant must—

(a) identify the witness to the court, unless at the prosecutor's request the court otherwise directs; and

(b) present to the court, unless it otherwise directs—

(i) the unedited witness statement from which the edited version has been prepared,

(ii) where the prosecutor is the applicant, the unedited version of any further prosecution evidence or material from which an edited version has been prepared, and

(iii) such further material as the applicant relies on to establish that the proposed order meets the conditions prescribed by section 88 of the 2009 Act.

(3) At any such hearing—

(a) the general rule is that the court must consider, in the following sequence—

(i) representations first by the applicant and then by each other party, in all the parties' presence, and then

(ii) information withheld from a defendant, and further representations by the applicant, in the absence of any (or any other) defendant; but

(b) the court may direct other arrangements for the hearing.

(4) Before the witness gives evidence, the applicant must identify the witness to the court—

(a) if not already done;

(b) without revealing the witness' identity to any other party or person; and

(c) unless at the prosecutor's request the court otherwise directs.

R18.20　Duty of court officer to notify the Director of Public Prosecutions

18.20 The court officer must notify the Director of Public Prosecutions of an application, unless the prosecutor is, or acts on behalf of, a public authority.

R18.21　Application to vary or discharge a witness anonymity order

18.21 (1) A party who wants the court to vary or discharge a witness anonymity order, or a witness who wants the court to do so when the case is over, must—

(a) apply in writing, as soon as reasonably practicable after becoming aware of the grounds for doing so; and

(b) serve the application on—

(i) the court officer, and

(ii) each other party.

(2) The applicant must—

(a) explain what material circumstances have changed since the order was made (or last varied, if applicable);

(b) explain why the order should be varied or discharged, taking account of the conditions for making an order; and

(c) ask for a hearing, if the applicant wants one.

(3) Where an application includes information that the applicant thinks might reveal the witness' identity, the applicant must—

(a) omit that information from the application that is served on a defendant;

[17] 1999 c. 23; section 45A was inserted by section 78 of the Criminal Justice and Courts Act 2015 (c. 2).
[18] 2003 c. 44.

(b) mark the information to show that it is only for the court and the prosecutor (if the prosecutor is not the applicant); and

(c) with that information include an explanation of why it has been withheld.

(4) Where a party applies to vary or discharge a witness anonymity order after the trial and any appeal are over, the party who introduced the witness' evidence must serve the application on the witness.

[Note. Under sections 91, 92 and 93 of the Coroners and Justice Act 2009, the court can vary or discharge a witness anonymity order—

(a) on an application, if there has been a material change of circumstances since it was made or previously varied; or

(b) on the court's own initiative, unless the trial and any appeal are over.]

Representations in response   R18.22

18.22 (1) This rule applies where a party or, where the case is over, a witness, wants to make representations about—

(a) an application for a witness anonymity order;

(b) an application for the variation or discharge of such an order; or

(c) a variation or discharge that the court proposes on its own initiative.

(2) Such a party or witness must—

(a) serve the representations on—

(i) the court officer, and

(ii) each other party;

(b) do so not more than 10 business days after, as applicable—

(i) service of the application, or

(ii) notice of the variation or discharge that the court proposes; and

(c) ask for a hearing, if that party or witness wants one.

(3) Where representations include information that the person making them thinks might reveal the witness' identity, that person must—

(a) omit that information from the representations served on a defendant;

(b) mark the information to show that it is only for the court (and for the prosecutor, if relevant); and

(c) with that information include an explanation of why it has been withheld.

(4) Representations against a witness anonymity order must explain why the conditions for making the order are not met.

(5) Representations against the variation or discharge of such an order must explain why it would not be appropriate to vary or discharge it, taking account of the conditions for making an order.

(6) A prosecutor's representations in response to an application by a defendant must include all information available to the prosecutor that is relevant to the conditions and considerations specified by sections 88 and 89 of the Coroners and Justice Act 2009.

Intermediary for a defendant
Appointment of intermediary to facilitate a defendant's participation   R18.23

18.23 (1) The court must exercise its power to appoint an intermediary to facilitate a defendant's effective participation in the trial where—

(a) the defendant's ability to participate is likely to be diminished by reason of—

(i) age, if the defendant is under 18, or

(ii) mental disorder (as defined in section 1(2) of the Mental Health Act 1983[19]), a significant impairment of intelligence and social functioning, or a physical disability or disorder; and

(b) the appointment is necessary for that purpose.

(2) In determining whether such an appointment is necessary, who to appoint and the duration or purpose of the appointment, the court must have regard to—

(a) the defendant's communication needs as reported to the court;

(b) the recommendations in any intermediary's report received by the court;

(c) any views that the defendant has expressed about—

(i) receiving the assistance of an intermediary,

(ii) other measures or arrangements to facilitate the defendant's effective participation in the trial;

---

[19] 1983 c. 20; section 1(2) was amended by sections 1, 55 and 56 of, and Schedule 11 to, the Mental Health Act 2007 (c. 12).

(d) the likely impact of the defendant's age, if under 18, level of intellectual ability or social functioning on the ability to—
   (i) give evidence, and
   (ii) understand what is said and done by the court and other participants;
(e) the likely impact on such participation and on such understanding of any mental disorder or other significant impairment of intelligence or social functioning;
(f) the adequacy of arrangements for questioning the defendant in the absence of an intermediary;
(g) any assistance that the defendant has received in the past—
   (i) while giving evidence in legal proceedings,
   (ii) while being questioned during the investigation of an alleged offence, or
   (iii) as a defendant in a criminal case;
(h) any assessment of the defendant's health by a mental health practitioner acting independently of the parties to assist the court;
(i) any expert medical opinion that the court may have received; and
(j) any other matter that the court thinks relevant.

(3) The court may exercise its power to appoint an intermediary—
   (a) for the duration of every hearing that the defendant is due to attend;
   (b) for the duration of any specified such hearing or hearings, or for the duration of a specified part of such a hearing; or
   (c) for a specified purpose during a hearing.

(4) Unless the court otherwise directs, the appointment of an intermediary extends to facilitating the defendant's communication with that defendant's legal representatives for the duration and for the purpose of the appointment.

(5) The court may decide whether to appoint an intermediary to facilitate a defendant's effective participation in the trial and whether to vary or discharge any such appointment—
   (a) on application or on the court's own initiative;
   (b) at a hearing, in public or in private, or without a hearing; and
   (c) in a party's absence, if that party—
      (i) applied for the appointment, variation or discharge, or
      (ii) has had at least 10 business days in which to make representations.

(6) The court must not exercise its power to vary or discharge a direction for the appointment of an intermediary unless satisfied that—
   (a) since the direction was made—
      (i) the defendant's communication needs have changed materially, or
      (ii) any other material circumstance has changed materially; and
   (b) the defendant will be able to participate effectively in the trial despite the variation or discharge of the direction.

R18.24 Application to vary or discharge the appointment of an intermediary for a defendant

18.24 (1) A party who wants the court to vary or discharge the appointment of an intermediary to facilitate a defendant's effective participation in the trial must—
   (a) apply in writing, as soon as reasonably practicable after becoming aware of the grounds for doing so; and
   (b) serve the application on—
      (i) the court officer, and
      (ii) each other party.

(2) The applicant must—
   (a) explain how the criteria listed in rule 18.23(6) are met (variation or discharge of appointment); and
   (b) ask for a hearing, if the applicant wants one, and explain why it is needed.

R18.25 Representations in response to application or proposal

18.25 (1) This rule applies where a party wants to make representations about—
   (a) an application or proposal for the appointment of an intermediary to facilitate a defendant's effective participation in the trial; or
   (b) an application or proposal for the variation or discharge of such an appointment.

(2) Such a party must—
   (a) serve the representations on—
      (i) the court officer, and
      (ii) each other party;

    (b) do so not more than 10 business days after, as applicable—
         (i)   service of the application, or
         (ii) notice of the appointment, variation or discharge that the court proposes; and
    (c) ask for a hearing, if that party wants one, and explain why it is needed.
(3) Representations against such an appointment, variation or discharge must explain why the
     criteria that apply are not met.

Duties of Intermediaries

Intermediary's duty to the court   R18.26

18.26 (1) This rule applies to an intermediary who accepts—
    (a) approval by the court for the purposes of section 29 of the Youth Justice and Criminal
         Evidence Act 1999[20] (Examination of witness through intermediary);
    (b) approval by the court for the purposes of section 33BA of the 1999 Act[21] (Examination of
         accused through intermediary); or
    (c) appointment by the court to facilitate a defendant's effective participation in the trial,
         when the defendant gives evidence or at any other time.
(2) The intermediary must help the court to achieve the overriding objective—
    (a) to the best of the intermediary's skill and understanding by—
         (i)   communicating to the witness or defendant (as the case may be) questions put to
               them,
         (ii) communicating to the questioner and the court the replies, and
         (iii) explaining such questions and answers so that they can be understood;
    (b) by assessing continually the witness' or the defendant's (as the case may be) ability to
         participate effectively and intervening if necessary;
    (c) where the intermediary is appointed to facilitate a defendant's effective participation, by
         explaining to the defendant, in terms the defendant can understand, what is said and done
         by the court and other participants; and
    (d) by actively assisting the court in fulfilling its duties under rule 3.2 (Case management;
         The duty of the court) and rule 3.9 (Case management; Ground rules hearing), in
         particular by—
         (i)   complying with directions made by the court, and
         (ii) at once informing the court of any significant failure (by the intermediary or another)
               to take any step required by such a direction.
(3) This duty overrides any obligation to the witness or to the defendant (as the case may be),
     or to the person by whom the intermediary is paid.

Declaration by intermediary   R18.27

18.27 (1) This rule applies where—
    (a) a video recorded interview with a witness is conducted through an intermediary; or
    (b) the court directs the examination of a witness or defendant through an intermediary.
(2) The intermediary must make a declaration—
    (a) before such an interview begins; and
    (b) before the examination begins (even if such an interview with the witness was conducted
         through the same intermediary).
(3) The declaration must be in these terms, or in any corresponding terms that the intermediary
     declares to be binding—

     "I swear by Almighty God [or I solemnly, sincerely and truly declare and affirm] that I shall
     faithfully communicate questions and answers and make true explanation of all matters and
     things required of me according to the best of my skill and understanding."

Content of intermediary's report   R18.28

18.28 (1) An intermediary's report must, in every case—
    (a) give details of the intermediary's qualifications, relevant experience and any accreditation;
    (b) identify the commissioner of the report;
    (c) identify those from whom the intermediary has obtained information material to the
         report;

---

[20] 1999 c. 23; section 29 was amended by paragraph 384 of Schedule 8 to the Courts Act 2003 (c. 39).
[21] 1999 c. 23; section 33BA is inserted by section 104(1) of the Coroners and Justice Act 2009 (c. 25), with effect from a date
to be appointed.

Criminal Procedure Rules

    (d) list the documents received or inspected by the intermediary which contained such information and give an indication of their content;

    (e) give the date or dates on which the intermediary met the witness or defendant, as the case may be, for the purpose of preparing the report;

    (f) describe the nature and duration of the intermediary's assessment, or assessments, of the witness or defendant;

    (g) by reference to examples drawn from the intermediary's assessment of the witness or defendant explain why in this particular case intermediary assistance is necessary;

    (h) include an evaluation of—

      (i) the impact of any condition or conditions which, whether in isolation or together, may adversely affect the witness' or the defendant's ability to communicate, and

      (ii) the extent, if any, to which that impact may be exacerbated by the trial;

    (i) if the intermediary is not able to reach an evaluation without qualifying it, state the qualification;

    (j) report the views of the witness or defendant, as the case may be, on receiving the assistance of an intermediary;

    (k) include in a summary of the intermediary's conclusions any recommendation, with reasons, for—

      (i) the approval or appointment of an intermediary,

      (ii) the manner and duration of any questioning of the witness or defendant, as the case may be, and

      (iii) arrangements for the way in which the intermediary, if approved or appointed, should participate; and

    (l) contain a statement that the intermediary—

      (i) understands an intermediary's duty to the court, and

      (ii) will comply with that duty if approved or appointed.

(2) Where the intermediary is asked to evaluate a defendant's communication needs the report must also—

    (a) include an evaluation of the extent to which any measures or arrangements beside the appointment of an intermediary will facilitate the defendant's effective participation in the trial; and

    (b) in the summary of the intermediary's conclusions include any recommendation, with reasons, for—

      (i) the duration and purpose of any appointment of an intermediary, and

      (ii) other measures or arrangements to help the defendant to participate effectively in the trial

Summary of eligibility for measures to which this Part applies

Special measures direction

Under section 16 of the Youth Justice and Criminal Evidence Act 1999[22], a witness is eligible for the assistance of a special measures direction given under section 19 of that Act if—

    (a) the witness is under 18; or

    (b) the witness has—

      (i) a mental disorder, or a significant impairment of intelligence and social functioning, or

      (ii) a physical disability or disorder

and the court considers that the completeness, coherence and accuracy (the 'quality') of evidence given by the witness is likely to be diminished by reason of those circumstances.

Under section 17 of the 1999 Act[23], a witness is eligible for such assistance if—

    (a) the court is satisfied that the quality of evidence given by the witness is likely to be diminished because of his or her fear or distress in connection with giving evidence, taking account particularly of—

      (i) the circumstances of the offence,

      (ii) the witness' age, social and cultural background, ethnic origins, domestic and employment circumstances, religious beliefs or political opinions,

      (iii) any behaviour towards the witness on the part of the defendant, the defendant's family or associates, or any other potential defendant or witness, and

      (iv) the witness' own views;

[22] 1999 c. 23.
[23] 1999 c. 23; section 17 was amended by section 99 of the Coroners and Justice Act 2009 (c. 25), paragraphs 1 and 2 of the Schedule to S.I. 2013/554 and section 46 of the Modern Slavery Act 2015 (c. 30).

(b) the witness is the complainant in respect of a sexual offence or other offence specified by the Act, and has not declined such assistance; or

(c) the offence is one of a list of offences involving weapons, and the witness has not declined such assistance.

Section 28 of the 1999 Act (video recorded cross-examination or re-examination) is not yet fully in force. With that exception, all the special measures listed in rule 18.1 potentially are available where the witness is eligible for assistance under section 16 of the Act. Those numbered (i) to (v) are available where the witness is eligible for assistance under section 17.

As a general rule, but with exceptions, the court must give a special measures direction—

(a) *under section 21 or 22 of the 1999 Act[24], where the witness—*

(i) *is under 18, or*

(ii) *was under that age when interviewed whether or not an application for a direction is made;*

(b) *under section 22A of the 1999 Act[25], where an application is made in the Crown Court for the evidence of a witness who is the complainant of a sexual offence to be admitted by means of a video recording of an interview with the witness in the place of examination-in-chief.*

Defendant's evidence direction

When the Coroners and Justice Act 2009(3) comes into force, under section 33BA of the 1999 Act the court can allow a defendant to give evidence through an intermediary if—

(a) *the defendant—*

(i) *is under 18, and the defendant's ability to participate effectively as a witness giving oral evidence is compromised by his or her level of intellectual ability or social functioning; or*

(ii) *suffers from a mental disorder or some other significant impairment of intelligence and social functioning and cannot participate effectively as a witness giving oral evidence for that reason; and*

(b) *the examination of the defendant through an intermediary is necessary to ensure that the defendant receives a fair trial.*

Witness anonymity order

Under section 86 of the Coroners and Justice Act 2009[26], a witness anonymity order is an order that specifies measures to be taken to ensure that the identity of a witness is not disclosed, such as withholding the witness' name from materials disclosed to a party to the proceedings, the use of a pseudonym, the screening of the witness from view, the modulation of the witness' voice, and the prohibition of questions that might reveal his or her identity. Before making such an order, the court must—

(a) *be satisfied that three conditions prescribed by the Act are met (section 88 of the 2009 Act); and*

(b) *have regard to considerations specified by the Act (section 89 of the 2009 Act).*

Intermediary for a defendant

In order to ensure the defendant's effective participation in his or her trial the court has an inherent power to appoint an intermediary to facilitate that participation, including during the giving of evidence by the defendant.

CRIMINAL PROCEDURE RULES   PART 19   EXPERT EVIDENCE

When this Part applies   R19.1

19.1 (1) This Part applies where a party wants to introduce expert opinion evidence.

(2) A reference to an 'expert' in this Part is a reference to a person who is required to give or prepare expert evidence for the purpose of criminal proceedings, including evidence required to determine fitness to plead or for the purpose of sentencing.

(3) Where evidence that is introduced as evidence of fact within a witness' direct knowledge includes expert opinion the court may direct that the requirements of rules 19.2 (Expert's duty to the court) and 19.3 (Introduction of expert evidence) apply, to the extent and with such adaptations as the court directs.

---

[24] 1999 c. 23; sections 21 and 22 were amended by sections 98, 100 and 178 of, and Part 3 of Schedule 23 to, the Coroners and Justice Act 2009 (c. 25).

[25] 1999 c. 23; section 22A was inserted by section 101 of the Coroners and Justice Act 2009 (c. 25).

[26] 2009 c. 25.

[Note. Expert medical evidence may be required to determine fitness to plead under section 4 of the Criminal Procedure (Insanity) Act 1964[1]. It may be required also under section 11 of the Powers of Criminal Courts (Sentencing) Act 2000[2], under Part III of the Mental Health Act 1983[3] or under Part 12 of the Criminal Justice Act 2003[4]. Those Acts contain requirements about the qualification of medical experts.]

R19.2   Expert's duty to the court

19.2   (1)   An expert must help the court to achieve the overriding objective —
        (a)   by giving opinion which is—
            (i)   objective and unbiased, and
            (ii)   within the expert's area or areas of expertise; and
        (b)   by actively assisting the court in fulfilling its duty of case management under rule 3.2, in particular by—
            (i)   complying with directions made by the court, and
            (iii)   at once informing the court of any significant failure (by the expert or another) to take any step required by such a direction.
    (2)   This duty overrides any obligation to the person from whom the expert receives instructions or by whom the expert is paid.
    (3)   This duty includes obligations—
        (a)   to define the expert's area or areas of expertise—
            (i)   in the expert's report, and
            (ii)   when giving evidence in person;
        (b)   when giving evidence in person, to draw the court's attention to any question to which the answer would be outside the expert's area or areas of expertise;
        (c)   inform all parties and the court if the expert's opinion changes from that contained in a report served as evidence or given in a statement; and
        (d)   to disclose to the party for whom the expert's evidence is commissioned anything—
            (i)   of which the expert is aware, and
            (ii)   of which that party, if aware of it, would be required to give notice under rule 19.3(3)(c).

[Note. The Practice Direction lists examples of matters that should be disclosed under this rule and rule 19.3(3)(c).]

R19.3   Introduction of expert evidence

19.3   (1)   A party who wants another party to admit as fact a summary of an expert's conclusions must serve that summary—
        (a)   on the court officer and on each party from whom that admission is sought; and
        (b)   as soon as practicable after the defendant whom it affects pleads not guilty.
    (2)   A party on whom such a summary is served must—
        (a)   serve a response stating—
            (i)   which, if any, of the expert's conclusions are admitted as fact, and
            (ii)   where a conclusion is not admitted, what are the disputed issues concerning that conclusion; and
        (b)   serve the response—
            (i)   on the court officer and on the party who served the summary, and
            (ii)   as soon as practicable, and in any event not more than 10 business days after service of the summary.
    (3)   A party who wants to introduce expert evidence otherwise than as admitted fact must—
        (a)   serve a report by the expert which complies with rule 19.4 (Content of expert's report) on—
            (i)   the court officer, and
            (ii)   each other party;
         (b)   serve the report as soon as practicable, and in any event with any application in support of which that party relies on that evidence;
        (c)   serve with the report—
            (i)   notice of anything of which the party serving it is aware which might reasonably be thought capable of undermining the reliability of the expert's opinion, or detracting from the credibility or impartiality of the expert, and

---

[1]   1964 c. 84; section 4 was substituted, together with section 4A, for section 4 as originally enacted, by section 2 of the Criminal Procedure (Insanity and Unfitness to Plead) Act 1991 (c. 25), and amended by section 22 of the Domestic Violence, Crime and Victims Act 2004 (c. 28).
[2]   2000 c. 6.
[3]   1983 c. 20.
[4]   2003 c. 44.

(ii) an explanation of how facts stated in the report are admissible as evidence if that is not explained by the report;

(d) if another party so requires, give that party a copy of, or a reasonable opportunity to inspect—

    (i) a record of any examination, measurement, test or experiment on which the expert's findings and opinion are based, or that were carried out in the course of reaching those findings and opinion, and

    (ii) anything on which any such examination, measurement, test or experiment was carried out.

(4) Unless the parties otherwise agree or the court directs, a party may not—

(a) introduce expert evidence if that party has not complied with paragraph (3); or

(b) introduce in evidence an expert report if the expert does not give evidence in person.

[Note. The Practice Direction sets out a form of notice for use in connection with this rule.

A party who accepts another party's expert's conclusions may admit them as fact under section 10 of the Criminal Justice Act 1967[5].

Under section 81 of the Police and Criminal Evidence Act 1984[6], and under section 20(3) of the Criminal Procedure and Investigations Act 1996[7], Criminal Procedure Rules may require the disclosure of expert evidence before it is introduced as part of a party's case and prohibit its introduction without the court's permission, if it was not disclosed as required.

Evidence of facts which are material to the opinions expressed in an expert report, or upon which those opinions are based, may be admissible if (i) they are within the expert witness' own direct knowledge, or (ii) as hearsay evidence within the meaning of section 114 of the Criminal Justice Act 2003[8] [9]: see also rule 19.4(b), (c), (d) and (e). Evidence of examinations etc. on which an expert relies may be admissible under section 127 of the 2003 Act

Under section 30 of the Criminal Justice Act 1988[10], an expert report is admissible in evidence whether or not the person who made it gives oral evidence, but if that person does not give oral evidence then the report is admissible only with the court's permission.]

Content of expert's report   R19.4

19.4   Where rule 19.3(3) applies, an expert's report must—

(a) give details of the expert's qualifications, relevant experience and accreditation;

(b) give details of any literature or other information which the expert has relied on in making the report;

(c) contain a statement setting out the substance of all facts given to the expert which are material to the opinions expressed in the report, or upon which those opinions are based;

(d) make clear which of the facts stated in the report are within the expert's own knowledge;

(e) where the expert has based an opinion or inference on a representation of fact or opinion made by another person for the purposes of criminal proceedings (for example, as to the outcome of an examination, measurement, test or experiment)—

    (i) identify the person who made that representation to the expert,

    (ii) give the qualifications, relevant experience and any accreditation of that person, and

    (iii) certify that that person had personal knowledge of the matters stated in that representation;

(f) where there is a range of opinion on the matters dealt with in the report—

    (i) summarise the range of opinion, and

    (ii) give reasons for the expert's own opinion;

(g) if the expert is not able to give an opinion without qualification, state the qualification;

(h) include such information as the court may need to decide whether the expert's opinion is sufficiently reliable to be admissible as evidence;

(i) contain a summary of the conclusions reached;

(j) contain a statement that the expert understands an expert's duty to the court, and has complied and will continue to comply with that duty; and

(k) contain the same declaration of truth as a witness statement.

---

[5]   1967 c. 80.

[6]   1984 c. 60; section 81 was amended by section 109(1) of, and paragraph 286 of Schedule 8 to, the Courts Act 2003 (c. 39).

[7]   1996 c. 25; section 20(3) was amended by section 109(1) of, and paragraph 378 of Schedule 8 to, the Courts Act 2003 (c. 39).

[8]   2003 c. 44

[9]   2003 c. 44; section 127 was amended by article 3 of, and paragraphs 45 and 50 of the Schedule to, S.I. 2004/2035.

[10]   1988 c. 33; section 30 was amended by section 47 of, and paragraph 32 of Schedule 1 to, the Criminal Procedure and Investigations Act 1996 (c. 25) and paragraph 60 of Schedule 3 and Schedule 37 to the Criminal Justice Act 2003 (c. 44).

[Note. Part 16 contains rules about written witness statements. Declarations of truth in witness statements are required by section 9 of the Criminal Justice Act 1967[11].]

R19.5   Expert to be informed of service of report

19.5   A party who serves on another party or on the court a report by an expert must, at once, inform that expert of that fact.

R19.6   Pre-hearing discussion of expert evidence

19.6   (1)   This rule applies where more than one party wants to introduce expert evidence.

     (2)   The court may direct the experts to—

         (a)   discuss the expert issues in the proceedings; and

         (b)   prepare a statement for the court of the matters on which they agree and disagree, giving their reasons.

     (3)   Except for that statement, the content of that discussion must not be referred to without the court's permission.

     (4)   A party may not introduce expert evidence without the court's permission if the expert has not complied with a direction under this rule.

[Note. At a pre-trial hearing, a court may make binding rulings about the admissibility of evidence and about questions of law under section 9 of the Criminal Justice Act 1987[12]; sections 31 and 40 of the Criminal Procedure and Investigations Act 1996[13]; and section 8A of the Magistrates' Courts Act 1980[14].]

R19.7   Court's power to direct that evidence is to be given by a single joint expert

19.7   (1)   Where more than one defendant wants to introduce expert evidence on an issue at trial, the court may direct that the evidence on that issue is to be given by one expert only.

     (2)   Where the co-defendants cannot agree who should be the expert, the court may—

         (a)   select the expert from a list prepared or identified by them; or

         (b)   direct that the expert be selected in another way.

R19.8   Instructions to a single joint expert

19.8   (1)   Where the court gives a direction under rule 19.7 for a single joint expert to be used, each of the co-defendants may give instructions to the expert.

     (2)   A co-defendant who gives instructions to the expert must, at the same time, send a copy of the instructions to each other co-defendant.

     (3)   The court may give directions about—

         (a)   the payment of the expert's fees and expenses; and

         (b)   any examination, measurement, test or experiment which the expert wishes to carry out.

     (4)   The court may, before an expert is instructed, limit the amount that can be paid by way of fees and expenses to the expert.

     (5)   Unless the court otherwise directs, the instructing co-defendants are jointly and severally liable for the payment of the expert's fees and expenses.

R19.9   Application to withhold information from another party

19.9   (1)   This rule applies where—

         (a)   a party introduces expert evidence under rule 19.3(3);

         (b)   the evidence omits information which it otherwise might include because the party introducing it thinks that that information ought not be revealed to another party; and

[11] 1967 c. 80; section 9 was amended by section 56 of, and paragraph 49 of Schedule 8 to, the Courts Act 1971 (c. 23), section 168 of, and paragraph 6 of Schedule 9 to, the Criminal Justice and Public Order Act 1994 (c. 33), section 69 of the Criminal Procedure and Investigations Act 1996 (c. 25), regulation 9 of, and paragraph 4 of Schedule 5 to, S.I. 2001/1090, paragraph 43 of Schedule 3 and Part 4 of Schedule 37 to the Criminal Justice Act 2003 (c. 44), section 26 of, and paragraph 7 of Schedule 2 to, the Armed Forces Act 2011 (c. 18) and section 80 of the Deregulation Act 2015 (c. 20). It is further amended by section 72 of, and paragraph 55 of Schedule 5 to, the Children and Young Persons Act 1969 (c. 54) and section 65 of, and paragraph 1 of Schedule 4 to, the Courts Act 2003 (c. 39), with effect from dates to be appointed.
[12] 1987 c. 38; section 9 was amended by section 170 of, and Schedule 16 to, the Criminal Justice Act 1988 (c. 33), section 6 of the Criminal Justice Act 1993 (c. 36), sections 72, 74 and 80 of, and paragraph 3 of Schedule 3 and Schedule 5 to, the Criminal Procedure and Investigations Act 1996 (c. 25), sections 45 and 310 of, and paragraphs 18, 52 and 54 of Schedule 36 and Part 3 of Schedule 37 to, the Criminal Justice Act 2003 (c. 44), article 3 of, and paragraphs 21 and 23 of S.I. 2004/2035, section 59 of, and paragraph 1 of Schedule 11 to, the Constitutional Reform Act 2005 (c. 4) and Part 10 of Schedule 10 to the Protection of Freedoms Act 2012 (c. 9). The amendment made by section 45 of the Criminal Justice Act 2003 (c. 44) is in force for certain purposes; for remaining purposes it has effect from a date to be appointed.
[13] 1996 c. 25; section 31 was amended by sections 310, 331 and 332 of, and paragraphs 20, 36, 65 and 67 of Schedule 36 and Schedule 37 to, the Criminal Justice Act 2003 (c. 44).
[14] 1980 c. 43; section 8A was inserted by section 45 of, and Schedule 3 to, the Courts Act 2003 (c. 39) and amended by SI 2006/2493 and paragraphs 12 and 14 of Schedule 5 to the Legal Aid, Sentencing and Punishment of Offenders Act 2012 (c. 10).

      (c) the party introducing the evidence wants the court to decide whether it would be in the public interest to withhold that information.

  (2) The party who wants to introduce the evidence must—

      (a) apply for such a decision; and

      (b) serve the application on—

         (i) the court officer, and

         (ii) the other party, but only to the extent that serving it would not reveal what the applicant thinks ought to be withheld.

  (3) The application must—

      (a) identify the information;

      (b) explain why the applicant thinks that it would be in the public interest to withhold it; and

      (c) omit from the part of the application that is served on the other party anything that would reveal what the applicant thinks ought to be withheld.

  (4) Where the applicant serves only part of the application on the other party, the applicant must—

      (a) mark the other part, to show that it is only for the court; and

      (b) in that other part, explain why the applicant has withheld it from the other party.

  (5) The court may—

      (a) direct the applicant to serve on the other party any part of the application which has been withheld; and

      (b) determine the application at a hearing or without a hearing.

  (6) Any hearing of an application to which this rule applies—

      (a) must be in private, unless the court otherwise directs; and

      (b) if the court so directs, may be, wholly or in part, in the absence of the party from whom information has been withheld.

  (7) At any hearing of an application to which this rule applies—

      (a) the general rule is that the court must consider, in the following sequence—

         (i) representations first by the applicant and then by the other party, in both parties' presence, and then

         (ii) further representations by the applicant, in the absence of the party from whom information has been withheld; but

      (b) the court may direct other arrangements for the hearing.

Court's power to vary requirements under this Part   **R19.10**

19.10 (1) The court may extend (even after it has expired) a time limit under this Part.

  (2) A party who wants an extension of time must—

      (a) apply when serving the report, summary or notice for which it is required; and

      (b) explain the delay.

CRIMINAL PROCEDURE RULES   PART 20   HEARSAY EVIDENCE

When this Part applies   **R20.1**

20.1   This Part applies in a magistrates' court and in the Crown Court where a party wants to introduce hearsay evidence, within the meaning of section 114 of the Criminal Justice Act 2003[1]

[Note. Under section 114 of the Criminal Justice Act 2003, a statement not made in oral evidence is admissible as evidence of any matter stated if—

      (a) a statutory provision makes it admissible;

      (b) a rule of law preserved by section 118 makes it admissible;

      (c) the parties agree to it being admissible; or

      (d) it is in the interests of justice for it to be admissible.

Under section 115 of the Act—

      (a) a "statement" means any representation of fact or opinion, by any means, and includes a representation in pictorial form; and

      (b) a "matter stated" is something stated by someone with the apparent purpose of—

      (c) causing another person to believe it, or

      (d) causing another person, or a machine, to act or operate on the basis that the matter is as stated.]

---

[1] 2003 c. 44.

Criminal Procedure Rules

R20.2   **Notice to introduce hearsay evidence**

20.2 (1) This rule applies where a party wants to introduce hearsay evidence for admission under any of the following sections of the Criminal Justice Act 2003—
   (a) section 114(1)(d) (evidence admissible in the interests of justice);
   (b) section 116 (evidence where a witness is unavailable);
   (c) section 117(1)(c)[2] (evidence in a statement prepared for the purposes of criminal proceedings);
   (d) section 121 (multiple hearsay).

(2) That party must—
   (a) serve notice on—
      (i)   the court officer, and
      (ii) each other party;
   (b) in the notice—
      (i)   identify the evidence that is hearsay,
      (ii)   set out any facts on which that party relies to make the evidence admissible,
      (iii) explain how that party will prove those facts if another party disputes them, and
      (iv)   explain why the evidence is admissible; and
   (c) attach to the notice any statement or other document containing the evidence that has not already been served.

(3) A prosecutor who wants to introduce such evidence must serve the notice not more than—
   (a) 20 business days after the defendant pleads not guilty, in a magistrates' court; or
   (b) 10 business days after the defendant pleads not guilty, in the Crown Court.

(4) A defendant who wants to introduce such evidence must serve the notice as soon as reasonably practicable.

(5) A party entitled to receive a notice under this rule may waive that entitlement by so informing—
   (a) the party who would have served it; and
   (b) the court.

[Note. The Practice Direction sets out a form of notice for use in connection with this rule.

The sections of the Criminal Justice Act 2003 listed in this rule set out the conditions on which hearsay evidence may be admitted under them.

If notice is not given as this rule requires, then under section 132(5) of the 2003 Act—

   (a) the evidence is not admissible without the court's permission;
   (b) if the court gives permission, it may draw such inferences as appear proper from the failure to give notice; and
   (c) the court may take the failure into account in exercising its powers to order costs.

This rule does not require notice of hearsay evidence that is admissible under any of the following sections of the 2003 Act—

   (a) section 117 (business and other documents), otherwise than as required by rule 20.2(1)(c);
   (b) section 118 (preservation of certain common law categories of admissibility);
   (c) section 119 (inconsistent statements);
   (d) section 120[3] (other previous statements of witness); or
   (e) section 127[4] (expert evidence: preparatory work): but see Part 19 for the procedure where a party wants to introduce such evidence.]

R20.3   **Opposing the introduction of hearsay evidence**

20.3 (1) This rule applies where a party objects to the introduction of hearsay evidence.
(2) That party must—
   (a) apply to the court to determine the objection;
   (b) serve the application on—
      (i)   the court officer, and
      (ii) each other party;

---

[2] 2003 c. 44; section 117 was amended by regulation 4 of, and paragraph 8 of Schedule 3 to, S.I. 2017/730 and section 10 of the Crime (Overseas Production Orders) Act 2019 (c. 5).
[3] 2003 c. 44; section 120 was amended by sections 112 and 178 of, and Schedule 23 to, the Coroners and Justice Act 2009 (c. 25).
[4] 2003 c. 44; section 127 was amended by article 3 of, and paragraphs 45 and 50 of the Schedule to, S.I. 2004/2035.

      (c) serve the application as soon as reasonably practicable, and in any event not more than 10 business days after—
          (i)   service of notice to introduce the evidence under rule 20.2,
          (ii) service of the evidence to which that party objects, if no notice is required by that rule, or
          (iii) the defendant pleads not guilty
        whichever of those events happens last; and
      (d) in the application, explain—
          (i)   which, if any, facts set out in a notice under rule 20.2 that party disputes,
          (ii) why the evidence is not admissible, and
          (iii) any other objection to the evidence.
  (3) The court—
      (a) may determine an application—
          (i)   at a hearing, in public or in private, or
          (ii) without a hearing;
      (b) must not determine the application unless the party who served the notice—
          (i)   is present, or
          (ii) has had a reasonable opportunity to respond;
      (c) may adjourn the application; and
      (d) may discharge or vary a determination where it can do so under—
          (i)   section 8B of the Magistrates' Courts Act 1980[5] (ruling at pre-trial hearing in a magistrates' court), or
          (ii) section 9 of the Criminal Justice Act 1987[6], or section 31 or 40 of the Criminal Procedure and Investigations Act 1996[7] (ruling at preparatory or other pre-trial hearing in the Crown Court).

Unopposed hearsay evidence   R20.4

20.4 (1) This rule applies where—
      (a) a party has served notice to introduce hearsay evidence under rule 20.2; and
      (b) no other party has applied to the court to determine an objection to the introduction of the evidence.
  (2) The court must treat the evidence as if it were admissible by agreement.

[Note. Under section 132(4) of the Criminal Justice Act 2003, rules may provide that evidence is to be treated as admissible by agreement of the parties if notice to introduce that evidence has not been opposed.]

Court's power to vary requirements under this Part   R20.5

20.5 (1) The court may—
      (a) shorten or extend (even after it has expired) a time limit under this Part;
      (b) allow an application or notice to be in a different form to one set out in the Practice Direction, or to be made or given orally; and
      (c) dispense with the requirement for notice to introduce hearsay evidence.
  (2) A party who wants an extension of time must—
      (a) apply when serving the application or notice for which it is needed; and
      (b) explain the delay.

CRIMINAL PROCEDURE RULES   PART 21   EVIDENCE OF BAD CHARACTER

When this Part applies   R21.1

21.1 This Part applies in a magistrates' court and in the Crown Court where a party wants to introduce evidence of bad character within the meaning of section 98 of the Criminal Justice Act 2003[1]

---

[5] 1980 c. 43; section 8B was inserted by section 45 of, and Schedule 3 to, the Courts Act 2003 (c. 39) and amended by paragraph 51 of Schedule 3, and Part 4 of Schedule 37, to the Criminal Justice Act 2003 (c. 44).
[6] 1987 c. 38; section 9 was amended by section 170 of, and Schedule 16 to, the Criminal Justice Act 1988 (c. 33), section 6 of the Criminal Justice Act 1993 (c. 36), sections 72, 74 and 80 of, and paragraph 3 of Schedule 3 and Schedule 5 to, the Criminal Procedure and Investigations Act 1996 (c. 25), sections 45 and 310 of, and paragraphs 18, 52 and 54 of Schedule 36 and Part 3 of Schedule 37 to, the Criminal Justice Act 2003 (c. 44), article 3 of, and paragraphs 21 and 23 of S.I. 2004/2035, section 59 of, and paragraph 1 of Schedule 11 to, the Constitutional Reform Act 2005 (c. 4) and Part 10 of Schedule 10 to the Protection of Freedoms Act 2012 (c. 9). The amendment made by section 45 of the Criminal Justice Act 2003 (c. 44) is in force for certain purposes; for remaining purposes it has effect from a date to be appointed.
[7] 1996 c. 25; section 31 was amended by sections 310, 331 and 332 of, and paragraphs 20, 36, 65 and 67 of Schedule 36 and Schedule 37 to, the Criminal Justice Act 2003 (c. 44).
[1] 2003 c. 44.

[Note. Under section 98 of the Criminal Justice Act 2003, evidence of a person's bad character means evidence of, or of a disposition towards, misconduct on that person's part, other than evidence that—

    (a) has to do with the alleged facts of the offence; or
    (b) is evidence of misconduct in connection with the investigation or prosecution.

Under section 100(1) of the Criminal Justice Act 2003, evidence of a non-defendant's bad character is admissible if—

    (a) it is important explanatory evidence;
    (b) it has substantial probative value in relation to a matter which—
        (i) is a matter in issue in the proceedings, and
        (ii) is of substantial importance in the context of the case as a whole; or
    (c) all parties to the proceedings agree to the evidence being admissible.

The section explains requirements (a) and (b). Unless the parties agree to the evidence being admissible, it may not be introduced without the court's permission.

Under section 101(1) of the Criminal Justice Act 2003, evidence of a defendant's bad character is admissible if—

    (a) all parties to the proceedings agree to the evidence being admissible;
    (b) the evidence is introduced by the defendant, or is given in answer to a question asked by the defendant in cross-examination which was intended to elicit that evidence;
    (c) it is important explanatory evidence;
    (d) it is relevant to an important matter in issue between the defendant and the prosecution;
    (e) it has substantial probative value in relation to an important matter in issue between the defendant and a co-defendant;
    (f) it is evidence to correct a false impression given by the defendant; or
    (g) the defendant has made an attack on another person's character.

Sections 102 to 106 of the Act supplement those requirements. The court must not admit evidence under (d) or (g) if, on an application by the defendant, the court concludes that to do so would be unfair.]

R21.2   **Content of application or notice**

21.2 (1) A party who wants to introduce evidence of bad character must—
    (a) make an application under rule 21.3, where it is evidence of a non-defendant's bad character;
    (b) give notice under rule 21.4, where it is evidence of a defendant's bad character.
  (2) An application or notice must—
    (a) set out the facts of the misconduct on which that party relies,
    (b) explain how that party will prove those facts (whether by certificate of conviction, other official record, or other evidence), if another party disputes them, and
    (c) explain why the evidence is admissible.

[Note. The Practice Direction sets out forms of application and notice for use in connection with rules 21.3 and 21.4.

The fact that a person was convicted of an offence may be proved under—

    (a) section 73 of the Police and Criminal Evidence Act 1984[2] (conviction in the United Kingdom); or
    (b) section 7 of the Evidence Act 1851[3] (conviction outside the United Kingdom).

See also sections 117 and 118 of the Criminal Justice Act 2003 (admissibility of evidence contained in business and other documents).

Under section 10 of the Criminal Justice Act 1967[4], a party may admit a matter of fact.]

R21.3   **Application to introduce evidence of a non-defendant's bad character**

21.3 (1) This rule applies where a party wants to introduce evidence of the bad character of a person other than the defendant.

---

[2] 1984 c. 60; section 73 was amended by section 90(1) of, and paragraphs 125 and 128 of Schedule 13 to, the Access to Justice Act 1999 (c. 22) and paragraph 285 of Schedule 8 to, the Courts Act 2003 (c. 39).
[3] 1851 c. 99.
[4] 1967 c. 80.

(2) That party must serve an application to do so on—
   (a)   the court officer; and
   (b)   each other party.
(3) The applicant must serve the application—
   (a)   as soon as reasonably practicable; and in any event
   (b)   not more than 10 business days after the prosecutor discloses material on which the application is based (if the prosecutor is not the applicant).
(4) A party who objects to the introduction of the evidence must—
   (a)   serve notice on—
         (i)   the court officer, and
         (ii) each other party
         not more than 10 business days after service of the application; and
   (b)   in the notice explain, as applicable—
         (i)   which, if any, facts of the misconduct set out in the application that party disputes,
         (ii) what, if any, facts of the misconduct that party admits instead,
         (iii) why the evidence is not admissible, and
         (iv) any other objection to the application.
(5) The court—
   (a)   may determine an application—
         (i)   at a hearing, in public or in private, or
         (ii) without a hearing;
   (b)   must not determine the application unless each party other than the applicant—
         (i)   is present, or
         (ii) has had at least 10 business days in which to serve a notice of objection;
   (c)   may adjourn the application; and
   (d)   may discharge or vary a determination where it can do so under—
         (i)   section 8B of the Magistrates' Courts Act 1980[5] (ruling at pre-trial hearing in a magistrates' court), or
         (ii) section 9 of the Criminal Justice Act 1987[6], or section 31 or 40 of the Criminal Procedure and Investigations Act 1996[7] (ruling at preparatory or other pre-trial hearing in the Crown Court).

[Note. The Practice Direction sets out a form of application for use in connection with this rule.

See also rule 21.5 (reasons for decisions must be given in public).]

Notice to introduce evidence of a defendant's bad character   **R21.4**

21.4 (1) This rule applies where a party wants to introduce evidence of a defendant's bad character.
     (2) A prosecutor or co-defendant who wants to introduce such evidence must serve notice on—
        (a)   the court officer; and
        (b)   each other party.
     (3) A prosecutor must serve any such notice not more than—
        (a)   20 business days after the defendant pleads not guilty, in a magistrates' court; or
        (b)   10 business days after the defendant pleads not guilty, in the Crown Court.
     (4) A co-defendant who wants to introduce such evidence must serve the notice—
        (a)   as soon as reasonably practicable; and in any event
        (b)   not more than 10 business days after the prosecutor discloses material on which the notice is based.
     (5) A party who objects to the introduction of the evidence identified by such a notice must—
        (a)   apply to the court to determine the objection;

---

[5] 1980 c. 43; section 8B was inserted by section 45 of, and Schedule 3 to, the Courts Act 2003 (c. 39) and amended by paragraph 51 of Schedule 3, and Part 4 of Schedule 37, to the Criminal Justice Act 2003 (c. 44).
[6] 1987 c. 38; section 9 was amended by section 170 of, and Schedule 16 to, the Criminal Justice Act 1988 (c. 33), section 6 of the Criminal Justice Act 1993 (c. 36), sections 72, 74 and 80 of, and paragraph 3 of Schedule 3 and Schedule 5 to, the Criminal Procedure and Investigations Act 1996 (c. 25), sections 45 and 310 of, and paragraphs 18, 52 and 54 of Schedule 36 and Part 3 of Schedule 37 to, the Criminal Justice Act 2003 (c. 44), article 3 of, and paragraphs 21 and 23 of S.I. 2004/2035, section 59 of, and paragraph 1 of Schedule 11 to, the Constitutional Reform Act 2005 (c. 4) and Part 10 of Schedule 10 to the Protection of Freedoms Act 2012 (c. 9). The amendment made by section 45 of the Criminal Justice Act 2003 (c. 44) is in force for certain purposes; for remaining purposes it has effect from a date to be appointed.
[7] 1996 c. 25; section 31 was amended by sections 310, 331 and 332 of, and paragraphs 20, 36, 65 and 67 of Schedule 36 and Schedule 37 to, the Criminal Justice Act 2003 (c. 44).

(b) serve the application on—
    (i) the court officer, and
    (ii) each other party
    not more than 10 business days after service of the notice; and
(c) in the application explain, as applicable—
    (i) which, if any, facts of the misconduct set out in the notice that party disputes,
    (ii) what, if any, facts of the misconduct that party admits instead,
    (iii) why the evidence is not admissible,
    (iv) why it would be unfair to admit the evidence, and
    (v) any other objection to the notice.
(6) The court—
(a) may determine such an application—
    (i) at a hearing, in public or in private, or
    (ii) without a hearing;
(b) must not determine the application unless the party who served the notice—
    (i) is present, or
    (ii) has had a reasonable opportunity to respond;
(c) may adjourn the application; and
(d) may discharge or vary a determination where it can do so under—
    (i) section 8B of the Magistrates' Courts Act 1980 (ruling at pre-trial hearing in a magistrates' court), or
    (ii) section 9 of the Criminal Justice Act 1987, or section 31 or 40 of the Criminal Procedure and Investigations Act 1996 (ruling at preparatory or other pre-trial hearing in the Crown Court).
(7) A party entitled to receive such a notice may waive that entitlement by so informing—
(a) the party who would have served it; and
(b) the court.
(8) A defendant who wants to introduce evidence of his or her own bad character must—
(a) give notice, in writing or orally—
    (i) as soon as reasonably practicable, and in any event
    (ii) before the evidence is introduced, either by the defendant or in reply to a question asked by the defendant of another party's witness in order to obtain that evidence; and
(b) in the Crown Court, at the same time give notice (in writing, or orally) of any direction about the defendant's character that the defendant wants the court to give the jury under rule 25.14 (Directions to the jury and taking the verdict).

[Note. The Practice Direction sets out a form of notice for use in connection with this rule.

See also rule 21.5 (reasons for decisions must be given in public).

If notice is not given as this rule requires, then under section 111(4) of the Criminal Justice Act 2003 the court may take the failure into account in exercising its powers to order costs.]

R21.5 Reasons for decisions

21.5 The court must announce at a hearing in public (but in the absence of the jury, if there is one) the reasons for a decision—
(a) to admit evidence as evidence of bad character, or to refuse to do so; or
(b) to direct an acquittal or a retrial under section 107 of the Criminal Justice Act 2003.

[Note. See section 110 of the Criminal Justice Act 2003.]

R21.6 Court's power to vary requirements under this Part

21.6 (1) The court may—
(a) shorten or extend (even after it has expired) a time limit under this Part;
(b) allow an application or notice to be in a different form to one set out in the Practice Direction, or to be made or given orally; and
(c) dispense with a requirement for notice to introduce evidence of a defendant's bad character.
(2) A party who wants an extension of time must—
(a) apply when serving the application or notice for which it is needed; and
(b) explain the delay.

CRIMINAL PROCEDURE RULES   PART 22   EVIDENCE OF A COMPLAINANT'S
PREVIOUS SEXUAL BEHAVIOUR

When this Part applies   R22.1

22.1   This Part applies in a magistrates' court and in the Crown Court where—

(i)   section 41 of the Youth Justice and Criminal Evidence Act 1999[1] prohibits the introduction of evidence or cross-examination about any sexual behaviour of the complainant of a sexual offence, and

(ii)   despite that prohibition, a defendant wants to introduce such evidence or to cross-examine a witness about such behaviour.

[Note. Section 41 of the Youth Justice and Criminal Evidence Act 1999 prohibits evidence or cross-examination about the sexual behaviour of a complainant of a sexual offence, subject to exceptions.

See also—

(a)   *section 42 of the 1999 Act[2], which among other things defines 'sexual behaviour' and 'sexual offence';*

(b)   *section 34, which prohibits cross-examination by a defendant in person of the complainant of a sexual offence (Part 23 contains relevant rules).]*

Exercise of court's powers   R22.2

22.2   The court—

(a)   must determine an application under rule 22.4 (Application for permission to introduce evidence or cross-examine)—
(i)   at a hearing in private, and
(ii)   in the absence of the complainant;

(b)   must not determine the application unless—
(i)   each party other than the applicant is present, or has had at least 10 business days in which to make representations, and
(ii)   the court is satisfied that it has been able to take adequate account of the complainant's rights;

(c)   may adjourn the application; and

(d)   may discharge or vary a determination where it can do so under—
(i)   section 8B of the Magistrates' Courts Act 1980[3] (ruling at pre-trial hearing in a magistrates' court), or
(ii)   section 9 of the Criminal Justice Act 1987[4], or section 31 or 40 of the Criminal Procedure and Investigations Act 1996[5] (ruling at preparatory or other pre-trial hearing in the Crown Court).

[Note. See also section 43 of the Youth Justice and Criminal Evidence Act 1999[6], which among other things requires an application under section 41 of the Act to be heard in private and in the absence of the complainant.

At a pre-trial hearing a court may make binding rulings about the admissibility of evidence and about questions of law under sections 31 and 40 of the Criminal Procedure and Investigations Act 1996[7] and section 8A of the Magistrates' Courts Act 1980[8].]

---

[1]   1999 c. 23.

[2]   1999 c. 23; section 42 was amended by paragraph 73 of Schedule 3 and Schedule 37 to the Criminal Justice Act 2003 (c. 44).

[3]   1980 c. 43; section 8B was inserted by section 45 of, and Schedule 3 to, the Courts Act 2003 (c. 39) and amended by paragraph 51 of Schedule 3, and Part 4 of Schedule 37, to the Criminal Justice Act 2003 (c. 44).

[4]   1987 c. 38; section 9 was amended by section 170 of, and Schedule 16 to, the Criminal Justice Act 1988 (c. 33), section 6 of the Criminal Justice Act 1993 (c. 36), sections 72, 74 and 80 of, and paragraph 3 of Schedule 3 and Schedule 5 to, the Criminal Procedure and Investigations Act 1996 (c. 25), sections 45 and 310 of, and paragraphs 18, 52 and 54 of Schedule 36 and Part 3 of Schedule 37 to, the Criminal Justice Act 2003 (c. 44), article 3 of, and paragraphs 21 and 23 of S.I. 2004/2035, section 59 of, and paragraph 1 of Schedule 11 to, the Constitutional Reform Act 2005 (c. 4) and Part 10 of Schedule 10 to the Protection of Freedoms Act 2012 (c. 9). The amendment made by section 45 of the Criminal Justice Act 2003 (c. 44) is in force for certain purposes; for remaining purposes it has effect from a date to be appointed.

[5]   1996 c. 25; section 31 was amended by sections 310, 331 and 332 of, and paragraphs 20, 36, 65 and 67 of Schedule 36 and Schedule 37 to, the Criminal Justice Act 2003 (c. 44).

[6]   1999 c. 23; section 43(3) was amended by section 109(1) of, and paragraph 384(g) of Schedule 8 to, the Courts Act 2003 (c. 39).

[7]   1996 c. 25; section 31 was amended by sections 310, 331 and 332 of, and paragraphs 20, 36, 65 and 67 of Schedule 36 and Schedule 37 to, the Criminal Justice Act 2003 (c. 44).

[8]   1980 c. 43; section 8A was inserted by section 45 of, and Schedule 3 to, the Courts Act 2003 (c. 39) and amended by SI 2006/2493 and paragraphs 12 and 14 of Schedule 5 to the Legal Aid, Sentencing and Punishment of Offenders Act 2012 (c. 10).

R22.3   **Decisions and reasons**

22.3   (1)   A prosecutor who wants to introduce the evidence of a complainant in respect of whom the court allows the introduction of evidence or cross-examination about any sexual behaviour must—

   (a)   inform the complainant of the court's decision as soon as reasonably practicable; and

   (b)   explain to the complainant any arrangements that as a result will be made for him or her to give evidence.

   (2)   The court must—

   (a)   promptly determine an application; and

   (b)   allow the prosecutor sufficient time to comply with the requirements of—

   (i)   paragraph (1), and

   (ii)   the code of practice issued under section 32 of the Domestic Violence, Crime and Victims Act 2004[9].

   (3)   The court must announce at a hearing in public—

   (a)   the reasons for a decision to allow or refuse an application under rule 22.4; and

   (b)   if it allows such an application, the extent to which evidence may be introduced or questions asked.

[Note. Under section 43 of the Youth Justice and Criminal Evidence Act 1999—

   (a)   the reasons for the court's decision on an application must be given in open court; and

   (b)   the court must state in open court the extent to which evidence may be introduced or questions asked.]

R22.4   **Application for permission to introduce evidence or cross-examine**

22.4.   (1)   A defendant who wants to introduce evidence or cross-examine a witness about any sexual behaviour of the complainant must—

   (a)   serve an application for permission to do so on—

   (i)   the court officer, and

   (ii)   each other party; and

   (b)   serve the application—

   (i)   as soon as reasonably practicable after becoming aware of the grounds for doing so, and in any event

   (ii)   not more than 10 business days after the prosecutor discloses material on which the application is based.

   (2)   The application must—

   (a)   identify the issue to which the defendant says the complainant's sexual behaviour is relevant;

   (b)   give particulars of—

   (i)   any evidence that the defendant wants to introduce, and

   (ii)   any questions that the defendant wants to ask;

   (c)   identify the exception to the prohibition in section 41 of the Youth Justice and Criminal Evidence Act 1999 on which the defendant relies; and

   (d)   give the name and date of birth of any witness whose evidence about the complainant's sexual behaviour the defendant wants to introduce.

R22.5   **Application containing information withheld from another party**

22.5.   (1)   This rule applies where—

   (a)   an applicant serves an application under rule 22.4 (Application for permission to introduce evidence or cross-examine); and

   (b)   the application includes information that the applicant thinks ought not be revealed to another party.

   (2)   The applicant must—

   (a)   omit that information from the part of the application that is served on that other party;

   (b)   mark the other part to show that, unless the court otherwise directs, it is only for the court; and

   (c)   in that other part, explain why the applicant has withheld that information from that other party.

   (3)   If the court so directs, the hearing of an application to which this rule applies may be, wholly or in part, in the absence of a party from whom information has been withheld.

   (4)   At the hearing of an application to which this rule applies—

   (a)   the general rule is that the court must consider, in the following sequence—

   (i)   representations first by the applicant and then by each other party, in all the parties' presence, and then

---

[9]   2004 c. 28; section 32 was amended by article 8 of, and paragraph 10 of the Schedule to, S.I. 2007/2128.

(ii) further representations by the applicant, in the absence of a party from whom information has been withheld; but

(b) the court may direct other arrangements for the hearing.

[Note. See section 43(3)(c) of the Youth Justice and Criminal Evidence Act 1999.]

Representations in response   R22.6

22.6. (1) This rule applies where a party wants to make representations about—

(a) an application under rule 22.4 (Application for permission to introduce evidence or cross-examine); or

(b) a proposed variation or discharge of a decision allowing such an application.

(2) Such a party must—

(a) serve the representations on—

(i) the court officer, and

(ii) each other party; and

(b) do so not more than 10 business days after, as applicable—

(i) service of the application, or

(ii) notice of the proposal to vary or discharge.

(3) Where representations include information that the person making them thinks ought not be revealed to another party, that person must—

(a) omit that information from the representations served on that other party;

(b) mark the information to show that, unless the court otherwise directs, it is only for the court; and

(c) with that information include an explanation of why it has been withheld from that other party.

(4) Representations against an application under rule 22.4 must explain the grounds of objection.

(5) Representations against the variation or discharge of a decision must explain why it should not be varied or discharged.

Special measures, etc. for a witness   R22.7

22.7 (1) This rule applies where the court allows an application under rule 22.4 (Application for permission to introduce evidence or cross-examine).

(2) Despite the time limits in rule 18.4 (Making an application for a direction or order)—

(a) a party may apply for a special measures direction or for the variation of an existing special measures direction not more than 10 business days after the court's decision; and

(b) the court may shorten the time for opposing that application.

(3) Where the court allows the cross-examination of a witness, the court must give directions for the appropriate treatment and questioning of that witness in accordance with rule 3.8(6) and (7) (setting ground rules for the conduct of questioning).

[Note. Special measures to improve the quality of evidence given by certain witnesses may be directed by the court under section 19 of the Youth Justice and Criminal Evidence Act 1999 and varied under section 20[10]. An application for a special measures direction may be made by a party under Part 18 or the court may make a direction on its own initiative. Rule 18.13(2) sets the usual time limit (10 business days) for opposing a special measures application.]

Court's power to vary requirements under this Part   R22.8

22.8. The court may shorten or extend (even after it has expired) a time limit under this Part.

CRIMINAL PROCEDURE RULES   PART 23   RESTRICTION ON
CROSS-EXAMINATION BY A DEFENDANT

General rules

When this Part applies   R23.1

23.1 This Part applies where—

(a) a defendant may not cross-examine in person a witness because of section 34 or section 35 of the Youth Justice and Criminal Evidence Act 1999[1] (Complainants in proceedings for sexual offences; Child complainants and other child witnesses); or

---

[10] 1999 c. 23; section 20(6) was amended by paragraph 384(a) of Schedule 8 to the Courts Act 2003 (c. 39).

[1] 1999 c. 23; section 35 was amended by sections 139 and 140 of, and paragraph 41 of Schedule 6 and Schedule 7 to, the Sexual Offences Act 2003 (c. 42), section 148 of, and paragraphs 35 and 36 of Schedule 26 to the Criminal Justice and Immigration Act 2008 (c. 4) and section 105 of the Coroners and Justice Act 2009 (c. 25).

(b) the court can prohibit a defendant from cross-examining in person a witness under section 36 of that Act[2] (Direction prohibiting accused from cross-examining particular witness).

[Note. Under section 34 of the Youth Justice and Criminal Evidence Act 1999, no defendant charged with a sexual offence may cross-examine in person a witness who is the complainant, either—

    (a) in connection with that offence; or
    (b) in connection with any other offence (of whatever nature) with which that defendant is charged in the proceedings.

Under section 35 of the 1999 Act, no defendant charged with an offence listed in that section may cross-examine in person a protected witness, either—

    (a) in connection with that offence; or
    (b) in connection with any other offence (of whatever nature) with which that defendant is charged in the proceedings.

A 'protected witness' is one who—

    (a) either is the complainant or is alleged to have been a witness to the commission of the offence; and
    (b) either is a child, within the meaning of section 35, or is due to be cross-examined after giving evidence in chief—
        (i) by means of a video recording made when the witness was a child, or
        (ii) in any other way when the witness was a child.

Under section 36 of the 1999 Act, where neither section 34 nor section 35 applies the court may give a direction prohibiting the defendant from cross-examining, or further cross-examining, in person a witness, on application by the prosecutor or on the court's own initiative. See also rules 23.3 to 23.7.]

R23.2 **Appointment of advocate to cross-examine witness**

23.2 (1) This rule applies where a defendant may not cross-examine in person a witness in consequence of—
    (a) the prohibition imposed by section 34 or section 35 of the Youth Justice and Criminal Evidence Act 1999; or
    (b) a prohibition imposed by the court under section 36 of the 1999 Act.
  (2) The court must, as soon as practicable, explain in terms the defendant can understand (with help, if necessary)—
    (a) the prohibition and its effect;
    (b) that if the defendant will not be represented by a lawyer with a right of audience in the court for the purposes of the case then the defendant is entitled to arrange for such a lawyer to cross-examine the witness on his or her behalf;
    (c) that the defendant must notify the court officer of the identity of any such lawyer, with details of how to contact that person, by no later than a date set by the court; and
    (d) that if the defendant does not want to make such arrangements, or if the defendant gives no such notice by that date, then—
        (i) the court must decide whether it is necessary in the interests of justice to appoint such a lawyer to cross-examine the witness in the defendant's interests, and
        (ii) if the court decides that that is necessary, the court will appoint a lawyer chosen by the court who will not be responsible to the defendant.
  (3) Having given those explanations, the court must—
    (a) ask whether the defendant wants to arrange for a lawyer to cross-examine the witness, and set a date by when the defendant must notify the court officer of the identity of that lawyer if the answer to that question is 'yes'; and
    (b) if the answer to that question is 'no', or if by the date set the defendant has given no such notice—
        (i) decide whether it is necessary in the interests of justice for the witness to be cross-examined by an advocate appointed to represent the defendant's interests, and
        (ii) if the court decides that that is necessary, give directions for the appointment of such an advocate.
  (4) The court may give the explanations and ask the questions required by this rule—
    (a) at a hearing, in public or in private; or
    (b) without a hearing, by written notice to the defendant.
  (5) The court may extend (even after it has expired) the time limit that it sets under paragraph (3)(a)—

---

[2] 1999 c. 23.

      (a) on application by the defendant; or

      (b) on its own initiative.

  (6) Paragraphs (7), (8), (9) and (10) apply where the court appoints an advocate.

  (7) The directions that the court gives under paragraph (3)(b)(ii) must provide for the supply to the advocate of a copy of—

      (a) all material served by one party on the other, whether before or after the advocate's appointment, to which applies—

          (i)   Part 8 (Initial details of the prosecution case),

          (ii)   in the Crown Court, rule 3.19 (service of prosecution evidence in a case sent for trial),

          (iii)   Part 16 (Written witness statements),

          (iv)   Part 19 (Expert evidence),

          (v)   Part 20 (Hearsay evidence),

          (vi)   Part 21 (Evidence of bad character), or

          (vii) Part 22 (Evidence of a complainant's previous sexual behaviour);

      (b) any material disclosed, given or served, whether before or after the advocate's appointment, which is—

          (i)   prosecution material disclosed to the defendant under section 3 (Initial duty of prosecutor to disclose) or section 7A (Continuing duty of prosecutor to disclose) of the Criminal Procedure and Investigations Act 1996[3],

          (ii)   a defence statement given by the defendant under section 5 (Compulsory disclosure by accused) or section 6 (Voluntary disclosure by accused) of the 1996 Act[4],

          (iii) a defence witness notice given by the defendant under section 6C of that Act[5] (Notification of intention to call defence witnesses), or

          (iv) an application by the defendant under section 8 of that Act[6] (Application by accused for disclosure);

      (c) any case management questionnaire prepared for the purposes of the trial or, as the case may be, the appeal; and

      (d) all case management directions given by the court for the purposes of the trial or the appeal.

  (8) Where the defendant has given a defence statement—

      (a) section 8(2) of the Criminal Procedure and Investigations Act 1996 is modified to allow the advocate, as well as the defendant, to apply for an order for prosecution disclosure under that subsection if the advocate has reasonable cause to believe that there is prosecution material concerning the witness which is required by section 7A of the Act to be disclosed to the defendant and has not been; and

      (b) rule 15.5 (Defendant's application for prosecution disclosure) applies to an application by the advocate as it does to an application by the defendant.

  (9) Before receiving evidence the court must establish, with the active assistance of the parties and of the advocate, and in the absence of any jury in the Crown Court—

      (a) what issues will be the subject of the advocate's cross-examination; and

      (b) whether the court's permission is required for any proposed question, for example where Part 21 or Part 22 applies.

(10) The appointment terminates at the conclusion of the cross-examination of the witness.

[Note. See section 38 of the Youth Justice and Criminal Evidence Act 1999[7]. Under section 38(8) the references in that section to a 'legal representative' are to a representative who is an advocate within the meaning of rule 2.2.

---

[3] 1996 c. 25; section 3 was amended by section 82 of, and paragraph 7 of Schedule 4 to, the Regulation of Investigatory Powers Act 2000 (c. 23), section 32 of, and paragraphs 20 and 21 of Schedule 36 to, the Criminal Justice Act 2003 (c. 44) and section 271 of, and paragraph 39 of Schedule 10 to, the Investigatory Powers Act 2016 (c. 25). Section 7A was inserted by section 37 of the Criminal Justice Act 2003 (c. 44) and was amended by section 271 of, and paragraph 39 of Schedule 10 to, the Investigatory Powers Act 2016 (c. 25).

[4] 1996 c. 25; section 5 was amended by section 119 of, and paragraph 126 of Schedule 8 to, the Crime and Disorder Act 1998 (c. 37), in respect of certain proceedings only, and by section 33 of, and paragraph 66 of Schedule 3, paragraphs 20 and 23 of Schedule 36 and Parts 3 and 4 of Schedule 37 to, the Criminal Justice Act 2003 (c. 44). Section 6 was amended by paragraphs 20 and 24 of Schedule 36 and Part 3 of Schedule 37 to the Criminal Justice Act 2003 (c. 44).) For transitional provisions and savings see paragraph (2) of Schedule 2 to S.I. 2005/950.

[5] 1996 c. 25; section 6C was inserted by section 34 of the Criminal Justice Act 2003 (c. 44).

[6] 1996 c. 25; section 8 was amended by section 82 of, and paragraph 7 of Schedule 4 to, the Regulation of Investigatory Powers Act 2000 (c. 23), section 38 of the Criminal Justice Act 2003 (c. 44) and section 271 of, and paragraph 39 of Schedule 10 to, the Investigatory Powers Act 2016 (c. 25).

[7] 1999 c. 23; section 38 was amended by section 109 of, and paragraph 384(f) of Schedule 8 to, the Courts Act 2003 (c. 39).

Under section 38(7) of the 1999 Act, where the court appoints an advocate Criminal Procedure Rules may apply with modifications any of the provisions of Part I of the Criminal Procedure and Investigations Act 1996. A summary of the disclosure requirements of the 1996 Act is at the end of Part 15 (Disclosure). Under section 5 of that Act, in the Crown Court the defendant must give a defence statement. Under section 6, in a magistrates' court the defendant may give such a statement but need not do so. Under section 6C, in the Crown Court and in magistrates' courts the defendant must give a defence witness notice indicating whether he or she intends to call any witnesses (other than him or herself) and, if so, identifying them. Under section 8 a defendant may apply for prosecution disclosure only if the defendant has given a defence statement.]

Application to prohibit cross-examination

R23.3 **Exercise of court's powers**

23.3 (1) The court may decide whether to impose or discharge a prohibition against cross-examination under section 36 of the Youth Justice and Criminal Evidence Act 1999—

(a) at a hearing, in public or in private, or without a hearing; and

(b) in a party's absence, if that party—

(i) applied for the prohibition or discharge, or

(ii) has had at least 10 business days in which to make representations.

(2) The court must announce, at a hearing in public before the witness gives evidence, the reasons for a decision—

(a) to impose or discharge such a prohibition; or

(b) to refuse to do so.

[Note. See section 37 of the Youth Justice and Criminal Evidence Act 1999[8].]

R23.4 **Application to prohibit cross-examination**

23.4 (1) This rule applies where under section 36 of the Youth Justice and Criminal Evidence Act 1999 the prosecutor wants the court to prohibit the cross-examination of a witness by a defendant in person.

(2) The prosecutor must—

(a) apply in writing, as soon as reasonably practicable after becoming aware of the grounds for doing so; and

(b) serve the application on—

(i) the court officer,

(ii) the defendant who is the subject of the application, and

(iii) any other defendant, unless the court otherwise directs.

(3) The application must—

(a) report any views that the witness has expressed about whether he or she is content to be cross-examined by the defendant in person;

(b) identify—

(i) the nature of the questions likely to be asked, having regard to the issues in the case,

(ii) any relevant behaviour of the defendant at any stage of the case, generally and in relation to the witness,

(iii) any relationship, of any nature, between the witness and the defendant,

(iv) any other defendant in the case who is subject to such a prohibition in respect of the witness, and

(v) any special measures direction made in respect of the witness, or for which an application has been made;

(c) explain why the quality of evidence given by the witness on cross-examination—

(i) is likely to be diminished if no such prohibition is imposed, and

(ii) would be likely to be improved if it were imposed; and

(d) explain why it would not be contrary to the interests of justice to impose the prohibition.

[Note. The Practice Direction sets out a form of application for use in connection with this rule.]

R23.5 **Application to discharge prohibition imposed by the court**

23.5 (1) A party who wants the court to discharge a prohibition against cross-examination which the court imposed under section 36 of the Youth Justice and Criminal Evidence Act 1999 must—

(a) apply in writing, as soon as reasonably practicable after becoming aware of the grounds for doing so; and

(b) serve the application on—

(i) the court officer, and

(ii) each other party.

[8] 1999 c. 23; section 37 was amended by section 109 of, and paragraph 384(e) of Schedule 8 to, the Courts Act 2003 (c. 39).

(2) The applicant must—
  (a) explain what material circumstances have changed since the prohibition was imposed; and
  (b) ask for a hearing, if the applicant wants one, and explain why it is needed.

[Note. Under section 37 of the Youth Justice and Criminal Evidence Act 1999, the court can discharge a prohibition against cross-examination which it has imposed—

  (a) on application, if there has been a material change of circumstances; or
  (b) on its own initiative.]

Application containing information withheld from another party   R23.6

23.6 (1) This rule applies where—
  (a) an applicant serves an application for the court to impose a prohibition against cross-examination, or for the discharge of such a prohibition; and
  (b) the application includes information that the applicant thinks ought not be revealed to another party.
(2) The applicant must—
  (a) omit that information from the part of the application that is served on that other party;
  (b) mark the other part to show that, unless the court otherwise directs, it is only for the court; and
  (c) in that other part, explain why the applicant has withheld that information from that other party.
(3) Any hearing of an application to which this rule applies—
  (a) must be in private, unless the court otherwise directs; and
  (b) if the court so directs, may be, wholly or in part, in the absence of a party from whom information has been withheld.
(4) At any hearing of an application to which this rule applies—
  (a) the general rule is that the court must consider, in the following sequence—
    (i) representations first by the applicant and then by each other party, in all the parties' presence, and then
    (ii) further representations by the applicant, in the absence of a party from whom information has been withheld; but
  (b) the court may direct other arrangements for the hearing.

[Note. See section 37 of the Youth Justice and Criminal Evidence Act 1999.]

Representations in response   R23.7

23.7 (1) This rule applies where a party wants to make representations about—
  (a) an application under rule 23.4 for a prohibition against cross-examination;
  (b) an application under rule 23.5 for the discharge of such a prohibition; or
  (c) a prohibition or discharge that the court proposes on its own initiative.
(2) Such a party must—
  (a) serve the representations on—
    (i) the court officer, and
    (ii) each other party;
  (b) do so not more than 10 business days after, as applicable—
    (i) service of the application, or
    (ii) notice of the prohibition or discharge that the court proposes; and
  (c) ask for a hearing, if that party wants one, and explain why it is needed.
(3) Representations against a prohibition must explain in what respect the conditions for imposing it are not met.
(4) Representations against the discharge of a prohibition must explain why it should not be discharged.
(5) Where representations include information that the person making them thinks ought not be revealed to another party, that person must—
  (a) omit that information from the representations served on that other party;
  (b) mark the information to show that, unless the court otherwise directs, it is only for the court; and
  (c) with that information include an explanation of why it has been withheld from that other party.

Criminal Procedure Rules

R23.8 **Court's power to vary requirements**

23.8 (1) The court may—

    (a) shorten or extend (even after it has expired) a time limit under rule 23.4 (Application to prohibit cross-examination), rule 23.5 (Application to discharge prohibition imposed by the court) or rule 23.7 (Representations in response); and

    (b) allow an application or representations required by any of those rules to be made in a different form to one set out in the Practice Direction, or to be made orally.

    (2) A person who wants an extension of time must—

    (a) apply when serving the application or representations for which it is needed; and

    (b) explain the delay.

CRIMINAL PROCEDURE RULES   PART 24   TRIAL AND SENTENCE IN A MAGISTRATES' COURT

R24.1 **When this Part applies**

24.1 (1) This Part applies in a magistrates' court where the court tries a case or the defendant pleads guilty.

    (2) Where the defendant is under 18, in this Part—

    (a) a reference to convicting the defendant includes a reference to finding the defendant guilty of an offence; and

    (b) a reference to sentence includes a reference to an order made on a finding of guilt.

[Note. A magistrates' court's powers to try an allegation of an offence are contained in section 2 of the Magistrates' Courts Act 1980[1]. In relation to a defendant under 18, they are contained in sections 45, 46 and 48 of the Children and Young Persons Act 1933[2].

See also section 18 of the Children and Young Persons Act 1963[3]), section 47 of the Crime and Disorder Act 1998[4] and section 27 of the Sentencing Act 2020[5].

The exercise of the court's powers is affected by—

    (a) the classification of the offence (and the general rule, subject to exceptions, is that a magistrates' court must try—

    (i) an offence classified as one that can be tried only in a magistrates' court (in other legislation, described as triable only summarily), and

    (ii) an offence classified as one that can be tried either in a magistrates' court or in the Crown Court (in other legislation, described as triable either way) that has been allocated for trial in a magistrates' court); and

    (b) the defendant's age (and the general rule, subject to exceptions, is that an allegation of an offence against a defendant under 18 must be tried in a magistrates' court sitting as a youth court, irrespective of the classification of the offence and without allocation for trial there).

Under sections 10, 14, 27A, 121 and 148 of the Magistrates' Courts Act 1980[6] and the Justices of the Peace Rules 2016[7], the court—

---

[1] 1980 c. 43; section 2 was substituted by section 44 of the Courts Act 2003 (c. 39) and amended by section 41 of, and paragraph 51 of Schedule 3 to, the Criminal Justice Act 2003 (c. 44).
[2] 1933 c. 12; section 45 was substituted by section 50 of the Courts Act 2003 (c. 39) and amended by section 15 of, and paragraph 20 of Schedule 4 to, the Constitutional Reform Act 2005 (c. 4); section 46 was amended by section 46 of, and Schedule 7 to, the Justices of the Peace Act 1949 (c. 101), section 72 of, and paragraph 4 of Schedule 5 to, the Children and Young Persons Act 1969 (c. 54), section 154 of, and paragraph 6 of Schedule 7 to, the Magistrates' Courts Act 1980 (c. 43), sections 68 and 100 of, and paragraph 1 of Schedule 8 and paragraph 40 of Schedule 11 to, the Criminal Justice Act 1991 (c. 53) and section 109 of, and paragraph 74 of Schedule 8 to, the Courts Act 2003 (c. 39); and section 48 was amended by section 79 of, and Schedule 9 to, the Criminal Justice Act 1948 (c. 58), section 132 of, and Schedule 6 to, the Magistrates' Courts Act 1952 (c. 55), section 64 of, and paragraph 12 of Schedule 3 and Schedule 5 to, the Children and Young Persons Act 1963 (c. 37), sections 72, 79 and 83 of, and Schedules 6, 9 and 10 to, the Children and Young Persons Act 1969 (c. 54), sections 68 and 100 of, and paragraph 1 of Schedule 8 and paragraph 40 of Schedule 11 to, the Criminal Justice Act 1991 (c. 53), section 106 of, and Schedule 15 to, the Access to Justice Act 1999 (c. 22) and section 109 of, and paragraph 75 of Schedule 8 to, the Courts Act 2003 (c. 39).
[3] 1963 c. 37; section 18 was amended by section 100 of, and paragraph 40 of Schedule 11 to, the Criminal Justice Act 1991 (c. 53) and section 168 of, and paragraph 5 of Schedule 9 to, the Criminal Justice and Public Order Act 1994 (c. 33).
[4] 1998 c. 37; section 47 was amended by section 165 of, and Schedule 12 to, the Powers of Criminal Courts (Sentencing) Act 2000 (c. 6), section 332 of, and Schedule 37 to, the Criminal Justice Act 2003 (c. 44) and article 2 of, and paragraph 59 of the Schedule to S.I. 2005/886.
[5] 2020 c. 17.
[6] 1980 c. 43; section 10 was amended by section 59 of, and paragraph 1 of Schedule 9 to, the Criminal Justice Act 1982 (c. 48), section 68 of, and paragraph 6 of Schedule 8 to, the Criminal Justice Act 1991 (c. 53) and section 47 of the Crime and Disorder Act 1998 (c. 37). Section 14 was amended by section 109 of, and paragraph 205 of Schedule 8 to, the Courts Act 2003 (c. 39). Section 27A was inserted by section 46 of the Courts Act 2003 (c. 39). Section 121 was amended by section 61 of the

(a) *must comprise at least two but not more than three justices, or a District Judge (Magistrates' Courts) (but a single member can adjourn the hearing);*

(b) *must not include any member who adjudicated at a hearing to which rule 44.2 applies (defendant's declaration of no knowledge of hearing);*

(c) *when reaching a verdict, must not include any member who was absent from any part of the hearing;*

(d) *when passing sentence, need not include any of the members who reached the verdict (but may do so).*

Under section 16A of the Magistrates' Courts Act 1980[8], the court may comprise a single justice where—

(a) *the offence charged is a summary offence not punishable with imprisonment;*

(b) *the defendant was at least 18 years old when charged or is a corporation;*

(c) *the court is satisfied that specified documents giving notice of the procedure under that section and containing other specified information have been served on the defendant; and*

(d) *the defendant has not served notice of an intention to plead not guilty, or of a desire not to be tried in accordance with that section.*

Under section 45 of the Children and Young Persons Act 1933[9] and under the Justices of the Peace Rules 2016, where the court is a youth court comprising justices each member must be authorised to sit as a member of that youth court.

Under section 150 of the Magistrates' Courts Act 1980[10], where two or more justices are present one may act on behalf of all.

Section 59 of the Children and Young Persons Act 1933[11] requires that—

(a) *the expressions 'conviction' and 'sentence' must not be used by a magistrates' court dealing with a defendant under 18; and*

(b) *a reference in legislation to a defendant who is convicted, to a conviction, or to a sentence, must be read as including a reference to a defendant who is found guilty of an offence, a finding of guilt, or an order made on a finding of guilt, respectively.*

Under section 14 of the Magistrates' Courts Act 1980, proceedings which begin with a summons or requisition will become void if the defendant, at any time during or after the trial, makes a statutory declaration that he or she did not know of them until a date after the trial began. See rule 44.2.

Under section 142 of the Magistrates' Courts Act 1980—

(a) *where a defendant is convicted by a magistrates' court, the court may order that the case should be heard again by different justices; and*

(b) *the court may vary or rescind an order which it has made when dealing with a convicted defendant,*

if in either case it appears to the court to be in the interests of justice to do so. See rule 44.3.

See also Part 32 (Breach, revocation and amendment of community and other orders). Rule 32.4 (Procedure on application by responsible officer) applies rules in this Part to the procedure with which that rule deals.]

General rules   R24.2

24.2 (1) Where this Part applies—

(a) the general rule is that the hearing must be in public; but

(b) the court may exercise any power it has to—

(i) impose reporting restrictions,

(ii) withhold information from the public, or

(iii) order a hearing in private; and

(c) unless the court otherwise directs, only the following may attend a hearing in a youth court—

(i) the parties and their legal representatives,

(ii) a defendant's parents, guardian or other supporting adult,

Criminal Justice Act 1988 (c. 33), section 92 of, and paragraph 8 of Schedule 11 to, the Children Act 1989 (c. 41), section 109 of, and paragraph 237 of Schedule 8 and Schedule 10 to, the Courts Act 2003 (c. 39). Section 148 was amended by section 109 of, and paragraph 248 of Schedule 8 to, the Courts Act 2003 (c. 39).

[7] S.I. 2016/709.

[8] 1980 c. 43; section 16A was inserted by section 48 of the Criminal Justice and Courts Act 2015 (c. 2).

[9] 1933 c. 12; section 45 was substituted by section 50 of the Courts Act 2003 (c. 39) and amended by section 15 of, and paragraph 20 of Schedule 4 to, the Constitutional Reform Act 2005 (c. 4).

[10] 1980 c. 43; section 150 has been amended but none is relevant to the note to this rule.

[11] 1933 c. 12; section 59 was amended by sections 79 and 83 of, and Schedules 9 and 10 to, the Criminal Justice Act 1948 (c. 58) and section 18 of the Costs in Criminal Cases Act 1952 (c. 48).

        (iii) a witness,

        (iv) anyone else directly concerned in the case, and

        (v) a representative of a news-gathering or reporting organisation.

(2) Unless already done, the justices' legal adviser or the court must—

    (a) read the allegation of the offence to the defendant;

    (b) explain, in terms the defendant can understand (with help, if necessary)—

        (i) the allegation, and

        (ii) what the procedure at the hearing will be;

    (c) ask whether the defendant has been advised about the potential effect on sentence of a guilty plea;

    (d) ask whether the defendant pleads guilty or not guilty; and

    (e) take the defendant's plea.

(3) The court may adjourn the hearing—

    (a) at any stage, to the same or to another magistrates' court; or

    (b) to a youth court, where the court is not itself a youth court and the defendant is under 18.

(4) Paragraphs (1) and (2) of this rule do not apply where the court tries a case under rule 24.9 (Single justice procedure: special rules).

[Note. See sections 10, 16A, 27A, 29 and 121 of the Magistrates' Courts Act 1980[12] and sections 46 and 47 of the Children and Young Persons Act 1933.

Where the case has been allocated for trial in a magistrates' court, part of the procedure under rule 24.2(2) will have taken place.

Part 6 contains rules about reporting, etc. restrictions. For a list of the court's powers to impose reporting and access restrictions, see the note to rule 6.1.

Under section 34A of the Children and Young Persons Act 1933[13], the court—

    (a) may require the defendant's parents or guardian to attend court with the defendant, where the defendant is under 18; and

    (b) must do so, where the defendant is under 16, unless satisfied that that would be unreasonable.

Part 7 contains rules about (among other things) the issue of a summons to a parent or guardian.

Part 46 (Representatives) contains rules allowing a parent, guardian or other supporting adult to help a defendant under 18.]

R24.3   Procedure on plea of not guilty

24.3 (1) This rule applies—

    (a) if the defendant has—

        (i) entered a plea of not guilty, or

        (ii) not entered a plea; or

    (b) if, in either case, it appears to the court that there may be grounds for making a hospital order without convicting the defendant.

(2) If a not guilty plea was taken on a previous occasion, the justices' legal adviser or the court must ask the defendant to confirm that plea.

(3) In the following sequence—

    (a) the prosecutor may summarise the prosecution case, concisely identifying the relevant law, outlining the facts and indicating the matters likely to be in dispute;

    (b) to help the members of the court to understand the case and resolve any issue in it, the court may invite the defendant concisely to identify what is in issue;

    (c) the prosecutor must introduce the evidence on which the prosecution case relies;

    (d) at the conclusion of the prosecution case, on the defendant's application or on its own initiative, the court—

        (i) may acquit on the ground that the prosecution evidence is insufficient for any reasonable court properly to convict, but

        (ii) must not do so unless the prosecutor has had an opportunity to make representations;

---

[12] 1980 c. 43; section 29 was amended by sections 68 and 100 of, and paragraph 6 of Schedule 8 and paragraph 40 of Schedule 11 to, the Criminal Justice Act 1991 (c. 53), section 168 of, and paragraph 41 of Schedule 10 to, the Criminal Justice and Public Order Act 1994 (c. 33) and section 41 of, and paragraph 51 of Schedule 3 to, the Criminal Justice Act 2003 (c. 44). Section 16A was inserted by section 48 of the Criminal Justice and Courts Act 2015 (c. 2).

[13] 1933 c. 12; section 34A was inserted by section 56 of the Criminal Justice Act 1991 (c. 53) and amended by section 107 of, and paragraph 1 of Schedule 5 to, the Local Government Act 2000 (c. 22).

    (e) the justices' legal adviser or the court must explain, in terms the defendant can understand (with help, if necessary)—
        (i)   the right to give evidence, and
        (ii) the potential effect of not doing so at all, or of refusing to answer a question while doing so;
    (f) the defendant may introduce evidence;
    (g) a party may introduce further evidence if it is then admissible (for example, because it is in rebuttal of evidence already introduced);
    (h) the prosecutor may make final representations in support of the prosecution case, where—
        (i)   the defendant is represented by a legal representative, or
        (ii) whether represented or not, the defendant has introduced evidence other than his or her own; and
    (i) the defendant may make final representations in support of the defence case.
  (4) Where a party wants to introduce evidence or make representations after that party's opportunity to do so under paragraph (3), the court—
    (a) may refuse to receive any such evidence or representations; and
    (b) must not receive any such evidence or representations after it has announced its verdict.
  (5) If the court—
    (a) convicts the defendant; or
    (b) makes a hospital order instead of doing so,
    it must give sufficient reasons to explain its decision.
  (6) If the court acquits the defendant, it may—
    (a) give an explanation of its decision; and
    (b) exercise any power it has to make—
        (i)   a behaviour order,
        (ii) a costs order.

[Note. See section 9 of the Magistrates' Courts Act 1980[14].

Under section 37(3) of the Mental Health Act 1983[15], if the court is satisfied that the defendant did the act or made the omission alleged, then it may make a hospital order without convicting the defendant.

Under section 35 of the Criminal Justice and Public Order Act 1994[16], the court may draw such inferences as appear proper from a defendant's failure to give evidence, or refusal without good cause to answer a question while doing so. The procedure set out in rule 24.3(3)(e) is prescribed by that section.

The admissibility of evidence that a party introduces is governed by rules of evidence.

Section 2 of the Criminal Procedure Act 1865[17] and section 3 of the Criminal Evidence Act 1898[18] restrict the circumstances in which the prosecutor may make final representations without the court's permission.

See rule 24.11 for the procedure if the court convicts the defendant.

Part 31 contains rules about behaviour orders.]

Evidence of a witness in person

R24.4

24.4 (1) This rule applies where a party wants to introduce evidence by calling a witness to give that evidence in person.
  (2) Unless the court otherwise directs—
    (a) a witness waiting to give evidence must not wait inside the courtroom, unless that witness is—
        (i)   a party, or
        (ii) an expert witness;
    (b) a witness who gives evidence in the courtroom must do so from the place provided for that purpose; and
    (c) a witness' address must not be announced unless it is relevant to an issue in the case.
  (3) Before the witness gives evidence—
    (a) the party who introduces the witness' evidence must explain how that evidence is admissible, unless it is only evidence of fact within the witness' direct knowledge; and
    (b) the witness must take an oath or affirm, unless other legislation otherwise provides.

---

[14] 1980 c. 43.
[15] 1983 c. 20; section 37(3) was amended by sections 1 and 55 of, and paragraphs 1 and 7 of Schedule 1 and Schedule 11 to, the Mental Health Act 2007 (c. 12). 37(3) was amended by sections 1 and 55 of, and paragraphs 1 and 7 of Schedule 1 and Schedule 11 to, the Mental Health Act 2007 (c. 12).
[16] 1994 c. 33; section 35 was amended by sections 35 and 120 of, and Schedule 10 to, the Crime and Disorder Act 1998 (c. 37). The Criminal Justice Act 2003 (c. 44) amendment to section 35 is not relevant to procedure in magistrates' courts.
[17] 1865 c. 18; section 2 was amended by section 10(2) of, and Part III of Schedule 3 to, the Criminal Law Act 1967 (c. 58).
[18] 1898 c. 36; section 3 was amended by section 1(2) of the Criminal Procedure (Right of Reply) Act 1964 (c. 34).

    (4) In the following sequence—
        (a) the party who calls a witness must ask questions in examination-in-chief;
        (b) every other party may ask questions in cross-examination; and
        (c) the party who called the witness may ask questions in re-examination.
    (5) If other legislation so permits, at any time while giving evidence a witness may refer to a record of that witness' recollection of events.
    (6) The justices' legal adviser or the court may—
        (a) ask a witness questions; and in particular
        (b) where the defendant is not represented, ask any question necessary in the defendant's interests.

[Note. Section 53 of the Youth Justice and Criminal Evidence Act 1999[19] provides that everyone is competent to give evidence in criminal proceedings unless unable to understand questions put or give intelligible answers. See also section 1 of the Criminal Evidence Act 1898[20].

Part 19 contains rules about the introduction of evidence of expert opinion. Part 20 contains rules about the introduction of hearsay evidence.

Sections 1, 3, 5 and 6 of the Oaths Act 1978[21] provide for the taking of oaths and the making of affirmations, and for the words that must be used. Section 28 of the Children and Young Persons Act 1963[22] provides that in a youth court, and where a witness in any court is under 18, an oath must include the words 'I promise' in place of the words 'I swear'. Under sections 55 and 56 of the Youth Justice and Criminal Evidence Act 1999, a person may give evidence without taking an oath, or making an affirmation, where that person (i) is under 14 or (ii) has an insufficient appreciation of the solemnity of the occasion and of the particular responsibility to tell the truth which is involved in taking an oath.

The questions that may be put to a witness—

    (a) by a party are governed by rules of evidence, for example—
        (i) the rule that a question must be relevant to what is in issue,
        (ii) the rule that the party who calls a witness must not ask that witness a leading question about what is in dispute, and
        (iii) the rule that a party who calls a witness may contradict that witness only in limited circumstances (see section 3 of the Criminal Procedure Act 1865)[23];
    (b) by the justices' legal adviser or the court are in their discretion, but that is subject to—
        (i) rules of evidence, and
        (ii) rule 1.3 (the application by the court of the overriding objective).

Under sections 34, 35 and 36 of the Youth Justice and Criminal Evidence Act 1999[24], a defendant who is not represented may not cross-examine a witness where—

    (a) the defendant is charged with a sexual offence against the witness;
    (b) the defendant is charged with a sexual offence, or one of certain other offences, and the witness is a child; or
    (c) the court prohibits the defendant from cross-examining the witness.

Part 23 contains rules relevant to restrictions on cross-examination.

Under section 139 of the Criminal Justice Act 2003[25], a witness may refresh his or her memory by referring to a record made before the hearing, either contained in a document made or verified by the witness, or in the transcript of a sound recording, if—

    (a) the witness states that it records his or her recollection of events at that earlier time; and
    (b) that recollection is likely to have been significantly better when the record was made than at the time of the hearing.

---

[19] 1999 c. 23.
[20] 1898 c. 36; section 1 was amended by section 1 of the Criminal Evidence Act 1979 (c. 16), section 78 of, and Schedule 16 to, the Criminal Justice Act 1982 (c. 48), sections 80(9) and 119(2) of, and Schedule 7 to, the Police and Criminal Evidence Act 1984 (c. 60), sections 31 and 168 of, and paragraph 2 of Schedule 10, and Schedule 11 to, the Criminal Justice and Public Order Act 1994 (c. 33), section 67 of, and paragraph 1 of Schedule 4, and Schedule 6 to, the Youth Justice and Criminal Evidence Act 1999 (c. 23) and sections 331 and 332 of, and paragraph 80 of Schedule 36, and Part 5 of Schedule 37 to, the Criminal Justice Act 2003 (c. 44).
[21] 1978 c. 19.
[22] 1963 c. 37; section 28 was amended by section 2 of the Oaths Act 1978 (c. 19) and section 100 of, and paragraph 40 of Schedule 11 to, the Criminal Justice Act 1991 (c. 53).
[23] 1865 c. 18.
[24] 1999 c. 23; section 35 was amended by sections 139 and 140 of, and paragraph 41 of Schedule 6 and Schedule 7 to, the Sexual Offences Act 2003 (c. 42) and section 148 of, and paragraphs 35 and 36 of Schedule 26 to, the Criminal Justice and Immigration Act 2008 (c. 4).
[25] 2003 c. 44.

In some circumstances, a witness may give evidence in accordance with special measures directed by the court under section 19 of the Youth Justice and Criminal Evidence Act 1999[26], or by live link under section 32 of the Criminal Justice Act 1988[27] or section 51 of the Criminal Justice Act 2003. Part 18 contains relevant rules.]

Evidence of a witness in writing   R24.5

24.5 (1) This rule applies where a party wants to introduce in evidence the written statement of a witness to which applies—

    (a) Part 16 (Written witness statements);

    (b) Part 19 (Expert evidence); or

    (c) Part 20 (Hearsay evidence).

    (2) That party must explain how the evidence is admissible unless it is—

    (a) evidence of fact within the direct knowledge of the person who made the written statement served under rule 16.4 (Written witness statement in evidence);

    (b) contained in an expert's report served under rule 19.3 (Introduction of expert evidence); or

    (c) identified as hearsay in a notice served under rule 20.2 (Notice to introduce hearsay evidence).

    (3) If the court admits such evidence—

    (a) the court must read the statement; and

    (b) unless the court otherwise directs, if any member of the public, including any reporter, is present, each relevant part of the statement must be read or summarised aloud.

[Note. See Parts 16, 19 and 20, and the other legislation to which those Parts apply. The admissibility of evidence that a party introduces is governed by rules of evidence.

A written witness statement to which Part 16 applies may only be introduced in evidence if there has been no objection within the time limit to which rule 16.4 refers.

An expert report to which Part 19 applies may only be introduced in evidence if it has been served in accordance with rule 19.3.

Rule 20.3 provides for opposing the introduction of hearsay evidence, including such evidence in a document. Where a witness gives evidence in person, a previous written statement by that witness may be admissible as evidence under section 119 (Inconsistent statements) or under section 120 (Other previous statements of witnesses) of the Criminal Justice Act 2003[28].]

Evidence by admission   R24.6

24.6 (1) This rule applies where—

    (a) a party introduces in evidence a fact admitted by another party; or

    (b) parties jointly admit a fact.

    (2) Unless the court otherwise directs, a written record must be made of the admission.

[Note. See section 10 of the Criminal Justice Act 1967[29]. The admissibility of evidence that a party introduces is governed by rules of evidence.]

Procedure on plea of guilty   R24.7

24.7 (1) This rule applies if—

    (a) the defendant pleads guilty; and

    (b) the court is satisfied that the plea represents a clear acknowledgement of guilt.

    (2) The court may convict the defendant without receiving evidence.

[Note. See section 9 of the Magistrates' Courts Act 1980[30].]

Written guilty plea: special rules   R24.8

24.8 (1) This rule applies where—

    (a) the offence alleged—

      (i) can be tried only in a magistrates' court, and

      (ii) is not one specified under section 12(1)(a) of the Magistrates' Courts Act 1980[31];

    (b) the defendant is at least 16 years old;

---

[26] 1999 c. 23.

[27] 1988 c. 33; section 32 was amended by section 55 of the Criminal Justice Act 1991 (c. 53), section 29 of, and paragraph 16 of Schedule 2 to, the Criminal Appeal Act 1995 (c. 35), section 62 of the Criminal Procedure and Investigations Act 1996 (c. 25), section 67 of, and Schedule 6 and paragraph 3 of Schedule 7 to, the Youth Justice and Criminal Evidence Act 1999 (c. 23) and paragraphs 24 and 26 of the Schedule to S.I. 2004/2035.

[28] 2003 c. 44; section 120 was amended by sections 112 and 178 of, and Schedule 23 to, the Coroners and Justice Act 2009 (c. 25).

[29] 1967 c. 80.

[30] 1980 c. 43.

[31] 1980 c. 43; section 12(1)(a) was amended by sections 308 and 332 of, and Part 12 of Schedule 37 to, the Criminal Justice Act 2003 (c. 44).

    (c) the prosecutor has served on the defendant—
        (i)   the summons or requisition,
        (ii) the material listed in paragraph (2) on which the prosecutor relies to set out the facts of the offence,
        (iii) the material listed in paragraph (3) on which the prosecutor relies to provide the court with information relevant to sentence,
        (iv) a notice that the procedure set out in this rule applies, and
        (v) a notice for the defendant's use if the defendant wants to plead guilty without attending court; and
    (d) the prosecutor has served on the court officer—
        (i)   copies of those documents, and
        (ii) a certificate of service of those documents on the defendant.

(2) The material that the prosecutor must serve to set out the facts of the offence is—
    (a) a summary of the evidence on which the prosecution case is based;
    (b) any—
        (i)   written witness statement to which Part 16 (Written witness statements) applies, or
        (ii) document or extract setting out facts; or
    (c) any combination of such a summary, statement, document or extract.

(3) The material that the prosecutor must serve to provide information relevant to sentence is—
    (a) details of any previous conviction of the defendant which the prosecutor considers relevant, other than any conviction listed in the defendant's driving record;
    (b) if applicable, a notice that the defendant's driving record will be made available to the court; and
    (c) a notice containing or describing any other information about the defendant, relevant to sentence, which will be made available to the court.

(4) A defendant who wants to plead guilty without attending court must, as soon as practicable and in any event no later than the business day before the hearing date—
    (a) serve a notice of guilty plea on the court officer; and
    (b) include with that notice—
        (i)   any representations that the defendant wants the court to consider, and
        (ii) a statement of the defendant's assets and other financial circumstances.

(5) A defendant who wants to withdraw such a notice must notify the court officer in writing before the hearing date.

(6) If the defendant does not withdraw the notice before the hearing date, then on or after that date—
    (a) to establish the facts of the offence and other information about the defendant relevant to sentence, the court may take account only of—
        (i)   information contained in a document served by the prosecutor under paragraph (1),
        (ii) any previous conviction listed in the defendant's driving record, where the offence is under the Road Traffic Regulation Act 1984[32], the Road Traffic Act 1988[33], the Road Traffic (Consequential Provisions) Act 1988[34] or the Road Traffic (Driver Licensing and Information Systems) Act 1989[35],
        (iii) any other information about the defendant, relevant to sentence, of which the prosecutor served notice under paragraph (1), and
        (iv) any representations and any other information served by the defendant under paragraph (4)
        and rule 24.11(3) to (9) inclusive must be read accordingly;
    (b) unless the court otherwise directs, the prosecutor need not attend; and
    (c) the court may accept such a guilty plea and pass sentence in the defendant's absence.

(7) With the defendant's agreement, the court may deal with the case in the same way as under paragraph (6) where the defendant is present and—
    (a) has served a notice of guilty plea under paragraph (4); or
    (b) pleads guilty there and then.

[*Note. The procedure set out in this rule is prescribed by sections 12 and 12A of the Magistrates' Courts Act 1980[36]. Under section 12(1)(a), the Secretary of State can specify offences to which the procedure will not apply. None has been specified.*]

---

[32] 1984 c. 27.
[33] 1988 c. 52.
[34] 1988 c. 54.
[35] 1989 c. 22.
[36] 1980 c. 43; section 12 was amended by section 45 of, and paragraph 1 of Schedule 5 to, the Criminal Justice and Public Order Act 1994 (c. 33), section 1 of the Magistrates' Courts (Procedure) Act 1998 (c. 15), section 109 of, and paragraph 203

Under section 1 of the Magistrates' Courts Act 1980[37] a justice of the peace may issue a summons requiring a defendant to attend court to answer an allegation of an offence. Under section 29 of the Criminal Justice Act 2003[38] a prosecutor authorised under that section may issue a written charge alleging an offence and a requisition requiring a defendant to attend court. Part 7 contains relevant rules.

See also rule 24.11(10)(a) under which the court must adjourn where the defendant is absent before passing a custodial sentence or imposing a disqualification.

For the court's power, where this rule applies, to take account of a previous conviction listed in a defendant's driving record, see section 13(3A) of the Road Traffic Offenders Act 1988[39].

The Practice Direction sets out forms of notice for use in connection with this rule.]

Single justice procedure: special rules   **R24.9**

24.9 (1) This rule applies where—

    (a) the offence alleged—

        (i) can be tried only in a magistrates' court, and

        (ii) is not one punishable with imprisonment;

    (b) the defendant is at least 18 years old or is a corporation;

    (c) the prosecutor has served on the defendant—

        (i) a written charge,

        (ii) the material listed in paragraph (2) on which the prosecutor relies to set out the facts of the offence,

        (iii) the material listed in paragraph (3) on which the prosecutor relies to provide the court with information relevant to sentence,

        (iv) a notice that the procedure set out in this rule applies,

        (v) a notice explaining the automatic online conviction option, if that will be available to the defendant, including explanations of penalties and liabilities, of where to obtain more details and of how to accept that option,

        (vi) a notice for the defendant's use if the defendant wants to plead guilty and wants to be sentenced by a single justice,

        (vii) a notice for the defendant's use if the defendant wants to plead guilty but wants the case dealt with at a hearing by a court comprising more than one justice, and

        (viii) a notice for the defendant's use if the defendant wants to plead not guilty; and

    (d) the prosecutor has served on the court officer—

        (i) copies of those documents, and

        (ii) a certificate of service of those documents on the defendant.

  (2) The material that the prosecutor must serve to set out the facts of the offence is—

    (a) a summary of the evidence on which the prosecution case is based;

    (b) any—

        (i) written witness statement to which Part 16 (Written witness statements) applies, or

        (ii) document or extract setting out facts; or

    (c) any combination of such a summary, statement, document or extract.

  (3) The material that the prosecutor must serve to provide information relevant to sentence is—

    (a) details of any previous conviction of the defendant which the prosecutor considers relevant, other than any conviction listed in the defendant's driving record;

    (b) if applicable, a notice that the defendant's driving record will be made available to the court; and

    (c) a notice containing or describing any other information about the defendant, relevant to sentence, which will be made available to the court.

---

of Schedule 8 to, the Courts Act 2003 (c. 39), section 308 of, and Part 12 of Schedule 37 to, the Criminal Justice Act 2003 (c. 44) and section 81 of the Deregulation Act 2015 (c. 20). Section 12A was inserted by section 45 of, and paragraph 2 of Schedule 5 to, the Criminal Justice and Public Order Act 1994 (c. 33) and amended by section 109 of, and paragraph 204 of Schedule 8 to, the Courts Act 2003 (c. 39).

[37] 1980 c. 43; section 1 was amended by section 68 of, and paragraph 6 of Schedule 8 to, the Criminal Justice Act 1991 (c. 53), sections 43 and 109 of, and Schedule 10 to, the Courts Act 2003 (c. 39), section 31 of, and paragraph 12 of Schedule 7 to, the Criminal Justice Act 2003 (c. 44) and section 153 of the Police Reform and Social Responsibility Act 2011. It is further amended by paragraphs 7 and 8 of Schedule 36 to, the Criminal Justice Act 2003 (c. 44), with effect from a date to be appointed.

[38] 2003 c. 44; section 29 has been brought into force for certain purposes only (see S.I. 2007/1999, 2008/1424, 2009/2879, 2010/3005, 2011/2188, 2012/825 and 2014/633). It was amended by section 50 of, and paragraph 130 of Schedule 4 to, the Commissioners for Revenue and Customs Act 2005 (c. 11), section 59 of, and paragraph 196 of Schedule 4 to, the Serious Organised Crime and Police Act 2005 (c. 15), section 15 of, and paragraph 187 of Schedule 8 to, the Crime and Courts Act 2013 (c. 22), S.I. 2014/834 and section 46 of the Criminal Justice and Courts Act 2015 (c. 2).

[39] 1988 c. 53; section 13(3A) was inserted by section 2 of the Magistrates' Courts (Procedure) Act 1998 (c. 15).

(4)   Not more than 15 business days after service on the defendant of the documents listed in
       paragraph (1)(c)—
       (a) a defendant who wants to plead guilty and wants to accept the automatic online
            conviction option, if that is offered, may do so;
       (b) a defendant who wants to plead guilty and wants to be sentenced by a single justice must
            serve a notice to that effect on the court officer and include with that notice—
            (i)   any representations that the defendant wants the court to consider, and
            (ii) a statement of the defendant's assets and other financial circumstances;
       (c) a defendant who wants to plead guilty but wants the case dealt with at a hearing by a court
            comprising more than one justice must serve a notice to that effect on the court officer; and
       (d) a defendant who wants to plead not guilty must serve a notice to that effect on the court
            officer.

(5)   If within 15 business days of service on the defendant of the documents listed in paragraph
       (1)(c) the defendant accepts the automatic online conviction option (if that is offered) and
       does not then withdraw that acceptance within the next 5 business days —
       (a) at the end of the fifth business day after acceptance the defendant is convicted of the
            offence and liable to each penalty and other payment specified for it; and
       (b) paragraphs (6) to (11) do not apply.

(6)   If within 15 business days of service on the defendant of the documents listed in paragraph
       (1)(c) the defendant serves a notice to plead guilty and to be sentenced by a single justice under
       paragraph (4)(b)—
       (a) the court officer must arrange for the court to deal with the case in accordance with that
            notice; and
       (b) the time for service of any other notice under paragraph (4) expires at once.

(7)   If within 15 business days of service on the defendant of the documents listed in paragraph
       (1)(c) the defendant wants to withdraw a notice served under paragraph (4)(b) (notice to plead
       guilty and to be sentenced by a single justice), paragraph (4)(c) (notice to plead guilty at a hear-
       ing) or paragraph (4)(d) (notice to plead not guilty), the defendant must either —
       (a) accept the automatic online conviction option, if that was offered; or
       (b) serve—
            (i)   notice of that withdrawal on the court officer, and
            (ii) any substitute notice under paragraph (4).

(8)   Paragraph (9) applies where by the date of trial the defendant has not—
       (a) served notice under paragraph (4)(c) or (d) of wanting to plead guilty at a hearing, or
            wanting to plead not guilty; or
       (b) given notice to that effect under section 16B(2) of the Magistrates' Courts Act 1980[40]
            (notice objecting to single justice procedure trial).

(9)   Where this paragraph applies—
       (a) the court may try the case in the parties' absence and without a hearing;
       (b) the court may accept any guilty plea of which the defendant has given notice under
            paragraph (4)(b); and
       (c) to establish the facts of the offence and other information about the defendant relevant
            to sentence, the court may take account only of—
            (i)   information contained in a document served by the prosecutor under paragraph
                   (1),
            (ii)   any previous conviction listed in the defendant's driving record, where the offence
                   is under the Road Traffic Regulation Act 1984, the Road Traffic Act 1988, the Road
                   Traffic (Consequential Provisions) Act 1988 or the Road Traffic (Driver Licensing
                   and Information Systems) Act 1989,
            (iii) any other information about the defendant, relevant to sentence, of which the
                   prosecutor served notice under paragraph (1), and
            (iv)   any representations and any other information served by the defendant under
                   paragraph (4)(b)
       and rule 24.11(3) to (9) inclusive must be read accordingly.

(10)   Paragraph (11) applies where—
       (a) the defendant serves on the court officer a notice under paragraph (4)(c) or (d); or
       (b) the court which tries the defendant under paragraph (9) adjourns the trial for the
            defendant to attend a hearing by a court comprising more than one justice.

---

[40] 1980 c. 43; section 16B was inserted by section 48 of the Criminal Justice and Courts Act 2015 (c. 2).

(11) Where this paragraph applies, the court must exercise its power to issue a summons and—

  (a) the rules in Part 7 apply (Starting a prosecution in a magistrates' court) as if the prosecutor had just served an application for a summons to be issued in the same terms as the written charge;

  (b) the rules in Part 8 (Initial details of the prosecution case) apply as if the documents served by the prosecutor under paragraph (1) had been served under that Part; and

  (c) except for rule 24.8 (Written guilty plea: special rules) and this rule, the rules in this Part apply.

[Note. The procedure set out in this rule is prescribed by sections sections 16A to 16L of the Magistrates' Courts Act 1980[41] and section 29 of the Criminal Justice Act 2003[42]. Under section 16A of the 1980 Act, the court may comprise a single justice. Under section 29 of the 2003 Act, a prosecutor authorised under that section may issue a written charge alleging an offence and a single justice procedure notice. Part 7 contains relevant rules.

Under section 1 of the Magistrates' Courts Act 1980[43]) a justice of the peace may issue a summons requiring a defendant to attend court to answer an allegation of an offence. Under sections 16C and 16D of the 1980 Act, a justice may issue a summons requiring a defendant to attend court in the circumstances listed in rule 24.9(10).

Under section 16K(1) of the Magistrates' Courts Act 1980 the time when a conviction takes effect after the defendant accepts the automatic online conviction option, if that is offered, is to be determined in accordance with Criminal Procedure Rules.

For the court's power, where this rule applies, to take account of—

  (a) information contained or described in a document served by the prosecutor under rule 24.9(1), see section 16F of the Magistrates' Courts Act 1980[44];

  (b) a previous conviction listed in a defendant's driving record, see section 13(3A) of the Road Traffic Offenders Act 1988[45].

The Practice Direction sets out forms of notice for use in connection with this rule.]

Application to withdraw a guilty plea   R24.10

24.10 (1) This rule applies where the defendant wants to withdraw a guilty plea.

  (2) The defendant must apply to do so—

  (a) as soon as practicable after becoming aware of the reasons for doing so; and

  (b) before sentence.

  (3) Unless the court otherwise directs, the application must be in writing and the defendant must serve it on—

  (a) the court officer; and

  (b) the prosecutor.

  (4) The application must—

  (a) explain why it would be unjust not to allow the defendant to withdraw the guilty plea;

  (b) identify—

  (i) any witness that the defendant wants to call, and

  (ii) any other proposed evidence; and

  (c) say whether the defendant waives legal professional privilege, giving any relevant name and date.

Procedure if the court convicts   R24.11

24.11 (1) This rule applies if the court convicts the defendant.

  (2) The court—

  (a) may exercise its power to require—

  (i) a statement of the defendant's financial circumstances,

---

[41] 1980 c. 43; sections 16E and 16F were inserted by section 48 of the Criminal Justice and Courts Act 2015 (c. 2). Sections 16G to 16L are inserted by section 3 of the Judicial Review and Courts Act 2022 (c. 35) with effect from a date to be appointed.

[42] 2003 c. 44; section 29 has been brought into force for certain purposes only (see S.I. 2007/1999, 2008/1424, 2009/2879, 2010/3005, 2011/2188, 2012/825 and 2014/633). It was amended by section 50 of, and paragraph 130 of Schedule 4 to, the Commissioners for Revenue and Customs Act 2005 (c. 11), section 59 of, and paragraph 196 of Schedule 4 to, the Serious Organised Crime and Police Act 2005 (c. 15), section 15 of, and paragraph 187 of Schedule 8 to, the Crime and Courts Act 2013 (c. 22), S.I. 2014/834 and section 46 of the Criminal Justice and Courts Act 2015 (c. 2).

[43] 1980 c. 43; section 1 was amended by section 68 of, and paragraph 6 of Schedule 8 to, the Criminal Justice Act 1991 (c. 53), sections 43 and 109 of, and Schedule 10 to, the Courts Act 2003 (c. 39), section 31 of, and paragraph 12 of Schedule 7 to, the Criminal Justice Act 2003 (c. 44) and section 153 of the Police Reform and Social Responsibility Act 2011. It is further amended by paragraphs 7 and 8 of Schedule 36 to, the Criminal Justice Act 2003 (c. 44), with effect from a date to be appointed.

[44] 1980 c. 43; section 16F was inserted by section 48 of the Criminal Justice and Courts Act 2015 (c. 2).

[45] 1988 c. 53; section 13(3A) was inserted by section 2 of the Magistrates' Courts (Procedure) Act 1998 (c. 15).

        (ii) a pre-sentence report; and

    (b) may (and in some circumstances must) remit the defendant to a youth court for sentence where—

        (i)   the defendant is under 18, and

        (ii) the convicting court is not itself a youth court.

(3) The prosecutor must—

    (a) summarise the prosecution case, if the sentencing court has not heard evidence;

    (b) identify any offence to be taken into consideration in sentencing;

    (c) provide information relevant to sentence, including any statement of the effect of the offence on the victim, the victim's family and others;

    (d) where it is likely to assist the court, identify any other matter relevant to sentence, including—

        (i)   the legislation applicable,

        (ii) any sentencing guidelines, or guideline cases,

        (iii) aggravating and mitigating features affecting the defendant's culpability and the harm which the offence caused, was intended to cause or might forseeably have caused, and

        (iv) the effect of such of the information listed in paragraph (2)(a) as the court may need to take into account; and

    (e) in a youth court, if the maker of a statement to which paragraph (3)(c) refers wishes to read that statement to the court, apply for a direction to which rule 24.2(1)(c) refers (attendance) and for any other direction that the prosecutor wants—

        (i)   when, or as soon as practicable after, the court convicts the defendant, and

        (ii) as a general rule, no later than 5 business days before the hearing at which sentence is due to be passed.

(4) The defendant must provide details of financial circumstances—

    (a) in any form required by the court officer;

    (b) by any date directed by the court or by the court officer.

(5) Where the defendant pleads guilty but wants to be sentenced on a different basis to that disclosed by the prosecution case—

    (a) the defendant must set out that basis in writing, identifying what is in dispute;

    (b) the court may invite the parties to make representations about whether the dispute is material to sentence; and

    (c) if the court decides that it is a material dispute, the court must—

        (i)   invite such further representations or evidence as it may require, and

        (ii) decide the dispute.

(6) Where the court has power to order the endorsement of the defendant's driving record, or power to order the defendant to be disqualified from driving—

    (a) if other legislation so permits, a defendant who wants the court not to exercise that power must introduce the evidence or information on which the defendant relies;

    (b) the prosecutor may introduce evidence; and

    (c) the parties may make representations about that evidence or information.

(7) Before the court passes sentence—

    (a) the court must—

        (i)   give the defendant an opportunity to make representations and introduce evidence relevant to sentence, and

        (ii) where the defendant is under 18, give the defendant's parents, guardian or other supporting adult, if present, such an opportunity as well; and

    (b) the justices' legal adviser or the court must elicit any further information relevant to sentence that the court may require.

(8) If the court requires more information, it may exercise its power to adjourn the hearing for not more than—

    (a) 3 weeks at a time, if the defendant will be in custody; or

    (b) 4 weeks at a time.

(9) When the court has taken into account all the evidence, information and any report available, the court must—

    (a) subject to paragraph (10), as a general rule, pass sentence there and then;

    (b) when passing sentence, explain the reasons for deciding on that sentence, unless neither the defendant nor any member of the public, including any reporter, is present;

    (c) when passing sentence, explain to the defendant its effect, the consequences of failing to comply with any order or pay any fine, and any power that the court has to vary or review the sentence, unless—

        (i)   the defendant is absent, or

        (ii) the defendant's ill-health or disorderly conduct makes such an explanation impracticable;

    (d) give any such explanation in terms the defendant, if present, can understand (with help, if necessary); and

    (e) consider exercising any power it has to make a costs or other order.

  (10) Despite the general rule—

    (a) the court must adjourn the hearing if—

        (i) the case started with a summons, requisition or single justice procedure notice,

        (ii) the defendant is absent, and

        (iii) the court considers passing a custodial sentence (where it can do so), or imposing a disqualification (unless it has already adjourned the hearing to give the defendant an opportunity to attend);

    (b) the court may defer sentence for up to 6 months;

    (c) the court may, and in some cases must, commit the defendant to the Crown Court for sentence;

    (d) if the prosecutor asks the court to commit the defendant to the Crown Court in respect of an offence so that a confiscation order can be considered—

        (i) the court must commit the defendant for that purpose, and

        (ii) sub-paragraph (e) applies; and

    (e) where this sub-paragraph applies—

        (i) the court may commit the defendant to the Crown Court to be dealt with there for any other offence of which the defendant has been convicted and with which the magistrates' court otherwise could deal, and

        (ii) if it does so, the court must state whether it would have committed the defendant to the Crown Court for sentence anyway under section 14, 16 or 16A of the Sentencing Act 2020[46].

[Note. See sections 9, 10 and 11 of the Magistrates' Courts Act 1980[47], and sections 31, 52, 59, 63, 124, 125 and 126 of the Sentencing Act 2020[48].

Under section 11(3A) of the 1980 Act, a custodial sentence passed in the defendant's absence does not take effect until the defendant is brought before the court.

Under sections 57D and 57E of the Crime and Disorder Act 1998[49], the court may require a defendant to attend a sentencing hearing by live link.

Under section 35 of the Sentencing Act 2020[50], the court may require a defendant who is an individual to provide a statement of assets and other financial circumstances if the defendant—

    (a) serves notice of guilty plea, where rule 24.8 (Written guilty plea: special rules) applies; or

    (b) is convicted.

Under section 20A of the Criminal Justice Act 1991[51], it is an offence for a defendant knowingly or recklessly to make a false or incomplete statement of assets or other financial circumstances, or to fail to provide such a statement, in response to a request by a court officer on behalf of the court.

Under section 30 of the Sentencing Act 2020 , the general rule (subject to exceptions) is that the court must obtain and consider a pre-sentence report—

    (a) where it is considering a custodial sentence or a community sentence;

---

[46] 2020 c. 17; section 16A was inserted by section 46 of, and paragraph 26 of Schedule 13 to, the Counter-Terrorism and Sentencing Act 2021 (c. 11).

[47] 1980 c. 43; section 10 was amended by section 59 of, and paragraph 1 of Schedule 9 to, the Criminal Justice Act 1982 (c. 48), section 68 of, and paragraph 6 of Schedule 8 to, the Criminal Justice Act 1991 (c. 53) and section 47 of the Crime and Disorder Act 1998 (c. 37). Section 11 was amended by section 123 of, and paragraph 1 of Schedule 8 to, the Criminal Justice Act 1988 (c. 33), section 168 of, and paragraph 39 of Schedule 10 to, the Criminal Justice and Public Order Act 1994 (c. 33), section 119 of, and paragraph 39 of Schedule 8 to, the Crime and Disorder Act 1998 (c. 37), section 304 of, and paragraphs 25 and 26 of Schedule 32 to, the Criminal Justice Act 2003 (c. 44) and section 54 of the Criminal Justice and Immigration Act 2008 (c. 4).

[48] 2020 c. 17.

[49] 1998 c. 37; sections 57A to 57E were substituted for section 57 as originally enacted by section 45 of the Police and Justice Act 2006 (c. 48), and amended by sections 106, 109 and 178 of, and Part 3 of Schedule 23 to, the Coroners and Justice Act 2009 (c. 25).

[50] 2020 c. 17.

[51] 1991 c. 53; section 20A was inserted by section 168 of, and paragraph 43 of Schedule 9 to, the Criminal Justice and Public Order Act 1994 (c. 33) and amended by sections 95 and 109 of, and paragraph 350 of Schedule 8 to, the Courts Act 2003 (c. 39) and section 44 of, and paragraph 26 of Schedule 16 to, the Crime and Courts Act 2013 (c. 22).

(b) where it thinks the defendant may pose a significant risk of causing serious harm to the public by
     further offending.

Under section 32(3) of the Sentencing Act 2020, where the court obtains a written pre-sentence report about a
defendant who is under 18, it may direct that information in it must be withheld, if it would be likely to create
a risk of significant harm to the defendant.

For the circumstances in which a magistrates' court may (and, in some cases, must) remit the defendant to a youth
court for sentence, section 25 of the Sentencing Act 2020.

The Sentencing Council may issue sentencing guidelines under section 120 of the Coroners and Justice Act
2009[52].

For the circumstances in which a court may (and, in some cases, must) order the endorsement of a defendant's
driving record, or the disqualification of a defendant from driving, see sections 34, 35 and 44 of the Road Traffic
Offenders Act 1988[53]. Under that legislation, in some circumstances the court has discretion not to make such
an order. See also rule 29.1.

The evidence that may be introduced is subject to rules of evidence.

In addition to the specific powers to which this rule applies, the court has a general power to adjourn a trial: see
rule 24.2.

Under section 52(4) of the Sentencing Act 2020, Criminal Procedure Rules may prescribe cases in which there
do not apply the court's usual duties to give reasons and explanations. Written notice of the effect of some sentences
is required by rule 28.2 (Notice of requirements of suspended sentence or community, etc. order), rule 28.3
(Notification requirements) and rule 30.2 (notice of fine or other financial order).

Under section 3 of the Sentencing Act 2020, if (among other things) the defendant consents, the court may defer
sentence for up to 6 months, for the purpose of allowing it to take account of the defendant's conduct after
conviction, or any change in the defendant's circumstances.

For the circumstances in which a magistrates' court may (and, in some cases, must) commit a defendant to the
Crown Court for sentence or for the making of other orders beyond a magistrates' court's powers, see—

(a) sections 14, 15, 16, 16A, 17, 18, 19 and 20 of the Sentencing Act 2020[54];
(b) the provisions listed in section 24 of the 2020 Act (including section 70 of the Proceeds of Crime Act
     2002[55]); and
(c) paragraph 11 of Schedule 16 to the 2020 Act.

See section 70(5) of the Proceeds of Crime Act 2002 for the court's power to make the statement to which this rule
refers.

See also rules 9.15 (Committal for sentence of offence related to an offence sent for trial) and 28.8 (Sentencing,
etc. after committal to the Crown Court). The note to rule 28.8 summarises the statutory provisions that apply.]

R24.12   **Procedure where a party is absent**

24.12 (1) This rule—

(a) applies where a party is absent; but
(b) does not apply where—
     (i)   the defendant has served a notice of guilty plea under rule 24.8 (Written guilty plea:
           special rules), or
     (ii) the court tries a case under rule 24.9 (Single justice procedure: special rules).

---

[52] 2009 c. 25.
[53] 1988 c. 53; section 34 was amended by section 29 of the Road Traffic Act 1991 (c. 40), section 3 of the Aggravated
Vehicle-Taking Act 1992 (c. 11), section 165 of, and paragraph 121 of Schedule 9 to, the Powers of Criminal Courts (Sen-
tencing) Act 2000 (c. 6), sections 56 and 107 of, and Schedule 8 to, the Police Reform Act 2002 (c. 30), section 25 of the Road
Safety Act 2006 (c. 49), article 2 of S.I. 2007/3480, paragraphs 2 and 5 of Schedule 27 to the Legal Aid, Sentencing and
Punishment of Offenders Act 2012 (c. 10), section 56 of, and paragraphs 9 and 12 of Schedule 22 to, the Crime and Courts
Act 2013 (c. 22) and section 177 of, and paragraph 90 of Schedule 21 to, the Coroners and Justice Act 2009 (c. 25). Section
35 was amended by section 48 of, and paragraph 95 of Schedule 4 to, the Road Traffic Act 1991 (c. 40), section 165 of, and
paragraph 122 of Schedule 9 to, the Powers of Criminal Courts (Sentencing) Act 2000 (c. 6) and section 177 of, and 90 of
Schedule 21 to, the Coroners and Justice Act 2009 (c. 25). Section 44 was amended by regulations 2 and 3 of, and paragraph
10 of Schedule 2 to, S.I. 1990/144 and sections 9, 10 and 59 of, and Schedule 7 to, the Road Safety Act 2006 (c. 49).
[54] 2020 c. 17; section 19 was amended by section 46 of, and paragraph 26 of Schedule 13 to, the Counter-Terrorism and
Sentencing Act 2021 (c. 11).
[55] 2002 c. 29; section 70 was amended by section 41 of, and paragraph 75 of Schedule 3 to, the Criminal Justice Act 2003 (c.
44), section 410 of, and paragraphs 181 and 195 of Schedule 24 to, the Sentencing Act 2020 (c. 17) and section 46 of, and
paragraph 19 of Schedule 13 to, the Counter-Terrorism and Sentencing Act 2021 (c. 11).

(2) Where the prosecutor is absent, the court may—

    (a) if it has received evidence, deal with the case as if the prosecutor were present; and

    (b) in any other case—

        (i) enquire into the reasons for the prosecutor's absence, and

        (ii) if satisfied there is no good reason, exercise its power to dismiss the allegation.

(3) Where the defendant is absent the general rule is that the court must proceed as if the defendant were present, and had pleaded not guilty (unless a plea already has been taken) but the general rule—

    (a) does not apply if the defendant is under 18;

    (b) is subject to the court being satisfied that—

        (i) any summons or requisition was served on the defendant a reasonable time before the hearing, or

        (ii) in a case in which the hearing has been adjourned, the defendant had reasonable notice of where and when it would resume; and

    (c) is subject also to rule 24.11(10)(a) (restrictions on passing sentence in the defendant's absence).

(4) Where the defendant is absent, the court—

    (a) must exercise its power to issue a warrant for the defendant's arrest and detention in the terms required by rule 13.3(3) (Terms of a warrant for detention or imprisonment), if it passes a custodial sentence; and

    (b) may exercise its power to issue a warrant for the defendant's arrest in any other case, if it does not apply the general rule in paragraph (3) of this rule about proceeding in the defendant's absence.

[Note. See sections 11, 15 and 16 of the Magistrates' Courts Act 1980[56].]

Under section 27 of the 1980 Act, where a magistrates' court dismisses an allegation of an offence classified as one that can be tried either in a magistrates' court or in the Crown Court (in other legislation, described as triable either way), that dismissal has the same effect as an acquittal in the Crown Court.

Under section 11 of the 1980 Act, the court may pass a custodial sentence in the defendant's absence if the case started with the defendant's arrest and charge (and not with a summons or requisition). Section 11(3A) requires that, in that event, the defendant must be brought before the court before being taken to a prison or other institution to begin serving that sentence: see also rule 13.3. Under section 7(1) of the Bail Act 1976[57], the court has power to issue a warrant for the arrest of a defendant released on bail who has failed to attend court when due to do so.

Under section 13 of the 1980 Act[58], the court has power to issue a warrant for the arrest of an absent defendant, instead of proceeding, where—

    (1) the case started with—

        (a) the defendant's arrest and charge, or

        (b) a summons or requisition, if—

            (i) the court is satisfied that that summons or requisition was served on the defendant a reasonable time before the hearing, or

            (ii) the defendant was present when the hearing was arranged; and

    (2) the offence is punishable with imprisonment; or

    (3) the defendant has been convicted and the court considers imposing a disqualification.]

Provision of documents for the court   R24.13

24.13 (1) A party who introduces a document in evidence, or who otherwise uses a document in presenting that party's case, must provide a copy for—

    (a) each other party;

    (b) any witness that party wants to refer to that document;

    (c) the court; and

    (d) the justices' legal adviser.

(2) Unless the court otherwise directs, on application or on its own initiative, the court officer must provide for the court—

    (a) any copy received under paragraph (1) before the hearing begins; and

---

[56] 1980 c. 43; section 14 was amended by section 109 of, and paragraph 205 of Schedule 8 to, the Courts Act 2003 (c. 39).

[57] 1976 c. 63.

[58] 1980 c. 43; section 13 was amended by section 45 of, and paragraph 3 of Schedule 5 to, the Criminal Justice and Public Order Act 1994 (c. 33), section 48 of the Criminal Procedure and Investigations Act 1996 (c. 25), section 3 of the Magistrates' Courts (Procedure) Act 1998 (c. 15), sections 31 and 332 of, and Part 12 of Schedule 37 to, the Criminal Justice Act 2003 (c. 44) and sections 54 and 149 of, and Part 4 of Schedule 28 to, the Criminal Justice and Immigration Act 2008 (c. 4).

        (b) a copy of the court officer's record of—

            (i)   information supplied by each party for the purposes of case management, including any revision of information previously supplied,

           (ii) each pre-trial direction for the management of the case,

          (iii) any pre-trial decision to admit evidence,

          (iv) any pre-trial direction about the giving of evidence, and

           (v) any admission to which rule 24.6 applies.

    (3) Where rule 24.8 (Written guilty plea: special rules) applies, the court officer must provide for the court—

        (a) each document served by the prosecutor under rule 24.8(1)(d);

        (b) the defendant's driving record, where the offence is under the Road Traffic Regulation Act 1984[59], the Road Traffic Act 1988[60], the Road Traffic (Consequential Provisions) Act 1988[61] or the Road Traffic (Driver Licensing and Information Systems) Act 1989[62];

        (c) any other information about the defendant, relevant to sentence, of which the prosecutor served notice under rule 24.8(1); and

        (d) the notice of guilty plea and any representations and other information served by the defendant under rule 24.8(4).

    (4) Where the court tries a case under rule 24.9 (Single justice procedure: special rules), the court officer must provide for the court—

        (a) each document served by the prosecutor under rule 24.9(1)(d);

        (b) the defendant's driving record, where the offence is under the Road Traffic Regulation Act 1984, the Road Traffic Act 1988, the Road Traffic (Consequential Provisions) Act 1988 or the Road Traffic (Driver Licensing and Information Systems) Act 1989;

        (c) any other information about the defendant, relevant to sentence, of which the prosecutor served notice under rule 24.9(1); and

        (d) any notice, representations and other information served by the defendant under rule 29.9(4)(b).

[Note. A written witness statement to which Part 16 applies may only be introduced in evidence if there has been no objection within the time limit to which rule 16.4 refers.

An expert report to which Part 19 applies may only be introduced in evidence if it has been served in accordance with rule 19.3.

See also rule 20.3 for the procedure where a party objects to the introduction of hearsay evidence, including such evidence in a document, and rules 21.3 and 21.4 for the procedure where a party objects to the introduction of evidence of bad character.

A direction about the giving of evidence may be made on an application to which Part 18 applies (Measures to assist a witness or defendant to give evidence).]

R24.14   Duty of justices' legal adviser

24.14 (1) A justices' legal adviser must attend the court and carry out the duties listed in this rule, as applicable, unless the court—

        (a) includes a District Judge (Magistrates' Courts); and

        (b) otherwise directs.

    (2) A justices' legal adviser must—

        (a) before the hearing begins, by reference to what is provided for the court under rule 24.13 (Provision of documents for the court) draw the court's attention to—

            (i)   what the prosecutor alleges,

           (ii) what the parties say is agreed,

          (iii) what the parties say is in dispute, and

          (iv) what the parties say about how each expects to present the case, especially where that may affect its duration and timetabling;

        (b) assist the court by—

            (i)   making a note of the substance of any oral evidence or representations, to help the court recall that information, and

---

[59] 1984 c. 27.
[60] 1988 c. 52.
[61] 1988 c. 54.
[62] 1989 c. 22.

Criminal Procedure Rules

    (ii) if the court rules inadmissible part of a written statement introduced in evidence, marking that statement in such a way as to make that clear.

(3) Where the defendant has no legal representative and indicates an intention to plead guilty a justices' legal adviser must, in terms the defendant can understand—

   (a) explain the procedures required by—

     (i) rule 24.7 (Procedure on plea of guilty), and

    (ii) rule 24.11 (Procedure if the court convicts); and

   (b) in particular explain—

     (i) the right to make representations about the facts alleged by the prosecutor,

    (ii) the right to offer mitigation, and

    (iii) the importance of providing information about financial and other personal circumstances so that the court can impose the most appropriate sentence.

(4) Where the defendant has served a notice of guilty plea to which rule 24.8 (Written guilty plea: special rules) applies, a justices' legal adviser must—

   (a) unless the court otherwise directs, if any member of the public, including any reporter, is present, read aloud to the court—

     (i) the material on which the prosecutor relies to set out the facts of the offence and to provide information relevant to sentence (or summarise any written statement included in that material, if the court so directs), and

    (ii) any written representations by the defendant; and

   (b) otherwise, draw the court's attention to—

     (i) what the prosecutor alleges, and any significant features of the material listed in paragraph (4)(a)(i), and

    (ii) any written representations by the defendant.

(5) Where the court tries a case under rule 24.9 (Single justice procedure: special rules), a justices' legal adviser must draw the court's attention to—

   (a) what the prosecutor alleges, and any significant features of the material on which the prosecutor relies to prove the alleged offence and to provide information relevant to sentence; and

   (b) any representations served by the defendant.

[Note. Section 28 of the Courts Act 2003[63] provides for the functions of a justices' legal adviser. See also rule 2.12 (Duties of justices' legal adviser) and sections 12 and 16A of the Magistrates' Courts Act 1980[64].

Under section 12(7ZA) of the 1980 Act[65], Criminal Procedure Rules may specify which of the documents listed in section 12(7) of that Act[66], if any, must be read aloud, and may require them to be read aloud only in circumstances specified in the rules.]

Duty of court officer and custodian

R24.15

24.15 (1) The court officer must—

   (a) serve on each party notice of where and when an adjourned hearing will resume, unless—

     (i) the party was present when that was arranged,

    (ii) the defendant has served a notice of guilty plea to which rule 24.8 (Written guilty plea: special rules) applies, and the adjournment is for not more than 4 weeks, or

    (iii) the court tries a case under rule 24.9 (Single justice procedure: special rules), and the adjourned trial will resume under that rule;

   (b) if the reason for the adjournment was to postpone sentence, include that reason in any such notice to the defendant;

   (c) unless the court otherwise directs, make available to the parties any written report to which rule 24.11 (Procedure if the court convicts) applies;

---

[63] 2003 c. 39; section 28 was amended by section 15 of, and paragraphs 308 and 327 of Schedule 4 to, the Constitutional Reform Act 2005 (c. 4).

[64] 1980 c. 43; section 12 was amended by section 45 of, and paragraph 1 of Schedule 5 to, the Criminal Justice and Public Order Act 1994 (c. 33), section 1 of the Magistrates' Courts (Procedure) Act 1998 (c. 15), section 109 of, and paragraph 203 of Schedule 8 to, the Courts Act 2003 (c. 39), section 308 of, and Part 12 of Schedule 37 to, the Criminal Justice Act 2003 (c. 44) and section 81 of the Deregulation Act 2015 (c. 20). Section 16A was inserted by section 48 of the Criminal Justice and Courts Act 2015 (c. 2).

[65] 1980 c. 43; section 12(7ZA) was inserted by section 81 of the Deregulation Act 2015 (c. 20).

[66] 1980 c. 43; section 12(7) was amended by section 81 of the Deregulation Act 2015 (c. 20).

      (d) where the court has ordered a defendant to provide information under section 25 of the Road Traffic Offenders Act 1988[67], serve on the defendant notice of that order unless the defendant was present when it was made;

      (e) serve on the prosecutor—

          (i) any notice of guilty plea to which rule 24.8 (Written guilty plea: special rules) applies, and

         (ii) any declaration served under rule 44.2 (Statutory declaration of ignorance of proceedings) that the defendant did not know about the case;

      (f) serve on the prosecutor notice of any hearing date arranged in consequence of such a declaration, unless—

          (i) the prosecutor was present when that was arranged, or

         (ii) the court otherwise directs;

      (g) serve on the prosecutor—

          (i) notice of any hearing date arranged in consequence of the issue of a summons under rule 24.9 (Single justice procedure: special rules), and in that event

         (ii) any notice served by the defendant under rule 24.9(2)(c) or (d) (notice of intention to plead guilty at a hearing or notice of intention to plead not guilty);

      (h) record the court's reasons for not proceeding in the defendant's absence where rule 24.12(3)(a) applies; and

      (i) give the court such other assistance as it requires.

(2) Where the court passes a sentence of immediate imprisonment or detention, or orders a suspended sentence of imprisonment to take effect, by this rule—

      (a) the court requires the defendant to provide, in writing or orally, his or her nationality; and

      (b) the custodian must obtain that information and record it

[Note. See sections 10, 11 and 12 of the Magistrates' Courts Act 1980[68].

Under section 25 of the Road Traffic Offenders Act 1988, where the court does not know a defendant's sex or date of birth, then on convicting the defendant of an offence involving obligatory or discretionary disqualification, the court must order the defendant to provide that information.

Under Part 5, the magistrates' court officer must record details of a case and of the court's decisions.]

Under section 86A of the Courts Act 2003[69], Criminal Procedure Rules must specify stages of proceedings at which the court must require the information to which rule 24.15(2) refers. A person commits an offence if, without reasonable excuse, that person fails to comply with such a requirement, whether by providing false or incomplete information or by providing no information.]

CRIMINAL PROCEDURE RULES   PART 25   TRIAL AND SENTENCE
IN THE CROWN COURT

[Note. Part 3 contains rules about case management that apply during preparation for trial and at trial. The rules in this Part must be read in conjunction with those rules.]

R25.1   **When this Part applies**

25.1   This Part applies in the Crown Court where the court tries a case or the defendant pleads guilty.

[Note. The Crown Court's powers to try an allegation of an offence are contained in sections 45 and 46 of the Senior Courts Act 1981[1].

The exercise of the court's powers is affected by—

      (a) the classification of the offence (and the general rule, subject to exceptions, is that the Crown Court must try—

         (i) an offence classified as one that can be tried only in the Crown Court (in other legislation, described as triable only on indictment), and

---

[67] 1988 c. 53; section 25 was amended by section 90 of, and paragraphs 140 and 142 of Schedule 13 to, the Access to Justice Act 1999 (c. 22), section 165 of, and paragraph 118 of Schedule 9 to, the Powers of Criminal Courts (Sentencing) Act 2000 (c. 6) and section 109 of, and paragraph 311 of Schedule 8 to, the Courts Act 2003 (c. 39).

[68] 1980 c. 43; section 10 was amended by section 59 of, and paragraph 1 of Schedule 9 to, the Criminal Justice Act 1982 (c. 48), section 68 of, and paragraph 6 of Schedule 8 to, the Criminal Justice Act 1991 (c. 53) and section 47 of the Crime and Disorder Act 1998 (c. 37).

[69] 2003 c. 39; section 86A was inserted by section 162 of the Policing and Crime Act 2016 (c. 3).

[1] 1981 c. 54.

   (ii) *an offence classified as one that can be tried either in a magistrates' court or in the Crown Court (in other legislation, described as triable either way) that has been allocated for trial in the Crown Court); and*

  (b) *the defendant's age (and the general rule is that an allegation of an offence against a defendant under 18 must be tried in a magistrates' court sitting as a youth court, irrespective of the classification of the offence and without allocation for trial there, unless the offence is—*

   (i) *one of homicide,*

   (ii) *one for which a convicted adult could be imprisoned for 14 years or more,*

   (iii) *one of certain specified offences involving firearms, or*

   (iv) *one of certain specified sexual offences).*

See sections 17 and 24 of the Magistrates' Courts Act 1980[2]) and section 51A of the Crime and Disorder Act 1998[3].

Under section 34A of the Children and Young Persons Act 1933[4], the court—

  (a) *may require the defendant's parents or guardian to attend court with the defendant, where the defendant is under 18; and*

  (b) *must do so, where the defendant is under 16,*

unless satisfied that that would be unreasonable. Part 46 (Representatives) contains rules allowing a parent, guardian or other supporting adult to help a defendant under 18.]

General powers and requirements   R25.2

25.2 (1) Where this Part applies, the general rule is that—

  (a) the trial must be in public, but that is subject to the court's power to—

   (i) impose a restriction on reporting what takes place at a public hearing, or public access to what otherwise would be a public hearing,

   (ii) withhold information from the public during a public hearing, or

   (iii) order a trial in private;

  (b) the court must not proceed if the defendant is absent, unless the court is satisfied that—

   (i) the defendant has waived the right to attend, and

   (ii) the trial will be fair despite the defendant's absence; and

  (c) the court must not sentence the defendant to imprisonment or detention unless—

   (i) the defendant has a legal representative,

   (ii) the defendant has been sentenced to imprisonment or detention on a previous occasion in the United Kingdom, or

   (iii) the defendant could have been represented under legal aid but is not because section 226(7), (8) of the Sentencing Act 2020[5] applies to him or her.

  (2) Before proceeding to trial the court must—

  (a) if more than one indictment has been preferred or proposed—

   (i) identify the indictment or indictments on which the prosecutor wants the defendant to be tried, and

   (ii) identify any indictment or count in an indictment on which the prosecutor does not want to proceed;

  (b) obtain the prosecutor's confirmation, in writing or orally, that each indictment on which the defendant is about to be tried sets out—

   (i) a statement of each offence that the prosecutor wants the court to try, and

   (ii) such particulars of the conduct constituting the commission of each such offence as the prosecutor relies upon to make clear what is alleged;

  (c) ensure that the defendant is correctly identified by each indictment on which the defendant is about to be tried;

---

[2] 1980 c. 43; section 24 was amended by paragraph 47 of Schedule 14 to the Criminal Justice Act 1982 (c. 48), sections 17, 68 and 101 of, and paragraph 6 of Schedule 8 and Schedule 13 to, the Criminal Justice Act 1991 (c. 53), paragraph 40 of Schedule 10, and Schedule 11, to the Criminal Justice and Public Order Act 1994 (c. 33), sections 47 and 119 of, and paragraph 40 of Schedule 8, to the Crime and Disorder Act 1998 (c. 37), paragraph 64 of Schedule 9 to the Powers of Criminal Courts (Sentencing) Act 2000 (c. 6), section 42 of, and paragraphs 1 and 9 of Schedule 3, and Part 4 of Schedule 37, to the Criminal Justice Act 2003 (c. 44) and sections 49 and 65 of, and paragraph 1 of Schedule 1 and Schedule 5 to, the Violent Crime Reduction Act 2006 (c. 38).

[3] 1998 c. 37; section 51A was inserted by paragraphs 15 and 18 of Schedule 3 to the Criminal Justice Act 2003 (c. 44) and amended by section 49 of, and paragraph 5 of Schedule 1 to, the Violent Crime Reduction Act 2006 (c. 38) and paragraph 6 of Schedule 21 to the Legal Aid, Sentencing and Punishment of Offenders Act 2012 (c. 10).

[4] 1933 c. 12; section 34A was inserted by section 56 of the Criminal Justice Act 1991 (c. 53) and amended by section 107 of, and paragraph 1 of Schedule 5 to, the Local Government Act 2000 (c. 22).

[5] 2020 c. 17.

(d) satisfy itself that each allegation has been explained to the defendant, in terms the defendant can understand (with help, if necessary); and

(e) invite any objection to the terms or validity of any indictment on which the defendant is about to be tried.

(3) The court may adjourn the trial at any stage.

See section 226(7), (8) of the Sentencing Act 2020, which applies to a defendant if—

(a) *representation was made available to the defendant for the purposes of the proceedings under Part 1 of the Legal Aid, Sentencing and Punishment of Offenders Act 2012 but was withdrawn because of the defendant's conduct or because it appeared that the defendant's financial resources were such that he or she was not eligible for such representation;*

(b) *the defendant applied for such representation and the application was refused because it appeared that the defendant's financial resources were such that he or she was not eligible for such representation; or*

(c) *having been informed of the right to apply for such representation and having had the opportunity to do so, the defendant refused or failed to apply.*

(4) Subject to paragraph (5), unless the court otherwise directs no further proceedings may be taken on an indictment or count in an indictment on which under this rule the prosecutor chooses not to proceed.

(5) Paragraph (4) does not apply to any count in an indictment which becomes a count in the indictment required by rule 25.16(3)(e) (substituted indictment for sentencing purposes).

Part 6 contains rules about reporting, etc. restrictions. For a list of the court's powers to impose reporting and access restrictions, see the note to rule 6.1.

Part 10 contains rules about the content and service of indictments. Under section 2(6ZA) of the Administration of Justice (Miscellaneous Provisions) Act 1933[6], no objection to the indictment may be taken after the trial commences by reason of any failure to observe those rules.]

R25.3   Application for ruling on procedure, evidence or other question of law

25.3 (1) This rule applies to an application—

(a) about—

(i) case management, or any other question of procedure, or

(ii) the introduction or admissibility of evidence, or any other question of law; and

(b) that has not been determined before the trial begins.

(2) The application is subject to any other rule that applies to it (for example, as to the time and form in which the application must be made).

(3) Unless the court otherwise directs, the application must be made, and the court's decision announced, in the absence of the jury (if there is one).

[Note. See also rule 3.21 (Pre-trial hearings in the Crown Court: general rules).]

R25.4   Procedure on plea of guilty

25.4 (1) This rule applies if—

(a) the defendant pleads guilty to an offence; and

(b) the court is satisfied that the plea represents a clear acknowledgement of guilt.

(2) The court need not receive evidence unless rule 25.16(4) applies (determination of facts for sentencing).

[Note. See also rule 3.32 (Arraigning the defendant on the indictment).]

R25.5   Application to vacate a guilty plea

25.5 (1) This rule applies where a party wants the court to vacate a guilty plea.

(2) Such a party must—

(a) apply in writing—

(i) as soon as practicable after becoming aware of the grounds for doing so, and

(ii) in any event, before the final disposal of the case, by sentence or otherwise; and

(b) serve the application on—

(i) the court officer, and

(ii) the prosecutor.

(3) Unless the court otherwise directs, the application must—

(a) explain why it would be unjust for the guilty plea to remain unchanged;

(b) indicate what, if any, evidence the applicant wishes to call;

---

[6] 1933 c. 36; section 2(6ZA) was inserted by section 116 of the Coroners and Justice Act 2009 (c. 25).

(c) identify any proposed witness; and

(d) indicate whether legal professional privilege is waived, specifying any material name and date.

Selecting the jury   R25.6

25.6 (1) This rule—

    (a) applies where—

        (i) the defendant pleads not guilty,

        (ii) the defendant declines to enter a plea and the court treats that as a not guilty plea, or

        (iii) the court determines that the defendant is not fit to be tried; but

    (b) does not apply where—

        (i) the court orders a trial without a jury because of a danger of jury tampering or where jury tampering appears to have taken place, or

        (ii) the court tries without a jury counts on an indictment after a trial of sample counts with a jury.

(2) The court must select a jury to try the case from the panel, or part of the panel, of jurors summoned by the Lord Chancellor to attend at that time and place.

(3) Where it appears that too few jurors to constitute a jury will be available from among those so summoned, the court—

    (a) may exercise its own power to summon others in the court room, or in the vicinity, up to the number likely to be required, and add their names to the panel summoned by the Lord Chancellor; but

    (b) must inform the parties, if they are absent when the court exercises that power.

(4) The court must select the jury by drawing at random each juror's name from among those so summoned and—

    (a) announcing each name so drawn; or

    (b) announcing an identifying number assigned by the court officer to that person, where the court is satisfied that that is necessary.

(5) If too few jurors to constitute a jury are available from the panel after all their names have been drawn, the court may—

    (a) exercise its own power to summon others in the court room, or in the vicinity, up to the number required; and

    (b) announce—

        (i) the name of each person so summoned, or

        (ii) an identifying number assigned by the court officer to that person, where the court is satisfied that that is necessary.

(6) The jury the court selects—

    (a) must comprise no fewer than 12 jurors; and

    (b) may comprise as many as 14 jurors to begin with, where the court expects the trial to last for more than 4 weeks.

(7) Where the court selects a jury comprising more than 12 jurors, the court must explain to them that—

    (a) the purpose of selecting more than 12 jurors to begin with is to fill any vacancy or vacancies caused by the discharge of any of the first 12 before the prosecution evidence begins;

    (b) any such vacancy or vacancies will be filled by the extra jurors in order of their selection from the panel;

    (c) the court will discharge any extra juror or jurors remaining by no later than the beginning of the prosecution evidence; and

    (d) any juror who is discharged for that reason then will be available to be selected for service on another jury, during the period for which that juror has been summoned.

(8) Each of the 12 or more jurors the court selects—

    (a) must take an oath or affirm; and

    (b) becomes a full jury member until discharged.

(9) The oath or affirmation must be in these terms, or in any corresponding terms that the juror declares to be binding on him or her—

'I swear by Almighty God [*or* I do solemnly, sincerely and truly declare and affirm] that I will faithfully try the defendant and give a true verdict according to the evidence.'

[Note. See sections 2, 5, 6, and 11 of the Juries Act 1974[7]. See also rule 38.7 (Discharging jurors).

---

[7] 1974 c. 23; section 2 was amended by section 61 of the Administration of Justice Act 1982 (c. 53) and Part 10 of Schedule 37 to the Criminal Justice Act 2003 (c. 44). Section 5 was amended by section 15 of, and paragraphs 77 and 78 of Schedule 4 to, the Constitutional Reform Act 2005 (c. 4). Section 6 was amended by paragraph 45 of Schedule 15 to the Criminal Justice

Under sections 44 and 46 of the Criminal Justice Act 2003[8], the court may try a case without a jury where there is a danger of jury tampering, or where jury tampering appears to have taken place. Under section 17 of the Domestic Violence, Crime and Victims Act 2004[9], the court may try sample counts with a jury and other counts without a jury. Part 3 (preparation for trial in the Crown Court) contains rules about an application for such a trial.

Sections 1, 3, 4, 5 and 6 of the Oaths Act 1978[10] provide for the taking of oaths and the making of affirmations, and for the words that must be used.

Part 26 contains other rules about jurors.]

R25.7 **Discharging jurors**

 25.7 (1) The court may exercise its power to discharge a juror at any time—
    (a) after the juror completes the oath or affirmation; and
    (b) before the court discharges the jury.
   (2) No later than the beginning of the prosecution evidence, if the jury then comprises more than 12 jurors the court must discharge any in excess of 12 in reverse order of their selection from the panel.
   (3) The court may exercise its power to discharge the jury at any time—
    (a) after each juror has completed the oath or affirmation; and
    (b) before the jury has delivered its verdict on each offence charged in the indictment.
   (4) The court must exercise its power to discharge the jury when, in respect of each offence charged in the indictment, either—
    (a) the jury has delivered its verdict on that offence; or
    (b) the court has discharged the jury from reaching a verdict.

[Note. See sections 16 and 18 of the Juries Act 1974[11].]

R25.8 **Objecting to jurors**

 25.8 (1) A party who objects to the panel of jurors must serve notice explaining the objection on the court officer and on the other party before the first juror's name or number is drawn.
   (2) A party who objects to the selection of an individual juror must—
    (a) tell the court of the objection—
     (i) after the juror's name or number is announced, and
     (ii) before the juror completes the oath or affirmation; and
    (b) explain the objection.
   (3) A prosecutor who exercises the prosecution right without giving reasons to prevent the court selecting an individual juror must announce the exercise of that right before the juror completes the oath or affirmation.
   (4) The court must determine an objection under paragraph (1) or (2)—
    (a) at a hearing, in public or in private; and
    (b) in the absence of the jurors, unless the court otherwise directs.

[Note. See section 29 of the Juries Act 1825[12] and section 12 of the Juries Act 1974[13].]

R25.9 **Procedure on plea of not guilty**

 25.9 (1) This rule applies where—
    (a) the defendant pleads not guilty; or
    (b) the defendant declines to enter a plea and the court treats that as a not guilty plea.
   (2) In the following sequence—
    (a) where there is a jury, the court must—
     (i) inform the jurors of each offence charged in the indictment to which the defendant pleads not guilty, and
     (ii) explain to the jurors that it is their duty, after hearing the evidence, to decide whether the defendant is guilty or not guilty of each offence;

Act 1988 (c. 33). Section 11 was amended by section 58 of, and paragraph 8 of Schedule 10 and Schedule 11 to, the Domestic Violence, Crime and Victims Act 2004 (c. 28).

[8] 2003 c. 44.
[9] 2004 c. 28.
[10] 1978 c. 19.
[11] 1974 c. 23; section 16 was amended by sections 121 and 170 of, and Schedule 16 to, the Criminal Justice Act 1988 (c. 33).
[12] 1825 c. 50; section 29 was amended by section 40 of, and paragraph 3 of Schedule 4 to, the Courts Act 1971 (c. 23). There are other amendments not relevant to this rule.
[13] 1974 c. 23; section 12 was amended by section 170 of, and Schedule 16 to, the Criminal Justice Act 1988 (c. 33).

(b)   the prosecutor may summarise the prosecution case, concisely outlining the facts and the matters likely to be in dispute;

(c)   where there is a jury, to help the jurors to understand the case and resolve any issue in it the court may—

    (i)   invite the defendant concisely to identify what is in issue, if necessary in terms approved by the court, and

    (ii) if the defendant declines to do so, direct that the jurors be given a copy of any defence statement served under rule 15.4 (Defence disclosure), edited if necessary to exclude any reference to inappropriate matters or to matters evidence of which would not be admissible;

(d)   the prosecutor must introduce the evidence on which the prosecution case relies;

(e)   subject to paragraph (3), at the end of the prosecution evidence, on the defendant's application or on its own initiative, the court—

    (i)   may direct the jury (if there is one) to acquit on the ground that the prosecution evidence is insufficient for any reasonable court properly to convict, but

    (ii) must not do so unless the prosecutor has had an opportunity to make representations;

(f)   subject to paragraph (4), at the end of the prosecution evidence, the court must ask whether the defendant intends to give evidence in person and, if the answer is 'no', then the court must satisfy itself that there has been explained to the defendant, in terms the defendant can understand (with help, if necessary)—

    (i)   the right to give evidence in person, and

    (ii) that if the defendant does not give evidence in person, or refuses to answer a question while giving evidence, the court may draw such inferences as seem proper;

(g)   the defendant may summarise the defence case, if he or she intends to call at least one witness other than him or herself to give evidence in person about the facts of the case;

(h)   in this order (or in a different order, if the court so directs) the defendant may—

    (i)   give evidence in person,

    (ii) call another witness, or witnesses, to give evidence in person, and

    (iii) introduce any other evidence;

(i)   a party may introduce further evidence if it is then admissible (for example, because it is in rebuttal of evidence already introduced);

(j)   the prosecutor may make final representations, where—

    (i)   the defendant has a legal representative,

    (ii) the defendant has called at least one witness, other than the defendant him or herself, to give evidence in person about the facts of the case, or

    (iii) the court so permits; and

(k)   the defendant may make final representations.

(3)   Paragraph (2)(e) does not apply in relation to a charge of murder, manslaughter, attempted murder, or causing harm contrary to section 18 or 20 of the Offences against the Person Act 1861[14] until the court has heard all the evidence (including any defence evidence), where the defendant is charged with—

(a)   any of those offences; and

(b)   an offence of causing or allowing a child or vulnerable adult to die or to suffer serious physical harm, contrary to section 5 of the Domestic Violence, Crime and Victims Act 2004[15].

(4)   Paragraph (2)(f) does not apply where it appears to the court that, taking account of all the circumstances, the defendant's physical or mental condition makes it undesirable for the defendant to give evidence in person.

(5)   Where there is more than one defendant, this rule applies to each in the order their names appear in the indictment, or in an order directed by the court.

(6)   Unless the jury (if there is one) has retired to consider its verdict, the court may allow a party to introduce evidence, or make representations, after that party's opportunity to do so under paragraph (2).

(7)   Unless the jury has already reached a verdict on a count, the court may exercise its power to—

(a)   discharge the jury from reaching a verdict on that count;

(b)   direct the jury to acquit the defendant on that count; or

---

[14]   1861 c. 100; section 18 was amended by the Statute Law Revision Act 1892 (c. 19), the Statute Law Revision (No 2) Act 1893 (c. 54) and section 10 of, and Part III of Schedule 3 to, the Criminal Law Act 1967 (c. 58). Section 20 was amended by the Statute Law Revision Act 1892 (c. 19).

[15]   2004 c. 28; section 5 was amended by section 1 of the Domestic Violence, Crime and Victims (Amendment) Act 2012 (c. 4).

(c) invite the jury to convict the defendant, if the defendant pleads guilty to the offence charged by that count.

[Note. See also rule 3.32 (Arraigning the defendant on the indictment).

Under section 6E of the Criminal Procedure and Investigations Act 1996[16], the court may make the direction for which rule 25.9(2)(c)(ii) provides, on application or on the court's own initiative.

The admissibility of evidence that a party introduces is governed by rules of evidence.

Under section 35 of the Criminal Justice and Public Order Act 1994[17], the court may draw such inferences as appear proper from a defendant's failure to give evidence, or refusal without good cause to answer a question while doing so. The procedure set out in rule 25.9(2)(f) and (4) is prescribed by that section.

Section 2 of the Criminal Evidence Act 1898[18] restricts the circumstances in which the defendant may summarise the defence case before introducing evidence.

Section 79 of the Police and Criminal Evidence Act 1984[19] requires a defendant who wishes to give evidence in person to do so before calling any other witness, unless the court otherwise permits.

Section 2 of the Criminal Procedure Act 1865[20] and section 3 of the Criminal Evidence Act 1898[21] restrict the circumstances in which the prosecutor may make final representations without the court's permission. See also section 1 of the Criminal Procedure (Right of Reply) Act 1964[22].

The procedure set out in rule 25.9(3) is prescribed by sections 6 and 6A of the Domestic Violence, Crime and Victims Act 2004[23].

Under section 17 of the Criminal Justice Act 1967[24], the court may direct the jury to acquit where the prosecutor offers no evidence.

See rule 25.14 for the procedure on taking the verdict and rule 25.16 for the procedure if the court convicts the defendant.]

R25.10 Defendant unfit to plead

25.10 (1) This rule applies where—
   (a) it appears to the court, on application or on its own initiative, that the defendant may not be fit to be tried; and
   (b) the defendant has not by then been acquitted of each offence charged by the indictment.
(2) The court—
   (a) must exercise its power to decide, without a jury, whether the defendant is fit to be tried; but
   (b) may postpone the exercise of that power until immediately before the opening of the defence case.
(3) Where the court determines that the defendant is not fit to be tried—
   (a) the court must exercise its power to appoint a person to put the case for the defence, taking account of all the circumstances and in particular—
      (i) the willingness and suitability (including the qualifications and experience) of that person,
      (ii) the nature and complexity of the case,
      (iii) any advantage of continuity of representation, and
      (iv) the defendant's wishes and needs;
   (b) the court must select a jury, if none has been selected yet; and
   (c) rule 25.9 (Procedure on plea of not guilty) applies, if the steps it lists have not already been taken, except that—
      (i) everything which that rule requires to be done by the defendant may be done instead by the person appointed to put the case for the defence,

[16] 1996 c. 25; section 6E was inserted by section 36 of the Criminal Justice Act 2003 (c. 44).
[17] 1994 c. 33; section 35 was amended by sections 35 and 120 of, and Schedule 10 to, the Crime and Disorder Act 1998 (c. 37) and paragraphs 62 and 63 of Schedule 36 to the Criminal Justice Act 2003 (c. 44).
[18] 1898 c. 36.
[19] 1984 c. 60.
[20] 1865 c. 18; section 2 was amended by section 10(2) of, and Part III of Schedule 3 to, the Criminal Law Act 1967 (c. 58).
[21] 1898 c. 36; section 3 was amended by section 1(2) of the Criminal Procedure (Right of Reply) Act 1964 (c. 34).
[22] 1964 c. 34; section 1 was amended by section 1 of, and the Schedule to, the Statute Law (Repeals) Act 1974 (c. 22).
[23] 2004 c. 28; section 6 was amended by section 3 of, and paragraphs 7 and 8 of the Schedule to, the Domestic Violence, Crime and Victims (Amendment) Act 2012 (c. 4) and section 6A was inserted by section 2 of that Act.
[24] 1967 c. 80; section 17 was amended by paragraph 42 of Schedule 36 to the Criminal Justice Act 2003 (c. 44).

(ii) under rule 25.9(2)(a), the court must explain to the jurors that their duty is to decide whether or not the defendant did the act or made the omission charged as an offence, not whether the defendant is guilty of that offence, and

(iii) rule 25.9(2)(e) does not apply (warning of consequences of defendant not giving evidence).

(4) Paragraphs (5) and (6) of this rule apply where—

  (a) the jury decides that the defendant did the act or made the omission charged as an offence;

  (b) the court makes a hospital order and a restriction order;

  (c) while the restriction order remains in effect the Secretary of State receives medical advice that the defendant can properly be tried and decides to remit the defendant to the Crown Court for trial; and

  (d) the Secretary of State so notifies the court officer.

(5) The prosecutor must serve on the court officer the medical report or reports by reference to which the defendant has been assessed as properly to be tried.

(6) The court must give directions—

  (a) for the return of the defendant to the court, which initial directions may be given—

    (i) without a hearing, or

    (ii) at a hearing, which must take place in the defendant's absence; and then

  (b) for the future conduct of the case, which further directions must be given—

    (i) at a hearing, and

    (ii) in the defendant's presence.

(7) Directions under paragraph (6)(a)—

  (a) may include directions under rule 3.10 (Directions for commissioning medical reports, other than for sentencing purposes) for the commissioning of any further report required by the court;

  (b) may set a timetable providing for the date by which representations about the future conduct of the case must be served; and

  (c) must set a date for a hearing under paragraph (6)(b).

(8) At the hearing under paragraph (6)(b)—

  (a) rule 3.21 (Pre-trial hearings in the Crown Court: general rules) applies even if a plea and trial preparation hearing has been conducted in the case before; and

  (b) among other things, the court must decide whether to grant or withhold bail.

[Note. See sections 4 and 4A of the Criminal Procedure (Insanity) Act 1964[25].

Under section 4 of the 1964 Act, the court must not determine the defendant's fitness to be tried except on the evidence of two or more registered medical practitioners, at least one of whom is approved as having special experience in the diagnosis or treatment of mental disorder. Under section 4A, if satisfied that the defendant did the act or made the omission charged as an offence the jury must make a finding to that effect, and if not so satisfied must acquit the defendant.

Under section 5A of the 1964 Act[26], where a hospital order and a restriction order have effect, and after consultation with the responsible clinician, the Secretary of State may remit a defendant for trial if satisfied that the defendant can properly be tried.]

Evidence of a witness in person   R25.11

25.11 (1) This rule applies where a party wants to introduce evidence by calling a witness to give that evidence in person.

(2) Unless the court otherwise directs—

  (a) a witness waiting to give evidence must not wait inside the courtroom, unless that witness is—

    (i) a party, or

    (ii) an expert witness;

  (b) a witness who gives evidence in the courtroom must do so from the place provided for that purpose; and

  (c) a witness' address—

    (i) must not be given in public unless the address is relevant to an issue in the case, and

    (ii) may be given in writing to the court, parties and jury.

---

[25] 1964 c. 84; sections 4 and 4A were substituted for section 4 as originally enacted by section 2 of the Criminal Procedure (Insanity and Unfitness to Plead) Act 1991 (c. 25), and amended by section 22 of the Domestic Violence, Crime and Victims Act 2004 (c. 28).

[26] 1964 c. 84; section 5A was inserted by section 24 of the Domestic Violence, Crime and Victims Act 2004 (c. 28), amended by section 15 of the Mental Health Act 2007 (c. 12) and repealed for certain purposes by paragraph 114 of Schedule 2 to the Sentencing (Pre-consolidation Amendments) Act 2020 (c. 9).

(3) Before the witness gives evidence—
  (a) the party who introduces the witness' evidence must explain how that evidence is admissible, unless it is only evidence of fact within the witness' direct knowledge; and
  (b) the witness must take an oath or affirm, unless other legislation otherwise provides.
(4) In the following sequence—
  (a) the party who calls a witness may ask questions in examination-in-chief;
  (b) if the witness gives evidence for the prosecution—
    (i) the defendant, if there is only one, may ask questions in cross-examination, or
    (ii) subject to the court's directions, each defendant, if there is more than one, may ask such questions, in the order their names appear in the indictment or as directed by the court;
  (c) if the witness gives evidence for a defendant—
    (i) subject to the court's directions, each other defendant, if there is more than one, may ask questions in cross-examination, in the order their names appear in the indictment or as directed by the court, and
    (ii) the prosecutor may ask such questions; and
  (d) the party who called the witness may ask questions in re-examination arising out of any cross-examination.
(5) If other legislation so permits, at any time while giving evidence a witness may refer to a record of that witness' recollection of events.
(6) The court may—
  (a) ask a witness questions; and in particular
  (b) where the defendant is not represented, ask a witness any question necessary in the defendant's interests.

[Note. Section 53 of the Youth Justice and Criminal Evidence Act 1999[27] provides that everyone is competent to give evidence in criminal proceedings unless unable to understand questions put or give intelligible answers. See also section 1 of the Criminal Evidence Act 1898[28].

Part 19 contains rules about the introduction of evidence of expert opinion. Part 20 contains rules about the introduction of hearsay evidence.

Sections 1, 3, 5 and 6 of the Oaths Act 1978[29] provide for the taking of oaths and the making of affirmations, and for the words that must be used. Section 28 of the Children and Young Persons Act 1963[30] provides that in a youth court, and where a witness in any court is under 18, an oath must include the words 'I promise' in place of the words 'I swear'. Under sections 55 and 56 of the Youth Justice and Criminal Evidence Act 1999, a person may give evidence without taking an oath, or making an affirmation, where that person (i) is under 14 or (ii) has an insufficient appreciation of the solemnity of the occasion and of the particular responsibility to tell the truth which is involved in taking an oath.

The questions that may be put to a witness—

  (a) by a party are governed by rules of evidence, for example—
    (i) the rule that a question must be relevant to what is in issue,
    (ii) the rule that the party who calls a witness must not ask that witness a leading question about what is in dispute, and
    (iii) the rule that a party who calls a witness may contradict that witness only in limited circumstances (see section 3 of the Criminal Procedure Act 1865)[31];
  (b) by the court are in its discretion, but that is subject to—
    (i) rules of evidence, and
    (ii) rule 1.3 (the application by the court of the overriding objective).

[27] 1999 c. 23.
[28] 1898 c. 36; section 1 was amended by section 1 of the Criminal Evidence Act 1979 (c. 16), section 78 of, and Schedule 16 to, the Criminal Justice Act 1982 (c. 48), sections 80(9) and 119(2) of, and Schedule 7 to, the Police and Criminal Evidence Act 1984 (c. 60), sections 31 and 168 of, and paragraph 2 of Schedule 10, and Schedule 11 to, the Criminal Justice and Public Order Act 1994 (c. 33), section 67 of, and paragraph 1 of Schedule 4, and Schedule 6 to, the Youth Justice and Criminal Evidence Act 1999 (c. 23) and sections 331 and 332 of, and paragraph 80 of Schedule 36, and Part 5 of Schedule 37 to, the Criminal Justice Act 2003 (c. 44).
[29] 1978 c. 19.
[30] 1963 c. 37; section 28 was amended by section 2 of the Oaths Act 1978 (c. 19) and section 100 of, and paragraph 40 of Schedule 11 to, the Criminal Justice Act 1991 (c. 53).
[31] 1865 c. 18.

Under sections 34, 35 and 36 of the Youth Justice and Criminal Evidence Act 1999[32], a defendant who is not represented may not cross-examine a witness where—

    (a)   the defendant is charged with a sexual offence against the witness;

    (b)   the defendant is charged with a sexual offence, or one of certain other offences, and the witness is a child; or

    (c)   the court prohibits the defendant from cross-examining the witness.

Part 23 contains rules relevant to restrictions on cross-examination.

Under section 139 of the Criminal Justice Act 2003[33], a witness may refresh his or her memory by referring to a record made earlier, either contained in a document made or verified by the witness, or in the transcript of a sound recording, if—

    (a)   the witness states that it records his or her recollection of events at that earlier time; and

    (b)   that recollection is likely to have been significantly better when the record was made than by the time the witness gives evidence in person.

In some circumstances, a witness may give evidence in accordance with special measures directed by the court under section 19 of the Youth Justice and Criminal Evidence Act 1999[34], or by live link under section 32 of the Criminal Justice Act 1988[35] or section 51 of the Criminal Justice Act 2003. Part 18 contains relevant rules.]

Evidence of a witness in writing   R25.12

25.12 (1)   This rule applies where a party wants to introduce in evidence the written statement of a witness to which applies—

    (a)   Part 16 (Written witness statements);

    (b)   Part 19 (Expert evidence); or

    (c)   Part 20 (Hearsay evidence).

    (2)   That party must explain how the evidence is admissible unless it is—

    (a)   evidence of fact within the direct knowledge of the person who made the written statement served under rule 16.4 (Written witness statement in evidence);

    (b)   contained in an expert's report served under rule 19.3 (Introduction of expert evidence); or

    (c)   identified as hearsay in a notice served under rule 20.2 (Notice to introduce hearsay evidence).

    (3)   If the court admits such evidence each relevant part of the statement must be read or summarised aloud, unless the court otherwise directs.

[Note. See Parts 16, 19 and 20, and the other legislation to which those Parts apply. The admissibility of evidence that a party introduces is governed by rules of evidence.

A written witness statement to which Part 16 applies may only be introduced in evidence if there has been no objection within the time limit to which rule 16.4 refers.

An expert report to which Part 19 applies may only be introduced in evidence if it has been served in accordance with rule 19.3.

Rule 20.3 provides for opposing the introduction of hearsay evidence, including such evidence in a document.

Where a witness gives evidence in person, a previous written statement by that witness may be admissible as evidence under section 119 (Inconsistent statements) or under section 120 (Other previous statements of witnesses) of the Criminal Justice Act 2003.]

Evidence by admission   R25.13

25.13 (1)   This rule applies where—

    (a)   a party introduces in evidence a fact admitted by another party; or

    (b)   parties jointly admit a fact.

    (2)   Unless the court otherwise directs, a written record must be made of the admission.

---

[32]   1999 c. 23; section 35 was amended by sections 139 and 140 of, and paragraph 41 of Schedule 6 and Schedule 7 to, the Sexual Offences Act 2003 (c. 42) and section 148 of, and paragraphs 35 and 36 of Schedule 26 to, the Criminal Justice and Immigration Act 2008 (c. 4).

[33]   2003 c. 44.

[34]   1999 c. 23.

[35]   1988 c. 33; section 32 was amended by section 55 of the Criminal Justice Act 1991 (c. 53), section 29 of, and paragraph 16 of Schedule 2 to, the Criminal Appeal Act 1995 (c. 35), section 62 of the Criminal Procedure and Investigations Act 1996 (c. 25), section 67 of, and Schedule 6 and paragraph 3 of Schedule 7 to, the Youth Justice and Criminal Evidence Act 1999 (c. 23) and paragraphs 24 and 26 of the Schedule to S.I. 2004/2035.

[Note. See section 10 of the Criminal Justice Act 1967[36]. The admissibility of evidence that a party introduces is governed by rules of evidence.]

R25.14   **Directions to the jury and taking the verdict**

25.14 (1)   This rule applies where there is a jury.

(2)   The court must give the jury directions about the relevant law at any time at which to do so will assist jurors to evaluate the evidence.

(3)   After following the sequence in rule 25.9 (Procedure on plea of not guilty), the court must—

(a)   to help the jury to come to a verdict—

(i)   give jurors directions about the relevant law, and

(ii)   summarise for them, to such extent as is necessary, the evidence relevant to the issues they must decide;

(b)   give those directions orally and, as a general rule, in writing as well;

(c)   direct the jury to retire to consider its verdict;

(d)   if necessary, recall the jury

(i)   to answer jurors' questions, or

(ii)   to give directions, or further directions, about considering and delivering its verdict or verdicts, including, if appropriate, directions about reaching a verdict by a majority;

(e)   in a case in which the jury is required to return a single verdict—

(i)   recall the jury (unless already recalled) when it informs the court that it has reached its verdict, and

(ii)   direct the delivery of that verdict there and then;

(f)   in a case in which the jury is required to return two or more verdicts—

(i)   recall the jury (unless already recalled) when it informs the court that it has reached a verdict or verdicts, and

(ii)   ask the jury whether its members all agree on every verdict required;

(g)   if the answer to that question is 'yes', direct the delivery of each of those verdicts there and then; and

(h)   if the answer to that question is 'no'—

(i)   direct the delivery there and then of any unanimous verdict that has been reached, or

(ii)   postpone the taking of any such verdict while the jury considers each other verdict required.

(4)   Directions to the jury under paragraph (3)(a) may include questions that the court invites jurors to answer in coming to a verdict.

(5)   The court may give the jury other assistance in writing.

(6)   When the court directs the jury to deliver its verdict or verdicts, the court must ask the foreman chosen by the jury, in respect of each count—

(a)   whether the jury has reached a verdict on which all the jurors agree;

(b)   if so, whether that verdict is guilty or not guilty;

(c)   if not, where the jury has deliberated for at least 2 hours and if the court decides to invite a majority verdict, then—

(i)   whether at least 10 (of 11 or 12 jurors), or 9 (of 10 jurors), agreed on a verdict,

(ii)   if so, is that verdict guilty or not guilty, and

(iii)   if (and only if) such a verdict is guilty, how many jurors agreed to that verdict and how many disagreed.

(7)   Where evidence has been given that the defendant was insane, so as not to be responsible for the act or omission charged as the offence, then under paragraph (5)(b) the court must ask whether the jury's verdict is guilty, not guilty, or not guilty by reason of insanity.

[Note. Under section 17 of the Juries Act 1974[37], the court may accept the verdict of a majority, as long as the jury has had at least 2 hours for deliberation.

Under section 6 of the Criminal Law Act 1967, the jury may convict a defendant of an offence other than one charged by the indictment if that offence is proved by the evidence.

The verdict to which rule 25.14(6) refers is provided for by section 2 of the Trial of Lunatics Act 1883[38]. The evidence required before such a verdict may be reached is prescribed by section 1 of the Criminal Procedure (Insanity and Unfitness to Plead) Act 1991[39].]

---

[36] 1967 c. 80.

[37] 1974 c. 23.

[38] 1883 c. 38; section 2 was amended by section 17 of, and Schedule 2 to, the Criminal Lunatics Act 1884 (c. 64) and sections 1 and 8 of the Criminal Procedure (Insanity) Act 1964 (c. 84).

[39] 1991 c. 25.

Conviction or acquittal without a jury   R25.15

25.15 (1) This rule applies where—
    (a) the court tries the case without a jury; and
    (b) after following the sequence in rule 25.9 (Procedure on plea of not guilty).
    (2) In respect of each count, the court must give reasons for its decision to convict or acquit.

[Note. Under sections 44 and 46 of the Criminal Justice Act 2003[40], the court may try a case without a jury where there is a danger of jury tampering, or where jury tampering appears to have taken place. Under section 17 of the Domestic Violence, Crime and Victims Act 2004[41], the court may try sample counts with a jury and other counts without a jury. Part 3 (preparation for trial in the Crown Court) contains rules about an application for such a trial.]

Procedure if the court convicts   R25.16

25.16 (1) This rule applies where the court convicts the defendant.
    (2) The court may exercise its power—
      (a) if the defendant is an individual—
        (i)   to require a pre-sentence report,
        (ii) to commission a medical report,
        (iii) to require a statement of the defendant's assets and other financial circumstances;
      (b) if the defendant is a corporation, to require such information as the court directs about the defendant's corporate structure and financial resources;
      (c) to adjourn sentence pending—
        (i)   receipt of any such report, statement or information,
        (ii) the verdict in a related case.
    (3) The prosecutor must—
      (a) summarise the prosecution case, if the sentencing court has not heard evidence;
      (b) identify in writing any offence that the prosecutor proposes should be taken into consideration in sentencing;
      (c) provide information relevant to sentence, including—
        (i)   any previous conviction of the defendant, and the circumstances where relevant,
        (ii) any statement of the effect of the offence on the victim, the victim's family or others;
      (d) identify any other matter relevant to sentence, including—
        (i)   the legislation applicable,
        (ii) any sentencing guidelines, or guideline cases,
        (iii) aggravating and mitigating features affecting the defendant's culpability and the harm which the offence caused, was intended to cause or might foreseeably have caused, and
        (iv) the effect of such of the information listed in paragraph (2) as the court may need to take into account; and
      (e) if the court so directs, where no single indictment contains every count on which the defendant is to be sentenced provide a substituted indictment for sentencing purposes that contains every such count and indicates—
        (i)   the indictment from which each such count derives,
        (ii) the defendant's plea to each such count,
        (iii) if a guilty plea, the date on which that plea was entered, and
        (iv) otherwise, the date on which the defendant was convicted on that count.
    (4) Where the defendant pleads guilty, the court may give directions for determining the facts on the basis of which sentence must be passed if—
      (a) the defendant wants to be sentenced on a basis agreed with the prosecutor; or
      (b) in the absence of such agreement, the defendant wants to be sentenced on the basis of different facts to those disclosed by the prosecution case.
    (5) Where the court has power to order the endorsement of the defendant's driving record, or power to order the defendant to be disqualified from driving—
      (a) if other legislation so permits, a defendant who wants the court not to exercise that power must introduce the evidence or information on which the defendant relies;
      (b) the prosecutor may introduce evidence; and
      (c) the parties may make representations about that evidence or information.
    (6) Before passing sentence—
      (a) the court must give the defendant an opportunity to make representations and introduce evidence relevant to sentence;

[40] 2003 c. 44.
[41] 2004 c. 28.

    (b) where the defendant is under 18, the court may give the defendant's parents, guardian or other supporting adult, if present, such an opportunity as well; and

    (c) if the court requires more information, it may exercise its power to adjourn the hearing.

(7) When the court has taken into account all the evidence, information and any report available, the court must—

    (a) as a general rule, pass sentence at the earliest opportunity;

    (b) when passing sentence—

      (i) explain the reasons,

      (ii) explain to the defendant its effect, the consequences of failing to comply with any order or pay any fine, and any power that the court has to vary or review the sentence, unless the defendant is absent or the defendant's ill-health or disorderly conduct makes such an explanation impracticable, and

      (iii) give any such explanation in terms the defendant, if present, can understand (with help, if necessary); and

    (c) deal with confiscation, costs and any behaviour order.

(8) The general rule is subject to the court's power to defer sentence for up to 6 months.

[Note. See sections 31, 52, 59, 63, 124, 125 and 126 of the Sentencing Act 2020[42].

Under sections 57D and 57E of the Crime and Disorder Act 1998[43] , the court may require a defendant to attend a sentencing hearing by live link.

Under section 30 of the Sentencing Act 2020, the general rule (subject to exceptions) is that the court must obtain and consider a pre-sentence report—

    (a) where it is considering a custodial sentence or a community sentence;

    (b) where it thinks the defendant may pose a significant risk of causing serious harm to the public by further offending.

Under section 32(3) of the Sentencing Act 2020, where the court obtains a written pre-sentence report about a defendant who is under 18, it may direct that information in it must be withheld, if it would be likely to create a risk of significant harm to the defendant.

Rule 28.8 of these Rules applies to commissions for medical reports.

Under section 35 of the Sentencing Act 2020, the court may require a defendant who is an individual to provide a statement of assets and other financial circumstances if the defendant is convicted.

Under section 20A of the Criminal Justice Act 1991[44], it is an offence for a defendant knowingly or recklessly to make a false or incomplete statement of assets or other financial circumstances, or to fail to provide such a statement, in response to a request by a court officer on behalf of the court.

The Sentencing Council may issue sentencing guidelines under section 120 of the Coroners and Justice Act 2009[45].

For the circumstances in which a court may (and, in some cases, must) order the endorsement of a defendant's driving record, or the disqualification of a defendant from driving, see sections 34, 35 and 44 of the Road Traffic Offenders Act 1988[46]. Under that legislation, in some circumstances the court has discretion not to make such an order. See also rule 29.1.

The evidence that may be introduced is subject to rules of evidence.

[42] 2020 c.17.

[43] 1998 c. 37; sections 57A to 57E were substituted for section 57 as originally enacted by section 45 of the Police and Justice Act 2006 (c. 48), and amended by sections 106, 109 and 178 of, and Part 3 of Schedule 23 to, the Coroners and Justice Act 2009 (c. 25). Section 57A was further amended by paragraphs 36 and 39 of Schedule 12 to the Legal Aid, Sentencing and Punishment of Offenders Act 2012 (c. 10).

[44] 1991 c. 53; section 20A was inserted by section 168 of, and paragraph 43 of Schedule 9 to, the Criminal Justice and Public Order Act 1994 (c. 33) and amended by sections 95 and 109 of, and paragraph 350 of Schedule 8 to, the Courts Act 2003 (c. 39) and section 44 of, and paragraph 26 of Schedule 16 to, the Crime and Courts Act 2013 (c. 22).

[45] 2009 c. 25.

[46] 1988 c. 53; section 34 was amended by section 29 of the Road Traffic Act 1991 (c. 40), section 3 of the Aggravated Vehicle-Taking Act 1992 (c. 11), section 165 of, and paragraph 121 of Schedule 9 to, the Powers of Criminal Courts (Sentencing) Act 2000 (c. 6), sections 56 and 107 of, and Schedule 8 to, the Police Reform Act 2002 (c. 30), section 25 of the Road Safety Act 2006 (c. 49), article 2 of S.I. 2007/3480, paragraphs 2 and 5 of Schedule 27 to the Legal Aid, Sentencing and Punishment of Offenders Act 2012 (c. 10), section 56 of, and paragraphs 9 and 12 of Schedule 22 to, the Crime and Courts Act 2013 (c. 22) and section 177 of, and paragraph 90 of Schedule 21 to, the Coroners and Justice Act 2009 (c. 25). Section 35 was amended by section 48 of, and paragraph 95 of Schedule 4 to, the Road Traffic Act 1991 (c. 40), section 165 of, and paragraph 122 of Schedule 9 to, the Powers of Criminal Courts (Sentencing) Act 2000 (c. 6) and section 177 of, and 90 of Schedule 21 to, the Coroners and Justice Act 2009 (c. 25). Section 44 was amended by regulations 2 and 3 of, and paragraph 10 of Schedule 2 to, S.I. 1990/144 and sections 9, 10 and 59 of, and Schedule 7 to, the Road Safety Act 2006 (c. 49).

In addition to the specific powers to which this rule applies, the court has a general power to adjourn a trial: see rule 25.2.

Part 28 contains rules about sentencing procedure in special cases. Part 31 contains rules about behaviour orders. Part 33 contains rules about confiscation and related orders. Part 45 contains rules about costs.

Under section 3 of the Sentencing Act 2020, if (among other things) the defendant consents, the court may defer sentence for up to 6 months, for the purpose of allowing it to take account of the defendant's conduct after conviction, or any change in the defendant's circumstances.]

Provision of documents for the court   R25.17

25.17 (1) Unless the court otherwise directs, a party who introduces a document in evidence, or who otherwise uses a document in presenting that party's case, must provide a copy for—
    (a) each other party;
    (b) any witness that party wants to refer to the document; and
    (c) the court.
  (2) If the court so directs, a party who introduces or uses a document for such a purpose must provide a copy for the jury.
  (3) Unless the court otherwise directs, on application or on its own initiative, the court officer must provide for the court—
    (a) any copy received under paragraph (1) before the trial begins;
    (b) a copy of the court officer's record of—
      (i)   information supplied by each party for the purposes of case management, including any revision of information previously supplied,
      (ii) each pre-trial direction for the management of the case,
      (iii) any pre-trial decision to admit evidence,
      (iv) any pre-trial direction about the giving of evidence, and
      (v)   any admission to which rule 25.13 (Evidence by admission) applies;
    (c) any other document served on the court officer for the use of the court; and
    (d) any evidence or other material prepared for the court.

Duty of court officer and custodian   R25.18

25.18 (1) The court officer must—
    (a) serve on each party notice of where and when an adjourned hearing will resume, unless that party was present when that was arranged;
    (b) if the reason for the adjournment was to postpone sentence, include that reason in any such notice to the defendant;
    (c) unless the court otherwise directs, make available to the parties any written report to which rule 25.16(2) applies (pre-sentence and medical reports);
    (d) where the court has ordered a defendant to provide information under section 25 of the Road Traffic Offenders Act 1988[47], serve on the defendant notice of that order unless the defendant was present when it was made;
    (e) give the court such other assistance as it requires, including—
      (i)   selecting jurors from the panel summoned by the Lord Chancellor, under rule 25.6 (Selecting the jury),
      (ii) taking the oaths or affirmations of jurors and witnesses, under rules 25.6 and 25.11 (Evidence of a witness in person),
      (iii) informing the jurors of the offence or offences charged in the indictment, and of their duty, under rule 25.9 (Procedure on plea of not guilty),
      (iv) retaining a copy of any written directions given to the jury under rule 25.14(2) or (3)(a),
      (v)   retaining a copy of any written material given to assist the jury under rule 25.14(5), and
      (vi) asking the jury foreman to deliver the verdict, under rule 25.14(6).

  (2) Where the court passes a sentence of immediate imprisonment or detention, or orders a suspended sentence of imprisonment to take effect, by this rule—
    (a) the court requires the defendant to provide, in writing or orally, his or her nationality; and
    (b) the custodian must obtain that information and record it

---

[47] 1988 c. 53; section 25 was amended by section 90 of, and paragraphs 140 and 142 of Schedule 13 to, the Access to Justice Act 1999 (c. 22), section 165 of, and paragraph 118 of Schedule 9 to, the Powers of Criminal Courts (Sentencing) Act 2000 (c. 6) and section 109 of, and paragraph 311 of Schedule 8 to, the Courts Act 2003 (c. 39).

[Note. See also section 82 of the Senior Courts Act 1981[48] (Duties of officers of Crown Court).

Under Part 5, the court officer must—

    (a) record details of a case and of the court's decisions; and

    (b) give public notice of specified details about a trial, including by such arrangements as the Lord Chancellor directs.

Under section 25 of the Road Traffic Offenders Act 1988, where the court does not know a defendant's sex or date of birth, then on convicting the defendant of an offence involving obligatory or discretionary disqualification, the court must order the defendant to provide that information.

Under section 86A of the Courts Act 2003, Criminal Procedure Rules must specify stages of proceedings at which the court must require the information to which rule 25.18(2) refers. A person commits an offence if, without reasonable excuse, that person fails to comply with such a requirement, whether by providing false or incomplete information or by providing no information.]

CRIMINAL PROCEDURE RULES   PART 26   JURORS

R26.1   **Appeal against officer's refusal to excuse or postpone jury service**

26.1   (1) This rule applies where a person summoned for jury service in the Crown Court, the High Court or the county court wants to appeal against a refusal by an officer on the Lord Chancellor's behalf—

        (a) to excuse that person from such service; or

        (b) to postpone the date on which that person is required to attend for such service.

    (2) The appellant must appeal to the court to which the appellant has been summoned.

    (3) The appellant must—

        (a) apply in writing, as soon as reasonably practicable; and

        (b) serve the application on the court officer.

    (4) The application must—

        (a) attach a copy of—

            (i) the jury summons, and

            (ii) the refusal to excuse or postpone which is under appeal; and

        (b) explain why the court should excuse the appellant from jury service, or postpone its date, as appropriate.

    (5) The court to which the appeal is made—

        (a) may extend the time for appealing, and may allow the appeal to be made orally;

        (b) may determine the appeal at a hearing in public or in private, or without a hearing;

        (c) may adjourn any hearing of the appeal; but

        (d) must not determine an appeal unless the appellant has had a reasonable opportunity to make representations in person.

[Note. See sections 9 and 9A of the Juries Act 1974[1].

Where a person summoned for jury service—

    (a) fails to attend as required; or

    (b) after attending as required, when selected under rule 25.6—

        (i) is not available, or

        (ii) is unfit for jury service by reason of drink or drugs

that conduct may be punished as if it were a contempt of court. See section 20 of the Juries Act 1974 and rules 48.5 to 48.8 (contempt of court). The maximum penalty which the court can impose is a fine of £1,000.]

R26.2   **Excusal from jury service by court**

26.2   At any time before a juror completes the oath or affirmation, the court may exercise its power to excuse him or her from jury service for lack of capacity to act effectively as a juror because of an insufficient understanding of English—

---

[48] 1981 c. 54; section 82 was amended by section 15 of, and paragraphs 114 and 135 of Schedule 4 to, the Constitutional Reform Act 2005 (c. 4) and sections 116 and 178 of, and Part 3 of Schedule 3 to, the Coroners and Justice Act 2009 (c. 25).
[1] 1974 c. 23; section 9 was amended by paragraphs 1, 3, 4, 5 and 6 of Schedule 33, and Part 10 of Schedule 37, to the Criminal Justice Act 2003 (c. 44) and paragraph 172 of Schedule 8 to the Courts Act 2003 (c. 39). Section 9A was inserted by section 120 of the Criminal Justice Act 1988 (c. 33) and amended by paragraphs 1, 7, 8, 9, 10 and 11 of Schedule 33 to the Criminal Justice Act 2003 (c. 44) and paragraph 172 of Schedule 8 to the Courts Act 2003 (c. 39).

(a) on the court's own initiative, or where the court officer refers the juror to the court; and

(b) after enquiry of the juror.

[Note. See section 10 of the Juries Act 1974[2].]

Provision of information for jurors   R26.3

26.3   The court officer must arrange for each juror to receive—

(a) by such means as the Lord Chancellor directs, general information about jury service and about a juror's responsibilities;

(b) written notice of the prohibitions against—

(i)   research by a juror into the case,

(ii) disclosure by a juror of any such research to another juror during the trial,

(iii) conduct by a juror which suggests that that juror intends to try the case otherwise than on the evidence, and

(iv) disclosure by a juror of the deliberations of the jury; and

(c) written warning that breach of those prohibitions is an offence, for which the penalty is imprisonment or a fine or both, and may be a contempt of court.

[Note. See sections 20A, 20B, 20C and 20D of the Juries Act 1974[3].

The Practice Direction sets out a form of notice for use in connection with this rule.]

Assessment of juror's availability for long trial, etc.   R26.4

26.4   (1) The court may invite each member of a panel of jurors to provide such information, by such means and at such a time as the court directs, about—

(a) that juror's availability to try a case expected to last for longer than the juror had expected to serve; and

(b) any association of that juror with, or any knowledge by that juror of—

(i)   a party or witness, or

(ii) any other person, or any place, of significance to the case.

(2) Where jurors provide information under this rule, the court may postpone the selection of the jury to try a case to allow each juror an opportunity to review and amend that information before that selection.

(3) Using that information, the court may exercise its power to excuse a juror from selection as a member of the jury to try a case, but the court must not—

(a) excuse a juror without allowing the parties an opportunity to make representations; or

(b) refuse to excuse a juror without allowing that juror such an opportunity.

Surrender of electronic communication devices by jurors   R26.5

26.5   (1) This rule applies where the court can order the members of a jury to surrender for a specified period any electronic communication devices that they possess.

(2) The court may make such an order—

(a) on application; or

(b) on its own initiative.

(3) A party who wants the court to make such an order must—

(a) apply as soon as reasonably practicable;

(b) notify each other party;

(c) specify for what period any device should be surrendered; and

(d) explain why—

(i)   the proposed order is necessary or expedient in the interest of justice, and

(ii) the terms of the proposed order are a proportionate means of safeguarding those interests.

[Note. See section 15A of the Juries Act 1974[4].]

Interpretation for a deaf juror   R26.6

26.6   (1) This rule applies where under section 9C of the Juries Act 1974(1) the court appoints one or more British Sign Language interpreters to enable a person who is deaf to act effectively as a juror.

---

[2] 1974 c. 23; section 10 was amended by section 168 of, and Schedule 11 to, the Criminal Justice and Public Order Act 1994 (c. 33) and sections 65 and 109 of, and paragraph 4 of Schedule 4 and Schedule 10 to, the Courts Act 2003 (c. 39).

[3] 1974 c. 23; sections 20A, 20B, 20C and 20D were inserted by sections 71, 72, 73 and 74 respectively of the Criminal Justice and Courts Act 2015 (c. 2).

[4] 1974 c. 23; section 15A was inserted by section 69 of the Criminal Justice and Courts Act 2015 (c. 2).

(2) Each such interpreter must take an oath or affirmation in these terms, or in any corresponding terms that the interpreter declares to be binding on him or her—

"I swear by Almighty God [or I do solemnly, sincerely and truly declare and affirm] that I will faithfully interpret all such matters and things as shall be required of me according to the best of my skill and understanding. I will enable communication among the jurors so that all may discharge their duties and I will not interfere in, influence or disclose the deliberations of the jury."

CRIMINAL PROCEDURE RULES   PART 27   RETRIAL AFTER ACQUITTAL
General
R27.1 When this Part applies

27.1 (1) Rule 27.2 applies where, under section 54 of the Criminal Procedure and Investigations Act 1996[1], the Crown Court or a magistrates' court can certify for the High Court that interference or intimidation has been involved in proceedings leading to an acquittal.

(2) Rules 27.3 to 27.7 apply where, under section 77 of the Criminal Justice Act 2003[2], the Court of Appeal can—

  (a) quash an acquittal for a serious offence and order a defendant to be retried; or

  (b) order that an acquittal outside the United Kingdom is no bar to the defendant being tried in England and Wales,

if there is new and compelling evidence and it is in the interests of justice to make the order.

Application for certificate to allow order for retrial
R27.2 Application for certificate

27.2 (1) This rule applies where—

  (a) a defendant has been acquitted of an offence;

  (b) a person has been convicted of one of the following offences involving interference with or intimidation of a juror or a witness (or potential witness) in any proceedings which led to the defendant's acquittal—

    (i) perverting the course of justice,

    (ii) intimidation etc. of witnesses, jurors and others under section 51(1) of the Criminal Justice and Public Order Act 1994[3], or

    (iii) aiding, abetting, counselling, procuring, suborning or inciting another person to commit an offence under section 1 of the Perjury Act 1911[4]; and

  (c) the prosecutor wants the court by which that person was convicted to certify for the High Court that there is a real possibility that, but for the interference or intimidation, the defendant would not have been acquitted.

(2) The prosecutor must—

  (a) apply in writing as soon as practicable after that person's conviction; and

  (b) serve the application on—

    (i) the court officer, and

    (ii) the defendant who was acquitted, if the court so directs.

(3) The application must—

  (a) give details, with relevant facts and dates, of—

    (i) the conviction for interference or intimidation, and

    (ii) the defendant's acquittal; and

  (b) explain—

    (i) why there is a real possibility that, but for the interference or intimidation, the defendant would not have been acquitted, and

    (ii) why it would not be contrary to the interests of justice to prosecute the defendant again for the offence of which he or she was acquitted, despite any lapse of time or other reason.

[1] 1996 c. 25.
[2] 2003 c. 44.
[3] 1994 c. 33; section 51 was amended by section 29 of, and paragraph 19 of Schedule 2 to, the Criminal Appeal Act 1995 (c. 35), section 67 of, and paragraphs 21 and 22 of Schedule 4 to, the Youth Justice and Criminal Evidence Act 1999 (c. 23), paragraphs 62 and 64 of Schedule 36 to the Criminal Justice Act 2003 (c. 44), section 45 of, and paragraph 36 of Schedule 17 to, the Crime and Courts Act 2013 (c. 22) and section 50 of, and paragraph 14 of Schedule 11 to, the Criminal Justice and Courts Act 2015 (c. 2). It is further amended by paragraph 11 of Schedule 36 to the Criminal Justice Act 2003 (c. 44), with effect from a date to be appointed.
[4] 1911 c.6.

(4) The court may—
  (a) extend the time limit under paragraph (2);
  (b) allow an application to be in a different form to one set out in the Practice Direction, or to be made orally; and
  (c) determine an application under this rule—
    (i) at a hearing, in private or in public; or
    (ii) without a hearing.
(5) If the court gives a certificate, the court officer must serve it on—
  (a) the prosecutor; and
  (b) the defendant who was acquitted.

[Note: See Section 54 of the Criminal Procedure and Investigations Act 1996 (Acquittals tainted by intimidation, etc.).

For the procedure on application to the High Court, see rules 77.6 to 77.15 of the Civil Procedure Rules 1998[5].]

Application to Court of Appeal to quash acquittal and order retrial
Application for reporting restriction pending application for order for retrial   **R27.3**

27.3 (1) This rule applies where—
  (a) no application has been made under rule 27.4 (Application for order for retrial);
  (b) an investigation by officers has begun into an offence with a view to an application under that rule; and
  (c) the Director of Public Prosecutions wants the Court of Appeal to make, vary or remove an order for a reporting restriction under section 82 of the Criminal Justice Act 2003 (Restrictions on publication in the interests of justice).
(2) The Director must—
  (a) apply in writing; and
  (b) serve the application on—
    (i) the Registrar, and
    (ii) the defendant, unless the court otherwise directs.
(3) The application must, as appropriate—
  (a) explain why the Director wants the court to direct that it need not be served on the defendant until the application under rule 27.4 is served;
  (b) specify the proposed terms of the order, and for how long it should last;
  (c) explain why an order in the terms proposed is necessary; and
  (d) explain why an order should be varied or removed.

[Note: For other rules about reporting restrictions, see Part 6.]

Application for order for retrial   **R27.4**

27.4 (1) This rule applies where—
  (a) a defendant has been acquitted—
    (i) in the Crown Court, or on appeal from the Crown Court, of an offence listed in Part 1 of Schedule 5 to the Criminal Justice Act 2003[6] (qualifying offences), or
    (ii) in proceedings elsewhere than in the United Kingdom of an offence under the law of that place, if what was alleged would have amounted to or included one of those listed offences; and
  (b) with the Director of Public Prosecutions' written consent, a prosecutor wants the Court of Appeal to make an order, as the case may be—
    (i) quashing the acquittal in the Crown Court and ordering the defendant to be retried for the offence, or
    (ii) declaring whether the acquittal outside the United Kingdom is a bar to the defendant's trial in England and Wales and, if it is, whether that acquittal shall not be such a bar.
(2) Such a prosecutor must—
  (a) apply in writing;
  (b) serve the application on the Registrar; and
  (c) not more than 2 business days later serve on the defendant who was acquitted—
    (i) the application, and

[5] S.I. 1998/3132; rules 77.6 to 77.15 were inserted by S.I. 2010/1953.
[6] 2003 c. 44; Part 1 of Schedule 5 was amended by section 26 of, and paragraph 3 of Schedule 2 to, the Corporate Manslaughter and Corporate Homicide Act 2007 (c. 19).

        (ii) a notice charging the defendant with the offence, unless the defendant has already been arrested and charged under section 87 of the Criminal Justice Act 2003[7] (arrest, under warrant or otherwise, and charge).

  (3) The application must—

    (a) give details, with relevant facts and dates, of the defendant's acquittal;

    (b) explain—

        (i) what new and compelling evidence there is against the defendant, and

        (ii) why in all the circumstances it would be in the interests of justice for the court to make the order sought;

    (c) include or attach any application for the following, with reasons—

        (i) an order under section 80(6) of the Criminal Justice Act 2003[8] (Procedure and evidence) for the production of any document, exhibit or other thing which in the prosecutor's opinion is necessary for the determination of the application,

        (ii) an order under that section for the attendance before the court of any witness who would be a compellable witness at the trial the prosecutor wants the court to order,

        (iii) an order for a reporting restriction under section 82 of the Criminal Justice Act 2003[9] (Restrictions on publication in the interests of justice); and

    (d) attach—

        (i) written witness statements of the evidence on which the prosecutor relies as new and compelling evidence against the defendant,

        (ii) relevant documents from the trial at which the defendant was acquitted, including a record of the offence or offences charged and of the evidence given, and

        (iii) any other document or thing that the prosecutor thinks the court will need to decide the application.

[Note. See sections 75, 76, 77, 80 and 82 of the Criminal Justice Act 2003[10]. Under Part 1 of Schedule 5 to that Act, the qualifying offences include murder and other serious offences against the person, offences of importation and exportation of Class A drugs, offences of causing explosions and other serious damage, terrorism offences and war crimes and other international offences.

The time limit for serving an application on the defendant is prescribed by section 80(2) of the 2003 Act. It may be extended but not shortened.]

R27.5 Respondent's notice

27.5 (1) A defendant on whom a prosecutor serves an application may serve a respondent's notice, and must do so if the defendant wants to make representations to the court.

  (2) Such a defendant must serve the respondent's notice on—

    (a) the Registrar; and

    (b) the prosecutor,

not more than 20 business days after service of the application.

  (3) The respondent's notice must—

    (a) give the date on which the respondent was served with the prosecutor's application;

    (b) summarise any relevant facts not contained in that application;

    (c) explain the defendant's grounds for opposing that application;

    (d) include or attach any application for the following, with reasons—

        (i) an extension of time within which to serve the respondent's notice,

        (ii) bail pending the hearing of the prosecutor's application, if the defendant is in custody,

        (iii) a direction to attend in person any hearing that the defendant could attend by live link, if the defendant is in custody,

        (iv) an order under section 80(6) of the Criminal Justice Act 2003 (Procedure and evidence) for the production of any document, exhibit or other thing which in the defendant's opinion is necessary for the determination of the prosecutor's application, or

        (v) an order under that section for the attendance before the court of any witness who would be a compellable witness at the trial the prosecutor wants the court to order; and

---

[7] 2003 c. 44.
[8] 2003 c. 44.
[9] 2003 c. 44.
[10] 2003 c. 44; section 76 was amended by S.I. 2012/1809.

(e) attach or identify any other document or thing that the defendant thinks the court will need to decide the application.

Application to Crown Court for summons or warrant

27.6 (1) This rule applies where—
   (a) the prosecutor has served on the Registrar an application under rule 27.4 (Application for order for retrial);
   (b) the defendant is not in custody as a result of arrest under section 88 of the Criminal Justice Act 2003[11] (Bail and custody before application); and
   (c) the prosecutor wants the Crown Court to issue—
      (i) a summons requiring the defendant to appear before the Court of Appeal at the hearing of the prosecutor's application, or
      (ii) a warrant for the defendant's arrest
   under section 89 of the 2003 Act[12] (Bail and custody before hearing).
   (2) The prosecutor must—
   (a) apply in writing; and
   (b) serve the application on the Crown Court officer.
   (3) The application must—
   (a) explain what the case is about, including a brief description of the defendant's acquittal, the new evidence and the stage that the application to the Court of Appeal has reached;
   (b) specify—
      (i) the decision that the prosecutor wants the Crown Court to make,
      (ii) each offence charged, and
      (iii) any relevant previous bail decision and the reasons given for it; and
   (c) propose the terms of any suggested condition of bail.

[Note. Under section 87 of the Criminal Justice Act 2003[13], in the circumstances prescribed by that section a justice of the peace may issue a warrant for the arrest of the defendant who was acquitted and that defendant may be charged with an offence that is to be the subject of an application to the Court of Appeal under rule 27.4.

Under section 88 of the 2003 Act, in the circumstances prescribed by that section a defendant who has been arrested and charged must be brought before the Crown Court and that court must either grant bail for that defendant to attend the Court of Appeal on the hearing of an application under rule 27.4, or remand the defendant in custody.

Under section 89 of the 2003 Act, where the prosecutor has made an application to the Court of Appeal under rule 27.4—

(a) if the defendant is in custody, the Crown Court must decide whether to remand him or her in custody to be brought before the Court of Appeal or to grant bail for that purpose; or

(b) if the defendant is not in custody, and if the prosecutor so applies, the Crown Court may either issue a summons for the defendant to attend the Court of Appeal or issue a warrant for the defendant's arrest.]

Application of other rules about procedure in the Court of Appeal

27.7 On an application under rule 27.4 (Application for order for retrial)—
   (a) the rules in Part 36 (Appeal to the Court of Appeal: general rules) apply with the necessary modifications;
   (b) rules 39.8, 39.9 and 39.10 (bail and bail conditions in the Court of Appeal) apply as if the references in those rules to appeal included references to an application under rule 27.4; and
   (c) rule 39.14 (Renewal or setting aside of order for retrial) applies as if the reference to section 7 of the Criminal Appeal Act 1968[14] were a reference to section 84 of the Criminal Justice Act 2003[15] (Retrial).

[Note. See also the notes to the rules listed in this rule.

---

[11] 2003 c. 44; section 88 is amended by section 148 of, and paragraphs 59 and 63 of Schedule 26 to, the Criminal Justice and Immigration Act 2008 (c. 4), with effect from a date to be appointed.
[12] 2003 c. 44.
[13] 2003 c. 44.
[14] 1968 c. 19; section 7 was amended by sections 43 and 170 of, and Schedule 16 to, the Criminal Justice Act 1988 (c. 33) and paragraph 44 of Schedule 36 to the Criminal Justice Act 2003 (c. 44).
[15] 2003 c. 44.

For the powers of the Court of Appeal that may be exercised by one judge of that court or by the Registrar, and for the right to renew an application for directions to a judge or to the Court of Appeal, see the Criminal Justice Act 2003 (Retrial for Serious Offences) Order 2005[16] and rule 36.5 (Renewing an application refused by a judge or the Registrar).

For rules governing applications for reporting restrictions, see Part 6. For rules governing proceedings in the Crown Court about bail, see Part 14.]

CRIMINAL PROCEDURE RULES   PART 28   SENTENCING PROCEDURES IN SPECIAL CASES AND ON COMMITTAL FOR SENTENCE, ETC.

[Note. See also—

(a)   *Part 24, which contains rules about the general procedure on sentencing in a magistrates' court;*
(b)   *Part 25, which contains rules about the general procedure on sentencing in the Crown Court;*
(c)   *Part 29 (Road traffic penalties);*
(d)   *Part 30 (Enforcement of fines and other orders for payment); and*
(e)   *Part 32 (Breach, revocation and amendment of community and other orders).]*

R28.1   Reasons for not following usual sentencing requirements

28.1   (1)   This rule applies where the court decides—
(a)   not to follow a relevant sentencing guideline;
(b)   not to make, where it could—
(i)   a reparation order (unless it passes a custodial or community sentence),
(ii)   a compensation order,
(iii)   a slavery and trafficking reparation order, or
(iv)   a travel restriction order;
(c)   not to order, where it could—
(i)   that a suspended sentence of imprisonment is to take effect,
(ii)   the endorsement of the defendant's driving record, or
(iii)   the defendant's disqualification from driving, for the usual minimum period or at all;
(d)   to pass a lesser sentence than it otherwise would have passed because the defendant has assisted, or has agreed to assist, an investigator or prosecutor in relation to an offence.
(2)   The court must explain why it has so decided, when it explains the sentence that it has passed.
(3)   Where paragraph (1)(d) applies, the court must arrange for such an explanation to be given to the defendant and to the prosecutor in writing, if the court thinks that it would not be in the public interest to explain in public.

[Note. See sections 52, 54 and 55 of the Sentencing Act 2020[1]; section 8(7) of the Modern Slavery Act 2015[2]; section 33(2) of the Criminal Justice and Police Act 2001[3]; paragraph 14(1) of Schedule 16 to the 2020 Act; section 47(1) of the Road Traffic Offenders Act 1988[4]; and section 74 of the 2020 Act.

For the duty to explain the sentence the court has passed, see section 52(1) of the 2020 Act and rules 24.119 (procedure where a magistrates' court convicts) and 25.16(7) (procedure where the Crown Court convicts).

Under section 59 of the 2020 Act, the court when sentencing must follow any relevant sentencing guideline unless satisfied that to do so would be contrary to the interests of justice.

For the circumstances in which the court may make—

(a)   *a reparation or compensation order, see sections 110 and 134 of the 2020 Act[5];*
(b)   *a slavery and trafficking reparation order, see section 8 of the 2015 Act;*
(c)   *a travel restriction order against a defendant convicted of drug trafficking, see sections 33 and 34 of the 2001 Act[6].]*

R28.2   Notice of requirements of suspended sentence and community, etc. orders

28.2   (1)   This rule applies where the court—
(a)   makes a suspended sentence order;

---

[16]   2003 S.I. 2005/679.
[1]   2020 c. 17.
[2]   2015 c. 30.
[3]   2001 c. 16.
[4]   1988 c. 53.
[5]   2009 c. 25; section 125 was repealed by section 413 of, and Schedule 28 to, the Sentencing Act 2020 (c. 17).
[6]   2001 c. 16; section 33 was amended by sections 39(3) and 39(4) of the Identity Cards Act 2006 (c. 15).

    (b) imposes a requirement under—
       (i) a community order,
      (ii) a youth rehabilitation order, or
     (iii) a suspended sentence order; or
    (c) orders the defendant to attend meetings with a supervisor.
(2) The court officer must notify—
    (a) the defendant of—
       (i) the length of the sentence suspended by a suspended sentence order, and
      (ii) the period of the suspension;
    (b) the defendant and, where the defendant is under 14, an appropriate adult, of—
       (i) any requirement or requirements imposed, and
      (ii) the identity of any responsible officer or supervisor, and the means by which that
          person may be contacted;
    (c) any responsible officer or supervisor, and, where the defendant is under 14, the appro-
      priate qualifying officer (if that is not the responsible officer), of—
       (i) the defendant's name, address and telephone number (if available),
      (ii) the offence or offences of which the defendant was convicted, and
     (iii) the requirement or requirements imposed; and
    (d) the person affected, where the court imposes a requirement—
       (i) for the protection of that person from the defendant, or
      (ii) requiring the defendant to reside with that person.
(3) If the court imposes an electronic monitoring requirement, the monitor of which is not the
    responsible officer, the court officer must—
    (a) notify the defendant and, where the defendant is under 16, an appropriate adult, of the
      monitor's identity, and the means by which the monitor may be contacted; and
    (b) notify the monitor of—
       (i) the defendant's name, address and telephone number (if available),
      (ii) the offence or offences of which the defendant was convicted,
     (iii) the place or places at which the defendant's presence must be monitored,
     (iv) the period or periods during which the defendant's presence there must be moni-
        tored, and
      (v) the identity of the responsible officer, and the means by which that officer may be
        contacted.

[Note. See sections 212(2) and 298(2) of the Sentencing Act 2020[7]; section 190(2) of the 2020 Act[8]; and section 1A(7) of the Street Offences Act 1959[9].

For the circumstances in which the court may—

    (a) make a suspended sentence order, see sections 264, 277, 286 and 288 of the 2020 Act[10];
    (b) make a community order (defined by section 200 of the 2020 Act), or a youth rehabilitation order (defined by section 173(1) of that Act), and for the identity and duties of responsible officers and qualifying officers, see generally Chapters 1 and 2 of Part 9 of the 2020 Act;
    (c) order the defendant to attend meetings with a supervisor, see section 1(2A) of the Street Offences Act 1959[11].

Under 174, 201 or 287 of the 2020 Act[12], the court may impose an electronic monitoring requirement to secure the monitoring of the defendant's compliance with certain other requirements (for example, a curfew or an exclusion).]

Notification requirements   R28.3
28.3 (1) This rule applies where, on a conviction, sentence or order, legislation requires the
       defendant—
    (a) to notify information to the police; or
    (b) to be included in a barred list.
   (2) The court must tell the defendant that such requirements apply, and under what legislation.

---

[7] 2003 c. 44; section 219 was repealed by section 413 of, and Schedule 28 to, the Sentencing Act 2020 (c. 17).
[8] 2008 c. 4.
[9] 1959 c. 57; section 1A was inserted by section 17(1) and (3) of the Policing and Crime Act 2009 (c. 26).
[10] 2008 c. 4; Schedule 1 was repealed by section 413 of, and Schedule 28 to, the Sentencing Act 2020 (c. 17).
[11] 1959 c. 57; section 1(2A) was inserted by section 17(1) and (3) of the Policing and Crime Act 2009 (c. 26).
[12] 2008 c. 4.

[Note. For the circumstances in which a defendant is required to notify information to the police, see—

    (a) Part 2 of, and Schedule 3 to, the Sexual Offences Act 2003[13] (notification for the period specified by section 82 of the Act[14] after conviction, etc. of an offence listed in Schedule 3 and committed in the circumstances specified in that Schedule);

    (b) Part 4 of the Counter Terrorism Act 2008[15] (notification after conviction of a specified offence of, or connected with, terrorism, for which a specified sentence is imposed).

For the circumstances in which a defendant will be included in a barred list, see paragraphs 1, 2, 7, 8 and 24 of Schedule 3 to the Safeguarding Vulnerable Groups Act 2006[16]. See also paragraph 25 of that Schedule[17].

These requirements are not part of the court's sentence.]

R28.4   **Variation of sentence**

     28.4   (1)   This rule—

         (a)   applies where a magistrates' court or the Crown Court can vary, rescind or set aside a sentence, penalty or order, other than an order to which rule 44.3 applies (Setting aside a conviction or varying a costs etc. order); and

         (b)   authorises the Crown Court, in addition to its other powers, to do so within the period of 56 days beginning with another defendant's acquittal or sentencing where—

             (i)   defendants are tried separately in the Crown Court on the same or related facts alleged in one or more indictments, and

             (ii)   one is sentenced before another is acquitted or sentenced.

       (2)   The court—

         (a)   may exercise its power—

             (i)   on application by a party, or on its own initiative,

             (ii)   at a hearing, in public or in private, or without a hearing; and

         (b)   must announce, at a hearing in public—

             (i)   a decision to vary or rescind a sentence or order, or to refuse to do so, and

             (ii)   the reasons for that decision.

       (3)   A party who wants the court to exercise that power must—

         (a)   apply in writing as soon as reasonably practicable after—

             (i)   the sentence, penalty or order that that party wants the court to vary, rescind or set aside, or

             (ii)   where paragraph (1)(b) applies, the other defendant's acquittal or sentencing;

         (b)   serve the application on—

             (i)   the court officer, and

             (ii)   each other party; and

         (c)   in the application—

             (i)   explain why the sentence, penalty or order should be varied, rescinded or set aside,

             (ii)   specify the variation that the applicant proposes, and

             (iii)   if the application is late, explain why.

       (4)   The court must not exercise its power in the defendant's absence unless—

         (a)   the court makes a variation—

             (i)   which is proposed by the defendant, or

             (ii)   the effect of which is that the defendant is no more severely dealt with under the sentence as varied than before; or

         (b)   the defendant has had an opportunity to make representations at a hearing (whether or not the defendant in fact attends).

       (5)   The court may—

         (a)   extend (even after it has expired) the time limit under paragraph (3), unless the court's power to vary or rescind the sentence cannot be exercised; and

         (b)   allow an application to be made orally.

[13] 2003 c. 42; Schedule 3 was amended by article 2 of S.I. 2007/296, section 63(2) of, and paragraph 63 of Schedule 6 to, the Serious Crimes Act 2007 (c. 27), section 148(1) of, and paragraphs 53 and 58 of Schedule 26 to, the Criminal Justice and Immigration Act 2008 (c. 4) and section 177(1) of, and paragraph 62 of Schedule 21 to, the Coroners and Justice Act 2009 (c. 25). Other amendments to Schedule 3 are not relevant to these Rules.

[14] 2003 c. 42; section 82 was amended by section 57 of the Violent Crime Reduction Act 2006 (c. 38).

[15] 2008 c. 28.

[16] 2006 c. 47; paragraphs 1, 2, 7 and 8 of Schedule 3 were amended by sections 81 and 89 of the Policing and Crime Act 2009 (c. 26). Paragraph 24 was amended by article 2 of S.I. 2008/3050.

[17] 2006 c. 47; paragraph 25 of Schedule 3 was amended by article 3 of S.I. 2008/3050 and section 81 of the Policing and Crime Act 2009 (c. 26).

(6) For the purposes of the announcement required by paragraph (2)(b), the court need not comprise the same member or members as the court by which the decision to be announced was made.

[Note. Under section 142 of the Magistrates' Courts Act 1980[18], in some cases a magistrates' court can vary or rescind a sentence or other order that it has imposed or made, if that appears to be in the interests of justice. The power cannot be exercised if the Crown Court or the High Court has determined an appeal about that sentence or order. See also rule 44.3 (Setting aside a conviction or varying a costs etc. order), which governs the exercise by a magistrates' court of the power conferred by section 142 of the 1980 Act in the circumstances to which that rule applies.

Under section 16M of the 1980 Act[19] a magistrates' court can set aside a penalty imposed under section 16I of the Act on a defendant who accepts the automatic online conviction option under section 16H if the amount of the penalty appears to the court to be unjust. If the court sets aside such a penalty it may impose any sentence that it could have imposed for the offence if the defendant had pleaded guilty at the first opportunity.

Under section 385 of the Sentencing Act 2020, the Crown Court can vary or rescind a sentence or other order that it has imposed or made. The power cannot be exercised—

(a) after the period of 56 days beginning with the sentence or order (but see the note below); or

(b) if an appeal or application for permission to appeal against that sentence or order has been determined.

Under section 385(7) of that Act, Criminal Procedure Rules can extend that period of 56 days where another defendant is tried separately in the Crown Court on the same or related facts alleged in one or more indictments.]

Application to vary or discharge a compensation, etc. order

R28.5

28.5 (1) This rule applies where on application by the defendant a magistrates' court can vary or discharge—

(a) a compensation order; or

(b) a slavery and trafficking reparation order.

(2) A defendant who wants the court to exercise that power must—

(a) apply in writing as soon as practicable after becoming aware of the grounds for doing so;

(b) serve the application on the magistrates' court officer;

(c) where the order was made in the Crown Court, serve a copy of the application on the Crown Court officer; and

(d) in the application, specify the order that the defendant wants the court to vary or discharge and explain (as applicable)—

(i) what civil court finding shows that the injury, loss or damage was less than it had appeared to be when the order was made,

(ii) in what circumstances the person for whose benefit the order was made has recovered the property for the loss of which it was made,

(iii) why a confiscation order, unlawful profit order or slavery and trafficking reparation order makes the defendant now unable to pay compensation or reparation in full, or

(iv) in what circumstances the defendant's means have been reduced substantially and unexpectedly, and why they seem unlikely to increase for a considerable period.

(3) The court officer must serve a copy of the application on the person for whose benefit the order was made.

(4) The court must not vary or discharge the order unless—

(a) the defendant, and the person for whose benefit it was made, each has had an opportunity to make representations at a hearing (whether or not either in fact attends); and

(b) where the order was made in the Crown Court, the Crown Court has notified its consent.

[Note. For the circumstances in which—

(a) the court may make a compensation order, see section 133 of the Sentencing Act 2020;

(b) the court may make a slavery and trafficking reparation order, see section 8 of the Modern Slavery Act 2015[20];

(c) a magistrates' court with power to enforce such an order may vary or discharge it under the 2020 Act, see section 143. (Under section 143(3), where the order was made in the Crown Court, the magistrates' court must first obtain the Crown Court's consent.)]

---

[18] 1980 c. 43; section 142 was amended by sections 26 and 29 of, and Schedule 3 to, the Criminal Appeal Act 1995 (c. 35).
[19] 1980 c. 43; section 16M is inserted by section 3 of the Judicial Review and Courts Act 2022 (c. 35) with effect from a date to be appointed.
[20] 2015 c. 30.

R28.6   Application to remove, revoke or suspend a disqualification or restriction

28.6 (1) This rule applies where, on application by the defendant, the court can remove, revoke or suspend a disqualification or restriction included in a sentence (except a disqualification from driving).

(2) A defendant who wants the court to exercise such a power must—
  (a) apply in writing, no earlier than the date on which the court can exercise the power;
  (b) serve the application on the court officer; and
  (c) in the application—
      (i) specify the disqualification or restriction, and
      (ii) explain why the defendant wants the court to remove, revoke or suspend it.

(3) The court officer must serve a copy of the application on the chief officer of police for the local justice area.

[Note. Part 29 contains rules about disqualification from driving. See in particular rule 29.2.

Part 34 (Appeal to the Crown Court) and Part 35 (Appeal to the High Court by case stated) contain rules about applications to suspend disqualifications pending appeal.

For the circumstances in which the court may—

  (a) remove a disqualification from keeping a dog, see section 4(6) of the Dangerous Dogs Act 1991[21]. The court may not consider an application made within 1 year of the disqualification; or, after that, within 1 year of any previous application that was refused.

  (b) revoke or suspend a travel restriction order against a defendant convicted of drug trafficking, see section 35 of the Criminal Justice and Police Act 2001[22]). The court may not consider an application made within 2 years of the disqualification, in any case; or, after that, before a specified period has expired.]

R28.7   Application for a restitution order by the victim of a theft

28.7 (1) This rule applies where, on application by the victim of a theft, the court can order a defendant to give that person goods obtained with the proceeds of goods stolen in that theft.

(2) A person who wants the court to exercise that power if the defendant is convicted must—
  (a) apply in writing as soon as practicable (without waiting for the verdict);
  (b) serve the application on the court officer; and
  (c) in the application—
      (i) identify the goods, and
      (ii) explain why the applicant is entitled to them.

(3) The court officer must serve a copy of the application on each party.

(4) The court must not determine the application unless the applicant and each party has had an opportunity to make representations at a hearing (whether or not each in fact attends).

(5) The court may—
  (a) extend (even after it has expired) the time limit under paragraph (2); and
  (b) allow an application to be made orally.

[Note. For the circumstances in which the court may order—

  (a) the return of stolen goods, see section 147 of the Sentencing Act 2020[23];

  (b) the defendant to give the victim of the theft goods that are not themselves the stolen goods but which represent their proceeds, see section 147(1)(b) of the 2020 Act.]

R28.8   Directions for commissioning medical reports for sentencing purposes

28.8 (1) This rule applies where for sentencing purposes the court requires—
  (a) a medical examination of the defendant and a report; or
  (b) information about the arrangements that could be made for the defendant where the court is considering—
      (i) a hospital order, or
      (ii) a guardianship order.

(2) The court must—
  (a) identify each issue in respect of which the court requires expert medical opinion and the legislation applicable;
  (b) specify the nature of the expertise likely to be required for giving such opinion;

---

[21] 1991 c. 65; section 4(6) was amended by section 109(1) of, and paragraph 353 of Schedule 8 to, the Courts Act 2003 (c. 39).
[22] 2001 c. 16; section 35 was amended by sections 39(3) of the Identity Cards Act 2006 (c. 15).
[23] 2020 c. 17.

(c) identify each party or participant by whom a commission for such opinion must be prepared, who may be—

    (i) a party (or party's representative) acting on that party's own behalf,

    (ii) a party (or party's representative) acting on behalf of the court, or

    (iii) the court officer acting on behalf of the court;

(d) where there are available to the court arrangements with the National Health Service under which an assessment of a defendant's mental health may be prepared, give such directions as are needed under those arrangements for obtaining the expert report or reports required;

(e) where no such arrangements are available to the court, or they will not be used, give directions for the preparation of a commission or commissions for an expert report or expert reports, including—

    (i) such directions as can be made about supplying the expert or experts with the defendant's medical records,

    (ii) directions about the other information, about the defendant and about the offence or offences alleged to have been committed by the defendant, which is to be supplied to each expert, and

    (iii) directions about the arrangements that will apply for the payment of each expert;

(f) set a timetable providing for—

    (i) the date by which a commission is to be delivered to each expert,

    (ii) the date by which any failure to accept a commission is to be reported to the court,

    (iii) the date or dates by which progress in the preparation of a report or reports is to be reviewed by the court officer, and

    (iv) the date by which each report commissioned is to be received by the court; and

(g) identify the person (each person, if more than one) to whom a copy of a report is to be supplied, and by whom.

(3) A commission addressed to an expert must—

(a) identify each issue in respect of which the court requires expert medical opinion and the legislation applicable;

(b) include—

    (i) the information required by the court to be supplied to the expert,

    (ii) details of the timetable set by the court, and

    (iii) details of the arrangements that will apply for the payment of the expert;

(c) identify the person (each person, if more than one) to whom a copy of the expert's report is to be supplied; and

(d) request confirmation that the expert from whom the opinion is sought—

    (i) accepts the commission, and

    (ii) will adhere to the timetable.

[Note. See also rule 3.10 (directions for commissioning medical reports in connection with fitness to participate in the trial, etc.).

For sentencing purposes the court may request a medical examination of the defendant and a report under—

    (a) section 35 of the Mental Health Act 1983[24], under which the court may order the defendant's detention in hospital to obtain a medical report;

    (b) section 36 of the 1983 Act[25], under which the Crown Court may order the defendant's detention in hospital instead of in custody pending trial or sentence;

    (c) section 37 of the 1983 Act[26], under which the court may order the defendant's detention and treatment in hospital, or make a guardianship order, instead of disposing of the case in another way

---

[24] 1983 c. 20; section 35 was amended by sections 1(4) and 10(1) and (2) of, and paragraphs 1 and 5 of Schedule 1 to, the Mental Health Act 2007 (c. 12) and section 208(1) of, and paragraphs 53 and 54 of Schedule 21 to, the Legal Services Act 2007 (c. 29).

[25] 1983 c. 20; section 36 was amended by sections 1(4), 5(1) and (2) and 10(1) and (3) of, and paragraphs 1 and 6 of Schedule 1 to, the Mental Health Act 2007 (c. 12) and section 208(1) of, and paragraphs 53 and 55 of Schedule 21 to, the Legal Services Act 2007 (c. 29).

[26] 1983 c. 20; section 37 was amended by sections 55 and 56 of, and paragraph 12 of Schedule 4 and Schedule 6 to, the Crime (Sentences) Act 1997 (c. 43), section 67 of, and paragraph 11 of Schedule 4 to, the Youth Justice and Criminal Evidence Act 1999 (c. 23), paragraph 90 of Schedule 9 to the Powers of Criminal Courts (Sentencing) Act 2000 (c. 6), section 304 of, and paragraphs 37 and 38 of Schedule 32 to, the Criminal Justice Act 2003 (c. 44), sections 49 and 65 of, and paragraph 2 of Schedule 1 and Schedule 5 to, the Violent Crime Reduction Act 2006 (c. 38), sections 1, 4, 10, 55 and paragraphs 1 and 7 of Schedule 1, and Part 1 of Schedule 11 to, the Mental Health Act 2007 (c. 12), sections 6 and 149 of, and paragraph 30 of Schedule 4, and Schedule 28 to, the Criminal Justice and Immigration Act 2008 (c. 4), sections 122 and 142 of, and paragraph 1 of Schedule 19 and paragraph 2 of Schedule 26 to, the Legal Aid, Sentencing and Punishment of Offenders Act 2012 (c. 10) and section 28 of, and paragraph 1 of Schedule 5 to, the Criminal Justice and Courts Act 2015 (c. 2). It is further amended by

(section 37(3) allows a magistrates' court to make such an order without convicting the defendant if satisfied that the defendant did the act or made the omission charged);

(d) *section 38 of the 1983 Act[27], under which the court may order the defendant's temporary detention and treatment in hospital instead of disposing of the case in another way;*

(e) *section 232 of the Sentencing Act 2020[28], under which the court must usually obtain and consider a medical report before passing a custodial sentence if the defendant is, or appears to be, mentally disordered;*

(f) *paragraphs 16 and 17 of Schedule 9 to the 2020 Act[29] (in the case of a defendant aged 18 or over), or paragraphs 28 and 29 of Schedule 6 to that Act (in the case of a defendant who is under 18), under which the court may impose a mental health treatment requirement.*

For the purposes of the legislation listed in (b), (c) and (d) above, the court requires the written or oral evidence of at least two registered medical practitioners, at least one of whom is approved as having special experience in the diagnosis or treatment of mental disorder. For the purposes of (a), (e) and (f), the court requires the evidence of one medical practitioner so approved.

Under section 11 of the Powers of Criminal Courts (Sentencing) Act 2000[30], a magistrates' court may adjourn a trial to obtain medical reports.

Part 19 (Expert evidence) contains rules about the content of expert medical reports.

For the authorities from whom the court may require information about hospital treatment or guardianship, see sections 39 and 39A of the 1983 Act[31].

The Practice Direction includes a timetable for the commissioning and preparation of a report or reports which the court may adopt with such adjustments as the court directs.

Payments to medical practitioners for reports and for giving evidence are governed by section 19(3) of the Prosecution of Offences Act 1985[32] and by the Costs in Criminal Cases (General) Regulations 1986[33], regulation 17 (Determination of rates or scales of allowances payable out of central funds), regulation 20 (Expert witnesses, etc.) and regulation 25 (Written medical reports). The rates and scales of allowances payable under those Regulations are determined by the Lord Chancellor.]

R28.9   Information to be supplied on committal to custody or admission to hospital or guardianship

28.9   (1)   This rule applies where the court—

     (a)   orders the defendant's committal to custody on withholding bail or on sentencing;

     (b)   orders the defendant's detention and treatment in hospital; or

     (c)   makes a guardianship order.

     (2)   Where paragraph (1)(a) applies, unless the court otherwise directs the court officer must, as soon as practicable, serve on or make available to the custodian any psychiatric, psychological or other medical report about the defendant received by the court for the purposes of the case.

---

section 148 of, and paragraph 8 of Schedule 26 to, the Criminal Justice and Immigration Act 2008 (c. 4) with effect from a date to be appointed.

[27] 1983 c. 20; section 38 was amended by section 49(1) of the Crime (Sentences) Act 1997 (c. 43), sections 1(4) and 10(1) and (5) of, and paragraphs 1 and 8 of Schedule 1 to, the Mental Health Act 2007 (c. 12) and section 208(1) of, and paragraphs 53 and 56 of Schedule 21 to, the Legal Services Act 2007 (c. 29).

[28] 2020 c. 17.

[29] 2003 c. 44; section 207 was amended by article 4(2) of, and paragraph 7 of Schedule 5 to, S.I. 2009/1182, article 14(a) and (b) of, and Part 1 of Schedule 5 to, S.I. 2010/813, section 72 of the Health and Social Care Act 2012 (c. 7), section 73 of the Legal Aid, Sentencing and Punishment of Offenders Act 2012 (c. 10) and section 62 of, and paragraph 48 of Schedule 5 to, the Children and Social Work Act 2017 (c. 16).

[30] 2000 c. 6.

[31] 1983 c. 20; section 39 was amended by sections 2(1) and 5(1) of, and paragraph 107 of Schedule 1 and Schedule 3 to, the Health Authorities Act 1995 (c. 17), section 2(5) of, and paragraphs 42 and 46 of Schedule 2 to, the National Health Service Reform and Health Care Professions Act 2002 (c. 17), section 31(1) and (2) of the Mental Health Act 2007 (c. 12), article 3 of, and paragraph 13 of the Schedule to, S.I. 2007/961 and section 55 of, and paragraphs 24 and 28 of Schedule 5 to, the Health and Social Care Act 2012 (c. 7). Section 39A was inserted by section 27(1) of the Criminal Justice Act 1991 (c. 53).

[32] 1985 c. 23; section 19(3) was amended by section 166 of the Criminal Justice Act 1988 (c. 33), section 7 of, and paragraph 8 of Schedule 3 to, the Criminal Procedure (Insanity and Unfitness to Plead) Act 1991 (c. 25), sections 40 and 67 of, and paragraph 4 of Schedule 7 to, the Youth Justice and Criminal Evidence Act 1999 (c. 23), section 165 of, and paragraph 99 of Schedule 9 to, the Powers of Criminal Courts (Sentencing) Act 2000 (c. 6) and section 378 of, and paragraph 107 of Schedule 16 to, the Armed Forces Act 2006 (c. 52).

[33] S.I. 1986/1335; regulation 17 was amended by regulations 2 and 13 of S.I. 2008/2448, regulation 20 was amended by regulations 2 and 14 of S.I. 2008/2448 and by regulations 4 and 7 of S.I. 2012/1804, and regulation 25 was amended by regulations 2 and 10 of S.I. 2009/2720.

(3) Where paragraph (1)(b) or (c) applies, unless the court otherwise directs the court officer must, as soon as practicable, serve on or make available to (as applicable) the hospital or the guardian—
    (a) a record of the court's order;
    (b) such information as the court has received that appears likely to assist in treating or otherwise dealing with the defendant, including information about—
        (i)   the defendant's mental condition,
        (ii) the defendant's other circumstances, and
        (iii) the circumstances of the offence.

[Note. Rule 13.3 provides for the terms of a warrant for detention or imprisonment. Rule 13.4 provides for the information that such a warrant must contain.

For the circumstances in which the court may order the defendant's detention and treatment in hospital, see sections 35, 36, 37, 38 and 44 of the Mental Health Act 1983[34]. For the circumstances in which the court may make a guardianship order, see the same section 37.]

Committal or remission, etc. for sentence

R28.10

28.10 (1) This rule applies where a magistrates' court or the Crown Court ('the transferring court')—
    (a) commits, remits or transfers a case to another court—
        (i)   for sentence, or
        (ii) for the defendant to be dealt with for breach of a deferred sentence, a conditional discharge, or a suspended sentence of imprisonment, imposed by that other court;
    (b) deals with a deferred sentence, a conditional discharge, or a suspended sentence of imprisonment, imposed by another court; or
    (c) makes an order that another court is, or may be, required to enforce.
(2) Unless the transferring court otherwise directs, the court officer must, as soon as practicable—
    (a) where paragraph (1)(a) applies, make available to the other court a record of any relevant—
        (i)   certificate of conviction,
        (ii)   magistrates' court register entry,
        (iii) decision about bail, for the purposes of section 5 of the Bail Act 1976[35],
        (iv)   note of evidence,
        (v)   statement or other document introduced in evidence,
        (vi)   medical or other report,
        (vii) representation order or application for such order,
        (viii) interim driving disqualification; and
        (ix)   statement by the court for the purposes of section 70(5) of the Proceeds of Crime Act 2002[36]
    (b) where paragraph (1)(b) or (c) applies, make available to the other court the transferring court's order; and
        (i)   the transmission from the convicting to the other court of notice of the convicting court's order, and
        (ii) the recording of that order at the other court;
    (c) in every case, notify the defendant and, where the defendant is under 16, a parent or guardian, of the location of the other court.

[Note. For the circumstances in which—

    (a) a magistrates' court may (and, in some cases, must) commit the defendant to the Crown Court for sentence, see rules 9.15 (Committal for sentence of offence related to an offence sent for trial), 24.11 (Procedure if the court convicts) and 28.12 (Sentencing, etc. after committal to the Crown Court) (the note to rule 28.12 summarises the statutory provisions that apply);

---

[34] 1983 c. 20; section 44 was amended by sections 10, 40 and 55 of, and Part 8 of Schedule 11 to, the Mental Health Act 2007 (c. 12).
[35] 1976 c. 63; section 5 was amended by section 65 of, and Schedule 12 to, the Criminal Law Act 1977 (c. 45), section 60 of the Criminal Justice Act 1982 (c. 48), paragraph 1 of Schedule 3 to the Criminal Justice and Public Order Act 1994 (c. 33), paragraph 53 of Schedule 9 to the Powers of Criminal Courts (Sentencing) Act 2000 (c. 6), section 129(1) of the Criminal Justice and Police Act 2001 (c. 16), paragraph 182 of Schedule 8 to the Courts Act 2003 (c. 39), paragraph 48 of Schedule 3, paragraphs 1 and 2 of Schedule 36, and Parts 2, 4 and 12 of Schedule 37 to the Criminal Justice Act 2003 (c. 44) and section 208 of, and paragraphs 33 and 35 of Schedule 21 to, the Legal Services Act 2007 (c. 27).
[36] 2002 c. 29; section 70 was amended by section 41 of, and paragraph 75 of Schedule 3 to, the Criminal Justice Act 2003 (c. 44), section 410 of, and paragraphs 181 and 195 of Schedule 24 to, the Sentencing Act 2020 (c. 17) and section 46 of, and paragraph 19 of Schedule 13 to, the Counter-Terrorism and Sentencing Act 2021 (c. 11).

    (b) *a magistrates' court may adjourn the case to another magistrates' court for sentence, see section 10 of the Magistrates' Courts Act 1980[37] and section 28 of the Sentencing Act 2020[38];*

    (c) *a magistrates' court or the Crown Court may (and, in some cases, must) adjourn the case to a youth court for sentence, see sections 25 and 26 of the 2020 Act;*

    (d) *a youth court may adjourn the case to a magistrates' court for sentence, see section 27 of the 2020 Act;*

    (e) *a magistrates' court may transfer a fine to be enforced to another court, see sections 89 and 90 of the 1980 Act[39].*

    (f) *the Crown Court may remit the defendant to a magistrates' court for sentence after committal for sentence to the Crown Court, or following a guilty plea in the Crown Court, see section 25A of the 2020 Act[40]. Under section 25A(3) of the Act, in deciding whether to remit a defendant the Crown Court must take into account (a) any other related offence before the Crown Court (whether the same, or a different, person is accused or has been convicted of the other offence), and (b) any allocation guideline.*

For the court's powers where it convicts a defendant who is subject to a deferred sentence, a conditional discharge, or a suspended sentence of imprisonment, imposed by another court, see section 10 of, and Schedules 2 and 16 to, the 2020 Act.

Under section 132 of the 2020 Act, a fine imposed or other sum ordered to be paid in the Crown Court is enforceable by a magistrates' court specified in the order, or from which the case was committed or sent to the Crown Court.

See also sections 212(4), 298(4) and 190(4) of the 2020 Act; and section 1A(9) of the Street Offences Act 1959[41].

See also rule 9.16 (Sending back or referring case for magistrates' court trial), which applies to the exercise of the Crown Court's powers under (a) section 46ZA of the Senior Courts Act 1981[42], and (b) paragraph 6 of Schedule 3 to the Crime and Disorder Act 1998[43].]

R28.11   **Application to review sentence because of assistance given or withheld**

  28.11 (1) This rule applies where the Crown Court can reduce or increase a sentence on application by a prosecutor in a case in which—

    (a) since being sentenced, the defendant has assisted, or has agreed to assist, an investigator or prosecutor in relation to an offence; or

    (b) since receiving a reduced sentence for agreeing to give such assistance, the defendant has failed to do so.

    (2) A prosecutor who wants the court to exercise that power must—

    (a) apply in writing as soon as practicable after becoming aware of the grounds for doing so;

    (b) serve the application on—

      (i) the court officer, and

      (ii) the defendant; and

    (c) in the application—

      (i) explain why the sentence should be reduced, or increased, as appropriate, and

      (ii) identify any other matter relevant to the court's decision, including any sentencing guideline or guideline case.

    (3) The general rule is that the application must be determined by the judge who passed the sentence, unless that judge is unavailable.

    (4) The court must not determine the application in the defendant's absence unless the defendant has had an opportunity to make representations at a hearing (whether or not the defendant in fact attends).

---

[37] 1980 c. 43; section 10 was amended by section 59 of, and paragraph 1 of Schedule 9 to, the Criminal Justice Act 1982 (c. 48), section 68 of, and paragraph 6 of Schedule 8 to, the Criminal Justice Act 1991 (c. 53) and section 47 of the Crime and Disorder Act 1998 (c. 37).

[38] 2020 c. 17.

[39] 1980 c. 43; section 89 was amended by section 47 of the Criminal Justice and Public Order Act 1994 (c. 33), paragraphs 95 and 107 of Schedule 13 to the Access to Justice Act 1999 (c. 22), paragraph 225 of Schedule 8 to the Courts Act 2003 (c. 39) and articles 46 and 49 of S.I. 2006/1737. Section 90 was amended by section 47(2) of the Criminal Justice and Public Order Act 1994 (c. 33), paragraph 226 of Schedule 8 to the Courts Act 2003 (c. 39) and articles 46 and 50 of S.I. 2006/1737.

[40] 2020 c. 17; section 25A was inserted by section 11 of the Judicial Review and Courts Act 2022 (c. 35).

[41] 1959 c. 57; section 1A was inserted by section 17(1) and (3) of the Policing and Crime Act 2009 (c. 26).

[42] 1981 c. 54; section 46ZA was inserted by section 11 of the Judicial Review and Courts Act 2022 (c. 35).

[43] 1998 c. 37; paragraph 6 of Schedule 3 was amended by sections 90 and 106 of, and paragraph 179 of Schedule 13 and Schedule 15 to, the Access to Justice Act 1999 (c. 22), sections 41 of, and paragraphs 15 and 20 of Schedule 3 to, the Criminal Justice Act 2003 (c. 44), S.I. 2005/886 and paragraphs 20 and 23 of the Schedule to the Courts and Tribunals (Judiciary and Functions of Staff) Act 2018 (c. 33).

[Note. Under section 73 of the Serious Organised Crime and Police Act 2005[44], the Crown Court may pass a lesser sentence than it otherwise would have passed because the defendant has assisted, or has agreed to assist, an investigator or prosecutor in relation to an offence.

Under sections 387 and 388 of the 2020 Act, where the Crown Court has sentenced a defendant a prosecutor may apply to the court—

    (a) to reduce the sentence, if the defendant subsequently assists, or agrees to assist, in the investigation or prosecution of an offence; or

    (b) to increase a reduced sentence to that which the court otherwise would have passed, if the defendant agreed to give such assistance but subsequently has knowingly failed to do so.

Such an application may be made only where the defendant is still serving the sentence and the prosecutor thinks it is in the interests of justice to apply.]

Sentencing, etc. after committal to the Crown Court

R28.12

28.12 (1) This rule applies where a magistrates' court commits the defendant to the Crown Court—

    (a) for sentence; or

    (b) to be dealt with under other powers available to the Crown Court after a defendant's conviction.

(2) Rule 25.16 (Trial and sentence in the Crown Court; Procedure if the court convicts) applies as if the defendant had been convicted in the Crown Court.

(3) As well as supplying the information required for sentencing purposes by rule 25.16(3), the prosecutor must identify any offence in respect of which the Crown Court cannot deal with the defendant in a way in which it could have done if the defendant had been convicted in the Crown Court, including—

    (a) an offence—

        (i) committed for sentence under section 18 or 19, as the case may be, of the Sentencing Act 2020[45], and

        (ii) in respect of which the magistrates' court did not state the opinion to which section 18(4) or 19(3) of that Act refers;

    (b) an offence committed for sentence under section 20 of the 2020 Act; and

    (c) an offence—

        (i) committed to the Crown Court under section 70 of the Proceeds of Crime Act 2002, and

        (ii) in respect of which the magistrates' court did not make the statement to which section 70(5) of that Act refers.

[Note. A magistrates' court may commit a convicted defendant to the Crown Court for sentence under—

    (a) section 14 of the Sentencing Act 2020 (Committal for sentence on summary trial of offence triable either way: adults and corporations) where the defendant is over 18 or is a corporation, the offence is one triable either way and the court is of the opinion that the offence of which the defendant has been convicted, or the combination of that offence and one or more offences associated with it, was so serious that the Crown Court should have the power to deal with the defendant in any way that that court could have done if the defendant had been convicted there;

    (b) section 16 of the 2020 Act (Committal for sentence of young offenders on summary trial of certain serious offences) where the defendant is under 18, the offence of which the defendant has been convicted is one to which section 16 refers (offences punishable with imprisonment for 14 years or more and certain sexual offences), and the court is of the opinion that the offence of which the defendant has been convicted, or the combination of that offence and one or more offences associated with it, was such that the Crown Court should have the power to impose a sentence of detention under section 250 of the Act;

    (c) section 16A of the 2020 Act[46] (Committal for sentence of young offenders on summary trial of certain terrorist offences) where the defendant is under 18, the offence of which the defendant has been convicted is one within section 252A of the Act[47] (terrorism offences attracting special sentence for offenders of particular concern) and the court is of the opinion that the offence of which the defendant has been convicted, or the combination of that offence and one or more offences associated

---

[44] 2020 c. 17.

[45] 2020 c. 17; section 19 was amended by section 46 of, and paragraph 26 of Schedule 13 to, the Counter-Terrorism and Sentencing Act 2021 (c. 11).

[46] 2020 c. 17; section 16A was inserted by section 46 of, and paragraph 26 of Schedule 13 to, the Counter-Terrorism and Sentencing Act 2021 (c. 11).

[47] 2020 c. 17; section 252A was inserted by section 22 of the Counter-Terrorism and Sentencing Act 2021 (c. 11).

with it, was such that the Crown Court should have the power to impose a sentence of detention for more than 2 years under section 252A;

(d)   section 18 of the 2020 Act (Committal for sentence on indication of guilty plea to offence triable either way: adult offenders) where the defendant is over 18 and the court has sent the defendant to the Crown Court for trial for a related offence;

(e)   section 19 of the 2020 Act (Committal for sentence on indication of guilty plea by child with related offences) where the defendant is under 18, the court has sent the defendant to the Crown Court for trial for a related offence, and the offence of which the defendant has been convicted is one to which section 19 refers (offences punishable with imprisonment for 14 years or more and certain sexual offences); or

(f)   section 20 of the 2020 Act (Committal in certain cases where offender committed in respect of another offence) where the court commits the defendant to the Crown Court for sentence for an offence under any of sections 14 to 19 of the Act, or under one of the other provisions to which section 20 refers, and—

(i)   if that offence is an indictable offence, then the court may also commit the defendant for sentence for any other offence, or

(ii)   if that offence is a summary offence, then the court may also commit the defendant for sentence for any other offence of which the court itself has convicted the defendant and which is punishable with imprisonment or disqualification from driving, and for any suspended sentence with which the committing court could deal.

A magistrates' court must commit a convicted defendant to the Crown Court for sentence under—

(a)   section 15 of the Sentencing Act 2020[48] (Committal for sentence of dangerous adult offenders) where the defendant is over 18, the offence of which the defendant has been convicted is one to which section 15 refers, and the court is of the opinion that an extended sentence of detention or imprisonment would be available in relation to the offence; or

(b)   section 17 of the 2020 Act[49] (Committal for sentence of dangerous young offenders) where the defendant is under 18, the offence of which the defendant has been convicted is one to which section 17 refers, and the court is of the opinion that an extended sentence of detention would be available in relation to the offence.

Under sections 21 and 22 of the Sentencing Act 2020[50] (Power of Crown Court on committal for sentence of offender under section 14, 15 or 18; Power of Crown Court on committal for sentence of person under 18 under section 16, 16A, 17 or 19), where the defendant is committed for sentence under any of sections 14 to 19 of that Act the Crown Court may deal with the defendant in any way in which it could have done if the defendant had been convicted in that court, unless—

(a)   the defendant was committed for sentence under section 18 or 19;

(b)   the magistrates' court did not state the opinion to which either section 18(4) or 19(3), whichever applies, refers (see also rule 9.15 (Committal for sentence for offence related to an offence sent for trial)); and

(c)   the defendant is not convicted in the Crown Court of any offence for which the magistrates' court sent the defendant for trial,

in which event the Crown Court may deal with the defendant only in a way in which the magistrates' court could have done.

Under section 23 of the 2020 Act (Power of Crown Court on committal for sentence under section 20), where the defendant is committed for sentence under section 20 of the Act the Crown Court may deal with the defendant only in a way in which the magistrates' court could have done except in relation to any suspended sentence committed under that section, in respect of which the Crown Court may exercise its usual powers on dealing with such a breach.

For other powers of a magistrates' court to commit a defendant to the Crown Court for sentence or otherwise to deal with the defendant, see—

(a)   the provisions listed in section 24 of the 2020 Act (Further powers to commit offender to the Crown Court to be dealt with); and

---

[48] 2020 c. 17; section 15 was amended by section 46 of, and paragraph 11 of Schedule 13 to, the Counter-Terrorism and Sentencing Act 2021 (c. 11).
[49] 2020 c. 17; section 17 was amended by section 46 of, and paragraph 26 of Schedule 13 to, the Counter-Terrorism and Sentencing Act 2021 (c. 11).
[50] 2020 c. 17; section 22 was amended by section 46 of, and paragraph 26 of Schedule 13 to, the Counter-Terrorism and Sentencing Act 2021 (c. 11).

(b) paragraph 11(2) of Schedule 16 to the 2020 Act, under which a magistrates' court may commit the
defendant to the Crown Court to be dealt with there if the magistrates' court convicts the defendant
of an offence during the operational period of a suspended sentence order made by the Crown Court.

The provisions listed in section 24 of the 2020 Act include section 70 of the Proceeds of Crime Act 2002[51]. Under
that section, if a magistrates' court commits a defendant to the Crown Court so that a confiscation order can be
considered then the court also may commit the defendant to the Crown Court to be dealt with there for any other
offence of which the defendant has been convicted and with which the magistrates' court otherwise could deal.
Under section 71 of the 2002 Act, the Crown Court may deal with the defendant in any way in which it could
have done if the defendant had been convicted in that court, unless the magistrates' court did not make the
statement to which section 70(5) refers. See also rule 24.11(10)(e), which refers to that statement.]

CRIMINAL PROCEDURE RULES   PART 29   ROAD TRAFFIC PENALTIES

[Note. Part 24 contains rules about the general procedure on sentencing in a magistrates' court. Part 25 contains
corresponding rules for the Crown Court.]

Representations about obligatory disqualification or endorsement   **R29.1**

29.1 (1) This rule applies—
  (a) where the court—
    (i) convicts the defendant of an offence involving obligatory disqualification from
          driving and section 34(1) of the Road Traffic Offenders Act 1988[1] (Disqualification
          for certain offences) applies,
    (ii) convicts the defendant of an offence where section 35 of the 1988 Act[2] (Disqualifi-
          cation for repeated offences) applies, or
    (iii) convicts the defendant of an offence involving obligatory endorsement of the
          defendant's driving record and section 44 of the 1988 Act[3] (Orders for endorsement)
          applies;
  (b) unless the defendant is absent.
  (2) The court must explain, in terms the defendant can understand (with help, if necessary)—
  (a) where paragraph (1)(a)(i) applies (obligatory disqualification under section 34)—
    (i) that the court must order the defendant to be disqualified from driving for a
          minimum of 12 months (or 2 or 3 years, as the case may be, according to the offence
          and the defendant's driving record), unless the court decides that there are special
          reasons to order disqualification for a shorter period, or not to order disqualification
          at all, and
    (ii) if applicable, that the period of disqualification will be reduced by at least 3 months
          if, by no later than 2 months before the end of the reduced period, the defendant
          completes an approved driving course;
  (b) where paragraph (1)(a)(ii) applies (disqualification under section 35)—
    (i) that the court must order the defendant to be disqualified from driving for a
          minimum of 6 months (or 1 or 2 years, as the case may be, according to the
          defendant's driving record), unless, having regard to all the circumstances, the court
          decides to order disqualification for a shorter period, or not to order disqualification
          at all, and
    (ii) that circumstances of which the court cannot take account in making its decision are
          any that make the offence not a serious one; hardship (other than exceptional
          hardship); and any that during the last 3 years already have been taken into account
          by a court when ordering disqualification for less than the usual minimum period, or
          not at all, for repeated driving offences;

---

[51] 2002 c. 29; section 70 was amended by section 41 of, and paragraph 75 of Schedule 3 to, the Criminal Justice Act 2003 (c.
44), section 410 of, and paragraphs 181 and 195 of Schedule 24 to, the Sentencing Act 2020 (c. 17) and section 46 of, and
paragraph 19 of Schedule 13 to, the Counter-Terrorism and Sentencing Act 2021 (c. 11).
[1] 1988 c. 53; section 34 was amended by section 29 of the Road Traffic Act 1991 (c. 40), section 3 of the Aggravated
Vehicle-Taking Act 1992 (c. 11), section 165 of, and paragraph 121 of Schedule 9 to, the Powers of Criminal Courts
(Sentencing) Act 2000 (c. 6), sections 56 and 107 of, and Schedule 8 to, the Police Reform Act 2002 (c. 30), section 25 of the
Road Safety Act 2006 (c. 49), article 2 of S.I. 2007/3480, paragraphs 2 and 5 of Schedule 27 to the Legal Aid, Sentencing and
Punishment of Offenders Act 2012 (c. 10), section 56 of, and paragraphs 9 and 12 of Schedule 22 to, the Crime and Courts
Act 2013 (c. 22) and section 177 of, and paragraph 90 of Schedule 21 to, the Coroners and Justice Act 2009 (c. 25).
[2] 2005 c. 15.
[3] 2005 c. 15; section 74 was amended by article 13 of, and paragraphs 1 and 19 of Schedule 15 to, S.I. 2010/976.

(c) where paragraph (1)(a)(iii) applies (obligatory endorsement), that the court must order the endorsement of the defendant's driving record unless the court decides that there are special reasons not to do so; and

(d) in every case, as applicable—

    (i) that the court already has received representations from the defendant about whether any such special reasons or mitigating circumstances apply and will take account of them, or

    (ii) that the defendant may make such representations now, on oath or affirmation.

(3) Unless the court already has received such representations from the defendant, before it applies rule 24.11 (magistrates' court procedure if the court convicts) or rule 25.16 (Crown Court procedure if the court convicts), as the case may be, the court must—

(a) ask whether the defendant wants to make any such representations; and

(b) if the answer to that question is 'yes', require the defendant to take an oath or affirm and make them.

[Note. For the circumstances in which the court—

(a) may, and in some cases must, order disqualification from driving under the Road Traffic Offenders Act 1988, see sections 26, 34, 35 and 36 of that Act[4];

(b) may, for some reasons or in some circumstances, abbreviate or dispense with a period of disqualification otherwise required by the 1988 Act, see sections 34(1) and 35(1), (4) of that Act;

(c) must usually order endorsement, see sections 9, 44 and 96 of, and Schedule 2 to, the 1988 Act.

For the circumstances in which the period of a disqualification from driving must or may be extended where the court also imposes a custodial sentence, see sections 35A and 35B of the 1988 Act[5].

For the circumstances in which the period of a disqualification from driving will be reduced if the defendant completes an approved driving course, see section 34A of the 1988 Act[6].]

R29.2 Application to remove a disqualification from driving

29.2 (1) This rule applies where, on application by the defendant, the court can remove a disqualification from driving.

(2) A defendant who wants the court to exercise that power must—

(a) apply in writing, no earlier than the date on which the court can exercise the power;

(b) serve the application on the court officer; and

(c) in the application—

    (i) specify the disqualification, and

    (ii) explain why the defendant wants the court to remove it.

(3) The court officer must serve a copy of the application on the chief officer of police for the local justice area.

[Note. For the circumstances in which the court may remove a disqualification from driving imposed under section 34 or 35 of the Road Traffic Offenders Act 1988, see section 42 of the Act[7]. The court may not consider

---

[4] 1988 c. 53; section 26 was substituted by section 25 of the Road Traffic Act 1991 (c. 40) and amended by paragraph 119 of Schedule 9 to the Powers of Criminal Courts (Sentencing) Act 2000 (c. 6), paragraphs 140 and 143 of Schedule 13 to the Access to Justice Act 1999 (c. 22), paragraph 2 of Schedule 2 to S.I. 1996/1974, paragraph 312 of Schedule 8 to the Courts Act 2003 (c. 39), paragraphs 32 and 34 of Schedule 5 to the Crime (International Co-operation) Act 2003 (c. 32) and sections 10 and 59 of, and paragraphs 30 and 32 of Schedule 3 and Schedule 7 to, the Road Safety Act 2006 (c. 49). Section 36 was substituted by section 32 of the Road Traffic Act 1991 (c. 40) and amended by paragraph 3 of Schedule 2 to S.I. 1996/1974, article 3 of S. I. 1998/1917, section 9(6) of, and paragraphs 2 and 7 of Schedule 7 to, the Road Safety Act 2006 (c. 49) and paragraphs 2 and 6 of Schedule 27 to the Legal Aid, Sentencing and Punishment of Offenders Act 2012 (c. 10). It is further amended by sections 10, 37 and 59 of, and paragraphs 30 and 39 of Schedule 3, and Schedule 7 to, the Road Safety Act 2006 (c. 49), with effect from a date to be appointed.

[5] 1988 c. 53; sections 35A and 35B were inserted by section 137 of, and paragraph 2 of Schedule 16 to, the Coroners and Justice Act 2009 (c. 25). Section 35A was amended by sections 89, 111 and 126 of, and paragraph 5 of Schedule 10, paragraph 1 of Schedule 14 and paragraph 4 of Schedule 21 to, the Legal Aid, Sentencing and Punishment of Offenders Act 2012 (c. 10) and sections 6 and 30 of, and paragraph 11 of Schedule 1 to, the Criminal Justice and Courts Act 2015 (c. 2).

[6] 1988 c. 53; section 34A was inserted by section 30 of the Road Traffic Act 1991 (c. 40). It was substituted by section 35 of the Road Safety Act 2006 (c. 49) for certain purposes, and for remaining purposes with effect from a date to be appointed. It is amended by section 177 of, and paragraphs 30 and 90 of Schedule 21 and paragraphs 30 and 31 of Schedule 22 to, the Coroners and Justice Act 2009 (c. 25), with effect from a date to be appointed.

[7] 1988 c. 53; section 42 was amended by section 48 of, and paragraph 98 of Schedule 4 to, the Road Traffic Act 1991 (c. 40), sections 9, 10 and 59 of, and paragraphs 2 and 8 of Schedule 2, paragraphs 30 and 40 of Schedule 3 and Schedule 7 to, the Road Safety Act 2006 (c. 49) and paragraph 90 of Schedule 21 to the Coroners and Justice Act 2009 (c. 25).

an application made within 2 years of the disqualification, in any case; or, after that, before a specified period has expired.]

Information to be supplied on order for endorsement of driving record, etc.   **R29.3**

29.3 (1) This rule applies where the court—

      (a) convicts the defendant of an offence involving obligatory endorsement, and orders there to be endorsed on the defendant's driving record (and on any counterpart licence, if other legislation requires)—

          (i) particulars of the conviction,

          (ii) particulars of any disqualification from driving that the court imposes, and

          (iii) the penalty points to be attributed to the offence;

      (b) disqualifies the defendant from driving for any other offence; or

      (c) suspends or removes a disqualification from driving.

    (2) The court officer must, as soon as practicable, serve on the Secretary of State notice that includes details of—

      (a) where paragraph (1)(a) applies—

          (i) the local justice area in which the court is acting,

          (ii) the dates of conviction and sentence,

          (iii) the offence, and the date on which it was committed,

          (iv) the sentence, and

          (v) the date of birth, and sex, of the defendant, where those details are available;

      (b) where paragraph (1)(b) applies—

          (i) the date and period of the disqualification, and

          (ii) the power exercised by the court; and

      (c) where paragraph (1)(c) applies—

          (i) the date and period of the disqualification,

          (ii) the date and terms of the order for its suspension or removal,

          (iii) the power exercised by the court, and

          (iv) where the court suspends the disqualification pending appeal, the court to which the defendant has appealed.

[Note. See sections 39(3), 42(5), 44A, 47 and 97A of the Road Traffic Offenders Act 1988[8].

Under section 25 of the 1988 Act[9], the court may order a defendant to disclose his or her date of birth, and sex, where that is not apparent (for example, where the defendant is convicted in his or her absence). Under section 27 of the 1988 Act[10], and under section 168 of the Sentencing Act 2020[11], the court may order a defendant to produce his or her driving licence, if not already produced.

For the circumstances in which the court—

    (a) must usually order endorsement, see sections 9, 44 and 96 of, and Schedule 2 to, the 1988 Act;

    (b) may, and in some cases must, order disqualification from driving under the 1988 Act, see sections 26, 34, 35 and 36 of that Act;

    (c) may order disqualification from driving under the 2020 Act, see sections 163 and 164 of that Act;

    (d) may suspend a disqualification from driving pending appeal, see sections 39 and 40 of the 1988 Act[12] (Part 34 (Appeal to the Crown Court) and Part 35 (Appeal to the High Court by case stated) contain relevant rules);

    (e) may remove a disqualification from driving imposed under section 34 or 35 of the 1988 Act, see section 42 of that Act (rule 29.2 applies).]

---

[8] 1988 c. 53; section 44A was inserted by section 9(1) and (3) of the Road Safety Act 2006 (c. 49). Section 97A was inserted by section 8 of the Road Safety Act 2006 (c. 49).

[9] 1988 c. 53; section 25 was amended by section 90 of, and paragraphs 140 and 142 of Schedule 13 to, the Access to Justice Act 1999 (c. 22), section 165 of, and paragraph 118 of Schedule 9 to, the Powers of Criminal Courts (Sentencing) Act 2000 (c. 6) and section 109 of, and paragraph 311 of Schedule 8 to, the Courts Act 2003 (c. 39).

[10] 1988 c. 53; section 27 was amended by regulations 2 and 3 of, and paragraph 3 of Schedule 2 to, S.I. 1990/144, section 48 of, and paragraph 91 of Schedule 4 to, the Road Traffic Act 1991 (c. 40), paragraphs 140 and 144 of Schedule 13 to the Access to Justice Act 1999 (c. 22), paragraph 120 of Schedule 9 to the Powers of Criminal Courts (Sentencing) Act 2000 (c. 6), section 16 of the Child Support, Pensions and Social Security Act 2000 (c. 19), paragraph 313 of Schedule 8 to the Courts Act 2003 (c. 39) and section 10 of, and paragraphs 30 and 33 of Schedule 3 and Schedule 7 to, the Road Safety Act 2006 (c. 49). It is further amended by paragraphs 52 and 53 of Schedule 32 to the Criminal Justice Act 2003 (c. 44) and section 58 of, and Part 4 of Schedule 7 to, the Welfare Reform Act 2009 (c. 24), with effect from dates to be appointed.

[11] 2020 c. 17.

[12] 1988 c. 53; section 40 was amended by sections 40 and 59 of, and paragraph 50 of Schedule 9 and paragraph 1 of Schedule 11 to, the Constitutional Reform Act 2005 (c.4).

R29.4 **Statutory declaration to avoid fine after fixed penalty notice**

29.4 (1) This rule applies where—

(a) a chief officer of police, or the Secretary of State, serves on the magistrates' court officer a certificate registering, for enforcement as a fine, a sum payable by a defendant after failure to comply with a fixed penalty notice;

(b) the court officer notifies the defendant of the registration; and

(c) the defendant makes a statutory declaration with the effect that there become void—

(i) the fixed penalty notice, or any associated notice sent to the defendant as owner of the vehicle concerned, and

(ii) the registration and any enforcement proceedings.

(2) The defendant must serve that statutory declaration not more than 21 days after service of notice of the registration, unless the court extends that time limit.

(3) The court officer must—

(a) serve a copy of the statutory declaration on the person by whom the certificate was registered;

(b) cancel any endorsement on the defendant's driving record (and on any counterpart licence, if other legislation requires); and

(c) notify the Secretary of State of any such cancellation.

[Note. See sections 72(1), (6), (6A), 73(1) and 74(2) of the Road Traffic Offenders Act 1988[13].

For the circumstances in which—

(a) a sum may be registered for enforcement as a fine after failure to comply with a fixed penalty notice, see sections 54, 55, 62, 63, 64, 70 and 71 of the 1988 Act[14];

(b) the registration may become void on the making of a statutory declaration by the defendant, see sections 72 and 73 of the 1988 Act[15]).

Under rule 2.11 (Taking of statutory declarations by court officers) a court officer may take the statutory declaration to which this rule refers.]

R29.5 **Application for declaration about a course or programme certificate decision**

29.5 (1) This rule applies where the court can declare unjustified—

(a) a course provider's failure or refusal to give a certificate of the defendant's satisfactory completion of an approved course; or

(b) a programme provider's giving of a certificate of the defendant's failure fully to participate in an approved programme.

(2) A defendant who wants the court to exercise that power must—

(a) apply in writing, not more than 20 business days after—

(i) the date by which the defendant was required to complete the course, or

(ii) the giving of the certificate of failure fully to participate in the programme;

(b) serve the application on the court officer; and

(c) in the application, specify the course or programme and explain (as applicable)—

(i) that the course provider has failed to give a certificate,

(ii) where the course provider has refused to give a certificate, why the defendant disagrees with the reasons for that decision, or

[13] 1988 c. 53; section 72(1) was amended by paragraphs 140 and 151 of Schedule 13 to, the Access to Justice Act 1999 (c. 22).
[14] 1988 c. 53; section 54 was amended by regulations 2(2) and 3 of, and paragraph 15 of Schedule 2 to, S.I. 1990/144, sections 48 and 83 of, and paragraph 103 of Schedule 4 and Schedule 8 to, the Road Traffic Act 1991 (c. 40), sections 76 and 108 of the Police Reform Act 2002 (c. 30) and sections 5, 9(6), 10 and 59 of, and paragraphs 1, 3 and 9 of Schedule 1 to, and paragraphs 2 and 14 of Schedule 2 to, the Road Safety Act 2006 (c. 49). Section 62 was amended by section 5 of, and paragraphs 1 and 7 of Schedule 1 to, the Road Safety Act 2006 (c. 49). Section 63 was amended by section 5 of, and paragraphs 1 and 8 of Schedule 1 to, the Road Safety Act 2006 (c. 49). Section 70 was amended by section 109 of, and paragraph 316 of Schedule 8 to, the Courts Act 2003 (c. 39) and sections 5, 9(6) and 59 of, and paragraphs 1 and 12 of Schedule 1, paragraphs 2 and 21 of Schedule 2 and paragraph 7 to, the Road Safety Act 2006 (c. 49). Section 71 was amended by section 63 of, and paragraph 25(1) of Schedule 3 to, the Vehicle Excise and Registration Act 1994 (c. 22), sections 90(1) and 106 of, and paragraphs 140 and 150(1) and (2) of Schedule 13, and table 7 of Schedule 15 to, the Access to Justice Act 1999 (c. 22), section 109(1) of, and paragraph 317(1) and (2) of Schedule 8 to, the Courts Act 2003 (c. 39) and section 9(6) of, and paragraphs 2 and 22 of Schedule 2 to, the Road Safety Act 2006 (c. 49).
[15] 1988 c. 53; section 72 was amended by regulations 2(2) and 3 of, and paragraph 20 of Schedule 2 to S.I. 1990/144, section 90 of, and paragraphs 140 and 151 of Schedule 13 to, the Access to Justice Act 1999 (c. 22) and sections 5, 9 10 and 59 of, and paragraphs 1 and 13 of Schedule 1, paragraphs 2 and 23 of Schedule 2, paragraphs 30 and 50 of Schedule 3 and Schedule 7 to, the Road Safety Act 2006 (c. 49). Section 73 was amended by section 90 of, and paragraphs 140 and 151 of Schedule 13 to, the Access to Justice Act 1999 (c. 22) and sections 5 and 59 of, and paragraphs 1 and 14 of Schedule 1 and Schedule 7 to, the Road Safety Act 2006 (c. 49).

(iii) where the programme provider has given a certificate, why the defendant disagrees with the reasons for that decision.

(3) The court officer must serve a copy of the application on the course or programme provider.

(4) The court must not determine the application unless the defendant, and the course or programme provider, each has had an opportunity to make representations at a hearing (whether or not either in fact attends).

[Note. For the circumstances in which the court may reduce a road traffic penalty on condition that the defendant attend an approved course, or take part in an approved programme, see sections 30A, 34A and 34D of the Road Traffic Offenders Act 1988[16].

Under sections 30B, 34B and 34E of the 1988 Act[17], the court that made the order, or the defendant's local magistrates' court, on application by the defendant may review a course or programme provider's decision that the defendant has not completed the course satisfactorily, or has not participated fully in the programme.]

Appeal against recognition of foreign driving disqualification   R29.6

29.6 (1) This rule applies where—

(a) a Minister gives a disqualification notice under section 57 of the Crime (International Co-operation) Act 2003[18]; and

(b) the person to whom it is given wants to appeal under section 59 of the Act[19] to a magistrates' court.

(2) That person ('the appellant') must serve an appeal notice on—

(a) the court officer, at a magistrates' court in the local justice area in which the appellant lives; and

(b) the Minister, at the address given in the disqualification notice.

(3) The appellant must serve the appeal notice within the period for which section 59 of the 2003 Act provides.

(4) The appeal notice must—

(a) attach a copy of the disqualification notice;

(b) explain which of the conditions in section 56 of the 2003 Act[20] is not met, and why section 57 of the Act therefore does not apply; and

(c) include any application to suspend the disqualification, under section 60 of the Act[21].

(5) The Minister may serve a respondent's notice, and must do so if—

(a) the Minister wants to make representations to the court; or

(b) the court so directs.

(6) The Minister must—

(a) unless the court otherwise directs, serve any such respondent's notice not more than 14 days after—

(i) the appellant serves the appeal notice, or

(ii) a direction to do so; and

(b) in any such respondent's notice—

(i) identify the grounds of opposition on which the Minister relies,

(ii) summarise any relevant facts not already included in the disqualification and appeal notices, and

---

[16] 1988 c. 53; section 30A is inserted by section 34(1) and (3) of the Road Safety Act 2006 (c. 49), with effect from a date to be appointed. Section 34A was inserted by section 30 of the Road Traffic Act 1991 (c. 40). It is amended by section 177(1) and (2) of, and paragraphs 30 and 90(1) and (3) of Schedule 21 and paragraphs 30 and 31 of Schedule 22 to, the Coroners and Justice Act 2009 (c. 25), with effect from a date to be appointed. Section 34D is inserted by section 15(1) of the Road Safety Act 2006 (c. 49), with effect from a date to be appointed. It is amended by section 177(1) of, and paragraph 90(1) and (5) of Schedule 21 to, the Coroners and Justice Act 2009 (c. 25), with effect from a date to be appointed.

[17] 1988 c. 53; section 30B is inserted by section 34(1) and (3) of the Road Safety Act 2006 (c. 49), with effect from a date to be appointed. Section 34B was inserted by section 30 of the Road Traffic Act 1991 (c. 40) and amended by paragraphs 140, 145 and 146 of Schedule 13 and Part V of Schedule 15 to, the Access to Justice Act 1999 (c. 22). Section 34B is substituted by section 35 of the Road Safety Act 2006 (c. 49), with effect from a date to be appointed. Section 34E is inserted by section 15(1) of the Road Safety Act 2006 (c. 49), with effect from a date to be appointed.

[18] 2003 c. 32; section 57 is in force in relation only to an offence of which an offender has been convicted in Ireland. For remaining purposes, it will come into force on a date to be appointed.

[19] 2003 c. 32; section 59 is in force in relation only to an offence of which an offender has been convicted in Ireland. For remaining purposes, it will come into force on a date to be appointed. Section 59 was amended by article 2 of, and paragraph 97 of the Schedule to, S.I. 2005/886.

[20] 2003 c. 32; section 56 is in force in relation only to an offence of which an offender has been convicted in Ireland. For remaining purposes, it will come into force on a date to be appointed.

[21] 2003 c. 32; section 60 is in force in relation only to an offence of which an offender has been convicted in Ireland. For remaining purposes, it will come into force on a date to be appointed. Section 60 was amended by section 40(4) of, and paragraph 79 of Schedule 9 to, the Constitutional Reform Act 2005 (c. 4).

        (iii) identify any other document that the Minister thinks the court will need to decide
           the appeal (and serve any such document with the notice).

(7) Where the court determines an appeal, the general rule is that it must do so at a hearing (which
    must be in public, unless the court otherwise directs).

(8) The court officer must serve on the Minister—

    (a) notice of the outcome of the appeal;

    (b) notice of any suspension of the disqualification; and

    (c) the appellant's driving licence, if surrendered to the court officer.

*[Note. Section 56 of the Crime (International Co-operation) Act 2003 sets out the conditions for recognition in
the United Kingdom of a foreign driving disqualification, and provides that section 57 of the Act applies where
they are met. Under section 57, the appropriate Minister may, and in some cases must, give the person concerned
notice that he or she is disqualified in the UK, too, and for what period.*

*Under section 59 of the 2003 Act, that person may appeal to a magistrates' court. If the court is satisfied that
section 57 of the Act does not apply in that person's case, the court must allow the appeal and notify the Minister.
Otherwise, it must dismiss the appeal.*

*The time limit for appeal under section 59 of the 2003 Act is the end of the period of 21 days beginning with
the day on which the Minister gives the notice under section 57. That period may be neither extended nor
shortened.*

Under section 60 of the 2003 Act, the court may suspend the disqualification, on such terms as it thinks fit.

*Under section 63 of the 2003 Act[22], it is an offence for a person to whom the Minister gives a notice under section
57 not to surrender any licence that he or she holds, within the same period as for an appeal.]*

CRIMINAL PROCEDURE RULES   PART 30   ENFORCEMENT OF FINES
AND OTHER ORDERS FOR PAYMENT

*[Note. Part 13 contains rules about warrants for arrest, detention or imprisonment, including such warrants
issued for failure to pay fines, etc.*

Part 24 contains rules about the procedure on sentencing in a magistrates' court.

*Part 28 contains rules about the exercise of a magistrates' court's powers to enforce an order made by another
court.]*

R30.1 When this Part applies

30.1 (1) This Part applies where a magistrates' court can enforce payment of—

    (a) a fine, or a sum that legislation requires the court to treat as a fine; or

    (b) any other sum that a court has ordered to be paid—

        (i) on a conviction, or

        (ii) on the forfeiture of a surety.

(2) Rules 30.7 to 30.9 apply where the court, or a fines officer, issues a warrant for an enforcement
    agent to take control of a defendant's goods and sell them, using the procedure in Schedule 12
    to the Tribunals, Courts and Enforcement Act 2007[1].

(3) In this Part—

    (a) 'defendant' means anyone liable to pay a sum to which this Part applies;

    (b) 'payment terms' means by when, and by what (if any) instalments, such a sum must be
        paid.

[Note. For the means by which a magistrates' court may enforce payment, see—

    (a) Part 3 of the Magistrates' Courts Act 1980[2]; and

    (b) Schedule 5 to the Courts Act 2003[3] and the Fines Collection Regulations 2006[4].

---

[22] 2003 c. 32; section 63 is in force in relation only to an offence of which an offender has been convicted in Ireland. For
remaining purposes, it will come into force on a date to be appointed. It was amended by sections 10(12) and 59 of, and
paragraphs 74 and 75 of Schedule 3, and Schedule 7 to, the Road Safety Act 2006 (c. 49).
[1] 2007 c. 15.
[2] 1980 c. 43.
[3] 2003 c. 39; Schedule 5 was amended by articles 2, 4, 6, 7 and 8 of S.I. 2006/1737, section 62 of, and paragraphs 148 and
149 of Schedule 13 to, the Tribunals, Courts and Enforcement Act 2007 (c. 15), section 80 of the Criminal Justice and
Immigration Act 2008 (c. 4), section 88 of the Legal Aid, Sentencing and Punishment of Offenders Act 2012 (c. 10), section
10 of, and paragraphs 24 and 27 of the Schedule to, the Prevention of Social Housing Fraud Act 2013 (c. 3), section 27 of the
Crime and Courts Act 2013 (c. 22) and section 56 of the Criminal Justice and Courts Act 2015 (c. 2). It is further amended
by section 26 of the Crime and Courts Act 2013 (c. 22) and paragraph 23 of Schedule 5 to the Modern Slavery Act 2015 (c.
30), with effect from dates to be appointed.

Under that Schedule and those Regulations, some enforcement powers may be exercised by a fines officer.

See also section 62 of, and Schedule 12 to, the Tribunals, Courts and Enforcement Act 2007. In that Act, a warrant to which this Part applies is described as 'a warrant of control'.]

Exercise of court's powers; duty of justices' legal adviser   R30.2

30.2 (1) The court must not exercise its enforcement powers unless—

    (a) the court officer has served on the defendant any collection order or other notice of—

       (i)   the obligation to pay,

       (ii) the payment terms, and

       (iii) how and where the defendant must pay; and

    (b) the defendant has failed to comply with the payment terms.

(2) A justices' legal adviser must ask such questions as may be needed to obtain information sufficient to allow the court to make such decisions as are required.

[Note. See section 76 of the Magistrates' Courts Act 1980[5]; and paragraphs 12 and 13 of Schedule 5 to the Courts Act 2003[6]. For the functions of a justices' legal adviser, see sections 28 and 29 of the Courts Act 2003[7] See also rule 2.12 (Duties of justices' legal adviser).]

Duty to give receipt   R30.3

30.3 (1) This rule applies where the defendant makes a payment to—

    (a) the court officer specified in an order or notice served under rule 30.2;

    (b) another court officer;

    (c) any—

       (i)   custodian of the defendant,

       (ii) supervisor appointed to encourage the defendant to pay, or

       (iii) responsible officer appointed under a community sentence or a suspended sentence of imprisonment; or

    (d) a person executing a warrant to which rule 13.6 (warrants for arrest, detention or imprisonment that cease to have effect on payment) or this Part applies.

(2) The person receiving the payment must—

    (a) give the defendant a receipt unless the method of payment generates an independent record (for example, a bank record); and

    (b) as soon as practicable transmit the payment to the court officer specified in an order or notice served under rule 30.2, if the recipient is not that court officer.

[Note. For the effect of payment to a person executing a warrant to which rule 13.6 applies, see that rule and sections 79[8] and 125(1)[9] of the Magistrates' Courts Act 1980.

For the circumstances in which the court may appoint a person to supervise payment, see section 88 of the 1980 Act[10].]

Appeal against decision of fines officer   R30.4

30.4 (1) This rule applies where—

    (a) a collection order is in force;

    (b) a fines officer makes a decision under one of these paragraphs of Schedule 5 to the Courts Act 2003—

       (i)   paragraph 22 (Application to fines officer for variation of order or attachment of earnings order, etc.),

---

[4] S.I. 2006/501.

[5] 1980 c. 43; section 76 was amended by section 7 of the Maintenance Enforcement Act 1991 (c. 17), section 78 of, and Schedule 16 to, the Criminal Justice Act 1982 (c. 48), and section 62(3) of, and paragraphs 45 and 46 of Schedule 13 to, the Tribunals, Courts and Enforcement Act 2007 (c. 15).

[6] 2003 c. 39; paragraph 13 was amended by articles 2, 4 and 15 of S.I. 2006/1737.

[7] 2003 c. 39; sections 28 and 29 were substituted by section 3 of, and paragraphs 25 and 26 of the Schedule to, the Courts and Tribunals (Judiciary and Functions of Staff) Act 2018 (c. 33).

[8] 1980 c. 43; section 79 was amended by paragraph 219 of Schedule 8 to the Courts Act 2003 (c. 39) and section 62 of, and paragraphs 45, 47 and 48 of Schedule 13 to, the Tribunals, Courts and Enforcement Act 2007 (c. 15).

[9] 1980 c. 43; section 125 was amended by section 33 of the Police and Criminal Evidence Act 1984 (c. 60), section 65(1) of the Criminal Justice Act 1988 (c. 33), sections 95(1), 97(4) and 106 of, and Part V of Schedule 15 and Table (8) to, the Access to Justice Act 1999 (c. 22), section 109(1) of, and paragraph 238 of Schedule 8 to, the Courts Act 2003 (c. 39) and sections 62(3), 86 and 146 of and paragraphs 45 and 57 of Schedule 23 to, the Tribunals, Courts and Enforcement Act 2007 (c. 15).

[10] 1980 c. 43; section 88 was amended by paragraph 53 of Schedule 14 to the Criminal Justice Act 1982 (c. 48), paragraph 68 of Schedule 9 to the Powers of Criminal Courts (Sentencing) Act 2000 (c. 6) and section 62 of, and paragraphs 45 and 54 of Schedule 13 to, the Tribunals, Courts and Enforcement Act 2007 (c. 15). It is further amended by paragraphs 58 and 64 of Schedule 7 to the Criminal Justice and Court Services Act 2000 (c. 43) with effect from a date to be appointed.

Criminal Procedure Rules

(ii) paragraph 31[11] (Application to fines officer for variation of reserve terms), or

(iii) paragraph 37[12] (Functions of fines officer in relation to defaulters: referral or further steps notice); and

(c) the defendant wants to appeal against that decision.

(2) Unless the court otherwise directs, the defendant must—

(a) appeal in writing not more than 10 business days after the decision;

(b) serve the appeal on the court officer; and

(c) in the appeal—

(i)   explain why a different decision should be made, and

(ii) specify the decision that the defendant proposes.

(3) Where the court determines an appeal the general rule is that it must do so at a hearing.

[Note. Under paragraph 12 of Schedule 5 to the Courts Act 2003, where a collection order is in force the court's powers to deal with the defendant's liability to pay the sum for which that order was made are subject to the provisions of that Schedule and to fines collection regulations.

For the circumstances in which a defendant may appeal against a decision to which this rule applies, see paragraphs 23, 32 and 37(9) of Schedule 5 to the 2003 Act[13]. The time limit for appeal is prescribed by those paragraphs. It may be neither extended nor shortened.]

R30.5   **Application to reduce a fine, vary payment terms or remit a courts charge**

30.5 (1) This rule applies where—

(a) no collection order is in force; and the defendant wants the court to—

(i)   reduce the amount of a fine, or

(ii) vary payment terms; or

(b) the defendant, a fines officer or an enforcement agent wants the court to remit a criminal courts charge.

(2) Unless the court otherwise directs, such a defendant, fines officer or enforcement agent must—

(a) apply in writing;

(b) serve the application on the court officer;

(c) if the application is to reduce a fine or vary payment terms, explain—

(i)   what relevant circumstances have not yet been considered by the court, and

(ii) why the fine should be reduced, or the payment terms varied; and

(d) if the application is to remit a criminal courts charge, explain—

(i)   how the circumstances meet the time limits and other conditions in section 50 of the Sentencing Act 2020[14], and

(ii) why the charge should be remitted.

(3) The court may determine an application—

(a) at a hearing, which may be in public or in private; or

(b) without a hearing.

[Note. See sections 75, 85 and 85A of the Magistrates' Courts Act 1980[15], sections 50 and 127 of the Sentencing Act 2020[16].

Under section 46 of the 2020 Act , a court must, at the times listed in sections 44 and 45 of that Act, order a defendant convicted of an offence to pay a charge in respect of relevant court costs. Under section 50 of the Act, a magistrates' court may remit the whole or part of such a charge, but—

(a) the court may do so only if it is satisfied that—

(i)   the defendant has taken all reasonable steps to pay the charge, having regard to his or her personal circumstances, or

(ii) collection and enforcement of the charge is impracticable;

---

[11] 2003 c. 39; paragraph 31 was amended by articles 2, 4 and 20 of S.I. 2006/1737.

[12] 2003 c. 39; paragraph 37 was amended by articles 2, 4 and 25(a) and (b) of S.I. 2006/1737.

[13] 2003 c. 39; paragraph 32 was amended by articles 2, 4 and 24(b) of S.I. 2006/1737.

[14] 2020 c. 17.

[15] 1980 c. 43; section 75 was amended by section 11 of, and paragraph 6 of Schedule 2 to, the Maintenance Enforcement Act 1991 (c. 17). Section 85 was substituted by section 61 of the Criminal Justice Act 1988 (c. 33) and amended by section 55 of, and paragraph 10(2) of Schedule 4 to, the Crime (Sentences) Act 1997 (c. 43), section 109(1) of, and paragraph 222 of Schedule 8 to, the Courts Act 2003 (c. 39) and section 179 of the Anti-social Behaviour, Crime and Policing Act 2014 (c. 12). It is further amended by paragraphs 25 and 28 of Schedule 32 to the Criminal Justice Act 2003 (c. 44) and section 26 of the Crime and Courts Act 2013 (c. 22), with effect from dates to be appointed. Section 85A was inserted by section 51(1) of the Criminal Justice Act 1982 (c. 48).

[16] 2020 c. 17.

(b) the court may not do so at a time when the defendant is in prison; and

(c) the court may not do so unless the periods specified by regulations under section 21E all have expired.]

Claim to avoid fine after penalty notice

R30.6

30.6 (1) This rule applies where—

    (a) a chief officer of police serves on the magistrates' court officer a certificate registering, for enforcement as a fine, a sum payable by a defendant after failure to comply with a penalty notice; and

    (b) the court or a fines officer enforces the fine.

  (2) A defendant who claims not to be the person to whom the penalty notice was issued must, unless the court otherwise directs—

    (a) make that claim in writing; and

    (b) serve it on the court officer.

  (3) The court officer must—

    (a) notify the chief officer of police by whom the certificate was registered; and

    (b) refer the case to the court.

  (4) Where such a claim is made—

    (a) the general rule is that the court must adjourn the enforcement for 28 days and fix a hearing; but

    (b) the court may make a different order.

  (5) At any such hearing, the chief officer of police must introduce any evidence to contradict the defendant's claim.

[Note. See section 10 of the Criminal Justice and Police Act 2001[17].

For the circumstances in which a sum may be registered for enforcement as a fine after failure to comply with a penalty notice, see sections 8 and 9 of the 2001 Act[18].]

Information to be included in a warrant of control

R30.7

30.7 (1) A warrant must identify—

    (a) each person to whom it is directed;

    (b) the defendant against whom it was issued;

    (c) the sum for which it was issued and the reason that sum is owed;

    (d) the court or fines officer who issued it, unless that is otherwise recorded by the court officer; and

    (e) the court office for the court or fines officer who issued it.

  (2) A person to whom a warrant is directed must record on it the date and time at which it is received.

  (3) A warrant that contains an error is not invalid, as long as—

    (a) it was issued in respect of a lawful decision by the court or fines officer; and

    (b) it contains enough information to identify that decision.

[Note. See sections 78 and 125ZA of the Magistrates' Courts Act 1980[19].]

Warrant of control: application by enforcement agent for extension of time, etc.

R30.8

30.8 (1) This rule applies where an enforcement agent wants the court to exercise a power under Schedule 12 to the Tribunals, Courts and Enforcement Act 2007[20], or under regulations made under that Schedule, to—

    (a) shorten or extend a time limit;

    (b) give the agent authority to—

      (i) enter premises which the agent would not otherwise have authority to enter,

      (ii) enter or remain on premises at a time at which the agent would not otherwise have authority to be there,

      (iii) use reasonable force, in circumstances in which the agent would not otherwise have authority to use such force,

---

[17] 2001 c. 16; section 10 was amended by paragraphs 1 and 10 of Schedule 23 to the Legal Aid, Sentencing and Punishment of Offenders Act 2012 (c. 10).

[18] 2001 c. 16; section 8 was amended by section 109(1) of, and paragraph 399 of Schedule 8 to, the Courts Act 2003 (c. 39). Section 9 was amended by section 109(1) of, and paragraph 400(1) (2) (3) and (4) of Schedule 8 to, the Courts Act 2003 (c. 39).

[19] 1980 c. 43; section 78 was amended by sections 37 and 46 of the Criminal Justice Act 1982 (c. 48) and paragraph 219 of Schedule 8 to, the Courts Act 2003 (c. 39). Section 125ZA was inserted by section 68 of the Tribunals, Courts and Enforcement Act 2007 (c. 15).

[20] 2007 c. 15

     (iv) sell goods by a method which the agent would not otherwise have authority to use, or

     (v) recover disbursements which the agent would not otherwise have authority to recover;

  (c) specify the manner in which goods which have not been sold must be disposed of.

(2) Such an enforcement agent must—

  (a) apply in writing;

  (b) serve the application on the court officer; and

  (c) pay any fee prescribed.

(3) The application must—

  (a) identify the power that the agent wants the court to exercise;

  (b) explain how the conditions for the exercise of that power are satisfied, including any condition that requires the agent to give another person notice of the application;

  (c) specify those persons, if any, to whom the agent has given notice in accordance with such a condition; and

  (d) propose the terms of the order that the agent wants the court to make.

(4) A person to whom the enforcement agent has given notice of an application and who wants to make representations to the court must—

  (a) serve the representations on—

     (i) the court officer,

     (ii) the enforcement agent, and

     (iii) any other person to whom the enforcement agent gave notice;

  (b) do so as soon as reasonably practicable and in any event within such period as the court directs; and

  (c) in the representations, propose the terms of the order that that person wants the court to make, and explain why.

(5) The court—

  (a) must not determine an application unless any person to whom the enforcement agent gave notice—

     (i) is present, or

     (ii) has had a reasonable opportunity to respond; but

  (b) subject to that, may determine an application—

     (i) at a hearing, which must be in private unless the court otherwise directs, or

     (ii) without a hearing.

[Note. See paragraphs 8, 15, 20, 21, 25, 31, 32 and 41 of Schedule 12 to the Tribunals, Courts and Enforcement Act 2007[21], regulations 6, 9, 13, 22, 25, 28, 29, 41 and 47 of the Taking Control of Goods Regulations 2013[22] and regulation 10 of the Taking Control of Goods (Fees) Regulations 2014[23]. Under paragraph 41 of that Schedule and regulation 41 of the 2013 Regulations, on an application for authority to sell goods otherwise than by public auction the enforcement agent must give notice to a creditor of the defendant in the circumstances described in those provisions.]

R30.9 **Warrant of control: application to resolve dispute**

30.9 (1) This rule applies where a defendant's goods are sold using the procedure in Schedule 12 to the Tribunals, Courts and Enforcement Act 2007 and there is a dispute about—

  (a) what share of the proceeds of those goods should be paid by the enforcement agent to a co-owner; or

  (b) the fees or disbursements sought or recovered by the enforcement agent out of the proceeds.

(2) An enforcement agent, a defendant or a co-owner who wants the court to resolve the dispute must—

  (a) apply in writing as soon as practicable after becoming aware of the grounds for doing so;

  (b) serve the application on—

     (i) the court officer,

     (ii) each other party to the dispute, and

     (iii) any other co-owner; and

  (c) pay any fee prescribed.

(3) The application must—

  (a) identify the warrant of control;

---

[21] 2007 c. 15. Paragraph 31 of Schedule 12 was amended by section 25(1), (5) of the Crime and Courts Act 2013 (c. 22). Paragraphs 60 and 66 of Schedule 12 were amended by paragraph 52 of Schedule 9 to the Crime and Courts Act 2013 (c. 22).
[22] S.I. 2013/1894.
[23] S.I. 2014/1.

      (b) specify the goods sold, the proceeds, and the fees and disbursements sought or recovered by the enforcement agent;

      (c) identify the power that the applicant wants the court to exercise;

      (d) specify the persons served with the application;

      (e) explain the circumstances of the dispute; and

      (f) propose the terms of the order that the applicant wants the court to make.

  (4) A person served with an application who wants to make representations to the court must—

      (a) serve the representations on—

          (i) the court officer,

          (ii) the applicant, and

          (iii) any other person on whom the application was served;

      (b) do so as soon as reasonably practicable and in any event within such period as the court directs; and

      (c) in the representations, propose the terms of the order that that person wants the court to make, and explain why.

  (5) The court—

      (a) must determine an application at a hearing, which must be in private unless the court otherwise directs;

      (b) must not determine an application unless each party—

          (i) is present, or

          (ii) has had a reasonable opportunity to attend.

[Note. See paragraph 50 of Schedule 12 to the Tribunals, Courts and Enforcement Act 2007[24], and regulations 15 and 16 of the Taking Control of Goods (Fees) Regulations 2014[25].]

CRIMINAL PROCEDURE RULES   PART 31   BEHAVIOUR ORDERS

[Note. See Part 3 for the court's general powers to consider an application and to give directions.]

When this Part applies   R31.1

31.1 (1) This Part applies where a magistrates' court or the Crown Court can—

      (a) make, vary, renew, discharge or revoke a civil order—

          (i) as well as, or instead of, passing a sentence, or in any other circumstances in which other legislation allows the court to make such an order, and

          (ii) that requires the defendant to do, or not do, something; or

      (b) require a person to enter into a recognisance—

          (i) to keep the peace and be of good behaviour, or

          (ii) (in the Crown Court only) to come up for judgment if called on.

  (2) In this Part—

      (a) 'behaviour order' means an order to which paragraph (1)(a) refers; and

      (b) 'bind over' means a requirement to which paragraph (1)(b) refers.

  (3) A reference to 'hearsay evidence' in this Part is a reference to evidence consisting of hearsay within the meaning of section 1(2) of the Civil Evidence Act 1995[1].

[Note. In the circumstances set out in the Acts listed beneath, the court can make a behaviour order—

    (a) on conviction, under—

        (i) section 14A of the Football Spectators Act 1989[2] (football banning orders),

        (ii) section 360 of the Sentencing Act 2020[3] (restraining orders),

        (iii) sections 1C and 1D of the Crime and Disorder Act 1998[4] (anti-social behaviour orders and interim anti-social behaviour orders),

---

[24] 2007 c. 15.

[25] S.I. 2014/1.

[1] 1995 c. 38.

[2] 1989 c. 37; section 14A was amended by section 1 of, and paragraphs 1 and 2 of Schedule 1 to, the Football (Disorder) Act 2000 (c. 25), section 86(5) of the Anti-Social Behaviour Act 2003 (c. 38), section 139(10) of the Serious Organised Crime and Police Act 2005 (c. 15) and sections 52(2) and 65 of, and paragraphs 1 and 2 of Schedule 3 and Schedule 5 to, the Violent Crime Reduction Act 2006 (c. 38).

[3] 2020 c. 17.

[4] 1998 c. 37; section 1C was inserted by section 64 of the Police Reform Act 2002 (c. 30) and amended by sections 83 and 86 of the Anti-social Behaviour Act 2003 (c. 38), sections 139, 140, 141 and 174 of, and Part 2 of Schedule 17 to, the Serious Organised Crime and Police Act 2005 (c. 15) and sections 123 and 124 of the Criminal Justice and Immigration Act 2008 (c. 4). Section 1D was inserted by section 65 of the Police Reform Act 2002 (c. 30) and amended by section 139 of the Serious Organised Crime and Police Act 2005 (c. 15). Each section was repealed on 20th October, 2014, by section 181 of, and

(iv)   *section 366 of the 2020 Act (parenting orders),*

(v)   *section 345 of the 2020 Act (sexual harm prevention orders),*

(vi)   *section 19 or 21 of the Serious Crime Act 2007[5] (serious crime prevention orders),*

(vii)   *section 331 of the 2020 Act (criminal behaviour orders),*

(viii) *section 14 of the Modern Slavery Act 2015[6] (slavery and trafficking prevention orders),*

(ix)   *section 19 of the Psychoactive Substances Act 2016[7] (prohibition orders),*

(x)   *section 20 of the Immigration Act 2016[8] (labour market enforcement orders),*

(xi)   *section 19 of the Offensive Weapons Act 2019[9] (knife crime prevention orders),*

(xii)   *section 342A of the 2020 Act[10] (serious violence reduction orders),*

(xiii) *section 376 of the 2020 Act[11] (requirement for parent or guardian of convicted young defendant to take proper care of the defendant and exercise proper control),*

(xiv)   *section 31(3) of the Domestic Abuse Act 2021[12] (domestic abuse protection orders);*

(xv)   *section 20 (2) of the Public Order Act 2023[13] (serious disruption prevention orders);*

(b) *on acquittal, under—*

(i)   *section 5A of the Protection from Harassment Act 1997[14] (restraining orders on acquittal),*

(ii)   *section 31(5) of the Domestic Abuse Act 2021 (domestic abuse protection orders on acquittal);*

(c) *on the making of a finding of not guilty by reason of insanity, or a finding of disability, under section 14 of the Modern Slavery Act 2015 (slavery and trafficking prevention orders);*

(d) *in proceedings for a genital mutilation offence, under paragraph 3 of Schedule 2 to the Female Genital Mutilation Act 2003[15] (female genital mutilation protection orders); and*

(e) *where the Crown Court allows an appeal against conviction, under section 31(6) of the Domestic Abuse Act 2021 (domestic abuse protection orders after appeal).*

Under section 1 of the Justices of the Peace Act 1361[16], section 1(7) of the Justices of the Peace Act 1968[17] and the inherent powers recognised by those provisions a magistrates' court or the Crown Court can bind over to keep the peace and be of good behaviour a person who or whose case is before the court, by requiring that person to enter into a recognisance (a formal undertaking to pay a specified sum in the event of failure to comply), or to give a surety, or both.

Under section 79 of the Senior Courts Act 1981[18] the Crown Court can release a convicted defendant pending sentence on a recognisance to come up for judgment if called on and meanwhile to be of good behaviour.

Section 1(2) of the Civil Evidence Act 1995 defines hearsay as meaning 'a statement made otherwise than by a person while giving oral evidence in the proceedings which is tendered as evidence of the matters stated'. Section 13 of that Act defines a statement as meaning 'any representation of fact or opinion, however made'.]

R31.2   Behaviour orders and bind overs: general rules

31.2   (1) The court must not make a behaviour order or impose a bind over unless the person to whom it is directed has had an opportunity—

(a) to consider—

(i)   what order is proposed and why, and

(ii) the evidence in support; and

(b) to make representations at a hearing (whether or not that person in fact attends).

(2) That restriction does not apply to making—

(a) an interim behaviour order, but unless other legislation otherwise provides such an order has no effect unless the person to whom it is directed—

---

paragraph 24 of Schedule 11 to, the Anti-social Behaviour, Crime and Policing Act 2014 (c. 12), subject to the saving provisions of section 33 of that Act.

[5] 2007 c. 27; section 21 was amended by section 48 of the Serious Crime Act 2015 (c. 9).

[6] 2015 c. 30.

[7] 2016 c. 2.

[8] 2016 c. 19.

[9] 2019 c. 17; section 19 comes into force on a date to be appointed.

[10] 2020 c. 17; section 342A is inserted by section 165 of the Police, Crime, Sentencing and Courts Act 2022 (c. 32) with effect from a date to be appointed.

[11] 2020 c. 17.

[12] 2021 c. 17; section 31 comes into force on a date to be appointed.

[13] 2023 c. 15; section 20 comes into force on a date to be appointed.

[14] 1997 c. 40; section 5A was inserted by section 12(5) of the Domestic Violence, Crime and Victims Act 2004 (c. 28) and amended by paragraph 144 of Schedule 24 to the Sentencing Act 2020 (c. 17).

[15] 2003 c. 31; Schedule 2 was inserted by section 73 of the Serious Crime Act 2015 (c. 9).

[16] 1361 c. 1.

[17] 1968 c. 69.

[18] 1981 c. 54.

       (i)   is present when it is made, or

       (ii) is handed a document recording the order not more than 5 business days after it is made; or

   (b) a domestic abuse protection order, but in that event the court must give the defendant an opportunity to make representations—

       (i)   as soon as is just and convenient, and

       (ii) at a hearing of which notice has been given to all parties.

(3) Where the court decides not to make, where it could—

   (a) a football banning order; or

   (b) a parenting order, after a person under 16 is convicted of an offence,

the court must announce, at a hearing in public, the reasons for its decision.

[Note. The Acts listed in the note to rule 31.1 impose requirements specific to each different type of behaviour order. Not all allow the court to make an interim behaviour order.

See section 14A(3) of the Football Spectators Act 1989[19], section 366 of the Sentencing Act 2020 and section 34 of the Domestic Abuse Act 2021[20].]

Application for behaviour order and notice of terms of proposed order: special rules

R31.3

31.3 (1) This rule applies where—

   (a) a prosecutor wants the court to make one of the following orders if the defendant is convicted—

       (i)   an anti-social behaviour order (but this rule does not apply to an application for an interim anti-social behaviour order),

       (ii)   a serious crime prevention order,

       (iii) a criminal behaviour order,

       (iv) a prohibition order,

       (v)   a knife crime prevention order,

       (vi) a serious violence reduction order, or

       (vii) a serious disruption prevention order;

   (b) a prosecutor proposes, on the prosecutor's initiative or at the court's request, a sexual harm prevention order if the defendant is convicted;

   (c) a prosecutor proposes a restraining order or domestic abuse protection order whether the defendant is convicted or acquitted; or

   (d) a prosecutor proposes a football banning order with additional requirements if the defendant is convicted.

(2) Where paragraph (1)(a) applies (order on application), the prosecutor must serve a notice of intention to apply for such an order on—

   (a) the court officer;

   (b) the defendant against whom the prosecutor wants the court to make the order; and

   (c) any person on whom the order would be likely to have a significant adverse effect, as soon as practicable (without waiting for the verdict).

(3) A notice under paragraph (2) must—

   (a) summarise the relevant facts;

   (b) identify the evidence on which the prosecutor relies in support;

   (c) attach any written statement that the prosecutor has not already served; and

   (d) specify the order that the prosecutor wants the court to make.

(4) A defendant served with a notice under paragraph (2) must—

   (a) serve notice of any evidence on which the defendant relies on—

       (i)   the court officer, and

       (ii) the prosecutor,

      as soon as practicable (without waiting for the verdict); and

   (b) in the notice, identify that evidence and attach any written statement that has not already been served.

(5) Where paragraph (1)(b) applies (sexual harm prevention order proposed), the prosecutor must—

   (a) serve a draft order on the court officer and on the defendant not less than 2 business days before the hearing at which the order may be made; and

---

[19] 1989 c. 37; section 14A was substituted, together with sections 14 and 14B-14J, for the existing sections 14-17, by section 1 of, and paragraphs 1 and 2 of Schedule 1 to, the Football (Disorder) Act 2000 (c. 25).

[20] 2021 c. 17; section 34 comes into force on a date to be appointed.

(b) in the draft order specify those prohibitions or requirements which the prosecutor proposes as necessary for the purpose of—
  (i) protecting the public or any particular members of the public from sexual harm from the defendant, or
  (ii) protecting children or vulnerable adults generally, or any particular children or vulnerable adults, from sexual harm from the defendant outside the United Kingdom.

(6) Where paragraph (1)(c) applies (restraining order or domestic abuse protection order proposed), the prosecutor must—
  (a) serve a draft order on the court officer and on the defendant as soon as practicable (without waiting for the verdict);
  (b) in a draft restraining order specify—
    (i) those prohibitions which, if the defendant is convicted, the prosecutor proposes for the purpose of protecting a person from conduct which amounts to harassment or will cause fear of violence, or
    (ii) those prohibitions which, if the defendant is acquitted, the prosecutor proposes as necessary to protect a person from harassment by the defendant; and
  (c) in a draft domestic abuse protection order, specify those requirements (including any prohibitions or restrictions) which the prosecutor proposes as necessary to protect the person for whose protection the order is made from domestic abuse or the risk of domestic abuse, including different kinds of abusive behaviour.

(7) Where paragraph (1)(d) applies (football banning order with additional requirements), the prosecutor must serve a draft order on the court officer and on the defendant not less than 2 business days before the hearing at which the order may be made.

(8) Where the prosecutor wants the court to make an anti-social behaviour order, a prohibition order, a criminal behaviour order or a domestic abuse protection order, the rules about special measures directions in Part 18 (Measures to assist a witness or defendant to give evidence) apply, but—
  (a) the prosecutor must apply when serving a notice under paragraph (2); and
  (b) the time limits in rule 18.4(a) do not apply.

[Note. The Practice Direction sets out a form of notice for use in connection with this rule.

The orders listed in rule 31.3(1)(a) may be made on application by the prosecutor. The orders to which rule 31.3(1)(b), (c) and (d) apply require no application and may be made on the court's own initiative. Under section 8 of the Serious Crime Act 2007 a serious crime prevention order may be made only on an application by the Director of Public Prosecutions or the Director of the Serious Fraud Office. See also paragraphs 2, 7 and 13 of Schedule 2 to the 2007 Act.

The court may give a special measures direction under the Youth Justice and Criminal Evidence Act 1999—

  (a) on an application for an anti-social behaviour, under section 1I of the Crime and Disorder Act 1998[21];
  (b) in proceedings for a prohibition order, under section 33 of the Psychoactive Substances Act 2016[22];
  (c) on an application for a criminal behaviour order, under section 340 of the Sentencing Act 2020[23]; and
  (d) in proceedings for a domestic abuse protection order, under section 49 of the Domestic Abuse Act 2021[24].

If a party relies on hearsay evidence, see also rules 31.6, 31.7, and 31.8.]

R31.4 **Evidence to assist the court: special rules**

31.4 (1) This rule applies where the court can make on its own initiative—
  (a) a football banning order;
  (b) a restraining order;
  (c) an anti-social behaviour order; or
  (d) a domestic abuse protection order.

---

[21] 1998 c. 37; section 1I was inserted by section 143 of the Serious Organised Crime and Police Act 2005 (c. 15), amended by paragraph 72 of Schedule 21 and Part 3 of Schedule 23 to the Coroners and Justice Act 2009 (c. 25) and repealed for specified purposes by paragraph 24 of Schedule 11 to the Anti-social Behaviour, Crime and Policing Act 2014 (c. 12).
[22] 2016 c. 2.
[23] 2020 c. 17.
[24] 2021 c. 17; section 49 comes into force on a date to be appointed.

(2) A party who wants the court to take account of evidence not already introduced must—
  (a) serve notice on—
    (i)   the court officer, and
    (ii) every other party,
    as soon as practicable (without waiting for the verdict); and
  (b) in the notice, identify that evidence; and
  (c) attach any written statement containing such evidence.

[Note. If a party relies on hearsay evidence, see also rules 31.6, 31.7, and 31.8.]

Application to vary, renew, discharge or revoke behaviour order   **R31.5**

31.5 (1) The court may vary, renew, discharge or revoke a behaviour order if—
  (a) the legislation under which it is made allows the court to do so; and
  (b) one of the following applies—
    (i)   the prosecutor,
    (ii)   the person to whom the order is directed,
    (iii) any other person protected or affected by the order,
    (iv)   the relevant authority or responsible officer,
    (v)   the relevant Chief Officer of Police,
    (vi)   the Director of Public Prosecutions, or
    (vii) the Director of the Serious Fraud Office.
  (2) A person applying under this rule must—
    (a) apply as soon as practicable after becoming aware of the grounds for doing so, explaining—
      (i)   why the order should be varied, renewed, discharged or revoked, as the case may be, by reference to the legislation under which it was made, and
      (ii) what, if any, material circumstances have changed since the court made the order or last determined an application to vary, renew, discharge or revoke it;
    (b) where the application is a second or subsequent application by the applicant in respect of the same order—
      (i)   give details of each previous application, and
      (ii) if the applicant wants the court to decide the application at a hearing, explain why;
    (c) in every case, serve the application on—
      (i)   the court officer, and
      (ii) the prosecutor (unless the prosecutor is the person applying under this rule);
    (d) unless the order was a restraining order or a domestic abuse protection order, serve the application on, as appropriate—
      (i)   the person to whom the order was directed, and
      (ii) any other person protected or affected by the order; and
    (e) serve the application on any other person if the court so directs.
  (3) A party who wants the court to take account of any particular evidence before making its decision must, as soon as practicable—
    (a) in every case, serve notice on—
      (i)   the court officer, and
      (ii) the prosecutor (unless the prosecutor is the party serving the notice);
    (b) unless the order was a restraining order or a domestic abuse protection order, serve the notice on, as appropriate—
      (i)   the person to whom the order was directed, and
      (ii) any other person protected or affected by the order;
    (c) serve the notice on any other person if the court so directs; and
    (d) in that notice identify the evidence and attach any written statement that has not already been served.
  (4) The court may decide an application under this rule—
    (a) at a hearing, in public or in private; or
    (b) without a hearing, if—
      (i)   the legislation under which the order was made so allows, or
      (ii) the court considers the application to be an abuse of the court's process.
  (5) But the court must not—
    (a) dismiss an application under this rule unless the applicant has had an opportunity to make representations; or
    (b) allow an application under this rule unless everyone required to be served, by this rule or by the court, has had at least 10 business days in which to make representations, including representations about whether there should be a hearing.

(6) The court officer must—
  (a) if the order was a restraining order or a domestic abuse protection order, serve the application under this rule on—
    (i) as appropriate, the person to whom the order was directed and any other person protected or affected by the order, and
    (ii) the relevant Chief Officer of Police;
  (b) serve the application on any other person if the court so directs;
  (c) serve any notice of evidence received by the court officer under paragraph (3) on—
    (i) each person, if any, on whom the court officer serves the application under this rule, and
    (ii) any other person if the court so directs; and
  (d) give notice of any hearing to—
    (i) the applicant, and
    (ii) any person required to be served, by this rule or by the court.

[Note. The legislation that gives the court power to make a behaviour order may limit the circumstances in which it may be varied, renewed, discharged or revoked and may require a hearing. Under section 22E of the Serious Crime Act 2007[25], where a person already subject to a serious crime prevention order is charged with a serious offence or with an offence of failing to comply with the order, the court may vary the order so that it continues in effect until that prosecution concludes.

Under section 26 of the Offensive Weapons Act 2019[26], where the court has made a knife crime prevention order the court may require the applicant and the defendant to attend one or more review hearings to consider whether the order should be varied or discharged. Where a requirement or prohibition imposed by the knife crime prevention order is to have effect after the end of one year from the date the order is made, the court must convene such a review on a specified date within the last 4 weeks of that year.

If a party relies on hearsay evidence, see also rules 31.6, 31.7 and 31.8.]

R31.6 Notice of hearsay evidence

31.6 (1) A party who wants to introduce hearsay evidence must—
  (a) serve notice on—
    (i) the court officer, and
    (ii) every other party directly affected; and
  (b) in that notice—
    (i) explain that it is a notice of hearsay evidence,
    (ii) identify that evidence,
    (iii) identify the person who made the statement which is hearsay, or explain why if that person is not identified, and
    (iv) explain why that person will not be called to give oral evidence.
  (2) A party may serve one notice under this rule in respect of more than one notice and more than one witness.

[Note. For the time within which to serve a notice of hearsay evidence, see rule 31.3(2) to (4), rule 31.4(2) and rule 31.5(3). See also the requirement in section 2 of the Civil Evidence Act 1995 for reasonable and practicable notice of a proposal to introduce hearsay evidence.

Rules 31.6, 31.7 and 31.8 broadly correspond with rules 3, 4 and 5 of the Magistrates' Courts (Hearsay Evidence in Civil Proceedings) Rules 1999[27], which apply in civil proceedings in magistrates' courts. Rule 3 of the 1999 Rules however includes a time limit, which may be varied by the court, or a justices' legal adviser, of 21 days before the date fixed for the hearing, for service of a hearsay notice.]

R31.7 Cross-examination of maker of hearsay statement

31.7 (1) This rule applies where a party wants the court's permission to cross-examine a person who made a statement which another party wants to introduce as hearsay.
  (2) The party who wants to cross-examine that person must—
    (a) apply in writing, with reasons, not more than 5 business days after service of the notice of hearsay evidence; and
    (b) serve the application on—
      (i) the court officer,

---

[25] 2007 c. 27; section 22E was inserted by section 49 of the Serious Crime Act 2015 (c. 9).
[26] 2019 c. 17; section 26 comes into force on a date to be appointed.
[27] S.I. 1999/681, amended by S.I. 2005/617.

(ii) the party who served the hearsay evidence notice, and

(iii) every party on whom the hearsay evidence notice was served.

(3) The court may decide an application under this rule with or without a hearing.

(4) But the court must not—

(a) dismiss an application under this rule unless the applicant has had an opportunity to make representations at a hearing (whether or not the applicant in fact attends); or

(b) allow an application under this rule unless everyone served with the application has had at least 5 business days in which to make representations, including representations about whether there should be a hearing.

[Note. See also section 3 of the Civil Evidence Act 1995.]

Credibility and consistency of maker of hearsay statement   **R31.8**

31.8 (1) This rule applies where a party wants to challenge the credibility or consistency of a person who made a statement which another party wants to introduce as hearsay.

(2) The party who wants to challenge the credibility or consistency of that person must—

(a) serve notice of intention to do so on—

(i) the court officer, and

(ii) the party who served the notice of hearsay evidence

not more than 5 business days after service of that hearsay evidence notice; and

(b) in the notice, identify any statement or other material on which that party relies.

(3) The party who served the hearsay notice—

(a) may call that person to give oral evidence instead; and

(b) if so, must serve notice of intention to do so on—

(i) the court officer, and

(ii) every party on whom the hearsay notice was served

not more than 5 business days after service of the notice under paragraph (2).

[Note. Section 5(2) of the Civil Evidence Act 1995 describes the procedure for challenging the credibility of the maker of a statement of which hearsay evidence is introduced. See also section 6 of that Act. The 1995 Act does not allow the introduction of evidence of a previous inconsistent statement otherwise than in accordance with sections 5, 6 and 7 of the Criminal Procedure Act 1865[28].]

Notice to supervisor of requirement for supervision or monitoring   **R31.9**

31.9 (1) This rule applies where—

(a) the legislation under which a behaviour order is made allows the court to impose a requirement for supervision or electronic monitoring; and

(b) the court imposes such a requirement.

(2) The court officer must—

(a) inform the person to be responsible for the supervision or monitoring ('the supervisor') of the defendant's name, address and, if available, telephone number, and as appropriate—

(i) details of the requirement to be supervised or monitored, and

(ii) details of the place at which the defendant's presence must be monitored and the period or periods during which the defendant's presence at that place must be monitored;

(b) inform the defendant of the supervisor's identity and the means by which the supervisor may be contacted; and

(c) notify the supervisor of any subsequent variation, renewal, discharge or revocation of the requirement.

[Note. The legislation that gives the court power to make a behaviour order may specify circumstances in which a requirement for supervision or electronic monitoring may be imposed. Under section 23 of the Public Order Act 2023[29] a serious disruption prevention order which imposes a requirement other than a notification requirement under section 24 of that Act[30] must similarly specify a supervisor.

---

[28] 1865 c. 18; section 6 was amended by section 10 of the Decimal Currency Act 1969 (c. 19), section 90 of, and paragraph 3 of Schedule 13 to, the Access to Justice Act 1999 (c. 22), section 109 of, and paragraph 47 of Schedule 8 to, the Courts Act 2003 (c. 39) and paragraph 79 of Schedule 36 and Schedule 37 to the Criminal Justice Act 2003 (c. 44). It is further amended by section 119 of, and Schedule 7 to, the Police and Criminal Evidence Act 1984 (c. 60), with effect from a date to be appointed.

[29] 2023 c. 15; section 23 comes into force on a date to be appointed.

[30] 2023 c. 15; section 24 comes into force on a date to be appointed.

Under section 347A of the Sentencing Act 2020[31] and under section 36 of the Domestic Abuse Act 2021[32] a sexual harm prevention order or a domestic abuse protection order, respectively, which imposes a requirement, other than an electronic monitoring requirement, on the defendant must specify the person or organisation responsible for supervising compliance with that requirement. Before including such a requirement in an order the court must receive evidence from that supervisor about the requirement's suitability and enforceability.

Under section 348A of the Sentencing Act 2020[33] and under section 37 of the Domestic Abuse Act 2021[34] a sexual harm prevention order or a domestic abuse protection order, respectively, which imposes an electronic monitoring requirement on the defendant must specify the person responsible for that monitoring. If there is a person other than the defendant without whose co-operation it would be impracticable to secure that monitoring, the requirement may not be imposed without that person's consent.]

R31.10   **Bind over: exercise of court's powers**

31.10 (1) Where the court can impose a bind over—
      (a) the court must decide, in this sequence—
          (i)   whether or not to do so and if so in what terms, and then
          (ii) the amount of the recognisance to require; and
      (b) the court may exercise its powers—
          (i)   on application or on the court's own initiative, and
          (ii) at a hearing in public, as a general rule, or, in exceptional circumstances, in private.
   (2) Before imposing a bind over the court must—
      (a) take into account, as well as any representations under rule 31.2 (Behaviour orders and bind overs: general rules)—
          (i)   any evidence introduced, and
          (ii) any admission made; and
      (b) satisfy itself so that it is sure that the criteria for the bind over are met.
   (3) Before deciding the amount of any recognisance to require the court must take into account, as well as any representations under rule 31.2, such information as is readily available about the financial circumstances of the person to be bound over.
   (4) As a general rule the court must not impose a bind over for more than 12 months.
   (5) If the court decides to impose a bind over—
      (a) the court must explain, in terms the person to be bound over can understand (with help if necessary)—
          (i)   the effect of the court's decision,
          (ii) the consequences of refusing to enter into a recognisance,
          (iii) the consequences of breaching the bind over, and
          (iv) the possibility of appeal; and
      (b) the court must announce its decision and reasons at a hearing in public.
   (6) A bind over must be in writing and must—
      (a) describe in ordinary language the conduct from which the person to be bound over must refrain;
      (b) specify the amount of the recognisance;
      (c) specify the duration of the bind over; and
      (d) identify any surety who is not the person to be bound over.
   (7) If the Crown Court requires the person to be bound over to come up for judgment, the bind over must also specify—
      (a) any date on which, and place and time at which, that person must attend court; or
      (b) the means by which that person will be given notice of such a date, place and time.
   (8) The court officer must serve the bind over as soon as practicable—
      (a) in every case, on the person bound by it; and
      (b) as applicable, on each party or other party.

[Note. Under section 1 of the Justices of the Peace Act 1361, section 1(7) of the Justices of the Peace Act 1968 and the inherent powers recognised by those provisions, before imposing a bind over the court must be satisfied that—

*   (a) a breach of the peace involving violence or a threat of immediate violence has occurred; or*
*   (b) there is a real risk of violence in the future perpetrated by—*

---

[31] 2020 c. 17; section 347A is inserted by section 175 of the Police, Crime, Sentencing and Courts Act 2022 (c. 32) with effect from a date to be appointed.
[32] 2021 c. 17; section 36 comes into force on a date to be appointed.
[33] 2020 c. 17; section 348A is inserted by section 178 of the Police, Crime, Sentencing and Courts Act 2022 (c. 32) with effect from a date to be appointed.
[34] 2021 c. 17; section 37 comes into force on a date to be appointed.

(i)   the person to be bound over, or

(ii) another person as a natural consequence of the conduct of the person to be bound over.]

Bind over: refusal or breach

R31.11

31.11 (1) Where a person to be bound over refuses to enter into a recognisance, the court must—

(a) consider such other steps as may be available, for example continuing or starting a prosecution; and

(b) treat committal to custody as a last resort.

(2) Where a person bound over is alleged to have breached a requirement, before the court forfeits the recognisance it must satisfy itself on the balance of probabilities that a breach has occurred.

(3) In addition to paragraph (1) or (2), as applicable, before committing to custody or forfeiting a recognisance the court must follow the procedure required by rule 48.8 (contempt of court by obstruction, disruption, etc.; procedure on enquiry) as if—

(a) the refusal or breach were a contempt of court; and

(b) the committal or forfeiture were a punishment for such a contempt.

[Note. Under section 1(7) of the Justices of the Peace Act 1968 if a person whom the court decides to bind over refuses to enter into a recognisance the court can commit that person to custody.

Payment of the sum due under a recognisance that is forfeit can be enforced under section 58 of the Magistrates' Courts Act 1980[35].]

Court's power to vary requirements under this Part

R31.12

31.12 Unless other legislation otherwise provides, the court may—

(a) shorten a time limit or extend it (even after it has expired);

(b) allow a notice or application to be given in a different form, or presented orally. And

(c) dispense with a requirement for service (even after service was required).

CRIMINAL PROCEDURE RULES   PART 32   BREACH, REVOCATION AND AMENDMENT OF COMMUNITY AND OTHER ORDERS

When this Part applies

R32.1

32.1   This Part applies where—

(a) the person responsible for a defendant's compliance with an order to which applies—

(i)   Schedule 5, 7, 10 or 16 to the Sentencing Act 2020[1], or

(ii) the Schedule to the Street Offences Act 1959[2],

wants the court to deal with that defendant for failure to comply;

(b) one of the following wants the court to exercise any power it has to revoke or amend such an order—

(i)   the responsible officer or supervisor,

(ii) the defendant, or

(iii) where the legislation allows, a person affected by the order; or

(c) the court considers exercising on its own initiative any power it has to revoke or amend such an order.

[Note. In the Sentencing Act 2020—

(a) Schedule 5 deals with the breach, revocation and amendment of reparation orders;

(b) Schedule 7 deals with the breach, revocation and amendment of youth rehabilitation orders;

(c) Schedule 10 deals with the breach, revocation and amendment of community orders; and

(d) Schedule 16 deals with the breach or amendment of suspended sentence orders, and the effect of a further conviction.]

Application by responsible officer or supervisor

R32.2

32.2   (1) This rule applies where—

(a) the responsible officer or supervisor wants the court to—

(i)   deal with a defendant for failure to comply with an order to which this Part applies, or

(ii) revoke or amend such an order; or

(b) the court considers exercising on its own initiative any power it has to—

---

[35] 1980 c. 43; section 58 was amended by section 17 of, and paragraphs 39 and 40 of Schedule 10 to, the Crime and Courts Act 2013 (c. 22).

[1] 2020 c. 17.

[2] 1959 c. 57; Schedule: Orders under section 1(2A) was inserted by section 17(1) and (4) of the Policing and Crime Act 2009 (c. 26).

  (i) revoke or amend such an order, and
  (ii) summon the defendant to attend for that purpose.
(2) Rules 7.2 to 7.4, which deal, among other things, with starting a prosecution in a magistrates' court, apply—
 (a) as if—
  (i) a reference in those rules to an allegation of an offence included a reference to an allegation of failure to comply with an order to which this Part applies, and
  (ii) a reference to the prosecutor included a reference to the responsible officer or supervisor; and
 (b) with the necessary consequential modifications.

R32.3 Application by defendant or person affected

32.3 (1) This rule applies where—
 (a) the defendant wants the court to exercise any power it has to revoke or amend an order to which this Part applies; or
 (b) where the legislation allows, a person affected by such an order wants the court to exercise any such power.
(2) That defendant, or person affected, must—
 (a) apply in writing, explaining why the order should be revoked or amended; and
 (b) serve the application on—
  (i) the court officer,
  (ii) the responsible officer or supervisor, and
  (iii) as appropriate, the defendant or the person affected.

R32.4 Procedure on application by responsible officer or supervisor

32.4 (1) Except for rules 24.8 (Written guilty plea; special rules) and 24.9 (Single justice procedure: special rules), the rules in Part 24, which deal with the procedure at a trial in a magistrates' court, apply—
 (a) as if—
  (i) a reference in those rules to an allegation of an offence included a reference to an allegation of failure to comply with an order to which this Part applies,
  (ii) a reference to the court's verdict included a reference to the court's decision to revoke or amend such an order, or to exercise any other power it has to deal with the defendant, and
  (iii) a reference to the court's sentence included a reference to the exercise of any such power; and
 (b) with the necessary consequential modifications.
(2) The court officer must serve on each party any order revoking or amending an order to which this Part applies.

CRIMINAL PROCEDURE RULES PART 33 CONFISCATION AND RELATED PROCEEDINGS
General rules

R33.1 Interpretation

33.1 In this Part: words and expressions used have the same meaning as in Part 2 of the Proceeds of Crime Act 2002 and:
'document' means anything in which information of any description is recorded;
'hearsay evidence' means evidence consisting of hearsay within the meaning of section 1(2) of the Civil Evidence Act 1995[1];
'restraint proceedings' means proceedings under sections 42 and 58(2) and (3) of the Proceeds of Crime Act 2002[2];
'receivership proceedings' means proceedings under sections 48, 49, 50, 51, 54(4), 59(2) and (3), 62 and 63 of the 2002 Act[3];

---

[1] 1995 c. 38.
[2] 2002 c. 29; section 42 was amended by sections 74(2) and 92 of, and paragraphs 1 and 23 of Schedule 8, and Schedule 14 to, the Serious Crime Act 2007 (c. 27). Section 58(2) was amended by section 62(3) of, and paragraphs 142 and 143 of Schedule 13 to, the Tribunals, Courts and Enforcement Act 2007 (c. 15).
[3] 2002 c. 29; sections 49, 62 and 63 were amended by sections 74 and 82(1) of, and paragraphs 1, 29 and 30 of Schedule 8 to, the Serious Crime Act (c. 27). Section 59(2) was amended by section 62(3) of, and paragraphs 142 and 144 of Schedule 13 to, the Tribunals, Courts and Enforcement Act 2007 (c. 15).

'witness statement' means a written statement signed by a person which contains the evidence, and only that evidence, which that person would be allowed to give orally.

Calculation of time   R33.2

33.2 (1) This rule shows how to calculate any period of time for doing any act which is specified by this Part for the purposes of any proceedings under Part 2 of the Proceeds of Crime Act 2002 or by an order of the Crown Court in restraint proceedings or receivership proceedings.

(2) A period of time expressed as a number of days shall be computed as clear days.

(3) In this rule 'clear days' means that in computing the number of days—

   (a) the day on which the period begins; and

   (b) if the end of the period is defined by reference to an event, the day on which that event occurs,

   are not included.

(4) Where the specified period is 5 days or less and includes a day which is not a business day that day does not count.

Court office closed   R33.3

33.3 When the period specified by this Part, or by an order of the Crown Court under Part 2 of the Proceeds of Crime Act 2002, for doing any act at the court office falls on a day on which the office is closed, that act shall be in time if done on the next day on which the court office is open.

Application for registration of Scottish or Northern Ireland order   R33.4

33.4 (1) This rule applies to an application for registration of an order under article 6 of the Proceeds of Crime Act 2002 (Enforcement in different parts of the United Kingdom) Order 2002[4].

(2) The application may be made without notice.

(3) The application must be in writing and may be supported by a witness statement which must—

   (a) exhibit the order or a certified copy of the order; and

   (b) to the best of the witness's ability, give full details of the realisable property located in England and Wales in respect of which the order was made and specify the person holding that realisable property.

(4) If the court registers the order, the applicant must serve notice of the registration on—

   (a) any person who holds realisable property to which the order applies; and

   (b) any other person whom the applicant knows to be affected by the order.

(5) The permission of the Crown Court under rule 33.10 (Service outside the jurisdiction) is not required to serve the notice outside England and Wales.

Application to vary or set aside registration   R33.5

33.5 (1) An application to vary or set aside registration of an order under article 6 of the Proceeds of Crime Act 2002 (Enforcement in different parts of the United Kingdom) Order 2002 may be made to the Crown Court by—

   (a) any person who holds realisable property to which the order applies; and

   (b) any other person affected by the order.

(2) The application must be in writing and may be supported by a witness statement.

(3) The application and any witness statement must be lodged with the Crown Court.

(4) The application must be served on the person who applied for registration at least 7 days before the date fixed by the court for hearing the application, unless the Crown Court specifies a shorter period.

(5) No property in England and Wales may be realised in pursuance of the order before the Crown Court has decided the application.

Register of orders   R33.6

33.6 (1) The Crown Court must keep, under the direction of the Lord Chancellor, a register of the orders registered under article 6 of the Proceeds of Crime Act 2002 (Enforcement in different parts of the United Kingdom) Order 2002.

(2) The register must include details of any variation or setting aside of a registration under rule 33.5 and of any execution issued on a registered order.

(3) If the person who applied for registration of an order which is subsequently registered notifies the Crown Court that the court which made the order has varied or discharged the order, details of the variation or discharge, as the case may be, must be entered in the register.

[4] S.I. 2002/3133.

R33.7   Statements of truth

33.7 (1) Any witness statement required to be served by this Part must be verified by a statement of truth contained in the witness statement.

(2) A statement of truth is a declaration by the person making the witness statement to the effect that the witness statement is true to the best of his knowledge and belief and that he made the statement knowing that, if it were tendered in evidence, he would be liable to prosecution if he wilfully stated in it anything which he knew to be false or did not believe to be true.

(3) The statement of truth must be signed by the person making the witness statement.

(4) If the person making the witness statement fails to verify the witness statement by a statement of truth, the Crown Court may direct that it shall not be admissible as evidence.

R33.8   Use of witness statements for other purposes

33.8 (1) Except as provided by this rule, a witness statement served in proceedings under Part 2 of the Proceeds of Crime Act 2002 may be used only for the purpose of the proceedings in which it is served.

(2) Paragraph (1) does not apply if and to the extent that—

(a) the witness gives consent in writing to some other use of it;

(b) the Crown Court gives permission for some other use; or

(c) the witness statement has been put in evidence at a hearing held in public.

R33.9   Service of documents

33.9 (1) Rule 49.1 (Notice required to accompany process served outside the United Kingdom and translations) shall not apply in restraint proceedings and receivership proceedings.

(2) An order made in restraint proceedings or receivership proceedings may be enforced against the defendant or any other person affected by it notwithstanding that service of a copy of the order has not been effected in accordance with Part 4 if the Crown Court is satisfied that the person had notice of the order by being present when the order was made.

R33.10   Service outside the jurisdiction

33.10 (1) Where this Part requires a document to be served on someone who is outside England and Wales, it may be served outside England and Wales with the permission of the Crown Court.

(2) Where a document is to be served outside England and Wales it may be served by any method permitted by the law of the country in which it is to be served.

(3) Nothing in this rule or in any court order shall authorise or require any person to do anything in the country where the document is to be served which is against the law of that country.

(4) Where this Part requires a document to be served a certain period of time before the date of a hearing and the recipient does not appear at the hearing, the hearing must not take place unless the Crown Court is satisfied that the document has been duly served.

R33.11   Certificates of service

33.11 (1) Where this Part requires that the applicant for an order in restraint proceedings or receivership proceedings serve a document on another person, the applicant must lodge a certificate of service with the Crown Court within 7 days of service of the document.

(2) The certificate must state—

(a) the method of service;

(b) the date of service; and

(c) if the document is served under rule 4.9 (Service by another method), such other information as the court may require when making the order permitting service by that method.

(3) Where a document is to be served by the Crown Court in restraint proceedings and receivership proceedings and the court is unable to serve it, the court must send a notice of non-service stating the method attempted to the party who requested service.

R33.12   External requests and orders

33.12 (1) The rules in this Part and in Part 42 (Appeal to the Court of Appeal in confiscation and related proceedings) apply with the necessary modifications to proceedings under the Proceeds of Crime Act 2002 (External Requests and Orders) Order 2005[5] in the same way that they apply to corresponding proceedings under Part 2 of the Proceeds of Crime Act 2002[6].

(2) This table shows how provisions of the 2005 Order correspond with provisions of the 2002 Act.

---

[5] S.I. 2005/3181.
[6] 2002 c. 29.

Article of the Proceeds of Crime Act 2002 (External Requests and Orders) Order 2005	Section of the Proceeds of Crime Act 2002
8	41
9	42
10	43
11	44
15	48
16	49
17	58
23	31
27	50
28	51
41	62
42	63
44	65
45	66

Confiscation proceedings

Statements in connection with confiscation orders   **R33.13**

33.13 (1) This rule applies where—
    (a) the court can make a confiscation order; and
    (b) the prosecutor asks the court to make such an order, or the court decides to make such an order on its own initiative.
  (2) Within such periods as the court directs—
    (a) if the court so orders, the defendant must give such information, in such manner, as the court directs;
    (b) the prosecutor must serve a statement of information relevant to confiscation on the court officer and the defendant; and
    (c) if the court so directs—
      (i)   the defendant must serve a response notice on the court officer and the prosecutor, and
      (ii) the parties must identify what is in dispute.
  (3) Where it appears to the court that a person other than the defendant holds, or may hold, an interest in property held by the defendant which property is likely to be realised or otherwise used to satisfy a confiscation order—
    (a) the court must not determine the extent of the defendant's interest in that property unless that other person has had a reasonable opportunity to make representations; and
    (b) the court may order that other person to give such information, in such manner and within such a period, as the court directs.
  (4) The court may—
    (a) shorten or extend a time limit which it has set;
    (b) vary, discharge or supplement an order which it has made; and
    (c) postpone confiscation proceedings without a hearing.
  (5) A prosecutor's statement of information must—
    (a) identify the maker of the statement and show its date;
    (b) identify the defendant in respect of whom it is served;
    (c) specify the conviction which gives the court power to make the confiscation order, or each conviction if more than one;
    (d) if the prosecutor believes the defendant to have a criminal lifestyle, include such matters as the prosecutor believes to be relevant in connection with deciding—
      (i)   whether the defendant has such a lifestyle,
      (ii) whether the defendant has benefited from his or her general criminal conduct,
      (iii) the defendant's benefit from that conduct, and
      (iv) whether the court should or should not make such assumptions about the defendant's property as legislation permits;

    (e) if the prosecutor does not believe the defendant to have a criminal lifestyle, include such matters as the prosecutor believes to be relevant in connection with deciding—

        (i) whether the defendant has benefited from his or her particular criminal conduct, and

        (ii) the defendant's benefit from that conduct; and

    (f) in any case, include such matters as the prosecutor believes to be relevant in connection with deciding—

        (i) whether to make a determination about the extent of the defendant's interest in property in which another person holds, or may hold, an interest, and

        (ii) what determination to make, if the court decides to make one.

(6) A defendant's response notice must—

    (a) indicate the extent to which the defendant accepts the allegations made in the prosecutor's statement of information; and

    (b) so far as the defendant does not accept an allegation, give particulars of any matters on which the defendant relies, in any manner directed by the court.

(7) The court must satisfy itself that there has been explained to the defendant, in terms the defendant can understand (with help, if necessary)—

    (a) that if the defendant accepts to any extent an allegation in a prosecutor's statement of information, then the court may treat that as conclusive for the purposes of deciding whether the defendant has benefited from general or particular criminal conduct, and if so by how much;

    (b) that if the defendant fails in any respect to comply with a direction to serve a response notice, then the court may treat that as acceptance of each allegation to which the defendant has not replied, except the allegation that the defendant has benefited from general or particular criminal conduct; and

    (c) that if the defendant fails without reasonable excuse to comply with an order to give information, then the court may draw such inference as it believes is appropriate.

[Note. Under section 6 of the Proceeds of Crime Act 2002[7], where a defendant is convicted of an offence the Crown Court must (with some exceptions)—

    (a) decide whether the defendant has 'a criminal lifestyle', within the meaning of the Act, or has benefited from particular criminal conduct;

    (b) decide the 'recoverable amount', within the meaning of the Act; and

    (c) make a confiscation order requiring the defendant to pay that amount.

Under section 14 of the 2002 Act[8], unless exceptional circumstances apply the court may postpone confiscation proceedings for a maximum of 2 years from the date of conviction, or until the end of a period of 3 months following the determination of an appeal by the defendant against conviction, if that is later.

Under section 16 of the 2002 Act[9], where the Crown Court is considering confiscation the prosecutor must give the court a statement of information which the prosecutor believes to be relevant to what the court must decide, within such period as the court directs. Under section 17 of the Act[10], where the prosecutor gives such a statement the court may order the defendant to respond and, if the defendant does not do so, then the court may treat the defendant as accepting the prosecutor's allegations. Under section 18[11], for the purpose of obtaining information to help it in carrying out its functions the court may at any time order the defendant to give it information specified in the order and, if the defendant does not do so, then the court may draw such inference as it believes appropriate. Under section 18A[12], for the purpose of obtaining information to help it to determine the extent of the defendant's interest in property the court may at any time order a person who the court thinks may hold an interest in that property to give it information specified in the order and, if that person does not do so, then the court may draw such inference as it believes appropriate.

[7] 2002 c. 29; section 6 was amended by paragraph 75 of Schedule 3 to the Criminal Justice Act 2003 (c. 44), section 74(2) of, and paragraphs 1 and 2 of Schedule 8 to, the Serious Crime Act 2007 (c. 27) and section 10 of, and paragraphs 11 and 12 of the Schedule to, the Prevention of Social Housing Fraud Act 2013 (c. 3).

[8] 2002 c. 29; section 14 was amended by section 74(2) of, and paragraphs 1 and 4 of Schedule 8 to, the Serious Crime Act 2007 (c. 27).

[9] 2002 c. 29; section 16 was amended by section 74(2) of, and paragraphs 1 and 5 of Schedule 8 to, the Serious Crime Act 2007 (c. 27) and section 2 of the Serious Crime Act 2015 (c. 9).

[10] 2002 c. 29; section 17 was amended by section 74(2) of, and paragraphs 1 and 6 of Schedule 8 to, the Serious Crime Act 2007 (c. 27).

[11] 2002 c. 29; section 18 was amended by section 74(2) of, and paragraphs 1 and 7 of Schedule 8 to, the Serious Crime Act 2007 (c. 27).

[12] 2002 c. 29; section 18A was inserted by section 2 of the Serious Crime Act 2015 (c. 9).

Under section 27 of the 2002 Act[13], special provisions apply where the defendant absconds.

Under section 97 of the Serious Organised Crime and Police Act 2005[14], the Secretary of State may by order provide for confiscation orders to be made by magistrates' courts.]

Application for compliance order

33.14 (1) This rule applies where—

    (a) the prosecutor wants the court to make a compliance order after a confiscation order has been made;

    (b) the prosecutor or a person affected by a compliance order wants the court to vary or discharge the order.

  (2) Such a prosecutor or person must—

    (a) apply in writing; and

    (b) serve the application on—

      (i) the court officer, and

      (ii) as appropriate, the prosecutor and any person who is affected by the compliance order (or who would be affected if it were made), unless the court otherwise directs.

  (3) The application must—

    (a) specify—

      (i) the confiscation order, and

      (ii) the compliance order, if it is an application to vary or discharge that order;

    (b) if it is an application for a compliance order—

      (i) specify each measure that the prosecutor proposes to ensure that the confiscation order is effective, including in particular any restriction or prohibition on the defendant's travel outside the United Kingdom, and

      (ii) explain why each such measure is appropriate;

    (c) if it is an application to vary or discharge a compliance order, as appropriate—

      (i) specify any proposed variation, and

      (ii) explain why it is appropriate for the order to be varied or discharged;

    (d) attach any material on which the applicant relies;

    (e) propose the terms of the order; and

    (f) ask for a hearing, if the applicant wants one, and explain why it is needed.

  (4) A person who wants to make representations about the application must—

    (a) serve the representations on—

      (i) the court officer, and

      (ii) the applicant;

    (b) do so as soon as reasonably practicable after service of the application;

    (c) attach any material on which that person relies; and

    (d) ask for a hearing, if that person wants one, and explain why it is needed.

  (5) The court—

    (a) may determine the application at a hearing (which must be in private unless the court otherwise directs), or without a hearing; and

    (b) may dispense with service on any person of a prosecutor's application for a compliance order if, in particular—

      (i) the application is urgent, or

      (ii) there are reasonable grounds for believing that to give notice of the application would cause the dissipation of property that otherwise would be available to satisfy the confiscation order.

[Note. See section 13A of the Proceeds of Crime Act 2002[15].]

Application for reconsideration

33.15 (1) This rule applies where the prosecutor wants the court, in view of fresh evidence—

    (a) to consider making a confiscation order where the defendant was convicted but no such order was considered;

    (b) to reconsider a decision that the defendant had not benefited from criminal conduct; or

    (c) to reconsider a decision about the amount of the defendant's benefit.

---

[13] 2002 c. 29; section 27 was amended by paragraph 75 of Schedule 3 to the Criminal Justice Act 2003 (c. 44) and section 74 of, and paragraphs 1 and 14 of Schedule 8 to, the Serious Crime Act 2007 (c. 27).

[14] 2005 c. 15; section 97 was amended by S.I. 2010/976.

[15] 2002 c. 29; section 13A was inserted by section 7 of the Serious Crime Act 2015 (c. 9).

    (2) The application must—
        (a) be in writing and give—
            (i) the name of the defendant,
            (ii) the date on which and the place where any relevant conviction occurred,
            (iii) the date on which and the place where any relevant confiscation order was made or varied,
            (iv) details of any slavery and trafficking reparation order made by virtue of any relevant confiscation order,
            (v) the grounds for the application, and
            (vi) an indication of the evidence available to support the application; and
        (b) where the parties are agreed on the terms of the proposed order include, in one or more documents—
            (i) a draft order in the terms proposed, and
            (ii) evidence of the parties' agreement.
    (3) The application must be served on—
        (a) the court officer; and
        (b) the defendant.
    (4) The court—
        (a) may determine the application without a hearing where the parties are agreed on the terms of the proposed order; but
        (b) must determine the application at a hearing in any other case.
    (5) Where this rule or the court requires the application to be heard, the court officer must arrange for the court to hear it no sooner than the eighth day after it was served unless the court otherwise directs.

[Note. See sections 19, 20 and 21 of the Proceeds of Crime Act 2002[16] and section 10 of the Modern Slavery Act 2015[17].]

R33.16 **Application for new calculation of available amount**

33.16 (1) This rule applies where the prosecutor or a receiver wants the court to make a new calculation of the amount available for confiscation.
    (2) The application—
        (a) must be in writing and may be supported by a witness statement;
        (b) must identify any slavery and trafficking reparation order made by virtue of the confiscation order; and
        (c) where the parties are agreed on the terms of the proposed order, must include in one or more documents—
            (i) a draft order in the terms proposed, and
            (ii) evidence of the parties' agreement.
    (3) The application and any witness statement must be served on the court officer.
    (4) The application and any witness statement must be served on—
        (a) the defendant;
        (b) the receiver, if the prosecutor is making the application and a receiver has been appointed; and
        (c) the prosecutor, if the receiver is making the application,
    (5) The court—
        (a) may determine the application without a hearing where the parties are agreed on the terms of the proposed order; but
        (b) must determine the application at a hearing in any other case.
    (6) Where this rule or the court requires the application to be heard, the court officer must arrange for the court to hear it no sooner than the eighth day after it was served unless the court otherwise directs.

[Note. See section 22 of the Proceeds of Crime Act 2002[18] and section 10 of the Modern Slavery Act 2015.]

R33.17 **Variation of confiscation order due to inadequacy of available amount**

33.17 (1) This rule applies where the defendant, the prosecutor or a receiver wants the court to vary a confiscation order because the amount available is inadequate.

---

[16] 2002 c. 29; sections 19, 20 and 21 were amended by section 74(2) of, and paragraph 1 and paragraphs 8, 9 and 10 respectively, of Schedule 8 to, the Serious Crime Act 2007 (c. 27). Sections 19 and 20 were further amended by paragraphs 16 and 17 of Schedule 5 to the Modern Slavery Act 2015 (c. 30).
[17] 2015 c. 30.
[18] 2002 c. 29; section 22 was amended by section 74(2) of, and paragraph 11 of Schedule 8 to, the Serious Crime Act 2007 (c. 27).

(2) The application—
    (a) must be in writing and may be supported by a witness statement;
    (b) must identify any slavery and trafficking reparation order made by virtue of the confiscation order; and
    (c) where the parties are agreed on the terms of the proposed order, must include in one or more documents—
        (i) a draft order in the terms proposed, and
        (ii) evidence of the parties' agreement.

(3) The application and any witness statement must be served on the court officer.

(4) The application and any witness statement must be served on—
    (a) the prosecutor;
    (b) the defendant, if the receiver is making the application; and
    (c) the receiver, if the defendant is making the application and a receiver has been appointed.

(5) The court—
    (a) may determine the application without a hearing where the parties are agreed on the terms of the proposed order; but
    (a) must determine the application at a hearing in any other case.

(6) Where this rule or the court requires the application to be heard, the court officer must arrange for the court to hear it no sooner than the eighth day after it was served unless the court otherwise directs.

[Note. See section 23 of the Proceeds of Crime Act 2002[19] and section 10 of the Modern Slavery Act 2015.]

Application by magistrates' court officer to discharge confiscation order   **R33.18**

33.18 (1) This rule applies where a magistrates' court officer wants the court to discharge a confiscation order because the amount available is inadequate or the sum outstanding is very small.

(2) The application must be in writing and give details of—
    (a) the confiscation order;
    (b) any slavery and trafficking reparation order made by virtue of the confiscation order;
    (c) the amount outstanding under the order; and
    (d) the grounds for the application.

(3) The application must be served on—
    (a) the defendant;
    (b) the prosecutor; and
    (c) any receiver.

(4) The court may determine the application without a hearing unless a person listed in paragraph (3) indicates, within 7 days after the application was served, that he or she would like to make representations.

(5) If the court makes an order discharging the confiscation order, the court officer must, at once, send a copy of the order to—
    (a) the magistrates' court officer who applied for the order;
    (b) the defendant;
    (c) the prosecutor; and
    (d) any receiver.

[Note. See sections 24 and 25 of the Proceeds of Crime Act 2002[20] and section 10 of the Modern Slavery Act 2015.]

Application for variation of confiscation order made against an absconder   **R33.19**

33.19 (1) This rule applies where the defendant wants the court to vary a confiscation order made while the defendant was an absconder.

(2) The application must be in writing and supported by a witness statement which must give details of—
    (a) the confiscation order;
    (b) any slavery and trafficking reparation order made by virtue of the confiscation order;
    (c) the circumstances in which the defendant ceased to be an absconder;
    (d) the defendant's conviction of the offence or offences concerned; and
    (e) the reason why the defendant believes the amount required to be paid under the confiscation order was too large.

(3) The application and witness statement must be served on the court officer.

---

[19] 2002 c. 29; section 23 was amended by section 74(2) of, and paragraph 12 of Schedule 8 to, the Serious Crime Act 2007 (c. 27) and section 8 of the Serious Crime Act 2015 (c. 9).
[20] 2002 c. 29; sections 24 and 25 were amended by section 109(1) of, and paragraphs 406(a) and 406(b), respectively, of Schedule 8 to, the Courts Act 2003 (c. 39).

(4) The application and witness statement must be served on the prosecutor at least 7 days before the date fixed by the court for hearing the application, unless the court specifies a shorter period.

[Note. See section 29 of the Proceeds of Crime Act 2002[21] and section 10 of the Modern Slavery Act 2015.]

R33.20   **Application for discharge of confiscation order made against an absconder**

33.20 (1) This rule applies where the defendant wants the court to discharge a confiscation order made while the defendant was an absconder and—
(a) the defendant since has been tried and acquitted of each offence concerned; or
(b) the prosecution has not concluded or is not to proceed.
(2) The application must be in writing and supported by a witness statement which must give details of—
(a) the confiscation order;
(b) the date on which the defendant ceased to be an absconder;
(c) the acquittal of the defendant if he or she has been acquitted of the offence concerned; and
(d) if the defendant has not been acquitted of the offence concerned—
(i) the date on which the defendant ceased to be an absconder,
(ii) the date on which the proceedings taken against the defendant were instituted and a summary of steps taken in the proceedings since then, and
(iii) any indication that the prosecutor does not intend to proceed against the defendant.
(3) The application and witness statement must be served on the court officer.
(4) The application and witness statement must be served on the prosecutor at least 7 days before the date fixed by the court for hearing the application, unless the court specifies a shorter period.
(5) If the court orders the discharge of the confiscation order, the court officer must serve notice on any other court responsible for enforcing the order.

[Note. See section 30 of the Proceeds of Crime Act 2002[22].]

R33.21   **Application for increase in term of imprisonment in default**

33.21 (1) This rule applies where —
(a) a court varies a confiscation order; and
(b) the prosecutor wants the court in consequence to increase the term of imprisonment to be served in default of payment.
(2) The application must be made in writing and give details of—
(a) the name and address of the defendant;
(b) the confiscation order;
(c) the grounds for the application; and
(d) the enforcement measures taken, if any.
(3) On receipt of the application, the court officer must—
(a) at once, send to the defendant and any other court responsible for enforcing the order, a copy of the application; and
(b) fix a time, date and place for the hearing and notify the applicant and the defendant of that time, date and place.
(4) If the court makes an order increasing the term of imprisonment in default, the court officer must, at once, send a copy of the order to—
(a) the applicant;
(b) the defendant;
(c) where the defendant is in custody at the time of the making of the order, the person having custody of the defendant; and
(d) any other court responsible for enforcing the order.

[Note. See section 39(5) of the Proceeds of Crime Act 2002[23].]

R33.22   **Compensation—general**

33.22 (1) This rule applies where a person who held realisable property wants the court to award compensation for loss suffered in consequence of anything done in relation to that property in connection with confiscation proceedings.
(2) The application must be in writing and may be supported by a witness statement.
(3) The application and any witness statement must be served on the court officer.

---

[21] 2002 c. 29.
[22] 2002 c. 29.
[23] 2002 c. 29; section 39(5) was amended by section 74(2) of, and paragraphs 1 and 21(2) of Schedule 8 to, the Serious Crime Act 2007 (c. 27).

(4) The application and any witness statement must be served on—
    (a) the person alleged to be in default; and
    (b) the person or authority by whom the compensation would be payable,
    at least 7 days before the date fixed by the court for hearing the application, unless the court directs otherwise.

[Note. See section 72 of the Proceeds of Crime Act 2002[24].]

Compensation—confiscation order made against absconder   R33.23

33.23 (1) This rule applies where—
    (a) the court varies or discharges a confiscation order made against an absconder;
    (b) a person who held realisable property suffered loss as a result of the making of that confiscation order; and
    (c) that person wants the court to award compensation for that loss.
    (2) The application must be in writing and supported by a witness statement which must give details of—
    (a) the confiscation order;
    (b) the variation or discharge of the confiscation order;
    (c) the realisable property to which the application relates; and
    (d) the loss suffered by the applicant as a result of the confiscation order.
    (3) The application and witness statement must be served on the court officer.
    (4) The application and witness statement must be served on the prosecutor at least 7 days before the date fixed by the court for hearing the application, unless the court specifies a shorter period.

[Note. See section 73 of the Proceeds of Crime Act 2002[25].]

Payment of money held or detained in satisfaction of confiscation order   R33.24

33.24 (1) An order under section 67 of the Proceeds of Crime Act 2002[26] requiring the payment of money to a magistrates' court officer ('a payment order') shall—
    (a) be directed to—
        (i)   the bank or building society concerned, where the money is held in an account maintained with that bank or building society, or
        (ii) the person on whose authority the money is detained, in any other case;
    (b) name the person against whom the confiscation order has been made;
    (c) state the amount which remains to be paid under the confiscation order;
    (d) state the name and address of the branch at which the account in which the money ordered to be paid is held and the sort code of that branch, if the sort code is known;
    (e) state the name in which the account in which the money ordered to be paid is held and the account number of that account, if the account number is known;
    (f) state the amount which the bank or building society is required to pay to the court officer under the payment order;
    (g) give the name and address of the court officer to whom payment is to be made; and
    (h) require the bank or building society to make payment within a period of 7 days beginning on the day on which the payment order is made, unless it appears to the court that a longer or shorter period would be appropriate in the particular circumstances.
    (2) In this rule 'confiscation order' has the meaning given to it by section 88(6) of the Proceeds of Crime Act 2002.

Application to realise seized property   R33.25

33.25 (1) This rule applies where—
    (a) property is held by a defendant against whom a confiscation order has been made;
    (b) the property has been seized by or produced to an officer; and
    (c) an officer who is entitled to apply wants a magistrates' court—
        (i) to make an order under section 67A of the Proceeds of Crime Act 2002[27] authorising the realisation of the property towards satisfaction of the confiscation order, or

[24] 2002 c. 29; section 72 was amended by section 50(6) of, and paragraph 97 of Schedule 4 to, the Commissioners for Revenue and Customs Act 2005 (c. 11), section 61 of the Policing and Crime Act 2009 (c. 26) and sections 15 and 55 of, and paragraphs 108 and 114 of Schedule 8 and paragraphs 14 and 19 of Schedule 21 to, the Crime and Courts Act 2013 (c. 22).
[25] 2002 c. 29.
[26] 2002 c. 29; section 67 was amended by section 109 of, and paragraph 409 of Schedule 8 to, the Courts Act 2003 (c. 39), section 74 of, and paragraph 33 of Schedule 8 to, the Serious Crime Act 2007 (c. 27), section 14 of the Serious Crime Act 2015 (c. 9) and section 26 of the Criminal Finances Act 2017 (c. 22).
[27] 2002 c. 29; section 67A was inserted by section 58 of the Policing and Crime Act 2009 (c. 26) and amended by section 14 of the Serious Crime Act 2015 (c. 9).

(ii) to determine any storage, insurance or realisation costs in respect of the property which may be recovered under section 67B of the 2002 Act[28].

(2) Such an officer must—

(a) apply in writing; and

(b) serve the application on—

(i) the court officer, and

(ii) any person whom the applicant believes would be affected by an order.

(3) The application must—

(a) specify the property;

(b) explain—

(i) the applicant's entitlement to apply,

(ii) how the proposed realisation meets the conditions prescribed by section 67A of the 2002 Act, and

(iii) how any storage, etc. costs have been calculated;

(c) attach any material on which the applicant relies; and

(d) propose the terms of the order.

(4) The court may—

(a) determine the application at a hearing, or without a hearing;

(b) consider an application made orally instead of in writing; and

(c) consider an application which has not been served on a person likely to be affected by an order.

(5) If the court authorises the realisation of the property, the applicant must—

(a) notify any person affected by the order who was absent when it was made; and

(b) serve on the court officer a list of those so notified.

[Note. Under section 67A of the Proceeds of Crime Act 2002, one of the officers listed in section 41A of the Act may apply to a magistrates' court for authority to realise property seized by such an officer if—

(a) a confiscation order has been made against the owner of the property;

(b) no receiver has been appointed in relation to that property; and

(c) any period allowed for payment of the confiscation order has expired.

Under section 67B of the 2002 Act, if a magistrates' court makes an order under section 67A then on the same or a subsequent occasion the court may determine an amount which may be recovered by the applicant in respect of reasonable costs incurred in storing or insuring the property, or realising it.]

R33.26 **Appeal about decision on application to realise seized property**

33.26 (1) This rule applies where on an application under rule 33.25 for an order authorising the realisation of property—

(a) a magistrates' court decides not to make such an order and an officer who is entitled to apply wants to appeal against that decision to the Crown Court, under section 67C(1) of the Proceeds of Crime Act 2002[29];

(b) a magistrates' court makes such an order and a person who is affected by that decision, other than the defendant against whom the confiscation order was made, wants to appeal against it to the Crown Court, under section 67C(2) of the 2002 Act; or

(c) a magistrates' court makes a decision about storage, etc. costs and an officer who is entitled to apply wants to appeal against that decision to the Crown Court, under section 67C(4) of the 2002 Act.

(2) The appellant must serve an appeal notice—

(a) on the Crown Court officer and on any other party; and

(b) not more than 21 days after the magistrates' court's decision, or, if applicable, service of notice under rule 33.25(5).

(3) The appeal notice must—

(a) specify the decision under appeal;

(b) where paragraph (1)(a) applies, explain why the property should be realised;

(c) in any other case, propose the order that the appellant wants the court to make, and explain why.

(4) Rule 34.11 (Constitution of the Crown Court) applies on such an appeal.

---

[28] 2002 c. 29; section 67B was inserted by section 58 of the Policing and Crime Act 2009 (c. 26).

[29] 2002 c. 29; section 67C was inserted by section 58 of the Policing and Crime Act 2009 (c. 26).

[Note. Under section 67C of the Proceeds of Crime Act 2002, an officer entitled to apply for an order under section 67A or 67B of that Act (authority to realise seized property towards satisfaction of a confiscation order; determination of storage, etc. costs) may appeal against a refusal to make an order, or against a costs determination; and a person affected by an order, other than the owner, may appeal against the order.]

Application for direction about surplus proceeds   R33.27

33.27 (1) This rule applies where—
    (a) on an application under rule 33.25, a magistrates' court has made an order authorising an officer to realise property;
    (b) an officer so authorised holds proceeds of that realisation;
    (c) the confiscation order has been fully paid; and
    (d) the officer, or a person who had or has an interest in the property represented by the proceeds, wants a magistrates' court or the Crown Court to determine under section 67D of the Proceeds of Crime Act 2002[30] —
        (i) to whom the remaining proceeds should be paid, and
        (ii) in what amount or amounts.
    (2) Such a person must—
    (a) apply in writing; and
    (b) serve the application on—
        (i) the court officer, and
        (ii) as appropriate, the officer holding the proceeds, or any person to whom such proceeds might be paid.
    (3) The application must—
    (a) specify the property which was realised;
    (b) explain the applicant's entitlement to apply;
    (c) describe the distribution proposed by the applicant and explain why that is proposed;
    (d) attach any material on which the applicant relies; and
    (e) ask for a hearing, if the applicant wants one, and explain why it is needed.
    (4) A person who wants to make representations about the application must—
    (a) serve the representations on—
        (i) the court officer,
        (ii) the applicant, and
        (iii) any other person to whom proceeds might be paid;
    (b) do so as soon as reasonably practicable after service of the application;
    (c) attach any material on which that person relies; and
    (d) ask for a hearing, if that person wants one, and explain why it is needed.
    (5) The court—
    (a) must not determine the application unless the applicant and each person on whom it was served—
        (i) is present, or
        (ii) has had an opportunity to attend or to make representations; but
    (b) subject to that, may determine the application—
        (i) at a hearing (which must be in private unless the court otherwise directs), or without a hearing,
        (ii) in the absence of any party to the application.

[Note. Under section 67D of the Proceeds of Crime Act 2002, a magistrates' court or the Crown Court may determine to whom, and in what proportions, any surplus proceeds of realisation must be distributed. Once a magistrates' court has made such a determination, the Crown Court may not do so, and vice versa.]

Seizure and detention proceedings

Application for approval to seize property or to search   R33.28

33.28 (1) This rule applies where an officer who is entitled to apply wants the approval of a magistrates' court, under section 47G of the Proceeds of Crime Act 2002[31] —
    (a) to seize property, under section 47C of that Act[32]; or

---

[30] 2002 c. 29; section 67D was inserted by section 58 of the Policing and Crime Act 2009 (c. 26).
[31] 2002 c. 29; section 47G was inserted by section 55 of the Policing and Crime Act 2009 (c. 26) and amended by section 55 of, and paragraphs 14 and 17 of Schedule 21 to, the Crime and Courts Act 2013 (c. 22) and section 13 of the Serious Crime Act 2015 (c. 9).
[32] 2002 c. 29; section 47C was inserted by section 55 of the Policing and Crime Act 2009 (c. 26) and amended by section 55 of, and paragraphs 14 and 16 of Schedule 21 to, the Crime and Courts Act 2013

    (b) to search premises or a person or vehicle for property to be seized, under section 47D, 47E or 47F of that Act[33].

(2) Such an officer must—
  (a) apply in writing; and
  (b) serve the application on the court officer.

(3) The application must—
  (a) explain—
    (i) the applicant's entitlement to apply, and
    (ii) how the proposed seizure meets the conditions prescribed by sections 47B, 47C and, if applicable, 47D, 47E or 47F of the 2002 Act[34];
  (b) if applicable, specify any premises, person or vehicle to be searched;
  (c) attach any material on which the applicant relies; and
  (d) propose the terms in which the applicant wants the court to give its approval.

(4) The court—
  (a) must determine the application—
    (i) at a hearing, which must be in private unless the court otherwise directs, and
    (ii) in the applicant's presence; but
  (b) may consider an application made orally instead of in writing.

[Note. Under section 47C of the Proceeds of Crime Act 2002, if any of the conditions listed in section 47B of the Act are met then one of the officers listed in section 47A may seize property other than cash or exempt property, as defined in the section, if that officer has reasonable grounds for suspecting that—

    (a) the property may otherwise be made unavailable for satisfying any confiscation order that has been or may be made against a defendant; or
    (b) the value of the property may otherwise be diminished as a result of conduct by the defendant or any other person.

Under sections 47D, 47E and 47F of the 2002 Act, such an officer may search premises, a person or a vehicle, respectively, for such property, on the conditions listed in those sections.

By sections 47C(6), 47D(2), 47E(4), 47F(6) and 47G of the 2002 Act, such an officer may seize property, and may search for it, only with the approval of a magistrates' court or, if that is impracticable, the approval of a senior officer (as defined by section 47G), unless in the circumstances it is not practicable to obtain the approval of either.]

R33.29 **Application to extend detention period**

33.29 (1) This rule applies where an officer who is entitled to apply, or the prosecutor, wants a magistrates' court to make an order, under section 47M of the Proceeds of Crime Act 2002[35], extending the period for which seized property may be detained.

(2) Such an officer or prosecutor must—
  (a) apply in writing; and
  (b) serve the application on—
    (i) the court officer, and
    (ii) any person whom the applicant believes would be affected by an order.

(3) The application must—
  (a) specify—
    (i) the property to be detained, and
    (ii) whether the applicant wants it to be detained for a specified period or indefinitely;
  (b) explain—
    (i) the applicant's entitlement to apply, and
    (ii) how the proposed detention meets the conditions prescribed by section 47M of the 2002 Act;
  (c) attach any material on which the applicant relies; and
  (d) propose the terms of the order.

(4) The court—
  (a) must determine the application—
    (i) at a hearing, which must be in private unless the court otherwise directs, and
    (ii) in the applicant's presence; but

---

[33] 2002 c. 29; sections 47D, 47E and 47F were inserted by section 55 of the Policing and Crime Act 2009 (c. 26).
[34] 2002 c. 29; section 47B was inserted by section 55 of the Policing and Crime Act 2009 (c. 26) and amended by section 13 of the Serious Crime Act 2015 (c. 9).
[35] 2002 c. 29; section 47M was inserted by section 55 of the Policing and Crime Act 2009 (c. 26) and amended by section 55 of, and paragraphs 14 and 18 of Schedule 21 to, the Crime and Courts Act 2013 (c. 22).

    (b) may—
        (i)   consider an application made orally instead of in writing,
        (ii) require service of the application on the court officer after it has been heard, instead of before.
  (5) If the court extends the period for which the property may be detained, the applicant must—
    (a) notify any person affected by the order who was absent when it was made; and
    (b) serve on the court officer a list of those so notified.

[Note. Under section 47M of the Proceeds of Crime Act 2002, one of the officers listed in that section, or the prosecutor, may apply to a magistrates' court for an order extending the period of 48 hours for which, under section 47J of the Act[36], property seized under section 47C may be detained.

On an application to which this rule applies, hearsay evidence within the meaning of section 1(2) of the Civil Evidence Act 1995 is admissible: see section 47Q of the 2002 Act[37].]

Application to vary or discharge order for extended detention   R33.30

33.30 (1) This rule applies where an officer who is entitled to apply, the prosecutor, or a person affected by an order to which rule 33.29 applies, wants a magistrates' court to vary or discharge that order, under section 47N of the Proceeds of Crime Act 2002[38].
  (2) Such a person must—
    (a) apply in writing; and
    (b) serve the application on—
        (i)   the court officer, and
        (ii) as appropriate, the applicant for the order, or any person affected by the order.
  (3) The application must—
    (a) specify the order and the property detained;
    (b) explain—
        (i)   the applicant's entitlement to apply,
        (ii) why it is appropriate for the order to be varied or discharged,
        (iii) if applicable, on what grounds the court must discharge the order;
    (c) attach any material on which the applicant relies;
    (d) if applicable, propose the terms of any variation; and
    (e) ask for a hearing, if the applicant wants one, and explain why it is needed.
  (4) A person who wants to make representations about the application must—
    (a) serve the representations on—
        (i)   the court officer, and
        (ii) the applicant;
    (b) do so as soon as reasonably practicable after service of the application;
    (c) attach any material on which that person relies; and
    (d) ask for a hearing, if that person wants one, and explain why it is needed.
  (5) The court—
    (a) must not determine the application unless the applicant and each person on whom it was served—
        (i)   is present, or
        (ii) has had an opportunity to attend or to make representations; but
    (b) subject to that, may determine the application—
        (i)   at a hearing (which must be in private unless the court otherwise directs), or without a hearing,
        (ii) in the absence of any party to the application.

[Note. Under section 47N of the Proceeds of Crime Act 2002, one of the officers listed in section 47M of the Act, the prosecutor, or a person affected by an order under section 47M, may apply to a magistrates' court for the order to be varied or discharged. Section 47N(3) lists the circumstances in which the court must discharge such an order.

On an application to which this rule applies, hearsay evidence within the meaning of section 1(2) of the Civil Evidence Act 1995 is admissible: see section 47Q of the 2002 Act.]

---

[36] 2002 c. 29; section 47J was inserted by section 55 of the Policing and Crime Act 2009 (c. 26).
[37] 2002 c. 29; section 47Q was inserted by section 55 of the Policing and Crime Act 2009 (c. 26).
[38] 2002 c. 29; section 47N was inserted by section 55 of the Policing and Crime Act 2009 (c. 26).

R33.31　**Appeal about property detention decision**

33.31 (1)　This rule applies where—

(a)　on an application under rule 33.29 for an order extending the period for which property may be detained—

(i)　a magistrates' court decides not to make such an order, and

(ii)　an officer who is entitled to apply for such an order, or the prosecutor, wants to appeal against that decision to the Crown Court under section 47O(1) of the Proceeds of Crime Act 2002[39];

(b)　on an application under rule 33.30 to vary or discharge an order under rule 33.29—

(i)　a magistrates' court determines the application, and

(ii)　a person who is entitled to apply under that rule wants to appeal against that decision to the Crown Court under section 47O(2) of the 2002 Act.

(2)　The appellant must serve an appeal notice—

(a)　on the Crown Court officer and on any other party; and

(b)　not more than 21 days after the magistrates' court's decision, or, if applicable, service of notice under rule 33.29(5).

(3)　The appeal notice must—

(a)　specify the decision under appeal;

(b)　where paragraph (1)(a) applies, explain why the detention period should be extended;

(c)　where paragraph (1)(b) applies, propose the order that the appellant wants the court to make, and explain why.

(4)　Rule 34.11 (Constitution of the Crown Court) applies on such an appeal.

[Note. Under section 47O of the Proceeds of Crime Act 2002, one of those entitled to apply for an order under section 47M of that Act (extension of detention of property) may appeal against a refusal to make an order, and one of those entitled to apply for the variation or discharge of such an order, under section 47N of that Act, may appeal against the decision on such an application.

On an appeal to which this rule applies, hearsay evidence within the meaning of section 1(2) of the Civil Evidence Act 1995 is admissible: see section 47Q of the 2002 Act.]

Restraint and receivership proceedings: rules that apply generally

R33.32　**Taking control of goods and forfeiture**

33.32 (1)　This rule applies to applications under sections 58(2) and (3) and 59(2) and (3) of the Proceeds of Crime Act 2002[40] for leave of the Crown Court to take control of goods or levy distress against property, or to exercise a right of forfeiture by peaceable re-entry in relation to a tenancy, in circumstances where the property or tenancy is the subject of a restraint order or a receiver has been appointed in respect of the property or tenancy.

(2)　The application must be made in writing to the Crown Court.

(3)　The application must be served on—

(a)　the person who applied for the restraint order or the order appointing the receiver; and

(b)　any receiver appointed in respect of the property or tenancy,

at least 7 days before the date fixed by the court for hearing the application, unless the Crown Court specifies a shorter period.

R33.33　**Joining of applications**

33.33　An application for the appointment of a management receiver or enforcement receiver under rule 33.56 may be joined with—

(a)　an application for a restraint order under rule 33.51; and

(b)　an application for the conferral of powers on the receiver under rule 33.57.

R33.34　**Applications to be dealt with in writing**

33.34　Applications in restraint proceedings and receivership proceedings are to be dealt with without a hearing, unless the Crown Court orders otherwise.

R33.35　**Business in chambers**

33.35　Restraint proceedings and receivership proceedings may be heard in chambers.

---

[39]　2002 c. 29; section 47O was inserted by section 55 of the Policing and Crime Act 2009 (c. 26).

[40]　2002 c. 29; section 58(2) was amended by section 62(3) of, and paragraphs 142 and 143 of Schedule 13 of the Tribunals, Courts and Enforcement Act 2007 (c. 15).

Criminal Procedure Rules

Power of court to control evidence R33.36

33.36 (1) When hearing restraint proceedings and receivership proceedings, the Crown Court may control the evidence by giving directions as to—

(a) the issues on which it requires evidence;

(b) the nature of the evidence which it requires to decide those issues; and

(c) the way in which the evidence is to be placed before the court.

(2) The court may use its power under this rule to exclude evidence that would otherwise be admissible.

(3) The court may limit cross-examination in restraint proceedings and receivership proceedings.

Evidence of witnesses R33.37

33.37 (1) The general rule is that, unless the Crown Court orders otherwise, any fact which needs to be proved in restraint proceedings or receivership proceedings by the evidence of a witness is to be proved by their evidence in writing.

(2) Where evidence is to be given in writing under this rule, any party may apply to the Crown Court for permission to cross-examine the person giving the evidence.

(3) If the Crown Court gives permission under paragraph (2) but the person in question does not attend as required by the order, his evidence may not be used unless the court gives permission.

Witness summons R33.38

33.38 (1) Any party to restraint proceedings or receivership proceedings may apply to the Crown Court to issue a witness summons requiring a witness to—

(a) attend court to give evidence; or

(b) produce documents to the court.

(2) Rule 17.3 (Application for summons, warrant or order: general rules) applies to an application under this rule as it applies to an application under section 2 of the Criminal Procedure (Attendance of Witnesses) Act 1965[41].

Hearsay evidence R33.39

33.39 Section 2(1) of the Civil Evidence Act 1995[42] (duty to give notice of intention to rely on hearsay evidence) does not apply to evidence in restraint proceedings and receivership proceedings.

Disclosure and inspection of documents R33.40

33.40 (1) This rule applies where, in the course of restraint proceedings or receivership proceedings, an issue arises as to whether property is realisable property.

(2) The Crown Court may make an order for disclosure of documents.

(3) Part 31 of the Civil Procedure Rules 1998[43] as amended from time to time shall have effect as if the proceedings were proceedings in the High Court.

Court documents R33.41

33.41 (1) Any order which the Crown Court issues in restraint proceedings or receivership proceedings must—

(a) state the name and judicial title of the person who made it;

(b) bear the date on which it is made; and

(c) be sealed by the Crown Court.

(2) The Crown Court may place the seal on the order—

(a) by hand; or

(b) by printing a facsimile of the seal on the order whether electronically or otherwise.

(3) A document purporting to bear the court's seal shall be admissible in evidence without further proof.

Consent orders R33.42

33.42 (1) This rule applies where all the parties to restraint proceedings or receivership proceedings agree the terms in which an order should be made.

(2) Any party may apply for a judgment or order in the terms agreed.

(3) The Crown Court may deal with an application under paragraph (2) without a hearing.

---

[41] 1965 c. 69; section 2 was substituted, together with sections 2 A to 2E, by section 66 of the Criminal Procedure and Investigations Act 1996 (c. 25) and amended by section 119 of, and paragraph 8 of Schedule 8 to, the Crime and Disorder Act 1998 (c. 37), section 109 of, and paragraph 126 of Schedule 8 to, the Courts Act 2003 (c. 39), paragraph 42 of Schedule 3 and Part 4 of Schedule 37 to the Criminal Justice Act 2003 (c. 44), section 169 of the Serious Organised Crime and Police Act 2005 (c. 15) and paragraph 33 of Schedule 17 to the Crime and Courts Act 2013 (c. 22).

[42] 1995 c. 38.

[43] S.I. 1998/3132; amending instruments relevant to this Part are S.I. 2000/221 and 2001/4015.

(4) Where this rule applies—
  (a) the order which is agreed by the parties must be drawn up in the terms agreed;
  (b) it must be expressed as being 'By Consent'; and
  (c) it must be signed by the legal representative acting for each of the parties to whom the order relates or by the party if he is a litigant in person.

(5) Where an application is made under this rule, then the requirements of any other rule as to the procedure for making an application do not apply.

R33.43 Slips and omissions

33.43 (1) The Crown Court may at any time correct an accidental slip or omission in an order made in restraint proceedings or receivership proceedings.

(2) A party may apply for a correction without notice.

R33.44 Supply of documents from court records

33.44 (1) No document relating to restraint proceedings or receivership proceedings may be supplied from the records of the Crown Court for any person to inspect or copy unless the Crown Court grants permission.

(2) An application for permission under paragraph (1) must be made on notice to the parties to the proceedings.

R33.45 Disclosure of documents in criminal proceedings

33.45 (1) This rule applies where—
  (a) proceedings for an offence have been started in the Crown Court and the defendant has not been either convicted or acquitted on all counts; and
  (b) an application for a restraint order under section 42(1) of the Proceeds of Crime Act 2002 has been made.

(2) The judge presiding at the proceedings for the offence may be supplied from the records of the Crown Court with documents relating to restraint proceedings and any receivership proceedings.

(3) Such documents must not otherwise be disclosed in the proceedings for the offence.

R33.46 Preparation of documents

33.46 (1) Every order in restraint proceedings or receivership proceedings must be drawn up by the Crown Court unless—
  (a) the Crown Court orders a party to draw it up;
  (b) a party, with the permission of the Crown Court, agrees to draw it up; or
  (c) the order is made by consent under rule 33.42.

(2) The Crown Court may direct that—
  (a) an order drawn up by a party must be checked by the Crown Court before it is sealed; or
  (b) before an order is drawn up by the Crown Court, the parties must lodge an agreed statement of its terms.

(3) Where an order is to be drawn up by a party—
  (a) he must lodge it with the Crown Court no later than 7 days after the date on which the court ordered or permitted him to draw it up so that it can be sealed by the Crown Court; and
  (b) if he fails to lodge it within that period, any other party may draw it up and lodge it.

(4) Nothing in this rule shall require the Crown Court to accept a document which is illegible, has not been duly authorised, or is unsatisfactory for some other similar reason.

R33.47 Order for costs

33.47 (1) This rule authorises the Crown Court, in addition to its other powers, to order a party to pay another party's costs in restraint or receivership proceedings.

(2) The court may make such an order—
  (a) on application by the party who incurred the costs; or
  (b) on its own initiative.

(3) A party who wants the court to make such an order must apply—
  (a) during the proceedings; or
  (b) as soon as practicable following the conclusion of the proceedings, and in any event within 28 days of that conclusion.

(4) Where the court is deciding whether to make such an order it has discretion as to—
  (a) whether costs are payable by one party to another;
  (b) the amount of those costs; and
  (c) when they are to be paid.

(5) If the court decides to make an order about costs—
  (a) the general rule is that the unsuccessful party must be ordered to pay the costs of the successful party; but
  (b) the court may make a different order.

(6) In deciding what order (if any) to make about costs, the court must have regard to all of the circumstances, including—
  (a) the conduct of all the parties; and
  (b) whether a party has succeeded on part of an application, even if he has not been wholly successful.

(7) The orders which the court may make include an order that a party must pay—
  (a) a proportion of another party's costs;
  (b) a stated amount in respect of another party's costs;
  (c) costs from or until a certain date only;
  (d) costs incurred before proceedings have begun;
  (e) costs relating to particular steps taken in the proceedings;
  (f) costs relating only to a distinct part of the proceedings; and
  (g) interest on costs from or until a certain date, including a date before the making of an order.

(8) Where the court would otherwise consider making an order under paragraph (7)(f), it must instead, if practicable, make an order under paragraph (7)(a) or (c).

(9) Where the court has ordered a party to pay costs, it may order an amount to be paid on account before the costs are assessed.

(10) The court may extend the time limit under paragraph (3)(b) even after it has expired

[Note. See section 52 of the Senior Courts Act 1981[44].]

Assessment of costs   R33.48

33.48 (1) Where the Crown Court has made an order for costs in restraint proceedings or receivership proceedings it may either—
  (a) make an assessment of the costs itself; or
  (b) order assessment of the costs under rule 45.11.

(2) In either case, the Crown Court or the assessing authority, as the case may be, must—
  (a) only allow costs which are proportionate to the matters in issue; and
  (b) resolve any doubt which it may have as to whether the costs were reasonably incurred or reasonable and proportionate in favour of the paying party.

(3) The Crown Court or the assessing authority, as the case may be, is to have regard to all the circumstances in deciding whether costs were proportionately or reasonably incurred or proportionate and reasonable in amount.

(4) In particular, the Crown Court or the assessing authority must give effect to any orders which have already been made.

(5) The Crown Court or the assessing authority must also have regard to—
  (a) the conduct of all the parties, including in particular, conduct before, as well as during, the proceedings;
  (b) the amount or value of the property involved;
  (c) the importance of the matter to all the parties;
  (d) the particular complexity of the matter or the difficulty or novelty of the questions raised;
  (e) the skill, effort, specialised knowledge and responsibility involved;
  (f) the time spent on the application; and
  (g) the place where and the circumstances in which work or any part of it was done.

Time for complying with an order for costs   R33.49

33.49 A party to restraint proceedings or receivership proceedings must comply with an order for the payment of costs within 14 days of—
  (a) the date of the order if it states the amount of those costs;
  (b) if the amount of those costs is decided later under rule 45.11, the date of the assessing authority's decision; or
  (c) in either case, such later date as the Crown Court may specify.

Criminal Procedure Rules

---

[44] 1981 c. 54; section 52 was amended by section 31 of, and Part II of Schedule 1 to, the Prosecution of Offences Act 1985 (c. 23), section 4 of the Courts and Legal Services Act 1990 (c. 41), article 3 and paragraphs 11 and 12(a) of the Schedule to S.I. 2004/2035 and section 59 of, and paragraph 26 of Schedule 11 to, the Constitutional Reform Act 2005 (c. 4). The Act's title was amended by section 59(5) of, and paragraph 1 of Schedule 11 to, the Constitutional Reform Act 2005 (c. 4).

R33.50 **Application of costs rules**

33.50 Rules 33.47, 33.48 and 33.49 do not apply to the assessment of costs in proceedings to the extent that section 11 of the Access to Justice Act 1999[45] applies and provisions made under that Act make different provision.

Restraint proceedings

R33.51 **Application for restraint order or ancillary order**

33.51 (1) This rule applies where the prosecutor, or an accredited financial investigator, makes an application under section 42 of the Proceeds of Crime Act 2002[46] for—

   (a) a restraint order, under section 41(1) of the 2002 Act; or

   (b) an ancillary order, under section 41(7) of that Act, for the purpose of ensuring that a restraint order is effective.

(2) The application may be made without notice if the application is urgent or if there are reasonable grounds for believing that giving notice would cause the dissipation of realisable property which is the subject of the application.

(3) An application for a restraint order must be in writing and supported by a witness statement which must—

   (a) give the grounds for the application;

   (b) to the best of the witness' ability, give full details of the realisable property in respect of which the applicant is seeking the order and specify the person holding that realisable property;

   (c) include the proposed terms of the order.

(4) An application for an ancillary order must be in writing and supported by a witness statement which must—

   (a) give the grounds for, and full details of, the application;

   (b) include, if appropriate—

     (i) any request for an order for disclosure of documents to which rule 33.40 applies (Disclosure and inspection of documents),

     (ii) the identity of any person whom the applicant wants the court to examine about the extent or whereabouts of realisable property,

     (iii) a list of the main questions that the applicant wants to ask any such person, and

     (iv) a list of any documents to which the applicant wants to refer such a person; and

   (c) include the proposed terms of the order.

(5) An application for a restraint order and an application for an ancillary order may (but need not) be made at the same time and contained in the same documents.

(6) An application by an accredited financial investigator must include a statement that, under section 68 of the 2002 Act[47], the applicant has authority to apply.

R33.52 **Restraint and ancillary orders**

33.52 (1) The Crown Court may make a restraint order subject to exceptions, including, but not limited to, exceptions for reasonable living expenses and reasonable legal expenses, and for the purpose of enabling any person to carry on any trade, business or occupation.

(2) But the Crown Court must not make an exception for legal expenses where this is prohibited by section 41(4) of the Proceeds of Crime Act 2002.

(3) An exception to a restraint order may be made subject to conditions.

(4) The Crown Court must not require the applicant for a restraint order to give any undertaking relating to damages sustained as a result of the restraint order by a person who is prohibited from dealing with realisable property by the restraint order.

(5) The Crown Court may require the applicant for a restraint order to give an undertaking to pay the reasonable expenses of any person, other than a person who is prohibited from dealing with realisable property by the restraint order, which are incurred in complying with the restraint order.

(6) An order must include a statement that disobedience of the order, either by a person to whom the order is addressed, or by another person, may be contempt of court and the order must include details of the possible consequences of being held in contempt of court.

---

[45] 1999 c. 22; section 11 was repealed by section 39 of, and paragraph 51 of Schedule 5 to, the Legal Aid, Sentencing and Punishment of Offenders Act 2012 (c. 10) with saving and transitional provisions made by regulations 6, 7 and 8 of S.I. 2013/534.

[46] 2002 c. 29; section 42 was amended by sections 74(2) and 92 of, and paragraphs 1 and 23 of Schedule 8, and Schedule 14 to, the Serious Crime Act 2007 (c. 27) and section 12 of the Serious Crime Act 2015 (c. 9).

[47] 2002 c. 29; section 68 was amended by section 50 of the Commissioners for Revenue and Customs Act 2005 (c. 11).

(7) Unless the Crown Court otherwise directs, an order made without notice has effect until the court makes an order varying or discharging it.

(8) The applicant for an order must—

    (a) serve copies of the order and of the witness statement made in support of the application on the defendant and any person who is prohibited by the order from dealing with realisable property; and

    (b) notify any person whom the applicant knows to be affected by the order of its terms.

Application for discharge or variation of restraint or ancillary order by a person affected by the order   **R33.53**

33.53 (1) This rule applies where a person affected by a restraint order makes an application to the Crown Court under section 42(3) of the Proceeds of Crime Act 2002 to discharge or vary the restraint order or any ancillary order made under section 41(7) of the Act.

(2) The application must be in writing and may be supported by a witness statement.

(3) The application and any witness statement must be lodged with the Crown Court.

(4) The application and any witness statement must be served on the person who applied for the restraint order and any person who is prohibited from dealing with realisable property by the restraint order (if he is not the person making the application) at least 2 days before the date fixed by the court for hearing the application, unless the Crown Court specifies a shorter period.

Application for variation of restraint or ancillary order by the person who applied for the order   **R33.54**

33.54 (1) This rule applies where the applicant for a restraint order makes an application under section 42(3) of the Proceeds of Crime Act 2002 to the Crown Court to vary the restraint order or any ancillary order made under section 41(7) of the 2002 Act (including where the court has already made a restraint order and the applicant is seeking to vary the order in order to restrain further realisable property).

(2) The application may be made without notice if the application is urgent or if there are reasonable grounds for believing that giving notice would cause the dissipation of realisable property which is the subject of the application.

(3) The application must be in writing and must be supported by a witness statement which must—

    (a) give the grounds for the application;

    (b) where the application is for the inclusion of further realisable property in a restraint order give full details, to the best of the witness's ability, of the realisable property in respect of which the applicant is seeking the order and specify the person holding that realisable property;

    (c) where the application is to vary an ancillary order, include, if appropriate—

        (i) any request for an order for disclosure of documents to which rule 33.40 applies (Disclosure and inspection of documents),

        (ii) the identity of any person whom the applicant wants the court to examine about the extent or whereabouts of realisable property,

        (iii) a list of the main questions that the applicant wants to ask any such person, and

        (iv) a list of any documents to which the applicant wants to refer such a person; and

    (d) include the proposed terms of the variation.

(4) An application by an accredited financial investigator must include a statement that, under section 68 of the 2002 Act, the applicant has authority to apply.

(5) The application and witness statement must be lodged with the Crown Court.

(6) Except where, under paragraph (2), notice of the application is not required to be served, the application and witness statement must be served on any person who is prohibited from dealing with realisable property by the restraint order at least 2 days before the date fixed by the court for hearing the application, unless the Crown Court specifies a shorter period.

(7) If the court makes an order for the variation of a restraint or ancillary order, the applicant must serve copies of the order and of the witness statement made in support of the application on—

    (a) the defendant;

    (b) any person who is prohibited from dealing with realisable property by the restraint order (whether before or after the variation); and

    (c) any other person whom the applicant knows to be affected by the order.

Application for discharge of restraint or ancillary order by the person who applied for the order   **R33.55**

33.55 (1) This rule applies where the applicant for a restraint order makes an application under section 42(3) of the Proceeds of Crime Act 2002 to discharge the order or any ancillary order made under section 41(7) of the 2002 Act.

(2) The application may be made without notice.

(3) The application must be in writing and must state the grounds for the application.

(4) If the court makes an order for the discharge of a restraint or ancillary order, the applicant must serve copies of the order on—

(a) the defendant;

(b) any person who is prohibited from dealing with realisable property by the restraint order (whether before or after the discharge); and

(c) any other person whom the applicant knows to be affected by the order.

Receivership proceedings

R33.56   Application for appointment of a management or an enforcement receiver

33.56 (1) This rule applies to an application for the appointment of a management receiver under section 48(1) of the Proceeds of Crime Act 2002[48] and an application for the appointment of an enforcement receiver under section 50(1) of the 2002 Act.

(2) The application may be made without notice if—

(a) the application is joined with an application for a restraint order under rule 33.51 (Application for restraint order or ancillary order);

(b) the application is urgent; or

(c) there are reasonable grounds for believing that giving notice would cause the dissipation of realisable property which is the subject of the application.

(3) The application must be in writing and must be supported by a witness statement which must—

(a) give the grounds for the application;

(b) give full details of the proposed receiver;

(c) to the best of the witness' ability, give full details of the realisable property in respect of which the applicant is seeking the order and specify the person holding that realisable property;

(d) where the application is made by an accredited financial investigator, include a statement that, under section 68 of the 2002 Act, the applicant has authority to apply; and

(e) if the proposed receiver is not a person falling within section 55(8) of the 2002 Act[49] and the applicant is asking the court to allow the receiver to act—

(i)   without giving security, or

(ii) before he has given security or satisfied the court that he has security in place,

explain the reasons why that is necessary.

(4) Where the application is for the appointment of an enforcement receiver, the applicant must provide the Crown Court with a copy of the confiscation order made against the defendant.

(5) The application and witness statement must be lodged with the Crown Court.

(6) Except where, under paragraph (2), notice of the application is not required to be served, the application and witness statement must be lodged with the Crown Court and served on—

(a) the defendant;

(b) any person who holds realisable property to which the application relates; and

(c) any other person whom the applicant knows to be affected by the application,

at least 7 days before the date fixed by the court for hearing the application, unless the Crown Court specifies a shorter period.

(7) If the court makes an order for the appointment of a receiver, the applicant must serve copies of the order and of the witness statement made in support of the application on—

(a) the defendant;

(b) any person who holds realisable property to which the order applies; and

(c) any other person whom the applicant knows to be affected by the order.

R33.57   Application for conferral of powers on a management receiver or an enforcement receiver

33.57 (1) This rule applies to an application for the conferral of powers on a management receiver under section 49(1) of the Proceeds of Crime Act 2002 or an enforcement receiver under section 51(1) of the 2002 Act.

(2) The application may be made without notice if the application is to give the receiver power to take possession of property and—

(a) the application is joined with an application for a restraint order under rule 33.51 (Application for restraint order or ancillary order);

(b) the application is urgent; or

---

[48] 2002 c. 29.

[49] 2002 c. 29; section 55(8) was amended by section 51(1) and (2) of the Policing and Crime Act 2009 (c. 26).

Criminal Procedure Rules

(c)   there are reasonable grounds for believing that giving notice would cause the dissipation of the property which is the subject of the application.
(3)   The application must be made in writing and supported by a witness statement which must—
    (a)   give the grounds for the application;
    (b)   give full details of the realisable property in respect of which the applicant is seeking the order and specify the person holding that realisable property;
    (c)   where the application is made by an accredited financial investigator, include a statement that, under section 68 of the 2002 Act, the applicant has authority to apply; and
    (d)   where the application is for power to start, carry on or defend legal proceedings in respect of the property, explain—
        (i)   what proceedings are concerned, in what court, and
        (ii)   what powers the receiver will ask that court to exercise.
(4)   Where the application is for the conferral of powers on an enforcement receiver, the applicant must provide the Crown Court with a copy of the confiscation order made against the defendant.
(5)   The application and witness statement must be lodged with the Crown Court.
(6)   Except where, under paragraph (2), notice of the application is not required to be served, the application and witness statement must be served on—
    (a)   the defendant;
    (b)   any person who holds realisable property in respect of which a receiver has been appointed or in respect of which an application for a receiver has been made;
    (c)   any other person whom the applicant knows to be affected by the application; and
    (d)   the receiver (if one has already been appointed),
    at least 7 days before the date fixed by the court for hearing the application, unless the Crown Court specifies a shorter period.
(7)   If the court makes an order for the conferral of powers on a receiver, the applicant must serve copies of the order on—
    (a)   the defendant;
    (b)   any person who holds realisable property in respect of which the receiver has been appointed; and
    (c)   any other person whom the applicant knows to be affected by the order.

Applications for discharge or variation of receivership orders, and applications for other orders   **R33.58**

33.58 (1)   This rule applies to applications under section 62(3) of the Proceeds of Crime Act 2002 for orders (by persons affected by the action of receivers) and applications under section 63(1) of the 2002 Act[50] for the discharge or variation of orders relating to receivers.
(2)   The application must be made in writing and lodged with the Crown Court.
(3)   The application must be served on the following persons (except where they are the person making the application)—
    (a)   the person who applied for appointment of the receiver;
    (b)   the defendant;
    (c)   any person who holds realisable property in respect of which the receiver has been appointed;
    (d)   the receiver; and
    (e)   any other person whom the applicant knows to be affected by the application,
    at least 7 days before the date fixed by the court for hearing the application, unless the Crown Court specifies a shorter period.
(4)   If the court makes an order for the discharge or variation of an order relating to a receiver under section 63(2) of the 2002 Act, the applicant must serve copies of the order on any persons whom he knows to be affected by the order.

Sums in the hands of receivers   **R33.59**

33.59 (1)   This rule applies where the amount payable under a confiscation order has been fully paid and any sums remain in the hands of an enforcement receiver.
(2)   The receiver must make an application to the Crown Court for directions as to the distribution of the sums in his hands.
(3)   The application and any evidence which the receiver intends to rely on in support of the application must be served on—
    (a)   the defendant; and
    (b)   any other person who held (or holds) interests in any property realised by the receiver,

---

[50] 2002 c. 29; section 63(1) was amended by section 74(2) of, and paragraphs 1 and 30 of Schedule 8 to, the Serious Crime Act 2007 (c. 27).

at least 7 days before the date fixed by the court for hearing the application, unless the Crown Court specifies a shorter period.

(4) If any of the provisions listed in paragraph (5) (provisions as to the vesting of funds in a trustee in bankruptcy) apply, then the Crown Court must make a declaration to that effect.

(5) These are the provisions—

  (a) section 82 of the Bankruptcy (Scotland) Act 2016[51];

  (b) section 306B of the Insolvency Act 1986[52]; and

  (c) article 279B of the Insolvency (Northern Ireland) Order 1989[53].

R33.60   **Security**

33.60 (1) This rule applies where the Crown Court appoints a receiver under section 48 or 50 of the Proceeds of Crime Act 2002 and the receiver is not a person falling within section 55(8) of the 2002 Act[54] (and it is immaterial whether the receiver is a permanent or temporary member of staff or on secondment from elsewhere).

(2) The Crown Court may direct that before the receiver begins to act, or within a specified time, he must either—

  (a) give such security as the Crown Court may determine; or

  (b) file with the Crown Court and serve on all parties to any receivership proceedings evidence that he already has in force sufficient security,

to cover his liability for his acts and omissions as a receiver.

(3) The Crown Court may terminate the appointment of a receiver if he fails to—

  (a) give the security; or

  (b) satisfy the court as to the security he has in force,

by the date specified.

R33.61   **Remuneration**

33.61 (1) This rule applies where the Crown Court appoints a receiver under section 48 or 50 of the Proceeds of Crime Act 2002 and the receiver is not a person falling within section 55(8) of the 2002 Act (and it is immaterial whether the receiver is a permanent or temporary member of staff or on secondment from elsewhere).

(2) The receiver may only charge for his services if the Crown Court—

  (a) so directs; and

  (b) specifies the basis on which the receiver is to be remunerated.

(3) Unless the Crown Court orders otherwise, in determining the remuneration of the receiver, the Crown Court shall award such sum as is reasonable and proportionate in all the circumstances and which takes into account—

  (a) the time properly given by him and his staff to the receivership;

  (b) the complexity of the receivership;

  (c) any responsibility of an exceptional kind or degree which falls on the receiver in consequence of the receivership;

  (d) the effectiveness with which the receiver appears to be carrying out, or to have carried out, his duties; and

  (e) the value and nature of the subject matter of the receivership.

(4) The Crown Court may refer the determination of a receiver's remuneration to be ascertained by the taxing authority of the Crown Court and rules 45.11 (Assessment and re-assessment) to 45.14 (Application for an extension of time) shall have effect as if the taxing authority was ascertaining costs.

(5) A receiver appointed under section 48 of the 2002 Act is to receive his remuneration by realising property in respect of which he is appointed, in accordance with section 49(2)(d) of the 2002 Act.

(6) A receiver appointed under section 50 of the 2002 Act is to receive his remuneration by applying to the magistrates' court officer for payment under section 55(4)(b) of the 2002 Act[55].

---

[51] 2016 asp 21.

[52] 1986 c. 45; section 306B was inserted by section 456 of, and paragraphs 1 and 16 of Schedule 11 to, the Proceeds of Crime Act 2002 (c. 29).

[53] S.I. 1989/2405 (N.I. 19); article 279B was inserted by section 456 of, and paragraph 20(3) of Schedule 11 to, the Proceeds of Crime Act 2002 (c. 29).

[54] 2002 c. 29; section 55(8) was amended by section 51(1) and (2) of the Policing and Crime Act 2009 (c. 26).

[55] 2002 c. 29; section 55(4)(b) was amended by paragraph 408 of Schedule 8 to, the Courts Act 2003 (c. 39).

Accounts   R33.62

33.62 (1) The Crown Court may order a receiver appointed under section 48 or 50 of the Proceeds of Crime Act 2002 to prepare and serve accounts.

(2) A party to receivership proceedings served with such accounts may apply for an order permitting him to inspect any document in the possession of the receiver relevant to those accounts.

(3) Any party to receivership proceedings may, within 14 days of being served with the accounts, serve notice on the receiver—

  (a) specifying any item in the accounts to which he objects;

  (b) giving the reason for such objection; and

  (c) requiring the receiver within 14 days of receipt of the notice, either—

    (i) to notify all the parties who were served with the accounts that he accepts the objection, or

    (ii) if he does not accept the objection, to apply for an examination of the accounts in relation to the contested item.

(4) When the receiver applies for the examination of the accounts he must at the same time lodge with the Crown Court—

  (a) the accounts; and

  (b) a copy of the notice served on him under this section of the rule.

(5) If the receiver fails to comply with paragraph (3)(c) of this rule, any party to receivership proceedings may apply to the Crown Court for an examination of the accounts in relation to the contested item.

(6) At the conclusion of its examination of the accounts the court must certify the result.

Non-compliance by receiver   R33.63

33.63 (1) If a receiver appointed under section 48 or 50 of the Proceeds of Crime Act 2002 fails to comply with any rule, practice direction or direction of the Crown Court, the Crown Court may order him to attend a hearing to explain his non-compliance.

(2) At the hearing, the Crown Court may make any order it considers appropriate, including—

  (a) terminating the appointment of the receiver;

  (b) reducing the receiver's remuneration or disallowing it altogether; and

  (c) ordering the receiver to pay the costs of any party.

Proceedings under the Criminal Justice Act 1988 and the Drug Trafficking Act 1994

[Note. The relevant provisions of the 1988 and 1994 Acts were repealed on 24th March 2003, but they continue to have effect in respect of proceedings for offences committed before that date.]

Statements, etc. relevant to making confiscation orders   R33.64

33.64 (1) Where a prosecutor or defendant—

  (a) serves on the magistrates' court officer any statement or other document under section 73 of the Criminal Justice Act 1988[56] in any proceedings in respect of an offence listed in Schedule 4 to that Act; or

  (b) serves on the Crown Court officer any statement or other document under section 11 of the Drug Trafficking Act 1994[57] or section 73 of the 1988 Act in any proceedings in respect of a drug trafficking offence or in respect of an offence to which Part VI of the 1988 Act applies,

that party must serve a copy as soon as practicable on the defendant or the prosecutor, as the case may be.

(2) Any statement tendered by the prosecutor to the magistrates' court under section 73 of the 1988 Act or to the Crown Court under section 11(1) of the 1994 Act or section 73(1A) of the 1988 Act must include the following particulars—

  (a) the name of the defendant;

  (b) the name of the person by whom the statement is made and the date on which it was made;

  (c) where the statement is not tendered immediately after the defendant has been convicted, the date on which and the place where the relevant conviction occurred; and

  (d) such information known to the prosecutor as is relevant to the determination as to whether or not the defendant has benefited from drug trafficking or relevant criminal

---

[56] 1988 c. 33; section 73 and Schedule 4 were repealed, with savings, by paragraphs 1 and 17 of Schedule 11 and Schedule 12 to, the Proceeds of Crime Act 2002 (c. 29).
[57] 1994 c. 37; section 11 was repealed, with savings, by paragraphs 1 and 25 of Schedule 11 and Schedule 12 to, the Proceeds of Crime Act 2002 (c. 29).

conduct and to the assessment of the value of any proceeds of drug trafficking or, as the case may be, benefit from relevant criminal conduct.

(3) Where, in accordance with section 11(7) of the 1994 Act or section 73(1C) of the 1988 Act, the defendant indicates in writing the extent to which he or she accepts any allegation contained within the prosecutor's statement, the defendant must serve a copy of that reply on the court officer.

(4) Expressions used in this rule have the same meanings as in the 1994 Act or, where appropriate, the 1988 Act.

R33.65   Postponed determinations

33.65 (1) Where an application is made by the defendant or the prosecutor—

(a) to a magistrates' court under section 72A(5)(a) of the Criminal Justice Act 1988[58] asking the court to exercise its powers under section 72A(4) of that Act; or

(b) to the Crown Court under section 3(5)(a) of the Drug Trafficking Act 1994[59] asking the Court to exercise its powers under section 3(4) of that Act, or under section 72A(5)(a) of the 1988 Act asking the court to exercise its powers under section 72A(4) of the 1988 Act, the application must be in writing and the applicant must serve a copy on the prosecutor or the defendant, as the case may be.

(2) A party served with a copy of an application under paragraph (1) must, within 28 days of the date of service, notify the applicant and the court officer, in writing, whether or not that party opposes the application, giving reasons for any opposition.

(3) After the expiry of the period referred to in paragraph (2), the court may determine an application under paragraph (1) —

(a) without a hearing; or

(b) at a hearing at which the parties may be represented.

R33.66   Confiscation orders—revised assessments

33.66 (1) Where the prosecutor or a receiver makes an application under section 13, 14, 15, 16 or 17 of the Drug Trafficking Act 1994[60] or section 74A, 74B, 74C or 83 of the Criminal Justice Act 1988[61], the application must be in writing and a copy must be served on the defendant.

(2) The application must include the following particulars—

(a) the name of the defendant;

(b) the date on which and the place where any relevant conviction occurred;

(c) the date on which and the place where any relevant confiscation order was made or, as the case may be, varied;

(d) the grounds on which the application is made;

(e) an indication of the evidence available to support the application; and

(f) a copy of any certificate issued by the High Court.

R33.67   Application to the Crown Court to discharge or vary order to make material available

33.67 (1) Where an order under section 93H of the Criminal Justice Act 1988[62] (order to make material available) or section 55 of the Drug Trafficking Act 1994[63] (order to make material available) has been made by the Crown Court, any person affected by it may apply in writing to the court officer for the order to be discharged or varied, and on hearing such an application the court may discharge the order or make such variations to it as the court thinks fit.

(2) Subject to paragraph (3), where a person proposes to make an application under paragraph (1) for the discharge or variation of an order, that person must give a copy of the application, not later than 48 hours before the making of the application—

(a) to a constable at the police station specified in the order; or

(b) to the office of the appropriate officer who made the application, as specified in the order,

---

[58] 1988 c. 33; section 72A was inserted by section 28 of the Criminal Justice Act 1993 (c. 36) and repealed, with savings, by sections 456 and 457 of, and paragraphs 1 and 17 of Schedule 11, and Schedule 12 to, the Proceeds of Crime Act 2002 (c. 29).

[59] 1994 c. 37; section 3 was repealed, with savings, by paragraphs 1 and 25 of Schedule 11 and Schedule 12 to, the Proceeds of Crime Act 2002 (c. 29).

[60] 1994 c. 37; sections 13, 14 and 15 were repealed, with savings, by paragraphs 1 and 25 of Schedule 11 and Schedule 12 to, the Proceeds of Crime Act 2002 (c. 29).

[61] 1988 c. 33; sections 74A, 74B and 74C were inserted by the Proceeds of Crime Act 1995 (c. 11), sections 5, 6 and 7 respectively, and repealed, with savings by paragraphs 1 and 17 of Schedule 11 and Schedule 12 to, the Proceeds of Crime Act 2002 (c. 29).

[62] 1988 c. 33; section 93H was inserted by section 11 of the Proceeds of Crime Act 1995 (c. 11) and repealed, with savings, by paragraphs 1 and 17 of Schedule 11 and Schedule 12 to, the Proceeds of Crime Act 2002 (c. 29).

[63] 1994 c. 37; section 55 was amended by paragraphs 1 and 25 of Schedule 11 and Schedule 12 to, the Proceeds of Crime Act 2002 (c. 29) and by paragraph 364 of Schedule 8 to the Courts Act 2003 (c. 39).

in either case together with a notice indicating the time and place at which the application for discharge or variation is to be made.

(3) The court may direct that paragraph (2) need not be complied with if satisfied that the person making the application has good reason to seek a discharge or variation of the order as soon as possible and it is not practicable to comply with that paragraph.

(4) In this rule:

'constable' includes a person commissioned by the Commissioners for [His] Majesty's Revenue and Customs;

'police station' includes a place for the time being occupied by [His] Majesty's Revenue and Customs.

Application to the Crown Court for increase in term of imprisonment in default of payment   R33.68

33.68 (1) This rule applies to applications made, or that have effect as made, to the Crown Court under section 10 of the Drug Trafficking Act 1994[64] and section 75A of the Criminal Justice Act 1988[65] (interest on sums unpaid under confiscation orders).

(2) Notice of an application to which this rule applies to increase the term of imprisonment or detention fixed in default of payment of a confiscation order by a person ('the defendant') must be made by the prosecutor in writing to the court officer.

(3) A notice under paragraph (2) shall—
   (a) state the name and address of the defendant;
   (b) specify the grounds for the application;
   (c) give details of the enforcement measures taken, if any; and
   (d) include a copy of the confiscation order.

(4) On receiving a notice under paragraph (2), the court officer must—
   (a) forthwith send to the defendant and the magistrates' court required to enforce payment of the confiscation order under section 140(1) of the Powers of Criminal Courts (Sentencing) Act 2000[66], a copy of the said notice; and
   (b) notify in writing the applicant and the defendant of the date, time and place appointed for the hearing of the application.

(5) Where the Crown Court makes an order pursuant to an application mentioned in paragraph (1) above, the court officer must send forthwith a copy of the order—
   (a) to the applicant;
   (b) to the defendant;
   (c) where the defendant is at the time of the making of the order in custody, to the person having custody of him or her; and
   (d) to the magistrates' court mentioned in paragraph (4)(a).

Drug trafficking—compensation on acquittal in the Crown Court   R33.69

33.69 Where the Crown Court cancels a confiscation order under section 22(2) of the Drug Trafficking Act 1994[67], the Crown Court officer must serve notice to that effect on the High Court officer and on the court officer of the magistrates' court which has responsibility for enforcing the order.

Contempt proceedings
Application to punish for contempt of court   R33.70

33.70 (1) This rule applies where a person is accused of disobeying—
   (a) a compliance order made for the purpose of ensuring that a confiscation order is effective;
   (b) a restraint order; or
   (c) an ancillary order made for the purpose of ensuring that a restraint order is effective.

(2) An applicant who wants the Crown Court to exercise its power to punish that person for contempt of court must comply with the rules in Part 48 (Contempt of court).

[64] 1994 c. 37; section 10 was repealed, with savings, by paragraphs 1 and 25 of Schedule 11 and Schedule 12 to, the Proceeds of Crime Act 2002 (c. 29).
[65] 1988 c. 33; section 75A was inserted by section 9 of the Proceeds of Crime Act 1995 (c. 11) and repealed, with savings, by paragraphs 1 and 17 of Schedule 11 and Schedule 12 to, the Proceeds of Crime Act 2002 (c. 29).
[66] 2000 c. 6; section 140 was amended by paragraphs 74 of Schedule 3 and Part 4 of Schedule 37 to the Criminal Justice Act 2003 (c. 44) and section 40(4) of, and paragraph 69 of Schedule 9 to, the Constitutional Reform Act 2005 (c. 4). It is further amended by sections 74 and 75 of, and paragraphs 160 and 194 of Schedule 8 to, the Criminal Justice and Court Services Act 2000 (c. 43) with effect from a date to be appointed.
[67] 1994 c. 37; section 22 was repealed, with savings, by paragraphs 1 and 25 of Schedule 11 and Schedule 12 to, the Proceeds of Crime Act 2002 (c. 29).

[Note. The Crown Court has inherent power to punish for contempt of court a person who disobeys its order: see section 45 of the Senior Courts Act 1981[68].]

CRIMINAL PROCEDURE RULES   PART 34   APPEAL TO THE CROWN COURT

R34.1   **When this Part applies**

34.1   (1)   This Part applies where—

(a)   a defendant wants to appeal under—

(i)   section 108 of the Magistrates' Courts Act 1980[1],

(ii)   section 45 of the Mental Health Act 1983[2],

(iii)   section 42 of the Counter Terrorism Act 2008[3];

(iv)   paragraph 10 of Schedule 5, paragraph 6(11) or 21(6) of Schedule 7, or paragraph 10(11), 14(8) or 23(6) of Schedule 10 to the Sentencing Act 2020[4];

(b)   the Criminal Cases Review Commission refers a defendant's case to the Crown Court under section 11 of the Criminal Appeal Act 1995[5]

(c)   a prosecutor wants to appeal under—

(i)   section 14A(5A) of the Football Spectators Act 1989[6], or

(ii)   section 147(3) of the Customs and Excise Management Act 1979[7]; or

(d)   a person wants to appeal under—

(i)   section 1 of the Magistrates' Courts (Appeals from Binding Over Orders) Act 1956[8],

(ii)   section 12(5) of the Contempt of Court Act 1981[9],

(iii)   regulation 3C or 3H of the Costs in Criminal Cases (General) Regulations 1986[10],

(iv)   section 22 of the Football Spectators Act 1989[11],

(v)   section 10 of the Crime and Disorder Act 1998[12],

(vi)   section 28(5)(b) of the Offensive Weapons Act 2019[13],

(vii)   section 366(9) of the Sentencing Act 2020,

(viii) section 342I(2) of the 2020 Act[14], or

(ix)   section 46(5) of the Domestic Abuse Act 2021[15].

(2)   A reference to an 'appellant' in this Part is a reference to such a party or person.

---

[68] 1981 c. 54. The Act's title was amended by section 59(5) of, and paragraph 1 of Schedule 11 to, the Constitutional Reform Act 2005 (c. 4).

[1] 1980 c. 43; section 108 was amended by sections 66(2) and 78 of, and Schedule 16 to, the Criminal Justice Act 1982 (c. 48), section 23(3) of the Football Spectators Act 1989 (c. 37), section 101(2) of, and Schedule 13 to, the Criminal Justice Act 1991 (c. 53), sections 119 and 120(2) of, and paragraph 43 of Schedule 8 and Schedule 10 to, the Crime and Disorder Act 1998 (c. 37), section 7(2) of the Football (Offences and Disorder) Act 1999 (c. 21), section 165(1) of, and paragraph 71 of Schedule 9 to, the Powers of Criminal Courts (Sentencing) Act 2000 (c. 6), section 1 of, and Schedule 3 to, the Football (Disorder) Act 2000 (c. 25), section 58(1) of, and paragraph 10 of Schedule 10 to, the Domestic Violence, Crime and Victims Act 2004 (c. 28), section 52(2) of, and paragraph 14 of Schedule 3 to, the Violent Crime Reduction Act 2006 (c. 38) and section 64 of, and paragraph 10 of Schedule 3 to, the Animal Welfare Act 2006 (c. 45).

[2] 1983 c. 20.

[3] 2008 c. 28.

[4] 2020 c. 17.

[5] 1995 c. 35.

[6] 1989 c. 37; section 14A(5A) was inserted by section 52 of, and paragraphs 1 and 3 of Schedule 3 to, the Violent Crime Reduction Act 2006 (c. 38).

[7] 1979 c. 2.

[8] 1956 c. 44; section 1 was amended by Part 1 of Schedule 7 to, the Criminal Justice Act 1967 (c. 80), Part 1 of Schedule 9 to, the Courts Act 1971 (c. 23) and Schedule 9 to, the Magistrates' Courts Act 1980 (c. 43).

[9] 1981 c. 49; section 12(5) was amended by section 165(1) of, and paragraph 83 of Schedule 9 to, the Powers of Criminal Courts (Sentencing) Act 2000 (c. 6).

[10] S.I. 1986/1335; regulation 3C was inserted by regulation 2 of The Costs in Criminal Cases (General) (Amendment) Regulations 1991 (SI 1991/789) and amended by regulation 5 of The Costs in Criminal Cases (General) (Amendment) Regulations 2004 (SI 2004/2408). Regulation 3H was inserted by regulation 7 of The Costs in Criminal Cases (General) (Amendment) Regulations 2004 (S.I. 2004/2408).

[11] 1989 c. 37; section 22 was amended by section 5 of the Football (Offences and Disorder) Act 1999 (c. 21), section 1 of, and paragraphs 9 – 11 and 17 of Schedule 2 to, the Football (Disorder) Act 2000 (c. 25) and section 109(1) and (3) of, and paragraph 335 of Schedule 8, and Schedule 10 to, the Courts Act 2003 (c. 39).

[12] 1998 c. 37; section 10 was amended by section 15 of, and paragraphs 276 and 277 of Schedule 4 to, the Constitutional Reform Act 2005 (c. 4), section 41 of the Crime and Security Act 2010 (c. 17) and section 17 of, and paragraph 52 of Schedule 9 to, the Crime and Courts Act 2013 (c. 22).

[13] 2019 c. 17; section 28 comes into force on a date to be appointed.

[14] 2020 c. 17; section 342I is inserted by section 165 of the Police, Crime, Sentencing and Courts Act 2022 (c. 32) with effect from a date to be appointed.

[15] 2021 c. 17; section 46 comes into force on a date to be appointed.

[Note. An appeal to the Crown Court is by way of re-hearing: see section 79(3) of the Senior Courts Act 1981[16]. For the powers of the Crown Court on an appeal, see section 48 of that Act.

A defendant may appeal from a magistrates' court to the Crown Court—

 (a) *under section 108 of the Magistrates' Courts Act 1980, against sentence after a guilty plea and after a not guilty plea against conviction, against a finding of guilt or against sentence;*
 (b) *under section 45 of the Mental Health Act 1983, where the magistrates' court makes a hospital order or guardianship order without convicting the defendant;*
 (c) *under paragraph 10 of Schedule 5, paragraph 6(11) or 21(6) of Schedule 7, or paragraph 10(11), 14(8) or 23(6) of Schedule 10 to the Sentencing Act 2020, where the magistrates' court—*

   (i) *deals with the defendant for breach of a reparation order, a youth rehabilitation order or a community order,*
   (ii) *except in some circumstances, amends a reparation order, or*
   (iii) *except in some circumstances, deals with an application to revoke a reparation order or a community order.*

 (d) *under section 42 of the Counter Terrorism Act 2008, where the magistrates' court decides that an offence has a terrorist connection.*

See section 13 of the Criminal Appeal Act 1995[17] for the circumstances in which the Criminal Cases Review Commission may refer a conviction or sentence to the Crown Court.

Under section 14A(5A) of the Football Spectators Act 1989, a prosecutor may appeal to the Crown Court against a failure by a magistrates' court to make a football banning order.

Under section 147(3) of the Customs and Excise Management Act 1979, a prosecutor may appeal to the Crown Court against any decision of a magistrates' court in proceedings for an offence under any Act relating to customs or excise.

Under section 1 of the Magistrates' Courts (Appeals from Binding Over Orders) Act 1956, a person bound over to keep the peace or be of good behaviour by a magistrates' court may appeal to the Crown Court.

Under section 12(5) of the Contempt of Court Act 1981, a person detained, committed to custody or fined by a magistrates' court for insulting a member of the court or another participant in the case, or for interrupting the proceedings, may appeal to the Crown Court.

Under regulation 3C of the Costs in Criminal Cases (General) Regulations 1986, a legal representative against whom a magistrates' court makes a wasted costs order under section 19A of the Prosecution of Offences Act 1985 and regulation 3B may appeal against that order to the Crown Court.

Under regulation 3H of the Costs in Criminal Cases (General) Regulations 1986, a third party against whom a magistrates' court makes a costs order under section 19B of the Prosecution of Offences Act 1985 and regulation 3F may appeal against that order to the Crown Court.

Under section 22 of the Football Spectators Act 1989, any person aggrieved by the decision of a magistrates' court making a football banning order may appeal to the Crown Court.

Under section 10 of the Crime and Disorder Act 1998 or under section 366(9) of the Sentencing Act 2020, a person in respect of whom a magistrates' court makes a parenting order may appeal against that order to the Crown Court.

Under section 28(5)(b) of the Offensive Weapons Act 2019 an applicant to a magistrates' court for the variation, renewal or discharge of a knife crime prevention order made by that court, or a respondent to such an application, may appeal to the Crown Court against the decision of the magistrates' court.

Under section 342I(2) of the Sentencing Act 2020 an applicant to a magistrates' court for the variation, renewal or discharge of a serious violence reduction order made by that court, or a respondent to such an application, may appeal to the Crown Court against the decision of the magistrates' court.

Under section 46(5), (7) of the Domestic Abuse Act 2021 an applicant to a magistrates' court for the variation or discharge of a domestic abuse prevention order made by that court, or a respondent to such an application, may appeal to the Crown Court against the decision of the magistrates' court.]

---

[16] 1981 c. 54. The Act's title was amended by section 59(5) of, and paragraph 1 of Schedule 11 to, the Constitutional Reform Act 2005 (c. 4).
[17] 1995 c. 35; section 13 was amended by section 321 of, and paragraph 3 of Schedule 11 to, the Armed Forces Act 2006 (c.52).

R34.2   **Service of appeal and respondent's notices**

34.2   (1)   An appellant must serve an appeal notice on—
        (a)   the magistrates' court officer; and
        (b)   every other party.
    (2)   The appellant must serve the appeal notice—
        (a)   as soon after the decision appealed against as the appellant wants; but
        (b)   not more than 15 business days after—
            (i)   sentence or the date sentence is deferred or the date of committal for sentence, whichever is earlier, if the appeal is against conviction or against a finding of guilt,
            (ii)   sentence, if the appeal is against sentence, or
            (iii)   the order or failure to make an order about which the appellant wants to appeal, in any other case.
    (3)   The appellant must serve with the appeal notice any application for the following, with reasons—
        (a)   an extension of the time limit under this rule, if the appeal notice is late;
        (b)   bail pending appeal, if the appellant is in custody; or
        (c)   the suspension of any disqualification imposed or order made in the case, where the magistrates' court or the Crown Court can order such a suspension pending appeal.
    (4)   Where both the magistrates' court and the Crown Court can grant bail or suspend a disqualification or order pending appeal, an application must indicate by which court the appellant wants the application determined.
    (5)   Where the appeal is against conviction or against a finding of guilt, unless the respondent agrees that the court should allow the appeal—
        (a)   the respondent must serve a respondent's notice on—
            (i)   the Crown Court officer; and
            (ii)   the appellant; and
        (b)   the respondent must serve that notice not more than 15 business days after service of the appeal notice.

[Note. Under sections 4 and 5 of the Sentencing Act 2020[18], a magistrates' court may defer passing sentence for up to 6 months.

Under section 113 of the Magistrates' Courts Act 1980[19], the magistrates' court may grant an appellant bail pending appeal. Under section 81(1)(b) of the Senior Courts Act 1981[20], the Crown Court also may do so. See also rule 14.7.

Under section 39 of the Road Traffic Offenders Act 1988[21], a court which has made an order disqualifying a person from driving may suspend the disqualification pending appeal. Under section 40 of the 1988 Act[22], the appeal court may do so. See also rule 29.2.

Under section 129 of the Licensing Act 2003[23], a court which has made an order to forfeit or suspend a personal licence issued under that Act may suspend the order pending appeal. Under section 130 of the 2003 Act[24], the appeal court may do so.]

R34.3   **Form of appeal and respondent's notices**

34.3   (1)   The appeal notice must—
        (a)   specify—
            (i)   the conviction or finding of guilt,
            (ii)   the sentence, or
            (iii)   the order, or the failure to make an order
           about which the appellant wants to appeal;
        (b)   summarise the issues;

---

[18]   2020 c. 17.
[19]   1980 c. 43; section 113 was amended by section 168 of, and paragraph 44 of Schedule 10 to, the Criminal Justice and Public Order Act 1994 (c. 33) and section 165 of, and paragraph 72 of Schedule 9 to, the Powers of Criminal Courts (Sentencing) Act 2000 (c. 6).
[20]   1981 c.54.
[21]   1988 c. 53.
[22]   1988 c. 53; section 40 was amended by sections 40 and 59 of, and paragraph 50 of Schedule 9 and paragraph 1 of Schedule 11 to, the Constitutional Reform Act 2005 (c.4).
[23]   2003 c. 17.
[24]   2003 c. 17; section 130 was amended by sections 40 and 59 of, and paragraph 78 of Schedule 9 and paragraph 1 of Schedule 11 to, the Constitutional Reform Act 2005 (c. 4).

(c) in an appeal against conviction or against a finding of guilt, to the best of the appellant's ability and to assist the court in fulfilling its duty under rule 3.2 (the court's duty of case management)—
  (i)   identify the witnesses who gave oral evidence in the magistrates' court,
  (ii) identify the witnesses who gave written evidence in the magistrates' court,
  (iii) identify the prosecution witnesses whom the appellant will want to question if they are called to give oral evidence in the Crown Court,
  (iv) identify the likely defence witnesses,
  (v)   give notice of any special arrangements or other measures that the appellant thinks are needed for witnesses,
  (vi) explain whether the issues in the Crown Court differ from the issues in the magistrates' court, and if so how, and
  (vii) say how long the trial lasted in the magistrates' court and how long the appeal is likely to last in the Crown Court;
(d) in an appeal against a sentence, order or failure to make an order—
  (i)   identify any circumstances, report or other information of which the appellant wants the court to take account, and
  (ii) explain the significance of those circumstances or that information to what is in issue;
(e) in an appeal against a finding that the appellant insulted someone or interrupted proceedings in the magistrates' court, attach—
  (i)   the magistrates' court's written findings of fact, and
  (ii) the appellant's response to those findings;
(f) say whether the appellant has asked the magistrates' court to reconsider the case; and
(g) include a list of those on whom the appellant has served the appeal notice.
(2) A respondent's notice must—
  (a) give the date on which the respondent was served with the appeal notice; and
  (b) to assist the court in fulfilling its duty under rule 3.2—
    (i)   identify the witnesses who gave oral evidence in the magistrates' court,
    (ii) identify the witnesses who gave written evidence in the magistrates' court,
    (iii) identify the prosecution witnesses whom the respondent intends to call to give oral evidence in the Crown Court,
    (iv) give notice of any special arrangements or other measures that the respondent thinks are needed for witnesses,
    (v)   explain whether the issues in the Crown Court differ from the issues in the magistrates' court, and if so how, and
    (vi) say how long the trial lasted in the magistrates' court and how long the appeal is likely to last in the Crown Court.
(3) Paragraph (4) applies in an appeal against conviction or against a finding of guilt where in the magistrates' court a party to the appeal—
  (a) introduced in evidence material to which applies—
    (i)   Part 16 (Written witness statements),
    (ii) Part 19 (Expert evidence),
    (iii) Part 20 (Hearsay evidence),
    (iv) Part 21 (Evidence of bad character), or
    (v)   Part 22 (Evidence of a complainant's previous sexual behaviour); or
  (b) made an application to which applies—
    (i)   Part 17 (Witness summonses, warrants and orders),
    (ii) Part 18 (Measures to assist a witness or defendant to give evidence), or
    (iii) Part 23 (Restriction on cross-examination by a defendant).
(4) If such a party wants to reintroduce that material or to renew that application in the Crown Court that party must include a notice to that effect in the appeal or respondent's notice, as the case may be.

[Note. The Practice Direction sets out forms of appeal and respondent's notices for use in connection with this rule.

In some cases, a magistrates' court can reconsider a conviction, sentence or other order and make a fresh decision. See section 142 of the Magistrates' Courts Act 1980[25].

See also rule 3.13 (Conduct of a trial or an appeal).]

---

[25] 1980 c. 43; section 142 was amended by sections 26 and 29 of, and Schedule 3 to, the Criminal Appeal Act 1995 (c. 35).

R34.4   **Duty of magistrates' court officer**

34.4   (1)   The magistrates' court officer must—

    (a)   arrange for the magistrates' court to hear as soon as practicable any application to that court under rule 34.2(3)(c) (suspension of disqualification or order pending appeal); and

    (b)   as soon as practicable notify the Crown Court officer of the service of the appeal notice and make available to that officer—

        (i)   the appeal notice and any accompanying application served by the appellant,

        (ii)   details of the parties including their addresses, and

        (iii)   a copy of each magistrates' court register entry relating to the decision under appeal and to any application for bail or for the suspension of a disqualification or order pending appeal.

  (2)   Where the appeal is against conviction or against a finding of guilt, the magistrates' court officer must make available to the Crown Court officer as soon as practicable—

    (a)   all material served on the magistrate's court officer to which applies—

        (i)   Part 8 (Initial details of the prosecution case),

        (ii)   Part 16 (Written witness statements),

        (iii)   Part 17 (Witness summonses, warrants and orders),

        (iv)   Part 18 (Measures to assist a witness or defendant to give evidence),

        (v)   Part 19 (Expert evidence),

        (vi)   Part 20 (Hearsay evidence),

        (vii)   Part 21 (Evidence of bad character),

        (viii)   Part 22 (Evidence of a complainant's previous sexual behaviour), or

        (ix)   Part 23 (Restriction on cross-examination by a defendant);

    (b)   any case management questionnaire prepared for the purposes of the trial;

    (c)   all case management directions given by the magistrates' court for the purposes of the trial; and

    (d)   any other document, object or information for which the Crown Court officer asks.

  (3)   Where the appeal is against sentence, the magistrates' court officer must make available to the Crown Court officer as soon as practicable any report received for the purposes of sentencing.

  (4)   Unless the magistrates' court otherwise directs, the magistrates' court officer—

    (a)   must keep any document or object exhibited in the proceedings in the magistrates' court, or arrange for it to be kept by some other appropriate person, until at least—

        (i)   6 weeks after the conclusion of those proceedings, or

        (ii)   the conclusion of any proceedings in the Crown Court that begin within that 6 weeks; but

    (b)   need not keep such a document if—

        (i)   the document that was exhibited is a copy of a document retained by the party who produced it, and

        (ii)   what was in evidence in the magistrates' court was the content of that document.

[Note. See also section 133 of the Criminal Justice Act 2003[26] (Proof of statements in documents).]

R34.5   **Duty of person keeping exhibit**

34.5   A person who, under arrangements made by the magistrates' court officer, keeps a document or object exhibited in the proceedings in the magistrates' court must—

    (a)   keep that exhibit until—

        (i)   6 weeks after the conclusion of those proceedings, or

        (ii)   the conclusion of any proceedings in the Crown Court that begin within that 6 weeks, unless the magistrates' court or the Crown Court otherwise directs; and

    (b)   provide the Crown Court with any such document or object for which the Crown Court officer asks, within such period as the Crown Court officer may require.

R34.6   **Reference by the Criminal Cases Review Commission**

34.6   (1)   The Crown Court officer must, as soon as practicable, serve a reference by the Criminal Cases Review Commission on—

    (a)   the appellant;

    (b)   every other party; and

    (c)   the magistrates' court officer.

  (2)   The appellant may serve an appeal notice on—

    (a)   the Crown Court officer; and

    (b)   every other party,

  not more than 15 business days later.

---

[26] 2003 c. 44.

(3) The Crown Court must treat the reference as the appeal notice if the appellant does not serve an appeal notice.

Preparation for appeal

R34.7

34.7 (1) The Crown Court may conduct a preparation for appeal hearing (and if necessary more than one such hearing) where—

(a) it is necessary to conduct such a hearing in order to give directions for the effective determination of the appeal; or

(b) such a hearing is required to set ground rules for the conduct of the questioning of a witness or appellant.

(2) Where under rule 34.3(4) a party gives notice to reintroduce material or to renew an application first introduced or made in the magistrates' court—

(a) no other notice or application to the same effect otherwise required by these Rules need be served; and

(b) any objection served by the other party in the magistrates' court is treated as renewed unless within 15 business days that party serves notice withdrawing it.

(3) Paragraphs (4) and (5) apply where—

(a) the appeal is against conviction or against a finding of guilt;

(b) a party wants to introduce material or make an application under a Part of these Rules listed in rule 34.3(3); and

(c) that party gives no notice of reintroduction or renewal under rule 34.3(4) (whether because the conditions for giving such a notice are not met or for any other reason).

(4) Such a party must serve the material, notice or application required by that Part not more than 21 days after service of the appeal notice.

(5) Subject to paragraph (4), the requirements of that Part apply (for example, as to the form in which a notice must be given or an application made and as to the time and form in which such a notice or application may be opposed).

Hearings and decisions

R34.8

34.8 (1) The Crown Court as a general rule must hear in public an appeal or reference to which this part applies, but—

(a) may order any hearing to be in private; and

(b) where a hearing is about a public interest ruling, must hold that hearing in private.

(2) The Crown Court officer must give as much notice as reasonably practicable of every hearing to—

(a) the parties;

(b) any party's custodian; and

(c) any other person whom the Crown Court requires to be notified.

(3) The Crown Court officer must serve every decision on—

(a) the parties;

(b) any other person whom the Crown Court requires to be served; and

(c) the magistrates' court officer and any party's custodian, where the decision determines an appeal.

(4) But where a hearing or decision is about a public interest ruling, the Crown Court officer must not—

(a) give notice of that hearing to; or

(b) serve that decision on,

anyone other than the prosecutor who applied for that ruling, unless the court otherwise directs.

[Note. See also Part 15 (Disclosure).]

Abandoning an appeal

R34.9

34.9 (1) The appellant—

(a) may abandon an appeal without the Crown Court's permission, by serving a notice of abandonment on—

(i) the magistrates' court officer,

(ii) the Crown Court officer, and

(iii) every other party

before the hearing of the appeal begins; but

(b) after the hearing of the appeal begins, may only abandon the appeal with the Crown Court's permission.

(2) A notice of abandonment must be signed by or on behalf of the appellant.

(3) Where an appellant who is on bail pending appeal abandons an appeal—

(a) the appellant must surrender to custody as directed by the magistrates' court officer; and

(b) any conditions of bail apply until then.

[Note. The Practice Direction sets out a form of notice of abandonment for use in connection with this rule.

Where an appellant abandons an appeal to the Crown Court, both the Crown Court and the magistrates' court have power to make a costs order against that appellant in favour of the respondent: see section 52 of the Senior Courts Act 1981[27] and section 109 of the Magistrates' Courts Act 1980[28]. Part 45 contains rules about costs on abandoning an appeal.]

R34.10   Court's power to vary requirements under this Part

34.10 The Crown Court may—

(a) shorten or extend (even after it has expired) a time limit under this Part;

(b) allow an appellant to vary an appeal notice that that appellant has served;

(c) direct that an appeal notice be served on any person; and

(d) allow an appeal notice or a notice of abandonment to be in a different form to one set out in the Practice Direction, or to be presented orally.

R34.11   Constitution of the Crown Court

34.11 (1) On the hearing of an appeal the general rule is that—

(a) the Crown Court must comprise—

(i) a judge of the High Court, a Circuit judge, a Recorder or a qualifying judge advocate, and

(ii) no less than two and no more than four justices of the peace, none of whom took part in the decision under appeal; and

(b) if the appeal is from a youth court, each justice of the peace must be qualified to sit as a member of a youth court.

(2) Despite the general rule—

(a) the Crown Court may include only one justice of the peace if—

(i) the presiding judge decides that otherwise the start of the appeal hearing will be delayed unreasonably, or

(ii) one or more of the justices of the peace who started hearing the appeal is absent; and

(b) the Crown Court may comprise only a judge of the High Court, a Circuit judge, a Recorder or a qualifying judge advocate if—

(i) the appeal is against conviction, under section 108 of the Magistrates' Courts Act 1980[29], and

(ii) the respondent agrees that the court should allow the appeal, under section 48(2) of the Senior Courts Act 1981[30].

(3) Before the hearing of an appeal begins and after that hearing ends—

(a) the Crown Court may comprise only a judge of the High Court, a Circuit judge, a Recorder or a qualifying judge advocate; and

(b) so constituted, the court may, among other things, exercise the powers to which apply—

(i) the rules in this Part and in Part 3 (Case management), and

(ii) rule 35.2 (stating a case for the opinion of the High Court, or refusing to do so).

[27] 1981 c. 54; section 52 was amended by section 31(5) of, and Part II of Schedule 1 to, the Prosecution of Offences Act 1985 (c. 23), section 4 of the Courts and Legal Services Act 1990 (c. 41), article 3 of, and paragraphs 11 and 12(a) of the Schedule to, S.I. 2004/2035, and section 59(5) of, and paragraph 26(1) and (2) of Schedule 11 to, the Constitutional Reform Act 2005 (c. 4). The Act's title was amended by section 59(5) of, and paragraph 1 of Schedule 11 to, the Constitutional Reform Act 2005 (c. 4).
[28] 1980 c. 43; section 109(2) was amended by section 109(1) of, and paragraph 234 of Schedule 8 to, the Courts Act 2003 (c. 39).
[29] 1980 c. 43; section 108 was amended by sections 66(2) and 78 of, and Schedule 16 to, the Criminal Justice Act 1982 (c. 48), section 23(3) of the Football Spectators Act 1989 (c. 37), section 101(2) of, and Schedule 13 to, the Criminal Justice Act 1991 (c. 53), sections 119 and 120(2) of, and paragraph 43 of Schedule 8 and Schedule 10 to, the Crime and Disorder Act 1998 (c. 37), section 7(2) of the Football (Offences and Disorder) Act 1999 (c. 21), section 165(1) of, and paragraph 71 of Schedule 9 to, the Powers of Criminal Courts (Sentencing) Act 2000 (c. 6), section 1 of, and Schedule 3 to, the Football (Disorder) Act 2000 (c. 25), section 58(1) of, and paragraph 10 of Schedule 10 to, the Domestic Violence, Crime and Victims Act 2004 (c. 28), section 52(2) of, and paragraph 14 of Schedule 3 to, the Violent Crime Reduction Act 2006 (c. 38), section 64 of, and paragraph 10 of Schedule 3 to, the Animal Welfare Act 2006 (c. 45) and section 54 of, and paragraphs 2 and 4 of Schedule 12 to, the Criminal Justice and Courts Act 2015 (c. 2).
[30] 1981 c. 54; section 48(2) was amended by section 156 of the Criminal Justice Act 1988 (c. 33).

[Note. See sections 73 and 74 of the Senior Courts Act 1981[31] (which allow rules of court to provide for the constitution of the Crown Court in proceedings on appeal), section 45 of the Children and Young Persons Act 1933[32] and section 9 of the Courts Act 2003[33]. Under section 8(1A) of the Senior Courts Act 1981[34], a qualifying judge advocate may not exercise the jurisdiction of the Crown Court on an appeal from a youth court.]

CRIMINAL PROCEDURE RULES   PART 35   APPEAL TO THE HIGH COURT BY CASE STATED

When this Part applies

R35.1

35.1 This Part applies where a person wants to appeal to the High Court by case stated—
- (a) under section 111 of the Magistrates' Courts Act 1980, against a decision of a magistrates' court; or
- (b) under section 28 of the Senior Courts Act 1981, against a decision of the Crown Court.

[Note. Under section 111 of the Magistrates' Courts Act 1980, 'any person who was a party to any proceeding before a magistrates' court or is aggrieved by the conviction, order, determination or other proceeding of the court may question the proceeding on the ground that it is wrong in law or is in excess of jurisdiction by applying to the justices composing the court to state a case for the opinion of the High Court on the question of law or jurisdiction involved'.

Under section 28 of the Senior Courts Act 1981, 'any order, judgment or other decision of the Crown Court may be questioned by any party to the proceedings, on the ground that it is wrong in law or is in excess of jurisdiction, by applying to the Crown Court to have a case stated by that court for the opinion of the High Court.'

Under section 28A of the 1981 Act[1], the High Court may 'reverse, affirm or amend the determination in respect of which the case has been stated; or remit the matter to the magistrates' court, or the Crown Court, with the opinion of the High Court, and may make such other order ... as it thinks fit.' Under that section, the High Court also may send the case back for amendment, if it thinks fit.]

Application to state a case

R35.2

35.2 (1) A party who wants the court to state a case for the opinion of the High Court must—
- (a) apply in writing, not more than 21 days after the decision against which the applicant wants to appeal; and
- (b) serve the application on—
  - (i) the court officer, and
  - (ii) each other party.

(2) The application must—
- (a) specify the decision in issue;
- (b) specify the proposed question or questions of law or jurisdiction on which the opinion of the High Court will be asked;
- (c) indicate the proposed grounds of appeal; and
- (d) include or attach any application for the following, with reasons—
  - (i) if the application is to the Crown Court, an extension of time within which to apply to state a case,
  - (ii) bail pending appeal, or
  - (iii) the suspension of any disqualification imposed in the case, where the court can order such a suspension pending appeal.

(3) A party who wants to make representations about the application must—
- (a) serve the representations on—
  - (i) the court officer, and
  - (ii) each other party; and

---

[31] 1981 c. 54; section 73 was amended by article 3 of, and paragraphs 11 and 12 of the Schedule to, S.I. 2004/2035 and section 26 of, and paragraph 2 of Schedule 2 to, the Armed Forces Act 2011 (c. 18). Section 74 was amended by sections 79 and 106 of, and Table (4) of Part V of Schedule 15 to, the Access to Justice Act 1999 (c. 22), article 3 of, and paragraphs 11 and 12 of the Schedule to S.I. 2004/2035, section 15 of, and paragraphs 114 and 133 of Schedule 4 to, the Constitutional Reform Act 2005 (c. 4) and section 26 of, and paragraph 3 of Schedule 2 to, the Armed Forces Act 2011 (c. 18). The Act's title was amended by section 59(5) of, and paragraph 1 of Schedule 11 to, the Constitutional Reform Act 2005 (c. 4).
[32] 1933 c. 12; section 45 was substituted by section 50 of the Courts Act 2003 (c. 39) and amended by section 15 of, and paragraph 20 of Schedule 4 to, the Constitutional Reform Act 2005 (c. 4).
[33] 2003 c. 39.
[34] 1981 c. 54; section 8(1A) was inserted by paragraph 1 of Schedule 2 to the Armed Forces Act 2011 (c. 18).
[1] 1981 c. 54; section 28A was inserted by section 1 of, and paragraph 9 of Schedule 2 to, the Statute Law (Repeals) Act 1993 (c. 50), and amended by section 61 of the Access to Justice Act 1999 (c. 22) and section 40 of, and paragraph 36 of Schedule 9 to, the Constitutional Reform Act 2005 (c. 4).

(b) do so not more than 10 business days after service of the application.
(4) The court—
    (a) may determine the application without a hearing; and
    (b) must determine the application not more than 15 business days after the time for service of representations under paragraph (3) has expired.
(5) If the court decides not to state a case, the court officer must serve on each party—
    (a) notice of that decision; and
    (b) the court's written reasons for that decision.

[Note. The time limit for applying to a magistrates' court to state a case is prescribed by section 111(2) of the Magistrates' Courts Act 1980. It may be neither extended nor shortened.

Under section 113 of the Magistrates' Courts Act 1980[2], the magistrates' court may grant an appellant bail pending appeal. Under section 81(1)(d) of the Senior Courts Act 1981[3], the Crown Court may do so. See also rule 14.7.

Where Part 34 (Appeal to the Crown Court) applies, an application to which this rule applies may be determined by a judge of the High Court, a Circuit judge, a Recorder or a qualifying judge advocate without justices of the peace: see rule 34.11 (Constitution of the Crown Court).

Under section 39 of the Road Traffic Offenders Act 1988[4], a court which has made an order disqualifying a person from driving may suspend the disqualification pending appeal. See also rule 29.2.

The Practice Direction sets out a form of application for use in connection with this rule.]

R35.3 **Preparation of case stated**

35.3 (1) This rule applies where the court decides to state a case for the opinion of the High Court.
(2) The court officer must serve on each party notice of—
    (a) the decision to state a case, and
    (b) any recognizance ordered by the court.
(3) Unless the court otherwise directs, not more than 15 business days after the court's decision to state a case—
    (a) in a magistrates' court, the court officer must serve a draft case on each party; or
    (b) in the Crown Court, the applicant must serve a draft case on the court officer and each other party.
(4) The draft case must—
    (a) specify the decision in issue;
    (b) specify the question(s) of law or jurisdiction on which the opinion of the High Court will be asked;
    (c) include a succinct summary of—
        (i) the nature and history of the proceedings,
        (ii) the court's relevant findings of fact, and
        (iii) the relevant contentions of the parties; and
    (d) if a question is whether there was sufficient evidence on which the court reasonably could reach a finding of fact—
        (i) specify that finding, and
        (ii) include a summary of the evidence on which the court reached that finding.
(5) Except to the extent that paragraph (4)(d) requires, the draft case must not include an account of the evidence received by the court.
(6) A party who wants to make representations about the content of the draft case, or to propose a revised draft, must—
    (a) serve the representations, or revised draft, on—
        (i) the court officer, and
        (ii) each other party; and
    (b) do so not more than 15 business days after service of the draft case.
(7) The court must state the case not more than 15 business days after the time for service of representations under paragraph (6) has expired.
(8) A case stated for the opinion of the High Court must—
    (a) comply with paragraphs (4) and (5); and
    (b) identify—

---

[2] 1980 c. 43; section 113 was amended by section 168 of, and paragraph 44 of Schedule 10 to, the Criminal Justice and Public Order Act 1994 (c. 33) and section 165 of, and paragraph 72 of Schedule 9 to, the Powers of Criminal Courts (Sentencing) Act 2000 (c. 6).
[3] 1981 c.54.
[4] 1988 c. 53.

(i)   the court that stated it, and

(ii) the court office for that court.

(9) The court officer must serve the case stated on each party.

[Note. Under section 114 of the Magistrates' Courts Act 1980[5], a magistrates' court need not state a case until the person who applied for it has entered into a recognizance to appeal promptly to the High Court. The Crown Court has a corresponding inherent power.

Under section 121(6) of the 1980 Act, the magistrates' court which states a case need not include all the members of the court which took the decision questioned.

For the procedure on appeal to the High Court, see Part 52 of the Civil Procedure Rules 1998[6] and the associated Practice Direction.]

Duty of justices' legal adviser   R35.4

35.4 (1) This rule applies—

(a) only in a magistrates' court; and

(b) unless the court—

(i)   includes a District Judge (Magistrates' Courts), and

(ii) otherwise directs.

(2) A justices' legal adviser must assist the court by—

(a) preparing and amending the draft case, and

(b) completing the case stated.

[Note. For the functions of a justices' legal adviser, see sections 28 and 29 of the Courts Act 2003[7]. See also rule 2.12 (Duties of justices' legal adviser).]

Court's power to vary requirements under this Part   R35.5

35.5 (1) The court may shorten or extend (even after it has expired) a time limit under this Part.

(2) A person who wants an extension of time must—

(a) apply when serving the application, representations or draft case for which it is needed; and

(b) explain the delay.

[Note. See also rule 35.2(2)(d)(i) and the note to rule 35.2.]

CRIMINAL PROCEDURE RULES   PART 36   APPEAL TO THE COURT
OF APPEAL: GENERAL RULES

When this Part applies   R36.1

36.1 (1) This Part applies to all the applications, appeals and references to the Court of Appeal to which Parts 37, 38, 39, 40, 41 and 43 apply.

(2) In this Part and in those, unless the context makes it clear that something different is meant, 'court' means the Court of Appeal or any judge of that court.

[Note. See rule 2.2 for the usual meaning of 'court'.

Under section 53 of the Senior Courts Act 1981[1], the criminal division of the Court of Appeal exercises jurisdiction in the appeals and references to which Parts 37, 38, 39, 40 and 41 apply.

Under section 55 of that Act[2], the Court of Appeal must include at least two judges, and for some purposes at least three.

---

[5] 1980 c. 43; section 114 was amended by section 90 of, and paragraphs 95 and 113 of Schedule 13 to, the Access to Justice Act 1999 (c. 22) and section 109 of, and paragraph 235 of Schedule 8 to, the Courts Act 2003 (c. 39).

[6] S.I. 1998/3132; Part 52 was inserted by S.I. 2000/221 and amended by paragraph 1 of Schedule 11 to the Constitutional Reform Act 2005 (c. 4) and S.I. 2003/2113, 2003/3361, 2006/3435, 2007/2204 and 2009/2092.

[7] 2003 c. 39; sections 28 and 29 were substituted by section 3 of, and paragraphs 25 and 26 of the Schedule to, the Courts and Tribunals (Judiciary and Functions of Staff) Act 2018 (c. 33).

[1] 1981 c. 54. The Act's title was amended by section 59(5) of, and paragraph 1 of Schedule 11 to, the Constitutional Reform Act 2005 (c. 4).

[2] 1981 c. 54; section 55 was amended by section 170 of, and paragraph 80 of Schedule 15 to, the Criminal Justice Act 1988 (c. 33), section 52 of the Criminal Justice and Public Order Act 1994 (c. 33) and section 58 of the Domestic Violence, Crime and Victims Act 2004 (c. 28). It is further amended by section 40 of, and paragraph 36 of Schedule 9 to, the Constitutional Reform Act 2005 (c. 4).

For the powers of the Court of Appeal that may be exercised by one judge of that court or by the Registrar, see sections 31, 31A, 31B, 31C and 44 of the Criminal Appeal Act 1968[3]; section 49 of the Criminal Justice Act 2003[4]; the Criminal Justice Act 2003 (Mandatory Life Sentences: Appeals in Transitional Cases) Order 2005[5]; the Serious Organised Crime and Police Act 2005 (Appeals under section 74) Order 2006[6]; the Serious Crime Act 2007 (Appeals under Section 24) Order 2008[7]; and the power conferred by section 53(4) of the 1981 Act.]

R36.2 Case management in the Court of Appeal

36.2 (1) The court and the parties have the same duties and powers as under Part 3 (Case management).

(2) The Registrar—

(a) must fulfil the duty of active case management under rule 3.2; and

(b) in fulfilling that duty may exercise any of the powers of case management under—

(i) rule 3.5 (the court's general powers of case management),

(ii) rule 3.12(3) (requiring a certificate of readiness), and

(iii) rule 3.13 (requiring a party to identify intentions and anticipated requirements) subject to the directions of the court.

(3) The Registrar must nominate a case progression officer under rule 3.4.

R36.3 Power to vary requirements

36.3 The court or the Registrar may—

(a) shorten a time limit or extend it (even after it has expired) unless that is inconsistent with other legislation;

(b) allow a party to vary any notice that that party has served;

(c) direct that a notice or application be served on any person; and

(d) allow a notice or application to be in a different form, or presented orally.

[Note. The time limit for serving an appeal notice—

(a) under section 18 of the Criminal Appeal Act 1968[8] on an appeal against conviction or sentence, and

(b) under section 18A of that Act[9] on an appeal against a finding of contempt of court

may be extended but not shortened: see rule 39.2.

The time limit for serving an application for permission to refer a sentencing case under section 36 of the Criminal Justice Act 1988[10] may be neither extended nor shortened: see rule 41.2(4).

The time limits in rule 43.2 for applying to the Court of Appeal for permission to appeal or refer a case to the Supreme Court may be extended or shortened only as explained in the note to that rule.]

---

[3] 1968 c. 19; section 31 was amended by section 21 of, and Schedule 2 to, the Costs in Criminal Cases Act 1973 (c. 14), section 24 of, and paragraph 10 of Schedule 6 to, the Road Traffic Act 1974 (c. 50), section 29 of the Criminal Justice Act 1982 (c. 48), section 170 of, and paragraphs 20, 29 and 30 of Schedule 15 to, the Criminal Justice Act 1988 (c. 33), section 4 of, and paragraph 4 of Schedule 3 to, the Road Traffic (Consequential Provisions) Act 1988 (c. 54), section 198 of, and paragraphs 38 and 40 of Schedule 6 to, the Licensing Act 2003 (c. 17), section 87 of the Courts Act 2003 (c. 39), paragraphs 86, 87 and 88 of Schedule 36 to the Criminal Justice Act 2003 (c. 44), section 48 of the Police and Justice Act 2006 (c. 48), section 47 of, and paragraphs 1, 9 and 11 of Schedule 8 to, the Criminal Justice and Immigration Act 2008 (c. 4) and section 177 of, and paragraph 69 of Schedule 21 to, the Coroners and Justice Act 2009 (c. 25). It is further amended by section 67 of, and paragraph 4 of Schedule 4 to, the Youth Justice and Criminal Evidence Act 1999 (c. 23), with effect from a date to be appointed. Section 31A was inserted by section 6 of the Criminal Appeal Act 1995 (c. 35) and amended by sections 87 and 109 of, and Schedule 10 to, the Courts Act 2003 (c. 39) and section 331 of, and paragraphs 86 and 88 of Schedule 36 to, the Criminal Justice Act 2003 (c. 44). Section 31B was inserted by section 87 of the Courts Act 2003 (c. 39). Section 31C was inserted by section 87 of the Courts Act 2003 (c. 39) and amended by sections 47 and 149 of, and paragraphs 1 and 12 of Schedule 8 and part 3 of Schedule 28 to, the Criminal Justice and Immigration Act 2008 (c. 4). Section 44 was amended by section 24(2) of, and paragraph 11 of Schedule 6 to, the Road Traffic Act 1974 (c. 50), section 170(1) of, and paragraphs 20 and 31 of the Criminal Justice Act 1988 (c. 33), section 4 of, and paragraph 4(2) of the Road Traffic (Consequential Provisions) Act 1988 (c. 54) and section 198(1), and paragraphs 38 and 41 of Schedule 6 to, the Licensing Act 2003 (c. 17).

[4] 2003 c. 44.

[5] S.I. 2005/2798.

[6] S.I. 2006/2135.

[7] S.I. 2008/1863.

[8] 1968 c. 19.

[9] 1968 c. 19; section 18A was inserted by section 170 of, and paragraphs 20 and 25 of Schedule 15 to, the Criminal Justice Act 1988 (c. 33).

[10] 1988 c. 33; section 36 was amended by section 272 of, and paragraphs 45 and 46 of Schedule 32 and paragraph 96 of Schedule 36 to, the Criminal Justice Act 2003 (c. 44), sections 49 and 65 of, and paragraph 3 of Schedule 1 and Schedule 5 to, the Violent Crime Reduction Act 2006 (c. 38), section 40 of, and paragraph 48 of Schedule 9 to, the Constitutional Reform Act 2005 (c. 4), sections 46, 148 and 149 of, and paragraphs 22 and 23 of Schedule 26 and Part 3 of Schedule 28 to, the Criminal Justice and Immigration Act 2008 (c. 4), paragraph 2 of Schedule 19 and paragraphs 4 and 5 of Schedule 26 to the Legal Aid, Sentencing and Punishment of Offenders Act 2012 (c. 10) and section 28 of, and paragraph 2 of Schedule 5 to, the Criminal Justice and Courts Act 2015 (c. 2). It is further amended by section 46 of the Criminal Justice and Immigration Act 2008 (c. 4) with effect from a date to be appointed.

Application for extension of time

36.4   A person who wants an extension of time within which to serve a notice or make an application must—

    (a) apply for that extension of time when serving that notice or making that application; and

    (b) give the reasons for the application for an extension of time.

Renewing an application refused by a judge or the Registrar

36.5   (1) This rule applies where a party with the right to do so wants to renew—

    (a) to a judge of the Court of Appeal an application refused by the Registrar; or

    (b) to the Court of Appeal an application refused by a judge of that court.

    (2) That party must—

    (a) renew the application in the form set out in the Practice Direction, signed by or on behalf of the applicant; and

    (b) serve the renewed application on the Registrar not more than 10 business days after—

        (i)   the refusal of the application that the applicant wants to renew; or

        (ii) the Registrar serves that refusal on the applicant, if the applicant was not present in person or by live link when the original application was refused.

[Note. The time limit of 10 business days under this rule is reduced to 5 business days where Parts 37, 38 or 40 apply: see rules 37.7, 38.10 and 40.7.

For the right to renew an application to a judge or to the Court of Appeal, see sections 31(3), 31C and 44 of the Criminal Appeal Act 1968, the Criminal Justice Act 2003 (Mandatory Life Sentences: Appeals in Transitional Cases) Order 2005[11], the Serious Organised Crime and Police Act 2005 (Appeals under section 74) Order 2006[12] and the Serious Crime Act 2007 (Appeals under Section 24) Order 2008.

A party has no right under section 31C of the 1968 Act to renew to the Court of Appeal an application for procedural directions refused by a judge, but in some circumstances a case management direction might be varied: see rule 3.6.

If an applicant does not renew an application that a judge has refused, including an application for permission to appeal, the Registrar will treat it as if it had been refused by the Court of Appeal.

Under section 22 of the Criminal Appeal Act 1968[13], the Court of Appeal may direct that an appellant who is in custody is to attend a hearing by live link.]

Hearings

36.6   (1) The general rule is that the Court of Appeal must hear in public—

    (a)   an application, including an application for permission to appeal; and

    (b)   an appeal or reference,

    but it may order any hearing to be in private.

    (2) Where a hearing is about a public interest ruling, that hearing must be in private unless the court otherwise directs.

    (3) Where the appellant wants to appeal against an order restricting public access to a trial, the court—

    (a)   may decide without a hearing—

        (i)   an application, including an application for permission to appeal, and

        (ii) an appeal; but

    (b)   must announce its decision on such an appeal at a hearing in public.

    (4) Where the appellant wants to appeal or to refer a case to the Supreme Court, the court—

    (a)   may decide without a hearing an application—

        (i)   for permission to appeal or to refer a sentencing case, or

        (ii) to refer a point of law; but

    (b)   must announce its decision on such an application at a hearing in public.

    (5) Where a party wants the court to reopen the determination of an appeal—

    (a)   the court—

        (i)   must decide the application without a hearing, as a general rule, but

        (ii) may decide the application at a hearing; and

    (b)   need not announce its decision on such an application at a hearing in public.

    (6) A judge of the Court of Appeal and the Registrar may exercise any of their powers—

    (a)   at a hearing in public or in private; or

    (b)   without a hearing.

---

[11] S.I. 2005/2798.

[12] S.I. 2006/2135.

[13] 1968 c. 19; section 22 was amended by section 48 of the Police and Justice Act 2006 (c. 48).

[Note. For the procedure on an appeal against an order restricting public access to a trial, see Part 40.

For the procedure on an application to reopen the determination of an appeal, see rule 36.15.]

R36.7 Notice of hearings and decisions

36.7 (1) The Registrar must give as much notice as reasonably practicable of every hearing to—
   (a) the parties;
   (b) any party's custodian;
   (c) any other person whom the court requires to be notified; and
   (d) the Crown Court officer, where Parts 37, 38 or 40 apply.

(2) The Registrar must serve every decision on—
   (a) the parties;
   (b) any other person whom the court requires to be served; and
   (c) the Crown Court officer and any party's custodian, where the decision determines an appeal or application for permission to appeal.

(3) But where a hearing or decision is about a public interest ruling, the Registrar must not—
   (a) give notice of that hearing to; or
   (b) serve that decision on,
   anyone other than the prosecutor who applied for that ruling, unless the court otherwise directs.

R36.8 Duty of Crown Court officer

36.8 (1) The Crown Court officer must—
   (a) where electronic arrangements have been made to receive and store information and documents for the Crown Court, as soon as practicable ensure that all such material is available to the Registrar in accordance with those arrangements; and
   (b) provide the Registrar with any document, object or information for which the Registrar asks, within such period as the Registrar may require.

(2) Where someone may appeal to the Court of Appeal, the Crown Court officer must keep any document or object exhibited in the proceedings in the Crown Court, or arrange for it to be kept by some other appropriate person, until—
   (a) 6 weeks after the conclusion of those proceedings; or
   (b) the conclusion of any appeal proceedings that begin within that 6 weeks,
   unless the court, the Registrar or the Crown Court otherwise directs.

(3) Where Part 37 applies (Appeal to the Court of Appeal against ruling at preparatory hearing), the Crown Court officer must as soon as practicable serve on the appellant a transcript or note of—
   (a) each order or ruling against which the appellant wants to appeal; and
   (b) the decision by the Crown Court judge on any application for permission to appeal.

(4) Where Part 38 applies (Appeal to the Court of Appeal against ruling adverse to prosecution), the Crown Court officer must as soon as practicable serve on the appellant a transcript or note of—
   (a) each ruling against which the appellant wants to appeal;
   (b) the decision by the Crown Court judge on any application for permission to appeal; and
   (c) the decision by the Crown Court judge on any request to expedite the appeal.

(5) Where Part 39 applies (Appeal to the Court of Appeal about conviction or sentence), the Crown Court officer must as soon as practicable serve on or make available to the Registrar—
   (a) any Crown Court judge's certificate that the case is fit for appeal;
   (b) the decision on any application at the Crown Court centre for bail pending appeal;
   (c) such of the Crown Court case papers as the Registrar requires; and
   (d) such transcript of the Crown Court proceedings as the Registrar requires.

(6) Where Part 40 applies (Appeal to the Court of Appeal about reporting or public access) and an order is made restricting public access to a trial, the Crown Court officer must—
   (a) immediately notify the Registrar of that order, if the appellant has given advance notice of intention to appeal; and
   (b) as soon as practicable provide the applicant for that order with a transcript or note of the application.

[Note. See also section 87(4) of the Senior Courts Act 1981[14] and rules 5.5 (Recording and transcription of proceedings in the Crown Court), 36.9 (duty of person transcribing record of proceedings in the Crown Court) and 36.10 (Duty of person keeping exhibit).]

---

[14] 1981 c. 54; section 87(4) was amended by articles 2 and 3 of, and paragraphs 11 and 17 of the Schedule to, S.I. 2004/2035.

Duty of person transcribing proceedings in the Crown Court   R36.9

36.9   A person who transcribes a recording of proceedings in the Crown Court under arrangements made by the Crown Court officer must provide the Registrar with any transcript for which the Registrar asks, within such period as the Registrar may require.

[Note. See also section 32 of the Criminal Appeal Act 1968[15] and rule 5.5 (Recording and transcription of proceedings in the Crown Court).]

Duty of person keeping exhibit   R36.10

36.10   A person who under arrangements made by the Crown Court officer keeps a document or object exhibited in the proceedings in the Crown Court must—
(a)   keep that exhibit until—
   (i)   6 weeks after the conclusion of the Crown Court proceedings, or
   (ii)   the conclusion of any appeal proceedings that begin within that 6 weeks,
unless the court, the Registrar or the Crown Court otherwise directs; and
(b)   provide the Registrar with any such document or object for which the Registrar asks, within such period as the Registrar may require.

[Note. See also rule 36.8(2) (Duty of Crown Court officer).]

Registrar's duty to provide copy documents for appeal or reference   R36.11

36.11   Unless the court otherwise directs, for the purposes of an appeal or reference—
(a)   the Registrar must—
   (i)   provide a party with a copy of any document or transcript held by the Registrar for such purposes, or
   (ii)   allow a party to inspect such a document or transcript,
on payment by that party of any charge fixed by the Treasury; but
(b)   the Registrar must not provide a copy or allow the inspection of—
   (i)   a document provided only for the court and the Registrar, or
   (ii)   a transcript of a public interest ruling or of an application for such a ruling.

[Note. Section 21 of the Criminal Appeal Act 1968 requires the Registrar to collect, prepare and provide documents needed by the court.]

Declaration of incompatibility with a Convention right   R36.12

36.12   (1)   This rule applies where a party—
(a)   wants the court to make a declaration of incompatibility with a Convention right under section 4 of the Human Rights Act 1998[16]; or
(b)   raises an issue that the Registrar thinks may lead the court to make such a declaration.
(2)   The Registrar must serve notice on—
(a)   the relevant person named in the list published under section 17(1) of the Crown Proceedings Act 1947[17]; or
(b)   the Treasury Solicitor, if it is not clear who is the relevant person.
(3)   That notice must include or attach details of—
(a)   the legislation affected and the Convention right concerned;
(b)   the parties to the appeal; and
(c)   any other information or document that the Registrar thinks relevant.
(4)   A person who has a right under the 1998 Act to become a party to the appeal must—
(a)   serve notice on—
   (i)   the Registrar, and
   (ii)   the other parties,
if that person wants to exercise that right; and
(b)   in that notice—
   (i)   indicate the conclusion that that person invites the court to reach on the question of incompatibility, and

---

[15]   1968 c. 19.
[16]   1998 c. 42; section 4 was amended by section 40 of, and paragraph 66 of Schedule 9 to, the Constitutional Reform Act 2005 (c. 4) and section 67 of, and paragraph 43 of Schedule 6 to, the Mental Capacity Act 2005 (c. 9).
[17]   1987 c. 38; section 9 was amended by section 170 of, and Schedule 16 to, the Criminal Justice Act 1988 (c. 33), section 6 of the Criminal Justice Act 1993 (c. 36), sections 72, 74 and 80 of, and paragraph 3 of Schedule 3 and Schedule 5 to, the Criminal Procedure and Investigations Act 1996 (c. 25), sections 45 and 310 of, and paragraphs 18, 52 and 54 of Schedule 36 and Part 3 of Schedule 37 to, the Criminal Justice Act 2003 (c. 44), article 3 of, and paragraphs 21 and 23 of S.I. 2004/2035, section 59 of, and paragraph 1 of Schedule 11 to, the Constitutional Reform Act 2005 (c. 4) and Part 10 of Schedule 10 to the Protection of Freedoms Act 2012 (c. 9). The amendment made by section 45 of the Criminal Justice Act 2003 (c. 44) is in force for certain purposes; for remaining purposes it has effect from a date to be appointed.

(ii) identify each ground for that invitation, concisely outlining the arguments in support.

(5) The court must not make a declaration of incompatibility—

    (a) less than 15 business days after the Registrar serves notice under paragraph (2); and

    (b) without giving any person who serves a notice under paragraph (4) an opportunity to make representations at a hearing.

R36.13   **Abandoning an appeal**

36.13 (1) This rule applies where an appellant wants to—

    (a) abandon—

      (i)   an application to the court for permission to appeal, or

      (ii) an appeal; or

    (b) reinstate such an application or appeal after abandoning it.

(2) The appellant—

    (a) may abandon such an application or appeal without the court's permission by serving a notice of abandonment on—

      (i)   the Registrar, and

      (ii) any respondent

    before any hearing of the application or appeal; but

    (b) at any such hearing, may only abandon that application or appeal with the court's permission.

(3) A notice of abandonment must be in the form set out in the Practice Direction, signed by or on behalf of the appellant.

(4) On receiving a notice of abandonment the Registrar must—

    (a) date it;

    (b) serve a dated copy on—

      (i)   the appellant,

      (ii) the appellant's custodian, if any,

      (iii) the Crown Court officer, and

      (iv) any other person on whom the appellant or the Registrar served the appeal notice; and

    (c) treat the application or appeal as if it had been refused or dismissed by the Court of Appeal.

(5) An appellant who wants to reinstate an application or appeal after abandoning it must—

    (a) apply in writing, with reasons; and

    (b) serve the application on the Registrar.

[Note. The Court of Appeal has power only in exceptional circumstances to allow an appellant to reinstate an application or appeal that has been abandoned.]

R36.14   **Grounds of appeal and opposition**

36.14 (1) If the court gives permission to appeal then unless the court otherwise directs the decision indicates that—

    (a) the appellant has permission to appeal on every ground identified by the appeal notice; and

    (b) the court finds reasonably arguable each ground on which the appellant has permission to appeal.

(2) If the court gives permission to appeal but not on every ground identified by the appeal notice the decision indicates that—

    (a) at the hearing of the appeal the court will not consider representations that address any ground thus excluded from argument; and

    (b) an appellant who wants to rely on such an excluded ground needs the court's permission to do so.

(3) An appellant who wants to rely at the hearing of an appeal on a ground of appeal excluded from argument by a judge of the Court of Appeal when giving permission to appeal must—

    (a) apply for permission to do so, with reasons, and identify each such ground;

    (b) serve the application on—

      (i)   the Registrar, and

      (ii) any respondent; and

    (c) serve the application not more than 10 business days after—

      (i)   the giving of permission to appeal, or

      (ii) the Registrar serves notice of that decision on the applicant, if the applicant was not present in person or by live link when permission to appeal was given.

(4) Paragraph (5) applies where one of the following Parts applies—
    (a) Part 37 (Appeal to the Court of Appeal against ruling at preparatory hearing);
    (b) Part 38 (Appeal to the Court of Appeal against ruling adverse to prosecution);
    (c) Part 39 (Appeal to the Court of Appeal about conviction or sentence); or
    (d) Part 40 (Appeal to the Court of Appeal about reporting or public access restriction).
(5) An appellant who wants to rely on a ground of appeal not identified by the appeal notice must—
    (a) apply for permission to do so and identify each such ground;
    (b) in respect of each such ground—
        (i) explain why it was not included in the appeal notice, and
        (ii) where Part 39 applies, comply with rule 39.3(2);
    (c) serve the application on—
        (i) the Registrar, and
        (ii) any respondent; and
    (d) serve the application—
        (i) as soon as reasonably practicable, and in any event
        (ii) at the same time as serving any renewed application for permission to appeal which relies on that ground.
(6) Paragraph (7) applies where a party wants to abandon—
    (a) a ground of appeal on which that party has permission to appeal; or
    (b) a ground of opposition identified in a respondent's notice.
(7) Such a party must serve notice on—
    (a) the Registrar; and
    (b) each other party,
before any hearing at which that ground will be considered by the court.

[Note. In some legislation, including the Criminal Appeal Act 1968, permission to appeal is described as 'leave to appeal'.

Under rule 36.5 (Renewing an application refused by a judge or the Registrar), if permission to appeal is refused the application for such permission may be renewed within the time limit (10 business days) set by that rule.]

Reopening the determination of an appeal   **R36.15**

36.15 (1) This rule applies where—
    (a) a party wants the court to reopen a decision which determines an appeal or reference to which this Part applies (including a decision on an application for permission to appeal or refer); or
    (b) the Registrar refers such a decision to the court for the court to consider reopening it.
(2) Such a party must—
    (a) apply in writing for permission to reopen that decision, as soon as practicable after becoming aware of the grounds for doing so; and
    (b) serve the application on the Registrar.
(3) The application must—
    (a) specify the decision which the applicant wants the court to reopen; and
    (b) explain—
        (i) why it is necessary for the court to reopen that decision in order to avoid real injustice,
        (ii) how the circumstances are exceptional and make it appropriate to reopen the decision notwithstanding the rights and interests of other participants and the importance of finality,
        (iii) why there is no alternative effective remedy among any potentially available, and
        (iv) any delay in making the application.
(4) The Registrar—
    (a) may invite a party's representations on—
        (i) an application to reopen a decision, or
        (ii) a decision that the Registrar has referred, or intends to refer, to the court; and
    (b) must do so if the court so directs.
(5) A party invited to make representations must serve them on the Registrar within such period as the Registrar directs.
(6) The court must not reopen a decision to which this rule applies unless each other party has had an opportunity to make representations.

[Note. The Court of Appeal has power only in exceptional circumstances to reopen a decision to which this rule applies.]

Criminal Procedure Rules

CRIMINAL PROCEDURE RULES　　PART 37　　APPEAL TO THE COURT OF APPEAL
AGAINST RULING AT PREPARATORY HEARING

R37.1　When this Part applies

37.1　(1)　This Part applies where a party wants to appeal under—

(a)　section 9(11) of the Criminal Justice Act 1987[1] or section 35(1) of the Criminal Procedure and Investigations Act 1996[2]; or

(b)　section 47(1) of the Criminal Justice Act 2003[3].

(2)　A reference to an 'appellant' in this Part is a reference to such a party.

[Note. Under section 9(11) of the Criminal Justice Act 1987 (which applies to serious or complex fraud cases) and under section 35(1) of the Criminal Procedure and Investigations Act 1996 (which applies to other complex, serious or long cases) a party may appeal to the Court of Appeal against an order made at a preparatory hearing in the Crown Court.

Under section 47(1) of the Criminal Justice Act 2003 a party may appeal to the Court of Appeal against an order in the Crown Court that because of jury tampering a trial will continue without a jury or that there will be a new trial without a jury.

Part 3 contains rules about preparatory hearings.

The rules in Part 36 (Appeal to the Court of Appeal: general rules) also apply where this Part applies.]

R37.2　Service of appeal notice

37.2　(1)　An appellant must serve an appeal notice on—

(a)　the Crown Court officer;

(b)　the Registrar; and

(c)　every party directly affected by the order or ruling against which the appellant wants to appeal.

(2)　The appellant must serve the appeal notice not more than 5 business days after—

(a)　the order or ruling against which the appellant wants to appeal; or

(b)　the Crown Court judge gives or refuses permission to appeal.

R37.3　Form of appeal notice

37.3　(1)　An appeal notice must be in the form set out in the Practice Direction.

(2)　The appeal notice must—

(a)　specify each order or ruling against which the appellant wants to appeal;

(b)　identify each ground of appeal on which the appellant relies, numbering them consecutively (if there is more than one) and concisely outlining each argument in support;

(c)　summarise the relevant facts;

(d)　identify any relevant authorities;

(e)　include or attach any application for the following, with reasons—

(i)　permission to appeal, if the appellant needs the court's permission,

(ii)　an extension of time within which to serve the appeal notice, or

(iii)　a direction to attend in person a hearing that the appellant could attend by live link, if the appellant is in custody;

(f)　include a list of those on whom the appellant has served the appeal notice;

(g)　attach—

(i)　a transcript or note of each order or ruling against which the appellant wants to appeal,

(ii)　all relevant skeleton arguments considered by the Crown Court judge,

(iii)　any written application for permission to appeal that the appellant made to the Crown Court judge,

(iv)　a transcript or note of the decision by the Crown Court judge on any application for permission to appeal, and

(v)　any other document or thing that the appellant thinks the court will need to decide the appeal and include or attach an electronic link to each such document that has

---

[1]　1947 c. 44; section 17 was amended by article 3(2) of S.I. 1968/1656.

[2]　1996 c. 25; section 35(1) was amended by section 45 of the Criminal Justice Act 2003 (c. 44). The amendment is in force for certain purposes, for remaining purposes it has effect from a date to be appointed. Section 35 was also amended by paragraphs 65 and 69 of Schedule 36 to the Criminal Justice Act 2003 (c. 44) and section 59 of, and paragraph 1 of Schedule 11 to, the Constitutional Reform Act 2005 (c. 4) and Part 10 of Schedule 10 to the Protection of Freedoms Act 2012 (c. 9).

[3]　2003 c. 44.

been made available to the Registrar under rule 36.8(1)(a) (Duty of Crown Court officer); and

(h) unless an authority identified by the grounds of appeal (see paragraph (2)(d)) is published by the Registrar as one frequently cited, include or attach—
   (i) an electronic copy of each authority so identified, or
   (ii) if two or more such authorities not so published are identified, electronic copies of each together in a single electronic document.

[Note. An appellant needs the court's permission to appeal in every case to which this Part applies unless the Crown Court judge gives permission.]

Crown Court judge's permission to appeal   R37.4

37.4 (1) An appellant who wants the Crown Court judge to give permission to appeal must—
   (a) apply orally, with reasons, immediately after the order or ruling against which the appellant wants to appeal; or
   (b) apply in writing and serve the application on—
      (i) the Crown Court officer, and
      (ii) every party directly affected by the order or ruling
      not more than 2 business days after that order or ruling.
   (2) A written application must include the same information (with the necessary adaptations) as an appeal notice.

[Note. For the Crown Court judge's power to give permission to appeal, see section 9(11) of the Criminal Justice Act 1987, section 35(1) of the Criminal Procedure and Investigations Act 1996 and section 47(2) of the Criminal Justice Act 2003.]

Respondent's notice   R37.5

37.5 (1) A party on whom an appellant serves an appeal notice may serve a respondent's notice, and must do so if—
   (a) that party wants to make representations to the court; or
   (b) the court so directs.
   (2) Such a party must serve the respondent's notice on—
   (a) the appellant;
   (b) the Crown Court officer;
   (c) the Registrar; and
   (d) any other party on whom the appellant served the appeal notice.
   (3) Such a party must serve the respondent's notice not more than 5 business days after—
   (a) the appellant serves the appeal notice; or
   (b) a direction to do so.
   (4) The respondent's notice must be in the form set out in the Practice Direction.
   (5) The respondent's notice must—
   (a) give the date on which the respondent was served with the appeal notice;
   (b) identify each ground of opposition on which the respondent relies, numbering them consecutively (if there is more than one), concisely outlining each argument in support and identifying the ground of appeal to which each relates;
   (c) summarise any relevant facts not already summarised in the appeal notice;
   (d) identify any relevant authorities;
   (e) include or attach any application for the following, with reasons—
      (i) an extension of time within which to serve the respondent's notice, or
      (ii) a direction to attend in person any hearing that the respondent could attend by live link, if the respondent is in custody;
   (f) identify any other document or thing that the respondent thinks the court will need to decide the appeal and include or attach an electronic link to each such document that has been made available to the Registrar under rule 36.8(1)(a) (Duty of Crown Court officer); and
   (g) unless an authority identified under paragraph (5)(d) is published by the Registrar as one frequently cited, include or attach—
      (i) an electronic copy of each authority so identified, or
      (ii) if two or more such authorities not so published are identified, electronic copies of each together in a single electronic document

Criminal Procedure Rules

R37.6   **Powers of Court of Appeal judge**

37.6   A judge of the Court of Appeal may give permission to appeal as well as exercising the powers given by other legislation (including these Rules).

[Note. See section 31 of the Criminal Appeal Act 1968[4] and section 49 of the Criminal Justice Act 2003[5].]

R37.7   **Renewing applications**

37.7   Rule 36.5 (Renewing an application refused by a judge or the Registrar) applies with a time limit of 5 business days.

R37.8   **Right to attend hearing**

37.8   (1)   A party who is in custody has a right to attend a hearing in public.

(2)   The court or the Registrar may direct that such a party is to attend a hearing by live link.

[Note. See rule 36.6 (Hearings).]

CRIMINAL PROCEDURE RULES   PART 38   APPEAL TO THE COURT OF APPEAL
AGAINST RULING ADVERSE TO PROSECUTION

R38.1   **When this Part applies**

38.1   (1)   This Part applies where a prosecutor wants to appeal under section 58(2) of the Criminal Justice Act 2003[1].

(2)   A reference to an 'appellant' in this Part is a reference to such a prosecutor.

[Note. Under section 58(2) of the Criminal Justice Act 2003 a prosecutor may appeal to the Court of Appeal against a ruling in the Crown Court. See also sections 57 and 59 to 61 of the 2003 Act.

The rules in Part 36 (Appeal to the Court of Appeal: general rules) also apply where this Part applies.]

R38.2   **Decision to appeal**

38.2   (1)   An appellant must tell the Crown Court judge of any decision to appeal—
(a)   immediately after the ruling against which the appellant wants to appeal; or
(b)   on the expiry of the time to decide whether to appeal allowed under paragraph (2).

(2)   If an appellant wants time to decide whether to appeal—
(a)   the appellant must ask the Crown Court judge immediately after the ruling; and
(b)   the general rule is that the judge must not require the appellant to decide there and then but instead must allow until the next business day.

[Note. If the ruling against which the appellant wants to appeal is a ruling that there is no case to answer, the appellant may appeal against earlier rulings as well: see section 58(7) of the Criminal Justice Act 2003.

Under section 58(8) of the 2003 Act the appellant must agree that a defendant directly affected by the ruling must be acquitted if the appellant (a) does not get permission to appeal or (b) abandons the appeal.

The Crown Court judge may give permission to appeal and may expedite the appeal: see rules 38.5 and 38.6.]

R38.3   **Service of appeal notice**

38.3   (1)   An appellant must serve an appeal notice on—
(a)   the Crown Court officer;
(b)   the Registrar; and
(c)   every defendant directly affected by the ruling against which the appellant wants to appeal.

(2)   The appellant must serve the appeal notice not later than—
(a)   the next business day after telling the Crown Court judge of the decision to appeal, if the judge expedites the appeal; or

---

[4] 1968 c. 19; section 31 was amended by section 21 of, and Schedule 2 to, the Costs in Criminal Cases Act 1973 (c. 14), section 24 of, and paragraph 10 of Schedule 6 to, the Road Traffic Act 1974 (c. 50), section 29 of the Criminal Justice Act 1982 (c. 48), section 170 of, and paragraphs 20, 29 and 30 of Schedule 15 to, the Criminal Justice Act 1988 (c. 33), section 4 of, and paragraph 4 of Schedule 3 to, the Road Traffic (Consequential Provisions) Act 1988 (c. 54), section 198 of, and paragraphs 38 and 40 of Schedule 6 to, the Licensing Act 2003 (c. 17), section 87 of the Courts Act 2003 (c. 39), paragraphs 86, 87 and 88 of Schedule 36 to the Criminal Justice Act 2003 (c. 44), section 48 of the Police and Justice Act 2006 (c. 48), section 47 of, and paragraphs 1, 9 and 11 of Schedule 8 to, the Criminal Justice and Immigration Act 2008 (c. 4) and section 177 of, and paragraph 69 of Schedule 21 to, the Coroners and Justice Act 2009 (c. 25). It is further amended by section 67 of, and paragraph 4 of Schedule 4 to, the Youth Justice and Criminal Evidence Act 1999 (c. 23), with effect from a date to be appointed.
[5] 2003 c. 44.
[1] 2003 c. 44.

(b) 5 business days after telling the Crown Court judge of that decision, if the judge does not expedite the appeal.

[Note. If the ruling against which the appellant wants to appeal is a public interest ruling, see rule 38.8.]

Form of appeal notice   R38.4

38.4 (1) An appeal notice must be in the form set out in the Practice Direction.

(2) The appeal notice must—

(a) specify each ruling against which the appellant wants to appeal;

(b) identify each ground of appeal on which the appellant relies, numbering them consecutively (if there is more than one) and concisely outlining each argument in support;

(c) summarise the relevant facts;

(d) identify any relevant authorities;

(e) include or attach any application for the following, with reasons—

(i) permission to appeal, if the appellant needs the court's permission,

(ii) an extension of time within which to serve the appeal notice,

(iii) expedition of the appeal, or revocation of a direction expediting the appeal;

(f) include a list of those on whom the appellant has served the appeal notice;

(g) attach—

(i) a transcript or note of each ruling against which the appellant wants to appeal,

(ii) all relevant skeleton arguments considered by the Crown Court judge,

(iii) any written application for permission to appeal that the appellant made to the Crown Court judge,

(iv) a transcript or note of the decision by the Crown Court judge on any application for permission to appeal,

(v) a transcript or note of the decision by the Crown Court judge on any request to expedite the appeal, and

(vi) any other document or thing that the appellant thinks the court will need to decide the appeal and include or attach an electronic link to each such document that has been made available to the Registrar under rule 36.8(1)(a) (Duty of Crown Court officer);

(h) unless an authority identified by the grounds of appeal (see paragraph (2)(d)) is published by the Registrar as one frequently cited, include or attach—

(i) an electronic copy of each authority so identified, or

(ii) if two or more such authorities not so published are identified, electronic copies of each together in a single electronic document

(i) include or attach—

(i) an electronic copy of any authority identified under paragraph (2)(d), or

(ii) if two or more such authorities are identified, electronic copies of each together in a single electronic document; and

(j) attach a form of respondent's notice for any defendant served with the appeal notice to complete if that defendant wants to do so.

[Note. An appellant needs the court's permission to appeal unless the Crown Court judge gives permission: see section 57(4) of the Criminal Justice Act 2003. For 'respondent's notice' see rule 38.7.]

Crown Court judge's permission to appeal   R38.5

38.5 (1) An appellant who wants the Crown Court judge to give permission to appeal must—

(a) apply orally, with reasons, immediately after the ruling against which the appellant wants to appeal; or

(b) apply in writing and serve the application on—

(i) the Crown Court officer, and

(ii) every defendant directly affected by the ruling

on the expiry of the time allowed under rule 38.2 to decide whether to appeal.

(2) A written application must include the same information (with the necessary adaptations) as an appeal notice.

(3) The Crown Court judge must allow every defendant directly affected by the ruling an opportunity to make representations.

(4) The general rule is that the Crown Court judge must decide whether or not to give permission to appeal on the day that the application for permission is made.

[Note. For the Crown Court judge's power to give permission to appeal, see section 57(4) of the Criminal Justice Act 2003.]

Rule 38.5(3) does not apply where the appellant wants to appeal against a public interest ruling: see rule 38.8(5).]

R38.6 Expediting an appeal

38.6 (1) An appellant who wants the Crown Court judge to expedite an appeal must ask, giving reasons, on telling the judge of the decision to appeal.

(2) The Crown Court judge must allow every defendant directly affected by the ruling an opportunity to make representations.

(3) The Crown Court judge may revoke a direction expediting the appeal unless the appellant has served the appeal notice.

[Note. For the Crown Court judge's power to expedite the appeal, see section 59 of the Criminal Justice Act 2003.

Rule 38.6(2) does not apply where the appellant wants to appeal against a public interest ruling: see rule 38.8(5).]

R38.7 Respondent's notice

38.7 (1) A defendant on whom an appellant serves an appeal notice may serve a respondent's notice, and must do so if—

(a) the defendant wants to make representations to the court; or

(b) the court so directs.

(2) Such a defendant must serve the respondent's notice on—

(a) the appellant;

(b) the Crown Court officer;

(c) the Registrar; and

(d) any other defendant on whom the appellant served the appeal notice.

(3) Such a defendant must serve the respondent's notice—

(a) not later than the next business day after—

(i) the appellant serves the appeal notice, or

(ii) a direction to do so

if the Crown Court judge expedites the appeal; or

(b) not more than 5 business days after—

(i) the appellant serves the appeal notice, or

(ii) a direction to do so

if the Crown Court judge does not expedite the appeal.

(4) The respondent's notice must be in the form set out in the Practice Direction.

(5) The respondent's notice must—

(a) give the date on which the respondent was served with the appeal notice;

(b) identify each ground of opposition on which the respondent relies, numbering them consecutively (if there is more than one), concisely outlining each argument in support and identifying the ground of appeal to which each relates;

(c) summarise any relevant facts not already summarised in the appeal notice;

(d) identify any relevant authorities;

(e) include or attach any application for the following, with reasons—

(i) an extension of time within which to serve the respondent's notice, or

(ii) a direction to attend in person any hearing that the respondent could attend by live link, if the respondent is in custody;

(f) identify any other document or thing that the respondent thinks the court will need to decide the appeal and include an electronic link to each such document that has been made available to the Registrar under rule 36.8(1)(a) (Duty of Crown Court officer); and

(g) include or attach—

(i) an electronic copy of any authority identified under paragraph (5)(d), or

(ii) if two or more such authorities are identified, electronic copies of each together in a single electronic document.

R38.8 Public interest ruling

38.8 (1) This rule applies where the appellant wants to appeal against a public interest ruling.

(2) The appellant must not serve on any defendant directly affected by the ruling—

(a) any written application to the Crown Court judge for permission to appeal; or

(b) an appeal notice,

if the appellant thinks that to do so in effect would reveal something that the appellant thinks ought not be disclosed.

(3) The appellant must not include in an appeal notice—

(a) the material that was the subject of the ruling; or

(b) any indication of what sort of material it is,

if the appellant thinks that to do so in effect would reveal something that the appellant thinks ought not be disclosed.

(4) The appellant must serve on the Registrar with the appeal notice an annex—

   (a) marked to show that its contents are only for the court and the Registrar;
   (b) containing whatever the appellant has omitted from the appeal notice, with reasons; and
   (c) if relevant, explaining why the appellant has not served the appeal notice.

(5) Rules 38.5(3) and 38.6(2) do not apply.

[Note. Rules 38.5(3) and 38.6(2) require the Crown Court judge to allow a defendant to make representations about (i) giving permission to appeal and (ii) expediting an appeal.]

Powers of Court of Appeal judge   R38.9

38.9 A judge of the Court of Appeal may—

   (a) give permission to appeal;
   (b) revoke a Crown Court judge's direction expediting an appeal; and
   (c) where an appellant abandons an appeal, order a defendant's acquittal, his release from custody and the payment of his costs,

as well as exercising the powers given by other legislation (including these Rules).

Renewing applications   R38.10

38.10 Rule 36.5 (Renewing an application refused by a judge or the Registrar) applies with a time limit of 5 business days.

Right to attend hearing   R38.11

38.11 (1) A respondent who is in custody has a right to attend a hearing in public.

   (2) The court or the Registrar may direct that such a respondent is to attend a hearing by live link.

[Note. See rule 36.6 (Hearings).]

CRIMINAL PROCEDURE RULES   PART 39   APPEAL TO THE COURT OF APPEAL ABOUT CONVICTION OR SENTENCE

When this Part applies   R39.1

39.1 (1) This Part applies where—

   (a) a defendant wants to appeal under—
      (i)   Part 1 of the Criminal Appeal Act 1968[1],
      (ii) section 274(3) of the Criminal Justice Act 2003[2],
      (iii) paragraph 14 of Schedule 22 to the Criminal Justice Act 2003[3], or
      (iv) section 42 of the Counter-Terrorism Act 2008[4];
   (b) the Criminal Cases Review Commission refers a case to the Court of Appeal under section 9 of the Criminal Appeal Act 1995[5];
   (c) a prosecutor wants to appeal to the Court of Appeal under section 14A(5A) of the Football Spectators Act 1989[6];
   (d) a party wants to appeal under section 389 of the Sentencing Act 2020[7];
   (e) a person found in contempt of court wants to appeal under section 13 of the Administration of Justice Act 1960[8] and section 18A of the Criminal Appeal Act 1968[9]; or

---

[1] 1968 c. 19.

[2] 2003 c. 44; section 274 was amended by section 40 of, and paragraph 82 of Schedule 9 to, the Constitutional Reform Act 2005 (c. 4).

[3] 2003 c. 44; paragraph 14 of Schedule 22 was amended by section 40 of, and paragraph 82 of Schedule 9 and paragraph 1 of Schedule 11 to, the Constitutional Reform Act 2005 (c. 4).

[4] 2008 c. 28.

[5] 1995 c. 35; section 9 was amended by section 58 of, and paragraph 31 of Schedule 10 to, the Domestic Violence, Crime and Victims Act 2004 (c. 28).

[6] 1989 c. 37; section 14A(5A) was inserted by section 52 of, and paragraphs 1 and 3 of Schedule 3 to, the Violent Crime Reduction Act 2006 (c. 38).

[7] 2020 c. 17.

[8] 1960 c. 65; section 13 was amended paragraph 40 of Schedule 8 to, the Courts Act 1971 (c. 23), Schedule 5 to, the Criminal Appeal Act 1968 (c. 19), paragraph 36 of Schedule 7 to, the Magistrates' Courts Act 1980 (c. 43), Schedule 7 to, the Supreme Court Act 1981 (c. 54), paragraph 25 of Schedule 2 to, the County Courts Act 1984 (c. 28), Schedule 15 to, the Access to Justice Act 1999 (c. 22), paragraph 13 of Schedule 9 to the Constitutional Reform Act 2005 (c. 4) and paragraph 45 of Schedule 16 to, the Armed Forces Act 2006 (c. 52).

[9] 1968 c. 19; section 18A was inserted by section 170 of, and paragraphs 20 and 25 of Schedule 15 to, the Criminal Justice Act 1988 (c. 33).

    (f)   a person wants to appeal to the Court of Appeal under—
        (i)   section 24 of the Serious Crime Act 2007[10],
        (ii) section 28(5)(a) of the Offensive Weapons Act 2019[11],
        (iii) section 342I(2) of the 2020 Act,
        (iv) section 46(5) of the Domestic Abuse Act 2021, or
        (v) regulation 3C or 3H of the Costs in Criminal Cases (General) Regulations 1986[12].
    (2) A reference to an 'appellant' in this Part is a reference to such a party or person.

[Note. Under Part 1 (sections 1 to 32) of the Criminal Appeal Act 1968, a defendant may appeal against—

    (a) a conviction (section 1 of the 1968 Act[13]);
    (b) a sentence (sections 9 and 10 of the 1968 Act[14]);
    (c) a verdict of not guilty by reason of insanity (section 12 of the 1968 Act);
    (d) a finding of disability or a finding that the defendant did the act or made the omission charged as an offence (section 15 of the 1968 Act[15];
    (e) a hospital order, interim hospital order or supervision order under section 5 or 5A of the Criminal Procedure (Insanity) Act 1964[16] (section 16A of the 1968 Act[17]).

See section 50 of the 1968 Act[18] for the meaning of 'sentence'.

Under section 274(3) of the 2003 Act, a defendant sentenced to life imprisonment outside the United Kingdom, and transferred to serve the sentence in England and Wales, may appeal against the minimum term fixed by a High Court judge under section 321 of the 2020 Act or under section 269 of the 2003 Act.

Under paragraph 14 of Schedule 22 to the Criminal Justice Act 2003 a defendant sentenced to life imprisonment may appeal against the minimum term fixed on review by a High Court judge in certain cases.

Under section 42 of the Counter Terrorism Act 2008 a defendant may appeal against a decision of the Crown Court that an offence has a terrorist connection.

---

[10] 2007 c. 27.

[11] 2019 c. 17; section 28 comes into force on a date to be appointed.

[12] S.I. 1986/1335; regulation 3C was inserted by regulation 2 of The Costs in Criminal Cases (General) (Amendment) Regulations 1991 (SI 1991/789) and amended by regulation 5 of The Costs in Criminal Cases (General) (Amendment) Regulations 2004 (SI 2004/2408). Regulation 3H was inserted by regulation 7 of The Costs in Criminal Cases (General) (Amendment) Regulations 2004 (SI 2004/2408).

[13] 1968 c. 19; section 1 was amended by section 154 of, and paragraph 71 of Schedule 7 to, the Magistrates' Courts Act 1980 (c. 43), paragraph 44 of Schedule 3 to the Criminal Justice Act 2003 (c. 44), section 1 of the Criminal Appeal Act 1995 (c. 35) and section 47 of, and paragraphs 1 and 2 of Schedule 8 to, the Criminal Justice and Immigration Act 2008 (c. 4).

[14] 1968 c. 19; section 9 was amended by section 170 of, and paragraph 21 of Schedule 15 to, the Criminal Justice Act 1988 (c. 33), section 119 of, and paragraph 12 of Schedule 8 to, the Crime and Disorder Act 1998 (c. 37), section 58 of the Access to Justice Act 1999 (c. 22) and section 271 of, and paragraph 44 of Schedule 3 and Schedule 37 to, the Criminal Justice Act 2003 (c. 44). Section 10 was amended by section 56 of, and paragraph 57 of Schedule 8 to, the Courts Act 1971 (c. 23), section 77 of, and paragraph 23 of Schedule 14 to, the Criminal Justice Act 1982 (c. 48), section 170 of, and paragraphs 20 and 22 of Schedule 15 and Schedule 16 to, the Criminal Justice Act 1988 (c. 33), section 100 of, and paragraph 3 of Schedule 11 to, the Criminal Justice Act 1991 (c. 53), sections 119 and 120 of, and paragraph 13 of Schedule 8 and Schedule 10 to, the Crime and Disorder Act 1998 (c. 37), section 58 of the Access to Justice Act 1999 (c. 22), section 67 of, and paragraph 4 of Schedule 4 and Schedule 6 to, the Youth Justice and Criminal Evidence Act 1999 (c. 23), sections 304, 319 and 322 of, and paragraphs 7 and 8 of Schedule 32 and Schedule 37 to, the Criminal Justice Act 2003 (c. 44) and section 6(2) of, and paragraph 4 of Schedule 4 to, the Criminal Justice and Immigration Act 2008 (c. 4).

[15] 1968 c. 19; section 15 was amended by section 7 of, and paragraph 2 of Schedule 3 to, the Criminal Procedure (Insanity and Unfitness to Plead) Act 1991 (c. 25), section 1 of the Criminal Appeal Act 1995 (c. 35) and section 58 of, and paragraph 4 of Schedule 10 to, the Domestic Violence, Crime and Victims Act 2004 (c. 28) and section 47 of, and paragraphs 1 and 5 of Schedule 8 to, the Criminal Justice and Immigration Act 2008 (c. 4).

[16] 1964 c. 84; section 5 was substituted, and section 5A inserted, by section 24 of the Domestic Violence, Crime and Victims Act 2004 (c. 28). Section 5A was amended by section 15 of the Mental Health Act 2007 (c. 12).

[17] 1968 c. 19; section 16A was inserted by section 25 of the Domestic Violence, Crime and Victims Act 2004 (c. 28).

[18] 1968 c. 19; section 50 was amended by section 66 of the Criminal Justice Act 1982 (c. 48), sections 100 and 101 of, and paragraph 4 of Schedule 11 and Schedule 13 to, the Criminal Justice Act 1991 (c. 53), section 79 of, and Schedule 5 to, the Criminal Justice Act 1993 (c. 36), section 65 of, and Schedule 1 to, the Drug Trafficking Act 1994 (c. 37), section 7 of the Football (Offences and Disorder) Act 1999 (c. 21), section 24 of, and paragraph 3 of Schedule 4 to, the Access to Justice Act 1999 (c. 22), section 165 of, and paragraph 30 of Schedule 9 to, the Powers of Criminal Courts (Sentencing) Act 2000 (c. 6), section 1 of, and Schedule 3 to, the Football (Disorder) Act 2000 (c. 25), section 456 of, and paragraphs 1 and 4 of Schedule 11 to, the Proceeds of Crime Act 2002 (c. 43), section 198 of, and paragraphs 38 and 42 of Schedule 6 to, the Licensing Act 2003 (c. 17), section 52 of, and paragraph 14 of Schedule 3 to, the Violent Crime Reduction Act 2006 (c. 38), paragraph 3 of Schedule 5 to the Legal Aid, Sentencing and Punishment of Offenders Act 2012 (c. 10) and section 85 of, and paragraph 3 of Schedule 4 to, the Serious Crime Act 2015 (c. 9). It is further amended by section 55 of, and paragraph 6 of Schedule 4 to, the Crime (Sentences) Act 1997 (c. 43), with effect from a date to be appointed.

See section 13 of the Criminal Appeal Act 1995[19] for the circumstances in which the Criminal Cases Review Commission may refer a conviction, sentence, verdict or finding to the Court of Appeal.

Under section 14A(5A) of the Football Spectators Act 1989 a prosecutor may appeal against a failure by the Crown Court to make a football banning order.

Under section 389 of the 2020 Act a prosecutor or defendant may appeal against a review by a Crown Court judge of a sentence that was reduced because the defendant assisted the investigator or prosecutor.

Under section 13 of the Administration of Justice Act 1960 a person in respect of whom an order or decision is made by the Crown Court in the exercise of its jurisdiction to punish for contempt of court may appeal to the Court of Appeal.

Under section 24 of the Serious Crime Act 2007 a person who is the subject of a serious crime prevention order, or the relevant applicant authority, may appeal to the Court of Appeal against a decision of the Crown Court in relation to that order. In addition, any person who was given an opportunity to make representations in the proceedings by virtue of section 9(4) of the Act may appeal to the Court of Appeal against a decision of the Crown Court to make, vary or not vary a serious crime prevention order.

Under section 28(5)(a) of the Offensive Weapons Act 2019 an applicant to the Crown Court for the variation, renewal or discharge of a knife crime prevention order made by that court, or a respondent to such an application, may appeal to the Court of Appeal against the decision of the Crown Court.

Under section 342I(2) of the Sentencing Act 2020 an applicant to the Crown Court for the variation, renewal or discharge of a serious violence reduction order made by that court, or a respondent to such an application, may appeal to the Court of Appeal against the decision of the Crown Court.

Under section 46(5), (7) of the Domestic Abuse Act 2021 an applicant to the Crown Court for the variation or discharge of a domestic abuse prevention order made by that court, or a respondent to such an application, may appeal to the Court of Appeal against the decision of the Crown Court.

Under regulation 3C of the Costs in Criminal Cases (General) Regulations 1986, a legal representative against whom the Crown Court makes a wasted costs order under section 19A of the Prosecution of Offences Act 1985[20] and regulation 3B may appeal against that order to the Court of Appeal.

Under regulation 3H of the Costs in Criminal Cases (General) Regulations 1986, a third party against whom the Crown Court makes a costs order under section 19B of the Prosecution of Offences Act 1985[21] and regulation 3F may appeal against that order to the Court of Appeal.

The rules in Part 36 (Appeal to the Court of Appeal: general rules) also apply where this Part applies.]

Service of appeal notice   R39.2

39.2 (1) The appellant must serve an appeal notice on the Registrar—
      (a) not more than 28 days after—
          (i)   the conviction, verdict, or finding,
          (ii) the sentence,
          (iii) the order (subject to paragraph (b)), or the failure to make an order, or
          (iv) the minimum term review decision under section 274(3) of, or paragraph 14 of Schedule 22 to, the Criminal Justice Act 2003
          about which the appellant wants to appeal;
      (b) not more than 15 business days after the order in a case in which the appellant appeals against a wasted or third party costs order; and
      (c) not more than 20 business days after the Registrar serves notice that the Criminal Cases Review Commission has referred a conviction to the court.
    (2) Unless the appeal notice includes grounds of appeal prepared by the person who was appointed to put the case for the defence under rule 25.10 (Defendant unfit to plead), paragraphs (3), (4) and (5) of this rule apply where the appeal is about—
      (a) a finding of disability under section 4 of the Criminal Procedure (Insanity) Act 1964[22],
      (b) a finding under section 4A of the 1964 Act that the defendant did the act or made the omission charged as an offence; or

---

[19] 1995 c. 35; section 13 was amended by section 321 of, and paragraph 3 of Schedule 11 to, the Armed Forces Act 2006 (c. 52).
[20] 1985 c. 23; section 19A was inserted by section 111 of the Courts and Legal Services Act 1990 (c. 41).
[21] 1985 c. 23; section 19B was inserted by section 93 of the Courts Act 2003 (c. 39).
[22] 1964 c. 84; section 4 was substituted, together with section 4A, for section 4 as originally enacted, by section 2 of the Criminal Procedure (Insanity and Unfitness to Plead) Act 1991 (c. 25), and amended by section 22 of the Domestic Violence, Crime and Victims Act 2004 (c. 28).

(c) a hospital order, interim hospital order or supervision order made under section 5 or 5A of the 1964 Act[23];

(3) The Registrar must refer the appeal notice to a judge of the Court of Appeal for the judge to give or refuse to give procedural directions under section 31B of the Criminal Appeal Act 1968[24].

(4) The judge may—

(a) give such procedural directions as the case requires where the appeal notice includes grounds of appeal that the judge considers reasonably arguable; or

(b) refuse to give such directions, in any other case.

(5) Such procedural directions may include—

(a) a direction for the appointment of a person to put the case for the appellant on appeal;

(b) a direction to commission medical evidence; and

(c) a direction for the reference of the case to the judge again to give, or to refuse to give, further directions.

[Note. The time limit for serving an appeal notice (a) on an appeal under Part 1 of the Criminal Appeal Act 1968 and (b) on an appeal against a finding of contempt of court is prescribed by sections 18 and 18A of the Criminal Appeal Act 1968. It may be extended, but not shortened.

For service of a reference by the Criminal Cases Review Commission, see rule 39.5.

[Under section 31C of the 1968 Act[25] a party has no right to renew to the Court of Appeal an application for procedural directions refused by a judge.]

R39.3 **Form of appeal notice**

39.3 (1) An appeal notice must—

(a) specify—

(i) the conviction, verdict, or finding,

(ii) the sentence, or

(iii) the order, or the failure to make an order about which the appellant wants to appeal;

(b) identify each ground of appeal on which the appellant relies (and see paragraph (2));

(c) identify the transcript that the appellant thinks the court will need, if the appellant wants to appeal against a conviction;

(d) identify the relevant sentencing powers of the Crown Court, if sentence is in issue;

(e) include or attach any application for the following, with reasons—

(i) permission to appeal, if the appellant needs the court's permission,

(ii) an extension of time within which to serve the appeal notice,

(iii) bail pending appeal,

(iv) a direction to attend in person a hearing that the appellant could attend by live link, if the appellant is in custody,

(v) the introduction of evidence, including hearsay evidence and evidence of bad character,

(vi) an order requiring a witness to attend court,

(vii) a direction for special measures for a witness,

(viii) a direction for special measures for the giving of evidence by the appellant, or

(ix) the suspension of any disqualification imposed, or order made, in the case, where the Court of Appeal can order such a suspension pending appeal;

(f) identify any other document or thing that the appellant thinks the court will need to decide the appeal and include or attach an electronic link to each such document that has been made available to the Registrar under rule 36.8(1)(a) (Duty of Crown Court officer); and

(g) unless an authority identified by the grounds of appeal (see paragraph (2)(f)) is published by the Registrar as one frequently cited, include or attach—

(i) an electronic copy of each authority so identified so identified, or

(ii) if two or more such authorities not so published are identified, electronic copies of each together in a single electronic document.

(2) The grounds of appeal must—

(a) include in no more than the first two pages a summary of the grounds that makes what then follows easy to understand;

---

[23] 1964 c. 84; section 5 was substituted, and section 5A inserted, by section 24 of the Domestic Violence, Crime and Victims Act 2004 (c. 28). Section 5A was amended by section 15 of the Mental Health Act 2007 (c. 12).

[24] 1968 c. 19; section 31B was inserted by section 87 of the Courts Act 2003 (c. 39).

[25] 1968 c. 19; section 31C was inserted by section 87 of the Courts Act 2003 (c. 39) and amended by sections 47 and 149 of, and paragraphs 1 and 12 of Schedule 8 and part 3 of Schedule 28 to, the Criminal Justice and Immigration Act 2008 (c. 4).

(b) in each ground of appeal identify the event or decision to which that ground relates;

(c) in each ground of appeal summarise the facts relevant to that ground, but only to the extent necessary to make clear what is in issue;

(d) concisely outline each argument in support of each ground;

(e) number each ground consecutively, if there is more than one;

(f) identify any relevant authority and—

(i) state the proposition of law that the authority demonstrates, and

(ii) identify the parts of the authority that support that proposition; and

(g) where the Criminal Cases Review Commission refers a case to the court, explain how each ground of appeal relates (if it does) to the reasons for the reference.

[Note. The Practice Direction sets out forms of appeal notice for use in connection with this rule.

In some legislation, including the Criminal Appeal Act 1968, permission to appeal is described as 'leave to appeal'.

An appellant needs the court's permission to appeal in every case to which this Part applies, except where—

(a) the Criminal Cases Review Commission refers the case;

(b) the appellant appeals against—

(i) an order or decision made in the exercise of jurisdiction to punish for contempt of court, or

(ii) a wasted or third party costs order; or

(c) the Crown Court judge certifies under sections 1(2)(a), 11(1A), 12(b), 15(2)(b) or 16A(2)(b) of the Criminal Appeal Act 1968[26], under section 81(1B) of the Senior Courts Act 1981[27], under section 14A(5B) of the Football Spectators Act 1989[28], or under section 24(4) of the Serious Crime Act 2007, that a case is fit for appeal.

A judge of the Court of Appeal may give permission to appeal under section 31 of the Criminal Appeal Act 1968[29].

See also rules 39.7 (Introducing evidence) and 39.8 (Application for bail, or to suspend a disqualification or order, pending appeal or retrial).]

Crown Court judge's certificate that case is fit for appeal   R39.4

39.4 (1) An appellant who wants the Crown Court judge to certify that a case is fit for appeal must either—

(a) apply orally, with reasons, immediately after there occurs—

(i) the conviction, verdict, or finding,

(ii) the sentence, or

(iii) the order, or the failure to make an order

about which the appellant wants to appeal; or

(b) apply in writing and serve the application on the Crown Court officer not more than 10 business days after that occurred.

(2) A written application must include the same information (with the necessary adaptations) as an appeal notice.

[Note. The Crown Court judge may certify that a case is fit for appeal under sections 1(2)(b), 11(1A), 12(b), 15(2)(b) or 16A(2)(b) of the Criminal Appeal Act 1968, under section 81(1B) of the Senior Courts Act 1981, under section 14A(5B) of the Football Spectators Act 1989 or under section 24(4) of the Serious Crime Act 2007.

See also rule 39.2 (service of appeal notice required in all cases).]

---

[26] 1968 c. 19; section 11(1A) was inserted by section 29 of the Criminal Justice Act 1982 (c. 48) and amended by section 47 of, and paragraphs 1 and 3 of Schedule 8 to, the Criminal Justice and Immigration Act 2008 (c. 4).

[27] 1981 c. 54; section 81(1B) was inserted by sections 29 and 60 of the Criminal Justice Act 1982 (c. 48). The Act's title was amended by section 59(5) of, and paragraph 1 of Schedule 11 to, the Constitutional Reform Act 2005 (c. 4).

[28] 1989 c. 37; section 14A(5B) was inserted by section 52 of, and paragraphs 1 and 3 of Schedule 3 to, the Violent Crime Reduction Act 2006 (c. 38).

[29] 1968 c. 19; section 31 was amended by section 21 of, and Schedule 2 to, the Costs in Criminal Cases Act 1973 (c. 14), section 24 of, and paragraph 10 of Schedule 6 to, the Road Traffic Act 1974 (c. 50), section 29 of the Criminal Justice Act 1982 (c. 48), section 170 of, and paragraphs 20, 29 and 30 of Schedule 15 to, the Criminal Justice Act 1988 (c. 33), section 4 of, and paragraph 4 of Schedule 3 to, the Road Traffic (Consequential Provisions) Act 1988 (c. 54), section 198 of, and paragraphs 38 and 40 of Schedule 6 to, the Licensing Act 2003 (c. 17), section 87 of the Courts Act 2003 (c. 39), paragraphs 86, 87 and 88 of Schedule 36 to the Criminal Justice Act 2003 (c. 44), section 48 of the Police and Justice Act 2006 (c. 48), section 47 of, and paragraphs 1, 9 and 11 of Schedule 8 to, the Criminal Justice and Immigration Act 2008 (c. 4) and section 177 of, and paragraph 69 of Schedule 21 to, the Coroners and Justice Act 2009 (c. 25). It is further amended by section 67 of, and paragraph 4 of Schedule 4 to, the Youth Justice and Criminal Evidence Act 1999 (c. 23), with effect from a date to be appointed.

R39.5 **Reference by Criminal Cases Review Commission**

39.5 (1) The Registrar must serve on the appellant a reference by the Criminal Cases Review Commission.

(2) The court must treat that reference as the appeal notice if the appellant does not serve such a notice under rule 39.2.

R39.6 **Respondent's notice**

39.6 (1) The Registrar—

(a) may serve an appeal notice on any party directly affected by the appeal; and

(b) must do so if the Criminal Cases Review Commission refers a conviction, verdict, finding or sentence to the court.

(2) Such a party may serve a respondent's notice, and must do so if—

(a) that party wants to make representations to the court; or

(b) the court or the Registrar so directs.

(3) Such a party must serve the respondent's notice on—

(a) the appellant;

(b) the Registrar; and

(c) any other party on whom the Registrar served the appeal notice.

(4) Such a party must serve the respondent's notice—

(a) not more than 10 business days after the Registrar serves—

(i) the appeal notice, or

(ii) a direction to do so; or

(b) not more than 20 business days after the Registrar serves notice that the Commission has referred a conviction.

(5) The respondent's notice must be in the form set out in the Practice Direction.

(6) The respondent's notice must—

(a) give the date on which the respondent was served with the appeal notice;

(b) identify each ground of opposition on which the respondent relies, numbering them consecutively (if there is more than one), concisely outlining each argument in support and identifying the ground of appeal to which each relates;

(c) identify the relevant sentencing powers of the Crown Court, if sentence is in issue;

(d) summarise any relevant facts not already summarised in the appeal notice;

(e) identify any relevant authorities;

(f) include or attach any application for the following, with reasons—

(i) an extension of time within which to serve the respondent's notice,

(ii) bail pending appeal,

(iii) a direction to attend in person a hearing that the respondent could attend by live link, if the respondent is in custody,

(iv) the introduction of evidence, including hearsay evidence and evidence of bad character,

(v) an order requiring a witness to attend court, or

(vi) a direction for special measures for a witness;

(g) identify any other document or thing that the respondent thinks the court will need to decide the appeal and include or attach an electronic link to each such document that has been made available to the Registrar under rule 36.8(1)(a) (Duty of Crown Court officer); and

(h) unless an authority identified under paragraph (6)(e) is published by the Registrar as one frequently cited, include or attach—

(i) an electronic copy of each authority so identified, or

(ii) if two or more such authorities not so published are identified, electronic copies of each together in a single electronic document.

[Note. The Practice Direction sets out the circumstances in which the Registrar usually will serve a defendant's appeal notice on the prosecutor.

See also rule 39.7 (Introducing evidence).]

R39.7 **Introducing evidence**

39.7 (1) The following Parts apply with such adaptations as the court or the Registrar may direct—

(a) Part 16 (Written witness statements);

(b) Part 18 (Measures to assist a witness or defendant to give evidence);

(c) Part 19 (Expert evidence);

(d) Part 20 (Hearsay evidence);

(e) Part 21 (Evidence of bad character); and

     (f) Part 22 (Evidence of a complainant's previous sexual behaviour).

(2) But the general rule is that—

    (a) a respondent who opposes an appellant's application or notice to which one of those Parts applies must do so in the respondent's notice, with reasons;

    (b) an appellant who opposes a respondent's application or notice to which one of those Parts applies must serve notice, with reasons, on—

       (i) the Registrar, and

      (ii) the respondent

        not more than 10 business days after service of the respondent's notice; and

    (c) the court or the Registrar may give directions with or without a hearing.

(3) A party who wants the court to order the production of a document, exhibit or other thing connected with the proceedings must—

    (a) identify that item; and

    (b) explain—

       (i) how it is connected with the proceedings,

      (ii) why its production is necessary for the determination of the case, and

     (iii) to whom it should be produced (the court, appellant or respondent, or any two or more of them).

(4) A party who wants the court to order a witness to attend to be questioned must—

    (a) identify the proposed witness;

    (b) explain—

       (i) what evidence the proposed witness can give,

      (ii) why that evidence is capable of belief,

     (iii) if applicable, why that evidence may provide a ground for allowing the appeal,

     (iv) on what basis that evidence would have been admissible in the case which is the subject of the application for permission to appeal or appeal, and

      (v) why that evidence was not introduced in that case; and

    (c) where the court can exercise a power to which Part 18 (Measures to assist a witness or defendant to give evidence) applies, provide any information that the court may need to assess—

       (i) the measure or measures likely to maximise so far as practicable the quality of the witness' evidence, and

      (ii) the witness' own views.

(5) Where the court orders a witness to attend to be questioned, the witness must attend the hearing of the application for permission to appeal or of the appeal, as applicable, unless the court otherwise directs.

(6) Where the court orders a witness to attend to be questioned before an examiner on the court's behalf, the court must identify the examiner and may give directions about—

    (a) the time and place, or times and places, at which that questioning must be carried out;

    (b) the manner in which that questioning must be carried out, in particular as to—

       (i) the service of any report, statement or questionnaire in preparation for the questioning,

      (ii) the sequence in which the parties may ask questions, and

     (iii) if more than one witness is to be questioned, the sequence in which those witnesses may be questioned; and

    (c) the manner in which, and when, a record of the questioning must be submitted to the court.

(7) Where the court orders the questioning of a witness before an examiner, the court may delegate to that examiner the giving of directions under paragraph (6)(a), (b) and (c).

[Note. An application to introduce evidence or for directions about evidence must be included in, or attached to, an appeal notice or a respondent's notice: see rules 39.3(1)(e)(v), (vi) and 39.6(6)(f)(iv), (v).

Under section 23 of the Criminal Appeal Act 1968[30], the Court of Appeal may order the production of a document, exhibit or other thing, may order a witness to attend to be examined before the court and may allow the introduction of evidence that was not introduced at trial. Under section 23(4), if it thinks it necessary or

Criminal Procedure Rules

---

[30] 1968 c. 19; section 23 was amended by sections 4 and 29 of, and paragraph 4 of Schedule 2 to, the Criminal Appeal Act 1995 (c. 35), section 48 of the Police and Justice Act 2006 (c. 48) and section 47 of, and paragraphs 1 and 10 of Schedule 8 to, the Criminal Justice and Immigration Act 2008 (c. 4).

expedient in the interests of justice the court may order the examination of a witness to be conducted before any judge, court officer or other person, and allow the admission of a record of that examination as evidence before the court.]

R39.8 **Application for bail, or to suspend a disqualification or order, pending appeal or retrial**

39.8 (1) This rule applies where—

(a) a party wants to make an application to the court about bail pending appeal or retrial; or

(b) an appellant wants to apply to the court to suspend a disqualification or order pending appeal.

(2) That party must serve an application in the form set out in the Practice Direction on—

(a) the Registrar, unless the application is with the appeal notice; and

(b) the other party.

(3) The court must not decide such an application without giving the other party an opportunity to make representations, including, in the case of a bail application, representations about any condition or surety proposed by the applicant.

[Note. See section 19 of the Criminal Appeal Act 1968[31], and section 3(8) of the Bail Act 1976[32] An application about bail or about the conditions of bail may be made either by an appellant or respondent.

Under section 81(1) of the Senior Courts Act 1981[33], a Crown Court judge may grant bail pending appeal only (a) if that judge gives a certificate that the case is fit for appeal (see rule 39.4) and (b) not more than 28 days after the conviction or sentence against which the appellant wants to appeal.

Under section 39 of the Road Traffic Offenders Act 1988[34], a court which has made an order disqualifying a person from driving may suspend the disqualification pending appeal. Under section 40 of the 1988 Act[35], the appeal court may do so. See also rule 29.2.

Under section 129 of the Licensing Act 2003[36], a court which has made an order to forfeit or suspend a personal licence issued under that Act may suspend the order pending appeal. Under section 130 of the 2003 Act[37], the appeal court may do so.]

R39.9 **Conditions of bail pending appeal or retrial**

39.9 (1) This rule applies where the court grants a party bail pending appeal or retrial subject to any condition that must be met before that party is released.

(2) The court may direct how such a condition must be met.

(3) The Registrar must serve a certificate in the form set out in the Practice Direction recording any such condition and direction on—

(a) that party;

(b) that party's custodian; and

(c) any other person directly affected by any such direction.

(4) A person directly affected by any such direction need not comply with it until the Registrar serves that person with that certificate.

(5) Unless the court otherwise directs, if any such condition or direction requires someone to enter into a recognizance it must be—

(a) in the form set out in the Practice Direction and signed before—

(i) the Registrar,

---

[31] 1968 c. 19; section 19 was substituted by section 29 of the Criminal Justice Act 1982 (c. 48) and was amended by section 170 of, and paragraphs 20 and 26 of Schedule 15 to, the Criminal Justice Act 1988 (c. 33), section 168 of, and paragraph 22 of Schedule 10 to, the Criminal Justice and Public Order Act 1994 (c. 33) and section 59 of, and paragraph 1 of Schedule 11 to, the Constitutional Reform Act 2005 (c. 4).

[32] 1976 c. 63; section 3(8) was amended by section 65 of, and Schedule 12 to, the Criminal Law Act 1977 (c. 45) and paragraph 48 of Schedule 3 to the Criminal Justice Act 2003 (c. 44).

[33] 1981 c. 54; section 81(1) was amended by sections 29 and 60 of the Criminal Justice Act 1982 (c. 48), section 15 of, and paragraph 2 of Schedule 12 to, the Criminal Justice Act 1987 (c. 38), section 168 of, and paragraph 19 of Schedule 9 and paragraph 48 of Schedule 10 to, the Criminal Justice and Public Order Act 1994 (c. 33), section 119 of, and paragraph 48 of Schedule 8 and Schedule 10 to, the Crime and Disorder Act 1998 (c. 37), section 165 of, and paragraph 87 of Schedule 9 and Schedule 12 to, the Powers of Criminal Courts (Sentencing) Act 2000 (c. 6), paragraph 54 of Schedule 3, paragraph 4 of Schedule 36 and Part 4 of Schedule 37 to the Criminal Justice Act 2003 (c. 44), articles 2 and 6 of S.I. 2004/1033 and section 177(1) of, and paragraph 76 of Schedule 21 to, the Coroners and Justice Act 2009 (c. 25).

[34] 1988 c. 53.

[35] 1988 c. 53; section 40 was amended by sections 40 and 59 of, and paragraph 50 of Schedule 9 and paragraph 1 of Schedule 11 to, the Constitutional Reform Act 2005 (c.4).

[36] 2003 c. 17.

[37] 2003 c. 17; section 130 was amended by sections 40 and 59 of, and paragraph 78 of Schedule 9 and paragraph 1 of Schedule 11 to, the Constitutional Reform Act 2005 (c. 4).

        (ii) the custodian, or

        (iii) someone acting with the authority of the Registrar or custodian;

    (b) copied immediately to the person who enters into it; and

    (c) served immediately by the Registrar on the appellant's custodian or vice versa, as appropriate.

(6) Unless the court otherwise directs, if any such condition or direction requires someone to make a payment, surrender a document or take some other step—

    (a) that payment, document or step must be made, surrendered or taken to or before—

        (i) the Registrar,

        (ii) the custodian, or

        (iii) someone acting with the authority of the Registrar or custodian; and

    (b) the Registrar or the custodian, as appropriate, must serve immediately on the other a statement that the payment, document or step has been made, surrendered or taken, as appropriate.

(7) The custodian must release the appellant where it appears that any condition ordered by the court has been met.

(8) For the purposes of section 5 of the Bail Act 1976[38] (record of decision about bail), the Registrar must keep a copy of—

    (a) any certificate served under paragraph (3);

    (b) a notice of hearing given under rule 36.7(1); and

    (c) a notice of the court's decision served under rule 36.7(2).

(9) Where the court grants bail pending retrial the Registrar must serve on the Crown Court officer copies of the documents kept under paragraph (8).

Forfeiture of a recognizance given as a condition of bail

R39.10

39.10 (1) This rule applies where—

    (a) the court grants a party bail pending appeal or retrial; and

    (b) the bail is subject to a condition that that party provides a surety to guarantee that he will surrender to custody as required; but

    (c) that party does not surrender to custody as required.

(2) The Registrar must serve notice on—

    (a) the surety; and

    (b) the prosecutor,

  of the hearing at which the court may order the forfeiture of the recognizance given by that surety.

(3) The court must not forfeit a surety's recognizance—

    (a) less than 5 business days after the Registrar serves notice under paragraph (2); and

    (b) without giving the surety an opportunity to make representations at a hearing.

[Note. If the purpose for which a recognizance is entered is not fulfilled, that recognizance may be forfeited by the court. If the court forfeits a surety's recognizance, the sum promised by that person is then payable to the Crown.]

Right to attend hearing

R39.11

39.11 A party who is in custody has a right to attend a hearing in public unless—

    (a) it is a hearing preliminary or incidental to an appeal, including the hearing of an application for permission to appeal;

    (b) it is the hearing of an appeal and the court directs that—

        (i) the appeal involves a question of law alone, and

        (ii) for that reason the appellant has no permission to attend; or

    (c) that party is in custody in consequence of—

        (i) a verdict of not guilty by reason of insanity, or

        (ii) a finding of disability.

---

[38] 1976 c. 63; section 5 was amended by section 65 of, and Schedule 12 to, the Criminal Law Act 1977 (c. 45), section 60 of the Criminal Justice Act 1982 (c. 48), paragraph 1 of Schedule 3 to the Criminal Justice and Public Order Act 1994 (c. 33), paragraph 53 of Schedule 9 to the Powers of Criminal Courts (Sentencing) Act 2000 (c. 6), section 129(1) of the Criminal Justice and Police Act 2001 (c. 16), paragraph 182 of Schedule 8 to the Courts Act 2003 (c. 39), paragraph 48 of Schedule 3, paragraphs 1 and 2 of Schedule 36, and Parts 2, 4 and 12 of Schedule 37 to the Criminal Justice Act 2003 (c. 44) and section 208 of, and paragraphs 33 and 35 of Schedule 21 to, the Legal Services Act 2007 (c. 27).

[Note. See rule 36.6 (Hearings) and section 22 of the Criminal Appeal Act 1968[39]. There are corresponding provisions in the Criminal Justice Act 2003 (Mandatory Life Sentences: Appeals in Transitional Cases) Order 2005[40], the Serious Organised Crime and Police Act 2005 (Appeals under section 74) Order 2006[41] and the Serious Crime Act 2007 (Appeals under Section 24) Order 2008[42]. Under section 22 of the 1968 Act and corresponding provisions in those Orders, the court may direct that an appellant who is in custody is to attend a hearing by live link.]

R39.12   **Power to vary determination of appeal against sentence**

39.12 (1)   This rule applies where the court decides an appeal affecting sentence in a party's absence.

(2)   The court may vary such a decision if it did not take account of something relevant because that party was absent.

(3)   A party who wants the court to vary such a decision must—

(a)   apply in writing, with reasons; and

(b)   serve the application on the Registrar not more than 5 business days after—

(i)   the decision, if that party was represented at the appeal hearing, or

(ii)   the Registrar serves the decision, if that party was not represented at that hearing.

[Note. Section 22(3) of the Criminal Appeal Act 1968 allows the court to sentence in an appellant's absence. There are corresponding provisions in the Criminal Justice Act 2003 (Mandatory Life Sentences: Appeals in Transitional Cases) Order 2005 and in the Serious Organised Crime and Police Act 2005 (Appeals under Section 74) Order 2006.]

R39.13   **Directions about re-admission to hospital on dismissal of appeal**

39.13 (1)   This rule applies where—

(a)   an appellant subject to—

(i)   an order under section 37(1) of the Mental Health Act 1983[43] (detention in hospital on conviction), or

(ii)   an order under section 5(2) of the Criminal Procedure (Insanity) Act 1964[44] (detention in hospital on finding of insanity or disability)

has been released on bail pending appeal; and

(b)   the court—

(i)   refuses permission to appeal,

(ii)   dismisses the appeal, or

(iii)   affirms the order under appeal.

(2)   The court must give appropriate directions for the appellant's—

(a)   re-admission to hospital; and

(b)   if necessary, temporary detention pending re-admission.

R39.14   **Renewal or setting aside of order for retrial**

39.14 (1)   This rule applies where—

(a)   a prosecutor wants a defendant to be arraigned more than 2 months after the court ordered a retrial under section 7 of the Criminal Appeal Act 1968[45]; or

(b)   a defendant wants such an order set aside after 2 months have passed since it was made.

(2)   That party must apply in writing, with reasons, and serve the application on—

(a)   the Registrar;

(b)   the other party.

[Note. Section 8(1) and (1A) of the Criminal Appeal Act 1968[46] set out the criteria for making an order on an application to which this rule applies.]

---

[39] 1968 c. 19; section 22 was amended by section 48 of the Police and Justice Act 2006 (c. 48).

[40] S.I. 2005/2798.

[41] S.I. 2006/2135.

[42] S.I. 2008/1863.

[43] 1983 c. 20; section 37(1) was amended by section 55 of, and paragraph 12 of Schedule 4 to, the Crime (Sentences) Act 1997 (c. 43) and section 304 of, and paragraphs 37 and 38 of Schedule 32 to, the Criminal Justice Act 2003 (c. 44).

[44] 1964 c. 84.

[45] 1968 c.19; section 7 was amended by sections 43 and 170 of, and Schedule 16 to, the Criminal Justice Act 1988 (c. 33) and section 331 of, and paragraph 44 of Schedule 36 to, the Criminal Justice Act 2003 (c. 44).

[46] 1968 c.19; section 8(1) was amended by section 56 of, and Part IV of Schedule 11 to, the Courts Act 1971 (c. 23) and section 43 of the Criminal Justice Act 1988 (c. 33). Section 8(1A) was inserted by section 43(4) of the Criminal Justice Act 1988 (c. 33).

CRIMINAL PROCEDURE RULES   PART 40   APPEAL TO THE COURT OF APPEAL ABOUT REPORTING OR PUBLIC ACCESS RESTRICTION

When this Part applies   R40.1

40.1 (1) This Part applies where a person directly affected by an order to which section 159(1) of the Criminal Justice Act 1988[1] applies wants to appeal against that order.

(2) A reference to an 'appellant' in this Part is a reference to such a party.

[Note. Section 159(1) of the Criminal Justice Act 1988 gives a 'person aggrieved' (in this Part described as a person directly affected) a right of appeal to the Court of Appeal against a Crown Court judge's order—

(a) under section 4 or 11 of the Contempt of Court Act 1981[2];

(b) under section 58(7) of the Criminal Procedure and Investigations Act 1996[3];

(c) restricting public access to any part of a trial for reasons of national security or for the protection of a witness or other person; or

(d) restricting the reporting of any part of a trial.

See also Part 6 (Reporting, etc. restrictions) and Part 18 (Measures to assist a witness or defendant to give evidence).

The rules in Part 36 (Appeal to the Court of Appeal: general rules) also apply where this Part applies.]

Service of appeal notice   R40.2

40.2 (1) An appellant must serve an appeal notice on—

(a) the Crown Court officer;

(b) the Registrar;

(c) the parties; and

(d) any other person directly affected by the order against which the appellant wants to appeal.

(2) The appellant must serve the appeal notice not later than—

(a) the next business day after an order restricting public access to the trial; or

(b) 10 business days after an order restricting reporting of the trial.

Form of appeal notice   R40.3

40.3 (1) An appeal notice must be in the form set out in the Practice Direction.

(2) The appeal notice must—

(a) specify the order against which the appellant wants to appeal;

(b) identify each ground of appeal on which the appellant relies, numbering them consecutively (if there is more than one) and concisely outlining each argument in support;

(c) summarise the relevant facts;

(d) identify any relevant authorities;

(e) include or attach, with reasons—

(i) an application for permission to appeal,

(ii) any application for an extension of time within which to serve the appeal notice,

(iii) any application for a direction to attend in person a hearing that the appellant could attend by live link, if the appellant is in custody,

(iv) any application for permission to introduce evidence, and

(v) a list of those on whom the appellant has served the appeal notice;

(f) attach any document or thing that the appellant thinks the court will need to decide the appeal and include or attach an electronic link to each such document that has been made available to the Registrar under rule 36.8(1)(a) (Duty of Crown Court officer); and

(g) include or attach—

(i) an electronic copy of any authority identified under paragraph (2)(d), or

(ii) if two or more such authorities are identified, electronic copies of each together in a single electronic document.

[Note. An appellant needs the court's permission to appeal in every case to which this Part applies.

---

[1] 1988 c. 33; section 159(1) was amended by section 61 of the Criminal Procedure and Investigations Act 1996 (c. 25).

[2] 1981 c. 49; section 4 was amended by section 57 of the Criminal Procedure and Investigations Act 1996 (c. 25), section 16 of, and Schedule 2 to, the Defamation Act 1996 (c. 31), paragraph 53 of Schedule 3 to the Criminal Justice Act 2003 (c. 44) and the Statute Law (Repeals) Act 2004 (c. 14).

[3] 1996 c. 25.

A Court of Appeal judge may give permission to appeal under section 31(2B) of the Criminal Appeal Act 1968[4].]

R40.4   **Advance notice of appeal against order restricting public access**

40.4   (1)   This rule applies where the appellant wants to appeal against an order restricting public access to a trial.

(2)   The appellant may serve advance written notice of intention to appeal against any such order that may be made.

(3)   The appellant must serve any such advance notice—

(a)   on—

(i)   the Crown Court officer,

(ii)   the Registrar,

(iii) the parties, and

(iv)   any other person who will be directly affected by the order against which the appellant intends to appeal, if it is made; and

(b)   not more than 5 business days after the Crown Court officer displays notice of the application for the order.

(4)   The advance notice must include the same information (with the necessary adaptations) as an appeal notice.

(5)   The court must treat that advance notice as the appeal notice if the order is made.

R40.5   **Duty of applicant for order restricting public access**

40.5   (1)   This rule applies where the appellant wants to appeal against an order restricting public access to a trial.

(2)   The party who applied for the order must serve on the Registrar—

(a)   a transcript or note of the application for the order; and

(b)   any other document or thing that that party thinks the court will need to decide the appeal.

(3)   That party must serve that transcript or note and any such other document or thing as soon as practicable after—

(a)   the appellant serves the appeal notice; or

(b)   the order, where the appellant served advance notice of intention to appeal.

R40.6   **Respondent's notice on appeal against reporting restriction**

40.6   (1)   This rule applies where the appellant wants to appeal against an order restricting the reporting of a trial.

(2)   A person on whom an appellant serves an appeal notice may serve a respondent's notice, and must do so if—

(a)   that person wants to make representations to the court; or

(b)   the court so directs.

(3)   Such a person must serve the respondent's notice on—

(a)   the appellant;

(b)   the Crown Court officer;

(c)   the Registrar;

(d)   the parties; and

(e)   any other person on whom the appellant served the appeal notice.

(4)   Such a person must serve the respondent's notice not more than 3 business days after—

(a)   the appellant serves the appeal notice; or

(b)   a direction to do so.

(5)   The respondent's notice must be in the form set out in the Practice Direction.

(6)   The respondent's notice must—

(a)   give the date on which the respondent was served with the appeal notice;

(b)   identify each ground of opposition on which the respondent relies, numbering them consecutively (if there is more than one), concisely outlining each argument in support and identifying the ground of appeal to which each relates;

(c)   summarise any relevant facts not already summarised in the appeal notice;

(d)   identify any relevant authorities;

(e)   include or attach any application for the following, with reasons—

(i)   an extension of time within which to serve the respondent's notice,

---

[4] 1968 c. 19; section 31(2B) was inserted by section 170 of, and paragraphs 20 and 30 of Schedule 15 to, the Criminal Justice Act 1988 (c. 33).

      (ii) a direction to attend in person any hearing that the respondent could attend by live link, if the respondent is in custody,

      (iii) permission to introduce evidence;

(f) identify any other document or thing that the respondent thinks the court will need to decide the appeal and include or attach an electronic link to each such document that has been made available to the Registrar under rule 36.8(1)(a) (Duty of Crown Court officer); and

(g) include or attach—

      (i) an electronic copy of any authority identified under paragraph (6)(d), or

      (ii) if two or more such authorities are identified, electronic copies of each together in a single electronic document.

Renewing applications   R40.7

40.7 Rule 36.5 (Renewing an application refused by a judge or the Registrar) applies with a time limit of 5 business days.

Right to introduce evidence   R40.8

40.8 No person may introduce evidence without the court's permission.

[Note. Section 159(4) of the Criminal Justice Act 1988 entitles the parties to give evidence, subject to procedure rules.]

Right to attend hearing   R40.9

40.9 (1) A party who is in custody has a right to attend a hearing in public of an appeal against an order restricting the reporting of a trial.

      (2) The court or the Registrar may direct that such a party is to attend a hearing by live link.

[Note. See rule 36.6 (Hearings). The court may decide an application and an appeal without a hearing where the appellant wants to appeal against an order restricting public access to a trial: rule 36.6(3).]

CRIMINAL PROCEDURE RULES   PART 41   REFERENCE TO THE COURT OF APPEAL OF POINT OF LAW OR UNDULY LENIENT SENTENCING

When this Part applies   R41.1

41.1 This Part applies where the Attorney General wants to—

(a) refer a point of law to the Court of Appeal under section 36 of the Criminal Justice Act 1972[1]; or

(b) refer a sentencing case to the Court of Appeal under section 36 of the Criminal Justice Act 1988[2].

[Note. Under section 36 of the Criminal Justice Act 1972, where a defendant is acquitted in the Crown Court the Attorney General may refer to the Court of Appeal a point of law in the case.

Under section 36 of the Criminal Justice Act 1988, if the Attorney General thinks the sentencing of a defendant in the Crown Court is unduly lenient he may refer the case to the Court of Appeal: but only if the sentence is one to which Part IV of the 1988 Act applies, and only if the Court of Appeal gives permission. See also section 35 of the 1988 Act[3] and the Criminal Justice Act 1988 (Reviews of Sentencing) Order 2006[4].

The rules in Part 36 (Appeal to the Court of Appeal: general rules) also apply where this Part applies.]

Service of notice of reference and application for permission   R41.2

41.2 (1) The Attorney General must serve any notice of reference and any application for permission to refer a sentencing case on—

(a) the Registrar; and

(b) the defendant.

---

[1] 1972 c. 71; section 36 was amended by section 31 of, and paragraph 8 of Schedule 1 to, the Prosecution of Offences Act 1985 (c. 23) and section 40 of, and paragraph 23 of Schedule 9 to, the Constitutional Reform Act 2005 (c. 4).

[2] 1988 c. 33; section 36 was amended by section 272 of, and paragraphs 45 and 46 of Schedule 32 and paragraph 96 of Schedule 36 to, the Criminal Justice Act 2003 (c. 44), sections 49 and 65 of, and paragraph 3 of Schedule 1 and Schedule 5 to, the Violent Crime Reduction Act 2006 (c. 38), section 40 of, and paragraph 48 of Schedule 9 to, the Constitutional Reform Act 2005 (c. 4), sections 46, 148 and 149 of, and paragraphs 22 and 23 of Schedule 26 and Part 3 of Schedule 28 to, the Criminal Justice and Immigration Act 2008 (c. 4), paragraph 2 of Schedule 19 and paragraphs 4 and 5 of Schedule 26 to the Legal Aid, Sentencing and Punishment of Offenders Act 2012 (c. 10) and section 28 of, and paragraph 2 of Schedule 5 to, the Criminal Justice and Courts Act 2015 (c. 2). It is further amended by section 46 of the Criminal Justice and Immigration Act 2008 (c. 4) with effect from a date to be appointed.

[3] 1988 c. 33; section 35(3) was amended by section 168 of, and paragraph 34 of Schedule 9 to, the Criminal Justice and Public Order Act 1994 (c. 33).

[4] S.I. 2006/1116.

  (2) Where the Attorney General refers a point of law—

      (a) the Attorney must give the Registrar details of—

          (i) the defendant affected,

          (ii) the date and place of the relevant Crown Court decision, and

          (iii) the relevant verdict and sentencing; and

      (b) the Attorney must give the defendant notice that—

          (i) the outcome of the reference will not make any difference to the outcome of the trial, and

          (ii) the defendant may serve a respondent's notice.

  (3) Where the Attorney General applies for permission to refer a sentencing case, the Attorney must give the defendant notice that—

      (a) the outcome of the reference may make a difference to that sentencing, and in particular may result in a more severe sentence; and

      (b) the defendant may serve a respondent's notice.

  (4) The Attorney General must serve an application for permission to refer a sentencing case on the Registrar not more than 28 days after the last of the sentences in that case.

[Note. The time limit for serving an application for permission to refer a sentencing case is prescribed by paragraph 1 of Schedule 3 to the Criminal Justice Act 1988[5]. It may be neither extended nor shortened.]

R41.3 **Form of notice of reference and application for permission**

  41.3 (1) A notice of reference and an application for permission to refer a sentencing case must give the year and number of that reference or that case.

      (2) A notice of reference of a point of law must—

          (a) specify the point of law in issue and indicate the opinion that the Attorney General invites the court to give;

          (b) identify each ground for that invitation, numbering them consecutively (if there is more than one) and concisely outlining each argument in support;

          (c) exclude any reference to the defendant's name and any other reference that may identify the defendant;

          (d) summarise the relevant facts; and

          (e) identify any relevant authorities.

      (3) An application for permission to refer a sentencing case must—

          (a) give details of—

             (i) the defendant affected,

             (ii) the date and place of the relevant Crown Court decision, and

             (iii) the relevant verdict and sentencing;

          (b) explain why that sentencing appears to the Attorney General unduly lenient, concisely outlining each argument in support; and

          (c) include the application for permission to refer the case to the court.

      (4) A notice of reference of a sentencing case must—

          (a) include the same details and explanation as the application for permission to refer the case;

          (b) summarise the relevant facts; and

          (c) identify any relevant authorities.

      (5) Where the court gives the Attorney General permission to refer a sentencing case, it may treat the application for permission as the notice of reference.

      (6) A notice of reference must include or attach—

          (a) an electronic link to each material document that has been made available to the Registrar under rule 36.8(1)(a) (Duty of Crown Court officer); and

          (b) unless an authority identified under paragraph (2)(e) or 4(c) is published by the Registrar as one frequently cited

            (i) an electronic copy of each authority so identified, or

            (ii) if two or more such authorities not so published are identified then electronic copies of each together in a single electronic document.

R41.4 **Respondent's notice**

  41.4 (1) A defendant on whom the Attorney General serves a notice of reference or an application for permission to refer a sentencing case may serve a respondent's notice, and must do so if—

      (a) the defendant wants to make representations to the court; or

      (b) the court so directs.

---

[5] 1988 c. 33.

Criminal Procedure Rules

(2) Such a defendant must serve the respondent's notice on—
    (a) the Attorney General; and
    (b) the Registrar.

(3) Such a defendant must serve the respondent's notice—
    (a) where the Attorney General refers a point of law, not more than 20 business days after—
       (i) the Attorney serves the reference, or
       (ii) a direction to do so; or
    (b) where the Attorney General applies for permission to refer a sentencing case, not more than 10 business days after—
       (i) the Attorney serves the application, or
       (ii) a direction to do so.

(4) Where the Attorney General refers a point of law, the respondent's notice must—
    (a) give the date on which the respondent was served with the notice of reference;
    (b) identify each ground of opposition on which the respondent relies, numbering them consecutively (if there is more than one), concisely outlining each argument in support and identifying the Attorney General's ground or reason to which each relates;
    (c) summarise any relevant facts not already summarised in the reference;
    (d) identify any relevant authorities; and
    (e) include or attach any application for the following, with reasons—
       (i) an extension of time within which to serve the respondent's notice,
       (ii) permission to attend a hearing that the respondent does not have a right to attend, or
       (iii) a direction to attend in person a hearing that the respondent could attend by live link, if the respondent is in custody.

(5) Where the Attorney General applies for permission to refer a sentencing case, the respondent's notice must—
    (a) give the date on which the respondent was served with the application;
    (b) say if the respondent wants to make representations at the hearing of the application or reference; and
    (c) include or attach any application for the following, with reasons—
       (i) an extension of time within which to serve the respondent's notice,
       (ii) permission to attend a hearing that the respondent does not have a right to attend, or
       (iii) a direction to attend in person a hearing that the respondent could attend by live link, if the respondent is in custody.

(6) A respondent's notice must include or attach—
    (a) an electronic link to each material document that has been made available to the Registrar under rule 36.8(1)(a) (Duty of Crown Court officer); and
    (b) unless an authority identified under paragraph 4(d) is published by the Registrar as one frequently cited—
       (i) an electronic copy of each authority so identified, or
       (ii) if two or more such authorities not so published are identified then electronic copies of each together in a single electronic document.

Variation or withdrawal of notice of reference or application for permission   R41.5

41.5 (1) This rule applies where the Attorney General wants to vary or withdraw—
    (a) a notice of reference; or
    (b) an application for permission to refer a sentencing case.

(2) The Attorney General—
    (a) may vary or withdraw the notice or application without the court's permission by serving notice on—
       (i) the Registrar, and
       (ii) the defendant
    before any hearing of the reference or application; but
    (b) at any such hearing, may only vary or withdraw that notice or application with the court's permission.

Right to attend hearing   R41.6

41.6 (1) A respondent who is in custody has a right to attend a hearing in public unless it is a hearing preliminary or incidental to a reference, including the hearing of an application for permission to refer a sentencing case.

(2) The court or the Registrar may direct that such a respondent is to attend a hearing by live link.

[Note. See rule 36.6 (Hearings) and paragraphs 6 and 7 of Schedule 3 to the Criminal Justice Act 1988. Under paragraph 8 of that Schedule, the Court of Appeal may sentence in the absence of a defendant whose sentencing is referred.]

R41.7   **Anonymity of defendant on reference of point of law**

41.7   Where the Attorney General refers a point of law, the court must not allow anyone to identify the defendant during the proceedings unless the defendant gives permission.

CRIMINAL PROCEDURE RULES   PART 42   APPEAL TO THE COURT OF APPEAL IN
CONFISCATION AND RELATED PROCEEDINGS

General rules

R42.1   **Extension of time**

42.1   (1)   An application to extend the time limit for giving notice of application for permission to appeal under Part 2 of the Proceeds of Crime Act 2002[1] must—

     (a)   be included in the notice of appeal; and

     (b)   state the grounds for the application.

     (2)   The parties may not agree to extend any date or time limit set by this Part or by the Proceeds of Crime Act 2002 (Appeals under Part 2) Order 2003[2].

R42.2   **Other applications**

42.2   Rules 39.3(2)(h) (Form of appeal notice) applies in relation to an application—

     (a)   by a party to an appeal under Part 2 of the Proceeds of Crime Act 2002 that, under article 7 of the Proceeds of Crime Act 2002 (Appeals under Part 2) Order 2003, a witness be ordered to attend or that the evidence of a witness be received by the Court of Appeal; or

     (b)   by the defendant to be given permission by the court to be present at proceedings for which permission is required under article 6 of the 2003 Order,

as it applies in relation to applications under Part I of the Criminal Appeal Act 1968[3] and the form in which rules 39.3 requires notice to be given may be modified as necessary.

R42.3   **Examination of witness by court**

42.3   Rule 36.7 (Notice of hearings and decisions) applies in relation to an order of the court under article 7 of the Proceeds of Crime Act 2002 (Appeals under Part 2) Order 2003 to require a personto attend for examination as it applies in relation to such an order of the court under Part I of the Criminal Appeal Act 1968.

R42.4   **Supply of documentary and other exhibits**

42.4   Rule 36.11 (Registrar's duty to provide copy documents for appeal or reference) applies in relation to an appellant or respondent under Part 2 of the Proceeds of Crime Act 2002 as it applies in relation to an appellant and respondent under Part I of the Criminal Appeal Act 1968.

R42.5   **Registrar's power to require information from court of trial**

42.5   The Registrar may require the Crown Court to provide the Court of Appeal with any assistance or information which it requires for the purposes of exercising its jurisdiction under Part 2 of the Proceeds of Crime Act 2002, the Proceeds of Crime Act 2002 (Appeals under Part 2) Order 2003 or this Part.

R42.6   **Hearing by single judge**

42.6   Rule 36.6(6) (Hearings) applies in relation to a judge exercising any of the powers referred to in article 8 of the Proceeds of Crime Act 2002 (Appeals under Part 2) Order 2003[4] or the powers in rules 42.12(3) and (4) (Respondent's notice), 42.15(2) (Notice of appeal) and 42.16(6) (Respondent's notice), as it applies in relation to a judge exercising the powers referred to in section 31(2) of the Criminal Appeal Act 1968[5].

R42.7   **Determination by full court**

42.7   Rule 36.5 (Renewing an application refused by a judge or the Registrar) applies where a single judge has refused an application by a party to exercise in that party's favour any of the powers listed in article 8 of the Proceeds of Crime Act 2002 (Appeals under Part 2) Order 2003, or the power in rule 42.12(3) or (4) as it applies where the judge has refused to exercise the powers referred to in section 31(2) of the Criminal Appeal Act 1968.

---

[1] 2002 c. 29.

[2] S.I. 2003/82.

[3] 1968 c. 19.

[4] S.I. 2003/82.

[5] 1968 c. 19; section 31(2) was amended by section 21 of, and Schedule 2 to, the Costs in Criminal Cases Act 1973 (c. 14), section 29 of the Criminal Justice Act 1982 (c. 48), section 170 of, and paragraphs 20 and 29 of Schedule 15 to, the Criminal Justice Act 1988 (c. 33), section 87 of the Courts Act 2003 (c. 39) and section 48 of the Police and Justice Act 2006 (c. 48).

Notice of determination and renewal of application for permission to appeal **R42.8**

42.8 (1) Paragraphs (2) and (3) of this rule apply where a single judge or the Court of Appeal has determined an application or appeal under the Proceeds of Crime Act 2002 (Appeals under Part 2) Order 2003 or under Part 2 of the Proceeds of Crime Act 2002.

(2) The Registrar must, as soon as practicable, serve notice of the determination on all of the parties to the proceedings.

(3) Where a single judge or the Court of Appeal has disposed of an application for permission to appeal or an appeal under section 31 of the 2002 Act[6], the Registrar must also, as soon as practicable, serve the order on the Crown Court officer and the court officer for the magistrates' court responsible for enforcing any confiscation order which the Crown Court has made (the 'enforcing court').

(4) Paragraphs (5) and (6) of this rule apply where—

    (a) a single judge has refused an application for permission to appeal under section 31 of the 2002 Act[7], and

    (b) the appellant renews that application, in time or with an application to extend the time within which to renew.

(5) The Registrar must, as soon as practicable, notify the court officer for the enforcing court, if any, of the service of that renewed application.

(6) Unless a single judge, the Court of Appeal or the enforcing court otherwise directs, pending disposal of the renewed application the court officer for the enforcing court must withhold the payment of any sum not yet paid—

    (a) which under section 13(6) of the 2002 Act[8] was directed to be paid out of sums recovered under a confiscation order, and

    (b) the payment of which is suspended pending appeal.

[Note. See also rule 42.11 (Notice of appeal) under which (i) the Registrar must notify the court officer for the enforcing court of the service of a notice of appeal, and (ii) that court officer must notify any person whose entitlement to payment of a sum is suspended by that appeal.

Under section 13 of the Proceeds of Crime Act 2002, if the Crown Court makes a confiscation order and one or more priority orders, as defined in that section, against the same defendant in the same proceedings then in some circumstances the court must direct that part or all of the priority order must be paid out of sums recovered under the confiscation order.

A compensation order under section 134 of the Sentencing Act 2020[9] is such a priority order. Under section 141(1) of the 2020 Act, a person in whose favour a compensation order is made is not entitled to receive the amount due until there is no further possibility of the order being varied or set aside on appeal (disregarding any power to grant leave to appeal out of time). Under section 141(2) of the 2020 Act, Criminal Procedure Rules may make provision about the way in which the enforcing court is to deal with money paid in satisfaction of a compensation order where the entitlement of the person in whose favour it was made is suspended.]

Record of proceedings and transcripts **R42.9**

42.9 Rule 5.5 (Recording and transcription of proceedings in the Crown Court) and rule 36.9 (Duty of person transcribing proceedings in the Crown Court) apply in relation to proceedings in respect of which an appeal lies to the Court of Appeal under Part 2 of the Proceeds of Crime Act 2002 as they apply in relation to proceedings in respect of which an appeal lies to the Court of Appeal under Part I of the Criminal Appeal Act 1968.

Appeal to the Supreme Court **R42.10**

42.10 (1) An application to the Court of Appeal for permission to appeal to the Supreme Court under Part 2 of the Proceeds of Crime Act 2002 must be made—

    (a) orally after the decision of the Court of Appeal from which an appeal lies to the Supreme Court; or

---

[6] 2002 c. 29; section 31 was amended by section 74 of, and paragraphs 1 and 16 of Schedule 8 to, the Serious Crime Act 2007 (c. 27).

[7] 2002 c. 29; section 31 was amended by section 74 of, and paragraphs 1 and 16 of Schedule 8 to, the Serious Crime Act 2007 (c. 27) and sections 3 and 85 of, and paragraph 27 of Schedule 4 to, the Serious Crime Act 2015 (c. 9).

[8] 2002 c. 29; section 13 was amended by section 54 of, and paragraph 11 of Schedule 12 to, the Criminal Justice and Courts Act 2015 (c. 2), section 6 of the Serious Crime Act 2015 (c. 9), section 410 of, and paragraph 182 of Schedule 24 to, the Sentencing Act 2020 (c. 17) and section 39 of, and paragraph 7 of Schedule 3 to, the Counter-Terrorism and Sentencing Act 2021 (c. 11).

[9] 2020 c. 17.

(b) in the form set out in the Practice Direction, in accordance with article 12 of the Proceeds of Crime Act 2002 (Appeals under Part 2) Order 2003 and served on the Registrar.

(2) The application may be abandoned at any time before it is heard by the Court of Appeal by serving notice in writing on the Registrar.

(3) Rule 36.6(6) (Hearings) applies in relation to a single judge exercising any of the powers referred to in article 15 of the 2003 Order, as it applies in relation to a single judge exercising the powers referred to in section 31(2) of the Criminal Appeal Act 1968.

(4) Rules 36.5 (Renewing an application refused by a judge or the Registrar) applies where a single judge has refused an application by a party to exercise in that party's favour any of the powers listed in article 15 of the 2003 Order as they apply where the judge has refused to exercise the powers referred to in section 31(2) of the 1968 Act.

(5) The form in which rule 36.5(2) requires an application to be made may be modified as necessary.

Confiscation: appeal by prosecutor or by person with interest in property

R42.11   Notice of appeal

42.11 (1) Where an appellant wishes to apply to the Court of Appeal for permission to appeal under section 31 of the Proceeds of Crime Act 2002[10], the appellant must serve a notice of appeal in the form set out in the Practice Direction on—

(a) the Crown Court officer;

(b) the defendant;

(c) the prosecutor, if the prosecutor is not the appellant; and

(d) any person who the appellant thinks is or may be someone—

    (i) holding an interest in property in which the Crown Court determined the extent of the defendant's interest under section 10A of the 2002 Act[11], and

    (ii) who is neither the defendant nor the appellant.

(2) When a notice of appeal is served on a respondent defendant, or other person under paragraph (1)(d), it must be accompanied by a respondent's notice in the form set out in the Practice Direction for the respondent to complete and a notice which—

(a) informs the respondent that the result of an appeal could be that the Court of Appeal would increase a confiscation order already imposed, make a confiscation order itself or direct the Crown Court to hold another confiscation hearing;

(b) informs the respondent of any right under article 6 of the Proceeds of Crime Act 2002 (Appeals under Part 2) Order 2003[12] to be present at the hearing of the appeal, although in custody;

(c) invites the respondent to serve any notice on the Registrar —

    (i) to apply to the Court of Appeal for permission to be present at proceedings for which such permission is required under article 6 of the 2003 Order, or

    (ii) to present any argument to the Court of Appeal on the hearing of the application or, if permission is given, the appeal, and whether the respondent wishes to present it in person or by means of a legal representative;

(d) draws to the respondent's attention the effect of rule 42.4 (Supply of documentary and other exhibits); and

(e) advises the respondent to consult a solicitor as soon as possible.

(3) The appellant must provide the Crown Court officer with a certificate of service stating that the appellant has served the notice of appeal on each respondent or explaining why it has not been possible to do so.

(4) The Crown Court officer must, as soon as practicable—

(a) notify the Registrar of the service of the notice of appeal;

(b) make available to the Registrar—

    (i) the notice of appeal and any accompanying application served by the appellant,

    (ii) details of the parties including their addresses, and

    (iii) details of the court officer for the magistrates' court responsible for enforcing any confiscation order which the Crown Court has made (the 'enforcing court').

(5) The Registrar must, as soon as practicable, notify the court officer for the enforcing court, if any, of the service of the notice of appeal.

---

[10] 2002 c. 29; section 31 was amended by section 74 of, and paragraphs 1 and 16 of Schedule 8 to, the Serious Crime Act 2007 (c. 27) and section 3 of the Serious Crime Act 2015 (c. 9).

[11] 2002 c. 29; section 10A was inserted by section 1 of the Serious Crime Act 2015 (c. 9).

[12] S.I. 2003/82.

(6) Where a person is entitled to receive a sum directed to be paid out of sums recovered under a confiscation order, the court officer for the enforcing court must, as soon as practicable, notify each such person of—

    (a) the appeal,

    (b) any suspension of that person's entitlement pending appeal, and

    (c) any power for the Court of Appeal to vary or set aside that person's entitlement on appeal.

[Note. See section 13 of the Proceeds of Crime Act 2002 and sections 134 and 141 of the Sentencing Act 2020. See also rule 42.8 (Notice of determination and renewal of application for permission to appeal) and the note to that rule.]

Respondent's notice
R42.12

42.12 (1) This rule applies where a respondent is served with a notice of appeal under rule 42.11.

    (2) If the respondent wishes to oppose the application for permission to appeal, the respondent must, not more than 10 business days after service of the notice of appeal, serve on the Registrar and on the appellant a notice in the form set out in the Practice Direction—

        (a) stating the date on which the notice of appeal was served;

        (b) summarising the respondent's response to the arguments of the appellant; and

        (c) specifying the authorities which the respondent intends to cite.

    (3) The time for giving notice under this rule may be extended by the Registrar, a single judge or by the Court of Appeal.

    (4) Where the Registrar refuses an application under paragraph (3) for the extension of time, the respondent is entitled to have the application determined by a single judge.

    (5) Where a single judge refuses an application under paragraph (3) or (4) for the extension of time, the respondent is entitled to have the application determined by the Court of Appeal.

Amendment and abandonment of appeal
R42.13

42.13 (1) The appellant may amend a notice of appeal served under rule 42.11 or abandon an appeal under section 31 of the Proceeds of Crime Act 2002—

        (a) without the permission of the court at any time before the Court of Appeal has begun hearing the appeal; and

        (b) with the permission of the court after the Court of Appeal has begun hearing the appeal, by serving notice in writing on the Registrar.

    (2) Where the appellant serves a notice abandoning an appeal under paragraph (1), the appellant must send a copy of it to—

        (a) each respondent served with the notice of appeal;

        (b) the Crown Court officer; and

        (c) the court officer for the magistrates' court responsible for enforcing any confiscation order which the Crown Court has made.

    (3) Where the appellant serves a notice amending a notice of appeal under paragraph (1), the appellant must send a copy of it to each respondent served with the notice of appeal.

    (4) Where an appeal is abandoned under paragraph (1), the application for permission to appeal or appeal must be treated, for the purposes of section 85 of the 2002 Act (Conclusion of proceedings), as having been refused or dismissed by the Court of Appeal.

Appeal about compliance, restraint or receivership order

Permission to appeal
R42.14

42.14 (1) Permission to appeal to the Court of Appeal under section 13B, section 43 or section 65 of the Proceeds of Crime Act 2002[13] may only be given where—

        (a) the Court of Appeal considers that the appeal would have a real prospect of success; or

        (b) there is some other compelling reason why the appeal should be heard.

    (2) An order giving permission to appeal may limit the issues to be heard and be made subject to conditions.

Notice of appeal
R42.15

42.15 (1) Where an appellant wishes to apply to the Court of Appeal for permission to appeal under section 13B, 43 or 65 of the Proceeds of Crime Act 2002 Act, the appellant must serve a notice of appeal in the form set out in the Practice Direction on the Crown Court officer.

    (2) Unless the Registrar, a single judge or the Court of Appeal directs otherwise, the appellant must serve the notice of appeal, accompanied by a respondent's notice in the form set out in the Practice Direction for the respondent to complete, on—

---

[13] 2002 c. 29; section 65 was amended by section 74 of, and paragraphs 1 and 32 of Schedule 8 to, the Serious Crime Act 2007 (c. 27). Section 13B was inserted by section 7 of the Serious Crime Act 2015 (c. 9).

(a) each respondent;

(b) any person who holds realisable property to which the appeal relates; and

(c) any other person affected by the appeal

as soon as practicable and in any event not later than 5 business days after the notice of appeal is served on the Crown Court officer.

(3) The appellant must serve the following documents with the notice of appeal—

(a) four additional copies of the notice of appeal for the Court of Appeal;

(b) four copies of any skeleton argument;

(c) one sealed copy and four unsealed copies of any order being appealed;

(d) four copies of any witness statement or affidavit in support of the application for permission to appeal;

(e) four copies of a suitable record of the reasons for judgment of the Crown Court; and

(f) four copies of the bundle of documents used in the Crown Court proceedings from which the appeal lies.

(4) Where it is not possible to serve all of the documents referred to in paragraph (3), the appellant must indicate which documents have not yet been served and the reasons why they are not currently available.

(5) The appellant must provide the Crown Court officer with a certificate of service stating that the notice of appeal has been served on each respondent in accordance with paragraph (2) and including full details of each respondent or explaining why it has not been possible to effect service.

R42.16   Respondent's notice

42.16 (1) This rule applies to an appeal under section 13B, 43 or 65 of the Proceeds of Crime Act 2002.

(2) A respondent may serve a respondent's notice on the Registrar.

(3) A respondent who—

(a) is seeking permission to appeal from the Court of Appeal; or

(b) wishes to ask the Court of Appeal to uphold the decision of the Crown Court for reasons different from or additional to those given by the Crown Court,

must serve a respondent's notice on the Registrar.

(4) A respondent's notice must be in the form set out in the Practice Direction and where the respondent seeks permission to appeal to the Court of Appeal it must be requested in the respondent's notice.

(5) A respondent's notice must be served on the Registrar not later than 10 business days after—

(a) the date the respondent is served with notification that the Court of Appeal has given the appellant permission to appeal; or

(b) the date the respondent is served with notification that the application for permission to appeal and the appeal itself are to be heard together.

(6) Unless the Registrar, a single judge or the Court of Appeal directs otherwise, the respondent serving a respondent's notice must serve the notice on the appellant and any other respondent—

(a) as soon as practicable; and

(b) in any event not later than 5 business days,

after it is served on the Registrar.

R42.17   Amendment and abandonment of appeal

42.17 (1) The appellant may amend a notice of appeal served under rule 42.15 or abandon an appeal under section 13B, 43 or 65 of the Proceeds of Crime Act 2002—

(a) without the permission of the court at any time before the Court of Appeal has begun hearing the appeal; and

(b) with the permission of the court after the Court of Appeal has begun hearing the appeal,

by serving notice in writing on the Registrar.

(2) Where the appellant serves a notice under paragraph (1), the appellant must send a copy of it to each respondent.

R42.18   Stay

42.18 Unless the Court of Appeal or the Crown Court orders otherwise, an appeal under section 13B, 43 or 65 of the Proceeds of Crime Act 2002 does not operate as a stay of any order or decision of the Crown Court.

R42.19   Striking out appeal notices and setting aside or imposing conditions on permission to appeal

42.19 (1) The Court of Appeal may—

(a) strike out the whole or part of a notice of appeal served under rule 42.15; or

(b) impose or vary conditions upon which an appeal under section 13B, 43 or 65 of the Proceeds of Crime Act 2002 may be brought.

(2) The Court of Appeal may only exercise its powers under paragraph (1) where there is a compelling reason for doing so.

(3) Where a party is present at the hearing at which permission to appeal was given, that party may not subsequently apply for an order that the Court of Appeal exercise its powers under paragraph (1)(b).

Hearing of appeals   R42.20

42.20 (1) This rule applies to appeals under section 13B, 43 or 65 of the Proceeds of Crime Act 2002.

(2) Every appeal must be limited to a review of the decision of the Crown Court unless the Court of Appeal considers that in the circumstances of an individual appeal it would be in the interests of justice to hold a re-hearing.

(3) The Court of Appeal may allow an appeal where the decision of the Crown Court was—

(a) wrong; or

(b) unjust because of a serious procedural or other irregularity in the proceedings in the Crown Court.

(4) The Court of Appeal may draw any inference of fact which it considers justified on the evidence.

(5) At the hearing of the appeal a party may not rely on a matter not contained in that party's notice of appeal unless the Court of Appeal gives permission.

CRIMINAL PROCEDURE RULES   PART 43   APPEAL OR REFERENCE TO THE SUPREME COURT

When this Part applies   R43.1

43.1 (1) This Part applies where—

(a) a party wants to appeal to the Supreme Court after—

(i) an application to the Court of Appeal to which Part 27 applies (Retrial following acquittal), or

(ii) an appeal to the Court of Appeal to which applies Part 37 (Appeal to the Court of Appeal against ruling at preparatory hearing), Part 38 (Appeal to the Court of Appeal against ruling adverse to prosecution), or Part 39 (Appeal to the Court of Appeal about conviction or sentence); or

(b) a party wants to refer a case to the Supreme Court after a reference to the Court of Appeal to which Part 41 applies (Reference to the Court of Appeal of point of law or unduly lenient sentencing).

(2) A reference to an 'appellant' in this Part is a reference to such a party.

[Note. Under section 33 of the Criminal Appeal Act 1968[1], a party may appeal to the Supreme Court from a decision of the Court of Appeal on—

(a) an application to the court under section 76 of the Criminal Justice Act 2003[2] (prosecutor's application for retrial after acquittal for serious offence). See also Part 27.

(b) an appeal to the court under—

(i) section 9 of the Criminal Justice Act 1987[3] or section 35 of the Criminal Procedure and Investigations Act 1996[4] (appeal against order at preparatory hearing). See also Part 37.

---

[1] 1968 c. 19; section 33 was amended by section 152 of, and Schedule 5 to, the Supreme Court Act 1981 (c. 54), section 15 of, and paragraph 3 of Schedule 2 to, the Criminal Justice Act 1987 (c. 38), section 36(1)(a) of the Criminal Procedure and Investigations Act 1996 (c. 25), section 456 of, and paragraphs 1 and 4 of Schedule 11 to, the Proceeds of Crime Act 2002 (c. 29), sections 47, 68 and 81 of the Criminal Justice Act 2003 (c. 44), by section 40 of, and paragraph 16 of Schedule 9 to, the Constitutional Reform Act 2005 (c. 4) and sections 74 and 92 of, and paragraph 144 of Schedule 8, and Schedule 14 to, the Serious Crime Act 2007 (c. 27).

[2] 2003 c. 44.

[3] 1987 c. 38; section 9 was amended by section 170 of, and Schedule 16 to, the Criminal Justice Act 1988 (c. 33), section 6 of the Criminal Justice Act 1993 (c. 36), sections 72, 74 and 80 of, and paragraph 3 of Schedule 3 and Schedule 5 to, the Criminal Procedure and Investigations Act 1996 (c. 25), sections 45 and 310 of, and paragraphs 18, 52 and 54 of Schedule 36 and Part 3 of Schedule 37 to, the Criminal Justice Act 2003 (c. 44), article 3 of, and paragraphs 21 and 23 of S.I. 2004/2035, section 59 of, and paragraph 1 of Schedule 11 to, the Constitutional Reform Act 2005 (c. 4) and Part 10 of Schedule 10 to the Protection of Freedoms Act 2012 (c. 9). The amendment made by section 45 of the Criminal Justice Act 2003 (c. 44) is in force for certain purposes; for remaining purposes it has effect from a date to be appointed.

[4] 1996 c. 25; section 35(1) was amended by section 45 of the Criminal Justice Act 2003 (c. 44). The amendment is in force for certain purposes, for remaining purposes it has effect from a date to be appointed. Section 35 was also amended by paragraphs 65 and 69 of Schedule 36 to the Criminal Justice Act 2003 (c. 44) and section 59 of, and paragraph 1 of Schedule 11 to, the Constitutional Reform Act 2005 (c. 4) and Part 10 of Schedule 10 to the Protection of Freedoms Act 2012 (c. 9).

      (ii) *section 47 of the Criminal Justice Act 2003[5] (appeal against order for non-jury trial after jury tampering.) See also Part 37.*

      (iii) *Part 9 of the Criminal Justice Act 2003[6] (prosecutor's appeal against adverse ruling). See also Part 38.*

      (iv) *Part 1 of the Criminal Appeal Act 1968[7] (defendant's appeal against conviction, sentence, etc.). See also Part 39.*

Under section 13 of the Administration of Justice Act 1960[8], a person found to be in contempt of court may appeal to the Supreme Court from a decision of the Court of Appeal on an appeal to the court under that section. See also Part 39.

Under article 12 of the Criminal Justice Act 2003 (Mandatory Life Sentence: Appeals in Transitional Cases) Order 2005[9], a party may appeal to the Supreme Court from a decision of the Court of Appeal on an appeal to the court under paragraph 14 of Schedule 22 to the Criminal Justice Act 2003[10] (appeal against minimum term review decision). See also Part 39.

Under article 15 of the Serious Organised Crime and Police Act 2005 (Appeals under Section 74) Order 2006[11], a party may appeal to the Supreme Court from a decision of the Court of Appeal on an appeal to the court under section 74 of the Serious Organised Crime and Police Act 2005[12] (appeal against sentence review decision). See also Part 39.

Under section 24 of the Serious Crime Act 2007[13], a party may appeal to the Supreme Court from a decision of the Court of Appeal on an appeal to that court under that section (appeal about a serious crime prevention order). See also Part 39.

Under section 36(3) of the Criminal Justice Act 1972[14], the Court of Appeal may refer to the Supreme Court a point of law referred by the Attorney General to the court. See also Part 41.

Under section 36(5) of the Criminal Justice Act 1988[15], a party may refer to the Supreme Court a sentencing decision referred by the Attorney General to the court. See also Part 41.

Under section 33(3) of the Criminal Appeal Act 1968, there is no appeal to the Supreme Court—

      (a) *from a decision of the Court of Appeal on an appeal under section 14A(5A) of the Football Spectators Act 1989[16] (prosecutor's appeal against failure to make football banning order). See Part 39.*

      (b) *from a decision of the Court of Appeal on an appeal under section 159(1) of the Criminal Justice Act 1988[17] (appeal about reporting or public access restriction). See Part 40.*

The rules in Part 36 (Appeal to the Court of Appeal: general rules) also apply where this Part applies.]

R43.2   Application for permission or reference

43.2 (1) An appellant must—

      (a) apply orally to the Court of Appeal—

          (i)   for permission to appeal or to refer a sentencing case, or

          (ii) to refer a point of law

         immediately after the court gives the reasons for its decision; or

---

[5] 2003 c. 44; section 47 was amended by section 59(5) of, and paragraph 1(2) of Schedule 11 to, the Constitutional Reform Act 2005 (c. 4).

[6] 2003 c. 44.

[7] 1968 c. 19.

[8] 1960 c. 65; section 13 was amended paragraph 40 of Schedule 8 to, the Courts Act 1971 (c. 23), Schedule 5 to, the Criminal Appeal Act 1968 (c. 19), paragraph 36 of Schedule 7 to, the Magistrates' Courts Act 1980 (c. 43), Schedule 7 to, the Supreme Court Act 1981 (c. 54), paragraph 25 of Schedule 2 to, the County Courts Act 1984 (c. 28), Schedule 15 to, the Access to Justice Act 1999 (c. 22), paragraph 13 of Schedule 9 to the Constitutional Reform Act 2005 (c. 4) and paragraph 45 of Schedule 16 to, the Armed Forces Act 2006 (c. 52).

[9] S.I. 2005/2798.

[10] 2003 c. 44; paragraph 14 of Schedule 22 was amended by section 40 of, and paragraph 82 of Schedule 9 and paragraph 1 of Schedule 11 to, the Constitutional Reform Act 2005 (c. 4).

[11] S.I. 2006/2135.

[12] 2005 c. 15.

[13] 2007 c. 27.

[14] 1972 c. 71; section 36(3) was amended by section 40 of, and paragraph 23 of Schedule 9 to, the Constitutional Reform Act 2005 (c. 4).

[15] 1988 c. 33; section 36(5) was amended by section 40(4) of, and paragraph 48(1) and (2) of Schedule 9 to, the Constitutional Reform Act 2005 (c. 4).

[16] 1989 c. 37; section 14A(5A) was inserted by section 52 of, and paragraphs 1 and 3 of Schedule 3 to, the Violent Crime Reduction Act 2006 (c. 38).

[17] 1988 c. 33; section 159(1) was amended by section 61 of the Criminal Procedure and Investigations Act 1996 (c. 25).

(b) apply in writing and serve the application on the Registrar and every other party not more than—

    (i) 14 days after the court gives the reasons for its decision if that decision was on a sentencing reference to which Part 41 applies (Attorney General's reference of sentencing case), or

    (ii) 28 days after the court gives those reasons in any other case.

(2) An application for permission to appeal or to refer a sentencing case must—

    (a) identify the point of law of general public importance that the appellant wants the court to certify is involved in the decision; and

    (b) give reasons why—

        (i) that point of law ought to be considered by the Supreme Court, and

        (ii) the court ought to give permission to appeal.

(3) An application to refer a point of law must give reasons why that point ought to be considered by the Supreme Court.

(4) An application must include or attach any application for the following, with reasons—

    (a) an extension of time within which to make the application for permission or for a reference;

    (b) bail pending appeal; or

    (c) permission to attend any hearing in the Supreme Court, if the appellant is in custody.

(5) A written application must be in the form set out in the Practice Direction.

[Note. In some legislation, including the Criminal Appeal Act 1968, permission to appeal is described as 'leave to appeal'.

Under the provisions listed in the note to rule 43.1, except section 36(3) of the Criminal Justice Act 1972 (Attorney General's reference of point of law), an appellant needs permission to appeal or to refer a sentencing case. Under those provisions, the Court of Appeal must not give permission unless it first certifies that—

(a) a point of law of general public importance is involved in the decision, and

(b) it appears to the court that the point is one which the Supreme Court ought to consider.

If the Court of Appeal gives such a certificate but refuses permission, an appellant may apply for such permission to the Supreme Court.

Under section 36(3) of the Criminal Justice Act 1972 an appellant needs no such permission. The Court of Appeal may refer the point of law to the Supreme Court, or may refuse to do so.

For the power of the court or the Registrar to shorten or extend a time limit, see rule 36.3. The time limit in this rule—

(a) for applying for permission to appeal under section 33 of the Criminal Appeal Act 1968 (28 days) is prescribed by section 34 of that Act[18]. That time limit may be extended but not shortened by the court. But it may be extended on an application by a prosecutor only after an application to which Part 27 applies (Retrial after acquittal).

(b) for applying for permission to refer a case under section 36(5) of the Criminal Justice Act 1988 (Attorney General's reference of sentencing decision: 14 days) is prescribed by paragraph 4 of Schedule 3 to that Act. That time limit may be neither extended nor shortened.

(c) for applying for permission to appeal under article 12 of the Criminal Justice Act 2003 (Mandatory Life Sentence: Appeals in Transitional Cases) Order 2005 (28 days) is prescribed by article 13 of that Order. That time limit may be extended but not shortened.

(d) for applying for permission to appeal under article 15 of the Serious Organised Crime and Police Act 2005 (Appeals under Section 74) Order 2006 (28 days) is prescribed by article 16 of that Order. That time limit may be extended but not shortened.

For the power of the Court of Appeal to grant bail pending appeal to the Supreme Court, see—

(a) section 36 of the Criminal Appeal Act 1968[19];

(b) article 18 of the Serious Organised Crime and Police Act 2005 (Appeals under Section 74) Order 2006[20].

---

[18] 1968 c. 19; section 34 was amended by section 88 of the Courts Act 2003 (c. 39), section 81 of the Criminal Justice Act 2003 (c. 44), and section 40(4) of, and paragraph 16 of Schedule 9 to, the Constitutional Reform Act 2005 (c. 4).

[19] 1968 c. 19; section 36 was amended by section 12 of, and paragraph 43 of Schedule 2 to, the Bail Act 1976 (c. 63), section 15 of, and paragraph 4 of Schedule 2 to, the Criminal Justice Act 1987 (c. 38), section 168 of, and paragraph 23 of Schedule 10 to, the Criminal Justice and Public Order Act 1994 (c. 33), section 36 of the Criminal Procedure and Investigations Act 1996 (c. 25), sections 47 and 68 of the Criminal Justice Act 2003 (c. 44) and section 40 of, and paragraph 16 of Schedule 9 to, the Constitutional Reform Act 2005 (c. 4).

[20] S.I. 2006/2135.

For the right of an appellant in custody to attend a hearing in the Supreme Court, see—

    (a) *section 38 of the Criminal Appeal Act 1968[21];*

    (b) *paragraph 9 of Schedule 3 to the Criminal Justice Act 1988[22];*

    (c) *article 15 of the Criminal Justice Act 2003 (Mandatory Life Sentences: Appeals in Transitional Cases) Order 2005[23];*

    (d) *article 20 of the Serious Organised Crime and Police Act 2005 (Appeals under Section 74) Order 2006[24].]*

R43.3   Determination of detention pending appeal, etc.

43.3   On an application for permission to appeal, the Court of Appeal must—

    (a) decide whether to order the detention of a defendant who would have been liable to be detained but for the decision of the court; and

    (b) determine any application for—

        (i) bail pending appeal,

        (ii) permission to attend any hearing in the Supreme Court, or

        (iii) a representation order.

[Note. For the liability of a defendant to be detained pending a prosecutor's appeal to the Supreme Court and afterwards, see—

    (a) *section 37 of the Criminal Appeal Act 1968[25];*

    (b) *article 19 of the Serious Organised Crime and Police Act 2005 (Appeals under Section 74) Order 2006[26].*

For the grant of legal aid for proceedings in the Supreme Court, see sections 14, 16 and 19 of the Legal Aid, Sentencing and Punishment of Offenders Act 2012[27].]

R43.4   Bail pending appeal

43.4   Rules 39.8 (Application for bail pending appeal or retrial), 39.9 (Conditions of bail pending appeal or re-trial) and 39.10 (Forfeiture of a recognizance given as a condition of bail) apply.

CRIMINAL PROCEDURE RULES   PART 44   REOPENING A CASE IN A MAGISTRATES' COURT

R44.1   When this Part applies

44.1   (1) (a) under section 14 or section 16E of the Magistrates' Courts Act 1980[1], the defendant makes a statutory declaration of not having found out about the case until after the trial began;

        (b) under section 16M of the 1980 Act the court can set aside a conviction; or

        (c) under section 142 of the 1980 Act[2], the court can—

           (i) set aside a conviction, or

           (ii) vary or rescind a costs order, or an order to which Part 31 applies (Behaviour orders).

R44.2   Statutory declaration of ignorance of proceedings

44.2   (1) This rule applies where—

        (a) the case started with—

           (i) an application for a summons,

           (ii) a written charge and requisition, or

           (iii) a written charge and single justice procedure notice; and

---

[21] 1968 c. 19; section 38 was amended by section 81 of the Criminal Justice Act 2003 (c. 44), and section 40(4) of, and paragraph 16 of Schedule 9 to, the Constitutional Reform Act 2005 (c. 4).

[22] 1988 c. 33; paragraph 9 of Schedule 3 was amended by section 40 of, and paragraph 48 of Schedule 9 to, the Constitutional Reform Act 2005 (c. 4).

[23] S.I. 2005/2798.

[24] S.I. 2006/2135.

[25] 1968 c. 19; section 37 was amended by section 65(1) of, and paragraph 39 of Schedule 3 to, the Mental Health (Amendment) Act 1982 (c. 51), section 148 of, and paragraph 23 of Schedule 4 to, the Mental Health Act 1983 (c. 20), section 58(1) of, and paragraph 5 of Schedule 10 to, the Domestic Violence, Crime and Victims Act 2004 (c. 28), section 40 of, and paragraph 16 of Schedule 9 to, the Constitutional Reform Act 2005 (c. 4) and section 47 of, and paragraphs 1 and 13 of Schedule 8 to, the Criminal Justice and Immigration Act 2008 (c. 4).

[26] S.I. 2006/2135.

[27] 2012 c. 10.

[1] 1980 c. 43; section 14 was amended by section 109 of, and paragraph 205 of Schedule 8 to, the Courts Act 2003 (c. 39). Section 16E was inserted by section 48 of the Criminal Justice and Courts Act 2015 (c. 2).

[2] 1980 c. 43; section 142 was amended by sections 26 and 29 of, and Schedule 3 to, the Criminal Appeal Act 1995 (c. 35).

(b) under section 14 or section 16E of the Magistrates' Courts Act 1980[3], the defendant makes a statutory declaration of not having found out about the case until after the trial began.

(2) The defendant must—

    (a) serve such a declaration on the court officer —

        (i) not more than 21 days after the date of finding out about the case, or

        (ii) with an explanation for the delay, if serving it more than 21 days after that date; and

    (b) serve with the declaration one of the following, as appropriate, if the case began with a written charge and single justice procedure notice—

        (i) a notice under rule 24.9(4)(b) (notice to plead guilty and be sentenced by a single justice), with any representations that the defendant wants the court to consider and a statement of the defendant's assets and other financial circumstances, as required by that rule,

        (ii) a notice under rule 24.9(4)(c) (notice of intention to plead guilty at a hearing before a court comprising more than one justice), or

        (iii) a notice under rule 24.9(4)(d) (notice of intention to plead not guilty).

(3) The court may extend that time limit, even after it has expired—

    (a) at a hearing, in public or in private; or

    (b) without a hearing.

(4) Where the defendant serves such a declaration, in time or with an extension of time in which to do so, and the case began with a summons or requisition—

    (a) the court must treat the summons or requisition and all subsequent proceedings as void (but not the application for the summons or the written charge with which the case began);

    (b) if the defendant is present when the declaration is served, the rules in Part 24 (Trial and sentence in a magistrates' court) apply as if the defendant had been required to attend the court on that occasion; and

    (c) if the defendant is absent when the declaration is served—

        (i) the rules in Part 7 apply (Starting a prosecution in a magistrates' court) as if the prosecutor had just served an application for a summons in the same terms as the original application or written charge;

        (ii) the court may exercise its power to issue a summons in accordance with those rules; and

        (iii) except for rule 24.8 (Written guilty plea: special rules), the rules in Part 24 then apply.

(5) Where the defendant serves such a declaration, in time or with an extension of time in which to do so, and the case began with a single justice procedure notice—

    (a) the court must treat the single justice procedure notice and all subsequent proceedings as void (but not the written charge with which the case began);

    (b) rule 24.9 (Single justice procedure: special rules) applies as if the defendant had served the notice required by paragraph (2)(c) of this rule within the time allowed by rule 24.9(4); and

    (c) where that notice is under rule 24.9(4)(c) (notice of intention to plead guilty at a hearing before a court comprising more than one justice) or under rule 24.9(4)(d) (notice of intention to plead not guilty), then—

        (i) if the defendant is present when the declaration is served, the rules in this Part apply as if the defendant had been required to attend the court on that occasion, or

        (ii) if the defendant is absent when the declaration is served, paragraph (6) of this rule applies.

(6) Where this paragraph applies, the court must exercise its power to issue a summons and—

    (a) the rules in Part 7 apply (Starting a prosecution in a magistrates' court) as if the prosecutor had just served an application for a summons in the same terms as the written charge;

    (b) except for rule 24.8 (Written guilty plea: special rules) and rule 24.9 (Single justice procedure: special rules), the rules in Part 24 apply.

[Note. Under sections 14 and 16E of the Magistrates' Courts Act 1980, proceedings which begin with a summons, requisition or single justice procedure notice will become void if the defendant, at any time during or after the trial, makes a statutory declaration that he or she did not know of them until a date after the trial began.

Under section 14(3) or section 16E(9) of the 1980 Act, the court which decides whether or not to extend the time limit for serving a declaration under this rule may comprise a single justice.

---

[3] 1980 c. 43; section 14 was amended by section 109 of, and paragraph 205 of Schedule 8 to, the Courts Act 2003 (c. 39). Section 16E was inserted by section 48 of the Criminal Justice and Courts Act 2015 (c. 2).

Under rule 2.11 (Taking of statutory declarations by court officers) a court officer may take the statutory declaration to which this rule refers.

The Practice Direction sets out a form of declaration for use in connection with this rule.]

R44.3　**Setting aside a conviction or varying a costs, etc. order**

44.3　(1)　This rule applies where the court can—

　　(a)　under section 16M of the Magistrates' Courts Act 1980 set aside a conviction under section 16H of the 1980 Act (conviction on accepting the automatic online conviction option); or

　　(b)　under section 142 of the 1980 Act—

　　　　(i)　set aside a conviction, or

　　　　(ii)　vary or rescind a costs order or an order to which Part 31 applies (Behaviour orders).

　(2)　The court may exercise its power—

　　(a)　on application by a party, or on its own initiative; and

　　(b)　at a hearing, in public or in private, or without a hearing.

　(3)　The court must not exercise its power in a party's absence unless—

　　(a)　the court makes a decision proposed by that party;

　　(b)　the court makes a decision to which that party has agreed in writing; or

　　(c)　that party has had an opportunity to make representations at a hearing (whether or not that party in fact attends).

　(4)　A party who wants the court to exercise its power must—

　　(a)　apply in writing as soon as reasonably practicable after the conviction or order that that party wants the court to set aside, vary or rescind;

　　(b)　serve the application on—

　　　　(i)　the court officer, and

　　　　(ii)　each other party; and

　　(c)　in the application—

　　　　(i)　explain why, as appropriate, the conviction should be set aside, or the order varied or rescinded,

　　　　(ii)　specify any variation of the order that the applicant proposes,

　　　　(iii)　identify any witness that the defendant wants to call, and any other proposed evidence,

　　　　(iv)　say whether the defendant waives legal professional privilege, giving any relevant name and date, and

　　　　(v)　if the application is late, explain why.

　(5)　The court may—

　　(a)　extend (even after it has expired) the time limit under paragraph (4), unless the court's power to set aside the conviction, or vary the order, can no longer be exercised; and

　　(b)　allow an application to be made orally.

[Note. Under section 142 of the Magistrates' Courts Act 1980—

　　(a)　where a defendant is convicted by a magistrates' court, the court may order that the case should be heard again by different justices; and

　　(b)　the court may vary or rescind an order which it has made when dealing with a convicted defendant,

if in either case it appears to the court to be in the interests of justice to do so.

The power cannot be exercised if the Crown Court or the High Court has determined an appeal about that conviction or order.

Under section 16M of the 1980 Act[4] a magistrates' court can set aside a conviction imposed on a defendant who accepts the automatic online conviction option under section 16H of the Act[5] if the conviction appears to the court to be unjust. Under section 16M (3) the court may comprise a single justice to set aside a conviction but must comprise two or more to refuse to do so.

See also rule 28.4 (Variation of sentence), which applies to an application under (i) section 16M(5) of the 1980 Act to set aside a penalty under section 16I[6], or (ii) section 142 of the Act to vary or rescind a sentence.]

---

[4]　1980 c. 43; section 16M is inserted by section 3 of the Judicial Review and Courts Act 2022 (c. 35) with effect from a date to be appointed.

[5]　1980 c. 43; section 16H is inserted by section 3 of the Judicial Review and Courts Act 2022 (c. 35) with effect from a date to be appointed.

[6]　1980 c. 43; section 16I is inserted by section 3 of the Judicial Review and Courts Act 2022 (c. 35) with effect from a date to be appointed.

CRIMINAL PROCEDURE RULES   PART 45   COSTS

General rules

When this Part applies   R45.1

45.1 (1) This Part applies where the court can make an order about costs under—

    (a) Part II of the Prosecution of Offences Act 1985[1] and Part II, IIA or IIB of The Costs in Criminal Cases (General) Regulations 1986[2];

    (b) section 109 of the Magistrates' Courts Act 1980[3];

    (c) section 52 of the Senior Courts Act 1981[4] and rule 45.6 or rule 45.7;

    (d) section 8 of the Bankers Books Evidence Act 1879[5];

    (e) section 2C(8) of the Criminal Procedure (Attendance of Witnesses) Act 1965[6];

    (f) section 36(5) of the Criminal Justice Act 1972[7];

    (g) section 159(5) and Schedule 3, paragraph 11, of the Criminal Justice Act 1988[8];

    (h) section 14H(5) of the Football Spectators Act 1989[9];

    (i) section 4(7) of the Dangerous Dogs Act 1991[10];

    (j) Part 3 of the Serious Crime Act 2007 (Appeals under Section 24) Order 2008[11]; or

    (k) Part 1 or 2 of the Extradition Act 2003[12].

(2) In this Part, 'costs' means—

    (a) the fees payable to a legal representative;

    (b) the disbursements paid by a legal representative; and

    (c) any other expenses incurred in connection with the case.

[Note. A costs order can be made under—

    (a) section 16 of the Prosecution of Offences Act 1985[13] (defence costs), for the payment out of central funds of a defendant's costs (see rule 45.4);

    (b) section 17 of the Prosecution of Offences Act 1985[14] (prosecution costs), for the payment out of central funds of a private prosecutor's costs (see rule 45.4);

    (c) section 18 of the Prosecution of Offences Act 1985[15] (award of costs against accused), for the payment by a defendant of another person's costs (see rules 45.5 and 45.6);

Criminal Procedure Rules

---

[1] 1985 c. 23.

[2] S.I. 1986/1335.

[3] 1980 c. 43; section 109(2) was amended by section 109 of, and paragraph 234 of Schedule 8 to, the Courts Act 2003 (c. 39).

[4] 1981 c. 54. The Act's title was amended by section 59(5) of, and paragraph 1 of Schedule 11 to, the Constitutional Reform Act 2005 (c. 4).

[5] 1879 c. 11.

[6] 1965 c. 69; section 2C was substituted with section 2, 2A, 2B, 2D and 2E, for the existing section 2 by section 66(1) and (2) of the Criminal Procedure and Investigations Act 1996 (c. 25).

[7] 1972 c. 71; section 36(5) was amended by section 40 of, and paragraph 23 of Schedule 9 to, the Constitutional Reform Act 2005 (c. 4).

[8] 1988 c. 33; paragraph 11 of Schedule 3 was amended by section 40 of, and paragraph 48 of Schedule 9 to, the Constitutional Reform Act 2005 (c. 4) and paragraph 11 and Part 4 of Schedule 7 to the Legal Aid, Sentencing and Punishment of Offenders Act 2012 (c. 10).

[9] 1989 c. 37; section 14H was substituted, together with sections 14, 14A-14G and 14J, for existing sections 14-17, by section 1 of, and paragraphs 1 and 2 of Schedule 1 to, the Football (Disorder) Act 2000 (c. 25).

[10] 1991 c. 65.

[11] S.I. 2008/1863.

[12] 2003 c. 41.

[13] 1985 c. 23; section 16 was amended by section 15 of, and paragraphs 14 and 15 of Schedule 2 to, the Criminal Justice Act 1987 (c. 38), section 150 of, and paragraph 103 of Schedule 15 to, the Criminal Justice Act 1988 (c. 33), section 7 of, and paragraph 7 of Schedule 3 to, the Criminal Procedure (Insanity and Unfitness to Plead) Act 1991 (c. 25), sections 69 and 312 of, and paragraph 57 of Schedule 3, and Part 4 of Schedule 37, to the Criminal Justice Act 2003 (c. 44), section 58 of, and Schedule 11 to, the Domestic Violence, Crime and Victims Act 2004 (c. 28), section 40 of, and paragraph 23 of Schedule 9 to, the Constitutional Reform Act 2005 (c. 4) and paragraphs 1 and 2 and Part 4 of Schedule 7 to the Legal Aid, Sentencing and Punishment of Offenders Act 2012 (c. 10).

[14] 1985 c. 23; section 17 was amended by section 40 of, and paragraph 41 of Schedule 9 to, the Constitutional Reform Act 2005 (c. 4) and paragraphs 1 and 4 and Part 4 of Schedule 7 to the Legal Aid, Sentencing and Punishment of Offenders Act 2012 (c. 10).

[15] 1985 c. 23; section 18 was amended by section 15 of, and paragraph 16 of Schedule 2 to, the Criminal Justice Act 1987 (c. 38), section 168 of, and paragraph 26 of Schedule 9 to, the Criminal Justice and Public Order Act 1994 (c. 33), sections 69 and 312 of the Criminal Justice Act 2003 (c. 44) and section 40 of, and paragraph 41 of Schedule 9 to, the Constitutional Reform Act 2005 (c. 4).

   (d)   *section 19(1) of the Prosecution of Offences Act 1985[16] and regulation 3 of the Costs in Criminal Cases (General) Regulations 1986, for the payment by a party of another party's costs incurred as a result of an unnecessary or improper act or omission by or on behalf of the first party (see rule 45.8);*

   (e)   *section 19A of the Prosecution of Offences Act 1985[17] (costs against legal representatives, etc.)—*

        (i)   *for the payment by a legal representative of a party's costs incurred as a result of an improper, unreasonable or negligent act or omission by or on behalf of the representative, or*

        (ii) *disallowing the payment to that representative of such costs (see rule 45.9);*

   (f)   *section 19B of the Prosecution of Offences Act 1985[18] (provision for award of costs against third parties) and regulation 3F of the Costs in Criminal Cases (General) Regulations 1986[19], for the payment by a person who is not a party of a party's costs where there has been serious misconduct by the non-party (see rule 45.10);*

   (g)   *section 109 of the Magistrates' Courts Act 1980, section 52 of the Senior Courts Act 1981 and rule 45.6, for the payment by an appellant of a respondent's costs on abandoning an appeal to the Crown Court (see rule 45.6);*

   (h)   *section 52 of the Senior Courts Act 1981 and—*

        (i)   *rule 45.6, for the payment by a party of another party's costs on an appeal to the Crown Court in any case not covered by (c) or (g),*

        (ii) *rule 45.7, for the payment by a party of another party's costs on an application to the Crown Court about the breach or variation of a deferred prosecution agreement, or on an application to lift the suspension of a prosecution after breach of such an agreement;*

   (i)   *section 8 of the Bankers Books Evidence Act 1879, for the payment of costs by a party or by the bank against which an application for an order is made (see rule 45.7);*

   (j)   *section 2C(8) of the Criminal Procedure (Attendance of Witnesses) Act 1965, for the payment by the applicant for a witness summons of the costs of a party who applies successfully under rule 17.7 to have it withdrawn (see rule 45.7);*

   (k)   *section 36(5) of the Criminal Justice Act 1972 or Schedule 3, paragraph 11, of the Criminal Justice Act 1988, for the payment out of central funds of a defendant's costs on a reference by the Attorney General of—*

        (i)   *a point of law, or*

        (ii) *an unduly lenient sentence*

           (see rule 45.4);

   (l)   *section 159(5) of the Criminal Justice Act 1988, for the payment by a person of another person's costs on an appeal about a reporting or public access restriction (see rule 45.6);*

   (m) *section 14H(5) of the Football Spectators Act 1989, for the payment by a defendant of another person's costs on an application to terminate a football banning order (see rule 45.7);*

   (n)   *section 4(7) of the Dangerous Dogs Act 1991, for the payment by a defendant of another person's costs on an application to terminate a disqualification for having custody of a dog (see rule 45.7);*

   (o)   *article 14 of the Serious Crime Act 2007 (Appeals under Section 24) Order 2008[20], corresponding with section 16 of the Prosecution of Offences Act 1985 (see rule 45.4);*

   (p)   *article 15 of the Serious Crime Act 2007 (Appeals under Section 24) Order 2008, corresponding with section 18 of the Prosecution of Offences Act 1985 (see rule 45.6);*

   (q)   *article 16 of the Serious Crime Act 2007 (Appeals under Section 24) Order 2008, corresponding with an order under section 19(1) of the 1985 Act (see rule 45.8);*

   (r)   *article 17 of the Serious Crime Act 2007 (Appeals under Section 24) Order 2008, corresponding with an order under section 19A of the 1985 Act (see rule 45.9);*

   (s)   *article 18 of the Serious Crime Act 2007 (Appeals under Section 24) Order 2008, corresponding with an order under section 19B of the 1985 Act (see rule 45.10);*

   (t)   *section 60 or 133 of the Extradition Act 2003 (costs where extradition ordered) for the payment by a defendant of another person's costs (see rule 45.4); or*

   (u)   *section 61 or 134 of the Extradition Act 2003[21] (costs where discharge ordered) for the payment out of central funds of a defendant's costs (see rule 45.4).*

See also the Criminal Costs Practice Direction.

---

[16] 1985 c. 23.

[17] 1985 c. 23; section 19A was inserted by section 111 of the Courts and Legal Services Act 1990 (c. 41).

[18] 1985 c. 23; section 19B was inserted by section 93 of the Courts Act 2003 (c. 39).

[19] S.I. 1986/1335; regulation 3F was inserted by regulation 7 of S.I. 2004/2408 and amended by regulations 2 and 5 of S.I. 2008/2448.

[20] S.I. 2008/1863.

[21] 2003 c. 41; sections 61 and 134 were amended by paragraphs 12, 13 and 16 and Part 4 of Schedule 7 to the Legal Aid, Sentencing and Punishment of Offenders Act 2012 (c. 10).

Part 39 (Appeal to the Court of Appeal about conviction or sentence) contains rules about appeals against costs orders made in the Crown Court under the legislation listed in (c) above.

Part 34 (Appeal to the Crown Court) and Part 39 (Appeal to the Court of Appeal about conviction or sentence) contain rules about appeals against costs orders made under the legislation listed in (e) and (f) above.

As to costs in restraint or receivership proceedings under Part 2 of the Proceeds of Crime Act 2002[22], see rules 33.47 to 33.50.

A costs order can be enforced—

(a) *against a defendant, under section 41(1) or (3) of the Administration of Justice Act 1970[23];*

(b) *against a prosecutor, under section 41(2) or (3) of the Administration of Justice Act 1970;*

(c) *against a representative, under regulation 3D of the Costs in Criminal Cases (General) Regulations 1986[24] or article 18 of the Serious Crime Act 2007 (Appeals under Section 24) Order 2008;*

(d) *against a non-party, under regulation 3I of the Costs in Criminal Cases (General) Regulations 1986[25] or article 31 of the Serious Crime Act 2007 (Appeals under Section 24) Order 2008[26].*

See also section 58, section 150(1) and Part III of the Magistrates' Courts Act 1980[27] and Schedule 5 to the Courts Act 2003[28].]

Costs orders: general rules   R45.2

45.2 (1) The court must not make an order about costs unless each party and any other person directly affected—

(a) is present; or

(b) has had an opportunity—

(i) to attend, or

(ii) to make representations.

(2) The court may make an order about costs—

(a) at a hearing in public or in private; or

(b) without a hearing.

(3) In deciding what order, if any, to make about costs, the court must have regard to all the circumstances, including—

(a) the conduct of all the parties; and

(b) any costs order already made.

(4) If the court makes an order about costs, it must—

(a) specify who must, or must not, pay what, to whom; and

(b) identify the legislation under which the order is made, where there is a choice of powers.

(5) The court must give reasons if it—

(a) refuses an application for a costs order; or

(b) rejects representations opposing a costs order.

(6) If the court makes an order for the payment of costs—

(a) the general rule is that it must be for an amount that is sufficient reasonably to compensate the recipient for costs—

(i) actually, reasonably and properly incurred, and

(ii) reasonable in amount; but

(b) the court may order the payment of—

(i) a proportion of that amount,

(ii) a stated amount less than that amount,

(iii) costs from or until a certain date only,

---

[22] 2002 c. 29.

[23] 1970 c. 31; section 41(3) was amended by section 62 of, and paragraph 35 of Schedule 13 to the Tribunals, Courts and Enforcement Act 2007 (c. 15) and section 17 of, and paragraph 52 of Schedule 9 to, the Crime and Courts Act 2013 (c. 22).

[24] S.I. 1986/1335; regulation 3D was inserted by article 2 of S.I. 1991/789 and amended by regulation 6 of S.I. 2004/2408.

[25] S.I. 1986/1335; regulation 3I was inserted by regulation 7 of S.I. 2004/2408.

[26] S.I. 2008/1863.

[27] 1980 c. 43; section 58 was amended by section 33 of, and paragraph 80 of Schedule 2 to, the Family Law Reform Act 1987 (c. 42); a relevant amendment was made to section 150(1) by paragraph 250 of Schedule 8, and Schedule 10 to, the Courts Act 2003 (c. 39).

[28] 2003 c. 39; Schedule 5 was amended by articles 2, 4, 6, 7 and 8 of S.I. 2006/1737, section 62 of, and paragraphs 148 and 149 of Schedule 13 to, the Tribunals, Courts and Enforcement Act 2007 (c. 15), section 80 of the Criminal Justice and Immigration Act 2008 (c. 4), section 88 of the Legal Aid, Sentencing and Punishment of Offenders Act 2012 (c. 10), section 10 of, and paragraphs 24 and 27 of the Schedule to, the Prevention of Social Housing Fraud Act 2013 (c. 3), section 27 of the Crime and Courts Act 2013 (c. 22) and section 56 of the Criminal Justice and Courts Act 2015 (c. 2). It is further amended by section 26 of the Crime and Courts Act 2013 (c. 22) and paragraph 23 of Schedule 5 to the Modern Slavery Act 2015 (c. 30), with effect from dates to be appointed.

(iv) costs relating only to particular steps taken, or

(v) costs relating only to a distinct part of the case.

(7) On an assessment of the amount of costs, relevant factors include—

    (a) the conduct of all the parties;

    (b) the particular complexity of the matter or the difficulty or novelty of the questions raised;

    (c) the skill, effort, specialised knowledge and responsibility involved;

    (d) the time spent on the case;

    (e) the place where and the circumstances in which work or any part of it was done; and

    (f) any direction or observations by the court that made the costs order.

(8) If the court orders a party to pay costs to be assessed under rule 45.11, it may order that party to pay an amount on account.

(9) An order for the payment of costs takes effect when the amount is assessed, unless the court exercises any power it has to order otherwise.

[Note. Under the powers to which apply rule 45.8 (Costs resulting from unnecessary or improper act, etc.) and rule 45.9 (Costs against a legal representative), specified conduct must be established for such orders to be made.

The amount recoverable under a costs order may be affected by the legislation under which the order is made. See, for example, section 16A of the Prosecution of Offences Act 1985[29].

Under section 141 of the Powers of Criminal Courts (Sentencing) Act 2000[30] and section 75 of the Magistrates' Courts Act 1980[31], the Crown Court and magistrates' court respectively can allow time for payment, or payment by instalments.]

R45.3   **Court's power to vary requirements**

45.3 (1) Unless other legislation otherwise provides, the court may—

    (a) extend a time limit for serving an application or representations under rules 45.4 to 45.10, even after it has expired; and

    (b) consider an application or representations—

        (i) made in a different form to one set out in the Practice Direction, or

        (ii) made orally instead of in writing.

(2) A person who wants an extension of time must—

    (a) apply when serving the application or representations for which it is needed; and

    (b) explain the delay.

[Note. The time limit for applying for a costs order may be affected by the legislation under which the order is made. See, for example, sections 19(1), (2) and 19A of the Prosecution of Offences Act 1985[32], regulation 3 of the Costs in Criminal Cases (General) Regulations 1986[33] and rules 45.8(4)(a) and 45.9(4)(a).]

Costs out of central funds

R45.4   **Costs out of central funds**

45.4 (1) This rule applies where the court can order the payment of costs out of central funds.

(2) In this rule, costs—

    (a) include—

        (i) on an appeal, costs incurred in the court that made the decision under appeal, and

        (ii) at a retrial, costs incurred at the initial trial and on any appeal; but

    (b) do not include costs met by legal aid.

(3) The court may make an order—

    (a) on application by the person who incurred the costs; or

    (b) on its own initiative.

---

[29] 1985 c. 23; section 16A was inserted by paragraphs 1 and 3 and Part 4 of Schedule 7 to the Legal Aid, Sentencing and Punishment of Offenders Act 2012 (c. 10).

[30] 2000 c. 6.

[31] 1980 c. 43, section 75 was amended by section 11 of, and paragraph 6 of Schedule 2 to, the Maintenance Enforcement Act 1991 (c. 17).

[32] 1985 c. 23; section 19 was amended by section 166 of the Criminal Justice Act 1988 (c. 33), section 45 of, and Schedule 6 to, the Legal Aid Act 1988 (c. 34), section 7 of, and paragraph 8 of Schedule 3 to, the Criminal Procedure (Insanity and Unfitness to Plead) Act 1991 (c. 25), section 24 of, and paragraphs 27 and 28 of Schedule 4 to, the Access to Justice Act 1999 (c. 22), sections 40 and 67 of, and paragraph 4 of Schedule 7 to, the Youth Justice and Criminal Evidence Act 1999 (c. 23), section 165 of, and paragraph 99 of Schedule 9 to, the Powers of Criminal Courts (Sentencing) Act 2000 (c. 6), section 378 of, and paragraph 107 of Schedule 16 to, the Armed Forces Act 2006 (c. 52), section 6 of, and paragraph 32 of Schedule 4 and paragraphs 1 and 5 of Schedule 27 to, the Criminal Justice and Immigration Act 2008 (c. 4) and paragraphs 22 and 23 of Schedule 5, and paragraphs 1 and 5 and Part 4 of Schedule 7, to the Legal Aid, Sentencing and Punishment of Offenders Act 2012 (c. 10). Section 19A was inserted by section 111 of the Courts and Legal Services Act 1990 (c. 41).

[33] S.I. 1986/1335; regulation 3 was amended by regulations 2 and 3 of S.I. 2008/2448.

(4) Where a person wants the court to make an order that person must apply as soon as practicable and—

    (a) on an application for a defendant's costs order—

        (i)   outline the type of costs and the amount claimed, if the applicant wants the court to direct an assessment; or

        (ii) specify the amount claimed, giving details, if the applicant wants the court to assess the amount itself; or

    (b) on an application for a prosecutor's costs order—

        (i)   apply in writing and serve it on the court officer (or, in the Court of Appeal, the Registrar), and

        (ii) in the application specify the amount claimed to the date of the application and provide the information listed in paragraph (5).

(5) The information required by paragraph (4)(b) is—

    (a) a summary of the items of work to date done by a solicitor;

    (b) a statement of the dates on which items of work were done, the time taken and the sums claimed;

    (c) details of any disbursements claimed, the circumstances in which they were incurred and the amounts claimed in respect of them, and

    (d) such further particulars, information and documents as the court may require.

(6) The general rule is that the court must make an order, but—

    (a) the court may decline to make a defendant's costs order if, for example—

        (i)   the defendant is convicted of at least one offence, or

        (ii) the defendant's conduct led the prosecutor reasonably to think the prosecution case stronger than it was;

    (b) the court may decline to make a prosecutor's costs order if, for example, the prosecution was started or continued unreasonably; and

    (c) the court may decline to make an order if the applicant fails to provide enough information for the court to decide whether to make an order at all and, if so, whether it should be for the full amount recoverable or for a lesser sum.

(7) If the court makes an order—

    (a) the general rule is that it must be for such amount as the court considers reasonably sufficient to compensate the applicant for any expenses properly incurred in the proceedings;

    (b) where the court considers there to be circumstances making it inappropriate for the applicant to recover that amount then the order must be for such lesser amount as the court considers just and reasonable;

    (c) the court may fix the amount to be paid in a case in which either—

        (i)   the recipient agrees the amount, or

        (ii) the court decides to allow a lesser sum than the full amount otherwise recoverable; and

    (d) if the court does not fix the amount itself it must direct an assessment under, as applicable—

        (i)   Part III of the Costs in Criminal Cases (General) Regulations 1986[34], or

        (ii) Part 3 of the Serious Crime Act 2007 (Appeals under Section 24) Order 2008[35].

(8) If the court makes a defendant's costs order—

    (a) the order may not require the payment of any amount in respect of fees payable to a legal representative, or disbursements paid by a legal representative (including expert witness costs), but if the defendant is an individual then an order may require payment of such an amount in a case—

        (i)   in a magistrates' court, including in an extradition case,

        (ii) in the Crown Court, on appeal from a magistrates' court,

        (iii) in the Crown Court, where the defendant has been sent for trial, the High Court gives permission to serve a draft indictment or the Court of Appeal orders a retrial and the defendant has been found financially ineligible for legal aid, or

        (iv) in the Court of Appeal, on an appeal against a verdict of not guilty by reason of insanity, or against a finding under the Criminal Procedure (Insanity) Act 1964[36], or on an appeal under section 16A of the Criminal Appeal Act 1968[37] (appeal against order made in cases of insanity or unfitness to plead);

[34] S.I. 1986/1335; relevant amending instruments are S.I. 1999/2096 and S.I. 2008/2448.
[35] S.I. 2008/1863.
[36] 1964 c. 84.
[37] 1968 c. 19; section 16A was inserted by section 25 of the Domestic Violence, Crime and Victims Act 2004 (c. 28).

     (b) any such amount may not exceed an amount specified by regulations made by the Lord Chancellor; and

     (c) an order which includes an amount in respect of fees payable to a legal representative, or disbursements paid by a legal representative, must include a statement to that effect.

   (9) If the court fixes the amount to be paid itself, it must do so subject to any restriction on the amount that is imposed by regulations made by the Lord Chancellor.

  (10) If the court directs an assessment, the order must specify any restriction on the amount to be paid that the court considers appropriate.

[Note. See also rule 45.2.

An order for the payment of costs out of central funds can be made—

    (a) for a defendant—
       (i)   on acquittal,
      (ii) where a prosecution does not proceed,
     (iii) where the Crown Court allows any part of a defendant's appeal from a magistrates' court,
     (iv) where the Court of Appeal allows any part of a defendant's appeal from the Crown Court,
      (v) where the Court of Appeal decides a prosecutor's appeal under Part 37 (Appeal to the Court of Appeal against ruling at preparatory hearing) or Part 38 (Appeal to the Court of Appeal against ruling adverse to prosecution),
     (vi) where the Court of Appeal decides a reference by the Attorney General under Part 41 (Reference to the Court of Appeal of point of law or unduly lenient sentence),
    (vii) where the Court of Appeal decides an appeal by someone other than the defendant about a serious crime prevention order, or
   (viii) where the defendant is discharged under Part 1 or 2 of the Extradition Act 2003;

(See section 16 of the Prosecution of Offences Act 1985 and regulation 14 of the Costs in Criminal Cases (General) Regulations 1986[38]; section 36(5) of the Criminal Justice Act 1972 and paragraph 11 of Schedule 3 to the Criminal Justice Act 1988; article 14 of the Serious Crime Act 2007 (Appeals under Section 24) Order 2008; and sections 61 and 134 of the Extradition Act 2003.)

    (b) for a private prosecutor, in proceedings in respect of an offence that must or may be tried in the Crown Court;

(See section 17 of the Prosecution of Offences Act 1985 and regulation 14 of the Costs in Criminal Cases (General) Regulations 1986.)

    (c) for a person adversely affected by a serious crime prevention order, where the Court of Appeal—
      (i) allows an appeal by that person about that order, or
     (ii) decides an appeal about that order by someone else.

(See article 14 of the Serious Crime Act 2007 (Appeals under Section 24) Order 2008.)

Where the court makes an order for the payment of a defendant's costs out of central funds, see also section 16A of the Prosecution of Offences Act 1985[39], sections 62A, 62B, 135A and 135B of the Extradition Act 2003[40] and regulations 4A and 7 of the Costs in Criminal Cases (General) Regulations 1986[41].]

Payment of costs by one party to another
R45.5 **Costs on conviction and sentence, etc.**

45.5 (1) This rule applies where the court can order a defendant to pay the prosecutor's costs if the defendant is—
    (a) convicted or found guilty;
    (b) dealt with in the Crown Court after committal for sentence there;
    (c) dealt with for breach of a sentence; or
    (d) in an extradition case—
      (i) ordered to be extradited, under Part 1 of the Extradition Act 2003,
     (ii) sent for extradition to the Secretary of State, under Part 2 of that Act, or

---

[38] S.I. 1986/1335; regulation 14 was amended by regulations 2 and 11 of S.I. 2008/2448.
[39] 1985 c. 23; section 16A was inserted by paragraphs 1 and 3 and Part 4 of Schedule 7 to the Legal Aid, Sentencing and Punishment of Offenders Act 2012 (c. 10) and amended by S.I. 2014/130.
[40] 2003 c. 41; sections 62A and 62B were inserted by paragraphs 12 and 15 and Part 4 of Schedule 7 to the Legal Aid, Sentencing and Punishment of Offenders Act 2012 (c. 10) and sections 135A and 135B were inserted by paragraphs 12 and 18 and Part 4 of that Schedule.
[41] S.I. 1986/1335; regulation 4A was inserted by regulations 4 and 5 of S.I. 2012/1804. Regulation 7 was substituted by regulations 4 and 6 of S.I. 2012/1804 and amended by S.I. 2013/2830.

(iii) unsuccessful on an appeal by the defendant to the High Court, or on an application by the defendant for permission to appeal from the High Court to the Supreme Court.

(2) The court may make an order—

    (a) on application by the prosecutor; or

    (b) on its own initiative.

(3) Where the prosecutor wants the court to make an order—

    (a) the prosecutor must—

       (i) apply as soon as practicable, and

       (ii) specify the amount claimed; and

    (b) the general rule is that the court must make an order if it is satisfied that the defendant can pay;

(4) A defendant who wants to oppose an order must make representations as soon as practicable.

(5) If the court makes an order, it must assess the amount itself.

[Note. See—

    (a) rule 45.2;

    (b) section 18 of the Prosecution of Offences Act 1985[42] and regulation 14 of the Costs in Criminal Cases (General) Regulations 1986; and

    (c) sections 60 and 133 of the Extradition Act 2003.

Under section 18(4) and (5) of the 1985 Act, if a magistrates' court—

    (a) imposes a fine, a penalty, forfeiture or compensation that does not exceed £5—

       (i) the general rule is that the court will not make a costs order against the defendant, but

       (ii) the court may do so;

    (b) fines a defendant under 18, no costs order against the defendant may be for more than the fine.

Part 39 (Appeal to the Court of Appeal about conviction or sentence) contains rules about appeal against a Crown Court costs order to which this rule applies.]

Costs on appeal   R45.6

45.6 (1) This rule—

    (a) applies where a magistrates' court, the Crown Court or the Court of Appeal can order a party to pay another person's costs on an appeal, or an application for permission to appeal; and

    (b) authorises the Crown Court, in addition to its other powers, to order a party to pay another party's costs on an appeal to that court, except on an appeal under—

       (i) section 108 of the Magistrates' Courts Act 1980[43], or

       (ii) section 45 of the Mental Health Act 1983[44].

(2) In this rule, costs include—

    (a) costs incurred in the court that made the decision under appeal; and

    (b) costs met by legal aid.

(3) The court may make an order—

    (a) on application by the person who incurred the costs; or

    (b) on its own initiative.

(4) A person who wants the court to make an order must—

    (a) apply as soon as practicable;

    (b) notify each other party;

    (c) specify—

       (i) the amount claimed, and

       (ii) against whom; and

---

[42] 1985 c. 23; section 18 was amended by section 15 of, and paragraph 16 of Schedule 2 to, the Criminal Justice Act 1987 (c. 38), section 168 of, and paragraph 26 of Schedule 9 to, the Criminal Justice and Public Order Act 1994 (c. 33), sections 69 and 312 of the Criminal Justice Act 2003 (c. 44) and section 40 of, and paragraph 41 of Schedule 9 to, the Constitutional Reform Act 2005 (c. 4).

[43] 1980 c. 43; section 108 was amended by sections 66(2) and 78 of, and Schedule 16 to, the Criminal Justice Act 1982 (c. 48), section 23(3) of the Football Spectators Act 1989 (c. 37), section 101(2) of, and Schedule 13 to, the Criminal Justice Act 1991 (c. 53), sections 119 and 120(2) of, and paragraph 43 of Schedule 8 and Schedule 10 to, the Crime and Disorder Act 1998 (c. 37), section 7(2) of the Football (Offences and Disorder) Act 1999 (c. 21), section 165(1) of, and paragraph 71 of Schedule 9 to, the Powers of Criminal Courts (Sentencing) Act 2000 (c. 6), section 1 of, and Schedule 3 to, the Football (Disorder) Act 2000 (c. 25), section 58(1) of, and paragraph 10 of Schedule 10 to, the Domestic Violence, Crime and Victims Act 2004 (c. 28), section 52(2) of, and paragraph 14 of Schedule 3 to, the Violent Crime Reduction Act 2006 (c. 38) and section 64 of, and paragraph 10 of Schedule 3 to, the Animal Welfare Act 2006 (c. 45).

[44] 1983 c. 20.

Criminal Procedure Rules

(d) where an appellant abandons an appeal to the Crown Court by serving a notice of abandonment—
  (i) apply in writing not more than 10 business days later, and
  (ii) serve the application on the appellant and on the Crown Court officer.
(5) A party who wants to oppose an order must—
  (a) make representations as soon as practicable; and
  (b) where the application was under paragraph (4)(d), serve representations on the applicant, and on the Crown Court officer, not more than 5 business days after it was served.
(6) Where the application was under paragraph (4)(d), the Crown Court officer may—
  (a) submit it to the Crown Court; or
  (b) serve it on the magistrates' court officer, for submission to the magistrates' court.
(7) If the court makes an order, it may direct an assessment under rule 45.11, or assess the amount itself where—
  (a) the appellant abandons an appeal to the Crown Court;
  (b) the Crown Court decides an appeal, except an appeal under—
    (i) section 108 of the Magistrates' Courts Act 1980, or
    (ii) section 45 of the Mental Health Act 1983; or
  (c) the Court of Appeal decides an appeal to which Part 40 applies (Appeal to the Court of Appeal about reporting or public access restriction).
(8) If the court makes an order in any other case, it must assess the amount itself.

[Note. See also rule 45.2.

A magistrates' court can order an appellant to pay a respondent's costs on abandoning an appeal to the Crown Court.

The Crown Court can order—

  (a) the defendant to pay the prosecutor's costs on dismissing a defendant's appeal—
    (i) against conviction or sentence, under section 108 of the Magistrates' Courts Act 1980, or
    (ii) where the magistrates' court makes a hospital order or guardianship order without convicting the defendant, under section 45 of the Mental Health Act 1983; and
  (b) one party to pay another party's costs on deciding any other appeal to which Part 34 (Appeal to the Crown Court) applies.

The Court of Appeal can order—

  (a) the defendant to pay another person's costs on dismissing a defendant's appeal or application to which Part 37 (Appeal to the Court of Appeal against ruling at preparatory hearing), Part 39 (Appeal to the Court of Appeal about conviction or sentence) or Part 43 (Appeal or reference to the Supreme Court) applies;
  (b) the defendant to pay another person's costs on allowing a prosecutor's appeal to which Part 38 (Appeal to the Court of Appeal against ruling adverse to the prosecution) applies;
  (c) the appellant to pay another person's costs on dismissing an appeal or application by a person affected by a serious crime prevention order;
  (d) one party to pay another party's costs on deciding an appeal to which Part 40 (Appeal to the Court of Appeal about reporting or public access restriction) applies.

See section 109 of the Magistrates' Courts Act 1980[45]; section 52 of the Senior Courts Act 1981[46] (which allows rules of court to authorise the Crown Court to order costs); section 18 of the Prosecution of Offences Act 1985; section 159(5) of the Criminal Justice Act 1988[47]; and article 15 of the Serious Crime Act 2007 (Appeals under Section 24) Order 2008[48].]

R45.7   Costs on an application
45.7 (1) This rule—
  (a) applies where the court can order a party to pay another person's costs in a case in which—
    (i) the court decides an application for the production in evidence of a copy of a bank record,
    (ii) a magistrates' court or the Crown Court decides an application to terminate a football banning order,

[45] 1980 c. 43; section 109(2) was amended by section 109 of, and paragraph 234 of Schedule 8 to, the Courts Act 2003 (c. 39).
[46] 1981 c. 54. The Act's title was amended by section 59(5) of, and paragraph 1 of Schedule 11 to, the Constitutional Reform Act 2005 (c. 4).
[47] 1988 c. 33.
[48] S.I. 2008/1863.

(iii) a magistrates' court or the Crown Court decides an application to terminate a disqualification for having custody of a dog,

(iv) the Crown Court allows an application to withdraw a witness summons, or

(v) the Crown Court decides an application relating to a deferred prosecution agreement under rule 11.5 (breach), rule 11.6 (variation) or rule 11.7 (lifting suspension of prosecution); and

(b) authorises the Crown Court, in addition to its other powers, to order a party to pay another party's costs on an application to that court under rule 11.5, 11.6 or 11.7.

(2) The court may make an order—

(a) on application by the person who incurred the costs; or

(b) on its own initiative.

(3) A person who wants the court to make an order must—

(a) apply as soon as practicable;

(b) notify each other party; and

(c) specify—

(i) the amount claimed, and

(ii) against whom.

(4) A party who wants to oppose an order must make representations as soon as practicable.

(5) If the court makes an order, it may direct an assessment under rule 45.11, or assess the amount itself.

[Note. See—

(a) rule 45.2;

(b) section 8 of the Bankers Books Evidence Act 1879[49];

(c) section 14H(5) of the Football Spectators Act 1989[50];

(d) section 2C(8) of the Criminal Procedure (Attendance of Witnesses) Act 1965[51]; and

(e) section 4(7) of the Dangerous Dogs Act 1991[52].

Section 52 of the Senior Courts Act 1981 allows rules of court to authorise the Crown Court to order costs.]

Costs resulting from unnecessary or improper act, etc.   **R45.8**

45.8   (1) This rule applies where the court can order a party to pay another party's costs incurred as a result of an unnecessary or improper act or omission by or on behalf of the first party.

(2) In this rule, costs include costs met by legal aid.

(3) The court may make an order—

(a) on application by the party who incurred such costs; or

(b) on its own initiative.

(4) A party who wants the court to make an order must—

(a) apply in writing as soon as practicable after becoming aware of the grounds for doing so and in any event no later than the end of the case;

(b) serve the application on—

(i) the court officer (or, in the Court of Appeal, the Registrar), and

(ii) each other party; and

(c) in that application specify—

(i) the party by whom costs should be paid,

(ii) the relevant act or omission,

(iii) the reasons why that act or omission meets the criteria for making an order,

(iv) the amount claimed, and

(v) those on whom the application has been served.

(5) Where the court considers making an order on its own initiative, it must—

(a) identify the party against whom it proposes making the order; and

(b) specify—

(i) the relevant act or omission,

(ii) the reasons why that act or omission meets the criteria for making an order, and

(iii) with the assistance of the party who incurred the costs, the amount involved.

(6) A party who wants to oppose an order must—

(a) make representations as soon as practicable; and

---

[49] 1879 c. 11.

[50] 1989 c. 37; section 14H was substituted, together with sections 14, 14A-14G and 14J, for existing sections 14-17, by section 1 of, and paragraphs 1 and 2 of Schedule 1 to, the Football (Disorder) Act 2000 (c. 25).

[51] 1965 c. 69; section 2C was substituted with section 2, 2A, 2B, 2D and 2E, for the existing section 2 by section 66(1) and (2) of the Criminal Procedure and Investigations Act 1996 (c. 25).

[52] 1991 c. 65.

(b) in reply to an application, serve representations on the applicant and on the court officer (or Registrar) not more than 5 business days after it was served.

(7) If the court makes an order, it must assess the amount itself.

(8) To help assess the amount, the court may direct an enquiry by—

(a) the Lord Chancellor, where the assessment is by a magistrates' court or by the Crown Court; or

(b) the Registrar, where the assessment is by the Court of Appeal.

(9) In deciding whether to direct such an enquiry, the court must have regard to all the circumstances including—

(a) any agreement between the parties about the amount to be paid;

(b) the amount likely to be allowed;

(c) the delay and expense that may be incurred in the conduct of the enquiry; and

(d) the particular complexity of the assessment, or the difficulty or novelty of any aspect of the assessment.

(10) If the court directs such an enquiry—

(a) paragraphs (3) to (8) inclusive of rule 45.11 (Assessment and re-assessment) apply as if that enquiry were an assessment under that rule (but rules 45.12 (Appeal to a costs judge) and 45.13 (Appeal to a High Court judge) do not apply);

(b) the authority that carries out the enquiry must serve its conclusions on the court officer as soon as reasonably practicable after following that procedure; and

(c) the court must then assess the amount to be paid.

[Note. See—

(a) rule 45.2;

(b) section 19(1) of the Prosecution of Offences Act 1985[53] and regulation 3 of the Costs in Criminal Cases (General) Regulations 1986[54]; and

(c) article 16 of the Serious Crime Act 2007 (Appeals under Section 24) Order 2008[55].

Under section 19(1), (2) of the 1985 Act and regulation 3(1) of the 1986 Regulations, the court's power to make a costs order to which this rule applies can only be exercised during the proceedings.

Under regulation 3(5) of the 1986 Regulations, if a magistrates' court fines a defendant under 17, no costs order to which this rule applies may be for more than the fine.

The Criminal Costs Practice Direction sets out a form of application for use in connection with this rule.]

Other costs orders

R45.9   Costs against a legal representative

45.9 (1) This rule applies where—

(a) a party has incurred costs—

(i)   as a result of an improper, unreasonable or negligent act or omission by a legal or other representative or representative's employee, or

(ii) which it has become unreasonable for that party to have to pay because of such an act or omission occurring after those costs were incurred; and

(b) the court can—

(i)   order the representative responsible to pay such costs, or

(ii) prohibit the payment of costs to that representative.

(2) In this rule, costs include costs met by legal aid.

(3) The court may make an order—

(a) on application by the party who incurred such costs; or

(b) on its own initiative.

(4) A party who wants the court to make an order must—

(a) apply in writing as soon as practicable after becoming aware of the grounds for doing so and in any event no later than the end of the case;

(b) serve the application on—

(i)   the court officer (or, in the Court of Appeal, the Registrar),

(ii)   the representative responsible,

(iii) each other party, and

(iv)   any other person directly affected; and

---

[53] 1985 c. 23.
[54] S.I. 1986/1335; regulation 3 was amended by regulations 2 and 3 of S.I. 2008/2448.
[55] S.I. 2008/1863.

(c) in that application specify—
   (i)   the representative responsible,
   (ii)   the relevant act or omission,
   (iii) the reasons why that act or omission meets the criteria for making an order,
   (iv)   the amount claimed, and
   (v)   those on whom the application has been served.
(5) Where the court considers making an order on its own initiative, it must—
   (a) identify the representative against whom it proposes making that order; and
   (b) specify—
      (i)   the relevant act or omission,
      (ii)   the reasons why that act or omission meets the criteria for making an order, and
      (iii) with the assistance of the party who incurred the costs, the amount involved.
(6) A representative who wants to oppose an order must—
   (a) make representations as soon as practicable; and
   (b) in reply to an application, serve representations on the applicant and on the court officer
        (or Registrar) not more than 5 business days after it was served.
(7) If the court makes an order—
   (a) the general rule is that it must do so without waiting until the end of the case, but it may
        postpone making the order; and
   (b) it must assess the amount itself.
(8) To help assess the amount, the court may direct an enquiry by—
   (a) the Lord Chancellor, where the assessment is by a magistrates' court or by the Crown
        Court; or
   (b) the Registrar, where the assessment is by the Court of Appeal.
(9) In deciding whether to direct such an enquiry, the court must have regard to all the
     circumstances including—
   (a) any agreement between the parties about the amount to be paid;
   (b) the amount likely to be allowed;
   (c) the delay and expense that may be incurred in the conduct of the enquiry; and
   (d) the particular complexity of the assessment, or the difficulty or novelty of any aspect of the
        assessment.
(10) If the court directs such an enquiry—
   (a) paragraphs (3) to (8) inclusive of rule 45.11 (Assessment and re-assessment) apply as if
        that enquiry were an assessment under that rule (but rules 45.12 (Appeal to a costs judge)
        and 45.13 (Appeal to a High Court judge) do not apply);
   (b) the authority that carries out the enquiry must serve its conclusions on the court officer as
        soon as reasonably practicable after following that procedure; and
   (c) the court must then assess the amount to be paid.
(11) Instead of making an order, the court may make adverse observations about the representa-
     tive's conduct for use in an assessment where—
   (a) a party's costs are—
      (i)   to be met by legal aid, or
      (ii)   to be paid out of central funds; or
   (b) there is to be an assessment under rule 45.11.

[Note. See—

   (a) rule 45.2;
   (b) section 19A of the Prosecution of Offences Act 1985[56];
   (c) article 17 of the Serious Crime Act 2007 (Appeals under Section 24) Order 2008[57].

Under section 19A(1) of the 1985 Act, the court's power to make a costs order to which this rule applies can only
be exercised during the proceedings.

The Criminal Costs Practice Direction sets out a form of application for use in connection with this rule.

Part 34 (Appeal to the Crown Court) and Part 39 (Appeal to the Court of Appeal about conviction or sentence)
contain rules about appeals against a costs order to which this rule applies.]

Costs against a third party   R45.10

45.10 (1) This rule applies where—
   (a) there has been serious misconduct by a person who is not a party; and
   (b) the court can order that person to pay a party's costs.

---

[56] 1985 c. 23; section 19A was inserted by section 111 of the Courts and Legal Services Act 1990 (c. 41).
[57] S.I. 2008/1863.

(2) In this rule, costs include costs met by legal aid.

(3) The court may make an order—

    (a) on application by the party who incurred the costs; or

    (b) on its own initiative.

(4) A party who wants the court to make an order must—

    (a) apply in writing as soon as practicable after becoming aware of the grounds for doing so;

    (b) serve the application on—

        (i) the court officer (or, in the Court of Appeal, the Registrar),

        (ii) the person responsible,

        (iii) each other party, and

        (iv) any other person directly affected; and

    (c) in that application specify—

        (i) the person responsible,

        (ii) the relevant misconduct,

        (iii) the reasons why the criteria for making an order are met,

        (iv) the amount claimed, and

        (v) those on whom the application has been served.

(5) Where the court considers making an order on its own initiative, it must—

    (a) identify the person against whom it proposes making that order; and

    (b) specify—

        (i) the relevant misconduct,

        (ii) the reasons why the criteria for making an order are met, and

        (iii) with the assistance of the party who incurred the costs, the amount involved.

(6) A person who wants to oppose an order must—

    (a) make representations as soon as practicable; and

    (b) in reply to an application, serve representations on the applicant and on the court officer (or Registrar) not more than 5 business days after it was served.

(7) If the court makes an order—

    (a) the general rule is that it must do so at the end of the case, but it may do so earlier; and

    (b) it must assess the amount itself.

(8) To help assess the amount, the court may direct an enquiry by—

    (a) the Lord Chancellor, where the assessment is by a magistrates' court or by the Crown Court; or

    (b) the Registrar, where the assessment is by the Court of Appeal.

(9) In deciding whether to direct such an enquiry, the court must have regard to all the circumstances including—

    (a) any agreement between the parties about the amount to be paid;

    (b) the amount likely to be allowed;

    (c) the delay and expense that may be incurred in the conduct of the enquiry; and

    (d) the particular complexity of the assessment, or the difficulty or novelty of any aspect of the assessment.

(10) If the court directs such an enquiry—

    (a) paragraphs (3) to (8) inclusive of rule 45.11 (Assessment and re-assessment) apply as if that enquiry were an assessment under that rule (but rules 45.12 (Appeal to a costs judge) and 45.13 (Appeal to a High Court judge) do not apply);

    (b) the authority that carries out the enquiry must serve its conclusions on the court officer as soon as reasonably practicable after following that procedure; and

    (c) the court must then assess the amount to be paid.

[Note. See—

    (a) rule 45.2;

    (b) section 19B of the Prosecution of Offences Act 1985 and regulation 3F of the Costs in Criminal Cases (General) Regulations 1986; and

    (c) article 18 of the Serious Crime Act 2007 (Appeals under Section 24) Order 2008.

The Criminal Costs Practice Direction sets out a form of application for use in connection with this rule.

Part 34 (Appeal to the Crown Court) and Part 39 (Appeal to the Court of Appeal about conviction or sentence) contain rules about appeals against a costs order to which this rule applies.]

Assessment of costs

Assessment and re-assessment   **R45.11**

45.11 (1) This rule applies where the court directs an assessment under—
    (a) rule 33.48 (Confiscation and related proceedings—restraint and receivership proceedings; rules that apply generally — assessment of costs);
    (b) rule 45.6 (Costs on appeal); or
    (c) rule 45.7 (Costs on an application).
  (2) The assessment must be carried out by the relevant assessing authority, namely—
    (a) the Lord Chancellor, where the direction was given by a magistrates' court or by the Crown Court; or
    (b) the Registrar, where the direction was given by the Court of Appeal.
  (3) The party in whose favour the court made the costs order ('the applicant') must—
    (a) apply for an assessment—
      (i) in writing, in any form required by the assessing authority, and
      (ii) not more than 3 months after the costs order; and
    (b) serve the application on—
      (i) the assessing authority, and
      (ii) the party against whom the court made the costs order ('the respondent').
  (4) The applicant must—
    (a) summarise the work done;
    (b) specify—
      (i) each item of work done, giving the date, time taken and amount claimed,
      (ii) any disbursements or expenses, including the fees of any advocate, and
      (iii) any circumstances of which the applicant wants the assessing authority to take particular account; and
    (c) supply—
      (i) receipts or other evidence of the amount claimed, and
      (ii) any other information or document for which the assessing authority asks, within such period as that authority may require.
  (5) A respondent who wants to make representations about the amount claimed must—
    (a) do so in writing; and
    (b) serve the representations on the assessing authority, and on the applicant, not more than 15 business days after service of the application.
  (6) The assessing authority must—
    (a) if it seems likely to help with the assessment, obtain any other information or document;
    (b) resolve in favour of the respondent any doubt about what should be allowed; and
    (c) serve the assessment on the parties.
  (7) Where either party wants the amount allowed to be re-assessed—
    (a) that party must—
      (i) apply to the assessing authority, in writing and in any form required by that authority,
      (ii) serve the application on the assessing authority, and on the other party, not more than 15 business days after service of the assessment,
      (iii) explain the objections to the assessment,
      (iv) supply any additional supporting information or document, and
      (v) ask for a hearing, if that party wants one;
    (b) a party who wants to make representations about an application for re-assessment must—
      (i) do so in writing,
      (ii) serve the representations on the assessing authority, and on the other party, not more than 15 business days after service of the application, and
      (iii) ask for a hearing, if that party wants one; and
    (c) the assessing authority—
      (i) must arrange a hearing, in public or in private, if either party asks for one,
      (ii) subject to that, may re-assess the amount allowed with or without a hearing,
      (iii) must re-assess the amount allowed on the initial assessment, taking into account the reasons for disagreement with that amount and any other representations,
      (iv) may maintain, increase or decrease the amount allowed on the assessment,
      (v) must serve the re-assessment on the parties, and
      (vi) must serve reasons on the parties, if not more than 15 business days later either party asks for such reasons.
  (8) A time limit under this rule may be extended even after it has expired—
    (a) by the assessing authority, or
    (b) by the Senior Costs Judge, if the assessing authority declines to do so.

Criminal Procedure Rules

R45.12   **Appeal to a costs judge**

45.12 (1)   This rule applies where—

    (a)   the assessing authority has re-assessed the amount allowed under rule 45.11; and

    (b)   either party wants to appeal against that amount.

(2)   That party must—

    (a)   serve an appeal notice on—

        (i)   the Senior Costs Judge,

        (ii)   the other party, and

        (iii)   the assessing authority

    not more than 15 business days after service of the written reasons for the re-assessment;

    (b)   explain the objections to the re-assessment;

    (c)   serve on the Senior Costs Judge with the appeal notice—

        (i)   the applications for assessment and re-assessment,

        (ii)   any other information or document considered by the assessing authority,

        (iii)   the assessing authority's written reasons for the re-assessment, and

        (iv)   any other information or document for which a costs judge asks, within such period as the judge may require; and

    (d)   ask for a hearing, if that party wants one.

(3)   A party who wants to make representations about an appeal must—

    (a)   serve representations in writing on—

        (i)   the Senior Costs Judge, and

        (ii)   the applicant

    not more than 15 business days after service of the appeal notice; and

    (b)   ask for a hearing, if that party wants one.

(4)   Unless a costs judge otherwise directs, the parties may rely only on—

    (a)   the objections to the amount allowed on the initial assessment; and

    (b)   any other representations and material considered by the assessing authority.

(5)   A costs judge—

    (a)   must arrange a hearing, in public or in private, if either party asks for one;

    (b)   subject to that, may determine an appeal with or without a hearing;

    (c)   may—

        (i)   consult the assessing authority,

        (ii)   consult the court which made the costs order, and

        (iii)   obtain any other information or document;

    (d)   must reconsider the amount allowed by the assessing authority, taking into account the objections to the re-assessment and any other representations;

    (e)   may maintain, increase or decrease the amount allowed on the re-assessment;

    (f)   may provide for the costs incurred by either party to the appeal; and

    (g)   must serve reasons for the decision on—

        (i)   the parties, and

        (ii)   the assessing authority.

(6)   A costs judge may extend a time limit under this rule, even after it has expired.

[Note. The Criminal Costs Practice Direction sets out a form for use in connection with this rule.]

R45.13   **Appeal to a High Court judge**

45.13 (1)   This rule applies where—

    (a)   a costs judge has determined an appeal under rule 45.12; and

    (b)   either party wants to appeal against the amount allowed.

(2)   A party who wants to appeal—

    (a)   may do so only if a costs judge certifies that a point of principle of general importance was involved in the decision on the review; and

    (b)   must apply in writing for such a certificate and serve the application on—

        (i)   the costs judge, and

        (ii)   the other party

    not more than 15 business days after service of the decision on the review.

(3)   That party must—

    (a)   appeal to a judge of the High Court attached to the [King's] Bench Division as if it were an appeal from the decision of a master under Part 52 of the Civil Procedure Rules 1998[58]; and

---

[58] S.I. 1998/3132.

      (b) serve the appeal not more than 15 business days after service of the costs judge's certificate under paragraph (2).

    (4) A High Court judge—

      (a) may extend a time limit under this rule even after it has expired;

      (b) has the same powers and duties as a costs judge under rule 45.12; and

      (c) may hear the appeal with one or more assessors.

[Note. See also section 70 of the Senior Courts Act 1981[59].]

Application for an extension of time   R45.14

45.14 A party who wants an extension of time under rule 45.11, 45.12 or 45.13 must—

      (a) apply in writing;

      (b) explain the delay; and

      (c) attach the application, representations or appeal for which the extension of time is needed.

CRIMINAL PROCEDURE RULES   PART 46   REPRESENTATIVES

Functions of representatives and supporters   R46.1

46.1 (1) Under these Rules, anything that a party may or must do may be done—

      (a) by a legal representative on that party's behalf;

      (b) by a person with the corporation's written authority, where that corporation is a defendant; or

      (c) with the help of a parent, guardian or other suitable supporting adult where that party is a defendant—

          (i) who is under 18, or

          (ii) whose understanding of what the case involves is limited

          unless other legislation (including a rule) otherwise requires.

    (2) A member, officer or employee of a prosecutor may, on the prosecutor's behalf—

      (a) serve on the magistrates' court officer, or present to a magistrates' court, an application for a summons or warrant under section 1 of the Magistrates' Courts Act 1980[1]; or

      (b) issue a written charge and requisition, or single justice procedure notice, under section 29 of the Criminal Justice Act 2003[2].

[Note. See also section 122 of the Magistrates' Courts Act 1980[3]. A party's legal representative must be entitled to act as such under section 13 of the Legal Services Act 2007[4].

Section 33(6) of the Criminal Justice Act 1925[5], section 46 of the Magistrates' Courts Act 1980[6] and Schedule 3 to that Act[7] provide for the representation of a corporation.

Sections 3 and 6 of the Prosecution of Offences Act 1985[8] make provision about the institution of prosecutions.

---

[59] 1981 c. 54. The Act's title was amended by section 59(5) of, and paragraph 1 of Schedule 11 to, the Constitutional Reform Act 2005 (c. 4).

[1] 1980 c. 43; section 1 was amended by section 68 of, and paragraph 6 of Schedule 8 to, the Criminal Justice Act 1991 (c. 53), sections 43 and 109 of, and Schedule 10 to, the Courts Act 2003 (c. 39), section 31 of, and paragraph 12 of Schedule 7 to, the Criminal Justice Act 2003 (c. 44) and section 153 of the Police Reform and Social Responsibility Act 2011. It is further amended by paragraphs 7 and 8 of Schedule 36 to, the Criminal Justice Act 2003 (c. 44), with effect from a date to be appointed.

[2] 2003 c. 44; section 29 has been brought into force for certain purposes only (see S.I. 2007/1999, S.I. 2008/1424 and S.I. 2009/2879). It was amended by section 50 of, and paragraph 130 of Schedule 4 to, the Commissioners for Revenue and Customs Act 2005 (c. 11) and section 59 of, and paragraph 196 of Schedule 4 to, the Serious Organised Crime and Police Act 2005 (c. 15).

[3] 1980 c. 43; section 122 was amended by section 125(3) of, and paragraph 25 of Schedule 18 to, the Courts and Legal Services Act 1990 (c. 41).

[4] 2007 c. 29.

[5] 1925 c. 86.

[6] 1980 c. 43.

[7] 1980 c. 43; Schedule 3 was amended by sections 25(2) and 101(2) of, and Schedule 13 to, the Criminal Justice Act 1991 (c. 53), section 47 of, and paragraph 13 of Schedule 1 to, the Criminal Procedure and Investigations Act 1996 (c. 25) (in relation to proceedings begun on or after 1 April 1997) and paragraph 51 of Schedule 3, and Part 4 of Schedule 37, to the Criminal Justice Act 2003 (c. 44).

[8] 1985 c. 23; section 3 was amended by section 15 of, and paragraph 13 of Schedule 2 to, the Criminal Justice Act 1987 (c. 38), paragraph 39 of Schedule 7 to the Police Act 1996 (c. 16), section 134 of, and paragraph 48 of Schedule 9 to, the Police Act 1997 (c. 50), section 164 of the Immigration and Asylum Act 1999 (c. 33), paragraph 10 of Schedule 7 to the Police Reform Act 2002 (c. 30), sections 86 and 92 of, and Schedule 3 to, the Anti-social Behaviour Act 2003 (c. 38), section 190 of the Extradition Act 2003 (c. 41), section 7 of the Asylum and Immigration (Treatment of Claimants, etc) Act 2004 (c. 19), section 40 of, and paragraph 41 of Schedule 9 to, the Constitutional Reform Act 2005 (c. 4), sections 59, 140 and 174 of, and paragraph 47 of Schedule 4 and Part 2 of Schedule 17 to, the Serious Organised Crime and Police Act 2005 (c. 15), sections

Section 223 of the Local Government Act 1972[9] allows a member or officer of a local authority on that authority's behalf to prosecute or defend a case before a magistrates' court, and to appear in and to conduct any proceedings before a magistrates' court.

Part 7 contains rules about starting a prosecution.]

R46.2 **Notice of appointment, etc. of legal representative: general rules**

46.2 (1) This rule applies—

    (a) in relation to—

        (i) a party who does not have legal aid for the purposes of a case, and

        (ii) a party to an extradition case in the High Court, whether that party has legal aid or not;

    (b) where such a party—

        (i) appoints a legal representative for the purposes of the case, or

        (ii) dismisses such a representative, with or without appointing another; and

    (c) where a legal representative for such a party withdraws from the case.

(2) Where paragraph (1)(b) applies, that party must give notice of the appointment or dismissal to—

    (a) the court officer;

    (b) each other party; and

    (c) where applicable, the legal representative who has been dismissed,

as soon as practicable and in any event within 5 business days.

(3) Where paragraph (1)(c) applies, that legal representative must—

    (a) as soon as practicable give notice to—

        (i) the court officer,

        (ii) the party whom he or she has represented, and

        (iii) each other party; and

    (b) where that legal representative has represented the defendant in an extradition case in the High Court, include with the notice—

        (i) confirmation that the defendant has notice of when and where the appeal hearing will take place and of the need to attend, if the defendant is on bail,

        (ii) details sufficient to locate the defendant, including details of the custodian and of the defendant's date of birth and custody reference, if the defendant is in custody, and

        (iii) details of any arrangements likely to be required by the defendant to facilitate his or her participation in consequence of the representative's withdrawal, including arrangements for interpretation.

(4) Any such notice—

    (a) may be given orally if—

        (i) it is given at a hearing, and

        (ii) it specifies no restriction under paragraph (5)(b) (restricted scope of appointment); but

    (b) must be in writing in any other case

(5) A notice of the appointment of a legal representative—

    (a) must identify—

        (i) the legal representative who has been appointed, with details of how to contact that representative, and

        (ii) all those to whom the notice is given;

    (b) may specify a restriction, or restrictions, on the purpose or duration of the appointment; and

    (c) if it specifies any such restriction, may nonetheless provide that documents may continue to be served on the represented party at the representative's address until—

        (i) further notice is given under this rule, or

        (ii) that party obtains legal aid for the purposes of the case.

7, 8 and 52 of, and paragraph 15 of Schedule 3 to, the Violent Crime Reduction Act 2006 (c. 38), section 74 of, and paragraph 149 of Schedule 8 to, the Serious Crime Act 2007 (c. 27), paragraph 171 of Schedule 16 to the Police Reform and Social Responsibility Act 2011 (c. 13), section 15 of, and paragraph 30 of Schedule 8 to, the Crime and Courts Act 2013 (c. 22) and article 3 of, and paragraphs 1 and 2 of the Schedule to, S.I. 2014/834.

[9] 1972 c. 70; section 223 was amended by paragraph 9 of Schedule 3 to the Solicitors Act 1974 (c. 47), section 134 of, and Schedule 10 to, the Police Act 1977 (c. 50), section 84 of, and paragraph 21 of Schedule 14 to, the Local Government Act 1985 (c. 51), section 237 of, and Schedule 13 to, the Education Reform Act 1988 (c. 40), section 120 of, and paragraph 17 of Schedule 22 and Schedule 24 to, the Environment Act 1995 (c. 25), paragraph 1 of Schedule 7 to the Police Act 1996 (c. 16), paragraphs 1 and 13 of Schedule 13 to the Local Government and Public Involvement in Health Act 2007 (c. 28), section 208 of, and paragraph 28 of Schedule 21 to, the Legal Services Act 2007 (c. 29), paragraphs 10 and 24 of Schedule 6 to the Local Democracy, Economic Development and Construction Act 2009 (c. 20), paragraphs 100 and 109 of Schedule 16 to the Police Reform and Social Responsibility Act 2011 (c. 13) and article 2 of, and paragraphs 1 and 2 of the Schedule to, S.I. 2001/3719.

(6) A legal representative who is dismissed by a party or who withdraws from representing a party must, as soon as practicable, make available to that party such documents in the representative's possession as have been served on that party.

Application to change legal representative (legal aid): general rules   R46.3

46.3 (1) This rule applies in a magistrates' court, the Crown Court and the Court of Appeal—

(a) in relation to a defendant who has legal aid for the purposes of a case; and

(b) where either—

(i) that defendant wants to select a legal representative (the 'proposed new representative') in place of the representative named in the legal aid representation order (the 'current representative') (see also rule 46.4), or

(ii) the current representative considers there to be a duty to withdraw from the case or no longer is able to represent the defendant through circumstances outside the representative's control (see also rule 46.5).

(2) The defendant or the current representative, as the case may be, must—

(a) apply in writing as soon as practicable after becoming aware of the grounds for doing so;

(b) serve the application on—

(i) the court officer,

(ii) the current representative, if the application is made by the defendant, and

(iii) the defendant, if the application is made by the current representative; and

(c) ask for a hearing, if the applicant wants one, and explain why it is needed.

(3) The court may determine the application—

(a) without a hearing, as a general rule; or

(b) at a hearing, if that is needed to resolve—

(i) matters in dispute, or

(ii) other matters unclear to the court.

(4) Unless the court otherwise directs, any hearing must be in private and in the absence of—

(a) the prosecutor,

(b) any co-defendant, and

(c) any legal representative or advocate of the prosecutor or a co-defendant.

(5) If the court allows the application, as soon as practicable—

(a) the current representative must make available to any new representative such documents in the current representative's possession as have been served on the defendant; and

(b) a new representative, if any, must serve notice of appointment on each other party.

(6) Paragraph (7) applies where—

(a) the court refuses an application under rule 46.4 and in response—

(i) the defendant declines further representation by the current representative or asks for legal aid to be withdrawn, or

(ii) the current representative declines further to represent the defendant; or

(b) the court allows an application under rule 46.5.

(7) If the court withdraws the defendant's legal aid—

(a) the court may specify the date on which that withdrawal will take effect; and

(b) the court officer must serve notice of the withdrawal on—

(i) the defendant,

(ii) the current representative, and

(iii) the prosecutor.

[Note. Under sections 16 and 19 of the Legal Aid, Sentencing and Punishment of Offenders Act 2012[10] and Part 2 of the Criminal Legal Aid (Determinations by a Court and Choice of Representative) Regulations 2013[11], a court before which criminal proceedings take place may determine whether an individual qualifies for legal aid representation in accordance with the 2012 Act.

Under regulation 13 of the 2013 Regulations, in relation to any proceedings involving co-defendants a represented person must select a representative who is also instructed by a co-defendant unless there is, or there is likely to be, a conflict of interest between the two defendants.

Under regulation 14 of the 2013 Regulations, once a representative has been selected the person who is represented has no right to select another in the place of the first unless the court so decides, in the circumstances set out in the regulation.

---

[10] 2012 c. 10.
[11] S.I. 2013/614.

Under regulation 9 of the 2013 Regulations, if a represented person declines to accept representation on the terms offered or requests that legal aid representation is withdrawn, or if the current representative declines to continue to represent that person, the court may withdraw legal aid.

See also regulation 11 of the 2013 Regulations, which requires that an application under regulation 14 (among others) must be made by the represented person, must be in writing and must specify the grounds.]

R46.4   **Application by defendant to change legal representative (legal aid)**

46.4 (1) An application by a defendant with legal aid to select a new representative in place of the current representative must—

(a) explain what the case is about, including what offences are alleged, what stage it has reached and what is likely to be in issue at trial;

(b) explain how and why the defendant chose the current representative;

(c) if an advocate other than the current representative has been instructed for the defendant, explain whether the defendant wishes to replace that advocate;

(d) explain, giving relevant facts and dates—

   (i) in what way, in the defendant's opinion, there has been a breakdown in the relationship between the defendant and the current representative such that neither that representative nor any colleague of theirs any longer can provide effective representation, or

   (ii) what other compelling reason, in the defendant's opinion, means that neither the current representative nor any such colleague any longer can provide effective representation;

(e) give details of any previous application by the defendant to replace a legal representative named in the legal aid representation order;

(f) state whether the defendant—

   (i) waives the legal professional privilege attaching to the defendant's communications with the current representative, to the extent required to allow that representative to respond to the matters set out in the application, or

   (ii) declines to waive that privilege and acknowledges that the court may draw such inferences as it thinks fit in consequence;

(g) explain how and why the defendant has chosen the proposed new representative;

(h) include or attach a statement by the proposed new representative which—

   (i) confirms that the proposed new representative is eligible and willing to conduct the case for the defendant,

   (ii) confirms that the proposed new representative can and will meet the current timetable for the case, including any hearing date or dates that have been set, if the application succeeds,

   (iii) explains what, if any, dealings the proposed new representative has had with the defendant before the present case,

   (iv) confirms that the proposed new representative has informed the current representative of the defendant's wish to select a new representative,

   (v) confirms that the proposed new representative has discussed the defendant's grounds for the proposed application with the current representative, and

   (vi) confirms that the proposed new representative has explained to the defendant what it means to waive the legal professional privilege attaching to the defendant's communications with the current representative and the potential consequences of not doing so; and

   (vii) ask for a hearing, if the defendant wants one, and explain why it is needed.

(2) The current representative must—

(a) respond in writing no more than 5 business days after service of the application; and

(b) serve the response on—

   (i) the court officer,

   (ii) the defendant, and

   (iii) the proposed new representative.

(3) The response must—

(a) if applicable, explain why the current representative—

   (i) considers there to be a duty to withdraw from the case in accordance with professional rules of conduct, giving details of the nature of that duty, or

   (ii) no longer is able to represent the defendant through circumstances outside the representative's control, giving details of the particular circumstances that render the representative unable to do so; or

(b) otherwise—
  (i) identify those matters, if any, set out in the application with which the current representative disagrees, and
  (ii) include any comments that the current representative thinks may assist the court.

[Note. There are forms of application and response for use in connection with this rule issued under the Practice Direction.]

Application by legal representative to withdraw (legal aid)   **R46.5**

46.5 An application by a current representative to withdraw from the case must—

(a) explain what the case is about, including what offences are alleged, what stage it has reached and what is likely to be in issue at trial; and
(b) explain why the current representative—
  (i) considers there to be a duty to withdraw from the case in accordance with professional rules of conduct, giving details of the nature of that duty, or
  (ii) no longer is able to represent the defendant through circumstances outside the representative's control, giving details of the particular circumstances that render the representative unable to do so.

CRIMINAL PROCEDURE RULES   PART 47   INVESTIGATION ORDERS AND WARRANTS
Section 1: general rules

When this Part applies   **R47.1**

47.1 This Part applies to the exercise of the powers listed in each of rules 47.4, 47.24, 47.35, 47.42, 47.46, 47.51, 47.54, 47.59, and 47.63

Meaning of 'court', 'applicant' and 'respondent'   **R47.2**

47.2 In this Part—
  (a) a reference to the 'court' includes a reference to any justice of the peace or judge who can exercise a power to which this Part applies;
  (b) 'applicant' means a person who, or an authority which, can apply for an order or warrant to which this Part applies; and
  (c) 'respondent' means any person—
    (i) against whom such an order is sought or made, or
    (ii) on whom an application for such an order is served.

Documents and recordings held by the court officer   **R47.3**

47.3 (1) Unless the court otherwise directs—
  (a) the court officer—
    (i) must either keep a written application, and a recording of any hearing of an application, or arrange for the whole or any part to be kept by some other appropriate person, including the applicant, subject to any conditions that the court may impose, and
    (ii) must arrange for any separate document to which rule 47.26(4) refers (information that the applicant thinks should be kept confidential) to be retained by the applicant, subject to any such condition; and
  (b) a person who, under such arrangements, keeps an application or recording or retains such a document must return it to the court if and when the court officer so requires.
  (2) Where the court makes an order when the court office is closed, the applicant must, not more than 72 hours later, serve on the court officer—
  (a) a copy of the order; and
  (b) any written material that was submitted to the court.
  (3) Where the court issues a warrant—
  (a) the applicant must return it to the court officer as soon as practicable after it has been executed, and in any event not more than 3 months after it was issued (unless other legislation otherwise provides); and
  (b) the court officer must—
    (i) keep the warrant for 12 months after its return, and
    (ii) during that period, make it available for inspection by the occupier of the premises to which it relates, if that occupier asks to inspect it.

[Note. See section 16(10) of the Police and Criminal Evidence Act 1984[1].]

---

[1] 1984 c. 60; section 16(10) was substituted by section 114 of the Serious Organised Crime and Police Act 2005 (c. 15).

Section 2: investigation orders

R47.4   **When this Section applies**

47.4   This Section applies where—

(a)   a Circuit judge can make, vary or discharge an order for the production of, or for giving access to, material under paragraph 4 of Schedule 1 to the Police and Criminal Evidence Act 1984[2], other than material that consists of or includes journalistic material;

(b)   for the purposes of a terrorist investigation, a Circuit judge can make, vary or discharge—

(i)   an order for the production of, or for giving access to, material, or for a statement of its location, under paragraphs 5 and 10 of Schedule 5 to the Terrorism Act 2000[3],

(ii)   an explanation order, under paragraphs 10 and 13 of Schedule 5 to the 2000 Act[4], or

(iii)   a customer information order, under paragraphs 1 and 4 of Schedule 6 to the 2000 Act[5];

(c)   for the purposes of—

(i)   a terrorist investigation, a Circuit judge can make, and the Crown Court can vary or discharge, an account monitoring order, under paragraphs 2 and 4 of Schedule 6A to the 2000 Act[6], or

(ii)   a terrorist financing investigation, a judge entitled to exercise the jurisdiction of the Crown Court can make, and the Crown Court can vary or discharge, a disclosure order, under paragraphs 9 and 14 of Schedule 5A to the 2000 Act[7];

(d)   for the purposes of an investigation to which Part 8 of the Proceeds of Crime Act 2002[8] or the Proceeds of Crime Act 2002 (External Investigations) Order 2014[9] applies, a Crown Court judge can make, and the Crown Court can vary or discharge—

(i)   a production order, under sections 345 and 351 of the 2002 Act[10] or under articles 6 and 12 of the 2014 Order,

(ii)   an order to grant entry, under sections 347 and 351 of the 2002 Act or under articles 8 and 12 of the 2014 Order,

(iii)   a disclosure order, under sections 357 and 362 of the 2002 Act[11] or under articles 16 and 21 of the 2014 Order,

(iv)   a customer information order, under sections 363 and 369 of the 2002 Act[12] or under articles 22 and 28 of the 2014 Order, or

---

[2] 1984 c. 60; paragraph 4 of Schedule 1 was amended by section 65 of, and paragraph 6 of Schedule 4 to, the Courts Act 2003 (c. 39).

[3] 2000 c. 11; paragraph 5 of Schedule 5 is amended by section 65 of, and paragraph 9 of Schedule 4 to, the Courts Act 2003 (c. 39), with effect from a date to be appointed. Paragraph 10 of Schedule 5 was amended by section 109(1) of, and paragraph 389 of Schedule 8 to, the Courts Act 2003 (c. 39) and it is further amended by section 65 of, and paragraph 9 of Schedule 4 to, the Courts Act 2003 (c. 39), with effect from a date to be appointed.

[4] 2000 c. 11; paragraph 13 of Schedule 5 was amended by section 65 of, and paragraph 9 of Schedule 4 to, the Courts Act 2003 (c. 39) and section 41(3)(d) of the Criminal Finances Act 2017 (c. 22).

[5] 2000 c. 11; paragraph 1 of Schedule 6 was amended by section 3 of, and paragraph 6 of Schedule 2 to, the Anti-terrorism, Crime and Security Act 2001 (c. 24). Paragraph 4 of Schedule 6 was amended by section 109(1) of, and paragraph 390 of Schedule 8 to, the Courts Act 2003 (c. 39).

[6] 2000 c. 11; Schedule 6A was inserted by section 3 of, and paragraph 1(1) and (3) of Part 1 of Schedule 2 to, the Anti-terrorism, Crime and Security Act 2001 (c. 24). Paragraph 4 was amended by section 41(5)(c) of the Criminal Finances Act 2017 (c. 22).

[7] 2000 c. 11; Schedule 5A was inserted by Schedule 2 to the Criminal Finances Act 2017 (c. 22).

[8] 2002 c. 29.

[9] S.I. 2014/1893.

[10] 2002 c. 29; section 345 was amended by section 75 of the Serious Crime Act 2007 (c. 27), section 169 of, and paragraphs 1 and 6 of Schedule 19 to, the Coroners and Justice Act 2009 (c. 25) and section 49 of, and paragraphs 1 and 4 of Schedule 19 to, the Crime and Courts Act 2013 (c. 22). Section 351 was amended by sections 74 and 77 of, and paragraphs 103 and 104 of Schedule 8 and paragraphs 1 and 6 of Schedule 10 to, the Serious Crime Act 2007 (c. 27), section 169 of, and paragraphs 1 and 9 of Schedule 19 to, the Coroners and Justice Act 2009 (c. 25), sections 66 and 112 of, and Part 5 of Schedule 8 to, the Policing and Crime Act 2009 (c. 26), sections 15 and 55 of, and paragraphs 108 and 136 of Schedule 8 and paragraphs 14 and 30 of Schedule 21 to, the Crime and Courts Act 2013 (c.22) and section 224 of, and paragraphs 1 and 11 of Schedule 48 to, the Finance Act 2013 (c. 29).

[11] 2002 c. 29; section 357 was amended by sections 74 and 77 of, and paragraphs 103 and 108 of Schedule 8 and paragraphs 1 and 10 of Schedule 10 to, the Serious Crime Act 2007 (c. 27), section 169 of, and paragraphs 1 and 13 of Schedule 19 to, the Coroners and Justice Act 2009 (c. 25), sections 15, 49 and 55 of, and paragraphs 108 and 139 of Schedule 8, paragraphs 1 and 8 of Schedule 19 and paragraphs 14 and 34 of Schedule 21 to, the Crime and Courts Act 2013 (c. 22) and article 3 of, and paragraphs 19 and 27 of Schedule 2 to, SI 2014/834. Section 362 was amended by section 74 of, and paragraphs 103 and 110 of Schedule 8 to, the Serious Crime Act 2007 (c. 27), section 169 of, and paragraphs 1 and 15 of Schedule 19 to, the Coroners and Justice Act 2009 (c. 25) and section 15 of, and paragraphs 108 and 140 of Schedule 8 to, the Crime and Courts Act 2013 (c. 22).

[12] 2002 c. 29; section 363 was amended by section 77 of, and paragraphs 1 and 11 of Schedule 10 to, the Serious Crime Act 2007 (c. 27), section 169 of, and paragraphs 1 and 16 of Schedule 19 to, the Coroners and Justice Act 2009 (c. 25) and section 49 of, and paragraphs 1 and 10 of Schedule 19 to, the Crime and Courts Act 2013 (c. 22). Section 369 was amended by section

(v) an account monitoring order, under sections 370, 373 and 375 of the 2002[13] Act or under articles 29, 32 and 34 of the 2014 Order;

(e) in connection with an extradition request, a Circuit judge can make an order for the production of, or for giving access to, material under section 157 of the Extradition Act 2003[14].

(f) a magistrates' court can make a further information order under section 22B of the Terrorism Act 2000[15] in connection with—

(i) an investigation into whether a person is involved in the commission of an offence under any of sections 15 to 18 of the 2000 Act[16],

(ii) determining whether such an investigation should be started, or

(iii) identifying terrorist property or its movement or use; and

(g) a magistrates' court can make a further information order under section 339ZH of the Proceeds of Crime Act 2002[17] in connection with—

(i) an investigation into whether a person is engaged in money laundering,

(ii) determining whether such an investigation should be started, or

(iii) an investigation into money laundering by an authority in a country outside the United Kingdom.

[Note. In outline, the orders to which these rules apply are—

(a) under the Police and Criminal Evidence Act 1984, a production order requiring a person to produce or give access to material, other than material that consists of or includes journalistic material;

(b) for the purposes of a terrorist investigation under the Terrorism Act 2000—

(i) an order requiring a person to produce, give access to, or state the location of material,

(ii) an explanation order, requiring a person to explain material obtained under a production, etc. order,

(iii) a customer information order, requiring a financial institution to provide information about an account holder,

(iv) an account monitoring order, requiring a financial institution to provide specified information, for a specified period, about an account held at that institution;

(c) for the purposes of a terrorist financing investigation under the Terrorism Act 2000, a disclosure order, requiring a person to provide information or documents, or to answer questions;

(d) for the purposes of an investigation to which Part 8 of the Proceeds of Crime Act 2002 or the Proceeds of Crime Act 2002 (External Investigations) Order 2014 applies—

(i) a production order, requiring a person to produce or give access to material,

(ii) an order to grant entry, requiring a person to allow entry to premises so that a production order can be enforced,

(iii) a disclosure order, requiring a person to provide information or documents, or to answer questions,

(iv) a customer information order, requiring a financial institution to provide information about an account holder,

(v) an account monitoring order, requiring a financial institution to provide specified information, for a specified period, about an account held at that institution;

(e) in connection with extradition proceedings, a production order requiring a person to produce or give access to material;

(f) under the Terrorism Act 2000, a further information order requiring a person to provide information related to a matter arising from a disclosure under section 21A of that Act[18] (Failure to

Criminal Procedure Rules

---

74 of, and paragraphs 103 and 111 of Schedule 8 to, the Serious Crime Act 2007 (c. 27), sections 15 and 55 of, and paragraphs 108 and 141 of Schedule 8, and paragraphs 14 and 35 of Schedule 21 to, the Crime and Courts Act 2013 (c. 22) and section 224 of, and paragraphs 1 and 14 of Schedule 48 to, the Finance Act 2013 (c. 29).

[13] 2002 c. 29; section 370 was amended by section 77 of, and paragraphs 1 and 12 of Schedule 10 to, the Serious Crime Act 2007 (c. 27), section 169 of, and paragraphs 1 and 17 of Schedule 19 to, the Coroners and Justice Act 2009 (c. 25) and section 49 of, and paragraphs 1 and 12 of Schedule 19 to, the Crime and Courts Act 2013 (c. 22). Section 375 was amended by section 74 of, and paragraphs 103 and 112 of Schedule 8 to, the Serious Crime Act 2007 (c. 27), sections 15 and 55 of, and paragraphs 108 and 142 of Schedule 8 and paragraphs 14 and 36 of Schedule 21 to, the Crime and Courts Act 2013 (c. 22) and section 224 of, and paragraphs 1 and 15 of Schedule 48 to, the Finance Act 2013 (c. 29).

[14] 2003 c. 41; section 157 was amended by section 174 of the Anti-social Behaviour, Crime and Policing Act 2014 (c. 12).

[15] 2000 c. 11; section 22B was inserted by section 37 of the Criminal Finances Act 2017 (c. 22).

[16] 2000 c. 11; section 17A was inserted by section 42 of the Counter-Terrorism and Security Act 2015 (c. 6).

[17] 2002 c. 29; section 339ZH was inserted by section 12 of the Criminal Finances Act 2017 (c. 22).

[18] 2000 c. 11; section 21A was inserted by section 3 of, and paragraph 5 of Schedule 2 to, the Anti-terrorism, Crime and Security Act 2001 (c. 24) and amended by regulation 2 of, and paragraphs 1 and 3 of Schedule 1 to, S.I. 2007/3398, section 59 of, and paragraphs 125 and 128 of, the Serious Organised Crime and Police Act 2005 (c. 15) and section 15 of, and paragraphs 67 and 72 of Schedule 8 to, the Crime and Courts Act 2013 (c. 22).

disclose: regulated sector) or under the law of a country outside the United Kingdom which corresponds with Part III of that Act (Terrorist property);

(g)   under the Proceeds of Crime Act 2002, a further information order requiring a person to provide information related to a matter arising from a disclosure under Part 7 of that Act (Money laundering) or under the law of a country outside the United Kingdom which corresponds with that Part of that Act.

These rules do not apply to an application for a production order under the Police and Criminal Evidence Act 1984 requiring a person to produce or give access to journalistic material: see paragraph 15A of Schedule 1 to the Act[19].

For all the relevant terms under which these orders can be made, see the provisions listed in rule 47.4.

Under section 8 of the Senior Courts Act 1981[20], a High Court judge, a Circuit judge, a Recorder, a qualifying judge advocate and a District Judge (Magistrates' Courts) each may act as a Crown Court judge.

When the relevant provisions of the Courts Act 2003 come into force, a District Judge (Magistrates' Courts) will have the same powers as a Circuit judge under the Police and Criminal Evidence Act 1984 and under the Terrorism Act 2000.

Under section 66 of the Courts Act 2003[21], in criminal cases a High Court judge, a Circuit judge, a Recorder and a qualifying judge advocate each has the powers of a justice of the peace who is a District Judge (Magistrates' Courts).

By section 341 of the Proceeds of Crime Act 2002[22], an investigation under Part 8 of the Act may be—

(a)   an investigation into (i) whether a person has benefited from criminal conduct, (ii) the extent or whereabouts of such benefit, (iii) the available amount in respect of that person, or (iv) the extent or whereabouts of realisable property available for satisfying a confiscation order made in respect of that person ('a confiscation investigation');

(b)   an investigation into whether a person has committed a money laundering offence ('a money laundering investigation');

(c)   an investigation into whether property is recoverable property or associated property (as defined by section 316 of the 2002 Act[23]), or into who holds the property or its extent or whereabouts ('a civil recovery investigation');

(d)   an investigation into the derivation of cash detained under the 2002 Act, or into whether such cash is intended to be used in unlawful conduct ('a detained cash investigation');

(e)   an investigation into the derivation of property detained under the 2002 Act, or into whether such property is intended to be used in unlawful conduct ('a detained property investigation');

(f)   an investigation into the derivation of money held in an account in relation to which an account freezing order made under the 2002 Act has effect, or into whether such money is intended to be used in unlawful conduct ('a frozen funds investigation');

(g)   an investigation for the purposes of Part 7 of the Coroners and Justice Act 2009[24] (criminal memoirs, etc.) into whether a person is a qualifying offender or has obtained exploitation proceeds from a relevant offence, or into the value of any benefits derived by such a person from such an offence or the amount available ('an exploitation proceeds investigation').

---

[19]   1984 c. 60; paragraph 15A of Schedule 1 was inserted by section 82 of the Deregulation Act 2015 (c. 20).

[20]   1981 c. 54; section 8 was amended by sections 65 and 109 of, and paragraph 259 of Schedule 8 to, the Courts Act 2003 (c. 39) and paragraph 1 of Schedule 2 to the Armed Forces Act 2011 (c. 18). The 1981 Act's title was amended by section 59(5) of, and paragraph 1 of Schedule 11 to, the Constitutional Reform Act 2005 (c. 4).

[21]   2003 c. 39; section 66 was amended by paragraph 6 of Schedule 2 to the Armed Forces Act 2011 (c. 18) and sections 17 and 21 of, and paragraphs 83 and 90 of Schedule 10 and paragraph 4 of Schedule 14 to, the Crime and Courts Act 2013 (c. 22).

[22]   2002 c. 29; section 341 was amended by section 75 of the Serious Crime Act 2007 (c. 27), section 169 of, and paragraphs 1 and 2 of Schedule 19 to, the Coroners and Justice Act 2009 (c. 25) and section 112 of, and paragraphs 99 and 110 of Schedule 7 to, the Policing and Crime Act 2009 (c. 26), section 49 of, and paragraphs 1, 2, 24 and 25 of Schedule 19 to, the Crime and Courts Act 2013 (c.22) and sections 38 and 85 of, and paragraph 55 of Schedule 4 to, the Serious Crime Act 2015 (c. 9).

[23]   2002 c. 29; section 316 was amended by paragraph 78 of Schedule 36 to the Criminal Justice Act 2003 (c. 44), section 109 of, and paragraphs 4 and 22 of Schedule 6 to, the Serious Organised Crime and Police Act 2005 (c. 15), section 74 of, and paragraphs 85 and 91 of Schedule 8 to, the Serious Crime Act 2007 (c. 27), article 12 of, and paragraphs 47 and 65 of Schedule 14 to, S.I. 2010/976, sections 15 and 48 of, and paragraphs 108 and 121 of Schedule 8 to, the Crime and Courts Act 2013 (c. 22), article 3 of, and paragraphs 19 and 25 of Schedule 2 to, SI 2014/834, section 85 of, and paragraph 54 of Schedule 4 to, the Serious Crime Act 2015 (c. 9) and article 8 of SI 2015/798.

[24]   2009 c. 25.

Under section 343 of the Proceeds of Crime Act 2002[25] —

    (a) *any Crown Court judge may make an order to which this Section applies for the purposes of a confiscation investigation, a money laundering investigation, a detained cash investigation, a detained property investigation or a frozen funds investigation;*

    (b) *only a High Court judge may make such an order for the purposes of a civil recovery investigation or an exploitation proceeds investigation (and these rules do not apply to an application to such a judge in such a case).*

As well as governing procedure on an application to the Crown Court, under the following provisions rules may govern the procedure on an application to an individual judge—

    (a) *paragraph 15A of Schedule 1 to the Police and Criminal Evidence Act 1984;*

    (b) *paragraph 10 of Schedule 5, paragraph 14 of Schedule 5A, paragraph 4 of Schedule 6 and paragraph 5 of Schedule 6A to the Terrorism Act 2000; and*

    (c) *sections 351, 362, 369, 375 and 446 of the Proceeds of Crime Act 2002.]*

Exercise of court's powers   R47.5

47.5 (1) Subject to paragraphs (2), (3) and (4), the court may determine an application for an order, or to vary or discharge an order—

    (a) at a hearing (which must be in private unless the court otherwise directs), or without a hearing; and

    (b) in the absence of—

        (i) the applicant,

        (ii) any respondent

        (iii) any other person affected by the order.

  (2) The court must not determine such an application in the applicant's absence if—

    (a) the applicant asks for a hearing; or

    (b) it appears to the court that—

        (i) the proposed order may infringe legal privilege, within the meaning of section 10 of the Police and Criminal Evidence Act 1984[26], section 348 or 361 of the Proceeds of Crime Act 2002[27] or article 9 of the Proceeds of Crime Act 2002 (External Investigations) Order 2014[28],

        (ii) the proposed order may require the production of excluded material, within the meaning of section 11 of the 1984 Act, or

        (iii) for any other reason the application is so complex or serious as to require the court to hear the applicant.

  (3) The court must not determine such an application in the absence of any respondent or other person affected, unless—

    (a) the absentee has had at least 2 business days in which to make representations; or

    (b) the court is satisfied that—

        (i) the applicant cannot identify or contact the absentee,

        (ii) it would prejudice the investigation if the absentee were present,

        (iii) it would prejudice the investigation to adjourn or postpone the application so as to allow the absentee to attend, or

        (iv) the absentee has waived the opportunity to attend.

  (4) The court must not determine such an application in the absence of any respondent who, if the order sought by the applicant were made, would be required to produce or give access to journalistic material, unless that respondent has waived the opportunity to attend.

  (5) The court officer must arrange for the court to hear such an application no sooner than 2 business days after it was served, unless—

    (a) the court directs that no hearing need be arranged; or

    (b) the court gives other directions for the hearing.

  (6) The court must not determine an application unless satisfied that sufficient time has been allowed for it.

  (7) If the court so directs, the parties to an application may attend a hearing by live link.

---

[25] 2002 c. 29; section 343 was amended by section 77 of, and paragraphs 1 and 3 of Schedule 10 to, the Serious Crime Act 2007 (c. 27), section 169 of, and paragraphs 1 and 4 of Schedule 19 to, the Coroners and Justice Act 2009 (c. 25) and sections 66 and 112 of, and Part 5 of Schedule 8 to, the Policing and Crime Act 2009 (c. 26).

[26] 1984 c. 60.

[27] 2002 c. 29; section 361 was amended by section 74 of, and paragraphs 103 and 109 of Schedule 8 to, the Serious Crime Act 2007 (c. 27).

[28] S.I. 2014/1893.

(8) The court must not make, vary or discharge an order unless the applicant states, in writing or orally, that to the best of the applicant's knowledge and belief—

    (a) the application discloses all the information that is material to what the court must decide; and

    (b) the content of the application is true.

(9) Where the statement required by paragraph (8) is made orally—

    (a) the statement must be on oath or affirmation, unless the court otherwise directs; and

    (b) the court must arrange for a record of the making of the statement.

(10) The court may—

    (a) shorten or extend (even after it has expired) a time limit under this Section;

    (b) dispense with a requirement for service under this Section (even after service was required); and

    (c) consider an application made orally instead of in writing.

(11) A person who wants an extension of time must—

    (a) apply when serving the application for which it is needed; and

    (b) explain the delay.

R47.6 Application for order: general rules

47.6 (1) This rule applies to each application for an order to which this Section applies.

(2) The applicant must—

    (a) apply in writing and serve the application on the court officer;

    (b) demonstrate that the applicant is entitled to apply, for example as a constable or under legislation that applies to other officers;

    (c) give the court an estimate of how long the court should allow—

      (i) to read the application and prepare for any hearing, and

      (ii) for any hearing of the application;

    (d) attach a draft order in the terms proposed by the applicant;

    (e) serve notice of the application on the respondent if any, unless the court otherwise directs; and

    (f) serve the application on any respondent to such extent, if any, as the court directs.

(3) A notice served on a respondent must—

    (a) specify the material or information in respect of which the application is made; and

    (b) identify—

      (i) the power that the applicant invites the court to exercise, and

      (ii) the conditions for the exercise of that power which the applicant asks the court to find are met.

(4) The applicant must serve any order made on a respondent.

R47.7 Application containing information withheld from a respondent or other person

47.7 (1) This rule applies where an application includes information that the applicant thinks ought to be revealed only to the court.

(2) The application must—

    (a) identify that information; and

    (b) explain why that information ought not to be served on a respondent or other person.

(3) At a hearing of an application to which this rule applies—

    (a) the general rule is that the court must consider, in the following sequence—

      (i) representations first by the applicant and then by the respondent if any and any other person, in the presence of them all, and then

      (ii) further representations by the applicant, in the others' absence; but

    (b) the court may direct other arrangements for the hearing.

R47.8 Application to vary or discharge an order

47.8 (1) This rule applies where one of the following wants the court to vary or discharge an order to which a rule in this Section refers—

    (a) an applicant;

    (b) a respondent; or

    (c) a person affected by the order.

(2) That applicant, respondent or person affected must—

    (a) apply in writing as soon as practicable after becoming aware of the grounds for doing so;

    (b) serve the application on—

      (i) the court officer, and

      (ii) the respondent, applicant, or any person known to be affected, as applicable;

    (c) explain why it is appropriate for the order to be varied or discharged;

    (d) propose the terms of any variation; and

    (e) ask for a hearing, if one is wanted, and explain why it is needed.

Application to punish for contempt of court   **R47.9**

47.9 (1) This rule applies where a person is accused of disobeying—

    (a) a production order made under paragraph 4 of Schedule 1 to the Police and Criminal Evidence Act 1984;

    (b) a production etc. order made under paragraph 5 of Schedule 5 to the Terrorism Act 2000;

    (c) an explanation order made under paragraph 13 of that Schedule;

    (d) an account monitoring order made under paragraph 2 of Schedule 6A to that Act;

    (e) a production order made under section 345 of the Proceeds of Crime Act 2002 or article 6 of the Proceeds of Crime Act 2002 (External Investigations) Order 2014;

    (f) an account monitoring order made under section 370 of the 2002 Act or article 29 of the 2014 Order; or

    (g) a production order made under section 157 of the Extradition Act 2003.

    (2) An applicant who wants the court to exercise its power to punish that person for contempt of court must comply with the rules in Part 48 (Contempt of court).

[Note. The Crown Court has power to punish for contempt of court a person who disobeys its order. See paragraphs 10(1) and 13(5) of Schedule 5, and paragraph 6(1) of Schedule 6A, to the Terrorism Act 2000; sections 351(7) and 375(6) of the Proceeds of Crime Act 2002 and articles 12(6) and 34(5) of the Proceeds of Crime Act 2002 (External Investigations) Order 2014; and section 45 of the Senior Courts Act 1981[29].

A Circuit judge has power to punish a person who disobeys a production order under the Police and Criminal Evidence Act 1984 as if that were a contempt of the Crown Court: see paragraph 15 of Schedule 1 to the Act[30].

Disobedience to an explanation order, to a disclosure order or to a customer information order under the Terrorism Act 2000 is an offence: see paragraph 14 of Schedule 5, paragraph 11 of Schedule 5A and paragraph 1(3) of Schedule 6, to the Act.

Disobedience to a disclosure order or to a customer information order under the Proceeds of Crime Act 2002 or under the Proceeds of Crime Act 2002 (External Investigations) Order 2014 is an offence: see sections 359 and 366 of the Act and articles 18 and 25 of the Order. Under section 342 of the Act[31] and under article 5 of the Order, subject to the exceptions for which those provide it is an offence to make a disclosure likely to prejudice an investigation or to interfere with documents relevant to it.

If a person fails to comply with a further information order under the Terrorism Act 2000 or under the Proceeds of Crime Act 2002 the magistrates' court may order that person to pay an amount not exceeding £5,000, which order may be enforced as if the sum due had been adjudged to be paid by a conviction: see section 22B(8), (9) of the Terrorism Act 2000[32] and section 339ZH((8), (9) of the Proceeds of Crime Act 2002[33].]

Orders under the Police and Criminal Evidence Act 1984

Application for a production order under the Police and Criminal Evidence Act 1984   **R47.10**

47.10 (1) This rule applies where an applicant wants the court to make an order to which rule 47.4(a) refers.

    (2) As well as complying with rule 47.6 (Application for order: general rules), the application must, in every case—

    (a) specify the offence under investigation (and see paragraph (3)(a));

    (b) describe the material sought;

    (c) identify the respondent;

    (d) specify the premises on which the material is believed to be, or explain why it is not reasonably practicable to do so;

    (e) explain the grounds for believing that the material is on the premises specified, or (if applicable) on unspecified premises of the respondent;

---

[29] 1981 c. 54. The Act's title was amended by section 59(5) of, and paragraph 1 of Schedule 11 to, the Constitutional Reform Act 2005 (c. 4).

[30] 1984 c. 60; paragraph 15 of Schedule 1 was amended by section 65 of, and paragraph 6 of Schedule 4 to, the Courts Act 2003 (c. 39).

[31] 2002 c. 29; section 342 was amended by section 77 of, and paragraphs 1 and 2 of Schedule 10 to, the Serious Crime Act 2007 (c. 27), regulation 3 of, and paragraphs 1 and 8 of Schedule 2 to, S.I. 2007/3398 and section 169 of, and paragraphs 1 and 3 of Schedule 19 to, the Coroners and Justice Act 2009 (c. 25).

[32] 2000 c. 11; section 22B was inserted by section 37 of the Criminal Finances Act 2017 (c. 22).

[33] 2002 c. 29; section 339ZH was inserted by section 12 of the Criminal Finances Act 2017 (c. 22).

Criminal Procedure Rules

(f) specify the set of access conditions on which the applicant relies (and see paragraphs (3) and (4)); and

(g) propose—

(i) the terms of the order, and

(ii) the period within which it should take effect.

(3) Where the applicant relies on paragraph 2 of Schedule 1 to the Police and Criminal Evidence Act 1984[34] ('the first set of access conditions': general power to gain access to special procedure material), the application must—

(a) specify the indictable offence under investigation;

(b) explain the grounds for believing that the offence has been committed;

(c) explain the grounds for believing that the material sought—

(i) is likely to be of substantial value to the investigation (whether by itself, or together with other material),

(ii) is likely to be admissible evidence at trial for the offence under investigation, and

(iii) does not consist of or include items subject to legal privilege or excluded material;

(d) explain what other methods of obtaining the material—

(i) have been tried without success, or

(ii) have not been tried because they appeared bound to fail; and

(e) explain why it is in the public interest for the respondent to produce the material, having regard to—

(i) the benefit likely to accrue to the investigation if the material is obtained, and

(ii) the circumstances under which the respondent holds the material.

(4) Where the applicant relies on paragraph 3 of Schedule 1 to the Police and Criminal Evidence Act 1984[35] ('the second set of access conditions': use of search warrant power to gain access to excluded or special procedure material), the application must—

(a) state the legislation under which a search warrant could have been issued, had the material sought not been excluded or special procedure material (in this paragraph, described as 'the main search power');

(b) include or attach the terms of the main search power;

(c) explain how the circumstances would have satisfied any criteria prescribed by the main search power for the issue of a search warrant; and

(d) explain why the issue of such a search warrant would have been appropriate.

[Note. See paragraphs 1 to 4 of Schedule 1 to the Police and Criminal Evidence Act 1984[36]. The applicant for an order must be a constable. Sections 10, 11 and 14 of the 1984 Act[37] define 'items subject to legal privilege', 'excluded material' and 'special procedure material'. The period within which an order takes effect must be specified in the order and, unless the court considers a longer period appropriate, must be 7 days from the date of the order.

See also the code of practice for searches of premises by police officers and the seizure of property found by police officers on persons or premises issued under section 66 of the Police and Criminal Evidence Act 1984[38].

The Practice Direction sets out forms of application, notice and order for use in connection with this rule.]

Orders under the Terrorism Act 2000

R47.11 **Application for an order under the Terrorism Act 2000**

47.11 (1) This rule applies where an applicant wants the court to make one of the orders to which rule 47.4(b) and (c) refers.

(2) As well as complying with rule 47.6 (Application for order: general rules), the application must—

(a) specify the offence under investigation;

[34] 1984 c. 60; paragraph 2 of Schedule 1 was amended by sections 111 and 113 of, and paragraph 43 of Schedule 7 to, the Serious Organised Crime and Police Act 2005 (c. 15).

[35] 1984 c. 60; paragraph 3 of Schedule 1 was amended by section 113 of the Serious Organised Crime and Police Act 2005 (c. 15).

[36] 1984 c. 60; paragraphs 1 and 4 of Schedule 1 were amended by section 65 of, and paragraph 6 of Schedule 4 to, the Courts Act 2003 (c. 39).

[37] 1984 c. 60; section 14 was amended by section 1177 of, and paragraph 193 of Schedule 1 to, the Corporation Tax Act 2010 (c. 4).

[38] 1984 c. 60; section 66 was amended by section 57 of the Criminal Justice and Court Services Act 2000 (c. 43), sections 110 and 174 of, and Schedule 17 to, the Serious Organised Crime and Police Act 2005 (c. 15) and section 115 of, and paragraph 21 of Schedule 9 to, the Protection of Freedoms Act 2012 (c. 9).

(b) explain how the investigation constitutes a terrorist investigation or terrorist financing investigation, as appropriate, within the meaning of the Terrorism Act 2000;[39]

(c) identify any respondent; and

(d) give the information required by whichever of rules 47.12 to 47.16 applies.

Content of application for a production etc. order under the Terrorism Act 2000   R47.12

47.12 (1) As well as complying with rules 47.6 and 47.11, an applicant who wants the court to make an order for the production of, or for giving access to, material, or for a statement of its location, must—

(a) describe that material;

(b) explain why the applicant thinks the material is—

    (i) in the respondent's possession, custody or power, or

    (ii) expected to come into existence and then to be in the respondent's possession, custody or power within 28 days of the order;

(c) explain how the material constitutes or contains excluded material or special procedure material;

(d) confirm that none of the material is expected to be subject to legal privilege;

(e) explain why the material is likely to be of substantial value to the investigation;

(f) explain why it is in the public interest for the material to be produced, or for the applicant to be given access to it, having regard to—

    (i) the benefit likely to accrue to the investigation if it is obtained, and

    (ii) the circumstances in which the respondent has the material, or is expected to have it; and

(g) propose—

    (i) the terms of the order, and

    (ii) the period within which it should take effect.

(2) An applicant who wants the court to make an order to grant entry in aid of a production order must—

(a) specify the premises to which entry is sought;

(b) explain why the order is needed; and

(c) propose the terms of the order.

[Note. See paragraphs 5 to 9 of Schedule 5 to the Terrorism Act 2000[40]. The applicant for a production, etc. order must be an 'appropriate officer' as defined by paragraph 5(6) of that Schedule. Where the applicant is a counter-terrorism financial investigator the application must be for the purposes of an investigation relating to 'terrorist property' as defined by section 14 of the 2000 Act. Under paragraphs 5 and 7 of Schedule 5 to that Act a production order may require a specified person—

(a) to produce to an appropriate officer within a specified period for seizure and retention any material which that person has in his or her possession, custody or power and to which the application relates; to give an appropriate officer access to any such material within a specified period; and to state to the best of that person's knowledge and belief the location of material to which the application relates if it is not in, and it will not come into, his or her possession, custody or power within the period specified; or

(b) where such material is expected to come into existence within the period of 28 days beginning with the date of the order, to notify a named appropriate officer as soon as is reasonably practicable after any material to which the application relates comes into that person's possession, custody or power, and then to produce that material to an appropriate officer; to give an appropriate officer access to it; and to state to the best of that person's knowledge and belief the location of material to which the application relates if it is not in, and it will not come into, his or her possession, custody or power within that period of 28 days.

Under paragraph 4 of Schedule 5 to the 2000 Act, 'legal privilege', 'excluded material' and 'special procedure material' mean the same as under sections 10, 11 and 14 of the Police and Criminal Evidence Act 1984.

The period within which an order takes effect must be specified in the order and, unless the court otherwise directs, must be—

(a) where the respondent already has the material, 7 days from the date of the order; or

(b) where the respondent is expected to have the material within 28 days, 7 days from the date the respondent notifies the applicant of its receipt.

---

[39] 2000 c. 11.

[40] 2000 c. 11; paragraphs 5, 6 and 7 of Schedule 5 were amended by section 65 of, and paragraph 9 of Schedule 4 to, the Courts Act 2003 (c. 39) and section 41 of the Criminal Finances Act 2017 (c. 22).

The Practice Direction sets out forms of application, notice and order for use in connection with this rule.]

R47.13 **Content of application for a disclosure order or further information order under the Terrorism Act 2000**

47.13 (1) As well as complying with rules 47.6 and 47.11, an applicant who wants the court to make a disclosure order must—

  (a) explain why the applicant thinks that—

    (i) a person has committed an offence under any of sections 15 to 18 of the Terrorism Act 2000[41], or

    (ii) property described in the application is terrorist property within the meaning of section 14 of the 2000 Act[42];

  (b) describe in general terms the information that the applicant wants a person to provide;

  (c) confirm that none of the information is—

    (i) expected to be subject to legal privilege, or

    (ii) excluded material;

  (d) explain why the information is likely to be of substantial value to the investigation;

  (e) explain why it is in the public interest for the information to be provided, having regard to the benefit likely to accrue to the investigation if it is obtained; and

  (f) propose the terms of the order.

(2) As well as complying with rule 47.6, an applicant who wants the court to make a further information order must—

  (a) identify the respondent from whom the information is sought and explain—

    (i) whether the respondent is the person who made the disclosure to which the information relates or is otherwise carrying on a business in the regulated sector within the meaning of Part 1 of Schedule 3A to the 2000 Act[43], and

    (ii) why the applicant thinks that the information is in the possession, or under the control, of the respondent;

  (b) specify or describe the information that the applicant wants the respondent to provide;

  (c) where the information sought relates to a disclosure of information by someone under section 21A of the 2000 Act[44] (Failure to disclose: regulated sector), explain—

    (i) how the information sought relates to a matter arising from that disclosure,

    (ii) how the information would assist in investigating whether a person is involved in the commission of an offence under any of sections 15 to 18 of that Act[45], or in determining whether an investigation of that kind should be started, or in identifying terrorist property or its movement or use, and

    (iii) why it is reasonable in all the circumstances for the information to be provided;

  (d) where the information sought relates to a disclosure made under a requirement of the law of a country outside the United Kingdom which corresponds with Part III of the 2000 Act (Terrorist property), and an authority in that country which investigates offences corresponding with sections 15 to 18 of that Act has asked the National Crime Agency for information in connection with that disclosure, explain—

    (i) how the information sought relates to a matter arising from that disclosure,

    (ii) why the information is likely to be of substantial value to the authority that made the request in determining any matter in connection with the disclosure, and

    (iii) why it is reasonable in all the circumstances for the information to be provided;

  (e) confirm that none of the information is expected to be subject to legal privilege; and

[41] 2000 c. 11; section 17A was inserted by section 42 of the Counter-Terrorism and Security Act 2015 (c. 6).
[42] 2000 c. 11.
[43] 2000 c. 11; Part 1 of Schedule 3A was inserted by section 3 of, and paragraph 5 of Schedule 2 to, the Anti-terrorism, Crime and Security Act 2001 (c. 24), substituted by article 2 of S.I. 2007/3288 and amended by articles 3 and 6 of, and paragraph 25 of Schedule 1 to, S.I. 2008/948, sections 183 and 237 of, and paragraph 1 of Schedule 18 and Part 29 of Schedule 25 to, the Localism Act 2011 (c. 20), regulation 79 of, and paragraph 3 of Schedule 4 to, S.I. 2011/99, article 2 of S.I. 2011/2701, article 2 of S.I. 2012/2299, article 2 of S.I. 2012/1534, regulation 46 of, and paragraph 40 of Schedule 2 to, S.I. 2013/3115, section 151 of, and paragraph 73 of Schedule 4 to, the Co-operative and Community Benefit Societies Act 2014 (c. 14), regulation 59 of, and paragraph 21 of Schedule 1 to, S.I. 2015/575, regulation 12 of S.I. 2016/680, regulation 2 of, and paragraph 11 of the Schedule to, S.I. 2017/80, regulation 109 of, and paragraph 4 of Schedule 7 to, S.I. 2017/692 and regulation 50 of, and paragraph 6 of Schedule 4 to, S.I. 2017/701.
[44] 2000 c. 11; section 21A was inserted by section 3 of, and paragraph 5 of Schedule 2 to, the Anti-terrorism, Crime and Security Act 2001 (c. 24) and amended by regulation 2 of, and paragraphs 1 and 3 of Schedule 1 to, S.I. 2007/3398, section 59 of, and paragraphs 125 and 128 of, the Serious Organised Crime and Police Act 2005 (c. 15) and section 15 of, and paragraphs 67 and 72 of Schedule 8 to, the Crime and Courts Act 2013 (c. 22).
[45] 2000 c. 11; section 17A was inserted by section 42 of the Counter-Terrorism and Security Act 2015 (c. 6).

    (f) propose the terms of the order, including—
        (i) how the respondent must provide the information required, and
        (ii) the date by which the information must be provided.

(3) Rule 47.8 (Application to vary or discharge an order) does not apply to a further information order.

(4) Paragraph (5) applies where a party to an application for a further information order wants to appeal to the Crown Court from the decision of the magistrates' court.

(5) The appellant must—
    (a) serve an appeal notice—
        (i) on the Crown Court officer and on the other party,
        (ii) not more than 15 business days after the magistrates' court's decision; and
    (b) in the appeal notice, explain, as appropriate, why the Crown Court should (as the case may be) make, discharge or vary a further information order.

(6) Rule 34.11 (Constitution of the Crown Court) applies on such an appeal.

[Note. See sections 22B, 22D and 22E of, and Schedule 5A to, the Terrorism Act 2000[46].

Under paragraph 9(6) of Schedule 5A to the 2000 Act the applicant for a disclosure order must be an 'appropriate officer', as defined by paragraph 5, who is, or who is authorised to apply by, a police officer of at least the rank of superintendent.

Under section 22B(12) of the 2000 Act the applicant for a further information order must be 'a law enforcement officer', as defined by section 22B(14), who is, or who is authorised to apply by, a 'senior law enforcement officer', defined by section 22B(14) as a police officer of at least the rank of superintendent, the Director General of the National Crime Agency or an officer of that Agency authorised by the Director General for that purpose.

Section 14 of the 2000 Act[47] defines terrorist property as money or other property which is likely to be used for the purposes of terrorism; proceeds of the commission of terrorism; and proceeds of acts carried out for the purposes of terrorism. Sections 15 to 18 of the Act create offences of fund raising for the purposes of terrorism; use or possession of property for the purposes of terrorism; funding terrorism; making an insurance payment in response to a terrorist demand; and facilitating the retention or control of terrorist property.

A disclosure order can require a lawyer to provide a client's name and address.

Under section 21A of the 2000 Act[48] a person engaged in a business in the regulated sector commits an offence where the conditions listed in that section are met and that person does not disclose, in the manner required by that section, knowledge or a suspicion that another person has committed or attempted to commit an offence under any of sections 15 to 18 in Part III of the Act. Part III of the Act also contains other disclosure provisions.

The Practice Direction sets out forms of application, notice and order for use in connection with this rule.]

Content of application for an explanation order under the Terrorism Act 2000   **R47.14**

47.14 As well as complying with rules 47.6 and 47.11, an applicant who wants the court to make an explanation order must—
    (a) identify the material that the applicant wants the respondent to explain;
    (b) confirm that the explanation is not expected to infringe legal privilege; and
    (c) propose the terms of the order.

[Note. See paragraph 13 of Schedule 5 to the Terrorism Act 2000[49]. The applicant for an explanation order may be a constable or, where the application concerns material produced to a counter-terrorism financial investigator, such an investigator.

An explanation order can require a lawyer to provide a client's name and address.

The Practice Direction sets out forms of application, notice and order for use in connection with this rule.]

---

[46] 2000 c. 11; sections 22B, 22D and 22E were inserted by section 37 to the Criminal Finances Act 2017 (c. 22). Schedule 5A was inserted by Schedule 2 to the Criminal Finances Act 2017 (c. 22).

[47] 2000 c. 11.

[48] 2000 c. 11; section 21A was inserted by section 3 of, and paragraph 5 of Schedule 2 to, the Anti-terrorism, Crime and Security Act 2001 (c. 24) and amended by regulation 2 of, and paragraphs 1 and 3 of Schedule 1 to, S.I. 2007/3398, section 59 of, and paragraphs 125 and 128 of, the Serious Organised Crime and Police Act 2005 (c. 15) and section 15 of, and paragraphs 67 and 72 of Schedule 8 to, the Crime and Courts Act 2013 (c. 22).

[49] 2000 c. 11; paragraph 13 of Schedule 5 was amended by section 65 of, and paragraph 9 of Schedule 4 to, the Courts Act 2003 (c. 39) and section 41(3)(d) of the Criminal Finances Act 2017 (c. 22).

R47.15 Content of application for a customer information order under the Terrorism Act 2000

47.15 As well as complying with rules 47.6 and 47.11, an applicant who wants the court to make a customer information order must—

(a) explain why it is desirable for the purposes of the investigation to trace property said to be terrorist property within the meaning of the Terrorism Act 2000;

(b) explain why the order will enhance the effectiveness of the investigation; and

(c) propose the terms of the order.

[Note. See Schedule 6 to the Terrorism Act 2000. The applicant for a customer information order must be a police officer of at least the rank of superintendent.

'Customer information' is defined by paragraph 7 of Schedule 6 to the 2000 Act. 'Terrorist property' is defined by section 14 of the Act.

The Practice Direction sets out forms of application, notice and order for use in connection with this rule.]

R47.16 Content of application for an account monitoring order under the Terrorism Act 2000

47.16 As well as complying with rules 47.6 and 47.11, an applicant who wants the court to make an account monitoring order must—

(a) specify—

  (i) the information sought,

  (ii) the period during which the applicant wants the respondent to provide that information (to a maximum of 90 days), and

  (iii) where, when and in what manner the applicant wants the respondent to provide that information;

(b) explain why it is desirable for the purposes of the investigation to trace property said to be terrorist property within the meaning of the Terrorism Act 2000;

(c) explain why the order will enhance the effectiveness of the investigation; and

(d) propose the terms of the order.

[Note. See Schedule 6A to the Terrorism Act 2000[50]. The applicant for an account monitoring order may be a police officer or a counter-terrorism financial investigator.

'Terrorist property' is defined by section 14 of the Act.

The Practice Direction sets out forms of application, notice and order for use in connection with this rule.]

Orders under the Proceeds of Crime Act 2002

R47.17 Application for an order under the Proceeds of Crime Act 2002

47.17 (1) This rule applies where an applicant wants the court to make one of the orders to which rule 47.4(d) refers.

(2) As well as complying with rule 47.6 (Application for order: general rules), the application must—

(a) identify—

  (i) any respondent, and

  (ii) the person or property the subject of the investigation;

(b) in the case of an investigation in the United Kingdom, explain why the applicant thinks that—

  (i) the person under investigation has benefited from criminal conduct, in the case of a confiscation investigation, or committed a money laundering offence, in the case of a money laundering investigation, or

  (ii) in the case of a detained cash investigation, a detained property investigation or a frozen funds investigation, the cash or property involved, or the money held in the frozen account, was obtained through unlawful conduct or is intended to be used in unlawful conduct;

(c) in the case of an investigation outside the United Kingdom, explain why the applicant thinks that—

  (i) there is an investigation by an overseas authority which relates to a criminal investigation or to criminal proceedings (including proceedings to remove the benefit of a person's criminal conduct following that person's conviction), and

  (ii) the investigation is into whether property has been obtained as a result of or in connection with criminal conduct, or into the extent or whereabouts of such property; and

(d) give the additional information required by whichever of rules 47.18 to 47.22 applies.

[50] 2000 c. 11; Schedule 6A was inserted by section 3 of, and paragraph 1(1) and (3) of Part 1 to, the Anti-terrorism, Crime and Security Act 2001 (c. 24) and amended by section 41(1), (5) of the Criminal Finances Act 2017 (c. 22).

[Note. See also the code of practice for those exercising functions as officers and investigators issued under section 377 of the 2002 Act[51], and the code of practice for prosecutors and others issued under section 377A of that Act[52].]

Content of application for a production order under the Proceeds of Crime Act 2002   **R47.18**

47.18 As well as complying with rules 47.6 and 47.17, an applicant who wants the court to make an order for the production of, or for giving access to, material, must—

    (a) describe that material;

    (b) explain why the applicant thinks the material is in the respondent's possession or control;

    (c) confirm that none of the material is—

        (i)   expected to be subject to legal privilege, or

        (ii) excluded material;

    (d) explain why the material is likely to be of substantial value to the investigation;

    (e) explain why it is in the public interest for the material to be produced, or for the applicant to be given access to it, having regard to—

        (i)   the benefit likely to accrue to the investigation if it is obtained, and

        (ii) the circumstances in which the respondent has the material; and

    (f) propose—

        (i)   the terms of the order, and

        (ii) the period within which it should take effect, if 7 days from the date of the order would not be appropriate.

[Note. See sections 345 to 350 of the Proceeds of Crime Act 2002[53] and articles 6 to 11 of the Proceeds of Crime Act 2002 (External Investigations) Order 2014[54]. Under those provisions—

    (a) 'excluded material' means the same as under section 11 of the Police and Criminal Evidence Act 1984; and

    (b) 'legal privilege' is defined by section 348 of the 2002 Act.

A Crown Court judge may make a production order for the purposes of a confiscation investigation, a money laundering investigation, a detained cash investigation, a detained property investigation or a frozen funds investigation.

The applicant for a production order must be an 'appropriate officer' as defined by section 378(1), (4) and (5) of the 2002 Act[55] and article 2(1) of the 2014 Order.

The Practice Direction sets out forms of application, notice and order for use in connection with this rule.]

Content of application for an order to grant entry under the Proceeds of Crime Act 2002   **R47.19**

47.19 An applicant who wants the court to make an order to grant entry in aid of a production order must—

    (a) specify the premises to which entry is sought;

    (b) explain why the order is needed; and

    (c) propose the terms of the order.

[Note. See section 347 of the Proceeds of Crime Act 2002 and article 8 of the Proceeds of Crime Act 2002 (External Investigations) Order 2014. The applicant for an order to grant entry must be an 'appropriate officer' as defined by section 378(1), (4) and (5) of the Act and article 2(1) of the 2014 Order.]

---

[51] 2002 c. 29; section 377 was amended by section 74 of, and paragraphs 103 and 114 of Schedule 8 to, the Serious Crime Act 2007 (c. 27), article 12 of, and paragraphs 47 and 67 of Schedule 14 to, SI 2010/976, sections 15 and 55 of, and paragraphs 108 and 143 of Schedule 8 and paragraphs 14 and 37 of Schedule 21 to, the Crime and Courts Act 2013 (c. 22) and section 224 of, and paragraphs 1 and 17 of Schedule 48 to, the Finance Act 2013 (c. 29).

[52] 2002 c. 29; section 377A was inserted by section 74 of, and paragraphs 103 and 115 of Schedule 8 to, the Serious Crime Act 2007 (c. 27) and amended by article 3 of, and paragraphs 19 and 28 of Schedule 2 to, SI 2014/834.

[53] 2002 c. 29; sections 345 and 346 were amended by section 75 of the Serious Crime Act 2007 (c. 27), section 169 of, and paragraphs 1, 6 and 7 of Schedule 19 to, the Coroners and Justice Act 2009 (c. 25) and section 49 of, and paragraphs 1, 4 and 5 of Schedule 19 to, the Crime and Courts Act 2013 (c. 22). Section 350 was amended by section 77 of, and paragraphs 1 and 5 of Schedule 10 to, the Serious Crime Act 2007 (c. 27), section 169 of, and paragraphs 1 and 8 of Schedule 19 to, the Coroners and Justice Act 2009 (c. 25) and sections 66 and 112 of, and Schedule 8 to, the Policing and Crime Act 2009 (c. 26).

[54] S.I. 2014/1893.

[55] 2002 c. 29; section 378 was amended by section 59 of, and paragraphs 168 and 175 of Schedule 4 to, the Serious Organised Crime and Police Act 2005 (c. 15), sections 74, 77 and 80 of, and paragraphs 103 and 116 of Schedule 8 and paragraphs 1 and 13 of Schedule 10 to, the Serious Crime Act 2007 (c. 27), sections 15, 49 and 55 of, and paragraphs 108 and 144 of Schedule 8 and paragraphs 1, 24, 27, 29 and 30 of Schedule 19 to, the Crime and Courts Act 2013 (c. 22) and section 224 of, and paragraphs 1 and 18 of Schedule 48 to, the Finance Act 2013 (c. 29).

R47.20   **Content of application for a disclosure order or further information order under the Proceeds of Crime Act 2002**

47.20 (1)   As well as complying with rules 47.6 and 47.17, an applicant who wants the court to make a disclosure order must—

(a)   describe in general terms the information that the applicant wants a person to provide;

(b)   confirm that none of the information is—

(i)   expected to be subject to legal privilege, or

(ii)   excluded material;

(c)   explain why the information is likely to be of substantial value to the investigation;

(d)   explain why it is in the public interest for the information to be provided, having regard to the benefit likely to accrue to the investigation if it is obtained; and

(e)   propose the terms of the order.

(2)   As well as complying with rule 47.6, an applicant who wants the court to make a further information order must—

(a)   identify the respondent from whom the information is sought and explain—

(i)   whether the respondent is the person who made the disclosure to which the information relates or is otherwise carrying on a business in the regulated sector within the meaning of Part 1 of Schedule 9 to the Proceeds of Crime Act 2002[56], and

(ii)   why the applicant thinks that the information is in the possession, or under the control, of the respondent;

(b)   specify or describe the information that the applicant wants the respondent to provide;

(c)   where the information sought relates to a disclosure of information under Part 7 of the Proceeds of Crime Act 2002 (Money laundering), explain—

(i)   how the information sought relates to a matter arising from that disclosure,

(ii)   how the information would assist in investigating whether a person is engaged in money laundering or in determining whether an investigation of that kind should be started, and

(iii)   why it is reasonable in all the circumstances for the information to be provided;

(d)   where the information sought relates to a disclosure made under a requirement of the law of a country outside the United Kingdom which corresponds with Part 7 of the 2002 Act, and an authority in that country which investigates money laundering has asked the National Crime Agency for information in connection with that disclosure, explain—

(i)   how the information sought relates to a matter arising from that disclosure,

(ii)   why the information is likely to be of substantial value to the authority that made the request in determining any matter in connection with the disclosure, and

(iii)   why it is reasonable in all the circumstances for the information to be provided;

(e)   confirm that none of the information is expected to be subject to legal privilege; and

(f)   propose the terms of the order, including—

(i)   how the respondent must provide the information required, and

(ii)   the date by which the information must be provided.

(3)   Rule 47.8 (Application to vary or discharge an order) does not apply to a further information order.

(4)   Paragraph (5) applies where a party to an application for a further information order wants to appeal to the Crown Court from the decision of the magistrates' court.

(5)   The appellant must—

(a)   serve an appeal notice on the Crown Court officer and on the other party not more than 15 business days after the magistrates' court's decision; and

(b)   in the appeal notice, explain, as appropriate, why the Crown Court should (as the case may be) make, discharge or vary a further information order.

(6)   Rule 34.11 (Constitution of the Crown Court) applies on such an appeal.

[Note. See sections 339ZH, 339ZJ, 339ZK, 357, 358 and 361 of the Proceeds of Crime Act 2002[57] and articles 16, 17 and 20 of the Proceeds of Crime Act 2002 (External Investigations) Order 2014[58].

---

[56]   2002 c. 29; Part 1 of Schedule 9 was substituted by articles 2 and 3 of S.I. 2007/3287 and amended by sections 183 and 237 of, and paragraph 2 of Schedule 18 and Part 29 of Schedule 25 to, the Localism Act 2011 (c. 20), regulation 79 of, and paragraph 3 of Schedule 4 to, S.I. 2011/99, article 3 of S.I. 2011/2701, article 3 of S.I. 2012/1534, article 3 of S.I. 2012/2299, regulation 46 of, and paragraph 41 of Schedule 2 to, S.I. 2013/3115, section 151 of, and paragraph 81 of Schedule 4 to, the Co-operative and Community Benefit Societies Act 2014 (c. 14), regulation 59 of, and paragraph 23 of Schedule 1 to, S.I. 2015/575, regulation 14 of S.I. 2016/680, regulation 2 of, and paragraph 13 of the Schedule to, S.I. 2017/80, regulation 109 of, and paragraph 6 of Schedule 7 to, S.I. 2017/692 and regulation 50 of, and paragraph 7 of Schedule 4 to, S.I. 2017/701.

[57]   2002 c. 29; sections 339ZH, 339ZJ and 339ZK were inserted by section 12 of the Criminal Finances Act 2017 (c. 22). Section 357 was amended by sections 74 and 77 of, and paragraphs 103 and 108 of Schedule 8 and paragraphs 1 and 10 of Schedule 10 to, the Serious Crime Act 2007 (c. 27), section 169 of, and paragraphs 1 and 13 of Schedule 19 to, the Coroners

Where the 2002 Act applies, a Crown Court judge may make a disclosure order for the purposes of a confiscation investigation or a money laundering investigation.

The applicant for a disclosure order must be a 'relevant authority' as defined by section 357(7) of the 2002 Act, or an 'appropriate officer' as defined by article 2(1) of the 2014 Order where the Order applies. Under section 362(6) of the Act[59], a relevant authority who under section 357(7) is an 'appropriate officer' (as defined by section 378(1), (4) and (5)[60]) may apply only if that person is, or is authorised to do so by, a 'senior appropriate officer' (as defined by section 378(2)).

Under section 339ZH(1), (12) the applicant for a further information order must be the Director General of the National Crime Agency or an officer of that Agency authorised by the Director General for that purpose.

A disclosure order can require a lawyer to provide a client's name and address.

Under sections 330, 331 and 332 in Part 7 of the 2002 Act[61] a person engaged in a business in the regulated sector commits an offence where the conditions listed in any of those sections are met and that person does not disclose, in the manner required by the relevant section, knowledge or a suspicion that another person is engaged in money laundering.

The Practice Direction sets out forms of application, notice and order for use in connection with this rule.]

Content of application for a customer information order under the Proceeds of Crime Act 2002   R47.21

47.21 As well as complying with rules 47.6 and 47.17, an applicant who wants the court to make a customer information order must—

(a) explain why customer information about the person under investigation is likely to be of substantial value to that investigation;

(b) explain why it is in the public interest for the information to be provided, having regard to the benefit likely to accrue to the investigation if it is obtained; and

(c) propose the terms of the order.

[Note. See sections 363, 364, 365 and 368 of the Proceeds of Crime Act 2002[62] and articles 22, 23, 24 and 27 of the Proceeds of Crime Act 2002 (External Investigations) Order 2014.

A Crown Court judge may make a customer information order for the purposes of a confiscation investigation or a money laundering investigation.

The applicant for a customer information order must be an 'appropriate officer' as defined by section 378(1), (4) and (5) of the 2002 Act and article 2(1) of the 2014 Order.

'Customer information' is defined by section 364 of the 2002 Act and article 2(1) of the 2014 Order.

and Justice Act 2009 (c. 25), sections 15, 49 and 55 of, and paragraphs 108 and 139 of Schedule 8, paragraphs 1 and 8 of Schedule 19 and paragraphs 14 and 34 of Schedule 21 to, the Crime and Courts Act 2013 (c. 22) and article 3 of, and paragraphs 19 and 27 of Schedule 2 to, SI 2014/834 and section 7(2) of, and paragraph 51 of Schedule 5 to, the Criminal Finances Act 2017 (c. 22). Section 358 was amended by section 169 of, and paragraphs 1 and 14 of Schedule 19 to, the Coroners and Justice Act 2009 (c. 25), section 49(a) of, and paragraphs 1 and 9 of Schedule 19 to, the Crime and Courts Act 2013 (c. 22) and section 7(3) of the Criminal Finances Act 2017 (c. 22). Section 361 was amended by section 74 of, and paragraphs 103 and 109 of Schedule 8 to, the Serious Crime Act 2007 (c. 27).

[58] S.I. 2014/1893.

[59] 2002 c. 29; section 362 was amended by section 74 of, and paragraphs 103 and 110 of Schedule 8 to, the Serious Crime Act 2007 (c. 27), section 169 of, and paragraphs 1 and 15 of Schedule 19 to, the Coroners and Justice Act 2009 (c. 25) and section 15 of, and paragraphs 108 and 140 of Schedule 8 to, the Crime and Courts Act 2013 (c. 22). It is further amended by section 7(4) of the Criminal Finances Act 2017 (c. 22), with effect from a date to be appointed.

[60] 2002 c. 29; section 378 was amended by section 59 of, and paragraphs 168 and 175 of Schedule 4 to, the Serious Organised Crime and Police Act 2005 (c. 15), sections 74, 77 and 80 of, and paragraphs 103 and 116 of Schedule 8 and paragraphs 1 and 13 of Schedule 10 to, the Serious Crime Act 2007 (c. 27), sections 15, 49 and 55 of, and paragraphs 108 and 144 of Schedule 8 and paragraphs 1, 24, 27, 29 and 30 of Schedule 19 to, the Crime and Courts Act 2013 (c. 22) and section 224 of, and paragraphs 1 and 18 of Schedule 48 to, the Finance Act 2013 (c. 29). It is further amended by paragraph 25 of Schedule 1, and paragraph 59 of Schedule 5, to the Criminal Finances Act 2017 (c. 22), with effect from dates to be appointed.

[61] 2002 c. 29; section 330 was amended by sections 102, 104, 105, 106 and 174 of, and Schedule 17 to, the Serious Organised Crime and Police Act 2005 (c. 15), article 2 of S.I. 2006/308, regulation 3 of, and paragraphs 1 and 2 of Schedule 2 to, S.I. 2007/3398 and section 15 of, and paragraphs 108 and 129 of Schedule 8 to, the Crime and Courts Act 2013 (c. 22). Section 331 was amended by sections 102 and 104 of the Serious Organised Crime and Police Act 2005 (c. 15) and section 15 of, and paragraphs 108 and 130 of Schedule 8 to, the Crime and Courts Act 2013 (c. 22). Section 332 was amended by sections 102 and 104 of the Serious Organised Crime and Police Act 2005 (c. 15) and section 15 of, and paragraphs 108 and 131 of Schedule 8 to, the Crime and Courts Act 2013 (c. 22).

[62] 2002 c. 29; section 363 was amended by section 77 of, and paragraphs 1 and 11 of Schedule 10 to, the Serious Crime Act 2007 (c. 27), section 169 of, and paragraphs 1 and 16 of Schedule 19 to, the Coroners and Justice Act 2009 (c. 25) and section 49 of, and paragraphs 1 and 10 of Schedule 19 to, the Crime and Courts Act 2013 (c. 22). Section 364 was amended by section 107 of the Serious Organised Crime and Police Act 2005 (c. 27) and article 2(1) of and paragraph 196 of Schedule 1 to, S.I. 2009/1941.

The Practice Direction sets out forms of application, notice and order for use in connection with this rule.]

R47.22 **Content of application for an account monitoring order under the Proceeds of Crime Act 2002**

47.22 As well as complying with rules 47.6 and 47.17, an applicant who wants the court to make an account monitoring order for the provision of account information must—

  (a) specify—

    (i) the information sought,

    (ii) the period during which the applicant wants the respondent to provide that information (to a maximum of 90 days), and

    (iii) when and in what manner the applicant wants the respondent to provide that information;

  (b) explain why the information is likely to be of substantial value to the investigation;

  (c) explain why it is in the public interest for the information to be provided, having regard to the benefit likely to accrue to the investigation if it is obtained; and

  (d) propose the terms of the order.

[Note. See sections 370, 371 and 374 of the Proceeds of Crime Act 2002[63] and articles 29, 30 and 33 of the Proceeds of Crime Act 2002 (External Investigations) Order 2014.

Where the 2002 Act applies, a Crown Court judge may make an account monitoring order for the purposes of a confiscation investigation, a money laundering investigation, a detained cash investigation, a detained property investigation or a frozen funds investigation.

The applicant for an account monitoring order must be an 'appropriate officer' as defined by section 378(1), (4) and (5) of the 2002 Act and article 2(1) of the 2014 Order.

'Account information' is defined by section 370 of the 2002 Act and article 29(3) of the 2014 Order.

The Practice Direction sets out forms of application, notice and order for use in connection with this rule.]

Orders under the Extradition Act 2003

R47.23 **Application for a production order under the Extradition Act 2003**

47.23 (1) This rule applies where an applicant wants the court to make an order to which rule 47.4(e) refers.

  (2) As well as complying with rule 47.6 (Application for order: general rules), the application must—

    (a) identify the person whose extradition is sought;

    (b) specify the extradition offence of which that person is accused;

    (c) identify the respondent; and

    (d) describe the special procedure or excluded material sought.

  (3) In relation to the person whose extradition is sought, the application must explain the grounds for believing that—

    (a) that person has committed the offence for which extradition is sought;

    (b) that offence is an extradition offence; and

    (c) that person is in the United Kingdom or is on the way to the United Kingdom.

  (4) In relation to the material sought, the application must—

    (a) specify the premises on which the material is believed to be;

    (b) explain the grounds for believing that—

      (i) the material is on those premises,

      (ii) the material consists of or includes special procedure or excluded material, and

      (iii) the material would be likely to be admissible evidence at a trial in England and Wales for the offence for which extradition is sought;

    (c) explain what other methods of obtaining the material—

      (i) have been tried without success, or

      (ii) have not been tried because they appeared bound to fail; and

    (d) explain why it is in the public interest for the respondent to produce or give access to the material.

  (5) The application must propose—

    (a) the terms of the order, and

    (b) the period within which it should take effect.

[63] 2002 c. 29; section 370 was amended by section 77 of, and paragraphs 1 and 12 of Schedule 10 to, the Serious Crime Act 2007 (c. 27), section 169 of, and paragraphs 1 and 17 of Schedule 19 to, the Coroners and Justice Act 2009 (c. 25) and section 49 of, and paragraphs 1 and 12 of Schedule 19 to, the Crime and Courts Act 2013 (c. 22).

[Note. See sections 157 and 158 of the Extradition Act 2003[64]. Under those provisions—

      (c) *'special procedure material' means the same as under section 14 of the Police and Criminal Evidence Act 1984; and*

      (d) *'excluded material' means the same as under section 11 of the 1984 Act.*

The applicant for a production order must be a constable.

The period within which an order takes effect must be specified in the order and, unless the court considers a longer period appropriate, must be 7 days from the date of the order.]

Section 3: investigation warrants

When this Section applies

R47.24

47.24 This Section applies where—

    (a) a justice of the peace can issue a warrant under—

        (i)   section 8 of the Police and Criminal Evidence Act 1984[65] or,

        (ii) section 2 of the Criminal Justice Act 1987[66];

    (b) a Circuit judge can issue a warrant under—

        (i)   paragraph 12 of Schedule 1 to the Police and Criminal Evidence Act 1984[67],

        (ii) paragraph 11 of Schedule 5 to the Terrorism Act 2000[68], or

        (iii) section 160 of the Extradition Act 2003[69];

    (c) a Crown Court judge can issue a warrant under—

        (i)   section 352 of the Proceeds of Crime Act 2002[70], or

        (ii) article 13 of the Proceeds of Crime Act 2002 (External Investigations) Order 2014[71]; and

    (d) a court to which these Rules apply can issue a warrant to search for and seize articles or persons under a power not listed in paragraphs (a), (b) or (c).

[Note. In outline, the warrants to which these rules apply are—

    (a) under the Police and Criminal Evidence Act 1984, a warrant authorising entry to, and the search of, premises for material, articles or persons;

    (b) under the Criminal Justice Act 1987, a warrant authorising entry to, and the search of, premises for documents sought by the Director of the Serious Fraud Office;

    (c) under the Terrorism Act 2000, a warrant authorising entry to, and the search of, premises for material sought for the purposes of a terrorist investigation;

    (d) under the Proceeds of Crime Act 2002 or under the Proceeds of Crime Act 2002 (External Investigations) Order 2014, a warrant authorising entry to, and the search of, premises for material sought for the purposes of a confiscation investigation, a money laundering investigation, a detained cash investigation or an external investigation;

    (e) under the Extradition Act 2003, a warrant authorising entry to, and the search of, premises for material sought in connection with the prosecution of a person whose extradition has been requested;

    (f) under other Acts, comparable warrants.

For all the relevant terms under which such warrants can be issued, see the provisions listed in this rule.

---

[64] 2003 c. 41; section 157 was amended by section 174 of the Anti-social Behaviour, Crime and Policing Act 2014 (c. 12).

[65] 1984 c. 60; section 8 was amended by paragraph 80 of Schedule 14 to the Immigration and Asylum Act 1999 (c. 33), sections 111, 113 and 114 of, and paragraph 43 of Schedule 7 to, the Serious Organised Crime and Police Act 2005 (c. 15) and section 86 of the Finance Act 2007 (c. 11).

[66] 1987 c. 38; section 2 was amended by sections 143 and 170 of, and paragraph 113 of Schedule 15 to, the Criminal Justice Act 1988 (c. 33), section 164 of the Criminal Justice and Public Order Act 1994 (c. 33), paragraph 20 of Schedule 3 to the Youth Justice and Criminal Evidence Act 1999 (c. 23), paragraph 23 of Schedule 2 to the Criminal Justice and Police Act 2001 (c. 16), paragraphs 11 and 12 of Schedule 5 to the Crime (International Co-operation) Act 2003 (c. 32) and section 12 of, and paragraphs 11, 12 and 13 of Schedule 1 to, the Criminal Justice Act 2003 (c. 44).

[67] 1984 c. 60; paragraph 12 of Schedule 1 was amended by section 65 of, and paragraph 6 of Schedule 4 to, the Courts Act 2003 (c. 39) and section 113 of the Serious Organised Crime and Police Act 2005 (c. 15).

[68] 2000 c. 11; paragraph 11 of Schedule 5 was amended by section 26 of the Terrorism Act 2006 (c. 11) and section 82 of the Deregulation Act 2015 (c. 20). It is further amended by section 65 of, and paragraph 9 of Schedule 4 to, the Courts Act 2003 (c. 39), with effect from a date to be appointed.

[69] 2003 c. 41; section 160 was amended by section 174 of the Anti-social Behaviour, Crime and Policing Act 2014 (c. 12).

[70] 2002 c. 29; section 352 was amended by sections 74, 76, 77 and 80 of, and paragraphs 103 and 105 of Schedule 8 and paragraphs 1 and 7 of Schedule 10 to, the Serious Crime Act 2007 (c. 27), section 169 of, and paragraphs 1 and 10 of Schedule 19 to, the Coroners and Justice Act 2009 (c. 25), sections 15, 49 and 55 of, and paragraphs 108 and 137 of Schedule 8, paragraphs 1 and 6 of Schedule 19 and paragraphs 14 and 31 of Schedule 21 to, the Crime and Courts Act 2013 (c. 22), section 224 of, and paragraphs 1 and 12 of Schedule 48 to, the Finance Act 2013 (c. 29), article 3 of, and paragraphs 19 and 26 of Schedule 2 to, SI 2014/834 and section 82 of the Deregulation Act 2015 (c. 20).

[71] S.I. 2014/1893.

Criminal Procedure Rules

Under section 8 of the Senior Courts Act 1981[72], a High Court judge, a Circuit judge, a Recorder, a qualifying judge advocate and a District Judge (Magistrates' Courts) each may act as a Crown Court judge.

When the relevant provisions of the Courts Act 2003 come into force, a District Judge (Magistrates' Courts) will have the same powers as a Circuit judge under the Police and Criminal Evidence Act 1984 and under the Terrorism Act 2000.

Under section 66 of the Courts Act 2003[73], in criminal cases a High Court judge, a Circuit judge, a Recorder and a qualifying judge advocate each has the powers of a justice of the peace who is a District Judge (Magistrates' Courts).

As well as governing procedure on an application to a magistrates' court or the Crown Court, under the following provisions rules may govern the procedure on an application to an individual Circuit or Crown Court judge—

    (a) paragraph 15A of Schedule 1 to the Police and Criminal Evidence Act 1984[74];
    (b) paragraph 11 of Schedule 5 to the Terrorism Act 2000;
    (c) section 352 of the Proceeds of Crime Act 2002; and
    (d) section 160 of the Extradition Act 2003.]

For a list of the types of investigation under Part 8 of the Proceeds of Crime Act 2002 and a list of the powers of judges in respect of each type, see the note to rule 47.4 (Section 2: Investigation orders; When this Section applies.]

R47.25 **Exercise of court's powers**

47.25 (1) The court must determine an application for a warrant—
    (a) at a hearing, which must be in private unless the court otherwise directs;
    (b) in the presence of the applicant; and
    (c) in the absence of any person affected by the warrant, including any person in occupation or control of premises which the applicant wants to search.
  (2) If the court so directs, the applicant may attend the hearing by live link.
  (3) The court must not determine an application unless satisfied that sufficient time has been allowed for it.
  (4) The court must not determine an application unless the applicant confirms, on oath or affirmation, that to the best of the applicant's knowledge and belief—
    (a) the application discloses all the information that is material to what the court must decide, including any circumstances that might reasonably be considered capable of undermining any of the grounds of the application; and
    (b) the content of the application is true.
  (5) If the court requires the applicant to answer a question about an application—
    (a) the applicant's answer must be on oath or affirmation;
    (b) the court must arrange for a record of the gist of the question and reply; and
    (c) if the applicant cannot answer to the court's satisfaction, the court may—
      (i) specify the information the court requires, and
      (ii) give directions for the presentation of any renewed application.
  (6) If the court considers information to which rule 47.26(4) refers (information that the applicant thinks should be kept confidential), the court must so record
  (7) Unless to do so would be inconsistent with other legislation, on an application the court may issue—
    (a) a warrant in respect of specified premises;
    (b) a warrant in respect of all premises occupied or controlled by a specified person;
    (c) a warrant in respect of all premises occupied or controlled by a specified person which specifies some of those premises; or
    (d) more than one warrant—
      (i) each one in respect of premises specified in the warrant,
      (ii) each one in respect of all premises occupied or controlled by a person specified in the warrant (whether or not such a warrant also specifies any of those premises), or
      (iii) at least one in respect of specified premises and at least one in respect of all premises occupied or controlled by a specified person (whether or not such a warrant also specifies any of those premises).

[72] 1981 c. 54; section 8 was amended by sections 65 and 109 of, and paragraph 259 of Schedule 8 to, the Courts Act 2003 (c. 39) and paragraph 1 of Schedule 2 to the Armed Forces Act 2011 (c. 18). The 1981 Act's title was amended by section 59(5) of, and paragraph 1 of Schedule 11 to, the Constitutional Reform Act 2005 (c. 4).
[73] 2003 c. 39; section 66 was amended by paragraph 6 of Schedule 2 to the Armed Forces Act 2011 (c. 18) and sections 17 and 21 of, and paragraphs 83 and 90 of Schedule 10 and paragraph 4 of Schedule 14 to, the Crime and Courts Act 2013 (c. 22).
[74] 1984 c. 60; paragraph 15A of Schedule 1 was inserted by section 82 of the Deregulation Act 2015 (c. 20).

(8) Paragraph (9) applies—
    (a) only in a magistrates' court; and
    (b) unless the court—
       (i) includes a District Judge (Magistrates' Courts), and
       (ii) otherwise directs.
(9) A justices' legal adviser must assist the court by completing the preparation of any warrant to be issued.

[Note. See section 15 of the Police and Criminal Evidence Act 1984[75] and section 2(4) of the Criminal Justice Act 1987[76]. Not all the powers to which the rules in this Section apply permit the issue of a warrant in respect of all premises occupied or controlled by a specified person: see, for example, rule 47.32 (Application for warrant under section 352 of the Proceeds of Crime Act 2002). For the functions of a justices' legal adviser, see sections 28 and 29 of the Courts Act 2003[77]. See also rule 2.12 (Duties of justices' legal adviser).]

Application for warrant: general rules

R47.26

47.26 (1) This rule applies to each application to which this Section applies.
(2) The applicant must—
    (a) apply in writing;
    (b) serve the application on—
       (i) the court officer, or
       (ii) if the court office is closed, the court;
    (c) demonstrate that the applicant is entitled to apply, for example as a constable or under legislation that applies to other officers;
    (d) give the court an estimate of how long the court should allow—
       (i) to read and prepare for the application, and
       (ii) for the hearing of the application; and
    (e) tell the court when the applicant expects any warrant issued to be executed.
(3) The application must disclose anything known or reported to the applicant that might reasonably be considered capable of undermining any of the grounds of the application.
(4) Where the application includes information that the applicant thinks should not be supplied under rule 5.7 (Supply to a party of information or documents from records or case materials) to a person affected by a warrant, where the application includes information that the applicant thinks should be kept confidential—
    (a) set out that information in a separate document, marked accordingly; and
    (b) in that document, explain why the applicant thinks that that information ought not to be supplied to anyone other than the court.
(5) The application must include—
    (a) a declaration by the applicant that to the best of the applicant's knowledge and belief—
       (i) the application discloses all the information that is material to what the court must decide, including anything that might reasonably be considered capable of undermining any of the grounds of the application, and
       (ii) the content of the application is true; and
    (b) a declaration by an officer senior to the applicant that the senior officer has reviewed and authorised the application.
(6) The application must attach a draft warrant or warrants in the terms proposed by the applicant.

Information to be included in a warrant

R47.27

47.27 (1) A warrant must identify—
    (a) the person or description of persons by whom it may be executed;
    (b) any person who may accompany a person executing the warrant;
    (c) so far as practicable—
       (i) the material, documents, articles or persons to be sought, and
       (ii) any information to be sought which may be stored electronically;
    (d) the legislation under which it was issued;
    (e) the name of the applicant;
    (f) the court that issued it, unless that is otherwise recorded by the court officer;

---

[75] 1984 c. 60; section 15 was amended by sections 113 and 114 of the Serious Organised Crime and Police Act 2005 (c. 15) and article 7 of S.I. 2005/3496.
[76] 1987 c. 38.
[77] 2003 c. 39; sections 28 and 29 were substituted by section 3 of, and paragraphs 25 and 26 of the Schedule to, the Courts and Tribunals (Judiciary and Functions of Staff) Act 2018 (c. 33).

      (g) the court office for the court that issued it; and

      (h) the date on which it was issued.

  (2) A warrant must specify—

      (a) either—

          (i) the premises to be searched, where the application was for authority to search specified premises, or

         (ii) the person in occupation or control of premises to be searched, where the application was for authority to search any premises occupied or controlled by that person; and

      (b) the number of occasions on which specified premises may be searched, if more than one.

  (3) A warrant must include, by signature, initial, or otherwise, an indication that it has been approved by the court that issued it.

  (4) Where a warrant comprises more than a single page, each page must include such an indication.

  (5) A copy of a warrant must include a prominent certificate that it is such a copy.

[Note. See sections 15 and 16 of the Police and Criminal Evidence Act 1984[78]. Not all the powers to which the rules in this Section apply permit the issue of a warrant in respect of all premises occupied or controlled by a specified person: see, for example, rule 47.32 (Application for warrant under section 352 of the Proceeds of Crime Act 2002).]

R47.28 **Application for warrant under section 8 of the Police and Criminal Evidence Act 1984**

  47.28 (1) This rule applies where an applicant wants a magistrates' court to issue a warrant or warrants under section 8 of the Police and Criminal Evidence Act 1984[79].

      (2) As well as complying with rule 47.26, the application must—

        (a) specify the offence under investigation (and see paragraph (3));

        (b) so far as practicable, identify the material sought (and see paragraph (4));

        (c) specify the premises to be searched (and see paragraphs (5) and (6));

        (d) state whether the applicant wants the premises to be searched on more than one occasion (and see paragraph (7)); and

        (e) state whether the applicant wants other persons to accompany the officers executing the warrant or warrants (and see paragraph (8)).

      (3) In relation to the offence under investigation, the application must—

        (a) state whether that offence is—

           (i) an indictable offence, or

          (ii) a relevant offence as defined in section 28D of the Immigration Act 1971[80]; and

        (b) explain the grounds for believing that the offence has been committed.

      (4) In relation to the material sought, the application must—

        (a) explain the grounds for believing that that material—

           (i) is likely to be of substantial value to the investigation (whether by itself, or together with other material),

          (ii) is likely to be admissible evidence at trial for the offence under investigation, and

         (iii) does not consist of or include items subject to legal privilege, excluded material or special procedure material; and

        (b) if that material may be stored in an electronic device or devices—

           (i) so far as practicable, describe each device or kind of device sought, and

          (ii) explain the grounds for believing that the material may be stored there.

      (5) In relation to premises which the applicant wants to be searched and can specify, the application must—

        (a) specify each set of premises;

        (b) in respect of each set of premises, explain the grounds for believing that material sought is on those premises; and

        (c) in respect of each set of premises, explain the grounds for believing that—

           (i) it is not practicable to communicate with any person entitled to grant entry to the premises,

          (ii) it is practicable to communicate with such a person but it is not practicable to communicate with any person entitled to grant access to the material sought,

---

[78] 1984 c. 60; section 16 was amended by paragraph 281 of Schedule 8 to the Courts Act 2003 (c. 39), section 2 of the Criminal Justice Act 2003 (c. 44), sections 113 and 114 of the Serious Organised Crime and Police Act 2005 (c. 15) and article 8 of S.I. 2005/3496.

[79] 1984 c. 60; section 8 was amended by paragraph 80 of Schedule 14 to the Immigration and Asylum Act 1999 (c. 33), sections 111, 113 and 114 of, and paragraph 43 of Schedule 7 to, the Serious Organised Crime and Police Act 2005 (c. 15) and section 86 of the Finance Act 2007 (c. 11).

[80] 1971 c. 77; section 28D was inserted by section 131 of the Immigration and Asylum Act 1999 (c. 33) and amended by sections 144 and 150 of the Nationality, Immigration and Asylum Act 2002 (c. 41).

(iii) entry to the premises will not be granted unless a warrant is produced, or

(iv) the purpose of a search may be frustrated or seriously prejudiced unless a constable arriving at the premises can secure immediate entry to them.

(6) In relation to premises which the applicant wants to be searched but at least some of which the applicant cannot specify, the application must—

    (a) explain the grounds for believing that—

        (i) because of the particulars of the offence under investigation it is necessary to search any premises occupied or controlled by a specified person, and

        (ii) it is not reasonably practicable to specify all the premises which that person occupies or controls which might need to be searched;

    (b) specify as many sets of premises as is reasonably practicable;

    (c) in respect of each set of premises, whether specified or not, explain the grounds for believing that material sought is on those premises; and

    (d) in respect of each specified set of premises, explain the grounds for believing that—

        (i) it is not practicable to communicate with any person entitled to grant entry to the premises,

        (ii) it is practicable to communicate with such a person but it is not practicable to communicate with any person entitled to grant access to the material sought,

        (iii) entry to the premises will not be granted unless a warrant is produced, or

        (iv) the purpose of a search may be frustrated or seriously prejudiced unless a constable arriving at the premises can secure immediate entry to them.

(7) In relation to any set of premises which the applicant wants to be searched on more than one occasion, the application must—

    (a) explain why it is necessary to search on more than one occasion in order to achieve the purpose for which the applicant wants the court to issue the warrant; and

    (b) specify any proposed maximum number of occasions.

(8) In relation to any set of premises which the applicant wants to be searched by the officers executing the warrant with other persons authorised by the court, the application must—

    (a) identify those other persons, by function or description; and

    (b) explain why those persons are required.

[Note. Under section 8 of the Police and Criminal Evidence Act 1984, where there are reasonable grounds for believing that an indictable offence has been committed a constable may apply to a justice of the peace for a warrant authorising a search for evidence on specified premises, or on the premises of a specified person. Under section 8(6) of the 1984 Act, section 8 applies also in relation to relevant offences as defined in section 28D(4) of the Immigration Act 1971 (some of which are not indictable offences).

Under section 23 of the 1984 Act[81], 'premises' includes any place, and in particular any vehicle, vessel, aircraft or hovercraft, any offshore installation, any renewable energy installation and any tent or moveable structure.

Under section 16(3) of the 1984 Act[82], entry and search under a warrant must be within 3 months from the date of its issue.

See also the code of practice for the search of premises issued under section 66 of the 1984 Act[83].

The Practice Direction sets out forms of application and warrant for use in connection with this rule.]

Application for warrant under section 2 of the Criminal Justice Act 1987   **R47.29**

47.29 (1) This rule applies where an applicant wants a magistrates' court to issue a warrant or warrants under section 2 of the Criminal Justice Act 1987[84].

(2) As well as complying with rule 47.26, the application must—

    (a) describe the investigation being conducted by the Director of the Serious Fraud Office and include—

        (i) an explanation of what is alleged and why, and

        (ii) a chronology of relevant events;

---

[81] 1984 c. 60; section 23 was amended by sections 103 and 197 of, and Part 1 of Schedule 23 to, the Energy Act 2004 (c. 20).

[82] 1984 c. 60; section 16(3) was amended by section 114 of the Serious Organised Crime and Police Act 2005 (c. 15).

[83] 1984 c. 60; section 66 was amended by section 57 of the Criminal Justice and Court Services Act 2000 (c. 43), sections 110 and 174 of, and Schedule 17 to, the Serious Organised Crime and Police Act 2005 (c. 15) and section 115 of, and paragraph 21 of Schedule 9 to, the Protection of Freedoms Act 2012 (c. 9).

[84] 1987 c. 38; section 2 was amended by sections 143 and 170 of, and paragraph 113 of Schedule 15 to, the Criminal Justice Act 1988 (c. 33); section 164 of the Criminal Justice and Public Order Act 1994 (c. 33), paragraph 20 of Schedule 3 to the Youth Justice and Criminal Evidence Act 1999 (c. 23), paragraph 23 of Schedule 2 to the Criminal Justice and Police Act 2001 (c. 16), paragraphs 11 and 12 of Schedule 5 to the Crime (International Co-operation) Act 2003 (c. 32) and section 12 of, and paragraphs 11, 12 and 13 of Schedule 1 to, the Criminal Justice Act 2003 (c. 44).

      (b) specify the document, documents or description of documents sought by the applicant (and see paragraphs (3) and (4)); and

      (c) specify the premises which the applicant wants to be searched (and see paragraph (5)).

(3) In relation to each document or description of documents sought, the application must—

      (a) explain the grounds for believing that each such document—

         (i) relates to a matter relevant to the investigation, and

        (ii) could not be withheld from disclosure or production on grounds of legal professional privilege;

      (b) explain the grounds for believing that—

         (i) a person has failed to comply with a notice by the Director to produce the document or documents,

        (ii) it is not practicable to serve such a notice, or

       (iii) the service of such a notice might seriously impede the investigation; and

      (c) if the document or documents may be stored in an electronic device or devices—

         (i) so far as practicable, describe each device or kind of device sought, and

        (ii) explain the grounds for believing that the document or documents may be stored there.

(4) In relation to any document or description of documents which the applicant wants to be preserved but not seized under a warrant, the application must—

      (a) specify the steps for which the applicant wants the court's authority in order to preserve and prevent interference with the document or documents; and

      (b) explain why such steps are necessary.

(5) In respect of each set of premises which the applicant wants to be searched, the application must explain the grounds for believing that a document or description of documents sought by the applicant is on those premises.

(6) If the court so directs, the applicant must make available to the court material on which is based the information given under paragraph (2).

[Note. Under section 2 of the Criminal Justice Act 1987, where the Director of the Serious Fraud Office is investigating a case of serious or complex fraud a member of that Office may apply to a justice of the peace for a warrant authorising a search of specified premises for documents relating to any matter relevant to the investigation. Under section 66 of the Courts Act 2003[85], a Circuit judge can exercise the power to issue a warrant.

Under section 16(3) of the Police and Criminal Evidence Act 1984, entry and search under a warrant must be within 3 months from the date of its issue.

The Practice Direction sets out forms of application and warrant for use in connection with this rule.]

R47.30   **Application for warrant under paragraph 12 of Schedule 1 to the Police and Criminal Evidence Act 1984**

47.30 (1) This rule applies where an applicant wants a Circuit judge to issue a warrant or warrants under paragraph 12 of Schedule 1 to the Police and Criminal Evidence Act 1984[86].

    (2) As well as complying with rule 47.26, the application must—

      (a) specify the offence under investigation (and see paragraph (3)(a));

      (b) specify the set of access conditions on which the applicant relies (and see paragraphs (3) and (4));

      (c) so far as practicable, identify the material sought and if that material may be stored in an electronic device or devices—

         (i) so far as practicable, describe each device or kind of device sought, and

        (ii) explain the grounds for believing that the material may be stored there;

      (d) specify the premises to be searched (and see paragraphs (6) and (7)); and

      (e) state whether the applicant wants other persons to accompany the officers executing the warrant or warrants (and see paragraph (8)).

    (3) Where the applicant relies on paragraph 2 of Schedule 1 to the Police and Criminal Evidence Act 1984[87] ('the first set of access conditions': general power to gain access to special procedure material), the application must—

      (a) specify the indictable offence under investigation;

[85] 2003 c. 39; section 66 was amended by paragraph 6 of Schedule 2 to the Armed Forces Act 2011 (c. 18) and sections 17 and 21 of, and paragraphs 83 and 90 of Schedule 10 and paragraph 4 of Schedule 14 to, the Crime and Courts Act 2013 (c. 22).

[86] 1984 c. 60; paragraph 12 of Schedule 1 was amended by section 65 of, and paragraph 6 of Schedule 4 to, the Courts Act 2003 (c. 39) and section 113 of the Serious Organised Crime and Police Act 2005 (c. 15).

[87] 1984 c. 60; paragraph 2 of Schedule 1 was amended by sections 111 and 113 of, and paragraph 43 of Schedule 7 to, the Serious Organised Crime and Police Act 2005 (c. 15).

(b) explain the grounds for believing that the offence has been committed;

(c) explain the grounds for believing that the material sought—

    (i) is likely to be of substantial value to the investigation (whether by itself, or together with other material),

    (ii) is likely to be admissible evidence at trial for the offence under investigation, and

    (iii) does not consist of or include items subject to legal privilege or excluded material;

(d) explain what other methods of obtaining the material—

    (i) have been tried without success, or

    (ii) have not been tried because they appeared bound to fail; and

(e) explain why it is in the public interest to obtain the material, having regard to—

    (i) the benefit likely to accrue to the investigation if the material is obtained, and

    (ii) the circumstances under which the material is held.

(4) Where the applicant relies on paragraph 3 of Schedule 1 to the Police and Criminal Evidence Act 1984[88] ('the second set of access conditions': use of search warrant power to gain access to excluded or special procedure material), the application must—

(a) state the legislation under which a search warrant could have been issued, had the material sought not been excluded or special procedure material (in this paragraph, described as 'the main search power');

(b) include or attach the terms of the main search power;

(c) explain how the circumstances would have satisfied any criteria prescribed by the main search power for the issue of a search warrant; and

(d) explain why the issue of such a search warrant would have been appropriate.

(5) Where the applicant relies on the second set of access conditions and on an assertion that a production order made under paragraph 4 of Schedule 1 to the 1984 Act[89] in respect of the material sought has not been complied with—

(a) the application must—

    (i) identify that order and describe its terms, and

    (ii) specify the date on which it was served; but

(b) the application need not comply with paragraphs (6) or (7).

(6) In relation to premises which the applicant wants to be searched and can specify, the application must (unless paragraph (5) applies)—

(a) specify each set of premises;

(b) in respect of each set of premises, explain the grounds for believing that material sought is on those premises; and

(c) in respect of each set of premises, explain the grounds for believing that—

    (i) it is not practicable to communicate with any person entitled to grant entry to the premises,

    (ii) it is practicable to communicate with such a person but it is not practicable to communicate with any person entitled to grant access to the material sought,

    (iii) the material sought contains information which is subject to a restriction on disclosure or an obligation of secrecy contained in an enactment and is likely to be disclosed in breach of the restriction or obligation if a warrant is not issued, or

    (iv) service of notice of an application for a production order under paragraph 4 of Schedule 1 to the 1984 Act may seriously prejudice the investigation.

(7) In relation to premises which the applicant wants to be searched but at least some of which the applicant cannot specify, the application must (unless paragraph (5) applies)—

(a) explain the grounds for believing that—

    (i) because of the particulars of the offence under investigation it is necessary to search any premises occupied or controlled by a specified person, and

    (ii) it is not reasonably practicable to specify all the premises which that person occupies or controls which might need to be searched;

(b) specify as many sets of premises as is reasonably practicable;

(c) in respect of each set of premises, whether specified or not, explain the grounds for believing that material sought is on those premises; and

(d) in respect of each specified set of premises, explain the grounds for believing that—

    (i) it is not practicable to communicate with any person entitled to grant entry to the premises,

    (ii) it is practicable to communicate with such a person but it is not practicable to communicate with any person entitled to grant access to the material sought,

---

[88] 1984 c. 60; paragraph 3 of Schedule 1 was amended by section 113 of the Serious Organised Crime and Police Act 2005 (c. 15).

[89] 1984 c. 60; paragraph 4 of Schedule 1 was amended by section 65 of, and paragraph 6 of Schedule 4 to, the Courts Act 2003 (c. 39).

(iii) the material sought contains information which is subject to a restriction on disclosure or an obligation of secrecy contained in an enactment and is likely to be disclosed in breach of the restriction or obligation if a warrant is not issued, or

(iv) service of notice of an application for a production order under paragraph 4 of Schedule 1 to the 1984 Act may seriously prejudice the investigation.

(8) In relation to any set of premises which the applicant wants to be searched by the officers executing the warrant with other persons authorised by the court, the application must—

(a) identify those other persons, by function or description; and

(b) explain why those persons are required.

[Note. Under paragraph 12 of Schedule 1 to the Police and Criminal Evidenced Act 1984, where the conditions listed in that paragraph and, if applicable, in paragraphs 12A and 14 of that Schedule[90] are fulfilled a constable may apply to a Circuit judge for a warrant authorising a search for evidence consisting of special procedure material or, in some cases, excluded material on specified premises or on the premises of a specified person.

Under section 16(3) of the 1984 Act[91], entry and search under a warrant must be within 3 months from the date of its issue.

See also the code of practice for the search of premises issued under section 66 of the 1984 Act.

The Practice Direction sets out forms of application and warrant for use in connection with this rule.]

R47.31   Application for warrant under paragraph 11 of Schedule 5 to the Terrorism Act 2000

47.31 (1) This rule applies where an applicant wants a Circuit judge to issue a warrant or warrants under paragraph 11 of Schedule 5 to the Terrorism Act 2000[92].

(2) As well as complying with rule 47.26, the application must—

(a) specify the offence under investigation;

(b) explain how the investigation constitutes a terrorist investigation within the meaning of the Terrorism Act 2000;

(c) so far as practicable, identify the material sought (see also paragraph (4)) and if that material may be stored in an electronic device or devices—

(i) so far as practicable, describe each device or kind of device sought, and

(ii) explain the grounds for believing that the material may be stored there;

(d) specify the premises to be searched (and see paragraph (5)); and

(e) state whether the applicant wants other persons to accompany the officers executing the warrant or warrants (and see paragraph (6)).

(3) Where the applicant relies on an assertion that a production order made under paragraph 5 of Schedule 5 to the 2000 Act[93] in respect of material on the premises has not been complied with—

(a) the application must—

(i) identify that order and describe its terms, and

(ii) specify the date on which it was served; but

(b) the application need not comply with paragraphs (4) or (5)(b).

(4) In relation to the material sought, unless paragraph (3) applies the application must explain the grounds for believing that—

(a) the material consists of or includes excluded material or special procedure material but does not include items subject to legal privilege;

(b) the material is likely to be of substantial value to a terrorist investigation (whether by itself, or together with other material); and

(c) it is not appropriate to make an order under paragraph 5 of Schedule 11 to the 2000 Act in relation to the material because—

(i) it is not practicable to communicate with any person entitled to produce the material,

---

[90] 1984 c. 60; paragraph 12A of Schedule 1 was inserted by section 113 of the Serious Organised Crime and Police Act 2005 (c. 15). Paragraph 14 of Schedule 1 was amended by sections 113 and 174 of, and Schedule 17 to, the Serious Organised Crime and Police Act 2005 (c. 15).

[91] 1984 c. 60; section 16(3) was amended by section 114 of the Serious Organised Crime and Police Act 2005 (c. 15).

[92] 2000 c. 11; paragraph 11 of Schedule 5 was amended by section 26 of the Terrorism Act 2006 (c. 11) and section 82 of the Deregulation Act 2015 (c. 20). It is further amended by section 65 of, and paragraph 9 of Schedule 4 to, the Courts Act 2003 (c. 39), with effect from a date to be appointed.

[93] 2000 c. 11; paragraph 5 of Schedule 5 is amended by section 65 of, and paragraph 9 of Schedule 4 to, the Courts Act 2003 (c. 39), with effect from a date to be appointed.

Criminal Procedure Rules

       (ii) it is not practicable to communicate with any person entitled to grant access to the material or entitled to grant entry to premises to which the application for the warrant relates, or

      (iii) a terrorist investigation may be seriously prejudiced unless a constable can secure immediate access to the material.

  (5) In relation to the premises which the applicant wants to be searched, the application must—

    (a) specify—

      (i) where paragraph (3) applies, the respondent and any premises to which the production order referred, or

      (ii) in any other case, one or more sets of premises, or any premises occupied or controlled by a specified person (which may include one or more specified sets of premises);

    (b) unless paragraph (3) applies, in relation to premises which the applicant wants to be searched but cannot specify, explain why—

      (i) it is necessary to search any premises occupied or controlled by the specified person, and

      (ii) it is not reasonably practicable to specify all the premises which that person occupies or controls which might need to be searched; and

    (c) explain the grounds for believing that material sought is on those premises.

  (6) In relation to any set of premises which the applicant wants to be searched by the officers executing the warrant with other persons authorised by the court, the application must—

    (a) identify those other persons, by function or description; and

    (b) explain why those persons are required.

[Note. Under paragraph 11 of Schedule 5 to the Terrorism Act 2000, where the conditions listed in that paragraph and in paragraph 12 of that Schedule[94] are fulfilled a constable may apply to a Circuit judge for a warrant authorising a search for material consisting of excluded material or special procedure material on specified premises or on the premises of a specified person.

Under section 16(3) of the 1984 Act, entry and search under a warrant must be within 3 months from the date of its issue.

See also the code of practice for the search of premises issued under section 66 of the 1984 Act.

The Practice Direction sets out forms of application and warrant for use in connection with this rule.]

Application for warrant under section 352 of the Proceeds of Crime Act 2002   R47.32

47.32 (1) This rule applies where an applicant wants a Crown Court judge to issue a warrant or warrants under—

    (a) section 352 of the Proceeds of Crime Act 2002[95]; or

    (b) article 13 of the Proceeds of Crime Act 2002 (External Investigations) Order 2014[96].

  (2) As well as complying with rule 47.26, the application must—

    (a) explain whether the investigation is a confiscation investigation, a money laundering investigation, a detained cash investigation, a detained property investigation, a frozen funds investigation or an external investigation;

    (b) in the case of an investigation in the United Kingdom, explain why the applicant suspects that—

      (i) the person under investigation has benefited from criminal conduct, in the case of a confiscation investigation, or committed a money laundering offence, in the case of a money laundering investigation, or

      (ii) in the case of a detained cash investigation, a detained property investigation or a frozen funds investigation, the cash or property involved, or the money held in the frozen account, was obtained through unlawful conduct or is intended to be used in unlawful conduct;

    (c) in the case of an investigation outside the United Kingdom, explain why the applicant believes that—

[94] 2000 c. 11; paragraph 12 of Schedule 5 was amended by Section 26 of the Terrorism Act 2006 (c. 11). It is further amended by section 65 of, and paragraph 9 of Schedule 4 to, the Courts Act 2003 (c. 39), with effect from a date to be appointed.

[95] 2002 c. 29; section 352 was amended by sections 74, 76, 77 and 80 of, and paragraphs 103 and 105 of Schedule 8 and paragraphs 1 and 7 of Schedule 10 to, the Serious Crime Act 2007 (c. 27), section 169 of, and paragraphs 1 and 10 of Schedule 19 to, the Coroners and Justice Act 2009 (c. 25), sections 15, 49 and 55 of, and paragraphs 108 and 137 of Schedule 8, paragraphs 1 and 6 of Schedule 19 and paragraphs 14 and 31 of Schedule 21 to, the Crime and Courts Act 2013 (c. 22), section 224 of, and paragraphs 1 and 12 of Schedule 48 to, the Finance Act 2013 (c. 29), article 3 of, and paragraphs 19 and 26 of Schedule 2 to, SI 2014/834 and section 82 of the Deregulation Act 2015 (c. 20).

[96] S.I. 2014/1893.

(i)   there is an investigation by an overseas authority which relates to a criminal investigation or to criminal proceedings (including proceedings to remove the benefit of a person's criminal conduct following that person's conviction), and

(ii) the investigation is into whether property has been obtained as a result of or in connection with criminal conduct, or into the extent or whereabouts of such property;

(d) indicate what material is sought (and see paragraphs (4) and (5));

(e) specify the premises to be searched (and see paragraph (6)); and

(f) state whether the applicant wants other persons to accompany the officers executing the warrant or warrants (and see paragraph (7)).

(3) Where the applicant relies on an assertion that a production order made under sections 345 and 351 of the 2002 Act[97] or under articles 6 and 12 of the 2014 Order has not been complied with—

(a) the application must—

(i)   identify that order and describe its terms,

(ii) specify the date on which it was served, and

(iii) explain the grounds for believing that the material in respect of which the order was made is on the premises specified in the application for the warrant; but

(b) the application need not comply with paragraphs (4) or (5).

(4) Unless paragraph (3) applies, in relation to the material sought the application must—

(a) specify the material and if that material may be stored in an electronic device or devices—

(i)   so far as practicable, describe each device or kind of device sought, and

(ii) explain the grounds for believing that the material may be stored there;

(b) give a general description of the material and explain the grounds for believing that it relates to the person, cash, property or money under investigation and—

(i)   in the case of a confiscation investigation, relates to the question whether that person has benefited from criminal conduct, or to any question about the extent or whereabouts of that benefit,

(ii) in the case of a money laundering investigation, relates to the question whether that person has committed a money laundering offence,

(iii) in the case of a detained cash investigation, a detained property investigation or a frozen funds investigation into the derivation of cash, property or money, relates to the question whether that cash, property or money is recoverable property,

(iv) in the case of a detained cash investigation, a detained property investigation or a frozen funds investigation into the intended use of cash, property or money, relates to the question whether that cash, property or money is intended by any person to be used in unlawful conduct, or

(v)   in the case of an investigation outside the United Kingdom, relates to that investigation.

(5) Unless paragraph (3) applies, in relation to the material sought the application must explain also the grounds for believing that—

(a) the material consists of or includes special procedure material but does not include excluded material or privileged material;

(b) the material is likely to be of substantial value to the investigation (whether by itself, or together with other material); and

(c) it is in the public interest for the material to be obtained, having regard to—

(i)   other potential sources of information, and

(ii) the benefit likely to accrue to the investigation if the material is obtained.

(6) In relation to the premises which the applicant wants to be searched, unless paragraph (3) applies the application must—

(a) explain the grounds for believing that material sought is on those premises;

(b) if the application specifies the material sought, explain the grounds for believing that it is not appropriate to make a production order under sections 345 and 351 of the 2002 Act or under articles 6 and 12 of the 2014 Order because—

(i)   it is not practicable to communicate with any person against whom the production order could be made,

---

[97] 2002 c. 29; section 345 was amended by section 75 of the Serious Crime Act 2007 (c. 27), section 169 of, and paragraphs 1 and 6 of Schedule 19 to, the Coroners and Justice Act 2009 (c. 25) and section 49 of, and paragraphs 1 and 4 of Schedule 19 to, the Crime and Courts Act 2013 (c. 22). Section 351 was amended by sections 74 and 77 of, and paragraphs 103 and 104 of Schedule 8 and paragraphs 1 and 6 of Schedule 10 to, the Serious Crime Act 2007 (c. 27), section 169 of, and paragraphs 1 and 9 of Schedule 19 to, the Coroners and Justice Act 2009 (c. 25), sections 66 and 112 of, and Part 5 of Schedule 8 to, the Policing and Crime Act 2009 (c. 26), sections 15 and 55 of, and paragraphs 108 and 136 of Schedule 8 and paragraphs 14 and 30 of Schedule 21 to, the Crime and Courts Act 2013 (c.22) and section 224 of, and paragraphs 1 and 11 of Schedule 48 to, the Finance Act 2013 (c. 29).

          (ii) it is not practicable to communicate with any person who would be required to comply with an order to grant entry to the premises, or

         (iii) the investigation might be seriously prejudiced unless an appropriate person is able to secure immediate access to the material; and

    (c) if the application gives a general description of the material sought, explain the grounds for believing that—

         (i) it is not practicable to communicate with any person entitled to grant entry to the premises,

         (ii) entry to the premises will not be granted unless a warrant is produced, or

         (iii) the investigation might be seriously prejudiced unless an appropriate person arriving at the premises is able to secure immediate access to them.

(7) In relation to any set of premises which the applicant wants to be searched by those executing the warrant with other persons authorised by the court, the application must—

    (a) identify those other persons, by function or description; and

    (b) explain why those persons are required.

[Note. Under section 352 of the Proceeds of Crime Act 2002 where there is a confiscation investigation, a money laundering investigation, a detained cash investigation, a detained property investigation or a frozen funds investigation, an 'appropriate officer' within the meaning of that section may apply to a Crown Court judge for a warrant authorising a search for special procedure material on specified premises, on the conditions listed in that section and in section 353 of the Act[98].

Under article 13 of the Proceeds of Crime Act 2002 (External Investigations) Order 2014, where there is an external investigation an 'appropriate officer' within the meaning of that article may apply to a Crown Court judge for a warrant authorising a search for special procedure material on specified premises, on the conditions listed in that article and in article 14 of the Order.

Under section 16(3) of the 1984 Act[99], as applied by article 3 of the Proceeds of Crime Act 2002 (Application of Police and Criminal Evidence Act 1984) Order 2015[100], entry and search under a warrant must be within 3 months from the date of its issue.

See also the code of practice for the search of premises issued under section 66 of the 1984 Act.

The Practice Direction sets out forms of application and warrant for use in connection with this rule.]

Application for warrant under section 160 of the Extradition Act 2003

R47.33

47.33 (1) This rule applies where an applicant wants a Circuit judge to issue a warrant or warrants under section 160 of the Extradition Act 2003[101].

(2) As well as complying with rule 47.26, the application must—

    (a) identify the person whose extradition is sought (and see paragraph (3));

    (b) specify the extradition offence of which that person is accused;

    (c) specify the material, or description of material, sought (and see paragraph (4)); and

    (d) specify the premises to be searched (and see paragraph (5)).

(3) In relation to the person whose extradition is sought, the application must explain the grounds for believing that—

    (a) that person has committed the offence for which extradition is sought;

    (b) that offence is an extradition offence; and

    (c) that person is in the United Kingdom or is on the way to the United Kingdom.

(4) In relation to the material sought, the application must—

    (a) explain the grounds for believing that—

         (i) the material consists of or includes special procedure or excluded material, and

         (ii) the material would be likely to be admissible evidence at a trial in England and Wales for the offence for which extradition is sought; and

    (b) if that material may be stored in an electronic device or devices—

         (i) so far as practicable, describe each device or kind of device sought, and

         (ii) explain the grounds for believing that the material may be stored there.

---

[98] 2002 c. 29; section 353 was amended by sections 74, 76, 77 and 80 of, and paragraphs 103 and 106 of Schedule 8 and paragraphs 1 and 8 of Schedule 10 to, the Serious Crime Act 2007 (c. 27), section 169 of, and paragraphs 1 and 11 of Schedule 19 to, the Coroners and Justice Act 2009 (c. 25), sections 15, 49 and 55 of, and paragraphs 108 and 138 of Schedule 8, paragraphs 1 and 7 of Schedule 19 and paragraphs 14 and 32 of Schedule 21 to, the Crime and Courts Act 2013 (c. 22), section 224 of, and paragraphs 1 and 13 of Schedule 48 to, the Finance Act 2013 (c. 29) and section 38 of the Serious Crime Act 2015 (c. 9) and paragraph 48 of Schedule 5 to the Criminal Finances Act 2017 (c. 22).

[99] 1984 c. 60; section 16(3) was amended by section 114 of the Serious Organised Crime and Police Act 2005 (c. 15).

[100] S.I. 2015/759.

[101] 2003 c. 41; section 160 was amended by section 174 of the Anti-social Behaviour, Crime and Policing Act 2014 (c. 12).

(5) In relation to the premises which the applicant wants to search, the application must explain the grounds for believing that—

(a) material sought is on those premises; and

(b) one or more of the following conditions is satisfied, namely—

   (i) it is not practicable to communicate with any person entitled to grant entry to the premises,

   (ii) it is practicable to communicate with such a person but it is not practicable to communicate with any person entitled to grant access to the material sought, or

   (iii) the material contains information which is subject to a restriction on disclosure or an obligation of secrecy contained in an enactment and is likely to be disclosed in breach of the restriction or obligation if a warrant is not issued.

(6) In relation to any set of premises which the applicant wants to be searched by the officers executing the warrant with other persons authorised by the court, the application must—

(a) identify those other persons, by function or description; and

(b) explain why those persons are required.

[Note. Under section 160 of the Extradition Act 2003, where a person's extradition is sought a constable may apply to a Circuit judge for a warrant authorising a search for special procedure material or excluded material on specified premises, on the conditions listed in that section.

Under section 16(3) of the 1984 Act, entry and search under a warrant must be within 3 months from the date of its issue.

See also the code of practice for the search of premises issued under section 66 of the 1984 Act.]

R47.34   **Application for warrant under any other power**

47.34 (1) This rule applies—

(a) where an applicant wants a court to issue a warrant or warrants under a power (in this rule, 'the relevant search power') to which rule 47.24(d) (other powers) refers; but

(b) subject to any inconsistent provision in legislation that applies to the relevant search power.

(2) As well as complying with rule 47.26, the application must—

(a) demonstrate the applicant's entitlement to apply;

(b) identify the relevant search power (and see paragraph (3));

(c) so far as practicable, identify the articles or persons sought (see also paragraph (4)) and if such an article may be stored in an electronic device or devices—

   (i) so far as practicable, describe each device or kind of device sought, and

   (ii) explain the grounds for believing that the article may be stored there;

(d) specify the premises to be searched (and see paragraphs (5) and (6));

(e) state whether the applicant wants the premises to be searched on more than one occasion, if the relevant search power allows (and see paragraph (7)); and

(f) state whether the applicant wants other persons to accompany the officers executing the warrant or warrants, if the relevant search power allows (and see paragraph (8)).

(3) The application must—

(a) include or attach the terms of the relevant search power; and

(b) explain how the circumstances satisfy the criteria prescribed by that power for making the application.

(4) In relation to the articles or persons sought, the application must explain how they satisfy the criteria prescribed by the relevant search power about such articles or persons.

(5) In relation to premises which the applicant wants to be searched and can specify, the application must—

(a) specify each set of premises; and

(b) in respect of each, explain how the circumstances satisfy any criteria prescribed by the relevant search power—

   (i) for asserting that the articles or persons sought are on those premises, and

   (ii) for asserting that the court can exercise its power to authorise the search of those particular premises.

(6) In relation to premises which the applicant wants to be searched but at least some of which the applicant cannot specify, the application must—

(a) explain how the relevant search power allows the court to authorise such searching;

(b) specify the person who occupies or controls such premises;

(c) specify as many sets of such premises as is reasonably practicable;

(d) explain why—

   (i) it is necessary to search more premises than those specified, and

   (ii) it is not reasonably practicable to specify all the premises which the applicant wants to be searched;

(e)   in respect of each set of premises, whether specified or not, explain how the circumstances satisfy any criteria prescribed by the relevant search power for asserting that the articles or persons sought are on those premises; and

(f)   in respect of each specified set of premises, explain how the circumstances satisfy any criteria prescribed by the relevant search power for asserting that the court can exercise its power to authorise the search of those premises.

(7)   In relation to any set of premises which the applicant wants to be searched on more than one occasion, the application must—

(a)   explain how the relevant search power allows the court to authorise such searching;

(b)   explain why the applicant wants the premises to be searched more than once; and

(c)   specify any proposed maximum number of occasions.

(8)   In relation to any set of premises which the applicant wants to be searched by the officers executing the warrant with other persons authorised by the court, the application must—

(a)   identify those other persons, by function or description; and

(b)   explain why those persons are required.

[Note. See, among other provisions, sections 15 and 16 of the Police and Criminal Evidence Act 1984[102], which apply to an application by a constable under any Act for a warrant authorising the search of specified premises, or the search of premises of a specified person, and to the execution of such a warrant. Unless other legislation otherwise provides, under section 16(3) of the 1984 Act entry and search under a warrant must be within 3 months from the date of its issue.

The Practice Direction sets out forms of application and warrant for use in connection with this rule.]

Section 4: orders for their retention or return of property

When this Section applies   R47.35

47.35 (1)   This Section applies where—

(a)   under section 1 of the Police (Property) Act 1897[103], a magistrates' court can—

(i)   order the return to the owner of property which has come into the possession of the police or the National Crime Agency in connection with an investigation of a suspected offence, or

(ii)   make such order with respect to such property as the court thinks just, where the owner cannot be ascertained; and

(b)   a Crown Court judge can—

(i)   order the return of seized property under section 59(4) of the Criminal Justice and Police Act 2001[104], or

(ii)   order the examination, retention, separation or return of seized property under section 59(5) of the Act.

(2)   In this Section, a reference to a person with 'a relevant interest' in seized property means someone from whom the property was seized, or someone with a proprietary interest in the property, or someone who had custody or control of it immediately before it was seized.

Exercise of court's powers   R47.36

47.36 (1)   The court may determine an application for an order—

(a)   at a hearing (which must be in private unless the court otherwise directs), or without a hearing; and

(b)   in a party's absence, if that party—

(i)   applied for the order, or

(ii)   has had at least 10 business days in which to make representations.

(2)   The court officer must arrange for the court to hear such an application no sooner than 10 business days after it was served, unless—

(a)   the court directs that no hearing need be arranged; or

(b)   the court gives other directions for the hearing.

(3)   If the court so directs, the parties to an application may attend a hearing by live link.

---

[102]   1984 c. 60; section 15 was amended by sections 113 and 114 of the Serious Organised Crime and Police Act 2005 (c. 15) and article 7 of S.I. 2005/3496. Section 16 was amended by paragraph 281 of Schedule 8 to the Courts Act 2003 (c. 39), section 2 of the Criminal Justice Act 2003 (c. 44), sections 113 and 114 of the Serious Organised Crime and Police Act 2005 (c. 15) and article 8 of S.I. 2005/3496.

[103]   1897 c. 30; section 1 was amended by sections 33 and 36 of, and Part III of Schedule 3 to, the Theft Act 1968 (c. 60), section 58 of the Criminal Justice Act 1972 (c. 71), section 192 of, and Part I of Schedule 5 to, the Consumer Credit Act 1974 (c. 39), the Statute Law (Repeals) Act 1989 (c. 43) and section 4 of the Police (Property) Act 1997 (c. 30).

[104]   2001 c. 16.

(4) The court may—

    (a) shorten or extend (even after it has expired) a time limit under this Section;

    (b) dispense with a requirement for service under this Section (even after service was required); and

    (c) consider an application made orally instead of in writing.

(5) A person who wants an extension of time must—

    (a) apply when serving the application or representations for which it is needed; and

    (b) explain the delay.

R47.37 Application for an order under section 1 of the Police (Property) Act 1897

47.37 (1) This rule applies where an applicant wants the court to make an order to which rule 47.35(1)(a) refers.

(2) The applicant must apply in writing and serve the application on—

    (a) the court officer; and

    (b) as appropriate—

        (i) the officer who has the property,

        (ii) any person who appears to be its owner.

(3) The application must—

    (a) explain the applicant's interest in the property (either as a person who claims to be its owner or as an officer into whose possession the property has come);

    (b) specify the direction that the applicant wants the court to make, and explain why; and

    (c) include or attach a list of those on whom the applicant has served the application.

[Note. Under section 1 of the Police (Property) Act 1897, the owner of property which has come into the possession of the police or the National Crime Agency in connection with the investigation of a suspected offence can apply to a magistrates' court for an order for its delivery to the claimant.]

R47.38 Application for an order under section 59 of the Criminal Justice and Police Act 2001

47.38 (1) This rule applies where an applicant wants the court to make an order to which rule 47.35(1)(b) refers.

(2) The applicant must apply in writing and serve the application on—

    (a) the court officer; and

    (b) as appropriate—

        (i) the person who for the time being has the seized property,

        (ii) each person whom the applicant knows or believes to have a relevant interest in the property.

(3) In each case, the application must—

    (a) explain the applicant's interest in the property (either as a person with a relevant interest, or as possessor of the property in consequence of its seizure, as appropriate);

    (b) explain the circumstances of the seizure of the property and identify the power that was exercised to seize it (or which the person seizing it purported to exercise, as appropriate); and

    (c) include or attach a list of those on whom the applicant has served the application.

(4) On an application for an order for the return of property under section 59(4) of the Criminal Justice and Police Act 2001, the application must explain why any one or more of these applies—

    (a) there was no power to make the seizure;

    (b) the property seized is, or contains, an item subject to legal privilege which is not an item that can be retained lawfully in the circumstances listed in section 54(2) of the Act[105];

    (c) the property seized is, or contains, excluded or special procedure material which is not material that can be retained lawfully in the circumstances listed in sections 55 and 56 of the Act; or

    (d) the property seized is, or contains, something taken from premises under section 50 of the Act, or from a person under section 51 of the Act, in the circumstances listed in those sections and which cannot lawfully be retained on the conditions listed in the Act.

(5) On an application for an order for the examination, retention, separation or return of property under section 59(5) of the 2001 Act, the application must—

    (a) specify the direction that the applicant wants the court to make, and explain why;

---

[105] 2001 c. 16; section 55 was amended by sections 456 and 457 of, and paragraphs 1 and 40 of Schedule 11 and Schedule 12 to, the Proceeds of Crime Act 2002 (c. 29). Section 56 was amended by article 364 of SI 2001/3649, section 12 of, and paragraph 14 of Schedule 1 to, the Criminal Justice Act 2003 (c. 44) and article 2 of, and paragraph 189 of Schedule 1 to, S.I. 2009/1941.

(b) if applicable, specify each requirement of section 53(2) of the Act (examination and return of property) which is not being complied with; and

(c) if applicable, explain why the retention of the property by the person who now has it would be justified on the grounds that, even if it were returned, it would immediately become appropriate for that person to get it back under—

(i) a warrant for its seizure, or

(ii) a production order made under paragraph 4 of Schedule 1 to the Police and Criminal Evidence Act 1984[106], section 20BA of the Taxes Management Act 1970[107] or paragraph 5 of Schedule 5 to the Terrorism Act 2000[108].

[Note. Under section 59 of the Criminal Justice and Police Act 2001, a person with a 'relevant interest' (see rule 47.35(2)) in seized property can apply in the circumstances listed in the Act to a Crown Court judge for an order for its return. A person who has the property in consequence of its seizure can apply for an order authorising its retention. Either can apply for an order relating to the examination of the property.]

Application containing information withheld from another party   **R47.39**

47.39 (1) This rule applies where—

(a) an applicant serves an application to which rule 47.37 (Application for an order under section 1 of the Police (Property) Act 1897) or rule 47.38 (Application for an order under section 59 of the Criminal Justice and Police Act 2001) applies; and

(b) the application includes information that the applicant thinks ought not be revealed to another party.

(2) The applicant must—

(a) omit that information from the part of the application that is served on that other party;

(b) mark the other part to show that, unless the court otherwise directs, it is only for the court; and

(c) in that other part, explain why the applicant has withheld that information from that other party.

(3) If the court so directs, any hearing of an application to which this rule applies may be, wholly or in part, in the absence of a party from whom information has been withheld.

(4) At any hearing of an application to which this rule applies—

(a) the general rule is that the court must consider, in the following sequence—

(i) representations first by the applicant and then by each other party, in all the parties' presence, and then

(ii) further representations by the applicant, in the absence of a party from whom information has been withheld; but

(b) the court may direct other arrangements for the hearing.

Representations in response   **R47.40**

47.40 (1) This rule applies where a person wants to make representations about an application under rule 47.37 or rule 47.38.

(2) Such a person must—

(a) serve the representations on—

(i) the court officer, and

(ii) the applicant and any other party to the application;

(b) do so not more than 10 business days after service of the application; and

(c) ask for a hearing, if that person wants one.

(3) Representations in opposition to an application must explain why the grounds on which the applicant relies are not met.

(4) Where representations include information that the person making them thinks ought not be revealed to another party, that person must—

(a) omit that information from the representations served on that other party;

(b) mark the information to show that, unless the court otherwise directs, it is only for the court; and

(c) with that information include an explanation of why it has been withheld from that other party.

---

[106] 1984 c. 60; paragraph 4 of Schedule 1 was amended by section 65 of, and paragraph 6 of Schedule 4 to, the Courts Act 2003 (c. 39).

[107] 1970 c. 9; section 20BA was inserted by section 149 of the Finance Act 2000 (c. 17).

[108] 2000 c. 11; paragraph 5 of Schedule 5 is amended by section 65 of, and paragraph 9 of Schedule 4 to, the Courts Act 2003 (c. 39), with effect from a date to be appointed.

R47.41 **Application to punish for contempt of court**

47.41 (1) This rule applies where a person is accused of disobeying an order under section 59 of the Criminal Justice and Police Act 2001.

(2) A person who wants the court to exercise its power to punish that person for contempt of court must comply with the rules in Part 48 (Contempt of court).

[Note. A Crown Court judge has power to punish a person who disobeys an order under section 59 of the 2001 Act as if that were a contempt of the Crown Court: see section 59(9) of the Act.]

Section 5: orders for the retention of fingerprints, etc.

R47.42 **When this Section applies**

47.42 This Section applies where—

(a) a District Judge (Magistrates' Court) can make an order under—

  (i) section 63F(7) or 63R(6) of the Police and Criminal Evidence Act 1984[109], or

  (ii) paragraph 20B(5) or 20G(6) of Schedule 8 to the Terrorism Act 2000[110]; and

(b) the Crown Court can determine an appeal under—

  (i) section 63F(10) of the Police and Criminal Evidence Act 1984, or

  (ii) paragraph 20B(8) of Schedule 8 to the Terrorism Act 2000.

[Note. Under the Police and Criminal Evidence Act 1984 or under the Terrorism Act 2000, an order may be made extending the period during which fingerprints, DNA profiles or samples may be retained by the police.]

R47.43 **Exercise of court's powers**

47.43 (1) The court must determine an application under rule 47.44, and an appeal under rule 47.45—

(a) at a hearing, which must be in private unless the court otherwise directs; and

(b) in the presence of the applicant or appellant.

(2) The court must not determine such an application or appeal unless any person served under those rules—

(a) is present; or

(b) has had an opportunity—

  (i) to attend, or

  (ii) to make representations.

R47.44 **Application to extend retention period**

47.44 (1) This rule applies where a magistrates' court can make an order extending the period for which there may be retained material consisting of—

(a) fingerprints taken from a person—

  (i) under a power conferred by Part V of the Police and Criminal Evidence Act 1984[111],

  (ii) with that person's consent, in connection with the investigation of an offence by the police, or

  (iii) under a power conferred by Schedule 8 to the Terrorism Act 2000[112] in relation to a person detained under section 41 of that Act;

(b) a DNA profile derived from a DNA sample so taken; or

(c) a sample so taken.

(2) A chief officer of police who wants the court to make such an order must—

(a) apply in writing—

  (i) within the period of 3 months ending on the last day of the retention period, where the application relates to fingerprints or a DNA profile, or

  (ii) before the expiry of the retention period, where the application relates to a sample;

(b) in the application—

  (i) identify the material,

  (ii) state when the retention period expires,

  (iii) give details of any previous such application relating to the material, and

  (iv) outline the circumstances in which the material was acquired;

(c) serve the application on the court officer, in every case; and

---

[109] 1984 c. 60; section 63D was inserted by section 1 of the Protection of Freedoms Act 2012 (c. 9). Section 63R was inserted by section 14 of that Act.

[110] 2000 c. 11; paragraph 20B of Schedule 8 was inserted by section 19 of, and paragraph 1 of Schedule 1 to, the Protection of Freedoms Act 2012 (c. 9) (for certain purposes, and for remaining purposes with effect from a date to be appointed) and amended by section 181 of, and paragraph 125 of Schedule 11 to, the Anti-social Behaviour, Crime and Policing Act 2014 (c. 12). Paragraph 20G of Schedule 8 was inserted by section 19 of, and paragraph 1 of Schedule 1 to, the Protection of Freedoms Act 2012 (c. 9) for certain purposes, and for remaining purposes with effect from a date to be appointed.

[111] 1984 c. 60.

[112] 2000 c. 11.

     (d) serve the application on the person from whom the material was taken, where—
        (i)   the application relates to fingerprints or a DNA profile, or
        (ii) the application is for the renewal of an order extending the retention period for a sample.

(3) An application to extend the retention period for fingerprints or a DNA profile must explain why that period should be extended.

(4) An application to extend the retention period for a sample must explain why, having regard to the nature and complexity of other material that is evidence in relation to the offence, the sample is likely to be needed in any proceedings for the offence for the purposes of—
     (a) disclosure to, or use by, a defendant; or
     (b) responding to any challenge by a defendant in respect of the admissibility of material that is evidence on which the prosecution proposes to rely.

(5) On an application to extend the retention period for fingerprints or a DNA profile, the applicant must serve notice of the court's decision on any respondent where—
     (a) the court makes the order sought; and
     (b) the respondent was absent when it was made.

[Note. See rule 47.42(a). The powers to which rule 47.44 applies may be exercised only by a District Judge (Magistrates' Courts).

The time limits for making an application under this rule are prescribed by sections 63F(8) and 63R(8) of the Police and Criminal Evidence Act 1984[113], and by paragraphs 20B(6) and 20G(8) of Schedule 8 to the Terrorism Act 2000[114]. They may be neither extended nor shortened.

Sections 63D and 63R of the 1984 Act[115], and paragraphs 20A and 20G of Schedule 8 to the 2000 Act[116], provide for the circumstances in which there must be destroyed the material to which this rule applies.

Section 63F of the 1984 Act, and paragraph 20B of Schedule 8 to the 2000 Act, provide for the circumstances in which fingerprints and DNA profiles may be retained instead of being destroyed. Under section 63F(7) and paragraph 20B(5), a chief officer of police to whom those provisions apply may apply for an order extending the statutory retention period of 3 years by up to another 2 years.

Section 63R of the 1984 Act and paragraph 20G of Schedule 8 to the 2000 Act provide for the circumstances in which samples taken from a person may be retained instead of being destroyed. Under section 63R(6) of the 1984 Act and paragraph 20G(6) of Schedule 8 to the 2000 Act, a chief officer of police to whom those provisions apply may apply for an order to retain a sample for up to 12 months after the date on which it would otherwise have to be destroyed. Under section 63R(9) and paragraph 20G(9), such an order may be renewed, on one or more occasions, for a further period of not more than 12 months from the end of the period when the order would otherwise cease to have effect.]

Appeal   R47.45

47.45 (1) This rule applies where, under rule 47.44, a magistrates' court determines an application relating to fingerprints or a DNA profile and—
     (a) the person from whom the material was taken wants to appeal to the Crown Court against an order extending the retention period; or
     (b) a chief officer of police wants to appeal to the Crown Court against a refusal to make such an order.

(2) The appellant must—
     (a) serve an appeal notice—
        (i)   on the Crown Court officer and on the other party, and
        (ii) not more than 15 business days after the magistrates' court's decision, or, if applicable, service of notice under rule 47.44(5); and
     (b) in the appeal notice, explain, as appropriate, why the retention period should, or should not, be extended.

(3) Rule 34.11 (Constitution of the Crown Court) applies on such an appeal.

---

[113] 1984 c. 60; section 63F was inserted by section 3 of the Protection of Freedoms Act 2012 (c. 9). Section 63R was inserted by section 14 of that Act.
[114] 2000 c. 11; paragraph 20B of Schedule 8 was inserted by section 19 of, and paragraph 1 of Schedule 1 to, the Protection of Freedoms Act 2012 (c. 9) (for certain purposes, and for remaining purposes with effect from a date to be appointed) and amended by section 181 of, and paragraph 125 of Schedule 11 to, the Anti-social Behaviour, Crime and Policing Act 2014 (c. 12). Paragraph 20G of Schedule 8 was inserted by section 19 of, and paragraph 1 of Schedule 1 to, the Protection of Freedoms Act 2012 (c. 9) for certain purposes, and for remaining purposes with effect from a date to be appointed.
[115] 1984 c. 60; section 63D was inserted by section 1 of the Protection of Freedoms Act 2012 (c. 9).
[116] 2000 c. 11; paragraph 20A of Schedule 8 was inserted by section 19 of, and paragraph 1 of Schedule 1 to, the Protection of Freedoms Act 2012 (c. 9) for certain purposes, and for remaining purposes with effect from a date to be appointed.

[Note. Under section 63F(10) of the Police and Criminal Evidence Act 1984, and under paragraph 20B(8) of Schedule 8 to the Terrorism Act 2000, the person from whom fingerprints were taken, or from whom a DNA profile derives, may appeal to the Crown Court against an order extending the retention period; and a chief officer of police may appeal to the Crown Court against the refusal of such an order.]

Section 6: investigation anonymity orders under the Coroners and Justice Act 2009

R47.46   **When this Section applies**

47.46 This Section applies where—
    (a) a justice of the peace can make or discharge an investigation anonymity order, under sections 76 and 80(1) of the Coroners and Justice Act 2009[117]; and
    (b) a Crown Court judge can determine an appeal against—
        (i) a refusal of such an order, under section 79 of the 2009 Act, or
        (ii) a decision on an application to discharge such an order, under section 80(6) of the 2009 Act.

[Note. Under the Coroners and Justice Act 2009, an investigation anonymity order may be made prohibiting the disclosure of information that identifies, or might identify, a specified person as someone who is, or was, willing to assist the investigation of an offence of murder or manslaughter caused by a gun or knife.]

R47.47   **Exercise of court's powers**

47.47 (1) The court may determine an application for an investigation anonymity order, and any appeal against the refusal of such an order—
    (a) at a hearing (which must be in private unless the court otherwise directs); or
    (b) without a hearing.
(2) The court must determine an application to discharge an investigation anonymity order, and any appeal against the decision on such an application—
    (a) at a hearing (which must be in private unless the court otherwise directs); and
    (b) in the presence of the person specified in the order, unless—
        (i) that person applied for the discharge of the order,
        (ii) that person has had an opportunity to make representations, or
        (iii) the court is satisfied that it is not reasonably practicable to communicate with that person.
(3) The court may consider an application or an appeal made orally instead of in writing.

R47.48   **Application for an investigation anonymity order**

47.48 (1) This rule applies where an applicant wants a magistrates' court to make an investigation anonymity order.
(2) The applicant must—
    (a) apply in writing;
    (b) serve the application on the court officer;
    (c) identify the person to be specified in the order, unless—
        (i) the applicant wants the court to determine the application at a hearing, or
        (ii) the court otherwise directs;
    (d) explain how the proposed order meets the conditions prescribed by section 78 of the Coroners and Justice Act 2009[118];
    (e) say if the applicant intends to appeal should the court refuse the order;
    (f) attach any material on which the applicant relies; and
    (g) propose the terms of the order.
(3) At any hearing of the application, the applicant must—
    (a) identify to the court the person to be specified in the order, unless—
        (i) the applicant has done so already, or
        (ii) the court otherwise directs; and
    (b) unless the applicant has done so already, inform the court if the applicant intends to appeal should the court refuse the order.

[Note. See section 77 of the Coroners and Justice Act 2009.]

R47.49   **Application to discharge an investigation anonymity order**

47.49 (1) This rule applies where one of the following wants a magistrates' court to discharge an investigation anonymity order—
    (a) an applicant; or
    (b) the person specified in the order.

[117] 2009 c. 25.
[118] 2009 c. 25.

(2) That applicant or the specified person must—
- (a) apply in writing as soon as practicable after becoming aware of the grounds for doing so;
- (b) serve the application on—
  - (i) the court officer, and as applicable
  - (ii) the applicant for the order, and
  - (iii) the specified person;
- (c) explain—
  - (i) what material circumstances have changed since the order was made, or since any previous application was made to discharge it, and
  - (ii) why it is appropriate for the order to be discharged; and
- (d) attach—
  - (i) a copy of the order, and
  - (ii) any material on which the applicant relies.

(3) A party must inform the court if that party intends to appeal should the court discharge the order.

[Note. See section 80 of the Coroners and Justice Act 2009.]

Appeal   **R47.50**

47.50 (1) This rule applies where one of the following ('the appellant') wants to appeal to the Crown Court—
- (a) the applicant for an investigation anonymity order, where a magistrates' court has refused to make the order; or
- (b) a party to an application to discharge such an order, where a magistrates' court has decided that application.

(2) The appellant must—
- (a) serve on the Crown Court officer a copy of the application to the magistrates' court; and
- (b) where the appeal concerns a discharge decision, notify each other party,

not more than 15 business days after the decision against which the appellant wants to appeal.

(3) The Crown Court must hear the appeal without justices of the peace.

[Note. See sections 79 and 80(6) of the Coroners and Justice Act 2009, and section 74 of the Senior Courts Act 1981[119].]

Section 7: investigation approval orders under the Regulation of Investigatory Powers Act 2000

When this Section applies   **R47.51**

47.51 This Section applies where a justice of the peace can make an order approving—
- (a) the grant or renewal of an authorisation, or the giving or renewal of a notice, under section 23A of the Regulation of Investigatory Powers Act 2000[120]; and
- (b) the grant or renewal of an authorisation under section 32A of the 2000 Act[121].

[Note. Under the Regulation of Investigatory Powers Act 2000, an order may be made approving a local authority officer's authorisation for the obtaining of information about the use of postal or telecommunications services, or for the use of surveillance or of a 'covert human intelligence source'.]

Exercise of court's powers   **R47.52**

47.52 (1) Rule 47.5 (Investigation orders; Exercise of court's powers) applies, subject to sections 23B(2) and 32B(2) of the Regulation of Investigatory Powers Act 2000[122].

(2) Where a magistrates' court refuses to approve the grant, giving or renewal of an authorisation or notice, the court must not exercise its power to quash that authorisation or notice unless the applicant has had at least 2 business days from the date of the refusal in which to make representations.

[Note. Under sections 23B(2) and 32B(2) of the Regulation of Investigatory Powers Act 2000, the applicant is not required to give notice of an application to any person to whom the authorisation or notice relates, or to such a person's legal representatives. See also sections 23B(3) and 32B(3) of the 2000 Act.]

---

[119] 1981 c. 54; section 74 was amended by sections 79 and 106 of, and Table (4) of Part V of Schedule 15 to, the Access to Justice Act 1999 (c. 22), article 3 of, and paragraphs 11 and 12 of the Schedule to S.I. 2004/2035 and section 15 of, and paragraphs 114 and 133 of Schedule 4 to, the Constitutional Reform Act 2005 (c. 4). The Act's title was amended by section 59(5) of, and paragraph 1 of Schedule 11 to, the Constitutional Reform Act 2005 (c. 4).

[120] 2000 c. 23; section 23A was inserted by section 37 of the Protection of Freedoms Act 2012 (c. 9).

[121] 2000 c. 23; section 32A was inserted by section 38 of the Protection of Freedoms Act 2012 (c. 9).

[122] 2000 c. 23; section 23B was inserted by section 37 and section 32B by section 38 of the Protection of Freedoms Act 2012 (c. 9).

R47.53   **Application for approval for authorisation or notice**

47.53 (1) This rule applies where an applicant wants a magistrates' court to make an order approving—

    (a) under sections 23A and 23B of the Regulation of Investigatory Powers Act 2000[123] —

        (i) an authorisation to obtain or disclose communications data, under section 22(3) of the 2000 Act[124], or

        (ii) a notice that requires a postal or telecommunications operator if need be to obtain, and in any case to disclose, communications data, under section 22(4) of the 2000 Act; or

    (b) under sections 32A and 32B of the Regulation of Investigatory Powers Act 2000[125], an authorisation for—

        (i) the carrying out of directed surveillance, under section 28 of the 2000 Act, or

        (ii) the conduct or use of a covert human intelligence source, under section 29 of the 2000 Act[126].

(2) The applicant must—

    (a) apply in writing and serve the application on the court officer;

    (b) attach the authorisation or notice which the applicant wants the court to approve;

    (c) attach such other material (if any) on which the applicant relies to satisfy the court—

        (i) as required by section 23A(3) and (4) of the 2000 Act, in relation to communications data,

        (ii) as required by section 32A(3) and (4) of the 2000 Act, in relation to directed surveillance, or

        (iii) as required by section 32A(5) and (6), and, if relevant, section 43(6A), of the 2000 Act[127], in relation to a covert human intelligence source; and

    (d) propose the terms of the order.

[Note. See also rule 47.5, under which the court may—

    (a) exercise its powers in the parties' absence; and

    (b) consider an application made orally.

Under section 23A(3) to (5) of the Regulation of Investigatory Powers Act 2000, on an application for an order approving an authorisation or notice concerning communications data (as defined in section 21 of the Act[128]), the court must be satisfied that—

    (a) the person who granted or renewed the authorisation, or who gave or renewed the notice, was entitled to do so;

    (b) the grant, giving or renewal met any prescribed restrictions or conditions;

    (c) at the time the authorisation or notice was granted, given or renewed, as the case may be, there were reasonable grounds for believing that to obtain or disclose the data described in the authorisation or notice was—

        (i) necessary, for the purpose of preventing or detecting crime or preventing disorder, and

        (ii) proportionate to what was sought to be achieved by doing so; and

    (d) there remain reasonable grounds for believing those things, at the time the court considers the application.

The Regulation of Investigatory Powers (Communications Data) Order 2010[129] specifies the persons who are entitled to grant, give or renew an authorisation or notice concerning such data, and for what purpose each may do so.

Under section 32A(3) and (4) of the Regulation of Investigatory Powers Act 2000, on an application for an order approving an authorisation concerning directed surveillance (as defined in section 26 of the Act[130]), the court must be satisfied that—

    (a) the person who granted the authorisation was entitled to do so;

[123] 2000 c. 23; sections 23A and 23B were inserted by section 37 of the Protection of Freedoms Act 2012 (c. 9).

[124] 2000 c. 23; section 22 was amended by section 112 of, and paragraphs 12 and 13 of Schedule 7 to, the Policing and Crime Act 2009 (c. 26).

[125] 2000 c. 23; sections 32A and 32B were inserted by section 38 of the Protection of Freedoms Act 2012 (c. 9).

[126] 2000 c. 23; section 29 was amended by section 8 of the Policing and Crime Act 2009 (c. 26).

[127] 2000 c. 23; section 43(6A) was inserted by section 38 of the Protection of Freedoms Act 2012 (c. 9).

[128] 2000 c. 23; section 21 was amended by section 88 of, and paragraphs 5 and 7 of Schedule 12 to, the Serious Crime Act 2007 (c. 27).

[129] S.I. 2010/480.

[130] 2000 c. 23; section 26 was amended by section 406 of, and paragraph 161 of Schedule 17 to, the Communications Act 2003 (c. 21).

(b) the grant met any prescribed restrictions or conditions;

(c) at the time the authorisation was granted there were reasonable grounds for believing that the surveillance described in the authorisation was—

(i) necessary, for the purpose of preventing or detecting crime or preventing disorder, and

(ii) proportionate to what was sought to be achieved by it; and

(d) there remain reasonable grounds for believing those things, at the time the court considers the application.

Under section 32A(5) and (6) of the Regulation of Investigatory Powers Act 2000, on an application for an order approving an authorisation of the conduct or use of a covert human intelligence source (as defined in section 26 of the Act), the court must be satisfied that—

(a) the person who granted the authorisation was entitled to do so;

(b) the grant met any prescribed restrictions or conditions;

(c) at the time the authorisation was granted there were reasonable grounds for believing that the conduct or use of a covert human intelligence source described in the authorisation was—

(i) necessary, for the purpose of preventing or detecting crime or preventing disorder, and

(ii) proportionate to what was sought to be achieved by it; and

(d) there remain reasonable grounds for believing those things, at the time the court considers the application.

Under section 43(6A) of the 2000 Act, on an application to approve the renewal of such an authorisation the court in addition must—

(a) be satisfied that, since the grant or latest renewal of the authorisation, a review has been carried out of the use made of the source, of the tasks given to him or her and of the information obtained; and

(b) consider the results of that review.

The Regulation of Investigatory Powers (Directed Surveillance and Covert Human Intelligence Sources) Order 2010[131] specifies the persons who are entitled to grant an authorisation concerning such surveillance or such a source, and for what purpose each may do so.

Under sections 23B(2) and 32B(2) of the 2000 Act, the applicant is not required to give notice of an application to any person to whom the authorisation or notice relates, or to such a person's legal representatives.]

Section 8: orders for access to documents, etc. under the Criminal Appeal Act 1995

When this Section applies   **R47.54**

47.54 This Section applies where the Crown Court can order a person to give the Criminal Cases Review Commission access to a document or other material under section 18A of the Criminal Appeal Act 1995[132].

[Note. Under section 18A of the Criminal Appeal Act 1995, on an application by the Criminal Cases Review Commission the court may order that the Commission be given access to a document or material in a person's possession or control if the court thinks that that document or material may assist the Commission in the exercise of any of their functions.]

Exercise of court's powers   **R47.55**

47.55 (1) Subject to paragraphs (2), (3) and (4), the court may determine an application by the Criminal Cases Review Commission for an order—

(a) at a hearing (which must be in private unless the court otherwise directs), or without a hearing; and

(b) in the absence of—

(i) the Commission,

(ii) the respondent, and

(iii) any other person affected by the order.

(2) The court must not determine such an application in the Commission's absence if—

(a) the Commission asks for a hearing; or

(b) it appears to the court that the application is so complex or serious as to require the court to hear the Commission.

(3) The court must not determine such an application in the absence of any respondent or other person affected, unless—

(a) the absentee has had at least 2 business days in which to make representations; or

(b) the court is satisfied that—

(i) the Commission cannot identify or contact the absentee,

---

[131] S.I. 2010/521.

[132] 1995 c. 35; section 18A was inserted by section 1 of the Criminal Cases Review Commission (Information) Act 2016 (c. 17).

Criminal Procedure Rules

    (ii) it would prejudice the exercise of the Commission's functions to adjourn or postpone the application so as to allow the absentee to attend, or

    (iii) the absentee has waived the opportunity to attend.

(4) The court must not determine such an application in the absence of any respondent who, if the order sought by the Commission were made, would be required to produce or give access to journalistic material, unless that respondent has waived the opportunity to attend.

(5) The court officer must arrange for the court to hear such an application no sooner than 2 business days after it was served, unless—

    (a) the court directs that no hearing need be arranged; or

    (b) the court gives other directions for the hearing.

(6) The court must not determine an application unless satisfied that sufficient time has been allowed for it.

(7) If the court so directs, the parties to an application may attend a hearing by live link.

(8) The court must not make an order unless an officer of the Commission states, in writing or orally, that to the best of that officer's knowledge and belief—

    (a) the application discloses all the information that is material to what the court must decide; and

    (b) the content of the application is true.

(9) Where the statement required by paragraph (8) is made orally—

    (a) the statement must be on oath or affirmation, unless the court otherwise directs; and

    (b) the court must arrange for a record of the making of the statement.

(10) The court may shorten or extend (even after it has expired) a time limit under this Section.

R47.56 Application for an order for access

47.56 (1) Where the Criminal Cases Review Commission wants the court to make an order for access to a document or other material, the Commission must—

    (a) apply in writing and serve the application on the court officer;

    (b) give the court an estimate of how long the court should allow—

        (i) to read the application and prepare for any hearing, and

        (ii) for any hearing of the application;

    (c) attach a draft order in the terms proposed by the Commission; and

    (d) serve the application and draft order on the respondent.

(2) The application must—

    (a) identify the respondent;

    (b) describe the document, or documents, or other material sought;

    (c) explain the reasons for thinking that—

        (i) what is sought is in the respondent's possession or control, and

        (ii) access to what is sought may assist the Commission in the exercise of any of their functions; and

    (d) explain the Commission's proposals for—

        (i) the manner in which the respondent should give access, and

        (ii) the period within which the order should take effect.

(3) The Commission must serve any order made on the respondent.

[Note. Under section 18A(3) of the Criminal Appeal Act 1995, the court may give directions for the manner in which access to a document or other material must be given, and may direct that the Commission must be allowed to take away such a document or material, or to make copies. Under section 18A(4) of the Act, the court may direct that the respondent must not destroy, damage or alter a document or other material before the direction is withdrawn by the court.]

R47.57 Application containing information withheld from a respondent or other person

47.57 (1) This rule applies where—

    (a) the Criminal Cases Review Commission serves an application under rule 47.56 (Application for an order for access); and

    (b) the application includes information that the Commission thinks ought not be revealed to a recipient.

(2) The Commission must—

    (a) omit that information from the part of the application that is served on that recipient;

    (b) mark the other part, to show that it is only for the court; and

    (c) in that other part, explain why the Commission has withheld it from that recipient.

(3) A hearing of an application to which this rule applies may take place, wholly or in part, in the absence of that recipient and any other person.

(4)   At a hearing of an application to which this rule applies—
    (a)   the general rule is that the court must consider, in the following sequence—
        (i)   representations first by the Commission and then by the other parties, in the presence of them all, and then
        (ii) further representations by the Commission, in the others' absence; but
    (b)   the court may direct other arrangements for the hearing.

Application to punish for contempt of court   R47.58

47.58 (1)   This rule applies where a person is accused of disobeying an order for access made under section 18A of the Criminal Appeal Act 1995.
     (2)   An applicant who wants the court to exercise its power to punish that person for contempt of court must comply with the rules in Part 48 (Contempt of court).

[Note. The Crown Court has power to punish for contempt of court a person who disobeys its order. See section 45 of the Senior Courts Act 1981[133].]

Section 9: orders for the extension of a moratorium period under the Proceeds of Crime Act 2002

When this Section applies   R47.59

47.59 (1)   This Section applies where the Crown Court can extend a moratorium period under section 336A of the Proceeds of Crime Act 2002[134].
     (2)   In this Section, 'respondent' means, as well as a person within the meaning of rule 47.2(c), an 'interested person' within the meaning of section 336D of the 2002 Act[135].

[Note. Under section 336A of the Proceeds of Crime Act 2002, the Crown Court may extend a moratorium period under section 335 or section 336 of the Act[136] by up to 31 days beginning with the day after the day on which the period otherwise would end.

Under sections 335 and 336 of the 2002 Act, a moratorium period is the period of 31 days starting with the day on which consent to the doing of an act is refused by a constable, a customs officer or the Director General of the National Crime Agency. The act to which those sections refer is one that would be an offence under section 327, 328 or 329 of the 2002 Act (money laundering offences) but for the making of a disclosure within the meaning of section 338 to such an officer in relation to that act. On the expiry of the moratorium period the person who made the disclosure will be treated as having the relevant officer's consent to the doing of the act and so will commit no offence by doing it.

The Crown Court may extend a moratorium period more than once, but the total period of extension may not exceed 186 days beginning with the day after the day on which the first 31 day period ended.

Under section 336D(3) of the 2002 Act, 'interested person' means the person who made the disclosure and any other person who appears to the person making an application under rule 47.61 to have an interest in the property that is the subject of that disclosure.]

Exercise of court's powers   R47.60

47.60 (1)   The court may determine an application to which rule 47.61 (Application for extension of moratorium period) applies—
    (a)   at a hearing (which must be in private unless the court otherwise directs), or without a hearing; and
    (b)   in the absence of—
        (i)   the applicant, and
        (ii) a respondent.
     (2)   The court must not determine such an application in the applicant's absence if the applicant asks for a hearing.
     (3)   The court must not determine such an application in the absence of a respondent unless—
    (a)   the absentee has had at least 2 business days in which to make representations; or
    (b)   the court is satisfied that—
        (i)   the applicant cannot identify or contact the absentee,

---

[133] 1981 c. 54. The Act's title was amended by section 59(5) of, and paragraph 1 of Schedule 11 to, the Constitutional Reform Act 2005 (c. 4).

[134] 2002 c. 29; section 336A was inserted by section 10 of the Criminal Finances Act 2017 (c. 22).

[135] 2002 c. 29; section 336D was inserted by section 10 of the Criminal Finances Act 2017 (c. 22).

[136] 2002 c. 29; section 335 was amended by section 10 of the Criminal Finances Act 2017 (c. 22). Section 336 was amended by paragraphs 168 and 173 of Schedule 4 to the Serious Organised Crime and Police Act 2005 (c. 15), paragraphs 108 and 133 of Schedule 8 to the Crime and Courts Act 2013 (c.22) and section 10 of the Criminal Finances Act 2017 (c. 22).

Criminal Procedure Rules

(ii) it would prejudice the investigation if the absentee were present,

(iii) it would prejudice the investigation to adjourn or postpone the application so as to allow the absentee to attend, or

(iv) the absentee has waived the opportunity to attend.

(4) The court officer must arrange for the court to hear such an application no sooner than 2 business days after notice of the application was served, unless—

(a) the court directs that no hearing need be arranged; or

(b) the court gives other directions for the hearing.

(5) If the court so directs, the parties to an application may attend a hearing by live link.

(6) The court must not extend a moratorium period unless the applicant states, in writing or orally, that to the best of the applicant's knowledge and belief—

(a) the application discloses all the information that is material to what the court must decide; and

(b) the content of the application is true.

(7) Where the statement required by paragraph (6) is made orally—

(a) the statement must be on oath or affirmation, unless the court otherwise directs; and

(b) the court must arrange for a record of the making of the statement.

(8) The court may—

(a) shorten or extend (even after it has expired) a time limit imposed by this rule;

(b) dispense with a requirement for service under this Section (even after service was required); and

(c) consider an application made orally instead of in writing.

R47.61 **Application for extension of moratorium period**

47.61 (1) This rule applies where an applicant wants the court to extend a moratorium period.

(2) The applicant must—

(a) apply in writing before the date on which the moratorium period otherwise would end;

(b) demonstrate that the applicant is entitled to apply as a senior officer within the meaning of section 336D of the Proceeds of Crime Act 2002;

(c) serve the application on the court officer;

(d) serve notice on each respondent that an application has been made; and

(e) serve the application on each respondent to such extent, if any, as the court directs.

(3) The application must specify—

(a) the disclosure in respect of which the application is made;

(b) the date on which the moratorium period began;

(c) the date and period of any previous extension of that period; and

(d) the date on which that period is due to end.

(4) The application must—

(a) describe the investigation being carried out in relation to that disclosure; and

(b) explain the grounds for believing that—

(i)   the investigation is being conducted diligently and expeditiously,

(ii) further time is needed for conducting the investigation, and

(iii) it would be reasonable in all the circumstances for the moratorium period to be extended.

(5) A respondent who objects to the application must—

(a) serve notice of the objection on—

(i)   the court officer, and

(ii) the applicant,

not more than 2 business days after service of notice of the application; and

(b) in that notice explain the grounds of the objection.

(6) The applicant must serve any order made on each respondent.

[Note. The Practice Direction sets out forms of application and notice of objection for use in connection with this rule.

Under section 336D of the Proceeds of Crime Act 2002, 'senior officer' means the Director General of the National Crime Agency or an authorised officer of that Agency, a police officer of at least the rank of inspector, an officer of HM Revenue and Customs or an immigration officer of equivalent rank, a senior member of the Financial Conduct Authority, the Director of the Serious Fraud Office or an authorised member of that Office, or an accredited financial investigator.

The time limit for making an application is prescribed by section 336A(3) of the Proceeds of Crime Act 2002. It may be neither extended nor shortened. Under section 336B(2) of the Act[137] the court must determine the application as soon as reasonably practicable. Under section 336C[138], where an application is made and not determined before the moratorium period otherwise would expire then that period is extended until (i) the application is determined, or (ii) the expiry of 31 days beginning with the day after the day on which that period expired, whichever occurs first.]

Application containing information withheld from a respondent   **R47.62**

47.62 (1) This rule applies where an application to extend a moratorium period includes an application to withhold information from a respondent.

    (2) The applicant must—

        (a) omit that information from any part of the application that is served on the respondent;

        (b) mark the other part to show that, unless the court otherwise directs, it is only for the court; and

        (c) in that other part, explain the grounds for believing that the disclosure of that information would have one or more of the following results—

            (i) evidence of an offence would be interfered with or harmed,

            (ii) the gathering of information about the possible commission of an offence would be interfered with,

            (iii) a person would be interfered with or physically injured,

            (iv) the recovery of property under this Act would be hindered, or

            (v) national security would be put at risk.

    (3) At any hearing of an application to which this rule applies—

        (a) the court must first determine the application to withhold information, in the respondent's absence and that of any legal representative of the respondent; and

        (b) if the court allows the application to withhold information, then in the following sequence—

            (i) the court must consider representations first by the applicant and then by the respondent, in the presence of both, and

            (ii) the court may consider further representations by the applicant in the respondent's absence and that of any legal representative of the respondent.

    (4) If the court refuses an application to withhold information from the respondent, the applicant may withdraw the application to extend the moratorium period.

[Note. See section 336B of the Proceeds of Crime Act 2002.]

Section 10: orders for access to electronic data under the Crime (Overseas Production Orders) Act 2019

When this Section applies   **R47.63**

47.63 (1) This Section applies where the Crown Court can make an overseas production order under section 1 of the Crime (Overseas Production Orders) Act 2019.[139]

    (2) In this Section, a reference to a person affected by such an order includes a person by whom or on whose behalf there is stored any journalistic data specified or described in the application for that order.

[Note. Under section 1 of the Crime (Overseas Production Orders) Act 2019, on an application by an appropriate officer (defined by section 2 of the Act) a Crown Court judge may order a person (in these rules, 'the respondent') to produce or give access to electronic data (by section 3, 'data stored electronically'), other than excepted such data, where, among other criteria listed in sections 1 and 4 of the Act, the judge is satisfied that—

    (a) there are reasonable grounds for believing that—

        (i) an indictable offence has been committed and proceedings in respect of the offence have been instituted or the offence is being investigated, or

        (ii) the order is sought for the purposes of a terrorist investigation within the meaning of the Terrorism Act 2000; and

    (b) there are reasonable grounds for believing that the respondent operates in, or is based in, a country or territory outside the United Kingdom which is a party to, or which participates in, a designated international co-operation arrangement.

---

[137] 2002 c. 29; section 336B was inserted by section 10 of the Criminal Finances Act 2017 (c. 22).
[138] 2002 c. 29; section 336C was inserted by section 10 of the Criminal Finances Act 2017 (c. 22).
[139] 2019 c. 5.

Criminal Procedure Rules

Section 3 of the 2019 Act defines 'excepted electronic data' as data stored electronically that is (a) an item subject to legal privilege, or (b) a personal record within the meaning of section 3(7) (medical, etc. records) which (i) was created in circumstances giving rise to a continuing obligation of confidence to an individual who can be identified from that record, or (ii) is held subject to a restriction on disclosure, or an obligation of secrecy, contained in an enactment. Where the respondent against whom an overseas production order is sought is a telecommunications operator, within the meaning of the Investigatory Powers Act 2016, 'excepted electronic data' also includes communications data within the meaning of the 2016 Act unless that communications data is comprised in, included as part of, attached to or logically associated with the electronic data sought. Where the investigation in aid of which an overseas production order is sought is a terrorist investigation other than a terrorist financing investigation within the meaning of the Terrorism Act 2000, 'excepted electronic data' does not include a confidential personal record.

Section 12 of the Act defines 'journalistic data' as electronic data that (a) was created or acquired for the purposes of journalism and (b) is stored by or on behalf of a person who created or acquired it for those purposes.]

R47.64 **Exercise of court's powers**

47.64 (1) Subject to paragraphs (2), (3) and (4), the court may determine an application under rule 47.68 for an overseas production order, or an application under rule 47.69 to vary or revoke an order—

    (a) at a hearing (which must be in private unless the court otherwise directs), or without a hearing; and

    (b) in the absence of—

        (i) the applicant,

        (ii) the respondent, and

        (iii) any other person affected by the order.

    (2) The court must not determine such an application in the applicant's absence if—

    (a) the applicant asks for a hearing; or

    (b) it appears to the court that—

        (i) the proposed order may require the production of excepted electronic data, within the meaning of section 3 of the Crime (Overseas Production Orders) Act 2019, or

        (ii) for any other reason the application is so complex or serious as to require the court to hear the applicant.

    (3) The court must not determine such an application in the absence of any respondent or other person affected unless—

    (a) the absentee has had at least 2 business days in which to make representations; or

    (b) the court is satisfied that—

        (i) the applicant cannot identify or contact the absentee,

        (ii) it would prejudice the investigation if the absentee were present,

        (iii) where journalistic data is sought, it would prejudice the investigation of another indictable offence or another terrorist investigation if the absentee were present,

        (iv) it would prejudice the investigation to adjourn or postpone the application so as to allow the absentee to attend, or

        (v) the absentee has waived the opportunity to attend.

    (4) The court must not determine such an application in the absence of any respondent who, if the order sought by the applicant were made, would be required to produce or give access to journalistic data, unless that respondent has waived the opportunity to attend.

    (5) The court officer must arrange for the court to hear such an application no sooner than 2 business days after notice of the application was served, unless—

    (a) the court directs that no hearing need be arranged; or

    (b) the court gives other directions for the hearing.

    (6) The court must not determine an application unless satisfied that sufficient time has been allowed for it.

    (7) If the court so directs, the parties to an application may attend a hearing by live link.

    (8) The court must not make, vary or revoke an order unless the applicant states, in writing or orally, that to the best of the applicant's knowledge and belief—

    (a) the application discloses all the information that is material to what the court must decide; and

    (b) the content of the application is true.

    (9) Where the statement required by paragraph (8) is made orally—

    (a) the statement must be on oath or affirmation, unless the court otherwise directs; and

    (b) the court must arrange for a record of the making of the statement.

    (10) The court may—

    (a) shorten or extend (even after it has expired) a time limit under this Section;

(b) dispense with a requirement for service under this Section (even after service was required); and

(c) consider an application made orally instead of in writing.

(11) A person who wants an extension of time must—

(a) apply when serving the application for which it is needed; and

(b) explain the delay.

Application for order   R47.65

47.65 (1) An applicant who wants the court to make an overseas production order must—

(a) apply in writing and serve the application on the court officer;

(b) demonstrate that the applicant is entitled to apply;

(c) give the court an estimate of how long the court should allow—

(i) to read the application and prepare for any hearing, and

(ii) for any hearing of the application;

(d) attach a draft order in the terms proposed by the applicant;

(e) serve notice of the application on the respondent and on any other person affected by the order, unless the court otherwise directs; and

(f) serve the application on the respondent and on any such other person to such extent, if any, as the court directs.

(2) A notice served on the respondent and on any other person affected by the order must—

(a) specify or describe the electronic data in respect of which the application is made; and

(b) identify—

(i) the power that the applicant invites the court to exercise, and

(ii) the conditions for the exercise of that power which the applicant asks the court to find are met.

(3) The application must—

(a) specify the designated international co-operation arrangement by reference to which the application is made;

(b) identify the respondent;

(c) explain the grounds for believing that the respondent operates in, or is based in, a country or territory outside the United Kingdom which is a party to, or participates in, that designated international co-operation arrangement;

(d) specify or describe the electronic data in respect of which the order is sought;

(e) explain the grounds for believing that the electronic data sought does not consist of or include excepted electronic data;

(f) briefly describe the investigation for the purposes of which the electronic data is sought and explain—

(i) the grounds for believing that an indictable offence has been committed which is under investigation or in respect of which proceedings have begun, or

(ii) how the investigation constitutes a terrorist investigation within the meaning of the Terrorism Act 2000;

(g) explain the grounds for believing that the respondent has possession or control of all or part of the electronic data sought;

(h) explain the grounds for believing that the electronic data sought is likely to be of substantial value to the investigation, or to the proceedings (as the case may be), whether by itself or together with other material;

(i) where paragraph (3)(f)(i) applies, explain the grounds for believing that all or part of the electronic data sought is likely to be relevant evidence in respect of the offence concerned;

(j) explain the grounds for believing that it is in the public interest for the respondent to produce or give access to the electronic data sought, having regard to—

(i) the benefit likely to accrue to the investigation, or to the proceedings (as the case may be), if that data is obtained, and

(ii) the circumstances under which the respondent has possession or control of any of that data;

(k) specify—

(i) the person, or the description of person, to whom the applicant wants the court to order that electronic data must be produced or made accessible, and

(ii) the period by the end of which the applicant wants the court to order that that electronic data must be produced or made accessible (which must be a period of 7 days beginning with the day on which the order is served on the respondent, unless the court otherwise directs); and

      (l) where the applicant wants the court to include a non-disclosure requirement in the order—

        (i) explain why such a requirement would be appropriate, and

        (ii) specify or describe when the applicant wants that requirement, if ordered, to expire.

(4) In the event that an overseas production order is made, the applicant must serve the order on the Secretary of State, or on a person prescribed by regulations, for service on the respondent.

(5) Where notice of the application was served on a respondent, in the event that the application is dismissed or abandoned the applicant must—

  (a) promptly so notify that respondent; and

  (b) where the application is dismissed, promptly inform that respondent if the court nonetheless orders that for a period that respondent must not—

    (i) conceal, destroy, alter or dispose of any of the electronic data specified or described in the application, or

    (ii) disclose the making of the application or its contents to any person.

[Note. See sections 1, 2, 4 and 5 of the Crime (Overseas Production Orders) Act 2019.

Under section 8 of the 2019 Act, an overseas production order may include a non-disclosure requirement obliging the respondent not to disclose the making of the order or its contents to any person except with the court's permission or with the written permission of the applicant (or an equivalent appropriate officer).

Under section 9 of the Act, an overseas production order may be served only by the Secretary of State or by a person prescribed by regulations made by the Secretary of State.

Under section 12 of the Act, if there are reasonable grounds for believing that the electronic data specified or described in the application consists of or includes journalistic data then unless the judge otherwise directs notice of the application must be served on (a) the person against whom the overseas production order is sought and (b) if different, the person by whom, or on whose behalf, the journalistic data is stored. The criteria for making such a direction correspond with those listed in rule 47.64(3)(b).

Under section 13 of the Act, following service of notice of an application for an overseas production order the respondent must not conceal, destroy, alter or dispose of any of the electronic data specified or described in the application, or disclose the making of the application or its contents to any person, except with the court's permission or with the written permission of the applicant (or an equivalent appropriate officer). Those obligations are superseded if an order is made. If the application is abandoned or dismissed, those obligations cease unless, in the event of dismissal, the court otherwise orders.

Section 14 of the Act provides for the means of service of notices and orders.

The Practice Direction sets out forms of application, notice and order for use in connection with this rule.]

R47.66   **Application to vary or revoke an order**

47.66 (1) The orders to which this rule applies are—

  (a) an overseas production order;

  (b) an order under section 8(4) of the Crime (Overseas Production Orders) Act 2019 maintaining an unexpired non-disclosure requirement;

  (c) an order under section 13(3) of the 2019 Act maintaining a duty not to conceal, destroy, alter or dispose of electronic data, and not to disclose the making or content of an application for an overseas production order; and

  (d) an order under section 13(4)(b) of the Act maintaining a duty not to conceal, destroy, alter or dispose of electronic data.

(2) This rule applies where one of the following wants the court to vary, to further vary or to revoke an order listed in paragraph (1)—

  (a) the applicant for that order, or an equivalent appropriate officer;

  (b) the respondent;

  (c) another person affected by the order; or

  (d) the Secretary of State.

(3) The applicant for the variation or revocation must—

  (a) apply in writing as soon as practicable after becoming aware of the grounds for doing so;

  (b) serve the application on—

    (i) the court officer, and

    (ii) as applicable, the applicant for the order, the respondent, any other person known to be affected and the Secretary of State,

  (c) attach a draft order in the terms proposed by the applicant; and

  (d) ask for a hearing, if one is wanted, and explain why it is needed.

(4) Where the applicant wants the court to vary, or further vary, an overseas production order, the application must—
  (a) specify or describe the electronic data in respect of which the varied order is sought (which may include electronic data not specified or described in the original order);
  (b) satisfy or, as the case may be, continue to satisfy, the requirements of rule 47.65(3)(a) and (c) to (i) (which may be done by reference to the original application); and
  (c) meet the requirements of rule 47.65(3)(j).
(5) Where the applicant wants the court to revoke an overseas production order, the application must—
  (a) explain why revocation is appropriate;
  (b) if the applicant wants the court, despite revocation, to maintain the requirement that for a period the respondent must not conceal, destroy, alter or dispose of any of the electronic data specified or described in the order—
    (i) explain why it would be appropriate to maintain that requirement, and
    (ii) specify or describe when the applicant wants that requirement, if maintained, to expire; and
  (c) if the order includes an unexpired non-disclosure requirement that the applicant wants the court, despite revocation, to maintain—
    (i) explain why it would be appropriate to maintain that requirement, and
    (ii) specify or describe when the applicant wants that requirement, if maintained, to expire.
(6) Where the applicant wants the court to vary, to further vary or to revoke an order under section 8(4), section 13(3) or section 13(4)(b) of the 2019 Act the application must—
  (a) explain—
    (i) what material circumstances have changed since the order was made, and
    (ii) why the order should be varied or revoked, as the case may be, as a result; and
  (b) if applicable, specify the variation proposed.
(7) The court officer must serve on the applicant for the overseas production order under rule 47.65 any order made on an application under this rule, and—
  (a) in the event that the court varies the overseas production order, the applicant under rule 47.65 must serve the order as varied on the Secretary of State, or on a person prescribed by regulations, for service on the respondent on whom the overseas production order first was served;
  (b) in any other event, the applicant under rule 47.65 must serve the order made on the application under this rule on every other person served under paragraph (3)(b).

[Note. See sections 7, 9, 11(1) and 18(2) of the Crime (Overseas Production Orders) Act 2019.

Under section 8(4) of the 2019 Act, where the court revokes an overseas production order which includes an unexpired non-disclosure requirement the court may order that the respondent is to remain subject to that requirement for a defined period.

Under section 13(3) of the Act, where the court dismisses an application for an overseas production order then the duty under section 13(1)(a) not to conceal, destroy, alter or dispose of any of the electronic data specified or described in the application, and under section 13(1)(b) not to disclose the making of the application or its contents to any person except with the court's permission or with the written permission of the applicant (or an equivalent appropriate officer), ceases to apply unless the court orders that a person served with notice of the application is to remain subject to that duty for a defined period.

Under section 13(4)(b) of the Act, where the court revokes an overseas production order before it is served then the duty under section 13(1)(a) not to conceal, destroy, alter or dispose of any of the electronic data specified or described in the application for the order ceases to apply unless the court orders that a person served with notice of the application is to remain subject to that duty for a defined period.

The Practice Direction sets out forms of application and order for use in connection with this rule.]

Application containing information withheld from a respondent or other person   **R47.67**

47.67 (1) This rule applies where an application under rule 47.65 or 47.66 includes information that the applicant thinks ought to be revealed only to the court.
(2) The application must—
  (a) identify that information; and
  (b) explain why that information ought not to be served on the respondent or another person.
(3) At a hearing of an application to which this rule applies—
  (a) the general rule is that the court must consider, in the following sequence—
    (i) representations first by the applicant and then by the respondent and any other person, in the presence of them all, and then
    (ii) further representations by the applicant, in the others' absence; but
  (b) the court may direct other arrangements for the hearing.

Criminal Procedure Rules

R47.68   **Application to punish for contempt of court**

    47.68 (1) This rule applies where a person is accused of disobeying an order made by the court under the Crime (Overseas Production Orders) Act 2019.

        (2) An applicant who wants the court to exercise its power to punish that person for contempt of court must comply with the rules in Part 48 (Contempt of court).

[Note. The Crown Court has power to punish for contempt of court a person who disobeys its order: see section 45 of the Senior Courts Act 1981[140]. Under section 11(4) of the Crime (Overseas Production Orders) Act 2019, an order made by a judge under the Act has effect as if it were an order of the Crown Court.]

CRIMINAL PROCEDURE RULES   PART 48   CONTEMPT OF COURT
General rules

R48.1   **When this Part applies**

    48.1 (1) This Part applies where the court can deal with a person for conduct—

        (a) in contempt of court; or

        (b) in contravention of the legislation to which rules 48.5 and 48.9 refer.

        (2) In this Part, 'respondent' means any such person.

[Note. For the court's powers to punish for contempt of court, see the notes to rules 48.5 and 48.9.]

R48.2   **Exercise of court's power to deal with contempt of court**

    48.2 (1) The court must determine at a hearing—

        (a) an enquiry under rule 48.8; and

        (b) an allegation under rule 48.9.

        (2) The court must not proceed in the respondent's absence unless—

        (a) the respondent's behaviour makes it impracticable to proceed otherwise; or

        (b) the respondent has had at least 10 business days' notice of the hearing, or was present when it was arranged.

        (3) If the court hears part of an enquiry or allegation in private, it must announce at a hearing in public—

        (a) the respondent's name;

        (b) in general terms, the nature of any conduct that the respondent admits, or the court finds proved; and

        (c) any punishment imposed.

R48.3   **Notice of suspension of imprisonment by Court of Appeal or Crown Court**

    48.3 (1) This rule applies where—

        (a) the Court of Appeal or the Crown Court suspends an order of imprisonment for contempt of court; and

        (b) the respondent is absent when the court does so.

        (2) The respondent must be served with notice of the terms of the court's order—

        (a) by any applicant under rule 48.9; or

        (b) by the court officer, in any other case.

[Note. By reason of sections 15 and 45 of the Senior Courts Act 1981[1], the Court of Appeal and the Crown Court each has an inherent power to suspend imprisonment for contempt of court, on conditions, or for a period, or both.]

R48.4   **Application to discharge an order for imprisonment**

    48.4 (1) This rule applies where the court can discharge an order for a respondent's imprisonment for contempt of court.

        (2) A respondent who wants the court to discharge such an order must—

        (a) apply in writing, unless the court otherwise directs, and serve any written application on—

            (i) the court officer, and

            (ii) any applicant under rule 48.9 on whose application the respondent was imprisoned;

        (b) in the application—

            (i) explain why it is appropriate for the order for imprisonment to be discharged, and

            (ii) give details of any appeal, and its outcome; and

        (c) ask for a hearing, if the respondent wants one.

---

[140] 1981 c. 54. The Act's title was amended by section 59(5) of, and paragraph 1 of Schedule 11 to, the Constitutional Reform Act 2005 (c. 4).

[1] 1981 c. 54.

[Note. By reason of sections 15 and 45 of the Senior Courts Act 1981, the Court of Appeal and the Crown Court each has an inherent power to discharge an order for a respondent's imprisonment for contempt of court in failing to comply with a court order.

Under section 97(4) of the Magistrates' Courts Act 1980[2], a magistrates' court can discharge an order for imprisonment if the respondent gives evidence.

Under section 12(4) of the Contempt of Court Act 1981[3], a magistrates' court can discharge an order for imprisonment made under that section.]

Contempt of court by obstruction, disruption, etc.

Initial procedure on obstruction, disruption, etc.   **R48.5**

48.5 (1) This rule applies where the court observes, or someone reports to the court—

    (a) in the Court of Appeal or the Crown Court, obstructive, disruptive, insulting or intimidating conduct, in the courtroom or in its vicinity, or otherwise immediately affecting the proceedings;

    (b) in the Crown Court, a contravention of—

        (i) section 3 of the Criminal Procedure (Attendance of Witnesses) Act 1965[4] (disobeying a witness summons); or

        (ii) section 20 of the Juries Act 1974[5] (disobeying a jury summons);

    (c) in a magistrates' court, a contravention of—

        (i) section 97(4) of the Magistrates' Courts Act 1980 (refusing to give evidence), or

        (ii) section 12 of the Contempt of Court Act 1981[6] (insulting or interrupting the court, etc.);

    (d) a contravention of section 9 of the Contempt of Court Act 1981[7] (without the court's permission, recording the proceedings, etc.); or

    (e) any other conduct with which the court can deal as, or as if it were, a criminal contempt of court, except failure to surrender to bail under section 6 of the Bail Act 1976[8].

  (2) Unless the respondent's behaviour makes it impracticable to do so, the court must—

    (a) explain, in terms the respondent can understand (with help, if necessary)—

        (i) the conduct that is in question,

        (ii) that the court can impose imprisonment, or a fine, or both, for such conduct,

        (iii) (where relevant) that the court has power to order the respondent's immediate temporary detention, if in the court's opinion that is required,

        (iv) that the respondent may explain the conduct,

        (v) that the respondent may apologise, if he or she so wishes, and that this may persuade the court to take no further action, and

        (vi) that the respondent may take legal advice; and

    (b) allow the respondent a reasonable opportunity to reflect, take advice, explain and, if he or she so wishes, apologise.

  (3) The court may then—

    (a) take no further action in respect of that conduct;

    (b) enquire into the conduct there and then; or

    (c) postpone that enquiry (if a magistrates' court, only until later the same day).

[Note. The conduct to which this rule applies is sometimes described as 'criminal' contempt of court.

---

[2] 1980 c. 43; section 97(4) was amended by sections 13 and 14 of, and paragraph 7 of Schedule 2 to, the Contempt of Court Act 1981 (c. 47) and section 17 of, and paragraph 6 of Schedule 3 and Part I of Schedule 4 to, the Criminal Justice Act 1991 (c. 53).

[3] 1981 c. 49.

[4] 1965 c. 69; section 3 was amended by section 56 of, and Part IV of Schedule 11 to, the Courts Act 1971 (c. 23) and sections 65 and 66 of the Criminal Procedure and Investigations Act 1996 (c. 25).

[5] 1974 c. 23; section 20 was amended by sections 37, 38 and 46 of the Criminal Justice Act 1982 (c. 48), section 170(1) of, and paragraph 46 of Schedule 15 to, the Criminal Justice Act 1988 (c. 33), paragraph 28 of Schedule 10 to, the Criminal Justice and Public Order Act 1994 (c. 33) and paragraphs 1 and 14 of Schedule 33 to, the Criminal Justice Act 2003 (c. 44).

[6] 1981 c. 49; section 12 was amended by section 78 of, and Schedule 16 to, the Criminal Justice Act 1982 (c. 48), section 17(3) of, and Part I of Schedule 4 to, the Criminal Justice Act 1991 (c. 53); section 65(3) and (4) of, and paragraph 6(4) of Schedule 3 to, the Criminal Justice Act 1993 (c. 36) and section 165 of, and paragraph 83 of Schedule 9 to, the Powers of Criminal Courts (Sentencing) Act 2000 (c. 6).

[7] 1981 c. 49.

[8] 1976 c. 63; section 6 was amended by sections 37, 38 and 46 of the Criminal Justice Act 1982 (c. 48), section 109 of, and paragraph 184 of Schedule 8 to, the Courts Act 2003 (c. 39) and section 15 of, and paragraph 48(1), (4) of Schedule 3 to, the Criminal Justice Act 2003 (c. 44).

By reason of sections 15 and 45 of the Senior Courts Act 1981, the Court of Appeal and the Crown Court each has an inherent power to imprison (for a maximum of 2 years), or fine (to an unlimited amount), or both, a respondent for contempt of court for the conduct listed in paragraph (1)(a), (b), (d) or (e). See also section 14 of the Contempt of Court Act 1981[9].

Under section 97(4) of the Magistrates' Courts Act 1980, and under sections 12 and 14 of the Contempt of Court Act 1981, a magistrates' court can imprison (for a maximum of 1 month), or fine (to a maximum of £2,500), or both, a respondent who contravenes a provision listed in paragraph (1)(c) or (d). Section 12(1) of the 1981 Act allows the court to deal with any person who—

> *(a)   wilfully insults the justice or justices, any witness before or officer of the court or any solicitor or counsel having business in the court, during his or their sitting or attendance in court or in going to or returning from the court; or*
> *(b)   wilfully interrupts the proceedings of the court or otherwise misbehaves in court.*

Under section 89 of the Powers of Criminal Courts (Sentencing) Act 2000[10], no respondent who is under 21 may be imprisoned for contempt of court. Under section 108 of that Act[11], a respondent who is at least 18 but under 21 may be detained if the court is of the opinion that no other method of dealing with him or her is appropriate. Under section 14(2A) of the Contempt of Court Act 1981[12], a respondent who is under 17 may not be ordered to attend an attendance centre.

Under section 258 of the Criminal Justice Act 2003[13], a respondent who is imprisoned for contempt of court must be released unconditionally after serving half the term.

Under sections 14, 15 and 16 of the Legal Aid, Sentencing and Punishment of Offenders Act 2012[14], the respondent may receive advice and representation in "proceedings for contempt committed, or alleged to have been committed, by an individual in the face of the court".

By reason of sections 15 and 45 of the Senior Courts Act 1981, the Court of Appeal and the Crown Court each has an inherent power temporarily to detain a respondent, for example to restore order, when dealing with obstructive, disruptive, insulting or intimidating conduct. Under section 12(2) of the Contempt of Court Act 1981[1], a magistrates' court can temporarily detain a respondent until later the same day on a contravention of that section.

Part 14 contains rules about bail.]

R48.6   Review after temporary detention

48.6   (1)   This rule applies in a case in which the court has ordered the respondent's immediate temporary detention for conduct to which rule 48.5 applies.

---

[9] 1981 c. 49; section 14 was amended by sections 77 and 78 of, and paragraph 60 of Schedule 14 and Schedule 16 to, the Criminal Justice Act 1982 (c. 48), section 65 of, and paragraphs 59 and 60 of Schedule 3 to, the Mental Health (Amendment) Act 1982 (c. 51), section 148 of, and paragraph 57 of Schedule 4 to, the Mental Health Act 1983 (c. 20), section 1 of the County Courts (Penalties for Contempt) Act 1983 (c. 45), section 17 of, and Parts 1 and V of Schedule 4 to, the Criminal Justice Act 1991 (c. 53), section 65 of, and paragraph 6 of Schedule 3 to, the Criminal Justice Act 1993 (c. 36), section 165 of, and paragraph 84 of Schedule 9 to, the Powers of Criminal Courts (Sentencing) Act 2000 (c. 6), section 1 of, and paragraph 19 of Schedule 1 to, the Mental Health Act 2007 (c. 12) and section 17 of, and paragraph 52 of Schedule 9 and paragraph 53 of Schedule 10 to, the Crime and Courts Act 2013 (c. 22). It is further amended by sections 6 and 149 of, and paragraph 25 of Schedule 4 and Part 1 of Schedule 28 to, the Criminal Justice and Immigration Act 2008 (c. 4), with effect from a date to be appointed.

[10] 2000 c. 6; section 89 was amended by paragraph 74 of Schedule 3, and Part 4 of Schedule 37, to the Criminal Justice Act 2003 (c. 44). It is further amended by section 74 of, and paragraphs 160 and 180 of Schedule 7 to, the Criminal Justice and Court Services Act 2000 (c. 43) with effect from a date to be appointed.

[11] 2000 c. 6; section 108 is repealed by sections 74 and 75 of, and paragraphs 160 and 188 of Schedule 7 and Schedule 8 to, the Criminal Justice and Court Services Act 2000 (c. 43), with effect from a date to be appointed.

[12] 1981 c. 49; section 14 was amended by section 65(1) of, and paragraphs 59 and 60 of Schedule 3 to, the Mental Health (Amendment) Act 1982 (c. 51), section 148 of, and paragraph 57 of Schedule 4 to, the Mental Health Act 1983 (c. 20), section 17(3) of, and Parts 1 and V of Schedule 4 to, the Criminal Justice Act 1991 (c. 53), section 65(3) and (4) of, and paragraph 6(5) of Schedule 3 to, the Criminal Justice Act 1993 (c. 36), section 165(1) of, and paragraph 84 of Schedule 9 to, the Powers of Criminal Courts (Sentencing) Act 2000 (c. 6), section 1(4) of, and paragraph 19 of Schedule 1 to, the Mental Health Act 2007 (c. 12) and section 17 of, and paragraph 52 of Schedule 9 and paragraph 53 of Schedule 10 to, the Crime and Courts Act 2013 (c. 22). It is further amended by sections 6(2) and 149 of, and paragraph 25 of Schedule 4 and Part 1 of Schedule 28 to, the Criminal Justice and Immigration Act 2008 (c. 4), with effect from a date to be appointed.

[13] 2003 c. 44; section 258 was amended by article 3 of S.I. 2005/643, section 34 of the Police and Justice Act 2006 (c. 4) and sections 117 and 121 of, and paragraphs 1 and 5 of Schedule 17 and paragraphs 1 and 8 of Schedule 20 to, the Legal Aid, Sentencing and Punishment of Offenders Act 2012 (c. 10).

[14] 2012 c. 10.

[15] 1981 c. 49; section 12(2) was amended by Part 1 of Schedule 4 to the Criminal Justice Act 1991 (c. 53).

(2) The court must review the case—
    (a) if a magistrates' court, later the same day; or
    (b) in the Court of Appeal or the Crown Court, no later than the next business day.
(3) On the review, the court must—
    (a) unless the respondent is absent, repeat the explanations required by rule 48.5(2)(a); and
    (b) allow the respondent a reasonable opportunity to reflect, take advice, explain and, if he or she so wishes, apologise.
(4) The court may then—
    (a) take no further action in respect of the conduct;
    (b) if a magistrates' court, enquire into the conduct there and then; or
    (c) if the Court of Appeal or the Crown Court—
        (i) enquire into the conduct there and then, or
        (ii) postpone the enquiry, and order the respondent's release from such detention in the meantime.

Postponement of enquiry   R48.7

48.7 (1) This rule applies where the Court of Appeal or the Crown Court postpones the enquiry.
    (2) The court must arrange for the preparation of a written statement containing such particulars of the conduct in question as to make clear what the respondent appears to have done.
    (3) The court officer must serve on the respondent—
        (a) that written statement;
        (b) notice of where and when the postponed enquiry will take place; and
        (c) a notice that—
            (i) reminds the respondent that the court can impose imprisonment, or a fine, or both, for contempt of court, and
            (ii) warns the respondent that the court may pursue the postponed enquiry in the respondent's absence, if the respondent does not attend.

Procedure on enquiry   R48.8

48.8 (1) At an enquiry, the court must—
    (a) ensure that the respondent understands (with help, if necessary) what is alleged, if the enquiry has been postponed from a previous occasion;
    (b) explain what the procedure at the enquiry will be; and
    (c) ask whether the respondent admits the conduct in question.
(2) If the respondent admits the conduct, the court need not receive evidence.
(3) If the respondent does not admit the conduct, the court must consider—
    (a) any statement served under rule 48.7;
    (b) any other evidence of the conduct;
    (c) any evidence introduced by the respondent; and
    (d) any representations by the respondent about the conduct.
(4) If the respondent admits the conduct, or the court finds it proved, the court must—
    (a) before imposing any punishment for contempt of court, give the respondent an opportunity to make representations relevant to punishment and a final opportunity to apologise;
    (b) in deciding how to deal with the respondent take into account—
        (i) the gravity of the contempt,
        (ii) the extent of any admission of the conduct and the stage at which that admission was made,
        (iii) any apology and the stage at which that apology was offered, and
        (iv) any period during which the respondent was detained pending the enquiry;
    (c) if imprisonment is imposed, impose the shortest period that is commensurate with the preservation of good order in the administration of justice;
    (d) explain, in terms the respondent can understand (with help, if necessary)—
        (i) the reasons for its decision, including its findings of fact, and
        (ii) the punishment it imposes, and its effect; and
    (e) if a magistrates' court, arrange for the preparation of a written record of those findings.
(5) The court that conducts an enquiry—
    (a) need not include the same member or members as the court that observed the conduct; but
    (b) may do so, unless that would be unfair to the respondent.

Contempt of court by failure to comply with court order, etc.

R48.9   **Initial procedure on failure to comply with court order, etc.**

48.9   (1)   This rule applies where—

(a)   a party, or other person directly affected, alleges—

(i)   in the Crown Court, a failure to comply with an order to which applies rule 33.70 (compliance order, restraint order or ancillary order), rule 47.9 (certain investigation orders under the Police and Criminal Evidence Act 1984[16], the Terrorism Act 2000[17], the Proceeds of Crime Act 2002[18], the Proceeds of Crime Act 2002 (External Investigations) Order 2014[19] and the Extradition Act 2003[20]), rule 47.41 (order for retention or return of property under section 59 of the Criminal Justice and Police Act 2001[21]) or rule 47.58 (order for access under section 18A of the Criminal Appeal Act 1995[22]),

(ii)   in the Court of Appeal or the Crown Court, any other conduct with which that court can deal as a civil contempt of court, or

(iii)   in the Crown Court or a magistrates' court, unauthorised use of disclosed prosecution material under section 17 of the Criminal Procedure and Investigations Act 1996[23]; or

(b)   the court deals on its own initiative with conduct to which paragraph (1)(a) applies.

(2)   Such a party or person must—

(a)   apply in writing and serve the application on the court officer; and

(b)   serve on the respondent—

(i)   the application, and

(ii)   notice of where and when the court will consider the allegation (not less than 10 business days after service).

(3)   The application must—

(a)   identify the respondent;

(b)   explain that it is an application for the respondent to be dealt with for contempt of court;

(c)   contain such particulars of the conduct in question as to make clear what is alleged against the respondent; and

(d)   include a notice warning the respondent that the court—

(i)   can impose imprisonment, or a fine, or both, for contempt of court, and

(ii)   may deal with the application in the respondent's absence, if the respondent does not attend the hearing.

(4)   A court which acts on its own initiative under paragraph (1)(b) must—

(a)   arrange for the preparation of a written statement containing the same information as an application; and

(b)   arrange for the service on the respondent of—

(i)   that written statement, and

(ii)   notice of where and when the court will consider the allegation (not less than 10 business days after service).

[Note. The conduct to which this rule applies is sometimes described as 'civil' contempt of court.

By reason of section 45 of the Senior Courts Act 1981[24], the Crown Court has an inherent power to imprison (for a maximum of 2 years), or fine (to an unlimited amount), or both, a respondent for conduct in contempt of court by failing to comply with a court order or an undertaking given to the court.

Under section 18 of the Criminal Procedure and Investigations Act 1996—[25]

(a)   the Crown Court can imprison (for a maximum of 2 years), or fine (to an unlimited amount), or both;

[16]   1984 c. 60.
[17]   2000 c. 11.
[18]   2002 c. 29.
[19]   S.I. 2014/1893.
[20]   2003 c. 41.
[21]   2001 c. 16; section 59 was amended by section 82 of the Deregulation Act 2015 (c. 20).
[22]   1995 c. 35; section 18A was inserted by section 1 of the Criminal Cases Review Commission (Information) Act 2016 (c. 17).
[23]   1996 c. 25; section 17 was amended by section 331 of, and paragraphs 20 and 33 of Schedule 36 to, the Criminal Justice Act 2003 (c. 44).
[24]   1981 c. 54.
[25]   1996 c. 25.

(b)   a magistrates' court can imprison (for a maximum of 6 months), or fine (to a maximum of £5,000), or both,

a person who uses disclosed prosecution material in contravention of section 17 of that Act. See also rule 15.8.

Under section 89 of the Powers of Criminal Courts (Sentencing) Act 2000, no respondent who is under 21 may be imprisoned for contempt of court. Under section 108 of that Act, a respondent who is at least 18 but under 21 may be detained if the court is of the opinion that no other method of dealing with him or her is appropriate. Under section 14(2A) of the Contempt of Court Act 1981, a respondent who is under 17 may not be ordered to attend an attendance centre.

Under section 258 of the Criminal Justice Act 2003, a respondent who is imprisoned for contempt of court must be released unconditionally after serving half the term.

The Practice Direction sets out a form of application for use in connection with this rule.

The rules in Part 4 require that an application under this rule must be served by handing it to the person accused of contempt of court unless the court otherwise directs.]

Procedure on hearing   **R48.10**

48.10 (1) At the hearing of an allegation under rule 48.9, the court must—
   (a) ensure that the respondent understands (with help, if necessary) what is alleged;
   (b) explain what the procedure at the hearing will be; and
   (c) ask whether the respondent admits the conduct in question.
(2) If the respondent admits the conduct, the court need not receive evidence.
(3) If the respondent does not admit the conduct, the court must consider—
   (a) the application or written statement served under rule 48.9;
   (b) any other evidence of the conduct;
   (c) any evidence introduced by the respondent; and
   (d) any representations by the respondent about the conduct.
(4) If the respondent admits the conduct, or the court finds it proved, the court must—
   (a) before imposing any punishment for contempt of court, give the respondent an opportunity to make representations relevant to punishment and a final opportunity to
apologise;
   (b) in deciding how to deal with the respondent take into account—
      (i)   the gravity of the contempt,
      (ii) the extent of any admission of the conduct and the stage at which that admission was
made, and
      (iii) any apology and the stage at which that apology was offered;
   (c) if imprisonment is imposed, impose the shortest period that is commensurate with the
preservation of good order in the administration of justice;
   (d) explain, in terms the respondent can understand (with help, if necessary)—
      (i)   the reasons for its decision, including its findings of fact, and
      (ii) the punishment it imposes, and its effect; and
   (e) if a magistrates' court, arrange for the preparation of a written record of those findings.

Introduction of written witness statement or other hearsay   **R48.11**

48.11 (1) Where rule 48.9 applies, an applicant or respondent who wants to introduce in evidence the
written statement of a witness, or other hearsay, must—
   (a) serve a copy of the statement, or notice of other hearsay, on—
      (i)   the court officer, and
      (ii) the other party; and
   (b) serve the copy or notice—
      (i)   when serving the application under rule 48.9, in the case of an applicant, or
      (ii) not more than 5 business days after service of that application or of the court's written
statement, in the case of the respondent.
(2) Such service is notice of that party's intention to introduce in evidence that written witness
statement, or other hearsay, unless that party otherwise indicates when serving it.
(3) A party entitled to receive such notice may waive that entitlement.

[Note. On an application under rule 48.9, hearsay evidence is admissible under the Civil Evidence Act 1995. Section 1(2) of the 1995 Act[26] defines hearsay as meaning 'a statement made otherwise than by a person while giving oral evidence in the proceedings which is tendered as evidence of the matters stated'. Section 13 of the Act[27] defines a statement as meaning 'any representation of fact or opinion, however made'.

Under section 2 of the 1995 Act[28], a party who wants to introduce hearsay in evidence must give reasonable and practicable notice, in accordance with procedure rules, unless the recipient waives that requirement.]

R48.12   Content of written witness statement

48.12 (1) This rule applies to a written witness statement served under rule 48.11.

(2) Such a written witness statement must contain a declaration by the person making it that it is true to the best of that person's knowledge and belief.

[Note. By reason of sections 15 and 45 of the Senior Courts Act 1981[29], the Court of Appeal and the Crown Court each has an inherent power to imprison (for a maximum of 2 years), or fine (to an unlimited amount), or both, for contempt of court a person who, in a written witness statement to which this rule applies, makes, or causes to be made, a false statement without an honest belief in its truth. See also section 14 of the Contempt of Court Act 1981[30].]

R48.13   Content of notice of other hearsay

48.13 (1) This rule applies to a notice of hearsay, other than a written witness statement, served under rule 48.11.

(2) Such a notice must—

(a) set out the evidence, or attach the document that contains it; and

(b) identify the person who made the statement that is hearsay.

R48.14   Cross-examination of maker of written witness statement or other hearsay

48.14 (1) This rule applies where a party wants the court's permission to cross-examine a person who made a statement which another party wants to introduce as hearsay.

(2) The party who wants to cross-examine that person must—

(a) apply in writing, with reasons; and

(b) serve the application on—

(i) the court officer, and

(ii) the party who served the hearsay.

(3) A respondent who wants to cross-examine such a person must apply to do so not more than 5 business days after service of the hearsay by the applicant.

(4) An applicant who wants to cross-examine such a person must apply to do so not more than 3 business days after service of the hearsay by the respondent.

(5) The court—

(a) may decide an application under this rule without a hearing; but

(b) must not dismiss such an application unless the person making it has had an opportunity to make representations at a hearing.

[Note. See also section 3 of the Civil Evidence Act 1995[31].]

R48.15   Credibility and consistency of maker of written witness statement or other hearsay

48.15 (1) This rule applies where a party wants to challenge the credibility or consistency of a person who made a statement which another party wants to introduce as hearsay.

---

[26] 1995 c. 38.
[27] 1995 c. 38.
[28] 1995 c. 38.
[29] 1981 c. 54.
[30] 1981 c. 49; section 14 was amended by sections 77 and 78 of, and paragraph 60 of Schedule 14 and Schedule 16 to, the Criminal Justice Act 1982 (c. 48), section 65 of, and paragraphs 59 and 60 of Schedule 3 to, the Mental Health (Amendment) Act 1982 (c. 51), section 148 of, and paragraph 57 of Schedule 4 to, the Mental Health Act 1983 (c. 20), section 1 of the County Courts (Penalties for Contempt) Act 1983 (c. 45), section 17 of, and Parts 1 and V of Schedule 4 to, the Criminal Justice Act 1991 (c. 53), section 65 of, and paragraph 6 of Schedule 3 to, the Criminal Justice Act 1993 (c. 36), section 165 of, and paragraph 84 of Schedule 9 to, the Powers of Criminal Courts (Sentencing) Act 2000 (c. 6), section 1 of, and paragraph 19 of Schedule 1 to, the Mental Health Act 2007 (c. 12) and section 17 of, and paragraph 52 of Schedule 9 and paragraph 53 of Schedule 10 to, the Crime and Courts Act 2013 (c. 22). It is further amended by sections 6 and 149 of, and paragraph 25 of Schedule 4 and Part 1 of Schedule 28 to, the Criminal Justice and Immigration Act 2008 (c. 4), with effect from a date to be appointed.
[31] 1995 c. 38.

(2) The party who wants to challenge the credibility or consistency of that person must—
 (a) serve notice of intention to do so on—
  (i) the court officer, and
  (ii) the party who served the hearsay; and
 (b) in it, identify any statement or other material on which that party relies.

(3) A respondent who wants to challenge such a person's credibility or consistency must serve such a notice not more than 5 business days after service of the hearsay by the applicant.

(4) An applicant who wants to challenge such a person's credibility or consistency must serve such a notice not more than 3 business days after service of the hearsay by the respondent.

(5) The party who served the hearsay—
 (a) may call that person to give oral evidence instead; and
 (b) if so, must serve notice of intention to do so on—
  (i) the court officer, and
  (ii) the other party
 as soon as practicable after service of the notice under paragraph (2).

[Note. Section 5(2) of the Civil Evidence Act 1995[32] describes the procedure for challenging the credibility of the maker of a statement of which hearsay evidence is introduced. See also section 6 of that Act[33].

The 1995 Act does not allow the introduction of evidence of a previous inconsistent statement otherwise than in accordance with sections 5, 6 and 7 of the Criminal Procedure Act 1865[34].]

Magistrates' courts' powers to adjourn, etc.   R48.16

48.16 (1) This rule applies where a magistrates' court deals with unauthorised disclosure of prosecution material under sections 17 and 18 of the Criminal Procedure and Investigations Act 1996[35].

(2) The sections of the Magistrates' Courts Act 1980 listed in paragraph (3) apply as if in those sections—
 (a) 'complaint' and 'summons' each referred to an application or written statement under rule 48.9;
 (b) 'complainant' meant an applicant; and
 (c) 'defendant' meant the respondent.

(3) Those sections are—
 (a) section 51[36] (issue of summons on complaint);
 (b) section 54[37] (adjournment);
 (c) section 55[38] (non-appearance of defendant);
 (d) section 97(1)[39] Superscript footnote number (summons to witness);
 (e) section 121(1)[40] (constitution and place of sitting of court); and
 (f) section 123[41] (defect in process).

(4) Section 127 of the 1980 Act[42] (limitation of time) does not apply.

[Note. Under section 19(3) of the Criminal Procedure and Investigations Act 1996[43], Criminal Procedure Rules may contain provisions equivalent to those contained in Schedule 3 to the Contempt of Court Act 1981[44] (which allows magistrates' courts in cases of contempt of court to use certain powers such courts possess in other cases).]

---

[32] 1995 c. 38.

[33] 1995 c. 38.

[34] 1865 c. 18; section 6 was amended by section 10 of the Decimal Currency Act 1969 (c. 19), section 90 of, and paragraph 3 of Schedule 13 to, the Access to Justice Act 1999 (c. 22), section 109 of, and paragraph 47 of Schedule 8 to, the Courts Act 2003 (c. 39) and paragraph 79 of Schedule 36 and Schedule 37 to the Criminal Justice Act 2003 (c. 44). It is further amended by section 119 of, and Schedule 7 to, the Police and Criminal Evidence Act 1984 (c. 60), with effect from a date to be appointed.

[35] 1996 c. 25; section 17 was amended by section 331 of, and paragraphs 20 and 33 of Schedule 36 to, the Criminal Justice Act 2003 (c. 44).

[36] 1980 c. 43; section 51 was substituted by section 47(1) of the Courts Act 2003 (c. 39).

[37] 1980 c. 43.

[38] 1980 c. 43.

[39] 1980 c. 43; section 97(1) was substituted by section 169(2) of the Serious Organised Crime and Police Act 2005 (c. 15).

[40] 1980 c. 43.

[41] 1980 c. 43.

[42] 1980 c. 43.

[43] 1996 c. 25; section 19(3) was amended by section 109 of, and paragraph 377 of Schedule 8 to, the Courts Act 2003 (c. 39) and section 15 of, and paragraph 251 of Schedule 4 to, the Constitutional Reform Act 2005 (c. 4).

[44] 1981 c. 49; Schedule 3 has been amended but the amendment is not relevant to this rule.

R48.17   **Court's power to vary requirements**

48.17 (1)   The court may shorten or extend (even after it has expired) a time limit under rule 48.11, 48.14 or 48.15.

(2)   A person who wants an extension of time must—

(a)   apply when serving the statement, notice or application for which it is needed; and

(b)   explain the delay.

CRIMINAL PROCEDURE RULES   PART 49   INTERNATIONAL CO-OPERATION

R49.1   **Notice required to accompany process served outside the United Kingdom and translations**

49.1 (1)   The notice which by virtue of section 3(4)(b) of the Crime (International Co-operation) Act 2003[1] (general requirements for service of process) must accompany any process served outside the United Kingdom must give the information specified in paragraphs (2) and (4) below.

(2)   The notice must—

(a)   state that the person required by the process to appear as a party or attend as a witness can obtain information about his rights in connection therewith from the relevant authority; and

(b)   give the particulars specified in paragraph (4) about that authority.

(3)   The relevant authority where the process is served—

(a)   at the request of the prosecuting authority, is that authority; or

(b)   at the request of the defendant or the prosecutor in the case of a private prosecution, is the court by which the process is served.

(4)   The particulars referred to in paragraph (2) are—

(a)   the name and address of the relevant authority, together with its telephone and fax numbers and e-mail address; and

(b)   the name of a person at the relevant authority who can provide the information referred to in paragraph (2)(a), together with his telephone and fax numbers and e-mail address.

(5)   The magistrates' court or Crown Court officer must send, together with any process served outside the United Kingdom—

(a)   any translation which is provided under section 3(3)(b) of the 2003 Act; and

(b)   any translation of the information required to be given by this rule which is provided to him.

(6)   In this rule 'process' has the same meaning as in section 51(3) of the 2003 Act.

R49.2   **Proof of service outside the United Kingdom**

49.2 (1)   A statement in a certificate given by or on behalf of the Secretary of State—

(a)   that process has been served on any person under section 4(1) of the Crime (International Co-operation) Act 2003 (service of process otherwise than by post);

(b)   of the manner in which service was effected; and

(c)   of the date on which process was served;

shall be admissible as evidence of any facts so stated.

(2)   In this rule 'process' has the same meaning as in section 51(3) of the 2003 Act.

R49.3   **Supply of copy of notice of request for assistance abroad**

49.3   Where a request for assistance under section 7 of the Crime (International Co-operation) Act 2003 is made by a justice of the peace or a judge exercising the jurisdiction of the Crown Court and is sent in accordance with section 8(1) of the 2003 Act, the magistrates' court or Crown Court officer shall send a copy of the letter of request to the Secretary of State as soon as practicable after the request has been made.

R49.4   **Persons entitled to appear and take part in proceedings before a nominated court, and exclusion of the public**

49.4   A court nominated under section 15(1) of the Crime (International Co-operation) Act 2003 (nominating a court to receive evidence) may—

(a)   determine who may appear or take part in the proceedings under Schedule 1 to the 2003 Act before the court and whether a party to the proceedings is entitled to be legally represented; and

---

[1]   2003 c. 32.

(b) direct that the public be excluded from those proceedings if it thinks it necessary to do so in the interests of justice.

Record of proceedings to receive evidence before a nominated court

49.5 (1) Where a court is nominated under section 15(1) of the Crime (International Co-operation) Act 2003 the magistrates' court or Crown Court officer shall enter in an overseas record—

  (a) details of the request in respect of which the notice under section 15(1) of the 2003 Act was given;

  (b) the date on which, and place at which, the proceedings under Schedule 1 to the 2003 Act in respect of that request took place;

  (c) the name of any witness who gave evidence at the proceedings in question;

  (d) the name of any person who took part in the proceedings as a legal representative or an interpreter;

  (e) whether a witness was required to give evidence on oath or (by virtue of section 5 of the Oaths Act 1978[2]) after making a solemn affirmation; and

  (f) whether the opportunity to cross-examine any witness was refused.

(2) When the court gives the evidence received by it under paragraph 6(1) of Schedule 1 to the 2003 Act to the court or authority that made the request or to the territorial authority for forwarding to the court or authority that made the request, the magistrates' court or Crown Court officer shall send to the court, authority or territorial authority (as the case may be) a copy of an extract of so much of the overseas record as relates to the proceedings in respect of that request.

[Note. As to the keeping of an overseas record, see rule 49.9.]

Interpreter for the purposes of proceedings involving a television or telephone link

49.6 (1) This rule applies where a court is nominated under section 30(3) (hearing witnesses in the UK through television links) or section 31(4) (hearing witnesses in the UK by telephone) of the Crime (International Co-operation) Act 2003.

(2) Where it appears to the justices' legal adviser or the Crown Court officer that the witness to be heard in the proceedings under Part 1 or 2 of Schedule 2 to the 2003 Act ('the relevant proceedings') is likely to give evidence in a language other than English, he shall make arrangements for an interpreter to be present at the proceedings to translate what is said into English.

(3) Where it appears to the justices' legal adviser or the Crown Court officer that the witness to be heard in the relevant proceedings is likely to give evidence in a language other than that in which the proceedings of the court referred to in section 30(1) or, as the case may be, 31(1) of the 2003 Act ('the external court') will be conducted, he shall make arrangements for an interpreter to be present at the relevant proceedings to translate what is said into the language in which the proceedings of the external court will be conducted.

(4) Where the evidence in the relevant proceedings is either given in a language other than English or is not translated into English by an interpreter, the court shall adjourn the proceedings until such time as an interpreter can be present to provide a translation into English.

(5) Where a court in Wales understands Welsh—

  (a) paragraph (2) does not apply where it appears to the justices' legal adviser or Crown Court officer that the witness in question is likely to give evidence in Welsh;

  (b) paragraph (4) does not apply where the evidence is given in Welsh; and

  (c) any translation which is provided pursuant to paragraph (2) or (4) may be into Welsh instead of English.

Record of television link hearing before a nominated court

49.7 (1) This rule applies where a court is nominated under section 30(3) of the Crime (International Co-operation) Act 2003.

(2) The magistrates' court or Crown Court officer shall enter in an overseas record—

  (a) details of the request in respect of which the notice under section 30(3) of the 2003 Act was given;

  (b) the date on which, and place at which, the proceedings under Part 1 of Schedule 2 to that Act in respect of that request took place;

  (c) the technical conditions, such as the type of equipment used, under which the proceedings took place;

---

[2] 1978 c. 19.

(d) the name of the witness who gave evidence;

(e) the name of any person who took part in the proceedings as a legal representative or an interpreter; and

(f) the language in which the evidence was given.

(3) As soon as practicable after the proceedings under Part 1 of Schedule 2 to the 2003 Act took place, the magistrates' court or Crown Court officer shall send to the external authority that made the request a copy of an extract of so much of the overseas record as relates to the proceedings in respect of that request.

[Note. As to the keeping of an overseas record, see rule 49.9.]

R49.8 Record of telephone link hearing before a nominated court

49.8 (1) This rule applies where a court is nominated under section 31(4) of the Crime (International Co-operation) Act 2003.

(2) The magistrates' court or Crown Court officer shall enter in an overseas record—

(a) details of the request in respect of which the notice under section 31(4) of the 2003 Act was given;

(b) the date, time and place at which the proceedings under Part 2 of Schedule 2 to the 2003 Act took place;

(c) the name of the witness who gave evidence;

(d) the name of any interpreter who acted at the proceedings; and

(e) the language in which the evidence was given.

[Note. As to the keeping of an overseas record, see rule 49.9.]

R49.9 Overseas record

49.9 (1) The overseas records of a magistrates' court shall be part of the register (within the meaning of section 150(1) of the Magistrates' Courts Act 1980[3]).

(2) The overseas records of any court shall not be open to inspection by any person except—

(a) as authorised by the Secretary of State; or

(b) with the leave of the court.

[Note. As to the making of court records, see rule 5.4.]

R49.10 Overseas freezing orders

49.10 (1) This rule applies where a court is nominated under section 21(1) of the Crime (International Co-operation) Act 2003[4] to give effect to an overseas freezing order.

(2) Where the Secretary of State serves a copy of such an order on the court officer—

(a) the general rule is that the court must consider the order no later than the next business day; but

(b) exceptionally, the court may consider the order later than that, though not more than 5 business days after service.

(3) The court must not consider the order unless—

(a) it is satisfied that the chief officer of police for the area in which the evidence is situated has had notice of the order; and

(b) that chief officer of police has had an opportunity to make representations, at a hearing if that officer wants.

(4) The court may consider the order—

(a) without a hearing; or

(b) at a hearing, in public or in private.

[Note. Under sections 20, 21 and 22 of the Crime (International Co-operation) Act 2003, a court nominated by the Secretary of State must consider an order, made by a court or other authority in a country outside the United Kingdom, the purpose of which is to protect evidence in the United Kingdom which may be used in proceedings or an investigation in that other country pending the transfer of that evidence to that country. The court may decide not to give effect to such an order only if—

(a) were the person whose conduct is in question to be charged with the offence to which the order relates, a previous conviction or acquittal would entitle that person to be discharged; or

(b) giving effect to the order would be incompatible with a Convention right, within the meaning of the Human Rights Act 1998.]

---

[3] 1980 c. 43; a relevant amendment was made to section 150(1) by paragraph 250 of Schedule 8, and Schedule 10 to, the Courts Act 2003 (c. 39).
[4] 2003 c. 32.

Overseas forfeiture orders

49.11 (1) This rule applies where—

(a) the Crown Court can—

(i) make a restraint order under article 5 of the Criminal Justice (International Co-operation) Act 1990 (Enforcement of Overseas Forfeiture Orders) Order 2005[5], or

(ii) give effect to an external forfeiture order under article 19 of that Order;

(b) the Director of Public Prosecutions or the Director of the Serious Fraud Office receives—

(i) a request for the restraint of property to which article 3 of the 2005 Order applies, or

(ii) a request to give effect to an external forfeiture order to which article 15 of the Order applies; and

(c) the Director wants the Crown Court to—

(i) make such a restraint order, or

(ii) give effect to such a forfeiture order.

(2) The Director must—

(a) apply in writing;

(b) serve the application on the court officer; and

(c) serve the application on the defendant and on any other person affected by the order, unless the court is satisfied that—

(i) the application is urgent, or

(ii) there are reasonable grounds for believing that to give notice of the application would cause the dissipation of the property which is the subject of the application.

(3) The application must—

(a) identify the property the subject of the application;

(b) identify the person who is or who may become the subject of such a forfeiture order;

(c) explain how the requirements of the 2005 Order are satisfied, as the case may be—

(i) for making a restraint order, or

(ii) for giving effect to a forfeiture order;

(d) where the application is to give effect to a forfeiture order, include an application to appoint the Director as the enforcement authority; and

(e) propose the terms of the Crown Court order.

(4) If the court allows the application, it must—

(a) where it decides to make a restraint order—

(i) specify the property the subject of the order,

(ii) specify the person or persons who are prohibited from dealing with that property,

(iii) specify any exception to that prohibition, and

(iv) include any ancillary order that the court believes is appropriate to ensure that the restraint order is effective; and

(b) where it decides to give effect to a forfeiture order, exercise its power to—

(i) direct the registration of the order as an order of the Crown Court,

(ii) give directions for notice of the order to be given to any person affected by it, and

(iii) appoint the applicant Director as the enforcement authority.

(5) Paragraph (6) applies where a person affected by an order, or the Director, wants the court to vary or discharge a restraint order or cancel the registration of a forfeiture order.

(6) Such a person must—

(a) apply in writing as soon as practicable after becoming aware of the grounds for doing so;

(b) serve the application on the court officer and, as applicable—

(i) the other party, and

(ii) any other person who will or may be affected;

(c) explain why it is appropriate, as the case may be—

(i) for the restraint order to be varied or discharged, or

(ii) for the registration of the forfeiture order to be cancelled;

(d) propose the terms of any variation; and

(e) ask for a hearing, if one is wanted, and explain why it is needed.

(7) The court may—

(a) consider an application

(i) at a hearing, which must be in private unless the court otherwise directs, or

(ii) without a hearing; and

(b) allow an application to be made orally.

[5] S.I. 2005/3180.

Criminal Procedure Rules

[Note. Under article 19 of the Criminal Justice (International Co-operation) Act 1990 (Enforcement of Overseas Forfeiture Orders) Order 2005, on the application of the Director of Public Prosecutions or the Director of the Serious Fraud Office the Crown Court may give effect to an order made by a court in a country outside the United Kingdom for the forfeiture and destruction, or other disposal, of any property in respect of which an offence has been committed in that country, or which was used or intended for use in connection with the commission of such an offence (described in the Order as an 'external forfeiture order').

Under article 5 of the 2005 Order, on the application of the Director of Public Prosecutions or the Director of the Serious Fraud Office the Crown Court may make a restraint order prohibiting any specified person from dealing with property, for the purpose of facilitating the enforcement of such a forfeiture order which has yet to be made.]

CRIMINAL PROCEDURE RULES   PART 50   EXTRADITION

Section 1: general rules

R50.1   When this Part applies

50.1   (1)   This Part applies to extradition under Part 1 or Part 2 of the Extradition Act 2003[1].

(2)   Section 2 of this Part applies to proceedings in a magistrates' court, and in that Section—

(a)   rules 50.3 to 50.7, 50.15 and 50.16 apply to extradition under Part 1 of the Act;

(b)   rules 50.3, 50.4 and 50.8 to 50.16 apply to extradition under Part 2 of the Act.

(3)   Section 3 of this Part applies where—

(a)   a party wants to appeal to the High Court against an order by the magistrates' court or by the Secretary of State; and

(b)   a party to an appeal to the High Court wants to appeal further to the Supreme Court under—

(i)   section 32 of the Act (appeal under Part 1 of the Act), or

(ii)   section 114 of the Act (appeal under Part 2 of the Act).

(4)   Section 4 of this Part applies to proceedings in a magistrates' court under—

(a)   sections 54 and 55 of the Act (Request for consent to other offence being dealt with; Questions for decision at consent hearing); and

(b)   sections 56 and 57 of the Act (Request for consent to further extradition to category 1 territory; Questions for decision at consent hearing).

(5)   In this Part, and for the purposes of this Part in other rules—

(a)   'magistrates' court' means a District Judge (Magistrates' Courts) exercising the powers to which Section 2 of this Part applies;

(b)   'presenting officer' means an officer of the National Crime Agency, a police officer, a prosecutor or other person representing an authority or territory seeking the extradition of a defendant; and

(c)   'defendant' means a person arrested under Part 1 or Part 2 of the Extradition Act 2003.

[Note. The Extradition Act 2003 provides for the extradition of a person accused or convicted of a crime to the territory within which that person is accused, was convicted or is to serve a sentence.

Under Part 1 of the Act (sections 1 to 68), the magistrates' court may give effect to a warrant for arrest issued by an authority in a territory designated for the purposes of that Part.

Under Part 2 of the Act (sections 69 to 141), the magistrates' court and the Secretary of State may give effect to a request for extradition made under a treaty between the United Kingdom and the requesting territory.

Under sections 67 and 139 of the Extradition Act 2003[2], a District Judge (Magistrates' Courts) must be designated for the purposes of the Act to exercise the powers to which Section 2 of this Part applies.

There are rights of appeal to the High Court from decisions of the magistrates' court and of the Secretary of State: see Section 3 of this Part.]

R50.2   Special objective in extradition proceedings

50.2   When exercising a power to which this Part applies, as well as furthering the overriding objective, in accordance with rule 1.3, the court must have regard to the importance of—

(a)   mutual confidence and recognition between judicial authorities in the United Kingdom and in requesting territories; and

---

[1] 2003 c. 41.

[2] 2003 c. 41; sections 67 and 139 were amended by section 15 of, and paragraphs 352 and 353 of Schedule 4 to, the Constitutional Reform Act 2005 (c. 4) and section 42 of, and paragraph 15 of Schedule 13 to, the Police and Justice Act 2006 (c. 48).

(b) the conduct of extradition proceedings in accordance with international obligations, including obligations to deal swiftly with extradition requests.

Section 2: extradition proceedings in a magistrates' court

Exercise of magistrates' court's powers   R50.3

50.3 (1) The general rule is that the magistrates' court must exercise its powers at a hearing in public, but—

    (a) that is subject to any power the court has to—

        (i) impose reporting restrictions,

        (ii) withhold information from the public, or

        (iii) order a hearing in private; and

    (b) despite the general rule the court may, without a hearing—

        (i) give any directions to which rule 50.4 applies (Case management in the magistrates' court and duty of court officer), or

        (ii) determine an application which these Rules allow to be determined by a magistrates' court without a hearing in a case to which this Part does not apply.

  (2) If the court so directs, a party may attend by live link any hearing except an extradition hearing under rule 50.6 or 50.13.

  (3) Where the defendant is absent from a hearing—

    (a) the general rule is that the court must proceed as if the defendant—

        (i) were present, and

        (ii) opposed extradition on any ground of which the court has been made aware;

    (b) the general rule does not apply if the defendant is under 18;

    (c) the general rule is subject to the court being satisfied that—

        (i) the defendant had reasonable notice of where and when the hearing would take place,

        (ii) the defendant has been made aware that the hearing might proceed in his or her absence, and

        (iii) there is no good reason for the defendant's absence; and

    (d) the general rule does not apply but the court may exercise its powers in the defendant's absence where—

        (i) the court discharges the defendant,

        (ii) the defendant is represented and the defendant's presence is impracticable by reason of his or her ill health or disorderly conduct, or

        (iii) on an application under rule 50.32 (Application for consent to deal with another offence or for consent to further extradition), the defendant is represented or the defendant's presence is impracticable by reason of his or her detention in the territory to which he or she has been extradited.

  (4) The court may exercise its power to adjourn—

    (a) if either party asks, or on its own initiative; and

    (b) in particular—

        (i) to allow there to be obtained information that the court requires,

        (ii) following a provisional arrest under Part 1 of the Extradition Act 2003, pending receipt of the warrant,

        (iii) following a provisional arrest with a warrant under Part 2 of the Act, pending receipt of the extradition request,

        (iv) following a provisional arrest without a warrant under Part 2 of the Act, pending receipt of evidence or information required by the court,

        (v) if the court is informed that the defendant is serving a custodial sentence in the United Kingdom,

        (vi) if it appears to the court that the defendant is not fit to be extradited, unless the court discharges the defendant for that reason,

        (vii) where a court dealing with a warrant to which Part 1 of the Act applies is informed that another such warrant has been received in the United Kingdom,

        (viii) where a court dealing with a warrant to which Part 1 of the Act applies is informed of a request for the temporary transfer of the defendant to the territory to which the defendant's extradition is sought, or a request for the defendant to speak to the authorities of that territory, or

        (ix) during a hearing to which rule 50.32 applies (Application for consent to deal with another offence or for consent to further extradition).

  (5) The court must exercise its power to adjourn if informed that the defendant has been charged with an offence in the United Kingdom.

Criminal Procedure Rules

(6) The general rule is that, before exercising a power to which this Part applies, the court must give each party an opportunity to make representations, unless that party is absent without good reason.

(7) The court may—

(a) shorten a time limit or extend it (even after it has expired), unless that is inconsistent with other legislation;

(b) direct that a notice or application be served on any person; and

(c) allow a notice or application to be in a different form to one set out in the Practice Direction, or to be presented orally.

(8) A party who wants an extension of time within which to serve a notice or make an application must—

(a) apply for that extension of time when serving that notice or making that application; and

(b) give the reasons for the application for an extension of time.

[Note. See sections 8A, 8B, 9, 21B, 22, 23, 25 and 44 of the Extradition Act 2003[3] (powers in relation to extradition under Part 1 of the Act) and sections 76A, 76B, 77, 88, 89 and 91 of the Act[4] (powers in relation to extradition under Part 2 of the Act). Under sections 9 and 77 of the Act, at the extradition hearing the court has the same powers (as nearly as may be) as a magistrates' court would have if the proceedings were the summary trial of an allegation against the defendant: see also rule 24.12(3) (Trial and sentence in a magistrates' court; procedure where the defendant is absent).

Under sections 206A to 206C of the 2003 Act[5], the court may require a defendant to attend by live link a preliminary hearing to which rule 50.5, 50.9 or 50.11 applies, any hearing for the purposes of rule 50.12 and the hearing to which rule 50.32 applies.

Part 6 contains rules about reporting and access restrictions.

Part 14 contains rules about bail. Rules 14.2(3) and 14.7(7)(c) allow an application to be determined without a hearing in the circumstances to which those rules apply.

The principal time limits are prescribed by the Extradition Act 2003: see rule 50.16.]

R50.4 Case management in the magistrates' court and duty of court officer

50.4 (1) The magistrates' court and the parties have the same duties and powers as under Part 3 (Case management), subject to—

(a) rule 50.2 (Special objective in extradition proceedings); and

(b) paragraph (2) of this rule.

(2) Rule 3.6 (Application to vary a direction) does not apply to a decision to extradite or discharge.

(3) Where this rule applies, active case management by the court includes—

(a) if the court requires information from the authorities in the requesting territory—

(i) nominating a court officer, the designated authority which certified the arrest warrant where Part 1 of the Extradition Act 2003 Act applies, a party or other person to convey that request to those authorities, and

(ii) in a case in which the terms of that request need to be prepared in accordance with directions by the court, giving such directions accordingly; and

(b) giving such directions as are required where, under section 21B of the Extradition Act 2003[6], the parties agree—

(i) to the temporary transfer of the defendant to the requesting territory, or

(ii) that the defendant should speak with representatives of an authority in that territory.

(4) Where this rule applies, active assistance by the parties includes—

(a) applying for any direction needed as soon as reasonably practicable; and

(b) concisely explaining the reasons for any application for the court to direct—

(i) the preparation of a request to which paragraph (3)(a) applies, or

(ii) the making of arrangements to which paragraph (3)(b) applies.

---

[3] 2003 c. 41; sections 8A and 8B were inserted by section 69 of the Policing and Crime Act 2009 (c. 26). Sections 9 and 44 were amended by paragraph 16 of Schedule 13 to the Police and Justice Act 2006 (c. 48). Section 21B was inserted by section 159 of the Anti-social Behaviour, Crime and Policing Act 2014 (c. 12). Section 22 was amended by section 71 of the Policing and Crime Act 2009 (c. 26). Section 23 was amended by paragraph 7 of Schedule 13 to the Police and Justice Act 2006 (c. 48) and section 71 of the Policing and Crime Act 2009 (c. 26).

[4] 2003 c. 41; sections 76A and 76B were inserted by section 70 of the Policing and Crime Act 2009 (c. 26). Section 77 was amended by paragraph 16 of Schedule 13 to the Police and Justice Act 2006 (c. 48). Section 88 was amended by section 71 of the Policing and Crime Act 2009 (c. 26). Section 89 was amended by paragraph 7 of Schedule 13 to the Police and Justice Act 2006 (c. 48) and section 71 of the Policing and Crime Act 2009 (c. 26).

[5] 2003 c. 41; sections 206A, 206B and 206C were inserted by section 78 of the Policing and Crime Act 2009 (c. 26).

[6] 2003 c. 41; section 21B was inserted by section 159 of the Anti-social Behaviour, Crime and Policing Act 2014 (c. 12).

(5) Where this rule applies, active assistance by the presenting officer includes—
- (a) taking reasonable steps to ensure that the defendant will be able to understand (with help, if necessary)—
  - (i) what is alleged by the warrant, if Part 1 of the 2003 Act applies, or
  - (ii) the content of the extradition request, if Part 2 of the Act applies; and
- (b) providing in writing identification of the equivalent offence or offences under the law of England and Wales for the conduct being relied on if—
  - (i) this is raised for the defence as an issue and the court considers it necessary to identify the equivalent offence or offences in writing, or
  - (ii) the defendant is not represented.
(6) The court officer must—
- (a) as soon as practicable, serve notice of the court's decision to extradite or discharge—
  - (i) on the defendant,
  - (ii) on the designated authority which certified the arrest warrant, where Part 1 of the 2003 Act applies, and
  - (iii) on the Secretary of State, where Part 2 of the Act applies; and
- (b) give the court such assistance as it requires.

[Note. Part 3 contains rules about case management which apply at an extradition hearing and during preparation for that hearing. This rule must be read in conjunction with those rules.

Under section 21B of the Extradition Act 2003 (Request for temporary transfer etc.), where Part 1 of the Act applies, and in the circumstances described in that section, the parties may agree to the defendant's temporary transfer to the requesting territory, or may agree that the defendant will speak to representatives of an investigating, prosecuting or judicial authority in that territory. On the making by a party of a request to such effect the court must if necessary adjourn the proceedings for 7 days while the other party considers it. If the parties then agree to proceed with the proposed transfer or discussion the court must adjourn the proceedings for however long seems necessary.]

Extradition under Part 1 of the Extradition Act 2003

Preliminary hearing after arrest   R50.5

50.5 (1) This rule applies where the defendant is first brought before the court after—
- (a) arrest under a warrant to which Part 1 of the Extradition Act 2003 applies; or
- (b) provisional arrest under Part 1 of the Act.
(2) The presenting officer must—
- (a) serve on the court officer—
  - (i) the arrest warrant, and
  - (ii) a certificate, given by the authority designated by the Secretary of State, that the warrant was issued by an authority having the function of issuing such warrants in the territory to which the defendant's extradition is sought; or
- (b) apply at once for an extension of time within which to serve that warrant and that certificate.
(3) An application under paragraph (2)(b) must—
- (a) explain why the requirement to serve the warrant and certificate at once could not reasonably be complied with; and
- (b) include—
  - (i) any written material in support of that explanation, and
  - (ii) representations about bail pending service of those documents.
(4) When the presenting officer serves the warrant and certificate, in the following sequence the court must—
- (a) decide whether the defendant is the person in respect of whom the warrant was issued;
- (b) explain, in terms the defendant can understand (with help, if necessary)—
  - (i) the allegation made in the warrant, and
  - (ii) that the defendant may consent to extradition, and how that may be done and with what effect;
- (c) give directions for an extradition hearing to begin—
  - (i) no more than 21 days after the defendant's arrest, or
  - (ii) if either party so applies, at such a later date as the court decides is in the interests of justice;
- (d) consider any ancillary application, including an application about bail pending the extradition hearing; and
- (e) give such directions as are required for the preparation and conduct of the extradition hearing.

[Note. See sections 4, 6, 7 and 8 of the Extradition Act 2003[7].

Under section 6 of the Act, following a provisional arrest pending receipt of a warrant the defendant must be brought before the court within 48 hours, and the warrant and certificate must be served within that same period. If they are not so served, the court may extend the time for service by a further 48 hours.

Under section 45 of the Act[8], a defendant's consent to extradition must be given before the court, must be recorded in writing, and is irrevocable. Consent may not be given unless the defendant has a legal representative with him or her when giving consent, or the defendant has failed or refused to apply for legal aid, or legal aid has been refused or withdrawn.

Part 14 contains rules about bail.]

R50.6 **Extradition hearing**

50.6 (1) This rule applies at the extradition hearing arranged by the court under rule 50.5.
  (2) In the following sequence, the court must decide—
    (a) whether the offence specified in the warrant is an extradition offence;
    (b) whether a bar to extradition applies, namely—
      (i)   the rule against double jeopardy,
      (ii)   absence of prosecution decision,
      (iii) extraneous considerations,
      (iv)   the passage of time,
      (v)   the defendant's age,
      (vi)   speciality,
      (vii) earlier extradition or transfer to the United Kingdom, or
      (viii) forum;
    (c) where the warrant alleges that the defendant is unlawfully at large after conviction, whether conviction was in the defendant's presence and if not—
      (i)   whether the defendant was absent deliberately, and
      (ii) if the defendant was not absent deliberately, whether the defendant would be entitled to a retrial (or to a review of the conviction, amounting to a retrial);
    (d) whether extradition would be—
      (i)   compatible with the defendant's human rights, and
      (ii) proportionate;
    (e) whether it would be unjust or oppressive to extradite the defendant because of his or her physical or mental condition;
    (f) after deciding each of (a) to (e) above, before progressing to the next, whether to order the defendant's discharge, and
    (g) whether to order the temporary transfer of the defendant to the territory to which the defendant's extradition is sought.
  (3) If the court discharges the defendant, the court must consider any ancillary application, including an application about—
    (a) reporting restrictions; or
    (b) costs.
  (4) If the court does not discharge the defendant, the court must—
    (a) exercise its power to order the defendant's extradition;
    (b) explain, in terms the defendant can understand (with help, if necessary), that the defendant may appeal to the High Court within the next 7 days; and
    (c) consider any ancillary application, including an application about—
      (i)   bail pending extradition,
      (ii) reporting restrictions, or
      (iii) costs.
  (5) If the court orders the defendant's extradition, the court must order its postponement where—
    (a) the defendant has been charged with an offence in the United Kingdom; or
    (b) the defendant has been sentenced to imprisonment or detention in the United Kingdom.

[Note. See sections 10, 11, 20, 21, 21B, 25, 26, 36A, 36B, 64 and 65 of the Extradition Act 2003[9].

---

[7] 2003 c. 41; section 6 was amended by section 77 of the Policing and Crime Act 2009 (c. 26). Section 7 was amended by paragraph 16 of Schedule 13 to the Police and Justice Act 2006 (c. 48) and section 77 of the Policing and Crime Act 2009 (c. 26). Section 8 was amended by paragraph 16 of Schedule 13 to the Police and Justice Act 2006 (c. 48) and section 155 of the Anti-social Behaviour, Crime and Policing Act 2014 (c. 12).
[8] 2003 c. 41; section 45 was amended by paragraphs 62 and 63 of Schedule 5 to the Legal Aid, Sentencing and Punishment of Offenders Act 2012 (c. 10) and section 163 of the Anti-social Behaviour, Crime and Policing Act 2014 (c. 12).
[9] 2003 c. 41; section 11 was amended by paragraphs 3 and 4 of Schedule 13 to the Police and Justice Act 2006 (c. 48), paragraphs 1 and 2 of Schedule 20 to the Crime and Courts Act 2013 (c. 22) and sections 156, 157, 158 and 181 of, and

Part 6 contains rules about reporting restrictions. Part 45 contains rules about costs.]

Discharge where warrant withdrawn   **R50.7**

50.7 (1) This rule applies where the authority that certified the warrant gives the court officer notice that the warrant has been withdrawn—

  (a) after the start of the hearing under rule 50.5; and

  (b) before the court orders the defendant's extradition or discharge.

  (2) The court must exercise its power to discharge the defendant.

[Note. See section 41 of the Extradition Act 2003.]

Extradition under Part 2 of the Extradition Act 2003

Issue of arrest warrant   **R50.8**

50.8 (1) This rule applies where the Secretary of State serves on the court officer—

  (a) an extradition request to which Part 2 of the Extradition Act 2003 applies;

  (b) a certificate given by the Secretary of State that the request was received in the way approved for the request; and

  (c) a copy of any Order in Council which applies to the request.

  (2) In the following sequence, the court must decide—

  (a) whether the offence in respect of which extradition is requested is an extradition offence; and

  (b) whether there is sufficient evidence, or (where the Secretary of State has so ordered, for this purpose) information, to justify the issue of a warrant of arrest.

  (3) The court may issue an arrest warrant—

  (a) without giving the parties an opportunity to make representations; and

  (b) without a hearing, or at a hearing in public or in private.

[Note. See sections 70, 71, 137 and 138 of the Extradition Act 2003[10].]

Preliminary hearing after arrest   **R50.9**

50.9 (1) This rule applies where a defendant is first brought before the court after arrest under a warrant to which rule 50.8 applies.

  (2) In the following sequence, the court must—

  (a) explain, in terms the defendant can understand (with help, if necessary)—

    (i) the content of the extradition request, and

    (ii) that the defendant may consent to extradition, and how that may be done and with what effect;

  (b) arrange for an extradition hearing to begin—

    (i) no more than 2 months later, or

    (ii) if either party so applies, at such a later date as the court decides is in the interests of justice;

  (c) consider any ancillary application, including an application about bail pending the extradition hearing; and

  (d) give any direction as is appropriate to the needs of the case about the introduction of evidence at the extradition hearing.

[Note. See sections 72 and 75 of the Extradition Act 2003[11].

Under section 127 of the 2003 Act[12] a defendant's consent to extradition must be given before the court, must be recorded in writing, and is irrevocable. Consent may not be given unless the defendant has a legal representative with him or her when giving consent, or the defendant has failed or refused to apply for legal aid, or legal aid has been refused or withdrawn.

Part 14 contains rules about bail.]

paragraph 104 of Schedule 11 to, the Anti-social Behaviour, Crime and Policing Act 2014 (c. 12). Section 21 was amended by paragraph 16 of Schedule 13 to the Police and Justice Act 2006 (c. 48). Section 21B was inserted by section 159 of the Anti-social Behaviour, Crime and Policing Act 2014 (c. 12), section 26 was amended by section 160 of that Act, sections 36A and 36B were inserted by section 161 of that Act and sections 64 and 65 were substituted by section 164 of that Act.

[10] 2003 c. 41; section 70 was amended by paragraphs 1 and 17 of Schedule 13 to the Police and Justice Act 2006 (c. 48). Section 71 was amended by paragraph 202 of Schedule 16 to the Armed Forces Act 2006 (c. 52). Section 137 was amended by sections 164 and 181 of, and paragraph 117 of Schedule 11 to, the Anti-social Behaviour, Crime and Policing Act 2014 (c. 12). Section 138 was amended by sections 164 and 181 of, and paragraph 118 of Schedule 11 to, the 2014 Act.

[11] 2003 c. 41; section 72 was amended by paragraph 16 of Schedule 13 to the Police and Justice Act 2006 (c. 48).

[12] 2003 c. 41; section 127 was amended by paragraphs 62 and 64 of Schedule 5 to the Legal Aid, Sentencing and Punishment of Offenders Act 2012 (c. 10).

R50.10 **Issue of provisional arrest warrant**

50.10 (1) This rule applies where a presenting officer wants a justice of the peace to issue a provisional arrest warrant under Part 2 of the Extradition Act 2003, pending receipt of an extradition request.

(2) The presenting officer must—

(a) serve an application for a warrant on the court officer; and

(b) verify that application on oath or affirmation.

(3) In the following sequence, the justice must decide—

(a) whether the alleged offence is an extradition offence; and

(b) whether there is sufficient evidence, or (where the Secretary of State has so ordered, for this purpose) information, to justify the issue of a warrant of arrest.

[Note. See sections 73, 137 and 138 of the Extradition Act 2003[13].]

R50.11 **Preliminary hearing after provisional arrest**

50.11 (1) This rule applies where a defendant is first brought before the court after arrest—

(a) under a provisional arrest warrant to which rule 50.10 applies; or

(b) under section 74A of the Extradition Act 2003[14], without a warrant.

(2) Where paragraph (1)(b) applies the court must first—

(a) on the basis of such evidence or information as is produced to the court, decide whether a warrant to which rule 50.10 applies would be issued if the defendant were not already under arrest; and

(b) if no such warrant would be issued, order the defendant's discharge.

(3) Unless the court orders the defendant's discharge under paragraph (2), the court must—

(a) explain, in terms the defendant can understand (with help, if necessary)—

(i) the allegation in respect of which the defendant has been arrested, and

(ii) that the defendant may consent to extradition, and how that may be done and with what effect; and

(b) consider any ancillary application, including an application about bail pending receipt of the extradition request.

[Note. See sections 74, 74A, 74B, 74C, 74D and 74E of the Extradition Act 2003[15]. Under section 127 of the Act, a defendant's consent to extradition must be given before the court, must be recorded in writing, and is irrevocable. Consent may not be given unless the defendant has a legal representative with him or her when giving consent, or the defendant has failed or refused to apply for legal aid, or legal aid has been refused or withdrawn.]

R50.12 **Arrangement of extradition hearing after provisional arrest**

50.12 (1) This rule applies when the Secretary of State serves on the court officer—

(a) a request for extradition in respect of which a defendant has been arrested—

(i) under a provisional arrest warrant to which rule 50.10 applies, or

(ii) under section 74A of the Extradition Act 2003, without a warrant;

(b) a certificate given by the Secretary of State that the request was received in the way approved for the request; and

(c) a copy of any Order in Council which applies to the request.

(2) Unless a time limit for service of the request has expired, the court must—

(a) give directions for an extradition hearing to begin—

(i) no more than 2 months after service of the request, or

(ii) if either party so applies, at such a later date as the court decides is in the interests of justice;

(b) consider any ancillary application, including an application about bail pending the extradition hearing; and

(c) give such directions as are required for the preparation and conduct of the extradition hearing.

[Note. See section 76 of the Extradition Act 2003.]

---

[13] 2003 c. 41; section 73 was amended by paragraph 203 of Schedule 16 to the Armed Forces Act 2006 (c. 52). Section 137 was amended by sections 164 and 181 of, and paragraph 117 of Schedule 11 to, the Anti-social Behaviour, Crime and Policing Act 2014 (c. 12). Section 138 was amended by sections 164 and 181 of, and paragraph 118 of Schedule 11 to, the 2014 Act.
[14] 2003 c. 41; section 74A was inserted by paragraphs 1 and 2 of the Schedule to the Extradition (Provisional Arrest) Act 2020 (c. 18).
[15] 2003 c. 41; sections 74B, 74C, 74D and 74E were inserted by paragraphs 1 and 2 of the Schedule to the Extradition (Provisional Arrest) Act 2020 (c. 18).

Extradition hearing

50.13 (1) This rule applies at the extradition hearing directed under rule 50.9 or rule 50.12.

(2) In the following sequence, the court must decide—

  (a) whether the documents served on the court officer by the Secretary of State include—

    (i) those listed in rule 50.8(1) or rule 50.12(1), as the case may be,

    (ii) particulars of the person whose extradition is requested,

    (iii) particulars of the offence specified in the request, and

    (iv) as the case may be, a warrant for the defendant's arrest, or a certificate of the defendant's conviction and (if applicable) sentence, issued in the requesting territory;

  (b) whether the defendant is the person whose extradition is requested;

  (c) whether the offence specified in the request is an extradition offence;

  (d) whether the documents served on the court officer by the Secretary of State have been served also on the defendant;

  (e) whether a bar to extradition applies, namely—

    (i) the rule against double jeopardy,

    (ii) extraneous considerations,

    (iii) the passage of time,

    (iv) hostage-taking considerations, or

    (v) forum;

  (f) where the request accuses the defendant of an offence, whether there is evidence which would be sufficient to make a case requiring an answer by the defendant if the extradition proceedings were a trial (unless the Secretary of State has otherwise ordered, for this purpose);

  (g) where the request accuses the defendant of being unlawfully at large after conviction, whether the defendant was—

    (i) convicted in his or her presence, or

    (ii) absent deliberately;

  (h) where the request accuses the defendant of being unlawfully at large after conviction, and the defendant was absent but not deliberately—

    (i) whether the defendant would be entitled to a retrial (or to a review of the conviction amounting to a retrial), and

    (ii) if so, whether there is evidence which would be sufficient to make a case requiring an answer by the defendant if the extradition proceedings were a trial (unless the Secretary of State has otherwise ordered, for this purpose);

  (i) whether extradition would be compatible with the defendant's human rights;

  (j) whether it would be unjust or oppressive to extradite the defendant because of his or her physical or mental condition; and

  (k) after deciding each of (a) to (j) above, before progressing to the next, whether to order the defendant's discharge.

(3) If the court discharges the defendant, the court must consider any ancillary application, including an application about—

  (a) reporting restrictions; or

  (b) costs.

(4) If the court does not discharge the defendant, the court must—

  (a) exercise its power to send the case to the Secretary of State to decide whether to extradite the defendant;

  (b) explain, in terms the defendant can understand (with help, if necessary), that—

    (i) the defendant may appeal to the High Court not more than 14 days after being informed of the Secretary of State's decision, and

    (ii) any such appeal brought before the Secretary of State's decision has been made will not be heard until after that decision; and

  (c) consider any ancillary application, including an application about—

    (i) bail pending extradition,

    (ii) reporting restrictions, or

    (iii) costs.

(5) If the Secretary of State orders the defendant's extradition, the court must order its postponement where—

  (a) the defendant has been charged with an offence in the United Kingdom; or

  (b) the defendant has been sentenced to imprisonment or detention in the United Kingdom.

[Note. See sections 78, 79, 84, 85, 86, 87, 91, 92, 137 and 138 of the Extradition Act 2003[16].

Part 6 contains rules about reporting restrictions. Part 45 contains rules about costs.]

R50.14   **Discharge where extradition request withdrawn**

50.14 (1) This rule applies where the Secretary of State gives the court officer notice that the extradition request has been withdrawn—
- (a) after the start of the hearing under rule 50.9 or 50.11; and
- (b) before the court—
  - (i) sends the case to the Secretary of State to decide whether to extradite the defendant, or
  - (ii) discharges the defendant.

(2) The court must exercise its power to discharge the defendant.

[Note. See section 122 of the Extradition Act 2003.]

Evidence at extradition hearing

R50.15   **Introduction of additional evidence**

50.15 (1) Where a party wants to introduce evidence at an extradition hearing under the law that would apply if that hearing were a trial, the relevant Part of these Rules applies with such adaptations as the court directs.

(2) If the court admits as evidence the written statement of a witness—
- (a) each relevant part of the statement must be read or summarised aloud; or
- (b) the court must read the statement and its gist must be summarised aloud.

(3) If a party introduces in evidence a fact admitted by another party, or the parties jointly admit a fact, a written record must be made of the admission.

[Note. The admissibility of evidence that a party introduces is governed by rules of evidence.

Under section 202 of the Extradition Act 2003[17], the court may receive in evidence—

(a) a warrant to which Part 1 of the Act applies;

(b) any other document issued in a territory to which Part 1 of the Act applies, if the document is authenticated as required by the Act;

(c) a document issued in a territory to which Part 2 of the Act applies, if the document is authenticated as required by the Act.

Under sections 84 and 86 of the Act, which apply to evidence, if required, at an extradition hearing to which Part 2 of the Act applies, the court may accept as evidence of a fact a statement by a person in a document if oral evidence by that person of that fact would be admissible, and the statement was made to a police officer, or to someone else responsible for investigating offences or charging offenders.

Under section 205 of the Act, section 9 (proof by written witness statement) and section 10 (proof by formal admission) of the Criminal Justice Act 1967[18] apply to extradition proceedings as they apply in relation to proceedings for an offence.]

Discharge after failure to comply with a time limit

R50.16   **Defendant's application to be discharged**

50.16 (1) This rule applies where a defendant wants to be discharged—
- (a) because of a failure—
  - (i) to give the defendant a copy of any warrant under which the defendant is arrested as soon as practicable after arrest,

---

[16] 2003 c. 41; section 79 was amended by paragraphs 4 and 5 of Schedule 20 to the Crime and Courts Act 2013 (c. 22). Section 103 was amended by section 160 of the Anti-social Behaviour, Crime and Policing Act 2014 (c. 12). Section 118A and 118B were inserted by section 161 of the 2014 Act. Section 137 was amended by sections 164 and 181 of, and paragraph 117 of Schedule 11 to, the 2014 Act. Section 138 was amended by sections 164 and 181 of, and paragraph 118 of Schedule 11 to, the 2014 Act.

[17] 2003 c. 41; section 202 was amended by paragraph 26 of Schedule 13 to the Police and Justice Act 2006 (c. 48).

[18] 1967 c. 80; section 9 was amended by section 56 of, and paragraph 49 of Schedule 8 to, the Courts Act 1971 (c. 23), section 168 of, and paragraph 6 of Schedule 9 to, the Criminal Justice and Public Order Act 1994 (c. 33), section 69 of the Criminal Procedure and Investigations Act 1996 (c. 25), regulation 9 of, and paragraph 4 of Schedule 5 to, S.I. 2001/1090, paragraph 43 of Schedule 3 and Part 4 of Schedule 37 to the Criminal Justice Act 2003 (c. 44), section 26 of, and paragraph 7 of Schedule 2 to, the Armed Forces Act 2011 (c. 18) and section 80 of the Deregulation Act 2015 (c. 20). It is further amended by section 72 of, and paragraph 55 of Schedule 5 to, the Children and Young Persons Act 1969 (c. 54) and section 65 of, and paragraph 1 of Schedule 4 to, the Courts Act 2003 (c. 39), with effect from dates to be appointed.

(ii) to bring the defendant before the court as soon as practicable after arrest under a warrant,

(iii) to bring the defendant before the court no more than 48 hours after provisional arrest under Part 1 of the Extradition Act 2003;

(iv) to give the defendant a copy of any certificate enabling provisional arrest without a warrant under section 74A of the 2003 Act as soon as practicable after arrest, or

(v) to bring the defendant before the court as soon as practicable after arrest under that section;

(b) because of a defect in a certificate enabling arrest without a warrant under section 74A of the 2003 Act;

(c) because there were no reasonable grounds on which there could have been issued a certificate enabling arrest without a warrant under section 74A of the 2003 Act;

(d) following the expiry of a time limit for—

(i) service of a warrant to which Part 1 of the 2003 Act applies, after provisional arrest under that Part of the Act (48 hours, under section 6 of the Act[19], unless the court otherwise directs),

(ii) service of an extradition request to which Part 2 of the Act applies, after provisional arrest under that Part of the Act (45 days, under section 74 of the Act[20], unless the Secretary of State has otherwise ordered for this purpose),

(iii) receipt of an undertaking that the defendant will be returned to complete a sentence in the United Kingdom, where the court required such an undertaking (21 days, under section 37 of the Act[21]),

(iv) making an extradition order, after the defendant has consented to extradition under Part 1 of the Act (10 days, under section 46 of the Act[22]),

(v) extradition, where an extradition order has been made under Part 1 of the Act and any appeal by the defendant has failed (10 days, under sections 35, 36 and 47 of the Act[23], unless the court otherwise directs),

(vi) extradition, where an extradition order has been made under Part 2 of the Act and any appeal by the defendant has failed (28 days, under sections 117 and 118 of the Act[24]),

(vii) the resumption of extradition proceedings, where those proceedings were adjourned pending disposal of another extradition claim which has concluded (21 days, under section 180 of the Act),

(viii) extradition, where extradition has been deferred pending the disposal of another extradition claim which has concluded (21 days, under section 181 of the Act), or

(ix) re-extradition, where the defendant has been returned to the United Kingdom to serve a sentence before serving a sentence overseas (as soon as practicable, under section 187 of the Act[25]); or

(e) because an extradition hearing does not begin on the date arranged by the court.

(2) Unless the court otherwise directs—

(a) such a defendant must apply in writing and serve the application on—

(i) the magistrates' court officer,

(ii) the High Court officer, where paragraph (1)(d)(v) applies, and

(iii) the prosecutor;

(b) the application must explain the grounds on which it is made; and

(c) the court officer must arrange a hearing as soon as practicable, and in any event no later than the second business day after an application is served.

[Note. See sections 4(4) & (5), 6(6) & (7), 8(7) & (8)[26], 35(5), 36(8), 37(7), 46(8)[27], 47(4), 72(5) & (6), 74(5), (6) & (10), 74D(10), 75(4), 76(5), 117(3), 118(7), 180(4) & (5), 181(4) & (5) and 187(3) of the Extradition Act 2003.]

[19] 2003 c. 41; section 6 was amended by section 77 of the Policing and Crime Act 2009 (c. 26).

[20] 2003 c. 41; section 74 was amended by paragraph 16 of Schedule 13 to the Police and Justice Act 2006 (c. 48).

[21] 2003 c. 41; section 37 was amended by paragraphs 9 and 10 of Schedule 13 to the Police and Justice Act 2006 (c. 48).

[22] 2003 c. 41; section 46 was amended by paragraph 16 of Schedule 13 to the Police and Justice Act 2006 (c. 48).

[23] 2003 c. 41; section 35 was amended by paragraph 9 of Schedule 13 to the Police and Justice Act 2006 (c. 48). Section 36 was amended by section 40 of, and paragraph 81 of Schedule 9 to, the Constitutional Reform Act 2005 (c. 4).

[24] 2003 c. 41; section 118 was amended by section 40 of, and paragraph 81 of Schedule 9 to, the Constitutional Reform Act 2005 (c. 4).

[25] 2003 c. 41; section 187 was amended by paragraph 15 of Schedule 13 to the Police and Justice Act 2006 (c. 48).

[26] 2003 c. 41; section 8 was amended by paragraph 16 of Schedule 13 to the Police and Justice Act 2006 (c. 48).

[27] 2003 c. 41; section 46 was amended by paragraph 16 of Schedule 13 to the Police and Justice Act 2006 (c. 48).

Section 3: appeal to the High Court

[Note. Under Part 1 of the Extradition Act 2003—

> *(a)   a defendant may appeal to the High Court against an order for extradition made by the magistrates' court; and*
>
> *(b)   the authority requesting the defendant's extradition may appeal to the High Court against an order for the defendant's discharge,*

(see sections 26 and 28 of the Act[28].

Under Part 2 of the 2003 Act—

> *(a)   a defendant may appeal to the High Court against an order by the magistrates' court sending a case to the Secretary of State for a decision whether to extradite the defendant;*
>
> *(b)   a defendant may appeal to the High Court against an order for extradition made by the Secretary of State; and*
>
> *(c)   the territory requesting the defendant's extradition may appeal to the High Court against an order for the defendant's discharge by the magistrates' court or by the Secretary of State,*

(see sections 103, 105, 108 and 110 of the Act[29].

In each case the appellant needs the High Court's permission to appeal (in the 2003 Act, described as 'leave to appeal').]

R50.17   **Exercise of the High Court's powers**

50.17 (1) The general rule is that the High Court must exercise its powers at a hearing in public, but—

   (a) that is subject to any power the court has to—
      (i)   impose reporting restrictions,
      (ii) withhold information from the public, or
      (iii) order a hearing in private;
   (b) despite the general rule, the court may determine without a hearing—
      (i)   an application for the court to consider out of time an application for permission to appeal to the High Court,
      (ii) an application for permission to appeal to the High Court (but a renewed such application must be determined at a hearing),
      (iii) an application for permission to appeal from the High Court to the Supreme Court,
      (iv) an application for permission to reopen a decision under rule 50.27 (Reopening the determination of an appeal), or
      (v)   an application concerning bail; and
   (c) despite the general rule the court may, without a hearing—
      (i)   give case management directions,
      (ii) reject a notice or application and, if applicable, dismiss an application for permission to appeal, where rule 50.31 (Payment of High Court fees) applies and the party who served the notice or application fails to comply with that rule, or
      (iii) make a determination to which the parties have agreed in writing.

   (2) If the High Court so directs, a party may attend a hearing by live link.

   (3) The general rule is that where the High Court exercises its powers at a hearing it may do so only if the defendant attends, in person or by live link, but, despite the general rule, the court may exercise its powers in the defendant's absence if—
   (a) the defendant waives the right to attend;
   (b) subject to any appeal to the Supreme Court, the result of the court's order would be the discharge of the defendant; or
   (c) the defendant is represented and—
      (i)   the defendant is in custody, or
      (ii) the defendant's presence is impracticable by reason of his or her ill health or disorderly conduct.

   (4) If the High Court gives permission to appeal to the High Court—
   (a) unless the court otherwise directs, the decision indicates that the appellant has permission to appeal on every ground identified by the appeal notice;

---

[28] 2003 c. 41; sections 26 and 28 were amended by section 160 of the Anti-social Behaviour, Crime and Policing Act 2014 (c. 12).
[29] 2003 c. 41; section 108 was amended by paragraphs 10 and 12 of Schedule 20 to the Crime and Courts Act 2013 (c. 22). Section 108 was further amended, and sections 103, 105 and 110 were amended, by section 160 of the Anti-social Behaviour, Crime and Policing Act 2014 (c. 12).

(b) unless the court otherwise directs, the decision indicates that the court finds reasonably arguable each ground on which the appellant has permission to appeal; and

(c) the court must give such directions as are required for the preparation and conduct of the appeal, including a direction as to whether the appeal must be heard by a single judge of the High Court or by a divisional court.

(5) If the High Court decides without a hearing an application for permission to appeal from the High Court to the Supreme Court, the High Court must announce its decision at a hearing in public.

(6) The High Court may—

(a) shorten a time limit or extend it (even after it has expired), unless that is inconsistent with other legislation;

(b) allow or require a party to vary or supplement a notice that that party has served;

(c) direct that a notice or application be served on any person; and

(d) allow a notice or application to be in a different form to one set out in the Practice Direction, or to be presented orally.

(7) A party who wants an extension of time within which to serve a notice or make an application must—

(a) apply for that extension of time when serving that notice or making that application; and

(b) give the reasons for the application for an extension of time.

[Note. The time limits for serving an appeal notice are prescribed by the Extradition Act 2003: see rule 50.19.]

Case management in the High Court

R50.18

50.18 (1) The High Court and the parties have the same duties and powers as under Part 3 (Case management), subject to—

(a) rule 50.2 (Special objective in extradition proceedings); and

(b) paragraph (3) of this rule.

(2) A master of the High Court, a deputy master, or a court officer nominated for the purpose by the Lord Chief Justice—

(a) must fulfil the duty of active case management under rule 3.2, and in fulfilling that duty may exercise any of the powers of case management under—

(i) rule 3.5 (the court's general powers of case management),

(ii) rule 3.12(3) (requiring a certificate of readiness), and

(iii) rule 3.13 (requiring a party to identify intentions and anticipated requirements) subject to the directions of a judge of the High Court; and

(b) must nominate a case progression officer under rule 3.4.

(3) Rule 3.6 (Application to vary a direction) does not apply to a decision to give or to refuse—

(a) permission to appeal; or

(b) permission to reopen a decision under rule 50.27 (Reopening the determination of an appeal).

Service of appeal notice

R50.19

50.19 (1) A party who wants to appeal to the High Court must serve an appeal notice on—

(a) in every case—

(i) the High Court officer,

(ii) the other party, and

(iii) the Director of Public Prosecutions, unless the Director already has the conduct of the proceedings;

(b) the designated authority which certified the arrest warrant, where Part 1 of the Extradition Act 2003 applies; and

(c) the Secretary of State, where the appeal is against—

(i) an order by the Secretary of State, or

(ii) an order by the magistrates' court sending a case to the Secretary of State.

(2) A defendant who wants to appeal must serve the appeal notice—

(a) not more than 7 days after the day on which the magistrates' court makes an order for the defendant's extradition, starting with that day, where that order is under Part 1 of the Extradition Act 2003; or

(b) not more than 14 days after the day on which the Secretary of State informs the defendant of the Secretary of State's decision, starting with that day, where under Part 2 of the Act—

(i) the magistrates' court sends the case to the Secretary of State for a decision whether to extradite the defendant, or

(ii) the Secretary of State orders the defendant's extradition.

(3) An authority or territory seeking the defendant's extradition which wants to appeal against an order for the defendant's discharge must serve the appeal notice—

    (a) not more than 7 days after the day on which the magistrates' court makes that order, starting with that day, if the order is under Part 1 of the Extradition Act 2003;

    (b) not more than 14 days after the day on which the magistrates' court makes that order, starting with that day, if the order is under Part 2 of the Act; or

    (c) not more than 14 days after the day on which the Secretary of State informs the territory's representative of the Secretary of State's order, starting with that day, where the order is under Part 2 of the Act.

[Note. See sections 26, 28, 103, 105, 108 and 110 of the Extradition Act 2003[30]. The time limits for serving an appeal notice are prescribed by those sections. They may be neither shortened nor extended, but—

    (a) if a defendant applies out of time for permission to appeal to the High Court the court must not for that reason refuse to consider the application if the defendant did everything reasonably possible to ensure that the notice was given as soon as it could be; and

    (b) a defendant may apply out of time for permission to appeal to the High Court on human rights grounds against an order for extradition made by the Secretary of State.

Under section 3 of the Prosecution of Offences Act 1985[31], the Director of Public Prosecutions may conduct extradition proceedings (but need not do so).]

R50.20   **Form of appeal notice**

50.20 (1) An appeal notice constitutes—

    (a) an application to the High Court for permission to appeal to that court; and

    (b) an appeal to that court, if the court gives permission.

(2) An appeal notice must be in writing.

(3) In every case, the appeal notice must—

    (a) specify—

        (i) the date of the defendant's arrest under Part 1 or Part 2 of the Extradition Act 2003, and

        (ii) the decision about which the appellant wants to appeal, including the date of that decision;

    (b) identify each ground of appeal on which the appellant relies;

    (c) summarise the relevant facts;

    (d) identify any document or other material that the appellant thinks the court will need to decide the appeal; and

    (e) include or attach a list of those on whom the appellant has served the appeal notice.

(4) If a defendant serves an appeal notice after the expiry of the time limit specified in rule 50.19 (Service of appeal notice)—

    (a) the notice must—

        (i) explain what the defendant did to ensure that it was served as soon as it could be, and

        (ii) include or attach such evidence as the defendant relies upon to support that explanation; and

    (b) where the appeal is on human rights grounds against an order for extradition made by the Secretary of State, the notice must explain why—

        (i) the appeal is necessary to avoid real injustice, and

        (ii) the circumstances are exceptional and make it appropriate to consider the appeal.

(5) Unless the High Court otherwise directs, the appellant may amend the appeal notice—

    (a) by serving on those listed in rule 50.19(1) the appeal notice as so amended; and

    (b) not more than 10 business days after service of the appeal notice.

---

[30] 2003 c. 41; section 108 was amended by paragraphs 10 and 12 of Schedule 20 to the Crime and Courts Act 2013 (c. 22). Section 108 was further amended, and sections 26, 28, 103, 105 and 110 were amended, by section 160 of the Anti-social Behaviour, Crime and Policing Act 2014 (c. 12).

[31] 1985 c. 23; section 3 was amended by section 15 of, and paragraph 13 of Schedule 2 to, the Criminal Justice Act 1987 (c. 38), paragraph 39 of Schedule 7 to the Police Act 1996 (c. 16), section 134 of, and paragraph 48 of Schedule 9 to, the Police Act 1997 (c. 50), section 164 of the Immigration and Asylum Act 1999 (c. 33), paragraph 10 of Schedule 7 to the Police Reform Act 2002 (c. 30), sections 86 and 92 of, and Schedule 3 to, the Anti-social Behaviour Act 2003 (c. 38), section 190 of the Extradition Act 2003 (c. 41), section 7 of the Asylum and Immigration (Treatment of Claimants, etc) Act 2004 (c. 19), section 40 of, and paragraph 41 of Schedule 9 to, the Constitutional Reform Act 2005 (c. 4), sections 59, 140 and 174 of, and paragraph 47 of Schedule 4 and Part 2 of Schedule 17 to, the Serious Organised Crime and Police Act 2005 (c. 15), sections 7, 8 and 52 of, and paragraph 15 of Schedule 3 to, the Violent Crime Reduction Act 2006 (c. 38), section 74 of, and paragraph 149 of Schedule 8 to, the Serious Crime Act 2007 (c. 27), paragraph 171 of Schedule 16 to the Police Reform and Social Responsibility Act 2011 (c. 13), section 15 of, and paragraph 30 of Schedule 8 to, the Crime and Courts Act 2013 (c. 22) and article 3 of, and paragraphs 1 and 2 of the Schedule to, S.I. 2014/834.

(6) Where the appeal is against an order by the magistrates' court—

  (a) if the grounds of appeal are that the magistrates' court ought to have decided differently a question of fact or law at the extradition hearing, the appeal notice must—

    (i) identify that question,

    (ii) explain what decision the magistrates' court should have made, and why, and

    (iii) explain why the magistrates' court would have been required not to make the order under appeal, if that question had been decided differently; and

  (b) if the grounds of appeal are that there is an issue which was not raised at the extradition hearing, or that evidence is available which was not available at the extradition hearing, the appeal notice must—

    (i) identify that issue or evidence,

    (ii) explain why it was not then raised or available,

    (iii) explain why that issue or evidence would have resulted in the magistrates' court deciding a question differently at the extradition hearing, and

    (iv) explain why, if the court had decided that question differently, the court would have been required not to make the order it made.

(7) Where the appeal is against an order by the Secretary of State—

  (a) if the grounds of appeal are that the Secretary of State ought to have decided differently a question of fact or law, the appeal notice must—

    (i) identify that question,

    (ii) explain what decision the Secretary of State should have made, and why, and

    (iii) explain why the Secretary of State would have been required not to make the order under appeal, if that question had been decided differently; and

  (b) if the grounds of appeal are that there is an issue which was not raised when the case was being considered by the Secretary of State, or that information is available which was not then available, the appeal notice must—

    (i) identify that issue or information,

    (ii) explain why it was not then raised or available,

    (iii) explain why that issue or information would have resulted in the Secretary of State deciding a question differently, and

    (iv) explain why, if the Secretary of State had decided that question differently, the order under appeal would not have been made.

[Note. The Practice Direction sets out a form of appeal notice for use in connection with this rule.]

Respondent's notice   R50.21

50.21 (1) A party on whom an appellant serves an appeal notice under rule 50.19 may serve a respondent's notice, and must do so if—

  (a) that party wants to make representations to the High Court; or

  (b) the court so directs.

(2) Such a party must serve any such notice on—

  (a) the High Court officer;

  (b) the appellant;

  (c) the Director of Public Prosecutions, unless the Director already has the conduct of the proceedings; and

  (d) any other person on whom the appellant served the appeal notice.

(3) Such a party must serve any such notice, as appropriate—

  (a) not more than 10 business days after—

    (i) service on that party of an amended appeal notice under rule 50.20(5) (Form of appeal notice), or

    (ii) the expiry of the time for service of any such amended appeal notice whichever of those events happens first; and

  (b) not more than 5 business days after service on that party of—

    (i) an appellant's notice renewing an application for permission to appeal, or

    (ii) a direction to serve a respondent's notice.

(4) A respondent's notice must—

  (a) give the date or dates on which the respondent was served with, as appropriate—

    (i) the appeal notice,

    (ii) the appellant's notice renewing the application for permission to appeal, or

    (iii) the direction to serve a respondent's notice;

  (b) identify each ground of opposition on which the respondent relies and the ground of appeal to which each such ground of opposition relates;

  (c) summarise any relevant facts not already summarised in the appeal notice; and

(d) identify any document or other material that the respondent thinks the court will need to decide the appeal.

[Note. Under rule 50.17, the High Court may extend or shorten the time limit under this rule.]

R50.22 **Renewing an application for permission to appeal, restoring excluded grounds, etc.**

50.22 (1) This rule—

    (a) applies where the High Court—

        (i) refuses permission to appeal to the High Court, or

        (ii) gives permission to appeal to the High Court but not on every ground identified by the appeal notice; but

    (b) does not apply where—

        (i) a defendant applies out of time for permission to appeal to the High Court, and

        (ii) the court for that reason refuses to consider that application.

(2) Unless the court refuses permission to appeal at a hearing, the appellant may renew the application for permission by serving notice on—

    (a) the High Court officer;

    (b) the respondent; and

    (c) any other person on whom the appellant served the appeal notice,

not more than 5 business days after service of notice of the court's decision on the appellant.

(3) If the court refuses permission to appeal, the renewal notice must explain the grounds for the renewal.

(4) If the court gives permission to appeal but not on every ground identified by the appeal notice the decision indicates that—

    (a) at the hearing of the appeal the court will not consider representations that address any ground thus excluded from argument; and

    (b) an appellant who wants to rely on such an excluded ground needs the court's permission to do so.

(5) An appellant who wants to rely at the hearing of an appeal on a ground of appeal excluded from argument must—

    (a) apply in writing, with reasons, and identify each such ground;

    (b) serve the application on—

        (i) the High Court officer, and

        (ii) the respondent; and

    (c) serve the application not more than 5 business days after—

        (i) the giving of permission to appeal, or

        (ii) the High Court officer serves notice of that decision on the applicant, if the applicant was not present in person or by live link when permission to appeal was given.

(6) Paragraph (7) applies where a party wants to abandon—

    (a) a ground of appeal on which that party has permission to appeal; or

    (b) a ground of opposition identified in a respondent's notice.

(7) Such a party must serve notice on—

    (a) the High Court officer; and

    (b) each other party,

before any hearing at which that ground will be considered by the court.

[Note. Under rule 50.17 (Exercise of the High Court's powers), the High Court may extend or shorten the time limits under this rule.

Rule 50.19 (Service of appeal notice) and the note to that rule set out the time limits for appeal.]

R50.23 **Appeal hearing**

50.23 (1) Unless the High Court otherwise directs, where the appeal to the High Court is under Part 1 of the Extradition Act 2003 the hearing of the appeal must begin no more than 40 days after the defendant's arrest.

(2) Unless the High Court otherwise directs, where the appeal to the High Court is under Part 2 of the 2003 Act the hearing of the appeal must begin no more than 76 days after the later of—

    (a) service of the appeal notice; or

    (b) the day on which the Secretary of State informs the defendant of the Secretary of State's order, in a case in which—

        (i) the appeal is by the defendant against an order by the magistrates' court sending the case to the Secretary of State, and

        (ii) the appeal notice is served before the Secretary of State decides whether the defendant should be extradited.

(3) If the effect of the decision of the High Court on the appeal is that the defendant is to be extradited—

    (a) the High Court must consider any ancillary application, including an application about—

        (i) bail pending extradition,

        (ii) reporting restrictions, or

        (iii) costs; and

    (b) the High Court is the appropriate court to order a postponement of the defendant's extradition where—

        (i) the defendant has been charged with an offence in the United Kingdom, or

        (ii) the defendant has been sentenced to imprisonment or detention in the United Kingdom.

(4) If the effect of the decision of the High Court on the appeal is that the defendant is discharged, the High Court must consider any ancillary application, including an application about—

    (a) reporting restrictions; or

    (b) costs.

[Note. Under sections 31 and 113 of the Extradition Act 2003[32], if the appeal hearing does not begin within the period prescribed by this rule or ordered by the High Court the appeal must be taken to have been dismissed by decision of the High Court.

Under section 103 of the Extradition Act 2003[33], a defendant's appeal against an order by the magistrates' court sending the case to the Secretary of State must not be heard until after the Secretary of State has decided whether to order the defendant's extradition.

Part 6 contains rules about reporting restrictions. Part 45 contains rules about costs.

See sections 36A, 36B, 118A and 118B Extradition Act 2003[34]. Where there is an appeal against an order for extradition, rules may provide that the appeal court may exercise the power under those sections to postpone the extradition.]

Early termination of appeal: order by consent, etc.   **R50.24**

50.24 (1) This rule applies where—

    (a) an appellant has served an appeal notice under rule 50.19; and

    (b) the High Court—

        (i) has not determined the application for permission to appeal, or

        (ii) where the court has given permission to appeal, has not determined the appeal.

(2) Where the warrant or extradition request with which the appeal is concerned is withdrawn—

    (a) the party or person so informing the court must serve on the High Court officer—

        (i) notice to that effect by the authority or territory requesting the defendant's extradition,

        (ii) details of how much of the warrant or extradition request remains outstanding, if any, and of any other warrant or extradition request outstanding in respect of the defendant,

        (iii) details of any bail condition to which the defendant is subject, if the defendant is on bail, and

        (iv) details sufficient to locate the defendant, including details of the custodian and of the defendant's date of birth and custody reference, if the defendant is in custody; and

    (b) paragraph (5) applies but only to the extent that the parties want the court to deal with an ancillary matter.

(3) Where a defendant with whose discharge the appeal is concerned consents to extradition, paragraph (5) applies but only to the extent that the parties want the court to—

    (a) give directions for that consent to be given to the magistrates' court or to the Secretary of State, as the case may be; or

    (b) deal with an ancillary matter.

(4) Paragraph (5) applies where the parties want the court to make a decision on which they are agreed—

    (a) determining the application for permission to appeal or the appeal, as the case may be;

    (b) specifying the date on which that application or appeal is to be treated as discontinued; and

    (c) determining an ancillary matter, including costs, if applicable.

---

[32] 2003 c. 41.

[33] 2003 c. 41; section 103 was amended by section 160 of the Anti-social Behaviour, Crime and Policing Act 2014 (c. 12).

[34] 2003 c. 41; sections 36A, 36B, 118A and 118B were inserted by section 161 of the Anti-social Behaviour, Crime and Policing Act 2014 (c. 12).

(5) The parties must serve on the High Court officer, in one or more documents—
    (a) a draft order in the terms proposed;
    (b) evidence of each party's agreement to those terms; and
    (c) concise reasons for the request that the court make the proposed order.

[Note. Under sections 42 and 124 of the Extradition Act 2003[35], where an appeal is pending in the High Court and the court is informed that the relevant warrant or extradition request has been withdrawn the court must—

    (a) order the defendant's discharge and quash the extradition order or decision, where the defendant has appealed against extradition;
    (b) dismiss the application for permission to appeal or the appeal, as the case may be, where the authority or territory requesting the defendant's extradition has appealed against the defendant's discharge.

Under sections 45 and 127 of the 2003 Act[36], a defendant in respect of whom no extradition order or decision has been made may give consent to extradition in the magistrates' court, or may give such consent to the Secretary of State if the case has been sent there.

Where the effect of the High Court's decision is that the defendant is to be extradited, sections 36 and 118 of the Act[37] set time limits for extradition after the end of the case.

Part 45 contains rules about costs.]

R50.25   **Application for permission to appeal to the Supreme Court**

50.25 (1) This rule applies where a party to an appeal to the High Court wants to appeal to the Supreme Court.
    (2) Such a party must—
      (a) apply orally to the High Court for permission to appeal immediately after the court's decision; or
      (b) apply in writing and serve the application on the High Court officer and every other party not more than 14 days after that decision.
    (3) Such a party must—
      (a) identify the point of law of general public importance that the appellant wants the High Court to certify is involved in the decision;
      (b) serve on the High Court officer a statement of that point of law; and
      (c) give reasons why—
        (i) that point of law ought to be considered by the Supreme Court, and
        (ii) the High Court ought to give permission to appeal.
    (4) As well as complying with paragraph (3), a defendant's application for permission to appeal to the Supreme Court must include or attach any application for the following, with reasons—
      (a) bail pending appeal; or
      (b) permission to attend any hearing in the Supreme Court, if the appellant is in custody.

[Note. See sections 32 and 114 of the Extradition Act 2003[38]. Those sections prescribe the time limit for serving an application for permission to appeal to the Supreme Court. It may be neither shortened nor extended.]

R50.26   **Determination of detention pending appeal to the Supreme Court against discharge**

50.26 On an application for permission to appeal to the Supreme Court against a decision of the High Court which, but for that appeal, would have resulted in the defendant's discharge, the High Court must—
    (a) decide whether to order the detention of the defendant; and
    (b) determine any application for—
      (i) bail pending appeal,
      (ii) permission to attend any hearing in the Supreme Court, or
      (iii) a representation order.

---

[35] 2003 c. 41; sections 42 and 124 were amended by article 3 of S.I. 2015/992.
[36] 2003 c. 41; sections 45 was amended by section 39 of, and paragraphs 62 and 63 of Schedule 5 to, the Legal Aid, Sentencing and Punishment of Offenders Act 2012 (c. 10) and section 163 of the Anti-social Behaviour, Crime and Policing Act 2014 (c. 12). Section 127 was amended by section 39 of, and paragraphs 62 and 64 of Schedule 5 to, the Legal Aid, Sentencing and Punishment of Offenders Act 2012 (c. 10).
[37] 2003 c. 41; sections 36 and 118 were amended by section 40 of, and paragraph 81 of Schedule 9 to, the Constitutional Reform Act 2005 (c. 4).
[38] 2003 c. 41; sections 32 and 114 were amended by paragraph 81 of Schedule 9 to the Constitutional Reform Act 2005 (c. 4) and section 42 of, and paragraph 8 of Schedule 13 to, the Police and Justice Act 2006 (c. 48).

[Note. See sections 33A and 115A of the Extradition Act 2003[39].

For the grant of legal aid for proceedings in the Supreme Court, see sections 14, 16 and 19 of the Legal Aid, Sentencing and Punishment of Offenders Act 2012[40].]

Reopening the determination of an appeal

R50.27

50.27 (1) This rule applies where a party wants the High Court to reopen a decision of that court which determines an appeal or an application for permission to appeal.

   (2) Such a party must—

     (a) apply in writing for permission to reopen that decision, as soon as practicable after becoming aware of the grounds for doing so; and

     (b) serve the application on the High Court officer and every other party.

   (3) The application must—

     (a) specify the decision which the applicant wants the court to reopen; and

     (b) give reasons why—

       (i) it is necessary for the court to reopen that decision in order to avoid real injustice,

       (ii) the circumstances are exceptional and make it appropriate to reopen the decision, and

       (iii) there is no alternative effective remedy.

   (4) The court must not give permission to reopen a decision unless each other party has had an opportunity to make representations.

Declaration of incompatibility with a Convention right

R50.28

50.28 (1) This rule applies where a party—

     (a) wants the High Court to make a declaration of incompatibility with a Convention right under section 4 of the Human Rights Act 1998[41]; or

     (b) raises an issue that appears to the High Court may lead to the court making such a declaration.

   (2) If the High Court so directs, the High Court officer must serve notice on—

     (a) the relevant person named in the list published under section 17(1) of the Crown Proceedings Act 1947[42]; or

     (b) the Treasury Solicitor, if it is not clear who is the relevant person.

   (3) That notice must include or attach details of—

     (a) the legislation affected and the Convention right concerned;

     (b) the parties to the appeal; and

     (c) any other information or document that the High Court thinks relevant.

   (4) A person who has a right under the 1998 Act to become a party to the appeal must—

     (a) serve notice on—

       (i) the High Court officer, and

       (ii) the other parties,

     if that person wants to exercise that right; and

     (b) in that notice—

       (i) indicate the conclusion that that person invites the High Court to reach on the question of incompatibility, and

       (ii) identify each ground for that invitation, concisely outlining the arguments in support.

   (5) The High Court must not make a declaration of incompatibility—

     (a) less than 15 business days after the High Court officer serves notice under paragraph (2); and

     (b) without giving any person who serves a notice under paragraph (4) an opportunity to make representations at a hearing.

Duties of court officers

R50.29

50.29 (1) The magistrates' court officer must—

     (a) keep any document or object exhibited in the proceedings in the magistrates' court, or arrange for it to be kept by some other appropriate person, until—

       (i) 6 weeks after the conclusion of those proceedings, or

       (ii) the conclusion of any proceedings in the High Court that begin within that 6 weeks;

---

[39] 2003 c. 41; sections 33A and 115A were inserted by section 42 of, and paragraphs 8 and 35 of Schedule 13 to, the Police and Justice Act 2006 (c. 48).
[40] 2012 c. 10.
[41] 1998 c. 42; section 4 was amended by section 40 of, and paragraph 66 of Schedule 9 to, the Constitutional Reform Act 2005 (c. 4) and section 67 of, and paragraph 43 of Schedule 6 to, the Mental Capacity Act 2005 (c. 9).
[42] 1947 c. 44; section 17 was amended by article 3(2) of S.I. 1968/1656.

(b) provide the High Court with any document, object or information for which the High Court officer asks, within such period as the High Court officer may require; and

(c) arrange for the magistrates' court to hear as soon as practicable any application to that court for bail pending appeal.

(2) A person who, under arrangements made by the magistrates' court officer, keeps a document or object exhibited in the proceedings in the magistrates' court must—

(a) keep that exhibit until—

(i) 6 weeks after the conclusion of those proceedings, or

(ii) the conclusion of any proceedings in the High Court that begin within that 6 weeks,

unless the magistrates' court or the High Court otherwise directs; and

(b) provide the High Court with any such document or object for which the High Court officer asks, within such period as the High Court officer may require.

(3) The High Court officer must—

(a) give as much notice as reasonably practicable of each hearing to—

(i) the parties,

(ii) the defendant's custodian, if any, and

(iii) any other person whom the High Court requires to be notified;

(b) serve a record of each order or direction of the High Court on—

(i) the parties,

(ii) any other person whom the High Court requires to be notified;

(c) if the High Court's decision determines an appeal or application for permission to appeal, serve a record of that decision on—

(i) the defendant's custodian, if any,

(ii) the magistrates' court officer, and

(iii) the designated authority which certified the arrest warrant, where Part 1 of the Extradition Act 2003 applies;

(d) where rule 50.24 applies (Early termination of appeal: order by consent, etc.), arrange for the High Court to consider the document or documents served under that rule; and

(e) treat the appeal as if it had been dismissed by the High Court where—

(i) the hearing of the appeal does not begin within the period required by rule 50.23 (Appeal hearing) or ordered by the High Court, or

(ii) on an appeal by a requesting territory under section 105 of the Extradition Act 2003[43], the High Court directs the magistrates' court to decide a question again and the magistrates' court comes to the same conclusion as it had done before.

[Note. See section 106 of the Extradition Act 2003[44].]

R50.30   **Constitution of the High Court**

50.30 (1) A master of the High Court or a deputy master, may exercise any power of the High Court to which the rules in this Section apply, except the power to—

(a) give or refuse permission to appeal;

(b) determine an appeal;

(c) reopen a decision which determines an appeal or an application for permission to appeal;

(d) grant or withhold bail; or

(e) impose or vary a condition of bail.

(2) Despite paragraph (1), such a master or deputy master may exercise one of the powers listed in paragraph (1)(a), (b), (d) or (e) if making a decision to which the parties have agreed in writing.

(3) A renewed application for permission to appeal to the High Court may be determined by—

(a) a single judge of the High Court other than the judge who first refused permission, or

(b) a divisional court.

(4) An appeal may be determined by—

(a) a single judge of the High Court; or

(b) a divisional court.

[Note. See sections 19 and 66 of the Senior Courts Act 1981[45].]

[43] 2003 c. 41; section 105 was amended by section 160 of the Anti-social Behaviour, Crime and Policing Act 2014 (c. 12).
[44] 2003 c. 41; section 106 was amended by section 42 of, and paragraph 8 of Schedule 13 to, the Police and Justice Act 2006 (c. 48).
[45] 1981 c. 54.

Payment of High Court fees   R50.31

50.31 (1) This rule applies where a party serves on the High Court officer a notice or application
    in respect of which a court fee is payable under legislation that requires the payment of such a
    fee.

(2) Such a party must pay the fee, or satisfy the conditions for any remission of the fee, when so
    serving the notice or application.

(3) If such a party fails to comply with paragraph (2), then unless the High Court otherwise
    directs—

   (a) the High Court officer must serve on that party a notice requiring payment of the fee due,
       or satisfaction of the conditions for any remission of that fee, within a period specified in
       the notice;

   (b) that party must comply with such a requirement; and

   (c) until the expiry of the period specified in the notice, the High Court must not exercise its
       power—

       (i) to reject the notice or application in respect of which the fee is payable, or

       (ii) to dismiss an application for permission to appeal, in consequence of rejecting an
           appeal notice.

*[Note. Section 92 of the Courts Act 2003[46] and the Civil Proceedings Fees Order 2008[47] require the payment of
High Court fees in cases to which this Section of this Part applies. Article 5 and Schedule 2 to the 2008 Order
provide for the remission of such fees in some cases.]*

Section 4: post-extradition proceedings

Application for consent to deal with another offence or for consent to further extradition   R50.32

50.32 (1) This rule applies where—

   (a) a defendant has been extradited to a territory under Part 1 of the Extradition Act 2003[48];
       and

   (b) the court officer receives from the authority designated by the Secretary of State a request
       for the court's consent to—

       (i) the defendant being dealt with in that territory for an offence other than one in
           respect of which the extradition there took place, or

       (ii) the defendant's further extradition from there to another such territory for an
           offence.

(2) The presenting officer must serve on the court officer—

   (a) the request; and

   (b) a certificate given by the designated authority that the request was made by a judicial
       authority with the function of making such requests in the territory to which the
       defendant was extradited.

(3) The court must—

   (a) give directions for service by a party or other person on the defendant of notice that the
       request for consent has been received, unless satisfied that it would not be practicable for
       such notice to be served;

   (b) give directions for a hearing to consider the request to begin—

       (i) no more than 21 days after the request was received by the designated authority, or

       (ii) at such a later date as the court decides is in the interests of justice; and

   (c) give such directions as are required for the preparation and conduct of that hearing.

(4) At the hearing directed under paragraph (3), in the following sequence the court must
    decide—

   (a) whether the consent requested is required, having regard to—

       (i) any opportunity given for the defendant to leave the requesting territory after
           extradition which the defendant did not take within 45 days of arrival there,

       (ii) if the defendant did not take such an opportunity, any requirements for consent
           imposed by the law of the requesting territory or by arrangements between that
           territory and the United Kingdom where the request is for consent to deal with the
           defendant in that territory for another offence, and

---

[46] 2003 c. 39; section 92 was amended by sections 15 and 59 of, and paragraphs 308 and 345 of Schedule 4 and paragraph 4
of Schedule 11 to, the Constitutional Reform Act 2005 (c. 4) and section 17 of, and paragraph 40 of Schedule 9 and paragraphs
83 and 95 of Schedule 10 to, the Crime and Courts Act 2013.

[47] S. I. 2008/1053; amended by S.I. 2013/1410, 2013/2302, 2014/874.

[48] 2003 c. 41.

(iii) if the defendant did not take such an opportunity, any requirements for consent imposed by arrangements between the requesting territory and the United Kingdom where the request is for consent to extradite the defendant to another territory for an offence; and

(b) if such consent is required, then—

(i) whether the offence in respect of which consent is requested is an extradition offence, and

(ii) if it is, whether the court would order the defendant's extradition under sections 11 to 25 of the Extradition Act 2003 (bars to extradition and other considerations) were the defendant in the United Kingdom and the court was considering extradition for that offence.

(5) The court must give directions for notice of its decision to be conveyed to the authority which made the request.

(6) Rules 50.3 (Exercise of magistrates' court's powers) and 50.4 (Case management in the magistrates' court and duty of court officer) apply on an application under this rule.

[Note. See sections 54, 55, 56 and 57 of the Extradition Act 2003[49].]

CRIMINAL PRACTICE DIRECTIONS 2023

Criminal Practice Directions 2023

Criminal Practice Directions 2023

The Criminal Practice Directions 2023, as presented by the Lord Chief Justice of England and Wales, came into force on 29 May 2023.

The text of the Practice Directions is presented as laid, accompanied by a corresponding paragraph number (e.g. **PD9.4** indicates **Practice Direction 9.4—Indications of sentence**).

1. GENERAL MATTERS
1.1 Introduction
PD1.1

1.1.1   This Practice Direction revokes the 2015 Criminal Practice Directions as amended.

1.1.2   Reference should continue to be made to the Practice Direction (Costs in Criminal Proceedings) 2015.

1.1.3   The Criminal Procedure Rules and the Criminal Practice Directions are the law.

1.1.4   They provide a code of current practice that is binding on the courts to which they are directed.

1.1.5   Participants must comply with the Rules and Practice Direction, and directions made by the court.

1.1.6   The Lord Chief Justice may issue forms for use with the Criminal Procedure Rules[1] and may amend or withdraw those forms. Unless a court otherwise directs any such form must be used in accordance with the relevant rule(s), these Practice Directions and any instructions in the form itself.[2]

2. OPEN JUSTICE
2.1 Overarching Principle
PD2.1

2.1.1   The general principle is that the administration of justice must be done in public, the public and the media have a right to attend all court hearings, and the media is able to report those proceedings fully and contemporaneously.[3]

2.1.2   The open justice principle is reflected in **CrimPR 6.2(1)** which requires the court, when exercising its powers in relation to reporting and access restrictions, to have regard to the importance of dealing with criminal cases in public and allowing a public hearing to be reported to the public.

2.2 Access to courts
PD2.2

2.2.1   It is the court's responsibility to ensure that members of the public can, in so far as possible, have access to courtrooms to observe proceedings.[4]

2.2.2   The court also has the responsibility to ensure that members of the public present in the court do not disrupt proceedings.

2.2.3   The court has an inherent power to restrict public access to the courtroom where it is **necessary** to do so in the interests of justice, for example to prevent disorder. Access may be restricted to prevent members of the public, as well as participants in the proceedings, from entering and leaving the courtroom during the following parts of proceedings:

a. Arraignment.
b. Empanelling and swearing in of the jury.
c. Oath taking or affirmation.
d. Return of verdict by a jury.
e. Passing of sentence.

2.2.4   It is unlawful to issue a blanket policy[5] for a court centre that restricts access during other parts of the proceedings. Unless the judge has specifically restricted access to the public gallery for good reason, the public can enter and leave the courtroom, provided they do so without disrupting proceedings.

---

[1] See **CrimPR 5.1.**
[2] Forms issued by the Lord Chief Justice under this paragraph are published at https://www.gov.uk/guidance/criminal-procedure-rules-forms.
[3] See *Khuja v Times Newspapers Ltd* [2019] AC 161.
[4] See **CrimPR r 6.4.**
[5] *R (on the application of Ewing) v Isleworth Crown Court* [2019] EWHC 288 (Admin).

2.2.5   In cases involving witnesses who are young or vulnerable the court should consider whether to restrict attendance by members of the public during that witness's evidence.

2.2.6   Facilities for reporting proceedings (subject to any legislative restrictions) must be provided. The court may restrict the number of reporters in the courtroom to such as is judged practicable and desirable. In ruling on any challenged claim to attend in the courtroom for the purpose of reporting, the court should be mindful of the public's general right to be informed about the administration of justice.

2.2.7   From 28 June 2022, courts have new powers to allow reporters and other members of the public to observe hearings remotely.[6]

2.2.8   Practice Guidance issued by the Lord Chief Justice and the Senior President of Tribunals and Remote Observation Guidance of hearings in the criminal courts issued by the President of the King's Bench Division provide detailed assistance on the approach that the courts should adopt.

PD2.3
2.3 Taking notes in court

2.3.1   The permission of the court is not required to take notes in court.

2.3.2   Where there are reasonable grounds to suspect that the taking of notes may be for an unlawful purpose, or that it may disrupt the proceedings, then court staff should make appropriate enquiries. The court has power to prohibit note-taking by a specified individual or individuals if it is necessary and proportionate.

2.3.3   Examples include:

     a. Where there is reason to believe that the taking of notes involves the transmission of live text-based communications without the required permission.
     b. Where there is reason to believe that notes are being taken in order to facilitate the contravention of a reporting restriction.

PD2.4
2.4 Live text-based communications

2.4.1   Members of the public require the court's permission to transmit live text-based communications from court; accredited journalists do not.

PD2.5
2.5 Sound recordings

2.5.1   Unauthorised recording of proceedings in court is a contempt of court and may be subject to forfeiture of the device.[7]

2.5.2   In exercising the court's unlimited discretion to grant, withhold or withdraw leave to use equipment for recording sound or to impose conditions as to the use of the recording, the following factors may be relevant:

     a. Any reasonable need on the part of the applicant for the recording to be made.
     b. The risk that the recording could be used for the purpose of briefing other witnesses.
     c. Any possibility that the use of the recording device would disturb the proceedings or distract or impact adversely on any witnesses or other participants.

2.5.3   The Court should always consider whether to impose conditions as to the use of any recording made. The identity and role of the applicant for leave and the nature of the subject matter of the proceedings may be relevant to this.

PD2.6
2.6 Access to material held by the court

2.6.1   The principle of open justice applies not only to physical presence and the viewing of proceedings, but in access to material held by the court.[8]

2.6.2   A request for access to documents used in a criminal case should first be addressed to the party who presented them to the court or who, in the case of a written decision by the court, received that decision.[9]

---

[6] Section 85A Courts Act 2003 as inserted by s.198 Police, Crime, Sentencing and Courts Act 2022. The regime is implemented by the Remote Observation and Recording (Courts and Tribunals) Regulations 2022.
[7] See s.9 Contempt of Court Act 1981 and **CrimPR 6.10**.
[8] *R (Guardian News and Media Ltd) v City of Westminster Magistrates' Court* [2012] EWCA Civ 420, [2013] QB 618.
[9] To note the protocol between the NPCC and CPS. Material should be sought under the relevant protocol before an application is made to the court.

2.6.3   The court may be asked to provide the public, including journalists, with access to information or documents (or copies)[10] held by the court and in some instances such applications will be challenged.

2.6.4   **CrimPR 5.8** requires court staff to supply some information on request without a judicial decision. The rule regulates the manner in which such requests for information should be made, and **CrimPR 5.10** the approach to be adopted by the Court in responding to requests referred by staff under **CrimPR 5.8(7)**.[11]

2.6.5   Where any material is supplied by the court it remains the responsibility of the recipient to ensure that they comply with any and all restrictions relating to it such as reporting restrictions.

2.6.6   There is no requirement for the court to consider the non-disclosure provisions of the Data Protection Act 2018 as the exemption under Sch 2 part 1 para 5 applies to all disclosure made under 'any enactment ... or by the order of a court', which includes under the Criminal Procedure Rules.

2.6.7   Under **CrimPR Part 5**, the same procedure applies to applications for access to information by reporters as to other members of the public. However, if the application is made by legal representatives instructed by the media, or by an accredited member of the media, who is able to produce in support of the application a valid Press Card, then there is a greater presumption in favour of providing the requested material. This approach respects the role of the press as a 'public watchdog' in a democratic society.[12]

2.6.8   Where an application is made by a reporter, the general principle is that the court should supply documents and information unless (a) there is a good reason not to, in order to protect the rights or legitimate interests of others, and/or (b) the request will not place an undue burden on the court.[13]

2.6.9   Court staff should verify the identity and press credentials of the applicant.

2.6.10   The supply of information[14] is at the discretion of the court, and court staff must ensure that they have received a clear direction from the court before providing any information or material[15] to a member of the public, including to the accredited media or their legal representatives.

Document Type	Considerations on Whether to Supply
Opening notes	Once placed before the court should usually be provided. Where there is no note, permission to obtain the transcript of the prosecution opening should usually be given.
Statements agreed under s.9 and admissions made under s.10 Criminal Justice Act 1967	Rule 5.10 considerations apply. A request by the media should usually be granted if they have been read aloud in entirety. If only summarised or read aloud in part then access may only be given to that part if proportionate to do so.
Statements of witnesses who give oral evidence	This should not usually be provided. Open justice is satisfied by public access to the hearing
Material disclosed under CPIA 1996	May only be supplied to the extent that the content is deployed at trial, when it becomes public.
An up to date, unmarked copy of the jury bundle and exhibits (including video footage shown to the jury)	Consider: i) whether access to the document is necessary to understand or report the case; ii) privacy of third parties; iii) reporting restrictions, and iv) risks of prejudice to a fair trial in this or any other case.

Criminal Practice Directions 2023

---

[10] For the purposes of this direction, 'document' includes images in photographic, digital including DVD format, video, CCTV or any other form.

[11] To note the protocol between HMCTS and the media.

[12] *Observer and Guardian v United Kingdom* (1992) 14 E.H.R.R. 153, Times November 27, 1991.

[13] *R (Guardian News and Media Ltd) v City of Westminster Magistrates' Court* [2012] EWCA Civ 420, [2013] QB 618 at [87].

[14] Under **CrimPR 5.8(7)** and **5.10**.

[15] Under **CrimPR 5.8(7)** and **5.10**.

Document Type	Considerations on Whether to Supply
Written notices, applications, replies (including any application for representation)	To the extent that evidence is introduced, or measures taken, at trial, the content becomes public at that hearing. A statutory prohibition against disclosure applies to an application for representation: ss.33, 34 and 35 LASPO Act 2012, but subject to the trial judge's permission.
Skeleton arguments and written submissions	Once placed before the court should usually be provided, but subject to the trial judge's permission.
Written decisions by the court, other than those read aloud in public or treated as if so read	If the only reason for delivering a decision that way is to promote efficiency and expedition then generally a copy should be provided if requested once the decision is final. Relevant reporting restrictions may mean a redacted version is supplied.
Victim Personal Statements	Usually confidential, even where reference has been made to it, or quoted from it in court.
Sentencing remarks	Subject to reporting restrictions, these should usually be provided, if the judge was reading from a prepared script which was handed out immediately afterwards; if not, then permission to obtain a transcript should usually be given.
Pre-sentence reports; medical reports; Reports and summaries for confiscation	Usually confidential, even where reference has been made to it, or quoted from it in court.
Transcripts	Transcripts of hearings in open court can be obtained for a fee from the transcription service provider. See paragraphs 2.6.18-2.6.22 below.
Means forms	Usually confidential, even where reference has been made to it, or quoted from it in court.

2.6.11   It may be convenient for copies to be provided electronically by advocates, as long as the documents are kept suitably secure. The media are expected to be aware of the limitations on the use to which such material can be put, for example that legal argument held in the absence of the jury must not be reported before the conclusion of the trial. Where material is to be given a wider circulation than the accredited media judicial superintendence is required.

2.6.12   Judges must not exercise an editorial judgment about 'the adequacy of the material already available to the paper for its journalistic purpose'.[16] The responsibility for complying with the Contempt of Court Act 1981 and any and all restrictions on the use of the material rests with the recipient.

Specific prohibitions against the provision of information

2.6.13   Various statutory provisions impose specific prohibitions against the provision of information, including the Rehabilitation of Offenders Act 1974, s.18 Criminal Procedure and Investigations Act 1996 (CPIA 1996) ('unused material' disclosed by the prosecution), ss.33, 34 and 35 Legal Aid, Sentencing and Punishment of Offenders Act 2012 (LASPO Act 2012) (privileged information furnished to the Legal Aid Agency) and reporting restrictions generally.[17]

2.6.14   Reports of allocation or sending proceedings are restricted by s.52A Crime and Disorder Act 1998. Only limited information, as specified in the statute, may be reported, whether it is referred to in the courtroom or not. The magistrates' court has power to order that the restriction shall not apply; if any defendant objects the court must apply the interests of justice test as specified in s.52A. The restriction ceases to apply either after all defendants indicate a plea of guilty, or after the conclusion of the trial of the last defendant to be tried. If the case does not result in a guilty plea, a finding of guilt or an acquittal, the restriction does not lift automatically and an application must be made to the court.

2.6.15   Extradition proceedings have some features in common with committal proceedings, but no automatic reporting restrictions apply.

---

[16] R (Guardian News and Media Ltd) v City of Westminster Magistrates' Court [2012] EWCA Civ 420, [2013] QB 618 at [82].
[17] Those most likely to be encountered are listed in the note to **CrimPR 5.8**.

2.6.16　Public Interest Immunity and the rights of a defendant, witnesses and victims under Article 6 and 8 European Convention on Human Rights may also restrict the power to release material to third parties.

Written decisions

2.6.17　Where the Criminal Procedure Rules allow for a determination without a hearing, the court should consider delivering the decision in writing, without a public hearing.

Transcripts

2.6.18　Statutory restrictions prohibit publication 'to the public at large or any section of the public', or some comparable formulation. They do not ordinarily prohibit a publication constituted only of the supply of a transcript to an individual applicant. However, any reporting restrictions will continue to apply to a recipient of the transcript, and where they apply the recipient must be alerted to them by the endorsement on the transcript of a suitable warning notice, to this or the like effect:

> 'WARNING: reporting restrictions may apply to the contents transcribed in this document, particularly if the case concerned a sexual offence or involved a child. Reporting restrictions prohibit the publication of the applicable information to the public or any section of the public, in writing, in a broadcast or by means of the internet, including social media. Anyone who receives a copy of this transcript is responsible in law for making sure that applicable restrictions are not breached. A person who breaches a reporting restriction is liable to a fine and/or imprisonment. For guidance on whether reporting restrictions apply, and to what information, ask at the court office or take legal advice.'

2.6.19　The default position is that the transcript is provided unredacted. It is good practice for the court to remind the recipient that reporting restrictions may apply, and that it is their responsibility to comply. Exceptionally, the judge may order that the transcript must be redacted before it is supplied to a recipient, or that the transcript must not be supplied to an applicant pending the supply of further information or assurances by that applicant, or at all, in exercise of the judicial discretion to which **CrimPR 5.5(2)** refers. If the judge orders that some content be redacted from the transcript, the transcribers should be directed to produce a version that complies with that order. The court will check that any redacted transcript complies before release.

2.6.20　A request for a transcript may be refused or be subject to appropriate redaction, for example, where circumstances cause staff reasonably to suspect that an applicant intends or is likely to disregard a reporting restriction that applies, despite the warning notice endorsed on the transcript, or reasonably to suspect that an applicant has malicious intentions towards another person. Given that the proceedings will have taken place in public, and despite any such suspicions, cogent and compelling reasons will be required to deny a request for transcript of such proceedings. The onus rests always on the court to justify such a denial, not on the applicant to justify the request. Even where there are reasons to suspect a criminal intent, the appropriate course may be to direct that the police be informed of those reasons rather than to direct that the transcript be withheld. Nevertheless, it may be appropriate in such a case for the request under **CrimPR 5.5** to be treated as a request under **CrimPR 5.8**; and then for the court to review that request under **CrimPR 5.10**.

2.6.21　Some of those applying for transcripts may be taken to be aware of the significance of reporting restrictions and thus unlikely to contravene any such restriction. Such applicants include public authorities within the meaning of s.6 Human Rights Act 1998[18] and public or private bodies exercising disciplinary functions in relation to practitioners of a regulated profession such as doctors, lawyers, accountants, etc. It would be only in the most exceptional circumstances that a court might refuse any such body access to an unredacted transcript of proceedings in public, irrespective of whether reporting restrictions do or do not apply.

2.6.22　**CrimPR Part 5** imposes no time limit on a request for the supply of a transcript. The assumption is that transcripts of proceedings in public in the Crown Court will continue to be available for as long as relevant records are maintained by the Lord Chancellor under the legislation to which **CrimPR 5.4** refers.[19]

---

[18] A definition which extends to government departments and their agencies, local authorities, prosecuting authorities, and institutions such as the Parole Board and the Sentencing Council.
[19] Sections 5 and 8 Public Records Act 1958.

3. SECURITY AT COURT

PD3.1

3.1 High risk defendants at court

3.1.1 [His] Majesty's Prison and Probation Service (HMPPS) must notify the listing officer of all:

    a. Category A prisoners;

    b. those on the Escape-List and Restricted Status prisoners; or

    c. other prisoners who have otherwise been assessed as presenting a significant risk of violence or harm.

3.1.2 The listing officer shall ensure that high risk prisoners will:

    a. as far as possible, have administrative and remand appearances listed by way of live link; and

    b. have priority for the use of live link equipment.

3.1.3 In all proceedings that require the appearance in person of a high-risk prisoner, the proceedings must be listed at an appropriately secure court building and in a court with a secure dock.

3.1.4 Where HMPPS consider that more extensive security measures than normal are required, they must submit a written application in support. The written application must be sent to the relevant court officer along with current, specific and credible evidence that the security measures sought are both necessary and proportionate to the identified risk and that the risk cannot be managed in any other way. The defence must be given the opportunity to make representations.

3.1.5 In determining the application, the court must consider whether the available security measures are sufficient taking account of the risk of prejudice to a fair trial.

3.1.6 Security measures the court should consider include:

    a. the use of live link;

    b. transferring the case to a more secure courtroom;

    c. the deployment of additional escort staff and/or police in the courtroom or building;

    d. securing the courtroom for all or part of the proceedings;

    e. the accused giving evidence from the secure dock;

    f. the use of approved restraints;[20]

    g. the deployment of armed police in the court building;[21]

    h. in exceptional circumstances, moving the hearing to a prison.

PD3.2

3.2 Armed police at court

Procedure for applications for armed police presence in the Royal Courts of Justice, Crown Courts and magistrates' court buildings

3.2.1 This Practice Direction applies to all criminal and extradition cases in which a police unit requests authorisation for presence of armed police officers in the Royal Courts of Justice, the Crown Court or magistrates' court buildings at any time, including during delivery of prisoners to court.

3.2.2 This Practice Direction does not apply to police officers carrying tasers, CS or PAVA incapacitant sprays as part of their operational equipment, when attending court buildings on routine court business, and when giving evidence.

Emergency situations

3.2.3 This Practice Direction does not apply in emergencies, when police must respond appropriately, according to their professional judgement.

Designated court centres

3.2.4 Applications may only be made for armed police presence in designated Crown Court and magistrates' court centres (see below). This list may be revised in consultation with the National Police Chiefs' Council (NPCC) and HMCTS.

3.2.5 The Crown Court centres designated for firearms deployment are:

    a. Northern Circuit: Carlisle, Chester, Liverpool, Preston, Manchester Crown Square & Manchester Minshull Street.

---

[20] The court should have regard to Article 3 ECHR, which prohibits degrading treatment, see *Ranniman v Finland* (1997) 26 EHRR 56. No prisoner should be handcuffed in court unless there are reasonable grounds for apprehending that they will be violent or will attempt to escape.

[21] The decision to deploy an armed escort is for the Chief Inspector of the relevant borough: the decision to allow the armed escort in or around the courtroom is for the Senior Presiding Judge.

Criminal Practice Directions 2023

    b. North Eastern Circuit: Bradford, Leeds, Newcastle upon Tyne, Sheffield, Teesside and Kingston-upon-Hull.

    c. Western Circuit: Bristol, Winchester and Exeter.

    d. South Eastern Circuit (not including London): Canterbury, Chelmsford, Ipswich, Luton, Maidstone, Norwich, Reading and St Albans.

    e. South Eastern Circuit (London only): Central Criminal Court, Woolwich, Kingston and Snaresbrook.

    f. Midland Circuit: Birmingham, Northampton, Nottingham and Leicester.

    g. Wales Circuit: Cardiff, Swansea and Caernarfon.

3.2.6   The magistrates' courts designated for firearms deployment are: Westminster Magistrates' Court and Belmarsh Magistrates' Court.

Preparatory work prior to applications in all cases

3.2.7   Before making any application for the presence of armed police officers in the court building, the officer should check with the court whether the prisoner can appear by live link.

3.2.8   Each requesting officer will attend the relevant court before an application is made to ensure there have been no changes to the premises and no circumstances which might affect security arrangements.

Applying to the Royal Courts of Justice

3.2.9   All applications relating to criminal and extradition cases must be sent to the Listing Office in which the case is due to appear. The application should be sent by email if possible and must be on the standard form.

3.2.10   The Listing Office will notify the President of the King's Bench Division (if the case is listed in the High Court) or the Vice-President of the Court of Appeal, Criminal Division (if the case is listed in that court), providing a copy of the email and any supporting evidence. The PKBD or V-P may ask to see the senior police officer concerned.

3.2.11   The PKBD or V-P will consider the application. The relevant Court Office will be notified of the decision and must immediately inform the police by telephone. The decision must then be confirmed by email to the police. If refused, the police must be informed.

Applying to the Crown Court

3.2.12   All applications, save for when a case listed in the High Court or Court of Appeal Criminal Division is to be heard in a Crown Court, should be sent to the Cluster Manager, or their deputy, by email if possible, and must be on the standard form. Where a case listed in the High Court or the Court of Appeal, Criminal Division is to be heard at a Crown Court, the procedure applicable to the Royal Courts of Justice should be followed, but with the relevant Resident Judge and the Presiding Judges being kept informed.

3.2.13   The Presiding Judges of the circuit and the Resident Judge will be notified by email, and supplied with a copy of the form and any supporting evidence. The Presiding Judge may ask to see the senior police officer concerned.

3.2.14   The Presiding Judge will consider the application. If the Presiding Judge approves the application, it should be forwarded to the Senior Presiding Judge's Office. The Senior Presiding Judge will make the final decision. The Presiding Judge will receive email confirmation of that decision.

3.2.15   The Presiding Judge will notify the appropriate court officer and the Resident Judge of the decision. The appropriate court officer will immediately inform the police of the decision by telephone. The decision must then be confirmed by email to the police.

Urgent applications to the Crown Court

3.2.16   If an application for the deployment of armed police arises as an urgent issue the Resident Judge has a discretion to agree such deployment without obtaining the consent of a Presiding Judge or the Senior Presiding Judge. In such a case:

    a. the Resident Judge should assess the facts and agree the proposed solution with a police officer of at least Superintendent level. That officer should agree the approach with the police Firearms Division;

    b. the Resident Judge must try to contact the Presiding Judge and/or Senior Presiding Judge by email and telephone. The Cluster Manager should be informed of the situation;

c. if the Resident Judge cannot obtain a response from the Presiding Judge or Senior Presiding Judge, the Resident Judge may grant the application if satisfied:

    i. that the deployment of armed officers is necessary;

    ii. that without such deployment there would be significant risk to public safety; and

    iii. that the case would have to be adjourned at significant difficulty or inconvenience.

3.2.17 The Resident Judge must keep the position under continual review, to ensure it remains appropriate and necessary. The Resident Judge must only authorise deployment of armed officers as an interim measure pending the decision of the Senior Presiding Judge which must be sought in the usual way.

Applying to the magistrates' courts

3.2.18 All applications should be directed, by email if possible, to the Chief Magistrate's Office, at Westminster Magistrates' Court and must be on the standard form.

3.2.19 The Chief Magistrate must consider the application and, if approved, it should be forwarded to the Senior Presiding Judge's Office. The Senior Presiding Judge will make the final decision. The Chief Magistrate will receive email confirmation of that decision and will then notify the requesting police officer and, where authorisation is given, the relevant magistrates' court of the decision. If refused, the police must be informed.

Urgent applications in the magistrates' courts

3.2.20 If the temporary deployment of armed police arises as an urgent issue, or if the Chief Magistrate is satisfied that there is a serious risk to public safety, then the Chief Magistrate will have a discretion to agree such deployment without having obtained the consent of the Senior Presiding Judge. In such a case:

a. the Chief Magistrate must assess the facts and agree the proposed solution with a police officer of at least Superintendent level. That officer should agree the approach with the police Firearms Division;

b. the Chief Magistrate must try to contact the Senior Presiding Judge by email and telephone. The Cluster Manager should be informed of the situation;

c. if the Chief Magistrate cannot obtain a response from the Senior Presiding Judge, the Chief Magistrate may grant the application if satisfied:

    i. that the deployment of armed officers is necessary;

    ii. that without such deployment there would be significant risk to public safety; and

    iii. that the case would have to be adjourned at significant difficulty or inconvenience.

3.2.21 The Chief Magistrate must keep the position under continual review and ensure it remains appropriate and necessary. The Chief Magistrate must ensure that the Senior Presiding Judge is notified of the full circumstances of the authorisation and any review.

4. Custody and Bail

PD4.1   ### 4.1 Forfeiture of monies lodged as security or pledged by a surety[22]

Key principles:

4.1.1 The court must have regard to the following key principles:

a. A security is the deposit of money, usually as a **pre-release** condition.

b. A surety **undertakes** to forfeit a sum if the accused fails to surrender as required.

c. Care must be taken to explain the obligations and consequences, before a surety or security is taken.

d. The surety or provider of a security has a duty to report to authorities if there is a concern that the accused will abscond. In those circumstances, the surety or security can apply to withdraw.

e. Upon failure to surrender, a surety or security should be given a reasonable but limited opportunity in which to seek to persuade the accused to surrender.

4.1.2 The court should not defer or adjourn a decision on enforcement of a surety or security until the accused appears before the court.

---

[22] The procedure is set out at **CrimPR 14.15**. Relevant forms for court staff are to be found on XHIBIT.

4.1.3   Before the court makes a decision on forfeiture, it should give sureties and securities an opportunity to make representations in person, through advocates or by statement.

4.1.4   As to forfeiture:

    a. The court should forfeit no more than necessary to maintain integrity/confidence in the system, but the starting point is forfeiture in full.

    b. An accused who absconds without warning their sureties does not release them from their responsibilities.

    c. Culpability or the lack of it is a factor, but is not a reason to reduce or set aside the surety's obligations.

    d. If a surety's financial circumstances alter in a way which would affect their ability to pay in the event it is called in, they should notify the court immediately.

Notifying sureties of hearing dates

4.1.5   If a surety has not been made continuous until trial, the surety must be reconfirmed before the renewal of bail at the end of a hearing. If the surety is not present, the accused may be remanded in custody until the recognisance is provided.

4.1.6   The Court must also notify sureties of the hearing dates at which the accused is ordered to appear as far in advance as possible.[23]

4.2 Failure to surrender to bail: consequences and penalties

PD4.2

Initiating Proceedings – Bail granted by a court

4.2.1   Where it appears that an accused has committed an offence under the Bail Act 1976, proceedings should be initiated either:

    a. by the court of its own motion;

    b. on application by the prosecutor.

4.2.2   The charge should be put to the accused, and they should be asked to enter a plea.

Timing of disposal

4.2.3   Courts should not, without good reason, adjourn the disposal of a failure to surrender offence contrary to ss.6(1) or 6(2) Bail Act 1976 until the conclusion of the proceedings in respect of which bail was granted. The court should deal with the accused as soon as practicable, taking into account when proceedings in respect of which bail was granted are expected to conclude, the seriousness of the offence for which the accused is already being prosecuted, the type of penalty that might be imposed for the Bail Act offence and other relevant circumstances.[24]

4.2.4   If the Bail Act offence is adjourned alongside the substantive proceedings, it is still necessary to consider imposing a separate penalty at the conclusion of the proceedings. Bail should usually be revoked in the meantime.

Conduct of Proceedings

4.2.5   Proceedings under s.6 Bail Act 1976 may be conducted either as a summary offence or as a criminal contempt of court. Where commenced by the police or prosecutor, the proceedings will be conducted by the prosecutor who, if the matter is contested, will call evidence. Where the court initiates proceedings, with or without a prosecutor's invitation, it may expect the prosecutor's assistance e.g. in cross-examining the accused, if required.

4.2.6   The burden of proof is on the accused to prove they had reasonable cause for failure to surrender to custody.[25]

Voluntary attendance at court after failure to attend

4.2.7   Where:

    a. the accused failed to attend court at the appointed time;

    b. a warrant has been issued for the accused's arrest for that failure; and

---

[23] See the observations of Parker LJ in *R v Crown Court at Reading ex parte Bello* [1992] 3 All ER 353.
[24] See the Sentencing Council Guideline.
[25] Section 6(3) Bail Act 1976.

c. the accused subsequently attends voluntarily, or indicates a wish to do so, e.g. by making enquiries of court staff,

the court may take any of the following courses of action:

    i.   if the accused is present, and the relevant personnel are available, arrange for the execution there and then of the warrant;

    ii. if the accused is present, deal there and then with the case as if consequent on the execution of the warrant;

    iii. arrange a resumed hearing in the accused's case at the next convenient opportunity, while warning the accused that the warrant remains liable to be executed in the meantime; and

    iv. withdraw the warrant and arrange a resumed hearing in the accused's case at the next convenient opportunity. The court should not withdraw an outstanding warrant unless the accused provides evidence of an established current residential address, a telephone number and, if available, an email address.

4.2.8 If an outstanding warrant is executed immediately, or if the court decides to deal at once with the accused as if consequent on arrest, then paragraphs 4.2.1-4.2.6 of this Practice Direction apply.

4.2.9 Only in exceptional circumstances should efforts be made to accommodate an accused who attends voluntarily and unexpectedly at a court building on any day other than a weekday on which a court is sitting at that building, or later than 12 noon on any such day.

4.2.10 If an outstanding warrant for the accused's arrest for failure to attend is executed or withdrawn, court staff must ensure this is notified to those responsible for national police records.

PD4.3
<h3 style="text-align:center">4.3 Bail during trial</h3>

4.3.1 During the trial it may be a proper exercise of discretion to refuse bail, e.g. if the accused cannot otherwise be kept apart from witnesses and jurors.

4.3.2 An accused who was on bail while on remand should not be refused bail during the trial unless, in the opinion of the court, the circumstances have changed to justify this refusal.

<h2 style="text-align:center">5. Trial Management</h2>

PD5.1
<h3 style="text-align:center">5.1 Defendant on bail: anticipated not guilty plea</h3>

5.1.1 Where the prosecutor does not anticipate a guilty plea at the first hearing in a magistrates' court:

a. it is essential that Initial Details of the Prosecution Case are sufficient to assist the court to identify real issues and give directions for an effective magistrates' court or Crown Court trial, and

b. the prosecution should provide in advance of the first hearing:

    i.   summary circumstances of the offence(s) including any interview account;

    ii. statements and exhibits the prosecution has identified as important for plea or initial case management, including CCTV relied upon and any Streamlined Forensic Report(s);

    iii. witness availability;

    iv. defendant's criminal record;

    v. Victim Personal Statement(s), if available;

    vi. an indication of any likely prosecution expert evidence;

    vii. information as to special measures, bad character or hearsay, where applicable.

5.1.2 In addition to material required by **CrimPR Part 8**, the Preparation for Effective Trial form must be fully completed in accordance with its published guidance. The form's directions and timetable apply unless the court otherwise orders.

5.1.3 In order to further the overriding objective the Better Case Management Form must be completed for cases sent to the Crown Court.

PD5.2
<h3 style="text-align:center">5.2 Case progression and trial preparation</h3>

Plea and Trial Preparation Hearing

5.2.1 In a case in which a magistrates' court has directed a Plea and Trial Preparation Hearing (PTPH):

a. an indictment should be uploaded at least seven days in advance of the hearing;

b. the time allowed for conduct of the PTPH must be sufficient for effective trial preparation.

5.2.2 If the first time a defendant indicates to their representative an intention to plead guilty is after being sent for trial but before the PTPH:

a. the defence representative must notify the Crown Court and prosecution immediately;

  b. the court will ensure there is sufficient time at the PTPH for sentence; and

  c. the case should be drawn to the attention of a judge for consideration as to the need for a pre-sentence report.

5.2.3 A judge must order a pre-sentence report where obliged to do under s.30 Sentencing Act 2020.

5.2.4 In all other circumstances a judge may order a pre-sentence report if it appears that either:

  a. there may be a realistic alternative to a custodial sentence; or

  b. the defendant may satisfy the criteria for classification as a dangerous offender; or

  c. there is some other appropriate reason for doing so.

5.2.5 The ordering of a pre-sentence report by the magistrates' court does not indicate the likelihood of any sentencing outcome. All options remain open in the Crown Court.

5.2.6 If at the PTPH the defendant pleads guilty and no pre-sentence report has been prepared, the court should if possible obtain a stand down report (if required).

5.2.7 Where the defendant was remanded in custody after being charged and sent for trial without service of Initial Details of the Prosecution Case:

  a. at least seven days before the PTPH the prosecutor should serve, as a minimum:

   i. summary circumstances of the offence(s) including any interview account;

   ii. statements and exhibits the prosecution has identified as important for plea or initial case management, including CCTV relied upon and any Streamlined Forensic Report(s);

   iii. witness availability;

   iv. defendant's criminal record;

   v. Victim Personal Statement(s), if available;

   vi. an indication of any likely prosecution expert evidence;

   vii. information as to special measures, bad character or hearsay, where applicable.

5.2.8 If at the PTPH the defendant does not plead guilty, the court should identify the issues in the case, and give appropriate directions for an effective trial.

Further case management hearing

5.2.9 After the PTPH further case management hearings may be required before the trial in order to:

  a. give directions for an effective trial;

  b. set ground rules for the conduct of the questioning of a witness or defendant;

  c. further the overriding objective.

5.2.10 If a further case management hearing is directed, a defendant in custody will not usually be expected to attend in person, unless the court directs otherwise.

Compliance courts

5.2.11 If a participant fails to comply with a case management direction, that participant may be required to attend the court to explain the failure. Unless the court otherwise directs, a defendant in custody will not usually be expected to attend and the hearings may be conducted by live link facilities or other electronic means, as the court may direct. Courts should maintain a record of any non-compliance.[26] It will be for the Presiding Judges, Resident Judge and Heads of Legal Operations (HoLO) to decide locally how often compliance courts should be held, depending on the scale and nature of the problem at each court centre.

Conduct of case progression hearings

5.2.12 As far as possible:

  a. case progression should be managed without a hearing in the courtroom;

  b. using electronic communication;[27]

  c. court staff should be nominated to conduct case progression as part of their role;[28]

  d. to aid effective communication the prosecution and defence should provide the court with details of who shall be dealing with the case at the earliest opportunity.

---

[26] See the Message from the Lord Chief Justice – Remote Attendance by Advocates in the Crown Court.

[27] In accordance with **CrimPR 3.5(2)(d)**.

[28] In accordance with **CrimPR 3.4(2)**.

Completion of Effective Trial Monitoring form

5.2.13 It is imperative that the Effective Trial Monitoring form is accurately completed by the parties for all cases listed for trial. Advocates must complete the form providing the relevant details.[29]

PD5.3   **5.3 Defendant's record**

5.3.1 The prosecution must provide up to date and accurate information about the defendant's record of previous convictions, cautions, reprimands, etc. in the Initial Details of the Prosecution Case. The record must be supplied to the court, the defence and (if applicable) Probation Service.

5.3.2 The record should usually be provided as a Police National Computer (PNC) printout, supplemented by Forms MG16/17 if the police hold convictions/cautions not shown on PNC.

5.3.3 If the defence object to the accuracy of the record, they should inform the prosecutor immediately.

PD5.4   **5.4 Trial adjournment in magistrates' court**

5.4.1 Parties and other participants must further the overriding objective and prepare cases so that they can proceed on the date set. Any change that may affect the listing of a case must be communicated between the parties and to the court as soon as reasonably practicable. Any communication must clearly identify the issue and any direction sought and should be referred to a legal adviser or case progression officer.

Change of plea

5.4.2 Where a defendant who previously has pleaded not guilty decides to enter a guilty plea, notice of that decision, and any basis of plea, must be given to the prosecution and court as soon as possible so that a decision can be taken about the need for witnesses to attend. Consideration must be given to whether the plea should be taken in advance of the date already set for trial and before the witnesses are de-warned.

Trial adjournment

5.4.3 It should be rare for applications to adjourn to be made on the day of trial, except in circumstances that could not have been foreseen. It may be necessary to hear a contested application to adjourn a trial either very shortly before or even on the date on which that trial is due to begin.

5.4.4 Section 10 of the Magistrates' Courts Act 1980 confers a discretionary power to adjourn. The starting point is that the trial should proceed.[30] The court must not be deterred from a prompt and robust determination. As an exercise of discretion, the High Court will only interfere with a decision on adjournment if there are compelling reasons so to do.

5.4.5 A court may be justified in refusing an adjournment even if that means the prosecutor is unable to prove the prosecution case or a part of it, or that the defendant is unable to explore an issue. Even in the absence of fault on the part of either party it may not be in the interests of justice to adjourn, notwithstanding that an imperfect trial may be the result.

5.4.6 The court must ensure that any adjournment is for as short a period as possible, for example by using time vacated by another trial or by conducting the hearing at another court or court centre. A just outcome may be achieved by a short adjournment to later on the same day. The shorter the time the more favourably the court may consider an application for an adjournment, but even a short adjournment must be justified.

Applications to vacate trials

5.4.7 Applications to vacate trials must be made promptly and in writing on the standard form, in advance of the date of trial. Any application should be served on each other party at the same time as it is served on the court. As a general rule, such an application will be dealt with outside the courtroom in advance of the hearing under **CrimPR 3.5** applying the preceding principles. The parties must provide full and accurate information to the court to enable it to assess where the interests of justice lie.[31]

---

[29] See Operational Guidance notes.
[30] See judgment of Gross LJ in *DPP v Petrie* [2015] EWHC 48 (Admin) and *R (DPP) v Sunderland Magistrates' Court, R (Kharaghan) v City of London Magistrates' Court* [2018] EWHC 229 (Admin).
[31] *R (on the application of F and another) v Knowsley Magistrates' Court* [2006] EWHC 695 (Admin); *R (Jones) v South East Surrey Local Justice Area* [2010] EWHC 916 (Admin), (2010) 174 JP 342; *DPP v Woods* [2017] EWHC 1070 (Admin).

5.4.8 Any application and any response should, as a minimum, include:

   a. a chronology of the case, recording the dates of compliance with any directions and of communication between the parties;
   b. an assessment of the interests of justice, addressing the factors identified above and indicating the likely effect should the court conclude that the trial should proceed on the date fixed;
   c. any restrictions on the future availability of witnesses;
   d. any likely changes to the number of witnesses or the way in which the evidence will be presented and any impact on the trial time estimate;
   e. any evidence supporting the reasons why an application to vacate is being made.

5.4.9 On receipt of an application, each other party should serve that party's response on the court and on the applicant within two business days unless the court otherwise directs. Any request for the matter to be determined at a hearing must be served with the application to vacate the trial (or with the response to that application), together with the reasons for that request, to enable the court to decide whether a hearing is needed.

5.4.10 In reaching a decision whether to adjourn the court must consider the following matters:

   a. That the court's duty is to deal justly with the case, which includes doing justice between the parties.
   b. The need for expedition and that delay is generally inimical to the interests of justice – it has the potential to bring the criminal justice system into disrepute.
   c. That proceedings in a magistrates' court should be simple and speedy.
   d. That applications for adjournments must be rigorously scrutinised and the court must have cogent reasons for adjourning.
   e. The need to review the history of the case.
   f. The need to examine the nature of the evidence and whether memories of relevant evidence are liable to fade.
   g. The interests of any co-defendant(s).
   h. The interests of any witness(es) who have attended, with particular emphasis on their age and/or vulnerability.
   i. The interest of the defendant(s) in resolving the matter without undue delay but also the public interest in ensuring that criminal charges are adjudicated upon thoroughly, with the guilty convicted as well as the innocent acquitted.
   j. The fact that the more serious the charge the greater the public interest in the trial proceeding and the greater the responsibility of the parties to have engaged in effective preparation.
   k. Where a defendant asks for an adjournment whether they will be able to present the defence fully without one and the extent to which the ability to do so may be compromised by an immediate trial.
   l. The court must consider the consequences of an adjournment on:
      i.   the ability of witnesses and defendants accurately to recall events;
      ii. the impact of adjournment on other cases;
      iii. the length of time it may take to list the case for trial.
   m. The court must also consider the nature and gravity of fault on the part of the applicant for the adjournment and who is responsible for it.

Absence of defendant

5.4.11 Where the reason for which the adjournment is sought relates to the absence of the defendant some particular issues arise.

5.4.12 **If the defendant is aged 18 or over:**

   a. the court shall proceed in the defendant's absence unless it appears to the court to be contrary to the interests of justice to do so;[32]
   b. proceeding in the absence of a defendant is the default position where the defendant is aware of the date of trial and no acceptable reason is offered for that absence;
   c. the court is not obliged to investigate if no reason is offered;
   d. the court will take into account all factors, including:
      i.   such reasons for absence as may be offered;
      ii. the reliability of the information supplied in support of those reasons;
      iii. the date on which the reasons for absence became known to the defendant and what action the defendant thereafter took in response;
      iv. that trial in absence can and sometimes does result in acquittal;

---

[32] Section 11 Magistrates' Courts Act 1980.

    v. that if convicted the defendant can ask that the conviction be re-opened in the interests of justice, for example if absence was involuntary;

    vi. if convicted the defendant has a right to a rehearing on appeal to the Crown Court;

  e. where the defendant provides a medical note to excuse non-attendance the court must assess the provenance and reliability of the information contained therein and if necessary summons the author to attend court. The court must give reasons explaining why it has decided to proceed or not to proceed with the trial on the date it is listed. The reasons must be specific to the case.

5.4.13 If the defendant is aged under 18:

  a. there is no presumption that the court should proceed in absence;

  b. the potential for an acquittal may still be a relevant factor;

  c. the potential for an application to re-open or appeal may also be a relevant matter;

  d. the age, vulnerability, or experience of the defendant should be taken into account;

  e. whether a parent or guardian is present, whether a parent or guardian ordinarily would be required to attend and whether such a person has attended a previous hearing;

  f. the court should consider the interests of any co-defendant in the case proceeding;

  g. the interests of any young and/or vulnerable witnesses who have attended.

Absence of witness

5.4.14 Where the court is asked to adjourn because a witness has failed to attend, the court must:

  a. rigorously investigate the steps taken to secure that witness's attendance, the fault for non-attendance is a relevant factor when deciding an application to adjourn;

  b. critically examine the reasons given for the absence and/or the likelihood of the witness attending should the case be adjourned;

  c. consider the relevance of the witness to the case, and whether the witness's statement can be agreed or admitted, in whole or part, as hearsay;

  d. consider whether proper notice has been given of the intention to call that witness;

  e. consider whether an absent witness can be heard later in the trial;

  f. where other witnesses have attended and the court has determined that the absent witness is required, consider hearing those witnesses who are present and adjourning the case part-heard, subject to that being possible within a reasonable timescale.

Need for additional evidence

5.4.15 It should rarely be the case that an application to adjourn based on a failure to serve evidence is made on the day of trial. The court is entitled to expect that evidence will have been served in good time and in accordance with the directions of the court. The court must consider whether the party who complains of the failure to serve evidence had informed the other party and the court in advance of the hearing. The court must conduct a rigorous inquiry into the nature of the evidence and must consider whether any of what is sought has been served, and if so when; the volume and the significance of what is sought; and the time likely to be needed for its consideration. In particular, the court must satisfy itself that any material still sought is relevant and that the party seeking it has a right to it.

5.4.16 In appropriate circumstances the court may refuse to admit evidence rather than adjourning the trial to allow it to be served.[33] Applications to adjourn in order to obtain expert evidence should be rigorously scrutinised and it may not be appropriate to adjourn where the opinion sought is speculative.[34]

Failure to comply with disclosure obligations

5.4.17 Where a defendant complains of a prosecution failure to disclose material that ought to have been disclosed the court must first establish whether either party is applying for an adjournment as a result. If an adjournment is sought, the court should consider whether the matter can be resolved by providing disclosure at that stage. If it cannot, the court should consider whether the parties have complied with their obligations and should consider the relevance of fault.

5.4.18 If the prosecutor has complied or purported to comply with initial disclosure obligations, no further material is disclosable and consequently, in the absence of a defence statement served in accordance with s.6 Criminal Procedure and Investigations Act 1996, no application to adjourn should be granted. If the defendant has served a defence statement and asks for further disclosure,

---

[33] *R v Boardman* [2015] EWCA Crim 175; [2015] 1 Cr. App. R. 33; [2015] Crim. L.R. 451.
[34] *R v Chabaan* [2003] EWCA Crim 1012.

in consequence of the prosecutor's allegedly inadequate response or in consequence of a failure to respond at all, the court application must be made under s.8 Criminal Procedure and Investigations Act 1996 and **CrimPR 15.5**. The court should consider hearing such an application immediately, provided that there is sufficient time available for the application itself and then for the defence to consider any material disclosed in consequence of it.

Managing trials within available court time

5.4.19 Where there is a risk of a trial being adjourned for lack of court time the court or legal adviser must assess the priority to be assigned to each trial listed for hearing that day based on:

a. the needs of the parties and witnesses;
b. whether the case has been adjourned before;
c. the seriousness of the offence;
d. giving priority to any cases in which the defendant is in custody by reason only of a trial due to be heard that day;
e. liaison between courtrooms to determine whether all listed trials might be heard through movement of cases.

5.4.20 Where a case is moved from one courtroom to another and as a result is assigned to a different advocate, the court must allow the fresh advocate adequate time in which to prepare. Courts should always begin a trial by reviewing the need for witnesses and the timetable set during pre-trial case management. The court must not adjourn a trial until it is clear that all other trials assessed as having an equal or higher priority for hearing that day will be effective.

5.4.21 The court is entitled to expect that parties will present their case within the time set during pre-trial case management. If more time is sought the court must keep in mind the need for the trial to be completed within the allocated time with minimal impact on other cases.

5.4.22 It is preferable to complete a trial on the date allocated but it may be appropriate to adjourn part-heard, particularly where it is possible to hear the majority of witnesses. Future listings may have to be moved to accommodate the case.

5.5 Use of live link   PD5.5

5.5.1 Where it is lawful and in the interests of justice to do so, courts should exercise their statutory and other powers to conduct hearings by live link. The Live Link in Criminal Courts Guidance issued by the Lord Chief Justice must be complied with.

Open justice and records of proceedings[35]

5.5.2 Open justice is the principal means by which courts are kept under scrutiny by the public. It follows that where a participant attends a hearing in public by live link then that person's participation must be, as nearly as possible, equally audible and, if applicable, equally visible to the public as it would be were that person physically present. Where electronic means of communication are used to conduct a hearing, records of the event must be maintained in the usual way.

5.6 Listing as a judicial responsibility and function   PD5.6

5.6.1 Listing is a judicial responsibility and function. The purpose is to ensure that all cases are brought to a hearing or trial in accordance with the interests of justice, that resources available for criminal justice are deployed as effectively as possible, and that cases are heard by an appropriate judge or bench with minimum delay.

5.6.2 The agreement reached between the Lord Chief Justice and the Secretary of State for Constitutional Affairs and Lord Chancellor ('the Concordat'), states that judges, working with HMCTS, are responsible for deciding on the assignment of cases to particular courts and the listing of those cases before particular judges. Therefore:

a. the Presiding Judges of each circuit have the overall responsibility for listing at all courts, Crown and magistrates', on their circuit;
b. subject to the supervision of the Presiding Judges, the Resident Judge at each Crown Court has the general responsibility within their court centre for the allocation of criminal judicial work, to ensure the just and efficient despatch of the business of the court or group of courts. This includes overseeing the deployment of allocated judges at the court or group, including the distribution of work between all the judges allocated to that court. A Resident Judge must appoint a deputy or deputies to exercise their functions when they are absent from the court centre. See also paragraph 5.6.5: Judicial responsibilities;

---

[35] See Ch 2, Open Justice.

Criminal Practice Directions 2023

    c. the listing officer in the Crown Court is responsible for carrying out the day-to-day operation of listing practice under the direction of the Resident Judge;

    d. in the magistrates' courts, the Judicial Business Group, subject to the supervision of the Presiding Judges of the circuit, is responsible for determining the listing practice in that area. The day-to-day operation of that listing practice is the responsibility of the HoLO with the assistance of the listing officer.

Key principles of listing

5.6.3 When setting the listing practice, the Resident Judge or the Judicial Business Group should take into account the following principles:

    a. Ensure the timely trial of cases and resolution of other issues (such as confiscation) so that justice is not delayed. The following factors are relevant:

        i. In general, each case should be tried within as short a time of its arrival in the court as is consistent with the interests of justice, the needs of victims and witnesses, and with the proper and timely preparation by the prosecution and defence of their cases in accordance with the directions and timetable set.

        ii. Priority should be accorded to the trial of young defendants, and cases where there are vulnerable or young witnesses. In *R v Barker*,[36] the Lord Chief Justice highlighted 'the importance to the trial and investigative process of keeping any delay in a case involving a child complainant to an irreducible minimum'.

        iii. Custody time limits (CTLs) must be observed.

        iv. Every effort must also be made to avoid delay in cases in which the defendant is on bail.

    b. Ensure that in the magistrates' court, unless impracticable, non-custody anticipated guilty plea cases are listed 14 days after charge, and non- custody anticipated not guilty pleas are listed 28 days after charge.

    c. Provide, when possible, for certainty and/or as much advance notice as possible, of the trial date; and take all reasonable steps to ensure that the trial date remains fixed and the trial can be effective on that date.

    d. Ensure that a judge or bench with any necessary authorisation and/or appropriate experience is available to try each case and, wherever desirable and practicable, there is judicial continuity, including in relation to post-trial hearings.

    e. Take account of the:

        i. efficient deployment of the judiciary in the Crown Court and the magistrates' courts taking into account relevant sitting requirements for magistrates;

        ii. proper use of the courtrooms available at the court;

        iii. provision in long and/or complex cases for adequate reading time for the judiciary;

        iv. facilities in the available courtrooms, including the security needs (such as a secure dock), size and equipment, such as live link facilities;

        v. proper use of jurors;

        vi. availability of legal advisers in the magistrates' courts;

        vii. need to return those sentenced to custody as soon as possible after the sentence is passed, and to facilitate the efficient operation of the prison escort contract;

        viii. need to list a hearing at a time that is convenient for court users (such as an early hearing time when a young witness is to be called, or a late hearing time when a prisoner is to be brought a long distance).

    f. Provide where practicable:

        i. the defendant and the prosecution with the advocate of their choice where this does not result in any unreasonable delay to the trial of the case; and,

        ii. for the efficient deployment of advocates, lawyers and associate prosecutors of the Crown Prosecution Service (CPS), and other prosecuting authorities, and of the resources available to the independent legal profession, for example by trying to group certain cases together.

    g. Meet the need for special security measures for category A and other high-risk defendants.[37]

    h. Ensure that proper time (including judicial reading time) is afforded to hearings.

    i. Consider the significance of ancillary proceedings, such as confiscation hearings, and the need to deal with such hearings promptly and, where possible, for such hearings to be conducted by the trial judge.

    j. Provide for government initiatives or approved projects.

---

[36] [2010] EWCA Crim 4.
[37] See further Ch 3. Security at Court.

5.6.4   Although the listing practice at each Crown Court centre and magistrates' court will take these principles into account, the listing practice adopted will vary from court to court depending particularly on the number of courtrooms and the facilities available, the location and the workload, its volume and type.

Judicial responsibilities

5.6.5   The Resident Judge (Crown Court), and the Judicial Business Group and the HoLO (magistrates' court), of each court is responsible for:

a. monitoring the general performance of the court and the listing practices;
b. ensuring that good practice is implemented throughout the court, such that all hearings commence on time;
c. ensuring that the reasons that a trial did not proceed on the date originally fixed are examined to see if there is any systemic issue;
d. monitoring the timeliness of cases and reporting any cases of serious concern to the Presiding Judge.

5.6.6   Each Judicial Business Group, subject to the overall jurisdiction of the Presiding Judge, is responsible for monitoring the workload and any changes that may impact on listing policies in the magistrates' courts.

5.7 Classification

PD5.7

5.7.1   The classification structure outlined below is solely for the purposes of trial in the Crown Court.

Offences are classified as follows:

5.7.2   Class 1: A:

a. Murder.
b. Attempted Murder.
c. Manslaughter.
d. Infanticide.
e. Child destruction (s.1(1) Infant Life (Preservation) Act 1929).
f. Abortion (s.58 Offences Against the Person Act 1861).
g. Assisting a suicide.
h. Cases including s.5 Domestic Violence, Crime and Victims Act 2004, as amended (if a fatality has resulted).
i. Soliciting, inciting, encouraging or assisting, attempting or conspiring to commit any of the above offences or assisting an offender having committed such an offence.

5.7.3   Class 1: B:

a. Genocide.
b. Torture, hostage-taking and offences under the War Crimes Act 1991.
c. Offences under ss.51 and 52 International Criminal Courts Act 2001.
d. An offence under s.1 Geneva Conventions Act 1957.
e. Terrorism offences (where offence charged is indictable only and took place during an act of terrorism or for the purposes of terrorism as defined in s.1 Terrorism Act 2000).
f. Piracy, under the Merchant Shipping and Maritime Security Act 1997.
g. Treason.
h. An offence under the Official Secrets Acts.
i. Incitement to disaffection.
j. Soliciting, inciting, encouraging or assisting, attempting or conspiring to commit any of the above offences or assisting an offender having committed such an offence.

5.7.4   Class 1: C:

a. Prison mutiny, under the Prison Security Act 1992.
b. Riot in the course of serious civil disturbance.
c. Serious gang-related crime resulting in the possession or discharge of firearms, particularly including a campaign of firebombing or extortion, especially when accompanied by allegations of drug trafficking on a commercial scale.
d. Complex sexual offence cases in which there are many complainants (underage, in care or otherwise particularly vulnerable) and/or many defendants who are alleged to have systematically groomed and abused them, often over a long period of time.
e. Cases involving people trafficking for sexual, labour or other exploitation and cases of human servitude.

f. Soliciting, inciting, encouraging or assisting, attempting or conspiring to commit any of the above offences or assisting an offender having committed such an offence.

5.7.5 Class 1: D:

a. Causing death by dangerous driving.
b. Causing death by careless driving.
c. Causing death by unlicensed, disqualified or uninsured driving.
d. Any Health and Safety case resulting in a fatality or permanent serious disability.
e. Any other case resulting in a fatality or permanent serious disability.
f. Soliciting, inciting, encouraging or assisting, attempting or conspiring to commit any of the above offences or assisting an offender having committed such an offence.

5.7.6 Class 2: A

a. Arson with intent to endanger life or reckless as to whether life was endangered.
b. Cases in which explosives, firearms or imitation firearms are used or carried or possessed.
c. Kidnapping or false imprisonment (without intention to commit a sexual offence but charged on the same indictment as a serious offence of violence such as under s.18 or s.20 Offences Against the Person Act 1861).
d. Cases in which the defendant is a police officer, member of the legal profession or a high profile or public figure.
e. Cases in which the complainant or an important witness is a high profile or public figure.
f. Riot otherwise than in the course of serious civil disturbance.
g. Child cruelty.
h. Cases including s.5 Domestic Violence, Crime and Victims Act 2004, as amended (if no fatality has resulted).
i. Soliciting, inciting, encouraging or assisting, attempting or conspiring to commit any of the above offences or assisting an offender having committed such an offence.

5.7.7 Class 2: B

a. Any sexual offence, with the exception of those included in Class 1C.
b. Kidnapping or false imprisonment (with intention to commit a sexual offence or charged on the same indictment as a sexual offence).
c. Soliciting, inciting, encouraging or assisting, attempting or conspiring to commit any of the above offences or assisting an offender having committed such an offence.

5.7.8 Class 2: C

a. Serious, complex fraud.
b. Serious and/or complex money laundering.
c. Serious and/or complex bribery.
d. Corruption.
e. Complex cases in which the defendant is a corporation (including cases for sentence as well as for trial).
f. Any case in which the defendant is a corporation with a turnover in excess of £1bn (including cases for sentence as well as for trial).
g. Soliciting, inciting, encouraging or assisting, attempting or conspiring to commit any of the above offences or assisting an offender having committed such an offence.

5.7.9 Class 3: All other offences not listed in the classes above.

Deferred Prosecution Agreements

5.7.10 Cases coming before the court under s.45 and Schedule 17 Crime and Courts Act 2013 must be referred to the President of the King's Bench Division who will allocate the matter to a judge from the list. Only the allocated judge may thereafter hear any matter or make any decision in relation to that case.

Criminal Cases Review Commission

5.7.11 Where the Criminal Cases Review Commission refers a case upon conviction from the magistrates' courts to the Crown Court, this shall be dealt with at a Crown Court centre designated by the Senior Presiding Judge.

PD5.8   **5.8 Referral of cases in the Crown Court to the Resident Judge and to the Presiding Judges**

5.8.1 This Practice Direction specifies:

a. cases which must be referred to a Presiding Judge for release; and

Criminal Practice Directions 2023

    b. cases which must be referred to the Resident Judge before being assigned to a judge, Recorder or qualifying judge advocate to hear.

5.8.2 It is applicable to all Crown Courts, but its application may be modified by the Senior Presiding Judge or the Presiding Judges, with the approval of the Senior Presiding Judge, through the provision of further specific guidance to Resident Judges in relation to the allocation and management of the work at their court.

5.8.3 This Practice Direction does not prescribe the way in which the Resident Judge gives directions as to listing policy to the listing officer; its purpose is to ensure that there is appropriate judicial control over the listing of cases. However, the Resident Judge must arrange with the listing officers a satisfactory means of ensuring that all cases are listed before judges, Recorders, qualifying judge advocates, or District Judges (Magistrates' Courts) of suitable seniority and experience, subject to the requirements of this Practice Direction.

5.8.4 In order to assist the Resident Judge and the listing officer, cases sent to the Crown Court should where possible include a brief case summary prepared by the prosecution, if the MG5 police summary uploaded to the Crown Court Digital Case System is insufficient, or does not adequately reflect the evidence. The prosecutor should ensure that any factors that make the case complex, or would lead it to be referred to the Resident Judge or a Presiding Judge are highlighted. The defence may also send submissions to the court, again highlighting any areas of complexity or any other factors that might assist in the case being allocated to an appropriate judge.

Cases in the Crown Court to be referred to the Resident Judge

5.8.5 All cases in Class 1A, 1B, 1C, 1D, 2A and 2C must be referred to the Resident Judge as must any case which appears to raise particularly complex, sensitive or serious issues.

5.8.6 Resident Judges should give guidance to the judges and staff of their respective courts as to which Class 2B cases should be referred to them following consultation with the Senior Presiding Judge. This will include any cases that may be referred to the Presiding Judge, see below. Class 2B cases to be referred to the Resident Judge are likely to be identified by the listing officer, or by the judge at the first hearing in the Crown Court. Any appeal against conviction and/or sentence from a Youth Court involving a Class 2B case must be brought to the attention of the Resident Judge as soon as practicable. Where not provided with the appeal papers, the list officer must obtain a full summary of the prosecution case so as to allow an informed allocation decision to be made.

5.8.7 Once a case has been referred to the Resident Judge, the Resident Judge should refer the case to the Presiding Judge, following the guidance below, or allocate the case to an appropriate category of judge, and if possible, to a named judge.

Cases in the Crown Court to be referred to a Presiding Judge

5.8.8 All cases in Class 1A, 1B and 1C must be referred by the Resident Judge to a Presiding Judge, as must a case in any class which is:

    a. an unusually grave or complex case or one in which a novel and important point of law is to be raised;

    b. a case where it is alleged that the defendant caused more than one fatality;

    c. a non-fatal case of baby shaking where serious injury resulted;

    d. a case where the defendant is a police officer, or a member of the legal profession or a high profile figure;

    e. a case which for any reason is likely to attract exceptional media attention;

    f. a case where a large organisation or corporation may, if convicted, be ordered to pay a very large fine;

    g. any case likely to last more than three months.

5.8.9 Resident Judges should refer any other case if they think it is appropriate to do so.

5.8.10 The Resident Judge should provide the Presiding Judge with a brief summary of the case, a clear recommendation by the Resident Judge about the judges available to try the case and any other comments. A written record of the decision and brief reasons for it must be made and retained.

5.8.11 Once a case has been referred to the Presiding Judge, the Presiding Judge may retain the case for trial by a High Court Judge, or release the case back to the Resident Judge, either for trial by a named judge, or for trial by an identified category of judge, to be allocated by the Resident Judge.

5.9 Authorisation of judges   PD5.9

5.9.1 Judges must be authorised by the Lord Chief Justice before they may hear certain types of case.

5.9.2 Judges (other than High Court Judges) to hear Class 1A cases must be authorised to hear such cases. Any judge previously granted a 'Class 1' or 'murder' authorisation is authorised to hear Class 1A cases. Judges previously granted an 'attempted murder' (including soliciting, incitement or conspiracy thereof) authorisation can only deal with these cases within Class 1A.[38]

5.9.3 Judges (other than High Court Judges) to hear sexual offences cases in Class 1C or any case within Class 2B must be authorised to hear such cases. Any judge previously granted a 'Class 2' or 'serious sex offences' authorisation is authorised to hear sexual offences cases in Class 1C or 2B.

5.9.4 It is a condition of the authorisation that it does not take effect until the judge has attended the relevant Judicial College course; the Resident Judge should check in the case of newly authorised judges that they have attended the course. Judges who have been previously authorised to try such cases must make every effort to ensure their training is up-to-date and maintained by attending the Serious Sexual Offences Seminar at least once every three years.

5.9.5 Cases in the magistrates' courts involving the imposition of very large fines:

a. Where a defendant appears before a magistrates' court for an either way offence, to which s.85 LASPO Act 2012 applies the case must be dealt with by a DJ(MC) who has been authorised to deal with such cases by the Chief Magistrate. See 5.16 below.
b. The authorised DJ(MC) must first consider whether such cases should be allocated to the Crown Court or, where the defendant pleads guilty, committed for sentence under s.14 Sentencing Act 2020, and must do so when the DJ(MC) considers the offence or combination of offences so serious that the Crown Court should deal with the defendant as if they had been convicted on indictment.
c. If an authorised DJ(MC) decides not to commit such a case the reasons must be recorded in writing to be entered onto the court register.

PD5.10

5.10 Allocation of business within the Crown Court

5.10.1 Cases in Class 1A may only be tried by:

a. a High Court Judge;[39]
b. a Circuit Judge authorised to try such cases and provided that the Presiding Judge has released the case for trial by such a judge; or
c. a Deputy Circuit Judge to whom the case has been specifically released by the Presiding Judge.

5.10.2 Cases in Class 1B may only be tried by:

a. a High Court Judge; or
b. a Circuit Judge provided that the Presiding Judge has released the case for trial by such a judge; or
c. a Deputy Circuit Judge to whom the case has been specifically released by the Presiding Judge.

5.10.3 Cases in Class 1C may only be tried by:

a. a High Court Judge; or
b. a Circuit Judge, or Deputy Circuit Judge, authorised to try such cases (if the case requires the judge to be authorised to hear sexual offences cases), provided that the Presiding Judge has released the case for trial by such a judge, or, if the case is a sexual offence, the Presiding Judge has assigned the case to that named judge.

5.10.4 Cases in Class 1D and 2A may be tried by:

a. a High Court Judge; or
b. a Circuit Judge, or Deputy Circuit Judge, or Deputy High Court Judge appointed under s.9(4) Senior Courts Act 1981, or a Recorder or a qualifying judge advocate, or a District Judge (Magistrates' Court), provided that either the Presiding Judge has released the case or the Resident Judge has allocated the case for trial by such a judge; with the exception that Class 2A 'a' cases may not be tried by a Recorder or qualifying judge advocate, Deputy High Court Judge appointed under s.9(4) Senior Courts Act 1981, or District Judge (Magistrates' Courts).

5.10.5 Cases in Class 2B may be tried by:

a. a High Court Judge; or

---

[38] Also see Terrorism Ch 13.
[39] All references to High Court Judge include those sitting in retirement.

    b. a Circuit Judge, or Deputy High Court Judge appointed under s.9(4) Senior Courts Act 1981, or Deputy Circuit Judge, or a Recorder or a qualifying judge advocate, or a District Judge (Magistrates' Court), authorised to try such cases and provided that either the Presiding Judge has released the case or the Resident Judge has allocated the case for trial by such a judge.

5.10.6   Cases in Class 2C may be tried by:

    a. a High Court Judge; or
    b. a Circuit Judge, or Deputy High Court Judge appointed under s.9(4) Senior Courts Act 1981, or Deputy Circuit Judge, or a Recorder or a qualifying judge advocate, or a District Judge (Magistrates' Court), with suitable experience (for example, with company accounts or other financial information) and provided that either the Presiding Judge has released the case or the Resident Judge has allocated the case for trial by such a judge.

5.10.7   Cases in Classes 1D, 2A and 2C will usually be tried by a Circuit Judge.

5.10.8   Cases in Class 3 may be tried by a High Court Judge, or a Circuit Judge, a Deputy Circuit Judge, or Deputy High Court Judge appointed under s.9(4) Senior Courts Act 1981, a Recorder or a qualifying judge advocate, or a District Judge (Magistrates' Court). A case in Class 3 shall not be listed for trial by a High Court Judge except with the consent of a Presiding Judge.

5.10.9   PTPHs should normally be heard by a Circuit Judge, but may, with the approval of the Resident Judge, be heard by any other judge qualified to sit in the Crown Court.

5.10.10 For cases in Class 1A, 1B or 1C, or any case that has been referred to the Presiding Judge, the preliminary hearing and PTPH must be conducted by a High Court Judge; by a Circuit Judge; or by a judge authorised by the Presiding Judges to conduct such hearings. In the event of a guilty plea before such an authorised judge, the case will be adjourned for sentencing and will immediately be referred to the Presiding Judge who may retain the case for sentence by a High Court Judge, or release the case back to the Resident Judge, either for sentence by a named judge, or for sentence by an identified category of judges, to be allocated by the Resident Judge.

5.10.11 Appeals from the Youth Court in relation to sexual offences shall be heard by:

    a. a Resident Judge; or
    b. a Circuit Judge nominated by the Resident Judge who is authorised under paragraph 5.9.3 to hear sexual offences in Class 1C or Class 2B; and
    c. no more than four magistrates, none of whom took part in the decision under appeal. The magistrates must have undertaken specific training to deal with youth matters.

5.10.12 No appeal against conviction and/or sentence from a Youth Court involving a Class 1C or Class 2B offence shall be heard by a Recorder save with the express permission of the Presiding Judge of the Circuit.

5.10.13 Allocation or committal for sentence following breach (such as a matter in which a community order has been made, or a suspended sentence passed), should, where possible, be listed before the judge who originally dealt with the matter or, if not, before a judge of at least the same seniority.

5.10.14 Applications for removal of a driving disqualification should be made to the location of the Crown Court where the order of disqualification was made. Where possible, the matter should be listed before the judge who originally dealt with the matter or, if not, before a judge of the same or higher level.

5.11 Listing of trials, custody time limits and transfer of cases   **PD5.11**

Estimates of trial length

5.11.1   Parties are under a duty to provide accurate time estimates for trial and other proceedings and accurate information about the availability of witnesses, and estimated times for their examination-in-chief and cross- examination.

5.11.2   The prosecutor must draw any custody time limits (CTL) to the attention of the court. A record of the CTL must be recorded in the court records. When a case is subject to a CTL all efforts must be made at the first hearing to list the case within the CTL and the judge should seek to ensure this.

Cases in the Crown Court that should usually have fixed trial dates

5.11.3 The cases where fixtures should be given will be set out in the listing practice applicable at the court, but should usually include the following:

    a. Cases in classes 1A, 1B, 1C, 2B and 2C.
    b. Cases involving vulnerable and intimidated witnesses (including domestic abuse cases), whether or not special measures have been ordered by the court.
    c. Cases where the witnesses are under 18 or have to come from overseas.
    d. Cases estimated to last more than a certain time – the period chosen will depend on the size of the centre and the available judges.
    e. Cases where a previous fixed hearing has not been effective.
    f. Re-trials.
    g. Cases involving expert witnesses.
    h. Cases involving an intermediary.

Custody Time Limits

5.11.4 Courts must list cases for trial within the CTL limits set by Parliament. The guiding principles are:

    a. At the first court hearing, the prosecution will inform the court when the CTL lapses.
    b. The CTL may only be extended in accordance with s.22 Prosecution of Offences Act 1985 and the Prosecution of Offences (Custody Time Limits) Regulations 1987 (as amended).
    c. If suitable, given priority and listed on a date not less than two weeks before the CTL expires, the case may be placed in a warned list.
    d. The CTL must be kept under continual review by the parties, HMCTS and the Resident Judge.
    e. If the CTL is at risk of being exceeded, an additional hearing should take place. In the Crown Court this should be listed before the Resident Judge or trial judge or other judge nominated by the Resident Judge.
    f. An application to extend the CTL in any case listed outside the CTL must be considered by the court whether or not it was listed with the express consent of the defence.
    g. Any application to extend CTLs must be considered as a matter of urgency. The reasons for needing the extension must be ascertained and fully explained to the court.
    h. Where courtroom or judicial availability is an issue, the court must itself list the case to consider the extension of any CTL. In the Crown Court the Delivery Director of the circuit or region must provide a statement setting out in detail what has been done to try to accommodate the case within the CTL both within that circuit or region and other circuits or regions.
    i. Where all parties and the court agree that the case will not be ready for trial before the expiration of the CTL, a date may be fixed outside the CTL. This may be done without prejudice to any application to extend the CTLs or with the express consent of the defence; this must be noted on the papers.

5.11.5 As legal argument may delay the swearing in of a jury, it is desirable to extend the CTL to a date later than the first day of the trial.

Re-trials ordered by the Court of Appeal

5.11.6 The Crown Court must comply with the directions of the Court of Appeal and cannot vary those directions without reference to the Court of Appeal.

5.11.7 In cases where a re-trial is ordered by the Court of Appeal the CTL is 112 days starting from the date that the new indictment is preferred i.e. from the date that the indictment is delivered to the Crown Court.

Changes to the date of fixed cases in the Crown Court

5.11.8 Once a trial date or window is fixed, it should not be vacated or moved without good reason.

5.11.9 The listing officer may, in circumstances determined by the Resident Judge, agree to the movement of the trial to a date to which the defence and prosecution both consent, provided the hearing is not delayed unduly. The prosecution must consider the impact on witnesses before agreeing to any change.

5.11.10 In all other circumstances, requests to adjourn or vacate fixtures or trial windows must be referred to the Resident Judge for their personal attention; the Resident Judge may delegate the decision to a named deputy.

Transferring cases from one Crown Court to another

5.11.11   Transfer between courts on the same circuit must be agreed by the Resident Judges of each court, subject to guidance from the Presiding Judges of the circuit.

5.11.12   Transfer of trials between circuits must be agreed between the Presiding Judges and Delivery Directors of the respective circuits.

5.11.13   Transfer of sentences between circuits must be agreed between the Resident Judges of the courts concerned.

5.12   Listing of hearings other than trials

5.12.1   A party who requests that a case be listed in court must ensure that the court office and any other party (save in a case where an application is being made by one party in the absence of others) is told the basis for the request. All relevant material must be served in good time, and include a time estimate for judicial reading time and for the hearing. The applicant must complete the application within the time estimate provided, unless there are exceptional circumstances.

5.12.2   Short hearings should not generally be listed before a judge such that they may delay the start or continuation of a trial at the Crown Court.

Confiscation and Related Hearings

5.12.3   Applications for restraint orders should be determined by the Resident Judge, or a judge nominated by the Resident Judge, at the Crown Court location at which they are lodged.

5.12.4   In order to prevent possible dissipation of assets of significant value, applications under the Proceeds of Crime Act 2002 should be considered urgent when lists are being fixed. In order to prevent potential prejudice, applications for the variation and discharge of orders, for the appointment of receivers, and applications to punish alleged breaches of orders as a contempt of court should similarly be treated as urgent and listed expeditiously.

5.12.5   It is important that confiscation hearings take place in good time after the defendant is convicted or sentenced.

Breach proceedings

5.12.6   Proceedings in respect of alleged breaches of community and other orders[40] should be dealt with at the court centre where the order was imposed.

5.12.7   An exception to that general rule should be made, however, to reflect the application of **CrimPR Part 1**, the overriding objective, and the key listing principles above, where the defendant's home is significantly closer to another court with jurisdiction to determine the proceedings, in which case those proceedings should be brought in that court. If the court in which the breach proceedings are brought was not the sentencing court, or the magistrates' court for the Crown Court centre at which the sentence was passed, then the authority by which the proceedings are instituted must explain the reasons for choosing it. Any dispute in the Crown Court over the proper venue should be determined by the relevant Presiding Judges.

Appeals from magistrates' courts

5.12.8   As a general rule, the hearing in the Crown Court of an appeal against conviction or sentence from a magistrates' court[41] should take place at the Crown Court centre to which that magistrates' court ordinarily sends cases for trial or commits for sentence.

5.12.9   There are two exceptions to that general rule, however, each of which reflects the application of **CrimPR Part 1**, the overriding objective, and the key listing principles above.

    a.   First, if on an appeal against conviction witnesses are required to give evidence in person then the appeal should be heard at the Crown Court centre which is the most conveniently situated for the majority of those witnesses. This exception is likely to apply where the defendant's conviction and sentence have been imposed at a magistrates' court distant from the place at which the offence occurred (this will be the case with many convictions under the single justice procedure). The information required of the parties to the appeal by **CrimPR 34.3** and by the associated appeal forms will be essential to determining the most appropriate venue for the appeal.

---

[40]   **CrimPR Part 32**.
[41]   An appeal to which **CrimPR Part 34** applies.

    b. Second, where the appeal is against sentence only, or if, exceptionally, on an appeal against conviction no witnesses are required to give evidence in person, then the appeal should be heard at the Crown Court centre which is the closest to the appellant's home. This exception is likely to apply where the appellant has been convicted and sentenced at a magistrates' court for the area in which the offence occurred but at a distance from the defendant's usual or present residence. This exception must not, however, be allowed to operate to the disadvantage of any victim of the offence who is expected to attend the sentencing in the Crown Court.

PD5.13   **5.13 Management of cases from the Organised Crime Division of the Crown Prosecution Service**

5.13.1   The Serious Economic, Organised Crime and International Directorate (SEOCID) of the CPS is responsible for prosecution of cases from the National Crime Agency (NCA). Typically, these cases involve more than one defendant, are voluminous and raise complex and specialised issues of law. It is recognised that if not closely managed, such cases have the potential to cost vast amounts of public money and take longer than necessary.

5.13.2   This section applies to all cases handled by the SEOCID.

Designated court centres

5.13.3   Subject to the overriding discretion of the Presiding Judges of the circuit, OCD cases should normally be heard at Designated Court Centres (DCC). The process of designating court centres for this purpose has taken into account geographical factors and the size, security and facilities of those court centres. The designated court centres are:

    a. Northern Circuit: Manchester, Liverpool and Preston.
    b. North Eastern Circuit: Leeds, Newcastle and Sheffield.
    c. Western Circuit: Bristol and Winchester.
    d. South Eastern Circuit (not including London): Reading, Luton, Chelmsford, Ipswich, Maidstone, Lewes and Hove.
    e. South Eastern Circuit (London only): Southwark, Blackfriars, Kingston, Woolwich, Croydon and the Central Criminal Court.
    f. Midland Circuit: Birmingham, Leicester and Nottingham.
    g. Wales Circuit: Cardiff, Swansea and Mold.

Selection of designated court centres

5.13.4   If arrests are made in different parts of the country and the OCD seeks to have all defendants tried by one Crown Court, the OCD will, at the earliest opportunity, write to the relevant court cluster manager with a recommendation as to the appropriate designated court centre, requesting that the decision be made by the relevant Presiding Judges. In the event that the designated court centre within one region is unable to accommodate a case, for example, as a result of a custody time limit expiry date, consideration may be given to transferring the case to a DCC in another region with the consent of the relevant Presiding Judges.

5.13.5   There will be a single point of contact person at the OCD for each HMCTS region, to assist listing co-ordinators.

5.13.6   The person for each HMCTS region will be the relevant cluster manager, with the exception of the South Eastern Circuit where the appropriate person will be the Regional Listing Co-ordinator.

Designation of the trial judge

5.13.7   The trial judge will be assigned by the Presiding Judge at the earliest opportunity, and in accordance with the allocation guidance above. Where the trial judge is unable to continue with the case, all further pre-trial hearings should be by a single judge until a replacement has been assigned.

Procedure after charge

5.13.8   Within 24 hours of the laying of a charge, a representative of the OCD will notify the relevant cluster manager of the following information to enable an agreement to be reached between that cluster manager and the reviewing CPS lawyer before the first appearance as to the DCC to which the case should be sent:

    a. the full name of each defendant and the name of their legal representatives, if known;
    b. the charges laid; and
    c. the name and contact details of the Crown Prosecutor with responsibility for the case.

Exceptions

5.13.9   Where it is not possible to have a case dealt with at a DCC, the OCD should liaise closely with the relevant cluster manager and the Presiding Judges to ensure that the cases are sent to the most appropriate court centre. This will, among other things, take into account the location of the alleged offending, convenience of the witnesses, travelling distance for OCD staff and facilities at the court centres.

5.13.10   In the event that it is allocated to a non-designated court centre, the OCD should be permitted to make representations in writing to the Presiding Judges within 14 days as to why the venue is not suitable. The Presiding Judges will consider the reasons and, if necessary, hold a hearing. The CPS may renew their request at any stage where further reasons come to light that may affect the original decision on venue.

5.13.11   Nothing in this annex should be taken to remove the right of the defence to make representations as to the venue.

5.14 General principles for the deployment of the judiciary in the magistrates' court   PD5.14

5.14.1   This distils the full deployment guidance issued in November 2012. Relevant sections dealing with allocation of magistrates' court work have been incorporated into this Practice Direction. It does not seek to replace the guidance.

Presumptions

5.14.2   The following illustrative non-exhaustive presumptions ('the Presumptions') provide a flexible framework for deployment of DJ(MC)s and magistrates. The system must be adapted to meet needs according to locality/caseload.

5.14.3   DJ(MC)s should generally be deployed in accordance with the Presumptions:

    a. Cases involving complex points of law and evidence.
    b. Cases involving complex procedural issues.
    c. Long cases (included on grounds of practicality).
    d. Interlinked cases (given the need for consistency, together with their likely complexity and novelty).
    e. Cases for which armed police officers are required in court, such as high-end firearms cases.
    f. A share of routine business, including case management and pre-trial reviews (considering the need for DJ(MC)s to have competence in all areas of work; equitable division of work between magistrates and DJ(MC)s, subject to the interests of justice).
    g. Where appropriate, in supporting the training of magistrates.
    h. Occasionally, in mixed benches of DJ(MC)s and magistrates (to improve collegiality and magistrates' case management skills).
    i. In the short-term tackling of particular local backlogs ('backlog busting'), sometimes in combination with magistrates from the local or (with the SPJ's approval) adjoining benches.

5.14.4   The following case classes necessitate DJ(MC)s and have been excluded from the above presumptions:

    a. Extradition.
    b. Terrorism.
    c. Prison Adjudications.
    d. Sex cases in the Youth Court.
    e. Cases where the defendant is likely to be sentenced to a very large fine, see 5.16 below.
    f. The Special Jurisdiction of the Senior District Judge (Chief Magistrate).

5.14.5   In formulating the Presumptions, the following considerations have been taken into account:

    a. Listing cases is a judicial function. In the magistrates' courts the Judicial Business Group, subject to the supervision of the Presiding Judges of the circuit, is responsible for determining day-to-day listing practice in that area. The operation of that listing practice is the responsibility of the HoLOs with the assistance of the listing officer.
    b. Equally, providing the training of magistrates is a responsibility of HoLOs.
    c. High profile cases should not be treated as a separate category, but to consider their listing in the light of the principles and presumptions. The circumstances surrounding high profile cases do not permit generalisation, save that they require sensitive handling. Listing decisions will benefit from good communication at local level between the HoLO, DJ(MC)s and the Bench Chair

d. Account must be taken of the need to maintain the competences of all members of the magistrates' court judiciary.

5.14.6   The Special Jurisdiction of the Senior District Judge (Chief Magistrate) concerns:

a. cases with a terrorism connection;
b. cases involving war crimes and crimes against humanity;
c. matters affecting state security;
d. cases brought under the Official Secrets Act;
e. offences involving royalty or Parliament;
f. offences involving diplomats;
g. corruption of public officials;
h. police officers charged with serious offences;
i. cases of unusual sensitivity.

5.14.7   Where cases fall within the category of the Special Jurisdiction they must be heard by:

a. the Senior District Judge (or if not available);
b. the Deputy Senior District Judge (or if not available);
c. a District Judge approved by the Senior District Judge or their deputy for the particular case.

5.14.8   Where it is in doubt whether a case falls within the Special Jurisdiction, reference should always be made to the Senior District Judge or Deputy Senior District Judge for clarification.

PD5.15   **5.15 Sexual offences in the Youth Court**

5.15.1   This section applies to all cases involving the allocation of an allegation of a sexual offence capable of being committed to the Crown Court for a sentence of long-term detention under s.250 Sentencing Code or included in s.249(1) Sentencing Code i.e. offences punishable in the case of a person aged 21 or over with imprisonment for 14 years or more; sexual assault; child sex offences committed by children or young person, sexual activity with a child family member; inciting a child family member to engage in sexual activity, irrespective of the gravity of the allegation, the age and/or antecedent history of the defendant.

5.15.2   This section does not alter the test that the Youth Court must apply when determining whether a case should be sent to the Crown Court for a potential sentence pursuant to s.250 Sentencing Code.

5.15.3   These cases can only be dealt with by an authorised DJ(MC).

Procedure

5.15.4   The determination of venue in the Youth Court is governed by s.24 MCA 1980 and s.51A Crime and Disorder Act 1998, which provide that the youth must be tried summarily unless charged with such a grave crime that long- term detention is a realistic possibility, or that one of the other exceptions to this presumption arises.

5.15.5   Such cases should be listed before an authorised DJ(MC), by live link if necessary, to make the allocation decision. The prosecution should notify the court in advance to ensure listing before an authorised DJ(MC). If jurisdiction is retained and the allegation involves actual, or attempted, penetrative activity, the case must be tried by an authorised DJ(MC). In all other cases, the authorised DJ(MC) must consider whether the case is so serious and/or complex that it must be tried by an authorised DJ(MC), or whether the case can be heard by any DJ(MC) or Youth Court Bench.

5.15.6   If it is not practicable for an authorized DJ(MC) to determine venue, any DJ(MC) or any Youth Court Bench may consider that issue. If jurisdiction is retained, appropriate directions may be given, but the case papers, including a detailed case summary and a note of any representations made by the parties, must be sent to an authorised DJ(MC) to consider. As soon as possible the authorised DJ(MC) must decide whether the case must be tried by an authorised DJ(MC), or whether the case is suitable to be heard by any DJ(MC) or Youth Court Bench; however, if the case involves actual, or alleged, penetrative activity, the trial must be heard by an authorised DJ(MC).

5.15.7   If the case must be tried by an authorised DJ(MC), all further procedural hearings should, so far as practicable, be heard by an authorised DJ(MC).

Cases remitted for sentence

5.15.8   All cases remitted for sentence for a sexual offence from the Crown Court to the Youth Court should be listed for sentence before an authorised DJ(MC).

Arrangements for an authorised DJ(MC) to be appointed

5.15.9   Where a case is to be tried by an authorised DJ(MC) but no such Judge is available, the Bench Legal Adviser should contact the Chief Magistrate's Office for an authorised DJ(MC) to be assigned.

5.16 Cases involving very large fines in the magistrates' court   PD5.16

5.16.1   An authorised DJ(MC) must deal with any allocation decision, trial and sentencing hearing in the following triable either way types of cases:

a. Involving a high risk of, or actual, death or significant, life-changing injury.
b. Involving substantial environmental damage or polluting material of a dangerous nature.
c. Where major adverse effect on human health or quality of life, animal health or flora has resulted.
d. Where major costs through clean-up, site restoration or animal rehabilitation have been incurred.
e. Where the defendant corporation has a turnover in excess of £10 million but does not exceed £250 million, and has acted in a deliberate, reckless or negligent manner.
f. Where the defendant corporation has a turnover in excess of £250 million.
g. Where the court will be expected to analyse complex company accounts.
h. Which are high profile or exceptionally sensitive.

5.16.2   The prosecution agency must notify the HoLO, where practicable, of any such case no fewer than seven days before the first hearing, to ensure an authorised DJ(MC) is available at the first hearing.

5.16.3   The HoLO shall contact the Chief Magistrate's Office to ensure an authorised DJ(MC) can be assigned to deal with such a case. If necessary, consideration should be given to arranging an appropriate DJ(MC)'s attendance via live link.

5.16.4   Where an authorised DJ(MC) is not appointed at the first hearing, the court shall adjourn the case. The court shall ask the accused for an indication of plea, but shall not allocate the case nor, if the accused indicates a guilty plea, impose sentence, commit for sentence, ask for a pre-sentence report or give any indication as to likely sentence that will be imposed. The HoLO shall ensure an authorised DJ(MC) is appointed for the following hearing.

5.16.5   When dealing with sentence, s.14 Sentencing Code 2020 can be invoked where, despite the magistrates' court having maximum fine powers available to it, the offence or combination of offences make it so serious that the Crown Court should deal with it as though the person had been convicted on indictment.

5.16.6   An authorised DJ(MC) should consider allocating the case to the Crown Court or committing the accused for sentence.

6. VULNERABLE PEOPLE AND WITNESS EVIDENCE

6.1 Vulnerable people in the courts   PD6.1

6.1.1   The court is required to take 'every reasonable step' to encourage and facilitate the attendance of witnesses and to facilitate the participation of any person, including the accused.[42] This includes enabling a witness or accused to give their best evidence, and enabling an accused to comprehend the proceedings. The pre-trial and trial process should, so far as necessary, be adapted to meet those ends.

6.1.2   Toolkits available through The Advocate's Gateway are a valuable resource. Advocates should consult and follow the relevant guidance whenever they prepare to question a young or otherwise vulnerable witness or accused. Judges should refer advocates to this material and use the toolkits themselves as an aid to case management.

6.1.3   'Vulnerability' may arise by reason of age, but also encompasses anyone who may not be able to participate effectively if reasonable steps are not taken to adapt the court process to their specific needs.

---

[42] CrimPR 3.8(3)(a) and (b).

Criminal Practice Directions 2023

6.1.4   Where there is a vulnerable witness or accused, consideration must be given to holding a 'ground rules hearing' (GRH). The greater the level of vulnerability the more important it will be to hold such a hearing. A GRH is required in all trials involving an intermediary. The arrangements for the trial must be discussed between the judge or magistrate(s), advocates and intermediary before the witness gives evidence. The intermediary must be present for the GRH but is not required to take the oath (the intermediary's declaration is made just before the witness gives evidence).

6.1.5   It is essential for a note of decisions reached in a GRH to be created. The judge must use this document to ensure that the agreed ground rules are complied with. The document should record any adaptations to the trial arrangements that are considered necessary. It should also record any arrangements made for the editing and judicial approval of questions to be asked in cross-examination, where appropriate. Where questions are to be committed to writing and subject to judicial editing, with or without input from an intermediary, then, as a general rule, the proposed questions must be shared with the other parties to the trial. This applies to both vulnerable witnesses and defendants, unless the judge directs otherwise. Where time limits have been set, or subject boundaries for questioning identified, they should also be recorded in an agreed note that is uploaded to the DCS.

6.1.6   The judge must stop over-rigorous or repetitive cross-examination of a child or vulnerable witness/defendant. Intervention by the judge, magistrate(s) or intermediary (if any) is minimised if questioning, taking account of the individual's vulnerability, is discussed in advance and ground rules are agreed and adhered to.

6.1.7   Where limitations on questioning are necessary and appropriate, they must be clearly defined. The judge has a duty to ensure that they are complied with and should provide the jury with an appropriate explanation. If the advocate fails to comply with the limitations, the judge should give relevant directions to the jury when that occurs and prevent further questioning that does not comply with the ground rules settled upon in advance.

6.1.8   Accommodating the needs of young and/or otherwise vulnerable people may require a radical departure from traditional cross-examination. The form and extent of appropriate cross-examination will vary from case to case. For adult non-vulnerable witnesses an advocate is expected to 'put the case' so that the witness will have the opportunity of commenting upon it and/or answering it. When the witness is young or otherwise vulnerable, the court may dispense with the normal practice and impose restrictions on the advocate 'putting the case', particularly where there is a risk of a young or otherwise vulnerable witness failing to understand, becoming distressed or acquiescing to leading questions.

6.1.9   Instead of exploring apparent inconsistencies in cross-examination it may, subject to discussion between the judge and the advocate(s), be appropriate for these to be identified to the jury after the witness's evidence. Where appropriate the judge should point out important inconsistencies after (instead of during) the witness's evidence. The judge should also remind the jury of these during summing up. The judge should be alert to alleged inconsistencies that are not in fact inconsistent, or are trivial, and thus do not need to be mentioned.

6.1.10   If there is more than one accused, the judge should not permit each advocate to repeat the questioning of a vulnerable witness. In advance of the trial, the advocates should divide the topics between them, with the advocate for one accused leading the questioning, and the advocate(s) for the other accused asking only ancillary questions relevant to their client's case, without repeating the questioning that has already taken place.

6.1.11   In a trial of a sexual offence, there is an obvious need for sensitivity in the nature of and way questions are asked of a complainant and/or accused. Judges should not permit advocates to ask the witness to point to a part of the witness's own body. Similarly, photographs of the witness's body should not be shown while the witness is giving evidence. If there is a need for a witness to identify a part of the body then the use of body maps will be appropriate.

PD6.2   6.2 Intermediaries

6.2.1   Intermediaries facilitate communication with witnesses and defendants who have communication needs. Their primary function is to improve the quality of evidence and aid understanding between the court, the advocates and the witness or defendant. Intermediaries are independent of parties and owe their duty to the court.[43]

---

[43] See **CrimPR 18.26**. Further information is in Intermediaries: Step by Step (Toolkit 16; The Advocate's Gateway, 2015) and chapter 2 of the Equal Treatment Bench Book (Judicial College, 2021).

Assessment

6.2.2   The process of appointment begins with assessment by an intermediary and a report. The report will make recommendations to address the communication needs of the witness or defendant during trial.[44]

Intermediaries for prosecution and defence witnesses

6.2.3   Intermediaries are a special measure available to witnesses under the Youth Justice and Criminal Evidence Act 1999 (YJCEA 1999). Witnesses deemed vulnerable in accordance with the criteria in s.16 YJCEA are eligible for the assistance of an intermediary when giving evidence pursuant to s.29 YJCEA 1999. These provisions do not apply to defendants.

Intermediaries for defendants

6.2.4   The court may direct the appointment of an intermediary to assist a defendant in reliance on its inherent powers.[45] There is however no presumption that a defendant will be so assisted and, even where an intermediary has the potential to improve the trial process, appointment is not mandatory.[46] The court must adapt the trial process to address a defendant's communication needs.[47]

6.2.5   Other measures designed to accommodate the needs of a vulnerable defendant will also need to be considered, whether or not an intermediary is appointed.[48]

6.2.6   The court may exercise its inherent powers to direct appointment of an intermediary to assist a defendant when giving evidence or for the entire trial. Terms of appointment are for the court.[49]

Ineffective directions for intermediaries to assist defendants

6.2.7   Directions for intermediaries to help defendants may be ineffective due to general unavailability, lack of suitable expertise, or non-availability for the purpose directed (for example, where the direction is for assistance during evidence, but an intermediary will only accept appointment for the entire trial). A trial will not necessarily be rendered unfair because a direction to appoint an intermediary for the defendant is ineffective. It remains the court's responsibility to adapt the trial process to address the defendant's communication needs. In such a case, a ground rules hearing should be convened to ensure every reasonable step is taken to facilitate the defendant's participation.[50]

Intermediaries for witnesses and defendants under 18

6.2.8   Communication needs (such as short attention span, suggestibility and reticence in relation to authority figures) are common to many witnesses and defendants under 18. Consideration must be given to the communication needs of all children and young people appearing in the criminal courts and to adapting the trial process to address any such needs.

6.2.9   Assessment by an intermediary should be considered for witnesses and defendants under 18 who seem liable to misunderstand questions or to experience difficulty expressing answers, including those who seem unlikely to be able to recognise a problematic question (such as one that is misleading or not readily understood), and those who may be reluctant to tell a questioner in a position of authority if they do not understand.

Attendance at ground rules hearing

6.2.10   Where the court directs questioning will be conducted through an intermediary the court must hold a ground rules hearing at which the intermediary is required to be present.[51]

---

[44]   See **CrimPR 18.28**.
[45]   See **CrimPR 18.23**. *C v Sevenoaks Youth Court* [2009] EWHC 3088 (Admin).
[46]   *R v Cox* [2012] EWCA Crim 549.
[47]   *R v Cox* [2012] EWCA Crim 549.
[48]   See **CrimPR 3.8(3)**, **(6)**, **(7)**. See **CrimPR 3.9(3)(b)**, *R v Cox, R (OP) v Ministry of Justice* [2014] EWHC 1944 (Admin) and *R v Rashid* [2017] EWCA Crim 2.
[49]   See **CrimPR 18.23**. See *R v R* [2015] EWCA Crim 1870, *OP v Secretary of State for Justice* [2014] EWHC 1944 (Admin).
[50]   See **CrimPR 3.9**.
[51]   See **CrimPR 3.9, 18.26(2)(d)**.

6.3 Pre-recording of cross-examination and re- examination for witnesses (s.28 YJCEA 1999)[52]

6.3.1   In any case where these provisions apply, careful attention must be paid to the court's case management powers and the obligations on the parties. Reference should be made to the joint protocol agreed between the police and the CPS.

6.3.2   In the Crown Court the Resident Judge may appoint a judicial lead who will be responsible for monitoring and supervision of the scheme.

6.3.3   Witnesses eligible for special measures under s.28 Youth Justice and Criminal Evidence Act 1999 (YJCEA 1999) should be identified promptly by the police. The police should discuss, with the witness or with the witness's parent or carer, the special measures that are available and the witness's needs, such that the most appropriate package of special measures can be identified. This may include use of a Registered Intermediary.

6.3.4   For timetabling of the case, it is imperative that the investigators and prosecutor commence the disclosure process at the start of the investigation. The Attorney General's Guidelines: Disclosure for Investigators, Prosecutors and Defence Practitioners must be followed, and if applicable, the 2013 Protocol and Good Practice Model on disclosure of information in cases of alleged child abuse and linked criminal and care directions.

6.3.5   Local Implementation Teams (LITs) should be established with all relevant agencies represented by someone of sufficient seniority. Their task will be to monitor the operation of the scheme and compliance with this Practice Direction and other relevant protocols. LITs should encourage all appropriate agencies to endorse and follow both the Protocol and the Good Practice Model. LITs should monitor compliance and issues should initially be raised at the LITs.

The first hearing in the magistrates' court

6.3.6   The prosecutor must formally notify the court and the defence at the first hearing (or as soon as possible thereafter if eligibility only becomes apparent following the first hearing):

a. that the case is eligible for special measures under s.28 YJCEA 1999; and
b. whether or not the prosecutor intends to apply for such a direction.

6.3.7   This Practice Direction applies only where the defendant indicates a not guilty plea or does not indicate a plea, and the case is sent for trial in the Crown Court, either with or without allocation.

6.3.8   In any case that is sent to the Crown Court for trial in which the prosecution has notified the court of its intention to make an application for special measures under s.28 YJCEA 1999, the timetable is that established by the Better Case Management initiative. The PTPH should be listed within 28 days of the date of sending from the magistrates' court.[53]

6.3.9   If the case is to be tried in the magistrates' court then a suitable timetable for the progress of the case must be set.

Before the Plea and Trial Preparation Hearing in the Crown Court

6.3.10   A transcript of the ABE interview and the application for special measures, including under s.28 YJCEA 1999, must be served on the Court and defence at least five business days prior to the PTPH. The report of any Registered Intermediary must be served with the application for special measures.

6.3.11   Any defence representations about the application for special measures must be served before the PTPH.

6.3.12   In a homicide case the timetable may need to be adapted at the first bail hearing in the Crown Court.

At the Plea and Trial Preparation Hearing

6.3.13   The court will hear the application, and if it is refused, this Practice Direction ceases to apply.[54]

---

[53] Section 10.2 of A protocol between the Association of Chief Police Officers, the Crown Prosecution Service and [His] Majesty's Courts and Tribunals Service to expedite cases involving witnesses under 10 years does not apply.
[54] Section 10.2 of A protocol between the Association of Chief Police Officers, the Crown Prosecution Service and [His] Majesty's Courts and Tribunals Service to expedite cases involving witnesses under 10 years will apply.
[55] The correct and timely application of the CPIA 1996 will be vital and close attention should be paid to the 2013 Protocol and Good Practice Model on Disclosure (November 2013) and the Attorney-General's Guidelines: Disclosure for Investigators, Prosecutors and Defence Practitioners.

6.3.14   The judge may hear submissions from the advocates and will rule on the application for special measures.

6.3.15   The judge will need to consider:

    a. whether any of the special measures, or a combination of them, would be likely to improve the quality of the witness's evidence, and if so;
    b. which of the special measures, or a combination of them would be likely to maximise, so far as practicable, the quality of evidence given by the witness.

6.3.16   The judge should bear in mind all the circumstances of the case, including any views expressed by the witness and whether the measure or measures might tend to inhibit such evidence being effectively tested.

6.3.17   The judge should pay careful regard to whether a s.28 special measures direction will in fact materially advance the date for the cross-examination and re-examination, so as to maximise, along with any other measures, the quality of the witness's evidence. This will involve detailed consideration of when the s.28 recording and the trial are likely to occur. This in turn will depend, amongst other things, on any waiting list to use the recording equipment, the likely length of the s.28 hearing and the availability of the judge, the advocates, the witness and a suitable courtroom.

6.3.18   Furthermore, if there have already been delays, for instance because of a lack of resources to facilitate the timely prerecording of the ABE interview (the examination-in-chief), that is a matter to which the judge should have regard when viewing the situation overall and deciding whether the s.28 special measure will improve and maximise the quality of the evidence. It may be necessary for the judge to revisit the decision if circumstances change.

6.3.19   Against that background, the judge should determine which, if any, of the measures, or combination of them, would be likely to improve so far as practicable the quality of the witness's evidence.

6.3.20   If the application is granted, the judge should make orders and give directions for preparation for the recorded cross-examination and re- examination hearing and advance preparation for the trial, including for disclosure of unused material.[55]

6.3.21   The orders made may include:

    a. service of the prosecution evidence within 50 days of sending;
    b. directions for service of witness requirements;
    c. service of initial disclosure under CPIA 1996, as soon as reasonably practical; in this context, this should be interpreted as being simultaneous with the service of the prosecution evidence, i.e. within 50 days of sending for both bail and custody cases. This will be within three weeks of the PTPH;
    d. orders on disclosure of material held by a third party;
    e. service of the defence statement; under the CPIA 1996, this must be served within 28 days of the prosecutor serving or purporting to serve initial disclosure;
    f. any editing of the ABE interview;
    g. the listing of a GRH (if the judge decides one is necessary). If one is to take place, depending on the circumstances of the case, this should be listed either at a convenient date prior to the recorded cross- examination and re-examination hearing, or it should take place immediately prior to the recording of the cross-examination and re- examination;
    h. service of the Ground Rules Hearing Form by the defence advocate;
    i. making arrangements for the witness to refresh their memory by viewing the recorded examination-in-chief ('ABE interview');
    j. making arrangements for the recorded cross-examination and re- examination hearing under s.28, including fixing a date, time and location;
    k. other special measures;
    l. where necessary, fixing a date for any further directions hearing whether at the conclusion of the recorded cross-examination and re- examination hearing or subsequently;
    m. provision by the prosecution of the paginated jury bundle, if possible, in advance of the s.28 hearing;
    n. fixing a date for trial.

Criminal Practice Directions 2023

---

[56] **Parts 21 and 22 of the CrimPR** apply to applications under s.100 and s.41 respectively.

6.3.22   The timetable should ensure the prosecution evidence and initial disclosure are served swiftly. The GRH, if one is ordered, will usually be soon after the deadline for service of the defence statement, with the recorded cross- examination and re-examination hearing about one week later. However, there must be time afforded for any further disclosure of unused material following service of the defence statement and for determination of any application under s.8 CPIA 1996. Subject to judicial discretion applications for extensions of time for service of disclosure by either party should generally be refused.

6.3.23   Where the defendant may be unfit to plead, a timetable for s.28 should usually still be set, save in cases where it is indicated that it is unlikely that there would be a trial if the accused is found fit.

6.3.24   As far as possible, without jeopardising the defendant's right to a fair trial, the timing and duration of the recorded cross-examination should take into account the needs of the witness.

6.3.25   An application for a witness summons to obtain material held by a third party, should be served in advance of the PTPH and determined at that hearing, or as soon as reasonably practicable thereafter. The timetable should accommodate any consequent hearings or applications, but it is imperative parties are prompt to obtain third party disclosure material. The prosecution must make the court and the defence aware of any difficulty as soon as it arises.

6.3.26   The needs of other witnesses should not be neglected. Witness and intermediary availability dates should be available for the PTPH.

6.3.27   Engagement with the Protocol is to be overseen by LITs. A single point of contact in each relevant agency can facilitate speedy disclosure.

Prior to ground rules hearing and hearing under s.28

6.3.28   It is imperative parties abide by orders made at the PTPH, including the completion and service of the Ground Rules Hearing Form by the defence advocate. Delays or failures must be reported to the judge as soon as they arise; this is the responsibility of each legal representative. If ordered the parties must provide a weekly update to the court Case Progression Officer, copied to the judge and parties, detailing the progress and any difficulties or delays in complying with orders. The court may order a further case management hearing if necessary.

6.3.29   Any applications in relation to bad character under ss.100 or 101 Criminal Justice Act 2003 or under s.41 of the YJCEA 1999 (evidence or cross- examination about complainants' sexual behaviour) or any other application which may affect the cross-examination must be made promptly, and responses submitted in time for the judge to rule on the application at the GRH.[56]

6.3.30   As a general rule children or otherwise vulnerable witnesses should undertake a court familiarisation visit, including an opportunity to practise on the live link/recording facilities, in advance of the s.28 hearing. If the witness is to give evidence from a remote site then a familiarisation visit should take place at that site. At the GRH the judge and advocates should consider appropriate arrangements for them to talk to the witness prior to cross- examination.

Ground rules hearing

6.3.31   Any appointed Intermediary must attend the GRH.

6.3.32   Depending on the circumstances of the case, the defence advocate at the GRH may be required to conduct the recorded cross-examination. See listing and allocation below on continuity of advocates and release from other cases.

6.3.33   Topics for discussion and agreement at the GRH will depend on the individual needs of the witness, and should be addressed in any intermediary report.

6.3.34   Depending on the circumstances of the case topics may include:

     a.   when the witness will view the ABE interview;
     b.   the overall length of cross-examination;
     c.   the relevance of toolkits;[57]
     d.   cross-examination by a single advocate in a multi-handed case;
     e.   any restrictions on the advocate's usual duty to 'put the defence case';
     f.   what explanation is to be given to the jury.

---

[57] Advocate's Gateway good practice guidance Toolkits.
[58] Or such other document as may be created in order to record the questions to be asked.

6.3.35   If a GRH is ordered (whether or not on a date in advance of the recorded cross-examination and re-examination), this may provide a convenient opportunity for the judge to:

    a.   rule on any application under s.100 or s.101 Criminal Justice Act 2003 or s.41 YJCEA 1999, or other applications that may affect the cross- examination;

    b.   decide how the witness may view exhibits or documents;

    c.   review progress in complying with orders made and make any necessary orders.

Recording of cross-examination and re-examination: hearing under s.28

6.3.36   This is the start of the trial, and the usual provisions relating to the attendance of an accused apply, as does the guideline on credit for a guilty plea. If the accused enters a guilty plea any reduction in respect of that shall reflect the day of the recorded cross-examination as being the first day of trial.

6.3.37   At the hearing, the witness will be cross-examined and re-examined, if required, via the live link from the courtroom to the witness suite (unless provision has been made for the use of a remote link) and the evidence will be recorded. It is the responsibility of the designated court clerk to ensure in advance that all of the equipment is working and to contact the provider's Service Desk if support is required. Any other special measures must be in place and any intermediary or supporter should sit in the live link room with the witness. The intermediary's role is transparent and therefore must be visible and audible to the judge and advocates at the cross-examination and in the subsequent replaying.

6.3.38   The judge, advocates and parties, including the accused, will usually assemble in the courtroom for the hearing. In some cases the judge and advocates may be in the witness suite with the witness, for example when questioning a very young child. The court will decide this on a case-by-case basis. The accused is entitled to communicate with their representative and should be able to hear the witness via the live link and see the proceedings: s.28(2). Whether the witness is screened or not will depend on the other special measures ordered, for example screens may have been ordered under s.23 YJCEA 1999. Where appropriate consideration may be given to having the courtroom cleared if the presence of people in the public gallery is assessed as having the potential to adversely affect the ability of the witness to give their best evidence.

After the recording

6.3.39   At the conclusion of the hearing, the judge must make orders, such as for any necessary editing of the recorded cross-examination, and set a timetable for progress. Any further orders made by the judge should be recorded and uploaded onto the relevant section of the DCS.

6.3.40   Under s.28(4) YJCEA 1999, the judge, on application of any parties or on the court's own motion, may direct that the recorded evidence is not admitted at trial, despite any previous direction. Such direction must be given promptly, preferably immediately after the conclusion of the examination.

6.3.41   Without exception, editing of the ABE interview/examination-in-chief or recorded cross-examination is prohibited without an order of the court.

6.3.42   The ability to record simultaneously from a court and a witness room and to play back the recording at trial will be provided in all Crown Courts as an additional facility within the existing Justice Video Service (JVS). Courts will book recording slots with the Service Desk who will launch the recording at the scheduled time when the court is ready. Recordings will be stored in a secure data centre for authorised access.

Preparation for trial

6.3.43   Recorded cross-examinations and re-examinations will be stored securely by the service provider so as to be accessible to the advocates and the court. It will not usually be necessary to obtain a transcript of the recorded cross-examination, but if it is difficult to comprehend, a transcript should be obtained and served. Where the Ground Rules Hearing Form[58] outlines questions to be put to the witness, answers to these questions may be recorded electronically by the judge during cross-examination. In combination the document and recording form a contemporaneous note of the hearing which can be served on the parties or uploaded to the DCS as an agreed record.

---

[59]   Subject to any relevant ticketing requirement.

6.3.44　No further cross-examination or re-examination of the witness may take place unless the criteria in s.28(6) are satisfied and the judge makes a further special measures direction under s.28(5). Any such further examination must be recorded via live link as described above.

6.3.45　Any application under s.28(5) must be in writing and be served on the court and the prosecution at least 28 days before the date of trial. The application must specify:

    a.　the topics on which further cross-examination is sought;
    b.　the material or matter of which the defence has become aware since the original recording;
    c.　why it was not possible for the defence to have obtained the material or ascertained the matter earlier; and
    d.　the expected impact on the issues before the court at trial.

6.3.46　The prosecution should respond in writing within five business days of the application. The judge may determine the application on the papers or order a hearing. Any further cross-examination ordered must be recorded via live link in advance of the trial and served on the court and the parties. These timescales may be varied for good reason on application to the judge.

Trial

6.3.47　In accordance with the judge's directions, the ABE interview/examination-in-chief and the recorded cross-examination and re-examination, edited as directed, should be played to the jury at the appropriate point within the trial.

6.3.48　If the matter was not addressed in advance, the judge should discuss with the advocates how any limitations on questioning should be explained to the jury at the time the evidence is received and/or in summing-up.

After conclusion of trial

6.3.49　Immediately after the trial, the ABE interview/examination-in-chief and the recorded cross-examination and re-examination should be stored securely.

Listing and allocation

6.3.50　Depending on the circumstances of the case, the judge may order that the defence advocate who appeared at the GRH must conduct the recorded cross-examination. When such an order is made, the judge and list office will make whatever reasonable arrangements are feasible to achieve this, assisted by the Resident Judge when necessary.

6.3.51　Although continuity of representation is to be encouraged, it is not mandatory for the advocate who conducted the s.28 cross-examination to represent the defendant at trial for the remainder of the trial.

6.3.52　When the timetable for the case is being set, advocates must have their up- to-date availability with them (in so far as is possible). When it has been ordered that the defence advocate who appeared at the GRH must conduct the recorded cross-examination, an advocate who is part-heard in another trial and is in difficulties in attending the s.28 hearing must inform the judges conducting the respective proceedings as soon as practicable. The judges shall resolve the conflict as regards the advocate's availability, taking into consideration the circumstances of the cases and the interests of justice (referring the issue, if necessary, to the Resident Judge(s)).

6.3.53　Depending on the circumstances of the case, the Resident Judge or the nominated lead judge may order that the GRH and the s.28 YJCEA 1999 hearing are to be listed before the same judge. Once the s.28 hearing has taken place, any judge, including appropriately authorised Recorders, can deal with the trial.[59]

6.3.54　Section 28 hearings should be listed at a time determined by the list officer, or as directed by the judge or Resident Judge, bearing in mind the circumstances of the witness as well the availability of the judge, the advocates and a courtroom with the relevant recording equipment. GRHs, if they are listed in advance of the day when the recorded cross-examination and re-examination is to occur, may be held at any time, including towards the end of the court day, to accommodate the advocates and the intermediary (if there is one) and to minimise disruption to other trials.

---

[52] This is to be read in connection with **CrimPR 18**.

Public, including media access, and reporting restrictions

6.3.55   Open justice is an essential principle of the common law. However, certain automatic statutory restrictions may apply, and the judge may consider it appropriate in the specific circumstances of a case to make an order applying discretionary restrictions. The parties to the proceedings, and interested parties such as the media, should have the opportunity to make representations before an order is made.

6.4 Vulnerable defendants   PD6.4

6.4.1   A GRH must always be considered in a case involving a young or otherwise vulnerable defendant.

6.4.2   Where one or more defendants is young or otherwise vulnerable consideration should be given to the following matters:

   a. The need to sit in a court in which communication is more readily facilitated.
   b. An opportunity for a vulnerable defendant to visit the courtroom, out of court hours, before the hearing so that they can familiarise themselves with it. Where an intermediary is being used to help the defendant communicate, the intermediary should accompany the defendant on any pre-trial visit.
   c. If the defendant's use of the live link is being considered, they should have an opportunity to have a practice session.
   d. The opportunity (subject to security arrangements) for a young or otherwise vulnerable defendant to sit with family or other supporting adult in a place which permits easy, informal communication with their legal representatives. This is especially important where vulnerability arises by reason of age. The court should ensure that a suitable supporting adult is available throughout the course of the proceedings.
   e. The need to timetable the case to accommodate the defendant's ability to concentrate.
   f. The impact on the non-vulnerable defendants in a multi-handed trial;
   g. In the Crown Court, the judge should consider whether robes and wigs should be worn, and should take account of the wishes of both a vulnerable defendant and any vulnerable witnesses.
   h. It is generally desirable that those responsible for the security of a vulnerable defendant who is in custody, especially if they are young, should not be in uniform, and that there should be no recognisable police presence in the courtroom save for good reason.
   i. Some cases against vulnerable defendants attract widespread public or media interest. In any such case, the assistance of the police should be enlisted to avoid the defendant being exposed to intimidation, vilification or abuse when attending the court. See further the Judicial College Guide on Press Reporting etc.
   j. Where appropriate the defence will provide information about the defendant's welfare.

Vulnerable defendant at trial

6.4.3   Consideration must be given to the need to ensure, by any appropriate means, that the defendant can comprehend and participate effectively in the trial process.

6.4.4   A vulnerable defendant who wishes to give evidence by live link, in accordance with s.33A YJCEA 1999, may apply for a direction to that effect; the procedure in **CrimPR 18.14 to 18.17** should be followed.

6.4.5   The court should be prepared to consider restricting attendance by members of the public in the courtroom to a small number, perhaps limited to those with an immediate and direct interest in the outcome. The court should rule on any challenged claim to attend. However, facilities for reporting the proceedings (subject to any reporting restrictions) must be provided. The court may restrict the number of reporters attending in the courtroom to such number as is judged practicable and desirable. In ruling on any challenged claim to attend in the courtroom for the purpose of reporting, the court should be mindful of the public's general right to be informed about the administration of justice.[60]

6.4.6   Where it has been decided to limit access to the courtroom, whether by reporters or generally, arrangements should be made for the proceedings to be relayed, audibly and if possible visually, to another room in the same court complex to which the media and the public have access if it appears that there will be a need for such additional facilities. Those making use of such a facility

Criminal Practice Directions 2023

---

[60] See Ch 2 Open Justice.

should be reminded that it is to be treated as an extension of the courtroom and that they are required to conduct themselves accordingly.

6.5 Appointment of advocates to cross-examine

6.5.1 Where statute prohibits a defendant from cross-examining in person[61] the court should consider the appointment, even on a provisional basis, of a legal representative to do so on their behalf.[62] It is essential that the role and status of the representative is clearly established at the earliest possible opportunity.

6.5.2 The court should require[63] the defendant to notify the court officer, by the date set by the court, whether the defendant:

a. will be represented by a legal representative for the purposes of the case generally, and if so by whom (in which event the court's provisional appointment has no effect);
b. will not be represented for the purposes of the case generally, but the defendant and the legal representative provisionally appointed by the court remain content with that provisional appointment (in which event the court's provisional appointment takes effect); or
c. will not be represented for the purposes of the case generally, but will arrange for a lawyer to cross-examine the relevant witness or witnesses on their behalf, giving that lawyer's name and contact details.

6.5.3 If the defendant fails to give notice by the due date then, unless it is apparent that they will, in fact, be represented for the purposes of the case generally, the court must confirm the provisional appointment and proceed accordingly.

Supply of case papers

6.5.4 It is essential for the court appointed advocate to establish what is in issue and to have access to all the necessary material.[64] In the Crown Court, the advocate may be given access to the Crown Court Digital Case System. Where relevant disclosable material is not available on that system it must be supplied to the advocate either by the defendant or by the prosecutor. The prosecutor should not disclose material to the advocate that is irrelevant to the task the advocate is to perform. In a magistrates' court, where the advocate has not been able to access[65] the material from some other source then the court may direct a member of the court staff to provide copies from the court's own records.

Obtaining information and observations from the defendant

6.5.5 A court appointed advocate must only engage with the defendant to the extent that is necessary to establish the issues to be dealt with in cross-examination(s). The advocate cannot and should not 'take instructions' from the defendant, in the usual sense.[66]

Extent of appointed advocate's duty

6.5.6 The court appointed advocate must fulfil both their professional and statutory duty.[67] Advocates will be alert to, and courts should keep in mind, the extent of the remuneration available to a cross-examination advocate.[68] Such an advocate who, having cross-examined, agrees to continue to represent a defendant may as a consequence not be entitled to any remuneration.

---

[61] By virtue of ss.34, 35 or 36 YJCEA 1999.
[62] Section 38(4), YJCEA 1999.
[63] **CrimPR 23**.
[64] **CrimPR 23.2(7)**.
[65] Such as when acting as the defendant's legal representative subject to a restriction on the purpose or duration of that appointment notified under **CrimPR 46.2(5)** – for example, pending the outcome of an application for legal aid or directly from the defendant by virtue of s.17(2)(a) CPIA 1996 or from the prosecutor.
[66] YJCEA 1999, s.38(5).
[67] See *Abbas v Crown Prosecution Service* [2015] EWHC 579 (Admin); [2015] 2 Cr. App. R. 11; see further Bar Council guidance.
[68] In assessing the amount of which the court has only a limited role: see s.19(3) Prosecution of Offences Act 1985, which empowers the Lord Chancellor to make regulations authorising payments out of central funds 'to cover the proper fee or costs of a legal representative appointed under s.38(4) YJCEA 1999 and any expenses properly incurred in providing such a person with evidence or other material in connection with his appointment', and also ss.19(3ZA) and 20(1A)(d) of the 1985 Act and the Costs in Criminal Cases (General) Regulations 1986, as amended.

6.6 Witness anonymity orders[69]

Application

6.6.1   An application for a witness anonymity order, whether by the prosecution or the defence, must be made as soon as reasonably practicable. The application does not have to have been determined in advance of the evidence being served. The witness statement setting out the proposed evidence should be redacted to prevent disclosure of the witness's identity.[70] The normal prosecution disclosure duties apply to the witness, albeit the material may have to be similarly redacted.

6.6.2   Where possible, the trial judge should determine the application. The judge will almost invariably require a defence statement to have been served. In the Crown Court, a recording of the hearing to determine the application will be made and the court must treat such a recording in the same way as the recording of an application for a public interest ruling.

6.6.3   On a prosecutor's application, the court is likely to be assisted by the attendance of a senior investigator or other person of comparable authority who is familiar with the case.

6.6.4   The court must scrutinise the confidential information to satisfy itself that the statutory conditions are met. If the court concludes that the only way this can be done is to hear from the witness, then exceptionally it may invite the applicant to call the proposed witness to be questioned by the court. Any such questioning should be carried out at such a time, and the witness brought to the court in such a way, as to prevent disclosure of their identity.

6.6.5   The court may, exceptionally, ask the Attorney General to appoint special counsel to assist.[71] Whether to accede to such a request is a matter for the Attorney General, and adequate time should be allowed for the consideration of such a request.

6.6.6   Before any order is made, the court must be satisfied of the qualifying conditions under the Coroners and Justice Act 2009.[72] If there is more than one anonymous witness, the nature of any link or the potential for collusion, should be investigated.

6.6.7   The court's decision on an application must be announced in the parties' presence and in public, providing such reasons as it is possible to give without revealing the witness's identity.[73] A record of the reasons must be kept.

An Anonymity Order

6.6.8   The order setting out the specific measures must be recorded in writing, approved by the court and issued on its behalf. An order made in a magistrates' court must be recorded in the court register.

6.6.9   On granting an order the following must be considered by the judge with the assistance of the court staff, so that the practical arrangements (**confidentially recorded**) are in place to ensure that the witness's anonymity is not compromised:

   a. Whether the evidence can be received by live link.
   b. Whether, and if so how, any pre-trial visit by the anonymous witness is to be arranged.
   c. How the witness will enter and leave the court building.
   d. Where the witness will wait until they give evidence.
   e. Provision for the prosecutor to speak to the anonymous witness before they give evidence.
   f. Provision for the anonymous witness to see their statement or view their ABEs.
   g. How the witness will enter and leave the courtroom.
   h. Provisions to disguise the identity of the anonymous witness whilst they give evidence (e.g. voice modulation, screens).
   i. Provisions for the anonymous witness to have any breaks required.
   j. Provisions to protect the anonymity of the witness in the event of an emergency such as a security alert.

6.6.10   The written record of the order must not disclose the identity of the witness. It is essential that the order clearly specifies which measures apply to which witness.

---

[70] As permitted by s.87(4) Coroners and Justice Act 2009.
[71] *R v H* [2004] UKHL 3, [2004] 2 A.C. 134 (at para [22]).
[72] Section 88 of the 2009 Act and see *R v Mayers and Others* [2008] EWCA Crim 2989, [2009] 1 W.L.R. 1915, [2009] 1 Cr. App. R. 30.
[73] And bearing in mind s.90(2) of the Act.
[74] See s.91 of the Act and **CrimPR 18.21**.

6.6.11 Should the application for anonymity be refused, the court should consider all appropriate arrangements that may assist in that witness being able to give evidence.

6.6.12 The court and the parties must keep under review whether the conditions for making an order continue to be met. Where the court considers the discharge or variation of an order, the procedure must, so far as is required, correspond to that indicated above.[74]

Retention of confidential material

6.6.13 If retained by the court, confidential material must be stored in secure conditions. Alternatively, subject to such directions as the court may give, such material may be committed to the safe keeping of the applicant or any other appropriate person.[75] If the material is released to any such person, the court must ensure that it will be available to the court at trial.

Arrangements at trial

6.6.14 At trial the greatest possible care must be taken to ensure that nothing will compromise the witness's anonymity. The arrangements for the witness must take account of the courtroom layout and means of access for the witness, for the defendant(s) and for members of the public. The risk of a chance encounter between the witness and someone who may recognise them, either then or subsequently, must be prevented.

PD6.7
6.7 Defendant's right to give or not to give evidence

6.7.1 Section 35(2) Criminal Justice and Public Order Act 1994 requires the court, at the appropriate time, to satisfy itself that the defendant knows they can give evidence and that a failure to do so may permit the drawing of adverse inferences.

If the defendant is legally represented

6.7.2 After the close of the prosecution case, if the defendant's representative requests a brief adjournment to advise the defendant on this issue the request should, ordinarily, be granted. When appropriate the judge should, in the presence of the jury, inquire of the representative in these terms:

> "Have you advised your client that the stage has now been reached at which they may give evidence and, if they choose not to do so, the jury may draw such inferences as appear proper from their failure to do so?"

6.7.3 If the representative replies to the judge that the defendant has been so advised, then the case shall proceed. If the representative replies that the defendant has not been so advised, then the judge shall direct the representative to do so and should adjourn briefly for this purpose, before proceeding further.

If the defendant is not legally represented

6.7.4 If the defendant is not represented, the judge shall, at the conclusion of the evidence for the prosecution, in the absence of the jury, indicate what will be said to the defendant in the presence of the jury and ask if the defendant understands and whether they would like a brief adjournment to consider their position.

6.7.5 When appropriate, and in the presence of the jury, the judge should say to the defendant:

> "Now is your chance to give evidence if you choose to do so. If you do give evidence it will be on oath [or affirmation], and you will be cross-examined like any other witness. If you do not give evidence the jury may hold it against you. If you do give evidence but refuse without good reason to answer the questions the jury may, as I have just explained, hold that against you. Do you now intend to give evidence?"

7. Expert Evidence

PD7.1
7.1 Admissibility generally

7.1.1 Expert opinion evidence is admissible in criminal proceedings if, in summary:

a. it is relevant to a matter in issue in the proceedings;

---

[75] See **CrimPR 18.6**.
[69] See ss.86-97 Coroners and Justice Act 2009, **CrimPR 18** and see also *R v Mayers and Others* [2008] EWCA Crim 2989 and *R v Donovan and Kafunda* [2012] EWCA Crim 2749.

b. it is needed to provide the court with information likely to be outside the court's own knowledge and experience;

c. the witness is competent to give that opinion; and

d. the expert opinion is sufficiently reliable to be admitted.

7.1.2 Factors which the court may take into account in determining the reliability of expert opinion, and especially of expert scientific opinion, include:

a. the extent and quality of the data on which the expert opinion is based;

b. the validity of the methodology employed by the expert;

c. if the expert's opinion relies on an inference from any findings, whether the opinion properly explains how safe or unsafe the inference is (whether by reference to statistical significance or in other appropriate terms);

d. if the expert's opinion relies on the results of the use of any method (for instance, a test, measurement or survey), whether the opinion takes proper account of matters, such as the degree of precision or margin of uncertainty, affecting the accuracy or reliability of those results;

e. the extent to which any material upon which the expert's opinion is based has been reviewed by others with relevant expertise (for instance, in peer-reviewed publications), and the views of those others on that material;

f. the extent to which the expert's opinion is based on material falling outside the expert's own field of expertise;

g. the completeness of the information which was available to the expert, and whether the expert took account of all relevant information in arriving at the opinion (including information as to the context of any facts to which the opinion relates);

h. if there is a range of expert opinion on the matter in question, where in the range the expert's own opinion lies and whether the expert's preference has been properly explained; and

i. whether the expert's methods followed established practice in the field and, if they did not, whether the reason for the divergence has been properly explained.

7.1.3 In addition, in considering reliability, and especially the reliability of expert scientific opinion,[76] the court must be astute to identify potential flaws in such opinion which detract from its reliability, for example:

a. being based on a hypothesis which has not been subjected to sufficient scrutiny (including, where appropriate, experimental or other testing), or which has failed to stand up to scrutiny;

b. being based on an unjustifiable assumption;

c. being based on flawed data;

d. relying on an examination, technique, method or process which was not properly carried out or applied, or was not appropriate for use in the particular case; or

e. relying on an inference or conclusion which has not been properly reached.

7.1.4 In order to enable full assessment of the reliability of any expert evidence relied upon, all potentially relevant information must be disclosed, both in relation to the expert and in relation to any corporation or other body with which the expert works, as an employee or in any other capacity; see the non-exhaustive list of examples below:[77]

a. any fee arrangement under which the amount or payment of the expert's fees is in any way dependent on the outcome of the case;

b. any conflict of interest of any kind, other than a potential conflict disclosed in the expert's report;

c. adverse judicial comment regarding a particular expert or corporation or other body for whom the expert works whether by a first instance tribunal or on appeal;

d. any case in which an appeal has been allowed by reason of a deficiency in the expert's evidence;

e. any adverse finding, disciplinary proceedings or other criticism by a professional, regulatory or registration body or authority, including the Forensic Science Regulator;

f. any such adverse finding or disciplinary proceedings against, or other such criticism of, others associated with the corporation or other body with which the expert works which calls into question the quality of that corporation's or body's work generally;

g. conviction of a criminal offence in circumstances that suggest:

i. a lack of respect for, or understanding of, the interests of the criminal justice system (for example, perjury; acts perverting or tending to pervert the course of public justice),

ii. dishonesty (for example, theft or fraud), or

---

[76] The court may be assisted by the Royal Society primers.
[77] **CrimPR 19.3(3)(c) and CrimPR 19.2(3)(d).**

iii. a lack of personal integrity (for example, corruption or a sexual offence);
h. lack of an accreditation or other commitment to prescribed standards where that might be expected;
i. a history of failure or poor performance in quality or proficiency assessments;
j. a history of lax or inadequate scientific methods;
k. a history of failure to observe recognised standards in the expert's area of expertise;
l. a history of failure to adhere to the standards expected of an expert witness in the criminal justice system.

7.1.5 In a case in which an expert, or a corporation or body with which the expert works, has been criticised without a full investigation, for example by adverse comment in the course of a judgment, those criticised must supply information about the conduct and conclusions of any independent investigation into the incident, and explain what steps, if any, have been taken to address the criticism.

7.1.6 Where matters ostensibly within the scope of the disclosure obligations come to the attention of the court without having been disclosed[78] then subject to any enquiry into the circumstances the potential for exclusion of that evidence will arise.[79]

PD7.2   **7.2 Declarations of truth in expert reports**

7.2.1 The statement and declaration[80] should be in the following terms, or in terms substantially the same as these:

"I (name) DECLARE THAT:

1. I understand that my duty is to help the court to achieve the overriding objective by giving independent assistance by way of objective, unbiased opinion on matters within my expertise, both in preparing reports and giving oral evidence. I understand that this duty overrides any obligation to the party by whom I am engaged or the person who has paid or is liable to pay me. I confirm that I have complied with and will continue to comply with that duty.
2. I confirm that I have not entered into any arrangement where the amount or payment of my fees is in any way dependent on the outcome of the case.
3. I know of no conflict of interest of any kind, other than any which I have disclosed in my report.
4. I do not consider that any interest which I have disclosed affects my suitability as an expert witness on any issues on which I have given evidence.
5. I will advise the party by whom I am instructed if, between the date of my report and the trial, there is any change in circumstances which affect my answers to points 3 and 4 above.
6. I have shown the sources of all information I have used.
7. I have exercised reasonable care and skill in order to be accurate and complete in preparing this report.
8. I have endeavoured to include in my report those matters, of which I have knowledge or of which I have been made aware, that might adversely affect the validity of my opinion. I have clearly stated any qualifications to my opinion.
9. I have not, without forming an independent view, included or excluded anything which has been suggested to me by others including my instructing lawyers.
10. I will notify those instructing me immediately and confirm in writing if for any reason my existing report requires any correction or qualification.
11. I understand that:
    (a) my report will form the evidence to be given under oath or affirmation;
    (b) the court may at any stage direct a discussion to take place between experts;
    (c) the court may direct that, following a discussion between the experts, a statement should be prepared showing those issues which are agreed and those issues which are not agreed, together with the reasons;
    (d) I may be required to attend court to be cross-examined on my report by a cross-examiner assisted by an expert.

---

[78] The rules require disclosure of what the expert, or the party who introduces the expert evidence, is aware. The rules do not require persistent or disproportionate enquiry, and courts will recognise that there may be occasions on which neither the expert nor the party has been made aware of criticism.
[79] For example under s.81 Police and Criminal Evidence Act 1984 or s.20 CPIA 1996.
[80] Required by **CrimPR 19.4(j) and (k)**.

(e)   I am likely to be the subject of public adverse criticism by the judge if the Court concludes that I have not taken reasonable care in trying to meet the standards set out above.

12. I have read **Part 19 of the Criminal Procedure Rules** and I have complied with its requirements.

13. I confirm that I have complied with the code of practice or conduct for experts of my discipline, namely [identify the code], in all respects save as identified in [schedule][annexe][x] to this report. That [schedule][annexe] gives details of the action taken to mitigate any risk of error that might arise as a result.

14. [For Experts instructed by the Prosecution only]

I confirm that I have read the CPS Guidance for Experts on Disclosure, Unused Material and Case Management which details my role and documents my responsibilities, in relation to revelation as an expert witness. I have followed the guidance and recognise the continuing nature of my responsibilities of disclosure. In accordance with my duties of disclosure, as documented in the guidance booklet, I confirm that:

(a)   I have complied with my duties to record, retain and reveal material in accordance with the Criminal Procedure and Investigations Act 1996, as amended;

(b)   I have compiled an Index of all material. I will ensure that the Index is updated in the event I am provided with or generate additional material;

(c)   in the event my opinion changes on any material issue, I will inform the investigating officer, as soon as reasonably practicable and give reasons.

I confirm that the contents of this report are true to the best of my knowledge and belief and that I make this report knowing that, if it is tendered in evidence, I would be liable to prosecution if I have wilfully stated anything which I know to be false or that I do not believe to be true."

7.3 Pre-hearing discussion of expert evidence   PD7.3

7.3.1 The court must give a direction for a pre-hearing discussion between experts in every case unless unnecessary.

7.3.2 The purpose of discussions between experts is to agree and narrow issues and in particular to identify:
a. the extent of the agreement between them;
b. the points of and short reasons for any disagreement;
c. action, if any, which may be taken to resolve any outstanding points of disagreement; and
d. any further material issues not raised and the extent to which these issues are agreed.

7.3.3 Any experts' meeting should be conducted in the manner most convenient and cost effective to those involved. The parties must agree an agenda that helps the experts to focus on the relevant issues. The agenda must not be in the form of leading questions and must promote an open discussion. No party may require or encourage an expert to avoid reaching agreement, or to defer reaching agreement, on any matter within the experts' competence.

7.3.4 If the legal representatives do attend:
a. they should not normally intervene in the discussion, except to answer questions put to them by the experts or to advise on the law; and
b. the experts may if they so wish hold part of their discussions in the absence of the legal representatives.

7.3.5 A statement must be prepared by the experts dealing with paragraphs (a) - (d) above. Individual copies of the statements must be signed or otherwise authenticated by the experts at the conclusion of the discussion, or as soon thereafter as practicable, and in any event within five business days. Copies of the statements must be provided to the parties no later than 10 business days after signing.

7.3.6 Experts must give their own opinions to assist the court and do not require the authority of the parties to sign a joint statement. The joint statement should include a brief re-statement that the experts recognise their duties, which should be in the following terms, or in terms substantially the same as these:

"We each DECLARE THAT:

1. We individually here re-state the Expert's Declaration contained in our respective reports that we understand our overriding duties to the court, have complied with them and will continue to do so.

2. We have neither jointly nor individually been instructed to, nor has it been suggested that we should, avoid reaching agreement, or defer reaching agreement, on any matter within our competence."

7.3.7   If an expert significantly alters an opinion, the joint statement must include a note or addendum by that expert explaining the change of opinion.

8. Jurors

PD8.1

8.1 Excusal

8.1.1   The judge has the power to excuse a person summoned for jury service, stand down a potential juror from the jury panel and discharge a juror during the trial in order to ensure fairness. A judge does not have the power to excuse, stand down or discharge jurors in order to influence the overall composition of the jury panel or jury.[81]

8.1.2   The Court has power[82] to excuse a potential juror:

    a. for insufficient understanding of English;
    b. whose personal circumstances render it unsuitable for them to serve,[83] whether or not an application has already been made to the jury summoning officer for deferral or excusal.[84]

8.1.3   The Court has a discretion to excuse a police or prison officer from serving on any particular jury. A judge must be informed at the stage of jury selection if any juror in waiting is in these categories. The juror summons warns jurors that the court staff should be informed of this type of employment.

8.1.4   In the case of police officers, the judge should conduct an inquiry of the parties to assess whether a police officer may serve as a juror. A serving police officer can serve provided there is no particular link between the case and where the officer is based. Factors to consider include:

    a. whether evidence from the police is in dispute and whether that dispute involves allegations against the police;
    b. whether the potential juror knows or has worked with the officers involved in the case;
    c. whether the potential juror has served or continues to serve in the same police units within the force as those dealing with the investigation of the case or is likely to have a shared local service background with police witnesses in a trial.

8.1.5   In the case of a serving prison officer, the judge should inquire whether the individual is employed at a prison linked to the case or has special knowledge of any person involved in a trial.

8.1.6   The judge must ensure that employees of prosecuting authorities do not serve on a trial prosecuted by their employer. They can serve on a trial prosecuted by another prosecuting authority.[85]

PD8.2

8.2 Standing jurors down

8.2.1   The Court has a common law discretion to stand down a potential juror for a particular trial.

8.2.2   The Court should stand down a potential juror who is personally concerned with the facts of the particular case, closely connected with a prospective witness, or has personal knowledge of the defendant.

8.2.3   The Court should consult with the advocates as to the questions, if any, it may be appropriate to ask potential jurors.[86] A copy of any questionnaire provided must be retained on the Digital Case System, if necessary in a secure area.[87]

---

[81] *R v Royston Ford* (1989) 89 Cr. App. R. 278.
[82] Section 10 Juries Act 1974.
[83] Subject to the capacity to make reasonable adjustments, in respect of which s.196 Police, Crime, Sentencing and Courts Act 2022 has made important changes in respect of jurors who require the services of a British Sign Language interpreter. See further Crim PR 26.6.
[84] *R v Mason* [1981] QB 881; *R v Jalil* [2008] EWCA Crim 2910.
[85] *R v Abdroikov* [2007] UKHL 37; *Hanif v UK* [2011] ECHR 2247; *R v L* [2011] EWCA Crim 65.
[86] Guidance on the topics for consideration in a questionnaire can be found in the 'Crown Court Compendium'. **CrimPR 26.4** governs the procedure in relation to jurors' availability for long trials.
[87] *Bermingham and Palombo* [2020] EWCA Crim 1662. If a 'paper' case the copy questionnaires will need to be retained on the court file.

8.2.4   The judge should release to the jury bailiff any potential juror who has been excused or stood down from serving on that trial, unless it is considered necessary to excuse that juror from further jury service at that time. Save in those circumstances, such a juror will be released back into the jury pool and may be asked to serve on another trial.

8.3 Swearing in jurors

PD8.3

8.3.1   Jurors may choose to take the juror oath by being sworn or by affirming. All jurors shall take the oath or affirmation in open court in the presence of one another. If jurors choose to swear the oath, they may choose the Holy Book on which to swear. The wording will depend on their faith as indicated to the court.

Preliminary instructions to jurors

8.3.2   After the jury has been sworn and the defendant has been put in their charge the judge must give directions to the jury that they are required to follow.[88]

8.3.3   Every member of the jury must also be provided with their own copy of the notice 'Your Legal Responsibilities as a Juror'. This notice outlines what is required of the juror during and after their time on the jury. The notice is not a substitute for the judge's directions, but is designed to reinforce what the judge outlines in the directions. The court clerk must ensure a record is made of the provision of the notice. Jurors should be advised to keep their copy of the notice with their summons during the trial. At the end of the trial they should retain the notice.

8.3.4   The judge must warn the jury of the consequences of breaching the legal directions given to them, by informing them as to the potential juror offences and the potential custodial sentences for breach.

8.3.5   The Court should ensure that the jury has clear guidance on the following:

   a. The need to try the case only on the evidence and remain faithful to their oath or affirmation.
   b. The prohibition on internet searches for matters related to the trial, issues arising or the parties or anyone else connected with the case, including the advocates and judge.
   c. The prohibition on discussing the case with anyone outside their own number or allowing anyone to talk to them about it, whether directly, by telephone, through internet facilities such as Facebook or Twitter or in any other way.
   d. The importance of taking no account of any media reports about the case.
   e. The collective responsibility of the jury for ensuring that the conduct of each member of the jury is consistent with the jury oath and the judicial directions.
   f. The duty to bring any concerns, including concerns about the conduct of other jurors, to the attention of the judge immediately, and not to wait until the case is concluded. The point must be made that, unless that is done while the case is continuing, it may not be possible to deal with the problem at all.
   g. The need to raise with the judge any situation in which a juror unexpectedly finds themselves in difficult professional or personal circumstances during the course of the trial.
   h. Any other legal directions relevant to the issues in the trial that the judge considers helpful to give at that stage.[89]

8.3.6   Trial judges should also instruct the jury on general matters which will include the time estimate for the trial and normal sitting hours.

8.3.7   Judges should consider reminding jurors of these instructions as appropriate at the end of each day and in particular when they separate after retirement.

8.4 Discharge of a juror during trial

PD8.4

8.4.1   The Court has a common law discretion to discharge a particular juror. Judges should exercise the power sparingly. The need to consider doing so may arise in a wide range of circumstances (e.g. an unexpected change in personal circumstances such as a family emergency or if it transpires during the trial that a juror is not competent to serve). The focus should be on whether the issue impacts on the ability of the juror to fulfil their task in accordance with their oath.

8.4.2   In longer trials, if the juror has a temporary problem affecting their jury service, it may well be possible to adjourn for a short period in order to allow the juror to deal with the issue. In shorter cases, it may be appropriate to discharge the juror and proceed with a reduced number of jurors.[90]

---

[88] *Taylor* v *The Queen* [2013] UKPC 8.
[89] See 8.5 below.
[90] The power is implicit in s.16(1) Juries Act 1974.

Criminal Practice Directions 2023

8.4.3 A juror can, if necessary, be discharged without appearing in open court.

PD8.5

8.5 Jury Directions and Written Material

Early provision of directions

8.5.1 The Court is required to provide directions about the relevant law at any time that will assist the jury to evaluate the evidence.[91] The judge may provide directions prior to any evidence being called, prior to the evidence to which the direction relates or shortly thereafter.

Oral and Written Directions

8.5.2 The Court must give the jury directions on the relevant law orally and, as a general rule, in writing as well.[92]

Written route to verdict

8.5.3 A route to verdict, which poses a series of legal questions the jury must answer in order to arrive at a verdict, may be provided as part of the written directions.[93] Each question should tailor the law to the issues and evidence in the case. The route to verdict may be presented (on paper or digitally) in the form of text, bullet points, a flowchart or other graphic.

Other written materials

8.5.4 Where the judge decides it will assist the jury, written materials should be provided. They may be presented (on paper or digitally) in the form of text, bullet points, a table, a flowchart or other graphic. Such written materials may be prepared by the parties at the direction of the judge, or by the judge. Where prepared by the parties at the direction of the judge, they will be subject to the judge's approval.

8.5.5 Examples of written materials that may be considered helpful to provide are chronologies, timelines, a family tree, non-controversial summaries of parts of the evidence and/or agreed expert evidence summaries.

8.5.6 Where a judge proposes to provide the jury with written material this should be shown to the parties in advance in order that they may make submissions and/or refer to the material when addressing the jury.

8.5.7 Consideration should be given as to whether guidance as to how to conduct deliberations should be given to the jury.[94]

8.5.8 Copies of all written materials provided to the jury, including all written legal directions, should be retained and/or uploaded to the DCS.

Summary of Evidence

8.5.9 The Court is required to summarise the evidence relevant to the issues to such extent as is necessary.[95]

Jury access to exhibits and evidence in retirement

8.5.10 The Court retains responsibility for deciding what material the jury should have in retirement and what they should not. Judges should invite submissions from the advocates.

PD8.6

8.6 Majority verdict

8.6.1 Before the jury retires the judge must direct the jury to this effect:

> "As you may know, the law permits me, in certain circumstances, to accept a verdict which is not the verdict of you all. Those circumstances have not as yet arisen, so that when you retire I must ask you to reach a verdict upon which each one of you is agreed.
>
> Should, however, the time come when it is possible for me to accept a majority verdict, I will give you a further direction."

---

[91] **CrimPR 25.14(2).**
[92] *R v AB* [2019] EWCA Crim 875; *R v Grant and others* [2021] EWCA Crim 1243, **CrimPR 25.14(3)(b).**
[93] **CrimPR 25.14(4).**
[94] See Appendix 9 to the Crown Court Compendium.
[95] **CrimPR 25.14(3)(a).**

8.6.2   Only a unanimous verdict can be accepted prior to the jury being given a majority direction.[96] Any enquiry as to verdict ahead of the giving of a majority direction should be in these terms:

> "Have you reached a verdict upon which you are all agreed? Please answer 'Yes' or 'No'."

If the answer is in the affirmative the verdict can be taken. If the answer is 'No' the jury should be sent out again, with a further direction to arrive if possible at a unanimous verdict.[97]

8.6.3   In the event that a majority direction is given (after at least two hours and 10 minutes of deliberation) and it becomes appropriate to enquire of the jury if they have reached a verdict the question should be put in these terms:

> "Have at least ten [where there are 11 or 12 jurors] or nine [where there are 10 jurors] of you agreed on your verdict?";
>
> If 'Yes', "Do you find the defendant guilty or not guilty? Please only answer 'Guilty' or 'Not Guilty'.";
>
> If the verdict is 'Not Guilty', there must be no enquiry as to whether
>
> unanimous or by a majority;
>
> If the verdict is 'Guilty', the jury must be asked "Is that the verdict of you all,
>
> or by a majority?";
>
> If 'Guilty' by a majority, the jury must be asked "How many of you agreed to the verdict and how many disagreed?"

8.6.4   At any stage when the jury is to be asked for a verdict the clerk will state in open court the cumulative total of the time the jury has been in retirement.

8.6.5   Where there are several counts, more than one defendant and/or alternative verdicts the above procedure will need to be adapted. A judge has a discretion in deciding when to accept partial verdicts; it may be better to give the majority direction before accepting any verdicts. If so the jury should be asked "Have you reached verdicts upon which you are all agreed in respect of all defendants and/or all counts?".

8.7 Jury irregularity   PD8.7

8.7.1   A jury irregularity is anything that may prevent one or more jurors from remaining faithful to their oath or affirmation.

8.7.2   A jury irregularity may involve contempt of court and/or the commission of an offence by or in relation to a juror. In such cases, the provision of a juror's details to the police is a matter for the judge.

Irregularity During Trial or Retirement

8.7.3   The primary concern of the judge should be the impact on the trial.

8.7.4   A jury irregularity should be drawn to the attention of the judge in the absence of the jury as soon as it becomes known. The judge should obtain, where possible, a written record of the matter that has been raised.

8.7.5   When the judge becomes aware of a jury irregularity, the judge must follow the procedure set out below:

STEP 1: Consider isolating juror(s)
STEP 2: Consult with advocates
STEP 3: Consider appropriate provisional measures
STEP 4: Seek to establish basic facts of jury irregularity
STEP 5: Further consult with advocates
STEP 6: Decide what to do in relation to conduct of trial
STEP 7: Consider ancillary matters (contempt in face of court and/or commission of criminal offence)[98]

---

[96] See s.71(4) Juries Act 1974 '…the Crown Court shall not accept such a verdict (i.e. by a majority) unless it appears to the court that the jury have had at least two hours for deliberation'. Conventionally the minimum time before giving a majority direction is two hours 10 minutes. This also applies to special verdicts under the Criminal Procedure (Insanity) Act 1964 and the questions to jurors will have to be suitably adjusted.

[97] If the number of jurors has been reduced to nine any verdict must be unanimous.

[98] Reference should be made to the most recent guidance 'Advisory Note: Contempt in the face of the Court' (2021).

STEP 1: Isolation

8.7.6   The judge must consider:

      a. whether the juror(s) concerned should be isolated from the rest of the jury, particularly if the juror(s) may have conducted research about the case;

      b. where two or more jurors are concerned, whether they should also be isolated from each other, particularly if one juror has made an accusation against another.

STEP 2: Consult with advocates

8.7.7   The judge must consult with the advocates and invite submissions about appropriate provisional measures (Step 3) and how to go about establishing the basic facts of the jury irregularity (Step 4).

8.7.8   The consultation should, unless there is good reason not to do so, be conducted:

      a. in open court;

      b. in the presence of the defendant; and

      c. with all parties represented.

8.7.9   If the jury irregularity involves a suspicion about the conduct of the defendant or another party, there may be good reason for the consultation to take place in the absence of the defendant or the other party. There may also be good reason for it to take place in private. If so, the proper location is in the courtroom, with the recording system operating, rather than in the judge's room.

8.7.10   If the jury irregularity relates to the jury's deliberations, the judge should warn all those present that it is an offence to disclose, solicit or obtain information about a jury's deliberations.[99] This would include disclosing information about the jury's deliberations divulged in court during consultation with the advocates (Step 2 and Step 5) or when seeking to establish the basic facts of the jury irregularity (Step 4). The judge should emphasise that the advocates, court staff and those in the public gallery would commit the offence by disclosing to another what is said in court about the jury's deliberations.

STEP 3: Consider appropriate provisional measures

8.7.11   The judge must consider appropriate provisional measures which may include surrender/seizure of electronic communications devices (including potentially those in the possession of a juror[100]) and taking the defendant into custody.

8.7.12   Having made an order for a juror to surrender a device, the judge may require a court security officer to search a juror to determine whether the juror has complied with the order.[101] It is contempt of court for a juror to fail to surrender an electronic communications device in accordance with an order for surrender.[102] Any electronic communications device surrendered or seized under these provisions should be kept safe by the court until returned to the juror or handed to the police as evidence.

8.7.13   If the defendant is on bail, and the jury irregularity involves a suspicion about the defendant's conduct, the judge should consider taking the defendant into custody. If that suspicion involves an attempt to suborn or intimidate a juror, the defendant should be taken into custody.

STEP 4: Seek to establish basic facts of jury irregularity

8.7.14   The judge should seek to establish the basic facts of the jury irregularity for the purpose of determining how to proceed in relation to the conduct of the trial. The judge's enquiries may involve having the juror(s) concerned write a note of explanation, or some further note, and/or questioning the juror(s). The judge may enquire whether the juror(s) feel able to continue and remain faithful to their oath or affirmation. If there is questioning, each juror should be questioned separately, in the absence of the rest of the jury, unless there is good reason not to do so. However, where there are circumstances internal to the jury, such as friction between members, the whole of the jury should be questioned in open court, through their foreman/woman, (if at the stage where one has been selected) as to their capacity to continue. It is not appropriate in such circumstances to separate and question an individual juror or jurors.[103]

---

[99] Section 20D(1) Juries Act 1974.
[100] Under s.15A(1) Juries Act 1974.
[101] Section 54A Courts Act 2003 contains the court security officer's powers of search and seizure.
[102] Section 15A(5) Juries Act 1974.
[103] *Orgles* [1994] 98 Cr. App. R. 185; *JC and others* [2013] EWCA Crim 368 para 29.

8.7.15   The enquiries should be conducted in open court; in the presence of the defendant; and with all parties represented unless there is good reason not to do so.[104]

STEP 5: Further consult with advocates

8.7.16   The judge must consult further with the advocates and invite submissions about how to proceed in relation to the conduct of the trial and what should be said to the jury (Step 6).

8.7.17   The consultation should be conducted in open court; in the presence of the defendant; and with all parties represented unless there is good reason not to do so.

STEP 6: Decide what to do in relation to conduct of trial

8.7.18   When deciding how to proceed, the judge may take time to reflect.

8.7.19   Considerations may include the stage the trial has reached. The judge should be alert to attempts by the defendant or others to disrupt the trial. In cases of potential bias, the judge should consider whether a fair minded and informed observer would conclude that there was a real possibility that the juror(s) or jury would be biased.[105]

8.7.20   In relation to the conduct of the trial, there are three possibilities:

1. Take no action and continue with the trial. If so, the judge should consider what, if anything, to say to the jury. Anything said should be tailored to the circumstances of the case.
2. Discharge the juror(s) concerned and continue with the trial. If so, the judge should consider what to say to the discharged juror(s) and the jurors who remain. All jurors should be warned not to discuss what has happened.
3. Discharge the whole jury. If so, the judge should consider what to say to the jury and they should be warned not to discuss what has happened.

8.7.21   If the judge is satisfied that jury tampering has then taken place, depending on the circumstances, the judge may continue the trial without a jury[106] or order a new trial without a jury.[107] Alternatively, the judge may order the trial to be relisted. If there is a real and present danger of jury tampering in the new trial, the prosecution may apply for a trial without a jury.[108]

STEP 7: Consider ancillary matters

8.7.22   A jury irregularity may also involve contempt in the face of the court and/or the commission of a criminal offence. The possibilities include the following:

a. Contempt in the face of the court by a juror.[109]
b. An offence by a juror[110] or a non-juror under the Juries Act 1974.
c. An offence by a juror[111] or a non-juror[112] other than under the Juries Act 1974.

Contempt in the face of the court by a juror

8.7.23   If a juror commits contempt in the face of the court, the juror's conduct may also constitute an offence. If so, the judge should decide whether to deal with the juror summarily under the procedure for contempt in the face of the court or refer the matter to the Attorney General's Office or the police.

---

[104] *R v KK and Others* [2020] 1 Cr. App. R. 29 at [80] to [81] and/or *Gabriel* [2020] EWCA Crim 998. As Davis LJ made clear in *Gabriel* a judge should have regard to the PD but '…as the Practice Direction itself makes clear, a judge has to decide what best to do where a jury irregularity occurs, and has to do so by reference to the context and to circumstances which arise in the particular case.'

[105] *Porter v Magill* [2001] UKHL 67, [2002] 2 AC 357.

[106] Section 46(3) Criminal Justice Act 2003.

[107] Section 46(5) Criminal Justice Act 2003.

[108] Section 44 Criminal Justice Act 2003.

[109] Non-jurors may commit the offence of disclosing, soliciting or obtaining information about the jury's deliberations: s.20D Juries Act 1974.

[110] Offences that may be committed by jurors are researching the case, sharing research, engaging in prohibited conduct or disclosing information about the jury's deliberations: ss.20A to 20D Juries Act 1974.

[111] A juror may commit an offence such as assault or theft.

[112] A non-juror may commit an offence in relation to a juror such as attempting to pervert the course of justice – for example, if the defendant or another attempts to suborn or intimidate a juror.

8.7.24   In the case of a minor and clear contempt in the face of the court, the judge may deal with the juror summarily.[113] The judge should also have regard to the Practice Direction regarding contempt of court updated in August 2020 (Practice Direction: Committal for Contempt of Court – Open Court), which emphasises the principle of open justice in relation to proceedings for contempt before all courts.

8.7.25   If a juror fails to comply with an order for surrender of an electronic communications device (see above), the judge should deal with the juror summarily following the procedure for contempt in the face of the court.

Offence by a juror or non-juror under the Juries Act 1974

8.7.26   If it appears that an offence under the Juries Act 1974 may have been committed by a juror or non-juror (and the matter has not been dealt with summarily under the procedure for contempt in the face of the court), the judge should contact the Attorney General's Office[114] to consider a police investigation, setting out the position neutrally. The officer in the case should not be asked to investigate.

8.7.27   If relevant to an investigation, any electronic communications device surrendered or seized pursuant to an order for surrender should be passed to the police as soon as practicable.

Offence by a juror or non-juror other than under the Juries Act 1974

8.7.28   If it appears that an offence, other than an offence under the Juries Act 1974, may have been committed by a juror or non-juror (and the matter has not been dealt with summarily under the procedure for contempt in the face of the court), the judge or a member of court staff should contact the police setting out the position neutrally. The officer in the case should not be asked to investigate.

8.7.29   If relevant to an investigation, any electronic communications device surrendered or seized pursuant to an order for surrender should be passed to the police as soon as practicable.

Other matters to consider

Jury deliberations

8.7.30   In light of the offence of disclosing, soliciting or obtaining information about a jury's deliberations,[115] great care is required if a jury irregularity relates to the jury's deliberations.

8.7.31   During the trial, there are exceptions to this offence that enable the judge (and only the judge) to:

a. seek to establish the basic facts of a jury irregularity involving the jury's deliberations (Step 4); and
b. disclose information about the jury's deliberations to the Attorney General's Office if it appears that an offence may have been committed (Step 7).

8.7.32   With regard to seeking to establish the basic facts of a jury irregularity involving the jury's deliberations (Step 4), it is to be noted that during the trial it is not an offence for the judge to disclose, solicit or obtain information about the jury's deliberations for the purposes of dealing with the case.[116]

8.7.33   With regard to disclosing information about the jury's deliberations to the Attorney General's Office if it appears that an offence may have been committed (Step 7), it is to be noted that during the trial:

a. it is not an offence for the judge to disclose information about the jury's deliberations for the purposes of an investigation by a relevant investigator into whether an offence or contempt of court has been committed by or in relation to a juror;[117] and
b. a relevant investigator means a police force or the Attorney General.[118]

8.7.34   If it is decided to discharge one or more jurors (Step 6), a minimum of nine jurors must remain if the trial is to continue.[119]

---

[113] The judge should follow the procedure in **CrimPR 48.5 to 48.8**.
[114] Attorney General's Office Contempt.SharedMailbox@attorneygeneral.gov.uk Tel: 020 7271 2492.
[115] Section 20D(1) Juries Act 1974.
[116] Sections 20E(2)(a) and 20G(1) Juries Act 1974.
[117] Section 20E(2)(b) Juries Act 1974.
[118] Section 20E(5) Juries Act 1974.
[119] Section 16(1) Juries Act 1974.

Preparation of statement by judge

8.7.35   If a jury irregularity occurs, and the trial continues, the judge should consider whether to prepare a statement that could be used in an application for leave to appeal or an appeal relating to the jury irregularity.[120]

Irregularity after the jury has been discharged

8.7.36   A jury irregularity that comes to light after the jury has been discharged may involve the commission of an offence by or in relation to a juror. It may also provide a ground of appeal.

Role of the trial judge or court

8.7.37   The judge has no jurisdiction in relation to a jury irregularity that comes to light after the jury has been discharged.[121] This will be when all verdicts on all defendants have been delivered or when the jury has been discharged from giving all verdicts on all defendants.

8.7.38   The judge has no power in relation to a jury irregularity that comes to light during an adjournment between verdict and sentence. The judge should proceed to sentence unless there is good reason not to do so.

8.7.39   A jury irregularity may come to light by a communication from a former juror.

8.7.40   If a jury irregularity comes to the attention of a judge or court after the jury has been discharged, and regardless of the result of the trial, the judge or a member of court staff should contact the Registrar of Criminal Appeals setting out the position neutrally. Any communication from a former juror should be forwarded to the Registrar.[122]

Role of the Registrar

8.7.41   If a jury irregularity comes to the attention of the Registrar after the jury has been discharged, and regardless of the result of the trial, the Registrar should consider if it appears that an offence may have been committed by or in relation to a juror. The Registrar should also consider if there may be a ground of appeal.

8.7.42   When deciding how to proceed, particularly in relation to a communication from a former juror, the Registrar may seek the direction of the Vice-President of the Court of Appeal (Criminal Division) (CACD) or another judge of the CACD in accordance with instructions from the Vice-President.

8.7.43   If it appears that an offence may have been committed by or in relation to a juror, the Registrar should contact the Private Office of the Director of Public Prosecutions through the Directors of Legal Services at the Crown Prosecution Service who will refer the matter to the relevant police force and invite the police to consider a police investigation.[123]

8.7.44   If there may be a ground of appeal, the Registrar should inform the defence.

8.7.45   If a communication from a former juror is not of legal significance, the Registrar should respond explaining that no action is required. An example of such a communication is if it is restricted to a general complaint about the verdict from a dissenting juror or an expression of doubt or second thoughts.

Role of the prosecution

8.7.46   If a jury irregularity comes to the attention of the prosecution after the jury has been discharged, which may provide a ground of appeal, the prosecution should notify the defence in accordance with their duties to act fairly and assist in the administration of justice.[124]

Role of the defence

8.7.47   If a jury irregularity comes to the attention of the defence after the jury has been discharged, which provides an arguable ground of appeal, an application for leave to appeal may be made.

---

[120]   See the remarks of Lord Hope in *R v Connors and Mirza* [2004] UKHL 2 at [127] and [128], [2004] 1 AC 1118, [2004] 2 Cr. App. R. 8.
[121]   *R v Thompson and others* [2010] EWCA Crim 1623, [2011] 1 WLR 200, [2010] 2 Cr. App. R. 27A.
[122]   penny.donnelly@criminalappealoffice.justice.gov.uk (Secretary) Tel 020 7947 6103 or generaloffice@criminalappealoffice.justice.gov.uk or 020 7947 6011.
[123]   DLS.Team@cps.gov.uk.
[124]   *R v Makin* [2004] EWCA Crim 1607, 148 SJLB 821.

Other matters to consider

Jury deliberations

8.7.48   If a possible jury irregularity comes to light after the jury has been discharged, there are exceptions to the offence of disclosing, soliciting or obtaining information about a jury's deliberations[125] that enable a judge, a member of court staff, the Registrar, the prosecution and the defence to disclose information about the jury's deliberations if it appears that an offence may have been committed by or in relation to a juror or if there may be a ground of appeal.

8.7.49   For example, it is to be noted that:

     a. after the jury has been discharged, it is not an offence for a person to disclose information about the jury's deliberations to defined persons if the person reasonably believes that an offence or contempt of court may have been committed by or in relation to a juror or the conduct of a juror may provide grounds of appeal;[126]

     b. the defined persons to whom such information may be disclosed are a member of a police force, a judge of the CACD, the Registrar of Criminal Appeals (the Registrar), a judge where the trial took place or a member of court staff where the trial took place who would reasonably be expected to disclose the information only to one of these defined persons;[127]

     c. after the jury has been discharged, it is not an offence for a judge of the CACD or the Registrar to disclose information about the jury's deliberations for the purposes of an investigation by a relevant investigator into (a) whether an offence or contempt of court has been committed by, or in relation to, a juror or (b) a juror's conduct may provide grounds of appeal;[128]

     d. a relevant investigator means a police force, the Attorney General, the Criminal Cases Review Commission (CCRC) or the CPS.[129]

8.7.50   Any discussion about a jury issue should, absent some good reason to proceed in private, be conducted in open court. Both sides must be present for any discussion unless there is some compelling reason for exclusion. All discussions must be recorded.

Investigation by the Criminal Cases Review Commission (CCRC)

8.7.51   If an application for leave to appeal, or an appeal, includes a ground of appeal relating to a jury irregularity, the Registrar may refer the case to the Full Court to decide whether to direct the CCRC to conduct an investigation under s.23A Criminal Appeal Act 1968.

8.7.52   If the Court directs the CCRC to conduct an investigation, directions should be given as to the scope of the investigation.

9. SENTENCING

PD9.1   **9.1 Guilty plea in the magistrates' courts**

9.1.1   Where a defendant enters or indicates a guilty plea in a magistrates' court, the court should consider whether a pre-sentence report is necessary. If so, a 'stand down' report is preferable.

PD9.2   **9.2 Pre-Sentence Reports on committal to Crown Court**

9.2.1   Where:

     a. a magistrates' court is considering committal for sentence; or

     b. the defendant has indicated an intention to plead guilty in a matter to be sent to the Crown Court,

the magistrates' court should request a pre-sentence report for the Crown Court if:

     i.   there may be a realistic alternative to a custodial sentence; or

     ii.   the defendant may satisfy the dangerous offender criteria; or

     iii.   there is some other appropriate reason for doing so.

9.2.2   The ordering of a pre-sentence report by the magistrates' court does not indicate the likelihood of any sentencing outcome. All options remain open in the Crown Court. The defendant should be reminded of this.

---

[125] Section 20D(1) Juries Act 1974.
[126] Section 20F(1) (2) Juries Act 1974.
[127] Section 20F(2) Juries Act 1974.
[128] Section 20F(4) Juries Act 1974.
[129] Section 20F(10) Juries Act 1974.

9.2.3   When a magistrates' court sends a case to the Crown Court for trial and the defendant indicates an intention to plead guilty, arrangements should be made to take the defendant's plea as soon as possible.

9.3 Pleas of guilty in the Crown Court   PD9.3

Where a guilty plea is offered to less than the whole indictment and the prosecution is minded to accept pleas tendered to some counts or to lesser alternative counts

9.3.1   If the judge is invited to approve a prosecutor's proposal to accept a plea to a lesser charge, or to only some of the charges, the judge's decision must be followed. If not invited to approve such a proposed course, it is open to the judge to indicate disagreement and invite the advocate to reconsider the matter and take instructions.

9.3.2   If the judge is of the opinion that the course proposed by the advocate may lead to injustice, the proceedings may be adjourned to allow for the following steps:

    a. The prosecution advocate must discuss the judge's observations with the Chief Crown Prosecutor or the senior prosecutor of the relevant prosecuting authority as appropriate, in an attempt to resolve the issue.

    b. Where the issue remains unresolved, the Director of Public Prosecutions or the Director of the relevant prosecuting authority should be consulted.

    c. In extreme circumstances the judge may decline to proceed with the case until the prosecuting authority has consulted with the Attorney General.

Where a guilty plea is offered on a limited basis

9.3.3   The following steps apply:

    a. A basis of plea that is proposed by a defendant must be in writing and uploaded to the Digital Case System. The prosecution response must also be uploaded.

    b. If the prosecution accepts the defendant's basis of plea, it must ensure that it is factually accurate and enables the judge to sentence appropriately.

    c. An 'agreed basis of plea' is always subject to the approval of the court, which will consider whether it appropriately reflects the evidence, whether it is fair and whether it is in the interests of justice.

    d. The document recording an 'agreed' basis must be signed by advocates for both sides, and made available to the judge prior to the case being opened.

    e. An agreed basis of plea that has been reached between the parties should not contain matters which are in dispute and any aspects upon which there is not agreement should be clearly identified.

    f. In resolving any disputed factual matters, the prosecution must consider its primary duty to the court and the interests of justice. If there are material factual disputes which could reasonably affect sentence then the prosecution must inform the court of this and not acquiesce or agree to any document containing material factual disputes.

    g. In some instances, the prosecution may consider that it lacks the evidence positively to dispute the defendant's account, for example, where the defendant asserts a matter outside the knowledge of the prosecution. This does not mean those assertions should be agreed. In such a case, the prosecution should test the defendant's evidence.

    h. The court must invite the parties to make representations about whether the dispute is material to sentence; and if the court decides that it is a material dispute, the court must invite such further representations or evidence as it may require and resolve the dispute.[130]

    i. A judge is entitled to insist that any evidence relevant to the facts in dispute (or upon which the judge requires further evidence for whatever reason) should be called.

    j. Where the disputed issue arises from facts which are within the exclusive knowledge of the defendant and the defendant is willing to give evidence in support of their case, the defence advocate should be prepared to call the defendant. If the defendant is not willing to testify, the judge may, subject to any explanation given, draw such inferences as appear appropriate.

    k. The decision whether or not a *Newton* hearing[131] is required is one for the judge. Evidence in a *Newton* hearing is called by the parties in the usual way and the criminal burden and standard of proof applies. The prosecutor should not leave the questioning to the judge, but should assist

---

[130] *R v Newton* (1982) 77 Cr. App. R. 13, (1982) 4 Cr. App. R. (S.) 388.
[131] See Crim PR 25.16.

the court by exploring the issues which the court requires to be explored. The rules of evidence should be followed, and judges should direct themselves appropriately.[132]

l. A judge is obliged to hold a *Newton* hearing unless sure that the basis of plea is manifestly false or the defendant declines to engage in the *Newton* hearing, whether by giving evidence or otherwise.

m. A basis of plea should not normally set out matters of mitigation. If there are mitigating factors that require resolution prior to sentence, the process does not amount to a *Newton* hearing. In so far as facts fall to be established the defence will have to discharge the civil burden to do so. Whether matters of mitigation need to be resolved is for the judge to determine.

Pleas of guilty in cases involving serious or complex fraud – basis of plea agreed by the prosecution and defence accompanied by joint submissions as to sentence[133]

9.3.4 In this part:

a. 'a plea agreement' means a written basis of plea agreed between the prosecution and defendant(s), supported by admissible documentary evidence or admissions under s.10 Criminal Justice Act 1967;

b. 'a sentencing submission' means sentencing submissions made jointly by the prosecution and defence as to the applicable sentencing range in the relevant sentencing guideline and any appropriate sentencing authorities relating to the plea agreement;

c. 'serious or complex fraud' includes, but is not limited to, allegations of fraud where two or more of the following are present:

    i.   the amount obtained or intended to be obtained exceeds £500,000;

    ii.   there is a significant international dimension;

    iii. the case requires specialist knowledge of financial, commercial, fiscal or regulatory matters such as the operation of markets, banking systems, trusts or tax regimes;

    iv. the case involves allegations of fraudulent activity against numerous victims;

    v.   the case involves an allegation of substantial and significant fraud on a public body;

    vi. the case is likely to be of widespread public concern;

    vii. the alleged misconduct endangered the economic well-being of the United Kingdom, for example by undermining confidence in financial markets.

Procedure

9.3.5 The procedure regarding agreed bases of plea outlined above, applies equally to the acceptance of pleas under this procedure. However, because the parties will have been discussing the plea agreement and the charges from a much earlier stage, it is vital that the judge is fully informed of all relevant background to the discussions, charges and the eventual basis of plea.

9.3.6 Where the defendant has not yet appeared before the Crown Court, the prosecutor must serve on the court and the parties and, where appropriate, upload to the DCS full details of the plea agreement and sentencing submission(s) at least seven days in advance of the defendant's first appearance. Where the defendant has already appeared before the Crown Court, the prosecutor must notify the court as soon as is reasonably practicable that a plea agreement and sentencing submissions are to be submitted in accordance with the Attorney General's Plea Discussion Guidelines. The court should set a date for the matter to be heard, and the prosecutor must send to the Court and/or upload to DCS full details of the plea agreement and sentencing submission(s) as soon as practicable, or in accordance with the directions of the court.

9.3.7 The details of the plea agreement must be sufficient to allow the judge to understand the facts of the case and the history of the plea discussions, to assess whether the plea agreement is fair and in the interests of justice, and to decide the appropriate sentence. The information required will include:

a. the plea agreement;

b. the sentencing submission(s);

c. all of the material provided by the prosecution to the defendant in the course of the plea discussions;

d. relevant material provided by the defendant, for example documents relating to personal mitigation; and

---

[132] See *R v Underwood* [2004] EWCA Crim 2256 para [6]-[10] for additional guidance.
[133] Guidance for prosecutors regarding the operation of this procedure is set out in the 'Attorney General's Guidelines on Plea Discussions in Cases of Serious or Complex Fraud', which came into force on 5 May 2009 and is referred to in this direction as the 'Attorney General's Plea Discussion Guidelines'.

e. the minutes of any meetings between the parties and any correspondence generated in the plea discussions.

The parties should be prepared to provide additional material at the request of the court.

9.3.8 To ensure that its consideration of the plea agreement and sentencing submissions does not cause any unnecessary further delay the court should at all times have regard to:

a. the length of time that has elapsed since the date of the occurrence of the events giving rise to the plea discussions;
b. the time taken to interview the defendant;
c. the date of charge and the prospective trial date (if the matter were to proceed to trial).

Status of plea agreement and joint sentencing submissions

9.3.9 Where a plea agreement and joint sentencing submissions are made the judge retains the absolute discretion to refuse to accept the plea agreement and to sentence otherwise than in accordance with the sentencing submissions made under the Attorney General's Plea Discussion Guidelines.

9.3.10 Sentencing submissions should draw the court's attention to any applicable range in any relevant guideline, and to any ancillary orders that may be applicable. Sentencing submissions should not include a specific sentence or agreed range other than the ranges set out in sentencing guidelines or authorities.

9.3.11 Prior to pleading guilty in accordance with the plea agreement, the defendant(s) may apply to the court for an indication of the likely maximum sentence under the procedure set out below (a '*Goodyear* indication').

9.3.12 If the defendant does not plead guilty in accordance with the plea agreement, or if a defendant who has pleaded guilty in accordance with a plea agreement, successfully applies to withdraw the plea,[134] the signed plea agreement may be treated as confession evidence, and may be used against the defendant at a later stage in those or any other proceedings. Any credit for a timely guilty plea may be lost. The court may exercise its discretion under s.78 Police and Criminal Evidence Act 1984 (PACE 1984) to exclude any such evidence.

9.3.13 Where a defendant has failed to plead guilty in accordance with a plea agreement, the case is unlikely to be ready for trial immediately. The prosecution may have been commenced earlier than it otherwise would have been, in reliance upon the defendant's agreement to plead guilty. This is likely to be a relevant consideration for the court in deciding whether or not to grant an application to adjourn or stay the proceedings to allow the matter to be prepared for trial in accordance with the protocol, Control and Management of Heavy Fraud and other Complex Criminal Cases or as required.

9.4 Indications of sentence[135]

PD9.4

9.4.1 When providing:

a. a '*Goodyear* indication' (a sentence indication under **CrimPR 3.31**) in the Crown Court; or
b. responding to a defendant's request for an indication under **CrimPR 3.16(3)(b)** in the magistrates' court;

the Court must not create or give the appearance of judicial pressure being placed on a defendant so as to promote a guilty plea.

In the Crown Court

9.4.2 An indication may be sought only when: (a) the plea is entered on the full facts of the prosecution case; or (b) a written basis of plea is agreed by the prosecution; or (c) if there is an issue between the prosecution and the defence, this is properly identified and the judge is satisfied that the issue is not material and does not require a *Newton* hearing to resolve.

9.4.3 Any advance indication given should be of the maximum sentence if a guilty plea were to be tendered at that stage of the proceedings only; the judge should not indicate the maximum possible sentence following conviction by a jury after trial.

---

[134] **CrimPR 25.5.**
[136] See paragraph 9.3.3 above.

9.4.4   The judge should only give a *Goodyear* indication if one is requested by the defendant, although the judge can, in an appropriate case, remind the defence advocate of the defendant's entitlement to seek an advance indication of sentence.

9.4.5   The judge has a discretion whether to give a *Goodyear* indication, and whether to give reasons for a refusal. If there is a dispute as to the basis of plea, such indications should not normally be given unless the judge concludes a *Newton* hearing is not required. If there is a basis of plea agreed by the prosecution and defence, it must be reduced into writing and a copy provided to the judge.[136]

9.4.6   The judge should not become involved in negotiations about the acceptance of pleas or any agreed basis of plea, nor should a request be made for an indication of the different sentences that might be imposed if various different pleas were to be offered.

9.4.7   There should be no prosecution opening nor should the judge hear mitigation. However, during the *Goodyear* application the prosecution advocate is expected to assist the court by ensuring that the court has received all of the prosecution evidence, any statement from the victim about the impact of the offence, and any relevant previous convictions. Where appropriate, the prosecution should refer to the relevant statutory powers of the court, relevant sentencing guidelines and authorities, and such other assistance as the court requires.

9.4.8   The prohibition against the Crown indicating its approval of a particular sentence applies in all circumstances when a defendant is being sentenced, including when the defence seeks a *Goodyear* indication or when joint sentencing submissions are made.

9.4.9   A *Goodyear* indication should be given in open court in the presence of the defendant but any reference to the hearing is not admissible in any subsequent trial, and reporting restrictions should normally be imposed.

In the magistrates' court

9.4.10   In accordance with **CrimPR 3.16** the defendant may seek an indication of whether a custodial or non-custodial sentence is more likely in the event of a guilty plea being forthcoming there and then.

9.4.11   If the defendant asks the court for such an indication, the prosecutor must:

a. provide any information relevant to sentence not yet served but which is available; and
b. identify any other matter relevant to sentence, including the legislation applicable, any sentencing guidelines or guideline cases and aggravating and mitigating factors.

9.4.12   The court is not obliged to give such an indication.

PD9.5   **9.5 Victim personal statements**

9.5.1   Victims of crime are invited to make a Victim Personal Statement (VPS).[137] The court will take the statement into account when determining sentence. In some circumstances, it may be appropriate for relatives of a victim to make a VPS, for example where the victim has died as a result of the relevant criminal conduct.

9.5.2   The decision about whether or not to make a VPS is entirely a matter for the victim; no pressure should be brought to bear, and no conclusion should be drawn if no statement is made. A VPS, or a further VPS, may be made at any time prior to the disposal of the case. A VPS after disposal is an exceptional step, should be confined to presenting up to date factual material, such as medical information, and should be used sparingly, most usually in the event of an appeal.

9.5.3   Evidence of the effects of an offence on the victim contained in the VPS or other statement, must be:

a. in a witness statement made under s.9 Criminal Justice Act 1967 or an expert's report; and
b. served in good time upon the defendant's solicitor or the defendant, if they are not represented.

9.5.4   Except where inferences can properly be drawn from the nature of or circumstances surrounding the offence, a sentencing court must not make assumptions unsupported by evidence about the effects of an offence on the victim.

---

[135] For the relevant principles see **CrimPR 3.31 (application for indication of sentence)** and *R v Goodyear* [2005] EWCA Crim 888.
[137] The revised Code of Practice for Victims of Crime gives further information about victims' entitlements within the criminal justice system, and the duties placed on criminal justice agencies when dealing with victims of crime.

9.5.5   The maker of a VPS may be cross-examined on its content.

9.5.6   At the discretion of the court, the VPS may also be read aloud or played in open court, in whole or in part, or it may be summarised. If the VPS is to be read aloud, the court should also determine who should do so. In making these decisions, the court should take account of the victim's preferences, and follow them unless there is good reason not to do so; examples include the inadmissibility of the content or the potentially harmful consequences for the victim or others.

9.5.7   Court hearings should not be adjourned solely to allow the victim to attend court to read the VPS. A VPS that is read aloud or played in open court in whole or in part ceases to be a confidential document. The VPS should be referred to in the course of the hearing.

9.5.8   The opinions of the victim or the victim's relatives as to what the sentence should be are not relevant, unlike the consequences of the offence on them, and should therefore not be included in the statement. If opinions as to sentence are included in the statement, then it is inappropriate for them to be referred to, and the court should have no regard to them.

Victims and others affected by serious crime

9.5.9   The court must have regard to those directly affected by serious crime. This applies to victims and those connected to them. The Code of Practice for Victims of Crime lists a range of people who are entitled to enhanced rights. Regard must be had to the needs of victims, their families and people connected to them. The trial process must not expose them to avoidable intimidation, humiliation or distress.

9.5.10   In so far as it is compatible with their status, if any, as witnesses, the court should consider the following measures:

    a. Practical arrangements being made in good time before the trial, such as seating for family members in the courtroom; if appropriate, in an alternative area, away from the public gallery.
    b. The provision of a warning if the evidence on a certain day is expected to be particularly distressing.
    c. Ensuring appropriate use of Victim Personal Statements.

Impact statements for businesses

9.5.11   If a victim, or one of those others affected by a crime, is a business, enterprise or other body (including a charity or public body, for example a school or hospital), a nominated representative may make an Impact Statement for Business (ISB). The ISB gives a formal opportunity for the court to be informed how a crime has affected a business or other body. The court will take the statement into account when determining sentence.

9.5.12   An ISB, or an updated ISB, may be made at any time prior to the disposal of the case. It will rarely be appropriate for an ISB to be made after disposal of the case but before an appeal.

9.5.13   A person making an ISB on behalf of such a business or body ('the nominated representative') must be authorised to do so on its behalf, either by nature of their position, as for example a director or owner or a senior official, or by having been suitably authorised by the owner or Board of Directors or governing body. The nominated representative must also be in a position to give admissible evidence about the impact of the crime on the business or body.

9.5.14   The ISB must be made in proper form, that is:

    a. as a witness statement made under s.9 Criminal Justice Act 1967 or an expert's report; and
    b. served in good time upon the defendant's solicitor or the defendant, if they are not represented.

9.5.15   The maker of an ISB can be cross-examined on its content.

9.5.16   The ISB and any evidence in support should be taken into account by the court, prior to passing sentence. The ISB should be referred to in the course of the hearing. Subject to the court's discretion, the contents of the statement may be summarised or read in open court. The views of the business or body should be taken into account in reaching a decision.

9.5.17   Opinions expressed as to what the sentence should be are not relevant. If opinions as to sentence are included in the statement, the court should have no regard to them and make no reference to them.

9.5.18   Except where inferences can properly be drawn from the nature of or circumstances surrounding the offence, a sentencing court must not make assumptions unsupported by evidence about the effects of an offence on a business or other body.

Community impact statement

9.5.19   A community impact statement may be prepared by the police to make the court aware of particular crime trends in the local area and the impact of these on the local community. Such statements must be made under s.9 Criminal Justice Act 1967 or an expert's report; and served in good time upon the defendant's solicitor or the defendant, if they are not represented.

9.5.20   The maker of such a statement can be cross-examined on its content.

9.5.21   A community impact statement and any evidence in support should be considered and taken into account by the court, prior to passing sentence. The statement should be referred to in the course of the sentencing hearing and/or in the sentencing remarks. Subject to the court's discretion, the contents of the statement may be summarised or read out in open court.

9.5.22   Account may be taken of such material but any opinions expressed in the documents as to what the sentence should be are not relevant, should not be referred to and the court should pay no attention to them.

9.5.23   Except where inferences can properly be drawn from the nature of or circumstances surrounding the offence, a sentencing court must not make assumptions unsupported by evidence about the effects of offending on the local community.

PD9.6   **9.6 Sentencing remarks in the Crown Court**

9.6.1   The provision of written sentencing remarks can be helpful, for example in the context of homicide, serious sexual offences or in the case of a young or otherwise vulnerable defendant, and is to be encouraged.

PD9.7   **9.7 Variation of sentence**

9.7.1   Where the Court varies sentence under s.142 Magistrates' Courts Act 1980 or s.385 Sentencing Act 2000 as appropriate, the making of the decision and the reasons for that decision always must be announced at a public hearing.[138]

10. Appeals to the Court of Appeal (Criminal Division)

PD10.1   **10.1 Guide to proceedings in the Court of Appeal, Criminal Division**

10.1.1   Parties must comply with the guidance set down by the Registrar in the Guide to Proceedings in the Court of Appeal, Criminal Division.

PD10.2   **10.2 Against conviction and sentence – the provision of notice to the prosecution**

10.2.1   On receipt of an appeal notice,[139] the Registrar of Criminal Appeals will notify the relevant prosecution authority, giving the case name, reference number and the trial or sentencing court.

10.2.2   If the court or the Registrar directs, or invites, the prosecution authority to serve a respondent's notice,[140] prior to the consideration of leave, the Registrar will also at that time serve on the prosecution authority the appeal notice containing the grounds of appeal and the transcripts, if available. If the prosecution authority is not directed or invited to serve a respondent's notice but wishes to do so, the authority should request the grounds of appeal and any existing transcript from the Criminal Appeal Office. Any respondent's notice received prior to the consideration of leave will be made available to the single judge.

10.2.3   The Registrar of Criminal Appeals will notify the relevant prosecution authority in the event that:

   a. leave to appeal against conviction or sentence is granted by the single judge; or
   b. the single judge or the Registrar refers an application for leave to appeal against conviction or sentence to the Full Court for determination; or
   c. there is to be a renewed application for leave to appeal against sentence only.

---

[138] See **CrimPR 28.4(1)(b)**.
[139] Served under **CrimPR 39.2**.
[140] Under **CrimPR 39.6**.

Criminal Practice Directions 2023

10.2.4   If the prosecution authority has not yet been served with the appeal notice and transcript, the Registrar will serve these with the notification, and if leave is granted, the Registrar will also serve the authority with the comments of the single judge.

10.2.5   The prosecution should notify the Registrar without delay if they wish to be represented at the hearing. Prosecutors should be aware that the case may be listed at short notice.

10.2.6   If the prosecution wishes to be represented at any hearing, the notification should include details of the advocate instructed and a time estimate.

10.2.7   In a renewed application for leave to appeal sentence that involves a fatality, where the prosecution is not represented and leave is granted, the court must consider adjourning the hearing so that the CPS may instruct an advocate, and the victim's family be given the opportunity to attend.

10.3 Listing of appeals against conviction and sentence in the Court of Appeal Criminal Division (CACD)   PD10.3

10.3.1   Arrangements for the fixing of dates for the hearing of appeals will be made by the Criminal Appeal Office Listing Officer, under the superintendence of the Registrar of Criminal Appeals who may give such directions as are deemed necessary.

10.3.2   Where possible, regard will be had to an advocate's existing commitments. However, in relation to the listing of appeals, the Court of Appeal takes precedence over all lower courts, including the Crown Court. Wherever practicable, a lower court will have regard to this principle when making arrangements to release an advocate to appear in the Court of Appeal. In case of difficulty the lower court should communicate with the Registrar. In general, an advocate's commitment in a lower court will not be regarded as a good reason for failing to accept a date proposed for a hearing in the Court of Appeal.

10.3.3   Similarly, when the Registrar directs that an appellant should appear by live link, the prison must give precedence to live links to the Court of Appeal over live links to the lower courts, including the Crown Court.

10.3.4   The copy of the Criminal Appeal Office summary provided to advocates will contain the summary writer's time estimate for the whole hearing including delivery of judgment. It will also contain a time estimate for the judges' reading time of the core material. The Listing Officer will rely on those estimates, unless the advocate for the appellant or the Crown provides different time estimates to the Listing Officer, in writing, within seven days of the receipt of the summary by the advocate. Where the time estimates are considered by an advocate to be inadequate, or where the estimates have been altered because, for example, a ground of appeal has been abandoned, it is the duty of the advocate to inform the Court promptly, in which event the Registrar will reconsider the time estimates and inform the parties accordingly.

10.3.5   The following target times are set for the hearing of appeals (subject to variation for vacations or expedited cases). Target times will run from the receipt of the appeal by the Listing Officer, as being ready for hearing.

Nature of Appeal	From receipt by Listing Officer to fixing of hearing date	From fixing of hearing date to hearing	Total time from receipt by Listing Officer to hearing
Sentence Appeal	14 days	14 days	28 days
Conviction Appeal	21 days	42 days	63 days
Conviction Appeal where witness to attend	28 days	52 days	80 days

10.3.6   'Appeal' includes an application for leave to appeal which requires an oral hearing.

10.4 Appeal notices containing grounds of appeal   PD10.4

10.4.1   Advocates should not settle grounds unless they consider that they are properly arguable. Grounds should be carefully drafted; the court is not assisted by grounds of appeal which are not properly set out and particularised.[141] The grounds must:

a. be concise;

---

[141] In accordance with **CrimPR 39.3**.

b. be presented in A4 page size and portrait orientation, in not less than 12 point font and in 1.5
    line spacing;
c. include in the appeal notice electronic links to relevant documents/digital evidence, identi-
    fying with particularity the sections of any such material the court needs to consider as well as
    where and how that is to be found.[142]

10.4.2   Defective grounds will be returned for revision within a directed period. Failure to revise might
         lead to the court refusing leave.

10.4.3   Where the appellant wants to appeal against conviction, transcripts must be identified.[143]

10.4.4   Fresh representatives must comply with the duty of due diligence explained in *R v McCook*.[144] To
         ensure compliance with this duty:

a. New legal representatives must confirm within the grounds of appeal that the duties set out in
    McCook and associated authorities have been complied with.
b. If privileged information is included within, or as an attachment, to the grounds of appeal
    (including but not limited to, explicit or implied complaints about the conduct of trial
    representatives), then a signed waiver of privilege must also be lodged with the grounds of
    appeal.
c. If trial representatives fail to respond to inquiries within a reasonable time, fresh representa-
    tives should instead seek other objective independent evidence to substantiate the factual basis
    for the grounds as far as they are able. A statement confirming that the trial representatives
    have failed to respond to their *McCook* inquiries must be lodged with the grounds of appeal,
    along with a signed waiver of privilege.
d. Fresh representatives must consider obtaining other objective independent evidence if the
    information provided by the trial representatives contradicts the appellant's instructions.
e. A signed waiver of privilege must also be lodged by new legal representatives in all fresh
    evidence cases, following the guidance in *R v Singh*.[145]

10.4.5   Where the appellant wants to rely on a ground of appeal that is not identified by the appeal
         notice, an application[146] is required. In *R v James and Others*[147] the Court of Appeal identified as
         follows the considerations that pertain and the criteria that the court will apply on any such
         application:

a. As a general rule all the grounds of appeal that an appellant wishes to advance should be
    lodged with the appeal notice, subject to their being perfected on receipt of transcripts from
    the Registrar.
b. The application for permission to appeal under s.31 Criminal Appeal Act 1968 is an
    important stage in the process. It must not be treated lightly or its determination in effect
    ignored merely because fresh representatives would have done or argued things differently to
    their predecessors. Fresh grounds advanced by fresh representatives must be particularly
    cogent.
c. As well as addressing the factors material to the determination of an application for an
    extension of time within which to renew an application for permission to appeal, if that is
    required,[148] the appellant or their representatives must address directly the factors which the
    court is likely to consider relevant when deciding whether to allow the substitution or addition
    of grounds of appeal. Those factors include (but this list is not exhaustive):
    i.   the extent of the delay in advancing the fresh ground or grounds;
    ii.   the reasons for that delay;
    iii. whether the facts or issues the subject of the fresh ground were known to the appellant's
          representatives when they advised on appeal;
    iv.   the interests of justice and the overriding objective in Part 1 of the **CrimPR**.

---

[142] See **CrimPR 39.3(1)(f)** & **(g)**, which in practice distinguish between documents on DCS and authorities in law reports.
[143] In accordance with **CrimPR 39.3(1)(c)**.
[144] [2014] EWCA Crim 734.
[145] [2017] EWCA Crim 466.
[146] Under **CrimPR 36.14(5)**.
[147] [2018] EWCA Crim 285.
[148] On an application under **CrimPR 36.14(5)**.

Criminal Practice Directions 2023

d. On the assumption that an appellant will have received advice on appeal from the trial advocate, who will have settled the grounds of appeal in the original appeal notice or who will have advised that there are no reasonably arguable grounds to challenge the safety of the conviction:

    i.   Fresh representatives should comply with the duty of due diligence explained in *R v McCook*.[149] Waiver of privilege by the appellant is very likely to be required.

    ii.   Once the trial lawyers have responded, the fresh representatives should again consider with great care their duty to the court and whether the proposed fresh grounds should be advanced as reasonably arguable and particularly cogent.

    iii.   The Registrar will obtain, before the determination of the application,[150] transcripts relevant to the fresh grounds and, where required, a respondent's notice relating to the fresh grounds.

e. While an application[151] will not require 'exceptional leave', and hence the demonstration of substantial injustice, the hurdle for the applicant is a high one nonetheless. A representation order would not usually be granted for such an application.

f. Permission to renew out of time an application for permission to appeal is not given unless the applicant can persuade the court that very good reasons exist. If that application to renew out of time is accompanied by an application to vary the grounds of appeal, the hurdle will be higher still.

g. Any application to substitute or add grounds will be considered by a fully constituted court and at a hearing, not on the papers.

h. Where a Court refuses a renewed application for permission to appeal,[152] it has the power to make a loss of time order or an order for costs in line with *R v Gray and Others*.[153] In that case the court said it would consider doing so when faced with an unmeritorious application, particularly if the single judge had given such an indication. By analogy with *R v Kirk*[154] (where the court refused an extension of time) the court has the power to order payment of the costs of obtaining the respondent's notice and any additional transcripts.

10.4.6   Applications must be lodged at the following address: applications@criminalappealoffice.justice.gov.uk.

10.5 Loss of time   PD10.5

10.5.1   Both the Court and the single judge have power, in their discretion, under the Criminal Appeal Act 1968 ss.29 and 31, to direct that part of the time during which an applicant is in custody after lodging their notice of application for leave to appeal should not count towards sentence.[155]

10.6 Criminal Appeal Office summaries   PD10.6

10.6.1   To assist the Court, the Criminal Appeal Office prepares summaries of the cases coming before it. These are entirely objective and do not contain any advice about how the Court should deal with the case or any view about its merits. They consist of two Parts, which may be combined in a single document.

10.6.2   Part I, which is provided to all of the advocates in the case, generally contains:

a. particulars of the proceedings in the Crown Court, including representation and details of any co-accused;

b. particulars of the proceedings in the Court of Appeal (Criminal Division);

c. the facts of the case, as drawn from the transcripts, appeal notice, respondent's notice, witness statements and / or the exhibits;

d. the submissions and rulings, summing up and sentencing remarks.

---

[149] [2014] EWCA Crim 734.
[150] Under **CrimPR 36.14(5)**.
[151] Under **CrimPR 36.14(5)**.
[152] Under **CrimPR 36.14(5)**.
[153] [2014] EWCA Crim 2372.
[154] [2015] EWCA Crim 1764.
[155] See on the loss of time orders *R v Gray and Others* [2014] EWCA Crim 2372.

10.6.3   The contents of the summary are a matter for the professional judgment of the writer, but an advocate wishing to suggest any significant alteration to Part I should write to the Registrar of Criminal Appeals. If the Registrar does not agree, the summary and the letter will be put to the Court for decision. The Court will not generally be willing to hear oral argument about the content of the summary.

10.6.4   Advocates may show Part I of the summary to their professional or lay clients (but to no one else) if they believe it would help to check facts or formulate arguments, but summaries are not to be copied or reproduced without the permission of the Criminal Appeal Office; permission for this will not normally be given in cases involving children, or sexual offences, or where the Crown Court has made an order restricting reporting.

10.6.5   Unless a judge of the High Court or the Registrar of Criminal Appeals gives a direction to the contrary, in any particular case involving material of an explicitly salacious or sadistic nature, Part I will also be supplied to appellants who seek to represent themselves before the Full Court, or who renew to the Full Court their applications for leave to appeal against conviction or sentence.

10.6.6   Part II, which is supplied to the Court alone, unless combined in a single document, contains:

     a. a summary of or electronic link to the grounds of appeal; and
     b. in appeals against sentence (and applications for such leave), summaries of or electronic links to the antecedent histories of the parties and of any relevant pre-sentence, medical or other reports.

10.6.7   All of the source material is provided to the Court and advocates are able to draw attention to anything in it which may be of particular relevance.

PD10.7

10.7 Criminal Appeal Office bundles and indexes for full court hearings

10.7.1   To assist the Full Court, the Criminal Appeal Office will, save where the summary is comprised of a single document, prepare an index to the bundle containing electronic links to the documents and material which the Registrar considers necessary to understand and determine the appeal for each member of the constitution. In exceptional circumstances, paper bundles may be provided.

10.7.2   The Registrar will not provide bundles where a party or the parties have been directed to prepare and lodge indexed bundles, or where an advocate has lodged indexed bundles of their own volition. Where an appellant who is not privately represented is directed to lodge indexed bundles, a Representation Order may be granted by the Court or the Registrar for this purpose.

10.7.3   Where digital or paper bundles are prepared by the Criminal Appeal Office, a copy of the index will be provided to the appellant, or if the appellant is represented, to the advocate. If the advocate or appellant considers that there is additional material which it is necessary to include in the bundle, they must notify the Registrar of this in writing.

10.7.4   Bundles lodged in response to a direction to do so, or of an advocate's own volition, should, wherever possible, be provided in pdf format with OCR (optical character recognition). All significant documents and all sections in bundles must be bookmarked for ease of navigation, with an appropriate description as the bookmark. An index or table of contents of the documents should be prepared. If practicable entries should be hyperlinked to the indexed document. Where, exceptionally, paper bundles are necessary unless otherwise directed, four copies of the indexed bundle should be lodged with the Registrar in good time before the hearing and in accordance with any direction as to the time by which they should be lodged. Bundles whether digital or paper should contain only documents and material which are necessary for the proper understanding of, and determination of, the issues involved in the appeal. The index and order of documents / material in the bundles should follow the order of the Registrar's template 'Index to Judge's Bundles' available from the Registrar on request.

PD10.8

10.8 Skeleton arguments and citation of authorities

10.8.1   Advocates should always ensure that the Court, and any other party as appropriate, has a single document containing all of the points that are to be argued.

10.8.2   In cases of an appeal against conviction, advocates must serve a skeleton argument when the appeal notice does not sufficiently outline the grounds of the appeal, particularly in cases where a complex or novel point of law has been raised. In an appeal against sentence it may be helpful for an advocate to serve a skeleton argument when a complex issue is raised.

10.8.3   Subject to any direction given by the court a skeleton argument[156] must:

    a. contain a numbered list of the points the advocate intends to argue, these should be grouped under each ground of appeal, and stated in no more than one or two sentences;

    b. be as succinct as possible;

    c. at the beginning of any document state the correct Criminal Appeal Office number and the date on which the document was served, and conclude with the advocates' names;

    d. define the issues;

    e. not normally exceed 15 pages (excluding front sheets and back sheets) and be concise;

    f. be presented in A4 page size and portrait orientation, in not less than 12 point font and in 1.5 line spacing;

    g. be set out in numbered paragraphs;

    h. be cross-referenced to any relevant document in any bundle prepared for the court;

    i. be self-contained;

    j. not include extensive quotations from documents or authorities.

10.8.4   Where it is necessary to refer to an authority, the skeleton argument must:

    a. cite the neutral citation number followed by the appropriate law report (taking the first in the hierarchy of law reporting should the case be reported in more than one place);[157] and

    b. state the proposition of law the authority demonstrates; and

    c. identify but not quote the parts of the authority that support the proposition.

10.8.5   If more than one authority is cited in support of a given proposition, the skeleton argument must briefly state why.

10.8.6   A chronology of relevant events will be necessary in most cases.

10.8.7   At the hearing the court may refuse to hear argument on a point unless it is included in a skeleton argument which (i) is served within the required time, and (ii) complies with the requirements of this Practice Direction (as varied, if applicable, by direction of the court). Any application for a variation, or further variation, of those requirements must give reasons, and such an application must accompany any skeleton argument that does not comply.

10.8.8   The Criminal Appeal Office may refuse to accept service of a document that fails to comply with the requirements in these Directions and may return that document to the advocate for amendment.

Citation of authority

10.8.9   Only an authority which establishes the principle should be cited. Reference should not be made to authorities which do no more than either (a) illustrate the principle or (b) restate it. The court is most unlikely to be prepared to look at an authority which does no more than illustrate or restate an established proposition.

10.8.10 Where a definitive Sentencing Council guideline is available, authorities decided before the issue of the guideline, and authorities after its issue which do not refer to it, will rarely be of assistance. An authority that does no more than uphold a sentence imposed at the Crown Court is unlikely to assist the court in deciding whether a sentence is manifestly excessive or wrong in principle.

10.8.11 When an authority is to be cited, whether in written or oral submissions, the advocate should always provide the neutral citation followed by the law report reference.

10.8.12 The following practice should be followed:

    a. Where a judgment is reported in the Official Law Reports (A.C., Q.B., Ch., Fam.) published by the Incorporated Council of Law Reporting for England and Wales or the Criminal Appeal Reports or the Criminal Appeal Reports (Sentencing), one of those two series of reports must be cited; either is equally acceptable. However, where a judgment is reported in the Criminal Appeal Reports or the Criminal Appeal Reports (Sentencing) that reference must be given in addition to any other reference.

---

[156] These requirements, save where specific to appeals, apply equally to skeleton arguments served in any proceedings to which the Practice Direction has application.

[157] Recognised hierarchy of law reporting: first, Official Law Reports (AC, QB, Ch, Fam) produced by the Incorporated Council of Law Reporting for England and Wales); second, All England Law Reports (All ER) or the Weekly Law Reports (WLR); third, authoritative specialist reports, which contain a headnote and are made by individuals holding a Senior Courts qualification; fourth, a judgment not reported in any of the reports listed above, but reported in other reports; fifth, an official transcript. The hierarchy of reporting applies in all courts to which the Practice Direction has application.

b. If a judgment is not reported in the Official Law Reports, the Criminal Appeal Reports or the Criminal Appeal Reports (Sentencing), but it is reported in an authoritative series of reports which contains a headnote and is made by individuals holding a Senior Courts qualification (for the purposes of s.115 Courts and Legal Services Act 1990), that report should be cited.

c. Where a judgment is not reported in any of the reports referred to above, but is reported in other reports, they may be cited.

d. Where a judgment has not been reported, reference may be made to the official transcript if that is available, not the handed-down text of the judgment, as this may have been subject to late revision after the text was handed down.

Provision of copies of judgments to the court

10.8.13 An electronic copy of any authority should be provided. Where there is more than one authority, they should be provided in a single electronic document.[158]

10.8.14 Authorities bundles should, wherever possible, be provided in pdf format with OCR (optical character recognition). All significant documents and all sections in bundles must be bookmarked for ease of navigation, with an appropriate description as the bookmark. An index or table of contents of the documents should be prepared. If practicable entries should be hyperlinked to the indexed document.

10.8.15 In providing materials for the Court, advocates should follow the detailed guidance issued by the Registrar of Criminal Appeals: The Court of Appeal Division Guide to Commencing Proceedings (2021).

Citation of Hansard

10.8.16 Where any party intends to refer to the reports of Parliamentary proceedings as reported in the Official Reports of either House of Parliament ('Hansard') in support of any such argument as is permitted by the decisions in *Pepper v Hart*[159] and *Pickstone v Freemans PLC*,[160] or otherwise, they must, unless the court otherwise directs, serve upon all other parties and the court copies of any such extract, together with a brief summary of the argument intended to be based upon such extract. No other report of Parliamentary proceedings may be cited.

10.8.17 Unless the court otherwise directs, service of the extract and summary of the argument shall be effected not less than five clear working days before the first day of the hearing, whether or not it has a fixed date. Advocates must keep themselves informed as to the state of the lists where no fixed date has been given. Service on the court shall be effected by sending electronically to the Registrar of Criminal Appeals.[161] If any party fails to do so, the court may make such order (relating to costs or otherwise) as is, in all the circumstances, appropriate.

PD10.9   10.9 Availability of judgments of the Court of Appeal

Availability of reserved judgments before handing down, corrections and applications consequential on judgment

10.9.1   Where judgment is to be reserved the Presiding Judge will, at the conclusion of the hearing, invite the views of the parties' legal representatives (or of a party, if unrepresented) as to the arrangements to be made for the handing down of the judgment.

10.9.2   Unless the court directs otherwise, the following provisions apply where the Presiding Judge is satisfied that the judgment will attract no special degree of confidentiality or sensitivity.

10.9.3   The court will provide a copy of the draft judgment to the parties' legal representatives (or of a party, if unrepresented) about three working days before handing down, or at such other time as the court may direct. Every page of every judgment which is made available in this way will be marked 'Unapproved judgment: No permission is granted to copy or use in court.'

10.9.4   The draft is supplied in confidence and on condition that:

a. neither the draft judgment nor its substance will be disclosed to any other person or used in the public domain; and

---

[158] See **CrimPR 39.3(1)(g)**.
[159] [1993] AC 593.
[160] [1989] AC 66.
[161] At the address advertised by HMCTS.

b. no action will be taken in response to the draft judgment (other than by the parties' legal representatives, or by a party if unrepresented, for the purpose of complying with para 10.9.5 or 10.9.6), before the judgment is handed down.

10.9.5   Unless the parties' legal representatives are told otherwise when the draft judgment is circulated, any proposed corrections to the draft judgment should be sent to the clerk of the judge who prepared the draft (or to the associate, if the judge has no clerk) with a copy to any other party's legal representatives, by 12 noon on the day before judgment is handed down.

10.9.6   If, having considered the draft judgment, the prosecution will be applying to the Court for a retrial or either party wishes to make any other application consequent on the judgment, the judge's clerk should be informed with a time estimate for the application by 12 noon on the day before judgment is handed down. This will enable the court to make appropriate listing arrangements and notify advocates to attend if the court so requires. There is no fee payable to advocates who attend the hand down hearing if not required to do so by the court. If either party is considering applying to the Court to certify a point for appeal to the Supreme Court, it would assist if the judge's clerk could be informed at the same time, although this is not obligatory as under s.34 Criminal Appeal Act 1968, the time limit for such applications is 28 days.

Communication to the parties including the defendant or the victim

10.9.7   The contents of the draft judgment must not to be communicated to the parties, including to the defendant, respondent or the victim (defined as a person entitled to receive services under the Code of Practice for Victims of Crime) until two hours before the listed time for pronouncement of judgment.

10.9.8   Judges may permit more information about the result of a case to be communicated on a confidential basis to the parties including to the defendant, respondent or the victim at an earlier stage if good reason is shown for making such a direction.

10.9.9   If, for any reason, the parties' legal representatives have special grounds for seeking a relaxation of the usual condition restricting disclosure to the parties, a request for relaxation of the condition may be made informally through the judge's clerk (or through the associate, if the judge has no clerk).

10.9.10 If the parties or their legal representatives are in any doubt about the persons to whom copies of the draft judgment may be distributed they should enquire of the judge or Presiding Judge.

10.9.11 Any breach of the obligations or restrictions in this section or failure to take reasonable steps to ensure compliance may be treated as contempt of court.

Restrictions on disclosure or reporting

10.9.12 Anyone who is supplied with a copy of the handed-down judgment, or who reads it in court, will be bound by any direction which the court may have given in a child case under ss.45 or 45A YJCEA 1999, or any other form of restriction on disclosure, or reporting, of information in the judgment.

10.9.13 Copies of the approved judgment can be ordered from the official shorthand writers, on payment of the appropriate fee.

11. INVESTIGATIVE ORDERS

11.1 Investigation orders and warrants

PD11.1

11.1.1   If an application is supplemented by oral or written information, on questioning by the court or otherwise, the court must keep a record in or annexed to the application form. If a sensitive information supplement is supplied and is not retained by the applicant,[162] this must be kept securely.

11.1.2   There are many powers of entry, search and seizure. If no application form has been issued for the warrant or order sought, another form should be adapted. The applicant must give the information required by the relevant legislation. If the court may be unfamiliar with that legislation then the applicant must provide a copy.

11.1.3   Wet ink judicial signatures are never needed.[163]

---

[162] See **CrimPR 47.3(1)**.
[163] **CrimPR 47.27(3)**.

Criminal Practice Directions 2023

PD11.2   **11.2 Investigation orders and warrants in the Crown Court**

11.2.1   This section covers applications made under:

      a. Schedule 1 PACE 1984;
      b. Section 2 Criminal Justice Act 1987;
      c. Drug Trafficking Act 1994;
      d. Part 8 Proceeds of Crime Act 2002;
      e. Schedule 5 Coroners and Justice Act 2009;
      f. Terrorism Act 2000.

11.2.2   It does **not** cover applications under the Extradition Act 2003, which are dealt with at Westminster Magistrates' Court or the High Court only.

Crown Court Centres

11.2.3   Investigators must give careful consideration to which Crown Court centre is most appropriate to hear the application, which must explain the rationale for choosing it. Relevant considerations include:

      a. where any subsequent proceedings are likely to be commenced;
      b. where a main suspect has some geographical connection; and/or
      c. where, in broad terms, the offending has taken place.

11.2.4   A court centre must not be chosen simply because it is most convenient or proximate to the investigator's location. Disputes over the proper venue for an application must be determined by the relevant Presiding Judges.

11.2.5   Where the investigation is complex, lengthy and/or involves multiple suspects, all applications must be made to one court centre. To ensure consistency, all subsequent applications arising out of the same or any connected investigation must be made to the same court centre and, where practicable, the same judge.

11.2.6   Judges can refuse to determine applications and request they be resubmitted (if necessary to another court) where:

      a. the application is not in the proper form;
      b. there is an inaccurate reading time estimate; and/or
      c. there is insufficient justification for the application to be made at that court centre.

Investigation Orders

11.2.7   Applications for investigation orders (e.g. production orders) can be determined without a hearing and, therefore, in the absence of the applicant.[164]

11.2.8   When permitted by the rules, and where the application has been submitted on the correct form, there is a presumption that the application will be dealt with without a hearing. The judge is always entitled to require a hearing to clarify omissions or ambiguity, or for any other reason.

11.2.9   It may not be appropriate for a court to deal with an application without a hearing in the following situations, subject to judicial discretion:

      a. Where the investigation involved covert activity or the application is based on material gathered covertly.
      b. Where the application is based on material which is especially sensitive and/or where it will be necessary to ensure the security at court of the material produced in support of the application.
      c. Where the case may result in substantial local and/or national public interest.
      d. Where the application is particularly lengthy, serious or complex.
      e. Where the application appears to relate to something akin to excluded material[165] such as sensitive personal records, or medical information.

11.2.10 Applications should be sent electronically to the designated secure email address at the relevant court centre.

---

[164] **CrimPR** 47.5(1)(a).
[165] PACE s.11.

11.2.11 Approved orders will be returned electronically to the applicant and an electronic copy must be securely saved by the court.

Investigation warrants

11.2.12 Applications for warrants must be heard with the applicant in attendance,[166] although that hearing can be by live link (including telephone).[167]

11.2.13 If the judge refuses the application, the judge may require further information. The Court will inform the applicant of the outcome and make necessary arrangements for any additional hearings that may be required.

11.2.14 If there is a particular urgency with any application, that fact should be made clear to the Court.

11.2.15 There is no requirement for any warrant to be signed by the judge with a 'wet ink' signature. An electronic record of any warrants that are made will be sent to the applicant.

Listing

11.2.16 To assist the listing process, the applicant must supply a realistic estimate of the reading time required. There must be adequate time allowed for the judge to read carefully the application and all the supporting evidence supplied with it. The judge will also require sufficient time to enable a short judgment to be given, where necessary, so that in the event of challenge in the Administrative Court there is an explanation of the reasons for the decision.

11.2.17 The covering email should stipulate whether there have been any previous applications in the same or any connected investigation and provide the name of the judge who granted any previous orders.

11.2.18 Where the judge directs a hearing at court, any additional material relied on by the applicant must be brought to court on the day of the hearing. Any additional material should not be retained by the court once the application has been determined, but must be taken away by the applicant at the end of the hearing and retained.

12. EXTRADITION

12.1 General matters and case management   PD12.1

General matters: expedition; Brexit developments

12.1.1   Extradition proceedings must be dealt with expeditiously, and in accordance with the Trade and Cooperation Agreement between the European Union and the European Atomic Energy Community, of the one part, and the United Kingdom of Great Britain and Northern Ireland, of the other part ('TCA') of the 24 December 2020 as amended, and where applicable the Council Framework Decision 2002/584/JHA of 13 June 2002 on the European arrest warrant and the surrender procedures between Member States ('Framework Decision').

12.1.2   Following the United Kingdom's exit from the European Union, the applicable surrender procedure will depend on whether the requested person was arrested pursuant to a European Arrest Warrant (EAW) before 31 December 2020. If so, the Framework Decision and the Extradition Act 2003 continue to apply in unamended form.[168] If not, a new system of surrender provided for in Title VII of Part 3 of the TCA and based on the new arrest warrant procedure will apply, as provided for in the amended Extradition Act 2003.

12.1.3   Part 3 of the TCA provides for ongoing law enforcement and judicial cooperation in criminal matters.[169]

12.1.4   Westminster Magistrates' Court directions must be followed. In particular:

  a. the court will give model case management directions, adapted to each individual case. These require parties to supply case management information, consistent with the overriding objective of the Criminal Procedure Rules;

  b. a requested person must identify issues at the first hearing so directions can be given to achieve a single, effective extradition hearing at the earliest possible date;

---

[166] **CrimPR 47.25(1)(a).**
[167] **CrimPR 47.25(2).**
[168] *Polakowski v WMC and various Judicial Authorities* [2021] EWHC 53 (Admin).
[169] Pages 312-329 in particular deal with Surrender (Title VII) and Mutual Assistance (Title VIII).

   c. if further information from the requesting authority is needed, the request must be formu-
      lated clearly and early, in comprehensible terms to ensure a prompt response;
   d. where such a request or other document, including a formal notice to the requested person of
      a post-extradition consent request, requires transmission to a requesting state, clear and
      realistic directions for transmission must be given and complied with. The court must be
      informed immediately of difficulties;
   e. skeleton arguments must comply with these Practice Directions and court directions. (10.8
      sets out the general requirements for skeleton arguments. Paragraphs 12.3.1 to 12.3.29 set out
      special requirements that apply to extradition appeals to the High Court.)

PD12.2   **12.2 General guidance under s.2(7A) Extradition Act 2003 (as amended)**

12.2.1   When considering under s.21A(3)(a) of the Act the seriousness of conduct alleged to constitute
         the extradition offence, the judge will determine the issue on the facts of each case as set out in the
         warrant, subject to paragraph 12.2.2 below.

12.2.2   Where the conduct alleged to constitute the offence falls into one of the categories in the table at
         paragraph 12.2.4 below, unless there are exceptional circumstances, the judge should generally
         determine that extradition would be disproportionate. It follows under the terms of s.21A(4)(b)
         of the Act that the judge must order the person's discharge.

12.2.3   The exceptional circumstances referred to above in paragraph 12.2.2 include:

   a. vulnerable victim;
   b. crime committed against someone because of their disability, gender- identity, race, religion or
      belief, or sexual orientation;
   c. significant premeditation;
   d. multiple counts;
   e. extradition also sought for another offence;
   f. previous offending history.

12.2.4   The table is as follows:

Category of offence	Examples
Minor theft – (not robbery/ burglary or theft from the person)	Where the theft is of a low monetary value and there is a low impact on the victim or indirect harm to others, for example: (a) theft of an item of food from a supermarket; (b) theft of a small amount of scrap metal from company premises; (c) theft of a very small sum of money.
Minor financial offences (forgery, fraud and tax offences)	Where the sums involved are small and there is a low impact on the victim and/or low indirect harm to others, for example: (a) failure to file a tax return or invoices on time; (b) making a false statement in a tax return; (c) dishonestly applying for a tax refund; (d) obtaining a bank loan using a forged or falsified document; (e) non-payment of child maintenance.
Minor road traffic, driving and related offences	Where no injury, loss or damage was incurred to any person or property, for example: (a) driving whilst using a mobile phone; (b) use of a bicycle whilst intoxicated.
Minor public order offences	Where there is no suggestion the person started the trouble and the offending behaviour was, for example: (a) non-threatening verbal abuse of a law enforcement officer or government official; (b) shouting or causing a disturbance, without threats; (c) quarrelling in the street, without threats.
Minor criminal damage (other than by fire)	For example, breaking a window.

Category of offence	Examples
Possession of a controlled substance (other than one with a high capacity for harm such as heroin, cocaine, LSD or crystal meth)	Where it was possession of a very small quantity and intended for personal use.

12.3 Management of appeal to the High Court

PD12.3

12.3.1 Applications for permission to appeal to the High Court under the Extradition Act 2003 must be started in the Administrative Court of the King's Bench Division at the Royal Courts of Justice in London.

12.3.2 A Lord or Lady Justice of Appeal ('LJ') appointed by the Lord Chief Justice will have responsibility to assist the President of the King's Bench Division with overall supervision of extradition appeals.

Definitions

12.3.3 The following definitions apply in this part:

    a. Where appropriate 'appeal' includes 'application for permission to appeal'.

    b. 'EAW' means European Arrest Warrant, and for the purpose of this direction should be read as synonymous with Arrest Warrants 'AW' under the TCA (although the distinctions in law should be noted).

    c. A 'nominated legal officer of the court' is a court officer assigned to the Administrative Court Office who is a barrister or solicitor and who has been nominated for the purpose by the Lord Chief Justice under **CrimPR 50.18**.

Forms

12.3.4 All application notices are made using form EX244.

12.3.5 The forms are to be used in the High Court, in accordance with **CrimPR 50.19, 50.20, 50.21** and **50.22**.

12.3.6 The forms may be amended or withdrawn from time to time, or new forms added, under the authority of the Lord Chief Justice.

Management of the Appeal

12.3.7 Where it is not possible for the High Court to begin to hear the appeal in accordance with time limits contained in **CrimPR 50.23(1) and (2)**, the court may extend the time limit if it believes it to be in the interests of justice to do so and may do so even after the time limit has expired.

12.3.8 The power to extend those time limits may be exercised by an LJ, a Single Judge of the High Court, a Master of the Administrative Court or a nominated legal officer of the court.

12.3.9 Case management directions setting down a timetable may be imposed upon the parties by an LJ, a Single Judge of the High Court, a Master of the Administrative Court or a nominated legal officer of the court. For the court's constitution and relevant powers and duties see s.4 Senior Courts Act 1981 and **CrimPR 50.18 and 50.30**.

Listing of Oral, Renewal and Substantive Hearings

12.3.10 Arrangements for the fixing of dates for hearings will be made by a Listing Officer of the Administrative Court under the direction of the judge with overall responsibility for supervision of extradition appeals.

12.3.11 An LJ, a Single Judge of the High Court, a Master of the Administrative Court or a nominated legal officer of the court may give such directions to the Listing Officer as they deem necessary with regard to the fixing of dates, including as to whether cases in the same/related proceedings or raising the same or similar issues should be heard together or consecutively under the duty imposed by **CrimPR 1.1(2)(e)**. Parties must alert the nominated court officer for the need for such directions.

12.3.12 Save in exceptional circumstances, regard will not be given to an advocate's existing commitments. This is in accordance with the spirit of the legislation that extradition matters should be dealt with expeditiously. Extradition matters are generally not so complex that an alternative advocate cannot be instructed.

Criminal Practice Directions 2023

12.3.13 If a party disagrees with the time estimate given by the court, they must inform the Listing Office within five business days of the notification of the listing and they must provide a time estimate of their own.

Expedited appeals

12.3.14 The court may direct that the hearing of an appeal be expedited.

12.3.15 The court will deal with requests for an expedited appeal without a hearing. Requests for expedition must be made in writing, either within the appeal notice, or by application notice, clearly marked with the Administrative Court reference number, which must be lodged with the Administrative Court Office or emailed to the appropriate email address[170] and notice must be given to the other parties.

12.3.16 Any requests for an expedited appeal made to an out of hours judge must be accompanied by:

    a. a detailed chronology;
    b. reasons why the application could not be made within court hours;
    c. any orders or judgments made in the proceedings.

Applications to vary notices

12.3.17 Any amendment to an appellant's or respondent's notice must be authorised by the Court in accordance with **CrimPR 50.17(6)(b)**:

    a. An application for permission to amend made before permission to appeal has been considered will be determined without a hearing.
    b. An application for permission to amend after permission to appeal has been granted and any submissions in opposition will normally be dealt with at the hearing unless there is any risk that the hearing may have to be adjourned. If there is any risk that the application to amend may lead the other party to seek time to answer the proposed amendment, the application must be made as soon as practicable and well in advance of the hearing. A failure to make timely applications for such an amendment is likely to result in refusal.
    c. Legal representatives or the appellant, if acting in person, must:
       i. inform the court at the time they make the application if the existing time estimate is affected by the proposed amendment; and
       ii. attempt to agree any revised time estimate no later than five business days after service of the application.

Out of time Renewals

12.3.18 Where an application for an extension of time to file a notice of renewal is refused (whether at a hearing or on paper), there is no jurisdiction for the court to entertain a renewed application at an oral hearing.

12.3.19 In such circumstances, the appellant may ask the court to reopen the application for permission to appeal, pursuant to the exceptional jurisdiction in **CrimPR 50.27**.[171]

Use of live links

12.3.20 When a party acting in person is in custody, the court office will request the institution to use live link for attendance at any oral or renewal hearing or substantive appeal. The institution must give precedence to all such applications in the High Court over live links to the lower courts, including the Crown Court.

Interpreters

12.3.21 It is the responsibility of the Listing Officer to ensure the attendance of an accredited interpreter when an unrepresented party in extradition proceedings is acting in person and does not understand or speak English.

12.3.22 Where a party who does not understand or speak English is legally represented it is the responsibility of that party's solicitors to instruct an interpreter if required for any hearing in extradition proceedings.

---

[170] crimex@administrativecourtoffice.justice.gov.uk.
[171] *Oleantu-Urshache v Judecatoris Bacau, Romania and Majewski v Polish Judicial Authority* [2021] EWHC 1437.

Disposing of applications and appeals by way of consent

12.3.23 **CrimPR 50.24** governs the submission of Consent Orders and lists the essential requirements for such orders. Any Consent Order, the effect of which will be to allow extradition to proceed, must specify the date on which the appeal proceedings are to be treated as discontinued, for the purposes of ss.36 or 118, as the case may be, Extradition Act 2003: whether that is to be the date on which the order is made or some later date.

12.3.24 A Consent Order may be approved by an LJ, a Single Judge of the High Court or, under **CrimPR 50.30(2)**, a nominated legal officer of the court. The order may, but need not, be pronounced in open court.[172] Once approved, the order will be sent to the parties and to any other person as required by **CrimPR 50.29(3)(b), (c)**.

12.3.25 A Consent Order to allow an appeal brought under s.28 Extradition Act 2003 must provide:

    a. for the quashing of the decision of the District Judge in Westminster Magistrates' Court discharging the Requested Person;

    b. for the matter to be remitted to the District Judge to hold fresh extradition proceedings;

    c. for any ancillary matter, such as bail or costs.

12.3.26 A Consent Order to allow an appeal brought under s.110 Extradition Act 2003 must provide:

    a. for the quashing of the decision of the Secretary of State for the Home Department not to order extradition;

    b. for the matter to be remitted to the Secretary of State to make a fresh decision on whether or not to order extradition;

    c. for any ancillary matter, such as bail or costs.

12.3.27 Where:

    a. a Consent Order is intended to dispose of an application for permission to appeal which has not yet been considered by the court, the order must make clear by what means that will be achieved, bearing in mind that an application for permission which is refused without a hearing can be renewed under **CrimPR 50.22(2)**. If the parties intend to exclude the possibility of renewal the order should declare either (i) that the time limit under **r.50.22(2)** is reduced to nil, or (ii) permission to appeal is given and the appeal determined on the other terms of the order;

    b. one of the parties is a child or protected party, the documents served under **CrimPR 50.24(5)** must include an opinion from the advocate acting on behalf of the child or protected party and, in the case of a protected party, any relevant documents prepared for the Court of Protection.

Fees

12.3.28 Applications to extend Representation Orders do not attract any fee.

12.3.29 Fees are payable for all other applications in accordance with the current Fees Order.

12.4 Representation Orders   PD12.4

12.4.1 Representation Orders may be granted by an LJ, a Single Judge of the High Court, a Master of the Administrative Court or a nominated legal officer of the court upon a properly completed CRM14 being lodged with the court. A Representation Order will cover a junior advocate and solicitors for the preparation of the Notice of Appeal to determination of the appeal.

12.4.2 Applications to extend Representation Orders may be granted by an LJ, a Single Judge of the High Court, a Master of the Administrative Court or a nominated court officer who may direct a case management hearing before an LJ, a Single Judge, or a Master of the Administrative Court. Since these applications do not attract a fee, parties may lodge them with the court by attaching them to an email addressed to the nominated legal officer of the court.

12.4.3 Applications to extend Representation Orders to cover the instruction of King's Counsel to appear either alone or with a junior advocate must be made in writing, either by letter or application notice, clearly marked with the Administrative Court reference number, which must be lodged with the Administrative Court Office or emailed to the appropriate email address.[173]

---

[172] **CrimPR 50.17(1)(c)(iii)**.
[173] crimex@administrativecourtoffice.justice.gov.uk.

12.4.4   The request must:

     a. identify the substantial novel or complex issues of law or fact in the case;
     b. explain why these may only be adequately presented by a King's Counsel;
     c. state whether a King's Counsel has been instructed on behalf of the respondent;
     d. explain any delay in making the request;
     e. be supported by advice from a junior advocate or King's Counsel.

12.4.5   Applications for prior authority to cover the cost of obtaining expert evidence must be made in writing, either by letter, clearly marked with the Administrative Court reference number, which must be sent or emailed to the Administrative Court Office.

12.4.6   The request must:

     a. confirm that the evidence sought has not been considered in any previous appeals determined by the appellate courts;
     b. explain why the evidence was not called at the extradition hearing in Westminster Magistrates' Court and what evidence can be produced to support that;
     c. explain why the new evidence would have resulted in the District Judge deciding a question at the extradition hearing differently and whether, if so, the District Judge would have been required to make a different order as to discharge of the requested person;
     d. explain why the evidence was not raised when the case was being considered by the Secretary of State for the Home Department or information was available that was not available at that time;
     e. explain why the new evidence would have resulted in the Secretary of State deciding a question differently, and if the question had been decided differently, the Secretary of State would not have ordered the person's extradition;
     f. state when the need for the new evidence first became known;
     g. explain any delay in making the request;
     h. explain what relevant factual, as opposed to expert evidence, is being given by whom to create the factual basis for the expert's opinion;
     i. explain why this particular area of expertise is relevant: for example why a child psychologist should be appointed as opposed to a social worker;
     j. state whether the requested person has capacity;
     k. set out a full breakdown of all costs involved including any VAT or other tax payable, including alternative quotes or explaining why none are available;
     l. provide a list of all previous extensions of the Representation Order and the approval of expenditure to date;
     m. provide a timetable for the production of the evidence and its anticipated effect on the time estimate and hearing date;
     n. set out the level of compliance to date with any directions order.

12.4.7   Experts must have direct personal experience of and proven expertise in the issue on which a report is sought; it is only if they do have such experience and it is relevant, that they can give evidence of what they have observed.

12.4.8   Where an order is granted to extend a Representation Order to obtain further evidence it will still be necessary for the party seeking to rely on the new evidence to satisfy the court hearing the application for permission or the substantive appeal that the evidence obtained should be admitted having regard to ss.27(4) and 29(4) Extradition Act 2003 and the judgment in *Szombathely City Court v Fenyvesi*.[174]

12.4.9   Applications to extend representation for the translation of documents must be made in writing, either by letter, clearly marked with the Administrative Court reference number, which must be sent to the Administrative Court Office.[175]

12.4.10 The request should:

     a. explain the importance of the document for which a translation is being sought and the justification for obtaining it;
     b. explain what it is believed to be contained in the document and the issues it will assist the court to address in hearing the appeal;
     c. confirm that the evidence sought has not been considered in any previous appeals determined by the appellate courts;

---

[174] [2009] EWHC 231 (Admin).
[175] The Royal Courts of Justice, Strand, London, WC2A 2LL or emailed to the appropriate email address crimex@administrativecourtoffice.justice.gov.uk.

    d. confirm that the evidence sought was not called at the extradition hearing in Westminster Magistrates' Court;

    e. explain why the evidence sought would have resulted in the District Judge deciding a question at the extradition hearing differently and whether, if so, the District Judge would have been required to make a different order as to discharge of the requested person;

    f. confirm that the new evidence was not raised when the case was being considered by the Secretary of State for the Home Department;

    g. explain why the new evidence sought would have resulted in the Secretary of State deciding a question differently, and if the question had been decided differently, the Secretary of State would not have ordered the person's extradition;

    h. confirm when the need for the new evidence first became known;

    i. explain any delay in making the request;

    j. explain fully the evidential basis for incurring the expenditure;

    k. explain why the appellant cannot produce the evidence themselves in the form of a statement of truth;

    l. set out a full breakdown of all costs involved including any VAT or other tax payable and the Legal Aid Agency contractual rates;

    m. provide a list of all previous extensions of the Representation Order and the expenditure to date.

12.4.11 Where an order is made to extend representation to cover the cost of the translation of documents it will still be necessary for the party seeking to rely on the documents as evidence to satisfy the court that it should be admitted at the hearing of the appeal having regard to ss.27(4) and 29(4) Extradition Act 2003 and the judgment in *Szombathely City Court v Fenyvesi*.[176]

PD12.5

12.5 Applications, etc

12.5.1 Extension or abridgement of time:

    a. Any party who seeks extension or abridgment of time for the service of documents, evidence or skeleton arguments must apply to the High Court on the appropriate form and pay the appropriate fee.

    b. Applications for extension or abridgment of time may be determined by an LJ, a Single Judge of the High Court, a Master of the Administrative Court or a nominated legal officer of the court.

    c. Applications for extension of time must include a witness statement setting out the reasons for non-compliance with any previous order and the proposed timetable for compliance.

    d. Any application made to an out of hours judge must be accompanied with:

        i.   a detailed chronology;

        ii. reasons why the application could not be made within court hours;

        iii. any orders or judgments made in the proceedings.

Representatives

12.5.2 **CrimPR Part 46** applies. Where under **CrimPR 46.2(1)(c)** a legal representative withdraws from the case then that representative should satisfy themselves that the requested person is aware of the time and date of the appeal hearing and of the need to attend, by live link if the court has so directed. If the legal representative has any reason to doubt that the requested person is so aware then they should promptly notify the Administrative Court Office.[177]

12.5.3 A legal representative must provide details of any arrangements likely to be required by the Requested Person to facilitate their participation in consequence of the representative's withdrawal, including arrangements for interpretation.[178]

Application to adjourn

12.5.4 Where a hearing date has been fixed, any application to vacate the hearing must be made on the appropriate form. A fee is required for the application if it is made within 14 days of the hearing date. The application must:

    a. explain the reasons why an application is being made to vacate the hearing;

    b. detail the views of the other parties to the appeal;

    c. include a draft order with the application notice.

---

[176] [2009] EWHC 231 (Admin).

[177] This may be filed by email to crimex@administrativecourtoffice.justice.gov.uk.

[178] **Crim PR 46.2(1)(c)**.

12.5.5   If the parties both seek an adjournment then the application must be submitted for consideration by an LJ, a Single Judge of the High Court or a Master of the Administrative Court. Exceptional circumstances must be shown if a date for the hearing has been fixed or the adjournment will result in material delay to the determination of the appeal.

12.5.6   An application to adjourn following a compromise agreement must be supported by evidence justifying exceptional circumstances and why it is in compliance with the overriding objective.

Variation of directions

12.5.7   Where parties are unable to comply with any order of the court they must apply promptly to vary directions before deadlines for compliance have expired and seek further directions. An application to vary directions attracts a fee and the application, to be submitted on the appropriate form, must:

   a. provide full and proper explanations for why the current and existing directions have not been complied with;
   b. detail the views of the other parties to the appeal;
   c. include a draft order setting out in full the timetable and directions as varied i.e. a superseding order which stands alone;
   d. if the application is made to an out of hours judge it must be accompanied by:
      i.   a detailed chronology;
      ii.   reasons why the application could not be made within court hours;
      iii. any orders or judgments made in the proceedings.

12.5.8   A failure to make the application prior to the expiry of the date specified in the order will generally result in the refusal of the application unless good reasons are shown.

Application to certify a point of law of general public importance

12.5.9   Where an application is made under **CrimPR 50.25(2)(b)** the application must be made on the appropriate form accompanied by the relevant fee.

12.5.10 Any response to the application must be made within 10 business days.

12.5.11 Where an application to certify is granted but permission to appeal to the Supreme Court is refused, it shall be for those representing the Requested Person to apply for an extension of the Representation Order to cover proceedings in the Supreme Court, if so advised.

12.5.12 The representation order may be extended by an LJ, a Single Judge of the High Court, a Master of the Administrative Court or a nominated legal officer of the court.

12.5.13 The result of the application to certify a point of law of general public importance and permission to appeal to the Supreme Court may be notified in advance to the legal representatives but legal representatives must not communicate it to the Requested Person until one hour before the pronouncement is made in open court.

12.5.14 There shall be no public announcement of the result until after it has been formally pronounced.

Application to reopen the determination of an appeal

12.5.15 An application under **CrimPR 50.27** to reopen an appeal must be referred to the court that determined the appeal, but may if circumstances require be considered by a judge or judges other than those who determined the original appeal.

Application to extend required period for removal pursuant to s.36 Extradition Act 2003

12.5.16 Where an application is made for an extension of the required period within which to extradite a Requested Person it must be accompanied by:

   a. a witness statement explaining why it is not possible to remove the Requested Person within the required period and the proposed timetable for removal;
   b. a draft order.

12.5.17 The application to extend time may be made before or after the expiry of the required period for extradition, but the court will scrutinise with particular care an application made after its expiry.

12.5.18 Where extensions of time are sought for the same reason in respect of a number of Requested Persons who are due to be extradited at the same time, a single application may be made to the court listing each of the Requested Persons for whom an extension is sought.

12.5.19 The application may be determined by an LJ, a Single Judge of the High Court, a Master of the Administrative Court or a nominated legal officer of the court and a single order listing those persons may be granted.

Application for directions ancillary to a discharge pursuant to ss.42 or 124 Extradition Act 2003

12.5.20 Where the High Court is informed that the warrant or extradition request has been withdrawn then unless ancillary matters are dealt with by Consent Order an application notice must be issued seeking any such directions. The notice of discharge of a Requested Person must be accompanied by:

a. the notification by the requesting state that the EAW has been withdrawn together with a translation of the same;

b. a witness statement containing:
   i.   details of whether the withdrawn EAW is the only EAW outstanding in respect of the Requested Person;
   ii. details of other EAWs outstanding in respect of the Requested Person and the stage which the proceedings have reached;
   iii. whether only part of the EAW has been withdrawn;
   iv. details of any bail conditions;
   v.   details of any institution in which the Requested Person is being detained, the Requested Person's prison number and date of birth.

12.5.21 The order for discharge may be made by an LJ, a Single Judge of the High Court, a Master of the Administrative Court or a nominated legal officer of the court.

12.5.22 It is the responsibility of the High Court to serve the approved order on the appropriate institution and Westminster Magistrates' Court.

12.6 Court papers

PD12.6

Skeleton arguments

12.6.1 The court on granting permission to appeal or directing an oral hearing for permission to appeal will give directions as to the filing of skeleton arguments. Unless the court has ordered otherwise:

a. the appellant's skeleton argument for an oral permission hearing must be filed and served not less than 7 days before the date of the hearing;

b. the appellant's skeleton argument for a final or rolled-up hearing must be filed and served not less than 14 days before the date of the hearing; and

c. the respondent's skeleton argument for a final or rolled-up hearing must be filed and served not less than 7 days before the date of the hearing.

12.6.2 Strict compliance is required with all time limits.

12.6.3 A skeleton argument must:

a. be concise, and in any event shall not, save with the permission of the court, exceed 10 pages (excluding front sheets and back sheets);

b. be printed on A4 paper in not less than 12 point font and 1.5 line spacing;

c. define the issues in the appeal;

d. be set out in numbered paragraphs;

e. be cross-referenced to any relevant document in the bundle;

f. be self-contained and not incorporate by reference material from previous skeleton arguments;

g. not include extensive quotations from documents or authorities.

12.6.4 Where it is necessary to refer to an authority, the skeleton argument must:

a. state the proposition of law the authority demonstrates; and

b. identify but not quote the parts of the authority that support the proposition.

12.6.5 If more than one authority is cited in support of a given proposition, the skeleton argument must briefly state why.

12.6.6 A chronology of relevant events will be necessary in most appeals.

12.6.7 Where a skeleton argument has been prepared in respect of an application for permission to appeal, the same skeleton argument may be relied upon in the appeal upon notice being given to the court or a replacement skeleton may be lodged not less than seven business days before the hearing of the appeal.

12.6.8   At the hearing the court may refuse to hear argument on a point not included in a skeleton argument filed within the prescribed time.

Hearing bundles

12.6.9   The hearing bundle should be agreed by the parties save where the Requested Person is acting in person. In those circumstances the court expects the Requesting State to prepare the bundle.

12.6.10 The hearing bundle must be prepared in electronic form in accordance with the Guidance on the Administrative Court website.

12.6.11 The hearing bundle must be paginated and indexed. It should only contain relevant documents and must not include duplicate documents.

12.6.12 Subject to any order made by the court, the following documents must be included in the appeal bundle:

     a. the Notice of Appeal and Grounds, or Application Notice and grounds;
     b. documents regarded as essential to the appeal, or application (for example the extradition request, the judgment of the District Judge, the Respondent's Notice etc.);
     c. any witness statements (or primary witness statement) relied on in support of the appeal or application; and
     d. a draft of the order the court is asked to make.

12.6.13 Hearing bundles should not exceed 20mb. If the documents required for the hearing exceed this size, the parties should prepare a core bundle containing the documents referred to at paragraph 12.6.12 above, and a further bundle (or bundles, none to exceed 20mb) containing the remaining documents. The appellant shall if requested by the Court, lodge a hard-copy version of the Hearing Bundle and/or the Authorities Bundle. The pagination of any hard-copy version must be the same as the pagination of the electronic bundle.

12.6.14 Hearing bundles must be lodged in accordance with the directions given by the court. In default of such directions:

     a. the hearing bundle for a renewal application must be lodged within 14 days of the date of the letter from the List Office confirming receipt of the renewed application for permission to appeal;
     b. the hearing bundle for a final or rolled-up hearing must be lodged 14 days before the date of the hearing.

12.6.15 Bundles lodged with the court will not be returned to the parties but will be destroyed in the confidential waste system at the conclusion of the proceedings and without further notification.

Authorities

12.6.16 A list of 'Frequently cited authorities' is published on the Administrative Court website. Copies of authorities on this list need not be provided to the judge hearing the application/appeal. Parties may assume that the judge will have a copy of the judgment; if any of these authorities is relied on parties need only cite the case and the relevant paragraph number(s).

12.6.17 Parties wishing to rely on any other authority must provide a copy of the case to the court in advance of the hearing. If the authority has been reported (for example in the Law Reports or All England Reports) parties must refer to and provide the reported version of the judgment in preference to a transcript of the judgment.

12.6.18 Unless the court has directed otherwise:

     a. authorities bundles containing all authorities to be relied on (save for those in the list of frequently cited authorities) must be lodged no later than 7 days prior to the date set for the hearing of the application/appeal; and
     b. all authorities bundles must be in electronic form and be prepared in accordance with the Guidance on the Administrative Court website.

PD12.7

12.7 Consequences of non-compliance with directions

12.7.1   Failure to comply with these directions will lead to applications for permission and appeals being dealt with on the material available to the court at the time when the decision is made.

12.7.2   Judges dealing with extradition appeals will seek full and proper explanations for any breaches of the rules and the provisions of this Practice Direction.

12.7.3 If no good explanation can be given immediately by counsel or solicitors, the senior partner or the departmental head responsible is likely to be called to court to explain any failure to comply with a court order. Where counsel or solicitors fail to obey orders of the court and are unable to provide proper and sufficient reasons for their disobedience they may anticipate the matter being formally referred to the President of the King's Bench Division with a recommendation that the counsel or solicitors involved be reported to their professional bodies.

12.7.4 The court may also refuse to admit any material or any evidence not filed in compliance with the order for directions or outside a time limit specified by the court.

12.7.5 A failure to comply with the time limits or other requirements for skeleton arguments will have the consequences specified in paragraph 12.6.8.

13. Case Management of Terrorism Cases

13.1 Application   PD13.1

13.1.1 For the purposes of this Practice Direction a case is a 'terrorism case' where:

a. one of the offences charged against any of the defendants is indictable only and it is alleged by the prosecution that there is evidence that it took place during an act of terrorism or for the purposes of terrorism as defined in s.1 Terrorism Act 2000. This may include, but is not limited to:
   i.   murder;
   ii. manslaughter;
   iii. an offence under s.18 Offences against the Person Act 1861 (wounding with intent);
   iv. an offence under s.23 or 24 of that Act (administering poison etc);
   v.   an offence under s.28 or 29 of that Act (explosives);
   vi. an offence under ss.2, 3 or 5 Explosive Substances Act 1883 (causing explosions);
   vii. an offence under s.1(2) Criminal Damage Act 1971 (endangering life by damaging property);
   viii. an offence under s.1 Biological Weapons Act 1974 (biological weapons);
   ix. an offence under s.2 Chemical Weapons Act 1996 (chemical weapons);
   x.   an offence under s.56 Terrorism Act 2000 (directing a terrorist organisation);
   xi. an offence under s.59 of that Act (inciting terrorism overseas);
   xii. offences under (v), (vii) and (viii) above given jurisdiction by virtue of s.62 of that Act (terrorist bombing overseas); and
   xiii. an offence under s.5 Terrorism Act 2006 (preparation of terrorism acts).
b. one of the offences charged is indictable only and includes an allegation by the prosecution of serious fraud that took place during an act of terrorism or for the purposes of terrorism as defined in s.1 Terrorism Act 2000, and the prosecutor gives a notice under s.51B Crime and Disorder Act 1998 (Notices in serious or complex fraud cases);
c. one of the offences charged is indictable only, and includes an allegation that a defendant conspired, assisted, encouraged or attempted to commit an offence under subparagraphs 13.1.1(a) or (b) above; or
d. it is a case (which can be indictable only or triable either way) that a judge of the terrorism cases list (see paragraph 13.2.1 below) considers should be a terrorism case. In deciding whether a case not covered by subparagraphs 13.1.1 (a), (b) or (c) above should be a terrorism case, the judge may hear representations from the CPS.

13.2 The terrorism cases list   PD13.2

13.2.1 All terrorism cases, wherever they originate in England and Wales, will be managed in a list known as the 'terrorism cases list' by such judges of the High Court as are nominated by the President of the King's Bench Division.

13.2.2 Such cases will be tried, unless otherwise directed by the President of the King's Bench Division, by a judge of the High Court as nominated by the President of the King's Bench Division, or an appropriately ticketed Crown Court judge.

13.2.3 The judges managing the terrorism cases referred to in paragraph 13.1.1 will be supported by the London and South Eastern Regional Co-ordinator's Office (the 'Regional Co-ordinator's Office') and the Case Progression Officer. An official of that office or an individual nominated by that office will act as the case progression officer for cases in that list.[179]

---

[179] For the purposes of **CrimPR 3.4**.

PD13.3

13.3 Procedure after charge

13.3.1 Immediately after a person has been charged in a terrorism case, anywhere in England and Wales, a representative of the CPS will notify the person on the 24-hour rota for special jurisdiction matters at Westminster Magistrates' Court of the following information:

     a. the full name of each defendant and the name of their solicitor or other legal representative, if known;

     b. the charges;

     c. the name and contact details of the Crown Prosecutor with responsibility for the case, if known; and

     d. confirmation that the case is a terrorism case.

13.3.2 The person on the 24-hour rota will then ensure that all terrorism cases wherever they are charged in England and Wales are listed before the Chief Magistrate or other District Judge designated under the Terrorism Act 2000. Unless the Chief Magistrate or other District Judge designated under the Terrorism Act 2000 directs otherwise, the first appearance of all defendants accused of terrorism offences will be listed at Westminster Magistrates' Court.

13.3.3 In order to comply with s.46 PACE 1984, if a defendant in a terrorism case is charged at a police station within the jurisdiction of Westminster Magistrates' Court, the defendant must be brought before Westminster Magistrates' Court as soon as is practicable and in any event not later than the first sitting after they are charged with the offence. If a defendant in a terrorism case is charged in a police station outside the jurisdiction of Westminster Magistrates' Court, unless the Chief Magistrate or other designated judge directs otherwise, the defendant must be removed to that area as soon as is practicable. They must then be brought before Westminster Magistrates' Court as soon as is practicable after their arrival in the area and in any event not later than the first sitting of Westminster Magistrates' Court after arrival in that area.

13.3.4 As soon as is practicable after charge a representative of the CPS will also provide the Regional Listing Co-ordinator's Office with the information listed in paragraph 4 above.

13.3.5 The Regional Co-ordinator's Office or the Case Progression Officer will then ensure that the Chief Magistrate and the Legal Aid Agency have the same information.

PD13.4

13.4 Cases to be sent to the Crown Court under s.51 Crime and Disorder Act 1998

13.4.1 In all terrorism cases, the magistrates' court case progression form for cases sent to the Crown Court under s.51 Crime and Disorder Act 1998 should not be used. Instead of the automatic directions set out in that form, the magistrates' court shall make the following directions to facilitate the preliminary hearing at the Crown Court:

     a. Three days prior to the preliminary hearing in the terrorism cases list, the prosecution must serve upon each defendant and the Regional Listing Co-ordinator and Case Progression Officer:

         i.   a preliminary summary of the case;

         ii.   the names of those who are to represent the prosecution, if known;

         iii.   an estimate of the length of the trial;

         iv.   a suggested provisional timetable which should generally include:

             • the general nature of further enquiries being made by the prosecution,

             • the time needed for the completion of such enquiries,

             • the time required by the prosecution to review the case,

             • a timetable for the phased service of the evidence,

             • the time for the provision of consent by the Attorney General if necessary,

             • the time for service of the detailed defence statement,

             • the date for the case management hearing, and

             • the estimated trial date;

         v.   a preliminary statement of the possible disclosure issues setting out the nature and scale of the issue, including the amount of unused material, the manner in which the prosecution intends to deal with these matters and a suggested timetable for discharging their statutory duty; and

         vi.   any information relating to bail and custody time limits.

     b. One day prior to the preliminary hearing in the terrorist cases list, each defendant must serve in writing on the Regional Listing Co-ordinator, the Case Progression Officer and the prosecution:

      i.   the proposed representation;

      ii.   observations on the timetable; and

      iii. an indication of plea and the general nature of the defence.

13.5 Cases to be sent to the Crown Court after the prosecutor gives notice under s.51B Crime and Disorder Act 1998

PD13.5

13.5.1 If a terrorism case is to be sent to the Crown Court after the prosecutor gives a notice under s.51B Crime and Disorder Act 1998 the magistrates' court should proceed as in paragraphs 11-13 above.

13.5.2 When a terrorism case is so sent the case will go into the terrorism list and be managed by a judge as described in paragraph 2 above.

13.6 The Plea and Trial Preparation Hearing at the Crown Court

PD13.6

13.6.1 At the PTPH, the judge will determine whether the case is one to remain in the terrorism list and if so, give directions setting the provisional timetable.

13.6.2 The Legal Aid Agency may attend the hearing by an authorised officer to assist the court.

13.7 Use of live links

PD13.7

13.7.1 Unless a judge otherwise directs, all Crown Court hearings prior to the trial will be conducted by live link for all defendants in custody.

13.8 Security

PD13.8

13.8.1 The police service and the prison service will provide the Regional Listing Co-ordinator's Office and Case Progression Officer with an initial joint assessment of the security risks associated with any court appearance by the defendant(s) within 14 days of charge. Any subsequent changes in circumstances or the assessment of risk which have the potential to impact upon the choice of trial venue will be notified to the Regional Listing Co-ordinator's Office and the Case Progression Officer immediately.

14. WELSH LANGUAGE IN COURT

14.1 General

PD14.1

14.1.1 The Welsh Language Act 1993 provides that in administration of justice in Wales, the English and Welsh languages should be treated equally.

14.1.2 If a defendant in a court in England asks to give/call evidence in Welsh, the case should not be transferred to Wales without consultation with the Presiding Judge.

14.1.3 Where such a transfer is considered appropriate the Welsh Language Unit should be contacted to discuss specific case requirements. A Welsh interpreter should be booked via:

    Welsh.language.unit.manager@justice.gov.uk Uned Iaith Gymraeg | Welsh Language Unit

    Gwasanaeth Llysoedd a Thribiwnlysoedd EM | HM Courts & Tribunals Service

    Canolfan Cyfiawnder Troseddol Caernarfon | Caernarfon Criminal Justice Centre

    Ffordd Llanberis | Llanberis Road Caernarfon

    Gwynedd LL55 2DF Ffôn | Tel. 0800 212 368

14.1.4 Issues of practicability should be discussed with the Welsh Language Liaison Judge:

    Ei Hanrhydedd y barnwr Mererid Edwards/ HHJ Mererid Edwards Barnwr Cyswllt I'r Gymraeg/ Welsh Language Liaison Judge HHJ.Mererid.Edwards@ejudiciary.net

    Canolfan Llysoedd Sifil Caerdydd / Cardiff Civil Justice Centre 2 Stryd y Parc / 2 Park Street

    Caerdydd / Cardiff CF10 1ET

    DX: 99500 CARDIFF 6

14.1.5 Legal representatives must inform the court when Welsh may be used by any witness or party, or in any document, to ensure appropriate listing arrangements.

14.1.6 The 'Magistrates' Courts' Protocol for Listing Cases where the Welsh Language is used' applies.[180]

---

[180] See also **CrimPR 24.14**.

Criminal Practice Directions 2023

14.1.7   If at the time of sending or lodging appeal to the Crown Court, it is known that Welsh might be used in the case, the court should be informed immediately, or as soon as it becomes known thereafter.

14.1.8   The law does not permit juror selection methods enabling discovery of whether a juror speaks Welsh, or to secure a bilingual jury, to try a case in which the Welsh language may be used.

PD14.2   **14.2 Witnesses**

14.2.1   When each witness is called, the court officer administering the oath/affirmation shall inform the witness that they may be sworn/affirm in Welsh/English. If Welsh is chosen, the witness should not be asked to repeat it in English.

PD14.3   **14.3 Opening/closing of Crown Courts**

14.3.1   Court opening and closing should be performed in Welsh and English, unless impracticable.

Index